DATE DUE

JUL 2 6 2006	

DEMCO, INC. 38-2931

Operations Management
A Value-Driven Approach

Operations Management

A Value-Driven Approach

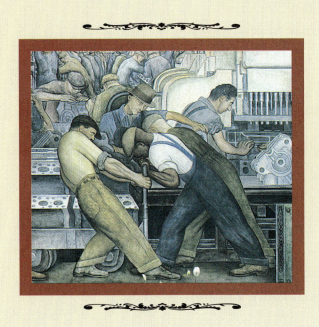

Steven A. Melnyk
Michigan State University

David R. Denzler
San Jose State University

Irwin McGraw-Hill

Boston, Massachusetts   Burr Ridge, Illinois   Dubuque, Iowa
Madison, Wisconsin   New York, New York   San Francisco, California   St. Louis, Missouri

Irwin/McGraw-Hill

*A Division of The **McGraw·Hill** Companies*

OPERATIONS MANAGEMENT: A VALUE-DRIVEN APPROACH

This book is printed on acid-free paper.

2 3 4 5 6 7 8 9 0 VNH VNH 9 0 9 8 7

ISBN 0-256-12381-0

Publisher: William Schoof
Acquisitions editor: John Weimeister
Project manager: Bob Lange
Marketing Manager: Colleen Suljic
Designer: Elm Street Publishing Services, Inc.
Photo research: Sarah Evertson/Image Quest
Compositor: Elm Street Publishing Services, Inc.
Typeface: 10/12 Palatino
Printer: Von Hoffmann Press, Inc.

          Library of Congress Cataloging-in-Publication Data

Melnyk, Steven A.
      Operations management: a value-driven approach / Steven A.
   Melnyk. David R. Denzler.
         p. cm.
      Includes bibliographical references and index.
      ISBN 0-256-12381-0
      1. Production management.   I. Denzler, David R.   II. Title.
   Ts155.M354   1996
   658.5–dc20   95-47182

COVER SOURCE: Photograph © The Detroit Institute of Arts, 1995.
   Gift of Edsel B. Ford.

http://www.mhcollege.com

To my four great teachers:

Stephen Melnyk (1924–1995)—my father,
who taught me to value education and knowledge.

A. R. (Bert) Wood (professor, University of Western Ontario)—
who taught me to be considerate and curious.

Bob Britney (professor, University of Western Ontario,
died 1994)—who taught me to be demanding of my research and
to look at things differently.

Gene Woolsey (professor, Colorado School of Mines)—
who taught me to learn by doing and to respect the practitioner
who makes his living through action and learning.

Steven A. Melnyk

To my great teachers:

Arthur H. Denzler and Jessie Y. Denzler—two parents
who taught me quality before TQM existed.

David R. Denzler

Preface

The last ten years have been periods of great change for the operations management field. This field has seen bewildering developments. Some of the most important developments include total quality management, just-in-time manufacturing, theory of constraints, lean manufacturing, time-based competition, mass customization, and the agile enterprise, to name a few. Each offers managers the promise of significant improvements in costs, quality, flexibility, and lead times. This period has also seen significant increases in the number of products offered and significant reductions in the time needed to introduce new products. For example, in the early 1980s, companies such as Chrysler, Ford, and General Motors took from five to eight years to design, build a prototype, and manufacture a new car. Even then the cars were often plagued by problems and defects in their first year—indications that they had been rushed into production. In late 1995, Ford announced its goal of going from drawing board to full production in about two years. Furthermore, each car would be fully debugged at the start of production rather than after two years of production.

Ten years ago, Japan and its operations management system represented the leading edge in terms of both thought and practice. Many managers and researchers traveled to Japan to learn about just-in-time manufacturing, the house of quality, the quality function deployment, and total quality management. Today, this situation has changed. Consider the following story.

> Traditionally the Japanese car market has been difficult to crack. This was the result of a mixture of protectionism, poor products, and half-hearted marketing. European and American firms could not seem to build the type of cars that the Japanese consumer wanted. Not only did these cars lack the required level of quality and right-hand drives, they also did not appeal to the typical Japanese buyer. This buyer was seen as wanting gadget-loaded cars—cars with power windows, power seats, dashboard TVs, and satellite-navigation systems. Now this same customer wants *"kakaku-hakai"* (price destruction) and high-quality, functional transportation. Japanese customers are now attracted by American products because these cars offer high quality at a low price. Aided by a weak dollar, Ford and Chrysler have reduced the price of their cars. For example, Chrysler's small Neon car will sell for about ¥1.5 million ($14,600) compared with similar Japanese products, which cost about ¥2 million. Suddenly, American products are attracting a lot of attention from the typical Japanese consumer.[1]

There has also been a rapid rate of change taking place in technology. Consider microcomputers, for example. In the early 1980s, a computer with a 8088/80826 chip with 1 MB of memory, a VGA card and monitor, and a 40 MB hard disk cost

---

[1]"Japan's Car Market: Auto Destruct," *The Economist,* November 4, 1995, pp. 69–70.

about $3,500 and was considered leading edge. Now, you can buy a Pentium 120 system with a super VGA card (and 1 MB memory on the card) and monitor, a quad speed CD drive, 16 MB of memory, a 1.2 GB hard disk, and multimedia capabilities for less than $2,500. This new desktop computer essentially offers all of the power of the early 1980s mainframe.

In the future we see the movement towards environmentally conscious manufacturing, global operations, virtual factories, and the increasing presence of knowledge workers. These developments emphasize that change is an integral element of the environment in which the operations manager must work. This change comes from such areas as technology, competitive actions, and the shifting expectations of our customers. These developments also emphasize the changing role of the worker. In the past, the employee was seen as simply a strong back and a pair of strong hands. Now we want employees who are intelligent, curious, and analytical, and who are problem solvers. We now see the employee as an important source of flexibility and innovation. Finally, these changes point to a reduction in the distance between the customer and the operations management system. We no longer want a factory that can build products at the lowest cost—instead, now we want systems that respond to the changing needs of our customers. We want to build what the customer wants, when it is wanted, in the amount wanted, and at the levels of cost and quality demanded by the customer.

Not only have these changes complicated life for the operations manager, they have also made the life of an operations management teacher more difficult. Just when we figured out how to effectively teach operations management (e.g., Operations Management—a TQM perspective), these changes force us to rethink our material and our approach to the topic. Many of the frameworks used to teach operations management have tended to be static. Using total quality management to teach operations management was fine as long as the operations management system was oriented primarily towards quality. But today, a new approach is needed. This book represents our thinking on this new approach.

We quickly became disillusioned with the traditional but limiting "planning, organizing, scheduling, controlling" frameworks found in most operations management books. We also rejected approaches that emphasize specific orientations, such as total quality management. Any book reflecting such an orientation runs the serious risk of becoming obsolete. We also rejected an extensively mathematical treatment, which made sense when the problems being solved by the operations manager were relatively stable. Such an approach is less applicable when the problems are constantly changing or poorly defined. We settled on an approach that emphasizes value and its role in the operations management system.

What is value? We view value as the subjective evaluation of the performance of a product, good, or service adjusted by cost. Performance consists of four major components: (1) functionality, (2) lead time, (3) quality, and (4) flexibility. Using this equation, we can generate different types of value, depending on whether we want to focus on performance, cost, or both cost and performance. Two firms making the same product can deliver very different types of value depending on which component of the value equation management wants to focus.

This value approach is interesting because it argues that everything we do is driven by value. Developments such as total quality management, time-based competition, and just-in-time manufacturing can be regarded as attempts to alter the value equation so that it favors one firm and its products (or processes) over another's. The value concept argues that people are not cost minimizers but value maximizers.

The value approach is attractive for a number of reasons. First, as a concept, value is fairly easy to understand and use. In fact, value is rather intuitive. Everyone thinks in terms of value. In class testing this concept, we found that students at both the undergraduate and graduate levels were able to quickly identify with the value approach and to understand its implications. Second, the value approach is simultaneously dynamic and stable. The components of value do not change much over time (i.e., cost, quality, lead time, flexibility, and function). However, how these components are weighted or emphasized over time does change. As new developments appear, the emphasis changes. With total quality management, the emphasis shifts to quality. With mass customization, the emphasis moves to flexibility. These changes in emphasis are triggered by internal changes (technological developments) and external changes (customer expectations, competitive actions, governmental actions). As a result, the value concept is flexible enough to allow updating for new developments without making the entire value-driven perspective obsolete. Third, value is fundamentally strategic in nature. Value is how we compete; our goal, as managers, is either to increase the level of value delivered by our system or to reduce waste. Value is also strategic in that it is a *relative* concept. That is, the goal of any value-driven enterprise is to identify and deliver superior value relative to that provided by the best alternative source. Operations managers also have to view their systems' effectiveness relative to that of other systems. This approach makes something like benchmarking (Chapter 5) a natural and logical activity.

The value approach also forces us to recognize the need for developing a true cross-functional perspective. For us to define value, we must know our customers (current and potential). The operations manager must work closely in such areas as marketing and strategy. To successfully work with such groups, we must break down the functional barriers that exist in many firms between these groups. The value perspective also forces us to recognize the importance of our suppliers. Our ability to deliver superior value is dependent not only on the capabilities of our internal operations management system but also on the capabilities of our suppliers. Finally, the value concept is consistent with the approach taken by such leading-edge companies as Hewlett-Packard and Siemens.

The value-driven approach found in this book is built on certain major themes:

- the need to understand and define in operational terms the concept of value
- the importance of processes within the value-driven enterprise
- the importance of rethinking the role of the human within the value-driven enterprise
- the role of capacity as both volume AND capabilities
- the need to present operations management in a forward-looking mode
- the need to see operations management as a living, breathing entity that is both interesting and challenging.

Our goal, in writing this book, has been to prepare the next generation of operations managers to successfully cope with the paradox of operations management—the twin goals of managing for stability but planning for change.

ORGANIZATION OF THE BOOK

Rather than structuring the book around the traditional elements of planning, organizing, controlling, and feedback, we follow in a logical way the aspects that must be grasped for students to understand the value-driven operations management system. First, they must understand why it is important that we change our way of looking at operations management. As operations managers, they will deal with frameworks (paradigms)—everything that we do reflects a paradigm. These frameworks are the vehicles by which we communicate with others and through which we view the world around us. Second, they must understand the concept of value and its elements. As operations managers, they will try to positively influence the definition of value offered by their firm. Third, they must understand the major perspectives and philosophies that permeate the study of operations management. These philosophies define ways of looking not only at the operations management system but also at the task of generating and delivering value to customers. Our students must understand these approaches in terms of the management models found in them and their general tools. Fourth, they must be familiar with the major activities and processes found in any operations management system. Finally, they must be prepared to deal with new trends and developments. They must be forward looking, because actions taken today will affect them in the future. Developments now emerging may become major influences on the shape of the operations management system in the future.

To be consistent with this logic and flow, the book is organized into seven parts. Part One, "**Operations Management: A Value-Driven Approach**," provides an overview of operations management, the challenges now facing operations management, needed changes in frameworks (from cost to value), and the way operations management fits within the corporate and competitive landscapes. Part Two, "**The Conceptual Foundation of the Value-Driven Approach**," defines value and then examines the attributes, or traits, associated with value (functionality, cost, quality, lead time, and flexibility). This part also includes a discussion of problem solving and decision making in operations management. We introduce the student to the basic process of management, managerial problem solving, and the major tools and concepts that effective operations managers draw on. In Part Three, "**Value as a Driver of OM Systems**," we look at the factors affecting the value-driven operations management system—the major managerial frameworks and tools used in the value-driven approach. Included in this part are a view of operations management as the task of building and managing processes, not products. Also included is a discussion of the human as an essential building block in the value-driven firm. This part also discusses two major approaches to the delivery of value—one using quality as a primary source of value (total quality management) and one continuously identifying and eliminating all sources of waste within the operations management system (just-in-time manufacturing). In Part Four, "**The Design of Value-Driven OM Systems**," we focus on the elements that must be considered when designing an operations management system, including demand management, product design, process design, and the design and management of the supply chain.

In Part Five, "**Planning Issues in Value-Driven OM Systems**," we look at planning within the value-driven operations management system. Here we address issues pertaining to overall planning and to capacity planning specifically. We shift to execution in Part Six, "**Execution in Value-Driven OM Systems**." Here we look at such topics as inventory management, materials management, capacity management, and shop-floor control (execution within the internal factory). In Part Seven, "**The Strategic Audit**," we try to identify where operations management is going in the future. We examine five emerging developments that appear to be defining the shape and structure of operations management in the future. The five developments are the challenge of vision, the challenge of being global, the challenge of being environmentally responsible, the challenge of knowledge, and the challenge of technology.

We end with these challenges because they are consistent with our view of operations management as a dynamic and ever-changing system. Students who will be successful operations managers must think about not only what is happening today but also what will be happening in the future. As Charles Kettering, the great industrialist, inventor, and philanthropist, once said, "My interest is in the future because I am going to spend the rest of my life there." This book is designed to help the student see that the end of the book is not the end of learning but only the start.

FEATURES OF THE BOOK

Several features of *Operations Management: A Value-Driven Approach* support the text beyond those found in traditional operations management texts:

- **Real-world case stories and vignettes are interwoven through the chapters.** Each chapter begins with a case (typically drawn from *Fortune* or *Business Week*), which sets the tone for the chapter and identifies its major themes. Numerous stories are also integrated into the discussion found in every chapter.
- **Comprehensive coverage.** The book covers all of the topics that are expected in a leading operations management textbook.
- **Forward-looking approach.** The book discusses such new topics as environmentally responsible operations, the emergence of the knowledge worker, core competencies, virtual corporations and the virtual factory, global operations, and the Internet.
- **Process-oriented perspective.** This book is the first to emphasize a process perspective. That is, we view nearly everything that happens within operations management as the result of a process (e.g., strategic planning process, manufacturing process, human resource planning process). To change processes to make them more effective requires that we first document them and analyze them. We provide the students with the tools for documentation and analysis, which are being used in the field.
- **Extensive and comprehensive treatment of the human element.** While most textbooks provide some analysis of the human in the system, this book provides a comprehensive treatment that draws on research in such fields as organizational behavior. This textbook deals with such topics as the knowledge worker, diversity within the workplace, and the problem of retaining critical employees.
- **Writing style.** The writing is consistent in both level and style and has been written to be easy to read. The extensive use of unusual examples, such as the dried jellyfish story in Chapter 2, illustrates that value is very situation specific.
- **Problem solving and management skills.** Operations managers and operations management students need to understand problem solving and management. As a result, Chapter 4 focuses on problem solving. We show the differences between problems, symptoms, causes, solutions, and effects. We

also show the differences between solutions that solve, resolve, and dissolve. Finally, we introduce the concept of the operations management toolkit—a set of tools and procedures that are common to nearly every situation encountered by the operations manager.

- **On-line support of the faculty.** With a home page on the Internet, the authors can answer questions, share teaching information, and distribute new stories in a timely fashion. For example, as new stories are identified, they will be posted to the Internet, along with hints on how they can be used. This service will be provided free to all professors using this book in class.

In addition to these content characteristics, a number of pedagogical features help the student learn and retain the material presented.

- Learning objectives and an opening vignette focus the student's attention on upcoming chapter content. The vignette is also woven throughout each chapter. Each vignette is continuously referred to as material and concepts are introduced in the chapter.
- "On the Job" boxes provide in-depth examples of problems and situations faced by operations managers. They illustrate how managers have coped with problems and introduced improvements, which are consistent with the value-driven perspective. "By the Way…" boxes explore unique operations management concepts in more detail. These boxes give students additional insight and more in-depth knowledge.
- Art exhibits are rendered in a modern computer style to provide a lively, interesting, and visual reading experience.
- Key quotations are placed in the text margin throughout to highlight concepts.
- Marginal definitions of key terms reinforce concepts.
- An end-of-chapter summary revisits the important terms and topics of the chapter. A list of key terms, with page numbers, is included for quick review at the end of the chapter.
- Numerous review and discussion questions follow each chapter, which can be used in the classroom or as homework. Special critical thinking questions in each chapter are challenging and thought-provoking and help students apply concepts.
- Cases at the end of each chapter illustrate the issues raised in the chapter and emphasize operations management principles and practices. Many are drawn from the industrial experiences of the authors.
- A glossary at the end of the book provides easy access to the marginal definitions.

LEARNING PACKAGE

- Instructor's Manual
- Video Instructor's Manual
- Test Bank
- Study Guide
- Excel templates
- PowerPoint
- Internet homepage

ACKNOWLEDGMENTS

This book is unique because it has tried to treat operations management as what it is—a fundamentally interesting and dynamic field. We have tried to show that effective and efficient operations management must be value driven. Writing this book has been challenging, demanding, and frustrating. This book reflects the work and influence not only of the authors but also of numerous other people who have played a wide range of roles. We recognize these people and thank them for everything that they have given—it is appreciated.

Personal Acknowledgments

Steven A. Melnyk: I would like to thank the following people. First of all, my partner and part-time editor, my wife, Christine Melnyk, who with this book gets her informal degree in Business with specialization in Operations Management. I also thank my two children, Charles and Beth, for their patience and understanding for those many nights that I spent working in my office on this book.

David R. Denzler: I recognize and acknowledge all of the support, encouragement, gentle prodding, and love that my wife, Cheryl Van Clark, has given me during the course of writing this book. The fact that this book has been written is due in large part to her. Thanks for everything.

General Acknowledgments

We would like to thank the reviewers, whose comments and insights have greatly contributed to this book: Ann Marucheck (University of North Carolina at Chapel Hill), Jack Hayya (Penn State University), Hank Kraebber (Purdue University), Al Raedels (Portland State University), and Dan Steele (University of South Carolina).

We also acknowledge the information that the survey respondents provided. Their valuable input helped us fine-tune our text:

Stephen Allen
Northeast Missouri State University

Steve Arendall
Union University

Avijit Banarjee
Drexel University

Robert Banis
University of Missouri—St. Louis

Proves Banks
SUNY, College at Buffalo

Habib Bazyari
Mississippi State University

Eli Bernicar
Pacific Lutheran University

Elizabeth Booth
Louisiana State University

William Breitling
Keuka College

Darrell Brown
University of Montana—Missoula

Thomas Callarman
Arizona State University—Tempe

Mark Coffin
Virginia Polytechnic Institute and State University

Adriel Collazo
University of Puerto Rico

Charles Crain
Miami University

George Cucore
Cheyney University of Pennsylvania

James Dauer
Elmhurst College

Eliot Elfner
St. Norbert College

Farzaneh Fazel
Illinois State University

Brenda Geren
Cleveland State Community College

Cengiz Haksever
Rider College

George Harding
Wilmington College

Lynn Hardt
Buena Vista College

Mark Hartley
College of Charleston

Peter Haug
Western Washington University

Ray Haynes
California State Polytechnic University

John Hillman
University of Mary Hardin-Baylor

Robert Jacobs
Indiana University

Jae Kim
Walla Walla College

Dennis Kroll
Bradley University

John Langley, Jr
University of Tennessee

Philip Lee
Campbellville College

Sang Lee
University of Nebraska

Bob Leone
Boston University

Catherine Lerme
Boston College

Binshan Lin
*Louisiana State University—
Shreveport*

John Mansuv
Wheeling Jesuit College

Paul Marlin
Quincy College

Kevin McCarthy
Shippensburg University

Peter Meenan
Loyola College

Joyce Mehring
University of Massachusetts—Lowell

Larry Meile
Babson College

Hokie Min
Northeastern University

George Muncrief
Ollu-Houston Weekend College

Jerry Murphy
Portland State University

Joao Neves
Trenton State College

John Nicholas
Loyola University (Chicago)

Conor O'Muirgheasa
University of Houston

Bill Omurtag
University of Missouri—Rolla

Behrooz Parkhideh
*California State University—
Northridge*

Paul Rackow
Fordham University, Rose Hill Center

Linda Ravindranath
Moorhead State University

Joe Sarris
University of Texas—Arlington

Mike Savoie
University of Tampa

Vijay Shah
Kent State University

Syed Shahabuddin
Central Michigan University

Musaffar Shaikh
Florida Institute of Technology

Bruce Sherony
Northern Michigan University

Stephen Shmanske
California State University—Hayward

Victor Sower
Sam Houston State University

Theresa Speck
St. Mary's College (Minnesota)

John Steelquist
Chaminade University

Robert Stephens
Georgia Southwestern College

Larry Struck
Central Washington University

Charles Teplitz
University of San Diego

Billy Thornton
Colorado State University

Duane Trojniak
Mercy College

Chen-Hua Chung
University of Kentucky

Evert Van Der Heide
Calvin College

B. J. Wall
Middle Tennessee State University

Scott Wallace
Xavier University

Ruth Wang
*California State University—
Sacramento*

Peter Ward
Ohio State University

Philip Weatherford
Embry-Riddle Aeronautical University

Scott Webster
University of Wisconsin

Nancy Weida
Bucknell University

Howard Weiss
Temple University

Ron Williams
Park College

Craig Wood
University of New Hampshire

David Woodruff
University of California—Davis

Imad Zbib
Central Missouri State University

We recognize the contributions of John Weimeister, our editor, and Bill Schoof, our publisher. These two people supported, prodded, and directed our efforts. Without their support, this book would have never become a reality. John Weimeister, especially, played a significant role, never wavering in his view that we should create an interesting and exciting book. We also recognize the work of Michele Heinz, Karen Hill, Sue Langguth, Melissa Morgan, Kelly Spiller, Madeline Strong Diehl, David Talley, and Abby Westapher of Elm Street Publishing Services. These people had the challenging task of editing a large document and condensing and polishing it. This process was not easy because this book represents our philosophy and way of life.

We recognize all of the people with whom we shared the ideas and contents of this book: Randall Schaefer (Spartan Motors); students of Management 303,

Management 800, and Management 803 (Michigan State University) and the students at San Jose State University who reviewed and commented on preliminary versions of chapters from this book; Art Halstead (father-in-law to Steven A. Melnyk and informal reviewer); Rob Handfield (Michigan State University); Phil Carter (Center for Applied Research—National Association of Purchasing Managers); Larry Fredendall (Clemson University); Bill Wassweiler (The J.D. Edwards Company); Mark Pagell (doctoral student, Michigan State University); Lonnie Herman and Sue Polhamus (secretaries at Michigan State University); and Linn Van Dynn (Michigan State University).

Steven A. Melnyk
David R. Denzler
November 1995

About the Authors

Steven A. Melnyk, CPIM, is Professor of Operations Management at Michigan State University, where he also teaches in the university's Advanced Management Program, and was cited as an outstanding faculty member by *Business Week's Guide to the Best Business Schools.* His research interests include MRPII, tool management and control, shop floor control, time-based competition, and environmentally responsible manufacturing. A member of APICS and NAPM, he has consulted with over 60 companies and has taught in several European countries.

In 1995 he was awarded a major grant to study environmentally conscious manufacturing from the National Science Foundation, to be shared by Michigan State University's Colleges of Business and Engineering.

In addition to *Operations Management: A Value-Driven Approach,* he is the lead author of *Shop Floor Control; Production Activity Control: A Practical Guide; Shop Floor Control: Principles, Practices and Case Studies; Computer Integrated Manufacturing: A Source Book;* and *Computer Integrated Manufacturing: Guidelines and Applications from Industrial Leaders.* He is also the editor of *Production and Inventory Control,* the first work devoted entirely to the study of tooling.

Dr. Melnyk sits on the review board for *Production and Inventory Management* and *Journal of Operations Management,* and is software editor for *APICS: The Performance Advantage.* His articles have appeared in national and international journals.

David R. Denzler is Professor of Manufacturing Management at San Jose State University's College of Business, where he helped build the manufacturing management program in 1986. He received his BSME from Lafayette College and his MBA and DBA from Washington University. His academic teaching background includes Purdue University's Krannert School of Industrial Administration and the University of Iowa.

Dr. Denzler, who prefers being called "Dave," has also had considerable work experience, including stints with Combustion Engineering, Weyerhauser Paper, American Forest Products, Rod McLellan Company, and Grotek, "a wholly owned tragic start-up," according to Dave.

His research interests involve applying stimulation and mathematical programming to operations planning and scheduling; his teaching interests lie in global supply chain management and in product design and development.

Dave is happily married to Cheryl Van Clark and is the proud parent of three soon-to-be independent children.

Contents in Brief

Contents

■ C H A P T E R   4

Decision Making in Operations Management

PART THREE

Value as a Driver of OM Systems

■ CHAPTER 5

Processes: The Building Blocks of the Value-Driven OM System

■ CHAPTER 6

Managing the Human Resource 240

Snapshot of Reality 241

■ CHAPTER 7

Total Quality Management: Frameworks and Standards   290

■ CHAPTER 8

Total Quality Management: Tools and Techniques

PART FOUR
The Design of Value-Driven OM Systems   383

■ CHAPTER 9
Just-in-Time Operations Management   384

Human Resource Management

Limits to Just-in-Time Manufacturing

Just-in-Time Manufacturing and Lean Production

Characteristics of Lean Production

Case 9.1 Good Guy Hospital $upply

Case 9.2 Roboworks, Inc.

On the Job JIT Shoes Too Big for Allen-Edmonds

On the Job Stop-and-Fix at Chevy

Appendix 9A Total Productive Maintenance

Demand Management and Demand Forecasting

Taking It in the Shorts

Demand Management in Operations Management

Demand Management in Service Organizations

Demand Management in Manufacturing Organizations

Demand Management and Product Development

Market Information Systems for Demand Management

Five-Step Demand Forecasting Process

Forecasting as a Process

Qualitative Demand Forecasts

Understanding Final-Product Demand and Demand for Components

Case 10.1 Happiness Express

On the Job Compaq's Crystal Ball

■ CHAPTER 12

Designing the Delivery Process   546

Arco Strikes It Rich with Innovative Service Delivery   547

■ CHAPTER 15

Capacity Management 692

PART SEVEN

The Strategic Audit

■ CHAPTER 19

Future Challenges for Operations Managers

PART ONE

Operations Management

A Value-Driven Approach

CHAPTER ONE

Operations Management
A Field in Transition

CHAPTER OBJECTIVES

[At the end of this chapter, you should be able to]

- Define *operations management* and describe its contribution to the well-being of both the customer and the company
- Discuss the link between operations management and value
- List the forces for change in the operations management system
- Review the set of mental models or paradigms that underlie operations management and their role in change
- Outline the major tenets and beliefs that characterize today's operations management system
- Demonstrate the links between the operations management system and other systems within the firm.

Compaq Redefines Its Business

In 1992, Compaq Computer Corporation was a company poised for disaster—but top managers seemed to be the last to know. One of the industry's biggest success stories, Compaq had carved a secure niche with its state-of-the-art computers. Riding high from a decade of heady success, Compaq executives were slow to react when the company began to post losses in 1991.

The source of this challenge to Compaq's market dominance was no secret. Consumers were shunning Compaq's pricey, glamorous models and buying less expensive clones at discount stores or through catalogs. But when faced with the necessity of competing in this new cost-sensitive environment, Compaq executives dragged their feet. They told the chairman that they couldn't get a proposed new, low-priced model out the door until the first quarter of 1993. Meanwhile, they believed the consumer would eventually return to the high-end models that had made Compaq's reputation.

Compaq's chairman, Benjamin M. Rosen, didn't agree. Rosen was a veteran of the industry, and he could read the writing on the wall. Compaq had to act—and it had to act fast. In a move that later shocked many Compaq employees, Rosen secretly recruited two middle managers to evaluate how fast a competitive low-cost machine could be launched.

SOURCES

Michael Allen, "Bottom Fishing: Developing New Line of Low-Priced PCs Shakes Up Compaq," *The Wall Street Journal,* June 15, 1992, pp. A1, A4.

Kelley Damore, "Volatile Desktop Market Comes to a Close," *Computer Reseller News,* December 12, 1994, pp. 35–38.

Posing as entrepreneurs, Rosen's operatives attended a computer trade show. There they found that the right, low-cost components already existed for Compaq to begin producing its new machines almost immediately.

Rosen's response was quick and decisive. First he fired Joseph R. "Rod" Canion, Compaq's cofounder and chief executive. Within the year, Compaq launched several models with prices under $1,000—beating such low-end rivals as Dell Computer Corporation at their own game. At the end of 1994, Compaq had regained its position as the number-one seller of desktop computers in the nation, shipping 4.8 million PCs worldwide.

For Compaq Computers, 1992 was an important year. It brought the shake-up of top management, along with a growing recognition that the firm's market had changed. Compaq had long claimed technological and quality leadership in the personal computer (PC) industry. Consistent with this assumption, most engineers and marketing people in the company denied that low-cost, low-quality products from clone makers such as Samsung and Packard-Bell could ever compete directly with Compaq.

Instead, the people at Compaq found themselves dislodged as the technological and quality leaders in the PC industry. The producers of low-cost clones often made machines of equal or better quality. Furthermore, the clone suppliers could also provide parts such as mother boards and hard drives faster, at lower cost, and with quality levels equal to or higher than those from existing Compaq suppliers or from Compaq's own factory. Mr. Rosen and others at Compaq learned that the company was no longer delivering the highest value to its customers.

This revelation forced them to reexamine the needs of customers and to redefine the attributes that a Compaq PC should offer. As a result, people at Compaq had to rethink the entire process of designing, building, and delivering personal computers. They had to change their manufacturing process to make it more efficient. They had to shift the emphasis of their operations management system technological leadership to value leadership.

By 1994, the changes that Compaq had considered in 1992 had begun to yield real benefits. Managers had succeeded in developing a truly value-driven operations management system that contributed to achievement of corporate objectives.

These changes are not unique to Compaq. Rather, they reflect a fundamental change in the way firms must sell to customers and the way they must design, build, and deliver products. As a result of these changes, many companies such as Compaq, IBM, Taco Bell, and Ford have had to rethink their operations management systems. This revelation has created a new way of looking at operations management. In this chapter, we introduce the field of operations management and the basics of this new view of the field.

To this end, we develop the following themes:

- Operations management is a business function concerning how firms make and provide goods and services.
- Operations management brings together three elements: customers/stakeholders, processes, and capacity.

- Operations management is fundamentally dynamic because it reacts to changes in underlying paradigms or mental models.
- The new model of operations management is based on value.
- This new model has important implications for analysis, management, design, control, and evaluation of the operations management system.

The rest of the book explores and expands on these themes. Understanding these ideas promotes a better understanding of why managers at Compaq needed to reinvent the firm and its operations management system. The rest of this book shows that operations management is not simply the study of making things; rather it is the dynamic study of how managers can consistently generate better value for customers.

WHAT IS OPERATIONS MANAGEMENT?

Operations management (OM) is a field of study that tries to understand, explain, predict, and change the organizational and strategic effects of the transformation process. In other words, OM deals with the effective and efficient management of the transformation process.

Effectiveness focuses on the extent to which the outputs of the transformation process satisfy the needs and expectations of customers in a way that contributes to the overall objectives and goals of the company. To evaluate effectiveness, managers ask, did we build something that the customer really wanted and deliver that product in a way that helped the firm to compete in the marketplace? **Efficiency** depends on costs incurred to deliver outputs; managers ask, how does the value of the inputs consumed to provide the output compare with the value or cost of the output? Effectiveness deals with issues of customer satisfaction and strategic positioning; efficiency concerns matters such as productivity, cost control, and variance analysis.

Effectiveness is *externally* evaluated. Customers, current and potential, assess the acceptability of the firm's products and its OM function. Chapter 2 will show how to measure effectiveness in terms of the *value* generated for the customer. In contrast, efficiency is often *internally* measured. Managers establish criteria against which to assess the performance of the OM function. They measure efficiency in such units as dollars or labor hours. Effectiveness is necessary for long-term survival; efficiency is important to short-term survival.

Exhibit 1.1 provides a good example of efficiency measures. The table compares the worker hours and dollars that different companies need to build cars. Efficiency ignores how well these cars really match what customers want, however.

An organization's transformation process creates at least two types of outputs: *physical goods* and *services*. A later section of the chapter discusses the differences between these outputs in greater detail.

operations management
A field of study that tries to understand, explain, predict, and change the organizational and strategic effects of the transformation process

effectiveness
The extent to which the outputs of a transformation process satisfy the needs and expectations of customers in a way that contributes to the overall objectives and goals of the company

efficiency
A measure of costs incurred to deliver outputs as compared with the value or cost of the outputs

"Effectiveness is doing the right things, whereas efficiency is doing things right."

Daniel Stamp, founder, Priority Management Systems

CUSTOMER, PROCESS, AND CAPACITY: FOUNDATIONS OF THE OM SYSTEM

Operations management integrates three major components into a cohesive and mutually supporting entity: customer, process, and capacity (see Exhibit 1.2).

[**E X H I B I T   1 . 1**]

Efficiency in Per-Unit Production Costs

In addition to labor and parts, total cost includes other manufacturing costs and non-manufacturing costs.

Company	Worker Hours	Labor Costs	Purchased Parts	Total Costs
Ford	50	$1,629	$3,066	$5,415
Chrysler	60	1,872	3,150	5,841
Toyota	36	928	4,124	6,126
Honda	40	1,031	4,346	6,618
Nissan	43	1,118	4,346	6,782
Mazda	45	1,161	4,346	6,826
General Motors	75	2,388	3,677	7,205

> " There is only one boss. The customer. And he can fire everybody in the company from the chairman on down, simply by spending his money somewhere else. "
>
> Sam Walton, founder, Wal-Mart

customer

Anyone who consumes the outputs of an OM system

Customer

The **customer** is anyone who consumes the outputs of the OM system. The customer is both a critical starting point and an ending point for the operations management system. Unless the firm has clearly identified its market segment and the customers in that segment, it cannot structure an effective or efficient operations management function. Knowledge of the customer allows a manager to accurately describe the firm's customers, what they want, what they are willing to pay, what they do not consider acceptable, and what they view as minimum acceptable levels of performance. This information helps the OM manager to design and run the OM system by identifying:

order winner

A trait in which the firm (and its OM function) must perform well relative to competitors to win orders

order qualifier

A trait in which the firm (and its OM function) must perform acceptably to be considered as a candidate to fill an order

order loser

A trait in which poor performance by the firm (and its OM function) can cause losses of current or future business

- **Order winners**[1]   Traits in which the firm and the OM function must perform well relative to competitors to win orders in the market. Order winners define how a firm wins orders and what the firm and its OM system must do well
- **Order qualifiers**   Traits such as lead times, cost, or quality in which the firm must perform acceptably to be considered as a candidate to fill a customer's order
- **Order losers**   Traits in which poor performance by the firm and its operations management function can cause losses of either current or future business

Order winners and order qualifiers form the basis for customers' expectations. The firm markets itself to customers by appealing to order winners and order qualifiers. Order losers, in contrast, result from customers' actual experiences with the firm and its OM process. They represent the gap between what the firm delivers and what customers expect. To understand the differences between these three kinds of traits, consider an example.

At midday, you decide that you need a quick lunch. You have only $6.00 and 45 minutes for lunch. Since you have captured one of the prized parking spots on campus, you would rather not have to drive anywhere. You could choose among several restaurants, some close and others far away. Some offer good meals, but slow service; others offer mediocre fast food. To decide, you first list all of your

[1]Terry Hill, *Manufacturing Strategy: Text and Cases* (Homewood, Ill.: Richard D. Irwin, 1989).

[EXHIBIT 1.2]

Major Components of the OM System

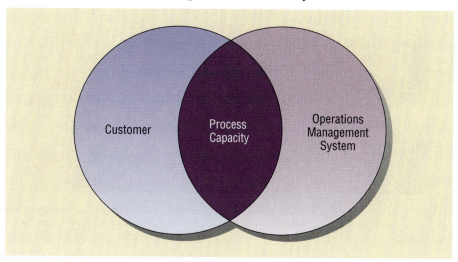

requirements for a restaurant. It must be close (within walking distance) with quick service and good, inexpensive food. You might also need a table since you will bring a book to read. These characteristics are the order qualifiers; you won't eat at any restaurant that does not satisfy them.

The analysis leaves a list of three possible restaurants. One offers hamburgers, fries, and so-so salads; another offers cheap Mexican food; the third sells pizza with a salad bar. Since you don't feel like eating heavy, you decide to have a salad at the third restaurant. You base your selection on the need for a light meal. That trait was the order winner.

When you go to the restaurant, you find the service slow and the food poorly prepared. As you leave, you promise yourself that you will never eat there again. The restaurant's poor food quality and service become order losers.

Once the firm delivers a product to the customer, he or she ultimately determines how well the system actually works and what areas need improvement as well as areas that require no significant change. The firm gains such information by soliciting feedback. This feedback can come from formal customer evaluations, customer complaints, repeat business, benchmarking (comparing its own products with the best in its target market), or external reviews by information providers like *Consumer Reports* or the J. D. Power rankings of car quality. However the firm gathers information, it becomes feedback for the OM system, identifying what the system is doing well and flagging potential problem areas. It also forms a basis for system revision and modification.

Ideally, the design, structure, and operation of the operations management function should accurately reflect what customers want and do not want. A system that has run in synch with what the customers have wanted in the past may no longer suit customers' current needs. This possibility became very real in the Compaq scenario presented at the start of this chapter. Before the 1992 shake-up, Compaq's operations management system was designed to deliver state-of-the-art technology to customers at premium prices. The system was not focused on such issues as lead time and cost, yet customers wanted competitively priced,

Since this man is not employed by the manufacturer of the product he is about to purchase, he is an external customer. Internal customers use the output of other departments within the producing firm.
SOURCE   M. Richards/PhotoEdit

high-quality products delivered quickly. Compaq's existing system could not meet those needs. The firm required a change in the structure and implementation of its operations management system.

Identifying Interested Parties.   Most people tend to associate the term *customer* with people who buy or use the outputs of the operations management system. This leads to the assumption that only customers become interested in the operations management system and its functions. However, different types of customers and other parties develop interests in an OM system's operation. Customers are individuals or groups of people (e.g., companies) who are interested in the output of the operations management system. They can be differentiated according to whether they are internal or external to the firm.

Internal versus External Customers.   People often think of producers and customers on a broad scale. Companies such as McDonald's, Kellogg, and Steelcase often represent producers, and consumers are individual people. However, within Kellogg or Steelcase, producers serve consumers. For example, a worker in the Seating Division of Steelcase, Inc. assembles office chairs. That worker needs upholstered seat cushions and seat backs from the upholstery department and chair frames from the metal fabrication department. The worker who assembles the chair is an internal customer consuming outputs from both the upholstery and metal fabrication departments. In turn, the assembler produces products (chairs) for internal customers in the shipping department of Steelcase. An **internal customer** is anyone who uses the output of another area or department within the producing firm.

In contrast, an **external customer** is anyone outside the boundaries of the producing firm who uses or buys its output. In the Steelcase example, a purchasing agent at Ford or an office supply store in Indianapolis might represent external customers. They use the output of Steelcase (the chair) while remaining outside Steelcase's corporate boundaries.

internal customer
Anyone who uses the output of another area or department within the producing firm

external customer
Anyone outside the corporate boundaries of the producing firm who uses its output

Producers often find it useful to differentiate external customers between intermediate customers and final customers. An intermediate customer buys the producer's output or interacts with it, but may not use it. Steelcase would view both the Ford purchasing agent and the shipping firm that transported the chair from its plant in Grand Rapids to Ford's offices in Oakville, Ontario, as intermediate customers. The person who finally sits in the chair is the final customer. The demands of intermediate customers may differ from those of final customers.

Linking internal customers to intermediate and then final, external customers gives a chain of customers. As one of its key objectives, the operations management system must identify and satisfy the needs and expectations of the customers in this chain.

Customers versus Stakeholders.   Compaq may serve a customer who buys a portable personal computer from a ComputerLand or MicroAge store for personal use. Another Compaq customer could be a firm that wants to supply all of its salespeople with portable personal computers to help them do their work out in the field. Customers buy more than physical products. Some buy capacity while others buy expertise; others buy access to the firm's entire delivery system.

Besides internal and external customers and intermediate and final customers, firms serve several other types of customers. *Current customers* are people who currently buy from the company. *Potential customers* represent a new market segment. This group may also include people who might benefit from new types of products or functions that a firm's system could provide.

A **stakeholder**, in contrast to a customer, is any person or group of people with an interest in the functions of an operations management system or firm and its well-being (financial and otherwise). Of the different types of stakeholders, five are the most important:

stakeholder
Any person or group with an interest in the firm and its well-being.

- *Financial stakeholders*   These stakeholders provide the firm needed financial resources. Stockholders, banks, and Wall Street investment firms are examples of financial stakeholders. These groups are interested in assessing the firm's strength as an investment and whether the firm provides its stockholders with an acceptable rate of return on their investments.

- *Resource stakeholders*   These stakeholders resemble financial stakeholders in that they provide needed resources. However, resource stakeholders provide physical resources (e.g., labor, materials, and equipment). A worker who provides labor and a supplier who provides access to its capacity and the parts produced by this capacity are the most common examples of this type of stakeholder. They become interested in the firm because they must decide whether to provide access to their resources. A potential employee may evaluate the firm to decide whether or not to accept a job offer; a supplier may evaluate the firm to decide whether or not to continue selling to it on credit.

- *Community stakeholders*   These stakeholders come from the community in which the firm and the operations management system operate. These people assess the firm's corporate citizenship and its contribution to the community and its surroundings. This group is interested in such issues as the level of employment, potential problems with pollution, and potential disruptions to the community (e.g., traffic jams and increased demands on community resources). They may also view the firm as a source of tax revenues and a consumer of community resources (e.g., water, waste management system, and tax breaks).

- *Societal stakeholders*   These stakeholders consider the effect of the firm's system on larger social goals. These goals can take the form of reductions in pollution, the production of safer products, employment opportunities for minorities, reductions in animal suffering, or preservation of endangered resources such as the Amazon rain forests.
- *Government stakeholders*   Units of government at the local, state/provincial, and national levels become stakeholders when they affect or shape the operations management function and its supervision. A government stakeholder has its greatest impact on the OM system when it acts either as a regulator or as an evaluator. As a regulator, the government establishes the rules and regulations under which the OM system must function. It identifies minimum acceptable standards for performance, and it limits what the firm can and cannot do. For example, the government defines criteria for a safe working environment. It also ensures that firms provide such environments for their employees.

The distinction between stakeholders and customers becomes blurred when stakeholders become consumers. For example, consider Ciba-Geigy, headquartered in Basel, Switzerland, a major chemical and pharmaceutical manufacturer that operates worldwide. Recently, under the leadership of its chairman, Heini Lippuner, it has begun to transform itself into an ethically and environmentally aware firm. This change in corporate orientation can be traced to the impact of its stakeholders, including employees and customers throughout the world. These stakeholders want to deal with and buy from a company that recognizes its responsibility to others and to the environment. These stakeholders have prompted Lippuner to lead Ciba-Geigy to develop a new vision for the company known as Vision 2000. The company is now working to disseminate throughout the world, both within the company and among its customers, a statement of its vision of what Ciba-Geigy must do to survive through 2000 and beyond:

> By striking a balance between our economic, social, and environmental responsibilities, we want to ensure the prosperity of our enterprise beyond the year 2000.
>
> We aim to generate appropriate financial results through sustainable growth and constant renewal of a balanced business structure, so that we justify the confidence of all those who rely on our company—stockholders, employees, business partners, and the public. We will not put our long-term future in danger by taking short-term profits.
>
> Ciba-Geigy is open and trustworthy toward society. Through our business activities we wish to make a worthwhile contribution to the solution of global issues and to the progress of mankind.
>
> Respect for the environment must be part of everything we do. We design products and processes to fulfill their purposes safely and with as little environmental impact as possible. We use natural resources and energy in the best possible way and reduce waste in all forms. It is our duty to dispose safely of all unavoidable waste using state-of-the-art technologies.[2]

Why differentiate between customers and stakeholders? Firms recognize that stakeholders and their demands or actions often influence the OM system and the operations manager. This book will focus primarily on customers. However, managers must remember the role of stakeholders. Like customers, stakeholders can significantly affect not only how the firm defines *value*, but also how it designs, implements, controls, and revises its processes and its capacity.

---

[2]James E. Liebig, *Merchants of Vision* (San Francisco, Calif.: Berrett-Koehler, 1994), pp. 83–84.

Major Components of a Process

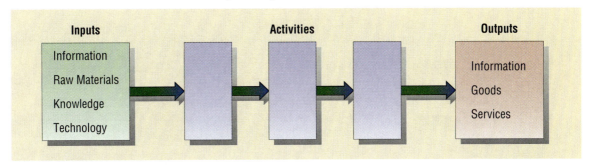

Once managers know what customers they serve and what those customers want from the operations management process, they can proceed to design a method of satisfying those demands and expectations. That design effort represents the second component of operations management—process.

Process

The firm's **process** is the sequence and organization (either formal or informal) of all activities it needs to convert inputs into outputs. A process draws together inputs, transformation activities, and outputs into a unified system (Exhibit 1.3). It identifies the resources that activities need (e.g., machines, material, labor, and information) and specifies stages at which the resources are needed and in what quantities. A process also describes the activities needed to convert inputs into outputs. For example, we use a stove and heat to convert a raw hamburger patty (an input) into a cooked hamburger (an output). Other activities transport or move items from one area to another. Still other activities store raw materials, work-in-process (begun but unfinished outputs), or completed work. Finally, some activities check or inspect work to make sure that it meets standards for quality, quantity, lead time, or timing.

Operations management processes can involve the production of a physical good or service. Workers follow processes to build chairs or give haircuts. Processes can also generate information. After placing an order for a book, you may call the bookstore to check on the status of your order. The storekeeper consults records to find that your book has just been shipped. This exchange produces no product or service, but it follows a process. The output of this process is information.

Every operations management system consists of processes. Some processes generate goods and services that firms sell to customers (resource management processes); others plan the next generation of goods and services or their associated processes (innovation processes) or plan where the firm as a whole should go (strategic management processes). Still others measure resources (measurement processes) or coordinate activities between a firm and its suppliers (supply-chain management processes). Exhibit 1.4 summarizes the various processes with strong links to the operations management system.

How operations managers structure processes influences the ability of the firm to serve its customers. We have all experienced organizations with complex, bureaucratic processes that seem incapable of providing a desired service in a timely manner.

process
The sequence and organization of all activities needed to convert inputs into outputs

Major Processes Linked to Operations Management

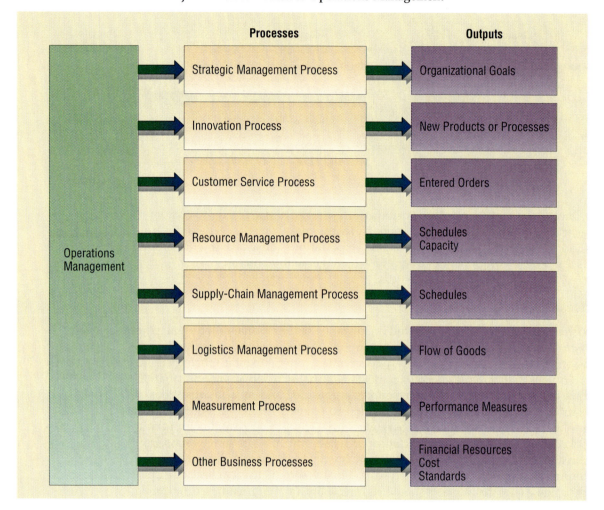

The design of a process should reflect what the customer wants. If the customer prizes quick response, then the process should be designed to respond quickly. Managers must identify and eliminate unnecessary or redundant steps, reduce distances between steps or activities, and diminish the time needed to complete each step.

This need for a fit between the process and the customer has important effects. It implies that if the customer changes, then the process might also have to change. This is the lesson that Compaq learned and the major reason for that company's shake-up.

Processes for Physical Goods versus Services.   Traditionally, the output of the operations management process has been described as either a good or a service. These two types of outputs are differentiated by the product's tangible or intangible nature. Exhibit 1.5 summarizes the differences between goods and services.

[**EXHIBIT 1.5**]

Characteristics of Goods and Services

Goods	Services
Tangible	Intangible
Can be inventoried	Cannot be inventoried
Little customer contact (separate consumption and production)	Extensive customer contact (simultaneous consumption and production)
Long lead times	Short lead times
Capital intensive	Labor intensive
Quality easily assess	Quality very difficult to assess

Goods.   A **good** is tangible, that is, it has a definite physical presence; it can be touched and stored (inventoried), and the firm can produce it in advance of customer demand. The book that you are now reading, your car, the television that you watch at night after you finish studying—these are all goods. The decision to produce goods affects the design and implementation of the operations management system in several ways.

good
A tangible product

First, because they can inventory goods, operations managers can separate the consumer of the product from the place where the firm produces it. Packard-Bell assembles its personal computers in Sacramento, California. From there, it can deliver the good to a customer in Albany, New York. Firms can locate manufacturing plants where it makes sense. For example, the first steel plants were located in the Pittsburgh, Pennsylvania, area for proximity to sources of iron ore and coal, two critical ingredients in steel.

Production of goods requires little contact with the customer. Firms often produce fairly standardized goods in advance of customer orders so they can respond quickly to orders.

The manufacturing processes for goods typically are very capital intensive, with machines working to make products. For example, in an auto assembly plant, robots attach windows to cars, and transfer lines move cars from one operation to another. The combination of a capital-intensive process and physical separation between the customer and the manufacturing process often results in long lead times.

Finally, operations managers can relatively easily establish quality standards for tangible goods and measure the products against these standards. For example, they can evaluate whether the good works (functionality), how long it works (reliability), how it operates under adverse conditions (durability), whether is it safe to use (safety), and how it appears (aesthetics). After setting standards for each of these traits, managers determine whether or not newly produced units meet the standards. A manufacturer of PCs can test the functionality of new units by turning on their power switches. If they boot up and operate correctly, they pass the functionality test. A car builder interested in aesthetics can measure the gaps between body panels to see if they fall within acceptable limits and examine paint jobs to ensure that the paint is uniformly applied.

Services.   In contrast to goods, **services** have no physical form. They are intangible. For example, at a restaurant, you buy not only food, but also the atmosphere in

service
An intangible product

which you eat. Because services are intangible, they cannot be stored. While goods manufacturing systems can accumulate and distribute inventory to smooth out imbalances between supply and demand, a producer of services must maintain enough production capacity to meet demand during peak periods. Otherwise, it must backlog the demand. When you go into a restaurant during its busy time, the greeter may ask you to wait in the lounge; you become part of a backlog of demand (i.e., customers sitting in the lounge, waiting to be served).

Because producers cannot inventory services, the production and consumption of the service must occur at the same time. In addition, the production process is often very visible to the customer. Customers observe the operation of the process and its structure because it routes them from one operation to another until they are served and sent on their way. The link between consumption and production tends to keep lead times shorter than those for tangible goods. If the lead times are long, customers are likely to leave the process without consuming the service. In other words, a long lead time can become an order loser.

Furthermore, service production often relies extensively on contact with the customer. Customers play a very important role in the delivery of a service, telling servers what they want, when they want it, and how they want the service delivered. As a result, production systems for services tend to be more flexible than manufacturing systems. Many restaurants encourage patrons to choose how their hamburgers are cooked.

Quality control is more difficult for services than for goods. Managers cannot really measure a service product and its attributes as they can in a manufacturing setting. After all, the product is intangible. Rather than evaluating products, service providers tend to evaluate methods of delivery. Because services are very labor intensive, managers evaluate how workers deliver the service to the customer. For example, a quality control inspector for McDonald's studies how counter workers greet customers who arrive to place orders, how they take orders, how they fill orders, and how they close out transactions (i.e., what they say when they give food to customers). This process defines quality to the service customer.

Because quality lies in the process, and given the labor-intensive nature of services, it becomes important to train workers in people skills (i.e., how to interact with customers) and how to deliver the service to customers.

Products.   Later in this chapter, the discussion of the total product experience will demonstrate that the boundary between goods and services is blurring. For this reason, we will refer to the output of any process as a **product**. This term covers both goods and services.

product

The output of any process (either a good or a service)

Capacity

capacity

What the firm can do effectively and efficiently

While processes describe how an operations management system works, **capacity** determines how much of what the system produces. To most people, *capacity* means how much output a firm can produce, often defined as a level of output per unit of time. This view of capacity, while important, is not comprehensive. It ignores the specific capabilities of the OM system and of the firm as a whole. The type of capacity, which results from a combination of equipment, work flows, and employee skill levels, determines what the firm can do efficiently and effectively and what it can do only poorly or not at all.

To understand capacity, compare Burger King and McDonald's. Burger King cooks in a flame-broiling process while McDonald's cooks on a grill. Burger King can offer you a flame-broiled hamburger; McDonald's cannot. However, because

McDonald's cooks on a grill, it can offer you pancakes in the morning; Burger King cannot. These differences result directly from the type of capacity that each company has. They may produce identical volume, but the capabilities inherent in that volume differ.

Each of the three components of operations management—customer, process, and capacity—is critical in creating an effective and efficient OM system. These elements are tightly interrelated. The manager faces the task of developing consistency and fit among these three elements. The type of process and the type and amount of capacity must support the needs of customers. Managers must align the operations management system with what customers want.

CHANGING PARADIGMS FOR CHANGING TIMES: OPERATIONS MANAGEMENT IN THE 21ST CENTURY

So far, we have defined *operations management* and identified some of its major elements. We have not yet really dealt with change like Compaq's need to redefine its operations management system. This need requires a new concept—the paradigm.

Operations management and management in general, consists of at least two elements. The first is general tools, procedures, and systems that define the overall framework of management. Customer, process, and capacity are the constants of operations management. A redefined operations management system must still define processes, serve customers, and draw on capacity. Specific applications of these tools, procedures, and systems are strongly influenced by the second element: underlying paradigms.

Paradigm Defined

Paradigms are critical to all firms and all operations managers. Stated in the simplest terms, **paradigms** are mental models or frameworks of thought. They represent sets of rules and regulations (either written or unwritten) through which managers view, understand, and interact with the world around them.[3] Paradigms define the perspectives from which managers evaluate, operate, and change the tasks of the OM function. Paradigms establish underlying belief structures for managers, and they set in place unstated but critical assumptions on which managers base decisions and actions. They help managers to identify what is acceptable and, more importantly, what is not acceptable. Paradigms also form the basis for value structures and beliefs.

paradigm
A mental model or framework of thought

Although OM managers have only recently become aware of the importance of paradigms, scientists have long understood their power. Science has realized that the universe changes only when the paradigms on which it is based change. The "By the Way" box discusses the importance of paradigms.

Compaq experienced the effects of a change in paradigms. It replaced old paradigms, or mental frameworks that it had relied on with a new set of paradigms. The new paradigms made the old ones obsolete. This observation is not new; others in such varied fields as science and college football have also experienced these changes (See the "On the Job" box).

---

[3]Joel Arthur Barker, *Paradigms: The Business of Discovering the Future* (New York: Harper Business, 1992), p. 32.

[BY THE WAY... POWER OF PARADIGMS]

You are what you know. Fifteenth-century Europeans "knew" that the sky was made of closed concentric crystal spheres, rotating around a central earth and carrying the stars and planets. That "truth" structured everything they did and thought, because it told them the truth. Then Galileo's telescope changed the truth.

As a result, 100 years later everybody "knew" that the universe was open and infinite, working like a giant clock. Architecture, music, literature, science, economics, art, politics—everything changed, mirroring the new world view created by the change in knowledge.

Today we live according to the latest version of how the universe functions. This view affects our behavior and thought, just as previous versions affected those who lived with them. Like the people of the past, we disregard phenomena that do not fit our view because they are "wrong" or outdated. Like our ancestors, we know the real truth.

At any time in the past, people have held a view of the way the universe works which was for them similarly definitive, whether it was based on myths or research. And at any time, that view they held was sooner or later altered by changes in the body of knowledge.

SOURCE   James Burke, *The Day the Universe Changed* (Boston, Mass.: Little, Brown, 1985), p. 9.

Rethinking Operations Management

" May you live in interesting times. "

Old Chinese Curse

Interesting times can seem like a curse because they often bring change and chaos. They are times when the old ways of doing things no longer apply and people need new approaches and perspectives. Compaq very evidently faced interesting times. The tactics and strategies that had made Compaq a success in the 1980s became inadequate in the changing times of the 1990s. In the field of operations management, interesting times require managers to rethink how they manage entire systems. This challenge is not unique to Compaq; other companies such as Boeing, Xerox, and Chrysler all face similar challenges.

In the 1990s, attention has focused more sharply on operations management topics such as quality, speed (in the form of time-based competition), and flexibility. As a result, the heroes of American industry are no longer firms that have generated the largest profits or sales increases. The new heroes are firms that have developed and implemented systems to achieve world-class levels of quality. These firms, such as Xerox, the Cadillac Division of General Motors, and Motorola, can compete, not only against the best in America, but against the best in the world.

The new heroes also include firms that have discovered the secret of speed. These firms have learned to develop new products faster and bring these products to the marketplace more quickly than their closest competitors. Other new heroes have reduced the time that they need to respond to customer orders. Hewlett-Packard has reduced the time it needs to develop and introduce new laser printers by over 50 percent—from 4.5 years to 22 months.[4] Intel, under chief executive officer Andrew Grove, now plans to introduce a new line of microprocessor chips every 2 years.[5] Motorola has reduced its delivery time for pagers

[4]Brian Dumaine, "How Managers Can Succeed through Speed," *Fortune,* February 13, 1989, pp. 54–59.
[5]Robert D. Hof, "Inside Intel," *Business Week,* June 1, 1992, pp. 86–94.

ON THE JOB

Paradigm Changes in College Football

When the small, no-name Catholic college took on the U.S. Military Academy in the fall of 1913, everyone fully expected Army to pull off yet another rout. The Black Knights on the Hudson (Army) were so formidable that they had trouble finding opponents, and the November 1 game promised to be a real yawner. Only second-rate reporters were sent to cover it, and some of them didn't even get Notre Dame's home town right. In their reports home, some sportswriters called it "South Bend, Illinois."

Army's team perfectly embodied the football strategy of its time, and it was considered practically unbeatable. In 1913, the primary offensive weapon was the run, and Army had the run down to a science. Quarterbacks were not the stars of the game like they are now—indeed, their main job at the time was handing off the ball to the runners. In 1913 quarterbacks had become so expendable that there was even talk of dropping the position altogether to make room for another running back.

Army dominated by virtue of its size—it had huge linemen to protect its runners and punch holes in the opponent's defense. Offense or defense, Army's game was the same—big linemen who played close up on the line. But Army's impenetrable line became a liability the minute the small, no-name college from the Midwest introduced its secret weapon. Late in the first half of the game, Notre Dame's quarterback, Gus Dorais, fired off a forward pass to a receiver named Knute Rockne, and the universe of football changed forever.

All David ever needed against Goliath was the right stone. Army's giant linemen were completely unable to protect their team against Notre Dame's forward pass. Again and again, Notre Dame completed passes, leaving Army's defense in tatters. Army's coaches panicked, trying in vain to get the passes ruled illegal. When Army finally tried to adjust to Notre Dame's passing game, Notre Dame used the pass to set up a running game. Army's linemen were baffled, without a clue. Meanwhile, Army's offense had become so totally predictable that Notre Dame's defense was a cinch.

When the dust finally settled, Notre Dame had beat Army by a score of 35 to 13, and the paradigm of college football had changed forever. Pretty soon the words "Notre Dame" shot fear into the hearts of college players everywhere, and *everybody* knew that South Bend was in Indiana!

SOURCE   Michael R. Steele, *Knute Rockne: A Bio-Bibliography* (Westport, Conn.: Greenwood Press, 1983), pp. 12–13.

from 3 weeks to 2 hours. Exhibit 1.6 lists other, similarly successful companies located in Europe.

Increasingly, managers, researchers, writers, and even government officials are educating North Americans about the strong link between manufacturing (one of the major forms of operations management) and the nation's economic health. People now realize that a nation needs a strong operations management/manufacturing function for a strong, dynamic, and vibrant economy.

Beginning with the Industrial Revolution, the United States was tremendously successful in developing mass manufacturing. In the 1990s, however, U.S. industry faces aggressive and efficient competitors from Japan, South Korea, Singapore, Germany, and Taiwan. These new competitors have succeeded not because they can rely on low-cost labor or abundant, low-cost capital. Rather, their success has come from their approach to the operations management problem. Instead of focusing on such traditional paradigms as large-scale production and cost reduction, these competitors have introduced new procedures and approaches such as

[EXHIBIT 1.6]

Successes in Europe

- Olivetti (typewriter production)—Throughput time reduced from 20 days to 3 days
- Michelin (steel cord)—Setup time reduced by 90 percent
- Uno a Erre (world leader in gold jewelry)—Production lead time reduced by 90 percent
- Fia Aviazione (parts for aircraft engines)—Lead time reduced by 50 percent
- Farmitalia Carlo Erba (pharmaceuticals)—Work-in-process reduced by 60 percent
- Lever Industries (detergents)—Working capital reduced by 50 percent
- Innocentia S. Eustachio (manufacturing equipment)—Lead time reduced by 30 percent

SOURCE   Giorgio Merli, *Total Manufacturing* (Cambridge, Mass.: Productivity Press, 1990), p. xxviii. English translation copyright © 1990 by Productivity Press, Inc., P. O. Box 13390, Portland, OR 97213-0390, (800) 394-6868. Reprinted by permission.

" To cherish traditions, old buildings, ancient cultures and graceful lifestyles is a worthy thing—but in the world of technology to cling to outmoded methods of manufacture, old product lines, old markets, or old attitudes among management and workers is a prescription for suicide. "

Sir Leuan Maddock, 1982
(Quoted in Richard N. Foster,
*Innovation: The Attacker's
Advantage* [New York: Summit
Books, 1986], p. 25.)

system simplification, *kaizen* or continuous improvement, total quality control, and just-in-time (JIT) manufacturing. These new developments, examined in greater detail in later chapters of this book, encourage managers to develop operations management systems that can meet or exceed customer expectations and desires. Instead of relying on new technology, automation, and computers, these new developments try to simplify systems. To compete against these new competitors, firms need new approaches and perspectives. The push to develop such perspectives has become part of the challenge facing the North American operations management student in 1995 and beyond.

BASIC BELIEFS OF THE NEW OPERATIONS MANAGEMENT FRAMEWORK

Certain basic beliefs underlie the new OM frameworks. This section discusses some of the most important tenets of the new frameworks.

- Operations management is ultimately responsible for the product delivered to the customer and the experience felt by the customer.
- Value, not cost, is critical to the success not only of the operations management function, but of the firm as a whole.
- People are critical to the success not only of the operations management function, but of the firm as a whole.
- The system is more than the sum of its parts.
- Prize simplicity; avoid unnecessary complexity.
- Systems can change if management wants them to change.

Value

It is not enough simply to meet the expectations of the customer. To succeed, firms must exceed these expectations. As Hal Mather, a well-known manufacturing consultant puts it, they must learn how to profitably delight their customers.

Traditionally, operations management has focused on cost. Every activity within the operations management function generates costs in some form. These costs are often identified and reported in dollar units. As a product moves through each stage in the OM process, activities increase costs. Workers withdraw raw materials from stores and add them to the product; workers use machine time; managers assign labor; the process consumes energy. To evaluate success, managers measure costs against the revenues. If revenues exceed costs, they conclude that the product and the operations management system have generated a positive income flow for the firm.

Most firms assign this accumulation and reporting of cost-related information to the accounting function. This may imply that price is outside the control of the operations manager and that this manager can influence only cost control and reduction. As a result, OM practitioners have long worked under the premise that they can improve corporate performance directly only by reducing costs. Larger reductions in cost mean better performance of the OM function and the firm.

Operations managers are now reevaluating the importance of cost. They understand that focusing on cost first and foremost can create problems. To reduce costs, a manager can decide not to spend money on such investments as preventive maintenance. As the condition of the equipment inevitably deteriorates, quality problems arise, overall costs increase, and lead times grow. To reduce costs further, the manager might invest less money in employee training and education, leaving workers less effective at dealing with problems they encounter on the shop floor. To save still more money, the firm may employ fewer workers, leaving remaining workers to cover the same work. Workers rush to finish, reducing quality even further. This sequence degenerates into a cost-driven vicious circle. It becomes increasingly clear that a product with the lowest cost is not always the most attractive to every buyer.

Rather, different people desire different characteristics in goods and services. Some customers view cost as less important than speed. When these people place orders, they expect to receive their goods quickly. Still others prize high quality. These people spend their time reading *Consumer Reports* and *Consumer Digest* before placing any order, looking for the product that offers the highest level of quality per dollar spent. Others are interested in flexibility; they want things done their way.

These various views of what makes a good or service acceptable or highly desirable to the customer fall together under the umbrella of **value**. Value, as Chapter 2 explains, is the customer's subjective evaluation, adjusted for cost, of how well a product meets or exceeds expectations. Operations managers now recognize their task as helping their firms to win new customers and retain existing customers by continually providing products that offer the highest levels of value to customers.

value
The customer's subjective evaluation, adjusted for cost, of how well a product meets or exceeds expectations

In accepting the need for a value-driven OM function, the operations manager must recognize certain realities. First, value is ultimately defined and assessed by the customer. As a result, the OM function and the firm need a clear idea of the specific group of customers they want to serve. The firm must always stay in touch with its customers.

Also, value is dynamic. Perceptions of value may change as a result of many factors: competitors' actions, government regulations, or changing customer preferences. For example, Wendy's was the first fast-food restaurant to introduce the drive-through window on a large scale. Competitors quickly copied this innovation. The operations manager must anticipate these changes in the definition of value and prepare to meet the new needs by changing the existing OM system, if necessary.

The opposite of value is waste. Any action that does not contribute to value may add to waste. Value and waste have come to drive the OM function.

Obvious value issued characterized the Compaq case presented at the start of this chapter. Compaq managers faced a change in customers' views of value. Compaq began in the early 1980s as the first company to offer a 100 percent IBM-compatible microcomputer. During this period, compatibility was critical to

Compaq's customers. They bought Compaq's products because the machines offered value. Over time, however, other producers of microcomputers, microprocessor chips, and computer components duplicated this capability. As a result, Compaq shifted its focus to quality and technological innovation since compatibility had lost its status as a source of value; it was simply expected. Compaq offered its customers state-of-the-art microcomputers, the definition of value at that time. Again, the actions of its competitors and suppliers over time forced Compaq to look for a new source of value. In 1992, managers' changes to the process of designing and building PCs were driven by value concerns, not by cost concerns.

Responsibility for the Product

moment of truth
The customer's perception based on continuing assessments of the product's value. The customer's most recent experience determines to a large extent how that customer sees the company.

Though a customer may be influenced by advertising, the customer's perception of the firm is shaped by actual experiences with the good or service at the moment of interacting with that good or service. This interaction is the **moment of truth**. The customer's experience determines much about whether he or she develops a favorable or poor view of the company. This highly subjective experience depends substantially on operations management because it ultimately produces the good or service that drives this interaction.

Every day, companies try repeatedly to shape your expectations and influence your buying behavior. On television, you see ads describing new car models, breakfast cereals, or restaurants. Ads in the local newspaper tell you about an airline's new, more convenient schedules with 12 daily flights to Chicago. These ads are trying to do more than simply to inform you; they are trying to develop a favorable predisposition in you toward the advertised products. When you are hungry, an advertiser wants you to think of its restaurant; when you need to go to Chicago, the airline wants you to consider its flights. However, these are only expectations.

When you do decide to try that new restaurant, you expect a good meal at a reasonable price delivered quickly within comfortable surroundings. When you fly with that airline, you expect convenience and reliability. From your first interaction with the firm, you begin to compare your expectations with the actual experience. If the actual experience meets or exceeds your expectations, you develop a favorable view of the company. ("Hey, this is a great place to come for a meal!") When the experience falls short of the expectation, you feel cheated. ("What's the use of 12 daily flights when half of them are canceled?"), you feel somehow cheated. Not only are you less likely to return, but you are also more likely to tell your friends about your bad experiences. You become a form of negative advertising.

Importance of People

Operations management systems draw heavily on technology in the form of computers, complex machinery, and automated equipment. However, OM systems are not technologically driven. Rather, they rely on humans (i.e., workers and managers) to generate most of their improvements and enhancements. Workers, by virtue of their experience with and understanding of the system, become the real experts. Every day that they work with a system, they learn about it. As they learn how it operates, they uncover shortcomings and identify opportunities for improvements. This insight poses two challenges for the operations manager. The first is to develop people and their skills so that they can contribute more to the continued growth and success of both the operations management function specifically and the firm as a whole. The second is to develop a mechanism by which to communicate and use this knowledge or expertise.

ON THE JOB

Eaton Learns the Value of Employee Input

For years, the unionized Eaton Corp. manufacturing plant in Lincoln, Illinois, was torn by labor-management strife. Morale suffered—and so did profits. But in 1992, Eaton reached out to its workers by asking them for their ideas on possible improvements. The company entrusted its workers with sales statistics and other sensitive corporate information. They were organized into teams and asked for their input in decision making. Managers were instructed to treat their people more or less as equals.

Encouraged to think more for themselves, workers consistently began to come up with effective, cost-saving innovations and improvements. But not everyone liked the new equality. When the engineering department was moved from its plush office to the shop floor, the department head and a colleague quit in protest.

On a typical day, a worker might suggest to a plant manager that welding electrodes could be sandblasted rather than machined and save the company $5,125 a year, or even more. Machine repairmen, tired of fixing the same equipment over and over, offered to build two new automated machines themselves. They were able to build the machines—which would have cost $350,000 and $250,000 if brought from the outside—for $80,000 and $93,000, respectively. Successfully designing and building the machines also gave the machinists a tremendous amount of pride and job satisfaction. "It's nice to start out with a concept and see it through, especially when it gets rid of monotonous work," explained machinist Rodney Romine.

Eaton's employees made more than 190 such suggestions in the first year of the new program and saved the company more than $1.4 million. First-quarter profits soared 30 percent above a year earlier. In return, workers were given $44,000 in "Eaton bucks," which they could trade for items such as sporting goods at the factory store. But even more importantly, workers began to care more deeply about doing a good job. "We're more or less our own bosses [now]," explained Romine.

When workers feel they have a stake in the well-being of the company, the company can only benefit. "If the company can't make money, you can't expect to have a job very long," said Romine. By valuing its workers, Eaton also found a way to generate more value for its customers.

SOURCE   Thomas F. O'Boyle, "Working Together: A Manufacturer Grows Efficient by Soliciting Ideas from Employees," *The Wall Street Journal,* June 5, 1992, p. A1, A5.

Recognizing the importance of people, managers must emphasize training as a corporate investment, empowerment (giving people the tools, knowledge, and authority they need to bring about changes), enfranchisement (expecting people to become the major agents of change), and teamwork (identifying the group as an effective problem-solving agent rather than individuals working in isolation). Making people important also requires an acceptance of cooperation, rather than conflict, as the preferred mode of operation. Emphasizing people assumes that everyone who works in the firm is fundamentally valuable and driven by the desires for survival (the need to earn enough to survive) and pride (to do a good job and to be part of a function or company that produces a good product). Everyone likes to identify with a winner.

Companies such as Motorola Corporation, Hewlett-Packard, Lincoln Electric, and Eaton Corporation (discussed in the "On the Job" box) are rediscovering the importance of employees as internal experts.

In stressing the importance of the human in the system, the focus of OM is changing from hardware and software to peopleware/knowledgeware. The increasing importance of workers is evident in a quote from an Eaton employee: "Our opinions matter here," says Luci Donaldson, an office clerk. "What we say counts—and it's not just to appease us."[6]

Goal-Directed Systems

system

A goal-driven group of interrelated activities linked together by means of a network or structure

Operations management deals with the design, management, and control of systems. A **system** can be defined as a goal-driven group of interrelated activities linked together by means of a network or structure. Everything in operations management involves systems. Systems help customers to place orders; systems release orders for filling; they deliver completed jobs to customers.

The description of systems as goal-driven recognizes that they are not random occurrences. Rather, they represent structures that have evolved to help managers achieve certain predetermined goals. The goal of operations management is to maximize value.

Systems are organized. Their activities display definite structures. The transformation process, as a system, has an inherent structure. Certain activities must precede others. For example, before building a product, the firm must generate plans and gather necessary inputs (materials, labor, and equipment). The design and description of this structure is one of the major tasks facing any operations manager.

Systems consist of interrelated activities. Something that occurs in one area often affects activities elsewhere. The ability of the OM function to build and deliver a quality product depends largely on the clarity and quality of product designs. It also depends on whether or not the shop floor includes enough capacity. (In an inescapable fact of OM life, quality and capacity utilization are negatively related. As the level of utilization increases, quality tends to fall. With insufficient capacity, workers try to met schedule commitments by spending less time on each unit of output. Without changes to the process, they must do less than the product demands, and quality must fall). Product quality is also influenced by the quality of supplies delivered by vendors and by the quality of the work force and the care with which they maintain equipment.

To view the operations management function as a system, one must recognize that each component does not operate in isolation. Rather, success depends on how the various processes help the OM function to achieve its overall objectives. One must always think in terms of structure and linkages. How is the entire process organized? How does a specific activity affect operations elsewhere? What other operations have important impacts on work in a given area?

A system's view requires managers to understand the process that binds together all of the elements of the system. Managers must manage systems rather than individual activities or elements within systems. They no longer control inventory; instead, they manage the processes that create inventory.

Simplicity

OM must go beyond even thinking of systems. One must ultimately think of simple systems. Simple systems are easy to understand, easy to operate, easy to teach, and easy to control. Simple systems are always effective because they create

---

[6]Thomas F. O'Boyle, "Working Together: A Manufacturer Grows Efficient by Soliciting Ideas from Employees," *The Wall Street Journal,* June 5, 1992, p. A5.

a direct bridge between need and response. They also respond most effectively to changes in needs with the shortest possible lead times. Complexity, on the other hand, creates confusion as it perpetuates itself. As a result, managers must continuously evaluate all of the processes and activities within the OM system to identify and eliminate or rethink all unnecessary activities and sources of complexity.

This tenet is often summarized by the acronym *KISS* for Keep It Simple, Stupid.

Change

The final belief that underlies modern operations management views all systems as subject to change. While all systems are fixed in the short term, they are still malleable over the long term. If the current system is not doing what managers want, they can and should change it. Change is always possible if managers are willing to invest the necessary time, effort, and resources. As a result, the principle of change views the operations manager as proactive within the OM environment.

"Nothing is permanent except change."

Heraclitus (540–475? B.C.)

 ## TRAITS OF THE VALUE-DRIVEN OM SYSTEM

Rethinking operations management reveals a system characterized by four critical traits:

- Emphasis on the total product experience
- Development of a system intended to generate and maintain a sustainable competitive advantage
- Simultaneous management of the technological, strategic, and human aspects of the operations management system
- Recognition that operations management is inherently dynamic

These four traits will reappear frequently in this book. They define part of the ongoing work of the effective and efficient operations management system.

Total Product Experience

Increasingly managers and customers see diminishing differences between goods and services. In reality, the marketplace includes very few pure goods and pure services. A commodity (e.g., milk, sugar, copper, or plastic forks) might be regarded as a pure good to be evaluated strictly based on its features and its price. However, most products are *hybrids,* mixtures of goods and services.

When you buy a new car, for example, you want to know not only whether the car is well-built, but also what services the dealer offers for repairs, body work, loaner cars, and parts. You do not simply buy a car; you also buy the support that comes with that car. Furthermore, the market offers few true services. Many service offers also include tangible products. McDonald's and Burger King, for example, sell tangible hamburgers along with intangible cooking services.

Understanding hybrid products leads managers to think in terms of the **total product experience**, the combination of tangibles (goods), intangibles (services, experiences, and outcomes) designed to win the customer's approval.[7] Customers do not think of services and goods separately; rather, both are part of one package that the firm delivers to the customer. The customer's experiences and impressions at the

total product experience
The combination of tangible and intangible product characteristics designed to win the customer's approval

[7]Karl Albrecht, *The Only Thing that Matters* (New York: Harper Business, 1992), p. 13.

Compact disc packaging, presentation, and the purchasing environment all shape this customer's perception of the product. His response to the total product experience will determine a favorable or unfavorable company image.   SOURCE   David Young-Wolff/PhotoEdit

moment of interacting with the total product experience determine how the person feels about the firm and the quality that it offers. Someone who has a bad meal at an expensive restaurant sees the quality of that restaurant as extremely poor.

The concept of the total product experience entails two issues. First, the difference between services and goods may not be as great as people may at first assume. Second, managers should view the two as part of a unified package.

Generating a Sustainable Competitive Advantage

An effective operations management system seeks to continually generate value for its targeted customers in order to develop and maintain a sustainable competitive advantage (Exhibit 1.7). The OM system must accept and pursue a concept of value that meets the needs and expectations of the firm's customers. Furthermore, the firm's OM system must generate a higher level of value for its customers than competitors through a system that builds a long-term position of strength for the firm in the marketplace.

OM System Management: Technological, Strategic, and Human Aspects

Operations management is more than technology. Seldom can a new machine or computer program solve an OM problem by itself. New equipment may be part of a solution, but technology, and the system that surrounds it, is only one part of OM. An integral element of any OM system is the person. Either individually or as part of a larger group, the person must affect any effort to identify and resolve problems or to implement a resulting solution. In addition, any new solution must be consistent with the strategic objectives and orientation of the firm as well as the activities of other groups within the firm (e.g., marketing and engineering).

[**E X H I B I T   1 . 7**]

Traits of a Sustainable Competitive Advantage

- Builds a long-term position of strength in the marketplace
- Closely identifies the firm and its market
- Gives the firm an appearance of "owning" the market
- Allows the firm to deliver products that embody better value faster than its competitors
- Allows the firm to force its competitors into reactive positions

Managers must simultaneously consider all of these facts. Ignoring any one aspect can damage the effectiveness of the OM function and its actions.

Operations Management as an Inherently Dynamic Pursuit

Each of the three elements in the operations management system (customer, process, and capacity) changes continuously. The customer changes with changes in expectations, education, income levels, competitors' actions, advertising, and government actions. In the early 1980s, quality became an important consideration in the automobile industry. Not all cars offered the same quality levels, and customers often based purchase decisions on such factors as quality ratings, reputations, and reviews. In the 1990s, quality levels are converging. Many Japanese-built cars offer quality no different from that of an American or European car. As a result, better quality is no longer as important as it was; customers now expect quality. Auto makers must now consider alternative tactics for attracting customers, often with significant impacts on their operations management systems.

Similarly, process and capacity change. Such changes reflect the effects of factors like changes in technology, introductions of new software products, new manufacturing management procedures (e.g., just-in-time manufacturing), and changes in availability and quality of resources (e.g., the overall literacy of the work force).

The dynamic nature of operations management greatly complicates the task of maintaining consistency among the three elements of the OM system. Without constant management involvement over time, dynamic events can cause the three components of the OM system to drift apart and become less consistent and supportive.

 ## OPERATIONS MANAGEMENT WITHIN THE FIRM

The operations management function, while critical to the overall success of the firm, is nevertheless simply one element. The typical firm brings together a number of diverse business processes, the most important of which typically include (in addition to the operations management function):

- Strategic planning
- Marketing
- Design and engineering
- Human resource management
- Purchasing

Bristol-Myers Squibb retains customer confidence and market superiority by utilizing interdepartmental teamwork to achieve common operational objectives.   SOURCE   Courtesy of Bristol-Myers Squibb Company

- Logistics management
- Finance
- Accounting

The firm needs each of these functions to achieve its objective of building a close fit between what the firm offers and what its targeted customers demand, expect, and want. Any firm that achieves this objective more effectively than competitors over time can command a profit. It can also assure its survival in the marketplace.

Each function within the firm plays an important part in achieving this objective. Each commands a share of company resources; each helps to define its capabilities and limitations; each provides information that can contribute to formulation of more effective corporate strategies. In the past, managers treated company functions as separate and, in many cases, autonomous entities. They encountered little interaction between functions. This view is now changing.

Increasingly, managers view company functions as intimately linked. Each function's actions affect the operation of the other functions. In turn, each is affected by actions elsewhere in the firm. The success of the human resource management function in identifying, recruiting, and selecting well-qualified workers has a major impact on the ability of the OM function to produce a high-quality product. This interdependence makes it critical to understand the roles played by each of the major functions in the firm.

Strategic Planning Function

Strategic planning by the firm's senior or upper-level managers provides the firm with an identity, a direction, and a sense of purpose. Strategic planning can be regarded as a process that generates a plan of action to develop and refine a competitive advantage for the firm.[8] It attempts to provide the firm with a unique and valuable competitive advantage over its rivals based on some combination of four

[8]Bruce D. Henderson, "The Origin of Strategy," in *Strategy: Seeking and Securing Competitive Advantage,* ed. by Cynthia A. Montgomery and Michael E. Porter (Cambridge, Mass.: Harvard Business Review, 1991), pp. 3–9.

critical elements: time, cost, quality, and flexibility. A sustainable competitive advantage emerges from development of a corporate mission and corporate goals.

A **corporate mission** is a statement that defines the firm both internally (i.e., to its workers) and externally (i.e., to its market, its competitors, and other groups such as the financial community and the government). To develop this sense of identity, the corporate mission answers questions such as:

corporate mission

A statement that defines the firm both internally and externally

- What business is the firm in?
- What business will it be in (in the future)?
- What business should it be in?
- What customers does it serve and what do they want?
- What customers should it serve (i.e., could any potential users benefit from the company's capabilities and products)?

The answers to these questions not only define the firm, but they also interpret the firm's perception of value (i.e., effectiveness).

The need to link the firm's self-definition to the customer and to value has led some to agree that this definition should answer three important questions:[9]

- Who does the firm satisfy? (What customer groups does it serve?)
- What does it satisfy (What customer needs does it address?)
- How does it satisfy customer needs? (What skills or distinctive competencies does it have?)

This approach to defining the firm focuses on the customer rather than the product or process. As such, it is very consistent with this book's orientation toward operations management.

To answer these strategic questions, strategic managers must build a consistent fit between the firm and its market. This requires a strong and accurate sense of internal capabilities. Managers must know what the firm does well and what it does poorly. A strong influence on defining these corporate capabilities comes from the operations management function, as the "By the Way" box illustrates. The type of production system that a firm has in place may strongly influence overall corporate capabilities.

The corporate mission must also define the customers that the firm wants to target. This can include current customers or potential future customers. The corporate mission guides efforts to build a tight, consistent fit between what the customer wants and what the firm can do. It tries to match wants with capabilities.

In addition, the corporate mission acts as a mechanism for unifying and coordinating the various functions and their activities. It identifies what the firm is and, more importantly, what it is not. The corporate mission also encourages functional activities that contribute to the firm's self-image and business definition, and it discourages those that do not.

More specific than the mission, **corporate goals** spell out explicitly what the firm wants to achieve. Corporate goals direct company actions toward achieving the corporate mission; they guide the formulation of strategy and its resulting implementation by the various functional units by describing in concrete terms what the firm wants to achieve. For example, a firm can state corporate goals in terms of market share, rate of return on investment, profit level, reputation, and technological leadership. Goals often specify time horizons over which the firm should complete them. Finally, corporate goals form part of the basis for perfor-

corporate goal

A statement in concrete terms of what the company wants to achieve

[9]Cyril Charney, *Time to Market: Reducing Product Lead Time* (Dearborn, Mich.: Society of Manufacturing Engineers, 1991), p. 26.

[BY THE WAY... IMPORTANCE OF THE FIT BETWEEN] PRODUCT AND DELIVERY SYSTEM

Recently, a major development in the fast-food industry has brought salad bars into former hamburger restaurants. This concept, pioneered by Wendy's, is very attractive to an increasingly health-conscious public. However, the introduction of the salad bar initially presented McDonald's with a major problem. McDonald's based its success on a production system that excels in delivering a quality product consistently and quickly. This system was not well suited a self-serve salad bar.

McDonald's built its system around the notion of portion control. McDonald's tightly controls the quantity and quality of everything that it sells. It tolerates no variability of any kind. It tries whatever it can to control or eliminate variance in the size of a hamburger patty, the amount of fries in a portion, etc. When soft drinks were dispensed by people who had to decide how much to fill, every soft-drink cup carried a line. The old saying taught that, "Below the line, you cheat the customer; above the line, you cheat yourself."

A self-serve salad bar defies the type of portion control demanded by McDonald's, creating a great deal of variance.

Someone might decide to make a salad with a lot of tomatoes while someone else might decide to go for a lot of cheese and croutons. McDonald's first attempts at introducing a salad bar failed because the self-serve concept did not fit with the capabilities of its delivery system. McDonald's could offer a salad only if it could maintain the same tight portion control that characterized the rest of the system. This happened when the firm introduced a prepackaged salad that offered the customer a healthy alternative in a form consistent with the capabilities of its delivery system.

mance measurement. For example, if a corporate goal commits the firm to becoming the highest-quality supplier of a certain product, then operations managers should measure their system's performance on how effectively it can build and deliver a quality product.

Together, the corporate mission and corporate goals give the firm a sense of cohesion and purpose. These strategic tools bind together the various functions to achieve a shared goal. Strategic planning does not address excellence in the individual functions. It does not focus narrowly on getting good employees or developing outstanding manufacturing systems, but rather on how the functions work together. As Casey Stengel, the legendary manager of the New York Yankees, once said, "It's easy to get good players. Gettin' 'em to play together—that's the hard part."

Strategic planning, like operations management, is inherently dynamic. It tries to influence activities both within the firm and in its environment (e.g., customers and competitors). In turn, it is influenced by both internal and external actions. If the OM function introduces a new system that gives the firm capabilities that are both valued by the customer and difficult for competitors to match, then corporate strategy may well change to take advantage of this new strength. Corporate strategy may also change in response to competitors' actions, government actions, changes in technology, and changes in customer expectations and demands. Ultimately, good strategic planning works to manage change rather than continuously reacting to it.

Marketing Function

Marketing manages the interface between the customer and the firm. It identifies the needs and expectations of the customer and communicates that information to the rest of the firm. It also helps to shape these expectations through activities such as advertising that communicate the capabilities of the firm to current and potential customers. Marketing also monitors interactions with the customer to identify and flag any changes in needs and expectations, and it tracks competitors to identify any actions that might adversely affect the firm's position in the marketplace (e.g., introduction of a new product or a change in pricing structure). In short, marketing represents the customer internally within the firm and it presents the firm to the customer externally.

Marketing plays a critical role in helping company managers identify the meaning of value to either current or future customers. It helps managers to restate this definition in terms that are meaningful to other functions such as operations management. Marketing may determine that the customer wants a product that provides the highest value for the money. Operations management might restate this view of value as the highest level of quality and the fastest response to changes in customer demands.

Design and Engineering Function

Design and engineering deals with the process of designing, implementing, maintaining, and refining product and process designs. This function is responsible for every activity from the first proposal for a new product or process to design to prototype to first run and ultimately to full production. For example, Intel's design and engineering function would be extensively involved in developing a new family of microchips. Ford's design and engineering function might handle installing a new assembly line.

Design and engineering also works to revise existing products and processes in light of continuing experience. No product or process design ever emerges completely correct from the drawing board. All designs should be viewed as fluid and likely to undergo changes. Designs change for many reasons: feedback from customers about product features, problems on the shop floor with either the product or the process, familiarity with the product or process that uncovers new opportunities for improvements, competitors' actions, changes in technology and government actions. The design and engineering function makes changes that improve either the product, by making it more attractive to the customer, or the process, by improving quality, reducing lead times, increasing flexibility, or decreasing the costs of production.

This work forms a strong link between design and engineering and operations management. The actions and decisions of design and engineering affect operations management in several critical ways. First, the product design affects the quantities and types of parts needed and the corresponding levels of inventories. This design also affects the time requirements and difficulty levels encountered on the shop floor. A well-designed product produced in a carefully conceived and installed system greatly simplifies the operations management function.

Product and process design determine capacity requirements and resource needs, including equipment, worker skills, types of tools, and amount of resources. In addition, it is easier and cheaper to correct problems at the design stage than on the shop floor once the product begins production, as Exhibit 1.8 illustrates.

[**EXHIBIT 1.8**]

Typical Costs of Design Changes in a Major Electronics Product

Time of Design Changes	Cost
Design phase	$ 1,000
Design testing phase	10,000
Process planning phase	100,000
Test production phase	1,000,000
Final production phase	10,000,000

SOURCE   Cyril Charney, *Time to Market: Reducing Product Lead Time* (Dearborn, Mich.: Society of Manufacturing Engineers, 1991), p. 26. Reprinted with permission of the Society of Manfuacturing Engineers (Dearborn, Mich.).

Changing a product design during the initial design phase costs about $1,000; the same change implemented during final production costs about $10 million—a 10,000-fold increase.

In addition to the product design, the process design determines such factors as the level of capacity available, the number of employees needed and their skill levels, the capabilities of the OM system, and the attributes of the process (i.e., cost, flexibility, lead time, and quality).

Human Resource Management Function

Human resource management handles the human side of company activities: recruiting, training, developing, evaluating, and controlling workers. An effective HRM function focuses on six key activities:[10]

- *Attraction*   Identifying job requirements within the organization; determining the number of people and skill mix needed, and assuring equal opportunities for qualified candidates
- *Selection*   Choosing people who best suit the needs of the firm
- *Retention*   Rewarding people for performance and keeping good people within the firm
- *Development*   Improving employee capabilities through training and education to develop the knowledge, skills, abilities, and other job-related traits of employees
- *Assessment*   Objectively evaluating job performance and behavior and attitudes relevant to the employee's job. At the heart of any assessment activity is performance measurement, which tells the employee what the firm values and what it does not. This communication influences what employees stress and what they ignore. As Oliver Wright once noted, "You get what you inspect, not what you expect."
- *Adjustment*   Maintaining compliance with the firm's personnel policies

Human resource management has an increasingly important impact on the operations management system and its performance. Operations management is beginning to benefit from the insights, suggestions, and ideas advanced by its work-

[10]Wayne F. Cascio, *Managing Human Resources,* 2d ed. (New York: McGraw-Hill, 1989), pp. 50–51.

ers. Managers are now recognizing employees as a major source of productivity gains. As reported in an earlier box, in 1992, the Eaton Corporation realized savings in excess of $1.4 million and a first-quarter profit increase of over 30 percent compared with the same period the previous year, despite erratic sales.[11] Employees fueled Eaton's progress through individual suggestions and group improvement activities. To tap these benefits, a firm needs good employees who are properly motivated and trained to work within its system. To obtain and retain such employees requires an effective and integrated human resource management function.

Purchasing Function

Purchasing deals with the firm as a buyer. Most firms pay anywhere from 50 to 80 percent of their cost of goods sold to purchase goods and services from outside suppliers, ranging from components for their products to energy to custodial and consulting services. The purchasing function identifies appropriate suppliers and works with them to ensure reliable supplies. Purchasing does not work simply to obtain goods and services from the cheapest sources. Rather, it works to identify suppliers who are consistent with the orientation of the firm and who can adequately support and enhance its efforts. If a company emphasizes quality, then it should look for suppliers who focus primarily on quality themselves.

Purchasing and operations management are closely linked. Ultimately, the performance of the OM system, measured by quality levels, lead time, cost, and flexibility, depends on inputs from the firm's suppliers, secured by the purchasing function. Suppliers act as a form of additional capacity for the firm, allowing it to increase production by freeing up some of its capacity. The firm can buy certain items more cheaply than it can make internally. Obtaining these items from suppliers allows it to devote the space and capacity to produce these items to production of other critical inputs. As a result, operations managers often refer to suppliers as **external plant**. Suppliers and purchasing, in turn, adhere to the same schedules and specifications that drive activities on the shop floor.

external plant
Capacity of external suppliers

Finally, suppliers represent a source of expertise for the firm. Nearly all North American firms feel pressure to reduce costs (primarily overhead) and streamline operations. In the past, firms have favored performing in house all of the major activities needed to deliver their products. In the automotive industry, companies such as General Motors and Ford have developed design departments not only for engines, but also for radios and brakes. The realization that external suppliers can often do a better job of designing and delivering these components has led companies to abandon their own design efforts in favor of purchasing them from other firms, reducing costs, speeding product development, and often improving quality.

Logistics Management Function

Logistics management deals with the movement and storage activities within the supply chain, beginning with the supplier and ending with the consumer. In its simplest form, the supply chain consists of three major components—the supplier, the firm, and the consumer. The supplier provides goods and services needed by the firm; the firm feeds the inputs from the supplier into the transformation

[11]O'Boyle, "Working Together," pp. A1, A5.

process to create its own products; the customer is the ultimate source of demand. These three elements are linked by flows of both information and goods. The customer places an order with the firm; the firm informs the customer whether and when it can fill the order.

This chain also includes storage points for goods and information, such as outside warehouses and stocking points within the firm (e.g., receiving docks). Storage facilities link the major elements along the supply chain (e.g., a warehouse in Chicago helps to bridge the distance between a customer in Iowa City and a factory in Detroit).

Logistics management links suppliers, the firm, and customers to provide spatial closure. This function plans, implements, and controls the efficient, cost-effective flow and storage of inventory and related information between the major elements along the supply chain.

Finance Function

Finance manages the financial resources of the firm. In this role, it acts as the interface between the firm and the financial community, including banks, investment firms, and individual and corporate stockholders. Finance raises funds and helps to determine how the firm can best distribute resources among its functions, and it measures how well functions use these resources. It also reports the company's financial performance to inform others (both within and outside the firm) of its own results and the creditworthiness of customers and suppliers. Reporting is an important task since the operations management system would suffer if it were to rely on suppliers from a vendor that faced bankruptcy.

Accounting Function

Accounting is one of the most misunderstood functions within the firm. Many view it as simply a system for tracking costs. Instead, accounting performs more of an information-gathering function. People within this function observe economic transactions such as movements of products on the shop floor or purchases of material and quantify this information. When the firm buys a new machine, accounting evaluates the transaction in dollar terms since this gives the closest thing that one can get to a universal measure. Dollar units allow comparisons between different functions and different departments, enhancing managers' ability to control operations. Aside from quantifying transactions, accounting also records and accumulates information over time, all with a reasonable level of accuracy.

The information generated by accounting, in turn, forms the basis for both written reports and decision making. Operations managers rely on this critical information to decide how much to build at one time (i.e., lot sizing) and to evaluate performance for individuals, departments, or the firm as a whole. For example, accounting information indicates how closely actual costs approach standard costs for a department. Accounting information also helps managers to determine the best structure for the transformation process, especially for decisions about adding equipment or introducing new technologies. Finally, accounting information helps managers to justify decisions to the rest of the firm. For example, they might defend a decision to introduce a new computer-based production and inventory control system based on the amount of money saved though reduced inventory levels or shorter lead times.

Importance of the Whole

Each functional activity discussed in this section is important. Each controls certain company resources; each influences how the firm defines and implements its vision of value. However, functional activities can satisfy the customer only when they work together. This book will not talk about operations management as independent of any other function; we will not say that operations management is the single most critical function in the firm; we will never talk about OM answers to value problems. Operations management is important, but it is not the only important function in the firm.

Operations management functions within a corporate framework. Every student must remember that generating value is a corporate activity. This book focuses on the tools, concepts, and frameworks to understand operations management and its role in satisfying customer needs and creating value. No one should ever ignore the corporate context in which operations management carries out these tasks.

COURSE ROAD MAP

The emphasis in this book is indicated by its title—*Operations Management: A Value-Driven Approach*. As the main title suggests, we introduce and explain theories, concepts, and analytical tools from the field of operations management. We deal with OM within a general management context. The subtitle, *A Value-Driven Approach*, indicates our unique effort to link the concepts and theories of OM to the task of generating value for the customer. The customer's values and expectations must permeate decision making in the OM system.

The book is divided into seven major parts (Exhibit 1.9). Part I, Operations Management: A Value-Driven Approach, consists of Chapter 1, which presents an overview of operations management, the challenges facing today's operations managers, the need for a change from a cost orientation to a focus on value, and the place of operations management within the corporate and competitive landscapes.

Part II examines the conceptual foundations of operations management. Chapter 2 defines *value* and Chapter 3 examines the attributes or traits that are frequently associated with value—response time or speed, quality, costs, and variety or flexibility. Part II concludes with Chapter 4, which discusses the major issues that an effective operations management system must address: developing a thorough understanding of management, managerial problem solving, and its evolution.

Part III discusses the forces that drive operations management functions in a globally competitive environment. Chapter 5 describes basic process flow analysis and some emerging management tools to enhance the effectiveness of operations management functions. Chapter 6 discusses the role of organization design in crafting an organization that can meet the needs of the firm and its workers, and it describes the critical and often overlooked role of people in the value-driven operations management system. Chapter 7 discusses managerial issues in total quality management, and Chapter 8 introduces tools and techniques most often associated with that management discipline. Chapter 9 describes just-in-time manufacturing, a value-based operating strategy that emphasizes continuing efforts to identify and eliminate waste at all levels and in all stages of the operations management system.

[**E X H I B I T   1 . 9**]

Course Map

Three of the four chapters in Part IV relate to designing of operations management systems. Chapter 10 examines the problem of predicting future demand through forecasting and understanding the processes that drive demand for a firm's goods and services. Chapter 11 deals with the product innovation process, including design and development of goods and services and, based on estimates of demand and product designs, design and development of systems to make and deliver products. Chapter 12 deals with the design of delivery services. Chapter 13 examines how successful firms have redefined their operations management systems to include suppliers in both the design and execution activities of operations management.

Part V deals with operations planning, one of the key functions of management. Chapter 14 describes the planning needs of an organization and then discusses some of the tools with which managers plan resource use within their functions. Chapter 15 deals exclusively with capacity management, one of the key decisions confronting most operations managers, especially those in service organizations.

Part VI deals with operations execution, that is, how firms ensure that their systems make decisions to keep things operating as they should. Chapter 16 examines inventory problems, basic inventory models, and inventory control systems. Chapter 17 focuses on materials requirement planning systems to effectively manage inventories for items with dependent demand. Chapter 18 examines how to schedule and sequence activities to achieve the efficiency and effectiveness goals of the organization.

Part VII includes only Chapter 19, which speculates about the operations management function of the next century. We present some trends that should affect the operations management system of the future by identifying and exploring five major challenges that are now emerging to shape operations management. These trends may reinvent operations management, and successful operations managers can survive and thrive in such a dynamic environment by continuously reinventing themselves. Operations management is never a solved problem, but a sequence of temporary solutions. This dynamic nature of operations management makes it an exciting and challenging field.

CHAPTER SUMMARY

This chapter has provided a broad overview and introduction to operations management. In discussing the scope and complexity of operations management, we have made the following points:

1. Operations management is now going through a period of change. Changes in customer expectations are forcing managers to rethink the answers to some of the most fundamental questions facing the firm. These changes have also spurred the development of new and more appropriate paradigms or mental frameworks.
2. The new frameworks have shifted the focus from cost to value. A firm can no longer just offer a low-cost product to customers. Rather, the operations management system and the firm as a whole face the challenge of profitably delighting the customer. Other features of these frameworks include an emphasis on people as critical resources and on developing a system that simplifies rather than complicates.
3. Operations managers try to understand, explain, predict, and change the transformation process to make it both efficient and effective.
4. Efficiency views the costs of the transformation process from an internal perspective. In contrast, effectiveness looks at whether the firm makes something for the customer that the customer really wants. Operations managers should try first to become effective and then work toward efficiency.
5. The value-driven operations management system is built on three components: customer, process, and capacity. All three elements must be aligned for the process to provide the products that customers want. To provide those products, the process (how the firm does things) must match capacity (what it can do and how much it can do). Keeping the three elements aligned is the major task facing the operations manager.
6. The customer is the starting and ending point for the operations management system. To design an effective transformation process, one must understand what the customer really desires and does not desire. In other words, one must identify the customer's order winners, order qualifiers, and order losers. This analysis extends to both internal and external customers. In addition to customers, one must satisfy stakeholders, parties who are interested in how the operations management function runs and its well-being. Stakeholders can be stockholders, banks, local governments, anyone who wants firms to produce environmentally sound products. The distinction between stakehold-

ers and customers is not definitive; customers often act as stakeholders. Operations managers must consider these various groups when they determine what constitutes value.

7. An effective value-driven system deals with neither a physical product nor a service exclusively. It deals with a total product experience that combines product, service, and the customer's experience.

8. One of the major objectives in developing an effective operations management system is to assure for the firm a sustainable competitive advantage. The system should provide the highest level of value for the customer while making it difficult for competitors to duplicate. Such an ever-changing system forces competitors to react, to struggle to catch up to a moving target.

9. Operations management should never be considered in isolation. Rather, the process of generating value requires the cooperation of a number of different functions within the firm. Operations management, for example, can never be effective without information about customers and competitors from marketing or direction from corporate strategy.

[KEY TERMS]

operations management 5	external customer 8	moment of truth 20
effectiveness 5	stakeholder 9	system 22
efficiency 5	process 11	total product experience 23
customer 6	good 13	corporate mission 27
order winner 6	service 13	corporate goal 27
order qualifier 6	product 14	external plant 31
order loser 6	capacity 14	
internal customer 8	paradigm 15	
	value 19	

[DISCUSSION QUESTIONS]

1. How would you define the operations management function in each of the following corporations?
   a. Marriott hotels
   b. Private golf and tennis club
   c. Ben & Jerry's Ice Cream
   d. Exxon Corporation

2. Use the university environment to illustrate how your school's dean might define *efficiency* and *effectiveness*. Now use a student perspective to illustrate these differences. What might explain the differences?

3. Select two products that you have recently purchased, one a manufactured good and one service. Review your process for making these purchase decisions, then identify your order winners, order qualifiers, and order losers in each case.

4. Think of two different business processes you encountered when you enrolled in college. Select one process, for example, the admissions process, and describe its inputs, activities, and outputs.

5. Consider the following processes that you frequently encounter as a college student:
   a. enrolling in college
   b. taking a class
   c. buying a ticket for a play, concert, or basketball game
   Describe each process and its input, activities, and outputs. What is being converted or transformed in each process? Identify the forms of capacity that you might expect to encounter in each process. Identify the customers and any stakeholders for each. Finally, for each process, identify a set of appropriate measures of performance.

6. Describe a paradigm shift that has happened in your life. Can you cite one that has occurred in the business world? In world affairs?

7. Consider three items normally found in a typical household. How might you and your parent value these items? Why might the values differ?
   a. cellular telephone
   b. Beatles poster
   c. television show "Roseanne"

8. Consider the following situations:
   a. You can buy and receive prescription eyeglasses in 1 hour.
   b. You can buy a personal computer containing a self-diagnostic program.
   c. You can communicate with your relatives in Peoria via the Internet.
   Each case presents a possible paradigm shift. Describe the underlying nature of the paradigm shift. What are the implications of each shift for the customer, the OM process, and the appropriate measures of performance? If you were a competitor dealing with these paradigm shifts, how could you respond?

9. Identify a system in your life. What are its inputs, activities, and outputs? How would you measure its performance?

10. Recall the last time you went to a fast-food restaurant such as McDonald's. Use this visit to illustrate the term *total product experience.*

11. The following firms have long been seen as having sustainable competitive advantages.
    a. Hewlett-Packard
    b. McDonald's
    c. Coca-Cola
    d. Xerox
    Go to the library and read about one of these companies. Also draw from your experience with that company to identify that company's competitive advantage. What about the company has given it a competitive advantage? Discuss how operations management, marketing, and human resource management relate to the company's competitive advantage.

12. Find a product that illustrates the principle of prizing simplicity. What about this product makes it prized? Can you name any other products where more is really less? Why?

13. General Motors and IBM once dominated their industries so strongly that the federal government mounted antitrust actions against them. How did these giants lose all or much of their sustainable competitive advantages? Can they regain their advantages? If so, how might they do so?

C A U T I O N

[C R I T I C A L   T H I N K I N G   R E Q U I R E D]

1. How might the concepts and topics covered in this chapter differ if we were writing this text for:
   a. students in an eastern European university?
   b. students in an Islamic, African university?
   c. students in a Mexico City university?
2. Why is the operations management function necessary? Is it necessary?

[S E L E C T E D   R E A D I N G S]

Albrecht, Karl. *The Only Thing that Matters.* New York: Harper Business, 1992.

Allen, Michael. "Bottom Fishing: Developing New Line of Low-Priced PCs Shakes Up Compaq." *Wall Street Journal,* June 5, 1992, pp. A1, A4.

Barker, Joel Arthur. *Paradigms: The Business of Discovering the Future.* New York: Harper Business, 1992.

Burke, James. *The Day the Universe Changed.* Boston, Mass.: Little, Brown, 1985.

Carlzon, Jan. *Moments of Truth: New Strategies for Today's Customer-Driven Economy.* New York: Harper & Row, 1987.

Cascio, Wayne F. *Managing Human Resources,* 2d ed. New York: McGraw-Hill, 1989.

Charney, Cyril. *Time to Market: Reducing Product Lead Time.* Dearborn, Mich.: Society of Manufacturing Engineers, 1991.

Cohen, Stephen S., and John Zysman,. *Manufacturing Matters: The Myth of the Post-Industrial Economy.* New York: Basic Books, 1987.

Damore, Kelley. "Volatile '94 for Desktop Market Comes to a Close." *Computer Reseller News,* December 12, 1994, pp. 35–38.

Davidow, William H., and Michael S. Malone. *The Virtual Corporation.* New York: Harper Business, 1992.

Dumaine, Brian. "How Managers Can Succeed through Speed." *Fortune,* February 13, 1989, pp. 54–59.

Foster, Richard N. *Innovation: The Attacker's Advantage.* New York: Summit Books, 1986.

Garwood, Dave and Michael Bane. *Shifting Paradigms: Reshaping the Future of Industry.* Marietta, Ga.: Dogwood Publishing, 1990.

Giffi, Craig, Aleda V. Roth, and Gregory M. Seal. *Competing in World Class Manufacturing: America's 21st Century Challenge.* Homewood, Ill.: Business One Irwin, 1990.

Hamel, Gary, and C. K. Prahalad. *Competing for the Future.* Cambridge, Mass.: Harvard Business School Press, 1994.

Hammer, Michael, and James Champy. *Reengineering the Corporation.* New York: Harper Business, 1993.

Harmon, Roy L., and Leroy D. Peterson. *Reinventing the Factory.* New York: Free Press, 1990.

Henderson, Bruce D. "The Origin of Strategy." In *Strategy: Seeking and Securing Competitive Advantage.* Ed. by Cynthia A. Montgomery and Michael E. Porter. Cambridge, Mass.: Harvard Business Review, 1991.

Hill, Terry. *Manufacturing Strategy: Text and Cases.* Homewood, Ill.: Richard D. Irwin, 1989.

Hof, Robert D. "Inside Intel." *Business Week,* June 1, 1992, pp. 86–94.

Kawasaki, Guy. *Selling the Dream.* New York: Harper Collins, 1991.

Liebig, James E. *Merchants of Vision.* San Francisco, Calif.: Berrett-Koehler, 1994.

Merli, Giorgio. *Total Manufacturing.* Cambridge, Mass.: Productivity Press, 1990.

Meyer, Christopher. *Fast Cycle Time: How to Align Purpose, Strategy, and Structure for Speed.* New York: Free Press, 1993.

O'Boyle, Thomas F. "Working Together: A Manufacturer Grows Efficient by Soliciting Ideas from Employees." *Wall Street Journal,* June 5, 1992, pp. A1, A5.

Peters, Tom. *The Tom Peters Seminar: Crazy Times Call for Crazy Organizations.* New York: Vintage Books, 1994.

Pine, B. Joseph, II. *Mass Customization: The New Frontier in Business Competition.* Cambridge, Mass.: Harvard Business School Press, 1993.

Plossl, George W. *Management in the New World of Manufacturing: How Companies Can Improve Operations to Compete Globally.* Englewood Cliffs, N.J.: Prentice-Hall, 1991.

Wheelwright, Steven C., and Kim B. Clark. *Revolutionizing Product Development: Quantum Leaps in Speed, Efficiency, and Quality.* New York: Free Press, 1992.

PART TWO

The Conceptual Foundation of the Value-Driven Approach

CHAPTER TWO

Value

CHAPTER OUTLINE

CHAPTER OBJECTIVES

[At the end of this chapter, you should be able to]

- Discuss the importance of value in determining the success of the OM system and the firm.
- Define *value*.
- List the four traits of value.
- List the attributes that most consumers associate with value.
- Explain the value equation.
- Review the five value-based strategies.
- Describe the concept of waste.
- Detail the relationships between the customer, value, the firm, key tasks for both the firm and the OM function, and the OM system.

Courtesy of Schwinn
Cycling & Fitness Inc.

Schwinn Re-enters the Race

For almost a hundred years, the name "Schwinn" was synonymous with value. A good bike enters the life of a child like a good friend, and generations of kids learned how to ride on Schwinn's sturdy, brightly colored bikes. Many of these same kids grew up to be parents—parents who wanted their kids to ride Schwinns.

That's why so many people were shocked when Schwinn announced that it was filing for bankruptcy protection in the fall of 1992. During the 1950s, Schwinn owned a solid 25 percent of the domestic market. But by 1992, its market share had dwindled to about 7 percent.

What went wrong? Schwinn had lost sight of the obvious—that the customer of the 1990s wanted very different things from the customer of the 1950s. While Schwinn was just coasting along, admiring the scenery, it got passed by some new kids on the block. Some of them were companies such as Huffy and Murray, whose low-end, kid-oriented bikes were sold at big discounters while Schwinn stubbornly kept selling out of small bike shops. As a result, Schwinn began to lose its name-recognition with kids.

But it was the mountain and road bikes that really left Schwinn in the dust. Companies such as Trek, Cannondale, and Specialized zoomed ahead in the rough terrain. Meanwhile, Schwinn was all but shut out of this pricey market by missing the boom's early stages.

SOURCES

Zapata Espinoza, "The Comeback Rig—Schwinn Bounces Back with a Hot, New Suspension Bike," *Mountain Bike,* February 1995, pp. 50–52.

Gary Strauss, "Schwinn Files for Chapter 11," *USA Today,* October 9, 1992, p. 1B.

But Schwinn wasn't out of the race completely. In 1993 the company emerged out of bankruptcy with a completely new image. A group of investors named the Scott Sports Group bought out all the rights to Schwinn, its name, and assets. Scott moved Schwinn's operations to Colorado, the capital of mountain biking. It then proceeded to completely reinvent the company, from marketing to product and operations management.

Schwinn's heightened sensitivity to its customer was reflected in the company's new motto: "fantastic value." With models such as the radical new FS, or Full Suspension, Schwinn has begun to wow industry reviewers, taking bicycle design into new territory. The new leadership successfully fought back to regain Schwinn's old magic, and once again there's nothing more thrilling to kids of all ages than the glint of a new Schwinn bike.

" The delivery of value to the customer is the nexus at which all aspects of commerce converge. It calls for a clear understanding of customer needs, products designed to meet those needs, intelligent application of technology, relentless focus on quality, cost control and productivity—and a pugnacious insistence on one-upping the competition. This is the most basic test of business effectiveness. Those who don't pass it may not be with us when the value decade is done. "

Stratford Sherman, "How to Prosper in the Value Decade," *Fortune,* November 30, 1992, p. 103.

Schwinn learned a hard lesson about the link between corporate survival and value. Emphasis on value binds the firm to its customers and strongly influences the structure and evaluation methods of the operations management system. Schwinn's experience illustrates certain lessons that are central not only to this chapter but to this entire textbook:

- Effective operations management systems are value-driven.
- Value links the customer, the firm, and the operations management system.
- Value is customer specific, not market or product specific.
- Value combines four major attributes: cost, quality, speed, and flexibility.
- The importance of attributes of value differ for different customers. (Huffy buyers accept moderate quality, but they place critical importance on low cost.)
- Value is dynamic; value today may not be value tomorrow.
- The operations manager faces the critical task of building consistency between what the customer wants and what the operations management system can deliver.

 CUSTOMERS, VALUE, AND OPERATIONS MANAGEMENT

Every firm faces two critical tasks. First, it must create customers, then it must keep the customers it creates. Both of these tasks are major undertakings that tax the firm's ingenuity and its resources. To create and keep customers, a firm cannot simply provide a good or service; it must offer those customers something that they value.

It can do this by giving customers an existing product for a lower price. As an alternative, it can try to attract customers by emphasizing quality. It can also try to attract customers by emphasizing speed (faster product development or delivery) or flexibility (as when Burger King urged "Have it your way"). Every

Value is subjective. The VCR that meets this man's needs and expectations may not meet those of another customer. Therefore, the operations management system must deliver goods that will be perceived as more valuable than their competitors'.   SOURCE   Mary Kate Denny/PhotoEdit

approach amounts to an attempt to offer customers a product that embodies something that they value. Given the importance of the concept of value, we have to define it carefully.

Value Defined

Value is simple to understand and to spot in action, but it is difficult to define. It is easy to understand because people know what they value and what they don't. Increasing attention in today's economy is making *value* the new watchword for both the customer and the firm:

> As the 1980s bonfire of the vanities recedes to a dim, distant glow, value is becoming the marketer's watchword for the 1990s. It's what customers are demanding—the right combination of product quality, fair price, and good service.
>
> *Value* means all that, but it's also important for what it doesn't mean. It doesn't mean high quality if it's only available at even higher prices. It doesn't necessarily mean cheap, if cheap means bare-bones or low grade. It doesn't mean high prestige, if the prestige is viewed as snobbish or self-indulgent. Instead, says Martyn Straw, an adman at Geer, DuBois Inc., agency for Jaguar Ltd., "value is the new prestige."[1]

Value is difficult to define because it is subjective. Value for one person may not suit another. We define **value** as the customer's subjective evaluation, adjusted for cost, of how well a good or service meets or exceeds expectations.

A simple notion underlies this view of value: customers do not care about the firm's maximizing its cost effectiveness or profit; rather, they want to maximize value. They buy products that offer the highest levels of value. The operations management system must design, build, and deliver goods and services that customers

value

The customer's subjective evaluation, adjusted for cost, of how well a good or service meets or exceeds expectations.

[1]Christopher Power, Walecia Konrad, Alice Z. Cuneo, and James B. Treece, "Value Marketing," *Business Week,* November 11, 1991, p. 132.

The United States still holds one secret weapon in its trade war with Japan—jellyfish. Jack Rudloe thinks so, anyway. Rudloe has high hopes that an American jellyfish industry could "penetrate the world market and reduce the trade deficit." He wants to export cannonball jellyfish, a Florida variety, to Japan and other Asian countries.

Rudloe and his wife Anne run a not-for-profit marine laboratory in Panacea, Florida, a coastal city off the Gulf of Mexico. He got the idea of starting an American jellyfish industry after noticing jellyfish being sold in Asian-American food markets. He found out that Malaysia and China export most of the dried jellyfish now sold in the United States. That didn't make sense to Rudloe when the coastal waters off Florida are teeming with the creatures.

It goes without saying that jellyfish are not currently part of the typical American's diet. Anyone who tried to sell them in

ON THE JOB

Value in the Jellyfish Industry

■

the United States in a big way would probably get stung. But jellyfish are in big demand in many Asian countries such as Malaysia, Japan, Taiwan, and Korea, and there is a small U.S. market among immigrants from those countries.

Rudloe thinks this untapped jellyfish market is one of the country's best-kept secrets. He has begun to get other people interested in the idea—including the U.S. Commerce Department, which awarded him an economic development grant to research how jellyfish are caught and processed in Asia.

The ideal processed jellyfish looks and tastes like a rubber band. "It has a crunch that just kind of goes through your head," explains Rudloe. "The Chinese call it 'music to the teeth.'" Since it has little taste of its own, the processed jellyfish is usually served shredded and marinated in soy sauce or sesame oil.

While the typical American customer might not value this particular commodity, there's a ready-made market in Asia. "All we have to do is find a way to market them," says Charles C. Thomas, head of Florida's Bureau of Seafood and Aquaculture. "Some people have a preference for things that we think are weird."

Meanwhile, it's not impossible that jellyfish won't catch on in the United States, too. After all, a lot of Americans weren't too fond of sushi when it was first introduced. Who knows? One day American kids might grow up on peanut butter and … jellyfish sandwiches?

SOURCE   Eric Morgenthaler, "U.S. Has Jellyfish That Nobody Wants Except Maybe in Asia," *The Wall Street Journal,* December 14, 1992, p. A1–A5.

perceive as offering more value than competitors' products. How they achieve this depends on traits or attributes that shape value:

- Value is ultimately defined by the customer.
- Managers face a critical task of articulating the demands and expectations of the customer.
- Value is dynamic.
- Value is best understood through a value equation.
- Value combines four major traits: speed, cost, quality, and flexibility. The importance of each of these traits depends on the customer's expectations.
- Value changes the way in which managers view and structure the delivery process.
- Value requires the operations manager to determine how well the firm can resolve the demands and expectations of the customer with the capabilities of its operations management system.

Understanding market segments and the demands of consumers is critical to successful operations management. This skateboard manufacturer must have a different operations strategy to meet the needs of a competitive teenager versus the desires of parents buying a first board for their young child.
SOURCE   Lawrence Migdale/Stock Boston

Value and the Customer

Value starts with the customer. One person's delicacy may disgust someone else. Consider Jack Rudloe's attempts to build a jellyfish industry in the United States reported in the "On the Job" box. Rudloe is learning the hard way that customer-specific value may make dried jellyfish a treat to a diner in Tokyo while patrons in a Minneapolis restaurant would rather starve.

The concept of value, however, applies everywhere, though its implementation and expression vary widely among markets and customers. At first glance, this statement seems fairly obvious, but it raises an important underlying issue. To compete on value, a firm must answer three critical questions.

Exactly Which Customers Determine Value?   Should managers evaluate input from the intermediate customer or the ultimate customer? A company like Huffy or Murray sells to customers as diverse as purchasing agents for department stores who decide whether to carry their bicycles, parents who buy the bicycles, and children who ride them. Each of these customers may expect different things. The purchasing agent may want to know the cost per bicycle, the terms of sale (e.g., the time between delivery and payment), reliability (e.g., the manufacturer's record in meeting its promised delivery dates), warranty, and return procedures. In contrast, the parent might decide based on price, durability, and ease of assembly. The child might focus on the bicycle's features (paint job, colors) and how fast it will go. Each customer sees value as something different. A company like Huffy or Murray doesn't sell to a single customer, but to a chain of customers.

What Target Market Does the Firm Serve?   Most firms do not think of serving individual customers. Rather, managers cater to market segments, groups of individual customers whose tastes and expectations make them seem more alike than different. Firms define market segments in many ways, but all must confront the trade-off between market size and ease of identifying exactly what a group of customers demand or expect.

To define a market segment for bicycles, a firm could lump together all bicycle buyers. Alternatively, it could define a market segment as everyone interested in a high-performance mountain bike. The first definition covers a huge group of customers who can generate a large volume of demand. However, it is difficult to build one bicycle that can satisfy every person in this market. This effort would produce a bike that the average customer would want. Many people may find this product good enough unless someone else comes out with a bicycle that more closely matches what they want. In contrast, the mountain bike market segment presents a better picture of what customers want to buy. They look first at performance, expecting light frames, rugged components, and pleasing designs. Such expensive bicycles will not appeal to someone who simply wants good, basic transportation.

The firm can refine its idea of what customers want at the cost of reducing the size of market. Instead of millions of bicycle riders, it now identifies thousands or maybe hundreds of potential customers. Serving a market of millions requires a different operations management system than serving a market of hundreds. Striking the right balance between market size and clarity of customer demands is not an easy task.

How Can a Firm Cope with Changes in Its Customer Base and Its Overall Market?   The customers who buy a company's output often change over time. Old customers leave; new customers replace them, bringing different expectations. Value for the old customers may no longer represent value to the new customers. The bicycle market shows the importance of changes in the customer base.

In 1980, the major type of bicycle sold was the road bike with its thin tires intended for use on paved roads. Every bicycle store offered a good selection of these bicycles. In the early 1980s, people such as Gary Fisher, Tom Ritchie, and Joe Breeze of Marin County, California, developed the mountain bike with wide, knobby tires and a small frame to stand up to rough, off-road use on walking trails and hilly paths. Instead of riding in the crouched, aerodynamic position of the road bike, the mountain biker rode in a fairly upright position. Instead of speed, mountain bikes were intended to offer recreation anywhere. The new machines attracted a new generation of bike owners.

After 10 years, in 1990, the bike market had changed. Estimates indicated that for every road bike sold, ten mountain bikes were sold. To survive in this new market, bicycle companies had to offer wide selections of mountain bike models. Those that failed to do so, such as Schwinn, faced disaster in the market.

Explicit and Latent Desires

explicit desire

A need that the customer recognizes and can describe

latent desire

A need that the customer recognizes and understands only vaguely

Once the firm has identified its customers and market segment, it must begin to understand what value means to them. Most situations feature two types of value. Customers express **explicit desires**, needs that they can describe when they know what they want in a good or service. Value may also depend on **latent desires** when customers know that they have a problem, but they may be unable to describe the solution. The firm must identify these latent desires and then provide a good or service that satisfies them. Essentially, the firm reacts to explicit desires; to satisfy latent desires, it must take a proactive initiative to anticipate the customer's recognition of a problem or an unfulfilled need.

The firm can try to anticipate these needs by viewing itself as a partner of the customer. It must commit to knowing its customers so well that it can determine what they want almost before they know themselves.[2] The customer then recognizes that the product satisfies their needs and that it offers value. Firms such as Nucor Steel, Landmark Graphics, and Schneider Nation trucking are recognized experts at anticipating and meeting latent desires.[3] Products like Xerox's photocopier and the Sony Walkman also satisfy latent desires.

Xerox and Latent Desires.   When Xerox management conceived the idea of a photocopier, they first offered it to IBM, which dismissed the concept, seeing no apparent need for it. Xerox had difficulty selling its photocopiers to other firms, as well. It managed to gain a foothold in the business market only by placing the photocopiers free of charge and collecting fees solely on the number of copies made at 5 cents each. Managers accepted this option since it wouldn't really cost them anything, they reasoned, because no one would use a Xerox machine when carbon paper seemed just as easy.

Xerox succeeded because its process and product met the needs of some real customers, secretaries. After secretaries learned how to operate the new photocopiers, they used them extensively. Compared with carbon copies, they found the Xerox process to be easier, less prone to error, quicker, and cleaner. Correcting an error on a carbon copy was a dirty, time-consuming, and frustrating experience. In contrast, they could correct errors on photocopies simply by running the corrected sheet through the machine again. Xerox turned an idea that IBM didn't want into a success because it identified and satisfied a latent desire.

Implications for Operations Management.   To make operations management a value-driven process, practitioners must accept the need to work closely with the marketing function. Marketing represents the needs and expectations of the customer within the firm and defines the market segment that the firm will try to satisfy. In addition, working closely with marketing allows the operations manager to educate that department (and, ideally, the rest of the firm) about what the operations management system can and cannot do.

Value and the Value Equation

Having identified a customer, the operations manager must next describe value for that person and determine how the operations management function can affect the perceived value of the firm's goods and services. The **value equation** offers one convenient way of approaching this task.

The notion of the value equation was developed by Procter & Gamble to describe the relationship between the various attributes of value. This equation can be written as follows:[4]

$$\text{Value} = \frac{\text{Performance}}{\text{Cost}} \qquad (2.1)$$

value equation
The mathematical expression of value as a ratio of performance to cost

---

[2]Myron Magnet, "Meet the New Revolutionaries," *Fortune*, February 24, 1992, pp. 94–101.

[3]Ibid.

[4]This concept comes from the value model introduced by Procter & Gamble CEO Edwin L. Artzt, Quality Forum VIII, October 1, 1992.

performance

A factor in the value equation that describes what a good or service does for the customer

quality

A factor in performance that represents how well a product meets a customer's expectations

speed

A factor in performance that describes how quickly the firm can deliver a product to the customer or design and produce a product

flexibility

A factor in performance that reflects how easily the firm can change the product to more closely match the needs of the customer

cost

The denominator in the value equation that measures all costs (objective and subjective) that the customer incurs to acquire, use, and dispose of a product

The value equation expresses value as a comparison of what a product can do against what it costs. **Performance** describes what the good or service does for the customer. Typically, performance is described in terms of three traits: quality, speed, and flexibility. **Quality** represents how well the good or service meets or exceeds the expectations of the customer at the time of purchase. **Speed** describes the time needed to deliver the good or service to the customer or the time that the firm needs to design and produce the good or service. **Flexibility** reflects how easily the firm can change the product to more closely match the needs of the customer (e.g., by adding or dropping options).

This discussion of performance presupposes the notion of the function of the product. The product must satisfy a real need, it must perform as promised, and it must offer the features that the customer wants. This condition underlies all expressions of value. Value-based competition must always create or enhance functionality by improving the other elements of value.

The three components of performance do not always carry equal weights. Rather, performance is a weighted sum of these variables based on subjective weights that reflect customers' priorities:

$$\text{Performance} = \beta_1 \times \text{Quality} + \beta_2 \times \text{Speed} + \beta_3 \times \text{Flexibility} \quad \textbf{(2.2)}$$

Many factors influence the values that customers assign to these parameters. These weights can change with customers' income or education levels or their cultures or nationalities. For example, dried jellyfish offers little value to most Americans, while someone from Taipei may view it as highly attractive and valuable.

More important, these weights often reflect customers' order winners, order qualifiers, and order losers, as discussed in Chapter 1. Using these three concepts, customers may well weight characteristics they see as order winners more heavily than order qualifiers or less important traits.

Cost, the denominator in the value equation, represents all costs (objective and subjective) that the customer incurs to acquire, use, and dispose of the good or service. Exhibit 2.1 shows the influence of the value equation on a set of guidelines to effective value marketing.

Implications for Operations Management.   The value equation is important for several reasons. First, it identifies the four components of value (cost, quality, speed, and flexibility) against which all managers must evaluate their operations management systems. We will refer repeatedly to this yardstick when introducing the various components of the operations management system.

Second, the value equation identifies the various ways in which the firm (and its operations management system) can create value for customers and compete in the marketplace. For example, managers might decide that their firm can compete most effectively by keeping performance constant and reducing cost. Alternatively, they could try to increase performance while keeping cost constant or to increase performance more than cost. The components of the value equation can change in many different ways to enhance value for the customer. Each of these ways identifies a different potential strategy for the firm (i.e., a different way of differentiating the firm from its competitors).

To understand how operations managers can use the value equation to define value and differentiate their companies, consider how Hewlett-Packard and Casio sell calculators. Hewlett-Packard competes on performance by designing new calculators that emphasize increasing performance levels while the cost to customers either remains the same or rises slightly. In contrast, Casio competes on cost by

[**E X H I B I T   2 . 1**]

How to Be a Value Marketer

Offer products that perform

This is just the price of entry. Consumers have lost patience with shoddy goods, and fashion won't distract them from flimsiness.

Give more than the consumer expects

Whether it's providing environmentally sound packaging or including air-conditioning in a car's standard price, offering pleasant— and useful—surprises will win customer loyalty.

Give guarantees

Offering an enhanced warranty and ponying up full refunds when problems arise can help to justify that higher price.

Avoid unrealistic pricing

Compaq found that out; it hewed too long to premium pricing that its basic product could not justify.

Give the customer the facts

Use your advertising to provide the kind of detailed information that today's sophisticated consumer demands.

Build relationships

Frequent-buyer plans, 800 numbers, and membership clubs can help to bind the consumer to your product and service.

SOURCE   Christopher Power, Walecia Konrad, Alice Z. Cuneo, and James B. Treece, "Value Marketing." Reprinted from November 11, 1991 issue of *Business Week* by special permission, copyright © 1991 by The McGraw-Hill Companies.

taking as given the feature sets defined by competitors and accepted by customers and working to reduce costs so that it can offer the same level of performance as competitors at a lower cost.

The value equation is important also because the four components of value can be combined to yield five major approaches for value-driven competition in the marketplace.

Any Time.   This strategy option focuses on time to create value for the customer. Time influences the actions of the customer as a resource, not a constraint. The firm and the OM system can enhance value by reducing lead time for the customer in many different ways:

- Reducing means and variances
- Managing both design and delivery lead times
- Reducing total system lead times
- Focusing on lead times for specific activities that interest the customer

Any Place.   This strategy option tries to reduce the distance between the customer and the supplier. In the future, successful firms will close the distance between customers and suppliers in several different ways. First, an increasing amount of production will take place at the customer's location. Customers will also play more active roles in the design, manufacturing, and delivery activities of their suppliers. Second, bringing together suppliers and customers will reduce the number of stages between customers and suppliers. Many firms will reduce these stages by eliminating unnecessary steps in the design and delivery process. Ultimately, the basic customer-supplier relationship must move from competition toward cooperation.

No Matter.   This strategy option describes a change in the way that customers view the firm's product as they use it. Suppliers no longer sell and customers no longer buy strictly physical goods. Intangible product characteristics such as security, goodwill, information, and service are beginning to play more important roles in company-customer relationships. When you buy a high-end bicycle such as a Serotta, you also buy continuing support. The dealer works with you to make sure that the bicycle fits you well, both before and after you buy it, and gives free periodic tune-ups to make sure that the bicycle continues to work well.

One of the first companies to recognize the importance of the no-matter strategy as a source of value was WordPerfect. This company became the leader in the market for DOS word-processing software by providing every user with access to toll-free telephone support. Besides a software package, WordPerfect users got the peace of mind of knowing that if they ever encountered problems that they couldn't solve, help was a telephone call away.

Mass Customization.   This strategy option describes a system that can customize products on a mass scale. Instead of building products for markets, mass customizers build products for individuals. They must be able to deliver acceptable products to these customers at prices not much higher than they would pay for standard products.

Panasonic in Japan can design a bike for a specific customer in 3 hours and build it within 3 days. This requires the OM system to manage 11,325,000 different options. Another good example of mass customization comes from a paint store, where you can blend a unique shade of paint to suit your specific needs.

Risk Reduction.   Simply stated, the strategy of risk reduction attracts customers by offering to eliminate or greatly reduce the risks of doing business. Risk reduction may focus on the transformation process itself. With companies increasingly moving toward systems that rely on less inventory and shorter lead times, suppliers can charge premium prices if they expose their customers to less risk. Typically, these systems are highly visible and under strict control. Such systems are designed to instill customer confidence by demonstrating control that assures on-time delivery of products that satisfy customers' quality and quantity needs.

Risk-reduction efforts may also focus on the product. A firm may try to provide a product that is easy to maintain, easy to use, and easy to repair. This approach to risk reduction tries to convince the customer that the firm can substantially reduce any risks associated with a purchase.

The value equation guides operations managers' efforts to develop a version of one of these strategies for their firm based on its customers' priorities at the time. The on-going work of value-driven management becomes more complicated, however, as those priorities change, requiring a redefinition of *value.*

▣ DYNAMIC NATURE OF VALUE

Customers' definitions of *value* change continually. Yesterday's thrilling innovation is considered simply acceptable today, and it may become inadequate tomorrow. These changes often result from changes in customer expectations and affect the various ß parameters in the value equation.

Forces That Drive Change

Customer expectations and value may change at any time for any of several reasons.

1. Familiarity.   Familiarity is the notion that exposure to something leads people to take it for granted. As a result, familiarity reduces the effect of a product trait or attribute as an order winner. Familiarity changes a unique order winner to a basic expectation that the customer expects in every product.

For example, in the early 1980s, the Japanese auto manufacturers increased their share of the North American car market by offering superior quality. Many customers viewed the superior quality of Japanese-built cars, combined with their moderate prices, as an order winner. However, the role of quality as an order winner has changed as North American auto manufacturers have matched or exceeded the quality levels of Japanese cars. This change combined with the repeated emphasis on quality in the press (e.g., the various consumer reporting services) has led customers to view quality as an order qualifier rather than an order winner.[5] They expect cars to offer a certain level of quality even to consider buying them.

Customers have become less sensitive to the whole issue of improved quality. Instead, they now look for faster delivery, easier product customization, and quicker introductions of new and better products as new sources of value.[6]

2. Income/Education.   As income levels increase, customers can afford to consider products that cost more, but also offer far higher levels of performance. Someone who earns $20,000 a year cannot afford a new Mercedes Benz. However, if that same person rises to a job that pays $100,000 a year, a Mercedes becomes a viable option. For similar reasons, higher levels of education increase customers' expectations. Education also tends to make customers more aware of the importance of performance.

3. Economic Conditions.   Changes in economic conditions affect people's perceptions of value. During a time of depressed economic conditions like the late

[5]Phillip L. Carter and Steven A. Melnyk, "Time-Based Competition: Building the Foundations for Speed," *APICS 35th International Conference Proceedings,* Montreal, Quebec, Canada, October 18–23, 1992, pp. 63–67.

[6]Joseph L. Bower and Thomas M. Hout, "Fast-Cycle Capability for Competitive Power," *Harvard Business Review,* November/December 1988; Brian Dumaine, "How Managers Can Succeed through Speed," *Fortune,* February 13, 1989, pp. 54–59; Brian Dumaine, "Earning More by Moving Faster," *Fortune,* October 7, 1991, pp. 89–94; George Stalk, Jr., "Time—The Next Source of Competitive Advantage," *Harvard Business Review,* July/August 1988; George Stalk, Jr. and Thomas H. Hout, *Competing against Time* (New York: Free Press, 1990); and Sara L. Beckman, "Manufacturing Flexibility: The Next Source of Competitive Advantage," in *Strategic Manufacturing,* ed. by Patricia E. Moody (Homewood, Ill.: Dow Jones-Irwin, 1990).

1980s and early 1990s, many people find themselves with either less money or with less secure economic futures. As a result, they buy lower-cost, more practical products. Value becomes especially critical in tough economic times.

4. Competitors' Actions and Corporate Strategies.   The three forces discussed so far reflect changes within the customer that affect expectations and assessments of value. Actions of others can also change customers' expectations. First, consider competitors' actions or changes in their corporate strategies.

As Chapter 1 pointed out, every firm tries as one of its major goals to develop, establish, and maintain a sustainable competitive advantage for itself. To do so, the firm must offer its customers something that its competitors do not. This effort often produces a series of moves and countermoves, each of which influences expectations and, ultimately, value. Each firm tries to offer or emphasize a feature of its good or service that its managers believe to be either unique, better than competitors' product features, or difficult to duplicate. Competitors respond by either matching or improving upon the new offering. This process of response and counter-response results in the "pugnacious insistence on one-upping the competition" described at the beginning of this chapter.[7]

Competitive sparring makes order winners into order qualifiers over time. For example, the Japanese car companies relied on quality in the form of better designed and built cars as an order winner. However, since the early 1980s, the North American car manufacturers have responded to this challenge by increasing their overall quality levels. As a result, in the 1990s, many agree that the quality gap between Japanese and North American cars is no longer significant. More important, most customers no longer give quality the importance that they once did. They expect to buy well-built cars. Quality has now become an order qualifier in the car market.

As order winners become order qualifiers, firms and managers search for new order winners, especially in areas where their systems excel but competitors' systems do not. In the 1990s, many of these new order winners involve time and flexibility. To understand this trend, consider the experiences of Intel.

Intel had become one of the largest manufacturers of microprocessor chips by developing and manufacturing the 80X86 family of chips which run most IBM-compatible microcomputers. Recently, Andy Grove, Intel's CEO, decided to emphasize speed as a way of securing the firm's place in the market. Intel will try to introduce a new family of chips that double power every 2 years to force cloners such as Advanced Micro Device (AMD) into a perpetual catch-up mode.[8]

Intel is working to generate value for customers by focusing on the performance side of the value equation. In the process, Intel is also affecting customer expectations. As customers see the speed and power of the next generation of chips, the previous generation's performance no longer seems adequate. The power of a 486 machine suddenly seems inadequate compared with the Pentium, which will in turn seem weak compared with new generations of computers. With Intel's speed-based strategy, by the time cloners have figured out through reverse engineering how to copy its latest generation of chips, Intel has introduced a new, more powerful generation. This leaves the cloners to build cheaper but obsolete chips.

The example of Intel also illustrates that a time-based advantage is valuable only when function is assured. This fact recently confronted Intel managers when

[7]Stratford Sherman, "How to Prosper in the Value Decade," *Fortune,* November 30, 1992, p. 103.
[8]Robert D. Hof, "Inside Intel," *Business Week,* June 1, 1992, pp. 86–94.

[BY THE WAY... PENTIUM HUMOR]
[FROM THE INTERNET]

Top Ten New Slogans for the Pentium (Apologies to David Letterman.)

9.9999973251:	It's a FLAW, dammit, not a bug.
8.9999163326:	It's close enough. We say so.
7.9999414610:	Nearly 300 correct opcodes
6.9999831538:	You don't need to know what's inside

5.9999835137:	Redefining the PC—and mathematics as well
4.9999999021:	We fixed it, really
3.9998245917:	Division considered harmful
2.9991523619:	Why do you think they call it *floating* point?
1.9999103517:	We're looking for a few good flaws
0.9999999998:	The errata inside

they faced a public relations disaster due to problems with the firm's newest and most powerful chip, the Pentium. Many firms relied on Pentium-based microcomputers to perform highly complex mathematical work such as design analysis in airplane manufacturing and computer graphics. In late 1994, however, Thomas Nicely, a mathematics professor at Lynchburg College in Virginia, discovered a problem with floating point division in the Pentium. Under certain circumstances, the chip would generate an error. When customers need double-digit accuracy, the Pentium would generate answers with roughly single-digit accuracy.

When this problem became widely known, Intel initially tried to stonewall, arguing that the problem occurred too infrequently to concern anyone but those doing complex mathematical analysis. After becoming the butt of numerous jokes (see the "By the Way" box, which reprints some responses from the Internet) and after losing several important customers such as IBM, however, Intel announced that it would replace the chip with a corrected model for any owner who asked. Intel learned that speed generates value only when a product works as promised.

Intel is not the only firm to have recognized the importance of a unique source of value. Exhibit 2.2 lists other firms that have succeeded in developing sustainable competitive advantages by linking strategy to value creation for the customer.

5. Government Actions. Government actions establish standards, or floors, for adequate performance. They set minimum performance levels that firms' goods and services must meet, helping to shape order qualifiers for many customers. These actions can take the form of new regulations or certification procedures. The government also collects and distributes information about company performance such as data about on-time arrivals and departures of airlines' flights at major airports.

Implications for Operations Management. The changeable nature of value has several important implications for the operations management system. First, the operations management system must be as dynamic as value. If customers look for value in lower costs, then operations managers must study their entire systems to identify and trim unnecessary costs. However, if the focus of value shifts to quality, they must manage their systems to enhance quality by identifying and eliminating

[**E X H I B I T   2 . 2**]

Value Marketers

Certain companies are leading the way in focusing on greater value. Among them:

Taco Bell: By reducing operating costs enough to make money on menu items under $1, it has reintroduced fast-food rivals to the notion of value.

Wal-Mart Stores: "The low price on the brands you trust." The motto says it all. Wal-Mart is now the world's largest retailer.

Southwest Airlines: By combining a consistently low price with friendly, but bare-bones service, it's the most successful carrier of its size.

Sara Lee: Its personal-products subsidiary prices its L'Eggs women's hoisery to beat store brands and still retain a quality image.

Toyota: From the $7,000 Tercel to the $42,000 Lexus, the Japanese carmaker consistently offers more features at reasonable price than most competitors.

activities that do not enhance quality (e.g., inspections) or that actually reduce quality (e.g., areas of the process that generate excess defects).

Inspections have received special attention recently. Inspections evaluate products of either previous steps in the OM process or the firm's suppliers to verify that they meet specifications for quality and delivery schedules. Ultimately, this step adds no value and customers are unwilling to pay extra for inspections. If the OM process or suppliers perform to specifications, inspections become unnecessary.

Some changes to an operations management system generate gradual and evolutionary improvements. By continuously studying a current system, operations managers can identify opportunities for improvements by introducing small changes to the existing system continuously. A later chapter will explore this concept of continuously introducing small improvements to a current system, now more commonly referred to as **kaizen**, a Japanese term for continuous improvement.[9] Improving the level of quality provided by suppliers might eliminate the need for an inspection; bringing two linked operations closer together might reduce component transportation times.

kaizen
A quality enhancement principle of continuously introducing small improvements to an existing OM system

Some changes generate sudden, large-scale, revolutionary improvements. When Henry Ford introduced the assembly line to the auto industry in the early 1900s, he revolutionized the process of building cars. Prior to the introduction of the assembly line for Ford's Model T, skilled and semi-skilled workers built cars at stationary work areas. Cars did not move; rather all of the materials and labor moved to each car. Only the rich could afford the output of this process. By introducing the assembly line, Henry Ford reduced the price of the Model T through the cost component of the value equation. As a result, more people could afford his cars. The introduction of the assembly line quickly made the earlier methods of car manufacturing obsolete. Henry Ford recognized the dynamic nature of value and its impact on the operations management system and, ultimately, the firm, as the "By the Way" box indicates.

[9]Masaaki Imai, *Kaizen—The Key to Japan's Competitive Success* (New York: Random House, 1986).

[**BY THE WAY... HENRY FORD ON THE CHANGEABLE NATURE OF OPERATIONS MANAGEMENT**]

If to petrify is success, all one has to do is to humor the lazy side of the mind; but if to grow is success, then one must wake up anew every morning and keep awake all day. I saw great businesses become but the ghost of a name because someone thought they could be managed just as they were always managed, and though the management may have been most excellent in its day, its excellence consisted in its alertness to its day and not in slavish following of its yesterdays. Life, as I see it, is not a location, but a journey. Even the man who most feels himself "settled" is not settled—he is probably sagging back. Everything is in flux, and was meant to be. Life flows. We may live at the same number of the street, but it is never the same man who lives there.

SOURCE   Henry Ford with Samuel Crowther, *My Life and Work*, (Garden City, N.J.: Doubleday, 1922).

The failure of Schwinn emphasizes the dynamic nature of value, the need for the operations management system to keep pace with these changes, and the cost of failure. Firms and operations management systems that do not keep pace are ultimately doomed to failure.

Implementing Change: Refinement versus Redefinition

How changes take place often reflects how companies try to develop their own competitive advantages. If everyone agrees on how to solve the value problem, then change often represents **refinement**. For example, if many competing firms agree that cost reduction is the key order winner for their customers, they will focus on activities that generate excessive or unnecessary costs. Managers identify firms that have reduced costs and study those firms' procedures and techniques. Managers then try to replicate others' success by implementing the same procedures and techniques in their own firms. They also try to improve on these procedures by continuously adjusting and fine-tuning them. This leads to refinement, a series of small, continuous improvements.

refinement
Incremental improvement of existing practices

However, if a firm decides to enhance value by emphasizing a different aspect of product performance that competitors ignore, then change occurs by **redefinition**. The nature of the value problem changes in such a situation, and operations managers must turn to new and different approaches. Radical and revolutionary changes generally accompany redefinition.

redefinition
Sudden, dramatic changes driven by new methods of enhancing value

Prior to Ford's introduction of the assembly line, most auto manufacturers were trying simply to produce well-built cars that worked. Cost was not especially important since cars were targeted to those who could afford to pay. Henry Ford redefined the problem that shaped the nature of his manufacturing process. Rather than producing well-built, functional cars, he attacked the problem of reducing the price of the car to allow more people to afford it. Ford could not solve this problem using the same old labor-intensive, expensive process; he had to invent a new process.

This discussion illustrates the development of a strong link among the customer, corporate strategy, and the operations management system. Corporate strategy identifies market segments to which the firm (and its underlying systems) will try to appeal. The firm tries to identify some feature or combination of features that represent value to those customers, who respond by buying (accepting the firm's view of value) or not buying. How the firm formulates this view of value shapes much of the OM system and its management. When this view of value changes, as it inevitably must, operations management methods must change to maintain a strong consistency between what the customers want and are willing to pay for and what the firm can offer.

Value and OM Capability

So far, we have considered the task of generating value from only one perspective—that of the customer. Previous sections have addressed the outcome, characterized by quality, cost, speed, and flexibility, that customers want and value. This narrow view assumes that managers can identify what the customer wants and then quickly and easily change the transformation system to make it consistent with these requirements. This assumption may not be valid. Assessing what an existing system can deliver often reveals a gap between current system strengths and customer expectations. To better understand the reasons for this gap and its impact on value, we must look more closely at the transformation process.

In the past, operations managers have tended to take a very narrow view of the transformation process solely in terms of volume. As noted in Chapter 1, evaluation of any transformation process tended to consider such output measures as numbers of hours (e.g., labor or machine hours) or units of output (e.g., cars, bicycles, gallons of paint). This view only looked at one aspect of the transformation process. It ignored the notion of the transformation process as **capability**. Exhibit 2.3 summarizes these two views.

capability

A task that a particular OM system can perform effectively

Each transformation process bundles together various capabilities. Each system can accomplish certain types of tasks, while it can perform other tasks only poorly. Simply stated, no system can be all things to all people; no one system can excel at all tasks or maximize every dimension of value (i.e., speed, cost, quality, and flexibility). Each system is uniquely suited to certain tasks; each excels in satisfying or exceeding the needs of certain types of customers. To better understand this concept of capability in the transformation process, consider the differences in OM processes of Huffy and Serotta Competition Bicycles.

Huffy's Capabilities.   Huffy builds bicycles primarily for the low end of the price range (i.e., $100 to $250). Sold primarily through toy stores and department stores, Huffy bicycles typically suit children or adults who take occasional rides through town. These buyers care little for performance issues such as low frame weight or state-of-the-art components, and they are not willing to pay premium prices for high-end features. They want low-cost, durable, no-frills bicycles that are not too heavy (making weight an order qualifier) and that will survive rough handling by children. They buy based on price and durability.

Huffy has designed a transformation process that excels at producing a durable bicycle at a low cost. To reduce costs, it strictly limits the number of models and variations in components. Huffy's factory is designed to build only a certain number of bicycle models, each in a limited range of frame sizes, using standard components. Emphasizing product standardization, Huffy relies extensively on automation to reduce costs, welding frames primarily by robots, for example. Automation enables Huffy to reduce labor costs since it can hire fewer workers with lower skill levels. Huffy's approach to manufacturing results in a

[**E X H I B I T   2 . 3**]

Capacity: Output and Capability

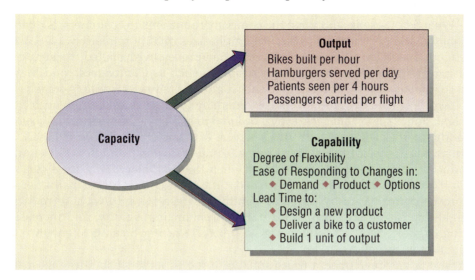

large fixed-cost base and relatively low variable costs to suit its need for high-volume production.

Huffy also designs its products to control costs. Instead of using high-quality, extremely durable metals such as chromoly steel, Huffy makes its bikes of lower grade, softer steel since most bicycle riders do not notice the difference and would not be willing to pay hundreds of dollars more for better-quality steel. Huffy holds its cables in place with plastic fasteners rather than the metal guides found on most midrange and high-end bicycles. It omits quick-release wheel fasteners in favor of simpler, more secure, and cheaper nut-and-bolt fasteners.

The combination of automation and product design creates a transformation process that excels at producing low-cost, durable bicycles in large quantities. However, these same factors also limit the transformation process. Huffy could not use this same process to meet the demands of buyers who want to pay more for hand-crafted, performance bicycles.

Capabilities of Serotta Competition Bicycles.   To build a performance bicycle requires a different set of skills and a different transformation process. Performance bicycles such as those of Serotta Competition Bicycles, Trek, Cannondale, or Specialized emphasize light weight. To reduce weight in a bicycle often requires a skilled worker to devote time, effort, and knowledge to careful filing to remove excess weight. Buyers of performance bicycles also demand much greater variety in components, sizes, and colors. Performance bicycles require the use of lighter and stronger materials (e.g., high-quality steel, carbon fiber, aluminum, titanium, or metal matrix materials). Finally, customers for performance bicycles tend to appreciate and demand evidence of craftsmanship in the construction of their bikes. All of these traits demand capabilities that Huffy's transformation process cannot match. Serotta's transformation process emphasizes these traits.

Serotta is a small bicycle manufacturing operation located in South Glen Falls, New York. The company offers many different types of machines, but specializes in road bicycles. It produces well-regarded road racing bikes, at one time supplying bicycles for the Coors Light Racing Team of Colorado. It sells mainly to people who want performance bicycles and are willing to pay for them. For example, a Serotta Legend TG, the company's lowest-priced bicycle, starts at about $1,850.

What Serotta sells, and what the company represents to customers, is quality, flexibility, and performance. The firm emphasizes quality in many ways—using premium materials, staffing its transformation process with skilled workers, purchasing premium components from suppliers such as Campagnolo and Mavic, and continually testing its bicycles in such high-stress situations as long-stage races.

Serotta enhances value for its customers by offering wide latitude in bicycle designs. For example, a bicycle can be ordered in any of 13 different paint schemes. In addition, the customer can outfit a bicycle with one of seven different road kits with various types of handlebars, stems, components, and saddles. If a regular, production bicycle is not good enough, then the customer can order a custom-built bicycle at a slightly higher price and with a longer lead time. Finally, Serotta improves performance by pursuing continuous research into ways of reducing weight, increasing strength and durability, enhancing rigidity, and increasing riding comfort. Serotta's experience with bicycle racing helps it to enhance the designs of its bicycles.

Serotta has developed a transformation process with capabilities that match the needs of customers who demand quality, flexibility, and performance in their bicycles. Unlike Huffy, which organizes its process around large runs of fairly standardized bicycles, Serotta produces small batches of bicycles that can differ widely in features like paint schemes and components. Instead of automation, Serotta relies on highly skilled workers using general-purpose equipment and tools. Each bicycle requires extensive, labor-intensive operations such as hand-brazing and filing of fittings.

Both Huffy and Serotta have developed transformation processes well-suited to their respective markets. Huffy's system excels at building low-cost, durable, standard bicycles in large volumes; Serotta's system effectively builds high-quality, high-performance bicycles in small quantities. Each system has inherent limitations. Huffy could no more build a high-performance bicycle using its current transformation system than Serotta could build a department store bicycle costing between $100 to $200.

Determinants of Process Capabilities.   The capabilities of a transformation system are the result of four assets managed by the operations management system (Exhibit 2.4):

- *Processes*   Systems (formal and informal) that the firm has developed for planning and controlling all flows of information or resources through the firm. Information flows may include orders from customers to the factory; other resource flows may include movements of bicycles through the various operations on the shop floor.
- *People*   All of the personnel employed by the firm. This resource includes all people engaged in all activities, including their intellectual resources, that involve the transformation process (e.g., supervisors and line workers).
- *Information*   All of the information that the operations management system draws on to build its products, process orders, improve efficiencies, respond to customer requests, design and test new products, and meet schedules, to name a few functions.

[E X H I B I T   2 . 4   ]

Four Assets of Operations Management

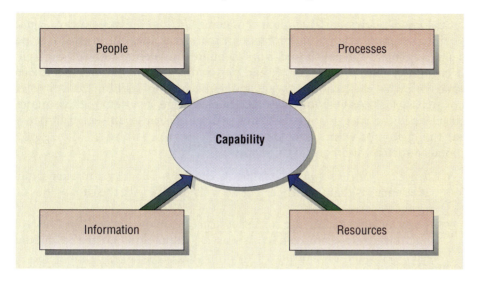

- *Resources*   A catch-all term that describes all remaining resources that help the operations management system to meet schedules, manage day-to-day operations, and respond to change. Resources can be either physical assets (e.g., machines, plants, locations) or financial assets (e.g., lines of credit).

The last three factors (people, information, and resources) are often grouped together under the broad heading of **capacity**.

Acting on these four assets are three major agents: technology, organization (the OM function's arrangement of people and activities as well as the resulting interrelationships), and strategy (Exhibit 2.5). Together these agents and assets shape the type of value that the operations management system can offer.

capacity

People, information, and other resources that help to determine the capabilities of an OM process

Capacity—Other Issues.   The short-term capabilities of the transformation system are essentially fixed, but they can change over the long term. Building and

[E X H I B I T   2 . 5   ]

Operations Management to Create Value

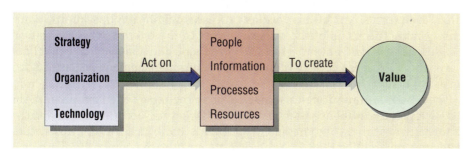

changing capabilities requires time and dedication of such corporate resources as money, labor, and effort. A firm can change existing capabilities or build new capabilities only by changing the appropriate assets and agents. This takes time and effort—it cannot be done over night.

Customers' views of value often change faster than the system can adjust its capability, creating a perpetual problem for managers. Ideally, an effective operations management system should work to build consistency between capabilities and customers. The OM system should perform best at operations that are compatible with what the customers want and value, but maintaining this consistency is not an easy task. As customers' expectations change, a system that has matched their needs in the past may may no longer forge the same consistent fit between what the customer wants and values and system capabilities. Managers can respond to such a gap in one of three ways:

- *Change the market segment*   Managers can try to identify a market segment with demands that the firm can effectively satisfy with the capabilities of its current system.
- *Change the capabilities of the current system*   By investing time and resources to acquire new resources or processes, managers can try to make the system's capabilities consistent with the market's changed demands.
- *Live with the mismatch*   In the short term, managers can decide to live with the mismatch by not investing any new resources in either changing the market segment or changing the capabilities of the existing system. This is a short-term response; over the long term, the gap between capabilities and customer expectations will reduce profits for the firm and encourage competitors to enter the market with systems that are more consistent with customer needs and desires.

Each option imposes a time penalty, and each requires resources to implement.

The changeability of customer needs forces operations managers to look at their systems in a different way. They must now think of an operations management system as a set of capabilities, and they must understand how these capabilities are shaped and changed by the processes and resources of the transformation process. They must also recognize the possibility that the firm will identify new demands and expectations of the customer that the capabilities of the current system cannot satisfy. Often this possibility forces managers to try to build needed capabilities in anticipation of new customer demands. Like any strategy, this one may fail to achieve the desired match. The dual problem is illustrated in Exhibit 2.6.

Implications for Operations Management.   When one views the transformation process as both output volume and capability, the understanding of operations management and its functions must change. First, an operations manager can no longer look at resources such as inventory, equipment, and workers in isolation. Rather, each forms part of the various processes within the operations management system. The focus of the analysis shifts to the overall process. Managers must describe the relevant processes, analyze them, and communicate that knowledge not only to other people within the operations management system, but to the firm as a whole.

They must communicate this knowledge to the rest of the firm because those processes greatly influence its capabilities. Marketing, accounting, finance, and top management must understand what drives the transformation process and creates the capabilities that give the firm its sustainable competitive advantage and allow it to meet the needs of its customers.

[**EXHIBIT 2.6**]

Value Problem: Matching Customer Demands with System Capabilities

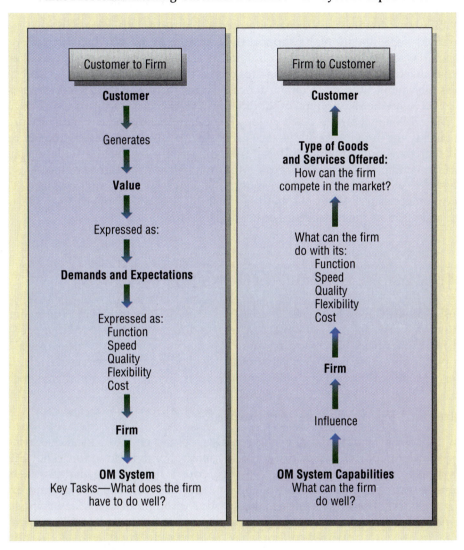

In analyzing the transformation process, the operations manager must begin to evaluate its capabilities. Adding a new machine may change more than the output level of the firm; it may also change the capabilities of the entire system. As for the initial analysis, the operations manager must update the rest of the firm (especially top managers) about changes in OM system capabilities and their implications for the firm.

As part of the manager's analysis of the transformation process and its capabilities, this effort must maintain an on-going link between customer-defined value and process capabilities. As new views of value evolve, the operations manager must restate them to specify the capabilities the firm will need to meet or exceed the resulting expectations. Similarly, as the firm develops new capabilities, the operations manager should identify the specific types of demands or expectations that the new system can satisfy.

Finally, the operations manager must remember that the capabilities of any transformation process react to forces outside the internal process and its resources. The capabilities of the firm's own transformation process depend on the capabilities of its suppliers. To compete on quality, a firm must not only develop capabilities within its transformation process that result in quality output; it must also make sure that suppliers support the transformation process with their own capabilities to produce quality goods. Quality leaders such as Motorola and Xerox have realized the importance of the capabilities of their supply chains (i.e., all suppliers who work with them either directly or indirectly) and the need for consistency between their suppliers' capabilities and their own.

Motorola, for example, has developed a system that can deliver a quality product quickly through its Six Sigma (6σ) program. The firm's managers quickly realized that they could maintain these capabilities only by dealing with suppliers that had similar systems. As a result, Motorola has now begun to reduce its supplier base, working only with suppliers that have 6σ programs in place. This requirement assures Motorola that the capabilities of its suppliers are consistent with and support the capabilities of its own transformation process.

WASTE AND OPERATIONS MANAGEMENT

Does adding labor to a product increase its value? Does increasing the material content in a product make it better? Does spending more time to build a product justify a higher price? Does adding more features make a product more useful? In the past, operations managers have often equated adding labor, materials, features, or time with increasing value, but this relationship no longer always holds.

Value and Resource Use: An Example

You decide that you need a new coffee maker, so you go to the local department store which offers a sale on two units of an identical brand and model. They differ only in rework; one of the coffee makers carries a note stating that production problems were identified during manufacturing and corrected by adding extra labor (rework). The other coffee maker passed through all manufacturing steps normally and passed all of the firm's product tests. Would you be willing to pay a higher price for the repaired coffee maker? Most people would answer a resounding *no*. Everyone wants a quality product; the repaired product was defective. Rather than pay more for a reworked product, people might expect a discount on its price.

Still, the repaired coffee maker absorbed more labor, material, and time, but this addition of resources didn't increase its value as compared to the normally produced product. To resolve this apparent contradiction, one must consider the notion of waste. The additional labor, material, and time for rework amounted to waste because they did not increase the product's value. Rather, they corrected a state that the customer would not accept (a defective product).

waste

Any activity or action that adversely affects the value equation for the customer

Waste Defined

The value-driven perspective of this book views value and waste as mirror images. **Waste** is any activity or action that adversely affects the value equation for the customer.

[**EXHIBIT 2.7**]

Two Objectives of Operations Management

Maximize Value

Undertake actions that maximize or enhance value and value creation.

Minimize Waste

Avoid or eliminate actions that reduce value or create waste.

Waste is a negative to be avoided or eliminated. Rather than increasing or enhancing value, waste reduces value. For example, managers for Serotta Competition Bicycles want to compete on quality, flexibility, and performance. Anything that reduces quality, decreases flexibility, or adversely affects performance is waste. Making a bicycle frame from steel that is too heavy creates waste, as does making an imperfectly aligned bicycle frame. Waste and value together define the major objectives of the effective operations management system (Exhibit 2.7).

Managers must view waste, like value, from the customer's perspective. Actions that some customers see as waste may generate value for others. As an example, consider inventory, items that a firm keeps in stock, from raw materials to products currently in production (work-in-process) and completed products sitting in stock. In general, operations managers view inventory as waste for several reasons. Inventory hides problems with the transformation process by allowing it to draw on stocks to avoid disruptions instead of correcting the causes of the problems. Inventory consumes corporate resources such as storage space, money to pay for it, people to count and manage it, etc. Inventory increases lead times because more inventory means that more work is in the system at any time, which means that it takes longer for any item to go from start to finish. Reducing the waste of inventory should result in shorter lead times, higher quality through improvements in the process, and lower costs, and this should equate to higher value. However, these relationships do not always hold.

Suppose that you need to travel in your car to an interview scheduled for the next day in a town about 130 miles away. The morning before the trip, you find that your car won't start. At a garage, the mechanic finds that it needs a small part that the mechanic happens to have in stock. You happily pay even a premium price for the part although you know that you are paying the mechanic to hold inventory which represents waste in most cases. In your case, however, the mechanic's inventory becomes a source of value because it reduces the lead time to repair your car. Without the inventory, you would have waited for the mechanic to order the part, increasing your lead time and perhaps forcing you to miss your interview.

As with value, one cannot identify waste without knowing what customers are willing to pay for.

"According to Henry Ford: Waste is any activity that does not add value."

Henry Ford, *Today and Tomorrow* (Cambridge, Mass.: Productivity Press, 1987).

"According to Forcier and Forcier: Waste defines the time, material, and energy not turned into valuable product."

Robert A. Forcier and Marsha M. Forcier, *Frontline Manufacturing* (Homewood, Ill.: Business One-Irwin, 1992), p. 72.

Categories of Waste

Operations management theorists have identified ten generic categories of waste:[10]

[10]Kiyoshi Suzaki, *The New Manufacturing Challenge* (New York: Free Press, 1987), pp. 12–18; and George W. Plossl, *Managing in the New World of Manufacturing* (Englewood Cliffs, N.J.: Prentice-Hall, 1991), pp. 50–51.

Bristol-Myers Squibb increased productivity of an anti-infective agent by reducing manufacturing cycle time. Faster production and delivery not only reduce waste, they can increase value by freeing employees to focus on other important activities.   SOURCE   Courtesy of Bristol-Myers Squibb Company

- *Waste of overproduction*   This waste occurs when the firm produces more goods than the market demands. Overproduction also takes place when the process gets ahead of the work; producing more than it needs creates extra inventory, requiring extra handling and extra space. All of these actions create costs for which the customer is not willing to pay.
- *Waste of waiting time*   This waste occurs when flows of materials and information become stalled. Any resource (material, information, etc.) that is not moving consumes resources without generating any offsetting value.
- *Waste of transportation*   This waste involves excessive handling or movement of goods as a result of such factors as poor layout, lack of coordination of processes, poor housekeeping, or inadequate methods of transportation.
- *Processing waste*   Excessive or unnecessary operations or actions also produce waste. Processing waste comes from doing more than is needed to build and deliver the product. Rework, correcting processing problems outside the normal process flow, falls into this category.
- *Inventory waste*   As discussed earlier, waste occurs when a process builds more than the firm needs to protect the system against problems such as excessively high scrap, shortages in vendor deliveries, and late arrivals of materials.
- *Waste of motion*   Some waste results from unnecessary human activity. This category separates motion from work and work from value. Efficiency requires reducing any unnecessary actions to achieve the motto, "Every step with a purpose and a purpose for every step."
- *Waste from product defects*   Creating defective products consumes resources, and correcting the defects consumes more. It also increases lead time by adding steps.
- *Waste of time*   Unnecessary delays or procrastination in decision making and taking action waste time which adversely affects the firm's ability to stay ahead of competitors in a rapidly changing environment.

[**EXHIBIT 2.8**]

Examples of Waste

- Inspections of incoming materials
- Illogical paper trails for materials orders
- Excessive handling of work on the shop floor
- Confusion on the floor
- Sequential design processes
- Some inventories
- Continuously working to correct acute problems in the process (fire-fighting)
- Excess idle capacity

- *Waste of human capabilities*   Every manager and worker brings certain skills, knowledge, and capabilities to the process. Ideally, the operations management system should make the fullest use of these capabilities, as unused capabilities become waste.
- *Waste from paperwork*   Unnecessary or redundant reports take time, consume resources (e.g., worker effort), and detract from value-adding activities.

These ten generic categories identify those general kinds of waste that adversely affect the value equation. One task of operations management is to identify specific examples of waste, categorize them appropriately, and then either reduce or eliminate them. Exhibit 2.8 lists some more specific forms of waste.

Waste and the Response of the Operations Management System

The operations manager can seldom target waste as a problem to attack. Rather, waste is a symptom of process problems. It acts like a thermometer. A higher level of waste (production of more scrap, a longer time to move an order through the system, etc.), indicates a larger problem (or problems). Typically, waste flags problems in the process, the resources (e.g., inadequate employee training), or the organization of the operations management system (e.g., an ineffective shop floor layout).

To eliminate waste of various types, the operations manager must first become familiar with the process. The manager must describe and understand the process to classify every action or activity into one of three categories:[11]

- *Value-adding activities*   Most of these activities involve work on the product. Activities add the most value in the transformation from input to output.
- *Waste-generating activities*   Activities that produce scrap, rework, and inspections are examples.
- *Nonvalue-adding but necessary activities*   Some necessary activities do not contribute to value. These are activities which have to take place. For example, whenever Serotta Competition Bicycles runs a new batch of frames, workers must set up the machines to process the order. By itself, this activity does not create value, but it represents necessary preparation for the value-adding activity (the actual process of building the bicycle frames).

"Japanese Perspective: Waste is "anything other than the minimum amount of equipment, materials, parts, space, and worker's time, which are absolutely essential to add value to the product.""

Fujio Cho of Toyota, quoted in Kiyoshi Suzaki, *The New Manufacturing Challenge* (New York: Free Press, 1987), p. 8.

---

[11]The chapter on Process Flow Analysis outlines tools and techniques for analyzing, describing, and understanding the various processes in the operations management system.

ON THE JOB

Rethinking at Frost, Inc.

■

Chad Frost is the president of a small manufacturing firm located in Grand Rapids, Michigan. This company with about 150 workers has been recognized as one of the leading practitioners of computer-integrated manufacturing (CIM). When he first took over the firm in the early 1980s, Frost saw no standards on the shop floor; everyone simply tried to do the best job possible. Three workers performed the same task at one station, each in a different way, though all did the best work they could. The amount of time required for the task and the quality level varied according to who was doing it.

Frost saw too much variability. His answer was to rethink. With the help of the workers, he identified the best single method of doing the task, making that method the standard for each of the three workers. Someone complained that this approach would stifle creativity. "Nonsense," said Frost. If someone had a better way of doing things, that person could prove to him and the area supervisor that the new method represented an improvement. The firm would then adopt the new method and make it the standard for the task. To Chad Frost, rethinking leads to simplification.

SOURCE   Steven A. Melnyk and Ram Narasimhan, *Computer-Integrated Manufacturing: Guidelines and Applications from Industrial Leaders* (Homewood, Ill.: Business One-Irwin, 1992), Chapter 10.

Another example of this category of activity is an inspection required by the customer of products and processes under tight control.

Assigning activities to these categories is not easy. Recognizing waste is an important management skill.[12] Often, attempts to categorize waste result in a new and temporary category: Don't Know. Managers don't always know whether a particular activity adds value, creates waste, or is necessary without adding value.

Once the operations manager has identified and categorized various activities, the next step is to change the process, the resources, or the organization to increase value and reduce waste. In general, this involves reducing or eliminating activities that generate waste, reducing the total time and steps needed for unavoidable, nonvalue-adding activities if possible, and keeping value-adding activities. To achieve these tasks, the manager can apply one of four actions to every activity in the process:

- *Keep*   The manager keeps any important or necessary activity since these typically add value. The current form of such an activity is appropriate and allows no obvious improvements.
- *Eliminate*   The activity serves no purpose and changing other steps in the process can eliminate it without adversely affecting the process. Typically, this action applies to nonvalue-adding activities.
- *Combine*   When two or more activities are distinct but similar, the manager can often eliminate one by combining them together into a single step.
- *Rethink/simplify*   This action suits any necessary activity that may be too complex and too time-consuming or experience too much variability.

[12]Robert A. Forcier and Marsha M. Forcier, *Frontline Manufacturing* (Homewood, Ill.: Business One-Irwin, 1992), p. 72.

Rethinking examines the process to identify a better way of completing the same activity. The "On the Job" box describes an interesting example of rethinking.

Value and waste are two hard taskmasters. They always drive and motivate the operations manager; they shape and influence the operations management system, its structure, its processes, and the resources that it consumes. The work of reducing waste and increasing value never ends. The twin goals of creating value and eliminating waste transforms operations management into a value-driven activity.

CHAPTER SUMMARY

This chapter has laid out many of the themes and issues that we will explore in greater detail in the rest of this book:

1. Effective operations management must begin with a clear understanding of the firm's customers, what they value now (both explicitly and latently) and what they are willing to pay for. To develop such an understanding, the firm and the operations management system must view themselves as partners to their customers. Managers must know the customers well enough to predict what they want almost before the customers know themselves.
2. Value, the major force that drives any effective operations management system, represents customers' subjective evaluation, adjusted for costs, of how well a good or service meets or exceeds their expectations.
3. The value equation (Value = Performance/Cost) links the operations management system to value. This equation identifies whether the firm should seek to enhance value by increasing performance, decreasing cost, increasing performance by more than any increase in costs, or some combination. Each strategy choice identifies a different set of critical capabilities that the operations management system must offer.
4. Four traits determine value: speed, quality, flexibility, and cost. Every action taken within the operations management system can be evaluated in terms of its effect on each of these traits.
5. The customer rates the importance of these four value traits as order winners, order qualifiers, or order losers.
6. Value is not a static concept. It changes continuously, often in response to competitors' actions, government regulations, customer familiarity, increasing income and education levels, or economic conditions. The operations management system must also be dynamic; a stagnant system cannot hope to survive in the long term.
7. An operations manager must evaluate an OM system based on both volume and capabilities. Capabilities allow a transformation system to excel at certain tasks while performing poorly on others.
8. The capabilities of any operations management system depend on the processes in place and its capacity (people, information, resources), technology, structure and strategy, so managers must be able to describe and evaluate these factors. Such evaluation will not only improve the management of the OM system, but also educate the rest of the firm about current system capabilities.
9. Changing a system's capabilities is a major undertaking, and the effects of the changes become evident only over time. To change capabilities, managers must invest in the factors that shape them.

10. The operations management system (and the firm as a whole) is most successful when it creates a close fit between what the customer wants and what the transformation system can do. Maintaining and building this consistency is one of the major responsibilities of any operations manager.
11. Besides enhancing the value generated by the operations management system, the operations manager must also work to reduce or eliminate waste.
12. Waste is any activity or action that adversely affects the value equation for the system's customers. In other words, waste increases costs, decreases quality, reduces flexibility, or increases lead times, all of which disappoint the customer.
13. Waste, like value, must be evaluated from the perspective of the system's customer.
14. All waste falls into one of ten categories (overproduction, waiting time, transportation, processing, inventory, motion, defects, time, people, and paperwork).
15. To reduce or eliminate waste, the operations manager must identify, describe, evaluate, and classify all of the activities in the OM process. Every activity either adds value, contributes to waste, or adds no value but remains necessary. Having identified and classified activities, the manager must try to eliminate or reduce waste-generating activities, reduce the time devoted to nonvalue-adding but necessary activities, and maintain value-adding activities.
16. The manager can eliminate waste in four ways: keep, eliminate, rethink, or combine activities.

Having established the two driving objectives of adding value and reducing waste, we will next discuss the four value traits (cost, speed, flexibility, and quality) and review the transformation system as a process. The next several chapters focus on these topics.

[KEY TERMS]

value 43	quality 48	refinement 55
explicit desire 46	speed 48	redefinition 55
latent desire 46	flexibility 48	capability 56
value equation 47	cost 48	capacity 59
performance 48	*kaizen* 54	waste 62

[DISCUSSION QUESTIONS]

1. How do the terms *cost* and *value* differ?
2. Think about a company that, like Schwinn, has had difficulty adjusting to changing market conditions. To what extent can you link these changes to changing customer values?
3. Discuss the impact of technological and demographic change since the time of your grandparents on the value of a watch. What do you think might happen to the watch market in the future?
4. About 30 years ago, Swanson Foods introduced the TV dinner. What factors do you think led to the development of this revolutionary product?
5. Discuss the relationship between a firm's market segment and what this chapter calls a *customer*.

6. Think about the way you get your morning cup of coffee (supposing that you drink coffee). What are your explicit desires for this beverage? How well does your current method of acquiring it satisfy these desires? What needs are being unmet? Do you have any latent desires for coffee? How might they be met?

7. Compare and contrast how your local convenience store and your local supermarket offer value to customers. Use the elements of the value equation as the basis for your answer.

8. You are considering purchasing a laptop computer. Compare and contrast the factors that would influence your decision to buy the same laptop from a nationally known mail-order house, Sears, a local computer store, and a classified ad offering to sell a "nearly new" machine?

9. Think about companies and products within your own area that compete on the basis of:
   a. any time
   b. any place
   c. no matter
   d. mass customization
   e. risk reduction
   Cite one firm and indicate what it does to achieve its goal.

10. Assume that you are the product manager for Chrysler's Neon subcompact car. How might each of the following factors influence your customers' demand for your car?
   a. familiarity
   b. income/education
   c. economic conditions
   d. competitors' actions and corporate strategies

11. In what ways do the following labels influence the value you might assign to the products?
   a. "Intel Inside" sticker on a desktop computer
   b. "Made in China" label on a Nike running shoe
   c. Union labor claim
   d. "Cruelty free" development claim (i.e., no animal testing)
   e. Recycled paper logo

12. How would you define *capacity* within a school of business?

13. Review your monthly household budget, then try to identify expenditures that seem to represent waste. Would all members of your household agree?

C A U T I O N

[C R I T I C A L   T H I N K I N G   R E Q U I R E D]

1. You and your significant other are together on Valentine's Day. As noon approaches, you satisfy your hunger with Big Macs at McDonald's. Both of you agree that lunch "hit the spot" (i.e., it met your immediate needs). That evening you are considering where to go for dinner. You don't have class that night and no hockey games are on the television. Why might a suggestion to go to McDonald's for dinner be a bad idea?

2. You must design a product for a market segment in which group norms strongly influence individual behavior. How would this fact alter the structure of your value chain? Please identify the groups to which your answer refers.

CASE 2.1

Starving Students Textbook Company

The consumer revolution is sweeping your campus and a friend sees an opportunity to delight his classmates by starting a for-profit textbook buying service. Your friend wants to bypass the normal college bookstore by offering students the following service:

1. Three weeks prior to the start of a semester, students place orders for new or used books. Used books will be bought from Follett's, the nation's largest used-book wholesaler.
2. Students would commit to these purchases by paying with either checks or major credit cards.
3. One week prior to the start of school, the textbooks would be delivered to a public warehouse. Temps would be hired through a local agency to pick individual student orders from the stacks of textbooks and then place the books and the invoices in heavy-duty plastic tote bags.
4. Two days prior to the start of classes, the firm would rent a van to transport orders to a near-

by business's parking lot where buyers could pick up their books.
5. By the second week of the semester, this business would shut down in time to start working on the first term papers.
6. Textbooks normally are sold in bookstores with a 25 percent profit margin. Your friend plans sell books for 10 percent less than the prices at the campus bookstore.

QUESTIONS

1. As a student, do you think that this service offers a good deal?
2. Why and/or why not?
3. How might existing sellers of books on campus respond to the new business?
4. In what other ways might your friend approach this business opportunity?

NOTE   A subsequent chapter will revisit this case to evaluate it as a viable business proposition.

[SELECTED READINGS]

Albrecht, Karl. *The Only Thing That Matters.* New York: Harper Business, 1992.

Carlzon, Jan. *Moments of Truth: New Strategies for Today's Customer-Driven Economy.* New York: Harper & Row, 1987.

Carter, Phillip L., and Steven A. Melnyk. "Time-Based Competition: Building the Foundations for Speed." *APICS: 35th International Conference Proceedings,* Montreal, Quebec, Canada, October 18–23, 1992, pp. 63–67.

Dumaine, Brian. "How Managers Can Succeed through Speed." *Fortune,* February 13, 1989, pp. 54–59.

——— "Earning More by Moving Faster." *Fortune,* October 7, 1991, pp. 89-94.

Ford, Henry, with Samuel Crowther. *My Life and Work.* Garden City, N.J.: Doubleday, 1922.

Imai, Masaaki. *Kaizen—The Key to Japan's Competitive Success.* New York: Random House, 1986.

Magnet, Myron. "Meet the New Revolutionaries." *Fortune,* February 24, 1992, pp. 94–101.

Pine, B. Joseph, II. *Mass Customization: The New Frontier in Business Competition.* Cambridge, Mass.: Harvard Business School Press, 1993.

Plossl, George W. *Management in the New World of Manufacturing: How Companies Can Improve Operations to Compete Globally.* Englewood Cliffs, N.J.: Prentice-Hall, 1991.

Power, Christopher, Walecia Konrad, Alice Z. Cuneo, and James B. Treece. "Value Marketing." *Business Week,* November 11, 1991.

Sherman, Stratford. "How to Prosper in the Value Decade." *Fortune,* November 30, 1992.

Stalk, George, Jr., and Thomas Hout. *Competing against Time.* New York: Free Press, 1990.

Suzaki, Kiyoshi. *The New Manufacturing Challenge.* New York: Free Press, 1987.

CHAPTER THREE

Identifying the Elements of Value

CHAPTER OBJECTIVES

[At the end of this chapter, you should be able to]

- List the components of the value equation.
- Explain how each component contributes to the overall value perceived by the customer.
- Review recent developments in value-based OM systems such as
  time-based competition and mass customization.
- Discuss such critical OM system paradigms as engineer to order,
  make to order, assemble to order, and make to stock.
- Trace the links existing among the value components of lead time,
  quality, and flexibility.
- Illustrate how the concept of customer service guides assignment
  of the relative weights of the components of the value equation.

Courtesy of
Oshkosh B'Gosh.

Cutting Costs in an Age of Disinflation

Look again at that pricetag. In a grand demonstration of the power of the consumer, the prices on many products are going down, not up. During 1994, Mercedes Benz pared its prices on some luxury cars by almost 15 percent, and Compaq slashed prices on some of its top-of-the-line computer models by 23 percent.

Welcome to the Age of Disinflation. Well-established companies are slashing their prices to respond to fierce pressure in the global marketplace. In this highly competitive atmosphere, corporate managers must find ways to lower prices while still increasing value to the customer.

This poses a tremendous challenge for the managers who cut their teeth on the old, inflation-ridden ways of the past. They are having to completely rethink their corporate strategies, revamping everything from manufacturing to marketing.

Take Oshkosh B'Gosh, for example. In 1994, the Wisconsin-based maker of quality children's clothing reduced the prices on its entire spring line by 6 to 8 percent. Oshkosh had to find inventive ways to lower its costs to make this possible. It completely overhauled its production facilities and invested in worker training. This ultimately helped Oshkosh to become a more flexible manufacturer—thereby reducing its costs.

SOURCE
Christopher Farrell,
Zachary Schiller,
Richard A. Melcher,
Geoffrey Smith, Peter
Burrows, and
Kathleen Kerwin,
"Stuck! How
Companies Cope
when They Can't
Raise Prices,"
Business Week,
November 15, 1993,
pp. 146–155.

Flexibility is the key in an age when product lifetimes are forever dwindling. Companies are redesigning products to make manufacturing them easier and faster, or eliminating features that don't add value for the customer. They are also redesigning their own organizational structures by stripping away barriers between departments and investing in high-tech information technologies.

The consumer of the 1990s doesn't just want lower prices. He or she wants more for less. "The management challenge of the 1990s is to reduce costs—and increase the perceived value of the product," explains Arthur L. Kelly, a private investor who sits on the board of directors for Deere, BMW, and Nalco Chemical. Or, as 1995 promotions for Target, the national discount retailer, put it: "Expect More. Pay Less."

Companies who feel the heat of the Age of Disinflation are scrambling to eliminate waste and constantly searching for ways to increase productivity. Any manager who doesn't is going to get left out in the cold.

DEFINING *VALUE* IN THE 1990s

To prosper in today's economy of disinflation, companies such as Compaq Computers, Burger King, Oshkosh, General Motors, and Philip Morris need to attract customers. Some do this by focusing on costs; others focus on quality, and still others try to make their products easier to use or build. In each case, managers must deal with the same fundamental problem: defining and implementing appropriate views of value. However they define value, the result involves four major elements:

- Speed, or lead time
- Flexibility
- Quality
- Cost

To succeed despite disinflation, managers have to put the value equation of Chapter 2 to work. This requires deciding how much emphasis to place on each of the four elements of value.

Before defining and implementing a unique version of the value equation, managers must understand, in operational terms, each of its components. As a result, the first part of this chapter focuses on interpreting those components, starting with the numerator (lead time, flexibility, and quality) and then moving on to the denominator (cost). This discussion will touch on such new developments as time-based competition (lead time), mass customization (flexibility), and alternative costing structures such as activity-based costing (ABC) and throughput costing.

The individual discussions of each element of value follow a consistent three-step process. First, we define the element and identify its attributes. Second, we discuss how managers can use that element to generate or enhance value for both the customer and the OM system. Third, we identify any recent developments centered on that element of value in the marketplace.

After examining the major components of value, the chapter concludes by discussing how to implement the value definition. This three-step process begins with establishing weights (β factors) consistent with the firm's view of how it and its OM system can compete in the marketplace and generate value for customers. The implementation process then communicates these views of value to both customers and employees, helping to form expectations. Finally, it measures the resulting performance against these expectations. These three activities constitute customer service.

This chapter addresses value-driven operations management as an integrated and focused system that emphasizes specific elements of the value equation at both at the strategic (long-term) and operational (day-to-day) levels. An effective value-driven operations management system must consistently measure performance against a set of standards that embody operational definitions of value to keep the system focused on delivering the level and type of value promised by the firm to its customers. Value-driven operations management continuously strives to close the loop between what customers want and what the operations management system can deliver.

REVISITING THE VALUE EQUATION

Chapter 2 introduced the value equation:

$$\text{Value} = \frac{\text{Performance}}{\text{Cost}} \qquad (3.1)$$

This equation expresses value as a ratio of what the product offers to its cost. Performance, the numerator, was defined as:

$$\text{Performance} = \beta_1 \times \text{Quality} + \beta_2 \times \text{Speed} + \beta_3 \times \text{Flexibility} \qquad (3.2)$$

This expresses performance as a weighted sum of three traits: quality, speed (lead time), and flexibility.

Equation 3.2 breaks down performance into two separate but linked tasks. The first defines the components of value in a way that makes sense to both customers and the operations management system in order to provide a type of value that the customer prizes. The second task assigns weights (i.e., the β factors) to the components. This step can proceed only after managers specify operational definitions for the components of value.

UNDERSTANDING LEAD TIME

Many describe the notion of lead time using terms like *speed, responsiveness, quickness,* and *reliability* (i.e., how closely an order's arrival time approaches the expected time). These terms describe various traits of lead time. More generally, **lead time** can be defined as the interval between the start and end of an activity or series of activities.

lead time
The interval between the start and end of an activity or series of activities

Managers can study lead times in two ways. They can look at them as individual events, perhaps evaluating how long the OM system takes to fill a specific order or design a specific product. Alternatively, they can look at the distributions of lead times. (See Exhibit 3.1.)

[**EXHIBIT 3.1**]

Lead Time Distribution

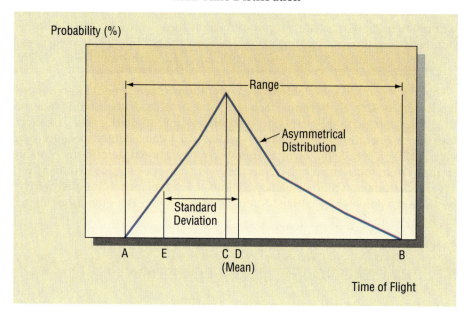

For example, an airline manager might measure how long a commercial jet takes to complete a particular flight. Over time, the manager can develop a history of such flights and summarize the information as a distribution. This distribution would present four specific pieces of information that would help the manager to evaluate the airline's OM system and its contribution to value:

mean

The expected value in a distribution

standard deviation

A statistical measure of the variability of a distribution

- *Mean* (Point D)   The **mean** denotes the expected value in the distribution. This is the amount of elapsed time that the manager expects for the typical jet flight on the chosen route. The mean differs from the mode (Point C), which has the most observations.
- *Standard deviation* (interval between Points D and E)   The **standard deviation** is an indicator of variability within the distribution. It is a statistic used to measure the degree of variability associated with a variable, which in this case is lead time. In general, a larger standard deviation indicates a less reliable mean and more difficulty in determining when an event will occur. (The issue of variability is discussed in greater detail in Chapter 9.) The standard deviation of the jet flight time distribution would indicate the reliability of the average flight time.

range

An indicator of dispersion within a distribution that also indicates whether the distribution is open ended or closed ended

shape

The symmetrical or asymmetrical form of a distribution

- *Range* (Interval between Points B and A)   Like the standard deviation, the **range** indicates the dispersion of a distribution and its predictability. However, the range also indicates whether the distribution is open ended (with no finite end points such as A or B) or closed ended (with finite ends that define both the lowest and highest values).
- *Shape*   As the term implies, **shape** describes the form of the distribution. In general, shapes can be classified as symmetrical and asymmetrical. The shape of a symmetrical distribution below the mean is identical to the shape above the mean. A symmetrical distribution indicates the same likelihood of a value either under or over the mean. The normal distribution is

a good example of a symmetrical distribution. In contrast, an asymmetrical distribution has a skewed shape. The mean divides the distribution into equal-sized chunks, but one side of an asymmetrical distribution tends to be more compact while the other tends to spread more widely. Again, shape indicates lead time predictability.

Changes in lead time tend to enhance value when they reduce its expected duration or its variability or both. As a result, operations managers typically focus efforts to improve lead times first on reducing mean lead time and then on reducing variance.

Lead Time Categories

At any point in time, the operations manager may have to control lead times in six major categories. These groupings cover all stages of planning and managing the value-driven OM system:

design lead time
The component of lead time devoted to producing a workable product design

Design Lead Time.   **Design lead time** measures the time needed to design a product. This covers all activities from the moment that managers first recognize a need in the marketplace until they deliver a design for production that is feasible to produce, acceptable (it satisfies the needs of customers), and consistent with the firm's strategic vision (it delivers a type of value that is consistent with how the firm competes in the marketplace). Besides new-product development activities, design lead time also measures efforts to revise and enhance existing products.

Actions and decisions to improve design lead time have major impacts on the OM system. Such actions affect, for example, inventories, types of capacity in the system (i.e., volume and capabilities), and costs of production. Furthermore, a firm can correct problems more easily and cheaply at this stage than after the product has been released to the transformation process. A useful rule of thumb states that a change during design might cost $1,000 to implement, but making the same change might cost $100,000 after design but before production and $10 million during production.[1]

Design lead time breaks down into the following stages:

- *Time from product concept to product design*   The product design process begins with recognition of a need, either explicit or latent, that no current product offering satisfies. Successful product designers recognize emerging needs quickly, describe them carefully, and then rapidly design products that satisfy them. This period defines a window of opportunity for the firm.[2]
- *Time from product design to prototype*   The product design process produces an intangible drawing or concept rather than a functioning physical product. Design lead time includes a period for making a prototype to determine whether a new product design really works as planned to meet customer needs.

    Traditionally, prototypes have helped managers to judge when to release products to their OM systems.[3] Recently, however, managers have come to view prototypes as learning tools that they can test to evaluate a design's fit with existing capabilities. Lessons learned feed back to the product design process until a prototype emerges of a product that the firm can introduce

---

[1]Christopher Meyer, *Fast Cycle Time* (New York: Free Press, 1993), p. 31.

[2]Marvin L. Patterson, *Accelerating Innovation* (New York: Van Nostrand Reinhold, 1992).

[3]Meyer, *Fast Cycle Time*, p. 223.

In the marketplace, companies recognize the value of time.   SOURCE   Courtesy of General Electric Information Services

to the market with confidence that it will offer value consistent with customer needs.

- *Time from prototype to job one*   A unique prototype made by skilled workers does not represent the conditions of full production. Design lead time includes a period for the transition from a prototype to the start of full, regular production. Operations managers usually refer to the first unit produced by the normal operations management system as job one. During this transition, they must design parts, manufacture tools, acquire or modify equipment, set time and cost standards, and establish the bill of materials (a list of parts needed to produce the product). Often this work requires input and cooperation from the firm's engineering, cost accounting, finance, and marketing functions as well as suppliers and customers. Problems that surface at this stage may return the process to its prototyping or product design stages.

[**E X H I B I T   3 . 2**]

Components of Design Lead Time

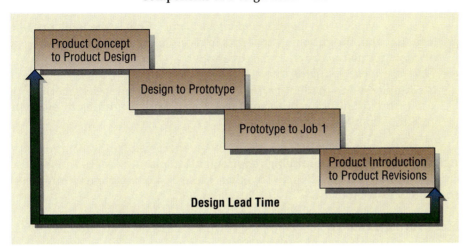

• *Time from product introduction to product revision*   After a product's introduction, customers provide feedback in the form of complaints, marketing survey responses, and actual product sales. Additional feedback comes from suppliers and company personnel. Operations managers review this feedback to identify any problems that need responses. This on-going component of design lead time keeps managers working continuously in an iterative process to revise the product design to meet customers' needs more effectively.

Together, the four components of design lead time define an integrated and iterative process. This measure determines how quickly the firm can introduce successful new products to the marketplace. (See Exhibit 3.2.)

Sourcing Lead Time   **Sourcing lead time** is the lead time associated with procuring the inputs to the product transformation process. This includes the following:

• *Time for supplier selection*   The firm consumes some lead time to identify and select suppliers for a product's components. Managers may spend time identifying potential vendors, evaluating them, and selecting final suppliers. This lead time identifies the pool of suppliers that will work with the operations management system. Supplier selection imposes a fixed cost for initial selection of potential suppliers and careful review of current suppliers to identify any that have failed to perform acceptably.

• *Time from supplier selection to supplier certification*   Operations managers often want to work with reliable suppliers that consistently deliver quality components and on schedule. Such suppliers eliminate the need for nonvalue-adding activities like inspections and receiving procedures as in-coming shipments can move directly to the shop floor. Supplier certification helps to ensure that suppliers will perform as expected by carefully evaluating their OM processes to ensure capabilities of consistently delivering quality components on time.

sourcing lead time
The components of lead time devoted to working with suppliers

- *Time from identifying a component requirement to placing an order*   This component of sourcing lead time describes the time that elapses from the moment managers identify a need until the supplier receives a purchase order or authorization to buy.
- *Time from supplier receipt of the order to delivery*   This is the total amount of lead time that the supplier consumes in receiving the order, scheduling production, filling the order, and delivering it.
- *Time for supplier-initiated revisions of parts and projects*   This is the time that the supplier takes to identify improvements to the purchaser's parts or projects, from identifying problems and formulating solutions to evaluating and implementing solutions.

In general, operations managers are most interested in the components of sourcing lead time from identifying requirements to placing orders and from supplier receipt of orders to delivery. Together, these two components form the supplier delivery lead time.

manufacturing lead time

The component of lead time devoted to producing the product within the firm's OM system

Manufacturing Lead Time.   Once the firm has designed the product, selected and scheduled suppliers, and initiated the flow of orders, it must make the product within its operations management system. This category of lead time, **manufacturing lead time**, can be broken into two major components:

- *Time from receipt of an order to the start of manufacturing*   When a customer places an order, a series of events begins with recording the order, entering it into the firm's database, verifying it, planning to identify component requirements and their timing and to place orders with suppliers, and scheduling to assign capacity to fill the order and set start and ending times or due dates. The OM system must accomplish all of these activities before it can start filling the order.
- *Time from start of manufacturing to entry into the distribution system*   This component measures the lead time from the moment that the OM system begins working on an order until it transfers the finished product to the distribution system for delivery.

Many students assume that manufacturing lead time consumes most of overall lead time, but this may not be the case. Manufacturing lead time is simply one of many components. It may or may not be the largest or most time-consuming.

distribution lead time

The component of lead time devoted to moving the product from the OM system to the customer

Distribution Lead Time.   **Distribution lead time** measures the time consumed by the distribution system. The distribution system is responsible for such activities as warehousing and selecting a mode of transportation. This component consists of only one element:

- *Time from entry into the distribution system to delivery to the customer*   This measures the interval from the moment that the transformation process finishes the product until that product reaches the customer. This includes time for packing the item, getting it ready for shipping, shipping transit time, and receiving at the customer's site.

Distribution lead time is critical for some companies such as mail-order software discounters, which must compete with local computer stores. In the past, customers made cost versus time trade-offs between these firms and the local stores. Mail-order suppliers offered great prices but customers had to wait for their software. Local stores charged higher prices for immediate delivery. The mail-order retailers have eliminated this time advantage, however, by developing marketing relationships with express shipping companies such as Federal Express. A customer in the eastern United States can often order software at a discount as late as 11 p.m. for delivery the next day before noon at a cost of $3 per order. These mail-order retailers have greatly reduced their distribution lead times.

Order Lead Time.   **Order lead time** results from links between the customer and the operations management system. This lead time consists of two major components:

- *Time from customer recognition of a need to receipt of an order at manufacturing* This element measures the entire period from the customer's recognition of an unfilled need until an order reaches the seller's OM system. This covers such activities as the customer identifying a product that will satisfy the need, placing an order, and receiving confirmation along with the seller's order-entry function.
- *Time from shipment to customer confirmation of delivery*   Once the seller has shipped a product, time elapses until the customer recognizes receipt. This lag is important in many corporate purchases where customers initiate payment only after confirming receipt of their orders. A shorter time lag brings payment more quickly.

order lead time
The component of lead time consumed by links between the customer and the OM system

Other Lead Times.   This last category is a general catch-all for components that do not fit easily into the other categories. In this book, we will focus attention on only one such component:

- *Time from customer complaint to company response*   As pointed out previously in the discussion of moments of truth, customers tend to form impressions of the firm and the operations management process every time they buy its products. When a customer complains about a problem with a product, his or her perception of the effectiveness of the firm's OM system is based on how quickly it responds to the complaint. This component of lead time measures the interval between the complaint and an offer of an acceptable resolution by the company. This emphasizes an *acceptable* resolution, because the time lag ends when the customer accepts a solution. In general, a longer lag makes the system seem less effective and raises the level of customer dissatisfaction.

These components sum to form the total product delivery lead time:

$$\text{Total product delivery lead time} = \begin{array}{l}\text{Design lead time} + \text{Supplier delivery lead time} +\\ \text{Manufacturing lead time} +\\ \text{Distribution lead time} + \text{Order lead time}\end{array}$$

Total Product Delivery Lead Time: Partitioning Lead Times

The last section identified the components of lead time; the **total product delivery lead time** (TPDLT) ties them together. This concept, first introduced by manufacturing consultant Gus Berger, measures the total lead time needed to bring a product to market, assuming no inventory anywhere within the supply chain (i.e., from the supplier through the operations management system to the distributor). In other words, the total product delivery lead time is the sum of all lead time components.

This concept becomes more useful when it is broken into two components. Internal lead time is the amount of total product delivery lead time that the com-

total product delivery lead time
The total lead time, including all components, needed to bring a product to market, assuming no inventory anywhere in the supply chain

pany consumes; customer lead time is the amount of lead time that the customer must accept. Internal lead time forces the company to absorb costs, while customers pay for costs created by external lead time. Internal lead times remain invisible to the customer, but they do affect his or her costs. In contrast, customer lead times are quite apparent to the customer. At a minimum, they create delays and inconvenience; at worst, they can increase the customer's costs.

Market Orientation and Total Product Delivery Lead Time.   Whether the customer or the firm bears the brunt of the total product delivery lead time depends on the market orientation of the product. In general, any product has one of four market orientations:

- Engineer to order (ETO)
- Make to order (MTO)
- Assemble to order (ATO)
- Make to stock (MTS)

These four categories describe both how a product provider makes a product and who bears the cost of lead time. They also determine how the operations management system can enhance value for both the firm and the customer.

Engineer to Order.   Products that firms **engineer to order** are unique because they allow extensive customization by the customer or because they have just started their product life cycles. Many examples of ETO products include a custom house, an oil tanker, some specialized industrial equipment, and a hand-built bicycle.

ETO products have the longest lead times of any product category because the total must include design lead time. Next, releasing the product for production requires unique orders from suppliers, which take time to arrive. After delivery, components must be assembled, and the product may have to pass inspection by the customer. Finally, it has to be shipped. Because the unique product requires an entirely new design, it is difficult to reduce lead times by carrying inventory, though the firm can carry some raw materials. For example, Serotta Competitive Bicycles from Chapter 2 may stock some specialized steel, but it would not keep stocks of components such as assembled, unpainted frames.

A producer of ETO products must wait for customers to place orders before beginning any activity. As a result, the customer bears the entire cost of the total product delivery lead time. In other words, the external lead time often exactly equals the total product delivery lead time.

Operations management systems for ETO products often compete on the basis of such traits as available capacity and flexibility (frequently a result of general-purpose equipment and highly skilled workers), along with close working relationships among the customer, designers, and the operations managers. A firm doesn't win or lose orders for ETO products on the basis of cost, but rather on the basis of the capability of the entire system to form potentially vague specifications into well-defined products and then produce them. Success depends on the firm's ability to reduce the customer's total product delivery lead time.

Make to Order.   **Make to order** products follow existing designs, but they cannot be stored economically. Such products may be too big or too expensive to store (like a jet airplane or a boat) or perishable (e.g., a meal at a fancy restaurant). A firm may not hold inventories of such products because they are subject to extensive user-customization. Whatever the reasons for keeping minimal inventories, production of MTO items closely resembles that of ETO items in that the process

engineer to order

A unique product that allows extensive user customization or that has just begun its product life cycle

make to order

A product built in response to a customer order following an existing design

This paint store clerk mixes and packages product based on individual customer needs. By assembling to order, companies avoid excess inventory and assure customer satisfaction.   SOURCE   Bonnie Kamin/ PhotoEdit

starts with a customer order. At this point, the customer must bear the entire cost of the lead time. Unlike ETO products, however, the customer does avoid design lead time; the company bears that cost.

Like ETO products, MTO products compete on the basis of flexibility, responsiveness, and capacity. Cost is typically an order qualifier. Make to order differs from engineer to order primarily in the importance of the producer's engineering capability. This function is critical within the engineer to order environment, but it does not affect a make to order product, which has already been designed when the customer places an order.

Assemble to Order.   Assemble to order products are essentially standard items that allow users to specify wide ranges of options. For example, you can buy paint in many different shades and colors. This large variety of product specifications makes it difficult to carry sufficient stocks to meet unpredictable customer demand. Furthermore, once a dealer mixes a specific color, it cannot reverse the process; if a store mixes a color that no one wants, it is stuck with the paint. In response, many firms assemble the end product to order. The paint store stocks a large supply of tints and a base color (usually white). No finished product exists until a customer specifies a color, at which time a worker adds tints to the base color to assemble the finished paint to order. By waiting until the customer specifies the exact color desired, the paint store avoids the problem of inventorying many premixed paints. In marketing, this approach is referred to as **postponement**. Successful sellers of assemble to order products must keep their assembly lead times as short as possible.

An assemble to order product results in a relatively long internal lead time. The firm absorbs the cost of time to design the product, select suppliers, order raw materials and components, and assemble components from inventory. The relatively short customer lead time is limited to the time needed to place the order and assemble the components into the desired end product.

assemble to order

A standard product assembled in response to a customer order to allow many user-specified options

postponement

Deferring final assembly of a product to allow the customer to specify options

[**EXHIBIT 3.3**]

Market Orientation and Internal and External Lead Time

Total Product Delivery Lead Time

- Engineer to Order
- Make to Order
- Assemble to Order
- Make to Stock

☐ Customer Lead Time   ☐ Internal Lead Time

make to stock

A standard product, often produced based on demand forecasts rather than known orders, that remains in inventory to await customer purchase

Make to Stock.   As the name implies, a seller must keep inventories of **make to stock** products available for purchase whenever the customer arrives. To meet this requirement for availability, firms often produce MTO items based on forecasts rather than known orders. This category tends to include standard, mature products. Make to stock products force the firm to absorb nearly all of the cost of lead time. The customer bears the cost of lead time only for placing the order and receiving it. As a general rule of thumb, make to stock products compete primarily on the basis of cost and availability. Examples of such products include most retail goods such as breakfast cereals, milk, shirts, jeans, and office desks.

Moving from ETO to MTS products, the shares of total product delivery lead time shift from 100 percent external lead time to almost all internal lead time, as Exhibit 3.3 illustrates. For each type of product, lead times affect value. Producers of ETO products feel strong incentives to reduce design and delivery lead times to attract customers. Reducing lead times for MTS products often reduces costs and, as the next section will show, improves quality and enhances flexibility. Again, these changes have positive impacts on the value equation.

Many service systems operate on an engineer or make to order basis, in part because there is no way to inventory the product being requested. Many restaurants stock ingredients in anticipation of a customer's arrival but must await a request. Whether the meal is engineered to order or make to order will depend on the degree of meal customization the chef practices. When the chef uses a recipe, then you have experienced a MTO meal. Burger King's "have it your way" slogan reflects the assemble to order approach. When you go to McDonald's, you normally experience a make to stock approach to food service.

Lead Time as a Source of Value

time to market

The total time that a firm takes to introduce a new product to the market or to revise an existing product

The previous section detailed a wide range of lead time components, but managers that emphasize customer-driven value must pay special attention to two types of lead times: time to market and time to product. **Time to market** measures the total time that a firm takes to conceive, design, produce, and deliver a new product to the market or to revise an existing product. When Chrysler tries to reduce the time it needs to successfully introduce a new car from 6 years to less than 3 years, its managers are working to reduce time to market.

[**EXHIBIT 3.4**]

Leading Time to Market Competitors

	Product	Old Time	New Time
Honda	Cars	5.0 years	2.0 years
AT&T	Phones	2.0 years	1.0 year
Navistar	Trucks	5.0 years	2.5 years
Hewlett-Packard	Printers	4.5 years	22.0 months

SOURCE   Brian Dumaine, "How Managers Can Succeed through Speed," *Fortune,* February 13, 1989, pp. 54–59. © 1989, Time, Inc. All rights reserved.

In contrast, **time to product** measures the time that the firm takes to respond to a customer order for an existing product. To reduce time to product, managers work to shrink the interval between the time that the customer recognizes a need and places an order until the customer takes delivery of the product.

In service systems, many customers judge the quality of a service largely on the firm's time to product performance. A dining experience is marred by slow service. Your shoe salesperson seems to have gotten lost in the back room. The operations manager thinks of this as a time to product problem. The customer calls it poor service.

Fast to Market.   Companies that compete by reducing their time to market follow **fast to market** strategies. A number of firms are now actively pursuing fast to market strategies, as Exhibit 3.4 illustrates. This lead-time-based strategy is most attractive to companies that deal with products in the introduction or growth stages of the product life cycle and to companies that compete by stressing continuous innovation. For example, a designer of fashion clothing might pursue a fast to market strategy, as might a computer hardware or software manufacturer. AT&T and MCI, two long-distance telephone companies, also try to be fast to market. These companies try to attract customers by offering new programs such as MCI's Friends and Families II™ and AT&T's True USA™ plan. These companies also work to maintain their current customers by responding quickly to any competitor's program. For example, AT&T has set a corporate goal of responding to any MCI initiative within 2 days.

These and other companies see fast to market as an attractive strategy for a number of reasons. First, they have found lead-time reductions very profitable. One study cited by Nicol found that a product introduced first 50 percent over budget generated higher profits than a product introduced on budget but 6 months late.[4] The first company could command a premium price for its product that offset the costs of exceeding the budget. The late firm could not command this premium and had to turn to price competition to win business away from the first mover. In addition, the cost of introducing a product later often equals or exceeds that of the

time to product

The time that the firm takes to respond to a customer order for an existing product

fast to market

A competitive strategy based on reducing time to market

[4]Ronald Nicol, "Time-Based Competition: A Systematic Approach to Business Improvement," in *Time-Based Competition: Going beyond JIT to Achieve a Competitive Advantage,* Society of Manufacturing Engineers seminar, Livonia, Mich., October 28–29, 1991.

firm that reaches the market first. As a result, a late firm faces lower initial prices and a longer product development cost recovery period.

Also, past experience has shown that consistently introducing new products faster than competitors can allow a firm to dominate the marketplace. Honda won the war with Yamaha for dominance of Japan's motorcycle market in the late 1970s and early 1980s by maintaining better product variety:

> In 18 months, Honda introduced 81 new motorcycle models in Japan. Yamaha was able to introduce only 34. This is even more startling when one considers that both competitors had only 60 models each in their entire product lines in the late 1970s. Yet taking these figures alone understates their effect on the market. When discontinued models are considered, Honda more completely refreshed its product line. Honda introduced 81 new models and discontinued 32 models for a total of 113 changes in its product line. Yamaha retired only 3 models and introduced 34 new models for a total of 37 changes. The consumer was seeing fresh Hondas and increasingly stale Yamahas.[5]

To understand how firms can compete based on a fast to market capability, consider an example. Company ABC and Company XYZ both design a new car telephone. Company ABC introduces its new line in 8 months while Company XYZ takes 12 months. Company ABC's 4-month lead time advantage over XYZ allows it to command a premium for its new car telephone that helps to cover its development costs. Furthermore, as soon as it has introduced its new product, Company ABC can begin working on the next generation, exploiting all of the new technology that has emerged since the start of development on the first generation.

In contrast, Company XYZ enters the market with a car telephone based on almost the same technology as the products of Company ABC. Unable to offer any performance advantage to its customers, Company XYZ must compete on cost. Like ABC, Company XYZ begins working on the next generation immediately after it introduces the new line, but ABC started 4 months earlier. As XYZ completes about one-third of its design process, ABC introduces its new generation, and XYZ has nothing comparable to offer. Customers see ABC as offering newer and better products faster, while they see XYZ offering stale technology.

Fast to Product Competition.   A company can also compete by reducing its time to product in a process referred to as **fast to product** competition, which emphasizes a speedy response to customer demand for an existing product. Many firms are now actively completing on this basis, as Exhibit 3.5 illustrates. These firms work to reduce the time interval from the customer's order until that order reaches the customer; this extends beyond the delivery time to the time that the customer can use the product. Like fast to market competition, a number of factors make fast to product competition very attractive.

First, many customers like fast to product suppliers, who make them spend less time waiting. Some customers are willing to pay premium prices to get their purchases sooner. This can increase revenues for the fast to product supplier.

Second, managers of fast to product competitors have found strong relationships between lead time and the other dimensions of value. They have found that reductions in lead time are correlated with:

fast to product

A competitive strategy based on reducing time to product

---

[5]James C. Abegglen and George Stalk, Jr., *Kaisha: The Japanese Corporation* (New York: Basic Books, 1985), pp. 49–50.

[**E X H I B I T   3 . 5**]

Leading Time to Product Competitors

	Product	Old Time	New Time
General Electric	Circuit breaker boxes	3 weeks	3 days
Motorola	Pagers	3 weeks	2 hours
Hewlett-Packard	Test equipment	4 weeks	5 days
Brunswick	Fishing reels	3 weeks	1 week
Matsushita	Washing machines	360 hours	2 hours
Harley-Davidson	Motorcycles	360 days	< 3 days

SOURCE   Brian Dumaine, "How Managers Can Succeed through Speed," *Fortune,* February 13, 1989, pp. 54–59. © 1989, Time, Inc. All rights reserved.

- *Increases in quality*   Reducing lead times requires the OM system to do things right the first time, every time. With shorter lead times, the firm tends to build products according to the latest specifications, so obsolete parts or out-of-date specifications cause fewer quality problems.
- *Reductions in inventory levels*   Shorter lead times reduce the amount of inventory in the system. The firm carries less work-in-process inventory because products pass through the OM system to customers more quickly, so the firm needs less storage space. For the same level of output, fast to product firms can operate physically smaller plants than slower competitors.
- *Improvements in flexibility*   As lead times fall, the firm can wait longer to build a product, which enhances its perceived flexibility. Furthermore, with shorter lead times, the firm tends to build in smaller lot sizes, so it can afford to build products in the exact quantities and to the specifications demanded by customers.
- *Reductions in cost*   Altogether, reductions in lead time, inventory, and physical space requirements combine with improvements in quality (less scrap, salvage, and rework) to lower operating costs.

These effects create an advantage for the fast to product firm. On one hand, it can command premium prices because it can deliver its products so quickly. On the other hand, its operating costs are usually lower than those of competitors. Fast to product competition becomes attractive because it can boost profits substantially.

To understand the operation of a fast to product firm, consider Motorola's Florida pocket pager plant. Plant managers initially considered trying to compete by emphasizing quality, product features, and cost against Japanese competitors such as NEC, Hitachi, and Fujitsu. Motorola managers dismissed quality as a basis for developing and maintaining a sustainable competitive advantage because it seemed difficult to compete with the Japanese on quality. They also dismissed adding product features for customers who had difficulty programming their VCRs. Cost was not seen as sufficiently important. However, another area seemed to offer a basis for developing a sustainable competitive advantage—speed. Motorola's competitors, located in Japan, had long supply lines. From its U.S. locations, Motorola did not see distance as much of a problem.

The firm designed and built an OM system that could produce pagers within two hours. If you want a Motorola pager, you call a toll-free number that connects

[**E X H I B I T   3 . 6**]

American Firms' Experience with Time-Based Competition

	Business	Delivery Time Advantage	Growth Difference	Performance Difference
Wal-Mart	Discount stores	80%	36 versus 12%	19 versus 9% profit
Century Door	Industrial doors	66	15 versus 5	10 versus 0.2% return on stock
Wilsonart	Decorative laminates	75	9 versus 3	40 versus 10% return on net assets
Thomasville	Furniture	70	12 versus 3	21 versus 11% return on assets

you with an operator in Chicago. About 20 minutes after the operator enters your order into the computer system, the order is kitted (i.e., workers have gathered the necessary parts) and sent out to the production line. Your pager can be built within 2 hours, and the firm usually sends it to you on the same day. You get a product built to your specifications without waiting a long time. Motorola also gains significant advantages—less inventory, less physical space, fewer quality problems, lower costs, and a sustainable competitive advantage.

Time-Based Competition: Competing on Lead Time

time-based competition

A strategy to enhance value by being faster to market or faster to product than competitors

Recently, firms such as Motorola have come to realize that time has value for many of their customers. As mentioned earlier, customers are often willing to pay premium prices for products that are designed and delivered quickly (assuming, of course, that those products work well and satisfy real customer needs). This strategy to target time as a major source of value is referred to as **time-based competition** (TBC). Active implementation of this strategy is bringing great success to companies in the United States (Exhibit 3.6) and Europe (Exhibit 3.7).

TBC manages lead times in three major ways. First, it addresses only those lead times that the customer values most. Second, reductions in lead times must reduce both mean and variance measures. Third, lead time reductions must be achieved through system analysis and changes in underlying processes rather than product-driven changes, that is, TBC cannot rely solely on excess resources (inventory, capacity, or skilled workers) to reduce lead times. Rather, TBC must implement a broad-based strategy to reduce lead times by changing the firm's processes and structures for designing, manufacturing, and delivering products for its customers.

TBC Strategies for Reducing Lead Times

A recent study of time-based competitors identified seven strategies for reducing either time to market or time to product:[6]

- Less of/System Simplification   ↓ process steps
- As One/System Integration   gaps between func. groups misplaced
- Same as/Standardization   reuse standard steps or parts

[6]Phillip L. Carter and Steven A. Melnyk, "Time-Based Competition: Building the Foundations for Speed," *APICS: 35th International Conference Proceedings,* Montreal, Quebec, Canada, October 18–23, 1992, pp. 63–67.

[**E X H I B I T   3 . 7**]

Time-Based Competition in Europe

- Olivetti (typewriter production): Throughput time reduced from 20 days to 3 days
- Michelin (steel cord): Setup time reduced by 90 percent
- Uno a Erre (world leader in gold jewelry): Production lead time reduced by 90 percent
- Fiat Aiazione (parts for aircraft engines): Lead time reduced by 50 percent
- Innocenti S. Eustachio (manufacturing equipment): Lead time reduced by 30 percent
- Europa Metalli (world leader in nonferrous metals): Setup time reduced by 70 percent

SOURCE   Giorgio Merli, *Total Manufacturing Management: Production Organization for the 1990s* (Cambridge, Mass.: Productivity Press, 1990), p. xxviii. English translation copyright © 1990 by Productivity Press, Inc. P. O. Box 13390, Portland, OR 97213-0390, (800) 394-6868. Reprinted by permission.

- At Once/Parallel Activities
- Watch It/Variance Control
- Better than/Automation
- More of/Excess Resources

Less of/System Simplification.   The first TBC strategy, **Less of/System Simplification**, is built around the simple premise that lead times result from processes. Such a process can consist of an individual activity (e.g., a person preparing an order form) or a series of linked processes (e.g., all of the steps needed to fill an order, from receipt of the order to delivery of the product). This process often changes over time for a number of reasons. To cope with a short-term problem such as a defective part from a supplier, managers might introduce an extra step such as an inspection to the process, increasing lead times. Unfortunately, these short-term changes often become institutionalized as accepted parts of the process. Even if the need for the step disappears (perhaps the supplier improves its quality level), the extra step remains.

A Less of/System Simplification strategy works to reduce lead times systematically. The first step identifies the affected processes and documents them. This step describes what actually takes place, as compared to what people think takes place. Analysis of the process identifies steps that no longer contribute to value, those that are either carried out inefficiently or no longer needed. The strategy works to improve inefficient steps by either rethinking (asking how to perform the same function more effectively) or combining two or more steps with similar goals into one. The remedy for unnecessary steps is elimination.

System Simplification produces a simpler process that requires fewer steps to complete. Such a process is easier to control, more predictable, and less time-consuming. It also simplifies training for others who are unfamiliar with the process. Managers frequently use techniques such as process flow analysis (discussed in Chapter 5) and setup reduction (Chapter 9) to simplify processes.

As One/System Integration.   When work is arranged sequentially, lead times increase for several reasons. First, the sequential arrangement of the processes lengthens lead times. Manufacturing can get the design for a new product only

Less of/System Simplification

A strategy for reducing lead times that tries to identify steps that can be eliminated, combined, or repositioned to create a simpler system that takes less time after it clears upstream departments, perhaps including product design, marketing, cost accounting, and styling. Second, strong barriers between functional areas often become "black holes" where orders or designs become lost or misplaced. Marketing may toss an order over the barrier to manufacturing, ending its responsibility for the order. However, just because marketing has passed on the order does not mean that manufacturing has received it or assumed responsibility for it. Finding lost orders increases lead times. Third, functional barriers may delay revisions in a sequential process and raise the cost of implementing them. Manufacturing problems often remain undiscovered in the conceptualization stage of product engineering to be uncovered only after the design function has firmed up the design and passed it on to the rest of the system. Once the errors are caught, the design must go through the entire sequential process again.

An **As One/System Integration** strategy tries to tear down these functional barriers and bring together interested parties to share necessary information and insights and coordinate their actions. This strategy can focus internally on bringing together various groups within the firm (e.g., purchasing, marketing, design, engineering, production, and inventory control). Alternatively, System Integration can focus externally on bringing together customers, suppliers, and the firm.

System Integration often works to improve a firm's organizational structure and information sharing. For example, a supplier can provide a customer with information about short-term capacity such as the amount of capacity available over a few weeks and the short-term load on that capacity. In turn, the customer can provide its short-term forecasts to the supplier. Exhibit 3.8 illustrates the results of System Integration. This strategy relies on procedures such as simultaneous engineering and process flow analysis. (How much shorter would class registration be if all steps could be handled by one person by computer?)

Same as/Standardization.   One way to reduce lead time is to nurture a minimalist focus on the minimum process necessary to complete a task. Instead of treating each task in a process or each part in a product as unique, the **Same as/Standardization** strategy can reduce lead times by reusing steps or parts that are common or standard. Standard processes eliminate the dual task in a fast to market competitor of designing a new product and learning or developing a new process. Instead, people work with a familiar process, freeing their attention to focus on designing the product within the context of the standard process. Similarly, people in a fast to product company respond to each order in the same way, reducing lead time and increasing predictability.

Standardizing parts or components allows workers to deliver new products faster by implementing ready solutions based on previously designed and built components for which costs, standards, bills of materials, and lead times are already known. Standardization frees workers to deal with unique parts and process components that offer value to customers. As a result, standardization significantly simplifies the overall design task.

At Once/Parallel Activities.   Unlike the other strategies, the **At Once/Parallel Activities** strategy focuses on the sequence of tasks in a process. In any process, tasks can appear either within or outside the **critical path**, the sequence of activities that define the minimum lead time needed to complete a task or project. Adding an activity to this path always increases lead times, but one can reduce lead times by moving any activity off of the critical path so that it occurs at the same time as, or in parallel with, the remaining activities on the critical path.

As One/System Integration

A strategy to reduce lead times by bringing together related activities, processes, and information flows

Same as/Standardization

A strategy to reduce lead times by trying to use standard processes or parts as much as possible, allowing people to focus on unique parts or process components

At Once/Parallel Activities

A strategy for reducing lead times by reorganizing sequential activities to occur in parallel, whenever possible

critical path

The sequence of activities that define the minimum lead time needed to complete a task or project

[**EXHIBIT 3.8**]

Impact of System Integration

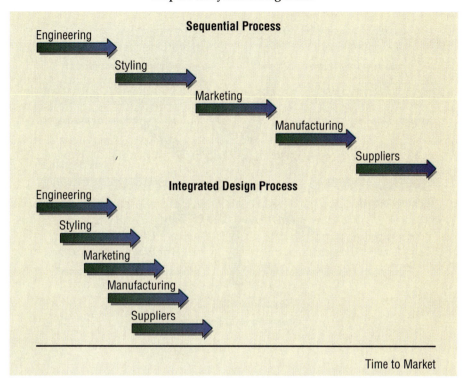

The Parallel Activities strategy tries to minimize the steps on the critical path. Often, value determines whether an activity forms part of the critical path or not. If a task contributes to value, as defined by the customer, then it may occur on the critical path. Whenever possible, this strategy moves nonvalue-adding activities off of the critical path.

Watch It/Variance Control.   The **Watch It/Variance Control** strategy focuses primarily on the predictability of the OM process. It attempts to control lead times by identifying activities or tasks with the highest levels of variance, measured by dispersion or spread in observed data. High variances characterize an unpredictable process. Managers often respond by stretching lead times to buffer or protect the system from problems created by high variability.

Variance Control identifies tasks with the highest variance and examines them to uncover the reasons for the variance. Attempts to eliminate or control variance focus on these causes. Typical tools for variance control include just-in-time manufacturing (Chapter 9), setup reduction (Chapter 9), and process flow analysis (Chapter 5). Reducing lead time variation often results in humans reducing their own "just in case" time buffers.

Better than/Automation.   The **Better than/Automation** strategy tries to reduce lead times by replacing older, less efficient procedures and technologies with newer, more efficient ones. This strategy is based on two important assumptions:

Watch It/Variance Control

A strategy to reduce lead times by identifying and eliminating or controlling activities that create variance within lead times

Better than/Automation

A strategy for reducing lead times through technology or automation

Impact of the Seven Strategies to Reduce Lead Times

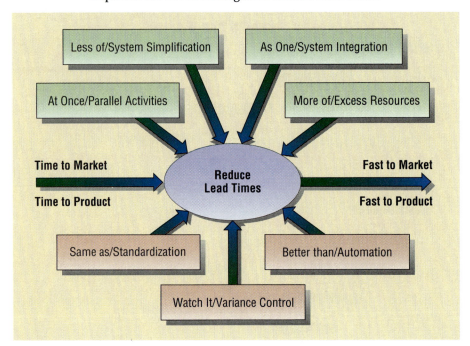

(1) that new technologies are inherently better and take less time, and (2) that problems with lead times result primarily from technology rather than process characteristics. The introduction of new technology or automation may or may not change the processes that use the technology.

For example, a firm might try to reduce time to market by building computer simulation models of a product before introducing it. The firm could also reduce the time needed for a customer to place an order by replacing a mailed document with a fax, computer network message, or electronic data interchange transaction. Instead of physically bringing people together for a meeting, a teleconference can often achieve the same objective.

More of/Excess Resources

A strategy to reduce lead times by deploying new resources in the form extra labor, equipment, materials, or tools to overcome lead time increases due to resource shortages

More of/Excess Resources.   The **More of/Excess Resources** strategy assumes that lead times grow because of resource constraints as orders must compete for access to scarce resources such as workers, machines, tools, or material. Two fairly simple actions can reduce these delays. First, the firm can introduce new resources, in the form of additional labor, unused machine capacity, and inventory. Most firms deploy such new resources at bottleneck sites, areas where resource shortages constrain process flows. A second Excess Resources response affects human resources by developing a highly skilled, cross-trained work force. Such workers can more easily accommodate variations in product mix or work load.

By combining these seven strategies, the operations manager can reduce the lead times needed to design new products or to deliver existing products (Exhibit 3.9). As a final example of some of these lead-time reducing strategies in action, consider *Fortune* magazine's description of the success of the redesigned Honda Accord:

A good candidate for Bargain of the Year, the Accord has been restyled to make it sportier and more expensive looking, but the base price starts at $14,130—same as on the 1993 model. To pull this off, Honda cut spending on engineering, development, and production by 50 percent—yes, five-oh. It even used some components made from designs 4 years old. The latest chariots are no hand-me-downs, however; *Automotive Industries* magazine reports that their new, powerful engines produce a ride so quiet that drivers may forget the motor is on. Honda expects to sell 320,000 of these Marysville, Ohio-built coupes and station wagons in the United States next year, up from 290,000 in 1993.[7]

FLEXIBILITY

Flexibility represents a relatively new strategic tool to enhance value and to promote effective competition in the marketplace. Many Japanese, European, and American firms now view flexibility as the next weapon in their strategic arsenals.

Many managers and students have formed only vague notions of flexibility, however, describing it with terms such as *responsiveness, speed of response,* and *adaptability*. In this book, **flexibility** means the ability of an operations management system to respond quickly to changes. These changes can be generated externally, as when the market begins demanding a different mix of products and a firm changes its schedule to provide the desired product mix. Change can also be generated internally, as when a machine breaks down and operations managers must rearrange the flow of products through the system to avoid disappointing customers.

The responsiveness of the operations management system can be described in terms of *range* and *time*.[8] Range describes the number of different possibilities that the operations management system can handle. For example, McDonald's process allows it to offer a more flexible breakfast menu than Burger King. Burger King organizes its process around a flame broiling cooking method while McDonald's relies on a grill. You can cook pancakes, omelets, and eggs on a grill; it is far more difficult to flame broil eggs.

After range, time is the second critical element of flexibility. This characteristic represents the amount of time a system needs to respond to a change with a new range of possibilities. As this response takes less time, the system becomes more flexible. Together, internally and externally generated changes along with a system's range and response time form the framework for understanding flexibility (Exhibit 3.10).

Flexibility attracts customers because it helps both them and the firm itself to deal with uncertainty. Competitors' actions can cause uncertainty, as when a competitor introduces a new product. To remain competitive, other firms must either match or beat this new product. Uncertainty can result when a customer wants the firm to accommodate changes in product mix or volume. Uncertainty can also derive from internal causes such as variances in material or equipment availability. Gerwin has listed some sources of uncertainty for the operations manager:[9]

- Market acceptance of product types
- Lengths of product life cycles

flexibility

The ability of an OM system to respond quickly, measured by range and time, to externally and internally generated changes

---

[7]Richard Sookdeo, "Oh Baby! What a Year for Products," *Fortune,* December 27, 1993, p. 91.

[8]Nigel Slack, "Flexibility as a Manufacturing Objective," *International Journal of Operations and Production Management* 3, no. 3 (1983), pp. 4–13.

[9]Donald Gerwin, "Manufacturing Flexibility: A Strategic Perspective," *Management Science* 39, no. 4 (April 1993), p. 406.

[EXHIBIT 3.10]

Conceptual Framework for Flexibility

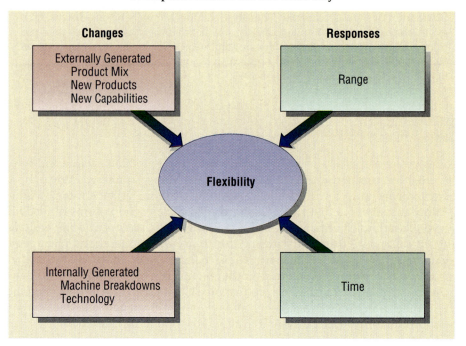

- Specific product characteristics
- Aggregate product demand
- Machine or equipment downtime
- Employee absenteeism
- Materials characteristics
- Rate of introduction of new processes and technologies

Types of Flexibility

As previously pointed out, flexibility depends on two traits: range and time. As for lead times, different range and time characteristics create many different types of flexibility. This section will explore seven categories of flexibility identified by Donald Gerwin:[10]

- Mix flexibility
- Changeover flexibility
- Modification flexibility
- Volume flexibility
- Rerouting/program flexibility
- Material flexibility
- Flexibility responsiveness

Mix Flexibility.   In the marketplace, a firm always faces uncertainty regarding the mix of products that customers want. As a result, firms typically offer multiple

---

[10]Gerwin, "Manufacturing Flexibility," pp. 395–410.

product lines, perhaps with numerous variations to allow customization. **Mix flexibility** is the ability of the operations management system to present a wide range of products or variants with fast setups. Mix flexibility allows the firm to respond quickly by changing from one product to another. This drastically reduces the need for inventory to act as a buffer and to protect against surprises.

Changeover Flexibility. In addition to the uncertain reception for a product among customers, a firm must also resolve doubts about the length of a product's life cycle. With product life cycles shrinking, today's managers must plan to quickly replace products that experience declining demand. **Changeover flexibility** is the ability to introduce a large variety of major design changes quickly within existing facilities. Changeover flexibility requires the OM system to reduce the amount of startup time it needs to work out problems and difficulties that arise in introducing a new product.

Modification Flexibility. Every product undergoes a process of continuous change and modification. Some changes answer customer requests for special modifications. Others result from marketplace feedback about features that customers value and those they do not. In addition, designers in most firms continually experiment with their products, adding features and dropping those that prove unwanted or too expensive relative to their contributions to perceived value. Managers must implement any such change within the operations management system. **Modification flexibility** is the ability of the transformation process to implement minor product design changes.

Range helps to describe this type of flexibility by identifying the number of different modifications that a system can accommodate, while the time trait captures the speed with which it can implement the changes. For a good example of modification flexibility, consider how effectively McDonald's and Burger King can respond to requests for specially cooked hamburgers. McDonald's organizes its OM system to turn out essentially standard products, so it takes longer to accommodate special requests. In contrast, Burger King's assemble to order system can easily make a hamburger to suit specific needs. While McDonald's inventories finished goods, Burger King inventories finished components in the form of cooked hamburger patties, buns, and condiments so workers can finish each burger to meet specific needs. As a result, modification flexibility is far higher at Burger King than at McDonald's.

Volume Flexibility. Managers must also resolve uncertainty about the quantity of a product that customers want. Some of this uncertainty comes from customers' scheduling practices, since many firms ship most of their output in the last week of every month, leaving suppliers to wonder until the end of the month what they will want for future production. Some uncertainty about quantities reflects demand fluctuations by customers (and their customers). **Volume flexibility** is the ability of the transformation process to accommodate variations in production quantity. The range of this type of flexibility describes the size of the variation in quantity that a system can accommodate without significantly higher costs; the time trait describes how quickly a system can respond to quantity variations. Volume flexibility might allow a process to produce 1,000 units in the same time per unit as it can produce 1 unit and to produce 1 unit for the same per unit cost as 1,000 units.

Rerouting/Program Flexibility. Any transformation process, from the kitchen at McDonald's to the Oshkosh B'Gosh factory, employs equipment, and some-

mix flexibility
The ability of an OM system to present a wide range of products or variants with fast setups

changeover flexibility
The ability of an OM system to introduce a large variety of major design changes quickly within existing facilities

modification flexibility
The ability of the transformation process to implement minor product design changes

volume flexibility
The ability of the transformation process to accommodate variations in production quantities

times needed equipment becomes unavailable, perhaps due to mechanical break-down. A breakdown increases lead times since the process must wait for repairs to complete the job, forcing customers to wait. Equipment also becomes unavailable during long production runs, when a single job occupies a machine until its completion. **Rerouting/program flexibility** is the ability of the OM system to reduce uncertainty of equipment availability by changing the route (i.e., the sequence of machines) through which a job flows.[11] If a machine breaks down, production can follow a different route through another machine. If a critical machine is occupied, a flexible system can change the process sequence and use another machine that is currently available. Rerouting/program flexibility helps managers to bypass bottlenecks.

Because rerouting/program flexibility often depends on alternative equipment, many operations managers measure this type of flexibility based on the number of alternate routes a system offers and the ease of changing from one to another. Higher rerouting/program flexibility reduces the cost (in terms of setup time and machine efficiency) to change a job's production route.

Material Flexibility.   Uncertainty can come from variations in the quality of materials from suppliers, since managers cannot always be sure that all inputs bring equal quality levels. For example, the amount of grapes that a winery needs for a given batch of wine is strongly influenced by the sweetness of the grapes. Sweeter grapes allow the winery to reduce the amount of grapes in a batch. The sweetness of grapes varies, however, with such factors as the time of harvest, the vineyard location, and the amounts of sunshine and rain during the growing season. As a result, the person who blends the grapes must test them and decide how much to use to achieve the desired taste.

Material flexibility describes the ability of the transformation process to adjust for unexpected variations in inputs. This kind of flexibility is often described in terms of the number of different variations and their magnitudes that the process can accommodate and the time it takes to respond.

Flexibility Responsiveness.   **Flexibility responsiveness** measures the ease and speed with which the firm can change its strategic objectives to respond to changes in the marketplace or in any other type of flexibility. This broad-based type of flexibility spans and affects the other six types of flexibility since it can dictate changes to them to maintain consistency between how the firm generates value for its customers and its system's capabilities.

Comments on the Categories of Flexibility.   The firm's consideration of the different types of flexibility should emphasize four critical points:

- *Selection of methods to improve flexibility should reflect how the firm competes.* Each type of flexibility generates value differently, so a firm should emphasize categories of flexibility that customers value most. For example, a firm that competes on the basis of reliable deliveries should identify rerouting/program flexibility as critical to its success. However, an appliance repair shop needs mix flexibility to respond to an unpredictable flow of customer needs.
- *No firm can excel on all seven dimensions of flexibility.* Trying to do everything risks mediocrity, making the system a jack of all trades, but a master of none.

rerouting/program flexibility
The ability of the OM system to reduce uncertainty of equipment availability by quickly and easily changing the route (i.e., the sequence of machines) through which a job flows

material flexibility
The ability of the transformation process to adjust for unexpected variations in inputs

flexibility responsiveness
The ability of the firm and its managers to change strategic objectives in response to changes in the marketplace

[11]We use both terms for this type of flexibility because both have been applied in the operations management literature.

[**EXHIBIT 3.11**]

Dimensions of Flexibility

Type of Flexibility	Type of Uncertainty	Strategic Objective
Mix flexibility	Market acceptance of product	Diverse product line
Changeover flexibility	Length of product life cycle	Product innovation
Modification flexibility	Specific product characteristics	Responsiveness to customers' specifications and needs
Volume flexibility	Aggregate product demand	Market share
Rerouting/program flexibility	Machine downtime/resource	Customers' due dates
Material flexibility	Material characteristics	Product quality
Flexibility responsiveness	Changes in other uncertainties	Strategic adaptability

SOURCE   Donald Gerwin, "Manufacturing Flexibility: A Strategic Perspective," *Management Science* 39, no. 4 (April 1993), p. 398. Reprinted by permission. Copyright 1993, The Institute of Management Sciences (currently INFORMS), 290 Westminster St., Providence, RI 02903, U.S.A.

- *Enhancing flexibility requires cooperation both inside and outside the firm.*   For example, a suitably designed product greatly enhances the ability of the operations manager to implement and compete on modification flexibility. To emphasize volume flexibility, a firm needs the support of suppliers. Success in enhancing mix or changeover flexibility depends on strong links with the internal marketing function and with customers.
- *Improving flexibility affects the other elements of value.*   Flexibility affects lead time and quality through the synergistic relationships among the three elements of the numerator of the value equation. Reductions in lead times affect flexibility; improvements in flexibility benefit quality; improvements in quality reduce lead times and enhance flexibility.

Exhibit 3.11 summarizes the relationships among sources of uncertainty, types of flexibility, and associated strategic objectives.

Flexibility as a Source of Value

Today's market links flexibility with value. Firms have found several beneficial effects from enhancing flexibility.

Consistency with Shorter Product Life Cycles.   Product life cycles are compressing, making all products increasingly like fashion goods that survive only for short times. Useful lives of products depend on factors other than durability such as customer tastes. Just like the demand for designer clothing, when tastes change, products leave the market. Examples of such products include toys (Mighty Morphin' Power Rangers), shoes (Air Jordans), breakfast cereals (oat bran recipes), and sports clothing. Flexibility helps a firm to cope with short and shrinking product life cycles.

Niche Marketing Opportunities.   We have discussed the fundamental shift from producing for broad-based markets to producing for individuals called *niche marketing.* Success in niche marketing is strongly linked to flexibility that allows the firm to produce in small lots, perhaps even to build each item for a specific customer. For example, Chrysler targets its Town and Country minivan at the high end of the market. Built in small quantities (less than 30,000 per year), these vans provide luxury buyers with desirable extras such as leather seats.

The movement toward niche market is evident in many different markets. For example, in 1980, only 88 brands of breakfast cereals were sold in the United States. This number has now grown to 200, including many variations on basic brands. To basic Cheerios, General Mills has added Honey Nut Cheerios, Apple Cinnamon Cheerios and Multi-Grain Cheerios, each targeted at a specific market segment. Coffee drinkers no longer simply drink the brand of their favorite company. Rather, they select from decaffeinated coffee, dark-roast blends, premium coffee, regional coffees, and coffee-house drinks, such as cappuccino and lattes, from the multitude of coffee-houses that have sprung up. Firms have found niche marketing very attractive, provided they have cultivated the right types of flexibility.

Premium Prices for Flexibility.   Flexibility allows a firm to fine-tune products to meet specific needs, justifying premium prices. Flexibility also helps firms to cope with uncertainty. In the marketplace, the customer can manage uncertainty by changing suppliers. However, uncertainty often requires firms to rely on such buffering mechanisms as inventory, increased lead times, or increased capacities, raising costs. Under these conditions, a flexible supplier can take over responsibility for dealing with uncertainty from the customer. Why worry about which items to stock if a supplier can provide needed items quickly? Customers are willing to pay premium prices for this kind of service.

Reductions in Lead Time.   Flexibility optimizes both range and time. Enhanced flexibility often translates directly into reduced lead time.

Improvements in Quality.   Flexibility requires a system to do everything right the first time. It leaves no room for error or for quality problems that affect its time dimension.

Reductions in Cost.   Flexibility reduces the need for inventory. Also, worker productivity improves as employees spend less time in nonvalue-adding activities such as correcting errors, filling inventories, and unnecessarily setting up and tearing down machines. These changes, together with shorter lead times and higher quality, translate into lower costs.

Mass Customization: Competing through Flexibility

mass customization
A corporate strategy designed to develop and maintain a sustainable competitive advantage by competing on the basis of flexibility

An entire corporate strategy designed around flexibility, **mass customization**, offers customers variety and customized products through flexibility and quick response times.[12] This strategy tries to generate value for customers by creating enough variety and opportunities for customization that nearly everyone finds almost exactly what he or she wants. Instead of forcing customers to compromise and buy products that come close enough to what they want, mass customization focuses on creating transformation and design processes that respond to the needs of the buyer. This requires an operations management system that is more productive with fewer resources than any previous type of operations management system (Exhibit 3.12). Mass customization is niche marketing taken to its logical conclusion.

[12]B. Joseph Pine II, *Mass Customization: The New Frontier in Business Competition* (Cambridge, Mass.: Harvard Business School, 1993), p. 44.

[**EXHIBIT 3 . 1 2**]

Evolution of Operations Management and Mass Customization

	Mass Production	Flexible Production	Mass Customization
Period of history	1900–1970	1971–2000	2001–2020
Typical number of machine tools	150	50–30	25–30
Typical number of products made	10–15	100–1,000	Unlimited
Proportion products reworked due to poor quality	25% or more	0.02% or less	Under 0.0005%

SOURCE   Otis Porter, "Custom-Made, Direct from the Plant." Reprinted from November 18, 1994 issue of *Business Week,* by special permission, copyright © 1991 by The McGraw-Hill Companies.

A number of companies have adapted this relatively new strategy for competition and the transformation process, including AT&T, Coke and Pepsi, breakfast cereal companies such as General Mills, fast-food companies such as McDonald's, manufacturers of computer modems such as U.S. Robotics, heavy manufacturing firms such as Caterpillar, and banking firms such as CitiCorp with its 15-minute mortgage program. Procter & Gamble produces babies' diapers in 13 different designs, each targeted to a specific age group, sex, and weight class. One of the most successful mass customizers has been Ross Operating Valve headquartered in Troy, Michigan:

> "I cannot train people quick enough to take care of all the potential new business," says David L. Ross, marketing director at Ross Operating Valve Company, a private 350-employee maker of pneumatic valves. At the Ross/Flex plant in Lavonia, GA, customers phone to discuss what valves they need with company engineers called *integrators*. The specs are entered into a CAD/CAM system to design a one-of-a-kind valve, and automated machine tools grind out the metal parts overnight.

Caterpillar Inc. generates value for its customers by producing a wide variety of construction machines and offering specialized customization. Mass customization is a flexible manufacturing response to customer needs.   SOURCE   Courtesy of Caterpillar Inc.

[**EXHIBIT 3.13**]

Corporate Implications of Mass Customization

Effects	Operations Management	Research and Development	Marketing	Finance and Accounting
Focus	Total process efficiency	Continuous incremental innovations	Gaining market share by fulfilling customer wants and needs, first domestically and then in export markets	Information useful to managers and workers
Positive effects	Low overhead and bureaucracy Optimum quality Elimination of waste Continuous process improvement Low inventory costs High labor productivity Integration of thinking and doing High utilization of and investment in worker skills Low total costs High production flexibility Greater variety at lower costs	Continuous improvements leading to eventual technological superiority Integration of innovation and production Frequent process innovations Low costs and short cycle times Mutually beneficial relationships with other firms Better fulfillment of customer wants and needs	Filling niches Responding quickly to changing customer needs Taking over markets High sales, both domestically and through exports Technology-intensive products	Sound long-term and short-term decisions Long-term supplier interdependence Low costs, high profits Long-term investment in capital, people, and technology Attention to competencies
Negative effects	Potential for a demanding, stressful environment	Potential for lack of breakthrough innovations	Becomes too enamored of technology	Ignores stockholders

SOURCE   Adapted and reprinted by permission of Harvard Business School Press from *Mass Customization: The New Frontier in Business Competition* by B. Joseph Pine II. Boston: 1993, pp. 111, 114, 118, 122. Copyright © 1993 by the President and Fellows of Harvard College.

Finished valves are delivered in as little as 72 hours, at a typical cost of $3,000. That's about one-hundredth the time and one-tenth the cost of traditional methods.[13]

The effects of mass customization extend beyond the operations management system to research and development, marketing, and finance and accounting (Exhibit 3.13). Success in implementing mass customization requires a change in focus from economies of scale, in which a firm builds more of a single item to reduce per-unit costs, to economies of scope, in which it tries to produce variety at almost the same cost and within almost the same time limits as building identical

[13]Otis Porter, "Custom-Made, Direct from the Plant," *Business Week,* November 18, 1994, p. 158.

ON THE JOB

Motorola Learns Quality the Hard Way

■

Motorola hasn't always been the champion of quality that it is today. Shortly after Motorola got started back in 1933, the company's Model 55 car radio became a hot seller—too hot, in fact.

The problem started small, like most problems do. Motorola's original Model 55 wasn't designed to carry enough power. Engineers tried adding a fuse, but it caused an annoying buzz. So engineers hooked up the radio directly to the car's battery. This would have worked fine, except for a tiny vibration.

Unfortunately, this tiny vibration could end up overloading a car's transformer and wiring. The overall effect could be quite dramatic, as Paul Galvin, Motorola's founder, learned after engineers testing radios set Galvin's car on fire twice in one month. Lots of people turn on the radio while waiting for their car's engine to warm up, but the Model 55 made things a little too warm. One Sioux City lawyer turned on his Model 55 radio while sitting in his car, and his car, garage, and half his house went up in flames. Finally, as if to add insult to injury, a Model 55 radio installed in a hearse set it on fire and, to the dismay of friends and family who would have liked a more traditional funeral, cremated the corpse inside.

SOURCE   Robert Hall, *The Soul of the Enterprise* (New York: Harper Business, 1993), p. 67.

items. Mass customization also relies on new relationships with suppliers. Rather than simple providers of goods and services, suppliers must become sources of expertise and resources. Instead of working alone to meet the challenge of flexibility, the operations manager must work with suppliers in on-going relationships that join their expertise and resources with those of the firm.

 QUALITY

Since the mid-1980s, quality has become the defining component of value in the views of many managers and customers. The Japanese automobile industry has made quality the major strategic tool for increasing its share of the American car market. Companies such as Xerox, Ford, Hewlett-Packard, and Florida Power and Light have relied on quality either to turn around their market performance or to enhance their positions in the marketplace. Motorola has joined this group after a rocky start on the road to quality, as described in the "On the Job" box. The U.S. Department of Commerce recognizes superior performance by American firms in improving quality with the Malcolm Baldrige National Quality Award. Increasingly, states are creating their own quality awards, but no one gives similar awards for superior flexibility or lead time.

Companies are making increasingly significant investments in quality initiatives. More than 87 percent of the largest American industrial corporations have

ON THE JOB

Customer Expectations of the Grateful Dead

For many fans, the Grateful Dead was not just a band, it was a way of life. Some people identified with the rock band so intensely that they seemed to plan their entire lives around concerts. Calling themselves "Deadheads," fans took entire summers off to follow the band around the country and the world.

The band did its part to accommodate and foster such loyalty. First, it knew its most loyal fans were adventurous vagabonds who didn't have a lot of money. It tried to sell its tickets at or below the average charged by other rock bands. It also sold its tickets through the mail and included a packet of information about inexpensive restaurants and places to stay near the concert site.

For true Deadheads, a Grateful Dead gig was an all-encompassing experience. Part of the draw was meeting other Deadheads, who descended on a city in a glorious caravan of psychedelic vans, campers, and buses. Concerts often lasted up to three and a half hours, and the band never played the same song twice, though it may have stayed in a given city for three or four nights.

Instead of barring recording at concerts, like most bands do, the Grateful Dead encouraged it. Many fans were able to finance their travels and the cost of concert tickets by selling these unofficial tapes along with other Deadhead paraphernalia such as tie-dyed T-shirts.

Through intimate knowledge of its customer, the Grateful Dead had consistently been able to meet and exceed the expectations of its fans. The Grateful Dead was big business—estimates of ticket revenues in 1992 topped $30 million. In December 1995, following the death of band leader Jerry Garcia, the remaining members disbanded, ending one of the most unusual microcosms to have evolved from a rock band.

SOURCE   James W. Dean, Jr., and James R. Evans, *Total Quality Management, Organization, and Strategy,* (St. Paul, Minn.: West, 1994), p. 8.

expanded their quality initiatives since 1987.[14] Some companies have begun to realize sizable returns on these investments. For example, in the early 1980s, Stanley, a 140-year-old manufacturer of tools decided to try to reverse large losses of market share by investing in quality. Over a 6-year period, it managed to reduce scrap, a major indicator of quality problems, from 15 percent to 3 percent. Since 1980, Stanley's profits have more than doubled. Monroe Auto Equipment mounted an all-out quality effort, raising productivity in its 36 plants by 26 percent from 1986 to 1990 and boosting annual sales to near $900 million—an increase of 70 percent. A recent shipment of 60,000 Monroe shock absorbers to Toyota was rated as having zero defects—an amazing achievement.[15]

As a final example of quality in action, the "On the Job" box discusses the Grateful Dead's continuous efforts to meet and exceed fans' expectations. Clearly, the Grateful Dead could attribute fan loyalty to recognition of the importance of quality.

In spite of its popularity, quality is not a well-understood concept. Confusion surrounds the distinction between what quality is and what it is not. Some managers see quality as nothing more than meeting specifications while others take a

[14]Marion Mills Steeples, *The Corporate Guide to the Malcolm Baldrige National Quality Award* (Milwaukee, Wis.: ASQC Quality Press, 1993), p. 5.

[15]Ibid., p. 6.

[**E X H I B I T   3 . 1 4**]

Five Views of Quality

1. Transcendental View

Neither mind nor matter, but a third entity independent of the two... Even though Quality cannot be defined, you know what it is.

A condition of excellence implying fine quality as distinct from poor quality... Quality is achieving or reaching for the highest standard as against being satisfied with the sloppy or fraudulent.

2. Product-Based View

Differences in quality amount to differences in the quantity of some desired ingredient or attribute.

Amounts of nonprice attributes contained in each unit of the priced attribute.

3. User-Based View

Capacity to satisfy wants.

In the final analysis of the marketplace, the quality of a product depends on how well it fits patterns of consumer preference.

Quality is fitness for use.

4. Manufacturing-Based View

Conformance to requirements.

The degree to which a specific product conforms to a design or specification.

5. Value-Based View

The degree of excellence at an acceptable price and the control of variability at an acceptable cost.

Best for certain customer conditions: (a) the actual use and (b) the selling price of the product.

SOURCE   David A. Garvin, *Managing Quality* (New York: Free Press, 1988), pp. 40–41. Copyright 1988 The McGraw-Hill Companies, Inc. All rights reserved.

much broader view. A recent series of commercials claimed that Mazda cars "just feel right"; the ads were talking about quality.

Garvin's review of the literature identifies five different definitions of quality. (See Exhibit 3.14.) Another author has defined it as "the integrity in delivering what a customer has a legitimate right to expect in view of what was promised at the time of the agreement to purchase."[16] This dynamic definition of quality recognizes that quality levels and expectations always move upward. For one variable, quality depends on time. A trip to McDonald's may represent a quality meal for a spouse on February 15, but not on February 14 (Valentine's Day).

Quality is not the same as product features; adding more features does not necessarily increase quality. Features are attributes designed into a product to help it meet the special needs of the customer, and they often help to define the market niche for a good or service.[17] Quality depends, however, on whether each product feature performs as the firm led the customer to believe that it should. A manufacturer can add features such as a CD-ROM drive, a larger hard disk, multimedia capabilities, an internal fax/modem, separate processors for computations and video, and a larger monitor to a microcomputer to better serve the needs of a buyer who wants to do multimedia presentations. However, the buyer assesses

[16]Myron Tribus, *Quality First* (Washington, D.C.: American Quality and Productivity Institute, 1988), p. 184.

[17]Ibid., p. 183.

quality whenever the computer offers the benefits of those features. When the CD-ROM drive works as expected and provides access to the necessary disks, it provides quality.

Finally, quality is described and understood in terms of certain traits and types. Traits identify aspects of the good or service that people can measure to assess quality. Types identify different categories of quality.

Attributes of Quality

If someone were to ask you to describe quality or how you would judge the quality of a product such as a microcomputer, you might reply by talking about such things as how long the computer would run before needing repair, whether it would run every time that you turned on the power switch, or whether it would be easy to use and maintain. These descriptions cite attributes of quality; they identify traits associated with quality that can be identified and, more importantly, measured. Attributes, however, are not the same as quality. Identifying every attribute of quality for a product would not describe that product's quality level. Seven general attributes contribute to quality:

- Functionality
- Reliability
- Durability
- Safety
- Serviceability
- Aesthetics
- Perceived quality

functionality

An attribute of quality that measures whether or not a product functions

Functionality.   **Functionality** gives a yes/no type of answer to the question whether or not a good or service performs as expected at the time of use. For example, a user judges the functionality of a computer at every power up. If the computer works when the user turns on the power, then it passes the test for functionality. If it fails to turn on or displays an error message, it fails this test. Other examples of functionality appear in Exhibit 3.15. Functionality is a moment of truth in action.

reliability

An attribute of quality that measures how long a product performs before it fails

Reliability.   **Reliability** measures how long a product performs before it fails. A package of light bulbs lists average lumen hours as such an indicator. An average lumen hours rating of 750, for example, indicates that a typical light bulb should light for 750 hours before it needs replacement. This figure indicates reliability. For another example, when a manufacturer of a computer hard disk reports a mean time between failures (MTBF) of 150,000 hours, it says that the user can expect trouble-free performance for an average of 150,000 hours.

durability

An attribute of quality that measures performance under adverse conditions

Durability.   **Durability**, like reliability, measures a product's performance over time, but with emphasis on performance under adverse conditions. Many product claims trumpet this attribute of quality. Olympus, for example, has claimed that its cameras have worked at the top of Mount Everest without any modification. Sears has always emphasized the ability of its Die Hard battery to work in sub-zero conditions or after all-night use.

Durability is important to many customers because it indicates the robustness of a product. Durable products encourage user confidence; a durable camera should withstand punishment such as falling off tables or down stairs without needing repairs.

[**E X H I B I T   3 . 1 5**]

Examples of Functionality

- Turning on the ignition in a car
- Turning on a light bulb
- Turning on a stereo
- Using a microwave oven
- Accessing an automated teller machine (ATM)

Safety.   **Safety** measures the likelihood of harm from a good or service. Safety is important to customers, as they showed when sales of Suzuki Samurai vehicles plummeted after a review in *Consumer Reports* cited a potential to turn over and roll under certain conditions. In contrast, companies such as Mercedes-Benz, Volvo, and Saab have built reputations for offering high-quality cars, in part, by offering high levels of safety.

> **safety**
> An attribute of quality that measures the likelihood of harm from a good or service

Gillette based its early growth on an appeal to safety. At the turn of the century, men shaved with straight razors. Shaving with such long, sharp blades required skill to avoid serious cuts. The straight razor was so dangerous that it had been used as a murder weapon, earning the nickname "cut-throat razor." Instead, Gillette developed a razor with the blade enclosed by a cage that exposed only a small edge, making cuts less likely and less dangerous. Gillette advertised its product as the Safety Razor.

Serviceability.   **Serviceability** measures such service-related traits as speed, courtesy, competence, and ease of repair. This trait is critical when a breakdown in equipment would be very expensive. For example, many newspaper reporters write their stories on computers. When a computer breaks down, then the reporter has lost not only the computer, but also the information stored on its hard disk. As a result, the reporter is likely to buy a computer from a manufacturer that can offer effective service. Companies such as Dell that offer on-site service and 24-hour turnaround times have been quite successful in selling to businesspeople and others who depend on their computers.

> **serviceability**
> An attribute of quality that measures a product's service-related traits

Aesthetics.   **Aesthetics** reflects a highly subjective assessment of how a product appears, feels, sounds, tastes, or smells.[18] A car buyer may evaluate aesthetic issues such as the fit and finish of the body panels or the smoothness of the paint job. When Mazda and Ford spend millions of dollars to determine the best places for the dials, knobs, and switches on a dashboard, they evaluate aesthetics.

> **aesthetics**
> An attribute of quality that subjectively measures a product's appearance, feel, sound, taste, or smell

Aesthetics are important because people want to buy products that both work and look "right." They judge the quality levels of restaurants and hotels, not simply on speedy service, but also on overall appearance and cleanliness.

To understand the importance of aesthetics, suppose that you have to buy a book for class. One of two books on the bookstore shelf is in perfect condition with no rips, tears, bent pages, or tears in the cover. The other book has a large scratch down the front cover. Both books have all of the actual text intact, and both are identically priced. Which book would you buy? Most people would buy the first book for its appearance (aesthetics).

[18]David A. Garvin, *Managing Quality* (New York: Free Press, 1988), p. 59.

Perceived Quality.   Customers do not always have complete information about the overall quality of a good or service. Such customers must base their assessments of quality on such factors as advertisements, media reports, reputations, and past experiences to indicate **perceived quality**. For example, if Hewlett-Packard were to announce a new generation of laser printers for computers, customers would likely welcome them as high-quality products. Since printers produced by Hewlett-Packard in the past have developed a reputation for durability, people would expect this new generation of printers to be equally durable. Similarly, people expect high-quality, well-built cars from Mercedes-Benz, Volvo, Cadillac, Saab, and Toyota—that is the reputation that these firms have built in the marketplace. This view is not based on actual experience with these products, but on subjective assessments of likely quality.

These seven attributes of quality give managers important help in identifying ways that their companies can compete on quality. Firms can compete by stressing different quality traits. In the microcomputer market, Dell competes on serviceability, while Hewlett-Packard and IBM compete on durability and perceived quality. By stressing attributes of quality different from those offered by competitors (provided that customers value identified differences), a firm can try to differentiate its products and make them unique.

perceived quality

An assessment of quality based on the reputation of the firm

Types of Quality

Earlier, this chapter identified different types of flexibility and different ways of competing on time; it can also outline different types of quality. Noritake Kano provides one useful way to categorize quality and understand its relationship to competition.[19] Kano breaks down quality into four categories:

indifferent quality

Quality that the customer does not notice or appreciate

- **Indifferent quality**   This is quality that the customer does not notice or appreciate. It generates no value for the customer. For example, a garnish on a dinner plate or a finger bowl, while nice, would probably not seem very important. Indifferent quality evokes a response like, "That's nice, but who cares?"

expected quality

Quality that the customer expects and demands

- **Expected quality**   This is quality that the customer expects and demands. For example, people expect cars to be safe and reliable, hotel rooms to be clean and quiet, and coffee to be hot. People notice expected quality only when it is missing. Lack of expected quality produces an order loser and a displeased customer.

one-dimensional quality

Quality that the customer expects, but that does not create an order loser when lacking

- **One-dimensional quality**   This category of quality resembles expected quality, but its absence does not necessarily create an order loser. For example, a restaurant server who is rude or slow may not cause customers to leave, though they might leave smaller tips. However, customers would leave if they observed insects cavorting in the food. The restaurant's slow service illustrates one-dimensional quality, while unsanitary conditions illustrate expected quality.

exciting quality

Quality that exceeds the customer's expectations, attracting favorable attention

- **Exciting quality**   This is quality that causes the customer to notice the firm. It is quality that exceeds customer expectations or pleasantly surprises customers, perhaps creating an order winner. Several examples illustrate this type of quality in action. When Lexus recalled its cars, an initial wave of snickering passed through the auto industry. After all, Lexus advertised its car as built by perfectionists for perfectionists. However, the management at

[19]Robert Hall, *The Soul of the Enterprise* (New York: Harper Business, 1993), p. 79.

[**E X H I B I T   3 . 1 6**]

Differences among the Four Types of Quality

Quality Type	Customer Reaction upon Discovering Presence of Quality	Customer Reaction upon Discovering Absence of Quality
Indifferent quality	That's nice, but who cares?	Is something missing?
Expected quality	This is what I expected.	Something is missing, and I won't buy again as a result.
One-dimensional quality	This is satisfactory, but it is not that important.	What a nuisance.
Exciting quality	This is really neat. I am going to buy again.	Is something missing?

Lexus turned a problem into an order winner by their response. They arranged to pick up the cars without inconvenience to the owners. Some owners dropped off their cars at dealerships in exchange for loaner cars. In other cases, the dealers arranged to pick up the cars from the owners at night. All cars were returned with full gas tanks, cleaned inside and outside, and with small gifts for the owners. This treatment represented quality that many owners who had previously driven Mercedes-Benz and BMW cars found very exciting. It surpassed their expectations.

Exhibit 3.16 summarizes the differences among these four types of quality.

Ford managers have developed another way of thinking about quality. They classify quality into two groups: **things gone wrong** (defects and errors) and **things gone right** (pleasing aesthetics, reliability, durability, good designs). Ford found that people will tolerate a number of things gone wrong if the number of things gone right greatly exceeds them.

things gone wrong/ things gone right
Ford's quality framework based on errors and defects versus product benefits

Managers work to improve performance by identifying areas of quality that offer the greatest opportunity for developing exciting, unexpected quality and for building up the number of things gone right. The areas of emphasis should differ from firm to firm; two firms cannot distinguish themselves by emphasizing the exact same attributes and types of quality.

Quality as a Source of Value

Many customers regard quality as an important source of value. Of the three components of the numerator of the value equation, quality was recognized first for its significant impact on the development and maintenance of a sustainable competitive advantage. This long-standing awareness of its importance has made quality something of an order qualifier, rather than an order winner. The experiences of such quality-oriented companies as Hewlett-Packard, Xerox, Motorola, and IBM have shown several effects on value of improvements in quality.

Improved Reputation.   Competing on quality has a positive impact on the reputation of a company. People buy from a company such as Motorola because they know of its reputation for quality as a winner of the Malcolm Baldrige National Quality Award, so they expect quality products. This same benefit applies to other companies that compete on quality (e.g., Xerox, Hewlett-Packard, and Cadillac).

Reputation provides important visibility and name recognition for such companies, and it gives them some freedom. Someone who has a problem with such a company's product is more likely to view the problem as an isolated occurrence, assuming that quality companies usually build quality products.

Easier Selling.   Increasingly, companies that compete on quality want to buy products from quality-oriented suppliers. For example, Motorola's quality-based Six Sigma program demands a level of quality consistent with 6δ or 6 standard deviations. Motorola's systems keep the customer's risk of getting a poor-quality product below 0.0000003 percent (i.e., 1 minus the probability of getting an acceptable product, or $1 - 0.9999997$). Stated another way, Six Sigma seeks to ensure that the firm produces fewer than three defective parts per million. Motorola recognizes that the quality of its products depends on the quality of its inputs from suppliers. As a result, Motorola has informed suppliers that they must implement their own versions of the Six Sigma program to keep Motorola's business.

Legal Implications.   By emphasizing quality, the firm benefits from demonstrating its concern about the effects of its goods and services and its actions to make them work well. This makes it easier for the firm to defend itself, should someone sue it for knowingly producing and selling an unsafe product.

Reduced Lead Times.   Lead times increase for any inspection or whenever the firm must assign workers, capacity, and material to correct quality-related problems in its products. By improving quality, the firm can eliminate these time-consuming activities and reduce lead times.

Enhanced Flexibility.   As it shrinks lead times, the emphasis on quality also enhances flexibility.

Improved Productivity.   The purpose of the operations management system is to enhance value and reduce waste. Devoting people and capacity to inspections, rework, scrap processing, or salvage (all direct results of quality problems), takes them away from work to enhance value or reduce waste. Using resources in these activities diverts them from value-adding activities to nonvalue-adding activities.

Reduced Floor Space Requirements.   A quality-driven transformation process needs less floor space for the same level of output than a quality-indifferent facility. Quality-driven processes need far less space for inventory to replace items that do not meet quality standards and for inspection and rework operations. A good example of the impact of quality on floor space requirements comes from Hewlett-Packard. An H-P plant manager decided to look at use of floor space in the plant. He colored a plant layout green in all areas where value-adding activities took place. He colored offices yellow and areas used for storing inventory brown. Finally, he used red for all rework and inspection areas. The manager viewed brown and red areas as nonvalue-adding, poor uses of space. The finished map showed about 50 percent of the plant either brown or red. This clarified an important goal—to reduce the amount of floor space devoted to red or brown activities. In the short term, the manager began to notice that the new layout could move more output through the door in less time and at a lower cost. He also noticed that eliminating the space for brown and red activities left space for future growth without adding onto the plant.

Reduced Cost.   Competing on quality introduces a paradox. In the short term, improving quality does increase costs since the firm must commit time and resources to identifying and eliminating quality problems. Sometimes it seems easier simply to hold some extra inventory or to add an inspection station or two. However, in the long term, eliminating quality-related problems reduces costs because it eliminates inspection and rework. Better quality saves the costs of fixing quality problems in the field and holds down the rate of product returns. Many operations managers now recognize that the highest-quality supplier is often the lowest-cost supplier.

Employee Pride.   Everyone, worker and manager, wants to be associated with a good company. Employees are motivated by knowledge that they produce some of the best products in the industry.

Clearly, lead time, flexibility, and quality are interdependent. To reduce lead time, a firm must emphasize quality; to become flexible, it must manage lead time. These three components of value also have a positive impact on costs, as careful evaluation of lead time, flexibility, and costs will drive costs downward. As a later section of this chapter will show, this relationship between lead time, flexibility, and quality on one hand and costs on the other cannot be worked successfully from the cost side. Often a focus on costs erodes quality, increases lead times, and inhibits flexibility.

Total Quality Management

Since the mid-1980s, the concept of quality has evolved into a broad-based corporate strategic system referred to as **total quality management** (TQM).[20] Total quality management views quality as something more than a corporate mandate or goal. TQM makes quality part of the corporate fabric, an integral element of the firm's competitive presence in the marketplace and its strategy for winning customers. Quality is not seen as a problem to solve, but rather as part of the solution. As Logothetis has defined it:

> Total quality management is a culture; inherent in this culture is a total commitment to quality and an attitude expressed by everybody's involvement in the process of continuous improvement of products and services, through the use of innovative scientific methods.[21]

This definition emphasizes four TQM principles (see also Exhibit 3.17):

- Commitment to quality
- Extensive use of scientific tools, technologies, and methods
- Total involvement in the quality undertaking
- Continuous improvement

total quality management

A culture that enfuses quality principles into every company activity

Commitment to Quality.   The notion of commitment implies resolution, dedication, and devotion to a theme or concept. TQM builds four types of commitment:

- Commitment to improvement
- Commitment to the customer

---

[20]Total quality management is covered in greater detail in Chapters 7 and 8 of this book.
[21]N. Logothetis, *Managing for Total Quality: From Deming to Taguchi and SPC* (Hertfordshire, U.K.: Prentice-Hall International, 1992), p. 5.

[**EXHIBIT 3.17**]

Four Principles of Total Quality Management

- Commitment of top management
- Commitment of the firm as a whole

Commitment to Improvement.   To successfully boost quality to the top of the company agenda, total quality management must foster a fundamental belief in the importance of quality. People within the firm must believe that quality can inspire an effective and efficient strategy for competing in the marketplace. They must accept that customers are attracted to quality and that they are willing to pay higher prices for something that lasts longer and over its life costs less.

Commitment to the Customer.   The second principle of TQM states that quality is an effective way of generating value for all customers. TQM targets all customers— internal, intermediate, and external to the firm.

Commitment of Top Management.   To succeed, TQM needs support and leadership from top management. Top managers must lead workers toward the goals of TQM, as they did at Xerox and Hewlett-Packard. At both firms, the CEOs (David Kearns at Xerox and John Young at Hewlett-Packard) played critical roles as champions for quality; each led the movement to quality through personal involvement and example. Top managers must work to create a corporate environment conducive to the acceptance of quality by emphasizing and directing resources toward:

- Training and education
- Proper working conditions
- Good incoming materials and equipment
- Adequate quality tools and systems
- Performance measurement systems that emphasize quality

Finally, top managers help to create the culture of quality. Without top management commitment, TQM becomes simply another fad.

Commitment of the Firm as a Whole.   Finally, the entire firm must commit to making TQM work. This corporate commitment recognizes that quality has many parents (e.g., operations management, suppliers, marketing, customers, engineering, accounting, and human resources management). All of these parents must involve themselves in all stages of the product's life, from concept to design to prototype to production to delivery to reinvention of the product. For TQM to work, everyone in the firm must be committed to quality; everyone must believe that quality is critical to the survival of the firm and to its ability to satisfy the needs of its customers.

Extensive Use of Scientific Tools, Technologies, and Methods.   Rather than relying on subjective guidelines and rules implemented by various people within the firm, total quality management recognizes and draws on more rigorous quality-related tools and theories. These tools rely extensively on statistics to differentiate random variation from underlying systematic changes. Workers can do nothing about random events, but changes in system performance require immediate attention because they threaten quality. Furthermore, scientific tools and theories provide a common language and a shared, proven method of identifying and describing quality-related problems and solving those problems.

Total Involvement in the Quality Undertaking.   Total quality management needs total involvement based on teamwork and empowerment to succeed. It relies on three different types of teamwork:

- *Vertical teamwork*   TQM requires on-going vertical cooperation between top management and functional groups. Actions on the shop floor or within engineering must contribute to the strategic orientation and goals of the firm.
- *Horizontal teamwork*   Horizontal teams bring together representatives from various functional groups. For example, to design a new car, a firm might form a design committee with representatives from engineering, operations management, purchasing, logistics, accounting, marketing, human resources, and, if possible, customers. Each member of this group would be affected by the design, and each could provide useful input to the design process.
- *Interorganizational teamwork*   The final type of teamwork brings together representatives of the firm with suppliers and customers. This type of teamwork ensures that the firm coordinates its quality activities with those of suppliers (e.g., so product designs call for inputs that suppliers can provide) and that these activities meet or exceed the expectations of customers.

Truly effective presupposes worker empowerment. Operations managers must empower or give authority to work teams to act on problems that they identify and to implement solutions that they generate. Empowerment comes from the operations manager's recognition of the need to transfer decision-making power to the people who are in actual contact with the problem. This changes the problem-solving process, as previous discussions of SAS and moments of truth have illustrated.

Continuous Improvement.   The final principle of total quality management, continuous improvement, transforms the drive toward quality into a never-ending journey. Every day, the firm must try to be better than it was the day before. Every day, the operations managers must encourage everyone within the organization to identify and act on opportunities for improvement. Effective continuous improvement needs the support of performance measurement methods.

Performance measurement systems help people to identify and measure, in quantitative terms, the sizes of improvements. This effort also keeps attention focused on quality. Reliable performance measurement must accurately assess progress toward intended objectives and behavior. As the "By the Way" box

[BY THE WAY... IMPORTANCE OF PERFORMANCE MEASUREMENT]

In a study of the problems at IBM, Paul Carroll examined the measurement system by which the firm's managers evaluated the quality of software development. This system measured quality in terms of the number of lines of code written per day, so programmers who wrote more lines of code were considered more productive. This encouraged programmers to write big, inefficient segments of code that ran more slowly because they took longer to read into memory and process. Large segments of code also required much more computer memory. This measurement system raised tensions between IBM and Microsoft when the two companies combined resources in the mid-1980s to work on OS/2:

One of the biggest fights the IBM and Microsoft developers had came when a Microsoft developer took a piece of IBM code that required 33,000 characters of space and rewrote it in 200 characters, 1/160th of the original space. That was considered rude. Other Microsoft developers then rewrote other parts of IBM's code to make it faster and smaller. That was even ruder. IBM managers then began complaining that, according to their measurement system, Microsoft hadn't been pulling its weight. Measured in lines of code, they said, Microsoft was actually doing *negative* work, meaning that Microsoft should have been paying IBM for the condensing it was doing.

SOURCE   Paul Carroll, *Big Blues: The Unmaking of IBM* (New York: Crown, 1993), p. 101.

indicates, performance measurement is important because you get what you inspect (or measure), not what you expect.

Of the three components in the value equation numerator, quality is the most fully developed. Interest in quality awakened in the beginnings of the 1980s in North America and as far back as the 1950s in Japan. Numerous companies have invested vast resources to implement quality-oriented systems and programs, and quality is the only component of value with its own national award. However, this long-standing interest in quality has made it an order qualifier for many markets.

 ## LEAD TIME, FLEXIBILITY, AND QUALITY: SUMMING UP THE NUMERATOR

Before considering the denominator of the value equation, cost, reflect on a few final observations. First, while the three components of value are interrelated, they focus on different activities. Quality focuses on activities that make a product better, though they also seem to improve lead times and flexibility. Improving lead times and flexibility require their own efforts, though they also boost quality.

Second, each dimension of value needs its own process. As the value-enhancement orientation shifts, perhaps from quality to lead time, the underlying processes must also change. This critical orientation toward process and its link to a specific type of value is one of this book's major building blocks.

Third, the three components of performance significantly affect costs. They produce cost reductions as by-products or residual effects. In the short term, in fact, value-enhancement actions increase costs. In the long term, however, they reduce costs by eliminating problems that cause long lead times, limited flexibility, and poor quality.

 ## COST: UNDERSTANDING THE DENOMINATOR

Having explored the numerator of the value equation, we now turn to the denominator, costs. Operations managers evaluate **cost**, measured in dollars, for its contributions in three important roles:

1. Reporting performance
2. Managing and evaluating operations
3. Enhancing value

Of these three contributions, most people are familiar with the first two. As explained in most introductory accounting textbooks, cost acts as both a common unit of measure and a means of comparing two different operations management systems. Analysts can draw conclusions about OM systems' performance by looking at either the costs they report or the profits they generate. Cost information supports comparisons even between systems that produce different outputs and compete in different ways. Furthermore, managers can identify potential operating problems by looking at cost variances (differences between actual and standard costs).

This book is most interested in the third role of cost—enhancing value. Cost reductions often translate directly into increases in value as they outweigh changes in performance.

cost

The denominator of the value equation which indicates what the customer must pay for a given level of performance

Understanding the Nature of Costs

Like lead time, flexibility, and quality, the term *costs* describes a variety of different elements. For example, a mention of costs could refer to one or more of several categories:

- *Acquisition cost*   The purchase price of a car, for example
- *Repair costs*   The cost of replacing a broken part
- *Maintenance costs*   The cost of oil changes and tune-ups
- *Operating costs*   The cost of gas and tires
- *Salvage/resale costs*   The cost recovered upon selling a car
- *Disposal costs*   The cost of disposing of a wrecked car

Furthermore, managers can break down costs to express them quantitatively (measured in dollars) or qualitatively (evaluating subjective effects). All of these elements of costs come together under the umbrella of total cost, to be discussed in greater detail in Chapter 4.

Cost as a Source of Value

Marketers know well that people like to buy things cheaply, but they do not like cheap things. This statement describes both the major attraction and the problem of emphasizing cost as the firm's major source of value. Customers want at least the same performance for a lower cost, not simply less for less. A cost-driven approach to value treats performance as given and focuses on reducing cost.

To achieve this objective, the operations management system must reexamine both the product (good or service) it offers and the processes by which it delivers the product. This reexamination seeks to identify product features that customers do not value highly or process traits that contribute unnecessarily to cost. These product and process features become candidates for elimination since the value they add does not justify their costs.

The danger of cost-driven value enhancement comes from the potential for abuse and an excessive emphasis on cost reduction. Such an approach stresses short-term savings while ignoring long-term implications. These actions often directly and negatively affect lead time, flexibility and quality. For example, to lower cost, a firm might use cheaper material that reduces quality. To save costs, management may decide to devote less time and resources to preventive maintenance of equipment and safety management. In the short term, these changes do save costs. However, in the long run, they reduce the availability of equipment and increase the burden of lost time due to on-the-job accidents.

Accounting for Overhead: Activity-Based Costing and Throughput Costing

Effective cost-driven value enhancement requires each product to bear its fair and accurate share of all costs the firm incurs to create it. Direct costs pose no major problem; managers simply record all of the labor, materials, and other resources directly used in creating a product and then assign these costs to the product. However, assigning overhead costs becomes more difficult. Overhead costs often reflect investments in technology (e.g., equipment and computer systems). Unlike direct costs, these expenses seldom vary with changes in output.

In the past, overhead costs did not pose major problems because they were smaller; labor accounted for much of a typical firm's costs. However, this situation has now changed in many areas of North America and Europe for several reasons. For one, labor has come to account for a smaller percentage of total costs, in some industries, less than 5 percent of total cost. Also, larger investments in automation and technology-intensive developments such as computer-integrated manufacturing (CIM) have raised fixed costs. Finally, labor has changed from a variable cost element to a fixed cost element.

These developments have complicated the process of assigning overhead costs. The new basis for overhead costs leaves no universal unit of measure for assigning them to specific products. Labor hours and machine hours no longer apply. To overcome this problem of assigning overhead costs, accountants and operations managers have developed activity-based costing and throughput costing. The following paragraphs will present a brief overview of these two procedures, leaving detailed discussions to an accounting text.

activity-based costing
A method of allocating costs to specific products based on breakdowns of cost drivers

Activity-Based Costing.   **Activity-based costing** (ABC) tries to trace costs to specific goods and services rather than arbitrarily allocating them on the basis of some universal measurement unit such as labor hours or machine hours. To do this, ABC identifies appropriate cost drivers, or quantifiable indicators of activities that reveal the sources of costs for products and services. Often, these drivers measure numbers of transactions in particular activities, as the examples in Exhibit 3.18 illustrate. For this reason, ABC is also called *transaction-based costing*.

Activity-based costing is now becoming common in North American and European companies, with increasing use by such companies as Hewlett-Packard and General Motors. Its increased popularity reflects the view that the profitabili-

[**EXHIBIT 3.18**]

Cost Drivers for Activity-Based Costing

Activity	Cost Driver	Rate
Material handling	Number of components	$0.25 per component
Engineering and design	Hours of engineering services	$100.00 per hour
Production setup	Number of setups	$55.00 per setup
Assembly (automated)	Number of components	$0.75 per component
Inspection	Hours of testing	$60.00 per hour of testing
Packaging and shipping	Number of orders	$4.50 per order shipped

SOURCE   Charles T. Horngren and Gary L. Sundem, *Introduction to Management Accounting*, 9th ed., p. 459. Copyright © 1993. Reprinted with permission of Prentice-Hall, Inc., River Saddle, NJ 07458.

ty of a product is best measured through its use. Proponents also claim that ABC helps firms to respond to changes in their product mixes, technologies, and processes. Furthermore, ABC forces managers to focus on activities that create costs rather than on end products. This focus reinforces a value-driven management method.

Throughput Costing.   **Throughput costing** assigns overhead costs in a very simple way that relates overhead to the amount of time that a good or service spends within the OM system. A product that takes longer to pass through the system must bear a greater share of its overhead costs. Conversely, an order that moves through the system more quickly bears a smaller share. The logic of this approach assumes that a product that spends a great deal of time in a system creates a relatively heavy burden for monitoring and control activities, raising the cost of these support activities, which drive indirect costs. Throughput costing often accompanies time-based competition.

throughput costing
A method of allocating costs to products based on how long they spend in the OM system

MANAGING BASED ON THE VALUE EQUATION: SOME FINAL COMMENTS

Value is a simple concept to talk about, but a very difficult one to implement. Effective value-driven management requires extreme precision. One cannot, for example, simply say that the firm will compete on the basis of flexibility. The earlier discussion outlined many different dimensions of flexibility. A decision to compete on flexibility defines an overall orientation and focus, but it demands elaboration to specify the type of flexibility on which to base competition. Only by specifying plans precisely can the operations manager and the OM system deliver the product promised by the firm and desired by the customer. A firm's definition of *value* influences the types of processes it builds, the investments it makes, the control systems it implements, and the way it measures performance. Without such clear and detailed definitions, the operations manager runs a very real risk of investing in unsuitable systems and processes that fail to deliver value as defined by the customer.

Roles of a Customer Service Policy

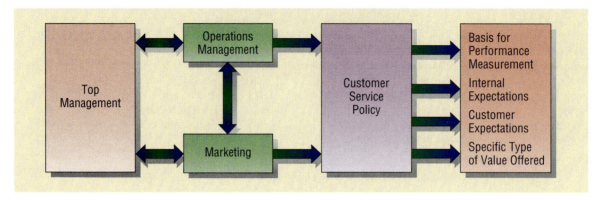

CUSTOMER SERVICE: INTEGRATING THE COMPONENTS OF VALUE

This chapter has considered separately each of the elements of the value equation and their interrelationships. The operations manager must combine these individual elements into a global statement of value. This process is critical to a firm that must meet the challenge of disinflation presented at the start of this chapter. A firm can avoid brutal price competition only by offering a vision of value that induces the customer to pay. In defining and implementing this vision of value, the firm performs **customer service**.

customer service

The firm's effort to define and implement its vision of value

The customer service policy bridges the gap between corporate strategy and the customer; it defines exactly how the firm will compete and the specific type of value that it will offer to its customers. The customer service policy performs four specific roles (see Exhibit 3.19):

- *Customer service defines the specific type of value that the firm will offer.*   At this stage, management provides weights (βs) to various components of the value equation which set its primary focus on quality, lead time, flexibility, or some unique combination. This critical weighting exercise influences how the firm will invest its resources to generate value for its customers. Note that a low β does not mean that the firm will ignore a component of value. Rather, it labels that component an order qualifier for which the firm will offer value considered acceptable by the customer. It may decide to match competitors on this component, but not to try to excel at it.
- *Customer service helps to shape customer expectations.*   It communicates to customers exactly what they can expect from the firm and the specific type of value that the firm promises to deliver.
- *Customer service communicates to people within the firm the type of value that they should try to deliver.*   This information guides employees' and managers' judgment of what to do to help the firm compete effectively.
- *Customer service forms the basis for evaluating performance.*   Effective performance measurement should be linked to the firm's basis for competition and the type of value it promises to the customer, rewarding any action consistent with these two goals and correcting any action contrary to them.

[**EXHIBIT 3.20**]

Customer Service Policy for Steelcase, Inc.

THE SCHEDULE MUST BE MET!

IT IS OUR BOSS! WE MUST FIGHT TO
THE ABSOLUTE LIMIT TO SHIP . . .

QUALITY PRODUCTS, ON TIME.

ANY ACTION IS WARRANTED TO ACCOMPLISH THIS END.

SOURCE   Steven A. Melnyk and Phillip L. Carter, *Shop Floor Control: Principles, Practices, and Case Studies* (Falls Church, Va.: American Production and Inventory Control Society, 1987), p. 122.

Exhibit 3.20 presents a good example of a customer service statement from Steelcase, a manufacturer of office furniture. This statement emphasizes lead time and quality. Cost, while important, cannot be allowed to jeopardize lead time and quality. Steelcase does not rank flexibility at the same level as quality and lead time, though flexibility may become more important in the future. This statement leads Steelcase to measure performance based on lead time and quality, perhaps by evaluating the elapsed time from receipt of an order until shipment of the correct products of acceptable quality. A performance measure based primarily on cost would be inappropriate because it would be inconsistent with the firm's customer service policy.

CHAPTER SUMMARY

The discussion of customer service has finished assembling the necessary elements to determine how to compete in today's age of disinflation. Managers try to develop an advantage over a firm's competitors by defining a specific, unique type of value that no one else can easily, quickly, and cheaply duplicate. To compete effectively in the age of disinflation requires an appreciation of the specific characteristics of the elements of value, how they are defined, and how they interact.

The chapter has raised these major issues:

1. To understand the concept of value, one must understand the components of the value equation: lead time, flexibility, quality, and cost.
2. Lead times measure elapsed times of OM processes. To compete on lead time, a firm must manage lead time variances and mean lead times.
3. The many different categories of lead time allow time-based competition based on two broad goals: being fast to market (moving quickly from concept

to finished product) or fast to product (moving quickly from the receipt of an order until the customer can use the product).

4. Determining how to compete on lead time requires a balance between the lead time that customers bear and the lead time that the firm absorbs. This balance differs for engineer to order, make to order, assemble to order, and make to stock products.

5. Time-based competition (TBC) emphasizes building and maintaining a sustainable competitive advantage by competing on the basis of lead time. This strategy is bringing success to companies such as Hewlett-Packard, Motorola, and Honda.

6. Firms reduce lead times through seven strategies: Less of/System Simplification, As One/System Integration, Same as/Standardization, At Once/ Parallel Activities, Watch It/Variance Control, Better than/Automation, and More of/Excess Resources. These strategies affect the other components of value: quality, flexibility, and cost.

7. Flexibility, the second component of value, describes the ability of the operations management system to respond quickly, measured by range and time, to externally and internally generated changes.

8. Flexibility breaks down into seven different types: mix flexibility, changeover flexibility, modification flexibility, volume flexibility, rerouting/program flexibility, material flexibility, and flexibility responsiveness. Each type of flexibility affects how a firm competes and the type of value it offers to customers.

9. Flexibility is at the heart of a mass customization strategy which focuses efforts to enhance value on improving flexibility.

10. Quality, the third component of value, is integrity in delivering what a customer has a legitimate right to expect in view of what was promised at the time of the agreement to purchase. Of the elements value, the concept of quality is both the most fully developed and the best known.

11. The seven attributes of quality identify specific product traits: functionality, reliability, durability, safety, serviceability, aesthetics, and perceived quality. These traits help managers to describe and measure quality, but they are not the same as quality.

12. The four different types of quality are indifferent quality, expected quality, one-dimensional quality, and exciting quality. This last category offers the firm a chance to develop order winners; the other types define either order losers or order qualifiers.

13. Total quality management is a corporate system for generating value based on quality. TQM invokes four principles: commitment to quality; extensive use of scientific tools, technologies, and methods; total involvement in the quality undertaking; and continuous improvement.

14. Cost, the denominator of the value equation, performs three major roles as a means of reporting performance, to aid in management and evaluation of operations, and to provide a source of value. This book emphasizes the last of these roles.

15. To compete on the basis of cost, a firm tries to provide products cheaply without providing cheap products. This keeps the performance component of the value equation (the numerator) constant while focusing attention on reducing costs.

16. Cost-driven efforts to enhance value can overemphasize cost reduction to stress short-term savings that adversely affect long-term performance.

17. Because of the increasing importance of overhead and indirect costs, accounting has tried to develop methods to more accurately assign these costs. Two

important methods are playing greater roles in operations management: activity-based costing and throughput costing.

18. A firm's customer service policy provides a mechanism to define specifically what type of value a firm and its transformation process generate for customers. It also communicates this view of value to both customers and employees. Finally, it should influence the firm's performance measures.

An understanding of value can lead to an understanding of the value-driven operations management system, but this also requires consideration of the roles of managers and problem solvers. Those two tasks are covered in the next chapter.

[KEY TERMS]

lead time   75
mean   76
standard deviation   76
range   76
shape   76
design lead time   77
sourcing lead time   79
manufacturing lead time
   80
distribution lead time   80
order lead time   81
total product delivery lead
   time   81
engineer to order   82
make to order   82
assemble to order   83
postponement   83
make to stock   84
time to market   84
time to product   85
fast to market   85
fast to product   86
time-based competition
   88

Less of/System
   Simplification   89
As One/System
   Integration   90
Same as/Standardization
   90
At Once/Parallel
   Activities   90
critical path   90
Watch It/Variance
   Control   91
Better than/Automation
   91
More of/Excess Resources
   92
flexibility   93
mix flexibility   95
changeover flexibility   95
modification flexibility
   95
volume flexibility   95
rerouting/program
   flexibility   96
material flexibility   96

flexibility responsiveness
   96
mass customization   98
functionality   104
reliability   104
durability   104
safety   105
serviceability   105
aesthetics   105
perceived quality   106
indifferent quality   106
expected quality   106
one-dimensional quality
   106
exciting quality   106
things gone wrong/things
   gone right   107
total quality management
   109
cost   113
activity-based costing   114
throughput costing   115
customer service   116

[DISCUSSION QUESTIONS]

1. Review the events of your daily life. Then identify activities in which you have experienced the following types of lead time:
   a. Manufacturing lead time
   b. Distribution lead time
   c. Product design lead time
   Would you value the goods or services provided in each case if the lead time had been significantly reduced? Why?
2. How might system variance have been a cause of lengthy lead time for your responses to the above question?

3. Consider products that you consume. Identify purchases made with firms with the following market orientation.
   a. Make to stock
   b. Make to order
   c. Assemble to order
   d. Engineer to order
   In each case, what are the conditions that enable or require a firm to adopt this market orientation?
4. Discuss how a firm's market orientation influences the following elements of value:
   a. Delivery speed; i.e., how quickly a customer gets the product
   b. Variety of the product offerings
   c. Design quality
   d. Cost of the good or service
5. Which market orientation would you consider for a standard product that has low, infrequent demand? What are the tradeoffs you would consider in making this decision?
6. For each of the following service operations, develop a lead time taxonomy as was done for manufacturing lead times. In each case, start with the customer's decision that he or she wants something, such as a pizza, and end with the service rendering transaction.
   a. Delivering a pizza
   b. Installing a second telephone line
   c. Securing a home mortgage
   d. Burying a much loved relative
7. The customer complaint resolution process is normally enhanced when a problem is swiftly resolved. Develop a lead time taxonomy for each of the following distressing situations:
   a. At a restaurant, there is a fly in your apple pie.
   b. There seems to be a bug in your Microsoft program.
   c. You think that your newly purchased computer has a defective Intel microprocessor.
   d. Your Mastercard statement has a $128.00 charge at your favorite restaurant, but you don't recall being there that day.
8. What percent of the items did you purchase over a year from firms competing on the basis of time? Which items were they? How did time influence your decision to buy that product? Was there a tradeoff in purchasing an item in a time-based competitive environment?
9. Explain how flexibility can be used to create a broader range of products or to produce and deliver goods or services quicker. Give examples.
10. Cite instances in your life in which the time or trouble to set up for an activity causes you to make more units than you might need. How might these setups be reduced?
11. Discuss instances where you or your family has paid a premium for products purchased from a flexible source. What were the tradeoffs involved?
12. Discuss the differences between design quality and quality of conformance. Try to map these two terms against what the text calls "Five Views of Quality."
13. Provide two examples of products whose quality is largely influenced by each of the following attributes:
    a. Functionality
    b. Reliability
    c. Durability
    d. Safety
    e. Serviceability
    f. Aesthetics
    g. Perceived quality
    Can you cite instances in which a product's attributes do not seem to fit together, such as a turbo-charged Yugo or an environmentally safe cigarette filter?

14. Name a service for which quality is the order winning criterion for your purchase decision. For this item, how would you classify the other elements of value?

15. Why is it necessary for statistical tools to be used in a firm committed to total quality management?

16. Select an item that is more than $500. How would you use the various cost categories discussed in this chapter to evaluate total cost of this product? How would you estimate these costs?

C A U T I O N

[**C R I T I C A L   T H I N K I N G   R E Q U I R E D**]

1. What are the downside risks associated with adopting a massive continuous improvement program?
2. In terms of value, why is the tenth candy bar less satisfying than the first?
3. How do expectations fit into the value equation?

C A S E   3 . 1

Steinway & Sons Piano

Steinway pianos have long been the premier brand among serious pianists. Franz Liszt called his Steinway "a glorious masterpiece." Gioacchino Rossini, a 19th-century composer, described the Steinway sound as "great as thunder, sweet as the fluting of a nightingale." In short, Steinway's product is the piano of choice for the vast majority of concert artists.

From its beginning, Steinways were a work of art. Jose Feghali, a classical pianist, illustrated this point when he remarked, "With the best pianos, you can walk into a room with 10 pianos and it's like playing 10 different instruments." The prices of the 5,000 or so pianos Steinway produces each year range from $10,000 for an upright to $62,000 for a special-order concert grand piano.

In the 1990s, Steinway & Sons encountered some problems. The firm was purchased by John and Robert Birmingham in a $53.5 million leverage buyout deal. John's previous experience involved making plastic windows for envelopes. Robert's most recent experience was with a mail-order business selling products with bear themes. Robert Birmingham said that they were delighted with the purchase because they viewed Steinway as a "great opportunity" given the firm's "a great name and a great tradition."

Steinway's craft-driven organization had not fared too well under its previous owner, CBS. The turmoil resulting from frequent management changes had reduced the consistency of Steinway's cherished reputation. Dealers complained that Steinways weren't of the same quality any more—they were often badly tuned and had sloppy finishes. Finally, in 1978, CBS hired a long-time piano industry executive who helped restore much of Steinway's reputation.

Now, a new set of outsiders owned them. That the owners liked classical music did not assure Steinway's 1,000 employees that they knew how to make classic quality pianos. To make matters worse, the Birmingham brothers were now talking about using their "extensive manufacturing experience" to streamline operations. One commented that the operation was "too reliant on a few craftsmen."

Soon modern manufacturing methods crept into the Steinway operation. A computer control system was introduced to keep track of parts and inventory. Eight million dollars was invested in new equipment to make the quality of small parts, such as piano hammers, more consistent. The loose-leaf binders that specified how pianos were to be built were replaced with engineering drawings. By the late 1980s, Steinway had entered the 20th century. John Birmingham lamented: "The music industry is made up largely of people enamored of music and the instruments they make, but they don't necessarily have great management skills."

As Steinway became more scientific, some stakeholders began to be concerned. Many of the older craftsmen found the new work environment not to their liking, and they left. Equally important, some within the industry began to be concerned that Steinway pianos were losing their personality. Some dealers and their customers even began to question the quality of Steinway's latest pianos. One classical pianist fumed that he had to use a 30-year-old Steinway because he could not find a new one he liked. Another dealer hired a consultant to review the quality of the pianos he had purchased from Steinway. He claimed that the soundboard, a key contributor to a piano's quality, had developed cracks. The consultant reported that this problem "indicated inadequate or improper controls over wood moisture content during various stages of manufacture." Subsequent study indicated that Steinway's new production quotas may have caused workers to pull wood from the conditioning rooms before it was ready to be bent, say, into a piano.

QUESTIONS

Assume that you are hired as a consultant to help Steinway deal with these latest problems. How could you use a value-driven approach to help this firm address these problems? What would you recommend?

[SELECTED READINGS]

Abegglen, James C., and George Stalk, Jr. *Kaisha: The Japanese Corporation.* New York: Basic Books, 1985.

Beckman, Sara L. "Manufacturing Flexibility: The Next Source of Competitive Advantage." In *Strategic Manufacturing,* ed. by Patricia E. Moody. Homewood, Ill.: Business One-Irwin, 1990.

Blackburn, Joseph D. *Time-Based Competition: The Next Battleground in American Manufacturing.* Homewood, Ill.: Business One-Irwin, 1991.

Bower, Joseph L., and Thomas Hout. "Fast-Cycle Capability for Competitive Power." *Harvard Business Review,* November/December, 1988.

Carroll, Paul. *Big Blues: The Unmaking of IBM.* New York: Crown, 1993.

Carter, Phillip L., and Steven A. Melnyk. "Time-Based Competition: Building the Foundations for Speed." *APICS: 35th International Conference Proceedings,* Montreal, Quebec, Canada, October 18–23, 1992. pp. 63–67.

Clark, Kim B., and Takahiro Fujimoto. *Product Development Performance.* Cambridge, Mass.: Harvard Business School Press, 1991.

Dean, James W., Jr., and James R. Evans. *Total Quality: Management, Organization, and Strategy.* St. Paul, Minn.: West, 1994.

DeMeyer, A., J. Nakane, J. G. Miller, and K. Ferdows. "Flexibility: The Next Competitive Battle." *Manufacturing Roundtable Research Report Series,* Boston University, School of Management, Boston, Mass., 1987

Dumaine, Brian. "How Managers Can Succeed through Speed." *Fortune,* February 13, 1989, pp. 54–59.
———. "Earning More by Moving Faster." *Fortune,* October 7, 1991, pp. 89–94.

Dunne, Jim, Joe Oldham, and Tony Swan. "Long-Term Test Cars." *Popular Mechanics,* November 1992, pp. 46–49.

Garvin, David A. *Managing Quality.* New York: Free Press, 1988.

Gerwin, Donald. "Manufacturing Flexibility: A Strategic Perspective." *Management Science* 39, no. 3 (April 1993), pp. 395–410.

Hall, Robert. *The Soul of the Enterprise.* New York: Harper Business, 1993.

Logothetis, N. *Managing for Total Quality: From Deming to Taguchi and SPC.* Hertfordshire, U.K.: Prentice-Hall International, 1992.

Merli, Giorgio. *Total Manufacturing Management: Production Organization for the 1990s.* Cambridge, Mass.: Productivity Press, 1990.

Merrills, Roy. "How Northern Telecom Competes on Time." *Harvard Business Review,* July/August 1989.

Nicol, Ronald. "Time-Based Competition: A Systematic Approach to Business Improvement." *Time-Based Competition: Going beyond JIT to Achieve a Competitive Advantage,* Society of Manufacturing Engineers seminar, Livonia, Mich., October 28–29, 1991.

Pine, B. Joseph, II. *Mass Customization: The New Frontier in Business Competition.* Cambridge, Mass.: Harvard Business School Press, 1993.

Slack, Nigel. "Flexibility as a Manufacturing Objective." *International Journal of Operations and Production Management* 3, no. 3 (1983), pp. 4–13.

Stalk, George, Jr. "Time—The Next Source of Competitive Advantage." *Harvard Business Review,* July/August 1988.

Stalk, George, Jr., and Thomas Hout, *Competing against Time.* New York: Free Press, 1990.

Stalk, George, Jr., Philip Evans, and Lawrence E. Shulman. "Competing on Capabilities: The New Rules of Corporate Strategy." *Harvard Business Review,* March/April 1992, pp. 57–69.

Steeples, Marion Mills. *The Corporate Guide to the Malcolm Baldrige National Quality Award.* Milwaukee, Wis.: ASQC Quality Press, 1993.

Swamidass, Paul M. *Manufacturing Flexibility* . Operations Management Association Monograph No. 2. Waco, Tex.: Schneider Group, January 1988.

Tribus, Myron. "Quality First." In *Selected Papers on Quality and Productivity Improvements.* Washington, D.C.: American Quality and Productivity Institute, 1988.

Turney, Peter B. B. *Common Cents: The ABC Performance Breakthrough.* Hillsboro, Ore.: Cost Technology, 1991.

CHAPTER FOUR

Decision Making in Operations Management

CHAPTER OBJECTIVES

[At the end of this chapter, you should be able to]

- List and explain the activities of management, decision making, and problem solving.
- Differentiate among the notions of problems, symptoms, and causes.
- Identify and apply the steps of OM's diagnostic and problem-solving models.
- Illustrate the role of models in decision making.
- Identify the eight forms of problems in operations management.
- Recognize the OM manager's three major problem-solving stances.
- Discuss the effects of constraints on OM decision making.
- Review the techniques in the operations management toolkit (OMT).

GE's Appliance Park: Decision Making and Problem Solving

WhEN THE CHAIRMAN OF A LARGE corporation like General Electric makes an important decision, it can mean the loss or gain of millions of dollars and affect the livelihoods of thousands of people. It may determine the future of entire factories and have a large impact on the cities in which they operate. That decision faced John F. Welch, Jr., as he contemplated the fate of Appliance Park, GE's sprawling five-factory complex located near Louisville.

Appliance Park was once a proud showcase for GE's most innovative appliances and manufacturing technology. But over the years GE had allowed Appliance Park's factories to become outdated, and by 1992 they were reporting losses of about $47 million.

Three of GE's U.S. appliance plants closed during the early 1990s, and Welch, GE's chairman, knew he would eventually have to make a decision about the 40-year-old factories at Appliance Park. But in 1992 the federal government forced his hand by announcing new energy standards for washing machines that would take effect in 1994. With less than two years to make improvements, Welch found himself charting the future of GE's washing machine division, and the fate of Appliance Park hung in the balance. Several options faced Welch—

✹

SOURCES

James R. Norman, "A
Very Nimble
Elephant," *Forbes*,
October 10, 1994,
pp. 88–92.

Zachary Schiller, "If
You Can't Stand the
Heat, Upgrade the
Kitchen," *Business
Week*, April 25, 1994,
p. 35.

Zachary Schiller,
"GE's Appliance
Park: Rewire or Pull
the Plug?" *Business
Week*, February 8,
1993, p. 30.

none of them easy or straightforward. He could risk an investment of as much as $70 million to overhaul the park's antiquated washing machine factories. However, as one GE executive put it, "To invest in a place that's losing money makes no business sense." Yet letting an outside contractor make GE's washers would mean slashing 1,500 jobs and endangering long-range prospects for Appliance Park.

To make this crucial decision, Welch and his high-level executives had to evaluate the impact of their various options on, not just one, but five factories. They had to separate the symptoms of problems from their causes. Most important, they had to isolate Appliance Park's real problem. Was it an unproductive work force, the age and condition of the equipment, some other cause not yet identified, or a combination of factors?

During tense mass meetings, management briefed workers about the situation. Realizing that their jobs hung in the balance, once-adversarial workers at Appliance Park became determined to make a difference. "Everybody is kind of pushing together now," said Rebecca Wells, an assembly-line worker. As Welch and other decision makers weighed their options, more than 1,500 people held their collective breaths.

The story of GE's Appliance Park shows management in action. Managers must solve problems; they must separate symptoms from the problems themselves and their causes. Managers also function as decision makers; to resolve the problems at Appliance Park, GE managers had to decide how to deploy the firm's resources (i.e., workers, money, management expertise, and equipment). For example, a decision to scrap the washing machine operation would force layoffs of hundreds of workers.

To analyze the problems at the Appliance Park, GE managers needed to follow a process to resolve a messy, unstructured situation into some kind of structure. They had to apply tools to analyze the situation and evaluate potential responses to resolve short-term problems such as loss of market share and decreasing profitability. To improve longer-term performance, they had to eliminate the original causes of these problems.

GE's experience with Appliance Park illustrates the importance of management techniques in the OM system. To become an effective operations manager, one must first understand the process of management and its role in problem solving. Managers are primarily decision makers who earn their salaries by cleaning up messes like the one in Appliance Park. This chapter focuses on the techniques that help managers to succeed in this challenging work.

GE could have written off Appliance Park as a failure and closed the plant. Instead, as a later section will detail, management staged a phenomenal turnaround. After losing $47 million in 1992, the facility generated projected profits of $40 million in 1994 and $80 million in 1995, due largely to the problem-solving and decision-making success of GE's operations managers.

MANAGEMENT METHODS IN OPERATIONS MANAGEMENT

The term *operations management* joins the concepts of operations, defined in Chapter 1 as a process with activities that transform inputs into desirable outputs, and management. Management involves a firm's activities to control, plan, monitor, and direct its actions to ensure that the outputs of its transformation process offer value to its targeted market segment. Management works to build and maintain consistency between what the transformation process can do and what customers expect (Exhibit 4.1). OM students must thoroughly understand the critical concept of management.

Management **Defined**

We define **management** as the process of directing resources and organizing activities to achieve organizational objectives. The key word *process* in this definition implies an on-going sequence of five intimately linked activities (see Exhibit 4.2):

- Planning
- Analyzing
- Organizing
- Directing/Implementing
- Controlling

management
The process of directing resources and organizing activities in achievement of corporate or organizational objectives

The notion of value drives these five activities. Managers plan, analyze, organize, direct, and control to keep the transformation process offering more value than competitors offer to customers.

Planning. **Planning** is the process of deciding what to do. For example, planning by managers at GE's Appliance Park focused on deciding what to do to restore the facility to profitability or to close it. Effective planning answers several questions:

planning
The process of deciding what to do

- *What* should the firm do? Planning must establish the goals and objectives that guide activities in the OM system.
- *When* must the firm achieve these goals and objectives? Planning must establish the time period over which the firm must achieve its established

[**E X H I B I T   4 . 1**]

Role of Management in Value-Driven OM System

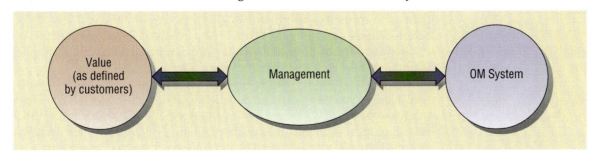

[**E X H I B I T   4 . 2**]

Five Functions of Management

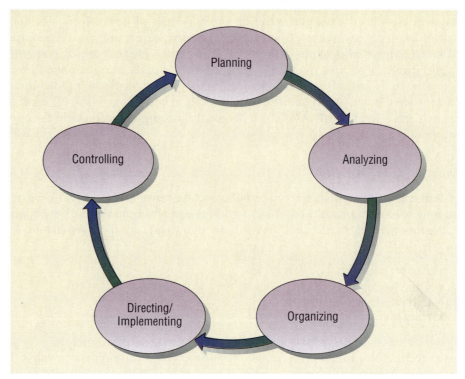

objectives or goals. GE's managers had to solve the problems at Appliance Park by 1994 to meet the new energy standards for washers.

- *Who* should act? Planning must identify individuals or groups involved in company activities to determine a plan's scope. The scope of GE's planning at Appliance Park was confined to the washing machine operation.
- *How* can the firm achieve its objectives and goals? Planning must identify the actions and their sequences that identified people should take to achieve established goals and objectives within the specified time. GE managers' planning focused on a choice between closing down the washing machine operation and buying from an outside supplier, investing in new equipment, and working with the union to improve worker productivity in the washing machine plant.
- *How* should the firm measure progress? Finally, planning must identify performance measures to govern evaluation of the effectiveness of chosen actions. These measures show managers involved in a situation (and others further away from it) how well they are carrying out plans. GE managers could specify several performance measures to gauge progress at Appliance Park, including reductions in costs, changes in market share, increases in profits, or changes in output per direct labor employee. A firm's performance measurement system serves an important communications function, telling employees what it expects of them. For example, a measurement system focused on cost signals to employees that the firm wants them to identify and pursue opportunities to reduce costs. Performance measures

ON THE JOB

Communicating Customer Satisfaction Behind the Scenes at SAS

■

Anyone who has ever missed a connection or lost luggage at an airport knows that travel by air can be very stressful. If an airline is not performing well, front-line personnel such as ticket agents typically get an earful from customers, while behind-the-scenes workers such as baggage handlers might never find out that something went wrong.

Since SAS caters to business travelers on very tight schedules, baggage handlers have a very important job. At Arlanda Airport in Stockholm, SAS wanted its passengers to be able to find their luggage on the conveyer belt the moment they set foot in baggage claim. In order to meet this goal, SAS baggage handlers needed important feedback about how well they were doing their jobs.

Jan Carlzon set up a system of performance measurement for baggage handlers at SAS to provide just that. Baggage handlers worked toward a clear target: getting luggage on the conveyer belt for immediate baggage claim. When they met this target, they received praise. When they missed it, they received constructive criticism. Most importantly, SAS's baggage handlers were no longer working in the dark. Even though they might never meet a customer face-to-face, they knew they were making a difference in the quality of their customers' lives.

SOURCE   Jan Carlzon, *Moments of Truth* (New York: Harper & Row, 1987), pp. 108–109.

also tell employees how the firm intends to compete in the marketplace. The story in the "On the Job" box of Jan Carlzon's attempt to develop a performance measurement system for baggage handlers at SAS Airlines illustrates the importance of this aspect of planning. Known throughout the world as a customer-oriented carrier, SAS has prospered by targeting business travelers—a very demanding set of customers.

Planning is a forward-looking activity.[1] Its time horizons can vary from long-term issues that will affect the firm or the OM system years into the future to short-term decisions like a grocery manager's assignment of employees to bagging, stocking, and checkstand duties on a particular day. These levels of planning differ in amounts of detail, time periods, and numbers of people or amounts of corporate resources affected. Managers develop plans at three levels:

- *Strategic Plans*   Typically dealing with long-term issues that affect an entire firm, managers tend to state these plans in very broad terms without much detail. For example, GE's long-term strategic plans require that it must command either the largest or second-largest market share in any business where it competes. The firm may divest any business unit that fails to achieve this strategic goal.
- *Operating Plans*   These plans typically affect specific units (e.g., the OM system). They elaborate on strategic plans, setting narrower goals in more detail and covering shorter time periods. A GE strategic plan may set goals to achieve over 10 years, while an operating plan for the Appliance Park

---

[1]John A. Wagner III and John R. Hollenbeck, *Management of Organizational Behavior* (Englewood Cliffs, N.J.: Prentice-Hall, 1992), p. 25.

By carefully analyzing data, managers like this Home Depot supervisor can correct problems and eliminate their recurrence.   SOURCE   Michael Newman/PhotoEdit

might cover a 1-year time horizon, stating near-term goals in detail to guide appropriate actions.

- *Tactical Plans*   These highly detailed plans cover month-to-month, week-to-week, or day-to-day time horizons. Managers at Appliance Park might specify how many washing machines a specific shift should produce. A tactical plan should state how many workers an operation needs, what stations they should staff, how long they should work, and what specific jobs they should do.

Good planning is a necessary function of management. Good planning makes good execution (and ultimately achievement of objectives and goals) possible.

analyzing

The process making sense of data that is often poorly structured, conflicting, inaccurate, or incomplete

Analyzing.   Like the other functions of management, **analyzing** is a process. It is the process of making sense of data that is often poorly structured, conflicting, incomplete, and inaccurate. In analyzing, managers separate relevant information from irrelevant clutter.

Managers analyze data for two purposes: correction and elimination. Correction pursues short-term improvements in operations; it tries to bypass problems but not necessarily to solve them completely. Elimination, on the other hand, represents a longer-term effort to solve problems and prevent them from ever occurring again. To clarify the difference between these two purposes of analyzing, consider a small shop that assembles microcomputers. After assembly, a test operation rejects over 15 percent of all computers due to hard-disk problems. In studying the problem, the manager learns that employees are breaking a fragile connector by inserting it the wrong way because nothing on the connector indicates the correct orientation.

As a correction step, the manager might increase hard-disk inventories so the worker at the test station could simply replace any defective hard disk. This would allow production to proceed, but it would not eliminate the problem, leaving the firm with high inventories and reject rates. As an elimination measure, the manager might decide to work with the supplier to improve the design of the connector. This kind of analyzing would eliminate the problem.

Organizing. In **organizing**, managers develop structures that combine interrelated tasks.[2] Organizing identifies and designs sequences for necessary tasks and allocates resources to these tasks. This allocation of resources includes assigning employees to work groups or teams, along with allocation of such resources as money, equipment, and land.

Organizing frequently divides resources of the OM system into departments or organizational units. Divisions between these organizational units can follow functional lines, joining activities, people, and equipment that perform the same or similar tasks into units. Bringing all process design engineers together into one group would create a functional organization. Alternatively, unit boundaries can separate products rather than functions. For example, a manufacturer of computer components might form a unit of everyone involved in designing and manufacturing hard disks, including engineers, OM workers, finance staff, and marketers. Organizing can also define units based on geographic locations, perhaps including all employees and operations located in a single state in one unit.

Steelcase Inc. organizes its manufacturing facilities in Grand Rapids, Michigan, by products. The Seating Division operates a plant to manufacture chairs and seats. Another plant builds desks, and a separate facility builds office computer furniture.

Directing/Implementing. The first three functions of management prepare company operations for **directing/implementing**, the action-oriented process of carrying out decisions made in the planning, analyzing, and organizing phases. Directing/implementing involves several important activities. First, managers communicate the goals and objectives of the firm (identified through planning) to the appropriate workers in readily understandable terms. For example, Jan Carlzon did not tell baggage handlers to ensure reliability or promptness because such terms would have carried no meaning; instead, he told them that the success of SAS depended on their success placing luggage on airport conveyors by the time passengers arrived, stating the promptness goal in terms that the workers could readily understand and implement.

In directing/implementing, managers commit resources secured by the organizing function. For example, if the GE's managers were to decide that obsolete equipment caused the problems at GE's Appliance Park, their directing/implementing work would involve investing money to buy new equipment. In directing/implementing, managers lead employees, influencing their behavior through action, example, or word, to work together to achieve company goals and objectives.

Controlling. Controlling generally follows directing/implementing. It is the process of measuring the results of previous decisions, comparing these results with expected results, and taking corrective action when necessary. SAS managers might control their baggage handling operation by stating performance targets (e.g., no customer will spend more than 5 minutes waiting for luggage) and then comparing actual performance to those standards. Controlling also involves comparing the firm's performance measures with customer satisfaction ratings, the ultimate performance measures. SAS might ask, "Did reduced time waiting for luggage raise customer satisfaction?" Both managers and baggage handlers need to know the results. If the operation fails to meet standards, then managers determine why and identify appropriate corrective actions as part of the controlling function.

organizing
The process of developing structures for necessary tasks and assigning resources to them

directing/implementing
The process of carrying out decisions made during planning, analyzing, and organizing

controlling
The process of measuring the results of previous decisions, comparing these results with expected results, and taking corrective action when necessary

---

[2]Wagner and Hollenbeck, *Management of Organizational Behavior,* p. 25.

Fayol's Fourteen Principles of Management

Division of Labor

Managers should divide a firm's work into specialized, simplified tasks. Matching task demand with work force skills will improve productivity. Separate management of work from its performance.

Authority and Responsibility

Authority is the right to give orders, and responsibility is the obligation to accept the consequences of using authority. One should accompany the other.

Discipline

Discipline is performing a task with obedience and dedication. It can be expected only when a firm's managers and subordinates agree on specific behaviors required by subordinates.

Unity of Command

Each subordinate should receive orders from only one hierarchical superior. Confusion from two or more superiors would undermine authority.

Unity of Direction

Each group of activities directed toward the same objective should have only one manager and only one plan.

Individual versus General Interests

The interests of individuals and the whole organization must be treated with equal respect. Neither can supersede the other.

Remuneration of Personnel

The pay received by employees must be fair and satisfactory to both them and the firm. Pay should be in proportion to personal performance, but employees' general welfare must not be threatened by unfair incentive-payment schemes.

SOURCE   Henri Fayol, *Industrial and General Administration*, trans. by J. A. Coubrough (Geneva, Switz.: International Management Institute, 1930).

One of the major roles of controlling is to provide feedback. Managers intend every action to contribute to achievement of a desired goal or objective. After formulating and implementing plans based on careful analysis and organization, they must assess the success of their plans. The results from the controlling function feed into future planning to create a continuous process of management, in which planning leads to action and action leads to more planning. This linkage between plan and action makes the manager more than an isolated planner—it makes the manager into a decision maker.

Functions of Management: Other Perspectives

The five principles of planning, analyzing, organizing, directing/implementing, and controlling are based on a set of functions first developed by Henri Fayol (1841–1925). While serving as the chief of a French mining firm, Fayol developed a list of 14 management principles that form the basis for modern management thought (Exhibit 4.3).

Centralization

Centralization, retention of authority by managers, is appropriate when managers desire greater control. Decentralization is appropriate, however, if subordinates' opinions, counsel, and expertise are needed.

Scalar Chain

The scalar chain is a hierarchical string extending from the uppermost manager to the lowest subordinate. The line of authority follows this chain, and it is the proper route for organizational communications.

Order

Order, a principle of "everything in its place," should be instilled whenever possible because it reduces waste of materials and efforts. Managers should design and staff to encourage order.

Equity

Equity means enforcing established rules with a sense of fair play, kindness, and justice. Management should guarantee equity because it increases members' loyalty, devotion, and satisfaction.

Stability of Tenure

Properly selected employees should be given the time needed to learn and adjust to their jobs. Lack of stability undermines organizational performance.

Initiative

Members should have the opportunity to think for themselves because this motivates performance and adds to the organization's pool of talent.

Esprit de Corps

Managers should harmonize the interests of organization members by resisting the urge to split up successful teams. They should rely on face-to-face communication to detect and correct misunderstandings immediately.

Even though Fayol formulated this list in the late 1800s, much of modern OM practice flows from these 14 principles. Fayol advanced these principles to help managers to improve the performance of any organization unit, from an entire company to its operations management function.

Fayol intended these principles as flexible and adaptable guidelines, not inviolable laws. He clearly recognized the importance of the human influence on management:

> [A]void the idea of rigidity, as there is nothing rigid or absolute in [management] matters; everything is a question of degree. The same principle is hardly ever applied twice in exactly the same way, because we have to allow for different and changing circumstances, for human beings who are equally different and changeable, and for the many other variable elements. The principles too are flexible, and can be adapted to meet every need: it is just a question of knowing how to use them.[3]

[3]Henri Fayol, *Industrial and General Administration,* trans. by J. A. Coubrough (Geneva, Switz.: International Management Institute, 1930), p. 19.

[**EXHIBIT 4.4**]

Which Kind of Manager Are You?

Old-Style Manager	New Manager
Self-image as manager or boss	Self-image as a sponsor, team leader, or internal consultant
Follows the chain of command	Deals with anyone necessary to get the job done
Works within a set organizational structure	Changes organizational structure in response to market changes
Makes most decisions alone	Invites others to join in decision making
Hoards information	Shares information
Tries to master one major discipline, such as marketing or finance	Tries to master a broad array of managerial disciplines
Demands long hours	Demands results

SOURCE   Brian Dumaine, "The New Non-Manager Managers," *Fortune,* February 22, 1993, pp. 80–84. © 1993, Time, Inc. All rights reserved.

New Managers

Changes in the field of operations management reflect continuous evolution in the theory and practice of management. Recent signs have suggested that management is transforming into a new practice where managers do not manage as much as they sponsor, facilitate, challenge, motivate, and cooperate with their employees.[4] (See Exhibit 4.4.) This new generation of manager suits the requirements of the value-based operations management system quite well.

 ## MANAGER AS PROBLEM SOLVER

So far we have explored the manager's role as decision maker. Managers also act as problem solvers, but before describing this role, we must clarify some potential confusion concerning symptoms, problems themselves, causes, and solutions.

Symptoms, Problems, Causes, and Solutions

GE's Appliance Park was losing both money and market share in 1992. Any manager assigned to this operation faced the initial task of determining whether these indicators of poor performance represented symptoms of some deeper problems or problems in their own right.

symptom
An indicator of some problem within a system

Symptoms. Most managers first recognize problems by noticing symptoms. **Symptoms** indicate that something is wrong, but they do not tell the reasons for the trouble. Physical symptoms such as a high thermometer reading might tell (1) whether or not someone is sick and (2) how sick that person is. The thermometer cannot indicate what is causing the patient's temperature to rise.

Managers often talk about symptoms when they use words such as *too much, too little,* or *not enough.* Exhibit 4.5 lists some examples of symptom statements. GE's losses of money and market share at Appliance Park were symptoms of problems

[4]Brian Dumaine, "The New Non-Manager Managers," *Fortune,* February 22, 1993, pp. 80–84.

[**E X H I B I T   4 . 5**]

Examples of Symptom Statements

- We have too much inventory in stock.
- Our scrap rate is too high.
- Our product return rate is too high.
- We do not have enough items in stock.
- Output per worker is too low.
- The number of employees absent on any given day is too high.

rather than problems themselves or causes. Performance data indicated that something was wrong, but not what or why.

Managers can never attack symptoms or resolve them directly. To eliminate symptoms, managers must identify and attack the causes of the symptoms. For example, if someone were running a fever (a symptom) as a result of a bacterial infection (the cause), one might try to reduce the fever with an ice bath. This would bring down the fever, but it would leave the infection unaffected and the symptom would return. An effective response to the symptom must attack the cause rather than the symptom itself.

Problems. Managers spend much of their time identifying, stating, and solving problems. Charles F. Kettering, one of the great innovators of 20th-century business and a major player in the growth of General Motors, once noted, "A problem well stated is a problem half solved." To help managers in the important work of solving problems, theorists have proposed several formal definitions of *problem:*[5]

- Felt difficulty
- Gap or obstacle to be circumvented
- Dissatisfaction with a purposeful state
- Something that fails to bring about a desired effect or result
- Perceived variance, or gap, between present conditions and some desired state of affairs
- Undesirable situation that may allow a solution by some agent, although probably with some difficulty

All of these definitions involve perception. A problem is something that people see or perceive as undesirable. This characteristic is important because people may not always agree about their views of problems. We define a **problem** as a perceived gap between a present situation and some desired situation. Because people's perceptions may differ, problem solving requires a clear understanding of and general agreement on a problem statement.

problem
A perceived gap between a present situation and some desired situation

GE's managers might state the problem at Appliance Park as a question: "Can we improve the efficiency of operations at the plant enough to bring its performance into line with the corporate goal of being either first or second in every market in which GE competes?" If so, the managers might proceed by trying to

[5]James R. Evans, *Creative Thinking in the Decision and Management Sciences* (Cincinnati, Ohio: South-Western, 1991), p. 11.

[**E X H I B I T   4 . 6**]

Spectrum of Problem Structures

identify changes that would improve performance; if not, they might decide to sell Appliance Park or close the plant.

OM problems vary widely, but operations managers can frequently group them together based on several traits:

- How well-structured they are
- Levels of company activities, from overall strategy to daily operations
- How urgent they are
- Activities on which they focus

Structures of Problems. At one end of the spectrum in Exhibit 4.6, a well-structured problem involves clear goals, well-understood means of achieving these goals, and complete and accurate information to identify and resolve the difficulty.[6] When they understand the reasons for such a gap between the current and desired future situations, managers can often adapt and apply ready-made, routine solutions.

When a car needs an oil change, the owner has a well-structured problem. To achieve the clear goals of keeping the car working well and preventing costly breakdowns, the owner knows that necessary actions include changing the oil regularly. After detecting the known conditions that require an oil change, perhaps by a glance at the calendar or the odometer, the owner applies the routine solution of changing the oil to create the desired situation—a well-maintained car.

At the other end of the spectrum, managers lack good information about an ill-structured problem. With a poor understanding of appropriate goals and the means to achieve them, they may have trouble assessing the size of the gap between the current and desired future situations, or even whether any gap exists. Doubts may obscure their view of necessary actions to correct the problem. An ill-structured problem imposes heavy burdens on managers, who must introduce structure into a chaotic situation. To solve such a problem, managers must assess current conditions, often gathering more information to do so, and they must identify necessary changes and the goals that these changes serve.

Between the extremes, managers have some information about a semistructured problem. They may know something about the current and desired future situations, but incomplete information leaves some uncertainty about the gap and the necessary actions to close it. Most OM problems are semistructured. GE managers faced such a problem in their efforts to improve operations at Appliance Park. They were uncertain whether observed symptoms had resulted from outmoded equipment, unproductive employees, or some other cause.

Strategic versus Operational Orientation. One problem may deal with a firm's overall strategy while another may deal with strictly operational isses. Problems at the

[6]Ibid., pp. 15–16.

operational end of this continuum affect strategy implementation actions such as responding to equipment breakdowns, controlling absenteeism, adjusting for late deliveries from suppliers, and assigning personnel to necessary tasks. These decisions affect how the firm carries out its competitive plans. At the other extreme, strategic problems affect how the firm formulates those plans and how it generates value for its customers. A typical operational problem has a relatively short time horizon, usually affecting operations on the day of the decision; a strategic problem usually has a very long time horizon, so today's actions affect the strategic position of the company far into the future.

Between these two extremes, some operational decisions can affect how a firm competes in the future. Again, many OM problems, including those at GE's Appliance Park, fall somewhere in this middle range.

Urgency of a Problem. An urgent problem requires immediate attention, while managers can deal with a less pressing problem when it is convenient. This spectrum runs from crises at one extreme to opportunity problems at the other. A crisis requires immediate action; failure to act poses a significant threat to the operations management system and, in some cases, to the entire firm. A firm pays a high price if managers ignore a crisis such as a strike or a major machine breakdown that jeopardizes schedules.

At the other extreme, opportunity problems create little urgency, and ignoring them exposes the firm to fairly low costs. The manager can resolve such problems whenever it is convenient. For example, a service station attendant may comment that your windshield wiper blades are worn. This creates no urgent problem, but you should respond at some time in the future. This is an example of an opportunity problem.

Fortunately, operations managers seldom face full-blown crises, but they can't often wait indefinitely, either.

Activity Focus. This final problem trait deals with the type of activity that it involves. Ackoff and Rivett have identified eight classes of problems:[7]

- *Queuing problems*   Queuing problems arise when people arrive at a service center. When customers arrive at a bank, they often have to wait in line for a teller, forcing bank managers to balance the cost of hiring excess, potentially idle tellers to reduce waiting times against the cost of longer customer waiting times due to staff shortages. Lines for bathrooms at sporting events create another queuing problem.
- *Allocation problems*   Allocation problems require managers to assign resources (labor, machines, tools, materials, etc.) to competing jobs in a way that maximizes overall efficiency, measured by total cost or profits.
- *Inventory problems*   Inventory problems require managers to control investments in idle resources (typically, stocks of materials), balancing the cost of holding inventory against the cost of shortages such as stockouts and setup costs for unplanned production runs to make needed supplies. Managers must decide how much inventory to hold, where to hold it, and when to order new supplies.
- *Sequencing problems*   Sequencing problems arise when jobs must wait for a resource (e.g., a machine). Managers must determine the order in which

[7]Russell L. Ackoff and Patrick Rivett, *A Manager's Guide to Operations Research* (New York: John Wiley & Sons, 1967), pp. 34–56.

jobs should flow based on their the priority or urgency levels, their due dates, how much work remains to complete each job, and how long they have waited.

- *Routing problems*   Routing problems arise when a resource (such as a vehicle or a machine) must visit a number of sites during a given time. Managers must set the order in which the resource visits the sites to maximize operating efficiencies, measured by distances traveled or time spent. Traveling sales representatives face a classical example of this problem.
- *Replacement problems*   Replacement problems require managers to plan to acquire and dispose of resources with finite useful lives (e.g., tools, car transmissions, bicycle chains). They must balance the potential costs of breakdowns against the costs of wasting unused resources.
- *Competition problems*   Competition problems arise when different parties or groups participate in an activity such as pricing or bidding. Managers must weigh likely actions and reactions to set a course for the firm. For example, if they decide to compete on the basis of quality, they must anticipate the reactions of competitors.
- *Search problems*   Search problems involve efforts to gather information, often through sampling and inspection. For example, a batch of parts from a supplier may include defective units; managers might decide to check every part in the batch to be certain of identifying any defects, but at a high price. Alternatively, they might decide to inspect a sample and estimate the number of defects in the batch based on their proportion in the sample. A sample size should balance the cost of the search (the inspection) against the cost of inaccurately assessing the batch's acceptability.

The categories of problem structure, strategic or operational orientation, urgency, and activity focus allow managers to classify and describe any problem. This helps them to formulate their response and to understand the special characteristics and requirements of each type of problem.

cause

A condition that creates or contributes to a gap between the current and desired future situations

Causes. The **cause** of a problem is anything that creates or contributes to a gap between the current and desired future situations. A cause is a source of observed symptoms. It is the condition that managers must identify and change to eliminate the symptoms.

Causes and symptoms are closely linked. Managers can often trace back many symptoms to only a few, common causes. On the other hand, different causes can create similar symptoms. Vague links between symptoms and causes complicate problem solving, since managers must often identify the most likely set of causes for observed symptoms based on available information and then take appropriate actions. Uncertainty over the relationship between symptoms and causes leaves the chance that managers may misidentify causes and take inappropriate actions. They can work to minimize this risk, but they can never avoid it entirely.

solution

A set of actions designed to close the gap between the current and desired future situations by changing the conditions that created or contributed to the gap

Solutions. The ultimate goal of any problem-solving process is to identify and implement a solution that will address causes and eliminate observed symptoms. In this book, **solution** refers to a set of actions designed to close the gap between the current and desired future situations by changing the conditions that created or contributed to the gap. Managers evaluate solutions by judging how feasible they are (i.e., how well they can work with existing conditions and technologies) and how well they can correct a problem in the short term and eliminate it in the long term.

Managers' Response to a Problem: Solve, Resolve, and Dissolve

A solution can affect an identified problem in one of three ways: it can solve the problem, it can resolve the problem, or it can dissolve the problem.[8] To solve a problem, managers try to identify the optimum solution for a given set of conditions. To resolve the problem, they look for a solution that is both acceptable to everyone and sufficiently effective, rather than the best possible solution. Resolve responses often draw on heuristics, or rules of thumb. Finally, an effort to dissolve a problem tries to eliminate the conditions that created the problem in the first place.

To understand the difference among these three approaches, consider an example. A firm makes a product to stock. The demand for the product is fairly regular at 1,200 units per month with little seasonal variation. It costs the firm $1 to keep 1 unit of the product in stock for 1 month. The cost to set up equipment to make the product amounts to $150 for every production run, a rather high cost. Managers want to know how much to produce in each production run to minimize total costs (i.e., the sum of costs for inventory and setup). To *solve* this problem, managers could apply a formula such as the economic order quantity model, discussed in detail in Chapter 16, to find an optimum order quantity of 600 units.[9]

Suppose, however, that the product is stored in 400-unit bins. Another solution would produce just enough to replenish a bin with each production run. This effort to *resolve* would simplify the problem by setting an order quantity of 400 units. It would not, however, set the optimum quantity.

For another solution, managers might ask why the setup cost for the product is so high. If they could reduce the setup cost far enough, they could produce only as much as they would need for each order as it arrived. By reducing the setup cost, they could eliminate the need to carry any inventory of the product, effectively *dissolving* the problem.

As a problem solver, the manager must deal with interrelationships among symptoms, problems, causes, and solutions. Symptoms indicate a situation that requires management attention. A problem statement clarifies these symptoms and gives them meaning. Based on the problem statement, managers examine the symptoms in order to identify underlying causes, and then they act to change those causes by implementing specific solutions. Jan Carlzon's experiences with SAS, described in the "On the Job" box, help to illustrate these problem-solving links.

This situation illustrates all of the elements of the discussion so far. Carlzon recognized unhappy passengers and unplanned delays as symptoms of a problem. The problem statement asked how to reduce the time that passengers at the Copenhagen airport needed to transfer from one flight to another. Carlzon traced the cause to the practice of treating planes for the Stockholm flight just like those for Danish domestic flights and servicing them at Concourse A where they landed.

---

[8]Russell L. Ackoff, *The Art of Problem Solving* (New York: John Wiley & Sons, 1978), pp. 39–40; and Evans, *Creative Thinking*, pp. 19–20.

[9]For now, note that the economic order quantity formula tries to set an order quantity that balances inventory holding costs against setup costs. If a problem satisfies its assumptions, then the model generates the optimal solution.

ON THE JOB

Symptoms Lead to Solutions at SAS

When dealing with a large problem, it's all too easy to miss the obvious. That's what Jan Carlzon found when he arrived early one morning at the Copenhagen Airport after a long red-eye flight from New York.

Carlzon didn't know he would be solving one of SAS Airline's most pressing problems that morning. All he knew at the time was that he needed to get to Stockholm and that his gate was a long way away—half a mile, to be exact.

Carlzon had his share of carry-on luggage to cart around, and like most international passengers who have traveled all night, he wasn't really in the mood for this unexpected trip to Concourse A. He felt his stress level rise as he realized that he had only a short time before his plane for Stockholm was supposed to take off.

"[W]hy is my plane at the other end of the airport?" Carlzon couldn't help asking an SAS employee. "All of us are going on to Stockholm."

Carlzon learned that SAS chose its departure gates based on what was most convenient for the planes—not the passengers. Carlzon's Stockholm plane had spent the morning flying on Danish domestic routes, and Concourse A was closer to this domestic terminal. Instead of moving the Stockholm plane on the ground to be closer to its connecting international passengers, SAS was forcing hundreds of harried travelers to run to meet the plane in another concourse.

As a result of Carlzon's input, SAS began to tow more planes from concourse to concourse at Copenhagen Airport. At one time, two-thirds of its passengers had to change concourses there; the airline reduced that figure to one-third. This not only made passengers happier and less harried, but it eliminated the need for some airplanes to delay takeoff while they waited for late passengers.

SOURCE   Jan Carlzon, *Moments of Truth* (New York: Harper & Row, 1987), pp. 53–54.

SAS developed a solution for the problem—moving airplanes closer together for the benefit of its passengers. This solution effectively dissolved the problem.

 PROBLEM-SOLVING PROCESS

As a problem solver, every manager must evaluate gaps between current and desired future situations, develop several courses of action designed to close this gap, and select one to implement. This statement of theory sounds fine, but it overlooks one major difficulty that frequently complicates management practice: managers must confront changing situations. A problem in one situation may turn out to be a symptom in another, and this inherent variability complicates the task of decision making. However, managers can deal with this variability and the resulting complexity as part of a formal problem-solving process. This five-step process, illustrated in Exhibit 4.7, provides a useful structure for dealing with any problem, from the most poorly structured to the most routine, well-structured problem.

[**E X H I B I T   4 . 7**]

Steps in the Problem-Solving Process

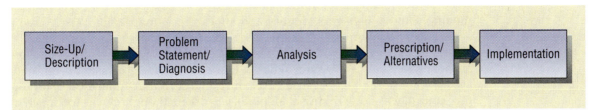

Size-up/Description

It may seem tempting to begin by trying to formulate a problem statement, but the process actually begins with structured information gathering in the **size-up/description** step. The problem solver should begin by gathering information for several reasons. First, the problem may not be clearly defined. Managers may perceive a gap between the current and desired future situations, but still lack a clearly defined notion of the current situation, leaving the problem ill-structured. (See Exhibit 4.8.)

    Frequently, managers begin problem solving knowing only that something is wrong, that they have a mess on their hands. They often have evidence of symptoms—orders shipping behind schedule, inventories rising, quality falling, customers complaining—but lack insight into the process that has produced those symptoms. Similarly, managers often must work to develop a clear image of the desired situation. They often know that they must act to improve conditions, but have no clear idea of what action to take. Different managers may disagree about the future situation that the firm should desire. Without a clear description of either the current or the desired situation, they cannot identify a problem to solve.

    The second reason for size-up/description is to confirm that managers have identified the right problem. They may fail to do so for many reasons. They may

size-up/description

The step in the problem-solving process at which managers gather information to accurately characterize a problem

[**E X H I B I T   4 . 8**]

Level of Problem Definition

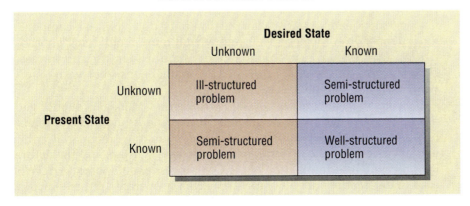

confuse symptoms with problems, as when they see high and increasing stock counts and conclude that they have a problem with inventories; high stock counts may actually be symptoms of problems elsewhere in the system such as high setup costs or poor supplier quality that requires large stocks to keep production moving. Unless managers identify and attack these underlying causes, they will achieve only temporary reductions in inventories.

Managers may fail to address the right problem for other reasons. One of the authors saw such a situation when a manager wanted to install a bar coding system for a store room because, he claimed, the current manual system for inventory control was not working at all because workers thought it was too much trouble to write down necessary information on withdrawal forms. The manager reasoned that a bar code reader would reduce the time and effort needed to record necessary information. An examination of the operation revealed, however, that workers would simply take what they wanted from the store room and leave without even a glance at the inventory forms, claiming that they would fill out the forms later. The bar coding system clearly would not improve inventory accuracy because it would require workers to do more than they were currently doing (nothing at all), but the real problem emerged when the manager revealed that he wanted a bar coding system because he saw one operate during a tour of another plant. The problems with inventory accuracy hid the real problem (the manager's desire for new equipment).

As a third reason for size-up/description, it can help managers to avoid wasting time working on problems that they think they can solve rather than those that they really should solve. This often occurs when they become proficient users of certain tools (e.g., spreadsheets, computer simulations, and linear programming), so they recast problems in terms that suit these tools.

Finally, size-up/description may reveal new problems that others in the organization have overlooked. Such problems often persist because people see the same situation every day, so they accept a problem as part of normal operations. Some structured information gathering during size-up/description forces a fresh look.

Information gathered during size-up/description covers such areas as:

- *Company Status*   Some problems may require information about the company's products, its financial health, and its methods for selling itself and its products in the marketplace.
- *Customers*   Information about who buys the company's products, how they place orders, and what they expect can be valuable. This review may reveal different markets, each with its own desires and requirements.
- *Order Winners, Order Qualifiers, and Order Losers*   Careful study can help managers to identify clearly what the firm must do better than competitors, what it must do sufficiently well, and what it must avoid doing poorly.
- *Critical OM Tasks*   A problem size-up should identify any necessary changes to make the actions of the OM system consistent with its order winners, order qualifiers, and order losers.
- *Real Events in the Operations Management System*   Managers should gather information about the transformation process and its methods for management and control. Depending upon the problem, they might collect information about how the system processes orders, staffing, and the nature of the process. This examination of the OM process should work to develop a clear understanding of how the system actually operates, rather than how it should operate.

Exhibit 4.9 lists some questions that might contribute to a size-up/description.

[**E X H I B I T   4 . 9**]

Critical Questions for Size-up/Description

- What is happening?
- What are the major indications of a problem?
- Who is involved in the situation?
- What does the firm provide for its customers?
- What does the operations management system offer the firm?
- Who are the firm's customers?
- What do customers really want from the firm and its operations management system?
- What does the firm have to do better than competitors to win orders from customers?
- What does it have to do as well as competitors to be considered as a supplier?
- What production process delivers the firm's goods and services to customers?
- What are the critical tasks in the process?
- What unique or special features are evident in customers, process, or product?
- So what?

Managers should collect this information, not simply to summarize common knowledge, but rather to uncover issues and facts that affect their formulation of a problem. Asking "Why is that?" can help to focus the investigation. If the answer does not reveal anything useful, then the subject of the question is not important and should be omitted. To illustrate the power of this question, consider an example. The production manager for a small fruit canning plant wonders whether it has enough capacity for the coming year. To examine collected information from a fresh point of view, the manager decides to ask "why is that":

- *Issue*   The plant may need more capacity to handle fresh fruit, which is available only from June to October.
- *Why is that?*   The fruit is both perishable and seasonal, so the plant must be ready to process it quickly.
- *Why is that?*   Since the fruit is perishable, it may spoil in storage if the plant cannot process it quickly because of delays in the manufacturing process or because of inability to meet peak demands during the summer.
- *Why is that?*   The plant needs enough capacity and an efficient process to make sure that it can meet peak demands and avoid delays in processing.

This line of logic focuses the manager's attention on the need for capacity. A problem size-up should gather this kind of information about capacity and related issues, since managers may overlook such a problem.

Tools for Size-Up/Description. Managers can rely on a number of tools and techniques to complete this process. The most important of these are:

- *Observation*   Simple observation offers one way to learn about a system. Spending time on the shop floor watching the process run can reveal critical information, provided the observer spends enough time to become familiar enough to understand completely everything that is taking place.
- *Participation*   Actually working in a system offers a second way to learn about that system.

- *Questionnaires*   Surveys of system participants can provide valuable information.
- *Interviews*   An analyst may talk to participants in person, by fax, by telephone, or even by e-mail over the Internet.
- *Written documents*   Annual reports, office memoranda, product records, and so on can shed light on an investigation, as the "On the Job" box illustrates.
- *Process mapping*   This tool, discussed in detail in Chapter 5, involves documenting the actual activities of a process using a set of standard symbols.
- *Check sheets*   This technique, to be discussed later in this chapter, helps the analyst to collect information such as types of defects and errors and their locations.
- *Benchmarking*   Benchmarking offers a set of tools and techniques by which the analyst can compare a system against the best practices either in the industry or overall.

Problem Statement/Diagnostics

**problem statement/
diagnostics**

The stage in the problem-
solving process in which
managers state the cur-
rent situation, listing
symptoms, causes, and
triggering events

Having become familiar with an OM system during size-up/description, managers can begin to identify the problem or problems that need attention during the **problem statement/diagnostics** phase. This phase involves a process of stating the current situation, listing symptoms, causes, and triggering events to develop a problem statement. Carefully specifying a problem allows the firm to avoid two major pitfalls: (1) solving the wrong problem and (2) wasting time and other resources addressing unimportant problems.[10] By accurately formulating the problem, managers identify the issues that any solutions must address.

A good problem statement should show the relationship between identified symptoms and the problem it describes. It should also distinguish between controllable variables and uncontrollable variables. Controllable variables are elements within the OM system that the decision maker can control. For example, controllable variables at Appliance Park might include the types of equipment that workers use, rules for scheduling work on the shop floor, and policies for assigning employees to specific tasks. In contrast, management has little or no control over uncontrollable variables. GE managers would have to treat the location of Appliance Park as an uncontrollable variable, at least in the short term.

Next, the problem statement should identify constraints in the situation, that is, limitations or requirements imposed on possible outcomes or alternative solutions.[11] Some constraints set time limits, as when top managers require that any solution must yield a positive payback within 5 years. Other constraints may limit possible alternatives. For example, if GE managers had to limit their attention to operations at Appliance Park, they could not consider any actions that would affect other operations within GE such as combining operations from other sites at the Appliance Park in order to improve operating efficiencies.

Finally, the problem statement should also identify desired outcomes and the values of those outcomes. The categories of solve, resolve, and dissolve can help to meet this requirement; the problem statement can specify whether a proposed solution represents an optimal solution (solve), a sufficient solution (resolve), or elimination of the problem through an attack on its causes (dissolve). The problem statement should identify the value of the solution because this specifies the benefits

[10]Charles Schwenk and Howard Thomas, "Formulating the Mess: The Role of Decision Aids in Problem Formulation," *OMEGA, The International Journal of Management Science* 11, no. 3 (1983), pp. 239–262.
[11]Evans, *Creative Thinking*, p. 14.

Managers who skip the size-up/description phase of problem solving do so at their own peril. Behind every dramatic turnaround story lies the arduous, and often untold, task of behind-the-scenes sweat and research.

Written documents provide one of the most obvious—yet overlooked—ways to understand the history of a problem. Many managers, eager to take action, jump in with both feet without first doing their homework. This is a common error, especially when a new leader feels pressure to tackle a high-profile problem.

When Lou Gerstner, Jr., took over as CEO of IBM Corp. in 1993, there was tremendous pressure on him to do something really dramatic. The $60 billion computer giant had been losing its stronghold in the industry, and Wall Street looked to Gerstner to take bold action.

ON THE JOB

IBM Remakes the Future by Studying Its Past

Gerstner did eventually take bold steps to begin remaking IBM's entire corporate culture. But at first he hesitated, taking no action that Wall Streeters could see, anyway. As a result, in his first year as CEO, Gerstner came under enormous fire for being "indecisive."

But behind the scenes, Gerstner was doing his homework. Instead of playing to his audience, Gerstner sat down and personally reviewed every plan-

ning document that had been written since the late 1970s. He knew a huge corporation like IBM couldn't be remade in a year, so he concentrated on solving short-term problems to give the corporation more stability while he tackled the more long-term problems.

Gerstner's strategy has begun to pay off. During 1994 and the first part of 1995, Gerstner got rid of many ingrained operating procedures and cut more than $6 billion in expenses. IBM's stock prices nearly doubled over that same period, and 1994 saw IBM's first profitable year since 1990.

Now Gerstner can begin to tackle the deeper changes he was called in to make. If Gerstner succeeds at remaking IBM's underlying culture, he'll do so partly by making use of the recorded thoughts and plans of many of those who have gone before him.

SOURCE   Michael A. Verespej, "Gutsy Decisions of 1994: Gerstner Looked Before Leaping," *Industry Week*, January 23, 1995, p. 36.

the firm will gain by addressing the problems and implementing the proposed solution. Any attempt to implement a solution must introduce some change, and this causes stress. The problem statement should show people what they will gain by making the proposed change as compared to letting the current situation continue.

The following questions should guide formulation of a problem statement:

- What symptoms are apparent?
- What problems are associated with these symptoms?
- What causes are creating these problems and their symptoms?
- What factors can decision makers control?
- What factors exceed decision makers' control and why?
- What changes would improve performance?
- Why should decision makers do anything about the problem?

In the problem statement/diagnostics stage, the problem-solving process builds critical agreement over the problem to address, which must precede any solution. A problem statement must clearly and unambiguously tell people what the proposal asks them to do. Remember the important advice quoted earlier: A problem well-stated is a problem half solved. According to Peter Drucker, a noted management consultant and writer:

> Indeed, the most common source of mistakes in management decisions is the emphasis on finding the right answer rather than the right question.... The important and difficult job is never to find the right answer, it is to find the right question. For there are few things as useless—if not dangerous—as the right answer to the wrong question.[12]

Tools. A later section of the chapter describes several tools for the problem statement/diagnostics stage.

Analysis

analysis

A step in the problem-solving process that explains the development of the current situation

The third problem-solving step, analysis, often overlaps with problem statement/ diagnostics. As its major task, **analysis** explains the development of the current situation. It details the relationships between features of that situation and outlines its problems, causes, and symptoms. By laying out causal relationships, analysis directs attention to changes needed to solve the problems described in the problem statement/diagnostics step. This forms a foundation on which to construct strategy alternatives in the following prescription/alternatives step.

Analysis often asks questions such as:

- What has happened?
- Why did it happen?
- What sequence of events caused observed problems and symptoms?
- What key factors have influenced these events?
- How can managers change these factors?

Tools. The analysis stage relies heavily on modeling, discussed in greater detail in a later section of this chapter. A model is a simplified representation of a real system. It includes only minimal detail on nonessential features of the problem or its solution, but it presents exhaustive information about critical features. Managers can build mathematical models using such management science tools as linear programming or computer simulation, or they can construct scaled-down physical models of systems they want to study.

For example, GE managers might have developed a computer model to simulate operations at Appliance Park as part of their analysis of the plant's transformation process. The model would have required complete, detailed information about essential decisions such as product scheduling while ignoring peripheral issues such as the weather.

Prescription/Alternatives

prescription/alternatives

A step in the problem-solving process that develops potential solutions to a problem

In the fourth step, **prescription/alternatives**, the problem-solving process focuses attention on developing a solution to the problem evaluated during size-up/description, formally stated in problem statement/diagnostics, and explained in analysis. Based on the results of analysis, managers identify problem features that they must attack or change to close the gap between the current and the desired future situations. They also establish criteria for an acceptable solution, specifying time limits (e.g., any solution must take no longer than 18 months to

[12]Peter F. Drucker, *The Practice of Management* (New York: Harper & Row, 1954), pp. 352–353.

implement), cost limits (e.g., any solution must provide a rate of return greater than 15 percent), and strategic emphasis (e.g., any solutions must reinforce the firm's position as the quality leader in its industry).

This step should not try to present a single solution, but rather a number of different alternatives. Managers should present each alternative in a brief statement about what changes it proposes, why and how those changes should improve operations, and the strengths and weaknesses of the alternative. This step frequently asks questions such as:

- What conditions must a solution alternative satisfy?
- What are the major features of each proposed alternative?
- How would each alternative improve operations and address the problem?
- What are the strengths and weaknesses of each alternative?
- Does the alternative propose a realistic solution to the problem?
- Does the alternative address all of the problem features and causes identified in the analysis step? If not, why not?

Tools. This step draws on tools such as computer simulation and payback analysis.

Implementation

In the final step, **implementation**, the problem-solving process formulates a single solution and puts it into practice. The previous four steps have carefully explored the current and desired future situations and developed a solution that will effectively close the gap between them. Implementation involves choosing one of the alternatives identified in the previous step or some combination of those alternatives when one cannot solve the problem by itself.

After selecting a solution alternative, managers must develop an implementation plan that describes how they intend to put it into practice. This plan lays out the changes that managers intend to make and the order in which they intend to introduce those changes for both short-term and long-term actions. The plan should describe short-term actions to improve the effects of the problem and long-term actions to eliminate or control its causes.

This step does not end when managers present an implementation plan, though. An effective response requires actual changes in company operations to successfully implement the chosen alternative. Much of this success depends on how completely people affected by the solution accept its changes. A solution that makes sense to managers may not gain acceptance by the people on the shop floor, especially if that solution will eliminate some of their jobs.

Practical experience identifies four principles that govern user acceptance of problem solutions:

- *Survival* Workers will usually accept a solution when they recognize that other alternatives (including doing nothing) will eliminate jobs. For example, one company's managers proposed to automate operations, reducing its employment from 500 to 350. To sell the idea to workers, the managers showed that the current system could offer 500 jobs, but only temporarily since it could not keep the company competitive and it would fail. Automation would offer fewer jobs, but more permanent ones since it would make the company far more competitive. The employees agreed to accept the change to automation.
- *Lack of Surprises* Employees tend to accept solutions that eliminate nasty surprises that a current system causes.

implementation
A step in the problem-solving process that puts a chosen solution alternative into practice

- *Simplicity* Workers tend to accept any solution that makes their jobs and their lives simpler.
- *Pride* Workers often accept solutions that help them to do their jobs better. They want to take pride in their work and will often welcome changes that improve it.

VanGundy has listed some questions that can help managers to evaluate a solution alternative and its chances for successful implementation:[13]

1. Does the firm have adequate resources (time, personnel, equipment, money, information, and so on) to implement the solution?
2. Do others demonstrate the motivation and commitment that successful implementation would require?
3. Will implementation have to overcome "closed thinking" and/or general resistance to change?
4. Will procedural obstacles inhibit implementation?
5. Will structural obstacles in the organization (e.g., inappropriate communications channels) complicate implementation?
6. What organizational or managerial policies will oppose implementation?
7. How much risk will those responsible for implementation willingly accept?
8. Could any ongoing power struggles within the organization (even those outside the scope of the solution) block implementation?
9. Could any interpersonal conflicts hinder implementation?
10. Is the general climate of the organization characterized by cooperation or distrust?

Problem-Solving Process—General Observations

Effective problem solving requires careful attention to each of the five steps in this process in order. The sequence of the steps is important, first, because it forms the process into a sort of checklist that helps managers to avoid ignoring or overlooking valuable information. Inexperienced problem solvers often try to move straight to problem statement in an attempt to quickly frame a decisive solution. This haste risks spending too little time on the critical size-up/description stage or even skipping it entirely. Time invested in sizing up a problem often pays returns in improved problem statements and more thorough understanding of a problem's background, which can help to smooth the implementation step. The five-step problem-solving process imposes some order on a potentially chaotic situation by providing a structure for understanding and responding to that situation.

The rest of this book develops tools and procedures for the problem-solving process to make it a value-driven activity. In identifying and addressing problems, operations managers (and all managers) work to increase the value generated by the OM system and the firm as a whole.

OPERATIONS MANAGEMENT TOOLKIT (OMT)

The chapter has focused on managers' decision-making activities and processes. To complete these activities and processes, every operations manager draws on a

---

[13]Arthur B. VanGundy, *Techniques of Structured Problem Solving* (New York: Van Nostrand Reinhold, 1981), p. 190.

basic set of conceptual tools and techniques in the **Operations Management Toolkit** (OMT):

- Total cost analysis
- Trade-off analysis
- Deming cycle (plan-do-check-act)
- Cause-and-effect analysis
- Pareto analysis
- Check sheets
- Model building

Operations Management Toolkit

A basic set of conceptual tools and techniques for completing the activities of operations management

These are the operations manager's equivalent of the carpenter's hammer, saw, and tape measure.

This list is not comprehensive, however; it omits some tools (such as simulation, linear programming, decision tree analysis, and queuing theory) that are more appropriately covered in a management science/operations research course.

Total Cost Analysis

Managers frequently repeat the old saying, "There is no such thing as a free lunch." Every action creates some sort of a cost. Some actions create large costs, while others create only small costs. Managers can measure some costs in dollars and cents while others are far more subjective. (What is the value to the firm of a good reputation?) To evaluate decisions, managers can rely on **total cost analysis**, a technique in which they identify all costs associated with a set of decisions and then choose the one with the lowest total cost.

The total cost of any decision consists of two major components, quantitative costs and qualitative costs:

total cost analysis

A decision-making technique in which managers identify all costs associated with a set of decisions and then choose the one with the lowest total cost

$$\text{Total cost} = \Sigma \text{ (Quantitative costs)} + \Sigma \text{ (Qualitative costs)} \qquad (4.1)$$

Quantitative Costs. Quantitative costs involve any cost that can be measured with repetition. For example, if scrap is too high, we can measure the number of units that have been thrown out and apply the dollar cost per unit to arrive at the cost in dollars. Managers can measure quantitative costs in monetary units with some degree of accuracy. Measurement of such costs follows a predetermined method, allowing others to easily reproduce results. One person could take raw cost data and use standard methods to calculate the same costs as someone else working with the same data. For example, if production of a pencil requires 7 inches of wood at $0.02 per inch, 7 inches of graphite at $0.03 per inch, glue at $0.05, and 1 minute of labor at $12.00 per hour, then the quantitative cost of producing that pencil should amount to $0.60. This information and the appropriate formula allow only one answer:

$$\begin{aligned}\text{Cost of pencil} &= \text{Cost of wood} + \text{Cost of graphite} + \text{Glue} + \text{Labor}\\ &= 7 \times \$0.02 + 7 \times \$0.03 + \$0.05 + \$12.00/60\\ &= \$0.60\end{aligned}$$

Quantitative costs break down into several major components:

- Variable costs
- Fixed costs
- Semivariable costs
- Relevant and irrelevant costs
- Opportunity costs

Relationship between Fixed and Variable Costs

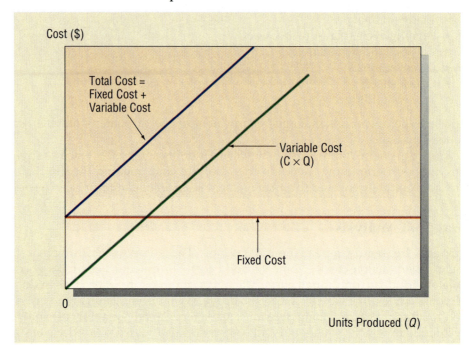

Variable costs are those that vary directly with output (i.e., Variable cost = Cost per unit × Number of units produced). Producing more units raises variable costs. This relationship can be either linear, in which costs rise a fixed amount with each new unit, or nonlinear, in which additional production makes the OM system either more or less efficient so costs rise by either a smaller or larger amount with each new unit. As we build more, we may become more efficient, resulting in a lower cost per unit at the higher output level. The pencil example included only linear variable costs.

The firm must pay fixed costs even if it produces no output. This category typically includes costs such as mortgage payments, debt interest payments, property taxes, and heat and light for facilities, etc. Exhibit 4.10 illustrates the relationship between fixed and variable costs.

Semivariable costs change in increments, creating a step-like pattern. Over a certain range, a semivariable cost acts like a fixed cost. Outside that range, the cost changes to a new level. In Exhibit 4.11, the semivariable cost remains essentially fixed over the range Q^* to Q^{**}. However, at a level of output beyond Q^{**}, the cost jumps upward.

To see why some costs behave in this way, suppose that a machine operator earns a wage for 8 hours per day, whatever the level of production. The operator can produce no more than 10 units an hour , so (ignoring overtime) at any level of output between 0 units and 80 units, the operator's pay represents a fixed cost. However, production of 81 units would require the firm to hire another operator, changing the level of fixed costs.

For another example, consider setup costs. To produce a different product, the firm incurs a cost for workers to set up equipment, so total cost varies with the new

[**EXHIBIT 4.11**]

Semivariable Costs

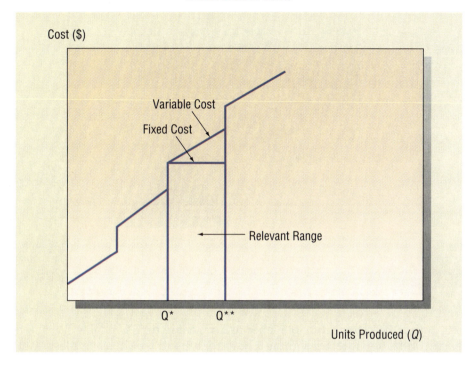

production. Over the production run, however, this cost remains fixed until the equipment must turn out a new product.

Besides fixed and variable costs, managers must separate relevant and irrelevant costs. Relevant costs are any costs that would change in response to an action or decision or any costs that would affect the outcome of the decision. Irrelevant costs, in contrast, remain independent of the decision.

Suppose, for example, that a worker does nothing but set up equipment. That worker earns a wage for 8 hours, and current production occupies only 60 percent of that time. A new inventory-control procedure would require an extra setup that would take 1½ hours. The labor cost of this extra setup is irrelevant to the decision about the new procedure because it would not change the setup worker's wage. This cost would remain fixed because the worker could accomplish the additional work within the normal day for which the firm is already paying; the extra setup cost would become relevant only if it were to force the firm to hire another worker. Another way of looking at this situation is to view the setup person as a sunk cost. The salary that person receives for eight hours a day is paid whether or not any work is done. (Sunk and fixed costs are discussed in greater detail in management accounting textbooks.)

Factors such as the level of capacity utilization can also affect the distinction between relevant and irrelevant costs. For example, a setup cost might be irrelevant at a low capacity utilization rate, when existing workers and equipment could accomplish the job without raising cash costs; the same cost could become relevant at a high capacity utilization rate, when the firm would have to hire more workers and buy more equipment to accomplish the job. A firm's capacity is finite at any

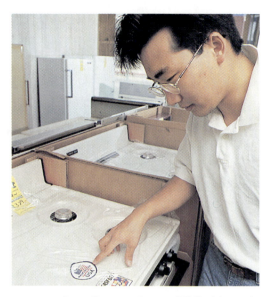

Many factors determine a customer's appliance preference. While this man's perception of value may increase due to the stove's country of manufacturer, another may find value in corporate reputation. These subjective considerations are important in the formulation of qualitative costs. SOURCE Michael Newman/PhotoEdit

point in time based on available labor and machine time available. With a high capacity utilization rate, consuming 1 hour for a setup would leave 1 less hour for production since the firm would lack idle capacity to assign to the new job. A setup would represent a real loss in such a situation, creating a relevant cost.

Opportunity costs, the last major component of quantitative costs, depend on the best alternative use of resources. An investment in inventory commits company resources so they are no longer available for other investments (e.g., adding capacity or simply earning interest in a bank account). Managers must carefully consider whether any investment offers a return that exceeds its opportunity cost, that is, the return that the same resources could earn if invested in some other activity or asset. Decisions about the best uses of resources hinge on opportunity costs.

Opportunity costs also have important influences on cash costs such as inventory carrying costs. Suppose that a plant manager must balance the needs of two separate operations, one of which wants to invest $10,000 in extra inventory. How should the manager evaluate the cost of this investment? The firm can borrow the money at an interest rate of 10 percent per year, but the second operation has returned about 25 percent per year on company resources invested in it. The true cost of the investment in inventory is not 10 percent per year, the cost of the loan, but 25 percent. To invest in inventory, the firm would have to forgo the return of 25 percent that the second operation could provide, so the inventory would have to provide a return in excess of this opportunity cost to yield a real benefit to the firm.

Qualitative Costs. Qualitative costs, in contrast to quantitative costs, reflect costs that managers cannot easily state in numerical terms. This includes some subjective considerations such as corporate reputation, public goodwill, an image as a good place to work, and the satisfaction of using environmentally responsible practices. The value of such a qualitative issue is difficult to specify because it depends on the decision maker's personal views and biases. One person may view something as a critical issue while another cares little.

To illustrate qualitative costs, consider an example. While browsing in a book store, you find an old book about the battle of Gettysburg that carries an inscription from someone who fought in that battle. How much does the inscription change the book's value? A Civil War buff might well pay much more for that book than for the same book without the inscription. Someone with no special interest in the Civil War might care little about the inscription. Both judgments of value are highly qualitative.

Some people may see little value in basing decisions on costs that are so difficult to measure and subjective. Managers evaluate qualitative costs, however, because they often become decisive in choices between alternatives with similar dollar costs. Managers may choose a more expensive option because they value its qualitative costs more than the difference between the options' quantitative costs. To allow for such a judgment, a complete total cost analysis should begin by identifying and measuring quantitative costs; it should then evaluate qualitative costs.

[PROBLEM 4.1]

Total Cost Analysis in Practice

You manage a plant that manufactures office furniture. In the past, the plant has packaged all shipments in cardboard because the materials are relatively cheap to buy. Its suppliers also use cardboard packaging for the same reason. Until recently, this practice was a part of business. You have now begun to question this practice. You have recognized that the cardboard removed from shipments causes a large mess on the shop floor, thus creating a serious housekeeping problem. Your customers must also store or dispose of the cardboard, and are complaining. In addition, increasingly crowded waste disposal sites have begun charging higher prices to accept cardboard waste. Finally, more customers are demanding environmentally friendly products, and top management expects this concern over "green" production methods to become a basic market demand—an order qualifier.

As a result, you have decided to look at alternatives for replacing cardboard containers for both incoming and outgoing shipments with reusable containers. These containers would take less storage space and cause fewer housekeeping problems. Returning them costs nothing because the trucks had returned empty before. They would also eliminate disposal problems. However, problems with the reusable containers begin with their cost. The plant could meet its shipping requirements by buying 10,000 reusable containers which would cost about $35 each. Furthermore, the new containers would require modifications to storerooms and trucks at a cost of $50,000. Training for employees (both within the plant and at suppliers' locations) would cost $20,000.

Currently, the plant uses 100,000 pounds of cardboard per year at $1.50 per pound. In addition, you estimate that hauling and disposing of the cardboard will cost $300 per 1,000 pounds at this year's price. The cost may increase to $450 next year. The cardboard increases housekeeping costs by $75,000 per year, and storage costs for cardboard waste run about $45,000 a year.

SOLUTION

You must decide between two alternatives: continuing to use cardboard or introducing reusable containers. To make this decision, you must first identify all quantitative costs attributable to each alternative.

Quantitative Costs of Cardboard Containers

- Acquisition costs:100,000 lbs. × $1.50 per lb. = $150,000
- Disposal costs:(100,000/1,000) × $300 per 1,000 lbs = $30,000
- Housekeeping costs: $75,000
- Storage costs: $45,000
- Total costs = Acquisition costs + Disposal costs + Housekeeping costs + Storage costs = 150,000 + 30,000 + 75,000 + 45,000 = $300,000

Quantitative Costs of Reusable Containers

- Acquisition costs:10,000 containers × $35 per container = $350,000
- Modifications to storerooms and trucks: $50,000
- Training costs: $20,000
- Total costs = Acquisition costs + Modifications + Training costs = 350,000 + 50,000 + 20,000 = $420,000

Based on quantitative costs, the current system is more cost efficient than switching to reusable containers. Not switching would save $120,000. Now consider the qualitative costs.

Qualitative Costs of Cardboard Containers

- Possibility of price increase for disposal of cardboard
- Risk of alienating customers who value environmentally conscientious manufacturing practices
- More housekeeping problems
- Larger storage space requirement

Qualitative Costs of Reusable Containers

- Smaller storage space requirement
- Fewer housekeeping problems
- Elimination of disposal problems
- Potential market benefits of environmentally conscientious manufacturing practices
- Reputation for leadership in the use of reusable containers
- Management and employees learning to manage flow of containers
- Employee resistance
- Tracking condition of reusable containers

In spite of the downside factors, the qualitative costs clearly favor the reusable containers. The third stage of the total cost analysis weighs quantitative costs against qualitative costs to determine the appropriate action. A decision to introduce reusable containers would state that their qualitative advantages would be worth at least $120,000 (the difference between the costs of the two alternatives), though this analysis does not specify a quantitative value. A decision to continue to use cardboard would indicate that the qualitative benefits of reusable containers are not worth the $120,000 difference between alternatives. This example illustrates an effective technique for cost-benefit analysis.   [■]

Total Cost Analysis—Other Comments. Total cost analysis considers the sum of all costs and benefits. Cost-benefit analysis weighs benefits against cost. The two terms are often used interchangeably. Total cost analysis is central to much of the decision making in operations management. Managers should evaluate the total costs of every action and decision, watching for links to value revealed by qualitative costs. Their view of strategic issues such as the importance of speed, product flexibility, environmentally responsible manufacturing, or good corporate citizenship often affect assessments of qualitative costs.

The widespread use of total cost analysis illustrates the fundamental value of this operations management tool. Total cost analysis is used to address the eight types of problems identified early in this chapter, and it underlies such basic operations management techniques as the economic order quantity model. It is also an integral part of trade-off analysis, described in the next section. In fact, much of operations management amounts to identifying and managing total costs to identify solution alternatives with the lowest total costs.

Trade-off Analysis

Consider two situations:

1. You must determine how much to order from a supplier. Every order costs $125 to process but, if you order more than you can use in any period, you pay $1 per unit per week in inventory holding costs. You must determine an order quantity that best balances the costs of not holding inventory (i.e., ordering costs) against the costs of holding inventory.
2. Your department operates two machines. The first requires only 10 minutes to set up to produce a different part, but it is operated manually so the operator takes 5 minutes to process each part. In contrast, the second machine is highly automated; setup takes 2 hours, but it can process each part in only 1 minute. You must determine under what conditions to process an order on each machine.

Many OM problems require managers to balance one set of costs against another. For example, to identify the best sample size in a search problem, one must balance the costs of inspecting each item in the sample against the risk of misjudging the quality of a batch of supplies. Raising the sample size improves the chance of accurately judging the batch's quality, but at the cost of more inspection. In a queuing problem, adding a server increases the cost of the firm's investment in resources, but it may reduce waiting time and save money.

Trade-off analysis offers one technique for balancing or trading off costs of different solution alternatives by identifying the indifference point between them. The indifference point specifies the conditions under which the two options yield the same result. In the machine allocation example above, the first machine had a shorter setup time, but a longer processing time while the second machine took longer to set up, but processed products more quickly. The solution must identify the processing quantity (Q^*) that takes the same total time on the first machine as on the second. This quantity defines the indifference point. Having identified this point, managers know that they should process any order quantity less than Q^* on the first machine and any quantity in excess of Q^* on the second.

trade-off analysis
A technique for choosing among decision alternatives based on the indifference point between them

This procedure relies on a carefully determined indifference point. The general procedure for determining this point is:

1. Identify the two decision alternatives.
2. Identify the costs associated with each option.
3. Determine the essential decision variable.
4. Write down the equation for the indifference point.

5. Solve for the indifference point.
6. Identify the decision zones.
7. Adjust for qualitative considerations.

To illustrate, consider the machine allocation example. First, the decision alternatives are the manual machine and the automated machine. To identify the costs associated with each alternative, recall that the manual machine setup takes 10 minutes and processing time per unit is 5 minutes; the automated machine takes 120 minutes to set up, and processing time is 1 minute. These costs depend on the number of units in a production run, so that is the essential decision variable. Indicating this number with the variable x, the equation for the indifference point is:

$$10 + 5x = 120 + 1x$$

The term left of the equal sign states the total processing time on the manual machine, while term right of the equal sign states the total processing time on the automated machine. Solving this equation for x (Step 5) gives an indifference point at 27.5 units. At that quantity, processing takes 147.5 minutes on either machine so the manager could assign the job to one as easily as the other. This information suggests that the manual machine should process any order with a quantity of 27 or fewer units, while the automated machine should process any order for 28 units or more.

The final step evaluates qualitative factors to which the decision maker can assign no objective, quantitative costs. As mentioned earlier, evaluation of such factors is highly subjective. Many qualitative factors might affect the machine allocation analysis. For example, a series of small orders might exceed the capacity of the manual machine, forcing some orders of fewer than 28 units onto the automated machine to stay within capacity limitations. Another qualitative consideration might involve the mechanical reliability and availability of the two machines. If the manual machine breaks down frequently (perhaps because it is older) or requires a lot of down time for preventive maintenance, many smaller orders might have to run on the automated machine. After adjusting the decision based on the indifference point for this qualitative information, managers arrive at a final decision rule.

Deming Cycle

Deming cycle

A sequence of plan-do-check-act designed to stabilize an OM system and identify opportunities for continuous improvement

The **Deming cycle** is also called the *Deming wheel* or the *PDCA cycle* (from the sequence plan-do-check-act).[14] Managers use this series of four separate but linked activities, illustrated in Exhibit 4.12, to stabilize a process and identify opportunities for continuous improvement:[15]

- *Plan* Managers identify a problem by studying the current situation to detect a gap between it and the desired future situation. A large gap can create significant opportunities for improvement; a small gap represents a chance for a continuous, incremental improvement. During this stage, managers also identify actions to improve the situation (i.e., close the gap). The step culminates in formulation of a plan for closing the recognized gap.
- *Do* Having formulated the plan, managers proceed in this step to implement it. Frequently, they begin by implementing a change at less than full scale in some kind of a pilot project to assess its larger-scale feasibility.

[14]W. Edwards Deming, *Out of the Crisis* (Cambridge, Mass.: MIT Center for Advanced Engineering Study, 1986), pp. 88–89.

[15]Howard Gitlow, Shelley Gitlow, Alan Oppenheim, and Rosa Oppenheim, *Tools and Methods for the Improvement of Quality* (Homewood, Ill.: Richard D. Irwin, 1989), pp. 159–160.

[**EXHIBIT 4.12**]

Deming Cycle

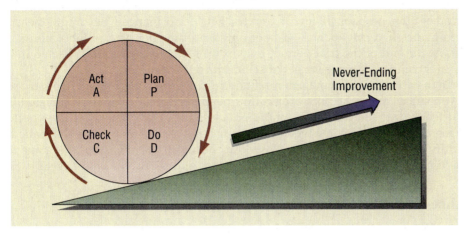

- *Check*   The primary activities of this third step involve monitoring and inspecting results. The people responsible for implementing the plan monitor its small-scale performance to try to answer two critical questions: whether the anticipated relationship between the manipulated variables and performance is occurring and whether the implementation is creating any downstream problems or improvements.[16]

  At this step, the manager compares the actual results of the implementation of the plan with desired results and studies reasons for any gap between them. Performance measurement becomes critical in this step because data must accurately reflect real events.
- *Act*   In the final stage, managers review information collected in the check step and take appropriate corrective action. The major objective of this step is to prevent any reoccurrence of problems addressed in the previous three stages. It also institutionalizes earlier changes and forms a starting point for the next round of the Deming cycle (the next iteration of the PDCA sequence).

The Deming cycle is a popular tool in operations management, especially in quality management.[17] However, this method can also help managers to address the eight types of OM problems identified earlier in this chapter, such as inventory problems. To better understand the Deming cycle, consider how it might help GE managers to address the problems at Appliance Park.

In the plan step, they try to identify the gap between what they see actually happening and what they want to happen and then develop an appropriate course of action. Suppose that their study uncovers some indication that problems with obsolete equipment have caused the poor performance at Appliance Park. Managers respond by evaluating the likely impact on plant performance of an investment to upgrade equipment. They then draw up a plan of action.

Next, in the do step, GE managers decide to implement the plan that they formulated in the previous step. Because some doubt remains that the expensive,

[16]Ibid., p. 20.

[17]James C. Benneyan and Alan D. Chute, CMA, "SPC, Process Improvements, and the Deming PDCA Circle in Freight Administration," *Production and Inventory Management* 34, no. 1 (1993), pp. 35–40.

new equipment will fully resolve the performance problems, they decide to upgrade equipment in an isolated production line on a trial basis. After training workers to operate the new, automated equipment, they restart operations.

In the check stage, the managers operate the renovated production line for a period of time, perhaps for a year, and track its performance. They might measure performance in terms such as cost per unit, lead time per unit, or labor hours per unit. At the end of the trial period, they examine the information collected in the trial and compare it against a set of standards or expectations.

In the act step, GE managers might decide to update equipment in other areas of Appliance Park if the pilot project improved performance on the renovated line sufficiently. If the new equipment did not close the performance gap as expected, the managers might review where the changes succeeded and where they failed to identify areas for future action. Based on the results of this step, the managers would most likely formulate a new set of plans and repeat the entire cycle.

Cause-and-Effect Diagrams

All of the previous discussions have simply assumed the difficult task of identifying causes that create observed symptoms. While managers can often readily identify symptoms (increasing costs, increasing scrap rates, decreasing quality, lengthening lead times), the root causes of those symptoms often remain elusive. This analysis becomes especially difficult when the relationship between a cause and a symptom does not follow a linear path. Poor equipment maintenance may seem to lead directly to an increasing defect rate, but the actual causes may act through less predictable sequences of interactions. Inadequate operator training combined with insufficient spare time and too few tools may lead to poor equipment maintenance which in turn leads to an increase in the defect rate.

cause-and-effect diagram

A problem-solving tool that visually represents relationships between symptoms and their root causes

Problem solvers need a mechanism for identifying potential causes and tracing back through complex interrelationships to identify the root causes of observed symptoms. **Cause-and-effect diagrams** provide this tool. They are also known as *C&E diagrams, fishbone diagrams* (because a completed diagram looks like the skeleton of a fish), or *Ishikawa charts*, in honor of Dr. Kaoru Ishikawa, who first developed this tool.[18] C&E diagrams are widely used throughout operations management, in both service and manufacturing operations. They facilitate and structure brainstorming work, encouraging people to share ideas and providing visual images of those ideas.

Exhibit 4.13 illustrates the structure of a C&E diagram. The vertical line separates the observed problem from possible causes on the left. The heavy horizontal arrow illustrates the root effect that the problem solver is trying to explain. Several branches join this root effect arrow with the labels *Materials, Work Methods, Labor,* and *Machine* to identify several basic categories of potential causes of the problem. Each of these branches supports smaller branches that represent specific elements of the category described in the major branch (contributing causes). For example, the Work Method branch could carry a twig labeled *Training*. From this twig, two even smaller twigs might carry the labels *Lack of Training* and *Ineffective Training*. Specifying potential causes within this structure illustrates their links to the symptoms of the problem.

This structure can also be stated as a sentence. To describe the links on the Work Methods branch, one might say that lack of training or ineffective training

[18]Kaoru Ishikawa, *Guide to Quality Control* (White Plains, N.Y.: Quality Resources, 1985), pp. 18–29.

[**E X H I B I T   4 . 1 3**]

Generic Cause-and-Effect Diagram

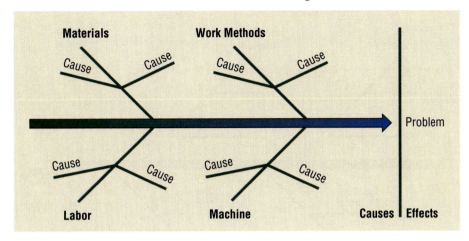

(i.e., too little time spent or poor methods of training) could create training problems. These problems, in turn, might contribute to problems with Work Methods, which might contribute to the root problem, a rising defect rate. This analysis would suggest that the manager can correct the defect-rate problem only by changing Work Methods through improvements in training. This would require further effort to isolate the cause as lack of training, ineffective training, or both.

This example illustrates the more common of the two major types of C&E diagrams, the dispersion analysis diagram. This type of diagram seeks to explain the causes of observed dispersion around or variation from expected results. Typically, problem solvers use this kind of diagram to answer questions such as:

- Why are measures of product quality falling?
- Why are finished product reject rates so high?
- Why must customers wait so long in line?
- Why are costs increasing?
- Why is output measured in units produced per hour falling?

Throughout this book, mentions of C&E diagrams will refer to dispersion analysis diagrams.

A second type of C&E diagram, the process classification diagram, tries explain the causes of problems by tracing through the activities in the production process.[19] This diagram presents main branches for various types of activities. For example, Exhibit 4.14 diagrams a problem with a bad toaster that could be caused at any of several work stations. The diagram links potential causes such as operator errors or poor tools to specific stages in the production process.

The choice between the two types of C&E diagrams depends on the nature of the problem and the process. If the potential causes of the problem are not specific to particular operations or production steps, then the dispersion analysis diagram is more appropriate. If the potential causes are linked to specific steps in the process, then the process classification diagram is more appropriate.

[19]Ibid., pp. 20–25.

[**EXHIBIT 4.14**]

Production Classification Diagram

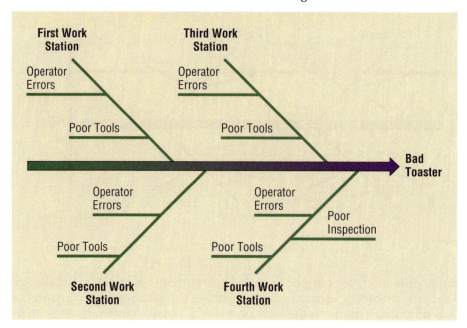

Constructing a C&E Diagram. The process of building a C&E diagram is fairly straightforward. It consists of the following steps:[20]

1. *Identify the Problem to Examine*   The process begins by clearly stating the problem or effect to examine in the diagram in a form acceptable to everyone involved. After noting the problem at the extreme right of the diagram, an arrow drawn from left to right illustrates the root effect. All causes that subsequent analysis identifies appear as branches linked to this arrow.

2. *Identify the Major Categories of Causes*   Next, identify the major categories of potential causes that could contribute to the effect under study. Represent them as main branches off the problem arrow, indicating the name of each category at the end of its branch. These main branches gather potential causes into groups to organize them and to begin to structure the analysis of cause-and-effect relationships. The categories often reflect issues identified in earlier study of the problem or such universal categories as Labor, Work Methods, Materials, Machines, and Measurement.

3. *Identify More Specific Causes*   On each main branch, place smaller branches, or twigs, to represent detailed causes that could contribute to the primary categories of causes. For each detailed cause, even smaller twigs can represent still more specific and detailed causes. Problem solvers often use brainstorming methods to identify major categories of causes and more detailed causes. This method seeks and records input from different people who are familiar with the problem under study to identify any

[20]Gitlow et al., *Tools and Methods*, pp. 383–385; and Ishikawa, *Guide to Quality Control*, pp. 19–20.

potential cause, from the most obvious to the most far fetched; later analysis eliminates unlikely possibilities to focus on the more likely ones.

4. *Circle Likely Causes*   After the diagram has been developed with sufficient care to ensure that it shows all potential causes, the next step is to review all of the causes and circle the most likely ones. Further analysis and data collection can then focus on those causes.

5. *Verify the Causes*   After identifying the most likely causes, ensure that they really lie at the heart of the problem using techniques such as Deming's PDCA cycle.

The best way of understanding how to use a C&E diagram is to actually develop one. See Problem 4.2.

[PROBLEM 4.2]

Developing a C&E Diagram

To develop a C&E diagram for Appliance Park, GE managers would begin by identifying the problem. They might begin by asking questions such as:

- Why are profits falling?
- Why are production costs increasing?
- Why is marketing share falling?
- Why is output per worker falling?

SOLUTION

Suppose that the problem solvers' analysis yields the problem statement "Increasing production costs." This becomes the label for the root effect arrow, as in Exhibit 4.15A.

In the second step, they would identify major categories of potential causes. The description at the start of the chapter identified several: Equipment (which may be obsolete), Work Practices, Labor, and Process Design (the system layout and production methods). The diagram could identify other potential causes, but these will make enough main branches for the example, as Exhibit 4.15B shows.

In the third step, the problem solvers would identify more detailed causes within the main categories. For example, one main branch in Exhibit 4.15C, Equipment, carries twigs for two more detailed causes, Maintenance and Age, indicating that old equipment and ineffective maintenance represent major equipment-related causes of increasing production costs. Ineffective mainte-

[EXHIBIT 4.15A]

Identifying the Root Effect

Increasing Production Costs

[E X H I B I T   4 . 1 5 B]

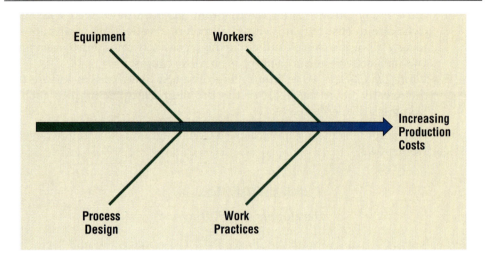

nance could result from either inadequate investments in maintenance or poor maintenance techniques. This diagram also presents some other potential causes and the structure of twigs that links them to main categories of causes and the problem itself.

In the fourth step, problem solvers examine the potential causes and circle those that seem most likely to cause the problem under study. Exhibit 4.15D

[E X H I B I T   4 . 1 5 C]

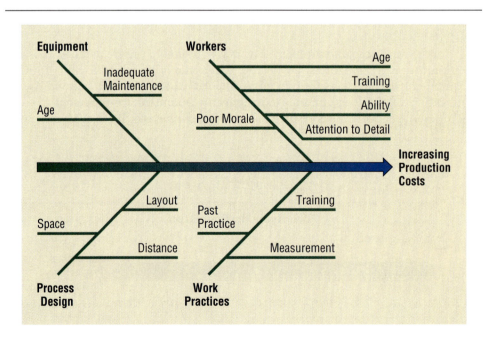

[EXHIBIT 4.15D]

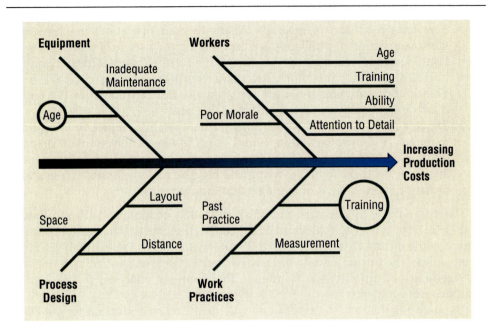

identifies two likely detailed causes: problems in work practices due to training and equipment problems related to the age of the machines. The problem
solvers would then target further study of these two causes, collecting data
about them and conducting more in-depth analysis, perhaps using tools such
as the Deming PDCA cycle. [■]

Benefits of Cause-and-Effect Diagrams. C&E diagrams offer several important
benefits:

- *Preparing them is educational.* C&E diagrams help everyone involved to
  develop a better understanding of all aspects of a problem and their interrelationships.
- *They help to guide discussions.* C&E diagrams help to focus discussions on
  specific causes and conditions, reducing the chance of straying from essential topics.
- *They help to direct data-collection activities.* By identifying potential causes and
  narrowing the list to the most likely ones, C&E diagrams help to target data
  collection on the most productive topics.
- *They can apply to any OM problem.* C&E diagrams offer a universal tool that
  can support study of any sort of problem, from quality issues to scheduling,
  layout, or lead time.

Pareto Analysis

Pareto analysis, one of the most important tools in the Operations Management
Toolkit, sets priorities for management action based on the assumption that 80

Pareto analysis

A problem-solving tool
that sets management
priorities based on the
assumption that 80 per-
cent of any gap between
expected and actual per-
formance results from 20
percent of an operation

percent of a gap between expected and actual performance results from 20 percent of an operation. This method reflects two simple but critical principles:

- *Everything is not equally important.* At any time, an operations manager may face many different problems, each competing for a share of time and attention. However, many problems often have relatively small impacts on the overall situation, while other, less numerous problems have critical effects. The operations manager must separate the critical few from the trivial many. Pareto analysis is well-suited to this task.
- *The best solutions get the biggest bang for the buck.* The effective operations manager concentrates attention and effort where the investment of time, effort, and money will yield the largest return. Pareto analysis helps to focus attention on these areas to wring the biggest payoff possible from every dollar or every minute of management time invested.

Pareto analysis began with the work of Italian economist Vilfredo Pareto (1848–1923). He observed that about 15 percent of the population earned about 80 percent of the income, leading to the 80-20 rule that governs Pareto analysis. Since Pareto's time, the impact of the vital few has been observed in such areas as time management and quality management.[21] In inventory analysis, the 80-20 rule underlies ABC analysis.

By manipulating and controlling events identified as critical under the 80-20 rule, Pareto analysis focuses management attention on the vital few activities that most affect overall system performance. It identifies those activities through a seven-step procedure:

1. *Identify categories about which to collect information.* An analysis of quality problems could specify categories that describe types of defects. Another problem might require categories based on inventory types or expense items; the categories should suit the problem under study. Data collection then structures information about these categories using another tool in the Operations Management Toolkit discussed in a later section, the check sheet.

2. *Decide on the time period to cover.* Next, the analysis must determine the period of time over which to collect information. This requires a trade-off between a shorter period, which would reduce the time and resources invested in gathering data, and a longer period, which would ensure that data would accurately represent the current situation. For example, a department store should not collect information about customer waiting times only on December 24, when waiting times are unusually long. A longer data collection period produces more representative information, but at the cost of a slower, more expensive process.

3. *Calculate total frequencies of variations by category for the time period.* To get these frequencies, problem solvers total the observed variations in the activities under study. A quality-related study would sum the number of product defects in each category. Summing the totals for all categories then gives the grand total. Dividing each category's variation frequency by the grand total and multiplying by 100 gives a percentage for that category.

[21]Richard I. Winwood, *Time Management* (Salt Lake City, Utah: Franklin Institute, 1990).

4. *Sort the categories in descending order based on their percentages.* This places the category with the highest percentage of variation at the top of the list of categories and the one with the lowest percentage at the bottom.

5. *Identify the vital few categories that account for most of the variation.* This step separates out the vital few categories based on the 80-20 rule. It identifies the 20 percent of the categories that account for around 80 percent of the total variation.

6. *Adjust the categories for any qualitative factors.* The previous steps identify a few categories of variation as vital based on quantitative data, but this type of data ignores information that cannot be counted or measured objectively. For example, a Pareto analysis of an inventory problem might measure inventory levels based on total dollars invested in inventory of each item. This would ignore such considerations as obsolescence, special storage requirements, or costs of stockouts (when the firm has no inventory to sell to a potential customer). Qualitative considerations could move a category near the bottom of the list up to the top.

7. *Present the data graphically, if appropriate.* The final step develops graphic illustrations of the results of the analysis, often using a bar graph or histogram. Typically, the horizontal axis of such a chart represents the categories of variation identified early in the analysis, arranged in descending order; the vertical axis represents the frequencies. In addition, the graph should present the cumulative frequency of variation for each category.

To illustrate Pareto analysis, consider Problem 4.3.

[**PROBLEM 4.3**]

Pareto Analysis in Action

The managers of a small, Midwestern firm are having difficulty maintaining a level of quality that satisfies customers. They have decided to collect information about product defects to identify the sources of the problem. In 2 weeks, data collection generates the following information:

Problem Areas	Number of Defects	Percentage of Defects
Caulking	377	29%
Fit	102	8
Appearance	90	7
Gaps	61	5
· Transformers	503	38
Coils	45	3
Controls	31	2
Other	112	8
Total	1,321	100%

NOTE Rounding errors may cause discrepancies. All data were reported without fractions: rounded to the nearest whole percentage.

Clearly, some problems are more critical than others. For example, defects in coils do not cause as many quality problems as defects in transformers. Pareto analysis can use this information to help the managers identify activities on which to focus their attention.

SOLUTION

Exhibit 4.16 presents the results of the first four steps of the Pareto analysis process. The categories identified in Step 1 outline the problem areas. After collecting data over a 2-week period (Step 2), the managers list the frequency of defects in each category. As described in the instructions for Step 3, they determine those frequency percentages by dividing each category's defect total by the overall total of 1,321 defects in all categories and multiplying the result by 100. For example, the frequency for percentage of caulking defects is:

$$\text{Frequency percentage of caulking defects} = \frac{\text{Number of caulking defects}}{\text{Total defects}} \times 100$$
$$= (377/1{,}321) \times 100$$
$$= 29 \text{ percent}$$

In Step 4, the managers sort the categories based on the frequency percentages in descending order.

Step 5 of the Pareto analysis reveals that defects in transformers and caulking together account for a large percentage of the total defects (67 percent). The third-largest category, Other, needs more study. Since it includes all defects that could not be assigned to one of the other seven categories, it does not give enough specific information for management action.

This analysis focuses management action on transformers and caulking. If the firm could reduce the number of defects in these two areas by 50 percent from 880 to 440, it would improve overall performance by over 33 percent (440/1,321). Before concentrating on transformers and caulking, we must determine if there are any relevant qualitative factors. To simplify our analysis, we assume there are not. In the final step, the managers graph the results, as in Exhibit 4.17.

This graph could also have been a cost Pareto chart in which the vertical axis would measure costs rather than defect frequency percentages. To calculate cost data, the managers would have multiplied the defect frequency for

[**E X H I B I T   4 . 1 6**   ]

Reasons for Defects

Problem Areas	Number of Defects	Percentage of Defects	Cumulative Frequency
Transformers	503	38%	38%
Caulking	377	29	67
Other	112	8	75
Fit	102	8	83
Appearance	90	7	90
Gaps	61	5	95
Coils	45	3	98
Controls	31	2	100
Total	1,321	100%	

NOTE   Rounding errors may cause discrepancies. All data was reported without fractions, rounded to the nearest whole percentage.

[**E X H I B I T   4 . 1 7**]

Pareto Chart

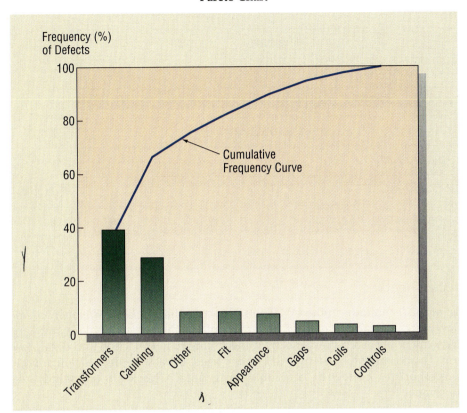

each category by the cost of such a defect. This would focus attention on the cost to the firm of defects in each category.   [■]

Benefits of Pareto Analysis. This technique is extremely powerful for several reasons. First, Pareto analysis draws attention to the vital few activities that affect performance most significantly. In Problem 4.3, it focused attention on problems with transformers and caulking. In such a simple problem, most people would reach the same conclusions without Pareto analysis, but practicing operations managers must study many more categories. When a complex OM process obscures the vital few activities, the power of Pareto analysis provides valuable help in sifting through massive amounts of data.

Second, Pareto analysis directs management efforts toward the best opportunities for improving operations. After acting to reduce defects in transformers and caulking, the managers in Problem 4.3 could repeat the Pareto analysis to gauge the effectiveness of their actions by looking for changes in the relative rankings of the problem areas and defect frequencies. Comparing the old and new Pareto charts would indicate their success and perhaps guide additional efforts to improve quality.

[**EXHIBIT 4.18**]

Attribute Check Sheet

Order Type	Frequency	Sum
Emergency order	✓✓✓✓✓✓✓✓✓✓✓✓✓	15
Nonemergency order	✓✓	42
Rework	✓✓✓✓✓✓✓✓✓✓✓✓✓✓✓✓✓✓✓✓✓✓✓✓✓✓✓✓	28
Safety stock	✓✓✓✓✓✓✓✓✓✓✓✓	12
Prototype job	✓✓✓✓✓✓✓	7
Other	✓✓✓✓✓	5

Check Sheets

Most of the techniques in the OM Toolkit assume that problem solvers have all of the accurate, logically organized information that they need. Actually, they must work to meet these requirements by undertaking data collection and data presentation. To accomplish these two tasks, they need an easy, rapid, efficient, and logical method for collecting and analyzing data. **Check sheets** satisfy these requirements.

A check sheet is a simple, widely used tool designed to facilitate collection of data in a form that allows problem solvers to use the information readily and analyze it almost automatically.[22] The check sheet lists a number of categories and leaves space for the manager to make a mark for each event in one of the categories. This information can support total cost calculations, trade-off analysis, Pareto analysis, and quality control methods. It can also help managers to address the eight kinds of OM problems described early in the chapter.

The three basic types of check sheets include attribute check sheets, variable check sheets, and location check sheets.[23] Nearly every other variant of check sheets is based on one of these three types.

Attribute Check Sheets. An attribute is simply a category such as a pass or fail rating for product quality. Attributes could also classify customers who pass through a bank by type; they could separate buyers of mountain bikes into novice riders, expert riders, professional racers, and so on. An attribute check sheet for Problem 4.3 might classify defects by type. The category designations in an attribute check sheet do not allow numerical comparisons, however. The attributes do not quantify relationships between categories; they simply indicate frequencies with which events in those categories occur.

Exhibit 14.18 shows an example of an attribute check sheet that indicates the types of jobs processed on a machine. After discussing their information needs

check sheet
A widely used method for collecting data by defining categories and making a mark for each event in each category

[22]Ishikawa, *Guide to Quality Control*, p. 34
[23]For a list of other variants of check sheets, see Ishikawa, *Guide to Quality Control*, Chapter 4.

[**EXHIBIT 4.19**]

Attribute Check Sheet with Order Arrival Time

Order Type	7 a.m.–9 a.m.	9 a.m.–11 a.m.	11 a.m.–1 p.m.	1 p.m.–3 p.m.	3 p.m.–5 p.m.	Sum
Emergency order	✓✓✓✓✓✓✓✓		✓		✓✓✓✓✓✓	15
Nonemergency order	✓✓✓✓✓✓	✓✓✓✓✓✓✓✓✓	✓✓✓✓✓✓✓✓✓	✓✓✓✓✓✓✓✓✓	✓✓✓✓✓✓✓✓✓	42
Rework	✓✓✓✓✓✓✓✓✓✓	✓✓	✓✓✓✓	✓✓✓	✓✓✓✓✓✓✓✓✓	28
Safety stock	✓✓	✓✓	✓	✓✓✓	✓✓	12
Prototype job			✓✓✓	✓✓✓	✓	7
Other	✓	✓✓		✓✓		5
	27	15	19	20	28	109

with the machine operator and the area supervisor, managers identified the following order categories: emergency customer orders, routine customer orders, rework (correcting defects in previously processed orders), safety stock orders (to fill inventory as protection against stockouts in times of unusually high demand), prototype orders (initial production of new designs), and other orders that do not fit in any of the designated categories.

Over the 1-week data collection period, the machine processed 109 jobs. After the largest category, routine customer orders, the machine processed large numbers of rework and emergency orders. Since rework to correct earlier mistakes fails to add value, the data might alert managers about a potential problem that merits further study. The check sheet provides a histogram that shows graphically the distribution of the machine's work load among job types. Finally, the information for this check sheet could support a Pareto analysis, since three of the six categories (routine customer orders, rework, and emergency orders) account for 78 percent of all work on the machine.

Exhibit 4.19 recasts this attribute check sheet to show when orders arrived, providing insight into the timing of the work load. For example, emergency orders clearly tend to arrive at either the start or the end of the shift. Rework shows the same pattern. In contrast, routine customer orders tend to flow in at a constant rate.

Variable Check Sheets. Variable check sheets represent continuous data. For example, a variable check sheet could show how the jobs arriving at a machine vary by processing times. Suppose that a machine's processing time spans a continuous range from 12 minutes 15 seconds to 121 minutes 45 seconds. A variable check sheet can break down this kind of continuous data to allow comparisons between values. A 30-minute job takes twice as long as a 15-minute job. Putting continuous data into categories shows how many events took place within a certain time period. For example, we might have the following processing times: 16.43 min., 16.44 min., 12.34 min., 15.33 min., 14.36 min., 17.45 min., 20.33 min.,

Variable Check Sheet

Processing Time (Minutes)	Number of Jobs	Sum
0–15	✓✓✓✓✓	6
15–30	✓✓✓✓✓✓✓✓	11
30–45	✓✓✓✓✓✓✓✓✓✓✓	15
45–60	✓✓✓✓✓✓✓✓✓✓✓✓✓✓	21
60–75	✓✓✓✓✓✓✓✓✓✓✓✓	19
75–90	✓✓✓✓✓✓✓✓✓	14
90–105	✓✓✓✓✓✓✓✓✓✓✓	17
105–120	✓✓✓	3
>120	✓✓✓	3
		109

21.36 min., 18.25 min., 25.18 min., 11.50 min., and 19.15 min. We would have a problem interpreting this data. We could count the observations (12 observations) or rearrange the data, but it is still difficult to uncover the underlying patterns in the data. However, we can use 3 categories: less then 15 minutes, 15–20 minutes, greater than 20 minutes, to generate these categories:

< 15 minutes:	3
15–20 minutes:	6
> 20 minutes:	3

Most of the jobs (50 percent) fall in the 15- to 20-minute range. Processing times also appear to be symmetrical. Categorization helps to highlight the underlying distribution of data better than simply dealing with the raw data.

The variable check sheet in Exhibit 4.20 shows a fairly symmetrical, bell-shaped distribution of processing time. This shows that slightly over 73 percent of all jobs take between 15 minutes and 90 minutes. This tool divides up a continuous variable (time) into a number of discrete categories.

Location Check Sheets. This type of check sheet identifies the locations of events. It can indicate where defects appear on a diagram of a part, for example, or where to insert parts.

Development of a check sheet begins with a decision about its purpose. For example, the attribute check sheet in Exhibit 4.18 was designed simply to report on the distribution of orders by category. The check sheet in Exhibit 4.19 added columns for time periods to suit its purpose of illustrating the distribution of arrival times of different types of jobs. The second step is to choose among an attribute check sheet, a variable check sheet, and a location check sheet.

Next, the problem solver specifies categories of events to track. Developing an attribute check sheet involves identifying categories about which to collect information. For a variable check sheet, the problem solver divides the chosen continuous variable (time, distance, cost, etc.) into a manageable number of meaningful categories. For example, the variable check sheet in Exhibit 4.20 divided the total time interval into nine categories of 15 minutes each. The location check sheet must identify the items to be located.

In laying out and producing the final check sheet, the problem solvers should consult the workers who will fill in the data. A machine operator who will fill in a check sheet can provide valuable input to its design and arrangement.

Finally, managers must designate an appropriate time period over which to collect information, specifying a period long enough to gather data representative of typical behavior. They then implement the check sheet study, collecting and storing data for analysis by operations managers.

Model Building

Effective problem solving requires the operations manager to overcome several obstacles, many of them related to information. A great deal of information generally surrounds any decision, some relevant and some trivial or at least nonessential. Also, even with this wealth of information, the decision maker may lack some necessary data.

The lack of structure in a situation may present a second obstacle. Links between variables are often not apparent, leaving serious confusion over the causes of particular symptoms.

Models building can help operations managers to overcome many of the obstacles in their problem solving. A **model** is an abstract representation of reality that simplifies actual events or situations. An effective model can help a problem solver to answer several questions:

model
An abstract representation of reality that simplifies actual events or situations

- *What*   A model identifies important elements in a problem or situation, separating factors that decision makers should consider from those that they can ignore and exclude from the model.
- *How*   A model also helps to specify relationships between elements of a situation, especially causes and effects. Models often designate independent variables to represent causes of particular symptoms. Dependent variables represent events that are influenced by independent, causal variables.
- *Why*   Some models even explain reasons for the relationships between causes and effects.
- *Under what conditions*   Models specify conditions such as when events occur, where they occur, and who makes things happen.

Problem solvers can choose among many different types of models.

Physical Models versus Conceptual Models. The word *model* often evokes images of tiny versions of houses or factories, clay-images of car models, or scaled-down airplane forms in wind tunnel tests. These are examples of physical models. While operations managers do make and use physical models, they rely on con-

These managers are using a computer spreadsheet as a conceptual model. By manipulating data within the model, they can forecast the effects of change upon the real business system.   SOURCE   Robert Rathe/ Stock Boston

ceptual models more often. A conceptual model is an abstract representation of logical or mathematical relationships in some system or process.[24] Once a model specifies these relationships, changing one element causes changes in other relationships. This indicates that similar reactions will occur in the real situation, assuming that the model represents the real system accurately (i.e., the relationships behave in the same way and the model omits no major variables).

Problem solvers create some conceptual models explicitly to represent certain situations. They also use implicit models, intellectual frameworks and abstractions through which they try to understand the world around them and interpret and react to data; these implicit models are often referred to as *mental models.* Changes in such models become critical when they stimulate paradigm shifts like those discussed in Chapter 1.

Prescriptive versus Descriptive Models. Problem solvers develop models for different reasons. A prescriptive model might help them to formulate a problem and arrive at a feasible solution to close a gap between the current and desired future situations. In contrast, a descriptive model would simply illustrate or describe system behavior. A cause-and-effect diagram is a type of descriptive model.

Analytical versus Simulation Models. Some problems allow managers to formulate relationships between variables precisely using mathematical terms and equations, so that solving the equations indicates an optimal solution. Specifying mathematical equations to represent a real situation creates an analytical model. The discussion of trade-off analysis included several examples of analytical models.

Some complex systems defy efforts to develop cost-effective and solvable analytical models. For these cases, a problem solver might create a simulation, that is,

[24]Averill M. Law and W. David Kelton, *Simulation Modeling and Analysis,* 2d ed. (New York: McGraw-Hill, 1991), p. 5.

a numerical exercise that shows how specific inputs affect measures of output or performance.[25] This exercise can rely on pencil-and-paper or computer calculations. Spreadsheet programs or simulation software packages help with this work.

Benefits of Models. Every manager relies on models, both carefully constructed, explicit statements of relationships and implicit mental images of basic understandings. Managers use models for several reasons:

- Models help them to control and manipulate the large number of details that surround problems or issues. A model clarifies the distinction between critical elements that require close attention and extraneous factors that often distort or confuse real relationships between inputs and outputs.
- Models allow managers to experiment with changes to see what effects they would have in real life. Without models, managers would have to make changes in real systems, a time-consuming and expensive process with a high cost of failure. A poor decision can even force a firm out of business. In addition, with long real-life time intervals between cause and effect, weeks or months may pass before the effect of an action becomes evident. Finally, real systems do not allow managers to control all aspects of a situation (e.g., worker reactions, competitors' actions, and economic conditions), potentially confusing or confounding observed results. In contrast, a change in a model that identifies a poor solution costs only the time and effort to manipulate the model.
- Models can help problem solvers to evaluate the effectiveness and efficiency of various alternatives, separating poor solutions from better ones.
- Models can improve communications, as managers often discuss systems using models. For example, this chapter discussed the problem-solving process by developing a model that set out the sequence of steps to follow to identify and respond to a problem.
- Models help to focus information-gathering activities. By identifying the key factors of a real situation, a model directs managers' attention to information that they need to make decisions.

Models are basic to operations management. Discussions of inventory, scheduling, and quality all rely on models. Managers use them to set inventory levels, design factory layouts, and identify the most appropriate levels of quality or lead times for a product. Effective operations managers must become good model builders.

Building a Model. The basic process for building a model involves addressing four questions:

1. What real-life problem must the model builder solve? The answer to this question identifies the scope of the model and its purpose.
2. What elements of the real situation are important and how are they related? The answer to this question specifies what the model must represent and how it must portray that information. The choice of key elements to model depends on the real-world problem or objective.
3. What data does the model require? An effective model must include certain inputs for independent variables, and collected data must accurately measure key elements.

---

[25]Law and Kelton, *Simulation Modeling and Analysis*, p. 6.

4. What major assumptions (implicit and explicit) does the model make? Are those assumptions reasonable? The answers to these questions determine how much the solutions or descriptions implied by the model depend on potentially faulty assumptions.

Whenever you must build a model, either as part of an exercise in this book or as a real-world decision maker, the answers to these questions can help you to evaluate your model and its effectiveness.

 APPLIANCE PARK REVISITED

The story at the beginning of this chapter related the near closure in 1992 of the washing machine production facility at GE's Appliance Park plant. Loss of the factory would have meant a devastating loss of some 1,500 jobs in Louisville. By 1994, however, everyone involved saw Appliance Park as a "classic transformation."[26] To turn around this facility, GE managers such as Richard Stonesifer, the head of the appliance operation, and Richard Burke, the manufacturing boss, studied a range of potential causes for the symptoms they observed and narrowed the list to target three areas for changes:

- Labor relations
- Inventory/manufacturing costs
- Product designs

Labor Relations

Appliance Park had been known as "Strike City, USA." Richard Burke set out to improve poor labor relations by forging a working relationship with Norman Mitchell, the president of Local 761 of the International Union of Electronics Workers. Together, they decided to work to move away from a situation described by Mitchell as "We'd kick them, then they'd kick us." Success would achieve survival of the operation and continued jobs for GE workers.

Both sides agreed to implement a 43-point program that incorporated a number of innovations, beginning with the introduction of work teams with strong voices in operational decisions. For example, when workers noted quality problems in supplied parts, they could complain directly to the suppliers. The new agreement eliminated piecework pay and stretched job definitions to reduce the number of classifications from 65 to 3, allowing workers to move freely between different jobs in the plant. Team decision making allowed GE to cut the number of supervisors.

Inventory/Manufacturing Costs

Together, management and the union attacked manufacturing costs with the goal of chopping them by about $60 million a year. They achieved this goal in part by reducing inventory requirements, raising inventory turnover from 5 times a year to 11 and saving some $500 million in working capital.

[26]James R. Norman, "A Very Nimble Elephant," *Forbes*, October 10, 1994, pp. 88–92.

Product Design

The working capital released by the reduction in manufacturing costs was spent on new product designs amounting to some $1 billion since 1992. In 1994 and 1995, for example, GE planned to introduce between 300 to 400 new appliance models, many targeted at specific markets and backed by major advertising campaigns. For example, GE aimed its Profile line of appliances at affluent customers with features such as soft handles on refrigerators, extra-large ovens in ranges, and fold-down racks in dishwashers. To save Appliance Park, GE became a master of niche marketing.

Far from closing down part of Appliance Park, GE hired some 700 new employees to handle the increased business, the first major hiring in over a decade. The changes turned a loss of $47 million in 1992 to a profit of $40 million in 1994 and a projected profit of $80 million in 1995. The firm planned to continue raising operating profits from 10 percent in 1994 to 15 percent annually over the following 3 years.

The Appliance Park case illustrates effective management problem solving. The turnaround required decision makers to differentiate carefully among causes, symptoms, problems, and effects. Then, with the help of the union and workers, they developed appropriate solutions and successfully implemented them.

 ## CHAPTER SUMMARY

In this chapter, we have explored the role of the operations manager as a manager, a decision maker, and a problem solver. We have examined the wider activity of management, its application to OM decisions, and the process of problem solving. Finally, we have presented the valuable techniques in the Operations Management Toolkit. This discussion has emphasized many important topics:

1. Operations managers must oversee the transformation process to ensure that it produces useful and desirable outputs that offer value to customers in the firm's targeted market segment.
2. Management is the process of directing resources and organizing activities to achieve corporate and organizational objectives. This work includes five interrelated activities: planning, analyzing, organizing, directing/implementing, and controlling.
3. In planning, a manager decides what to do. Good planning provides important preparation for good execution.
4. Managers formulate three different types of plans: strategic plans, operating plans, and tactical plans.
5. Analyzing is the process of making sense of information that is often ill-structured, inaccurate, or incomplete. Analyzing works to correct problems in an OM system or the firm or to eliminate the causes of the problem.
6. Organizing is the process of providing structure and assigning resources to achieve the goals set in planning and analyzing.
7. Directing/implementing carries out the plans that managers formulate in their planning, analyzing, and organizing activities.
8. Controlling measures the results of directing/implementing, compares these results with expected results, and takes necessary corrective actions.
9. Management is changing. Increasingly, managers are acting as team leaders and sharing information and decision-making authority. The new manager is a coordinator rather than a commander.

Value-Driven OM Decision Process

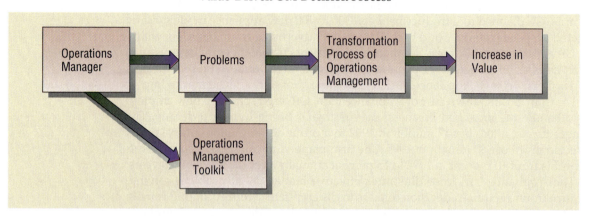

10. Effective problem solvers recognize the differences among symptoms (indicators of problems with a system), problems (perceived gaps between the current and desired future situations), causes (conditions that create problems), and solutions (actions designed to close gaps between the current and desired future situations).

11. Operations managers encounter eight basic types of problems: queuing problems, allocation problems, inventory problems, sequencing problems, routing problems, replacement problems, competition problems, and search problems.

12. To respond to a problem, a manager can *solve* it (follow the best solution), *resolve* it (follow a solution that will correct the situation well enough), or *dissolve* it (eliminate the original causes of the problem).

13. Operations managers can rely on a rather standard process to solve their firms' problems in five major steps: size-up/description, problem statement/diagnostics, analysis, prescription/alternatives, and implementation.

14. Operations managers use techniques from the Operations Management Toolkit to complete the problem-solving process; these techniques include total cost analysis, trade-off analysis, the Deming cycle, cause-and-effect analysis, Pareto analysis, check sheets, and model building. Each of these tools provides a method for structuring problems and focusing attention on critical elements.

15. Ultimately operations management consists of a process of enhancing the value created by the transformation process. (See Exhibit 4.21.)

[**K E Y   T E R M S**]

[DISCUSSION QUESTIONS]

1. Assume that a recently deceased relative's will leaves you a Burger Queen restaurant in Nutley, New Jersey. Your experience in this business is limited to a 6-month stint as a McDonald's French fry cook and a lifetime of chomping hamburgers. Based on what you have learned in this chapter, prepare a list of the management activities that you will have to master as the new owner of the restaurant.

2. Illustrate the activities of each of the five functions of management at GE's Appliance Park. If you feel that you lack certain facts, make assumptions to develop a likely story. How would you measure the effectiveness of each activity that you describe?

3. Think about a structured problem that you have faced and an unstructured one. Clearly define each problem in a short paragraph, describing the current situation when you recognized the problem and the future situation that you desired at that time. What symptoms might someone have mistaken for the real problem? How should you have measured progress toward solving each problem?

4. The opening story in Chapter 1 described how Compaq's CEO assigned two employees to a secret research project without telling their managers or the other top managers. Which of Fayol's 14 principles of management did this move violate? Were the CEO's actions acceptable?

5. Discuss how emerging telecommunications technology is affecting management practices in American businesses. If Henri Fayol were alive today, do you think that he would approve or disapprove of these emerging changes in management structure?

6. Within the past few years, you may have decided to enter a particular college. How might you have made this decision using the five-stage problem-solving process described in this chapter?

7. A college student must normally declare a major. Use this decision as an example to illustrate the structure of the problem-solving process described in this chapter. How might that process have helped you make this decision? How could the process be improved to help you make this decision?

8. Many college students complain that they cannot graduate in 4 years because they can't get into the necessary courses. Is this a symptom or a problem? Why? Which of the techniques in the Operations Management Toolkit would you choose to identify or explain the true problem? Illustrate the application of this tool to the problem.

9. A book publisher allows students to choose whether to purchase a new, nicely bound textbook for $65, a loose-leaf, unbound version for $35, or a used book for about $50. At the end of the semester, the bookstore will pay you 60 percent of the price of a bound book that you bought new, 40 percent for one that you purchased used, and nothing for a loose-leaf version. Write a total cost analysis equation that will identify the least-cost alternative. What other information would you want to make this decision?

10. In the table below, cite an illustration of each type of problem in a service company and a manufacturer:

Problem Type	Service Example	Manufacturing Example
Queuing problem		
Allocation problem		
Inventory problem		
Sequencing problem		
Routing problem		
Replacement problem		
Competition problem		

Which quantitative tools should managers use to study each problem?

11. Select two of the problems you listed for Question 10 and explain how company managers might solve, resolve, and dissolve the problems.
12. A firm must choose between two manufacturing alternatives. It estimates demand for the product of 100,000 units, plus or minus 20,000 units. The relevant costs for the two proposed alternatives are:

	Alternative 1	Alternative 2
Unit revenue	$ 0.50 per unit	$ 0.50 per unit
Direct material	0.20 per unit	0.15 per unit
Direct labor	0.10 per unit	0.05 per unit
Variable overhead	0.05 per unit	0.05 per unit
Fixed overhead per year (including depreciation)	10,000	25,000

   a. Determine the break-even volume for each alternative.
   b. Determine the profitability of each alternative at sales of 80,000, 100,000, and 120,000 units.
   c. What other issues might you consider in deciding between the alternatives?
13. Student absenteeism may be a problem in one of your classes. Develop a check sheet to help reveal the reason for the absenteeism. The check sheet might track attributes such as the student's seating location within the class, gender, the day of the week, or whatever you think might be important.
14. Prepare a cause-and-effect diagram to explain why you did not do well in some endeavor. This diagram could explain your performance in a course, an exam, a marriage, or a job situation. How could this analysis help you to understand your performance?
15. In sports, winners are determined by game scores. Select one sport and use performance statistics reported on your local newspaper's sports page for at least 25 games to explain why one team outperformed others. Avoid obvious data such as a baseball team's runs scored or a basketball team's field goals made. Specify which tools or techniques discussed in this chapter helped your analysis.
16. Prepare a cause-and-effect diagram to explore possible reasons why most individuals eat three meals each day.

C A U T I O N

[CRITICAL THINKING REQUIRED]

1. Of the management tools discussed in this chapter, which one or ones have you used most in your life, perhaps without knowing that you were using problem-solving techniques? Why have you relied on those techniques? Have you found it easy or difficult to explain your analysis to others? Why?
2. Explain your view of the influence of computers and information networks on management techniques for identifying, analyzing, and solving problems.

CASE 4.1

Down on the Line

Hanna muttered to herself on the way to her boss's assignment to, "Go down to the rework line and find out what is causing our final-assembly quality problems." With a B.S. degree in management, she had to stand with a clipboard and assess the defects of each rework unit as it came to the line. She knew, however, that her boss was under pressure due to growing quality problems on the final-assembly line. The company's top managers really didn't understand or care about shop-floor operations. One said, "Assembly is just making big things out of small ones—what is so difficult about that?"

After watching the line operation for a while, Hanna decided to collect some data. On her clipboard, she noted the nature of each quality defect and the likely cause. In the first day, she found 100 defects on 86 units diverted to the rework area (since some had more than one observed defect), distributed as follows:

Defect	Assigned Cause	Number of Defects
Missed operations	Workmanship	13
Paint scratches	Workmanship	9
Wrong part installed	Production control	12
Part failure	Purchasing/ vendor	2
Sheet metal gaps	Workmanship	11
Misalignment	Workmanship	6

Obviously, workmanship was a good place to start.

Armed with this data, Hanna approached Henry, the line supervisor, and received a somewhat defensive response: "These defects aren't really the responsibility of my people! We get all the blame, but you ought to see the stuff we have to work with. Of course, there are gaps and misalignment, but you ought to talk to the fabrication shop about that." He attributed the missed operations and paint scratches to workers rushing to keep up with the fast pace of the assembly line. "Sure, we could keep up if everything fit together well, but that just isn't always true," he said.

Hanna then went to see Holly, fabrication shop supervisor, who agreed that some of the department's output "may occasionally be a tad off spec." She argued, however, that the company had to expect variation with the unreasonable quality specifications set by engineers and the old tools and equipment the workers had to use. Also, she complained, "half the time production control is sending us rush orders and we are making the parts out of the closest thing we have to part specifications. And those paint scratches aren't happening here. We get them that way from our suppliers." Hanna shook her head and continued on to purchasing.

The purchasing manager, Horace, was delighted to see that top management finally was addressing the problem. He was tired of taking the heat when the people in receiving really had the responsibility of assuring that suppliers delivered parts that met specifications. Surface finish specs left no excuse for paint scratches, assuming, Horace hinted, that parts really were arriving with scratches.

Hanna suspected that her hunt was futile, so she decided to hold a meeting involving all of the area supervisors. Hanna has asked you, her good friend, how to conduct the meeting and any subsequent problem-solving program.

QUESTIONS

1. What advice would you give Hanna?
2. Which of the tools and techniques discussed in this chapter might help her? Why?

CASE 4.2

Cadence Design Systems

Joe Costello, the chief executive officer of Cadence Design Systems, had a problem. While microchip sales had begun to skyrocket in the early 1990s, sales of his firm's electronic design-automation systems seemed to be stagnating. In 1992, gross sales of $418 million and net income of $55.4 million made Cadence the market leader in the market for electronic design-automation equipment. In 1993, however, sales declined to $368.6 million, resulting in a $12.8 million loss.

After considerable soul searching, Costello concluded that the problem lay more with the firm's organizational structure than with its technology. The firm's one-size-fits-all approach had worked well in the past, but he sensed that standardization was driving a wedge between employees and valued customers. Customer satisfaction had declined and some of the customers' wrath was falling on the firm's best design engineers.

The nature of Cadence's product did not help matters. Whereas Microsoft *Windows* for the PC requires 3 million lines of software code, one of Cadence's microprocessor-design systems might take 30 million lines of code. Also, each major customer's program was requiring increasing customization. Cadence's customer service engineers were frustrated by their inability to adequately solve or resolve customers' technical questions and complaints. One said that he spent 75 percent of his time responding to customer complaints, and most wanted to return to their old system-design jobs.

Costello decided to reassign Cadence's technical experts to consulting teams and make them become integral parts of customers' product-design teams. They helped each customer to create a suitable mix of standard and custom design tools, trained designers how to use the tools, and turned customers' factories into efficient product-innovation systems, for which they coined the term *design factories*. As one Cadence application engineer said, "Before we were more like water boys than quarterbacks. Now we're part of the team."

The new role created a win-win situation for both Cadence staffers and customers. Cadence applications engineers became consultants to customers' design engineers, ensuring that they were using the right electronic design-automation tools. In this position, the Cadence reps could quiz customers to keep the product lines targeted correctly and to help customers use the products effectively.

Cadence created an image of knowing all the answers by developing expertise in the area of customers' needs. Their work with customers helps Cadence applications engineers to advise its design people to keep their work focused on developing new products capable of meeting the market's future needs.

These organizational changes returned Cadence to growth and profitability, According to Dataquest, it now has 18.4 percent of the $1.8 billion market for electronic design-automation systems. Recently, it won a $75 million, 5-year contract to take over internal chip-design work for Unisys at Rancho Bernardo, California. Cadence no longer thinks of itself as a maker of design-automation tools; it plans to become the market's premier provider of chip-design services.

QUESTIONS

1. Describe Joe Costello's problem-solving method.
2. How has Cadence's value equation changed? What caused the changes?
3. What risks does each party take in the Unisys deal?

[S E L E C T E D   R E A D I N G S]

Ackoff, Russell L., and Patrick Rivett. *A Manager's Guide to Operations Research.* New York: John Wiley & Sons, 1967.

Ackoff, Russell L. *The Art of Problem Solving.* New York: John Wiley & Sons, 1978.

Carlzon, Jan. *Moments of Truth.* New York: Harper & Row, 1987.

De Bono, Edward. *Six Thinking Hats.* Boston, Mass.: Little, Brown, 1985.

Deming, W. Edwards. *Out of the Crisis.* Cambridge, Mass.: MIT Center for Advanced Engineering Study, 1986.

Drucker, Peter F. *The Practice of Management.* New York: Harper & Row, 1954.

Dumaine, Brian. "The New Non-Manager Managers." *Fortune,* February 22, 1993, pp. 80–84.

Evans, James R. *Creative Thinking in the Decision and Management Sciences.* Cincinnati, Ohio: South-Western, 1991.

Fayol, Henri. *Industrial and General Administration.* Trans. by J. A. Coubrough. Geneva, Switz.: International Management Institute, 1930.

Gitlow, Howard, Shelley Gitlow, Alan Oppenheim, and Rosa Oppenheim. *Tools and Methods for the Improvement of Quality.* Homewood, Ill.: Richard D. Irwin, 1989.

Ishikawa, Kaoru. *Guide to Quality Control.* White Plains, N.Y.: Quality Resources, 1985.

Law, Averill M., and W. David Kelton. *Simulation Modeling and Analysis,* 2d ed. New York: McGraw-Hill, 1991.

Schwenk, Charles, and Howard Thomas. "Formulating the Mess: The Role of Decision Aids in Problem Formulation." *OMEGA: The International Journal of Management Science* 11, no. 3 (1983), pp. 239–262.

VanGundy, Arthur B. *Techniques of Structured Problem Solving.* New York: Van Nostrand Reinhold, 1981.

Wagner, John A., and John R. Hollenbeck. *Management of Organizational Behavior.* Englewood Cliffs, N.J.: Prentice-Hall, 1992.

Winwood, Richard I. *Time Management.* Salt Lake City, Utah: Franklin Institute, 1990.

PART THREE

Value as a Driver of OM Systems

CHAPTER FIVE

Processes
The Building Blocks of the Value-Driven OM System

CHAPTER OUTLINE

CHAPTER OBJECTIVES
[At the end of this chapter, you should be able to]

- Define *process* and list the major categories of activities in all OM processes.
- Identify the types of outputs that all processes generate.
- Explain the relationship between capacity (expressed as a volume measure) and the operation of a process.
- Illustrate the role of a bottleneck in a process.
- Outline the key OM processes and discuss the transformation process in detail.
- Apply process flow analysis to document and analyze the structure and operation of a process.
- Demonstrate how benchmarking helps operations managers to assess current conditions and direct change.
- Show how business process reengineering (BPR) can improve the effectiveness and efficiency of a process.

Courtesy of IBM
Corporation

Humanizing the Process at IBM Austin

IN THE 1980S, PLANTS LIKE IBM'S
manufacturing complex in Austin, Texas, rushed to install robots in an
effort to reduce labor costs. In the 1990s, they're tearing out the robots
and putting the people back in. "We found that when you designed a
process so simply that a robot could do it, a human can do it even faster
and more flexibly," explained Pedro Berdion, an IBM consultant.

In an age when "agility" and "flexibility" have become the new
corporate catchwords, companies have rediscovered the value of their
people. Robots lock a manufacturing system into a fixed configuration,
but people can be trained to do a variety of different processes.
Companies like IBM used to look first to technology and expensive
machinery to solve their problems. Now they're closely examining
underlying processes and redesigning them from the ground up,
putting humans as the central component.

To prepare for its radical restructuring a few years ago, IBM Austin
mapped all steps associated with developing a product. This helped
analysts simplify the process and eliminate redundant steps. They then
found vital points where agreements were achieved and decisions were
made. They charted these points and discussed them with everyone
from line workers on up.

> By giving its line workers the big picture, IBM Austin has made them partners in its efforts to become more competitive. This kind of worker participation pays off on a basic day-to-day level. Now if an assembly line gets loaded with the wrong parts, workers are able to spot it in a matter of minutes. In the old days, such a mistake might have gone past the plant's automated inspection equipment until thousands of defective circuit boards were made.
>
> By creatively combining processes like manufacturing and inspection, IBM Austin has become a model for other American manufacturers. In the new competitive atmosphere of the global marketplace, technology and markets are changing continuously, and companies need to design processes that can respond quickly to these changes in customer needs. They're finding out that developing a top-notch, well-trained work force is the key to their success.

SOURCE
Jon Van, "Involved at IBM: Errors Drop after Workers Get Big Picture," *Chicago Tribune,* July 26, 1992, Section 7, pp. 1–2.

IBM Austin highlights processes as the fundamental building blocks of operations management. Processes link activities, consume resources, and define and shape the exact type of value offered by every OM system and ultimately every firm. Managers of an effective value-driven OM system know that they can change its behavior or the characteristics of its products only by altering its underlying processes. This makes operations management a process-driven activity. In the text we explore in detail the link between process and value.

PROCESSES IN THE OM SYSTEM

People deal with OM processes every day, whether or not they notice. At a restaurant, a server offers a menu and takes the diner's order as part of the ordering process. The manufacturing process in the kitchen prepares the order. Finally, the order delivery process moves the food from the kitchen to the table.

Although processes are central to a company's success, since they determine how it delivers value to the customer, still they stir deep confusion in many managers. Processes involve activities, but they are not the same as activities. Processes draw on structures and resources, but they are not simply structures or collections of resources. A **process** is a collection of activities that transforms inputs into an output that offers value to the customer.[1] This definition emphasizes six major traits:

1. A process is a collection of activities.
2. A process transforms inputs (physical resources and information) into outputs (goods, services, or information).
3. Structure and capacity determine the resources that the process requires to accomplish its transformation, making issues such as bottlenecks important.

process

A collection of activities that transform inputs into an output that offers value to the customer

---

[1]Michael Hammer and James Champy, *Reengineering the Corporation* (New York: Harper Business, 1993), p. 35.

[EXHIBIT 5.1]

Five Major Categories of Process Activities

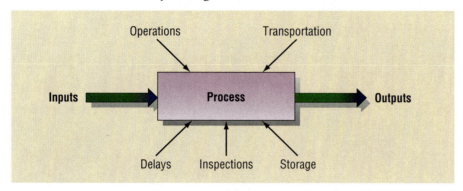

4. A process creates an output which can range from delivery of an existing product through design and delivery of a new product to generation of information.
5. Managers evaluate a process based on the level of value (measured by time, quality, cost, and flexibility) that it generates. Techniques for measuring performance are called *metrics.*
6. Processes are linked to other processes both vertically and horizontally, making them interdependent. This creates a need for careful attention to the interfaces between processes.

Categories of Activities within a Process

In a process, many things may happen at once. To construct one circuit board, the IBM Austin process had to identify and locate the right parts, move them to the assembly line, assemble them, verify that the assembled board worked, and then move it on to the next operation. These activities fall into five distinct categories (Exhibit 5.1):

- Operation
- Transportation
- Inspection
- Delay
- Storage

Operation. An **operation** is any activity that causes a change or transformation to an input. Operations occur whenever:

- *An activity intentionally changes one or more of the major traits of an input.* An operation to assemble a circuit board changes it by adding components and make the board resemble its desired end state more closely.
- *Information is communicated.* An operation might retrieve information for building a circuit board from a corporate database or identify the necessary parts to build a circuit board.
- *Planning or calculations occur.* An operation might determine how many circuit boards to build over the next week or month.

operation
A process activity that causes a change or transformation to an input

By loading these finished products onto the truck, this worker is aiding in the transportation process. The process will be complete when the truck delivers the finished product to the customer.   SOURCE Richard Pasley/Stock Boston

Operations are the major sources of value in nearly all systems. They also generate waste.

transportation

A process activity that moves an object

Transportation.   Transportation is any activity that moves an object from one place to another. A transportation activity changes only the location of a part without transforming its characteristics. A transportation activity might ship a completed circuit board from the IBM Austin plant to a customer in Tennessee. A move is not considered a transportation activity, however, when it is an integral part of an operation or inspection. For example, as part of an operation to assemble a circuit board, a worker might pick up a batch of chips and move them to the work area.

inspection

A process activity that checks or verifies the results of another activity

Inspection.   **An **inspection activity checks or verifies the results of another activity. An inspection might examine a part to identify it as the right one or compare it against a standard. Employees at the IBM Austin plant conduct inspections through an automated system that checks the quality of the parts.

Standards that guide inspection activities can take several different forms:

1. *Internally generated standards*   An inspection might compare actual production times against standard times calculated as part of the company's cost accounting process.
2. *Externally generated standards*   Parties outside the firm can set standards, including customers, the government, or official organizations (e.g., Underwriters Laboratories). The International Standards Organization (ISO) Standards are discussed in Chapters 7 and 8.
3. *Benchmarking standards*   Benchmarking is a technique, discussed later in the chapter, by which managers base their own performance standards on those of other firms with the best practices in some area of company operations.

delay

A process activity that results from interference with the process

Delay.   **A **delay is an activity that results from interference with the process. For example, an order may have to wait at a machine because other, more urgent orders displace it. The machine must finish processing the other orders before

[**EXHIBIT 5.2**]

Indicators of the Five Categories of Activities

Process Classification	Major Action/Result
Operation	Produce, do, accomplish, make, use
Transportation	Move, change location
Inspection	Verify, check, make sure, measure
Delay	Interfere, temporary stop
Storage	Keep, safeguard

completing the new order. A delay may also occur while an order waits for the arrival of other information or goods. A delay would occur when a circuit board has to wait for a late deliver of microchips. An unanticipated problem like a machine breakdown or accident can also cause a temporary delay. In these situations, a delay is a temporary stoppage. It describes a good or service temporarily at rest.

Storage. **Storage** is an activity that places an item under some kind of control so that access requires appropriate authorization. Storage activities can place tools or materials in stock rooms located on the shop floor; they can also represent warehousing or placing items in holding/receiving areas.

A storage is any activity in which an item is kept under control. To get access to this activity requires that appropriate authorization. For example, whenever you put money in a bank, what you have done is to put the money into storage. Why? Because if you want to get your money out, you need to first give the teller at the bank a withdrawal form. This withdrawal form can take the form of a withdrawal slip, a check, or an ATM (Automated Teller Machine) transaction. Without the appropriate authorization, the bank will not release any money to you.

Storage resembles a delay, but they differ in the need for control. Storage must include control of an item; if the same item sits uncontrolled awaiting use, the activity amounts to a delay. Inventory of a microchip in an IBM stockroom represents storage rather than a delay because access to it requires authorization, perhaps indicated by a pick ticket (a document that authorizes the holder to withdraw a specific item from stock for use in production). That same microchip meets a delay as it waits in a bin near a machine that will install it in a circuit board.

These five categories can classify nearly every activity in any process. A later section of this chapter describes their essential role in a valuable management technique, process flow analysis. To assign categories to unusual activities that seem to fall outside these limits, refer to the word associations listed in Exhibit 5.2.

Inputs, Outputs, and Processes

Activities in the five categories link the inputs of a process to its outputs. These links create a structure designed to manage and control flows. Efforts to understand a process must begin with its flows, inputs, and structure.

Flows. Most systems consist of two basic types of resource flows: information flows and physical flows. **Information flows** result from efforts to manage data

storage
A process activity that places an item under some kind of control

information flow
An exchange of data that supports efforts to manage a process

within a process. These efforts create and distribute a predictable range of information exchanges:

- *Order status exchanges*   Information flows when people ask and answer questions about the locations in the process of particular orders and their placement in the work schedule.
- *Order definition exchanges*   Some information exchanges relate to necessary activities, components, and design criteria to complete an order.
- *Work flow exchanges*   Information flows specify the necessary operations to build a product and their exact sequence.
- *Order evaluation exchanges*   A process carries information about its performance and how well its products have met or exceeded expectations.

Information flows form critical communication links both internally (between the OM system and other company functions) and externally (between the firm and its customers and suppliers).

physical flow

A movement of tangible inputs through the activities of a process to become outputs

Physical flows carry tangible inputs like materials and components through the activities of a process to become outputs. Physical flows create visible, tangible movement through process work stations, as when a circuit board moves along a production line. In contrast, information flows move invisibly.

Activities in the five categories described earlier (operation, transportation, inspection, delay, and storage) affect both information and physical flows. Activities might store information in a database, check it for accuracy, move it by fax, computer network, or electronic data interchange (EDI) system. Operations managers control both kinds of flows to keep processes transforming inputs into outputs.

Inputs.   Inputs are resources that either initiate process activities or contribute to the transformation that makes products for customers. Activities use some inputs directly, as when a microchip becomes part of a circuit board. They use other inputs indirectly, as when equipment or a building contribute to the transformation without becoming part of the final product.

Even a simple process relies on a wide and extremely complex range of inputs, some more apparent than others:

- *Materials*   Materials can be anything from steel in a car's body panels to staples that hold together the production orders that set the schedule for the car's production.
- *Energy*   Many process activities require power such as electricity as an input.
- *Information*   Operations managers need inputs of product-specific and process-specific information. Product-specific information describes how to create the firm's product or service (i.e., its parts, the order in which the process needs them, and the sequence of operations). Process-specific information describes the capabilities and limitations of the current process (i.e., available machine hours and labor hours, functions of available equipment, skills of employees) and the current or projected work load of that capacity.

  Knowledge, the expertise of line employees, customer service personnel, managers, and even customers and suppliers, is an essential part of the information input to a process. Knowledge often plays a critical role in improving either the product or the process. Chapters 6 and 19 discuss this resource in more detail.
- *Management*   Efforts of company personnel to plan, analyze, organize, direct, and control the transformation process represent process inputs.

[**EXHIBIT 5.3**]

Sequential Positioning of Activities

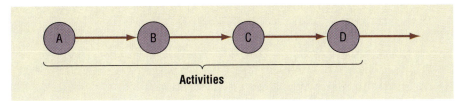

Activities

- *Technology* This term describes the system of physical means by which the OM system generates the goods and services it needs.[2] In other words, technology consists of all the equipment, automation, computers, and similar tools used by the process. Technology includes hard automation (specialized equipment) and soft automation (flexible, easily reprogrammable equipment).
- *Facilities* Facilities are the buildings, other structures, and grounds that house process activities.
- *Labor* Every process requires inputs of human resources, either directly or indirectly, to carry out process activities.
- *Drivers* A process cannot operate without specific objectives and directions to drive its activities. For example, drivers determine the volume of product a process builds, the mix of products, the timing of process activities, order arrival rates, and standards for quality, cost, lead time, and flexibility that the product must meet or exceed. Drivers describe what the customers want and govern the firm's allocation of resources among its orders. Ultimately, drivers move a process from rest into action.

Structure. Structure deals with the organization of inputs, activities, and outputs of a process. Operations managers define this structure by ordering activities, positioning them, and linking them.

Ordering Activities. Activities rarely occur randomly. Some must occur before others for the process to flow smoothly. The requirements of the process determine this precedence or sequence of activities. For example, a cook must make pancake batter before cooking it on the griddle. A process that can operate only in a specific sequence requires **strict precedence**; the cook cannot possibly make pancakes before preparing the batter.

    Other activities can occur in more than one sequence, allowing **nonstrict precedence**. For example, an IBM assembly process could insert microchips in many different sequences. Whether a process requires strict or nonstrict precedence of activities, operations managers must order activities carefully to achieve effective performance measured by lead time, cost, quality, and flexibility.

Positioning Activities. Ordering determines the sequence of activities over an entire process, while positioning organizes activities in relation to each other. A process can position most activities either sequentially or in parallel. Sequential positioning places activities one after another, as in Exhibit 5.3. A pancake cook

strict precedence
A particular sequence of activities that a process needs to flow smoothly

nonstrict precedence
An order of process activities that allows more than one sequence

[2]Steven A. Melnyk and Ram Narasimhan, *Computer-Integrated Manufacturing: Guidelines and Applications from Industrial Leaders* (Homewood, Ill.: Business One-Irwin, 1992), p. 332

[EXHIBIT 5.4]

Parallel Positioning of Activities

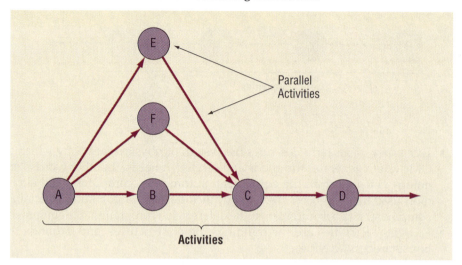

might position activities sequentially, opening the recipe book, gathering the ingredients, mixing them, cooking the batter on the griddle, and delivering the pancakes to the waiting customer. Sequential positioning gives a total process lead time equal to the sum of the lead times of the individual activities.

Sequential positioning also limits the responsiveness of a process when it must cope with changes. Any change must often be introduced at the initial activity and carry in sequence through all of the other activities. In addition, when a problem caused early in the process becomes evident only later, correcting it requires returning to the activity where the problem was created and moving the solution back through each later step.

In contrast, parallel positioning organizes activities to occur simultaneously as much as possible, as illustrated in Exhibit 5.4. For example, the pancake cook might organize the cooking and consumption activities in parallel so customers can eat one batch while the next is cooking. Parallel positioning tends to reduce lead times, determining total process lead time by the sequence of activities with the longest lead time (often referred to as a *bottleneck*).

Linking Activities.   Links result from the relationships created as activities are positioned. A **spatial link** represents the distance, measured in feet, meters, inches, or similar units, between two activities. Locating two related activities closer to one another should reduce the time needed to move components, tools, or other resources between them.

Physical links represent tangible connections between related activities. For example, an automobile assembly line physically links activities by placing work stations in a specific configuration and moving cars past them in a set order. Physical links often reduce lead time. Also, lead time shows less variability (the difference between actual lead times and their means) because the physical connections allow little or no diversion from the standard sequence. After the initial expense of building a physically linked production line (a fixed cost), it can also generate lower variable costs than less tightly linked processes.

spatial link

The distance between two related activities

physical link

A tangible connection between related activities

Determinants of Process Performance

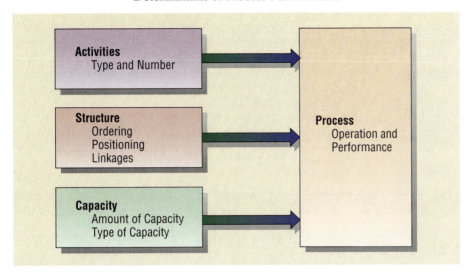

Physical links also limit flexibility, however. If some change requires activities to occur in a different sequence, one must often change physical links, tearing up existing production lines and building new ones. This consumes considerable time and money.

The performance of any process depends substantially on the resource flows defined by links between activities and their sequence. Inputs also have significant effects. The capacity of the process joins with these elements to determine the performance of a process. (See Exhibit 5.5.)

CAPACITY AND PROCESS

An earlier chapter discussed capacity as both the volume of output that a transformation process can produce and the specialized capabilities of the process. This section discusses the effects of capacity as output volume; later chapters will discuss specific capabilities in more detail.

Capacity affects process performance because it determines the resources available to all activities. A circuit board assembly operation needs capacity like tools, machines, and labor; a transportation activity to move a batch of parts needs a pallet or a cart; a storage activity needs floor space, storage shelves, a clerk, and inventory for a stock room. Exhibit 5.6 gives examples of the capacity needs of the five types of activities.

The productive benefits of resources are limited by their capacities: the number of hours of machine time available, the number of parts that a cart can carry, the floor space in a stock room. The speed of an activity bears an especially strong relationship to capacity; insufficient capacity can substantially increase lead time, as when an activity to transport 30 parts must use a cart that can carry only 20, forcing a worker to make two trips.

Capacity limits are also significant sources of delay in processes. A delay occurs whenever an order must wait for access to a limited resource to continue

[**EXHIBIT 5.6**]

Capacity Needs of Process Activities

Process Activity	Associated Capacity
Operation	Tools, labor, machine capacity
Transportation	Pallets, carts, fork-lift trucks, trucks, trains
Inspection	Inspectors, inspection stations, gages, robots or machine-vision equipment
Delay	Space on shop floor, bins, carts, racks, computer disks
Storage	Floor space, racks, bins, stockroom clerks, computer disk

moving through the process. Finite capacity may create competition for limited resources, forcing some demand on the process to wait and increasing lead time.

Calculating Capacity

Operations managers measure capacity as a rate of output per unit of time. Stated another way, capacity equals "the rate at which work is withdrawn from the system."[3] In other words, capacity is the volume of output that a process can produce in its operation or inspection activities, hold in its delay or storage activities, or carry in its transportation activities. This level of output can be measured by a figure for either resource availability (i.e., machine hours, labor hours, tools, or square feet of floor space available) or potential output (number of parts that the process can produce, dollars worth of products it can produce, etc.).

maximum capacity

The largest amount of output that a process can generate; also called *design capacity*

Our method of calculating capacity focuses on the maximum capacity of a process, otherwise known as the *design capacity*.[4] **Maximum capacity** states the largest amount of output that a process can generate. Often this gives a theoretical upper limit rather than a practical level of production. The two-step procedure calculates the maximum capacity of any process by first calculating the capacity of its activities and then calculating the capacity of the entire process. The positioning or organization of activities has a powerful effect on the capacity calculation for the overall process.

Capacity Calculation in a Sequentially Positioned Process.   The capacity of a sequentially positioned process depends on that of the activity with the least capacity. This activity determines the maximum overall capacity since the process must pass through its capacity to reach completion.

Exhibit 5.7 shows a circuit board assembly process with four sequentially positioned operations. The maximum capacity for this process, 275 boards per hour, is based on the capacity of Operation C, which has the lowest capacity. Although Operation B can produce 125 more boards per hour, the process cannot exploit this excess capacity because Operation C can accept only 275 boards an hour.

---

[3]John H. Blackstone, Jr., *Capacity Management* (Cincinnati, Ohio: South-Western, 1989), p. 7.

[4]Later chapters will discuss two additional measures, effective capacity and demonstrated capacity. The linkage with capacity is discussed in Chapter 16.

[**E X H I B I T   5 . 7**]

Maximum Capacity in a Sequentially Positioned Process

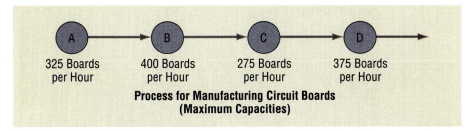

Process for Manufacturing Circuit Boards
(Maximum Capacities)

Capacity Calculation in a Parallel Positioned Process.   The maximum process capacity changes for operations organized in parallel. If the parallel tasks represent the same type of activity, then their cumulative capacity equals the sum of their individual capacities.

Exhibit 5.8 revises the circuit board assembly process to show a second operation made up of three parallel operations, each performing the same type of task. The total capacity for this second operation is not 90 boards (the single-operation minimum) but 400 boards (the sum of the capacities of Operations E, F, and B). The maximum capacity for the overall process remains at 275 boards per hour, however, because the work must still flow through Operation C.

Identifying the Bottlenecks.   By any method of calculating the capacities of activities, the capacity of any process is ultimately constrained by the capacity of

[**E X H I B I T   5 . 8**]

Maximum Capacity in a Parallel Positioned Process

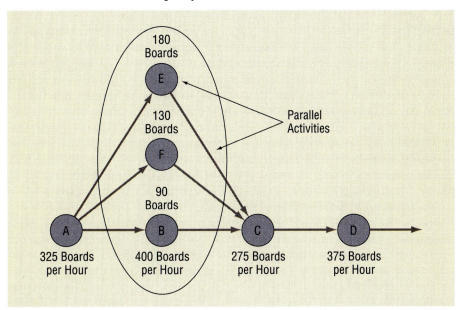

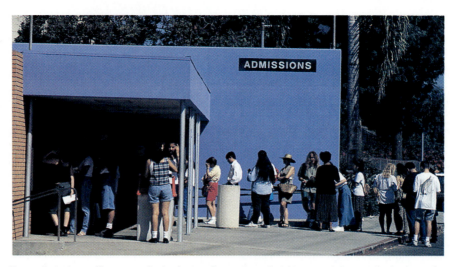

A college admissions office must obtain data to determine admission requirements and status of capacity. The data they collect will be used to determine if more capacity and resources are needed.   SOURCE David Young-Wolff/PhotoEdit

bottleneck

The lowest-capacity operation in a process

unavoidable activities with the lowest capacities. Operations managers refer to lowest-capacity operations as *limiting* or *bottleneck operations,* or simply **bottlenecks**. Such an activity often becomes a critical operation since it effectively sets the pace for the output of the entire process.

Bottlenecks also dictate company investment strategies. A manager cannot increase the output of a process by investing in higher capacity of operations other than bottlenecks because this would only create unusable excess capacity. Effective investment strategies focus on changing the capacities of activities at bottlenecks. Therefore, effective management of the operations management system centers on bottleneck activities.

Other Determinants of Capacity.   The discussion so far has focused on the role of activity capacity in overall process capacity. Input can affect capacity, as well, when a process must adapt for extensive variation in materials and other inputs. For example, a university must accommodate students with a wide range of skills taking diverse courses. Students who need extensive guidance consume more resources than more independent students and require more capacity in the system. An oil refinery must accommodate variations in crude oil that affect its capacity to produce gasoline. Refining crude oil with low sulfur content (called *sweet* crude) takes fewer steps and less time than refining high-sulfur, *sour* crude; sour crude corrodes processing equipment, reducing its productive life, and requires more processing to remove the sulfur, so refining it demands higher capacity. Managers must consider the characteristics of current inputs when they calculate capacities for these kinds of processes.

Finally, the calculation of the capacity of a process must consider its ability to accommodate changes in the product mix. An inflexible process loses capacity when it must change from one product to another to respond to a change in the product mix. A more flexible process with short changeover times can make this adjustment with little loss in time and capacity. Operations managers frequently correct capacity calculations for differences in flexibility of product mix by defining a theoretical typical product and assuming a typical product mix.

General Guidelines for Calculating Capacity.   To complete a detailed calculation of capacity for a process, operations managers rely on some version of a four-step method:

1. *Describe the general flow of activities within the process.* In laying out the process, the manager tries to identify and describe its activities and their organization.[5] This analysis must determine which are organized in sequence and which in parallel.

2. *Establish the time period.* A capacity measurement refers to a specific period of time, so the calculation must establish a time standard (e.g., a month, week, day, or year) and measure the capacity of every activity in the process over that exact time period. No meaningful comparison is possible between data for different periods, and analysis becomes very difficult, as well.

3. *Establish a common unit for measuring and comparing capacities.* Next, a calculation for the overall capacity of a process must report activity capacities in some common unit of measurement. For example, a calculation of circuit board assembly capacity at IBM Austin might measure the capacity of separate activities in different ways. The calculation could state the capacity of a machine that inserts chips into boards as some number of chips inserted per minute or per hour. However, it might report the capacity of a machine that wave solders boards (i.e., floats them across a pool of hot solder) as some number of boards soldered per minute or per hour. Different units of measurement prevent meaningful comparisons, so the analysis must identify a common unit of measurement in which to state the capacity of every stage in the process, perhaps boards processed per hour at IBM.

4. *Identify the maximum capacity for the process.* Next, we have to determine the overall maximum capacity for the entire process. As described earlier, this calculation begins by determining the maximum capacities for the individual activities; usually these are relatively straightforward calculations. Based on these figures, the calculation finds an overall maximum capacity for the entire process based on sequentially positioned and parallel positioned processes.

To better understand this process, consider the example in Problem 5.1.

[**P R O B L E M   5 . 1**]

Process Capacity at Zug Island Steel

Zug Island operates a mill that makes steel for a variety of uses. You have been hired as a consultant to evaluate the current state of operations of the coking oven, blast furnace, and basic oxygen furnace (BOF) departments.

In the first stage of the process, a coking oven changes coal from a nearby coal dump into coke. The coke is left to cool in a heap and then moved to a pile near the blast furnace. Currently, the coke oven has a design capacity of 71,000 tons of coke per year.

The blast furnace converts coke from the pile and iron pellets, also from a nearby pile, into pig iron. The pig iron is moved to a staging area to cool. The

---

[5]Later in this chapter, the section on Process Flow Analysis will introduce a set of graphical tools for diagraming processes to aid this analysis.

blast furnace uses 1.5 tons of coke and 2.3 tons of iron pellets to make every ton of pig iron, with a design capacity of 55,000 tons of pig iron per year.

In the next step, the BOFs convert pig iron into steel, which is taken to a soaking pit to await the next stage of processing. The BOFs require 0.8 tons of pig iron and 1.2 tons of scrap and chemicals to produce a ton of steel. They have a design capacity of 68,000 tons of steel per year.

Over the last year, the plant produced 60,000 tons of steel. You have been asked to calculate the capacity of the production process at Zug Island, stating results in tons of finished product (i.e., tons of steel). Also, the company is considering increasing the capacity of the blast furnace from 55,000 tons to 70,000 tons of pig iron per year, citing two major reasons. First, managers see a need to balance capacity across processes. Second, the change seems very attractive economically, with a return on investment significantly above the firm's requirement. What is your evaluation of this proposed change?

SOLUTION

Initially, this problem seems complex with many different activities and capacities stated in varying units such as pig iron tons, steel tons, and coke tons. The four-step procedure makes it accessible, however.

1. Exhibit 5.9 lays out three operations (the coking oven, the blast furnace, and the basic oxygen furnaces) and six storage activities within the steel making process. The process is organized basically sequentially, as the coking oven feeds the blast furnace which feeds the basic oxygen furnaces. Therefore, the overall capacity for this process depends on that of the lowest-capacity activity.
2. The most appropriate time period for the capacity calculation is 1 year since all data are stated in annual units.
3. To establish a common unit of measure, the calculation must convert the first two units—coke tons and pig iron tons—to steel tons to satisfy the company's requirements for the capacity data. As Exhibit 5.10 shows, to convert the output of the coke oven (measured in coke tons) into pig iron tons, divide the number of coke tons by 1.5 because the blast furnace needs 1.5 tons of coke to create a ton of pig iron. Similarly, to convert steel tons to coke tons, multiply the output of the BOF (in steel tons) by 0.8 (because it takes 0.8 tons of pig iron to make a ton of steel) and that result by 1.5 (because it takes 1.5 tons of coke to make a ton of pig iron).
4. Finally, Exhibit 5.11 calculates the maximum capacity for each operation. This shows a maximum capacity for the steel-making process of 59,166.67 steel tons per year. The coke oven is the bottleneck for the process, since it generates the lowest output, measured in any units. The coke oven cannot produce enough coke to keep the blast furnace and BOFs operating at capacity, constraining the overall output of the process. The maximum capacities of the blast furnace and the BOFs are fairly well-balanced.

This capacity calculation indicates that the blast furnace is not the bottleneck, so the proposed investment in expanding its capacity would not improve the overall capacity of the process. In fact, at the higher capacity, the blast furnace would be used only 67.6 percent of the time, found by dividing the coking oven's output of 59,166.76 steel tons by the new blast furnace output of 87,500

[**E X H I B I T   5 . 9**]

Process Flow for Zug Island Steel

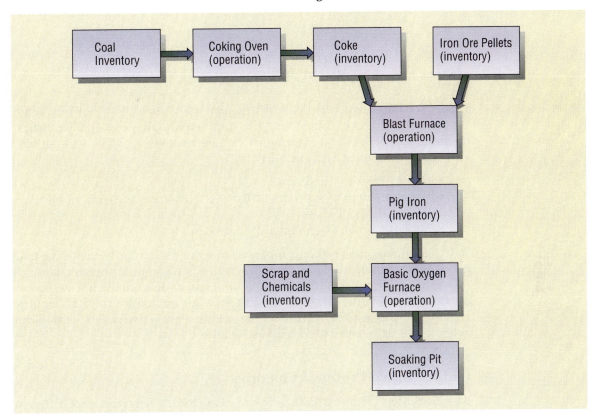

[**E X H I B I T   5 . 10**]

Converting between Units of Capacity Measurement

Unit of Capacity	Convert to Coke Tons	Convert to Pig Iron Tons	Convert to Steel Tons
Output of coke oven (CO)	No conversion	(CO output)/1.5	(CO output)/(1.5 × 0.8)
Output of blast furnace (BF)	BF output × 1.5	No conversion	BF output/0.8
Output of basic oxygen furnace (BOF)	BOF output × 1.5 × 0.8	BOF output × 0.8	No conversion

[**E X H I B I T   5 . 11**]

Calculating Maximum Capacity

Unit of Capacity	Maximum Coke Tons	Maximum Pig Iron Tons	Maximum Steel Tons
Output of coke oven (CO)	71,000	47,333	59,167
Output of blast furnace (BF)	82,500	55,000	68,750
Output of basic oxygen furnace (BOF)	81,600	54,400	68,000

steel tons.[6] Based on this calculation, Zug Island should target any investment in capacity at the coke ovens, assuming that the decision would be based strictly on capacity needs.   [▪]

MAJOR PROCESS OUTPUTS

Earlier sections have evaluated process activities, structures that link activities, process inputs, and capacity. Outputs complete the range of characteristics that distinguish processes and determine their effectiveness. Any OM process can generate up to three basic types of outputs:

- *Goods*   Physical products
- *Services*   Intangible products that save customers the work of meeting certain needs themselves
- *Information*   Data generated by a process

These three categories encompass a wide range of outputs, including tangible goods like computers and intangible services like computer repairs. Designs for new products or processes represent outputs separate from the finished goods, as do shipping schedules for incoming supplies or outgoing products, inquiries to customers to assess their levels of satisfaction, corporate and OM department goals, and even internal production schedules.

Output-Based Process Categories

Based on their outputs, managers can characterize, analyze, and differentiate processes to define eight categories: strategic management processes, innovation processes, customer service processes, resource management processes, supply chain management processes, logistics management processes, measurement processes, and other supporting processes.

Strategic Management Process.   This type of process identifies, formulates, and implements an organization's strategic vision of value and its overall objectives and goals. To generate this output, it must manipulate inputs of information about the organization's unique capabilities, the market's needs, the outputs of rival organizations, and the potential costs and benefits of closing the gap between what customers are getting and what they want.

Innovation Process.[7]   This type of process generates new product and process designs. It includes activities to identify a concept or idea, describe that concept, and complete development of the new product or process. Operations managers often group these activities into narrower, supporting processes:

- *Product design process*   The processes involved in designing and building new products, such as IBM's new laptop computer, for the marketplace.

---

[6]The denominator, 87,500, results from dividing the new maximum capacity for the blast furnace, 70,000 tons, by 0.8 to arrive at the new maximum capacity in steel tons.

[7]Marvin L. Patterson, *Accelerating Innovation* (New York: Van Nostrand Reinhold, 1993).

- *Process design process*   The processes involved in designing and delivering new processes.
- *System design process*   The processes and activities involved in designing and delivering new systems, such as a new computer for an operations management system.

Customer Service Process.   This type of process determines how the organization or its OM system interfaces with customers, especially external customers. Many supporting processes contribute to this work:

- *Order entry and processing/promising*   This supporting process enters orders from customers into the OM system and provides information about completion and delivery schedules.
- *Forecasting*   This supporting process gathers and analyzes information to project the product mixes, quantities, and timing that customers will demand in the future.
- *Demand management*   This supporting process matches customers' needs identified through the previous two processes with the capabilities of the firm and its OM system to ensure that the firm makes credible commitments about due dates, quantities, and quality levels to customers.

Resource Management Process.   This type of process combines the outputs of the strategic management process (company objectives) and the customer service process (customer orders) to determine the firm's resource needs (capacity, labor, tools, and materials). Supporting processes include:

- *Planning*   This supporting process works with inputs of company objectives and customer orders to develop estimates of demands on company resources and to compare these demands with the current and projected levels of available resources to identify any unmet needs.
- *Acquisition*   When planning identifies a resource shortage, this subprocess works to gather the needed resources. Acquisition can make short-term changes (e.g., increasing capacity through scheduling overtime work or expediting existing orders from suppliers), or it can make long-term changes (e.g., expanding current facilities or building a new plant).
- *Scheduling*   This supporting process assigns company resources to meet competing demands by setting priorities for orders and other demands on the OM system and then assigning resources from the highest-priority to the lowest-priority demands.
- *Implementation*   This supporting process carries out the resource management decisions developed in the earlier subprocesses, releasing orders to the OM system; routing them to specific workers and machines; requisitioning materials and tools; and building the ordered products.

Supply Chain Management Process.   This type of process recognizes that no firm's OM system can ever achieve complete self-sufficiency. Every OM system depends on inputs from suppliers through the supply chain, so resource management must extend beyond immediate links to direct suppliers to reach all sources of the firm's inputs beginning with raw materials. Managers are looking further beyond direct suppliers as they come to understand the influence on their own firms' performance of activities throughout the supply chain. Also, besides materials, components, and services, suppliers can offer expertise, market information, and access to new technology. Supporting processes include:

- *Supplier selection/communication*   Activities in this supporting process focus on identifying potential suppliers, selecting those that offer the best value, and maintaining ongoing relationships with the chosen vendors.
- *Supply base development*   This subprocess extends the communication activity to work in depth with direct suppliers to ensure that their capabilities and capacity levels will continue to support the firm's needs.
- *Supplier/OM system scheduling and interfacing*   This subprocess coordinates the firm's daily operations with those of suppliers.
- *Insourcing/outsourcing*   This subprocess addresses the make-or-buy decision, in which the operations manager must weigh the effectiveness of making a needed component internally (insourcing) against that of outsourcing it from a supplier. This decision must adjust a comparison of costs between the two options to reflect the component's importance to the OM process, the quality levels and reliability of suppliers, and the match between the requirements of making the needed component and the capabilities of the firm and its OM system.

Logistics Management Process.   All but the smallest OM systems must solve problems that arise from physical or spatial separation. IBM, for example, produces its goods at factories throughout the world from components supplied by other firms across great distances. The firm's logistics management process works to close these geographic gaps by implementing the lowest-cost combinations of subprocesses like warehousing and transshipping (which temporarily store inputs), transportation links, logistics inventory (inputs in transit through the logistics system), and order delivery/communication (flows of information and goods to meet customer needs). A few subprocesses are especially critical:

- *Logistics system design*   Goods flow through the logistics management system in various stages of completion, including work-in-process at work stations and finished components in storage areas such as warehouses. Warehouses, for example, can both serve a traditional storage function and help to coordinate transportation by consolidating small, outbound loads into larger loads, which are cheaper to ship, or by breaking up large, incoming loads into smaller shipments for individual customers. Recently, many firms have given warehouses narrower transshipping functions, breaking up large, homogeneous loads from suppliers immediately into smaller loads for individual stores or other operations; goods often spend very little time in storage at such a warehouse.

  This supporting process develops the initial design for the entire logistics management system, detailing levels and locations of inventory within the system; the number, locations, and functions of warehouses; modes, amounts, and timing of transportation capacity; and specifications, locations, and amounts of order communication technologies.
- *Management of logistics inventory*   This supporting process looks for opportunities to improve the movement and storage of goods. It adjusts levels of work-in-process inventory and lead times, the amounts and time periods to store inventory in warehouses, modes of transportation, and communication methods used to pass information through the system to reduce the time and cost that goods generate as they pass through the logistics system.
- *Performance measurement*   This subprocess determines appropriate and accurate measures of performance for activities in the logistics management process. An old saying often attributed to Oliver Wight, a well-known

manufacturing consultant, highlights the importance of the measurement process: "You get what you inspect, not what you expect." Performance measurement communicates to everyone within the firm and the OM system what they must do well. Cost-based performance measures encourage people to work at reducing costs; quality-based measures focus attention on maintaining high quality.

Performance measurement can refer to internally generated standards from the firm's own cost accounting or engineering systems, for example. Many operations managers have begun to compare their systems' performance against the best practices in their industries or product classes; benchmarking is a popular technique for making this comparison.

Other supporting processes.   The preceding seven processes are central to operations management, but other processes support it indirectly. Operations managers rely on accounting for accurate and timely cost data, finance for evaluations of the financial impacts of alternative investments, and marketing for information about customer needs.

Management Implications of Output-Based Process Categories

These eight processes (shown earlier in Exhibit 1.4) are basic to any operations management system. Smaller, more focused subprocesses apply the larger processes to the firm's specific situation, often in complex networks of activities with interfaces that cross boundaries between company departments. These interfaces require special management attention to maintain overall coordination. For example, without careful organization, important customer orders can disappear as one department or area completes its work and passes on responsibility to another.

Also, operations managers evaluate every process based on standards for time, cost, and flexibility. To improve any one of these performance measures, they must change the process itself. A later section of this chapter will discuss process flow analysis, a powerful technique for identifying necessary changes.

 ## EVALUATING PROCESSES—ESTABLISHING THE LINK TO VALUE

Chapters 2 and 3 discussed the value-oriented perspective for assessing organizational and OM system performance. Most firms express the concept of value by referring to its components: lead time, quality, flexibility, and cost; each of these characteristics bears a strong relationship to the firm's OM process. For example, lead time, the total interval a process requires from start to finish, depends strongly on process characteristics:

Process Trait	Impact on Lead Times
Number of steps	More steps = Longer lead time
Physical locations of activities	Closer activities = Shorter lead time
Organization of activities	Sequential organization = Longer lead time; Parallel organization = Shorter lead time
Composition of activities	More moves, storage activities, delays, and inspections = Longer lead time and more time for nonvalue-adding activities

Measuring Overall Effectiveness

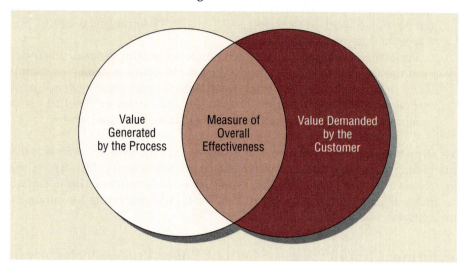

The other components of value bear similar relationships to the details of the process, so the organization of the process powerfully affects the type of value that the firm can offer to customers. This critical notion underlies a central premise of value-driven operations management: To change the type of value delivered by a given process, the operations manager must change the process itself.

This relationship suggests a system for measuring the performance of a process by assessing its contribution to value. This becomes essential feedback to tell organization members whether they have delivered the intended level of value and to help them identify potential problem areas by highlighting the largest gaps between what the system should have delivered and what it actually delivered.

The overlap between the value that customers want and the value that the process generates indicates its overall effectiveness (Exhibit 5.12). Operations managers have developed several more specific criteria for judging the effectiveness of their processes based on cost performance, lead-time performance, flexibility, and value content.

Cost Performance

Managers have developed several cost-based measures to indicate the efficiency of a process.

- *Contribution margin*   Contribution margin measures the difference between revenues generated by a process and the variable cost to the firm of operating that process. (These concepts are taught in introductory accounting courses.)
- *Variance*   A variance figure measures the difference between planned, standard costs and actual costs, so it indicates how efficiently the process has implemented plans.
- *Ratio of direct to indirect labor*   Rising indirect costs raise fixed costs, increasing the break-even point and inhibiting the flexibility of the process

[EXHIBIT 5.13]

Indirect Labor and Fixed Costs

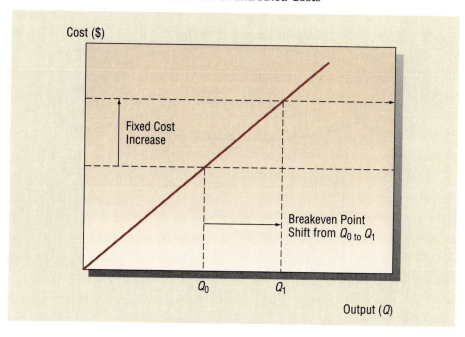

(Exhibit 5.13). A low ratio of direct to indirect labor indicates this kind of inefficiency, while a high ratio suggests efficient cost performance.

- *Inventory turnover*   This measure identifies how long inventory stays within the process before customers buy it. A lower value indicates that inventory stays longer within the system, raising the cost to the OM process for holding costs, storage costs, and working capital.
- *Paperwork burden*   Carlos del Rio of SmithKline Beecham Pharmaceuticals developed a measure of the paperwork burden of a process after observing a direct link between costs, system complexity, and paperwork.[8]
- *Level of scrap/rejects/rework*   Scrap, rejects, and rework consume process capacity and materials to correct the underlying defects without returning any offsetting revenue. This waste reduces process efficiency.

Lead-Time Performance

Operations managers typically measure lead-time performance by evaluating the number and types of activities involved in a process. More steps generally cause longer lead times. Delays and storage activities also increase lead times since costs accumulate without any change in value. To spot excessive lead times, operations managers look for several traits, including large numbers of steps, many delays or storage activities, numerous inspections, numerous exceptions to the standard process, large distances between operations, and many physical links in a sequentially organized process.

[8]Brian H. Maskell, *Performance Measurement for World Class Manufacturing* (Cambridge, Mass.: Productivity Press, 1991), pp. 280–282.

[**EXHIBIT 5.14**]

Summary: Links between Process and Value

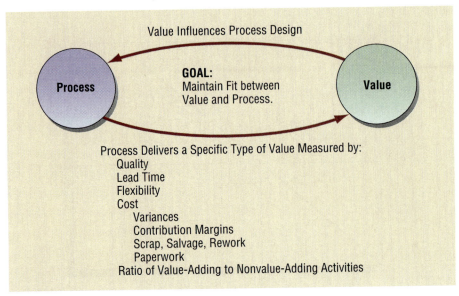

Flexibility Performance

Operations managers evaluate the flexibility of a process by measuring the number of steps, since many steps usually inhibits flexibility. They also look for automation, since extensive hard automation reduces flexibility, and for physical links (e.g., conveyor belts) between activities. Physical links move work-in-process quickly from one activity to the next, but they also increase changeover time between runs for different products.

Value Content

To judge the value added by a process, the operations manager can divide its steps between activities that add value and those that do not. This helps to achieve the ultimate objective of developing processes with high proportions of value-adding activities. To judge progress toward this goal, managers can count the value-adding activities and then divide by the total number of activities:

$$\frac{\Sigma(\text{Activities that add value})}{\Sigma(\text{Process Activities})} \qquad\qquad \textbf{(5.1)}$$

A similar calculation could divide the time spent in activities that add value by the total time of the process.

Either calculation presupposes that the analyst can separate activities that add value from those that do not. One way of making this distinction focuses on the type of activity. Of the five categories of activities, one might argue that only operations add value, since only operations actually change a product, ideally to add value. This method would recast the Equation 5.1 as:

$$\frac{\Sigma(\text{Operations})}{\Sigma(\text{Operations} + \text{Transportation} + \text{Storage activities} + \text{Delays} + \text{Inspections})}$$

[**EXHIBIT 5.15**]

Subprocesses within the Larger Process

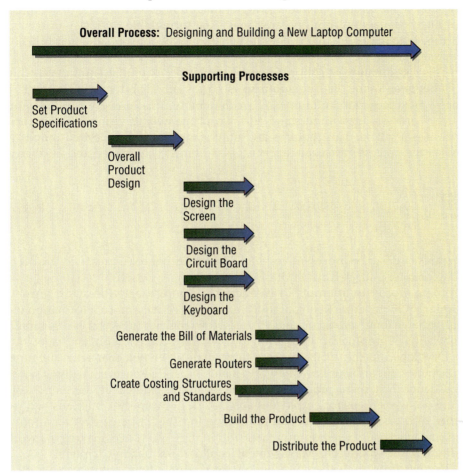

Overall Process: Designing and Building a New Laptop Computer

Supporting Processes

Set Product
Specifications

Overall
Product
Design

Design the
Screen

Design the
Circuit Board

Design the
Keyboard

Generate the Bill of Materials

Generate Routers

Create Costing Structures
and Standards

Build the Product

Distribute the Product

However this analysis breaks down the process and its activities, operations managers ultimately want to push the fraction in either Equation 5.1 or 5.2 toward a value of 1, which would indicate that all steps add value.

Exhibit 5.14 summarizes the elements of the strong, continuous link between the process, including its structure and design, and value.

PROCESS INTERFACES

The earlier discussion of categories of processes detailed many small subprocesses that carry out certain tasks or achieve certain objectives as part of larger processes. For example, IBM relied on an innovation process to speed up the OM process by which it designed and launched a new laptop computer. Exhibit 5.15 divides this process into a number of separate subprocesses for activities like designing keyboards, circuit boards, and video screens; establishing specifications; generating the bill of materials; and creating cost structures and standards.

Coordinating all of these subprocesses involves more than structuring or organizing individual processes. The manager must bring together and coordinate subprocesses from different parts of the firm; engineering staff may design the laptop computer while operations management must implement that design to build the computer. Managers from one area may face formidable obstacles in trying to coordinate activities and to change the behavior of people outside their functional boundaries.

This coordination of subprocesses also requires careful attention to the interfaces between them. As one subprocess hands off a job to another, the larger process must preserve continuity and accountability. Finally, every person involved in every process must understand and accept the overall vision of value for the process as a whole. This requires an initial statement of the desired output and goals of the process measured in terms of lead time, cost, quality, and flexibility.

PROCESS FLOW ANALYSIS—TOOLS FOR MAPPING AND ANALYZING PROCESSES

Attempts to describe processes verbally, like those that have preceded this section of the chapter, suffer from limitations of language. Descriptive language risks becoming wordy in attempts to characterize complex activities with imprecise meanings. Often, a quick look at a visual aid can convey more information more clearly than a long verbal passage. Process flow analysis (PFA) takes advantage of the benefits of graphic representation to solve this problem with language.

Developed in the 1950s, process flow analysis helped managers define and implement standards for flows of work, materials, and paperwork within their systems.[9] Since then, managers have used the technique extensively for work design, laying out work areas for employees and determining specific methods and techniques of work. Managers are now recognizing the value of PFA as a tool for studying any type of process anywhere within the OM system, making it a worthy addition to the Operations Management Toolkit described in Chapter 4.

process flow analysis
A technique for documenting activities in a detailed, compact, and graphic form to help the manager to understand the process and to highlight potential improvements

Process flow analysis is a technique for documenting activities in a detailed, compact, and graphic form to help the manager to understand the process and highlight potential improvements. Process flow analysis essentially generates a blueprint of a process that supplies all of the information that an analyst needs. This tool helps to close the gaps between the process that company manuals describe (which often does not exist), the process that people think exists (which tends to depend on personal perspective), the process that actually exists, and the process that generates the most possible value (what should exist). It underlies more recent developments such as business process reengineering which help managers to restructure and redefine the processes within their firm.

Process flow analysis consists of five steps:

1. Identify and categorize process activities
2. Document the process as a whole
3. Analyze the process and identify opportunities for improvement
4. Recommend appropriate changes to the process
5. Implement the changes

[9]Roland H. Raeker, "New Times, Old Tools," *APICS 35th International Conference Proceedings,* Montreal, Quebec, Canada, October 8–23, 1992, p. 255.

[**EXHIBIT 5.16**]

Activity Symbols

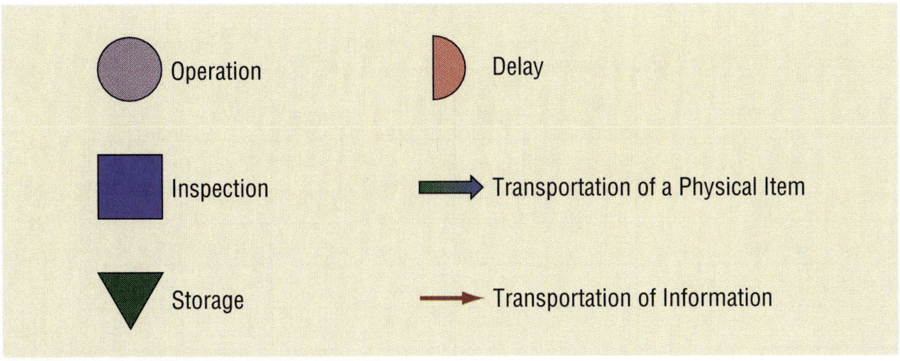

- ○ Operation
- □ Inspection
- ▽ Storage
- ◗ Delay
- → Transportation of a Physical Item
- → Transportation of Information

Identify and Categorize Process Activities

An earlier section described five categories of activities: operation, transportation, inspection, storage, and delay. Process flow analysis defines special symbols for each of these kinds of activities (Exhibit 5.16).

Circles represent operations, an easy device to remember since the symbol looks like the first letter in *operation*. Inspections are denoted by squares. A triangle standing on its point represents a storage activity, resembling a storage bin. A large capital *D* represents a delay, and an arrow indicates a transportation. A heavy solid arrow represents a physical transportation (e.g., an activity that moves parts from one operation to another), while a narrow arrow indicates an information flow. These symbols replace words with pictures that facilitate an immediate understanding of a specific activity.

Document the Process as a Whole

To document a process the analyst traces the activities, identifies the type of each, and assigns the proper symbol to each, placing the symbols in the order in which the activities occur. The result should describe the process as currently implemented, rather than the official version or some individual's image of the process.

Process flow analysis arranges symbols on one of five charts:

- General process chart
- Process flow chart
- Process flow diagram
- Assembly process chart
- Flow chart

Each chart focuses attention on a different aspect of the process, but all describe the process in terms of the same performance measures:

1. Number of steps (broken down by category)
2. Distance covered
3. Time required
4. Value orientation of the activities (value-adding or not)

[**EXHIBIT 5.17**]

Sample General Process Chart

Activities	Current		Proposed		Difference	
	No.	Total Time	No.	Total Time	No.	Total Time
Operations (◯)						
Inspections (◼)						
Transportations (⇒)						
Storage Periods (▼)						
Delays (◗)						
Distance (feet/meters)						

5. Number of departmental boundaries crossed
6. Number of people who touch or come into contact with the order

Each of these six measures relates to the four components of value: lead time, cost, quality, and flexibility. For example, a longer distance raises the expected lead time and reduces the flexibility of the process. The first three measures indicate traditional criteria for process activities, while the last three are relatively new and reflect the value-adding orientation of modern operations management. (These last three do not always appear in every chart.)

general process chart

A summary process flow analysis chart that indicates time required for and distance covered by activities in each category

General Process Chart.   The **general process chart** simply summarizes the current process, the proposed new process, and expected improvements from proposed changes (Exhibit 5.17). This chart characterizes the process by describing the amount of time that activities in each category take overall, the number of activities by category, and the distance that activities in each category cover.[10] The summary provided by the general process chart indicates with a single glance major problems in the existing process, measured in activity time, frequency of occurrence, or total time. This condenses a great deal of information into a small space, but the summary information needs augmentation by other, more detailed charts.

Process Flow Chart.   The general process chart does not place activities in sequence, a very important omission in a complex problem-solving and decision-making effort. For example, two processes with the same mix of activities would have identical summary data on the general process chart, although one may place all delays and inspections at the beginning of the process while the second places them at the end. A set of changes that would prove highly effective for one process might have a different effect for the other. Process flow analysis needs a tool to develop a detailed understanding of a sequence of activities, the process flow chart (Exhibit 5.18).

[10]Note that this distance measurement indicates the physical distance that an order or part moves in units such as inches, feet, or centimeters. If a part moves from one floor of a building to another, the distance measurement states the actual vertical and horizontal distance it covers in the move.

[**EXHIBIT 5.18**]

Sample Process Flow Chart

Process Flow Chart

Page ____ of ____

Overall Description of Process Charted: _____

Date Charted: _____   Charted by: _____

Check Appropriate Box: Current Process: ☐   Proposed Process: ☐

Distance (feet/ Meters)	Time (average)	Symbol	Person Involved	Value Code V/W/N/?	Description of Activity (indicate outcome)
		● ■ → ◗ ▼			
		● ■ → ◗ ▼			
		● ■ → ◗ ▼			
		● ■ → ◗ ▼			
		● ■ → ◗ ▼			
		● ■ → ◗ ▼			
		● ■ → ◗ ▼			
		● ■ → ◗ ▼			
		● ■ → ◗ ▼			
		● ■ → ◗ ▼			
		● ■ → ◗ ▼			
		● ■ → ◗ ▼			
		● ■ → ◗ ▼			
		● ■ → ◗ ▼			
		● ■ → ◗ ▼			
		● ■ → ◗ ▼			

For each line, fill in the required information (and also fill in the appropriate symbol).
Next, connect the symbols to show the flow through the process.

NOTE The value code indicates whether the activity adds value (V), generates waste (W), does not add value but remains necessary (N), or has an unknown effect on value (?).

process flow chart

A process flow analysis tool that categorizes each activity and details time requirements, briefly describes the activity, and presents other appropriate information

The user fills in the required information and the appropriate symbol for each activity on one line of a **process flow chart** and then connects the symbols to show the flow through the process. The completed chart describes the exact sequence and placement of activities with several important pieces of information for each:

- *Activity category*   The chart identifies each activity as an operation, transportation, inspection, delay or storage.
- *Distance and time requirements*   The chart reports the physical distance an individual activity covers and the amount of time it takes measured as a standard time, mean observed time, or variance or standard deviation of observed times. The last two statistics often provide valuable insights because they indicate the reliability or predictability of the activity.
- *Number of people*   Data about staffing needs for an activity can indicate overall costs. Counting the workers involved in operations gives an idea of direct costs; other workers contribute to overhead costs, the fastest-growing cost component in most firms.
- *Value code*   Recall from Chapter 2 that every activity can add value, add no value but remain necessary (e.g., equipment setup or an inspection required by a customer), or generate waste; the process flow chart may include a code to place each activity in one of these groups.[11] A question mark for this code indicates uncertainty about the activity's impact on value.
- *Brief description*   This information elaborates on the symbol designation. An *O* symbol indicates an operation, but process flow analysis requires a more specific description to separate an activity that takes an order over the phone, for example, from one to cut material to fill the order. The chart should also indicate the analyst's recommendation to keep the activity as is, eliminate it entirely, combine it with another, similar activity, or rethink it, following the options identified in Chapter 2.

The basic process flow chart covers at least the activity category, the time requirement, and the description for each activity. The chart may present the other pieces of information listed to further enhance understanding.

The process flow chart suits certain situations especially well. It can help an operations manager to study a single process organized to create a certain output at one specific point in time. It does not, however, illustrate simultaneous processes. For example, a process flow chart could represent a process for converting oranges to juice, but it could not detail the entire process of creating a can of orange juice, in which one process makes cans while another grows oranges and another extracts juice. An assembly process chart, discussed later in this section, would more effectively illustrate the overall process.

The process flow chart also suits a process with no variation, such as production that does not meet specifications and requires rework. Only defective products would require these additional steps, and a single process flow chart cannot capture separate processes for good parts and bad parts. Each variation of a process needs its own chart.

A process flow chart can effectively represent a sequentially organized process because it places separate activities one after another. It cannot show two or more simultaneous activities like those in a process organized in parallel.

Process Flow Diagram.   The process flow analysis techniques discussed so far identify activities, describe their organization and sequence, and categorize them

[11]Raeker, "New Times."

ON THE JOB

Tightening Production at Titeflex

■

In 1988, Titeflex seemed more like a paper-pushing factory than a $50 million manufacturer of industrial hoses. Titeflex's redundant production system had everyone awash in paperwork, from the president on down.

The paperwork headache started the minute an order came in the door of the Springfield, Massachussetts, plant. Once entered into Titeflex's computer system, a new order generated paperwork for purchasers, production schedulers, stockers, inspectors, engineers, and cost reviewers. The resultant confusion was sorted out in seemingly endless meetings for three to five weeks before a hose was ever made.

But once an order entered production, the paperwork avalanche really started rolling. Part of the order went to the basic hose-manufacturing area, and another part went to a fittings process spread over five departments. Completed components moved on to another department for cleaning, then through at least three more departments for final assembly. But the hose did not stop there; it still had to get through the 50-person quality assurance department and finally on to shipping.

Keeping track of all these movements required mountains of paperwork. To make matters worse, every hose snaked through the stockroom at least six times. (On the master flow chart, someone with a sense of humor labelled it "Spaghetti Junction.") All together, manufacturing took at least six weeks on top of the three to five weeks for preproduction planning—and that was when everything went smoothly.

Things have changed! Processes are completely rewired. Now new orders feed into an administrative cell (called a Genesis Team), consisting of six people with their desks in a tight circle. Players include a contracts administrator (the voice of Titeflex to the outside customer); applications engineers, who immediately review each order from an engi-

neering stand-point; a design engineer, determining manufacturing requirements; and a draftsman to draw up new designs if necessary. Little paperwork is created, and the whole order-entry process consumes as few as 10 minutes for something routine and no more than two to five days for a novel and intricate request.

The rest of the operation (the factory) has been organized into de facto "small businesses" (manufacturing cells) of 5 to 15 people each. Before an order is released to the factory floor, the Genesis Team communicates directly with the Business Development Teams (BDTs). Immediately after order release, the BDTs begin manufacturing and now perform their own quality control. When the component builders finish, their output goes to the stockroom (the *only* trip through the stockroom), and from there to final assembly.

Total manufacturing time now varies from two days to one week. Crash orders go to a lightning-fast Rapid Development Team, which can handle the whole works—from order entry to the shipping dock—in as little as three or four hours.

SOURCE   Tom Peters, "Before and After: Trimming Fat from Production, *Chicago Tribune*, January 28, 1991, Section 4, p. 6.

for detailed study. This information may underemphasize spatial relationships, however. Most processes move something from activity to activity, so physical layouts can powerfully affect the distance that each activity must cover and its lead time, handling requirements, costs, and quality.

The description in the "On the Job" box of operations at Titeflex demonstrates the importance of spatial relationships. Before the change in the layout, orders traveled through a maze of departments, consuming time and increasing the potential for errors at every step. On the shop floor, the confused product flows took every order through the stock room six times. General process charts and process flow charts cannot accurately illustrate these kinds of physical movements to reveal problems.

process flow diagram

A process flow analysis tool in which the analyst draws physical flows through related activities

The **process flow diagram** offers a tool for this kind of analysis by presenting a picture of a plant layout on which the analyst draws movements of orders from one activity or area to another. The resulting diagram measures process performance in units of time and distance. This fairly straightforward analysis must take care to measure all distances over which activities move work, both horizontally and vertically when activities occupy different floors or levels of a facility. This diagram assumes that moving products over distances, both horizontally and vertically, takes time and consumes resources that affect the overall process flow analysis.

Labels on the process flow diagram indicate areas or activities that correspond to the list on the process flow chart, creating a strong, complementary relationship between these tools. The process flow chart details the nature of process activities while the process flow diagram maps out their physical flows. Together, they help the operations manager to clearly see how a process actually operates.

Exhibit 5.19 presents a process flow diagram for a blood-donation process. Clearly, the process flows in a strongly sequential pattern in which donors move in order from one station to the next. Analysis of a process flow diagram looks for excessive and unnecessary movements. These may show up as long moves between activities, criss-crosses in paths as orders move back and forth across the shop floor, repeated movements between two activities, or other illogical or convoluted flows. An effective, efficient process eliminates criss-crosses and locates sequential, high-volume activities close together to minimize move times.

Assembly Process Charts.   The process flow analysis tools explored so far focus on individual processes. However, many processes combine components produced by various subprocesses. IBM Austin builds a microcomputer by combining a motherboard, a case, memory chips and cards, other circuit boards, disk drives, and other components, each of them the product of some subprocess. Effective, efficient assembly of the microcomputer requires careful management of both the final assembly process and the various subprocesses that feed components into it.

assembly process chart

A process flow analysis tool that depicts activities in subprocesses and how they flow together to form the overall process

Process flow analysis offers the **assembly process chart** as a tool for this work. Exhibit 5.20 lays out separate subprocesses from top to bottom and shows how they flow together to form the overall process. The movement down the diagram shows the exact sequence of the various activities. It also indicates when the overall process and each subprocess must finish their work to complete an order on schedule. This vertical movement indicates time requirements, while the horizontal layout illustrates subprocesses. This chart also shows the most critical processes, indicated by the longest sequences of activities, and how the smaller subprocesses support the critical ones.

Of the four process flow analysis tools discussed so far, the assembly process chart offers the richest information, since it shows the entire system with all of its subprocesses in a single picture. The assembly process chart also allows the operations manager to combine information about the structure of a process with information about its capacity. For every activity, the chart can present information about both effective and maximum capacity. For operations, it can detail equipment and labor capacity; for storage activities, it can state the amounts of space available; for transportation activities, it can report carrying capacity. Including this information helps to highlight bottlenecks.

[**EXHIBIT 5.19**]

Sample Process Flow Diagram

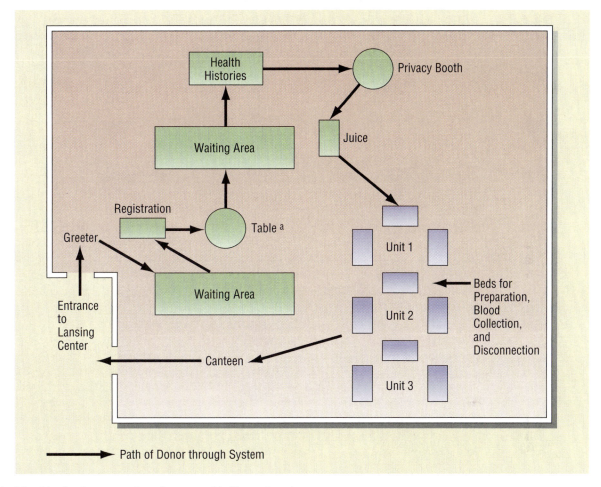

[a] At this table, the donor completes forms provided by registration.

Flow Charts. As a simpler alternative to the assembly process chart, operations managers can prepare flow charts. **Flow charts** typically depict activities in a sidelong arrangement showing movement from left to right through the process. A flow chart can help to clarify any loops in a process (i.e., a series of activities that must be repeated because of errors such as quality problems). This additional information comes at a cost due to the loss of a time indicator. An assembly process chart shows the time requirements of a process as it moves from top to bottom. Loops in a flow chart obscure time flows.

To understand how a flow chart works, suppose that managers at Zug Island Steel, from the earlier problem, add a process step to test every batch of steel on completion. The new process routes any inadequate batches to a secondary soaking pit where they await a return to the blast furnace for further processing. These reworked batches have priority over all other types of orders.

Exhibit 5.9 illustrated this process flow. Exhibit 5.21 then recasts the process using the standard symbols of process flow analysis for the various activities. The

flow chart

A graphic representation of process flows

[EXHIBIT 5.20]

Sample Assembly Process Chart

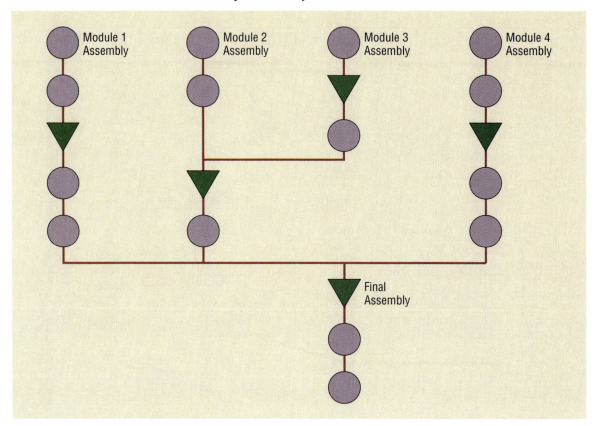

second chart highlights an important decision about the amount of detail to include. It shows iron pellets as an inventory, but this input actually comes from a subprocess that transforms raw iron ore. As a general rule, the focus of the study dictates whether or not to chart the subprocess that makes such a transformation. For an analysis of the flow of output through the steel-making process without any indications of problems with shortages of iron ore, the study should probably omit the subprocess of converting iron ore to iron pellets. The benefit of the additional detail does not justify its cost.

The designation of the secondary soaking pit as a delay assumes that the wait is temporary and the process requires no formal authorization to move this steel to another activity. From the discussion earlier in the chapter, recall that any formal system of control over the steel in the secondary soaking pit would change it to a storage activity.

Exhibit 5.21 provides a clear picture of the flow of a batch through the system, allowing careful analysis of the contribution of each activity and subprocess to the overall process. Note that the loop that takes defective steel back through the blast furnace complicates the lead time calculation. Lead time for a batch now depends on whether the inspection accepts or rejects it.

[**EXHIBIT 5.21**]

Finished Flow Chart for Zug Island Steel

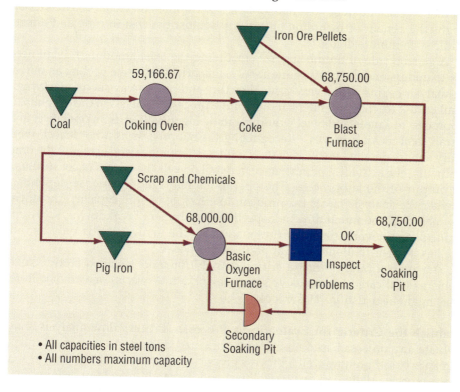

Guidelines for Process Flow Analysis

Process flow analysis can become a very complex and time-consuming task, but some general guidelines can make it simpler and easier to manage.

Set Boundaries for the Inquiry.   Before analyzing any process, first identify limits within which to confine the investigation. In general, indications of problems should guide this decision. The analysis need not extend to processes that are working well. Instead of modeling the entire steel-making process including the subprocess for producing iron ore pellets, the flow chart in Exhibit 5.21 simply presented the last step in this process; the chart ignored how the iron ore pellets reached the point at which they joined the process under study. A separate analysis could return to the overlooked subprocess in more detail if it were to become necessary.

 Comparatively long lead times can indicate processes that merit study. Some analysts may focus on processes with the highest variability in lead times. Others may target processes with the largest numbers of exceptions, defects, or other variations in routine activities.

 Study boundaries have important implications for the choice of process flow analysis tools. More tightly confined processes suit more formal tools such as process flow charts or process flow diagrams. Larger processes with many subprocesses suit either assembly process charts or flow charts, since these tools map the interactions between two or more processes.

Identify Minimum Acceptable Levels of Detail.   Any process flow analysis must continually determine how much detail to model. The study must obviously include some activities that take large blocks of time, but the analyst must decide whether to present steps that take only a few minutes or seconds. This decision weighs the benefit of including an activity against the cost in time and effort to handle such minute detail.

A general rule of thumb suggests including the least amount of detail necessary to understand the process. In practice, this principle is like peeling an onion—the analysis begins with a very general picture and peels away successive layers of detail until it reaches an understanding of the process. Analysis of the coke-making subprocess at Zug Island Steel would begin by identifying it as an operation in the overall steel-making process. Recognizing the subprocess as a bottleneck would justify a more detailed analysis of its activities, stripping away a layer of the onion. Evaluating the activities' performance in detail reveals the causes of constraints on the output of the subprocess. The operations manager's response depends on whether the analysis traces the problem to a lack of overall capacity, insufficient raw materials, too much time in inspections, equipment breakdowns, scheduling conflicts, or uneven quality in raw materials. The analysis adds only as much detail as it needs to identify the appropriate response.

The analyst might target a critical activity for more detailed study. Quality problems (indicated by excessive scrap, rework, and rejects) or variance in lead times might also justify a closer look.

Establish the Criteria for Evaluating a Process.   Process flow analysis should evaluate any process based on customer-oriented criteria. As always, judge performance based on how well a process gives customers what they value. If a customer expects quality (an order qualifier) and demands speed (an order winner), then the analyst must evaluate the ability of the firm's process to deliver a quality product quickly.

Include Every Step in a Process.   This guideline may seem obvious, but both students and practicing managers often overlook implicit or hidden delays. Suppose, for example, that an ordering process begins with a telephone operator taking information over the phone. The operator then passes order information once a day to a supervisor who reviews it for accuracy and completeness. This seems like a fairly straightforward three-step process composed of an operation (the operator taking the order) followed by transportation of accumulated orders to the supervisor followed by an inspection.

This breakdown omits delays in the process, however, as each order waits for transportation to the supervisor and as it waits again for the supervisor to select and inspect it. In addition, the inspection process produces two piles of orders as output, one for complete and accurate orders and one for incomplete or inaccurate ones. Both piles represent additional delays, as part of a more complex process, indicated by the flow chart in Exhibit 5.22. Ignoring these delays would make the image of the process inaccurate.

Lead Times in Process Flow Analysis

The number of activities in a process powerfully affects the length of time required for completion of the process, but a complete analysis must evaluate other factors, as well. In general, lead time is influenced by three process traits:

Complete Flow Chart for the Order-Taking Process

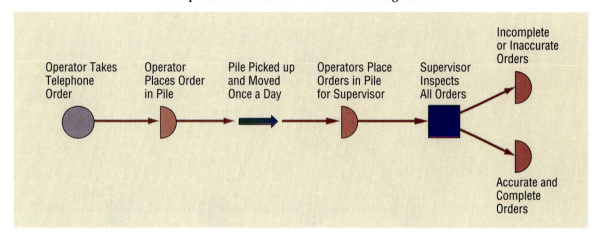

- Time required for each activity
- Process structure
- Amount of capacity for each activity

Time for Each Activity.   Each step in a process, every storage activity, operation, or movement, takes time, and these time requirements vary by type of activity. For example, the time required to complete an operation depends on the amount of setup *(S)* or preparation it needs, the number of pieces in a production batch *(Q),* the run time for each item in the batch *(R),* and the efficiency of the worker running the operation *(E).*[12] With these bits of information, an analyst could calculate the expected time for a given operation for a given order quantity:

$$\text{Lead time} = (\text{Run time} + \text{Setup time}) \times \text{Efficiency} \qquad \textbf{(5.3)}$$
$$= (R \times Q + S) \times E$$

Suppose, for example, that an operation to insert chips into a circuit board takes 1 second per chip. The average board contains 15 chips and each batch usually includes 30 boards. The operation requires a 5-minute setup time. The time standards apply to a normal, experienced operator, but the current operator is a new employee with an efficiency rating of 80 percent. This example gives a total lead time for a single operation of:

$$\text{Lead Time} = [(15 \text{ chips} \times 1 \text{ sec./chip} \times 30 \text{ boards}) + 300] \times 1/0.8$$
$$= (450 \text{ sec. per batch} + 300) \times 1/0.8$$
$$= 937.5 \text{ seconds or } 15.6 \text{ minutes}$$

This calculation assumes that the operator's efficiency rating affects both processing time and setup. In addition, it expresses efficiency as a reciprocal (1/0.8) to reflect the lower efficiency of the inexperienced worker; if an experienced operator

---

[12]As noted previously, efficiency is defined by the output of the normal employee. A worker with an efficiency rating of 125 percent could produce 1.25 units of output in the same time that a normal worker could produce 1.00 unit.

Lead Time Calculations for Parallel versus Sequential Organization

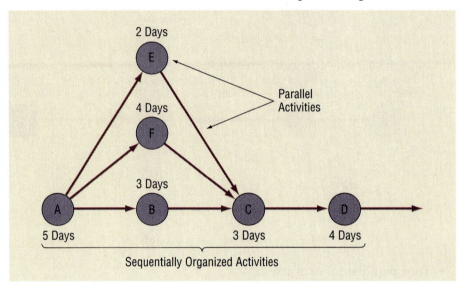

takes 1.00 minute to complete a single unit, the the worker who is 80 percent efficient should take $(1/0.8) \times 1.00$, or 1.25 minutes.

Process flow analysis calculates lead times for inspections just like those for operations. For transportation activities, however, the average lead time varies depending on three factors: (1) the amount to be moved (relative to the size of any container, if applicable), (2) the distance to cover, and (3) the speed of the move. The first factor determines the number of trips, while the second and third factors determine how long each trip should take.

For example, to transport 175 circuit boards between two operations 250 feet apart, a worker needs a cart that carries 100 circuit boards. A one-way trip takes about 5 minutes, and only one cart is available. The lead time to transport the 175 circuit boards would be 20 minutes (2 round trips of 10 minutes each), the same as the lead time to transport 200 boards.

Lead times for storage and delay activities are determined by the demand for the items in storage or delayed. If an order arrives for an item immediately as it enters the stock room, then the storage activity consumes no lead time. However, if the same item sits in the stock room for 3 weeks, the lead time for the storage activity is 3 weeks.

Process Structure.   Process flow analysis determines the lead times for activities organized in parallel as the lead time of the longest single activity. The total lead time for a group of activities organized in sequence is the sum of the individual activities' lead times. Exhibit 5.23 illustrates these differences. Activities B, E, and F are organized in parallel; their total lead time of 4 days reflects the individual lead time of Activity F, the longest of the three. The sequential organization of Activities A, (B,F,E), C, and D gives a total lead time equal to the sum of the individual lead times, 16 days.

[**EXHIBIT 5.24**]

Lead Time Distribution

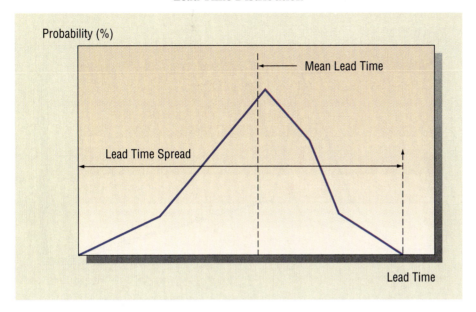

Amount of Capacity for Each Activity.   Capacity affects lead time in two ways: (1) through the processing time to complete the activity, and (2) through waiting time. Processing time, a critical determinant of the rate at which a job moves through an activity, depends on the amount of capacity available to process the job. A process with low capacity can complete operations or other activities only slowly. Waiting times become important when orders are ready to begin activities, but other orders already occupy machines and other resources. For example, a batch of circuit boards might arrive at an inspection station while the inspector is busy checking another batch; the newly arrived job has to wait until the inspection completes other jobs that arrived earlier. This waiting time increases lead time.

Other Issues Involving Lead Times.   The discussion of lead times has assumed mean or average lead times. This satisfies most requirements, but analysts must accept that single values such as means do not give truly accurate measures of lead times. Rather, distributions like the one in Exhibit 5.24 offer the best descriptions of lead times. The spread of a distribution (the difference between the upper and lower points) indicates the predictability of lead times. A wider spread suggests less predictable values, and a narrower spread inspires more confidence. Operations managers measure these spreads by such statistics as range (subtracting the lowest value from the highest), variance, and standard deviation.

In addition to the spread, the shape of a distribution provides information about what will happen to a job. For example, the two distributions in Exhibit 5.25 have similar means and spreads, but their shapes differ. The symmetrical shape of Distribution A indicates the same likelihood of a job being completed either early or late. Distribution B indicates early completion of many jobs with a few taking a long time. An accurate study of lead times must look beyond mean values to consider the spreads and shapes of lead time distributions.

[EXHIBIT 5.25]

Shapes of Lead Time Distributions

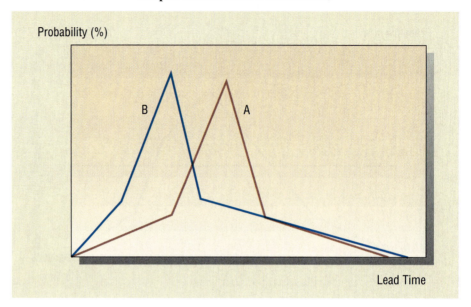

Process flow analysis highlights three options for reducing lead times. The operations manager can try first to simplify a process by eliminating or consolidating activities; a process with fewer steps often takes less lead time. Second, the operations manager can try to reduce lead time by increasing capacity to speed processing within activities. Finally, the manager can reorganize the process to replace sequential organization for activities with parallel organization.

 ## CHANGING PROCESSES: A VALUE-DRIVEN PERSPECTIVE

Value guides the efforts of operations managers to analyze any process. This section explores that link in greater detail, and it suggests a method for changing and improving a process to more effectively enhance value.

An operations manager follows a four-step procedure to examine and change a processes to maximize value:

- Setting standards
- Evaluating the process
- Determining dispositions of specific activities
- Determining positions of remaining activities

Setting Standards

The effort to implement value-driven changes to a process begins by establishing the criteria by which to judge the value that the current process delivers to its customers. Two methods for this work, customer surveys and benchmarking, generate

[E X H I B I T   5 . 2 6]

Translating Customer Expectations into Process Evaluation Criteria

		Process Evaluation Matrix		
Explicit Demand	**Latent Demand**	**Customer Demands**		**Process Criteria**
		Order Winners	Process Evaluation	Number of Steps
				Parallel versus Sequential Process
		Order Qualifiers		Distance
				Inspections/Delays
		Order Losers		Capacity/ Availability

similar outputs: (1) criteria by which to assess the contribution of each activity in the process to value and (2) descriptions of expected outputs.

Ideally, setting standards should identify what customers expect of the process and how they judge value; this determines the operations manager's criteria for value contributions of activities. Expected outputs describe what each activity should do or produce to add value to the process. Accurate judgments require fairly concrete specifications for outputs; Titeflex might specify that the order-taking process should quickly process and enter new orders, for example. The standards set in this step determine the ultimate effectiveness of the process.

Surveying Customers.   The order winners, order qualifiers, and order losers discussed in Chapter 1 suggest a framework for establishing customer expectations. As Exhibit 5.26 indicates, customer surveys first identify order winners, order qualifiers, and order losers. Operations managers then determine standards that indicate how effectively the firm's process supplies the first two and avoids the third. For example, customer surveys may identify speed and responsiveness as order winners. To help the firm compete on these two dimensions, an effective process would have to feature fewer steps, relatively few delays or storage activities (which unnecessarily increase lead time), short distances between activities, few transportation activities, short setups relative to processing times (since setups consume capacity without generating value), and parallel rather than sequential organization patterns for activities.

Customer surveys must separate explicit demands (expected quality) from latent demands (exciting quality). Recall that an explicit demand represents a problem that customers recognize with a solution that they can describe clearly; a latent demand results from a recognizable problem with no clear solution. The difference between explicit and latent demands guide the future orientation of the process. Explicit demands define what the process must do now to solve a known

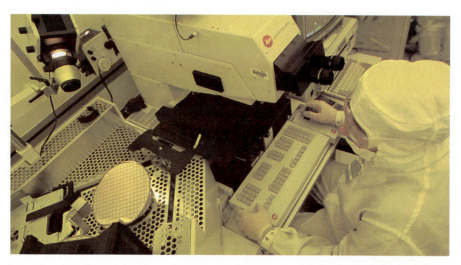

Intel uses benchmarking to compare the processes used in the production of its silicon chips with those used by other well-known manufacturers. In this way, Intel is able to evaluate the effectiveness of its practices.   SOURCE   Ed Kashi

problem with a specified product. In contrast, latent demands define what the process must do in the future because the problem and the product to solve it require clarification.

These concepts underlie the process evaluation matrix in Exhibit 5.26. Operations managers can use this matrix to formulate criteria by which to assess the value that the process generates.

Benchmarking.   In addition to customer surveys, operations managers can practice benchmarking to establish standards for evaluating processes. **Benchmarking** compares a company's own practices against similar practices of firms recognized as the most effective at some task. This relatively new process is attracting increasing attention and acceptance from managers in industry. A recent survey found that:[13]

benchmarking

Comparing a company's own practices against similar practices of firms recognized as the most effective at some task

- 79 percent of companies believe they must benchmark to survive
- 95 percent of companies claim they don't know how to benchmark
- 28 percent of companies see benchmarking as a fad
- 79 percent of companies believe that small firms can afford the expense

A number of advocates are stirring interest in benchmarking. To win the Malcolm Baldrige Quality Award, the highest recognition for quality processes by a U.S. firm, a company must practice benchmarking. Many successful companies such as Xerox, Hewlett-Packard, Ford, Chrysler, Intel, and Motorola maintain extensive benchmarking efforts. For industry giants and many smaller firms, benchmarking is now becoming a fact of life.

Some see benchmarking as a copying exercise to identify the best practices in the field, copy them, and improve on them.[14] Others interpret benchmarking as a search for the best possible practice to achieve superior performance.[15]

[13]Eugene E. Sprow, "Benchmarking: It's Time to Stop Tinkering with Manufacturing and Start Clocking Yourself against the Best," *Manufacturing Engineering* 111, no. 3 (September 1993), p. 58.

[14]Sprow, "Benchmarking."

[15]Gregory H. Watson, *The Benchmarking Workbook* (Cambridge, Mass.: Productivity Press, 1992), p. 5.

Effective benchmarking requires a well-defined process of its own, though different practitioners set their own sequences of steps. For example, Gerald Balm identified 21 distinct steps in the benchmarking process developed by IBM's Rochester, Minnesota, facility:

ON THE JOB

Benchmarking Process

■

1. Determine what to benchmark.
2. Identify key performance variables to measure.
3. Estimate the cost of a benchmarking study and obtain management approval.
4. Select a benchmarking team and provide training in the technique.
5. Complete a detailed analysis of the firm's own process or business practice.
6. Decide on methods such as phone surveys, mailed questionnaires, personal visits, or some combination.
7. Develop questions to ask through these methods.
8. Identify companies against which to benchmark.
9. Identify contacts within the companies.
10. Collect internal and public domain data on the appropriate companies, processes, or business practices.
11. Analyze existing information to determine additional data needs.
12. Plan the specific methods for the benchmarking study.
13. Collect data by performing phone, mail, or personal interviews as planned.
14. Analyze the data, projecting future performance levels of the benchmarked companies.
15. Develop recommendations from the study's conclusions.
16. Prepare an implementation plan and budgets for the recommendations.
17. Identify appropriate performance standards for supporting departments or functions in the new process.
18. Present the plan to management for approval.
19. Upon approval, communicate the plan and performance requirements to the supporting departments.
20. Implement the plan, monitor progress, and conduct periodic management reviews.
21. Periodically, review market conditions to assure that goals and objectives remain valid.

SOURCE Gerald J. Balm, *Benchmarking: A Practitioner's Guide for Becoming and Staying the Best* (Schaumburg, Ill.: QPMA Press, 1992).

However one defines the term, certain important traits characterize all versions of benchmarking. It is a well-defined process or sequence of activities. It looks beyond the firm's own industry to identify the best practices in any firm anywhere. By comparing its own practices against the best possible practices, the benchmarking firm seeks to identify gaps between its current process (defined through analytical procedures like process flow analysis) and the process it should implement (defined by the best practices). It works to develop an insider's view of another company's operations to highlight distinctions between the practices of the two companies.

Benchmarking evaluates best practices selectively, recognizing that some apply to the firm's own situation while others do not. It then reviews these best practices to look for additional potential improvements. Rather than copying other firms' solutions automatically, benchmarking aims to learn from others' experience to avoid the pain and time required to repeat those experiences.

Ultimately, like the customer survey, benchmarking represents a customer-driven quest for value. Tom Carter, vice president of quality at Alcoa, states, "We

[**E X H I B I T   5 . 2 7**]

Focuses of Benchmarking

Benchmark Type	Focus	Team	Guidelines
Product	Dissecting products	Designers, operations managers, and manufacturing engineers	Requires no site visit and provides hard, historical, and short-lived design information. Any process information only implicated.
Process	Manufacturing processes	Manufacturing engineers, specialists and operations managers	Requires site visits, focuses on specific functions, and requires some humility, admitting ways are not necessarily the best.
Best practices	Management processes	Staff and middle management	Combines visits and industry observations to look beyond an industry to combine process and management practices.
Strategic	Management directions	Top management	Long term, and seldom based on site visits or sharing, but on presumed information, and is very uncertain and subjective to other benchmarking efforts.

Other Types of Benchmarking

Tactical	Strategic focus not particularly industry-specific
Industry	Focused on general characteristics of an industry
Generic	Focused on general, not industry-specific, business practices
Competitive	Focused only on head-to-head competitors
Functional	Isolates specific business or operations management functions
Performance	Focuses on numerical characteristics of specific products or processes

SOURCE   Eugene E. Sprow, "Benchmarking: It's Time to Stop Tinkering with Manufacturing and Start Clocking Yourself against the Best," *Manufacturing Engineering* 111, no. 3 (September 1993), p. 58. Reprinted with permission of the Society of Manufacturing Engineers (Dearborn, Michigan).

benchmark for a purpose: to add value."[16] Benchmarking is fueled by the belief that the search for best practices will eventually lead to superior performance.

In fact, benchmarking provides a strong complement to the customer survey rather than an alternative. The customer survey tells the manager what customers expect; benchmarking tells the manager what other organizations are doing successfully. Each provides essential information aimed at process improvement that the other does not.

A benchmarking exercise generally does not cover the entire range of another company's processes. Exhibit 5.27 details some narrower focuses for typical benchmarking efforts; the choice between them is strongly influenced by the needs of the organization. For example, a firm that confronts potential changes in its business might conduct strategic benchmarking to examine other firms outside its industry to identify significant business trends that it might otherwise have overlooked.[17]

Evaluating the Process

After setting standards by customer surveys and benchmarking, the effort to change the process continues by assigning each activity documented through process flow analysis to one of four categories:

[16]Ibid., p. 33.

[17]Ibid., p. 8.

- *Value-adding*   The activity contributes to value.
- *Nonvalue-adding but necessary*   The activity adds no value, but a customer demands it (e.g., a required inspection of all components before shipment of an order).
- *Waste-creating*   The activity consumes resources but generates no value for the customer.
- *Uncertain (?)*   Current information leaves the operations manager unsure about the category in which a specific activity fits. This temporary changes when more information suggests reclassification in one of the first three categories.

The effort to assign activities to categories can draw on a powerful technique called the *Five Whys*.[18] This technique asks why a process includes an activity or how the activity contributes to value. The initial response may be fairly shallow, but repeated questioning (often through up to five times) moves the investigation beyond obvious information to fully define what characteristics of the activity add value or create waste, or what makes a nonvalue-adding activity necessary.

This step should complete the classification of every activity in a process. The change process continues by determining the dispositions of those activities.

Determining the Disposition of Activities

Change disposes of every activity in one of four ways:

- *Keep*   This decision leaves intact any current value-adding activity that analysis designates as both efficient and effective, so no improvements seem appropriate.
- *Combine*   This decision joins a value-adding activity with others that do the same or similar things to improve the efficiency of the process.
- *Rethink*   This decision reevaluates an inefficient value-adding or nonvalue-adding but necessary activity to maintain any contribution to value while enhancing process efficiency.
- *Eliminate*   This decision applies to any activity that creates only waste to improve speed (by dropping unnecessary steps) and enhance the ability of the process to deliver value.

The disposition exercise identifies and eliminates activities that do not contribute to value while enhancing the efficiency of the revised process.

Determining the Positions of Remaining Activities

In every process, one set of activities determines the overall process lead time. Operations managers typically refer to this important sequence of activities as the critical path of the process. Adding activities to the critical path increases the overall lead time of the process; removing activities from the critical path reduces overall lead time.

The change initiative can position each activity either on the critical path or parallel to the critical path. As discussed earlier, organizing activities sequentially produces a longer process lead time than organizing them in parallel.

---

[18]Kenneth A. Wantuck, *Just in Time for America* (Southfield, Mich.: KWA Media, 1989), p. 53.

The four-step change effort should develop a process with a high value content that consumes less time, space, and resources than the initial process. The new process should be both effective and efficient.

BUSINESS PROCESS REENGINEERING

The change process discussed in the previous section emphasizes analysis and revision of existing processes to eliminate waste-generating activities and enhance the efficiency with which the remaining activities add value. A more radical approach, **business process reengineering** (BPR), seeks to develop processes that generate the highest level of value for customers without restrictions of any prior process. Since BPR was first developed by Michael Hammer, it has been successfully used at such companies as Ford, IBM Credit, Capital Holdings, Kodak, Bell Atlantic, and Taco Bell. BPR is increasingly being redefined as business process redesign to denote that it includes both major and minor changes.

BPR is not a new concept. Henry Ford used BPR to make cars. Alfred P. Sloan used a similar process to introduce the concept of annual model changes in the automotive industry, and Frank Perdue used it to revolutionize the chicken industry.

Hammer and Champy describe business process reengineering as, "the fundamental rethinking and radical redesign of business processes to achieve dramatic improvements in critical contemporary measures of performance, such as cost, quality, service, and speed."[19] Like process flow analysis, business process reengineering is process-oriented. It begins, not with the existing process, but with a precise image of the outputs that customers want. It then develops a process that delivers those exact outputs. BPR focuses not on what is, but on what should be.

Business process reengineering advocates a rethinking exercise with three steps: a vision statement, an impact statement, and an implementation phase to reengineer the process.

business process reengineering
A technique for implementing radical change in a process by defining the sequence of activities that most effectively deliver the output that customers want

Vision Statement

A BPR vision statement describes the ideal state of a process. This image of what should be sharply outlines the goal toward which all activities should carry the process.

Impact Statement

While the vision statement identifies what should be, the impact statement describes the implications of maintaining the current process for both the OM system and the firm as a whole. The impact statement identifies the costs to everyone of doing things just as they have been done in the past. This often-disturbing picture motivates the radical change of BPR. The "On the Job" box gives an example of the importance of an impact statement.

[19]Michael Hammer and James Champy, *Reengineering the Corporation* (New York: Harper Business, 1993), p. 32.

Cone Drive produces double-enveloping worm gears and speed reducers in a small batch-manufacturing process. It competes in a mature and very competitive market against many Japanese and Taiwanese firms.

In the early 1980s, the management at Cone Drive recognized a need to replace the company's current process with a comprehensive computer-integrated manufacturing (CIM) system. The new system would improve the productivity of every employee, but flat demand for the firm's products meant that it would also reduce its need for employees. Managers estimated that the plant would need fewer than 250 of its 550 current employees.

ON THE JOB

Cone Drive Involves Employees in Impact Statement

■

To justify the need for these changes, managers presented an impact statement to employees. The statement argued that without the changes, the firm could preserve all 550 jobs, but only for the short term. Because the current process did not work as efficiently as those of competitors,

over the long term, Cone Drive would become progressively less competitive until other firms eventually forced it out of the market. The impact statement pointed out that the current process could not protect the jobs of any of the firm's 550 employees for very long.

It then discussed the impact of the proposed changes. The firm would become more productive and competitive so it could indefinitely protect the jobs of fewer employees. Long-term security for 250 employees could come only at the cost of the jobs of 300 coworkers. The employees, who were members of a union, decided to favor long-term survival over short-term gains; they agreed with management about the need for CIM.

SOURCE   Steven A. Melnyk and Ram Narasimhan, *Computer-Integrated Manufacturing: Guidelines and Applications from Industrial Leaders* (Homewood, Ill.: Business One-Irwin, 1992), Chapter 7.

Reengineering the Process

Like process flow analysis, business process reengineering is process-oriented. Its redesign of a process emphasizes ambitious changes. Small changes from fine-tuning an existing system do not satisfy BPR. Rather, it advocates large improvements in performance. For example, Ford applied BPR to its accounts payable department and reduced its staff for processing vendor invoices from 500 people to 125 people and its turnaround time for processing invoices from a period of months to days.[20]

Such dramatic changes require a rule-breaking process. BPR challenges people's cherished assumptions regarding the need for specialization, sequential organization of activities, and timing. To identify radical alternatives to reduce time and eliminate steps in the process, BPR uses information creatively, relying heavily on technologies like CD-ROMs, laser discs, and other computer-based systems.

Principles of Business Process Reengineering

BPR applies a standard set of principles to rethink a process and create an entirely new sequence of activities. When possible, it combines several jobs into one, simi-

[20]Ibid., pp. 39–44, p. 47.

lar to the process flow analysis response to combine activities, as discussed earlier. This often moves decision making from managers to people who actually perform tasks.

BPR tries to arrange process steps in natural sequences. This principle arranges work in a sequence governed by what needs to be done and which activities need to follow others. A similar principle calls for a process to perform work at the most sensible location. For example, Navistar, a major manufacturer of trucks, turned over the task of managing its tire inventory to a supplier, Goodyear. Goodyear has more expertise than Navistar at managing tire warehouses, and it can most effectively ensure that Navistar's process gets the Goodyear, Bridgestone, and Michelin tires that it needs when it needs them.

Rather than developing several processes to perform slightly different tasks, BPR tries to develop multiple versions of a single process. One process may offer a range of options to match the needs of different markets. For example, IBM Credit's process for issuing credit has three versions. For straightforward cases, an automatic, computer-based process handles the records. For moderately difficult determinations, deal structurers make decisions on their own. In really difficult cases, deal structurers receive advice from specialists.[21]

BPR always tries to devote the minimum possible resources to checking and control work. Most inspection activities add cost without adding value. Whenever possible, BPR reduces or eliminates them. It also tries to minimize resources devoted to reconciling inconsistent data. For example, BPR would try to prevent discrepancies between physical inventory counts and inventory data in a computer system by assigning the person who controls the inventory to maintain the computer records.

Even this brief discussion demonstrates the radical, far-reaching goals of business process reengineering. It aims to change not only the process, but also people's roles in the new process and the nature of the organization within which the redesigned process functions. It changes the role of the operations manager from a commander who tells people exactly what to do to a leader and a coach who teaches workers to perform tasks themselves and then supports their efforts to do so.

Business Process Reengineering at Taco Bell

Taco Bell, a fast-food restaurant chain with a Mexican and southwestern menu, has used BPR extensively.[22] Management saw the chain's growth rate of –16 percent between 1978 and 1982 as unacceptable, especially since its industry had grown by 6 percent over that period. In 1983, when John Martin took over as chief executive officer for Taco Bell, he observed a strong feeling that the company did not know what it wanted to be. The future looked uncertain, as Taco Bell was slipping backward fast.

As the first step in trying to turn around Taco Bell, management decided to talk with customers. They found that customers did not want fancy facilities and playgrounds. Rather they wanted good food, served fast and hot, in a clean environment, at an affordable price. Nothing else that the chain could provide had much value to them.

In this information, Taco Bell management heard a call to reduce the cost of everything outside the chain's direct cost of goods sold, including marketing and facility designs. The firm's BPR exercise totally redesigned the process by which its

---

[21]Ibid., p. 55.
[22]Ibid., Chapter 11.

restaurants prepared and delivered food to offer customers what they had said they wanted—good food delivered hot and fast in a clean setting.

In the past, each store had prepared food on site. This required a large kitchen that consumed a lot of space, leaving less space for customer seating. Managers highlighted this fact because, they reasoned, customer seating generates revenue. The kitchen also increased overhead costs, which contradicted the firm's stated goal of reducing costs. Finally, employees viewed the kitchen as an undesirable place to work; it was hot, dirty, and somewhat dangerous since employees had to work with hot grease and sharp knives.

The kitchen study concluded that restaurants should concentrate on retailing food rather than manufacturing it, so managers developed the K-Minus system, which removed kitchens from individual restaurants. In the place of the kitchen, each restaurant includes a smaller food preparation area where workers assemble food (meat, beans, corn tortilla shells, and so on) prepared at central commissaries and delivered. A hot-water system heats meat and beans and workers combine them with other preprocessed ingredients in response to customer orders.

The K-Minus system pushed 15 hours of work out of each Taco Bell restaurant for systemwide savings of 11 million labor-hours per year. K-Minus saved Taco Bell about $7 million in 1992.[23] In addition, it brought a number of other benefits:

- Better quality control
- Better employee morale through eliminations of the drudgery of food preparation
- Fewer employee accidents and injuries
- Big savings in utility costs
- More time to spend on the customer
- Better control of food costs

Business process reengineering helped Taco Bell to grow from a $500 million regional company in 1982 to a $3 billion national company in 1992.

Fine-Tuning versus Rethinking: When to Apply Business Process Reengineering

This chapter has explored a spectrum of options to enhance the effectiveness and efficiency of any process. At one end of this spectrum, fine-tuning methods try to improve existing processes by introducing incremental changes. At the other end, business process reengineering makes far more radical changes, perhaps even throwing out the current process in favor of an entirely new one. The operations manager must decide where to start along this spectrum from incremental fine-tuning to dramatic changes through BPR.

Much of this decision depends on the size of the gaps between the output of the current process, customers' definitions of value, and the output of competitors' processes. In general, substantial gaps justify business process reengineering because they indicate serious inadequacy of the current process. In particular, superior processes of competitors often take away a firm's customers and provoke a crisis that demands drastic action rather than incremental modifications of the current process. Small gaps between the output of the current process and customer demands encourage incremental improvements rather than highly disruptive reengineering.

[23]Ibid., p. 178.

CHAPTER SUMMARY

At the heart of every OM system, processes define the firm's capabilities and the specific type of value that it can deliver to customers. The importance of processes to operations management demanded a fairly extensive and detailed chapter with some critical lessons:

1. A process is a collection of activities that convert various inputs into an output that customers value.
2. Processes are characterized by activities (i.e., operations, storage activities, transportation activities, delays, and inspections), structures (organization schemes of activities), and capacity (the volume of work that the process can generate).
3. A process can organize activities sequentially (one after another) or in parallel (simultaneously).
4. Capacity, an integral characteristic of every process, can be defined as a rate of output per unit of time. Every activity adds capacity to a process, and lead time grows whenever capacity cannot keep up with demand.
5. The maximum level of output from any process is determined by the activity (or activities) with the lowest capacity. Attempts to increase output and decrease lead time focus on such activities, known as *bottlenecks*.
6. The operations manager can reduce lead time and increase output in three ways: increasing the physical capacity, eliminating activities to free up the capacity they consume, or reorganizing sequentially arranged tasks in parallel.
7. Any firm maintains processes to accomplish such tasks as strategic planning, product innovation, resource management, supply chain management, logistics management, and measurement.
8. Process flow analysis is a graphic technique to study and improve processes using symbols and charts to map process flows. PFA tools include the general process chart, process flow chart, process flow diagram, and assembly process chart (along with its variant, the flow chart). These charts describe the number and types of activities in a process, their organization, the time they require, and the distance they cover.
9. Operations managers judge processes by cost, time, flexibility, and value-content criteria.
10. Value ultimately drives any truly effective process, so operations managers assess the contribution to value of a process and each activity through a four-step process. The first step sets standards against which to evaluate the process by surveying customers and benchmarking. The next step determines whether each activity in the process adds value, generates waste, or adds no value but remains necessary, or whether the value contribution remains unknown. After classifying each activity in this way, process flow analysis determines whether to keep each activity, combine it with others, eliminate it, or rethink it. Finally, PFA determines the position of each retained activity in the new process sequence, either on or off of the critical path.
11. Business process reengineering analyzes processes in a far more radical way, identifying the desired outputs of the process and then designing the best possible process to deliver these outputs without concern for the existing process.

The operations manager cannot underestimate the importance of the process. To compete effectively in the marketplace, a firm must always maintain a tight fit between what its process can deliver and what customers want and demand.

[KEY TERMS]

process 186	strict precedence 191	process flow chart 212
operation 187	nonstrict precedence 191	process flow diagram 214
transportation 188	spatial link 192	assembly process chart
inspection 188	physical link 192	214
delay 188	maximum capacity 194	flow chart 215
storage 189	bottleneck 196	benchmarking 224
information flow 189	process flow analysis 208	business process
physical flow 190	general process chart 210	reengineering 228

[DISCUSSION QUESTIONS]

1. Define the processes that you follow from the time you decide to leave for class until you return home. Illustrate the activities in a process flow chart.

2. In what ways would a distance learning system change the process you detailed in Question 1? Prepare a process flow diagram describing the new sequence of activities and their spatial arrangement. How might the value content of this process differ from that of the process in Question 1?

3. When is an item at rest outside a storage activity?

4. How would you define the capacity of your school of business? In what way does capacity influence the value of your college experience?

5. You are making your weekly trip to the Hi-Value Supermarket and to the local Wal-Mart. Use a process flow chart to describe your decision-making process about what to buy and where to buy it. What inputs did you use in helping you make these weekly decisions? How could an advanced consumer information system have made your process easier?

6. When is the capacity of a process with parallel activities defined by that parallel path with the least capacity? Give an illustration.

7. Assume the following roles and then indicate whether or not you would adopt either a benchmarking or a business process reengineering approach to your firm's operations:
   a. You are the new CEO of Kmart.
   b. You are the new CEO of Wal-Mart.
   c. You are the new manager of Wal-Mart's Porterville, California, distribution center.
   d. You are the new manager of Kmart's Garden Center.

8. Your eyeglass frame-making firm is considering one of two distribution alternatives. The first is make all shipments from your Chicago plant to one of three regional warehouses located in Philadelphia, Chicago, and Reno. All orders from eyeglass retailers would be shipped from these sites. The second alternative would be to create one warehouse in Memphis, Tennessee and ship all orders via Federal Express.

   Prepare a process flow chart of each alternative. What additional information would you need to ascertain which alternative will provide the best value to your customers? Is this different from a lower cost solution? Why?

9. Rabbi Murphy's Bagel Shops is a chain of bagel eateries supported by a central bakery. Most raw materials are delivered to RMB's bakery where the ingredients are inspected for quality and then stored in the raw materials warehouse, which is located on the bakery's second floor. The second floor is also where the ingredients are measured into batch quantities before being inserted into the bagel dough blender. Two-hundred pound batches of each bagel blend are mixed for about one hour. The mixed dough is

then extruded into bagel shapes and placed on flat baking pans. The full pans are placed in "shipping racks" which are then sent about fifty yards to the shipping area.

Each day, the shops order bagel blanks in increments of the number on each flat baking pan. The shipping department rearranges the number of each type of bagels on each shipping rack to assure that the number shipped to a given bagel shop matches the number ordered. Each shop's filled shipping rack are segregated by the delivery department to assure that the incoming trucks can be accurately and quickly loaded. Loading a truck requires approximately 20 minutes.

The bagel dough rises during the transportation process for about forty minutes. The truck are scheduled to arrive at each bagel shop at 5 o'clock in the morning. There the bagel shop crew unloads each shipping rack, places any surface ingredients, i.e., poppy seeds, to the bagel trays as needed, and then places them either into the shop's ovens or the raw bagel storage area. It takes approximately 40 minutes to cook most bagels. Trays of cooked bagels are removed from the ovens and placed in the bagel cooling area.

Once sufficiently cooled, the fresh bagels are placed into the retail area displays which are designed to send bagel-scented air in the direction of the customer-seating area. Fresh bagels are cooked each morning as needed. Unsold bagels are packaged into six-pack bags and sold at a discount after 2 PM.

a. Prepare a process flow chart of the above business.

b. Indicate the operations in which value is being added.

10. Prepare a process flow diagram of your college's physical layout. What factors do you think were involved in arranging your school as it was done? How could the value of your education process be increased by rearranging this process layout?

11. Use your curriculum with its prerequisites to illustrate the use of assembly process chart. How would a student's limited financial resources influence the nature of this chart?

12. Describe the role of performance measurement in business process analysis. How does value enter into this process? Does it cause any problems?

13. Your school of business wants to dramatically enhance its reputation within its region. Create a vision statement to help all school stakeholders understand the direction of the proposed business process reengineering process. Then prepare the corresponding impact statement. Then outline the process that you think the school would need to take to implement a business process reengineering program for your school.

14. After considering a business process reengineering approach, your school's faculty decides that an incremental approach might be better. How would a benchmarking approach be applied to the same problem described in Question 13? Prepare a program designed to enhance the value of your school's business degree by 50 percent five years from now.

C A U T I O N

[C R I T I C A L   T H I N K I N G   R E Q U I R E D]

1. The great cartoon philosopher, Pogo, once said, "We have met the enemy and it is us!" More recently, quality guru W. Edwards Deming said: "It is not the people, it is the process." Discuss the merits of each statement in the context of the materials discussed in Chapter 5.

2. Discuss the role emerging information technology will play in the college-level learning processes by the year 2000. What factors will limit these processes?

CASE 5.1

Evergreen Products

The top managers of Evergreen Products of Dubuque, Iowa, have hired you as a consultant to give advice on a problem. The managers want your help to understand their situation and to develop suggestions for improvements.

Evergreen Products manufactures a line of decorative pots and plant-care tags for a market segment consisting primarily of small to medium-sized florists and grocery stores. Both the pots and the tags are relatively inexpensive to make, and the firm sells them at a high markup (60 percent). Evergreen managers feel that their customers value quick delivery and high quality above all, but the firm has not met these needs lately.

Customers place orders in one of two ways. In the first, a customer notices low stock and calls in an order. The customer gives the Evergreen sales clerk a customer number and quantities and types of products needed. The clerk records this information on a sheet and sets a due date about 5 working days after placement of the order, though customers' needs dictate actual delivery dates. No hard-and-fast rule governs this decision.

Once each day, a sales account manager gathers all sales orders and checks them to ensure complete and accurate information and to approve the customer's credit rating. Acceptable orders go into a pile to await pickup the next morning. The account manager returns any unacceptable or incomplete order to the person who took it, who must correct the problem within a reasonable period of time. The corrected order repeats the process. Each order takes about half a day to move from sales clerk to account manager and about 1 hour to clear the account manager. Some form of error appears on 40 percent of orders.

In the second order-placement procedure, the company's traveling sales representatives visit customers and check their inventories. They fill out orders to replenish these stocks and phone them in about once every day, though timing varies depending on their schedules. Since the firm rates each salesperson's performance based on the total dollar sales generated, they have built-in incentives to carefully track their clients' inventories.

A sales rep's order goes to the sales account manager and follows much the same process as orders that customers place by phone. On average, an order placed through a sales rep is delayed about half a day, though this can reach 2 days.

Once an order clears the sales account manager, it goes to the day's pile in accounting. A worker there enters the order into the accounting system, an important step that marks the beginning of the billing process. The order takes an average of half a day to pass through accounting, but this time can range up to 2 days, after which it goes to the shop floor scheduler.

The scheduler reviews all orders for accuracy and completeness, setting aside any problem orders to be returned to the sales account manager for correction. The scheduler typically returns about 15 percent of the orders received each day. The scheduler releases acceptable orders to the shop floor, where production typically takes 1 day. The time can vary depending on the time of year, however, as high volume at Christmas, Valentine's Day, Easter, Mother's Day, and similar holidays drastically increase pressure on the shop floor, which runs on average at 80 percent utilization. The shop floor is held accountable for meeting all quoted customer due dates.

Evergreen's top managers are concerned with poor performance on the shop floor. They complain about high and growing inventories, excessive overtime, missed delivery dates, and growing customer dissatisfaction. They want your advice about replacing the current shop floor scheduler.

QUESTIONS

1. What are the desired outcomes for Evergreen? That is, what does Evergreen wish to accomplish with its order-entry system? How would you judge whether the order entry system is working well or poorly? How is it doing now?
2. What do the customers want from Evergreen? What type of problems do Evergreen's existing customers pose? Why?
3. Describe the steps in the process. Where do problems disrupt the order-entry process? Why?
4. If nothing goes wrong, how long should an order take to successfully pass through order entry? How long should it take if problems arise? (Assume that the order has to go through a rework cycle only once.)
5. What specific improvements would you suggest for the order-entry process at Evergreen?

CASE 5.2

Midas Gold Corporation

You are the purchasing director for Midas Gold Corporation, a small Midwestern fruit-juice that produces a line of premium, limited-run fruit juice (Slogan: Midas Juice—You'll be touched by the Gold). As one of your responsibilities, you review all requests for capital equipment that cost $10,000 or more. Recently, you have received a request from the production department to purchase an additional stamping machine. This machine will double the capacity of the tin shop from its current level of 80,000 lids (design capacity) to 160,000 lids. Every can needs two lids. Production managers also claim that the new machine will balance the line and improve output dramatically.

In reviewing the request, you decide to examine the production process. You find a fairly straightforward process that starts by squeezing the juice from the fruit and storing it in tanks. On average, these tanks hold 4,000 gallons available at any time. Under ideal circumstances, this amount fills 40,000 cans per month.

The can-making process has two stages. In the first, the cans are made in two steps involving two departments. The tin department makes lids with a current capacity of 80,000. The stamping department converts sheets of tin into the can bodies. The tin department uses 4,000 sheets of tin per month, and each sheet produces 12 can bodies. The bodies and lids are assembled in the filling department where they are filled and sealed. The design capacity of the filling department is 50,000 cans per month.

QUESTIONS

1. What is your response to the request for the new machine?
2. Identify any concerns that you have. (*Hint:* Think about the process and its design capacities when answering this question.)

CASE 5.3

United Computer Systems

"Our customers are madder than a nest of hornets and, to be honest, I don't blame them. What we are asking them to do is not acceptable. We sell them a package and bill them but we ask them to wait for the documentation. That's like selling them a car without giving them the keys. We have got to improve things." With these words, Jose Flechette, the manager of the software fulfillment center of United Computer Systems (UCS) of Southfield, Michigan, dismisses you from his office. Your task is to suggest ways of improving performance in the software fulfillment center (SFC).

SFC generates, packages, and ships the documentation for all UCS software packages. These packages are primarily banking oriented and are highly technical and complex. They run on DOS, Windows and PICK operating systems. The documentation must accompany all software sold by

UCS, as it is difficult to use by commercial-banking and management information system users. Because of frequent changes in the software and the costs of storing documentation that will likely soon be obsolete, management is concerned about inventory costs and the costs of discarding obsolete manuals. As a result, a low stock policy (low levels of inventory which are replenished frequently) is followed.

At present, the order fill rate (completed orders filled on time) is 43 percent. It takes three to four weeks to fill incomplete orders. This delay in filling incomplete orders has resulted in many customer complaints as well as a heavy Federal Express bill.

In checking the order fulfillment center and its operation, you find that the orders are generated once a week by marketing and then passed on to

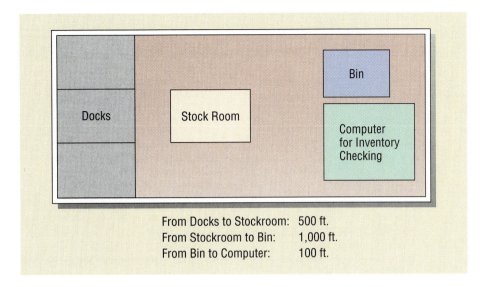

From Docks to Stockroom: 500 ft.
From Stockroom to Bin: 1,000 ft.
From Bin to Computer: 100 ft.

the SFC. SFC dates the arriving orders and puts them in a bin on the floor. Fillers select the orders from the bin. They enter the documentation numbers into the computer, which tells them where the manuals are located. They write this information down and go to the locations. They pull the manuals and write down the amount pulled on bin cards. If a manual is not available, they note the absence on the order cards. If the manual is available, they take it to a center processing location (the dock) where they put the manuals into a shipping box. They continue to move from the processing location to the floor until all of the components have been pulled.

You notice that everyone manages the process differently. Some pull one manual and then go to the dock, while others pull all that they can before going to the dock. The same lack of uniformity also applies to the recording of shortages. Some record and communicate shortages as they are identified, while others wait until the entire order has been picked. Currently, the fillers are evaluated on the amount of time spent picking and filling orders (i.e., they must be able to justify spending 8 hours on the job).

What recommendations do you offer Jose Flechette on improving operations in the SFC? Why are there problems? Provide a complete solution (i.e., don't jump to the conclusion). In your answer, focus on the following issues:

- Who are your customers? What do they want? Identify the order winners, order qualifiers, and order losers.
- Compare the customers' definition of value with what the system is currently organized to achieve.
- What should an effectively operating SFC deliver as desired outcomes?
- Describe the current process. What are the problems with this current process? Use any process flow analysis tools which are relevant to document process.
- Drawing on the strategies for enhancing value as introduced in Chapter 3 (i.e., More of, Less of, Better than, At once, etc.), what general changes would you introduce to improve performance in the short term? In the long term?
- How would you measure performance in the SFC?
- If you were asked to do a business process reengineering exercise on the SFC, what elements would you have to provide that are so far missing?

Assume the following information:

1. All of the manuals are in stock when the picker goes out.

2. The computer used for checking inventory records is located next to the bin where the orders are stored.
3. The bin where the orders are located is positioned at the other end of the building from the dock.
4. The average order consists of five sets of manuals, and the pickers return to the dock after picking up two sets of manuals.
5. The locations are written down for all the manuals when the order is first pulled.

[SELECTED READINGS]

Andrews, Dorine C., and Susan K. Stalick. *Business Reengineering: The Survival Guide.* Englewood Cliffs, N.J.: Yourdon Press, 1994.

Balm, Gerald J. *Benchmarking: A Practitioner's Guide for Becoming and Staying the Best.* Schaumburg, Ill.: QPMA Press, 1992.

Blackstone, John H., Jr. *Capacity Management.* Cincinnati, Ohio: South-Western, 1989.

Currid, Cheryl, and Company. *Reengineering ToolKit: 15 Tools and Technologies for Reengineering Your Organization.* Rocklin, Calif.: Primag, 1994.

Davidow, William H., and Michael S. Malone. *The Virtual Corporation.* New York: Harper Business, 1992.

Hammer, M. "Reengineering Work: Don't Automate, Obliterate." *Harvard Business Review,* July/August 1990, pp. 104–112.

Hammer, Michael, and James Champy. *Reengineering the Corporation.* New York: Harper Business, 1993.

Hansen, Gregory A. *Automating Business Process Reengineering: Breaking the TQM Barrier.* Englewood Cliffs, N.J.: Prentice-Hall, 1994.

Harrington, H. James. *Business Process Improvement: The Breakthrough Strategy for Total Quality, Productivity, and Competitiveness.* New York: McGraw-Hill, 1991.

Maskell, Brian H. *Performance Measurement for World Class Manufacturing.* Cambridge, Mass.: Productivity Press, 1991.

Melan, Eugene H. *Process Management: Methods for Improving Products and Service.* New York: McGraw-Hill, 1993.

Melnyk, Steven A., and Ram Narasimhan. *Computer-Integrated Manufacturing: Guidelines and Applications from Industrial Leaders.* Homewood, Ill.: Business One-Irwin, 1992.

Melnyk, Steven A., and William R. Wassweiler. "Business Process Reengineering: Understanding the Process, Responding to the Right Needs." *APICS: 37th International Conference Proceedings.* San Diego, Calif., October 30–November 4, 1994, pp. 115–120.

Raeker, Roland H. "New Times, Old Tools." *APICS: 35th International Conference Proceedings.* Montreal, Quebec, Canada, October 18–23, 1992, pp. 255–258.

Rummler, G. A., and A. P. Brache. *Improving Performance: How to Manage the White Space on the Organization Chart.* San Francisco, Calif.: Jossey-Bass, 1990.

Senge, Peter. *The Fifth Discipline: The Art and Practice of Learning Organizations.* New York: Doubleday, 1990.

Sprow, Eugene E. "Benchmarking: It's Time to Stop Tinkering with Manufacturing and Start Clocking Yourself against the Best." *Manufacturing Engineering* 11, no. 3 (September 1993).

Watson, Gregory H. *The Benchmarking Workbook.* Cambridge, Mass.: Productivity Press, 1992.

CHAPTER SIX

Managing the Human Resource

CHAPTER OBJECTIVES

[At the end of this chapter, you should be able to]

- Describe the forces driving change in operations management.
- Explain how an understanding of those forces underlies any effort to manage change.
- List the best practices by which successful organizations have helped their workers to deal with social and technical change.
- Apply some traditional OM tools and some new tools to assess a current situation and evaluate potential responses designed to move the organization toward its objectives.

Jim Pickerell /
Woodfin Camp &
Associates

Snapshot of Reality

THE MORNING PASSENGERS HEADED downtown on a Chicago commuter train did not seem ready to delight customers. The only smile in the crowd came from a chuckling, middle-aged man deeply immersed in the comics section of the morning paper.

Perhaps the train represents an unfair snapshot of the American worker. Still, these are the people that customers encounter in stores, at work, and behind the counters at government agencies.

A charitable observer might see them as just one cup of coffee away from being likable, effective employees. A cynic might repeat a comment from one manager who came to believe in reincarnation after seeing employees come to life at quitting time each day.

Operations managers must meet the challenge of helping each employee reach his or her full potential as a caring, competent individual. This requires a work environment in which each individual understands his or her role in the organization, knows how to perform this role effectively, and, most importantly, cares enough to do the work well. The work environment must also provide the parts, tools, and information that the worker needs to perform the work, along with a healthy and acceptably pleasant workplace. The work environment should inspire a feeling in workers that the organization is a good place to work and one where employees can grow to their full potential through fair opportunities for training and advancement.

This tough assignment competes for attention with other management responsibilities, but successful management of the human resource is essential for long-run organizational success. For example, McDonald's has developed business processes that allow it to meet or exceed customers' expectations. Its purchasing function virtually guarantees quality raw materials, and its logistics system reliably delivers them to restaurants quickly and in good condition. Its French-friers make even a new employee an error-free cook. At the moment of truth, however, all of this work fails to satisfy customers if counter workers serve food without a smile or in an unpleasant environment.

People commonly believe that operations managers spend all of their time tinkering with robots, computers, and expert systems. To be sure, these technological tools are having important impacts on businesses, but they have not eliminated the essential role of humans in organizations; in fact, workers have become more important than ever, though their roles are changing. Therefore, operations managers must look past the declining importance of direct labor costs to recognize that the importance of their work managing human resources has never been greater.

As late as the 1960s, many operations managers took the narrow focus of the best practices of early manufacturing management with the goal of extracting the most work possible from a firm's laborers. Taylor, Gantt, the Gilbreaths, and others researched methods, tools, and work procedures to enhance the efficiency of a firm's direct labor force. The managers of the day referred to employees as *laborers* or *hands,* unmistakably demonstrating what contribution they most valued. Since that time, the task of managing humans within the OM function has outgrown a limited concern for workers' physiological contributions. Indeed, this concern must pass beyond the boundaries of the operations management function since the success of today's organization often depends on effective cross-functional and inter-company cooperation.

In Chapter 6, we explore the complex interface between the operations management and human resource management functions through which they work together to develop and implement policies and practices that transform the firm's workers into experts in customer service. Three themes will drive this chapter:

1. The manager must design the work of every employee to directly or indirectly support the ultimate goal of the organization: to please customers.
2. An organization must design all of its systems and processes to recognize and respond effectively to change in its behavioral, technological, consumer, social, and legal environments.
3. An organization must create an environment that fosters close cooperation between people with diverse cultural and functional perspectives to help them to work together for their common good.

Styles of human resource management vary to fit individual circumstances, but these issues appear to be universal.

We will begin this chapter's discussion by describing some important human resource challenges facing American businesses. The next section will discuss some of the best practices of firms that have successfully responded to some of these challenges. The final section describes some of the tools that management practitioners have developed to help them design organizations that can meet the challenges of competition, employee effectiveness, and customer satisfaction.

 ## MAJOR CHANGES IN THE WORKPLACE

Chapter 1 discussed the evolution of operations management practices in response to changes in technology, consumer preferences, and social values. This process continues today, so current planning for human roles in an organization must anticipate operating conditions in coming decades. In this section, we will discuss some of the conditions that firms will likely encounter over time. This analysis assumes that:

1. The trend toward mass customization will overtake an even larger segment of goods and services than it currently affects, but not all products.
2. The rate and scope of technological change will increase. Since firms cannot easily change their work forces overnight, human resource management should set a planning horizon about 10 years into the future.

These assumptions should help managers to anticipate many difficult challenges in the decade to come. The following sections review some of these developments.

Declining Employee Commitment

North American culture is posing an increasingly serious challenge to the ability of a firm to inspire emotional and intellectual commitments in its workers. In days gone by, management could demand and expect a fair day's work for a fair day's pay, with a judgment of fairness that focused on efficiency. How can today's operations manager measure efficiency in an environment increasingly dominated by knowledge workers? What criteria govern the evaluation of an empowered employee who has been taught to do anything necessary to please a customer or to improve some aspect of a job? Employee performance standards have switched from efficiency toward effectiveness, but too many organizations retain their efficiency-based performance evaluation systems.

A traditional management style may simplify performance measurement, but it may also limit a firm's ability to secure strong commitments from workers. United Parcel Service has successfully implemented a work measurement program that encourages workers to improve their productivity. UPS has reaped gains from a system that mandates additional training and closer supervision for workers whose performance ratings fall in the lowest 15 percent of all workers. Still, such traditional carrot-and-stick systems often fail to inspire worker commitment.

For example, a toothbrush manufacturer's industrial engineering department automatically recorded the performance of each operator of injection molding machines that made plastic toothbrush handles, displaying a real-time statistical distribution of each employee's work times on a monitor in the department. The display color-coded these distributions of employee performance times with green for performance within standard, yellow for sub-par times, and red for downtime when the machines were not operating. No employees achieved outstanding performance. The industrial engineers did little with this information because the union contract prohibited including information about inferior production performance in the employee evaluation process. Traditional motivation techniques based on reward and punishment could offer no improvement in such a dysfunctional worker/management relationship.

Concern over the perception of an evolving malaise extends outside company management. Author David Halberstam reports the lament of Douglas Fraser, the former president of the United Auto Workers union:

> It is one of the ironies of American society that success and affluence loosen ties between men and institutions. When he [Fraser] was young and poor, everyone had been united by hardship. He first started noticing the change in the attitude of the younger workers in the late sixties and early seventies. It was not something that happened overnight, he was sure it was cumulative, but at some point he and a few of the other members of his generation realized that there was something of a crisis. Part of the change, he believed, was the effect of Vietnam and Watergate; there was a new skepticism, even cynicism, about all institutions. It had begun with the children of the upper middle class and had taken less than a decade to work itself into the children of the working class. By the early seventies it was a problem for factory managers and union representatives. There was a new iconoclasm, a change in the nature of loyalties and a new view of work and of money.[1]

Fraser also told the story of a new graduate from Chrysler's die-making apprenticeship program who had a terrible attendance record. The man worked diligently 4 days a week in a plant that required overtime. Someone asked him why he worked only 4 days a week, and the man responded, "Because I can't make it on 3 days' pay." Such comments exasperated even a zealous union leader who recalled "what it was like during the Depression."[2]

The task of winning commitments from employees starts with effective organizational design and careful selection of individual employees. This never-ending process requires ongoing appraisals of the current systems, workers, and environmental changes. Employee training and retraining are critical and should be carefully targeted to meet the needs of both individual workers and the firm. Employee happiness certainly does not guarantee success, but a disgruntled work force can drive an organization into decline.

" It takes a whole village to raise a child. "

African Proverb

This quest for employee commitment must recognize human limits, however. Recently, a hard-driving CEO lost his job at a Fortune 500 firm after the entire top management team threatened to quit en masse. For one thing, they complained that the CEO insisted that they wear beepers 24 hours a day, 7 days a week. By the standards of the 1990s, this represented an oppressive management demand, and the board of directors agreed that the firm should not expect employees to place its needs so far above the needs of their families. Good workers seek out firms that demonstrate concern for them and their families. The Family Leave Act of 1993 codified the existing practices of firms with leading-edge human resource policies to allow workers time off in case of health-related needs of family members.

To counter the stories of disinterested workers, one could cite many examples of workers with the healthy willingness to extend themselves for their employers. Pride in workmanship thrives in organizations that design their processes to elicit and nurture employee contributions. We must reiterate, however, that managers must carefully weigh the commitment that they expect from workers, since this

[1]David Halberstam, *The Reckoning* (New York: William Morrow, 1986), p. 486.
[2]Ibid, p. 488.

question has become a key organizational design issue. Excessive demands draw negative responses, while weak commitments waste resources. Both managers and employees must understand the need for extra effort to meet well-stated customer service objectives.

Declining Employer Commitment

Many authors have attributed much of the success of Japanese firms to their practice of committing to life-long employment for workers. These comments often criticize a lack of a similar commitment by American business, but both positions stretch the truth. To a certain degree, the life-long employment promise results from a sort of village mentality that many Japanese accept as a part of their social obligations. Many older Japanese executives recall the harsh conditions of the post–World War II era. Those conditions spawned social contracts based on corporate unions' acceptance that workers' wages depended on the well-being of the firm. Conversely, Japanese firms accepted the obligation to employ workers until retirement in exchange for strong commitments to perform well. As a result, firms willingly invested in workers who would certainly remain to provide the benefit of the training. Also, social norms supported many honors for the most senior employees, and such practices inspired strong employee commitments.

Many reports overlook limits on these laudable practices, however, which often apply only to the permanent workers of first-tier Japanese firms. Most of these firms also hire large groups of temporary workers to buffer against fluctuating human resource requirements. Since even the leading Japanese firms usually buy inputs from other firms rather than making them in-house, and since they often practice just-in-time production methods, their own sales volume variation frequently disrupts production of smaller suppliers, which seldom commit to life-long employment. Finally, ample evidence confirms that Japanese firms operating plants in the United States do not always demonstrate the same commitment to their American employees. Matsushita and Sanyo both recently shifted their television production facilities from Illinois and Arkansas to Mexico, leaving many workers behind.

Life-long employment practices are not limited to Japan. Leading-edge American firms have fully demonstrated solid commitments to their workers. IBM maintained its traditional no-layoff policy until recently, despite a declining business climate. Motorola requires the approval of its chairman before laying off any worker with 10 years or more of seniority. Further, each of these firms invests routinely in employee development, requiring every employee to spend about 40 hours in training per year. These firms and thousands of others recognize that their employees hold the key to their future success.

Still, a recent move away from permanent, full-time staffing may represent erosion in companies' long-term commitments to at least some of their employees. Many North American firms now hire large numbers of temporary workers to keep their labor-cost structures flexible. In 1994, the largest private employer in America was not General Motors or Wal-Mart, but Manpower, Inc., a provider of temporary workers. Many firms are using temp agencies both to hire people temporarily and as a way to assess people's performance before hiring them permanently. To get entry-level jobs in many Silicon Valley firms, workers often must start off as employees of those firms' temp agencies. Book publishers have relied for a long time on free-lance help to meet seasonal demand for labor. Most eventually find full-time jobs with their customers, but some accept the uncertainty as the price of independence.

[BY THE WAY... LIFETIME EMPLOYMENT AND THE BRAVE NEW WORKPLACE]

I first met Louie at his 50th birthday party. It was a happy event attended by most of his immediate family and close friends. Louie proudly recalled how America had been good to him. His two children had successfully married, and he and his wife were proud grandparents. They lived comfortably in a ranch-style home situated on a three-acre rural plot. Louie still enjoyed his work in the meter reading department of Pacific Gas and Electric after 32 years with the firm, starting work right out of high school.

Shortly after the party, Louie experienced a jolt. PG&E was becoming lean, or so the managers said, and he had been identified as a candidate for the firm's early retirement program. They made him an attractive offer, but he really did not want to go. "I still like my job," he said. If he declined the current offer, however, his bosses implied that future offers would not be as good. Louie's world changed overnight. "I thought that when you worked for a utility, you had a job for life," he reflected.

A lot of workers like Louie face uncertainty in America today. Many large firms are staffing at leaner levels and declaring human workers redundant. The term *lay off* often deceives because it implies that a job may wait for the worker to return to after the layoff. Not for Louie!

As firms such as IBM and Digital Equipment Corporation have encountered difficulties responding to changes in the marketplace, even long-term employees have lost the certainty of continuing employment. Despite the best intentions, these fine employers could not continue to honor their commitments to life-long employment. In 1993, Pacific Gas and Electric, the nation's largest public utility, announced that it would lay off 11 percent of its employees, an uncharacteristic move in the stable utility industry. PG&E blamed its decision in part on declining demand for its services. Also, its employees suffered when a public-interest group used benchmarking techniques to argue in a utility-rate case that PG&E's staffing levels were substantially higher than those at utilities elsewhere in the country. The resulting adverse rulings on rate requests contributed to PG&E's decision to reduce its commitment to life-long employment. The "By the Way" box discusses one employee's experience with layoffs.

In books such as Rosebeth Moss Kanter's *When Giants Learn to Dance* and Davidson and Malone's *The Virtual Corporation*,[3] certain popular management theories may try to justify weaker commitments to current employees. These theories often observe that people today live in a change-driven world that may make long-term employer and employee commitments unwise. They advise firms to form short-term business alliances that can respond quickly to fast-moving markets and then dissolve when the perceived market opportunities vanish.

Such a theory may lead to a somewhat schizophrenic attitude toward employees. Recognizing that process capabilities come largely from employee skills, a firm's **organizational design** should emphasize nurturing these skills and direct-

organizational design
The management task of defining relationships between jobs that help workers to accomplish the organization's objectives

---

[3]Rosebeth Moss Kanter, *When Giants Learn to Dance: Mastering the Challenge of Strategy, Investment, and Careers in the 1990s* (New York: Simon & Schuster, 1989); William H. Davidson and Michael S. Malone, *The Virtual Corporation: Structuring and Revitalizing the Corporation for the 21st Century* (New York: HarperBusiness, 1992).

ON THE JOB

**Three Countries'
Responses to Downsizing**

■

In a recent PBS broadcast, correspondent Hedrick Smith compared the responses of steel makers in Japan, Germany, and the United States to patterns of declining employment needs. Nippon Steel felt a moral obligation to its employees, so it was creating new businesses to create work for people displaced from steel-making operations. The firm built an amusement park where a blast furnace had stood, training steel workers to maintain and manage this service-oriented business.

German firms shared an obligation to help dislocated steel workers with the government.

Since German firms tend to stick to their knitting, they couldn't redeploy workers outside their declining businesses as Nippon Steel had. The national government stepped in with grants and loans to support the redeployment of plant, equipment, and employees. Workers were retrained and employed in the new firms, often at the same locations.

The chairman of United States Steel saw the problem as the responsibility of individual workers, and possibly the government, with familiar results. Displaced American steel workers may be finding employment, but not at wages anywhere near what they were making in their former vocations. These people show up as statistics in the news, but their families, friends, and former coworkers know them as real people.

SOURCE   Excerpted from Hedrick Smith, "Challenge to America," Public Broadcasting Service, January 5, 1994.

ing their development toward enhancing value. Much of the benefit would accrue to future temporary partners, however. Also, an unanticipated shift in technologies could force the firm to acquire new talents in the marketplace. Kanter argues that future employees should think of themselves as intellectual knights-errant whose careers consist of sequences of assignments to kingdoms most in need of their services. These issues are discussed in Chapter 19.

Such an arrangement would naturally erode loyalty in both employee and employer, though it would stimulate business for temporary employee agencies and executive head hunters. Team building might become quite difficult in an environment of such fluid career moves. The "On the Job" box discusses company responses to declining need for full-time steel workers in three countries.

Increased Employee Diversity

North American workplaces have always employed a diverse group of workers. Consider Henry Ford's situation in 1914:

> Language was a real problem in the Ford workplace. A survey carried out in November of 1914 showed that only 29 percent of Ford workers were American born—and that the 71 percent of foreigners came from no less than 22 different national groups. English-language classes based on the direct, Berlitz method became compulsory for all foreign-born Ford workers who wanted to earn their profit-sharing bonuses. At the end, successful students went through a ritual that was part church service, part rite of initiation.[4]

[4]Robert Lacey, *Ford: The Men and the Machine* (New York: Ballentine, 1986), p. 134.

Today, managers strive to understand and embrace each employee's history and build an organizational culture that identifies the shared goals of the firm.   SOURCE   Tom McCarthy/PhotoEdit

corporate culture

The set of values that guide the decisions of a company's staff as they work to achieve its objectives

This quote might draw a nod from a Silicon Valley executive who stated to the authors that his firm needed "to communicate to employees who came from 56 different nationalities—and that is if you count people from India as one nationality." Gender and lifestyle characteristics of workers have also become more diverse. Every increase in diversity brings new and varied values into the workplace.

In the past, organizations have tried to minimize the effect of diversity by creating **corporate cultures** with unique values. However, changes in North American societies and legal systems have diminished the ability of managers to impose their values over those of others. To view these changes in perspective, consider that in 1912, Henry Ford created the Ford Sociological Department with investigators who would visit the homes of his workers to assure that they were not "frittering their share of Ford's profits away on extravagances and wild living."[5]

For years, IBM has rigorously screened prospective employees to assure that newly hired workers fit reasonably well with its corporate culture. One California firm has hired immigrants exclusively from one valley in Mexico with a reputation for producing the best workers.

For much of this century, many large firms, and the nation as a whole, sought to *Americanize* workers of diverse backgrounds, justified by an appeal to the familiar image of the United States as a cultural melting pot. Other organizations dealt with diversity by segregating workers according to ethnic and/or gender identities. For example, in its early years, Bethlehem Steel made staffing decisions largely along ethnic lines. Germans worked as tool and die makers, Irish as maintenance workers, and African-Americans in the less desirable jobs.[6] Skeptics might call this a divide-and-conquer solution to problems with communication in a department. Elsewhere, industrial engineers commonly classified repetitive work requiring good hand dexterity but minimal hard labor as "ideally suited for women."[7]

[5]Ibid., p. 132.
[6]John Strohmeyer, *Crisis at Bethlehem Steel* (Bethesda, Md.: Adler & Adler, 1986), p. 23.
[7]Franklin G. Moore, *Production Management* (Homewood, Ill.: Richard D. Irwin, 1961), p. 315.

In the past, a lack of ethnic, gender, or lifestyle diversity (or a tendency to ignore that diversity) freed managers to focus more narrowly on the tasks of business. In these early times, even a firm with a solid, long-standing commitment to its employees often failed to deal effectively with worker diversity. People should not judge firms' past actions, acknowledged as benevolent at the time, by 1990s values. Everyone must accept the realities of the 1990s, however, which require businesses that operate in North America to deal effectively with worker diversity. Two simple reasons force this issue to the attention of the manager:

1. Laws now prohibit many practices of the past, and society tolerates them less easily.
2. No modern firm can afford to allow feelings of being undervalued to limit its employees' potential.

Worker diversity lies like an iceberg below the surface; most employees will mask hurt feelings, but discord reduces their motivation to perform.

On the other hand, managers need to understand that some negative feelings have nothing to do with their own actions. Employees sometimes bring anger to work with them. One cannot expect individuals who have suffered unfair treatment in the past to leave behind all of their feelings when the firm hires them. Part of today's management challenge involves understanding each employee's history and respecting, or even celebrating, individual differences while building an organizational culture that invites each person to identify with the shared goals of the firm and to understand his or her role in accomplishing them.

Age Diversity.   After the Great Depression and World War II, a demographic time bomb began ticking, creating a serious threat to most industrial nations. Members of the Baby Boom generation, people born between 1946 and 1964, number about 76 million and represent approximately one-third of the U.S. population. As the Baby Bust generation followed, birth rates fell to approximately one-half of the prior period's rates. Until 2000, the annual growth rate in the U.S. labor force will average 1 percent, the slowest growth rate that the country has experienced except during the Great Depression. By 2000, 51 percent of the work force will be middle aged, that is, between the ages of 35 and 54 years old.

As one adverse consequence of this demographic anomaly, firms will have to choose among fewer and probably lower-skilled workers entering the work force. Younger workers will probably have fewer skills because they have spent more time in school taking general courses, and less time learning vocational skills on the job or in technical programs. Older workers changing careers will also generally have fewer skills because they will likely not have spent time in training for their new careers. Organizations will need to become proficient at transforming raw, often-demanding talent into employees with useful job skills and suitable behavioral perspectives to work effectively with men and women of all ages and lifestyles. To attract the best of the declining numbers of new workers, a firm will need to cultivate a reputation as a good place to work.

The demographic shift also compounds the potential age-diversity problem of conflicts between the values of younger and older workers. Younger employees often approach work in ways that seem foreign to older workers, perhaps favoring short-term benefits over longer-term benefits. They respond to authority differently, and they tend to express their views much more vocally. Older workers can insist inflexibly on familiar routines, and they often accept conditions that they consider simple realities of the workplace. They frequently show more interest than their younger colleagues in benefits geared to long-term needs such as health care and retirement income. To control potential conflict, managers will need to build more flexibility into organizational cultures and benefit programs to satisfy the diverse values of employees.

The Green movement advocates recapping worn tires as a less expensive alternative to buying new ones that reduces piles of unwanted tire carcasses. In the same way, today's firms must make employee revitalization part of accepted business practices, since it minimizes the financial pinch of early retirement obligations and large groups of retirees. People have often quoted the saying "You can't teach an old dog new tricks," but managers are discovering that it applies only to uninspired dogs whose creative spirits were damaged in early training.

Like any solution, employee revitalization has mixed impacts. Retention of older workers reduces the opportunities for advancement for younger ones, perhaps stirring conflicts. It may also increase employee commitment among young workers, however, when they see the firm treat older employees well and come to expect similar treatment.

Increasingly Turbulent Business Environment

Business organizations will have to deal with the issues discussed so far in an environment that increasingly is characterized by one word—*change*. Every business will feel a unique impact, but most will need to respond to some common change drivers:

- Increased need to design, manufacture, and market goods and services internationally
- Increased need to design, manufacture, and market customized goods and services
- Increased pressure to decrease times to market for new products along with compressed product life cycles
- Increased pressure to create lean organizations in order to remain competitive during the late stages of product life cycles
- Stronger impact of information technology on the nature of work, workers, and organization structures

" The pace of work these days isn't easy to live with, but welcome to the 90s. Intel didn't create this world, we're just supplying the tools with which we can all work ourselves to death. Exhausting as it is, it's highly preferable to being unemployed. "

Andy Grove, Intel CEO

We have mentioned the plight of employees who lose formerly secure jobs when their firms must downsize. Even firms with winning business strategies must carefully deploy their human resources. By any standard, Intel has been an American success story, growing to become the world's major supplier of electronic components to the computer industry. Each generation of its microchips from the 80286 to the 80386, 80486, and now the Pentium has followed a more compressed product life cycle, as illustrated in Exhibit 6.1. In addition, competitive conditions often force Intel to discount prices in the late stages of its products' life cycles.

Changes in product life cycles have forced changes in employment practices at chip fabrication plants. During the early years, such a plant needs technical personnel to master leading-edge manufacturing processes. As processes stabilize, the demand for these services declines as the maturing products need fewer engineering changes. Intel works to redeploy these human resources to facilities that make new products with state-of-the-art designs and equipment. This employee-redeployment strategy severely strains Intel's human resource management program, since it requires continuous work to upgrade their skills. It also requires employees and their families to anticipate relocations as part of a manufacturing

[**EXHIBIT 6.1**]

Representative Product Life Cycles of Intel Chips

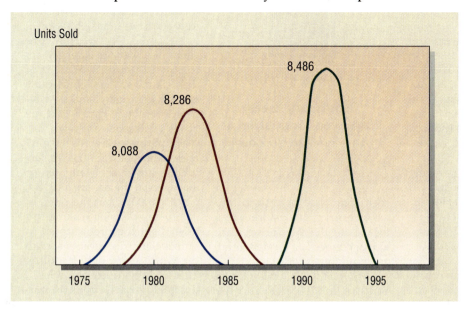

SOURCE   Intel.

career with Intel. Since Intel manufactures its products worldwide, international assignments are common.

The information highway and related technologies are also changing organizational relationships. Something as simple as a beeper can empower employees to interact with others, including customers, outside the formal chain of command. These kinds of interactions will profoundly affect quality management. Retail store chains are now setting up information networks designed to maximize their insight into both what customers are buying and what they say they want to buy. Levi Strauss is developing a system that will take detailed customer measurements in a discreet way and then custom-make jeans to fit individual variations in body shapes; this amazing customization costs only a $12 premium. Burger King plans a system to dispatch a mobile pizza wagon that will make a specific order while in transit to the delivery location. Customers might even be able to say "I'll have my regular order," prompting the computer to retrieve product specifications based on a telephone number and a database of recent ordering patterns.

Innovations like these will determine how organizations structure their activities. New applicants may seem to offer the best hope of finding the novel skills that firms will need, but changing demographics may force them to hire and develop high-school dropouts. Older people and immigrants may also become key employees with additional training. On the other hand, firms may avoid the need to develop some necessary skills internally by accessing outside capabilities through the information highway.

These and other, unforeseen problems will challenge operations managers throughout the 1990s and in future decades. The work will not be easy, but rich rewards await firms and managers when they develop organizations that nur-

ON THE JOB

Teamwork Frees Employee Motivation at the San Diego Zoo

■

Until recently at the San Diego Zoo, the wild animals weren't the only ones plotting their escape. Many employees felt like they were in cages, too. Though their cages were figurative, not literal, the effect was the same: The employees felt they were trapped in rigid, dead-end jobs, without the power to make a difference.

In an effort to raise the quality of life for both animals and employees, zoo management decided to radically restructure the way the zoo saw itself. Instead of a place that merely displayed wild animals, the San Diego Zoo transformed itself into an organization that could delight its customers by creatively educating visitors about the animals and their habitats.

Zoo officials got rid of traditional cages and spent millions of dollars to create "bioclimatic zones" where the animals could feel at home. The employees of each zone were organized into work teams to brainstorm ideas for making the zoo a better place to work as well as for delighting and educating visitors.

At two of these zones, Gorilla Tropics and Tiger River, the work teams began to function as separate organizations, with team members or immediate supervisors making almost all the decisions on hiring, vacations, and budgets. "It is like managing your own business here," one team member explained.

Not all employees were immediately enamored with the new arrangement, however. Some cynically saw the work teams as a way for management to squeeze more work out of them. But even the skeptics came around eventually, and now almost everybody agrees that the zoo is a better place to work.

Employees were not the only ones to benefit from the restructuring, however. Many senior managers at the zoo are also top-notch curators, but the press of day-to-day decision making had kept them too preoccupied to pursue their true vocations. With the work teams now handling most of these operating details, the curators can focus on their areas of expertise.

As for the animals, one can only assume they are much happier, too.

SOURCE   R. Jacob, "Absence of Management," *The American Way*, February 15, 1993.

ture individuals and environments that respect diversity, accept change as a way of life, and devote vigorous energies to better serving customers. Besides financial success, managers gain great personal pride from association with networks of vital individuals, and they enhance their feelings of security by improving the survival prospects for their organizations, though nothing can really guarantee success anymore.

To avoid carrying a pessimistic image of today's changing environment, consider the story in the "On the Job" box about the San Diego zoo's solution to some contemporary problems.

 ## KEYS TO MANAGING HUMANS IN ORGANIZATIONS

In the first part of this chapter, we described the human resource management challenges that face the operations manager in the 1990s. In this section, we present a five-step procedure designed to guide the organization's development of a human resource environment that brings the needs of employees and those of the firm into at least partial alignment. The five steps are:

1. Study the environment.
2. Articulate key success factors.
3. Identify performance gaps.
4. Initiate a corrective organizational development program.
5. Monitor progress and recommend additional adjustments.

The logic of this procedure closely resembles the basis of the continuous-improvement tools studied earlier. A spirit of exploration and discovery should guide the process. A firm must undertake meticulous, strategic reviews of its human resource policies to purge outdated social and behavioral assumptions.

Step 1: Study the Environment

An old principle of sales, "you gotta know the territory," has never lost its relevance over decades of repetition. To create an organization that can respond effectively to emerging challenges, the operations manager must fully understand four distinct characteristics of the human resource territory:

- What customers expect from the organization
- Forecasted technological advances and related skills
- Employees' cultures, aspirations, values, capabilities, and even past experiences that may influence their future behavior
- Current and anticipated social values and their likely impacts on the organization

This framework assumes that an ongoing operation is working to keep its human resource policies up to date. An entirely new firm would have more freedom since it could select the location and applicants that suit its situation the best prior to conducting this study.

Customer Expectations.   This discussion presumes and reinforces the requirement covered in earlier chapters to delight customers. Remember, however, that the moment of truth in a typical service operation occurs when a customer interacts with a company employee. That customer's impression of the company's service depends in part on how well the total experience exceeded expectations. In addition to managing product delivery, the service firm must try to manage the customer's expectations by resisting the compelling temptation to promise more than it can deliver.

Chapter 3 explained that the best and least expensive place to catch poor quality is at the source. This is especially important in services. Since no firm can prevent all inadvertent mistakes, every firm must empower employees to take rapid corrective action. Even a small unresolved problem can destroy a customer's total experience.

Technological Advances.   The need to evaluate current and likely future technological changes results from their potential impacts on the organization and the demands they will place on company personnel. Engineers long ago abandoned their slide rules and T-squares in favor of powerful computer workstations and sophisticated computer-assisted design (CAD) software. In services, smart cash registers have eliminated the need for employees with math skills to calculate

Technical advances, such as teleconferencing, have drastically changed the way companies do business. These advances directly impact organizations and the demands placed on employees.   SOURCE   Courtesy of Hewlett Packard Company

sales tax and customers' change. Automated teller machines can free bank tellers from routine transactions. In some neighborhoods, bilingual ATM machines reduce banks' needs for human employees with these skills. Even college instruction can be partially automated through the use of multimedia software, increasing instructional effectiveness.

Employees' Attitudes.   Understanding employees is the most difficult part of the initiative to study the environment. In the past, American managers have assumed that employees bore responsibility for understanding and adapting themselves to the corporate culture. American society's image of itself as a melting pot seemed to presume a single, shared vision of common goals. While some still advocate this as a laudable goal, contemporary events now require organization structures that at least accommodate diversity. Some argue that firms should even celebrate it, but every firm must respect it.

national culture

The set of shared assumptions and attitudes that guide the behaviors and beliefs of people from a particular country

Geert H. Hofstede has given some insight into the impact of **national culture** on an organization. This behavioral scientist has studied the differences in social norms and values between national cultures and the effects of these similarities and differences on people's attitudes and behaviors. Hofstede collected responses from 116,000 IBM employees in 40 countries. His research indicated that four characteristics described most differences among national cultures:

- *Uncertainty avoidance*   People's degree of comfort with ambiguous situations and unpredictable future outcomes
- *Masculinity–femininity*   A culture's orientation toward values that emphasize independence, aggressiveness, dominance, and physical strength
- *Individualism–collectivism*   The emphasis of a culture's norms and values on either satisfying personal needs or looking after the needs of the group
- *Power distance*   People's acceptance of differences in power and status among themselves

[**EXHIBIT 6.2**]

Comparison of Cultural Characteristics

National Culture	Uncertainty Avoidance	Masculinity/ Femininity	Individualism/ Collectivism	Power Distance
Canada	48	52	80	39
France	86	43	71	68
Great Britain	35	66	89	35
Germany	65	66	67	60
Greece	112	57	35	60
Italy	75	70	76	50
Japan	92	95	46	54
Mexico	82	69	30	81
Singapore	8	48	20	74
Taiwan	69	45	17	58
United States	46	62	91	40

SOURCE   Geert H. Hofstede, "Motivation, Leadership, and Organization: Do American's Theories Apply Abroad?" *Organizational Dynamics* 9, (1980), pp. 42-63. Reprinted with permission of the author.

Hofstede's data indicated distinct national differences in cultural characteristics. Exhibit 6.2 presents some of this data. Larger numbers signify stronger tendencies toward uncertainty avoidance, masculinity, individualism, and power distance.

The IBM survey data bank analysis looked at differences in answers between nations, not at absolute scores. Cross-cultural studies need matched samples: respondents from different cultures who are functionally equivalent in other respects than their (national) culture. The IBM respondents were unusually well-matched, being from the same company, the same jobs, the same technology, the same education levels, and the same age brackets.

This matching made the national component in their value differences stand out unusually clearly. The validity of the IBM scores as measures of national differences, moreover, was thoroughly validated against non-IBM data about the same countries. The obvious differences reinforce the effect of the ethnic blend of a firm's work force on its organization structure. Hofstede's research raises a number of questions. Which national culture welcomes change the most easily, that is, which has the lowest uncertainty avoidance? Which tolerates change the least? Which national culture seems most conducive to teamwork? Which national culture seems most receptive to rigid, hierarchical management structures, indicated by high power distance values? Which seems least tolerant of such structures? How does U.S. culture compare to attitudes in other countries?

An operations manager may want to ask questions that relate more directly to the company's operations. What characteristics should the human resources department target in recruiting staff for an organization with few layers of management and widely distributed authority in which workers accept change as a way of life and work together effectively in teams? Does American society include individuals with those traits? Can the firm train workers who do not fit this profile to perform effectively? Could management create an organization that nurtures the desirable traits of newly hired employees and develops needed traits?

Hofstede's research cannot give definitive answers to so many questions, but it does illustrate the futility of trying to develop an organization based on one set of cultural assumptions. Any attempt to fit diverse individuals into a single mold risks wasting the potential of many employees. No firm may fully realize all of its employees' potential, but different situations induce different people to commit themselves more energetically. A firm should craft an organizational design flexible enough to accommodate diverse characteristics of workers with varying national origins, genders, education levels, ages, and lifestyles. In the next section, we will present some practical guidelines for dealing with such diversity.

Changes in Social Values.   Finally, the manager's study of the firm's environment must assess the likely impact of external forces. Social issues, such as debates over government-sponsored health care and environmental protection, can powerfully influence an organization's structure. The statewide health-care program in Hawaii requires every employer to insure each full-time employee, defined as someone who works more than 19 hours per week (though some coverage may vary in proportion to hours worked). This mandate may tempt a manager of a Hawaiian hotel to limit as many employees as possible to part-time status. In a largely service-oriented economy, however, the manager would have to weigh the cost of health insurance against the cost of an employee perception that the firm cares more about the bottom line than the well-being of the workers and their families.

" The way your employees feel is ultimately the way your customers feel. "

Karl Albrecht

Step 2: Articulate Key Success Factors

Managers work primarily to keep an organization's ongoing activities sharply focused on adding value. The judgment of which activities actually add value hinges on an understanding of the strategic **mission** of the firm and the role of each individual and department in accomplishing that mission.

mission

The common, driving vision that underlies specific objectives and gives the organization its reason for existing

Consider the old tale of two stone cutters. The first stone cutter seems to work with great skill, but with a dour look. When asked what he was doing, he replied, "I am chiseling this damn granite rock into a building block." A second, equally adept stone cutter appeared to be enjoying the work. To the same question, the second worker chirped, "You see, I am a member of this team that is building a cathedral, and my part is to create these key components." Too many North American workers seem to display the attitude of the first stone cutter. Worse yet, many recognize that they perform useful tasks, but no one seems to value their services. Humorous management quips such as "My way or the highway" actually help to make workers feel like replaceable cogs in production-driven systems.

To avoid this miserable situation, a manager must accept a key responsibility of articulating the organization's mission to all workers and of working diligently to transform this mission into a shared vision that encompasses everyone whose services contribute to achievement of organizational goals. The manager must express the mission statement in whatever language workers understand and as often as necessary to communicate a basic understanding of what is important, reinforced as appropriate by body language. Transforming understood goals into shared goals is the more difficult task, especially if all communications move downward from supervisor to worker. The phrase "everyone whose services contribute to achievement of organizational goals" intentionally stretches to include the roles of a firm's suppliers and customers in ongoing refinement, and redefinition if necessary, of the organization's mission statement.

key success factor

Something that the firm must do well to accomplish its stated mission. Key success factors can be recast into Order Winners, Order Qualifiers, and Order Losers.

Similarly, the term **key success factors** includes everything that an organization must do well in order to accomplish its stated mission. This concept helps

ON THE JOB

**Motto for SAS:
Whatever It Takes**

One morning, a frantic passenger approached an agent outside an SAS boarding station. The traveler had left his ticket in his hotel room and the flight was scheduled to leave in half an hour. Based on prior experience, the customer knew that no one ever gets on a plane without a ticket, and he dreaded missing his flight.

The agent expressed empathy and asked the name of the hotel where the customer had left the ticket and where he planned to stay the next night. She then issued a temporary boarding pass and promised to forward the remaining portion of this ticket to the hotel at his next destination. The unbelieving customer smiled, thanked the agent, and sat down relieved.

The agent immediately telephoned the hotel, where an employee confirmed that the ticket had been left exactly where the traveler said it was. The airline paid a courier service to deliver the ticket to the airport, and it arrived prior to the departure of the flight, amazing the grateful customer once again.

SOURCE   Jan Carlzon, *Moments of Truth: New Strategies for Today's Customer-Driven Economy* (New York: Harper & Row, 1987).

managers to set priorities, much as order winners, order qualifiers, and order losers guided judgments of priorities for processes and activities in earlier chapters. To illustrate the application of this concept, consider how Scandinavian Airlines (SAS) used its mission statement to identify key success factors.

SAS commits itself to the mission of becoming the world's best airline for business travelers. This clear, precise statement led managers to ask what business travelers expect and, more importantly, what they might want beyond the normal services associated with air travel. While these customers expressed a desire to be pampered, they identified convenient departures as their most important need. They preferred smaller, more frequent flights to single, jumbo-jet flights. This led SAS to park its Airbus jets and fly smaller, less economical aircraft. In further comparisons of its ongoing activities against its key success factors, SAS discovered mismatches between its stated goals and its expenditures for staffing, training, and investment. The firm decided to empower employees to do anything necessary to delight customers. The "On the Job" box illustrates how empowerment of SAS employees inspired actions designed to delight customers.

Clearly, no firm can separate its product or process design from its organization design. Product design formulates specifications for the goods or services that the firm believes will delight its customers. Process design must then specify both human resources and production resources to deliver what the product design promises.

Shadowing the continuous-improvement methodology, the procedure for establishing key success factors begins with an explicit description of the value added by a change and a list of manufacturing and business processes needed to deliver value to the customer. SAS identified the customer/agent interaction at the boarding gate as a key link in the system to satisfy customers. The airline searched for a way to manage that interaction to give virtually all of its business travelers service that would match or exceed their expectations.

[E X H I B I T   6 . 3]

Customer Service Map

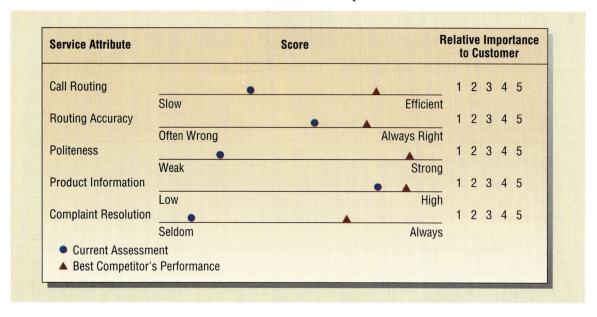

Step 3: Identify Performance Gaps

Step 2 of the human resource management process identifies key success factors, or driving forces that determine whether or not an organization succeeds. Step 3 then employs a functional mapping technique to graphically depict gaps between the current system and the system that the firm needs to accomplish its stated mission. Most people are familiar with maps that guide travelers. General aviation requires a different set of maps, with different information, and a politician would want a map showing voter precincts and perhaps data about political party affiliations. A manager uses a functional map to display a picture of the firm's performance judged against its key success factors.

Assume that Step 2 identified in-house customer service as a key success factor for a firm. In this key business process, employees respond to questions, requests, and complaints from current customers. Exhibit 6.3 presents a chart that the firm might distribute to customers to gauge its performance at this critical task. While managers may wonder exactly how well this chart measures performance, they cannot wait for a perfect or precise tool to begin their improvement initiative, and they cannot improve the process until they measure its current performance to determine just what needs improvement.

Clearly, the firm is providing adequate product information and its routing accuracy is reasonably good. This is good news if customers also identify these two areas as extremely important to them. (No one wants to be directed either to the wrong person or to someone who lacks sufficient product information to resolve a dispute.) The effectiveness with which customer service personnel resolve customers' complaints is not winning many friends, however. This could cause severe problems, since the customer's total experience defines quality, especially in services.

Industrial engineers have developed a number of tools for identifying gaps between current systems and desired systems. In part, these tools serve to determine the most efficient way to perform a task. As a second purpose, they help to establish labor standards that managers can use to plan work, evaluate workers' performance, and perhaps set a base level in an incentive program such as a piecework compensation. Later in this chapter, we will describe many of these tools in deeper detail. For now, they underscore the need for methods to discover how employees actually do their jobs.

Employees may view the tools of this discovery process as part of a traditional time-and-motion study. They may well resent such an effort and resist it, expecting their input to make their own lives less pleasant.

Step 4: Initiate a Corrective Organizational Development Program

Having identified key success factors in Step 2 and gaps between the current and desired systems in Step 3, the human resource management process must continue by implementing an **organizational development** program to specify appropriate changes. Knowing what the firm needs to do is not enough; organizational success depends on motivating and training employees in essential skills. This requires careful application of the knowledge gained in Step 1 about the firm's environment because corrective actions must harmonize with that environment to produce the intended effects.

organizational development

An orchestrated, companywide process of revising procedures and relationships to close a gap between current and desired performance

Success stories abound of the powers of teamwork, employee empowerment, and other innovative approaches for managing employees. For every success story, businesses probably experience ten anonymous failures. Some changes fail because they make the wrong revisions, but most failures result from insufficient attention to planning for implementation. This results in dismissing comments like, "We tried that and it didn't work." More likely the failures end in silence because no managers want to admit that they tried worker empowerment or another trendy technique but could not make it work.

Ralph Stayer's experience, reported in the "On the Job" box, is not uncommon. Gross underestimation of an organization's problem is routine. All too often we allocate too much time to making decisions and too little time to thinking through how best to implement the changes.

Step 5: Monitor Progress and Recommend Additional Adjustments

A new solution often creates a new problem, or perhaps more than one new problem. The fifth step in the human resource management process recognizes this general truth by monitoring results to confirm that company actions are achieving the desired effects and to identify new potential process improvements. This resembles the controlling function of management, as discussed in Chapter 4, or the check function in the Deming cycle (plan-do-check-action).

Monitoring human resource development accomplishes three things. First, it verifies the effectiveness of actions taken to correct system deficiencies or to capitalize on business opportunities. Simply put, the manager asks whether a change that the firm tried has worked. Second, monitoring looks for new phenomena, either unanticipated effects of planned actions or effects of some external force. Surprises like these may create new opportunities or pose new threats for an organization.

The third benefit of monitoring, and perhaps the most important, is the change in organizational behavior that it produces. Simply beginning to monitor some

ON THE JOB

Taking Responsibility for Quality at Johnsonville Sausage

■

In 1980 Ralph Stayer became frustrated with the high level of apathy he found among most of his employees at Johnsonville Sausages. They seemed bored and didn't really care about their jobs, so they were making a lot of stupid mistakes. He knew he had to motivate them to care more, or his company would not survive a serious competitive challenge.

But in looking for solutions, Stayer initially missed an important source of the problem—himself. Unknowingly, Stayer had conditioned his employees to depend on him to solve their problems for them over the years. It took an employee survey to reveal to Stayer that he, in a sense, was the real problem. His authoritarian management style had trained employees not to care.

Like the supporters of many good theories, Stayer found that it was a lot easier to agree with the idea of "empowerment" than it was to put it into practice. "Deep down I was still in love with my own control," Stayer realized later. After five years of unsuccessfully trying to push reform, Stayer finally realized that his employees had to want more responsibility—he couldn't just give it to them. So Stayer stopped trying to directly control his employees, and instead he coached them to manage themselves. He concentrated his energies on improving processes to enhance product quality.

Stayer at first asked top managers to taste-test the product each day, but he found that this did not help his employees deepen their commitment to quality.

So he asked the employees themselves to do the taste-tests. They assumed responsibility for making sure that only top-quality sausages left the plant. Stayer also began forwarding customer complaints to the employees, and employees soon began to collect data and resolve most quality problems on their own.

When his newly empowered employees began complaining about other employees who were not as committed, Stayer suggested that they set up performance standards. With help from human resource professionals, the employees eventually took over most personnel tasks.

One step at a time, empowerment came to infuse the culture at Johnsonville Sausage. Rather than try to dictate how that would happen, Ralph Stayer learned that sometimes, the best way to lead is to step back. By letting go and allowing his employees call the shots, Stayer finally achieved his goal: "To create an environment where people insisted on being responsible."

SOURCE   Ralph Stayer, "How I Learned to Let My Workers Lead," *Harvard Business Review*, November/December 1990.

---

aspect of company activities often causes people within the organization to react. Monitoring some process may bring it to the attention of company personnel. They may well ask why it behaves as it does, what could have caused observed events, how the firm might correct a problem or create more favorable reactions. Without any program to monitor results, these thought processes often do not occur.

The "On the Job" box suggests another beneficial effect of performance monitoring: behavior modification. If managers dictate standards of performance, it is not hard to predict worker behavior. Positive monitoring may affect the system in a beneficial way, helping to align individuals' behavior with that of the organization. Monitoring that provokes fear may motivate some uncommitted but creative individual to figure a way around the new constraint.

Only through the committed efforts of workers can the firm exploit the potential of its other resources. The five-step process outlined in the preceding sections

ON THE JOB

Schwab's Blackboard Magic

■

The performance of a Carnegie Steel mill perplexed Charles Schwab. Its superintendent was a bright, well-qualified engineer. Its equipment was among the firm's best. Yet the productivity of the plant hovered close to the bottom. On his next visit, Schwab toured the plant but was unable to identify the problem.

Partly out of frustration, Schwab asked the plant guard to get him a chalk board, which was placed conspicuously near the workers' gate. As the workers from the first shift left, he asked a worker "How many pours [of steel] did you do today?" The response was, "Three, sir." He placed a large number 3 on the board and left.

The number on the chalk board piqued the interest of the night crew. They asked, "What does this mean?" The plant guard simply related Schwab's request and subsequent action. "Well, we can beat that!" stated a night shift operator, and they did, proudly writing a 4 on the board to show off to the day shift. This exchange led to a rivalry that continued until that mill had reached 12 pours per shift, in excess of the output of the best mills.

SOURCE   Arthur H. Denzler.

aims at ensuring diligent, effective work by developing an organization that inspires employees to perform as well as they possibly can. To carry out this process, however, managers must understand and apply the conceptual tools described in the next section.

PRINCIPLES OF ORGANIZATIONAL DESIGN

In this final section, we describe some of the tools that operations managers can use to keep human resources as effective as possible. This discussion begins with techniques for crafting an organizational design that resolves companywide concerns. The focus then shifts to some more detailed issues that arise in designing individual jobs. Managers must complete both tasks, especially if the firm's operations extend across the globe.

Building a Change-Oriented Organization

The importance of this activity changes with variations in the turbulence of a firm's business environment. A staid business with few competitive threats and a stable work force may not need to focus acutely on building systems that can respond to change. Any business with respectable sales growth and profit margins will attract competition, however, and unforeseen threats often blind-side those who make the smug assumption that everything will remain constant.

A healthy sense of vulnerability can help a firm to combat smugness. In nature, constant wariness of potential danger helps animals to survive. The leader of a successful firm can also benefit from a keen sense of wariness. Bill Gates, the CEO of

Microsoft, sends memos to his employees warning them that unseen new competitors are sowing the seeds of their highly successful firm's destruction.

The best way to deal with change is to predict it and prepare a response. This requires close relationships with customers, suppliers, employees, and relevant technologies. An appreciation of the thrill of discovery contributes to this work, helping the firm to track what its customers want along with the needs and preferences of competitors' customers. The firm must also try to anticipate technical and social changes that will affect its operations.

A change-accepting culture stimulates and reinforces this awareness of new developments by encouraging experimentation without recrimination. Thomas Edison encouraged discovery by reminding associates that he had learned more from his mistakes than from his successes. An organization culture should support individuals when they constructively challenge conventional wisdom and protect them from jeopardizing their positions within the organization.

Building a Learning Organization

Seeing the need for adaptability is easy, but in creating an organization design that helps both individuals and the firm as a whole to adapt to change, the operations manager faces an arduous task. Some even dismiss this goal as impossible, but more committed firms have succeeded. Peter Senge of MIT argues that organizations, like individuals, can and often do suffer from learning disorders. "Learning disabilities are tragic in children, but they are fatal in organizations," he states. "Because of them, few corporations live even half as long as a person—most die before they reach the age of forty."[8] Unfortunately, most organizations confuse learning with experience. The "By the Way" box illustrates the importance of new learning to an organization's continuing success. In the following section, we will describe how firms can avoid certain mindsets that lead to organizational failure.

Senge's concept of a learning organization provides a conceptual framework for understanding why some organizations seem unable to adopt team-oriented, change-accepting management styles. In *The Fifth Discipline,* Senge points out that "the team that became great didn't start out great—it learned how to produce extraordinary results."[9] A firm that learns faster than its competitors, he suggests, can gain an important competitive advantage. Furthermore, he argues, learning thrives most when it pervades an organization. Firms can no longer rely on a Henry Ford or a Jack Welch to identify and dispense correct decisions from on high.

Senge argues that five so-called *disciplines* create an organization that can "truly learn":

- *Systems thinking*   A learning organization needs a conceptual system, a body of knowledge, and carefully developed analytical tools to fully understand patterns of events. The organization needs a formal process for seeing the big picture beyond the clutter of details.
- *Personal mastery*   The learning organization's spiritual foundation enables it to continually clarify and deepen its vision of its realm, to focus its energies on areas that matter, to develop the ability to see reality objectively, and to cultivate the patience needed for timely decision making. Senge's concept of personal mastery involves a reciprocal relationship between the individual

---

[8]Peter Senge, *The Fifth Discipline* (New York: Doubleday, 1990), p. 18.
[9]Ibid, p. 10.

[BY THE WAY... HIGH COST OF SUCCESS]

At a meeting of senior executives from one of Detroit's Big Three auto makers, a consultant was discussing the implications of just-in-time OM techniques on purchasing functions. As part of this presentation, he suggested that his audience might want to review the assumptions of their firm's cost control systems. After he concluded, a crusty executive said, "Young man, are you suggesting that we scrap a control system that we have developed and refined over the past 50 years?" The consultant thought for moment and then said, "Oh, I think that you should keep it if nothing in your industry has changed in the last 30 years."

Although this response may not have increased the consultant's chances of securing an ongoing relationship with the company, his point was right on target. A firm must not blindly assume that traditionally successful decisions and practices will remain effective in the future. Learning based on experience alone can blind an organization to new conditions and developments. Today's success can cause tomorrow's organizational learning disorder.

and the organization, "a special spirit of an enterprise made up of learners." This discipline directs people's energies toward achieving important goals by "living our lives in the service of our highest aspirations."

- *Mental models*   Mental models are paradigms, as discussed in Chapter 1. Senge emphasizes the importance of these "deeply ingrained assumptions, generalizations, or even pictures or images that influence how we understand the world and how we take action." Mental models form many barriers within people's minds, as embodied in sayings like "You can't teach an old dog new tricks." People in a learning organization need open, disciplined minds to look inward at their own assumptions, to objectively evaluate external conditions, and then to judiciously probe the underlying assumptions that support their mental models. Most importantly, Senge notes that "learningful" conversations occur "when people expose their own thinking effectively and make that thinking open to the influence of others."
- *Building shared vision*   This practice involves developing common "pictures of the future that foster genuine commitment and enrollment rather than compliance." Leaders of a learning organization must accept that even a sincerely benevolent attempt to dictate a vision is counterproductive. Ralph Stayer learned this painful lesson when he unilaterally decided to empower his employees. Years later, he had a great organization, but it wasn't quite the one he envisioned. Why should it be?
- *Team learning*   Senge's fifth discipline starts with a dialogue in which the members of the team can suspend assumptions and enter into a genuine "think together." Others might call this an *open conversation.* As an interesting aside, Senge discusses the Greek word *dia-logos* which referred to a free flow of meaning through a group, allowing the group to discover insights that individuals alone could not. Furthermore, he notes that "the word *discussion* has its roots with percussion and concussion, literally a heaving of ideas back and forth in a winner-takes-all competition."

[**E X H I B I T   6 . 4**]

Laws of the Fifth Discipline

1. Today's problems come from yesterday's solutions.
2. When you push harder, the system pushes back harder.
3. Behavior grows better before it grows worse; this suggests a possible time lag between short-term benefit and longer-term problem.
4. The easy way out usually leads back in.
5. The cure can be worse than the disease.
6. Faster is slower; all natural systems, from ecosystems to animals in organizations, have intrinsically optimal rates of growth far below the fastest possible growth rate.
7. Cause and effect are not closely related in time and space.
8. Small changes can produce big results, but the areas of highest leverage are often the least obvious.
9. You can have your cake and eat it, but not at the same time.
10. Dividing an elephant in half does not produce two small elephants.
11. There is no blame.

SOURCE   Peter Senge, *The Fifth Discipline* (New York: Doubleday, 1990). Copyright © 1990 by Peter M. Senge. Used by permission of Doubleday, a division of Bantam Doubleday Dell Publishing Group, Inc.

If Senge's "learning organization" were a machine, he might have called these building blocks *necessary technologies.* Since the learning organization involves humans, however, he calls them *disciplines.* This term is an apt choice, since the five principles require humans to behave in a manner that might strain most people's abilities. Remember, however, that Senge observed that a great team doesn't simply emerge, but rather it learns to accomplish things that it could not accomplish before.

Senge describes how to approach common organizational problems through disciplined systems thinking. Exhibit 6.4 lists the 11 laws of his fifth discipline, in part because they give a good example of how to use humor to illustrate serious points. The last law is the most important because fear of blame is a root cause of organizational intransigence.

Senge's criticism is not limited to outdated mental models. North American managers often enthusiastically adopt popular programs such as just-in-time manufacturing, total quality management, employee empowerment, and the Deming cycle without fully evaluating the effects of those programs throughout their organizations. Certainly, these approaches can offer benefits, but OM systems do not improve just because operations managers repeat trendy slogans. Genuine systems thinking enables managers to see their organization as a whole rather than from the limited perspective of a functional department or a TQM enthusiast.

Senge's book explains the difficulty of quickly changing an existing firm's product design and development process to a cross-functional, team-driven system. His five disciplines make sense, but getting an existing organization to practice them requires that people "unlearn" beliefs, habits, and values that have helped them to survive. Before he retired, Donald Peterson, then the CEO of Ford, was visiting John Young, then the CEO of Hewlett-Packard. At the end of a facility tour, Peterson stated that he envied Young because the HP organization did not have to unlearn all of the bad habits that Peterson had inherited at Ford. Most people are similarly encumbered with such baggage, and Senge's work can help to liberate human thinking as part of a life-long learning experience.

[**E X H I B I T   6 . 5**]

Impact of Fear at Work

Issue	Responses (percent)
Negative feelings about the organization	29%
Negative impact on quality or productivity	27
Negative feelings about oneself	19
Negative emotions	12
Other negative effects	11
Positive effects	2

SOURCE   Kathleen D. Ryan and David K. Oesterich, *Driving Fear Out of the Workplace: How to Overcome the Invisible Barriers to Quality, Productivity, and Innovation,* Table 5, p. 157. (San Francisco: Jossey-Bass, 1991). Copyright © 1991 by Jossey-Bass, Inc., Publishers.

Charles Savage's similarly titled book, *The Fifth Dimension,* addresses many of the same issues in the context of information theory. Each book covers essentially the same principle by which an organization can break down barriers that separate functional fiefdoms to create cross-functional teams capable of working together to think through and implement solutions to an organization's problems.

Building a Fear-Free Organization

One of Deming's 14 Points for Management urges an organization to drive out fear as much as possible. When employees feel free to tell the truth about problems in the workplace without repercussions, then their ideas concerning innovation, quality, and productivity will flourish. Ralph Stayer at Johnsonville Sausage learned, however, that an existing organization cannot instantly blossom into a fear-free, empowered environment. Exhibit 6.5 lists results of a field study that asked employees how fear affected their feelings, relationships, quality of work, and productivity. The consequences of these negative feelings commonly include increases in unproductive political and self-protective behavior.

The same survey asked respondents to list qualities of an organization that would create a fear-free environment. They responded with the following attributes:

- Mutual helpfulness and trust
- Members helping one another to remain objective
- Members sharing feedback on both strengths and opportunities for improvement
- Members influencing one another's ideas and decisions
- Humor and members' enjoyment of one another's company
- Creative, synergistic problem solving with results greater than the sum of the inputs
- Respect for differences in backgrounds and talents; reliance on one another's expertise
- Willingness and ability to work through conflicts and disagreements
- Commitments to common goals and one another's success
- Intimate rapport and honesty between members
- Straightforward communications

If one accepts these attributes as characteristics of a fair, well-managed organization, then fear in an organization signals bad management, perhaps due in part to causes outside the organization.

leadership
An organizational quality that unifies members in pursuit of common goals and sustains vigorous motivation and commitment

These attributes represent necessary conditions for a change-driven organization, but they omit one component: leadership. The definition of **leadership** remains elusive. An effective leader can move a group toward accomplishing a stated mission, provided the members all value its goals. Unfortunately, some styles of leadership rely heavily on fear. Few of the soldiers who served under General George Patton in World War II recognized many of the positive organizational attributes listed above. Fear can drive people toward short-term results, but it fails to unify workers in pursuit of common goals or to sustain vigorous motivation and commitment.

unproductive fear
Concern for individual failure that causes waste by limiting the effectiveness of the group

Fear of outside threats shared by an entire organization can be useful if it prevents complacency, as when Bill Gates tries to keep Microsoft "running scared." Too many managers create **unproductive fear**, however, or fear that causes waste by limiting the effectiveness of the group in working to achieve the goals of the organization. Unproductive fear makes employees risk-averse and promotes political infighting designed to protect individuals and their chances of survival.

A change-driven organization encourages discovery without unproductive fear. Such an organization needs leaders who can direct, coordinate, and inspire members to accept and strive to achieve its shared goals.

Dealing with Diversity

Earlier in the chapter, we described the efforts of most North American firms to eliminate diversity by forcing employees to adopt rigid sets of workplace values. Some firms may manage to maintain this trend, especially small firms or firms in regions with relatively homogeneous populations. Most firms, however, face serious challenges in their efforts to form teams of individuals with diverse values, and success can depend on an effective response. Accommodating diversity often requires a comprehensive review of corporate policies and practices to identify and adjust those that contradict employees' needs.

This review might logically start with recognition that employees want individualized treatment, just as customers increasingly demand customized products. One size does not fit all in human resource management any more than in the garment industry. A manager who tries to treat everyone equally will encounter obstacles in a diverse workplace because people have different needs.

Instead, a firm must develop a flexible style of management that tolerates and benefits from individuality. It must develop policies, systems, and practices that allow managers to focus on performance and on individual differences in styles, needs, preferences, motivators, and rewards. Jamieson and O'Mara list several components of such a system:[10]

- Setting goals and standards for work
- Clarifying tasks and roles
- Observing and/or coaching performance
- Providing feedback and performance evaluation
- Identifying training and development requirements
- Rewarding good performance

[10]D. Jamieson and J. O'Mara, *Managing Work Force 2000* (San Francisco: Jossey-Bass, 1991).

At first glance, these activities may seem no different from traditional human resource management practices. Jamieson and O'Mara argue, however, that the firm must individualize each activity for each employee.

Similarly, Peter Senge argues that most organizations build fear into their systems because they focus on what he calls *detailed complexity*, in which traditional goal setting and resulting performance-appraisal practices focus too heavily on mastery of detailed, individual tasks, leading to narrow, linear interpretations of performance, as in piecework compensation systems. This focus often convinces the work force that the firm cares about nothing but production.

Senge distinguishes this limited perspective from *dynamic complexity*, which shifts the emphasis from linear cause-and-effect chains toward networks of relationships between individuals and the system. Feedback no longer flows strictly in a top-to-bottom path, instead following reciprocal flows of influence, each of which acts as both cause and effect. This forms part of Senge's image of the learning organization. Others refer to this practice as **coaching**.

coaching
A management style that acknowledges and respects networks of relationships between individuals and the organization

Practicing managers see little new thought in these theorists' revelations. Good managers have always treated workers as individuals, often succeeding despite formal procedures and policies that mandate equal treatment for all. While such formal procedures provide an illusion of fairness, managers must usually stretch them to fit daily realities or even to selectively ignore them to accomplish anything. Unions have long used a threat to work to contract, or to strictly observe work rules, using the folly of formal systems to demonstrate their power. Likewise, good managers selectively adapt set rules to achieve a strong working relationships with their employees and expect the occasional "bad day" or performance fluctuations.

Tools for Managing a Diverse Work Force.   The earlier discussion of Hofstede's studies outlined differences among national cultures. Diversity-conscious managers should evaluate the implications of these differences for their firm's planning and control system.

For example, many international companies have established low-value-added assembly plants in Badong, Indonesia, an island 12 miles east of Singapore. These plants recruit many young women from small Indonesian villages much as Massachusetts textile mills did from small New England villages during America's industrial revolution. The workers live in strictly supervised company housing to assure their families that they will be eligible for marriage when they return to their largely Moslem villages.

Far away, Disney has opened its Euro-Disney World outside Paris. Disney has encountered resistance in its attempts among the largely French work force to promote the image of wholesome good cheer and eager customer service that it demands at its American theme parks.

Clearly, these two situations require dramatically different management styles. Likewise, McDonald's employs different management practices for its Moscow unit, where workers earn wages comparable to those of Russian physicians, than for U.S. outlets, where most employees view their jobs as temporary stopovers in their journeys toward more fulfilling careers. Effective managers have long known that no two situations are alike, and an effective organization designer needs to learn the same lesson and evaluate the idiosyncrasies of the work force culture and then create effective policies, procedures, and systems for this environment.

Based on their field studies, Jamieson and O'Mara have formalized the principles of successful management of diversity. Success begins with effective traditional management skills. To build on that foundation, the manager must develop five skills for working with a changing work force:[11]

1. *Empower others.* A manager must share power and information, solicit input, and reward performance. Activities focus on managing more as a coach than as a boss, encouraging participation, and sharing accountability.
2. *Develop others.* Through coaching, modeling desired behaviors, mentoring, and providing opportunities for growth, an effective manager delegates responsibility fully to those who have the ability to do the work. Activities focus on questioning and counseling employees on their interests, preferences, and careers and then working to satisfy individual training needs.
3. *Value diversity.* Self-reflection is necessary to understand one's own assets, liabilities, and biases. Activities focus on viewing diversity as an asset, understanding diverse cultural practices, facilitating integration among individuals, and helping others to identify their own needs and options.
4. *Work for change.* An effective manager supports employees by adapting policies, systems, and practices to help meet their needs. Activities focus on monitoring and influencing organizational change.
5. *Communicate responsibility.* An effective manager demonstrates a commitment to workers as individuals. Activities focus on clearly communicating expectations, asking questions to increase one's own understanding, listening with empathy, clarifying distortions due to cultural and linguistic differences, and providing ongoing feedback with sensitivity to individual differences.

Managing diversity requires competence at both traditional management tasks and these more specialized skills. Real effectiveness requires an organization design that embodies these skills and encourages them in individual managers.

Policy Deployment

As a fundamental task, managers must develop systems that help to align the interests of the firm's employees with the stated goals of the organization. Once the organization has articulated these goals, managers must internalize them throughout the organization so that individual members from top to bottom know how their jobs contribute to accomplishment of larger goals. In his book describing Japan's *kaizen* management system, Masaaki Imai describes this process as policy deployment.

standard of performance
An indicator of organizational policy to guide the efforts of an individual manager

Many North American firms set **standards of performance** for key members of management to carry policy throughout the organizations. The processes for developing these standards are often not nearly as meticulous as the policy deployment efforts of Japanese firms. More importantly, they do not normally encompass lower levels of management and hourly employees. In a poorly managed organization with inferior policy deployment, employees may say that they don't really understand what management wants them to do.

Job Design

As another major task, managers must design jobs that divide up the work they want employees to perform. This process should create a system that effectively accomplishes the mission of the firm through daily contributions of individuals. In

[11]Ibid.

short, **job design** decides *who* will perform each task, *how* each employee will complete his or her work, and *where* each job will take place.

Staffing Individual Jobs.   In a sense, the *who* part of the job design function amounts to a make-or-buy decision. Managers decide whether to assign firm employees to perform necessary activities or to buy the outputs of those activities from other organizations. Once job design determines which activities to assign to in-house personnel, the manager must continue to select the workers and other resources that will perform the job most effectively.

The operations manager must determine whether the nature of the needed work suits high-volume, repetitive manufacturing methods. If so, the firm may accomplish its mission by hiring largely unskilled workers, each doing a single, narrow job. This **specialization strategy** may allow the organization to train low-wage applicants quickly and still develop proficient workers. For example, McDonald's automated French fry equipment enables an employee to make first-class fries within the first hour on the job. Likewise, Henry Ford achieved high levels of productivity using unskilled, immigrant labor since he had to train each worker to do only a small fraction of the work of assembling an automobile.

Earlier chapters have warned of limited flexibility in such a system. In addition, job specialization often leaves workers bored and dissatisfied. A manager cannot assume, however, that all individuals dislike the repetition of a specialized division of labor. Some even seem to enjoy monotony that frees them from job-related thoughts, making few demands and imposing little or no responsibility. Such workers may bring their hands to the job, but little else. If the firm can offer only this limited work, then it must recruit employees that suit the conditions. Such minimal skills cannot do much to make a firm a world-class competitor, however.

Much more frequently, firms try to enhance their job designs to provide a more demanding, less monotonous workplace. This effort can seek to enhance either the duties of individual jobs or the settings in which workers perform those duties. **Job enlargement** enhances a job by stretching its limits horizontally to include more tasks. For example, job enlargement might assign a worker on an assembly line to complete a number of assembly steps rather than one or two more repetitive tasks. At the extreme, job enlargement might assign a worker or a small team to assemble an entire product. Two-person teams at Harley Davidson assemble some low-volume motorcycles, and Volvo and Mercedes-Benz have implemented limited team-assembly programs.

Another method to enhance the work environment, **job rotation**, cycles workers through different jobs during a shift. This requires more broadly trained workers, but it also promotes a broader understanding of a firm's operations. If some jobs impose harder physical demands or other requirements, job rotation can distribute undesirable tasks evenly throughout a work crew. This benefit may sacrifice some efficiency if a less proficient worker staffs a bottleneck operation.

Job enrichment, also called *vertical job enlargement*, expands the scope of a worker's activities to include tasks that require different skill levels. A machine operator may work constantly to fabricate a part, leaving a janitor to clean up the work area, a setup worker to place fittings and set machine controls, a maintenance worker to grease and adjust equipment, and an inspector to check the quality of the output. A job enrichment program would train a single individual or a small team to perform some or all of these activities. This assumes that an individual can learn more skills and wants to assume broader responsibilities. Job enrichment, like other job enhancement programs, hopes to improve the effectiveness of workers, who perceive an increase in company trust and more meaningful work.

job design
Assigning specific tasks and company resources to particular workers to create a system that effectively accomplishes the mission of the firm through daily contributions of individuals

specialization strategy
Staffing narrow jobs with low-wage, quickly trained workers as part of a high-volume, repetitive manufacturing system

job enlargement
A technique of enhancing a job by assigning more tasks to a single worker

job rotation
A technique of enhancing a job by cycling workers through different tasks during a shift

job enrichment
A technique of enhancing a job by expanding the scope of its activities to include tasks that require different skill levels

Work Methods.   When job design specifies *how* a worker should perform a set of tasks, it finds the right work methods. Frederick Taylor, the father of the scientific management movement, called this standard *the one best way* to do a job. Essentially, job design seeks to organize tasks in the most appropriate manner, which depends on the business situation. If customers strive for cost, then effectiveness will demand efficiency. The firm must first be effective and be efficient second. Most systems must measure these two goals to develop performance requirements for job design.

Frederick Taylor spent much of his early career studying how to organize work. He proposed six steps as a logical basis for efficient manufacturing practices:[12]

1. *Assign all responsibility for organizing work to managers rather than workers.* Managers should do all the thinking necessary to plan work, leaving workers to carry out those plans.
2. *Through scientific methods, determine the one best way to perform each task.* Managers should design each worker's job to follow this one best way by specifying a set of standard methods for completing the task.
3. *Select the person most suited to each job to perform that job.* Managers should match the abilities of individual workers to the demands of particular jobs.
4. *Train the worker to perform the job correctly.* Managers should train workers to perform their jobs according to scientifically determined standards.
5. *Monitor work performance to ensure that workers follow specified procedures correctly and achieve appropriate results.* Managers should control activities to guarantee that every worker always performs every job in the one best way.
6. *Provide further support by planning work assignments and eliminating interruptions.* Managers can keep their workers producing at high levels by shielding them from distractions that interfere with job performance.

Taylor seemed to assume that workers either did not care or lacked sufficient intelligence to learn the tools of scientific management. This may have been the result of his early experience applying his theories. He often complained about workers "soldiering" (a term denoting laziness; serving in the military was not seen as a desirable career) on the job. This assessment may have been appropriate for some employees, but unfortunately Taylor's views spread to become a popular doctrine (see the Charlie Chaplin photograph).

To carry out Taylor's six-step scientific management method, he had to develop a number of analytical tools. Studies to determine the one best way to do a task led to the development of the current field of industrial engineering. In the early years, evaluations of job designs focused primarily on efficiency. Industrial engineers tried to determine the method that could correctly complete a job in the fewest possible units of labor. This type of analysis led to the development of work measurement methods to quantify labor inputs as data for efficiency estimates.

Following Taylor's first step, firms hired or trained members of management to determine the one best way to do each task. They used methods such as process flow analysis, described in Chapter 5, to develop detailed insight into the flow of work and the processes, people, and equipment that perform it. This analysis identified the goals of a unit under study, its essential quality standards, and current practices, if any.

Most Taylor-era studies focused heavily on the relationship between the worker, the machine, and the work they performed. It broke down work into the

---

[12]Frederick Taylor, *The Principles of Scientific Management* (New York: Norton, 1911), pp. 34–40.

One view of traditional job design: Charlie Chaplin in *Modern Times*.   SOURCE   The Bettmann Archive.

minimum rational work unit, a single, continuous, and distinct motion of a worker or machine. The detail of such a breakdown depended on the purpose of the study and the workplace setting. To reduce the labor requirement for a highly repetitive activity to produce a standard part, the analyst would need a minutely detailed breakdown.

To collect data for the operating time for each minimum rational work unit, an industrial engineer (IE) (ideally, a knowledgeable one) timed a worker with a stopwatch. The observation sheet for such a time study in Exhibit 6.6 illustrates a number of IE practices. Note that the observer, Craig Clifton, took ten measurements in seconds, timing each of the six operations with a stopwatch. He also estimated the rate at which the operator was working. For example, he judged that the worker as walking at a 90 percent rate, a pace 10 percent slower than what a firm could normally expect from an employee. To determine normal standards, industrial engineers routinely watch films of employees working at various paces to keep their estimates consistent. Clifton then adjusted the average time of his observations for his estimate of the observed pace to calculate the minutes per cycle for each operation.

Note that the observer made a judgment call on the fourth time element. During the sixth observation, he recorded an outlier, that is, a measurement well outside that operation's normal range, when the worker dropped the bag. Since this is not typical, he deleted this observation before calculating the operation's normal time.

At the bottom of the worksheet, it allows an additional adjustment to the time for the entire job to allow for delays. The adjustments for personal and fatigue delays and normal delays reflect standard numbers for any industrial engineering study. Workers or their representatives may dispute these allowances as unreasonable, an especially important consideration if the firm will base performance evaluations or bonus calculations on the resulting standards.

As a final result, the exhibit shows a time standard for this operation of 0.600 minutes. The firm could use this information to estimate the cost of this task. Since the study gives a standard time for the bag-filling task of 36 seconds, a worker could fill about 100 bags an hour working constantly without interruptions. If the worker costs the firm $7.50 per hour including fringe benefits, then it pays $7.50/100 or 7.5 cents for direct labor to fill each bag.

minimum rational work unit

A single, continuous, and distinct motion of a worker or machine in a scientific management study

[**EXHIBIT 6.6**]

Sample Time Study Observation Sheet

Operation: Filling Coffee Bags	**Date:** 3/4/04	**Operator:** Arthur Henry
Department: Whole Bean	**Shift:** Day	
Part No.	**Study:** Budget Review	**Observer:** Craig Clifton
Size: 1 Pound Bags	**Sheet:** 1 of 1	.....
		.....
Remarks: Mr. Henry said that this was his second week on the job.		

ELEMENT DESCRIPTION	: 1: 2: 3: 4: 5: 6: 7: 8: 9:10	: Rating:Normal	: Min/cycle
1. Get Empty Bag	: 3: 4: 3: 3: 4: 2: 3: 2: 3: 3	: 100%: 3.0	sec:.050
2. Walk to Bin	: 5: 6: 5: 7: 5: 5: 6: 4: 7: 5	: 90%: 6.11	sec:.102
3. Fill Coffee Bag	:12:13: 9:11:12:11: 9:12:13: 9	: 100%:11.1	sec:.185
4. Seal Bag Flap	: 5: 5: 6: 5: 4:12: 5: 5: 6: 5	: 100%: 5.0	sec:.083
5. Affix Label	: 3: 3: 4: 3: 3: 3: 3: 2: 3: 3	: 100%: 3.0	sec:.050
6. Hand to Customer	: 2: 2: 3: 2: 4: 3: 4: 6: 3: 2	: 100%: 3.1	sec:.052
		Total Normal 31.31	sec:.522 min
			.....
ALLOWANCES			.....
Personal and Fatigue	10%		.....
Delays	5%		.....
STANDARD TIME = 0.522 min. × 1.15 = 0.600 minutes, or 36 seconds			

The firm could use this time standard in a number of other ways. Planners might compare the standard time to demand estimates to provide a rough estimate of the number of bag fillers it should hire. As a later section will explain, the time standard might become the basis for an incentive system, or the industrial engineering department might base a comparison between alternative methods on their time standards.

Firms collect time standard data by a variety of methods. One firm might film or videotape workers rather than assigning an individual with a stopwatch to observe them directly. Another might observe the nature of the tasks and then apply some **predetermined motion-time measurement system**, which applies a set database of elemental time standards for certain common motions. Such a system might specify a time to move a 4-pound object horizontally 6 inches to an exact location using one hand. Since even a simple task generally requires many basic motions, this method requires considerably more work and skill than traditional methods to develop accurate time standards. While it eliminates the need to perform time studies on the shop floor, workers may doubt that a standard model presents a fair and accurate model of their particular work.

predetermined motion-time measurement system

A method for developing time standards based on a set database of elemental time standards for certain common motions

Yet another firm might estimate time standards based on **work sampling**, which makes random observations of an operation. To estimate of the amount of time during which a given line is actually making products, work sampling would dictate a sequence of steps:

1. Decide what to measure and its intended use. This might involve setting preliminary time standards or performance estimates.
2. Set a level of statistical confidence for the data.
3. Through statistical techniques, determine the sample size necessary to reach the desired confidence level.
4. Develop a sampling plan that indicates exactly when to take samples. This step lays out a time horizon and assigns specific random numbers to each period of time.
5. At the specified times, observe the worker or process under study. After completing the observations, estimate the proportion of time that the worker or process is behaving in a specified manner and calculate the appropriate confidence interval.

Work sampling can observe activities directly or record data by some computer-driven device. Many computer-integrated manufacturing systems can generate transaction logs that indicate a machine's status at any point in time.

A trusting relationship with employees allows a much simpler method of gathering time estimate data. The manager can simply ask them how long a task or process takes under normal circumstances. This kind of trust can save the firm the cost of industrial engineers and less obvious costs created by worker aggravation when they feel that a member of management is spying on them. No industrial engineers set standards at Kawasaki's Lincoln, Nebraska, plant. Workers keep track of how long their work takes and try to improve aggregate productivity by 1 percent each month.

Learning Curve.   The Japanese managers at Kawasaki's Lincoln plant adjusted their planning process to recognize that as people gain experience at a task, they can complete it in less time. This rule assumes that conditions encourage learning, or at least permit it. Senge's concept of the learning organization describes the conditions that contribute to such an environment.

Unfortunately, conditions in some organizations actually restrict learning. If either the formal or informal organization has established a standard output rate, then the formal organization loses the potential financial benefits of learning. (The informal organization within a firm arises from the needs, experiences, and past performance of the firm; it constitutes an unofficial way of work that may be at odds with the formal organization.) Such a standard may relax pressure on workers, perhaps indirectly benefiting the organization if this frees workers to devote more effort to improving product quality or achieving a more reliable output rate. However, lack of an incentive to improve the output rate may diminish the rate at which an organization learns. This phenomenon led W. Edwards Deming, the quality guru, to label rigid standards a *prescription for mediocrity*. At Kawasaki, both the managers and the workers understand that the competitive environment would allow no firm to freeze its current level of productivity with rigid time standards.

The learning curve is an analytical tool designed to quantify the rate at which cumulative experience allows an organization to reduce the amount of resources it must expend to accomplish a task. As early as 1925, managers had noticed the learning curve. The commander at Wright-Patterson Air Force Base in Dayton,

work sampling

A method of developing time standards based on statistically determined random observations of a worker or process

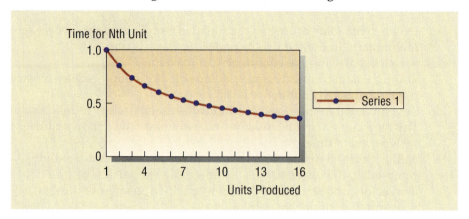

Learning Curve with 80 Percent Learning Rate

Ohio, noted that workers performing manufacturing operations at the base "exhibited a definite learning pattern." He noted that most aircraft manufacturing tasks experienced what he called an 80 percent learning rate, meaning that workers need 20 percent fewer hours to make a part each time their cumulative experience making that part doubled. Thus, if the first part took 100 minutes, the second would require 80 minutes, the fourth would require 64 minutes, and so on.

An operations manager can express the relationship between the amount of time it takes an organization with a learning rate percentage of r to produce the nth item as an equation:

$$T_n = T_1(n^b) \quad \text{where } b = \log_{10}r/\log_{10}2 \tag{6.1}$$

Thus, the cost to produce the eighth part in the earlier example would be:

$$T_8 = (100)(8^{-0.322}) = 51.2 \quad \text{since } b = \log_{10}(0.80)/\log_{10}(2) = -0.322$$

Exhibit 6.7 graphs the reduction in unit time required to produce each item when an organization has an 80 percent learning rate. Appendix 6A at the back of this chapter presents a table for selected learning rates. Another appears in the spreadsheet file titled LEARNCURVETAB on the student disk.

The learning curve contributes to time estimates by formally recognizing that initial labor costs may not accurately represent future costs. However, operations managers must evaluate learning curve expectations carefully. Expectations may lose validity if the workers who carry a project through the pilot stages of production give way to less skilled workers for regular production. Also, the organization's culture must support learning to derive any benefits from the learning curve.

Selecting the learning rate value poses another problem. To estimate this rate for a new product, industrial engineers often try to identify similar products and assess their learning rates. They may also evaluate the complexity of the process, since a more complex process offers greater potential learning. In addition, they may look for outside effects on the pace of a process, such as a machine, a labor contract, etc.

Rather than trying to estimate a particular learning rate, an operations manager may find a more interesting question in methods for influencing the existing learning rate. An unusually high learning rate, perhaps around 95 percent, may indicate a defect in the organization's culture that inhibits learning, or it could indicate simply that excellent production methods and training programs maximized productivity early in the project. An unusually low learning rate, perhaps around 75 percent, may indicate that a project began with insufficient planning and worker training, or it could indicate that highly motivated workers are straining to improve. Only through careful analysis of individual circumstances can managers develop an accurate picture of a process.

[**PROBLEM 6.1**]

Estimating Learning Curve Benefits

A firm must set a bid on a contract to make 12 units of a new product. Engineering analysis indicates that the nature of this product and its manufacturing processes resemble those for the firm's current Model 206, so the firm decides to base its bid on the 85 percent learning rate it experienced on that model. If engineers estimate that the first unit will require 10 hours of labor, how many hours will the firm take to make all 12 units?

SOLUTION

Find the unit times for an 85 percent learning rate in Appendix A or the spreadsheet named LEARNCURVETAB on the student disk.

Unit Produced	Unit Time	Hours per Unit	Cumulative Hours Required
1	1.0000	10.0 hrs.	10.00 hrs.
2	0.8500	8.50	18.50
3	0.7729	7.73	26.23
4	0.7225	7.23	33.45
5	0.6857	6.86	40.31
6	0.6570	6.57	46.88
7	0.6337	6.34	53.22
8	0.6141	6.14	59.36
9	0.5974	5.97	65.33
10	0.5828	5.83	71.16
11	0.5699	5.70	76.86
12	0.5584	5.58	82.44

This table indicates that the last unit will require 5.58 hours, raising the total number of hours needed to make all 12 units to 82.44 hours.   [▪]

Continuing operations may require an operations manager to consider another concept, the unlearning curve. This curve measures the rate at which workers lose the benefit of experience whenever they must interrupt production on a given item. This becomes a common problem when a firm organizes work in batches. As one of the forms of waste discussed in earlier chapters, this phenomenon may require managers to understand and plan for loss of familiarity by individuals or organizations to minimize the cost to the firm.

Process Analysis Design Tools.   Chapter 5 introduced process flow analysis, a powerful tool for evaluating work methods. Process analysis includes some additional tools to study alternative ways to complete a particular task. Like most scientific management tools, this analysis begins with current work methods. Industrial

[**EXHIBIT 6.8**]

Process Analysis Design Tools

Tool	Purpose of Study	Target of Study
Process flow chart	Understand process, identify delays & problems	Overall system analysis
Operations chart	Understand methods and search for simplifications	Operator at fixed work station
Worker-machine chart	Understand man-machine interfaces, identify delays	Operator interaction with machine
Crew activity chart	Understand crew interfaces and identify conflicts and delays	Crew interactions

engineers have developed several tools to study different types of work situations, as shown in Exhibit 6.8.

Each analytical tool suits a particular purpose. Process flow analysis seeks primarily to gain an overview of the sequence of operations, the locations of delays, and, in some cases, physical distances traveled. Exhibit 6.9 illustrates a process for requisitioning petty cash. It embodies another process flow analysis application as described in Chapter 5.

After documenting the present work flow, the analysis continues with a thorough review of the justification for each activity. The operations manager asks why the current process includes its activities and whether the firm could improve effectiveness by eliminating some or shifting responsibilities to other workers or activities. This stage must also consider the current work methods for completing a task and whether other methods could produce better results.

In some situations, analysis of a process must monitor more than one aspect of its activities. Some activities require two or more individuals to work together as a team. In others, interactions between a human and a machine become important. Exhibit 6.10 shows a worker-machine chart, which illustrates the functions of both a worker and a machine over time. The worker's data alone indicates inactivity while the machine fills the bag. A worker-machine chart shows how a machine contains a worker's activities and how the worker constrains the machine's activities.

The information provided by charts such as these clarifies how both the operator and the machine interact over a production cycle. Time when the machine sits idle waiting for the operator to complete a task represents lost production. In contrast, if the operator often must wait for a machine to complete its operation, the manager may see a candidate for some form of job enrichment. Managers must face the challenge of improving processes to eliminate this kind of waste.

A crew activity chart indicates how various work teams interact with each other. In a format that closely resembles a worker-machine chart, it places columns for two workers or teams side by side and lists their activities down the columns to indicate interrelationships.

Location Decisions.   Job design and process management overlap to determine *where* work takes place. As a job enters a system, someone must make a job triage decision, directing it to a job shop or a higher-volume assembly line, for example.

[**EXHIBIT 6.9**]

Process Flow Chart for Petty Cash Disbursement

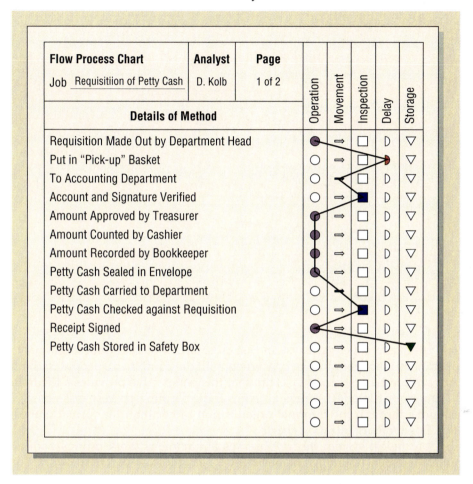

Flow Process Chart	Analyst	Page	Operation	Movement	Inspection	Delay	Storage
Job Requisitiion of Petty Cash	D. Kolb	1 of 2					
Details of Method							
Requisition Made Out by Department Head			●	⇒	□	D	▽
Put in "Pick-up" Basket			○	⇒	□	●	▽
To Accounting Department			○	⇒	□	D	▽
Account and Signature Verified			○	⇒	■	D	▽
Amount Approved by Treasurer			●	⇒	□	D	▽
Amount Counted by Cashier			●	⇒	□	D	▽
Amount Recorded by Bookkeeper			●	⇒	□	D	▽
Petty Cash Sealed in Envelope			●	⇒	□	D	▽
Petty Cash Carried to Department			○	⇒	□	D	▽
Petty Cash Checked against Requisition			○	⇒	■	D	▽
Receipt Signed			●	⇒	□	D	▽
Petty Cash Stored in Safety Box			○	⇒	□	D	▼
			○	⇒	□	D	▽
			○	⇒	□	D	▽
			○	⇒	□	D	▽
			○	⇒	□	D	▽

SOURCE   Elias M. Awad, *Systems Analysis and Design* (Burr Ridge, Ill.: Richard D. Irwin, 1979), p. 113. © 1979 by Richard D. Irwin, Inc. Reprinted by permission.

Operations managers must determine which machines should handle each job, and which workers should operate those machines. The location decision within job design may contribute significantly to workers' satisfaction with the job setting. Many firms arrange work stations in *U*-shaped cells, for example, in order to facilitate worker communications. In addition to creating a more congenial work setting, shop floor layouts may also enhance worker cooperation. Chapter 12 on process design will cover these issues in more detail.

 # SOCIOTECHNICAL PERSPECTIVE

A less technical method of job design called **sociotechnical systems perspective** views work in the context of the informal organization. This method studies the interfaces between humans and technology, viewing any OM system as both a

sociotechnical systems perspective

A method of studying the interfaces between humans and technology and emphasizing interactions outside formal organizational relationships

[**EXHIBIT 6.10**]

Worker-Machine Chart

Product: Ground Whole Bean Coffee   *Operator: Arthur Henry*
Process: Coffee Grinding

Step	Employee	Time (in seconds)	Machine
1	Grasps empty coffee bag	3 sec.	
2	Measures 1 pound of coffee beans	5	
3	Pours whole beans into grinder	5	Receives coffee beans
4		15	Grinds coffee beans
5	Empties ground coffee into bag	5	Dispenses ground coffee
6	Seals bag using end flaps	3	

Summary

	Operator	Machine
Busy	21 sec.	25 sec.
Idle	15	11
Total	36	36

social system and a technical system. Sociotechnical systems advocates argue that an operations manager must be concerned with the equipment, people, and interactions within the system. They claim that this perspective provides a theoretical explanation for the effectiveness of teams in performing process tasks based on interactions through the informal organization rather than the formal one commonly shown on organization charts.

Sociotechnical system theory observes autonomous work groups within an organization, each assuming responsibility for a significant part of the work. Some managers, those at lower levels, resist the idea of workers self-organizing to accomplish work in the way they see fit, but effective front-line supervisors long have relied on natural leaders among operating employees to finish the work they need to do. Shop-floor-level union representatives often function in this capacity. The sociotechnical system perspective urges managers to accept and understand informal, autonomous groups and to integrate them into the plant's system of governance, as appropriate.

INCENTIVE SYSTEMS

Besides simply paying compensation for work, incentive systems seek to induce employees to act in ways that contribute to the organization's success. Incentives align the interests of specific sets of employees with those of the organization. Sales representatives receive commissions to encourage increased sales. Firms intend executives' incentive packages to ultimately enhance the wealth of shareholders. Clerical workers with exemplary performance records often earn additional days off as rewards. Group or individual incentive pay programs often encourage factory workers to produce better-quality products.

Most early worker incentive programs were negatively oriented KITA programs (an acronym for *kick in the ass*) directed largely at what Frederick Herzberg has referred to as *labor activities*. He has noted that people labor "to avoid the growing pains of deprivation, while they work to create products that express growing levels of ability."[13] Similarly, Maslow's hierarchy of needs may help explain why incentive systems help to motivate workers with few viable economic alternatives. Financial incentives help people achieve the security to move to self-actualization (the highest level in Maslow's hierarchy).

Selecting the right set of incentives to motivate employees is a key task that requires answers to a number of difficult questions:

1. What does the firm want its employees to do?
2. How many groups will need separate incentives?
3. What type of incentive will be most effective for each group? Would individual or group incentives work more effectively? Should the firm offer money, stock, perks, etc.? Should it distribute incentives weekly, monthly, or annually? What performance measures should drive incentives— cost, sales, profits, or something else?
4. How can managers assure fair distribution of incentives among groups?
5. Can they change the program to suit future situations?

Any incentive system can actually erode performance if it limits the flexibility of the management system and reduces the firm's ability to respond to changing competitive situations. Hourly workers often view changes in an incentive system rather warily, and sales reps and executives may not welcome new standards. Human nature often resists change, but a firm must avoid the trap of leading employees to believe that change won't occur. A learning organization must adapt to change of every kind!

The requirement for fairness is critical to the effectiveness of any incentive program. In general, managers should tie rewards to performance measures that workers believe they can significantly influence. For example, sawmill workers may doubt that they can affect the profitability of a mill since profits depend on the spread between its cost for logs and its income from lumber sales, both of which lie outside workers' control. Incentives based on scrap rates or cost control might motivate employees more effectively than profit-based incentives. If, however, the worker could see a real stake in the well-being of the enterprise, overall mill profitability might be a more appropriate measure, though it would risk alienating workers instead of motivating them.

Many firms disperse stock through employee stock ownership plans (ESOPs) as a means of aligning the interests of the firm and its employees, but this, too, risks unintended consequences. In many startup operations, workers accept considerable risk along with their jobs and most readily identify with the goals of the enterprise. In more traditional firms, work groups may not see a direct, immediate link between their performance and the stock market's view of the value of the company's stock. Many workers view subsidized stock purchase programs as part of retirement savings, and they may doubt the portfolio management practice on concentrating so much of their future income on a single firm, even their employer. Long-term IBM employees must have felt discouraged when the shares they had accumulated over their careers declined from the 1980s' $130 to around $54 in 1993. By October 1995 the stock had rebounded to $92.50, still a far cry from its peak. People take money issues extremely personally!

---

[13]Frederick Herzberg, *The Motivation of Work* (New York: John Wiley & Sons, 1950).

ON THE JOB

Teamwork Gives Levi's the Right Fit

Like many garment manufacturers of the past, clothing giant Levi Strauss & Company used to drive its employees to work harder using piecework incentive systems. A good employee was a quiet employee, and as one Levi president recently admitted, "We encouraged people not to think."

Now all that's changing as Levi's strives to remain competitive in the new global marketplace. The traditional assembly line at Levi's has been replaced by Japanese-style teams that *encourage* employees to think. Organized into work teams of 3 to 38 people, employees are paid based on their group performance. Team leaders make decisions about how many garments workers will make each day, who will do each job, and how long he or she will carry out each task.

Empowered workers may also make decisions about what incentives they would like to receive as well. Some workers chose to receive higher wages if their work teams exceed production quotas. Workers at Levi's Blue Ridge, Georgia, plant chose to go home early once their plant reached its weekly quota.

This incentive and Levi's new work team approach has helped bring about some impressive statistics at Blue Ridge:

Levi's Productivity Push

Old Method	Team Concept
Part flow time, cutting to shipping	
6–7 days	2 days
Laundering	
5–6 days	1 day
Errors	
3 per 100	<1 per 100

Employees at Blue Ridge earn early quitting times in about one of every four weeks. This means that the company's overall labor costs remain stable while production costs and work-in-process inventories have declined. Meanwhile, overall component flow time has been cut in half.

Empowerment hasn't been easy on everyone at Levi's. Some employees don't like working in groups, and many middle and lower managers had trouble giving up some authority. Levi's lost 1 to 2 percent of its workers due to dissatisfaction with the new system, and it could stand to lose another 20 percent over the next five years. Still, top management has declared the change a success—so much so that Levi's intends to invest $60 million to convert its other 27 sewing plants to the new work team system.

SOURCE "Levi Strauss Adopts Team-Based Manufacturing," *San Francisco Chronicle*, January 11, 1993.

Over the years, firms have proposed and implemented many incentive plans in attempts to motivate hourly workers. Early in this century, many firms compensated employees based on individual piecework incentive systems. Much of the interest in time and motion studies focused on determining the amount of work that a firm could fairly expect from a competent employee doing a job correctly. In the 1930s, a number of firms started to develop group incentive systems. The most famous of these, the Scanlon Plan, sought to encourage cooperation between workers and management by giving workers shares of cost reductions they achieved. The workers formed committees to actively seek out areas for improvement. Ironically, the Wagner Act, part of the New Deal labor legislation of that decade, prohibited management-labor committees if their purposes could be construed as thwarting employee unionization activities.

A most successful incentive program at the Lincoln Electric Company in Cleveland, Ohio, has lasted since the early 1900s because workers recognized its provisions as fair, yet flexible enough to adjust to fit current competitive threats. Lincoln's system works through individual piecework-based compensation, profit sharing, and individual report cards. Most workers' piecework rates change to reflect routine time and motion studies. Employees also receive the bulk of the firm's profits through an annual profit-sharing bonus. The Lincoln bonuses make front-page news in Cleveland during the first week of every December because they routinely approach the amounts of employees' annual wages.

Individual report cards, key determinants of individuals' bonuses, evaluate workers' productivity, the quality of their work, their attendance records during the year, and assessments of their "cooperativeness." Employee ratings range from 70 to 130, and total scores must average 100. Thus the highest-rated employees can receive a bonus almost twice as large as that of the lowest-rated employee. Lincoln has developed an effective, successful program, but not all individuals want to work in such a competitive environment.

Despite all of the clever incentive systems that companies have conceived, praise and respect remain the most universally accepted employee incentive system. Without them, most incentive systems will fail. Employees who receive respectful, appreciative treatment will surprise their managers in many small ways, and without expecting financial rewards. Levi Strauss & Company has experienced this benefit, as the "On the Job" box reports.

CHAPTER SUMMARY

In this chapter, we covered a wide variety of issues that arise when a firm tries to create an organization that can reliably delight customers, satisfy employees, and generate sufficient cash flow to meet the goals of the enterprise.

1. A central challenge of management is to create a work environment in which each individual knows his or her role in the organization and how to fulfill that role, and in which everyone cares enough to want to perform well.
2. This work environment must also provide the tools that workers need to perform their jobs, a healthy and reasonably pleasant workplace, and the parts, ingredients, and information that workers need to do quality work. This work environment should build a reputation for the firm with workers as a good place to work and one that offers a fair opportunity for training and advancement to employees with the potential to improve.
3. Managers face some difficult challenges in their efforts to create or maintain systems that create desirable work environments, driven by a number of competitive forces that influence companies' human resource policies.
4. Diversity in the work force poses an especially important challenge and/or opportunity. Age, gender, lifestyle, and racial diversity bring a broad spectrum of values into an organization, and good companies routinely respond with sensitivity.
5. Effective competitors respond to competitive challenges by enhancing their organizational designs in a five-step method in which managers study the firm's environment, articulate key success factors, identify performance gaps, and initiate corrective organizational development programs; they then monitor progress and recommend additional adjustments.
6. This chapter's method for evaluating and improving an organization design may seem like a relatively direct application of the scientific method or the Deming cycle, but a formal procedure helps managers to recognize the need to

analyze and adjust human resource practices along with other business processes.

7. Today's best practices for developing human resource management systems for the 1990s and beyond include creating change-accepting organizations, though fear may limit this goal without effective measures to prevent it.

8. Some firms are developing management skills specifically intended to deal with all kinds of diversity. These practices supplement long acknowledged good management practices rather than replace them.

9. In particular, the coaching style of management empowers employees to make more operating decisions than traditional styles allow.

10. Attempts to individualize human resource practices and policies may conflict with traditional values of treating all employees equally.

11. Over the years, organizational theorists and industrial engineers have developed tools like scientific management methods that have served managers well in the past. Today's managers must constantly review and reevaluate their methods, however, to assure that their behavioral assumptions remain appropriate for their competitive environments.

12. Throughout the chapter, we have illustrated weaknesses in one-size-fits-all solutions. They seldom work any better in human resource management than in clothing design.

[KEY TERMS]

organizational design 246	coaching 267	minimum rational work
corporate culture 248	standard of performance	unit 271
national culture 254	268	predetermined motion-
mission 256	job design 269	time measurement
key success factor 256	specialization strategy	system 272
organizational	269	work sampling 273
development 259	job enlargement 269	sociotechnical systems
leadership 266	job rotation 269	perspective 277
unproductive fear 266	job enrichment 269	

[DISCUSSION QUESTIONS]

1. Develop a set of classifications to describe the diversity of people on your dormitory floor, your apartment, or your neighborhood. Project the effects of attributes in each classification on the organizational structure of a pizza delivery service.

2. Compare and contrast your own attitude toward a permanent job with those of your parents. How do they differ? What experiences may have influenced these differences in attitudes?

3. In his book *What Color Is Your Parachute?* Richard Boles argues that everyone should maintain an "inventory" of his or her skills and be prepared to answer the question, "What would you do if you lost your job tomorrow?"

a. If you currently are working, prepare an inventory of job skills that you believe you could offer your next employer.

b. If you are a full-time student and not working, think about the inventory of skills that you are accumulating to offer a future employer. What have you done or what are you doing to add to this inventory? How have you tried to ensure that you will be able to offer skills that businesses will want?

4. Assume that you have just been hired to manage individuals in each of the low-prestige occupations listed below. What techniques from this chapter might help you to build a world-class organization with these workers as members? Describe your proposed operation.

a. janitors who clean your classrooms at night

b. pickers on your community's recycling line

c. kitchen workers at a grade-school cafeteria

5. A worker from one of the teams on an assembly line that you manage complains that communication by coworkers in a language other than English limits his or her ability to enthusiastically serve on the area's quality improvement team. The employee has no history of causing trouble, producing good but not outstanding performance. As the area supervisor, respond to this complaint.

6. Prepare a worker-machine chart for the following interactions:

a. a bank customer depositing two checks at an automated teller machine

b. a young mother buying gasoline at a no-service filling station where a philosophy student hides in a cashier's booth behind bullet-proof glass. Describe the contribution to value (or the reduction in value) of being able to pay for the gas via credit card at the pump.

c. a student trying to register for classes through your university's automated enrollment system

7. An OM system makes the first unit of a new product in 20 minutes, and managers believe that over time the system should experience a learning rate of 80 percent.

a. How long should the system take to make the tenth unit?

b. How many total hours should it take to make those ten units?

8. In Question 8, the firm estimates that it will sell 100 units during the first year of production. The product's cost structure is as follows:

Material costs	$10.00 per unit
Labor rate	$8.00 per hour
Labor overhead	$2.50 per hour
Other production overhead	15% of sales
Selling costs	15% of sales
General and administration costs	20% of sales

a. What price should the firm set to realize a 20 percent pretax profit on sales during the first year? (*Hint:* We strongly recommend that the student use a spreadsheet to solve this problem.)

b. What pretax profit margin will the firm earn on the 100th unit?

9. What can a firm do to minimize the loss due to unlearning if it must organize its manufacturing process for batch production? You may use a manufacturing process for pancakes as an illustration in your response.

C A U T I O N

[C R I T I C A L   T H I N K I N G   R E Q U I R E D]

1. Job rotation assigns an hourly worker to perform a variety of jobs; cross-functional training rotates an executive through a variety of job assignments over time. How do the goals of these activities differ? Do they differ?
2. How might the advent of the information highway influence the work content of the following jobs:
   a. university professor
   b. pizza-delivery service order taker
   c. family doctor
   d. college dating-service manager

Keep responses polite, please!

C A S E   6 . 1

Bully Boy Packaging

Bully Boy was the premier packager of organic soil amendments serving the southern California markets for lawn and garden products. Its location near the dairies of Chino, California, gave it a strategic competitive advantage.

Bully Boy's plant manager faced a dilemma, despite the reputation of the plant as one of the most efficient packaging processes in the industry. Each of the plant's bagging lines consists of four work stations. At the first, a worker places a bag over a filler spout, actuates a level to drop a precisely measured amount of product into the bag, and passes it to the next station. There, a second worker places the filled bag into a thermal sealer to close the top of the plastic bag. The worker then places the bag on a conveyor to the next station where the other two workers snatch the filled, sealed bags and neatly stack them on wooden pallets that carry 50 bags each. The workers earn an hourly wage that is approximately $1 above minimum wage plus a group bonus based on weekly production. Each week's bonus represents about 40 percent of each worker's weekly wage.

An equipment maker's sales representative has demonstrated to your boss a new, highly automated, form-and-fill packaging system that con-

verts rolls of printed bag stock into bags immediately prior to filling each bag and automatically sealing the top. The economic benefits of this new system should permit the firm to recover its investment in about 2 years.

The plant manager has observed, however, that the form-and-fill lines seem incompatible with the firm's existing group incentive system. The new packaging line would eliminate half of the shop-floor jobs, perhaps discouraging remaining workers. Worse yet, the machine rather than a worker determines the speed at which the product is packaged. Further, the system would provide its best return on investment if the firm were to concentrate all production at one plant and place a smaller bag line nearby. This evaluation assumes that the new line would run two shifts a day during the busy season; the company has not run two shifts before.

Q U E S T I O N

1. As the Bully Boy plant manager, what analysis would you want to make before deciding whether to purchase the form-and-fill machine?

CASE 6.2

United Parcel Service

United Parcel Service has long been recognized as a winning competitor. UPS is the largest transportation company in the United States with sales of $17.8 billion and earnings of $809 million in 1993. Its rigid management system is renowned for producing employee efficiency and for effective service to customers who need dependable, low-cost deliveries of small parcels. With 128,000 ugly, brown trucks and 458 aircraft, UPS controls more than 75 percent of the market for domestic, ground deliveries of parcels. Its share of the air-express delivery market, about 25 percent, amounts to about one-half of the share of Federal Express. In September 1994, UPS was one of only nine U.S. firms with AAA bond ratings.

For most of its life, UPS has competed mainly with the U.S. Postal Service. By using traditional management tools to design inflexible work methods, UPS came to dominate the small-parcel market by offering efficient, reliable, low-cost service. Its industrial engineers knew exactly how many workers the firm would need to deliver a given volume of packages on any day. Their studies determined the best way for each worker to perform each activity down to the most minute detail. For example, the process specified a 3-feet-per-second walking pace for delivery workers, and it directed them to hold truck keys "teeth up with the third finger." The system taught drivers to knock on doors rather than ring bells because customers respond more quickly. The common sight of double-parked UPS trucks has led some to suspect that driver training specifies this tactic. Supervisors with stopwatches and clipboards routinely travel with workers who post sub-par performance times to help them "better understand" their duties. In short, Frederick Taylor would be proud of UPS.

Until recently, UPS workers, who are members of the Teamsters Union and earn in excess $40,000 per year, seemed to accept this highly regimented system. The company's steady growth seemed to assure job security, and most managers came up through the ranks, so they had worn the shoes of the people they managed. The corporation's founder expressed a creed of advancement from within: "You can't be a big man until you show competence as a small man." UPS managers' compensation included shares of the privately held firm with a stock price set by the board of directors, and shareholders were free to sell stock back to the company at any time. UPS paid employees well, provided meaningful opportunities for advancement and outstanding job security, and respected each individual, if not individual differences in performance.

Lately, however, UPS workers have begun to feel stress due to evolving competition. A fierce competitor, UPS has responded vigorously to every threat to its market share from competitors. The success of Federal Express led the company to introduce air-express delivery service. UPS also has developed its own computer-based parcel tracking system to match this service feature pioneered by Federal Express. When FedEx acquired Emery Air Freight, UPS quickly increased its weight and size limits for parcels. The firm has spent in excess of $2 billion to update its technology to better serve its customers and to meet competitive threats.

As a consequence, UPS drivers have had to learn how to deliver new services, some of which require additional lifting. Others require speedier deliveries and more thorough knowledge of UPS package tracing systems. Some of the new services place new demands on drivers, and the company also expects them to explain the services to customers. One driver commented, "Its tough enough making your deliveries when they got us doing all these show and tells." Even pilots have complained that the firm's performance-driven programs cause them to fly under "dangerous or seriously impaired conditions 15 percent to 31 percent of the time."

Management contends that "these worker complaints don't reflect so much an increase in the workload as in the degree of difficulty of many jobs." UPS's productivity actually declined last year as domestic volume fell 0.6 percent while employment remained steady. Some of the new systems did introduce time-saving technologies, however, which reduced troublesome paperwork.

Still, drivers respond that many of the new services are time sensitive. Last year, UPS expanded its guarantee of 10:30 a.m. delivery for overnight letters to most of the country. This new guarantee often forces drivers to make duplicate runs over their territories, a morning run to deliver the overnight letters and a later run to deliver the rest of the parcels. One driver contended that the total number of packages per day had increased from 160 to about 220, many of them oversized and heavier packages.

In partial recognition of this change in work, UPS has started to hire more skilled and college-educated workers. Historically, it had hired high school graduates. Also, as elsewhere in North America, the diversity of UPS's work force has greatly increased, bringing in employees who tolerate rigid work rules less easily. One Teamsters local "demanded limits on driver supervision, workloads, and harassment by managers." They supported their argument with a study showing that "UPS employees scored in the 91st percentile of U.S. workers for job stress, while many suffered from anxiety, phobias, or back strain." UPS management branded the report as "biased and unscientific." The dispute was settled with new contract language stating that management "shall not intimidate, harass, coerce, or overly supervise any employee."

UPS contends that it must offer new services to remain competitive and that its productivity-enhancement programs are necessary to remain profitable in an environment that does not allow the firm to increase the prices for its services.

Besides, UPS managers claim, much of this new labor unrest results from "muscle flexing by an embattled Teamsters Union leadership." Ron Carey, the newly elected head of the union, disagreed. Based on experience as a UPS driver, he observed that "It's a very strained relationship right now, much more so than ever before."

QUESTIONS

1. How does UPS compete in its marketplace? What does it have to do to succeed? What factors are causing UPS to change the way that it competes in the marketplace?
2. In the past, from a human resource management perspective, what did UPS do to improve its performance in the marketplace? Why was it successful?
3. How have the changes in the marketplace (resulting from the introduction of new competitors) affected the UPS approach to the management of its people?
4. Why have these changes created problems for UPS? What are the issues at stake for both UPS and the teamsters?
5. What actions would you recommend to UPS management? In your answer, please focus specifically on the human resource management issues.

SOURCE   Frank Robert, "As UPS Tries to Deliver More to Its Customers, Labor Problem Grows, " *The Wall Street Journal*, May 23, 1994.

[SELECTED READINGS]

Drucker, Peter. *The Practice of Management.* New York: Harper & Row, 1954.

Finly, R. E., and H. R. Ziobro. *The Manufacturing Man and His Job.* New York: American Management Assoc., 1966.

Imai, Masaaki. *Kaizen.* New York, Random House, 1989.

D. Jamieson and J. O'Hara. *Managing Work Force 2000.* San Francisco: Jossey-Bass, 1991.

McGregor, Douglas. *The Human Side of Enterprise.* New York: McGraw-Hill, 1960.

Ryan, K. D., and D. K. Oesterich. *Driving Fear Out of the Workplace.* San Francisco: Jossey-Bass, 1991.

Senge, Peter. *The Fifth Discipline: The Art and Practice of the Learning Organization.* New York: Doubleday, 1990.

Taylor, Frederick. *The Principles of Scientific Management.* New York: Norton, 1911.

Turkel, Studs. *Working: People Talk about What They Do All Day and How They Feel about What They Do.* New York: Avon, 1972.

APPENDIX   6A

Selected Learning Rates

	95 percent		90 percent		85 percent		80 percent	
Unit No.	Unit Time	Total Time	Unit Time	Total Time	Unit Time	Total Time	Unit Time	Total Time
1	1.0000	1.000	1.0000	1.000	1.0000	1.000	1.0000	1.000
2	0.9500	1.950	0.9000	1.900	0.8500	1.850	0.8000	1.800
3	0.9219	2.872	0.8462	2.746	0.7729	2.623	0.7021	2.502
4	0.9025	3.774	0.8100	3.556	0.7225	3.345	0.6400	3.142
5	0.8877	4.662	0.7830	4.339	0.6857	4.031	0.5956	3.738
6	0.8758	5.538	0.7616	5.101	0.6570	4.688	0.5617	4.299
7	0.8659	6.404	0.7439	5.845	0.6337	5.322	0.5345	4.834
8	0.8574	7.261	0.7290	6.574	0.6141	5.936	0.5120	5.346
9	0.8499	8.111	0.7161	7.290	0.5974	6.533	0.4929	5.839
10	0.8433	8.954	0.7047	7.994	0.5828	7.116	0.4765	6.315
11	0.8374	9.792	0.6946	8.689	0.5699	7.686	0.4621	6.777
12	0.8320	10.624	0.6854	9.374	0.5584	8.244	0.4493	7.227
13	0.8271	11.451	0.6771	10.052	0.5480	8.792	0.4379	7.665
14	0.8226	12.274	0.6696	10.721	0.5386	9.331	0.4276	8.092
15	0.8184	13.092	0.6626	11.384	0.5300	9.861	0.4182	8.511
16	0.8145	13.907	0.6561	12.040	0.5220	10.383	0.4096	8.920
17	0.8109	14.717	0.6501	12.690	0.5146	10.898	0.4017	9.322
18	0.8074	15.525	0.6445	13.334	0.5078	11.405	0.3944	9.716
19	0.8042	16.329	0.6392	13.974	0.5014	11.907	0.3876	10.104
20	0.8012	17.130	0.6342	14.608	0.4954	12.402	0.3812	10.485
21	0.7983	17.929	0.6295	15.237	0.4898	12.892	0.3753	10.860
22	0.7955	18.724	0.6251	15.862	0.4844	13.376	0.3697	11.230
23	0.7929	19.517	0.6209	16.483	0.4794	13.856	0.3644	11.594
24	0.7904	20.307	0.6169	17.100	0.4747	14.331	0.3595	11.954
25	0.7880	21.095	0.6131	17.713	0.4701	14.801	0.3548	12.309
26	0.7858	21.881	0.6094	18.323	0.4658	15.267	0.3503	12.659
27	0.7836	22.665	0.6059	18.929	0.4617	15.728	0.3461	13.005
28	0.7815	23.446	0.6026	19.531	0.4578	16.186	0.3421	13.347
29	0.7794	24.226	0.5994	20.131	0.4541	16.640	0.3382	13.685
30	0.7775	25.003	0.5963	20.727	0.4505	17.091	0.3346	14.020
31	0.7756	25.779	0.5933	21.320	0.4470	17.538	0.3310	14.351
32	0.7738	26.553	0.5905	21.911	0.4437	17.981	0.3277	14.679
33	0.7720	27.325	0.5877	22.498	0.4405	18.422	0.3244	15.003
34	0.7703	28.095	0.5851	23.084	0.4374	18.859	0.3213	15.324
35	0.7687	28.864	0.5825	23.666	0.4345	19.294	0.3184	15.643
36	0.7671	29.631	0.5800	24.246	0.4316	19.725	0.3155	15.958
37	0.7655	30.396	0.5776	24.824	0.4289	20.154	0.3127	16.271
38	0.7640	31.160	0.5753	25.339	0.4262	20.580	0.3100	16.581
39	0.7625	31.923	0.5730	25.972	0.4236	21.004	0.3075	16.888
40	0.7611	32.684	0.5708	26.543	0.4211	21.425	0.3050	17.193
41	0.7597	33.444	0.5687	27.111	0.4187	21.844	0.3026	17.496
42	0.7584	34.202	0.5666	27.678	0.4163	22.260	0.3002	17.796
43	0.7570	34.959	0.5646	28.243	0.4140	22.674	0.2979	18.094

Unit No.	95 percent		90 percent		85 percent		80 percent	
	Unit Time	Total Time	Unit Time	Total Time	Unit Time	Total Time	Unit Time	Total Time
44	0.7558	35.715	0.5626	28.805	0.4118	23.086	0.2958	18.390
45	0.7545	36.469	0.5607	29.366	0.4096	23.496	0.2936	18.684
46	0.7533	37.222	0.5588	29.925	0.4075	23.903	0.2915	18.975
47	0.7521	37.975	0.5570	30.482	0.4055	24.309	0.2895	19.265
48	0.7509	38.725	0.5552	31.037	0.4035	24.712	0.2876	19.552
49	0.7498	39.475	0.5535	31.590	0.4015	25.113	0.2857	19.838
50	0.7486	40.224	0.5518	32.142	0.3996	25.513	0.2838	20.122
51	0.7475	40.971	0.5501	32.692	0.3978	25.911	0.2820	20.404
52	0.7465	41.718	0.5485	33.241	0.3960	26.307	0.2803	20.684
53	0.7454	42.463	0.5469	33.787	0.3942	26.701	0.2786	20.963
54	0.7444	43.208	0.5453	34.333	0.3925	27.094	0.2769	21.239
55	0.7434	43.951	0.5438	34.877	0.3908	27.484	0.2753	21.515
56	0.7424	44.693	0.5423	35.419	0.3891	27.873	0.2737	21.788
57	0.7414	45.435	0.5409	35.960	0.3875	28.261	0.2721	22.060
58	0.7405	46.175	0.5395	36.499	0.3860	28.647	0.2706	22.331
59	0.7395	46.915	0.5381	37.037	0.3844	29.031	0.2691	22.600
60	0.7386	47.653	0.5367	37.574	0.3829	29.414	0.2676	22.868
61	0.7377	48.391	0.5353	38.109	0.3814	29.796	0.2662	23.134
62	0.7368	49.128	0.5340	38.643	0.3800	30.176	0.2648	23.399
63	0.7359	49.864	0.5327	39.176	0.3785	30.554	0.2635	23.662
64	0.7351	50.599	0.5314	39.708	0.3771	30.931	0.2621	23.924
65	0.7342	51.333	0.5302	40.238	0.3758	31.307	0.2608	24.185
66	0.7334	52.067	0.5290	40.767	0.3744	31.682	0.2596	24.445
67	0.7326	52.799	0.5278	41.294	0.3731	32.055	0.2583	24.703
68	0.7318	53.531	0.5266	41.821	0.3718	32.427	0.2571	24.960
69	0.7310	54.262	0.5254	42.346	0.3706	32.797	0.2559	25.216
70	0.7302	54.992	0.5243	42.871	0.3693	33.166	0.2547	25.471
71	0.7295	55.722	0.5231	43.394	0.3681	33.534	0.2535	25.724
72	0.7287	56.451	0.5220	43.916	0.3669	33.901	0.2524	25.977

Unit No.	95 percent		90 percent		85 percent		80 percent	
	Unit Time	Total Time	Unit Time	Total Time	Unit Time	Total Time	Unit Time	Total Time
73	0.7280	57.179	0.5209	44.437	0.3657	34.267	0.2513	26.228
74	0.7272	57.906	0.5198	44.957	0.3645	34.632	0.2502	26.478
75	0.7265	58.632	0.5188	45.475	0.3634	34.995	0.2491	26.727
76	0.7258	59.358	0.5177	45.993	0.3623	35.357	0.2480	26.975
77	0.7251	60.083	0.5167	46.510	0.3611	35.718	0.2470	27.222
78	0.7244	60.808	0.5157	47.025	0.3601	36.078	0.2460	27.468
79	0.7237	61.531	0.5147	47.540	0.3590	36.437	0.2450	27.713
80	0.7231	62.254	0.5137	48.054	0.3579	36.795	0.2440	27.957
81	0.7224	62.977	0.5127	48.567	0.3569	37.152	0.2430	28.200
82	0.7217	63.698	0.5118	49.078	0.3559	37.508	0.2420	28.442
83	0.7211	64.420	0.5109	49.589	0.3548	37.863	0.2411	28.683
84	0.7204	65.140	0.5099	50.099	0.3539	38.217	0.2402	28.924
85	0.7198	65.860	0.5090	50.608	0.3529	38.570	0.2393	29.163
86	0.7192	66.579	0.5081	51.116	0.3519	38.922	0.2384	29.401
87	0.7186	67.298	0.5072	51.624	0.3510	39.272	0.2375	29.639
88	0.7180	68.016	0.5063	52.130	0.3500	39.622	0.2366	29.875
89	0.7174	68.733	0.5055	52.635	0.3491	39.972	0.2357	30.111
90	0.7168	69.450	0.5046	53.140	0.3482	40.320	0.2349	30.346
91	0.7162	70.166	0.5038	53.644	0.3473	40.667	0.2341	30.580
92	0.7156	70.882	0.5029	54.147	0.3464	41.013	0.2332	30.813
93	0.7150	71.597	0.5021	54.649	0.3455	41.359	0.2324	31.046
94	0.7145	72.311	0.5013	55.150	0.3446	41.704	0.2316	31.277
95	0.7139	73.025	0.5005	55.650	0.3438	42.047	0.2308	31.508
96	0.7134	73.738	0.4997	56.150	0.3429	42.390	0.2301	31.738
97	0.7128	74.451	0.4989	56.649	0.3421	42.732	0.2293	31.967
98	0.7123	75.163	0.4981	57.147	0.3413	43.074	0.2285	32.196
99	0.7117	75.875	0.4973	57.644	0.3405	43.414	0.2278	32.424
100	0.7112	76.586	0.4966	58.141	0.3397	43.754	0.2271	32.651

CHAPTER SEVEN

Total Quality Management
Frameworks and Standards

CHAPTER OUTLINE

CHAPTER OBJECTIVES

[At the end of this chapter, you should be able to]

- Trace the evolution of total quality management (TQM) beyond a simple emphasis on quality.
- Explain the four major axioms of TQM: commitment to quality; extensive use of scientific tools, technologies, and methods; total involvement in the quality undertaking; and continuous improvement.
- Describe the impact of TQM pioneers like Deming, Juran, Crosby, and Imai on the development of TQM.
- Present the results of attempts to formalize TQM principles.
- Report on new developments in TQM.

Human Face of Quality at L.L. Bean

WHAT'S WORSE THAN BEING STRANDED in a canoe without a paddle? Being stranded without a canoe. That's what one sales representative at L.L. Bean thought when he received a complaint from a New York customer that a canoe hadn't arrived in time for a weekend trip. So the dutiful employee strapped a canoe on his car and personally drove it hundreds of miles from the company's offices in Maine to save the customer's canoe trip.

This incident provided L.L. Bean executives with a dramatic good news/bad news scenario. The good news was that their individual employees were committed to going out of their way to provide quality customer service. The bad news was how very far this employee had to go out of his way. Far from being reassuring, the incident left management with a disturbing question: Why wasn't the canoe shipped on time in the first place?

The resultant soul-searching set L.L. Bean on the path to Total Quality Management (TQM). An investigation revealed that, although L.L. Bean employees had the mind-set for quality, they often didn't have the authority to carry it out. They also didn't have the "big picture" and needed a wider knowledge about processes throughout the company to help them prevent problems.

SOURCE

Dawn Anfuso, "At
L.L. Bean, Quality
Starts with People,"
Personnel Journal, 73,
no. 1 (January 1994),
p. 60.

Rather than focus on improving *processes* first, as many companies might, L.L. Bean set about improving its employee training and development. But even before that, it came up with a clearly stated definition of what it wanted to achieve with its TQM system and communicated that to all of its employees.

L.L. Bean's TQM definition reads: "Total quality involves managing an enterprise to maximize customer satisfaction in the most efficient and effective way possible by totally involving people in improving the way work is done." Now in its sixth year, that emphasis on human resources has helped L.L. Bean reengineer every process in the company. The implementation of TQM has boosted profits, enhanced safety, and reduced backlogs. Best of all, customer satisfaction is up, too—and intrepid sales representatives no longer have to drive hundreds of miles to save their customers' canoe trips.

The ability to rejuvenate, as L.L. Bean did, is one of the defining traits of TQM. For some companies, new energy from TQM has meant the difference between survival and extinction. For example, the CEO of Xerox turned to TQM upon discovering that the firm's major competitors could set selling prices on their photocopiers near the cost to Xerox of building its products. Xerox faced competitive disaster when other firms could beat its prices so badly, not with loss-leader prices, but with prices that returned fair profits to the manufacturers.[1] TQM saved Xerox from collapse and failure.

total quality management

A program to focus all organizational activities on enhancing quality for customers by redirecting the corporate culture and implementing management and statistical tools

Total quality management establishes an organizationwide focus on quality, merging the development of a quality-oriented corporate culture with intensive use of management and statistical tools aimed at designing and delivering quality products to customers. TQM can dramatically improve corporate practices and performance. Motorola, one of the leading practitioners of TQM, is now approaching its goal of 60 defects or less per 1 billion units of its products. Over a decade ago, Hewlett-Packard, another TQM practitioner, found defects in 4 of every 1,000 soldered computer components. It set a goal of cutting this defect rate in half, but a vigorous TQM effort actually reduced the rate to 2 per 1 million soldered components. Now, aggressive practitioners such as Xerox, Hewlett-Packard, and Stanley Tools have targeted an ambitious new goal of offering perfect products to customers, with no defects at all in design, manufacturing, or delivery.

In this chapter, we explore the management underpinnings of total quality management. The presentation begins with an overview of the historical development of the TQM movement. In a subsequent section, we then describe the strategic thrust and total corporate undertaking that characterize that movement and discuss the change in corporate culture and thinking that successful implementation produces.

An organization cannot view total quality management as a Japanese development or as an American or European concept. Rather, in later sections we show the effects of the writings and teachings of Deming, Juran, Crosby, and Imai on current thinking about quality and TQM. To truly understand TQM, one must understand the contributions of these four pioneers.

---

[1]A firm creates a loss leader when it sets a price that generates a loss rather than a profit to attract initial customers who then buy other products with higher prices that generate profits.

We then review an accelerating movement toward formalizing TQM methods. This formalization has given shape to systems of certification and measurement based on quality criteria, typified by the ISO 9000 standards. It has also led to programs like the Malcolm Baldrige National Quality Award in the United States to recognize firms that have developed outstanding quality-driven systems. Both certification programs and quality awards seek to measure quality-related performance and to identify firms that have excelled by those measures.

The dynamic nature of quality and total quality management have spurred development of new standards such as ISO 14000. Late in the chapter, we discuss these changes, along with the merger between TQM and concern for the environment that has given rise to total quality environmental management.

TOTAL QUALITY MANAGEMENT: AN OVERVIEW[2]

This discussion of TQM can review the roots and development of this movement, but no single chapter can possibly cover all of its methods and implications. Total quality management has inspired an explosion of theory and knowledge in recent times, as reported in numerous books, newspaper and magazine articles, and even mailing lists. This chapter presents an overview to provide a basis for the reader's continued exploration of this fascinating and dynamic topic.

The idea that total quality management could be so complex may surprise some. It represents a relatively new operations management development to most North American and European managers, who first encountered its concepts in the early 1980s. However, TQM has a long history in Japan, where it was first developed, refined, and used extensively.

World War II devastated the Japanese economy. The country had gained a reputation for building inferior copies of products designed elsewhere, until the phrase "Made in Japan" had become synonymous for poor quality. In 1946, even making a telephone call across town could become an adventure, with unreliable equipment and uncertain coverage. After the war, Japanese managers searched for ways to restructure their firms and the country's economy as a whole.

W. Edwards Deming saw this situation when he worked as a statistician with the American Occupation Force. He and his fellow TQM leaders, including Joseph Juran, brought the seeds of a new management theory to Japan. They advocated merging statistical techniques with management tools and frameworks to create the theory that would transform that nation's economy—total quality management.

Interest in this theory spread with news of Japan's success with TQM, reinforced by reports of improvements at such early North American implementors as Hewlett-Packard, Xerox, and Motorola. The emphasis in TQM on the basic principles of customer satisfaction, employee empowerment, powerful management and statistical tools has dramatically reoriented firms and altered their structures.

The image of traditional business organization resembles a pyramid (Exhibit 7.1). At its base, operating employees interact routinely with customers, so they see the daily problems and difficulties of the firm's system. From this close vantage point, they can offer the clearest insight into the tasks and activities that it must accomplish to produce a good or service. The employees, in turn, support progressively smaller layers of management from supervisors to lower-level managers, middle managers, and top managers. Ultimately, this entire pyramid

---

[2]In this section, we summarize many of the points raised previously in Chapter 3.

Traditional Organizational Structure

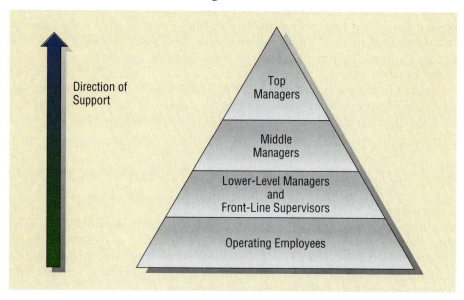

culminates with the leader of the organization, typically the owner, president, or CEO. From this high perch, the top leader must guide the entire organization and formulate the strategic vision that drives and directs its actions.

TQM challenges this organizational structure in the belief that it directs support in the wrong direction. Operating employees have the closest contact with

TQM View of the Organizational Structure

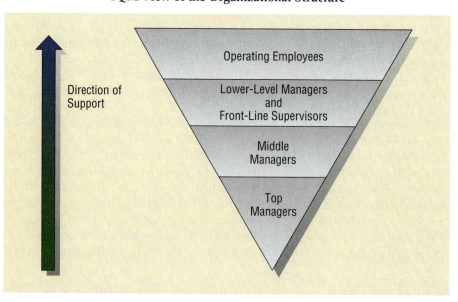

ON THE JOB

Corporate Structure at the Moment of Truth

■

If SAS managers truly intended to dedicate themselves to orienting the company toward each customer's individual needs, they had to abandon any search for answers in rule books and instructions from distant corporate offices. They had to place responsibility for ideas, decisions, and actions with the people who represented SAS during the 15 seconds of customer interactions that became moments of truth. This group included ticket agents, flight attendants, baggage handlers, and all other front-line employees. If those workers had to wait for an decision on an individual problem to flow down the organizational chain of command, then those 15 golden seconds would elapse without a response, and the firm would have lost an opportunity to earn a loyal customer.

Carlzon observed that this orientation turned the traditional corporation upside down, but he saw the radical change as necessary. He described the traditional corporate structure as a pyramid capped by the chief executive and a number of highly qualified vice presidents, all well-educated, skilled specialists in finance, production, exports, and sales, who tried to make all the decisions necessary to run the company. The crush of minute decisions occupied all of their time, forcing them to deal with intermediaries to convey these decisions throughout the company. At the bottom of the pyramid, both blue-collar and white-collar foot soldiers dealt daily with the customers. Though they knew the most about the company's front-line operations, they were typically powerless to respond to the individual situations that constantly arose.

SOURCE   Jan Carlzon, *Moments of Truth* (Cambridge, Mass.: Ballinger, 1987).

customers, and they work with the details of the processes that generate the firm's goods and services. Operating employees, not top or intermediate-level managers, determine the quality level that the firm offers. They know more than anyone about the firm's problems and the effects that the solutions must achieve. As a result, TQM advocates believe, the entire organization should support the operating employees. This view turns the traditional organization upside down (Exhibit 7.2), assigning managers the responsibility of supporting employees. Jan Carlzon of SAS Airlines has articulated this view, as the "On the Job" box reports.

Defining the TQM Concept

Operations managers must develop a thorough understanding of a technique with the power to upend the organization of both the firm and the OM function. Logothetis describes total quality management as "a culture; inherent in this culture is a total commitment to quality and attitude expressed by everybody's involvement in the process of continuous improvement of products and services, through the use of innovative scientific methods."[3] This definition highlights four major TQM axioms, illustrated in Exhibit 7.3.

[3]Nickolas Logothetis, *Managing for Total Quality: From Deming to Taguchi and SPC* (Hertfordshire, U.K.: Prentice-Hall International, 1992), p. 5.

[**EXHIBIT 7.3**]

Major Axioms of TQM

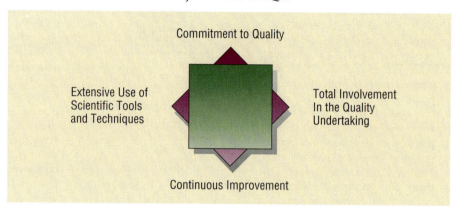

Commitment to Quality

Extensive Use of
Scientific Tools
and Techniques

Total Involvement
In the Quality
Undertaking

Continuous Improvement

Commitment to Quality.   Successful total quality management requires a fundamental belief in and commitment to quality at four different levels. First, everyone in the organization must make a *commitment to producing quality products*. This springs from unquestioning acceptance that quality offers a viable focus for developing and maintaining a sustainable competitive advantage in the marketplace. Everyone has to trust that customers want quality enough to buy from a firm that offers it, even at a higher price than competitors' products.

Organization members must make a *commitment to customers*. A customer is anyone anywhere who consumes or uses the output of a process. This commitment requires every representative of a firm to maintain and deliver quality at every interchange or transaction with either customers or suppliers.

TQM demands a *commitment by top managers*. Top managers must take actions that support the organization's move toward TQM, allocate resources to that move, and become champions of TQM within the firm.

Finally, TQM requires a *commitment of the firm as a whole*. For TQM to work, everyone who contributes to the firm's product, including employees, managers, and suppliers, must accept quality as a critical component of both the survival of the firm and its ability to satisfy its customers.

Extensive Use of Scientific Tools, Technologies, and Methods.   Total quality management requires an organization to replace subjective procedures and rules with powerful statistical tools. Statistics can help the TQM practitioner to identify and ignore random variations to focus instead on systematic changes in the process or product.

Total Involvement in the Quality Undertaking.   TQM can succeed only through teamwork and empowerment. Teamwork brings together people from different functional areas into groups that can enrich the decision-making process with information from many different perspectives. Empowerment gives both responsibility for delivering quality and authority to identify problems and then formulate and implement solutions to employees who have direct contact with a problem. Empowerment frees employees from the need to ask for permission from a manager; they simply do whatever they must to solve the problem. The "On the Job" box presents a good example of empowerment.

ON THE JOB

**Empowerment Cures
Small Business Woes**

■

Corporate America has had almost a decade to adjust to the TQM ideals of empowerment and teamwork. As these ideas filter down into smaller, family-owned businesses, the transformations are no less dramatic—or successful.

Take Growing Green, Inc., of St. Louis, for example. Teri Pesapane started the small gift shop, plantscaping, and plant care business with her husband Joel back in 1973 with just $3,200 from their savings. In the beginning, the husband and wife team were able to handle all aspects of the business, with Teri closing the deals and Joel making the deliveries.

As the business grew, the Pesapanes took on additional employees, and by 1988 their business boasted revenues of $700,000 and a staff of 16. But instead of enjoying the success, the Pesapanes found they had a crisis on their hands, both personally and professionally. Employee turnover was high, morale was low, and the Pesapanes felt they

couldn't go anywhere for even a weekend because their business might fall apart.

"Employees couldn't make decisions," explained one longtime employee. "We had to check with Joel about every detail—from what to spray a plant with to whether a large ficus tree needed to be fertilized."

The Pesapanes realized they had to give up some control. After attending a seminar on work team management, they divided the company into small action teams. The sales team brings in new business, operations handles plant installations, service

maintains plants at customer sites, and an administrative team handles billing and other financial matters. Senior-level employees from each of these teams make up a management team. Teri and Joel no longer involve themselves in the daily decision making of their work teams. Instead, they act as sounding boards and provide "big picture" leadership.

The new system works so well that the Pesapanes even venture out of the country these days. When they come back, they find that, not only has their business not fallen apart, but their sales team has brought in new contracts. With 250 clients and revenues of about $1 million, it's clear that Growing Green has benefited from implementing the same TQM culture that has rejuvenated America's larger corporations. And that's been personally satisfying to everyone involved. "We want our people to grow, just like our plants," explained Joel.

SOURCE   Barbara Buchholz and Margaret Crane, "Nurturing the Team Spirit at Growing Green," *Your Company*, Spring 1995, p. 11.

Continuous Improvement.   The fourth axiom of total quality management requires never-ending improvement. TQM inspires members of an organization to improve something, no matter how small, every day. Later discussions of just-in-time manufacturing develop this notion of ongoing improvement under the name *kaizen*.

Tools of Total Quality Management

Total quality management draws on two distinct sets of tools to guide and promote the advance of quality: management tools and statistical tools. **Management tools for quality** form theoretical frameworks and mental models that act as magnifying glasses through which managers can examine processes that affect the firm's design and delivery of quality. These tools also provide numerous general guidelines and rules of thumb. Management tools most clearly show the influence

management tools for quality
Theoretical frameworks and mental models through which managers examine and influence OM processes to enhance quality

of TQM pioneers such as Deming, Juran, and Crosby. This chapter focuses primarily on understanding these management tools.

In contrast, the next chapter presents the more technical **statistical tools for quality**. They help managers to assess their control of processes and to identify and describe problems within those processes and the likely causes. Control charts, run charts, and scatterplots are examples of such tools.

In general, managers rely most heavily on management tools while operating workers use statistical tools. This does not imply that operating workers never use management tools—they do. In fact, both groups use both sets of tools to facilitate progress toward the goal of total quality management: defining and consistently delivering quality to customers.

statistical tools for quality

Formal, scientific indicators through which managers assess their control of OM processes and identify problems and likely causes

Pioneers of TQM Management Tools

Four people have led the development of the current set of management tools within total quality management.

- Dr. W. Edwards Deming articulated his 14 points for management, 5 deadly sins and diseases, the theory of variance, and the role of management.
- Dr. Joseph Juran outlined the habit of quality, quality trilogy, and universal breakthrough sequence.
- Philip B. Crosby enumerated absolutes for quality management and 14 steps for quality improvement.
- Masaaki Imai explained the principle of *kaizen*, or continuous improvement.

 ## DEMING AND THE ORIGINS OF QUALITY MANAGEMENT

To many, the name W. Edwards Deming is synonymous with quality and total quality management. Along with Juran, Deming exposed Japanese managers to the fundamental concepts of quality production. Deming first envisioned quality management as an organizationwide activity rather than a technical task for inspectors or a specialized quality-assurance group. He identified quality as a management responsibility, observing that managers must create the systems and processes that generate quality.

Finally, Deming made the initial insight that a firm could never inspect quality into a product. A quality product combines a good design with effective production methods. Only by meeting both of these conditions could a firm assure quality.

Deming created a set of guidelines for achieving quality that could change every aspect of an organization's management. He realized that an organization's very survival depended on making such changes rather than assuming that past success assured continued operations. When someone asked Deming to justify the need for his TQM recommendations, he answered, "You do not have to do this—survival is not compulsory."[4]

Historical Background

Born in Sioux City, Iowa, in 1900, W. Edwards Deming earned a bachelor's degree in physics from the University of Wyoming and a doctorate in mathematical

---

[4]Logothetis, *Managing for Total Quality*, p. 61.

W. Edwards Deming is the father of Total Quality Management. His belief that quality management should involve the total organization revolutionized business management systems worldwide.
SOURCE   UPI/Bettmann

physics from Yale University. From the time he left Yale in 1928 until 1939, he worked for the U.S. Department of Agriculture as a mathematical physicist, gaining his first experience with the theories and practices of statistical science and statistical control. Also during this time, Deming encountered the work of Walter Shewhart on variability within the manufacturing process. Shewhart saw the need to gain control over this variability as a critical management task. Deming would expand on the importance of variability in his theory of variance.

From 1939 to 1945, Deming was involved extensively with the American Bureau of the Census and the U.S. weapons industry. Both benefited from his expertise in the techniques of sampling and statistical control, but Deming also found few managers willing to accept his idea of improving quality by correctly diagnosing the most important sources of variation in a process and then controlling or eliminating them.

The United States emerged from World War II as one of the few countries in the world with its industrial capacity intact. At the same time, the world hurried to rebuild and repair the effects of the war. Also, wartime deprivation had stirred a strong pent-up demand for consumer goods. The combination of strong demand and reduced production capacity of potential competitors left U.S. managers in a position to sell everything that they could produce, of whatever quality. If one customer declined to buy a product with poor quality, someone else would willingly pay for it. As a result, Deming's lessons fell on deaf ears in North America. He found a more receptive audience in Japan, however.

World War II devastated the Japanese economy, as American bombers had shattered its manufacturing base. Japanese managers lacked the capacity to meet even basic demands, and they welcomed news of a new way of organizing and managing their rebuilt manufacturing systems. They listened carefully to Deming and other teachers and learned a great deal about quality.

Deming first visited Japan in 1946 as a representative of the Economic and Scientific Section of the U.S. Department of War. Thousands of Japanese managers attended Deming's courses on statistical process control, which began in 1950 in

[**EXHIBIT 7.4**]

Deming's 14 Points for Management (Adapted)

1. Create consistency of purpose for continual improvement of product and service.
2. Adopt the new philosophy for economic stability.
3. Cease dependency on inspection to achieve quality.
4. End the practice of awarding business on price tag alone.
5. Improve constantly and forever the system of production and service.
6. Institute training on the job.
7. Adopt and institute modern methods of supervision and leadership.
8. Drive out fear.
9. Break down barriers between departments and individuals.
10. Eliminate the use of slogans, posters, and exhortations.
11. Eliminate work standards and numerical quotas.
12. Remove barriers that rob the hourly worker of the right to pride in workmanship.
13. Institute a vigorous program of education and retraining.
14. Define top management's permanent commitment to ever-improving quality and productivity.

SOURCE   Adapted from *Out of the Crisis* by W. Edwards Deming by permission of MIT and the W. Edwards Deming Institute. Published by MIT, Center for Advanced Engineering Study, Cambridge, MA 02139. Copyright 1986 by W. Edwards Deming.

Deming Prize

Annual award by the Japanese government to recognize active contributions to development of quality management tools to promotion of quality improvement programs

response to an invitation from the Union of Japanese Scientists and Engineers (JUSE). In his initial contacts with JUSE, Deming spoke directly to the top managers of leading Japanese industrial firms such as Sony, NEC, and Hitachi. This exposure to top management strengthened his impact on industry, fostering critical commitments to the notion of quality and to the TQM methods. This experience explains Deming's insistence on top managers' leadership of successful TQM initiatives.

Recognizing Deming's important effect on the performance of Japanese firms, that country created the **Deming Prize** in 1951. This annual award recognizes a company or individual for active contributions to the development of quality management tools or to the spread and implementation of quality improvement programs. Past recipients have included Nissan, Toyota, Nissan Steel, and the Playboy Club of Tokyo. The Japanese government acknowledged Deming's own contributions by awarding him the nation's highest decoration, the Second Order Medal of the Sacred Treasure, in 1960.

Despite his success and high reputation in Japan, few North Americans had heard of Deming as late as 1979. An American television show aired on June 24, 1980, spread news of his achievements and those of Conway, the president of Nashua Corporation and the first major American promoter of Deming's principles.[5] Since then, numerous companies have discovered and practiced those principles, including Texas Instruments, Procter & Gamble, Ford Motor Company, Dow Chemical, General Motors, and Motorola. W. Edwards Deming died in December 1993.

Deming's 14 Points for Management

Deming succinctly summarized his views on management and its relationship with quality in his 14 points for management (Exhibit 7.4). Altogether, these guidelines

[5]Ibid., p. 28.

describe a fundamental basis for an organization's culture. They define a process by which managers actively seek out bad practices and habits and replace them with better, more effective practices.

1. Create consistency of purpose for continual improvement of product and service.   Deming's first point calls for long-term thinking by managers at all levels to promote a clear vision of the firm, its customers, its method for delivering value to its customers, and the role of quality in that method. Managers must also ensure that employees understand this vision and move continuously toward it. This point emphasizes the danger of short-term problem-solving activities that can allow the firm to drift in increments away from its quality objectives and its vision over time. Finally, this point calls for managers to focus attention sharply on long-term efforts to reduce unnecessary variance in their OM system.

2. Adopt the new philosophy for economic stability.   The second point recognizes the need for a new philosophy to keep the firm and its OM function alive and growing in today's competitive environment. Basic survival requires managers to accept the need for continuous change and innovation, taking full advantage of every available resource. One important resource is the intelligence of its entire work force. In today's dynamic business climate, a small group of managers can no longer expect to identify problems and then recommend and implement potential solutions. Rather, managers must share both responsibility and authority for problem solving and decision making with employees, reducing organizational layers to enhance the responsiveness of the entire organization.

3. Cease dependency on inspection to achieve quality.   Traditionally, operations managers have viewed inspections as necessary but wasteful activities. They acknowledged defects as inherent to any product and process, so they could hope to prevent those defects from reaching customers only by inspecting each item. Deming pointed out the error in this view, since inspections increase costs rather than reduce them and create more problems than they solve.

First, inspections are no more perfect than other activities, so they allow defective products to pass. Second, inspections correct symptoms in the form of defects, leaving the causes intact to create more symptoms. Third, inspections rarely increase value for customers. Fourth, inspections often form bottlenecks that restrict the flow of products through the OM system. Finally, inspections create complacency, divide responsibility for quality between operators and inspectors, and reduce overall concern for quality. Inspections create gaps between people and processes that create the defects and people and processes that catch the defects, with important implications for the firm as described in the "On the Job" box. While some very limited conditions may make inspection unavoidable, in general, inspection is never an adequate substitute for a well-designed product built by a carefully designed and controlled process incorporating quality components provided by qualified suppliers.

4. End the practice of awarding business on price tag alone.   This principle emphasizes the need for a total cost assessment of any purchase. Low dollar prices often buy low quality, which can actually raise overall costs through increased expenses for inspection, scrap and rework, inventory to replace defective items, and employee frustration. Managers must identify and assess all of the effects and costs created by every purchase and buy from the supplier that offers the lowest total cost. In most cases, those will be the suppliers that offer the highest quality.

ON THE JOB

Inspection at Consolidated Diesel Corporation

Consolidated Diesel Corporation of Whitakers, North Carolina, manufactured small diesel engines as a joint venture between Cummins and J. I. Case Tractor. From the outset, the plant was designed expressly to manufacture a quality diesel engine every time. The initial plant layout placed a single inspection station at the end of the final assembly line, where inspectors would hook up finished engines to a computer that would run a battery of tests. If this revealed a problem, inspectors could repair the engine and send it on its way immediately.

The plant managers discovered that inspection staff became very good at correcting symptoms. Their efforts to fix defects in the engines did nothing to eliminate the underlying prob-

lem, however. If an inspector found an improperly tightened screw in a clamp, that problem was likely occur in the next engine, as well. The person who created the problem never knew of its existence.

To remedy this process failure, the employees recommended removing any engine with a

defect, no matter how small, from the line and returning it to the area that created the defect. The engine waited behind the operator until he or she corrected the defect, which had be done before the operator could take a lunch or coffee break. A waiting engine acted as a visual signal of a process problem, and the number of defective engines indicated the severity of the problem. The system returned a defective engine to the operator quickly, helping people to determine what caused the problem before making more mistakes.

This system gave every operator an incentive to make each engine right the first time, every time.

SOURCE   Steven A. Melnyk and Phillip L. Carter, *Shop Floor Control: Principles, Practices, and Case Studies* (Falls Church, Va.: American Production and Inventory Control Society, 1987), pp. 279–323.

5. Improve constantly and forever the system of production and service.   To build a system that can consistently produce a quality product, managers must identify and eliminate waste and variability throughout the system. This analysis must extend beyond the performance of the OM system itself to encompass other systems to which it has links (e.g., purchasing, transportation, product and process engineering, facility maintenance, accounting, human resource management, and customer service). Each process affects quality, so each can generate waste. Managers must study both the defects created by those processes and the processes themselves. Finally, the entire organization must view its quest for quality as a continuing journey. As long as processes produce waste or variance, they leave room for improvement.

6. Institute training on the job.   Most firms view training as a requirement when an employee is first hired. Later, they implicitly and wrongly assume that the employee no longer needs any training. The critical need to learn never ends. To support employees' efforts to improve performance by identifying waste and variance, the firm must expose them to new and different types of training to develop their understanding of standards for acceptable work, statistical tools and techniques, and the problem-solving process. This training must cover essential skills like how to use a control chart along with more general education about the basic characteristics of quality and its importance to the firm's success or even survival.

7. Adopt and institute modern methods of supervision and leadership.   Total quality management changes the traditional role of supervision. Supervisors cease being commanders who simply tell their employees what to do and expect them to carry out these instructions. Supervisors and managers must now see themselves as teachers, coaches, and facilitators who support the activities of workers in immediate contact with process problems. Supervisors and managers must recognize the implicit messages that their actions send to workers and consistently reinforce the importance of employees, the role of quality, and the need for teamwork. Managers must treat errors as cherished opportunities to learn about processes and systems rather than as occasions to cast blame. Finally, supervisors and managers must encourage and promote teamwork and reward innovation and initiative. TQM defines a leader as someone who leads by example.

8. Drive out fear.   Deming identified fear as a major obstacle to improved efficiency and effectiveness and a major barrier to change and survival. Fear affects an OM system in many ways. Some people are afraid to ask questions and reveal weaknesses in their knowledge; other people fear cooperating because it may leave them vulnerable to opportunistic threats from others. Fear of the perceived cost of failure, such as poor performance reviews or even termination, prevents some people from challenging current practices or trying new techniques. Finally, many people simply fear change because it forces them to deal with new and unfamiliar methods in place of known and comfortable, if inefficient, methods.

To drive out fear, managers must create an environment that encourages people to ask questions, report problems, and try new ideas. Employees must know that the firm will not punish them if new ideas fail. Managers must demonstrate the importance of trying something new that offers a chance for a major leap in effectiveness rather than sticking with safe methods that offer only stable or declining benefits.

9. Break down barriers between departments and individuals.   Many organizations tolerate weaknesses because they look at problems within strict functional limits and ignore insights and concerns raised by related functional areas. As a result, firms often optimize activities within a function but fail to exploit potential gains from organizationwide changes. An engineer designing a portable phone might implement a solution to make it lighter in weight, even though that solution would make it more difficult to build. This narrow search for improvement ignores inputs and insights from other groups that might make the final product more valuable overall. Input from operations managers could save the cost of designing a lighter phone that simply costs too much to build.

Interdisciplinary teams can enhance quality and effectiveness of efforts to design and build products as compared with a strictly functionally oriented process. Such teams more reliably identify potential problems throughout the OM process, and they help to spread information and education throughout the firm. Such a team would quickly educate the engineer who designed the phone about the impact of that design in the marketplace and on manufacturing, shipping and receiving, and suppliers. Management must encourage teamwork by making changes such as moving work stations closer together, assigning people to teams, and changing the performance measurement system to reward group performance rather than individual results.

10. Eliminate the use of slogans, posters, and exhortations.   Slick messages may insult employees rather than motivate them. Such blatant motivational pushes implicitly assume that workers could give more effort or work harder. Most workers truly want to do good jobs. Quality problems usually come from limits in the current system. Rather than insulting workers with promotional messages designed to make them work harder, managers should give them the tools and training they need to work smarter.

11. Eliminate work standards and numerical quotas.   TQM sets one ultimate task for any employee: to produce quality products. Numerical standards and quotas focus attention on quantities instead. Attempts to meet reasonable quotas lead to complacency over time since workers achieve their goals and need do no more. Excessively demanding quotas either discourage workers who can never meet them or induce workers to compromise quality standards to make their numbers. In either case, the unreasonable quotas cause fear and frustration. Finally, any quota, reasonable or not, leaves room for improvement. As a result, setting some artificial numerical goal distracts attention from the larger goal of encouraging continuous improvement. TQM need not eliminate all numerical standards. Rather, it balances any such standards against the need to improve continuously and to eliminate waste.

12. Remove barriers that rob the hourly worker of the right to pride in workmanship.   TQM begins with an OM system full of both obvious and subtle barriers and obstacles to good workmanship. Its principles guide managers in the task of identifying these barriers and obstacles and taking appropriate actions to eliminate them.

13. Institute a vigorous program of education and retraining.   Continual training keeps the work force up to date with information about new developments, changes in product designs and machinery, new tools and procedures, and innovative techniques. In addition, this investment in continuing training and education also sends an important message to the work force that managers value them as important assets well worth efforts to keep well-maintained and productive. Investments in training represent the firm's ongoing commitment to its employees.

14. Define top management's permanent commitment to ever-improving quality and productivity.   Top managers' actions communicate the true importance of quality and TQM throughout the firm. This critical commitment encourages many managers and employees to follow top managers toward personal and organizational success. For TQM to succeed, a firm's president and vice presidents must publicly demonstrate their vigorous commitments to continuous quality improvement and innovation; they must openly practice what they preach.

Consider the example set by John A. Young, Hewlett-Packard's president and CEO. In the early 1980s, the company, which had built a reputation for quality products, discovered that reactions to quality problems tied up as much as 25 percent of its manufacturing assets. Young decided that Hewlett-Packard had to make a significant commitment to quality to maintain its position of market leadership. He set a very demanding goal for this initiative: a tenfold reduction in the field failure rates of the company's products within 10 years.[6] More importantly, however, Young then directed each plant and division manager to set more detailed targets designed to move the firm toward this broad objective. He then reviewed each manager's progress toward these goals regularly. All of this sent a very clear

[6]David A. Garvin, *Managing Quality* (New York: Free Press, 1988), p. 28.

In the early 1980s, Hewlett-Packard CEO John A. Young defined the company's commitment to quality by creating a quality objective. Over the next 10 years, Hewlett-Packard significantly reduced field failure rates.   SOURCE   Courtesy of Hewlett-Packard Company

message throughout the ranks: Hewlett-Packard values quality, and employees must take whatever actions are necessary to meet corporate quality objectives.

Deming used his 14 points for management to emphasize the critical role of managers in total quality management. He saw managers rather than workers or equipment as the real obstacle to TQM, often pointing out that 85 percent of quality problems could be traced to management, while workers were responsible for the remaining 15 percent. In the mid-1980s, one analyst has claimed, the percentage of problems caused by managers increased to 94 percent.[7] The samples of Deming quotes in Exhibit 7.5 underscore the importance he assigned to the role of management.

Deming's Theory of Variance

Most of Deming's work revolves around his **theory of variance**. This theory views variations from standard activities as a major source of problems for all OM processes and most firms. Variance causes unpredictability, which increases uncertainty and reduces control over the processes. TQM assigns managers the task of finding the sources of this variance and eliminating it to significantly improve OM system performance through a process of continuing improvement.

Variance can come from many sources. Activities within the OM system can disrupt standard work flows, as can the actions of such groups as marketing, engineering, purchasing, and accounting. Managers can categorize all variances as either controlled or uncontrolled. A **controlled variance** responds to efforts by a worker to correct or manage the activity; an **uncontrolled variance** reflects the impact of some factor outside the control of the employee, who cannot correct it.

Workers or managers can correct a variance by either changing its common causes or removing its special causes. **Common causes** reflect systematic problems in an OM process, including weaknesses in product design, failure to match incoming components to needs, equipment malfunctions, poor facilities maintenance,

---

theory of variance
Deming's central premise that variations from standard activities cause many problems for all OM processes and most firms

controlled variance
A variation from a standard process that a worker can correct or manage

uncontrolled variance
A variation from a standard process due to the impact of some factor outside the control of the employee

common cause
A systematic problem that produces variance in an OM process

[7]Logothetis, *Managing for Total Quality*, p. 27.

[**E X H I B I T 7 . 5**]

W. Edwards Deming on Current Management Practice

- It would be a mistake to export American Management to a friendly country. America is the world's most underdeveloped nation!
- The wealth of a nation depends on its people, management, and government, more than its natural resources.
- The right Quality and Uniformity are foundations of commerce, prosperity, and peace.
- The workers are handicapped by the system, and the system belongs to the management.
- Defects are not free; somebody makes them and gets paid to make them!
- When will management learn that they have a moral obligation to protect investment and safeguard jobs?
- Management needs training to learn about the company.
- The job of management is not supervision but leadership.
- The big problem in leadership and training arises from a standard of what is acceptable work and what is not.
- Putting out fires is not improvement.
- When managers visit other companies seeking examples, one can only hope that they will enjoy the ride because this is the only thing they will be getting out of it!
- Absenteeism is a function of poor management. If people feel important to a job, they will come to work.
- Slogans, exhortations, and posters with targets to be met (without providing the means to meet them), are directed to the wrong people. They take no account of the fact that most of the trouble comes from the system.

SOURCE   Logothetis, *Managing for Total Quality*, pp. 56–57.

special cause

A short-term source of variance in an OM process

and incomplete or inaccurate routing documents and bills of material. In contrast, **special causes** reflect short-term sources of variance in an OM process that operators could correct. Special causes might include problems such as a lack of knowledge or skill, worker inattention, or a bad batch of incoming materials. Correcting common causes requires a management response, while shop-floor personnel must correct special causes.

Differentiating variances as either controlled or uncontrolled and as results of either common or special causes defines the matrix of responsibility in Exhibit 7.6.

[**E X H I B I T 7 . 6**]

Categories of Variances

	Common Cause	Special Cause
Controlled Variance	Management	Employee
Uncontrolled Variance	Management	Management

This table reemphasizes the pivotal role of managers in TQM since they bear responsibility for three of the four cells.

Deming's Deadly Diseases and Sins

Deming recognized that implementation of his 14 points would strain managers' skills and determination. Successful application of these guidelines can completely transform an OM system and even an entire firm. As an initial step toward TQM, managers can first eliminate certain bad practices, or **five deadly diseases and sins**, as Deming called them.

five deadly diseases and sins
Deming's list of bad practices that managers must address early in a TQM initiative

Lack of Constancy.   Once a firm's managers commit themselves to quality, they can never allow any variation in this message. They must judge quality by absolute rather than relative standards. At one small plant, for example, the plant manager stated vehemently that no one should ever compromise quality. As the end of one month approached, however, a customer called desperate for a rush order to meet its own shipping commitment and willing to take any product that the plant could ship irrespective of the quality. The plant could not offer a batch of acceptable parts, but the plant manager decided to ship parts of inferior quality to fill the order. At that moment, the manager effectively told the plant that schedule requests took precedence over quality, essentially destroying the quality program.

Concentration on Short-Term Profits.   A process that focuses on short-term profits encourages short-term thinking and short-term actions. Managers may cut costs in the short term while sacrificing the long-term thinking and planning that total quality management demands and raising costs overall.

Overreliance on Performance Appraisals.   A performance appraisal system or any similar program for rating the merit of individual employees can hinder the implementation of TQM by encouraging rivalry, fear, and short-term thinking. It can also undermine teamwork and mutual respect. Finally, performance appraisals tend to emphasize output measures like units shipped rather than indicators of effectiveness of the processes that create those outputs (e.g., a monthly reduction in defects).

Job Hopping.   This disease results from constant movements of managers from one position to another. Job hopping exposes managers to a beneficial diversity of experiences, but excessive rotation of assignments encourages short-term thinking and inhibits the ability of the manager to understand the long-term implications of actions. By the time a manager learns about a new position, the duration of the assignment may leave little time for new decisions. He or she may have to move to a new job long before all of the implications and effects of some actions have become evident. As one manager in the automobile industry noted, "With all of this job hopping, my job amounts to defusing the land mines that the last manager left and planting land mines for the next one."

Overemphasis on Visible Figures.   The final disease results when managers evaluate performance by looking only at measures that they can easily capture. TQM requires them to evaluate the total effect of any action by reviewing both quantitative information like the number of defects or the percentage of jobs shipped late and qualitative data like expressions of customer satisfaction or employee perceptions about the company. TQM measures total cost, as discussed in Chapter 4, to assess performance.

[**EXHIBIT 7.7**]

Deming Wheel[a]

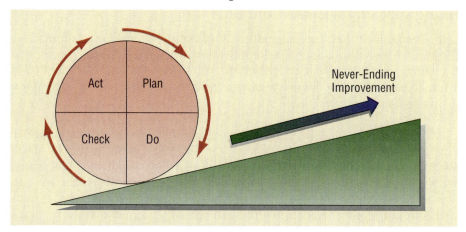

[a]Also referred to as the *Deming cycle* or *PDCA cycle.*

Deming and Total Quality Management: Some Final Comments

To successfully practice total quality management in a firm, top managers must take the first step, accepting and committing to the guidelines and points that form the basis of TQM. The firm can then begin to implement TQM using the Deming wheel, illustrated in Exhibit 7.7 (also discussed in Chapter 4). The Deming wheel breaks down all actions into four interlinked steps: plan-do-check-act. This keeps the firm moving along a path of continuous improvement, driven by the need to identify and eliminate waste and variance in any form.

Finally, TQM is not a crusade that the operations manager can win acting alone; success requires an organizationwide effort. TQM defines a philosophy for the entire firm and everyone in it.

JURAN AND TOTAL QUALITY MANAGEMENT

After Deming, Dr. Joseph Juran has had the greatest impact on the theory and practice of quality management. Besides writing 12 books on the subject, Juran has pioneered training manuals for managers and spoken across the world on quality. With Deming, Juran was part of the initial group of lecturers invited to Japan in the early 1950s, and he has also been awarded the Second Order of the Sacred Treasure by the Emperor of Japan.

Juran's contribution to total quality management centers on four themes:

- Compelling definitions of *quality* and the *cost of quality* (COQ)
- Quality habit
- Quality trilogy
- University breakthrough sequence

Juran's concepts have promoted the development of the theory and practice of TQM by beginning on the shop floor and working up to the level of top management.

Quality Defined and the Cost of Quality

Rather than defining the term by references to conformance to specifications (a definition based on quality-control criteria), Juran defined *quality* as **fitness for use**. This broad definition accommodates variations in levels of quality, so it does not force the same level of quality for every situation. Instead, the appropriate level of quality matches the use that customers intend for the good or service. A student who wants to travel from home to lecture halls may not need a Rolls-Royce; an Escort may offer adequate quality.

Fitness for use results from five major product traits: quality of design, quality of conformance, availability, safety, and field use.[8] *Quality of design* reflects the suitability of a product's design concept and specifications for its intended use. L.L. Bean pursues quality of design when it builds its products with unique features, functions that users want, and resilient materials. These design strengths differentiate its products from those of its competitors.

Quality of conformance reflects how well an actual product achieves the intentions of its design, determined by conditions like the firm's choice of an OM process, employee capabilities, equipment condition, and the feasibility of the design. *Availability* reflects an absence of problems that could affect the product's use. Reliability, or the probability of a breakdown, affects availability, as does ease of maintenance and repair. *Safety* reflects the threat of harm to the user of the product. Finally, *field use* represents the condition of the product once it reaches the customer's hands, which depends on such characteristics as packaging, storage, and field support and maintenance.

To make a product with these five traits, managers must carefully control quality over the entire product life cycle from concept to design to prototype to production to phase-out or renewal. Like Deming's methods, Juran advocated appropriate statistical tools for each quality trait.

Juran's approach to quality emphasizes active involvement in daily operations. It presents specific tests and desired outcomes, making it a valuable shop-floor tool. This may present a problem, however, since shop-floor workers deal with issues that top managers may find mundane. In an attempt to get the attention of top managers, Juran developed the concept of the **cost of quality** (COQ).

This system developed an accounting system and an application of the total cost analysis method discussed in Chapter 4 to state all of the costs associated with defective products in dollars and cents. These include the costs of making, finding, repairing, or avoiding defects. To simplify data analysis, Juran divided all costs among four categories:

- *Internal failure costs*   Costs that result from detection of quality defects in products prior to shipment to customers, including scrap, salvage, rework, excess inventory, and inspection
- *External failure costs*   Costs that result from identifying defects in products after they reach customers, including complaint adjustments, loss of goodwill, returned materials, and field service or repairs
- *Appraisal costs*   Costs the result from examinations to assess products' quality levels, including incoming material inspections, product and process inspections, inspection staff, and maintenance of test equipment

fitness for use

Joseph Juran's definition of *quality* which incorporates quality of design, quality of conformance, availability, safety, and field use

cost of quality

Juran's method of stating all of the costs associated with defective products in dollars and cents, including internal failure costs, external failure costs, appraisal costs, and prevention costs

[8]Artemis March, "A Note on Quality: The Views of Deming, Juran, and Crosby," in *Readings in Total Quality Management*, ed. by Harry Costin (New York: Harcourt Brace, 1994), p. 143.

- *Prevention costs*   Costs that result from efforts to prevent defects and limit failure and appraisal costs, including quality planning, new-product reviews, training, process control, periodic improvement projects, and continuous improvement

On-going measurement of the cost of quality clearly highlights the attraction of improvements. In particular, the cost of poor quality control, captured by the sum of internal and external failure costs, often becomes surprisingly large, sometimes accounting for 50 to 80 percent of the overall COQ. Measurements of the COQ also provide guidelines for investments in prevention. In general, managers should continue to invest in prevention until additional investments would raise the total cost of quality.

Quality Habit

habit of quality

An unwavering focus, routinely adjusted and reinforced, on the need for quality

Juran set an ultimate goal for a total quality management program of starting the OM system and the firm as a whole on a process of continuous improvement. Slogans and exhortations cannot accomplish such thorough change. Rather, TQM requires an unwavering focus on the need for better quality. This focus, routinely adjusted and reinforced, should develop into a **habit of quality** that emphasizes objective results and the lessons that those results teach. To help the firm develop this quality habit, Juran advocated a four-stage process:[9]

1. Establish specific goals that identify what organization members should do and why.
2. Establish plans for reaching those goals with enough detail to guide people's actions from beginning to end.
3. Assign clear responsibilities for meeting the goals.
4. Base rewards on results.

In another parallel with Deming, Juran identified management action as the key to success in developing the quality habit. Therefore, he assigned responsibility for TQM primarily to managers rather than workers.

Quality Trilogy

quality trilogy

The set of actions that encompass everything that the firm must do to define quality, including quality planning, quality control, and quality improvement

Juran broke down the requirements for successful total quality management into three major activities, the **quality trilogy**: quality planning, quality control, and quality improvements. These actions encompass everything that the firm must do to define quality (i.e., determine fitness for use), ensure that the OM process delivers a quality product, and facilitate further quality improvements. Together, the three stages of the quality trilogy (Exhibit 7.8) define a sequence of events similar to the Deming wheel, which is discussed in Chapter 4.

Quality Planning.   Juran observed that quality does not happen by accident; rather, it results directly from good planning. He proposed a four-step quality-planning sequence:

1. Recognize what customers the firm or functional area serves, and understand their needs. This fairly broad image of customers includes both external and internal customers. L.L. Bean managers must track both the person who phones in an order and the worker who picks the items and

---

[9]Logothetis, *Managing for Total Quality*, p. 64.

[**E X H I B I T   7 . 8**]

Quality Trilogy

packs the shipment, since this person represents an internal customer of the worker who takes the order over the phone.

2. Restate the needs of customers into terms that everybody within the firm or functional area can understand, and then develop a product design that meets those needs.

3. With the product design completed, effectively structure the process that produces it, and keep that process operating correctly.

4. With the process established and proven, transfer responsibility for it to the OM system.

These four steps create a cross-functional quality planning procedure that guides product and process design toward both quality and cost objectives. Planners should justify actions on the basis of both improvements to quality and reductions in costs.

Quality Control.   Juran recognized that any process, once implemented, may suffer deterioration. TQM requires vigilant quality control to detect variance and bring the process back into conformance. This function relies heavily on TQM's statistical tools and techniques, as discussed in the next chapter. Quality control emphasizes the important goal of keeping the OM process in continuous control to assure predictable results, both to facilitate routine management and to provide a stable base for further efforts to improve quality.

Quality Improvement.   While quality control pursues the goal of maintaining an existing level of quality, the quality habit pushes the firm onward to the next, higher level of quality. Quality improvement focuses on this goal, seeking to achieve quality breakthroughs that move the firm to a new level of performance. These breakthroughs reflect long-term thinking and planning by managers as part of the universal breakthrough sequence.

Universal Breakthrough Sequence

Juran's universal breakthrough sequence identifies a set of actions directed toward achieving major leaps in quality. This sequence specifies general actions that can apply to any situation or organizational problem, either within or outside operations management. The effective application of this sequence absolutely requires prior management acceptance of responsibility for improvement. Juran asserted that all breakthroughs follow a universal sequence beginning with proof of need, then proceeding through project identification, organizing for improvement, the diagnostic journey, remedial action, and resistance to change, to culminate in actions to hold onto gains.

Proof of Need.   The first step in the universal breakthrough sequence creates awareness of a need for change, that is, recognition that some fault in the current process requires an immediate response. This step identifies costs of not changing that exceed the costs of change. Efforts to promote awareness may have to overcome resistance from people familiar with the problem who have come to accept it as part of the routine. Often they simply overlook some costs created by the problem. An advocate of improvement can often add urgency to concerns over chronic waste by stating its effects as amounts of money lost. Everyone in a firm understands an amount measured in dollars, so this tactic can help to spread acute awareness of a problem. Other units of measurement, such as statistical process control data, can be used, provided that everyone in the target audience understands them clearly.

Project Identification.   The next step in the universal breakthrough sequence identifies specific projects to bring about improvements. Project identification creates a critical concentration for improvement efforts in specific projects, which then become catalysts for breakthroughs. People achieve breakthroughs by working on concrete conditions and actions that can show real benefits. Also, a string of projects completed successfully over time marks a path toward improvement goals, keeping alive a feeling of real progress. Finally, projects foster accumulation of experience, which Juran views as essential to total quality development.

To maximize the important benefits of project identification, managers must carefully choose projects to undertake. They should concentrate efforts on projects with high, and highly visible, potential payoffs. Pareto analysis and cause-and-effect analysis, discussed in Chapter 4, provide tools for identifying such projects.

Organizing for Improvement.   In the next step, the universal breakthrough sequence organizes for successful completion of the chosen projects. Organization begins with a committee of top managers with responsibility for supervising the overall quality improvement initiative, providing direction, and allocating necessary resources to project teams. The organizing step then assigns workers to task forces to undertake specific projects. With these committees in place, organizers must then institute detailed work policies and procedures and identify milestones against which to judge progress. Finally, they must define the conditions that successful projects will achieve.

Diagnostic Journey.   At this stage, the universal breakthrough sequence traces back from symptoms to find underlying causes. Project committees determine whether observed problems result from systematic causes (underlying faults in the system), random causes, or purposeful, willful disruptions. Further, they categorize the causes they find as under the control of either operating workers or managers.

Remedial Action.   The project teams then work to identify and implement changes to correct the causes of quality problems. They first identify the range of available alternatives and select the most appropriate. They then proceed to implement that alternative. As they act to correct existing problems, the teams should watch for opportunities for preventive maintenance programs to keep new problems from arising.

All of this work requires open communications and feedback among different groups, people, and departments to encourage a clear understanding of all the major criteria for quality (definitions, product specifications, test requirements, etc.). Standardization of language and vocabulary enhance effective communication.

This stage also includes actions to allocate responsibility for implementation and to introduce testing and inspection. (Unlike Deming, Juran accepted inspection as a necessary evil.) Effective implementation also must separate the vital few problems and solutions from the trivial many.

Resistance to Change.   The universal breakthrough sequence explicitly recognizes that change almost always attracts resistance. Typically, social or cultural forces drive resistance, but sometimes simple fear of the unknown can make people uneasy about change. Anticipating resistance, managers should encourage wide participation in TQM projects; people who work on those projects are more likely to accept their outcomes and take ownership of responsibility for success. Managers can also rely on time to overcome resistance; most people will accept change over time.

Holding onto Gains.   Having overcome resistance and brought about the breakthrough, managers face a final challenge of preventing any return to old, inferior practices and procedures. They can solidify gains by changing the overall process to make it consistent with the new, higher level of quality. They make the change part of the new routine by establishing new standards, increasing training, and developing new control systems with reliable early warning signals, statistical techniques, feedback loops, data systems, and rules for decision making. After setting a new quality standard, managers prepare to repeat this sequence of events to achieve continuing quality breakthroughs.

Juran versus Deming

Juran and Deming shared similar points of view on many subjects. Both agreed on the important role of top managers in TQM, and both recognized a crisis of quality in manufacturing. Both agreed on the importance of both internal and external customers, the importance of continuous improvement, and the need for effective training and tools.

However, these two pioneers viewed some aspects of TQM from different perspectives: Deming is more process oriented while Juran is more concerned about the output.

- Deming believed that everyone within the firm (including operating employees) must contribute to successful implementation of total quality management; Juran emphasized middle managers as key players in this change.
- Deming set a goal of perfect quality; Juran advocated accepting lower quality if the benefits of achieving perfection would not justify the costs.
- Juran focused on quantitative costs more than Deming, who emphasized more subtle indicators of quality.
- Deming identified variance as the target of TQM initiatives; Juran tolerated variance more willingly.

In many ways, Juran continued and extended traditional ways of thinking about quality while Deming advocated a break with tradition and a new approach to quality management.

 ## PHILIP B. CROSBY AND TOTAL QUALITY MANAGEMENT

Philip B. Crosby, the third major influence on the management tools of total quality management, started his career as a line inspector, working his way up to corporate vice president and quality director of ITT. He was a management consultant, chairman of Philip Crosby Associates, and the director of Crosby's Quality College in Winter Park, Florida. Crosby contributed three major ideas to TQM:

- Absolutes for quality management
- 14 steps for quality improvement
- Quality vaccine

Following Deming, Crosby addressed his message to top management. In quality management, he saw a viable strategy for corporate survival and growth. Further, he denied that a firm must invest large sums to improve quality; rather, such investments save money. As a result, Crosby asserted, a quality management program will generate savings that ultimately will pay for itself. This line of reasoning leads to Crosby's conclusion that, ultimately, quality is free.

He advocated a more ambitious goal than simply eliminating problems through improved inspections. Rather, managers should strive for a goal of zero defects. They should design and build products with the objective from the outset of generating products without any defects. Finally, Crosby urged managers to set a corporate tone that denies the inevitability of defects, which contrasts his position with Juran's.

Absolutes for Quality Management

absolutes for quality management
Four laws proposed by Philip B. Crosby as fundamental elements of any effective TQM system

Crosby identified four laws, called **absolutes for quality management**, that define the fundamental elements of any effective TQM system.

Quality Is Conformance to Requirements, Not Goodness. Crosby recognized only one sensible definition of *quality* based on exactly what the customer wants. A firm produces quality only when its good or service meets or exceeds customers' expectations. Managers must ensure that everyone within the firm understands these requirements. They must then provide the tools necessary to achieve those requirements.

Quality Systems Amount to Prevention. The path to successful quality management must begin with a thorough study and evaluation of current processes in which managers identify every opportunity for quality problems to disrupt a process and eliminate those opportunities. Such a study employs essential statistical tools, such as statistical process control, discussed in the next chapter.

Zero Defects Define the Performance Standard. Any effective TQM system sets a goal of zero defects. More than a slogan, the call for zero defects promotes a comprehensive method for designing, producing, and delivering a good or service that tries to eliminate any possibility for defects. It also advocates a corporate environment that accepts no possibility of errors.

Measurement of Quality Is the Price of Nonconformance.   To make quality a strategic issue, managers must measure it. They must continuously assess the cost of failing to achieve quality goals in dollar units, since top managers understand financial information most completely. Quality measurement should center on the costs of doing things wrong (rejects, inspections, warranty repairs, field service complaints, satisfying unhappy customers, salvage, rework, etc.). These costs, which can run as high as 20 percent to 40 percent of most firms' total operating costs, represent the **price of nonconformance** (PONC).

Once top managers understand the high costs of poor quality, they feel strong motivation to improve operations. This information encourages them to make necessary investments in quality training and education, improved product and process design, and better buyer-supplier relations. The costs of these efforts is the **price of conformance** (POC).

Crosby's 14 Steps for Quality Improvement

Like Deming and Juran, Crosby viewed the march toward quality as a never-ending journey. Before beginning this journey, managers must first assess their firm's current quality culture. The management maturity grid in Exhibit 7.9 can aid this self-assessment by positioning the firm in one of five states of quality awareness and quality culture:

- *Uncertainty*   The firm remains unaware of the importance of quality as a strategic imperative.
- *Awakening*   Managers understand the importance of quality, but they have not yet acted to improve it.
- *Enlightenment*   Managers openly acknowledge the importance of quality and the corporate need for improvement, and they have begun to take concrete action to improve overall quality by establishing a formal program.
- *Wisdom*   Managers have established a quality management program that is working well, identifying problems early and routinely pursuing corrective actions. The program emphasizes prevention rather than appraisal.
- *Certainty*   Quality has become an unavoidable component of the current management structure. The entire system is designed to ensure that the firm can attain its goal of zero defects. Any problems are both infrequent and truly random events.

Once managers have determined their firm's position on the grid, they can begin improving quality by implementing Crosby's **14 steps for quality improvement**. This program emphasizes prevention and elimination of process faults rather than inspection (the dissolve mode of problem solving identified in Chapter 4). The program seeks to improve product quality by changing the corporate culture. Detailed statistical tools, while important, remain secondary to this general change in culture. The program accepts no standard short of zero defects—designing and building products free of any quality problem.

The 14 steps begin with an echo from Deming's work:

1. *Management commitment*   Managers must believe in the importance of quality and demonstrate a real commitment to improvement throughout the organization by aligning their statements, actions, policies, and

price of nonconformance
The costs of poor quality in the form of rejected products, inspections, repairs, and unhappy customers

price of conformance
The cost of investments in training, product and process design, and buyer-seller relationships to improve quality

14 steps for quality improvement
A program of quality management that advocates a change in corporate culture to achieve a goal of zero defects

[**EXHIBIT 7.9**]

Management Maturity Grid

Categories of Quality	Stage I: Uncertainty	Stage II: Awakening
Management's understanding and attitudes toward quality	Does not see quality as either a management or strategic issue	Supports quality in theory, but remains unwilling to take the actions necessary to really improve it
Quality organization status	Treats quality as an operations management or engineering function alone; orients quality activities largely toward inspections	Appoints quality leader, but limits quality activities to appraisal of failure, primarily in operations management and engineering
Problem handling	Addresses problems as they occur; resolves symptoms leaving underlying causes untouched	Establishs teams to attack major problems but possesses a short-term orientation
Cost of quality as a percentage of sales	Reported: Unknown Actual: 20.0–40.0 percent	Reported: 5.0 percent Actual: 18.0 percent
Quality improvement actions	Nothing organized	Driven by slogans and mottoes; short-term frame
Summary of company's quality position	We know that we have a quality problem, but we don't know why	Why do we always have to have quality problems?

SOURCE   Philip B. Crosby, *Quality Is Free*, McGraw-Hill, New York, 1979. Copyright © 1979. Reprinted with permission of The McGraw-Hill Companies.

procedures with the principles of TQM. Managers identify and eliminate any gaps between the current product and what customers want. All discussions and meetings must address quality as a high-priority agenda item.

2. *Quality improvement team*   The program continues by establishing a team with clear access to top management to guide the process of quality improvement. The team should unite members from groups throughout the firm in an effort to change the attitudes and actions of the people in the company. The team should play a role in establishing all educational and quality-oriented policy activities, leading to larger work coordinating and supervising the change in corporate culture.

3. *Quality measurement*   The program continues by establishing clear measures of quality stated in meaningful terms that relate specifically to individual activities. For example, a measure for the operations management function might state the percentage of production time lost due to inadequate operator training or poor equipment maintenance. These measures allow the program to map and monitor progress.

4. *Cost of quality evaluation*   The program now identifies the price of nonconformance and the price of conformance by collecting data on cost components. Differences between these costs indicate the relative sizes of different opportunities for quality improvement.

Stage III: Enlightenment	Stage IV: Wisdom	Stage V: Certainty
Actively learning about quality and coming to support it	Participate in quality activities and lead through example	Sees quality as necessary to corporate survival and growth
Establishes quality department that reports to top management, with the department's leader actively involved in company management	Makes quality manager an officer of the company and shifts emphasis from appraisal to inspection	Assigns quality manager seat on the board of directors, emphasizes prevention as the main quality activity, and zero defects as the goal
Resolves problems in an orderly fashion with regular corrective action	Identifies problems early in the process	Studies and structures systems to eliminate opportunities for problems by design
Reported: 8.0 percent Actual: 12.0 percent	Reported: 6.5 percent Actual: 8.0 percent	Reported: 2.5 percent Actual: 2.5 percent
14-step program implemented	Continuing 14-step program	Regular on-going quality-improvement activities
We are identifying and eliminating our quality problems with intense success because managers support the new quality-improvement programs now in place.	We routinely prevent quality problems from occurring.	We no longer have a quality problem and we know why we have been so successful. However, we are not going to stop. We can always do better.

5. *Quality awareness*   Next, the program promotes awareness of quality throughout the company, perhaps requiring improvements to communication channels. The quality improvement team must carefully coordinate slogans with appropriate actions to maintain credibility.

6. *Corrective action*   The team proceeds by identifying and studying problems in the OM system. They first bring observed problems to supervisor, helping them to resolve as many as possible. The team carries any remaining problems to higher levels for resolution, always advocating the goal of prevention over correction.

7. *Zero-defects planning*   Managers must plan how to move the company from correcting problems to totally eliminating them to achieve zero defects. This transition requires a total commitment to the zero-defect principle by top managers.

8. *Employee education*   The TQM program must train managers and employees at all levels to fulfill their roles in quality improvement. Along with Deming, Crosby believed that education should pervade all levels of the company. Furthermore, it must accommodate the company's unique situation. Crosby emphasized the importance of successful education as the primary catalyst for change. Though he places it in Step 8, it is an integral element of Step 1 (management commitment) and Step 2 (quality improvement team).

9. *Zero-defects day*   Crosby recommended scheduling a particular date as zero-defects day. This day marks a major turning point in the life of the company when it begins moving toward its goal of zero defects. This day signals to everyone that their work must meet a new, higher standard of performance and that expectations have risen significantly.

10. *Goal setting*   To achieve zero defects, a firm must establish goals that represent progress toward this target. These goals guide performance measurement and evaluation, and they keep quality in its necessary place at the forefront of organizational priorities.

11. *Error cause removal*   The TQM program should encourage employees to identify any problems that prevent them from producing error-free work. All employees should accept responsibility for identifying problems, correcting them, and preventing them from recurring.

12. *Recognition*   The TQM program should include public, nonfinancial expressions of appreciation to employees and managers whose actions have helped the firm achieve or exceed its quality goals and objectives. This recognition motivates others in the firm and sets examples for all to imitate.

13. *Quality council*   Crosby recommended formation of a quality council, a group of quality professionals and team leaders who meet regularly to share experiences, information about problems, and ideas for solutions. This council can also coordinate actions between groups and facilitate learning.

14. *Do it all over again!*   Because the march toward quality is a never-ending journey, the final step returns the program to the beginning to repeat the entire process. This action renews everyone's commitment to quality and identifies a new round of opportunities for improvements.

These steps present several similarities and differences between Crosby's method and those advocated by Deming and Juran. Like Deming and Juran, Crosby advocated a continuing process of total quality management; TQM becomes part of an organization's everyday life. Like the others, Crosby urged elimination of quality-related defects and creation of a quality-oriented corporate culture. Finally, Crosby also stressed the pivotal role of top managers.

Crosby differed from Deming and agreed with Juran in his view that managers play more important roles than workers. He also disputed Deming's Point 10 and accepted slogans, mottoes, and posters as both appropriate and useful. Finally, Crosby recommended performance measures and performance goals, a position that contradicts Deming's Point 11.

Quality Vaccine

quality vaccine

Crosby's image of a TQM regimen that improves the health of the firm and corrects its problems

Crosby advocated making TQM an integral part of an organization's activities through his concept of the quality vaccine. The **quality vaccine** describes a corporate quality management regimen that improves the overall health of the firm and corrects many of its pressing problems. Integrity, the first of three major vaccine components illustrated in Exhibit 7.10, represents an honest attempt by management to eliminate bureaucracy, improve performance, and satisfy customers in the most effective way possible. This concept captures the importance of the firm's commitment to offer products that are right the first time, every time.

The second component, communication, represents the flow of information, both internally between functional departments and externally between the firm

[**E X H I B I T   7 . 1 0**]

Major Components of Crosby's Quality Vaccine

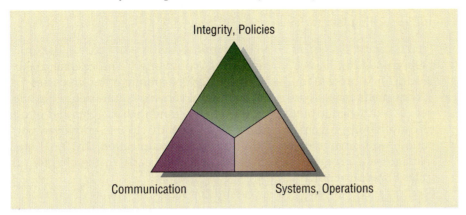

and its customers and suppliers. The vaccine requires regular exchanges of information about quality problems, performance on quality characteristics, progress toward quality goals, and opportunities for quality improvement.

The final component of the quality vaccine consists of systems and operations designed to maintain the firm's new quality environment. By applying the quality vaccine, top managers reorient their firm's culture toward total quality management.

IMAI AND *KAIZEN*

Kaizen is a Japanese name for a formal system to promote continuous improvement initially developed as part of just-in-time manufacturing techniques.[10] Masaaki Imai described the elements of *kaizen* in great detail in a 1986 book, citing the system as an important basis for the success of many leading Japanese firms.[11] Currently, Imai chairs the board of the Cambridge Corporation, an international management consulting organization based in Tokyo.

Understanding *Kaizen*

Kaizen begins with the notion that an organization can assure its long-term survival and success only when every member, in the OM system and throughout the firm, actively pursues opportunities to identify and implement improvements every day. *Kaizen* sets no conditions for the sizes of improvements. In fact, it often favors small, incremental improvements over large innovations. Pursuit of small improvements keeps people thinking about the process and its current operation. They identify potential improvements by understanding the functions of the current system and its weaknesses or relative inefficiencies. Furthermore, small improvements gain returns for the firm without the need for large, initial

---

[10]This concept is discussed in greater detail in Chapter 9 on just-in-time manufacturing.

[11]Masaaki Imai, *Kaizen: The Key to Japan's Competitive Success* (New York: Random House, 1986).

investments to fund major innovations like a new, automated assembly line. An old saying nicely describes the quality-improvement perspective of *kaizen:* "Every day and in every way, we are getting better and better."

Kaizen refines its emphasis on daily, incremental improvement to develop three guiding principles:

- *Process view of the system* The basic unit of analysis in *kaizen* is the process, as discussed in Chapter 5. This analysis could affect a process for making a product or a process for designing a product, among other processes.
- *Success comes from people* Any successful *kaizen* program relies heavily on people's knowledge of their firms' processes and their insights and intuition to conceive improvements. Success requires discipline, employee participation, skill development, and effective communication. The total quality management program at L.L. Bean, described early in the chapter, illustrates *kaizen* in action.
- *Constant sense of urgency* A successful *kaizen* program depends on unceasing awareness of the need for change. Everyone must feel that they can improve their performance and never accept a current process, however good, as sufficient. Complacency and overconfidence drain the energy from *kaizen.* In response to a question about his struggles to improve late in his career, Satchel Paige, a great baseball pitcher and popular wit, replied, "Never look behind yourself. You never know what might be gaining on you."

 ## TOTAL QUALITY MANAGEMENT: SUMMARIZING THE MANAGEMENT TOOLS

Exhibit 7.11 illustrates the contributions of Deming, Juran, Crosby, and Imai to the current practice of total quality management. While these pioneers have disagreed on details, they offer a unified message on certain important themes, which form the basic tenets of TQM.

Quality is not a tactical tool, but a strategic goal that an organization must achieve to survive and grow. Anyone who doubts the truth of this statement must quickly revise this opinion after measuring all of the costs created by poor quality.

The importance of quality forces an organization to extend responsibility for quality beyond any single functional area to spread TQM throughout its ranks, since every member affects the quality that the OM system delivers to customers. Those members do not define quality, however; instead, they work to fulfill customers' definition.

The most effective quality management programs emphasize prevention of defects over inspection intended to catch them before they reach customers. To reliably improve quality, an organization must understand and improve the process that generates it. Success in this effort requires continuous improvement. An organization can always deliver a little better quality.

Effective quality management requires the support and commitment of managers, from the top down, to inspire and direct the actions of employees who must ultimately deliver quality. Quality improves when an organization focuses its corporate culture on the goal of building quality into its most essential structures. Workers can deliver quality only if their managers supply appropriate tools and adequate education and training in the use of those tools.

[**E X H I B I T   7 . 1 1**]

Major Contributors to TQM Management Tools

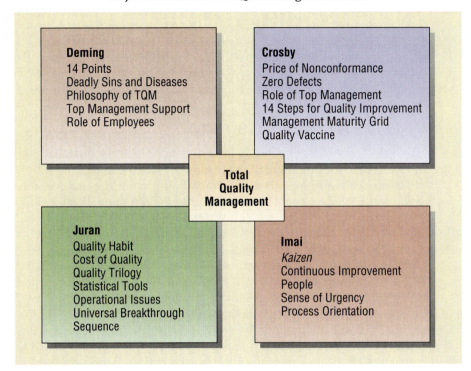

Quality management is a continuing process. Its critical importance requires vigilant protection from compromises driven by short-term considerations or actions. Daily details can overshadow the more distant goals of TQM unless some formal system sets clear specifications for quality as a standard for routine activities and as a basis for competition. National and international programs like ISO 9000 and the Malcolm Baldrige National Quality Award define such specifications.

ISO 9000 AND THE BALDRIGE AWARD: FORMALIZING THE SEARCH FOR QUALITY

In the past, organizations have treated quality management primarily as a management decision in which managers determine the level of quality that their firm will offer and then sell to appropriate customers. Increasingly, however, government agencies, customers, and the firms themselves have come to recognize the potential importance of quality. Quality-oriented firms tend to incur low costs, and they also tend to reduce buyers' risk of faulty products or late deliveries. They have become the most reliable suppliers of products and the most productive contributors to their nations' economies.

This increased awareness of quality has inspired two recent developments that have major implications for operations managers and OM systems: ISO 9000 standards and the Malcolm Baldrige National Quality Award. These national and international programs have formalized systems for evaluating the ability of any firm to consistently design, produce, and deliver a quality product. In the process, they have established a new set of hurdles for firms to clear. An organization that wants to do business in Europe, for example, should plan to become certified under ISO 9000. Motorola expects all of its North American suppliers to apply for the Malcolm Baldrige Award and to strive to meet its standards.

In this section, we explore the implications of these important sets of standards for operations managers. We begin by examining ISO 9000, proceed to discuss the Malcolm Baldrige Award, and then finish by comparing the two programs.

Formalized Process Control in ISO 9000

ISO 9000

A set of internationally accepted standards for business quality adopted in 1987 by the International Organization for Standardization

ISO 9000 defines a set of internationally accepted standards for business quality adopted in 1987 by the International Organization for Standardization (ISO).[12] The ISO 9000 standards identify activities and traits that govern the acceptability of products and that customers expect of a supplier to demonstrate its effective control of its processes. ISO 9000 certification assures customers that a firm has designed and managed its processes to assure delivery of a quality product.

Actually, ISO 9000 spans five documents (ISO 9000 through ISO 9004) that state a wide range of standards that a firm must meet to gain certification. ISO 9001 through ISO 9003 enumerate standards for all firms while ISO 9004 and the ISO 9000-*X* family provide guidelines specific to particular industries. Exhibit 7.12 summarizes the relationships of these documents.

Of the three general documents, ISO 9001 reaches the most comprehensive scope and sets the most demanding requirements for processes and auditing. It covers all aspects of the design, manufacturing, delivery, installation, and servicing process, requiring complete documentation of every affected process in a candidate for certification. In contrast, ISO 9002 deals with narrower issues limited to purchasing, production, and installation, while ISO 9003 sets still less demanding requirements limited to the production process. In general, ISO 9003 amounts to a subset of ISO 9002, and ISO 9002 amounts to a subset of ISO 9001. Exhibit 7.13 summarizes these differences.

Elements of ISO 9000.   ISO 9000 sets standards for 20 specific elements of a firm's quality program. To become certified, the firm must pass a rigorous audit to assure compliance with all of these standards. Section 4 of the ISO 9000 document gives the details:

- *Management responsibility*   The audit must identify someone at a high level within the firm who carries responsibility for the effectiveness of the entire quality management process and for delivery of goods and services that meet or exceed each buyers' specifications and other expectations (Section 4.1).[13]
- *Quality system*   The candidate for certification must have a formal quality system in place to ensure that all delivered goods meet customers' specifications (Section 4.2).
- *Contract review*   The candidate must have a formal process in place to review all accepted contracts and orders to ensure agreement between what marketing or sales personnel sold and what the OM system delivers to the customer (Section 4.3).

---

[12]John T. Rabbit and Peter A. Bergh, *The ISO 9000 Book* (White Plains, N.Y.: Quality Resources, 1993), p. 9.

[13]The section numbers noted in parentheses refer to relevant subsections of ISO 9000, Section 4.

[**EXHIBIT 7.12**]

ISO 9000 Family of Documents

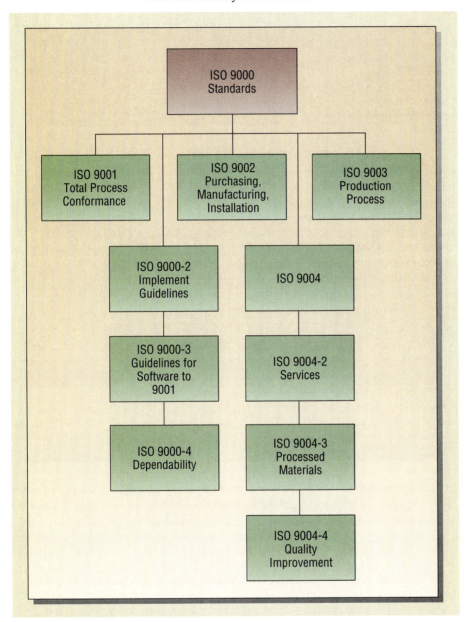

SOURCE   John T. Rabbit and Peter A. Bergh, *The ISO 9000 Book* (White Plains, N.Y.: Quality Resources, 1993), p. 10.

- *Design control*   The candidate must have a formal, documented process in place to verify that a product design fulfills its intended use and backs up sales/marketing claims for the product's function. The candidate must also maintain processes to manage engineering changes to the product design (Section 4.4).

[**EXHIBIT 7.13**]

Scope of ISO 9001, ISO 9002, and ISO 9003

Requirement	ISO 9001	ISO 9002	ISO 9003
Management responsibility	x	x[a]	x[b]
Quality system	x	x	x[b]
Contract review	x	x	
Design control	x		
Document control	x	x	x[b]
Purchasing	x	x	
Purchasing supplied products	x	x	
Product identification	x	x	x[b]
Process control	x	x	
Inspection and testing	x	x	x[b]
Test equipment	x	x	x[b]
Control of nonconforming products	x	x	x[b]
Corrective action	x	x	
Storage and handling	x	x	x[b]
Quality records	x	x	x[b]
Internal quality audits	x	x[a]	
Training	x	x[a]	x[b]
Servicing	x		
Statistical techniques	x	x	x[b]
Packaging and delivery	x	x	x[b]
Test status	x	x	x[b]

[a]Less stringent requirement than ISO 9001
[b]Less stringent requirement than ISO 9002

SOURCE   Michael Breen, Bob Jud, and Pablo E. Pareja, *An Introduction to ISO 9000* (Dearborn, Mich.: Society of Manufacturing Engineers, Reference Publication Division, 1993), p. 2. Reprinted with permission of the Society of Manufacturing Engineers (Dearborn, Michigan).

- *Document control*   The candidate must specify processes and procedures to document all of the information needed to build, service, and maintain the product (Section 4.5).
- *Purchasing*   The candidate must maintain systems and procedures to ensure consistency in time, quantity, quality, and types of products between the needs of the firm and the supplies acquired by purchasing (Section 4.6).
- *Purchasing of supplied products*   The candidate must have processes and systems in place to govern the storage and maintenance of all purchased components and to identify and correct any problems in purchased materials (Section 4.7).
- *Product identification and traceability*   The candidate must document processes for identifying, tracing, and monitoring all parts and products in the OM system to ensure that actual production uses the parts specified in the product design (Section 4.8).
- *Process control*   The candidate must demonstrate procedures within the OM process to control and maintain quality and to flag and correct potential process problems, perhaps including process tools from the Operations Management Toolkit described in Chapter 4 such as check sheets, Pareto analysis, cause-and-effect diagrams, etc. (Section 4.9).

- *Inspection and testing*   The candidate must maintain procedures to make sure that the product actually works as promised (Section 4.10).
- *Inspection, measuring, and test equipment*   The candidate must follow specific procedures to maintain and verify the accuracy of the testing and inspection equipment (Section 4.11).
- *Inspection and test status*   The candidate must provide some standard documentation to inform customers that their products have undergone tests and the results of the tests (Section 4.12).
- *Control of nonconforming products*   The candidate must document systematic procedures for identifying and correcting defects in products (Section 4.13).
- *Corrective actions*   The candidate must demonstrate procedures to correct any problems that become evident (Section 4.14).
- *Handling, storage, packaging, and delivery*   The candidate must follow specific procedures and systems to assure safe handling, storage, packaging, and delivery of finished goods from the end of the manufacturing line to the hands of the customer (Section 4.15).
- *Quality records*   The candidate must implement standard procedures to document the quality of all products that it makes at every stage from raw material to product delivery (Section 4.16).
- *Internal quality audits*   The candidate's internal systems must ensure that the entire process operates within control and that employees act to correct problems identified in any such internal audit (Section 4.17).
- *Training*   The candidate must maintain systems and procedures to properly train all employees, including procedures to measure the effectiveness of training (Section 4.18).
- *Servicing*   The candidate must follow systematic processes for servicing products after their release for use in the field (Section 4.19).
- *Statistical techniques*   The candidate must demonstrate its use of statistical techniques (e.g., control charts, histograms, scatterplots) to maintain control and ensure quality, and training programs must teach workers how to use these techniques (Section 4.20).

During the certification audit, the auditor evaluates the candidate's implementation of each standard. This includes a review of written procedures for carrying out each standard process and verification that all organization members understand the written procedures that affect them. The audit also looks for evidence that employees actually follow the procedures. The audit evaluates methods for responding to any deviations from procedures that emerge and determines who in the organization ensures compliance with procedures.

Clearly, ISO 9000 certification requires a rigorous evaluation. To pass the detailed audit, a firm must reexamine every aspect of its processes for designing, building, storing, and delivering a quality product. This time-consuming process can take anywhere from 3 to 24 months to implement, depending on the initial level of compliance of the firm's systems.[14] Why should a firm subject itself to such a burden?

Benefits of ISO 9000 Certification.   An organization must consider submitting to the compliance audit if customers demand certification as a condition of making any purchases. Many firms now demand this certification of suppliers, making it an important order qualifier.

[14]Rabbit and Bergh, *ISO 9000 Book*, pp. 77–78.

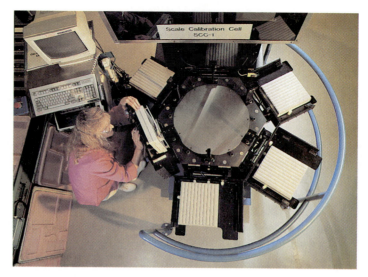

Pitney Bowes is only one of the thousands of companies with ISO 9000 certification, viewed as quality assurance in the international market.   SOURCE   Scott R. Goodwin, Inc.

More specifically, three forces are boosting the impetus for ISO 9000 certification:

- International competitiveness and customer demands
- Market realities and perceptions
- Internal organizational health

Each of these forces creates a strong benefit of ISO 9000 certification and an equally heavy cost of noncompliance.

International Competitiveness and Customer Demands.   Increasingly, firms recognize the need for certification to sell products to customers in Europe, including Great Britain. On December 31, 1992, the major European countries began moving toward a shared goal of removing all barriers to trade among themselves to establish a common market, the European Economic Community (EC), that will unify 19 countries with a total population of over 380 million people. As part of this process, the EC established the European Council for Standardization (CEN) to establish a single set of standards for manufacturers to simplify free trade among the member states. This council accepted the provisions of ISO 9000 verbatim, so a company must often follow these standards to have any hope of selling to EC customers. Certification has become a minimum requirement for trade.

ISO 9000 standards represent minimum requirements outside the EC, as well. Every major industrial nation in the world has accepted these standards, and the U.S. Department of Defense and NATO are incorporating them into purchasing requirements. Finally, they are also becoming part of the Good Manufacturing Practices Standards now under construction to define specifications for manufacturing practices.

In short, ISO 9000 certification has become a necessary condition to sell to customers in major markets. Certification may not represent an order winner, but it is rapidly becoming a universal order qualifier. As of April 1994, over 2,500 American companies and over 30,000 European firms had accepted this reality and become ISO certified. This requirement represents a simple cost of doing business in today's world.

[**EXHIBIT 7.14**]

Past Winners of the Malcolm Baldrige National Quality Award

	Manufacturing	Small Business	Service
1988	Motorola, Westinghouse Commercial Fuel Division	Globe Metallurgical	None awarded
1989	Xerox Corp. Business Products and Systems, Milliken & Co.	None awarded	None awarded
1990	Cadillac Div. of GM, IBM Rochester	Wallace Co.	Federal Express
1991	Solectron Corp., Zytec Corp.	Marlow Industries	None awarded
1992	AT&T Network Systems, Texas Instruments	Granite Rock Co.	AT&T Universal Card Services, The Ritz-Carlton Hotel Co.
1993	Eastman Kodak Co.	Ames Rubber Corp.	None awarded
1994	None awarded	Wainwright Industries	AT&T Consumer Communication Service, GTE Directories

Market Realities and Perceptions.   A noncertified company faces increasing difficulty competing against ISO 9000-certified firms. Certification makes a competitor seem like a better, more reliable vendor. A noncertified firm must win orders over competitors whose processes meet a number of details and that have passed rigorous audits. Media reports in newspapers, television, and such popular business magazines as *Business Week* and *Fortune* reinforce this perception of better quality from ISO 9000-certified firms.

Internal Organizational Health.   Finally, ISO 9000-certified firms have benefited from improvements in their internal organizational health in the course of the process. To pass the audit, people within the firm re-examine and critically challenge their practices and weed out inefficiencies. This activity helps to relieve pent-up organizational frustration, and it invites employees to assume responsibility for improving both operations and the formal quality process. This empowers people and raises effectiveness. Finally, the certification process improves communication links between functional areas within the firm. It forces people to forge agreements on such important issues as the firm's definition of value and its identification of its target market. All of these activities relieve internal stress and boost morale and effectiveness.

Malcolm Baldrige National Quality Award: Recognizing Outstanding Quality

In many ways, the Malcolm Baldrige National Quality Award is the American equivalent of Japan's Deming Prize. In Chapter 1, we described this award, presented annually to U.S.companies that best represent the successfully implementation of quality in the design, production, and delivery of products for the marketplace. The Baldrige Award recognizes companies that represent the most effective pursuit and attainment of total quality. The list of past winners in Exhibit 7.14 includes many firms from the elite of American industry. These firms have also posted some of the best performances in American industry, as the "By the Way" box reports.

[BY THE WAY... THE LINK BETWEEN FINANCIAL PERFORMANCE AND QUALITY]

Top U.S. performers in the quality arena are also tops in the stock market, according to a study by the U.S. Commerce Department. Winners of the Malcolm Baldrige National Quality Award outperformed the Standard & Poor's 500 index by almost three to one in the stock market, according to a study by the department's National Institute of Standards and Technology, the unit which oversees the award program.

The study traced the stock performance of the 11 public companies that won the award from 1988 to 1993. These companies returned a hypothetical 92 percent, including reinvested dividends, compared with a 33 percent return from the S&P 500 index. The study was conducted by assuming a $1,000 investment in each winner compared with an equivalent investment in the S&P 500.

Not all winners dazzled investors, however. Westinghouse Electric Corp. stock prices declined by 50 percent, while Solectron Corp. of Milpitas rose 527 percent between the first business day in April of the year the company won the prize, through October 3, 1994.

SOURCE "Baldrige Winners Outperform S&P 500," *San Jose Mercury News*, February 25, 1995, p. 4D.

The Malcolm Baldrige National Quality Award emerged as a response to the competitive challenges facing U.S. businesses in the early 1980s. Recognizing declining productivity in American industry, President Ronald Reagan signed legislation in October 1982 mandating a national study and conference on productivity. Conferences by the National Advisory Council for Quality (NACQ), the American Productivity Center (now the American Productivity and Quality Center or APQC), and others reached consensus on a recommendation that the U.S. government should sponsor a national quality award along the lines of Japan's Deming Prize. A bill to establish such an award passed the House of Representatives on June 8, 1987, with the strong support of Secretary of Commerce Malcolm Baldrige, confirming the strategic importance of quality to the welfare of American industry. When Malcolm Baldrige was killed in a rodeo accident, the award was renamed in his honor. (The "By the Way" box presents a brief biography of Baldrige.)

Goals and Procedures of the Malcolm Baldrige National Quality Award. The National Quality Award is intended to recognize and encourage improvements in quality and productivity by:

- Stimulating companies to attain excellence in quality for the pride of achievement and improved profitability
- Recognizing outstanding companies and disseminating the experiences of these firms to teach others about quality and its impact on corporate performance
- Establishing guidelines for quality assessment by organizations in business, government, and other areas
- Gathering detailed information from award winners about how to manage for superior quality by changing corporate cultures and practices

These objectives are designed to support two results-oriented goals: delivery of ever-improving value to customers and improvement of overall corporate performance,

[BY THE WAY... MALCOLM BALDRIGE: A BRIEF BIOGRAPHY]

Malcolm Baldrige was nominated as Secretary of Commerce by President Reagan on December 11, 1980, and confirmed by the United States Senate on January 22, 1981.

During his tenure, Baldrige played a major role in developing and carrying out administration trade policy. He took the lead in resolving difficulties in technology transfers with China and India. Baldrige held the first cabinet-level talks with the Soviet Union in seven years, which paved the way for increased access by U.S. firms to the Soviet market. He was highly regarded by the world's preeminent leaders.

Leading the administration's effort to pass the Export Trading Company Act of 1982, Baldrige was named by the president to chair a cabinet-level trade strike force to search out unfair trading practices and recommend ways to end those practices. He was the leader in the reform of the nation's antitrust laws.

Baldrige's award-winning managerial excellence contributed to the long-term improvement in the economy and the efficiency and effectiveness of government. Within the Commerce Department, Baldrige reduced the budget by more than 30 percent and administrative personnel by 25 percent.

Baldrige worked during his boyhood as a ranch hand and earned several awards as a professional team roper on the rodeo circuit. He was Professional Rodeo Man of the Year in 1980 and was installed in the National Cowboy Hall of Fame in Oklahoma City in 1984.

Malcolm Baldrige died July 25, 1987, in a rodeo accident in California. His service as Secretary of Commerce was one of the longest in history. He was possibly the most colorful Secretary of Commerce and one of the most beloved.

SOURCE   Steeples, *The Corporate Guide to the Malcolm Baldrige National Quality Award,* p. 11.

contributing to survival and growth. The Malcolm Baldrige National Quality Award joins people from the private and public sectors in a review-and-evaluation process administered by the National Institute of Standards and Technology (NIST). This four-stage process involves independent review by outsiders, on-site visits, and judges' reviews. The entire review and evaluation process is driven by the following fundamental beliefs about TQM:[15]

- Customers define quality.
- Senior corporate leaders must create clear quality values and build them into company operations.
- Excellent quality evolves from well-designed and well-executed systems and processes.
- Firms must integrate continuous improvement into the management of all systems and processes.
- Companies must develop detailed goals and strategic and operational plans to achieve quality leadership.
- Quality-improvement efforts must include initiatives to reduce response times for all operations.

[15]Marion Mills Steeples, *The Corporate Guide to the Malcolm Baldrige National Quality Award* (Homewood, Ill.: Business One-Irwin, 1993), pp. 19–20.

- Operations and decisions of the company must be based on fact.
- All employees must be appropriately trained, developed, and involved in quality-improvement activities.
- Quality systems must emphasize design quality and error prevention as key elements.
- Companies must communicate quality requirements to suppliers and work to elevate their performance.

Based on these beliefs, the award examination defines seven categories on which the award review evaluates each applicant's performance. The applicant can earn up to 1,000 points over all of the examination categories. Exhibit 7.15 lists the categories and their assigned weights, clearly demonstrating the Baldrige award's emphasis on results and customer satisfaction.

Benefits of the Malcolm Baldrige National Quality Award Program.   Achieving excellent scores in the Baldrige Award's numerous categories represents a significant accomplishment. Many firms apply every year, but no more than six can be recognized (at most, two each in the manufacturing, services, and small-firm divisions). Why would a firm undertake this very expensive application process with such short odds of winning?

Self-Assessment Tool.   The process of applying for the Baldrige Award often has results more important than the selection of the winner. As they apply the award's categories to company processes, both managers and employees learn much about their own operations and their success in serving their customers. This self-assessment can yield dramatic and important insights.

Baldrige Effect.   In general, for every application received, over 2,000 firms request guidelines and applications. Many firms never really intend to apply for the award; instead, their managers use its categories and evaluation process as guidelines for improving their processes.

Sharing Information.   All winners of the Baldrige Award agree to work actively teaching others about quality and about their firms' experiences with quality. This leads to beneficial exchanges of information through war stories and through formal education and training programs.

ISO 9000 versus the Malcolm Baldrige National Quality Award

So far in this section, we have presented two formal research methods designed to improve and assure quality. In general, the Baldrige Award imposes far more demanding and far more comprehensive standards. It forces managers to look at both internal and external operations and at the role of quality in strategic planning. It also deals with the firm's competitive position in the marketplace, explicitly recognizing the critical role of the customer in any judgment of quality.

In contrast, the ISO 9000 standards do not consider the relationship between quality and strategic planning in any depth. Also, they extend only to the firm's internal operations, processes, and procedures. In short, an ISO 9000–certified firm cannot count on winning, or even scoring well, in the Malcolm Baldrige National Quality Award program.

[**E X H I B I T   7 . 1 5**]

Baldrige Award Examination Categories and Point Values

1994 Examination Categories/Items	Point Values
1.0 *Leadership*	90[a]
1.1 Senior executive leadership	45
1.2 Management for quality	25
1.3 Public responsibility and corporate citizenship	20[a]
2.0 *Information and Analysis*	75
2.1 Management of information and data	20[a]
2.2 Competitive comparisons and benchmarking	15[a]
2.3 Analysis and uses of company-level data	40
3.0 *Strategic Planning*	55
3.1 Strategic development	35
3.2 Strategy deployment	20[a]
4.0 *Human Resource Development and Management*	140[a]
4.1 Human resource planning and evaluation	20
4.2 High-performance work systems	45[a]
4.3 Employee education, training, and development	50[a]
4.4 Employee well-being and satisfaction	25
5.0 *Process Management*	140
5.1 Design and introduction of products and services	40
5.2 Process management: product and service production and delivery	40[a]
5.3 Process management: support services	30
5.4 Management of supplier performance	30
6.0 *Business Results*	250[a]
6.1 Product and service quality results	70
6.2 Company operational and financial results	130[a]
6.3 Supplier quality results	45[a]
7.0 *Customer Focus and Satisfaction*	250[a]
7.1 Customer and market knowledge	30[a]
7.2 Customer relationship management	30[a]
7.3 Customer satisfaction determination	30
7.4 Customer satisfaction results	100[a]
7.6 Customer satisfaction comparison	60[a]
Total Points	1,000

[a]Weighting changed from the 1993 criteria.

Recent Developments in the Formalized Search for Quality: ISO 14000

To keep current in the dynamic process of formalizing the search for quality, an operations manager must track continuous changes. By 1996, a new set of ISO 14000 standards will be introduced to advance the ISO 9000 standards into new areas of organizational activities. The new standards are conceived as an internationally applied set of measures to assess a company's environmental responsibility. These standards will begin as a set of voluntary guidelines and a certification program based on:

- *Management systems*   Standards for systems development and integration and to introduce environmental concerns into general business
- *Operations*   Standards for consumption of natural resources and energy
- *Environment-related systems*   Standards for measuring, assessing, and managing emissions, effluents, and other waste streams

Building on the success and visibility of the ISO 9000 standards, ISO 14000 should promote green manufacturing principles and practices extremely effectively.

Formalized Search for Quality: Some Final Comments

Even successful implementation of the standards of ISO 9000, 14000 (discussed in Chapter 19), or the Malcolm Baldrige National Quality Award cannot guarantee continued success for any firm. In 1993, the Wallace Company filed for Chapter 11 bankruptcy protection, 3 years after winning the Malcolm Baldrige National Quality Award. In addition, the time-consuming application process requires an investment of significant amounts of money. Some companies have spent up to $1 million in preparing their briefs for the award review. Creating the documentation required to meet ISO 9001 standards exposes a firm to significant costs, as well. As a result, both programs have been criticized as excluding many small firms.

In addition, both ISO 9000 and the Baldrige Award have been criticized for goal-oriented rather than process-oriented criteria. Both rate success based on achievement of a specific goal, but neither has defined the next goal or challenge. Once a firm wins the Baldrige Award, what should it do next? The answers that firms like Xerox and Motorola find for this question will significantly affect their long-term growth and viability.

TOTAL QUALITY ENVIRONMENTAL MANAGEMENT

total quality environmental management

A technique that applies the tools and techniques of TQM to the problem of improving corporate environmental responsibility

TQM cannot stop and accept its current version as definitive. In one recent development, some managers and consultants have begun to apply the principles of TQM to evaluation of companies' environmental responsibility. Firms can apply the same principles, frameworks, tools, and techniques that they now use for total quality management to the problem of improving corporate environmental responsibility. This application of TQM principles and frameworks to the environmental problem is now referred to as **total quality environmental management** or TQEM. The familiar goal of this system is to create better-run companies by inducing them to operate in more environmentally responsible ways.

CHAPTER SUMMARY

We began this chapter by reviewing L.L. Bean's experience in transforming and improving its processes through total quality management. In the rest of the chapter, we explored the details of TQM management tools and their effects on the firm and its employees, especially the operations manager:

1. Total quality management strives to achieve a sustainable competitive advantage by emphasizing superior quality by focusing company actions on customer satisfaction, employee empowerment, and powerful management and statistical tools.

2. Successful TQM turns an organizational structure upside down, assigning managers the role of supporting the activities of operating employees, who are most familiar with the firm's quality problems and most likely to recognize opportunities for improvement.

3. Four pioneers made especially significant contributions to the theory underlying TQM: W. Edwards Deming, Joseph Juran, Philip B. Crosby, and Masaaki Imai. Deming developed his 14 points of management, 5 deadly sins and diseases, and the theory of variance, and he highlighted for the first time the importance of top management support and involvement. Juran promoted the habit of quality, the cost of quality calculation, the quality trilogy, and the universal breakthrough sequence. Crosby has advocated absolutes for quality management and his 14 steps in quality improvement as well as the management maturity grid. Imai has articulated the notion of continuous improvement.

4. Increasingly, sets of formal standards guide evaluations of quality systems, and ISO 9000 and the Malcolm Baldrige National Quality Award program define the most significant of these standards. Both of these programs effectively define minimum acceptable standards for quality among the most important industrial customers.

5. ISO 9000 certifies that a firm has passed a rigorous audit to confirm that its major processes have been documented, that everyone associated with those processes understands correct procedures, and that people routinely follow these procedures. The increasing importance of ISO 9000 seems likely to make certification a near-universal order qualifier in important markets in Europe and elsewhere.

6. The Malcolm Baldrige National Quality Award, the American equivalent of Japan's Deming Prize, is presented annually to a maximum of six companies. Based on standards broader than those of ISO 9000, the Baldrige Award emphasizes results, planning for quality throughout an organization, and customer involvement and satisfaction.

7. TQM is a dynamic concept subject to constant change. One evolutionary development, total quality environmental management, applies TQM techniques to evaluate a firm's environmental responsibility. Also, expanded standards in ISO 14000 encompass environmental concerns within the concept of quality.

TQM promotes a broad, cross-functional strategy for generating value through profound changes in a firm's corporate culture and management goals. Success requires a firm to carry this initiative to employees throughout the firm, arming them with the statistical tools and techniques they need to achieve the objectives of TQM. In the next chapter, we examine the most important of these tools and techniques.

[KEY TERMS]

total quality management	management tools for	statistical tools for quality
292	quality 297	298

[D I S C U S S I O N   Q U E S T I O N S]

1. A common proverb used in business is: "That which is not measured is not managed." In what ways does total quality management agree and disagree with this statement?

2. Why is the orientation of the "Direction of Support" arrow in Exhibit 7.2 an important element of the total quality management approach? Is the Japanese business culture be more amenable to this orientation? Explain.

3. The SAS tale illustrates why employee empowerment is an essential element of total quality management in services. Cite instances where the service provider empowered its employee to go the extra mile to totally delight you. Then indicate an instance where the opposite happened. What programs should have been in place to prevent substandard service?

4. You have been commissioned to create a local equivalent of the Deming Prize for your college's campus. The winner will receive free campus parking for one academic year. Prepare a list of criteria for use in deciding who on your campus is most worthy of this award. How would you propose that these factors be measured? Should they be?

5. The eighth of Deming's Fourteen Points of Management states that a firm must "drive out fear." Discuss the practicality of this tenet. Can an effective TQM program be realized in an organization in which employees experience fear?

6. Discuss the conditions under which inspecting a good or service is not waste. What products would you be willing to pay more for because their performance is assured through some inspection process? Cite a product for which this condition previously existed but that you now are willing to buy without inspection.

7. Exhibit 7.7 uses a two-dimensional problem classification scheme to restate Deming's statement that 85 percent of business problems are attributable to management. Which item(s) in the Manager's Toolkit could you use to help classify these?

8. Compare and contrast Frederick Taylor's scientific methods of management and Deming's PDCA cycle.

9. You have been appointed head of quality control for your organization (a firm you have worked at or your college). During the first month, you interview disciples of Deming, Juran, and Crosby. Each seems to be equally affable and competent. Which consultant would you hire for your organization? Why?

10. Place each of the following organizations on Crosby's Management Maturity Grid.
    a. The management of your favorite fast food outlet
    b. Your college's financial aid office
    c. The United States' post office—your local branch
    d. Your local computer store
    What would it take for each of these organizations to move "up the grid"?

11. As a star operations management student, you try to apply *kaizen* at your work. An experienced supervisor retorts, "*kaizen*—that is just another one of those Japanese fads—I'll wait for next year's." Is the supervisor's interpretation incorrect? Why do you think she might feel that way?

12. Why are export-oriented countries, such as Germany and Japan, on the leading edge of the quality movement?

C A U T I O N

[C R I T I C A L   T H I N K I N G   R E Q U I R E D]

1. "TQM is great, but don't try to apply it to your home life." Is there wisdom in this statement? Why?
2. Apply Juran's five dimensions of quality to the domestic use of nuclear power to electrify homes and industry. Is it a useful construct for debating the merits of this technology? Is there any other quality construct that is more useful? Why?

CASE 7.1

Advanced Laser Technology, Inc.

Punita Bigolow and her husband have a small, highly successful firm that serves a narrow niche of medical applications of laser technologies. The firm has only four customers, but each is a leading player in the emerging medical-electronics technology markets. Each firm has told Bigolow that it is pleased with her product, service, and ability to provide leading edge technology.

Bigolow's problem begins in the form of a memo. One of her major customers has just decided to seek ISO 9000 certification. As the customer has grown, it needs ISO 9000 certification to effectively compete in international markets. Bigolow understands this logic so far.

The next paragraph reads:

As part of our ISO 9000 certification process, we will expect each of our key suppliers to become ISO 9000 certified. While we realize that this may impose some hardships on you, we are firmly convinced that the end result will be goods and services of world class quality.

What little Bigolow knows about ISO 9000 is that this new requirement would pose an enormous problem for Advanced Laser Technology. Her firm has five employees: herself, her engineer husband, two technicians, and one secretary. How will ALT be able to document all that it did?

It seems to be a catch-22 situation. If Bigolow and her husband divert their attention to document all 20 aspects of Section 4 of ISO 9000, then the firm risks losing its competitive edge in this fast-changing technological field. If ALT hires a consultant to help with this certification process, it risks diverting both management attention and critical cash resources. As she reflects on this dilemma, Bigolow wonders, "How does this add value?"

QUESTION

What would you recommend to Bigolow?

[SELECTED READINGS]

Bhote, Keri R. *Strategic Supplier Management: A Blueprint for Revitalizing the Manufacturer-Supplier Partnership*. New York: American Management Association, 1989.

Breen, Michael, Bob Jud, and Pablo E. Pareja. *An Introduction to ISO 9000*. Dearborn, Mich.: Society of Manufacturing Engineers, Reference Publication Division, 1993.

Carlzon, Jan. *Moments of Truth*. Cambridge, Mass.: Harper & Row, 1989.

Crosby, Philip B. *Quality Is Free*. New York: McGraw-Hill, 1979.

Dean, James W. Jr., and James R. Evans. *Total Quality: Management, Organization, and Strategy*. Minneapolis/St. Paul, Minn.: West, 1994.

Deming, W. Edwards. *Quality, Productivity, and Competitive Position*. Cambridge, Mass.: MIT Center for Advanced Engineering Study, 1982.

———. *Out of Crisis*. Cambridge, Mass.: MIT Center for Advanced Engineering Study, 1986.

"Does the Baldrige Award Really Work?" *Harvard Business Review*, January/February 1992, pp. 126–147.

Garvin, David A. *Managing Quality*. New York: Free Press, 1988.

Hall, Robert, ed. *Manufacturing Report 21: The Future of Japanese Manufacturing*. Wheeling, Ill.: Association for Manufacturing Excellence, 1990.

Imai, Masaaki. *Kaizen: The Key to Japan's Competitive Success*. New York: Random House, 1986.

Juran, Joseph M., and Frank M. Gryna, Jr. *Quality Planning and Analysis*. New York: McGraw-Hill, 1980.

Logothetis, N. *Managing for Total Quality: From Deming to Taguchi and SPC*. Hertfordshire, U.K.: Prentice-Hall International, 1992.

Makower, Joel. *The E Factor*. New York: Times Books, 1993.

Maskell, Brian. *Performance Measurement for World-Class Manufacturing*. Cambridge, Mass.: Productivity Press, 1991.

21st Manufacturing Enterprise Strategy: An Industry-Led View, 2 volumes. Ann Arbor, Mich.: National Center for Manufacturing Sciences, November 1991.

Rabbit, John T., and Peter A. Bergh. *The ISO 9000 Book*. White Plains, N.Y.: Quality Resources, 1993.

Senge, Peter M. *The Fifth Discipline*. New York: Doubleday, 1990.

Steeples, Marion Mills. *The Corporate Guide to the Malcolm Baldrige National Quality Award*. Homewood, Ill.: Business One-Irwin, 1993.

Tribus, Myron, ed. *Quality First: Selected Papers on Quality and Productivity Improvements*. Washington, D.C.: American Quality and Productivity Institute, 1988.

Zemke, Ron. "A Bluffer's Guide to TQM." *Training*, April 1993, pp. 48–55.

CHAPTER EIGHT

Total Quality Management
Tools and Techniques

CHRYSLER STALLS ON DEFECTS

Tools and Variables

Nature of Variables

Process Tools

Check Sheets • Pareto Analysis • Cause-and-Effect Diagrams • Process Flow Analysis • Histograms • Process Capability Measures: C_p and C_{pk} • Control Charts • Scatterplots • Plan-Do-Check-Act Cycles • Brainstorming • Putting the Tools Together

Design Tools

Quality Function Deployment/House of Quality • Concurrent Engineering • Hoshin Management • Comments on the TQM Design Tools

CHAPTER SUMMARY

Case 8.1 THE BULLY BOY BAGGING LINE

On the Job DISNEY BRAINSTORMS NEW PATHS TO QUALITY

On the Job WHAT TQM DID FOR MOTOROLA

[At the end of this chapter, you should be able to]

- Differentiate attribute data from variable data to determine appropriate inputs for TQM statistical tools.
- Explain the principles and applications of ten major process-analysis tools found in most successful TQM systems: Pareto analysis, check sheets, cause-and-effect diagrams, process flow analysis, histograms, measures of process spread and variability, control charts, plan-do-check-act cycles, scatterplots, and brainstorming.
- Apply these tools to analyze common quality-related problems in operations management.
- Describe the conditions under which each tool becomes most effective.
- Show the benefits of integrated systems of quality tools such as Motorola's Six Sigma program.
- Define the functions and benefits of three major quality-oriented design tools: quality function deployment/house of quality, concurrent engineering, and Hoshin management.

J. Polimeni/
Liaison International

Chrysler Stalls on Defects

URING 1994 CHRYSLER WAS RIDING high on the car industry boom. It was selling out of nearly every automobile it built and had a tight 45-day inventory supply. But when Robert J. Eaton, Chrysler's chairman, put his foot on the accelerator, he knew he was in trouble. While test-driving a prototype Cirrus sedan at Chrysler's proving grounds north of Phoenix, Eaton heard a disturbing clatter from the accelerating V-6 engine. He also noticed that the dashboard's plastic pieces did not fit together neatly, and neither did the trim.

It's hard enough to woo skeptical baby boomers away from Japanese cars without such defects. Eaton returned from his test-drive in March determined to boost the quality of Chrysler cars. He ordered that production of the Cirrus and its cousin, the Dodge Stratus, be delayed until fixes could be made.

Eaton was taking a risk with this delay. The market for family sedans is one of the industry's most lucrative, and bad timing could leave Chrysler out in the cold. But Eaton knew that even one minor defect could turn off a potential customer forever.

The task ahead of Eaton and Chrysler was enormous. Eaton and other top management had worked hard to infuse a culture of TQM throughout Chrysler. But creating a "culture" for quality is not enough. Eaton's employees obviously needed better tools for bringing it about.

S O U R C E
David Woodruff,
"Bug Control at
Chrysler," *Business
Week,* August 22,
1994, p. 26.

While Chrysler's minivans were earning top rankings in the all-important J.D. Power & Associates quality ratings for trucks, all of its car models were performing below average.

To compound this problem, executives weren't finding out about a lot of problems until customers were surveyed—45 days after driving away in their cars. For high-volume models, those 45 days could mean about 30,000 unhappy buyers.

Obviously, Chrysler needed a better audit system to catch problems before cars left dealer lots. But more importantly, plant employees needed better analytic and statistical tools to put Chrysler's culture of quality into practice *before* the cars even went to market.

The Chrysler example shows how essential empowerment is. Empowerment combines authority and knowledge. Authority allows or even encourages employees to make changes in the system to improve its effectiveness. Knowledge gives them the training and analytical tools they need to make those changes and motivates them to carry their ideas to success. In this chapter, we discuss the TQM tools that workers use to measure and improve quality.

In the first section of the chapter, we discuss the types of data that TQM practitioners must recognize and manipulate. In the next section, we discuss several popular statistical tools for meaningful analysis of this data. In another section, we describe Motorola's Six Sigma standards, which integrate statistical tools into a unified TQM program. Toward the end of the chapter, we describe tools that help operations managers to design processes to produce quality outputs.

 ## TOOLS AND VARIABLES

Total quality management relies heavily on contributions from empowered employees, but employees remain powerless, whatever strategy choices managers have made, without access to appropriate tools. Bill Conway of the Nashua Corporation made this point effectively when speaking with some top-management visitors from Ford:

> Conway started the meeting with a challenge. "Suppose I ask two of you successful vice presidents at Ford to enter a contest. The winner will win a trip around the world for his whole family. I know that both of you are totally motivated and dedicated, by virtue of your exalted positions at Ford. The contest is to see who can drive a nail into this wall. One of you will get a hammer, the other nothing but management encouragement! Who do you think will win?" The answer was obvious. Motivation is important, management encouragement is important. But employees at all levels must have tools. They must be the *right* tools.[1]

Rather than hammers and other physical tools, TQM empowers managers and employees by providing analytical techniques and procedures. These conceptual and statistical tools help people to measure and improve the quality levels of their

[1]Keri R. Bhote, *Strategic Supplier Management: A Blueprint for Revitalizing the Manufacturer-Supplier Partnership* (New York: American Management Association, 1989), p. 168.

firm's processes for designing and producing a good or service. These tools indicate how well the firm controls its OM processes. If they reveal poor control, they also help to identify likely sources of the problems.

In general, these tools fall into two major categories: process tools and design tools. With **process tools,** employees assess conditions in existing processes to detect problems that require intervention and to regain any lost control. Shop-floor workers frequently apply these tools. In contrast, **design tools** aid employees in conceiving and developing effective new products and processes. This analysis focuses on preventing problems or reducing their likelihood and integrating the needs and expectations of the customer into new processes.

Nature of Variables

To apply process and design tools, TQM practitioners need input data. In general, the tools help employees to manipulate data. Without this data, or with the wrong kind of data, the tools are useless.

Analysts can measure process conditions with either variable data or attribute data. **Variable data** measures quantifiable process conditions. Workers can count this type of data, and its order represents both relative and absolute magnitudes. Examples of variable data include the sizes of holes in a reinforcing plate, the number of typographical errors per page, the hardness of steel, and the serving temperature of hamburgers in the serving bins of a fast-food restaurant.

To understand the meaning of the concept of magnitude, consider an example. You work in the receiving department of a plant processing inputs of components from suppliers. You check for defects in a sample of 50 units from each batch. If you find more than 15 percent defects in a sample (i.e., 8 or more bad units), you reject the batch and return it to the supplier. Otherwise, you accept the batch. Exhibit 8.1 summarizes data for 20 batches.

Counting the defects in each batch has led you to accept 15 batches and reject 5, for a total acceptance rate of 75 percent. The number of defects becomes a variable in this exercise because the exhibit can arrange the data in increasing order of magnitude, starting with 0 defects on March 10 and reaching 12 defects on March 8. Furthermore, you can make meaningful comparisons of the data. The first sample had 2 defects; the second had 4. The first batch had fewer defects than the second (half as many). Each number has an absolute magnitude, and the relative magnitudes may become important, as well.

In contrast, **attribute data** measures qualitative conditions of a process (pass/fail, go/no-go, good/bad). Exhibit 8.1 presents attribute data in the last column, "Action," which describes the decision based on the variable data. Comparisons with attribute data yield only limited insights. If you could see only the first and last columns of Exhibit 8.1, you could determine that the first two batches were acceptable, but you could not say how good the samples seemed or make any comparisons between them. The attribute data indicates nothing about any differences between the first and second batches. Even when such data indicate a difference, as between the second and third samples, you could conclude only that the second must have had seven or fewer defects while the third must have had eight or more defects.

Variable and attribute measures are linked. An analyst can convert variable data into attribute data, as when a sample with eight defects gains the attribute of a reject while a batch with three defects gains the attribute of an acceptable batch. The relationship usually runs only one way, however; attribute data indicates little or nothing about variables. The accept/reject decision indicates only whether or

process tools

Statistical TQM tools that help employees to assess conditions in existing processes to detect problems and regain lost control

design tools

Statistical TQM tools that help employees to conceive and develop effective new processes

variable data

Data that quantifies some process condition, allowing the analyst to count it and make comparisons

attribute data

Data that indicates some qualitative condition of a process

[**EXHIBIT   8.1**   ]

Variable Data for Defects per Batch

Date of Batch	Number of Defects per 50	Action
3/7	2	Accept
3/7	4	Accept
3/7	8	Reject
3/8	12	Reject
3/8	3	Accept
3/8	7	Accept
3/8	5	Accept
3/8	10	Reject
3/9	4	Accept
3/9	4	Accept
3/9	9	Reject
3/10	0	Accept
3/11	1	Accept
3/11	2	Accept
3/11	9	Accept
3/11	2	Accept
3/14	6	Accept
3/14	3	Accept
3/14	11	Reject
3/14	7	Accept

not a sample included more than a set number of defects. This distinction may become important because some of the tools presented in this chapter need variable data while others can manipulate either variable or attribute measures.

 ## PROCESS TOOLS

Most TQM systems rely heavily on ten major process tools. This list covers the traditional or first-generation TQM tools:

- Check sheets
- Pareto analysis
- Cause-and-effect diagrams
- Process flow analysis
- Histograms
- Measures of process spread and variability
- Control charts
- Plan-do-check-act cycles
- Scatterplots
- Brainstorming

We discussed check sheets, Pareto analysis, cause-and-effect diagrams, and plan-do-check-act cycles in Chapter 4, and we covered process flow analysis in Chapter 5.

TQM practitioners use each of these tools to evaluate their control of a process or system and to identify problems, uncover the most likely causes of

[**EXHIBIT 8.2**]

TQM Tool Applications

Activity	Typical Process Tools Used

Gain process control
   Eliminate special causes
   Observe causes of inherent variation
	Cause-and-effect diagrams; C_p/C_{pk}; Check sheets;
	   Histograms

Determine process capability	C_p/C_{pk}; Histograms; Check sheets
Maintain process control	Control charts; Scatterplots; Histograms
Improve process capabilities	Casue-and-effect diagrams; Checksheets; Histograms; Process flow analysis; Brainstorming; Plan-do-check-act

those problems, and assess the effects of any corrective actions. While each tool can provide powerful insights by itself, combinations of them generate more accurate pictures of processes. Each tool reveals a part of a problem, but none can fully describe its features alone; each tool complements information and insight from the others.

The complementary strengths of these tools suggest combinations for different TQM stages. TQM begins with gaining process control. It then applies appropriate analytical tools to determine process capabilities, maintain process control, and improve process capabilities. Exhibit 8.2 lists combinations of the ten process tools for each of these stages. Individual subsections discuss the tools and their roles in a comprehensive program of total quality management.

Check Sheets

As Chapter 4 explained, check sheets provide a systematic means of collecting and analyzing data. They can generate categories of defects and the number of occurrences per category. In the example from Exhibit 8.1, as you discovered a defective item, you could simply add a check to an existing row if you had seen the same type of defect previously or add a new row if you had not seen a similar defect before. Each week's check sheets would then indicate the types of defects discovered during that week and the number of occurrences of each.

In this way, check sheets support defective-item checks by summarizing information about types of defects and their percentages. They also support defect-location checks by indicating specific locations of defects on individual units of process output. Data collected over a number of parts may direct attention toward a systematic cause of defects in a particular location.

TQM systems also employ check sheets for production process distribution checks. These types of check sheets track continuous, variable data for characteristics like the sizes, weights, or diameters of process outputs. This data, perhaps restated in a histogram, provides a control gauge for the process that generates the outputs.

A check sheet can help a TQM analyst to dig deeper by tracking the causes of defects. This defective-cause check sheet expands on the information of the previous types of check sheets, which indicate occurrences of problems, but say little about their causes and effects. By arranging a check sheet with separate categories for defects from separate shifts, machines, or operators, the analyst can narrow down the causes and target corrective actions.

Engineers at Chrysler would use check sheets to gather several kinds of data in the process of improving the quality of the Cirrus. They might begin with a defective-item check sheet to determine the types of defects in the car and frequency of each type. A defect-location check sheet might indicate where on the car a particular type of defect occurs, leading the search for a cause to process activities that contact the car at that point. If the information gained from these check sheets points to a problem with a particular part, the engineers could evaluate its process traits using a production process distribution check sheet. Finally, the engineers could narrow their search to the most important potential causes and effects of these quality problems using a defective-cause check sheet.

Pareto Analysis

Chapter 4 also described Pareto analysis, a method for identifying and separating the vital few process events from the trivial many. This tool begins by specifying as many potential causes of a problem as possible. The analysis then assigns each cause a value based on some appropriate unit of measure to indicate its contribution to the problem. Pareto analysis could measure such a contribution as a dollar cost, a percentage of defects in a sample, or a percentage of time devoted to correcting defects, among other measures.

By ranking these values from highest to lowest, Pareto analysis highlights the causes most closely associated with the problem. These ranks also set priorities for corrective action, targeting the first improvements at the cause that accounts for the highest dollar costs or the largest percentage of defects. After eliminating that cause as a potential source of problems, TQM continues by addressing the next one on the list. Tackling causes in rank order eliminates the most likely causes of problems first. Problem 8.1 applies Pareto analysis to a hypothetical TQM problem to show how it works.

[**P R O B L E M   8 . 1**]

Pareto Analysis of Pear Defects

Pear Computers, a small Midwestern manufacturer of personal computers, has built a reputation for innovation, flexible product configurations, on-time delivery, and quality. Recently, however, quality has slipped. Final inspections of the new Pear 6000 model have revealed problems in an unacceptably high number of computers. Some computers have refused to boot up, while others have run for the first 5 hours of the 48 burn-in, then shut down after generating error messages. After talking with assembly workers, Bob Feller, the operations manager in charge of the assembly line, has identified possible causes of these problems and gathered information about the frequency of problems. Over a 4-week test period, 15,000 computers are assembled. Defects are traced to these causes:

Potential problems	Number of occurrences	Percentage	Rank
Chips inserted incorrectly	43	3.97	8
CPU chip/memory chips popping out during burn-in	117	10.79	4
Traces cut on motherboard during assembly	78	7.20	6
Loose power connections	150	13.84	3

Connections not made on motherboard	34	3.14	9
Dust in critical areas	90	8.30	5
Incorrect components	51	4.70	7
Motherboard incorrectly seated	15	1.38	10
Motherboard damaged during installation	245	22.60	2
CPU damaged during assembly	261	24.08	1
	1,084	100.00	

A chart of the data constructed using Pareto analysis shows that the last two causes together account for about 47 percent of all defects (Exhibit 8.3). This chart suggests that Bob should begin his improvement efforts in these two areas. Just by eliminating the causes of damage to the CPU during assembly, he could reduce defects from 1,084 to 823. To accomplish this improvement, however, Bob must understand more specifically how this damage occurs.   [■]

Cause-and-Effect Diagrams

TQM uses cause-and-effect (C&E) diagrams, also introduced in Chapter 4, to generate and organize detailed information about the results of specific subprocesses or activities. They help users to look more deeply at individual problems and the relationships of their potential causes. C&E diagrams also help to direct problem-solving and data-collection efforts toward the most likely causes of observed defects. Problem 8.2 develops a cause-and-effect diagram for the TQM study from Problem 8.1.

[**E X H I B I T 8 . 3**]

Pareto Analysis for Pear Computers

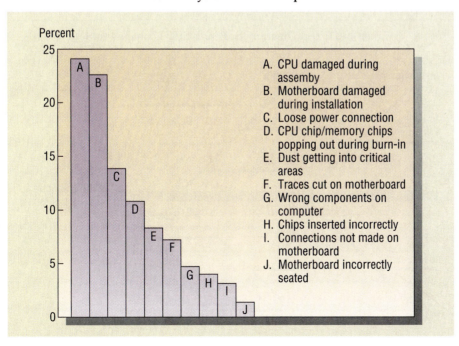

A. CPU damaged during assemby
B. Motherboard damaged during installation
C. Loose power connection
D. CPU chip/memory chips popping out during burn-in
E. Dust getting into critical areas
F. Traces cut on motherboard
G. Wrong components on computer
H. Chips inserted incorrectly
I. Connections not made on motherboard
J. Motherboard incorrectly seated

[**PROBLEM 8.2**]

Cause-and-Effect Diagrams for Pear

Pareto analysis has told Bob Feller that damage to the CPU during assembly has caused more defects in the Pear computers produced by his OM process than any other cause. He has constructed the cause-and-effect diagram in Exhibit 8.4 to try to pinpoint the specific cause of this damage.

This diagram identifies four categories of potential causes: equipment, employees, CPU chips, and inspection. More specific causes in these four categories guide Bob's analysis and data-collection activities. In particular, they identify targets for more detailed process flow analysis.   [■]

Process Flow Analysis

In Chapter 5, we discussed process flow analysis as a method of graphically representing the activities in a process, the exact tasks of these activities, and their organization or structure within the process. In TQM, a PFA graph leads to a better understanding of an overall process and its potential problems. By graphing out the process, a TQM practitioner can study its details and uncover causes of variance and opportunities for improvement.

For example, after Bob Feller completes a cause-and-effect diagram, he might continue with a process flow analysis of the activities involved in inserting the CPU during computer assembly. By diagraming the process using the symbols described in Chapter 5, he can spot variance, or differences in times to carry out an activity. He can also look for confusion in activity flows or disruptions that force employees to spend more time than necessary on a certain task because of problems with either the procedures or the components (e.g., the CPU or the computer case).

[**EXHIBIT 8.4**]

Cause and Effect Diagram for Pear's CPU Damage Problem

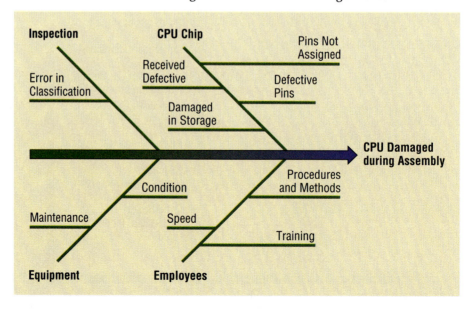

[**E X H I B I T   8 . 5**]

Sample Histogram

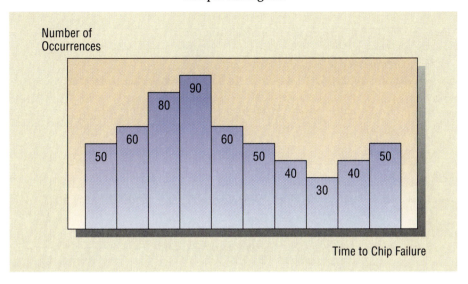

Number of
Occurrences

Time to Chip Failure

Histograms

Variance arises in every activity or process, since no human system can function exactly the same way all the time. Operations managers can tightly control some variance, as they do in highly automated processes. Some variance defies efforts to control it, however. A **histogram** graphically displays data gathered during the operation of a process to show the extent and type of variance within the system. Exhibit 8.5 shows an example.

A histogram analyzes and graphically displays quantitative rather than qualitative data. TQM practitioners use histograms to display information about process and activity performance like how long donors take to give blood, the sizes of mounting holes in successive units of a part, or the weights of assembled dashboard panels. Histograms are most effective when they display information with some natural order, such as the number of defects found. Without a natural order for different data categories, the shape of a histogram depends on the order in which the analyst arranges the categories.

Histograms help operations managers to achieve deeper insight into the characteristics of data distributions associated with activities. L.L. Bean managers from the story in Chapter 7 might construct a histogram to represent data collected by measuring the time it takes to serve customers over the telephone. Chrysler managers might construct a histogram with data about dashboard panels.

Practitioners of total quality management use histograms to summarize data and display patterns. They know that any set of observations must display some variation. Histograms present graphic pictures that quickly summarize this variation.

All variation displays some pattern. Histograms show patterns effectively, helping researchers to recognize and understand process characteristics through their data. Patterns in histograms capture three critical traits of distributions:

- *Center of the distribution* This point usually coincides with the mean of the overall distribution. The theoretical or desired mean (often written as μ) should fall at the center of the histogram's graphic picture of the distribution.

histogram
A TQM statistical tool that graphically displays data gathered during the operation of a process to show the extent and type of variance within the system

[**EXHIBIT 8.6**]

Common Shapes of Distributions

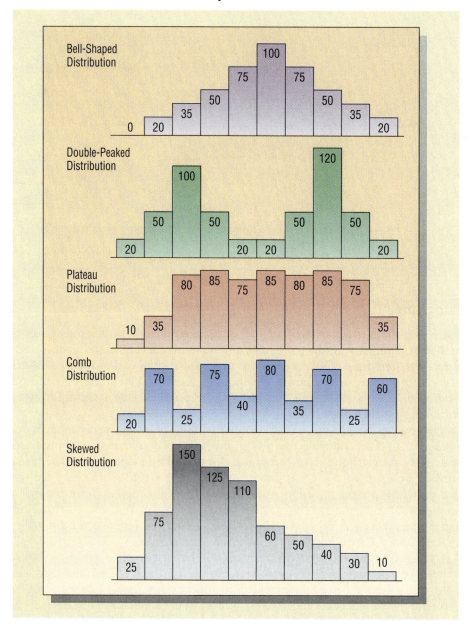

SOURCE   Reprinted from *Guide to Quality Control* by Kaoru Ishikawa, copyright 1992 Asian Productivity Organization, with permission of the publisher, Asian Productivity Organization. Distributed in North America by Quality Resources, New York, NY.

Any gap between these two points may indicate the amount of bias in the distribution, that is, an uneven distribution of data around the true mean.

- *Width of the distribution*   In statistics, the difference between the highest and lowest values in a distribution is its range. A histogram graphically shows the range as the width of a distribution, which often indicates how predictably the activity that generated the distribution operates. A wider distribution represents a less predictable activity; a narrower distribution indicates a more predictable activity.

- *Shape of the distribution*   The overall shape of a distribution often indicates different problems in the data or influences on the overall distribution

The histograms in Exhibit 8.6 show five different types of distributions, and each indicates a very different type of behavior. Most students are familiar with the normal, bell-shaped distribution. This symmetrical distribution indicates a natural spread of data from a single stable process. In contrast, the double or twin-peaked distribution often results from a combination of two normal distributions, perhaps because the analyst has gathered data from two distinct processes.

The plateau distribution shows a flat region with no distinct peak. This pattern usually results from a combination of multiple data sets, each of which may have a normal distribution. The means of the various distributions occur evenly across a particular range, defining a flat region.

The comb distribution, in contrast, shows multiple peaks and troughs, indicating wide variation commonly associated with errors. Besides defects in the process, this variation could indicate errors due to faulty measurements of process characteristics, errors in data collection, rounding errors, or poor grouping of data into categories for the histogram. In some cases, the comb distribution may also represent an extreme version of the plateau distribution.

Finally, the skewed distribution shows an asymmetrical pattern of data. The narrow tail of a positively skewed distribution extends to the right, as in Exhibit 8.6. The tail of a negatively skewed distribution extends to the left. Such patterns often suggest some limit restraining data on one side of the distribution. For example, if Bob Feller were to measure the number of defective microchips per 1,000 CPUs, he would probably generate a positively skewed histogram because zero defects forms a natural lower limit near which much of the data should fall.

Histograms are easy to construct, but more difficult to interpret. To get meaningful data, one must select the category sizes carefully. Too many categories spread data too thinly across the histogram, breaking down potential patterns into scattered points; too few categories lump together conflicting data, obscuring patterns that might otherwise emerge. Exhibit 8.7 gives some general guidelines for choosing numbers of categories.

Also, meaningful histograms need data points that accurately represent typical and current conditions in the process. For example, if a histogram charts data from

[**EXHIBIT 8.7**]

Guidelines for Histogram Categories

Number of Data Points in the Sample	Number of Categories
Less than 50	5–7
50–100	6–10
100–250	7–12
Over 250	10–20

SOURCE   Kaoru Ishikawa, *Guide to Quality Control* (White Plains, N.Y.: Quality Resources, 1982), p. 8.

a process before some change, then the analyst risks drawing conclusions based on biased information. In addition, only by collecting data for a sufficiently large sample, at least 30 observations, can an analyst make reasonable judgments based on a histogram.

Even after observing all of these requirements, a TQM practitioner should draw only tentative conclusions or findings from analysis of histograms. Wise analysts generally look for several different explanations for observed data and carefully test these explanations through further analysis.

Process Capability Measures: C_p and C_{pk}

Histograms effectively illustrate variance and highlight patterns, but they ignore expectations or demands for limits on variance in products or processes. A customer, or an engineer intent on designing a product or process to satisfy a customer, may define certain specifications for acceptable levels of variance. The **specification width** (S) sets this desired level of variance as the interval between the lower and upper limits on performance data for a product or process, determined by either a customer or a design engineer. The actual distribution of performance data should fall within this interval.

Similarly, the **process width** (P) sets limits for the variability of a process. This width measures the interval between the lower and upper ends of the distribution of process performance data.

Based on these two measures of variance, TQM practitioners calculate a measure of process variability, C_p:

$$C_p = \frac{\text{Specification width}}{\text{Process width}} = \frac{S}{P} \qquad (8.1)$$

The specification width has both upper and lower limits. Most process distributions are open-ended, however, with only lower limits on performance data, so statisticians often set limits at 3 standard deviations (3σ) on each side of the mean. The resulting range encompasses over 99 percent of a normal distribution.

To illustrate the application of C_p, Exhibit 8.8 shows three different distributions of process performance data. All have the same specification width (40 – 20 = 20). Distribution A shows process variance that exceeds the limits set by the specification width. The resulting C_p value of 0.67 indicates that this process meets specifications only 67 percent of the time. Such unacceptably wide process variance requires management intervention to reduce it. In Distribution B, however, the process width equals the specification width for a C_p value of 1.0. While this represents a gain in control over Distribution A, it is only a marginal improvement. Any slight disruption or problem in the process will send it outside acceptable limits, indicated by a C_p value less than 1.0.

Distribution C indicates significantly better process performance. The process width remains well within the limits set by the specification width, giving a C_p value of 1.67. The gaps between the most extreme process performance data and the limits set for acceptable performance represent a cushion of protection or safety margin. Distribution C shows a 40 percent safety margin, indicated by the inverse of the C_p value (P/S). Distribution C's specification width is 40% larger than the process width. This implies that a process can increase 40 percent and still remain within the specification limits.

In general, a larger C_p value indicates a more reliable and predictable process and a higher probability that the process will satisfy or exceed customers'

specification width

The interval between the lower and upper limits on performance data for a product or process

process width

The interval between the lower and upper ends of the distribution of process performance data

C_p

A TQM statistical tool that indicates the variability of a process

[**EXHIBIT 8.8**]

Sample Distributions and C_p Measures

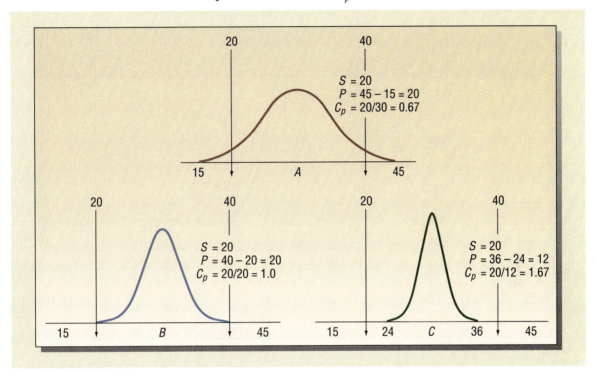

requirements. In fact, some buyers use C_p values as part of their supplier-selection mechanisms. Before placing an order, such a firm requires evidence that the seller's process can met or exceed some minimum C_p value (e.g., 2.0). C_p also serves as an indicator of process capability.[2] This statistic measures the capability of the process to meet or exceed the needs of the customer, represented by the specification width.

Improving on C_p: C_{pk}.   The C_p value effectively measures process variation or capability, but only for a process with a centered distribution of performance data. That statistic's calculation assumes that the mean of the process distribution coincides with the midpoint of the specification width. The distribution in Exhibit 8.9 shows the risk of this assumption. This distribution has the same process width as Distribution C from Exhibit 8.8 and the specification width remains the same, so both distributions give identical C_p values. While Distribution C showed a process under control with a fairly large safety margin, however, the distribution in Exhibit 8.9 shows a process far out of control. The second distribution is centered on the lower specification limit rather than the midpoint of the specification width (30). This indicates that 50 percent of the output of this process is unacceptable.

The C_{pk} value adjusts for any difference between the center of a distribution and the midpoint of the specification width by adding a correction factor to the calculation. Mathematically, C_{pk} equals:

C_{pk}
A TQM statistical tool of the variability of a process, adjusted for any deviation of the center of the distribution of process performance data from the midpoint of the specification width

[2]Ibid., pp. 172–174.

Deceptive C_p Value

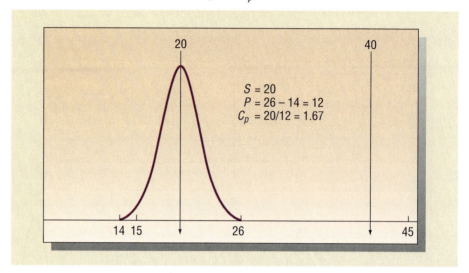

$$S = 20$$
$$P = 26 - 14 = 12$$
$$C_p = 20/12 = 1.67$$

$$C_p = S/P$$

$$K = \frac{abs\ [D - \bar{X}]}{S/2}$$

$$C_{pk} = (1 - K) \times C_p$$

(8.2)

S and P still stand for the specification width and process width, respectively. D represents the design center of the specification width, the target value for performance data, while $\bar{X}$ is the process average. When D equals $\bar{X}$, then C_{pk} is identical to C_p.

To calculate the C_{pk} value for the distribution in Exhibit 8.9, set D equal to 30, the midpoint of the specification width; $\bar{X}$ equals 20. Although the C_p value remains at 1.67, K equals absolute $[38 - 30]/(20/2)$. These figures give a C_{pk} value of 0.334, indicating an unreliable process that cannot meet customers' needs regularly. Many companies, TQM leaders Xerox and Motorola among them, target a C_{pk} value of 2.0 as a minimum requirement for their own processes and those of potential suppliers.

A C_{pk} value effectively measures both the variability and the capability of a process because it tracks both variance (spread) in performance data and divergence of the distribution mean from the target value. A high C_{pk} value indicates low variance and a properly centered distribution of performance data. In this way, the statistic forces both managers and employees to recognize the importance of both reducing variance in performance and also keeping performance aimed at the right target. They can often move performance toward the center of the acceptable range simply by adjusting the process. Reducing variance, on the other hand, requires fundamental changes to the process that generates the observed variation. For relations with outside suppliers, C_{pk} offers a convenient and effective method of specifying acceptable quality on critical traits.[3]

---

[3]Ibid., p. 175.

[**PROBLEM 8.3**]

Calculating C$_{pk}$

A manager is studying a manufacturing process with the following characteristics shown below:

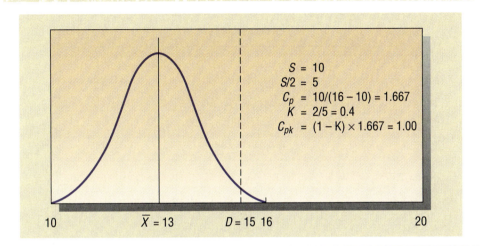

$$S = 10$$
$$S/2 = 5$$
$$C_p = 10/(16 - 10) = 1.667$$
$$K = 2/5 = 0.4$$
$$C_{pk} = (1 - K) \times 1.667 = 1.00$$

10       $\bar{X} = 13$ $D = 15$ 16   20

What is its process capability?

$$C_p = S/P = (20 - 10)/(16 - 10) = 10/6 = 1.667$$
$$C_{pk} = (1 - K)C_p = (0.4) \times 1.667 = 1.00$$
$$\text{since } K = \text{abs}[D - \bar{X}]/(s/2) = \text{abs}[15 - 13]/5 = 0.40$$

You can see that there is little margin for error since a slight shift in the process to the left will likely result in goods being produced with the measured variable less than 10. How many? That will depend on how much the distribution has shifted to the left and the subsequent sequence of random events. [■]

Control Charts

The TQM statistical tools discussed so far have presented basically static information. Histograms and check sheets, for example, consolidate data to show an overall picture of a process at one time. Pareto analysis identifies and rank orders potential problem areas in a current process. However, none of these tools accurately represents changes in performance data over time or the responses of data over time to variations in materials, employees, equipment condition, or methods. TQM practitioners track process performance over time and assess the operations manager's control of a process based on control charts. Most readers treat statistical process control (SPC) and control charts as synonymous.

A **control chart** plots data collected over time across a set of limits for the upper and lower boundaries of acceptable performance (Exhibit 8.10). Sample statistics that fall between these two limits indicate acceptable performance; any points that fall outside these limits indicate problems with the process that generated the performance data. Operations managers consider points outside acceptable limits as indicators of a need to intervene to improve the operation of the process. They typically set performance boundaries to correspond to a given

control chart
A TQM statistical tool that displays performance data as points across a set of limits for the upper and lower boundaries of acceptable process performance

Limits of Acceptable Performance for Process Control

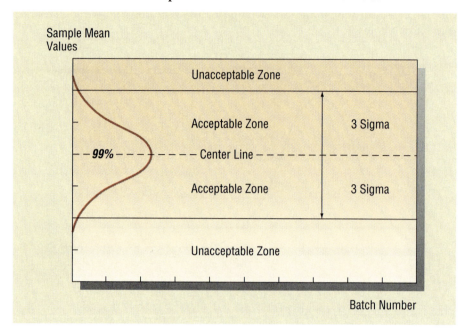

confidence interval (usually 99 percent or 3σ on either side of the mean or center of the distribution). They attribute divergence from the mean of any points that fall between the upper and lower limits to random variations; points outside the limits indicate underlying systematic problems with the process.

TQM practitioners construct five different types of control charts, listed in Exhibit 8.11. Each type of chart suits a particular type of data. Continuous data can

Control Charts and Data Types

Type of Data	Appropriate Control Chart	Data Measures
Continuous/indiscrete	$\bar{x} - \bar{R}$	Measurement (inches, mm)
		Volume
		Product weight
		Power consumed
Discrete	pn^a	Number of defects
	p	Fraction defective
	u	Number of pin holes per area in different sized pieces of plated sheet
	c	Number of pin holes in a fixed area

[a]Probability of defect × Number in batch

SOURCE   Reprinted from *Guide to Quality Control* by Kaoru Ishikawa, copyright 1992 Asian Productivity Organization, with permission of the publisher, Asian Productivity Organization. Distributed in North America by Quality Resources, New York, NY.

[**EXHIBIT 8.12**]

Hard-Disk Seek Times (millisecond)

Sample No.	1	2	3	4	5	$\bar{x}$	R
1	12.2[a]	12.3	12.4	11.8	12.7	12.3	0.9
2	12.3	12.1	11.8	12.2	12.3	12.1	0.5
3	12.4	12.7	12.3	12.5	12.3	12.4	0.4
4	12.5	12.3	12.3	12.1	12.1	12.3	0.4
5	12.1	12.4	11.9	12.0	12.3	12.1	0.5
6	12.6	11.8	12.2	11.9	11.9	12.1	0.8
7	11.8	12.1	12.5	12.8	12.5	12.3	1.0
8	12.5	12.8	12.0	12.5	11.9	12.3	0.9
9	12.1	12.3	12.0	11.9	12.1	12.1	0.4
10	11.2	12.3	11.8	11.7	11.9	11.8	1.1
11	11.7	12.2	12.2	11.7	12.1	12.0	0.5
12	12.4	12.2	12.1	12.1	12.1	12.2	0.3
13	11.7	12.1	11.9	11.8	11.9	11.9	0.4
14	11.8	12.2	12.2	12.1	12.2	12.1	0.4
15	11.9	12.3	11.8	11.9	12.1	12.0	0.5
16	12.3	12.4	13.0	12.3	12.2	12.4	0.8
17	11.9	12.6	12.6	12.9	12.1	12.4	0.9
18	11.9	12.0	12.7	12.7	11.9	12.2	0.8
19	11.4	11.6	12.4	11.9	11.8	11.8	1.0
20	11.6	11.8	12.4	12.3	11.2	11.9	1.2

[a]Nominal Mean Seek Time = 12 ms.

vary anywhere within a particular range (e.g., holes can be any size). Discrete data states some quantity that people can count such as the number of defective units in a batch or the fraction of defective products in a sample. In this section, we will deal primarily with continuous data and the $\bar{x} - R$ control chart, one of the most common control charts.

Constructing an $\bar{x} - R$ Chart.   This type of control chart actually combines two charts. The $\bar{x}$ chart compares the mean for a sample of performance data, $\bar{x}$, against preset upper and lower control limits to gauge the level of control of a process. The R chart calculates a range for each data sample and compares this range to a control interval to verify that the sample data does not indicate a large and unacceptable change. The first chart, based on mean values, could hide a large gap between the largest and smallest observations in the sample if extremely low values were to offset extremely high values. A sufficiently large difference would indicate some sudden change in performance and a need for employee or management intervention. The R chart supplements the $\bar{x}$ chart by checking for this kind of a gap.

TQM practitioners follow a 10-step process to construct and use an $\bar{x} - R$ chart. To illustrate this process, we will present an example with data from Exhibit 8.12. Bob Feller of Pear Computer wants to track hard-disk seek times to make sure that he has the process that builds these components under control. To make this assessment, he decides to build a control chart:

1. *Initialize the system and collect data to calculate performance limits.* The data from which the analyst calculates the control limits for both charts

should come from a process known to be under control. TQM practitioners often gather this kind of data from processes just after major overhauls, when they know that they can rely on smooth operations. The nature of this data should match that of the process that the control chart will monitor. In general, this data should reflect about 100 observations of the process.

2. *Group observations into samples.* Next, the analyst groups observations into coherent samples that share some common trait (e.g., data from a single production run or from one day or shift). For each sample, the control-limit calculation requires the number of observations (n). In general, a larger sample size allows the analyst to calculate tighter limits, leaving a smaller gap between the upper and lower limits. However, this increased precision comes at the cost of gathering more data. The variable k denotes the number of samples needed for the control-limit calculation. Exhibit 8.12 groups the 100 data points into 20 samples of 5 observations, so n equals 5 and k equals 20.

3. *For each sample, find the sample mean.* For each sample, the analyst should calculate the sample mean to one-decimal-point accuracy using the following formula:

$$\bar{x} = \frac{\sum_{i=1}^{n} x_i}{n}$$

For the first sample from Exhibit 8.12, sum the five data points (12.2 + 12.3 + 12.4 + 11.8 + 12.7, or 61.4) and divide by 5 to arrive at 12.28 or 12.3 after rounding. Repeating this calculation for each sample gives the 20 sample means.

4. *For each sample, find the range,* R. The range measures the difference between the largest and smallest values. For the first sample in Exhibit 8.12, R equals 12.7 minus 11.8, or 0.9. The analyst must repeat this calculation for every sample.

5. *Calculate the overall mean,* $\bar{\bar{x}}$. Summing the sample means, $\bar{x}$, and dividing by the total number of samples gives the mean for the entire data set. From the data in Exhibit 8.12, the sample means sum to 843.2, so the overall mean equals 12.14 (242.7/20). This number defines the center line for the control chart.

6. *Calculate the mean range* ($\bar{R}$). The R chart needs a center line, as well. To define this line, sum the R values from all of the samples and divide by the number of samples to arrive at the mean R, or $\bar{R}$. The range values for the data samples in Exhibit 8.12 sum to 13.7, so the mean R is 0.69 (13.7/20). Besides defining the center line for the R chart, $\bar{R}$ also helps the analyst to estimate the upper and lower control limits, since the range gives an estimate of a sample's standard deviation ($\sigma/\sqrt{n}$).

7. *Compute control limits.* To calculate the positions of the control limit lines, the analyst enters values from Exhibit 8.13 in the equations:

$\bar{x}$ Control chart:

Central line $= \bar{\bar{x}}$

Lower control limit $= \bar{\bar{x}} - A_2 \bar{R}$

Upper control limit $= \bar{\bar{x}} + A_2 \bar{R}$

Values for Setting Control Limit Lines

n	A_2	D_4	D_3
2	1.880	3.267	0.000
3	1.023	2.575	0.000
4	0.729	2.282	0.000
5	0.577	2.115	0.000
6	0.483	2.004	0.000
7	0.419	1.924	0.076
number in each sample	$\bar{X}$ limits 99 percent	$\bar{R}$ limit Upper end	$\bar{R}$ limit Lower end

R Control chart:

Central line $= \bar{R}$

Lower control limit $= D_3\,\bar{R}$

Upper control limit $= D_4\,\bar{R}$

After entering these values and the product performance data from Exhibit 8.12, these equations give the control limits for the chart, as summarized in Exhibit 8.14.

8. *Construct the control charts.* With this information, the analyst can construct the control charts. By convention, the center line appears as a solid line and broken or dotted lines mark the control limits.

9. *Plot the $\bar{X}$ and R values on the appropriate control charts.* With the center line and control limits established, the analyst can plot the data for the sample means and ranges on the appropriate charts. Dots represent $\bar{X}$ points and small xs represent R values. Exhibit 8.15 shows the resulting charts. After plotting the data, the analyst circles any outliers, or points above or below the control limits, in either control chart. These circled points indicate unusual variance that requires intervention to improve process control.

10. *Annotate the control charts, if necessary.* In the final step, the analyst notes on the charts such information as the $\bar{X}$ and R values, the n value, the numerical values for the control limits, and other information about the nature of the data. This step completes the control charts.

Control Limits for Example Control Charts

Data Points	$\bar{x}$ Chart	$\bar{R}$ Chart
Central line	12.14 ms	0.69
Lower control limit	$12.14 - 0.577 \times 0.69 = 11.74$	0.00
Upper control limit	$12.14 + 0.577 \times 0.69 = 12.54$	$2.115 \times 0.69 = 1.459$

[**EXHIBIT 8.15**]

$\bar{X}$ and R Chart for the Example Data Set

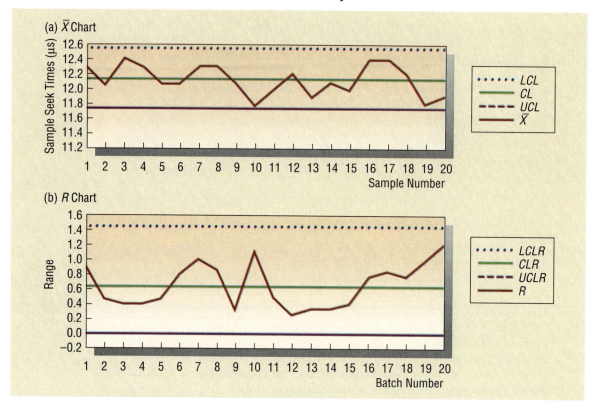

Interpreting Control Charts. Usually, control charts point out problems as places where sample means or range values appear outside the control lines. This signals managers or workers to stop the process to identify and correct the underlying problems that caused the faulty data. Control charts may also indicate a need for intervention in the process in three other conditions, however.

Trends. A control chart indicates a trend when successive points seem to fall along a line moving either upward or downward. A trend in control chart data indicates some continuing change in the process. This signal may warrant intervention before the trend line crosses control limits to generate an actual defect.

Runs. Truly random variations should not form any pattern in the distribution of data around the central lines. However, runs in a process place points in apparent cycle about the central line, defining a run of points above the central line followed by a run of points below. Such cycles indicate systematic problems in the process that require attention.

Hugging. Hugging occurs when various points appear so closely grouped around the central line that they seem to show no variation in the data. Hugging usually indicates some intervention in the process to limit or eliminate variation. In other words, some action is masking the natural variation in the process. The TQM practitioner must uncover and remove this limiting force, due to employee action or

[EXHIBIT 8.16]

Data for Scatterplot of Conveyor Speed versus Cut Length

Sample Number	Conveyor Speed (cm./sec.)	Cut length (mm.)	Sample Number	Conveyor Speed (cm./sec.)	Cut length (mm.)
1	8.1	1,046	26	8.0	1,040
2	7.7	1,030	27	5.5	1,013
3	7.4	1,039	28	6.9	1,025
4	5.8	1,027	29	7.0	1,020
5	7.6	1,028	30	7.5	1,022
6	6.8	1,025	31	6.7	1,020
7	7.9	1,035	32	8.1	1,035
8	6.3	1,015	33	9.0	1,052
9	7.0	1,038	34	7.1	1,021
10	8.0	1,036	35	7.6	1,024
11	8.0	1,026	36	8.5	1,029
12	8.0	1,041	37	7.5	1,015
13	7.2	1,029	38	8.0	1,030
14	6.0	1,010	39	5.2	1,010
15	6.3	1,020	40	6.5	1,025
16	6.7	1,024	41	8.0	1,030
17	8.2	1,034	42	6.9	1,031
18	8.1	1,036	43	7.6	1,034
19	6.6	1,023	44	6.5	1,034
20	6.5	1,011	45	5.5	1,020
21	8.5	1,030	46	6.0	1,025
22	7.4	1,014	47	5.5	1,023
23	7.2	1,030	48	7.6	1,028
24	5.6	1,016	49	8.6	1,020
25	6.3	1,020	50	6.3	1,026

SOURCE   Reprinted from *Guide to Quality Control* by Kaoru Ishikawa, copyright 1992 Asian Productivity Organization, with permission of the publisher, Asian Productivity Organization. Distributed in North America by Quality Resources, New York, NY.

whatever cause, to reveal the true operation and natural variation in the process. Hugging prevents the analyst from judging whether the process as currently constituted really operates under control or some outside force is taking unusual measures to produce acceptable results.

Scatterplots

To refine this insight, TQM constructs scatterplots to determine if a perceived relationship really exists between two process characteristics, and the direction of the relationship (whether increases in one seem related to increases or decreases in the other).

A **scatterplot** graphically illustrates the relationship between variables, typically based on quantitative data. Scatterplots reveal bivariate relationships, that is, relationships between pairs of variables, such as number of defects per batch against changes in the speed of the production line, or production time per unit against hours of training.

Exhibit 8.16 shows data for a scatterplot that compares the speed of a conveyor line and the lengths of cut metal tubing. The analysis seeks to determine

scatterplot

A TQM statistical tool that graphically illustrates the relationship between two quantitative variables whether a certain range of speeds facilitates consistent cuts of raw material to a certain length. The analyst has collected data for the lengths of 50 cut pieces along with the speed of the line for each.

The scatterplot for the data (Exhibit 8.17) seems to suggest a positive relationship between the conveyor speed and the cut length; an increase in conveyor speed seems associated with longer pieces. The relationship does not seem especially strong, indicated by the large space covered by the points. A tight block of points approximating a diagonal line sloping upward to the right would indicate a strong positive relationship. To determine the significance of the relationship between conveyor speed and cut length, further analysis would include a statistical test such as a linear regression. This would, in fact, indicate a statistically significant relationship between the two variables.

Scatterplots can give TQM practitioners a lot of information about the nature of the relationship between process performance variables. A group of points that seem to form a horizontal or vertical line indicate no relationship. Points that approximate a line from the upper left to the lower right indicate a negative relationship. Points which seem to fall along an arc indicate a nonlinear relationship.

In addition, tightly grouped points indicate a strong relationship, while loosely scattered points suggest a weak relationship. This information can help to confirm or deny hypothetical causes of observed effects. If a scatterplot shows no relationship between the supposed cause and effect, then the analyst can return to the cause-and-effect diagram to look for other possible causes. To apply the power of scatterplots carefully, the analyst must interpret them with care.

Plan-Do-Check-Act Cycles

We discussed this tool in Chapter 4 under the name *Deming cycle*. It describes the sequence of events and actions by which managers or workers can solve problems and improve quality continuously over time. Recall that the PDCA cycle consists of four major activities:

- *Plan*   This activity defines the problem to solve, identifies the most likely cause, and develops a plan of action aimed at correcting the problem.
- *Do*   This activity implements the plan developed in the previous stage.
- *Check*   After implementing the plan, this activity determines whether or not it has generated the desired result. In addition, this activity watches for unplanned problems elsewhere in system or previously hidden problems uncovered by the newly implemented changes.
- *Act*   Based on the information generated in the check stage, this activity undertakes appropriate corrective action as needed.

The PDCA cycle then repeats to identify another set of problems to examine and solve, driving continuous improvement.

The PDCA cycle might provide a framework within which Pear Computer could address its problem with defective computers. Recall that Pareto analysis revealed damage to CPUs during assembly as the largest contributing factor to the observed rate of defects. Cause-and-effect analysis then uncovered a number of potential causes. Next, data collection, perhaps using check sheets, would break down defects into the categories identified in the cause-and-effect diagram. Suppose that this data suggests potential problems with the CPU chip itself and with employees' procedures and methods for handling and inserting the chips (perhaps a subject for more Pareto analysis). Discussions with the employees responsible for the design, receipt, and installation of the CPUs, perhaps in the

[**EXHIBIT 8.17**]

Scatterplot for Conveyor Speed versus Cut Length

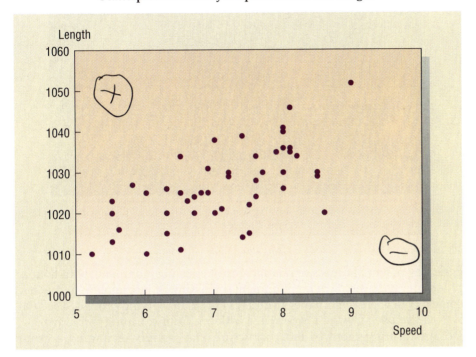

form of a brainstorming session as described in the next section, leads the problem-solving effort toward difficulties with properly aligning the microchip pins. The TQM team decides to design a new device for chip installation to eliminate the problem. All of the process up to this point fall into the plan stage of the PDCA cycle.

After making the new device, the team must train workers to use it, after which, the workers introduce it into daily production. This implementation of the TQM team's solution completes the do stage of the cycle.

In the check stage, the team monitors the number of defects observed in inspection. After gathering enough data (perhaps 3 weeks' worth), they compare the new defect data with the old data. If inspections now find fewer defects due to problems with the CPU, then the new chip-installation device becomes a standard part of the production routine. The check stage also includes consideration of other problems that prevent the process from completing quality computers, leading back to the beginning of the PDCA cycle.

Continued efforts to spot and fix bugs in implementation of the new production method form part of the act stage of the PDCA cycle. This stage also identifies new problems that require solutions, as the cycle repeats, moving the entire process toward its ultimate goal of producing a perfect computer the first time every time.

Brainstorming

Brainstorming, the final TQM tool to be discussed in this section, helps people uncover hidden quality issues and generally facilitates creativity within the total quality management process. **Brainstorming** encourages people to envision and

brainstorming
A TQM tool that encourages people to envision and suggest any potential causes or relationships, reserving judgment about their accuracy for later analysis

This video service company uses brainstorming sessions to uncover hidden quality issues and increase creativity within the total quality management process.   SOURCE   Ferry/Liaison International

suggest any potential causes or relationships, reserving judgment about their accuracy for later analysis. This nonjudgmental massing of information and ideas has become a critical element in the entire TQM problem-solving process. The "On the Job" box discusses Disney's experience with one brainstorming technique.

Brainstorming requires more structure than simply arranging a group of people around a table or in a room and telling them to generate ideas. In practice, such an approach does not work. First, this may fail to draw contributions from normally quiet people. Instead, a vocal few may dominate the discussion. Second, the bandwagon effect may derail progress when someone suggests something that seems highly plausible, leading the group to abandon their search for ideas in the belief, often mistaken, that they have uncovered the one critical factor. Further discussion may then focus on implementing this narrow idea. Finally, some group members may fear eventual criticism of their contributions, leading them to decline to participate so the group generates fewer ideas than it could.

These problems often prevent brainstorming sessions from achieving their goal of identifying all possible causes, including new ideas that no one had previously conceived. One suggested solution from Myron Tribus is known as nominal group technique.[4] This technique consists of five steps:

1. *Silent generation of ideas*   The group works individually in silence for a period of time (e.g., 15 to 30 minutes). During this time, each member writes a list of possible answers to a question posed by the group leader.
2. *Round robin feedback*   The group leader then asks each person in succession, typically following an order based on seating arrangements, to present only one idea from his or her list. One group member takes notes, writing down each idea as presented with no editing. When someone has no more ideas to offer, that person says "I pass." The leader continues to poll the group in sequence until everyone in the group has passed.

[4]Myron Tribus and Yoshikazu Tsuda, "The Quality Imperative in the New Economic Era," in *Quality First: Selected Papers on Quality and Productivity Improvement by Dr. Myron Tribus* (Washington, D.C.: National Society of Professional Engineers, 1988), pp. 209–210.

ON THE JOB

**Disney Brainstorms New
Paths to Quality**

■

The TQM technique's emphasis on continuous improvement requires its practitioners to constantly rethink old ways of doing things. The brainstorming method can encourage the kind of risk taking, imagination, and creativity that a team needs to solve urgent quality problems.

Companies with products as diverse as insurance, data transactions, and corn chips have taken brainstorming one step further using a method called *storyboarding*. Based on Walt Disney's revolutionary invention of the storyboard in 1928 to improve animation quality, storyboarding has gone on to help companies like Frito-Lay and Rockwell Hanford Operations to resolve pressing quality problems.

Long before the term "Total Quality Management" was even thought of, Walt Disney wanted to improve the quality of his animation by using four times as many frames per second as other studios. This created an organizational headache, however, as thousands of drawings piled up in his studio. So, Disney directed his artists to pin their drawings on the wall in sequence. This enabled them to judge progress at a glance and determine which scenes weren't working. The story was told on a wall covered with a special kind of board—hence, *storyboard*.

A Disney executive in the 1970s refined this concept and began using it as a tool for solving complex problems. Like simple brainstorming, the problem is stated in simple terms and posted where brainstorming participants can see it during their discussion. But aspects of the problem are tacked up on the wall beneath this statement under headings such as "Recruiting High-Quality Employees" or "Differentiating Our Product from Competitors." During the discussion, ideas are written on note cards so they can be posted and moved around. This enables brainstorming participants to visualize how aspects of the problems are interconnected.

Storyboarding takes longer than simple brainstorming, but it can be used to solve highly complex problems. The storyboard technique has become a cornerstone of Frito-Lay's creative problem-solving program and has been used to solve quality problems at hospitals and information system design corporations alike.

SOURCE   James M. Higgins, "Storyboard Your Way to Success," *Training & Development*, June 1995, pp. 13–17.

3. *Group clarification of ideas*   The group then works together in a free-flowing discussion to clarify ideas noted during the previous step and to group together similar ideas. An idea joins such a cluster only with the consent of the group members who initially suggested it. The group leader must invite participation to ensure that no one dominates the discussion.

4. *Individual voting*   After a full discussion, each group member chooses the ideas that seem best in a voting procedure. If the group has generated N ideas, each member may cast $(1 + 0.5N)$ votes. If the final list included 24 ideas, each group member would select the 13 most promising ones. (The calculation always rounds the number of votes upward in case of a fraction.) This step continues as each member arranges his or her chosen ideas in order from most important to least important. The group leader tallies the votes for each idea.

5. *Pareto analysis*   In Pareto analysis of the final vote totals, the group focuses on the most popular ideas first.

[**EXHIBIT 8.18**]

Process Tools and the Quality Process

Quality Process Activity	Questions	Appropriate Tools
Problem awareness	Is something wrong with the process?	Histograms C_p and C_{pk} Control charts Check sheets
Problem analysis/ cause identification	What is causing an observed problem?	Brainstorming Pareto analysis Cause-and-effect diagrams Process flow analysis Check sheets
Cause assessment	Is this a hypothetical cause really generating an identified problem?	Scatterplots Process flow analysis Histograms Plan-do-check-act cycles
Problem resolution	How can an operations manager implement a solution? Where does the TQM process go next?	Subsequent Pareto analysis Check sheets Plan-do-check-act cycles Brainstorming Process flow analysis Control charts Histograms

Putting the Tools Together

The earlier sections have presented the ten statistical tools of TQM separately, and practitioners can use them that way. However, they promote overall success of the TQM process most effectively when they reinforce one another as part of an integrated campaign to improve process control. Altogether, these ideas empower employees at any level to identify problems, uncover the underlying causes, and bring about improvement. Exhibit 8.18 shows how these tools help a TQM program to attack different parts of the process to improve and maintain quality. The next "On the Job" box shows how Motorola used TQM.

Six Sigma

Motorola's TQM program which seeks to guarantee that 99.99966 percent of all products that the firm builds meet applicable standards

Interest in Motorola's **Six Sigma** quality program has spread outside the firm and its groups of suppliers and customers. This program represents an emerging trend in TQM that is leading firms to actively pursue quality and process-improvement goals rather than passively responding to problems as they occur.

Six Sigma also represents an attempt to change fundamental organizational paradigms, as discussed in Chapter 1. The new standards declare 99 percent quality an outdated and insufficient goal. Six Sigma promotes a new set of expectations about acceptable practices among customers, organization members, and suppliers. Finally, Six Sigma explicitly recognizes that superior quality requires an integrated corporate endeavor rather than an isolated OM initiative.

ON THE JOB

What TQM Did for Motorola

◼

Once you get good at something, such as TQM, there is no turning back. Consider what happened when Motorola gain statistical control of its processes but still was not satisfied. Using TQM tools they achieved plus or minus three sigma (3σ) quality levels. Motorola then developed a new system to achieve higher levels of quality of at least six sigma (6σ).

Why a six sigma level of quality? At this level, 99.99966 percent of all products will be "good." Furthermore, for every extra 9 after the decimal point (see Exhibit 8.19), there is a corresponding 10-fold *reduction* in nonconformities.

Motorola's six sigma program improves quality by changing the processes used in the design and delivery of products. In this respect, the six sigma program is like the process capability tools of C_p and C_{pk}. However, unlike these tools, six sigma improves the various processes by actively involving all the design and de-livery functions. It also draws on a wide range of tools, including:

- Design for manufacturability
- Statistical process control (SPC)
- Supplier SPC (the application of SPC at the supplier's site)
- Participative management practices
- Part standardization and supplier certification
- Computer simulation

These tools identify and attack all the forms of variance that can affect quality, and customers who want quality products will receive higher levels of value.

 DESIGN TOOLS

In this chapter, we have discussed many statistical tools for evaluating and guiding improvements in existing processes. Managers need not wait for old systems to fail, however, before they begin to address process variance and quality. In TQM design tools, they have a set of procedures and techniques that can help them to design either a product or a process to ensure consistent quality. TQM practition-ers use design tools to prevent quality problems by eliminating potential causes of

[**EXHIBIT 8.19**]

Quality Confidences Levels

Quality Confidence	Quality Risk	Total Defects (parts per million, PPM)	PPM Change Factor
0.9	0.1	100,000	29,411
0.99	0.01	10,000	2,941
0.999	0.001	1,000	294
0.9999	0.0001	100	29
0.99999	0.00001	10	3
0.999999	0.000001	1	0.3

variance in either products or processes and to enhance customer awareness, ensuring that product or process designs accommodate customers' needs and requirements. They also involve other areas of the firm:

- Marketing must identify exactly what the targeted customers want and are willing to pay for.
- Accounting contributes product costing support.
- Purchasing must identify outside resources that might enhance the product or process development activities.
- Engineering and R&D must identify what is technically possible.
- Organizational design must provide the type of learning organization to effectively utilize TQM design tools.

In this section, we discuss three of the many design tools available to the operations manager:

- Quality function deployment/house of quality
- Concurrent engineering
- Hoshin management (planning for breakthroughs)

Quality Function Deployment/House of Quality

quality function deployment

A set of methods to identify all of the major requirements of a firm's customers and to evaluate how well the designs of products and OM processes meet or exceed those requirements

Any effective TQM system needs input about customers' expectations to ensure that the firm can meet its ultimate objective of profitably delighting the customer. One tool to gather this input, **quality function deployment** (QFD), specifies a set of methods to identify all of the major requirements of a firm's customers and to evaluate how well the designs of products and OM processes meet or exceed those requirements. In many ways, QFD acts as a set of communication and translation tools.

Since its development in 1966 in Japan and its introduction into the United States, managers at such firms as Ford, General Motors, Motorola, Xerox, Kodak, IBM, Procter & Gamble, Hewlett-Packard, and AT&T have successfully implemented QFD. In 1992, Cadillac made quality function deployment an integral element of its new-product planning and design process. In 1994, Ford introduced a new program, Ford 2000, to design and build cars, vans, and trucks that would offer the highest possible value to its customers. QFD lies at heart of this program.

QFD tries to eliminate the gap between what customers want in a new product and what the product must deliver. Often this technique helps TQM practitioners to clearly identify customers' major demands. QFD incorporates these expectations, stated in the customers' own words, as the voice of the customer (VOC). The method then classifies these expectations as order winners, order losers, and order qualifiers and as indicators of expected or one-dimensional quality and exciting quality.

As discussed in Chapter 3, *expected quality* refers to statements of product traits that customers expect to find in a product (usually not articulated until missing). These traits usually represent order qualifiers or order losers; customers may not appreciate them explicitly, but failure to meet these expectations causes customer dissatisfaction. In contrast, *exciting quality* refers to traits that customers do not expect. They do not notice the lack of such traits, but special characteristics can excite them and induce them to choose one product over another. Unlike expected quality, customers often have difficulty describing exciting quality. In general, exciting quality enhances the value of a product while expected quality maintains value. The QFD process provides a structure to help managers to identify both

Focus groups like this one enable companies to obtain direct customer input. Defining customer expectations is one key to profitable consumer satisfaction.   SOURCE   Michael Newman/PhotoEdit

expected and exciting quality and to focus process design and implementation specifically to meet these needs.

The whole company designs and communicates what matters most to the customer. The many benefits attributed directly to QFD include improved teamwork, reduced lead time for product development, lower product costs, fewer changes after the design stage, and higher quality. Finally, the QFD process helps to integrate a firm's TQM effort by unifying four major functional strategies: (1) marketing, (2) sales, (3) product design, and (4) OM process.

QFD Process.   The QED process can be stated in its simplest form as four linked matrixes. In many cases, these four matrixes represent an important subset. The four-step process of quality function deployment generates four matrixes (see Exhibit 8.20). In the first stage, the **customer requirements planning matrix** identifies customer requirements and translates these requirements into a set of technical product features. This first stage joins together marketing, operations management, and engineering to identify both expected and exciting quality.

In the second step, QFD generates a **technical features deployment matrix** which translates the technical product features identified in the columns of the

customer requirements planning matrix

A tool of quality function deployment that identifies customer requirements and translates these requirements into a set of technical product features

technical features deployment matrix

A tool of quality function deployment that translates the technical product features identified in the columns of the customer requirements planning matrix into design requirements for critical product components

[EXHIBIT 8.20]

Customer Requirements Planning Matrix

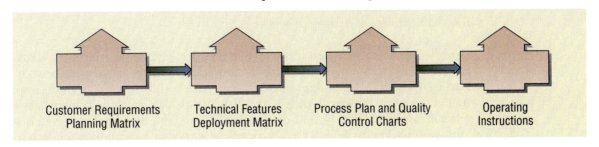

Customer Requirements Planning Matrix → Technical Features Deployment Matrix → Process Plan and Quality Control Charts → Operating Instructions

[**EXHIBIT 8.21**]

House of Quality

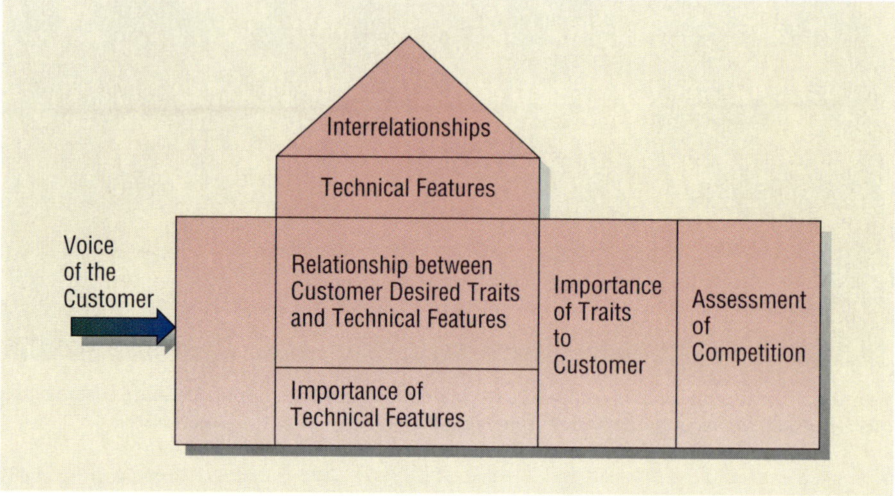

SOURCE   Glenn Mazur, QFD Institute Executive Director.

process plan and quality control chart

A quality function deployment tool that translates the columns of the technical features deployment matrix into critical process and product parameters and appropriate process control limits

operating instruction

A statement in quality function deployment that translates critical process and product parameters into specifications for operations to be performed by plant personnel

customer requirements planning matrix into design requirements for critical product components. In the third step, QFD translates the columns of the technical features deployment matrix into critical process and product parameters and appropriate process control limits through **process plan and quality control charts**. In the fourth and final step, QFD generates matrixes of **operating instructions** that translate critical process and product parameters into specifications for operations to be performed by plant personnel. This step ensures that the activities of people on the shop floor contribute to the firm's efforts to meet the requirements set down in the process and product parameters. At each step in this process, QFD generates requirements (listed in the rows of the matrixes) and translates these requirements into supporting actions to meet those requirements (listed in the columns of the matrixes).

Because of its structure, QFD users often call the customer requirements planning matrix the *house of quality* (HOQ), a term coined by Mr. Sawada of Toyota Auto Body when a correlation matrix (roof) was added in a reliability study. Most companies view it as the most important of the four QFD matrixes, so we will focus our attention on its construction and interpretation.

House of Quality.   The house of quality relates customer-defined product traits to the technical product and process requirements needed to support and generate these features. Exhibit 8.21 shows the graphic layout of this chart. QFD generates this map through a six-step process.

Identify Customer Attributes.   The first step seeks to place statements of what customers want from a product along the left edge of the chart to form rows in the house of quality. If possible, these statements should express quantity requirements in the customers' own words. The chart designates requirements as order winners, order qualifiers, and order losers or as components of expected quality and exciting quality. Success in this analysis requires a clear understanding of the firm's customers and their priorities. The chart may have to accommodate different priorities of various customer groups (e.g., corporate purchasing agent, retail store buyer, and final user).

Identify Supporting Technical Characteristics.   Next, QFD lists the technical characteristics that a product needs to meet or exceed the customer requirements and expectations identified earlier. These features form the columns along the top of the house of quality, and they indicate the characteristics that the product design will need, as described by the people who will develop that design. Ideally, these traits should be measurable to indicate their contributions to the customer requirements.

The roof of the house of quality, as shown in Exhibit 8.21, indicates important interrelationships between pairs of technical features. The strengths of these inter-relationships are denoted by three symbols. A green circle identifies a very strong relationship; a red circle denotes a strong relationship; a blue triangle indicates a weak relationship. These three symbols represent numerical values based on which QFD evaluates product feature alternatives. In general, a green circle carries a value of 9, a red circle carries a value of 3, and a blue triangle carries a value of 1. This roof helps the designers to understand how changes in one technical feature may influence other features. Depending on the application, the roof may or may not be present.

Correlate Customer Attributes with Supporting Technical Features.   In this important step, QFD explores the relationship or fit between customer requirements and technical product features. The house of quality documents these relationships in the major matrix at the center of the diagram. Again, the symbols from the roof of the HOQ indicate the strengths of these relationships to show how well various product features satisfy customers' needs or expectations.

This step also evaluates the extent to which the firm can increase value by achieving exciting quality rather than expected quality in particular product features. Any technical feature without a positive relationship to a customer requirement does not really add value; it becomes a candidate for elimination or at least detailed re-examination. This step forces designers to verify that each technical feature they want to add will satisfy a real customer need.

Assign Priorities to Customer Requirements and Technical Features.   Next, QFD assigns weights to the previously identified customer requirements to indicate their relative importance to customers. The weights can reflect either priorities identified in marketing studies or focus groups or simply consensus judgments of management, the most dangerous approach as it makes the rash assumption that management understands the customer. In Exhibit 8.22, the weights appear in the column labeled "Importance Rating."

At the same time, QFD assigns weights to the customer requirements (these are called sales points) to reflect their importance to product performance. These weights can reflect priorities based on strengths that the firm will stress in its competitive strategy or how it intends to generate value for customers. In other words, these weights reflect the importance of product features to the strategic vision of the firm.

Evaluate Competitors' Stances and Products.   In the fifth step, QFD evaluates the firm's own product against those of competitors from the customer's perspective. This comparison identifies potential weaknesses in rival products and indicates the strength of the firm's proposed product relative to rivals.

[**E X H I B I T   8 . 2 2**]

Coffee Maker House of Quality

Whats versus Hows	Acidity	Brewing Time	Brewing Temp.	Water Heat Rate	Full Cycle Time	Wattage	Number of Parts to Clean	Importance Rating	Competition	Current Product—MC	BU	BR	Target	Improvement Ratio	Sales Point	Absolute Weight	Demanded Quality Weight
Strong Relationship: ● 9 / Medium Relationship: ● 3 / Weak Relationship: ▲ 1																	
Coffee tastes good																	
Full-flavor coffee	●	●	●					5		3	2	5	5	1.7	1.5	13	29
Rich aroma	▲		●					4		2	2	4	4	2.5	1.0	10	23
Hot coffee		▲	●	●	▲	●		4		4	4	3	4	1.0	1.0	4	9
Ready quickly		●	●	●	●	●		3		3	4	2	4	1.3	1.0	4	9
Easy to clean	▲						●	4		3	1	4	5	1.7	1.2	8	19
Doesn't drip							●	3		2	3	3	3	1.5	1.0	5	10
Absolute Weight	303	355	408	56	93	112	262										
Quality Characteristic Weight	19	22	26	4	6	7	16										
Competitive Assessment																	
Current Product—MC	5.7	60	192	85	75	100	4										
BU	5.8	40	195	100	50	120	7										
BR	5.6	75	185	60	95	100	3										
Plan	5.6	45	195	100	60	120	2										
Unit	pH	Sec./Cup	Degrees F	Deg./Cup/Min.	Sec./Cup	Watts	Number										

SOURCE   © 1991 Glenn Mazur, QFD Institute Executive Director.

Identify Technical Characteristics to Deploy in the Final Product Design.   Finally, QFD identifies the technical features that the firm will build into the final design of the product, based on what it takes to ouperform the competition on the most critical technical characteristics. These characteristics usually appear in a row or column labeled "Deployment" or "Plan" and identify those features of interest to the customer where the competition is better perceived and consistent with the strategic stance of the firm.

House of Quality: A Example.   The best way of understanding the use of the house of quality is to apply it to a small example.[5] Coffee MC wants to develop a design for a new coffee maker to compete with products from Company BU and Company BR. The design process begins with input from marketing to identify product benefits that customers want.[6] Previous studies have uncovered four traits that dominate customers' evaluation of coffee makers:

- *Good taste*   This statement is hard to define, but further study finds a strong correlation with three traits: (1) full flavor, (2) rich aroma, and (3) hot coffee.
- *Ready quickly*   This characteristic reflects how long a coffee maker takes to brew coffee from the moment that the customer flips the switch until the first cup is ready.
- *Easy to clean*   This characteristic measures the difficulty of cleaning the coffee maker.
- *Doesn't drip*   This characteristic reflects the desire for a coffee maker that does not continue to drip unless a pot is in place.

This information defines the rows of the house of quality in Exhibit 8.22. The solid shading in the row for the attribute "coffee tastes good" means that the analysis does not define it directly, but in subcategories in the following three rows. For each row, the chart assigns an importance rating, often reflecting the results of a customer survey, among other considerations. Ratings run from 1 for unimportant attributes to 5 for extremely important attributes. Only the attribute "full flavor coffee" earns this high rating, indicating that customers would really value a coffee maker that could offer full flavor. This deduction illustrates the transition from product traits desired by customers to features designed into the coffee maker.

Next, the chart evaluates the current MC model against competitors from BU and BR. Clearly, it does not compare well with those rival products. BU offers an attractive ability to make coffee quickly and to keep it hot. In contrast, BR scores well on the characteristics of flavor and ease of cleaning. Having assessed both the current model and competing products, the analysis determines targets for traits that would make the new coffee maker most desirable. The chart shows that the product design should emphasize flavor and easy cleaning.

Comparing these targets with the current values for each customer benefit determines the improvement ratio. For example, for the "rich aroma" trait, the chart shows a target weight of 5 while the current model scores only a 2. The new coffee maker model will have to improve performance on this trait 2.5 times (or 250 percent) over the existing coffee maker. The sales point values identify the importance of each trait to the firm's sales or marketing effort. The absolute weight reflects the impact of the importance rating, the improvement ratio, and the sales point. It is determined by multiplying together the numbers for each trait (e.g., the trait "full flavor coffee" gets a score of $5 \times 1.7 \times 1.5 = 12.75$, or 13 rounding to the nearest integer). The last column, demanded quality weight, indicates the relative importance of each customer trait. (Note that these numbers sum to 100, allowing for slight variation due to rounding errors.)[7]

---

[5]We express our gratitude for the help offered by Glenn Mazur of the QFD Institute in Ann Arbor, Mich. Glenn provided the example offered in this section and he helped to acquaint us with the theory and application of QFD and the house of quality.

[6]Note that customers buy benefits while makers produce features.

[7]The value for each row is obtained by summing the absolute weights and dividing each row's absolute weight by this sum. This generates a number of points out of 100 (a percentage) for each row. The demanded quality weight for full flavor coffee is 13/44, or 29.5, while the value for easy to clean is 8/44, or 19.

Having identified what customers want and what the new coffee maker model should offer to give customers the highest possible value, the chart must translate these traits to design specifications. These specifications indicate how the coffee maker will achieve the product traits that earlier analysis determined to be important. The house of quality displays these specifications as columns. Exhibit 8.22 identifies seven possible specifications, beginning with acidity and ending with the number of parts. For each column, the exhibit also identifies the appropriate units for measuring each design specification. For example, the pH level indicates acidity while brewing time is measured in seconds per cup.

For each column, the three symbols (green circle, red circle, and blue triangle) indicate the strength of the relationship between the design specification and the customer-demanded trait. Again, absolute weights indicate the importance of each trait, and the quality characteristic weights convert absolute weights to scores out of a total of 100. The next three rows then evaluate each of the competing products.

Finally, the row labeled "plan" gives desired scores for the product specifications. To meet or exceed customers' expectations, the new coffee maker model should make coffee with a pH value of 5.6, take 45 seconds per cup to brew, serve the coffee at 195 degrees, produce the first cup of coffee within 60 seconds, and require the user to clean only two parts. The house of quality indicates that such a design will meet customers' need for a coffee maker that produces a flavorful cup of coffee and that is easy to clean.

This analysis might not yield a satisfactory design in the first trial, but the design process could repeat the house of quality analysis to guide subsequent redesign, as well. Throughout the process, this method places customer desires in control of product design and the definitions of value.

Concurrent Engineering

The house of quality technique often accompanies a second TQM design tool, concurrent engineering, also called *simultaneous engineering*. A later chapter will discuss this technique in more detail in another context, but for now, we will treat it as an example of the At Once/System Integration process strategy discussed in Chapter 3.

concurrent engineering
A TQM design tool that brings together representatives from all of the functions involved in designing, producing, delivering, and selling a product to contribute to its initial design

Concurrent engineering brings together representatives from all of the functions involved in designing, producing, delivering, and selling a product to contribute to its initial design. Typically, this forms a team with members from marketing, operations management, purchasing, logistics, human resource management, and finance. In seeking input from these people at the design stage, concurrent engineering tries to achieve several critical objectives.

First, the cross-functional team can spot a variety of potential problems in the product design on paper or within a computer-aided design (CAD) system. Changes made at this stage cost less and take less time than changes made later in the product introduction process. Phillips Petroleum refers to this fact as the "1-10-100 rule." A problem caught in the design stage costs $1 to correct; once released to the shop floor, the same correction costs $10; once defective products reach the hands of the customer, the correction costs $100.

Second, concurrent engineering can improve the overall quality of the product as it reduces the production cost. Costs fall because the design team identifies and eliminates potential problems at the design stage. This reduces the time required to solve those problems at a later stage in the OM system, reduces errors and therefore the burden of reworking rejects, and shrinks inventory needs since the process no longer must hold stock to cover problems in the product.

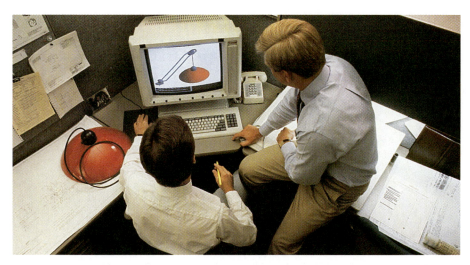

Including representatives from several key departments on the product design team often reveals potential product problems. Design changes cost far less to implement than changes made during the product introduction process.   SOURCE   Tim Bieber Inc./The Image Bank

Third, while concurrent engineering does take longer to complete a design, it can often reduce the total time from design to full-scale production. This speeds overall time to market as part of a fast to market competitive strategy. This shows how a firm can integrate TQM methods into the core of its competitive strategy, making continuous, incremental improvement a fundamental organizational activity.

Hoshin Management

Another TQM design tool tries to formalize planning for dramatic breakthroughs in quality improvement, rather than routine progress in small steps. Large jumps in product and process quality often bring sudden, significant improvements in a firm's competitive position in the marketplace. To achieve these stunning developments, the TQM structure incorporates a new planning structure, Hoshin management.

Like other design tools, **Hoshin management** tries to enable the organization to plan for and achieve higher levels of quality, equating higher quality with higher levels of customer value. However, unlike other TQM tools, Hoshin management works toward dramatic, strategic breakthroughs for the organization. To achieve this objective, five key principles guide Hoshin management:

Hoshin management
A TQM design tool that works toward dramatic, strategic breakthroughs for the organization

- It defines a planning and implementation process organized to foster continuous improvement through the PDCA cycle.
- It identifies the key functions and systems within the firm that need to be improved for the firm to achieve its strategic objectives.
- It encourages appropriate cross-functional and vertical participation in planning to execution for and achieving yearly objectives.
- It bases all planning and execution on fact.
- Its goals and action plans reflect the true capabilities of the organization.

Exhibit 8.23 shows how total quality management integrates Hoshin management with its other tools and techniques. Hoshin management draws information from the daily data-collection process and hunts for indications of needed and

Integrating Hoshin Management with Other TQM Components

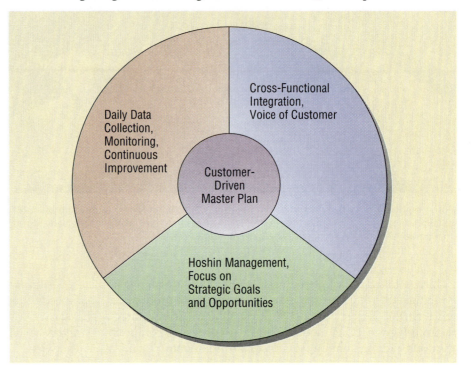

NOTE   The above is a simplified, modified version of the TQM wheel developed by GOAL/QPC, 13 Broad St., Metheun, MA 01844-1953.

possible quality breakthroughs. Once implemented, these breakthroughs drive the process for further continuous improvements. Hoshin management also implements a cross-functional process to listen to the voice of the customer and to identify opportunities for strategic breakthroughs. Potential gains in exciting quality that correspond to explicit customer demands define likely areas for a strategic breakthroughs, while improvements in expected quality or areas of latent customer demands may relate more closely to small, continuous improvements.

Hoshin Management Process.   Hoshin management begins with a long-term corporate vision that identifies the firm's market and its method for serving this market over the following 3 to 5 years. This vision answers the question, how will the firm deliver value to its customers? Within this long-term plan, Hoshin management identifies areas within the firm that either help or hinder its achievement of this vision and the associated objectives.

This long-term planning becomes a quest for strategic breakthroughs because it continually pursues opportunities to offer a type of value that competitors could not match or could match only with difficulty. Hoshin management actively seeks either new forms of demand within the firm's existing customer base or demands from new groups of customers.

Hoshin management then refines the long-term plan's general statements of organizational intentions into a 1-year plan that specifies a few key objectives that the firm must achieve within the following year. It then assigns those objectives to the appropriate departments and functions, which then develop detailed plans and objectives aimed at implementing the 1-year plan. At each level within each function, further planning identifies areas for improvement that contribute directly to the achievement of the 1-year plan.

The organization then implements the plans generated from this process. Regular reviews (monthly or quarterly) may lead to changes in plans, if necessary. A preliminary review of the overall yearly plan occurs 2 to 3 months before the end of the year to determine whether or not the organization seems likely to achieve the objectives of the yearly plan and to begin the process of developing the next 1-year plan.

In short, Hoshin management tries to raise the sights of TQM from minute, routine details to encourage a strongly strategic orientation. This system has brought success to companies such as Hewlett-Packard and Florida Power & Light, the first non-Japanese winner of the Deming Prize.

Comments on the TQM Design Tools

In this section, we have touched on some of the design tools of total quality management. This section could not cover every potential tool exhaustively, and we have had to omit some valuable tools like design for experiments, failure mode effects analysis, fault tree analysis, product liability analysis, and the Shainin diagnostic tools. We intend this brief overview to show how TQM design tools can help managers to develop products and processes that consistently meet or exceed customers' needs and expectations.

Despite the need to present these tools in separate sections, they become most effective when managers use them together to provide complementary information about a situation. Quality function deployment and the house of quality, for example, formally incorporate the voice of the customer into the product/process design process, forcing designers to link the features that their products will offer to the customer requirements that those features should satisfy. Effective quality function deployment and house of quality requires input and evaluations from a cross-functional design team, however, one of the major features of concurrent engineering.

Finally, TQM practitioners must understand that the process of developing high-value products and processes is fundamentally dynamic, producing constant streams of change driven by strategy. Hoshin management propels the TQM system forward to generate important strategic breakthroughs for the firm.

 ## CHAPTER SUMMARY

We began this chapter by looking at Chrysler's development of its new Cirrus model. The company discovered just before the car's scheduled introduction that it could not meet the quality standards set by Chrysler and expected by its customers. To correct the problems, Chrysler had to implement a refinement effort based on various process and design tools. In this chapter, we explored many of these tools, which TQM practitioners consider integral to their management methods, covering many important developments:

1. While management frameworks are important to TQM, success depends on giving people the right tools and teaching them how to use those tools. Practitioners use process tools to assess current conditions in processes, identify potential problems, and bring the processes back under control. They use design tools to ensure quality and reliable performance in new products and processes.

2. TQM tools can manipulate either attribute or variable data. Variable data can be measured and compared while attribute data describes states (pass/fail, go/no-go, good/bad) or locations. Variable data can always be converted into attribute data, but attribute data may indicate only general limits for variable data.

3. Ten important TQM process tools include Pareto analysis, check sheets, cause-and-effect diagrams, process flow analysis, histograms, measures of process spread and variability (C_p and C_{pk}), PDCA cycles, scatterplots, and brainstorming. While any of these tools can advance a TQM effort by itself, they are most effective when used together.

4. Check sheets provide a highly useful means of collecting and analyzing data.

5. Pareto analysis identifies and focuses attention on the vital few process characteristics as compared to the trivial many. Pareto analysis targets improvement efforts at the elements of a process that account for the largest percentage of quality-related problems.

6. Cause-and-effect diagrams generate and organize comprehensive information about causes of observed events.

7. Process flow analysis graphically portrays the activities in a process, the exact nature of these activities, and their organization within the process.

8. Histograms graphically capture and display information about distributions of process performance data. The shapes of these distributions can reveal much about the behavior of the underlying processes.

9. The two measures of process spread and capability, C_p and C_{pk}, capture the extent to which a process can meet or exceed a customer's requirements, represented by the specification width.

10. Control charts determine the extent of management control of a process and flag conditions that require outside intervention.

11. Scatterplots graphically illustrate the nature of relationships between two variables.

12. Plan-do-check-act cycles, or Deming wheels, describe sequences of events and actions needed to solve problems and improve quality continuously over time.

13. Brainstorming provides a structured method by which people can uncover and evaluate all potential causes and conditions related to a specific problem.

14. Motorola's Six Sigma quality program signifies a new trend that leads managers to do more than simply control and manage an existing process. Six Sigma tries to actively change an existing process to allow a dramatically higher level of control and quality.

15. The first of three major design tools, quality function deployment (including house of quality analysis), formally bridges the gap between customer requirements and technical product features, forcing designers to consider the match between customer desires and the firm's methods for competing in the marketplace.

16. Concurrent engineering gathers input from all of the critical company functions affected by a product, bringing them together into a cross-functional team during the design stage.

17. Hoshin management keeps TQM from drowning in detail by pursuing strategic organizational breakthroughs.

Taken together, the TQM tools display a definite trend. Increasingly, managers are moving beyond the task of controlling existing processes to work on understanding fundamental relationships between process elements and their ultimate impacts on quality. Accompanying this change, TQM practitioners are taking increasingly proactive attitudes, working to improve processes and products through integrated efforts that join together people from marketing, engineering, purchasing, finance, and operations management. Organizational success now requires these people to deliver more than expected quality; they must now offer exciting quality. Driving this change in focus is the customer's pursuit of value.

This chapter and the previous one have described TQM as a wide-ranging, cross-functional quest to generate value. An operations manager need not consider TQM as the only option, however. Another OM methodology, just-in-time manufacturing, emphasizes waste elimination and tight process control, as the next chapter will explain.

[KEY TERMS]

process tools 341	control chart 353	technical features
design tools 341	scatterplot 359	deployment matrix 367
variable data 341	brainstorming 361	process plan and quality
attribute data 341	Six Sigma 364	control chart 368
histogram 347	quality function	operating instruction 368
specification width 350	deployment 366	concurrent engineering
process width 350	customer requirements	372
C_p 350	planning matrix 367	Hoshin management 373
C_{pk} 351		

[DISCUSSION QUESTIONS]

1. As the quality control manager of a local food chain, you have adopted total quality management. One of your jobs is to track the number of customer complaints received on the chain's 800-ShapeUp telephone line. The number of complaints received per day typically has had a mean of 40 calls and a standard deviation of 5. This week, the number of calls has been: 17 on Monday, 12 on Tuesday, 8 on Wednesday, 15 on Thursday, and 21 on Friday. Is this process under control? What actions would you recommend? Why?

2. For the following check sheet, assume that o indicates a surface scratch, an x indicates a blowhole, a D indicates a defective finish, a * indicates an improper shape, and a ? indicates other defects. How would you analyze the check sheet?

	Worker	Mon.	Mon	Tue.	Tue.	Wed.	Wed.	Thur.	Thur.	Fri.	Fri.
		A.M.	P.M.	A.M.	P.M.	A.M.	P.M.	A.M.	P.M.	A.M.	P.M.
Machine 1	1	oox*	ox	oxx	oooxx xo	ooooo xxxo	ooxx	oooo	oxx	oo	oDxx
Machine 2	2	oxx*	oooxx*	ooooo xx	oooxx	ooooo oxx*	ooooo x*	ooooox x	ooox**	ooxx*	ooooo

Conduct a Pareto analysis of this data. Is stratification appropriate for this type of a problem? How would you stratify the data to identify variables that will have an important effect on the observed results?

3. Construct an $\overline{X} - R$ chart for the following data set:

Subgroup No.	6:00	10:00	14:00	18:00	22:00	$\overline{x}$	R
1	14.0	12.6	13.2	13.1	12.1	13.00	1.9
2	13.2	13.3	12.7	13.4	12.1	12.94	1.3
3	13.5	12.8	13.0	12.8	12.4	12.90	1.1
4	13.9	12.4	13.3	13.1	13.2	13.18	1.5
5	13.0	13.0	12.1	12.2	13.3	2.72	1.2
6	13.7	12.0	12.5	12.4	12.4	12.60	1.7
7	13.9	12.1	12.7	13.4	13.0	13.02	1.8
8	13.4	13.6	13.0	12.4	13.5	13.18	1.2
9	14.4	12.4	12.2	12.4	12.5	12.78	2.2
10	13.3	12.4	12.6	12.9	12.8	12.80	0.9
11	13.3	12.8	13.0	13.0	13.1	13.04	0.5
12	13.6	12.5	13.3	13.5	12.8	13.14	1.1
13	13.4	13.3	12.0	13.0	13.1	12.96	1.4
14	13.9	13.1	13.5	12.6	12.8	13.18	1.3
15	14.2	12.7	12.9	12.9	12.5	13.04	1.7
16	13.6	12.6	12.4	12.5	12.2	12.66	1.4
17	14.0	13.2	12.4	13.0	13.0	13.12	1.6
18	13.1	12.9	13.5	12.3	12.8	12.92	1.2
19	14.6	13.7	13.4	12.2	12.5	13.28	2.4
20	13.9	13.0	13.0	13.2	12.6	13.14	1.3
21	13.3	12.7	12.6	12.8	12.7	12.82	0.7
22	13.9	12.4	12.7	12.4	12.8	12.84	1.5
23	13.2	12.3	12.6	13.1	12.7	12.78	0.9
24	13.2	12.8	12.8	12.3	12.6	12.74	0.9
25	13.3	12.8	12.0	12.3	12.2	12.72	1.1
				Σ of $\overline{x}$		323.50	33.8
				Grand mean $(\overline{\overline{x}})$		12.94	1.41

4. The section on scatterplots discussed problems with data hugging some desired center value as people continually take extraordinary measures to intervene in the operation of a system to keep it on target. Why does TQM discourage this practice?

5. Describe a procedure for applying house of quality analysis in the task of reengineering a process.

6. Why must statistical tools be an integral part of any total quality management program?

7. A friend asks, "How are you doing?" You respond, "Fine." What inputs went into your response? Prepare a list of the top ten inputs you used to determine your overall state. Which can be transformed into variable data or attribute data? How would you measure them?

8. Which process tool presented in this chapter is most appropriate for the following situations:

   a. Automobiles coming off the final assembly line have what are commonly called "fit and finish" defects; slight paint scratches, misaligned parts, etc.

   b. Employee absenteeism is running 30 percent higher at one plant over a firm's other plants.

    c. You have been asked to explain why units of blood and blood components needed in different types of surgery vary so widely, even within a given type of surgery.

    d. Each time you try on clothing at a retail store, you are not sure what size will fit best. Assume that the mass and configuration of your body have not changed.

    How should data be collected for each process tool?

9. List the advantages and disadvantages of using attributes to measure the performance of a process. What do you gain when you measure performance as a continuous variable?

10. The price of textbooks seems to be on an upward spiral. Use one of the process tools to help explain what is happening.

11. Discuss the pros and cons of having the operator of a machine analyze the control chart measurements of the production process.

12. The chapter noted that although inspections are not always value-adding activities, there are conditions under which they are needed. What conditions lead to a situation where inspections are required?

13. Explain to a golfing buddy in his terms what Motorola's Six Sigma Quality standard means.

C A U T I O N

[C R I T I C A L   T H I N K I N G   R E Q U I R E D]

1. Develop house of quality charts for:
   a. New mountain bicycle
   b. Introductory operations management course
   c. New candy bar

   In your analysis, indicate characteristics that represent (i) expected quality and (ii) exciting quality.

2. As the quality control czar of your household, you have been asked to solve a complex problem found in most homes—the single sock gremlin. A flaw in many household laundry processes results in either the loss of one sock or the arrival of an undeclared single sock from an unknown source.

   a. Develop a cause-and-effect diagram and any other appropriate SPC tools that might shed light on this mystery.

   b. Prepare a list of some of the possible corrective actions.

C A S E   8 . 1

The Bully Boy Bagging Line

The manager reviewed the production on the firm's large bag packaging line. There seemed to be much more variation in quality than she normally noticed. After calling for a summary of data from production control, she received the following data for the last 16 work weeks.

Date	Day	Number of Workers	Number of Bags Produced	Number of Bad Bags
1	Monday	4	2997	59
2	Tuesday	5	4349	173
3	Wednesday	5	2866	114
4	Thursday	5	2772	110
5	Friday	3	1934	19
6	Saturday	3	1211	12
7	Monday	5	3761	150
8	Tuesday	5	3924	156
9	Wednesday	5	4913	196
10	Thursday	5	4049	161
11	Friday	5	3465	138
12	Saturday	4	1720	34
13	Monday	4	2201	44
14	Tuesday	5	3269	130
15	Wednesday	5	4345	173
16	Thursday	5	2454	98
17	Friday	5	3726	149
18	Saturday	4	2733	54
19	Monday	5	3934	157
20	Tuesday	5	3016	120
21	Wednesday	5	3420	136
22	Thursday	5	2727	109
23	Friday	5	3328	133
24	Saturday	0	0	0
25	Monday	4	2574	51
26	Tuesday	4	2524	50
27	Wednesday	5	3012	120
28	Thursday	5	2412	96
29	Friday	4	2291	45
30	Saturday	3	1429	14
31	Monday	4	2481	49
32	Tuesday	5	3010	120
33	Wednesday	5	4634	185
34	Thursday	5	3352	134
35	Friday	5	2274	90
36	Saturday	0	0	0
37	Monday	5	3540	141
38	Tuesday	5	3854	154
39	Wednesday	5	3163	126
40	Thursday	4	3040	60
41	Friday	4	3153	63
42	Saturday	4	1804	18
43	Monday	5	2873	114
44	Tuesday	5	3439	137
45	Wednesday	4	3352	67
46	Thursday	4	3607	72
47	Friday	4	3127	62
48	Saturday	0	0	0

Date	Day	Number of Workers	Number of Bags Produced	Number of Bad Bags
49	Monday	5	2399	95
50	Tuesday	5	2699	107
51	Wednesday	5	2995	119
52	Thursday	5	3115	124
53	Friday	5	3520	140
54	Saturday	3	1712	17
55	Monday	4	2611	52
56	Tuesday	5	2450	98
57	Wednesday	5	4360	174
58	Thursday	5	2491	99
59	Friday	5	3307	132
60	Saturday	0	0	0
61	Monday	4	2390	47
62	Tuesday	4	3007	60
63	Wednesday	4	2979	59
64	Thursday	4	2173	43
65	Friday	4	2346	46
66	Saturday	0	0	0
67	Monday	5	3666	146
68	Tuesday	4	3510	70
69	Wednesday	4	2032	40
70	Thursday	4	2319	46
71	Friday	3	1900	19
72	Saturday	3	1537	15
73	Monday	4	2086	41
74	Tuesday	5	3596	143
75	Wednesday	5	2418	96
76	Thursday	5	2571	102
77	Friday	3	2288	22
78	Saturday	3	1441	14
79	Monday	4	2358	47
80	Tuesday	5	3661	146
81	Wednesday	5	3449	137
82	Thursday	5	3952	158
83	Friday	5	3749	149
84	Saturday	0	0	0
85	Monday	4	2717	54
86	Tuesday	4	3069	61
87	Wednesday	4	2197	43
88	Thursday	3	1623	16
89	Friday	3	1903	19
90	Saturday	0	0	0
91	Monday	4	1824	36
92	Tuesday	4	3797	75
93	Wednesday	5	3810	152
94	Thursday	5	2767	110
95	Friday	5	2106	84
96	Saturday	3	1436	14

QUESTIONS

1. What does this data tell you?

2. Which tools did you use to determine what is happening?

3. What management actions are appropriate?

[SELECTED READINGS]

AT&T. *Statistical Quality Control Handbook,* 11th ed. Charlotte, N.C.: Delmar, 1985.

Bhote, Keri R. *Strategic Supplier Management: A Blueprint for Revitalizing The Manufacturer-Supplier Partnership.* New York: American Management Association, 1989.

Dean, James W., Jr., and James R. Evans. *Total Quality: Management, Organization, and Strategy.* Minneapolis/St. Paul, Minn.: West, 1994.

Deming, W. Edwards. *Quality, Productivity, and Competitive Position.* Cambridge, Mass.: MIT Center for Advanced Engineering Study, 1982.

Deming, W. Edwards. *Out of Crisis.* Cambridge, Mass.: MIT Center for Advanced Engineering Study, 1986.

Garvin, David, A. *Managing Quality.* New York: Free Press, 1988.

Gitlow, Howard, Shelly Gitlow, Alan Oppenheim, and Rosa Oppenheim. *Tools and Methods for the Improvement of Quality.* Homewood, Ill.: Richard D. Irwin, 1989.

Hall, Robert, ed. *Manufacturing Report 21: The Future of Japanese Manufacturing.* Wheeling, Ill.: Association for Manufacturing Excellence, 1990.

Imai, Masaaki. *Kaizen: The Key to Japan's Competitive Success.* New York: Random House, 1986.

Ishikawa, Kaoru. *Guide to Quality Control.* White Plains, N.Y.: Quality Resources, 1982.

Ishikawa, Kaoru. *What Is Total Quality Control? The Japanese Way.* Englewood Cliffs, N.J.: Prentice-Hall, 1985.

Juran, Joseph M., and Frank M. Gryna, Jr. *Quality Planning and Analysis.* New York: McGraw-Hill, 1980.

Klippel, Warren H., ed. *Statistical Quality Control.* Dearborn, Mich.: Society of Manufacturing Engineers, 1984.

Logothetis, N. *Managing for Total Quality: From Deming to Taguchi and SPC.* Hertfordshire, U.K.: Prentice-Hall International, 1992.

Mizuno, Shigerua, and Yoji Akao, eds. *QFD: The Customer-Driven Approach to Quality Planning and Deployment.* Hong Kong: Nordica International, 1994.

21st Manufacturing Enterprise Strategy: An Industry-Led View, vol. 1. Ann Arbor, Mich.: National Center for Manufacturing Sciences, 1991.

21st Manufacturing Enterprise Strategy: An Industry-Led View, vol. 2. Ann Arbor, Mich.: National Center for Manufacturing Sciences, 1991.

Steudel, Harold J., and Paul Destruelle. *Manufacturing in the Nineties.* New York: Van Nostrand Reinhold, 1992.

Tribus, Myron. *Quality First: Selected Papers on Quality and Productivity Improvements.* Washington, D.C.: American Quality and Productivity Institute, 1988.

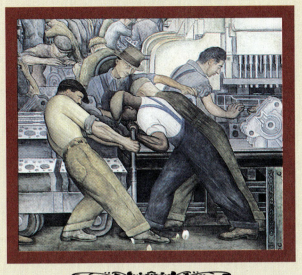

PART FOUR

The Design of Value-Driven OM Systems

CHAPTER NINE

Just-in-Time Operations Management

CHAPTER OBJECTIVES

[At the end of this chapter, you should be able to]

- Define the term *just-in-time manufacturing*.
- Trace the historical roots of JIT manufacturing.
- Identify the major objectives and goals in an effective JIT system.
- Differentiate between types of JIT systems.
- Describe JIT procedures.
- Outline the implications of JIT for functional areas outside operations management such as marketing, strategy development, and accounting.
- Illustrate the application of JIT concepts and practices across all operating environments and settings.
- Demonstrate the relationship between JIT manufacturing and lean production.

Harley-Davidson Rules the JIT Road

FOR YEARS, PEOPLE CONSIDERED THE small puddle of oil that collected under a parked Harley-Davidson motorcycle as a badge of honor. But when some less-expensive, better-made cycles from Honda, Yamaha, and Suzuki roared onto the scene, people no longer seemed to find the famous Harley oil leak cute. At least not if Harley-Davidson's near-failure during the early 1980s was any indication.

Harley applied for government protection from its Japanese rivals, but its managers knew this was only a short-term solution. They viewed that oil leak as a symptom of a serious problem with quality, and the company could no longer glide along on the momentum of its mystique.

Harley managers decided that it was better to face their problems, and they instituted a Japanese-style just-in-time manufacturing system called *Material as Needed*, or *MAN*. With MAN, Harley slashed product lead times from about 360 days to less than three. It reduced inventory by 50 percent and scrap and rework by 68 percent. Its productivity increased 50 percent in a system that required 25 percent less space.

In addition to these improvements in efficiency, Harley's MAN system freed up cash that had been tied up in inventory. Managers used this capital to pay off debt from the company's leveraged buyout.

S O U R C E
Peter C. Reid, *Well-Made in America— Lessons from Harley-Davidson on Being the Best*, (New York: McGraw-Hill, 1990), p. 11

> Meanwhile, consumers discovered that the quality of a new Harley-Davidson motorcycle was better than ever, and no one really seemed to miss that famous oil leak.

In addition to Harley-Davidson, many other companies have implemented just-in-time manufacturing with great success. Among the success stories are many prominent North American producers of a broad range of products, including:

- Black & Decker, a leading maker of appliances and power tools
- Hutchinson Technology, a custom manufacturer of computer components and complex electronic assemblies[1]
- Ford, General Motors, and Chrysler, the "Big Three" auto manufacturers
- Xerox, a star in document-management systems
- Hewlett-Packard, an innovative maker of computers and electronic devices
- Steelcase, a producer of popular office furniture systems

JUST-IN-TIME MANUFACTURING DEFINED

just-in-time manufacturing

An organizationwide quest to produce output within the minimum possible lead time and at the lowest possible total cost by continuously identifying and eliminating all forms of waste and variance

Just-in-time manufacturing is an organizationwide quest to produce output within the minimum possible lead time and at the lowest possible total cost by continuously identifying and eliminating all forms of waste and variance. JIT encourages managers to plan and implement a smooth, integrated flow of production activities that produce components just as subsequent activities need them, from raw materials through suppliers' and the firm's own OM processes to finished products.

This definition highlights waste as the critical focus of just-in-time manufacturing and the relationship of waste to variance. It emphasizes the need to implement just-in-time manufacturing throughout the organization rather than stopping at the boundaries of the operations management function. Finally, it points out the development of JIT beyond its origins as a well-defined set of procedures and techniques to become an overall organizational orientation to eliminating waste and reducing variance.

Why the interest in JIT? In many ways, JIT represents a complete implementation of the value-driven perspective emphasized in this book. It requires a broad reorganization of operations to evolve a vital transformation system that embodies the notions of value and waste control throughout its design, structure, and management. The JIT mandate reaches beyond operations management and the shop floor to affect organizationwide systems for employee reimbursement, product design, buyer-supplier relationships, and performance measurement and evaluation. Full implementation of JIT produces a complex, interlinked web of activities, all of which emphasize continuous improvement.

JIT manufacturing becomes a continuing journey rather than a single destination. The route may have to change as implementation proceeds depending on the organization's environment and internal reactions. The spreading interest and

---

[1]Edward J. Hay, *The Just-in-Time Breakthrough* (New York: John Wiley & Sons, 1988), pp. 4–11.

importance of JIT have made it a compelling force in business today. An operations manager must develop a thorough understanding of both the underlying concept and the specific techniques and procedures associated with JIT.

OVERVIEW OF JUST-IN-TIME MANUFACTURING

Just-in-time manufacturing has been the source of considerable confusion in both the academic and practitioner communities. JIT manufacturing is used for many activities, including:

- *Inventory Reduction.* JIT is a system for reducing inventory levels at all levels within the operations management system.
- *Quality Control Improvement.* JIT provides a procedure for improving quality both within the firm (at the level of the shop floor) and outside the firm (within the chain of vendors supplying the firm and its transformation system).
- *Lead Time Reduction.* With JIT, lead time components such as setup and move times are significantly reduced.
- *Vendor Control/Performance Improvement.* JIT gives the buying organization greater power in the buyer-supplier relationship. The firm moves from a situation where multiple suppliers are used for most parts to a situation where only one or two suppliers are used for most parts. With fewer suppliers, the buying organization has more power because it is making larger purchases from each vendor. Second, the buying organization now imposes tighter requirements on each supplier in terms of delivery and quality.
- *Continuous Improvement.* JIT describes a never-ending approach to operations management. Existing problems corrected; new problems identified. The Japanese term *kaizen*, discussed in earlier chapters, describes this view of JIT.
- *Total Preventive Maintenance.* JIT emphasizes preventive maintenance to reduce the risk of equipment breakdowns.
- *Strategic Gain.* JIT provides the firm's management with a means of developing, implementing, and maintaining a sustainable competitive advantage in the marketplace.

Each of these perspectives allows an operations manager to see only part of just-in-time manufacturing. Each highlights a different aspect of the concept, but none gives a complete picture by itself.

Waste in JIT Manufacturing

At its heart, JIT works to reduce waste. Recall from Chapter 2 that waste is any organizational activity or action that does not contribute to value. This definition encompasses seven basic forms of waste, listed in Exhibit 9.1. JIT manufacturing systems attempt to uncover and eliminate examples of any of these types of waste.

Managers in a JIT manufacturing system view waste as a symptom of some problem rather than a problem in its own right. In other words, they see waste as a residual outcome of some process defect, so they can never really attack it directly. An earlier chapter cited inventory as one of the most common examples of waste. Operations managers often view some inventory as waste, first, because inventory consumes resources. It raises costs directly, when the process devotes materials, capacity, and time to generating products that provide no immediate return from

Seven Types of Waste

- Waste from Overproduction (e.g., building more than is demanded)
- Waste from Waiting Time (jobs waiting to be processed)
- Transportation Waste (jobs being unnecessarily moved)
- Process Waste (excessive or unnecessary operations)
- Inventory Waste (building more to protect against system problems)
- Waste of Motion (unnecessary or excessive human activity)
- Waste from Product Defects (waste due to scrap, rework, salvage)

sales revenue, and indirectly, when it devotes floor space to stockrooms and worker and computer time to tracking levels of inventory.

Second, inventory hides problems created by poor quality, long lead times, and ineffective designs. For example, suppose that 50 percent of the units of some component suffer from quality problems; if the firm keeps enough units in stock, it need not place special urgency on correcting these quality problems. If one selected component is defective, workers can simply throw it aside and take another one.

This use of inventory as a buffer can mask many problems in a process. In addition to quality defects, it offers one way to overcome long order lead times or unreliable delivery schedules, since production can continue to draw down stock levels until new shipments arrive. Inventory can help a system to protect against rising costs by buying large quantities in advance of component price increases. Operations managers could also cope with these problems by increasing the system's own lead time to wait for new shipments or by maintaining extra capacity to speed production when those shipments finally arrive. The firm cannot eliminate the need for inventory (or for some other wasteful response), however, unless it first eliminates the problems that the inventory helped to solve.

Exhibit 9.2 graphically illustrates how inventory and other buffering techniques protect an OM system from its own inherent problems. The exhibit shows several basic obstacles to the system's smooth progress: unreliable deliveries from suppliers, poor quality, excessive machine breakdowns, high employee absenteeism, poor housekeeping that delays material movements, long setups that require large order quantities, poor system scheduling, and inefficient material handling. All of these problems threaten the ability of the system to generate output. Instead of solving these problems, the operations manager could increase the level of inventory to float the output past them. A higher inventory level covers up more underlying problems and reduces the urgency of solving them, but only at the cost of the resources that the firm consumes to produce and store the additional units.

In the same way, reducing the inventory level exposes underlying problems that threaten system performance. Instead of raising inventory levels again, JIT advocates identifying these underlying obstacles and removing them. This action orientation makes just-in-time manufacturing a powerful tool for improving effectiveness.

Remember, however, that waste is defined in relation to value. Finished goods inventory often represents a form of waste, but recall the example from an earlier chapter when a garage kept in stock a needed part for a broken down car, allowing

Inventory as Buffer to Bypass Problems

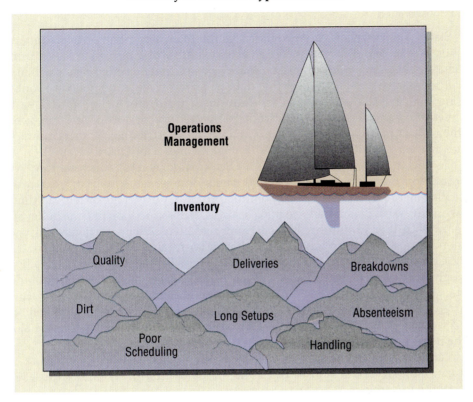

a lucky student to reach a job interview on time. This inventory of repair parts added value for the customer, so one could not label it waste.

To distinguish waste from a value-adding resource, JIT can call on a tool from Chapters 2 and 5 and classify activities as:

- Value-adding
- Waste-generating
- Nonvalue-adding but required (e.g., some equipment setups)
- Unknown

JIT manufacturing requires careful analysis to determine whether unknown activities add value or generate waste, eliminate or reduce waste-generating activities, reduce nonvalue-adding but required activities, and maintain value-adding activities. These critical distinctions give new importance to the disposal options discussed in earlier chapters: keep, combine, eliminate, or rethink.

Waste and Variance.   Variance measures the overall predictability of an OM process and its subprocesses as the dispersion of a distribution of process performance data about its mean. Mathematically, variance can be defined as:

$$\text{Variance} = \frac{\Sigma(x_i - \bar{x})^2}{n - 1} \tag{9.1}$$

where

n = number of observations
$\bar{x}$ = sample average
$x_i = i^{\text{th}}$ observation

Stated another way, variance indicates the likely size of an error in data prediction. Variance indicates how far an actual value will differ, on average, from a predicted value. In general, higher variance means that an actual result will likely differ more from expectations or that data will show a wider dispersion about the mean, making that mean less valuable as a predictor of an actual value. Conversely, a smaller variance indicates more predictable overall performance. In Exhibit 9.3, Distribution A shows less variance than Distribution B, so its mean provides a better indicator of a likely result than the mean for Distribution B.

To see the effect of variance on OM system waste, suppose that ABC Corporation promises to deliver components on average 10 working days after receiving an order, while XYZ Corporation promises an average order lead time of 25 working days. This difference makes ABC Corporation look like the better supplier until further study reveals that it may actually deliver a particular shipment of goods anywhere from 5 days to 65 days after receiving the order. In contrast, XYZ Corporation has consistently delivered goods between 23 and 27 days. Even though ABC can promise a shorter mean lead time, its lead times for individual orders would show greater variance, requiring as much as 65 days' worth of wasteful inventory for safety stock. The lower variance and higher reliability of XYZ would drastically reduce the need for the protection of safety stocks, making it the better supplier for a JIT manufacturing plant.

Variance indicates simply and clearly the seriousness of waste within an OM system. Higher variance raises costs and stretches lead times. Many causes can contribute to variance:

- Unexpected changes in schedules
- Inaccurate scheduling practices
- Ineffective manufacturing planning and control
- Scrap, salvage, and rework
- Employee absenteeism
- Inefficient lot sizes
- Variability of process activities
- Accidents

As a major goal, JIT manufacturing works to identify the causes of system variance and to either eliminate or control these causes. By attacking the sources of variance, JIT manufacturing can reduce the dependency of the OM system on wasteful buffers like excessive inventory, long lead times, and idle capacity for emergencies.

Organizationwide Commitment to JIT Manufacturing

JIT is not some independent initiative of the operations manager; rather it spreads throughout an organization because waste and variance, its central enemies, originate from many causes in many functional areas both within and outside the OM system. For example, high scrap and rework rates indicate waste on many shop floors. (Scrap denotes units of output that fail to satisfy quality standards in ways that workers cannot correct, so the firm must pay to dispose of them or sell them at a loss; rework indicates units of output with quality defects that workers

Variances of Two Distributions

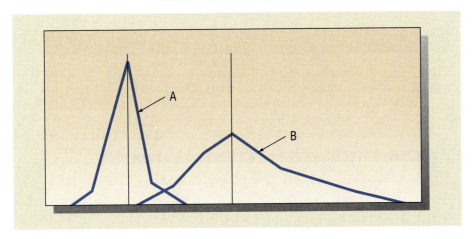

can correct in extra processing steps.) Study to identify the causes of a high scrap or rework rate, perhaps using a cause-and-effect diagram, might identify a range of potential contributing factors:

- *Product design*   Scrap can result from defects in the product concept or design, usually the primary responsibility of a product engineering department.
- *Process design*   A poorly conceived manufacturing process could create unnecessary scrap; responsibility for this function rests with a process engineering department.
- *Faulty components from suppliers*   Defects in finished products often depend significantly on the quality of parts obtained from suppliers by the purchasing department.
- *Poorly trained or improperly selected employees*   Workers who lack necessary skills could well raise scrap and rework rates. Human resource management must recruit and select the right workers and operations management must train them well.
- *Poor condition of equipment*   Worn-out or improperly maintained production equipment cannot produce output with consistently high quality. A facilities management department often shares responsibility for maintenance with the operations management function; finance participates in justifying purchases of new equipment.
- *Badly targeted performance measurement system*   If the firm evaluates the performance of operations managers and workers on the basis of criteria such as minimizing costs or maximizing output, the system may create no real incentive for anyone to reduce scrap and rework. Top managers or accounting staff often set these performance measures.
- *Inadequate capacity*   Scrap and rework increase when the OM system must rush to complete assigned work because it lacks sufficient time or capacity. Lack of capacity may result from poor planning by operations managers or when time standards for planning, generated by either process or product engineering, understate the actual time requirements of production.

[**E X H I B I T   9 . 4**]

Potential Causes of High Scrap or Rework Levels

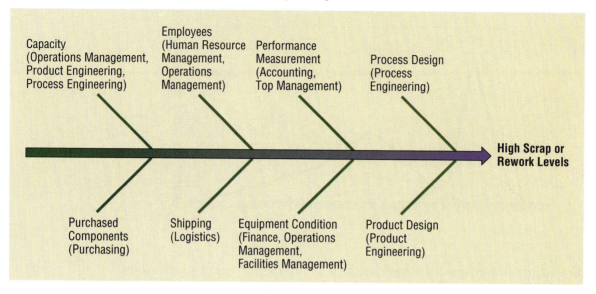

• *Damage in shipping or storage*   Scrap and rework can result from problems encountered either in shipping components from suppliers or in storing them in warehouses. A logistics department handles these activities.

Exhibit 9.4 illustrates the wide range of potential causes for a problem of high scrap and rework levels in an operations management system. An attempt to solve the problem by focusing on the OM system alone would ignore these other influences, making success difficult. To eliminate waste on the shop floor, operations managers must trace its cause wherever it lies in the organization. JIT manufacturing would attack this waste as an organizationwide problem and responsibility.

JIT as a Philosophy

To understand JIT, a student must do more than master a well-defined set of techniques. Rather, one must approach JIT as a general philosophy of pursuing smooth, integrated production flows to eliminate waste and enhance value. As a philosophy, JIT manufacturing sets some general objectives and outlines ideas for achieving them without identifying specific, limited sets of tools, procedures, or techniques. The objectives of JIT methods focus on eliminating waste and maximizing value. However, the definition of value varies in different situations, so implementation of those methods must guarantee flexibility.

Not all companies are successful in implementing JIT. The "On the Job" box shows Allen-Edmond's unsuccessful attempt. Differences in willingness to accept JIT as a philosophy may explain the differences in success in implementing JIT systems at the two companies. The changes that improved motorcycle-manufacturing operations may have failed terribly in the shoe-making plant. Each firm must produce different types of value and deal with different types of waste.

ON THE JOB

JIT Shoes Too Big for Allen-Edmonds

■

Large American companies have been reaping the benefits of the Japanese "Just-in-Time" (JIT) production method for years now. But smaller companies such as Allen-Edmonds Shoe Corp. are finding those shoes hard to fill.

"It really flopped miserably," says John Stollenwerk of recent attempts to implement JIT at his Allen-Edmonds plants. Stollenwerk, the company's president and largest shareholder, had watched larger companies successfully use JIT methods to speed production, boost customer satisfaction, and save money. Designed to streamline production and eliminate waste, the JIT strategy relies on supplying work stations with only the exact amount of material needed at the exact time it is required. Among other advantages, this eliminates the need for warehousing raw materials and unfinished product, freeing up valuable resources. But when Allen-Edmonds recently tried to jump on the JIT bandwagon, it lost $1 million. What happened?

JIT works miracles for large companies that produce huge volumes of the same item. By contrast, Allen-Edmonds relies more on traditional craftsmanship to produce mostly limited runs of expensive shoes. It makes 41,000 variations of men's and women's shoes, further diversified by style, color, and size.

The company's initial foray into JIT techniques had been encouraging. Allen-Edmonds automated its main plant in Port Washington, Wisconsin, in 1988 by building a conveyer belt between work stations, eliminating the need for workers to ferry unfinished shoes back and forth in carts. This $180,000 investment cut the production inventory of unfinished shoes from 5,000 pairs to 1,200 pairs, freeing up $400,000 in capital. It also cut production time from three and a half days down to eight hours.

But the euphoria ended when Allen-Edmonds tried to bring JIT to its Lake Church plant six miles away. Since JIT works by instilling a concern for quality and teamwork, Stollenwerk changed the entire pay structure at Lake Church from piecework to hourly wages. But many seamstresses there had worked for years by the piece, and they prided themselves on their speed. When they began to be paid by the hour, they felt betrayed and productivity *dropped*. When losses reached $1 million, Stollenwerk went back to paying his workers by the piece.

Stollenwerk concedes that his company has made modest improvements in reducing inventory overhead and speeding up production at Port Washington thanks to JIT methods. But the JIT shoe won't entirely fit companies like Allen-Edmonds until efficiency experts figure out how to tailor JIT for smaller manufacturers with more limited production runs.

SOURCE   Barbara Marsh, "Allen-Edmonds Shoe Tries 'Just-in-Time' Production," *The Wall Street Journal*, March 4, 1993, p. B2.

Benefits of Just-in-Time Manufacturing

North American managers first learned of the concept of just-in-time manufacturing in October 1980 at a seminar in Dearborn, Michigan, organized by the Automotive Interest Action Group (AIAG). Managers in the auto industry were initially drawn to JIT because it resolved several paradoxes that they had encountered in comparing their OM systems with Japanese manufacturing practices.

First, they wanted to understand the cost advantage of Japanese competitors over their North American counterparts (Exhibit 9.5). In 1980, a customer could buy a Japanese car more cheaply than a comparable Ford or GM. They tried to explain the cost gap based on differences in wages between Japanese and North

[**EXHIBIT 9.5**]

Japanese Cost Advantage in Car Production

Cost Component	Japanese Advantage
Labor productivity	$1,000
Labor and wage rate	740
Depreciation	200
Warranty	100
Inventory carrying costs	60
Freight and duties	−500
Materials, energy, and other costs	−200
Total	$1,400

American workers, but they discovered that this difference accounted for only $740 of the $1,400 total cost difference.

Further, two other cost categories (freight and duties and materials, energy, and other costs) offset this wage rate differential. The Japanese firms incurred $500 in costs that domestic competitors did not have to pay to transport cars from Japan and to cover import fees. Also, in resource-poor Japan, firms incurred higher energy costs because all sources of fuel came from overseas, as did resources such as iron ore and petroleum for plastics manufacturing. These elements added $700 to the average cost of a Japanese car, eliminating all but $40 of the cost difference due to wages.

Some attributed the $1,400 comparative price advantage for Japanese cars to production in newer plants. With most of its production capacity rebuilt after the destruction of World War II, Japanese producers were operating newer plants with more beneficial depreciation rates. (Older North American car plants had already been depreciated.) Yet, depreciation only accounted for $200 of the $1,400 difference.

Higher labor productivity, lower inventory costs, and lower warranty costs seemed to account for the Japanese cost advantage. Japanese cars were less expensive because the workers who built them worked smarter, indicated by their higher productivity. In addition, the firms held less inventory, and the cars themselves offered higher quality, generating lower warranty costs.

Comparisons between North American and Japanese workers across industries reinforced the claim that the cost difference resulted from differences in productivity (Exhibit 9.6). On average, these comparisons found that American processes took 1.5 times as many steps as Japanese processes to complete the same output. Careful study revealed the reason for higher productivity and lower costs at Japanese firms: just-in-time manufacturing methods.

The first North American students of JIT were also attracted by reports of results at firms that had successfully implemented its principles and concepts. For example, one study evaluated the operations of 21 U.S. suppliers to Japanese-managed electronics and automotive companies in the United States. As compared with non-JIT suppliers, the JIT practitioners had generated:[2]

[2]Craig Giffi, Aleda V. Roth, and Gregory M. Seal, *Competing in World-Class Manufacturing: America's 21st Century Challenge* (Homewood, Ill.: Business One-Irwin, 1990), pp. 221–222.

[**E X H I B I T   9 . 6**]

Japanese Edge in Manufacturing

Industry	Manufacturing Labor Steps	Steps Index[a]
Automobiles	1,200	1.98
Fork-lift trucks	900	1.82
Auto engines	250	1.62
Auto transmissions	200	1.41
Color televisions	80	1.15
Steel sheets	17	1.00

[a]Number of U.S. steps divided by number of Japanese steps.

SOURCE   *Business Week*, June 8, 1987, p. 134.

- *Shorter lead times*   The study found that 70 percent of the JIT suppliers had reduced their lead times, as compared to only 30 percent of the non-JIT suppliers, allowing them to respond more quickly to changing customer requirements.
- *Lower defect rates*   On average, JIT suppliers had 50 percent lower defect rates than non-JIT suppliers. In addition, non-JIT suppliers had to add extra inspections steps just to guarantee acceptable levels of quality to their customers, further increasing overall costs and lead times.
- *Less raw materials inventory*   Over 50 percent of the JIT suppliers had reduced their need for raw material inventories, as compared to only 9 percent of the non-JIT suppliers.
- *Less work-in-process inventory*   Of the JIT suppliers, 43 percent had reduced their need for work-in-process stocks, as compared to 9 percent of the non-JIT suppliers.
- *Less finished goods inventory*   Also, 29 percent of the JIT suppliers operated with less finished goods inventory, as compared to only 18 percent of the non-JIT suppliers.
- *Flexible work forces*   JIT suppliers reported that 67 percent of their workers knew two or more jobs and 45 percent knew three or more, as compared to 54 percent and 34 percent, respectively, in non-JIT systems. Companies reported that more flexible workers brought benefits like less worker idle time, reduced overhead, fewer layoffs due to demand fluctuations in specific product lines, and increased responsiveness.

Exhibit 9.7 lists some other benefits attributed to JIT systems and practices.

Many North American managers found JIT attractive in the early 1980s because it offered a new, fundamentally active framework for the task of operations management to replace the reactive model that they had employed. For the first time, just-in-time manufacturing challenged accepted facts of life that before had seemed eternal and unchanging. JIT leaves no fact of life immune to change.

It treats setups, for example, as variable rather than fixed requirements; managers can reduce the time spent making equipment ready if they will spend the time and effort. Among JIT leaders, Toyota has demonstrated this principle by reducing a setup that took 6 hours in a typical U.S. plant down to about 12

[**E X H I B I T   9 . 7**]

Additional Benefits of Just-in-Time Manufacturing Systems

- Elimination of unpleasant surprises (e.g., late supplier deliveries, unacceptable quality) within the operations management system
- Reduction in computer system needs
- Significant improvements in quality
- Reduction in customer-related problems
- Substantial reduction in level of inventory, especially work in process
- Tightening of system variability
- Shorter lead times
- Enhancements in system flexibility
- Reduction in floor space needs
- Improvements in communication
- Release of pressure on receiving docks and incoming inspection areas
- Improvements in employee morale

minutes.[3] Such reductions in setup times do not require extensive involvement of engineers; they come from active involvement by people who work with equipment daily.

JIT also showed large potential gains from reducing scrap, salvage, and rework. It showed how to work with suppliers who were providing unacceptable quality levels, for example, to significantly improve quality in both inputs and finished products. If the suppliers failed to demonstrate avid interest in helping to implement JIT, it advocated replacing them with more willing competitors.

JIT's proactive stance attracted many managers because it revealed their operations in a different light. They were excited by the opportunities it promised to identify potential improvements that they had previously overlooked.

 ## HISTORICAL ROOTS OF JUST-IN-TIME MANUFACTURING

The history of just-in-time manufacturing traces back directly to the Toyota Production System developed by that firm's vice president, Taiichi Ohno.[4] Toyota implemented this system in response to several developments in its business environment. First, the worldwide oil crisis of 1973 raised costs dramatically for Japanese firms, especially international competitors such as Toyota, which lacked any domestic sources of petroleum supplies. To offset their rising energy costs, these firms had to use resources more efficiently and productively. They could no longer afford to rely on wasteful inventory to buffer the effects of problems.

Also, just-in-time manufacturing solved production problems cheaply, a critical strength for firms, again including Toyota, that lacked the capital resources of North American competitors. In rebuilding after World War II, Japanese firms could not base their systems on computers and electronic technology. With these

[3]Robert W. Hall, *Zero Inventories* (Homewood, Ill.: Dow Jones-Irwin, 1983), p. 13.

[4]Yasuhiro Monden, *Toyota Production System* (Norcross, Ga.: Industrial Engineering and Management Press, 1983), p. v.

Ford Motor Company produced its first automobiles on static production lines. After 1913, moving assembly lines were developed, which resulted in a drastic decrease of production time per vehicle.
SOURCE   From the Collections of Henry Ford Museum & Greenfield Village

expensive tools out of reach, managers had to rely on the decision-making and problem-solving skills of workers to attack problems of waste and productivity that they saw in their daily routines. The resulting emphasis on the human role in the OM system has become one of the hallmarks of just-in-time manufacturing. In fact, the initial reports on JIT called it a "just-in-time and respect-for-human system."[5]

The rigors of international competition, a third development that drove Toyota to implement JIT, forced the premiere Japanese firms to compete worldwide on cost and productivity. Survival depended on their ability to provide high levels of value at low cost. Together with rising energy costs and scarce capital, this competitive threat pushed Toyota and other Japanese firms toward the simple, efficient practices of JIT systems. Ironically, however, they developed those systems by adapting manufacturing practices transplanted from American firms.

American Roots of JIT

Ohno's just-in-time manufacturing system traces its lineage back to two distinctly American institutions: Henry Ford's mass production system and the supermarket. The pioneers of mass production and assembly-line technology first conceived many of the techniques that form the basis of JIT. The image of the supermarket became Ohno's vision of an ideal operations management system.

Ford's Mass Production System in JIT.   As an earlier chapter described, Henry Ford was only one among many competitors when he introduced his car to the market in 1886. He dominated those competitors for a time, in the process transforming the auto industry and the entire U.S. economy, by moving beyond the standard practice of hand-crafting cars in small batches for rich buyers. Ford succeeded by making the car available to a mass market. Expressed in the value equation, he increased value primarily by reducing cost:

[5]Y. Sugimori, K. Kusunoki, F. Cho, and S. Uchikawa, "Toyota Production System and Kanban System—Materialization of Just-in-Time and Respect-for-Human System," *International Journal of Production Research* 15, no. 6 (1977), pp. 553–564.

$$\text{Value} = \frac{\text{Performance}^{\uparrow}}{\text{Cost}^{\downarrow\downarrow}}$$ **(9.2)**

$$\text{Performance}^{\uparrow} < \text{Cost}^{\downarrow\downarrow}$$

" They can have any color they want, as long as it's black. "

Henry Ford

Ford's mass production system raised value by reducing cost more quickly than the market-driven rate of improvements in performance. To reduce cost, for example, Ford eliminated options like color choices and focused instead on standardization and interchangeable parts.

To control and reduce costs, Ford built large factories to produce identical cars at the lowest price possible. He extended his control over costs and their variations by managing the entire supply chain within his own organization. Ford employees mined iron ore in the firm's own pits. Ford ships and tractors transported the ore to the company's docks where Ford cranes unloaded it. Ford steel mills processed the iron ore to make steel plate from which Ford factories built the Model T. Henry Ford and his employees controlled every step.

Ford's determination to reduce the cost of his car drove him to reduce the time of production, as well. While old methods of hand building took days to assemble a finished car, Ford factories could turn out a Model T in hours. Inventory never sat unused for long. Ford boasted that iron ore unloaded at his River Rouge plant became steel components in a Ford truck rolling off the assembly line within 48 hours.

Finally, Ford constantly searched for process innovations. He and his employees continually challenged themselves to build cars and components at lower costs with less labor time and less waste of material and other resources. This preoccupation foreshadowed later tactics of just-in-time systems:

- *Concern with waste*   Henry Ford viewed waste as the bitter enemy of any effective OM system, since it created costs without adding value to the product. Ford saw any action that did not add to value as a contribution to waste. The crusade to eliminate waste led Ford engineers to set rigid specifications for shipping containers for certain incoming parts, for example, demanding a definite type of wood in carefully dimensioned strips. The factory returned containers that failed to satisfy these requirements to the suppliers, even if the parts inside them met standards. The containers were so important because after emptying them, workers knocked them apart and installed the strips of wood as floor boards in Model T cars.
- *Emphasis on continuous improvement*   Ford recognized no single, best way of doing things that would remain constant over time. Rather, he proclaimed, "Our own attitude is that we are charged with discovering the best way of doing everything, and that we must regard every process employed ... as purely experimental."[6] Following this principle, Ford insisted that his systems improve continuously.
- *Setup reduction*   To keep his system working well, Ford recognized the need to minimize setups, since the unavoidable costs do not contribute directly to value. As a result, engineers located tools near work sites to minimize delays in finding them. The engineers also arranged to deliver all tools and materials to waist-high storage locations to reduce unproductive stooping to the floor to pick up a tool or part.[7]
- *Emphasis on improved housekeeping*   Dirt decreased employee productivity, made the workplace dangerous, and caused people to spend valuable time

[6]Henry Ford, *Today and Tomorrow* (Cambridge, Mass.: Productivity Press, 1989), pp. 52–53.
[7]Ibid., p. 103.

looking for needed tools or materials among the clutter. As a result, Ford required a clean, well-organized workplace, equating good housekeeping with high employee morale and productivity.

- *Level product scheduling*   Uneven, fluctuating schedules caused variations in work flows that created confusion, complicated time management, and obscured opportunities for improvements. Ford instituted level schedules, building the same number of cars every day, to avoid these costly problems.
- *Respect for people*   Henry Ford pioneered the modern concern for creating a workplace that maximized the productivity of labor, the most important resource of any firm in his view. He later wrote, "Materials are less important than human beings—although we have not yet come quite around to thinking in that fashion."[8] He wanted the work in his plants to enhance the value of this precious resource.

To promote this view, Ford introduced a number of innovations in worker-company relationships. The Henry Ford Trade School offered skills training for well-paying occupations to orphans and widows' sons, and Ford invested in a hospital system to guarantee his workers the best possible health care. Also, he paid his workers $5 per day, double the average wage of the time. This generous compensation attracted the best workers and created a new market for Ford cars among his own well-paid employees. The high wages also allowed workers to afford the necessities of healthy living, reducing the cost of absenteeism due to illness. Finally, Ford invested in technology to reduce the physical strain and stress on workers. Company policy disapproved of physically demanding work that machines could perform more effectively than humans. Ford wanted his employees to work hard, not by heavy lifting, but by applying their minds and skills to solve production problems.

Decades after Ford built his mass production system, Ohno incorporated many of these and other Ford innovations into Toyota's JIT system. Early in the century, Ford was advocating and implementing practices very similar to the just-in-time manufacturing principles driving many North American and Japanese firms today.

Supermarkets and JIT Manufacturing.   Despite the similarities in principles, the core of Ohno's vision of an ideal OM system came not from the large and efficient Ford facility at River Rouge, Michigan, but from American supermarkets. Ohno has described his discovery and application of this retailing innovation:

> In 1956, I toured U.S. production plants at General Motors, Ford, and other machinery companies. But my strongest impression was the extent of the supermarkets' prevalence in America. The reason for this was that by the late 1940s, at Toyota's machine shop that I managed, we were already studying the U.S. supermarket and applying its methods to our work…. We made a connection between supermarkets and the just-in-time system….
>
> A supermarket is where a customer can get (1) what is needed, (2) at the time needed, (3) in the amount needed. From the supermarket, we got the idea of viewing the earlier processes in the production line as a kind of store. The later process (the customer) goes to the earlier process (the supermarket) to acquire the required parts (the commodities) at the time and in the quantity needed. The earlier process immediately produces the quantity just taken (restocking the shelves). We hoped that this would help us approach our just-in-time goal, and … we actually applied the system to our machine shop at the main plant.[9]

---

[8]Ibid., p. 92.

[9]William H. Davidow and Michael S. Malone, *The Virtual Corporation* (New York: Harper Business, 1992), pp. 119–120.

The supermarket model held many attractions for JIT advocates like Ohno. It showed that a system could keep inventory to a minimum and succeed based on active customer service. Furthermore, in this system, the need for products determined what moved onto the shelves. Finally, this system strived to keep products moving continuously from suppliers to customers. These characteristics greatly shaped the historical development of just-in-time manufacturing and helped managers to formulate its objectives.

OBJECTIVES OF JUST-IN-TIME MANUFACTURING

Following Ohno's supermarket-based model, just-in-time manufacturing pursues a very specific goal: to provide the right amount of product at the right time with the right quality level at the right place. As in all value-driven operations management, customer demand always determines what is right. JIT tries to build only what internal and external customers want when they want it. To guide daily operations, managers can restate this broad goal of JIT as a series of smaller, more focused objectives:

1. Produce only the products (goods or services) that customers want.
2. Produce products only as quickly as customers want to use them.
3. Produce products with perfect quality.
4. Produce in the minimum possible lead times.
5. Produce products with features that customers want, and no others.
6. Produce with no waste of labor, materials, or equipment; designate a purpose for every movement to leave zero idle inventory.
7. Produce with methods that reinforce the occupational development of workers.

These seven objectives have some very important implications for the entire OM system.

Operations Management under JIT

To achieve the objectives of JIT, operations managers must build several critical characteristics into their processes and subprocesses.

Small Order Sizes.   Small orders help the system to build what customers want in the desired amounts. Also, processes can produce small orders with shorter lead times, since they complete jobs and move on to others more quickly, which speeds the firm's response to customer demand. Ultimately, JIT aims to produce products in a standard lot size of 1 unit.

Short Lead Times.   The goal of reducing lead times must extend beyond the effects of small orders. Short lead times position the OM system to deliver what customers actually want when and where they want it, basing production on actual customer demand. In contrast, long lead times force the system to base production on a potentially flawed forecast, raising the risk of holding unsold finished goods inventory or losing sales when demand outpaces supply. Further, a longer lead time makes forecasters look further ahead in time, exposing the process to larger forecasting error. Short lead times also help to keep costs low, and they enforce a healthy discipline on the entire OM system because any disruption in the production flow quickly shows up as unsatisfied customers.

Worker Planning, Production, and Problem-Solving.   Just-in-time manufacturing redefines and greatly expands the role of the employee by combining the traditional planning responsibilities of management with the execution responsibilities of employees. The mandate to minimize lead times cannot tolerate delays while employees wait for others to analyze and solve problems that arise. Rather, every worker must make quick decisions and solve problems, both to keep production moving and to exploit their day-to-day familiarity with the system to resolve its disruptions. JIT merges planning and execution in the hands of operating employees. It forces managers to relinquish to workers the power and authority to implement necessary changes to resolve problems.

Intolerance for Ineffectiveness.   JIT leaves no slack for poor performance that produces quality defects, late deliveries, or equipment breakdowns. It requires employees to identify any cause of longer lead times or increased system variance and eliminate it before it disrupts the flow of production throughout the OM system and disappoints customers. Life without the buffers of inventory, safety capacity, or increased lead times requires an organization to aggressively attack any causes of problems that contribute to the need for these buffers.

 ## MAJOR TOOLS AND TECHNIQUES OF JIT MANUFACTURING

Just-in-time manufacturing works at two different levels. As a large-scale, organizationwide philosophy, it directs everyone's efforts at identifying and eliminating waste in the firm. This broad-based, strategic orientation can be referred to as *JIT* (in capital letters), *corporate JIT,* or **Big JIT**. On the other hand, practitioners can focus on various analytical tools and techniques that are frequently associated with just-in-time manufacturing. Often this tactical orientation can be seen as *jit, shop-floor JIT,* or **Little JIT**.

Big JIT
Just-in-time manufacturing as a large-scale, organizationwide philosophy

In this section, we cover the tactical tools of Little JIT. Specifically, we examine:

Little JIT
Just-in-time manufacturing as a set of tactically oriented, analytical tools

- Kanban or pull scheduling
- Level, mixed-model scheduling
- Setup reduction
- Poka-yoke (fool-proofing)
- Quality at the source
- Flexible/cross-trained workers
- Group technology
- Focused factories
- Statistical process control
- Standardization
- Supplier partnerships
- *Kaizen*

In addition, Appendix 9A covers total productive maintenance. Remember throughout these discussions that each technique intends primarily to help managers to achieve the seven objectives of JIT.

Kanban or Pull Scheduling

Kanban

A system of control cards that govern material movements through an OM system within JIT

To build only what customers demand when they demand it, just-in-time manufacturing needs a scheduling system that can immediately and clearly communicate the demands of the customer to the delivery system. The **Kanban** or **pull scheduling** system does this. In its simplest meaning, the word *Kanban* is the Japanese term for a card. In JIT, Kanban is a name for a system of control cards that govern material movements through an OM system. By extension, the name also denotes an overall system for day-to-day production and inventory control. In this section, *Kanban* refers to a system of control cards.

The Kanban control system relies on visual signals such as control cards, empty squares on the floor or a shelf, or even colored golf balls to control the withdrawal and replenishment of materials and components during processing. (Exhibit 9.8 gives some examples of Kanban signals and their meanings.) Kanbans send urgent signals for workers to initiate specific actions immediately, perhaps beginning production of a certain part or transferring inventory. A certain type of Kanban sends a prespecified signal. In this way, Kanban creates a paperless system by which a later stage of production can order specific materials or components from either internal or external suppliers; cards or other signals replace more traditional paper orders. A Kanban system can reach across organizational boundaries to forge real-time links with both customers and suppliers.

Pull versus Push Scheduling.   Kanban creates a pull system for scheduling production as an internal or external customer's signal pulls output from a supplier as needed. In contrast, a push scheduling system might direct a worker to move output on to the next work center immediately upon finishing a prescheduled job. This may lead to piles of inventories waiting unproductively at various points within the system, perhaps obscuring bottlenecks. Quality tends to fall then as workers try to clear out the work piling up at their stations. Kanban seeks to set up a smooth flow of materials at various stages of completion through the firms, and ultimately from raw material to customer use.

withdrawal Kanban

A card or other signal that accompanies an order and authorizes a worker to take parts or materials necessary to fill the order

production Kanban

A card or other signal that accompanies an empty bin or other transportation option and authorizes a worker to produce parts to resupply a later stage of production

Toyota's Kanban System.   To understand how Kanban works, look at Toyota's implementation of the concept.[10] This system defines two basic types of Kanbans: production Kanbans and withdrawal Kanbans (also known as *conveyance Kanbans*). Many firms use only **withdrawal Kanbans**, which give signals that authorize someone to withdraw a standard lot of a specific type of item. This Kanban is typically attached to a container of parts undergoing processing at a specific operation. If a worker processing the job runs out of a part, the withdrawal Kanban that accompanied the job gives that person the authority to take an empty bin to a replenishment area to exchange for a full bin. To govern later material flows, the worker reattaches the withdrawal Kanban to the filled bin.

In contrast, a **production Kanban** authorizes a worker to replenish an empty bin. When an empty bin arrives at a work station with a production Kanban attached, the worker sees a signal to build a new batch of items to fill the bin. The production Kanban specifies the type of parts and the amount to build, typically the amount that will fit in a container or a truck or cart load.

---

[10]Y. Monden, "What Makes the Toyota Production System Really Tick?" *Industrial Engineering* 13, no. 1 (1981), pp. 36–46.

[**EXHIBIT 9.8**]

Examples of Kanbans

Golf balls: When a golf ball rolls up to a work station the operator builds a product indicated by the color of the golf ball.

Cards: Information might state the amount and type of item to produce, a stock location, or a process.

Taped square on the floor: When the square empties, fill it.

Metal triangle on a pile: When removed products expose the metal triangle, build more.

Carts or trucks: When an empty cart arrives, fill it.

Containers: When a container empties to a line painted inside, refill it.

Exhibit 9.9 illustrates how the two kinds of Kanbans control interactions between work stations.[11] Work Center A supplies inputs for Work Center B, and several containers carry parts through a storage area between them. This storage area typically contains one container of each type of part. Since the storage area is full in Exhibit 9.9A, Work Center A sits idle rather than building parts that its internal customer does not currently need. Exhibit 9.9B shows an empty bin in Work Center B with a withdrawal Kanban attached. To get more parts to finish production, the operator at Work Center B returns the empty bin to the storage area and exchanges it for a container filled with the needed parts with a production Kanban attached. The worker moves the withdrawal Kanban, which gives authority to take the parts, from the empty bin to the full one. He or she then moves the production Kanban to the empty bin and returns with the full bin to Work Center B.

In Exhibit 9.9C, the empty bin returns to Work Center A where the production Kanban signals the operator to produce the standard complement of parts to refill the bin and return it to the storage area. If no empty bins await the operator at Work Center A at the end of this cycle, production stops.

This example shows why Kanban is called a *pull system*. Work Center B pulls needed parts from the storage area, which effectively pulls replacement parts from Work Center A. This pull system responds quickly and automatically to pre-existing demand. This prevents unneeded production from building up inventory. In contrast, a push system creates supply in the hope that well-timed demand will promptly consume it. Any disruption of this necessarily imprecise timing creates wasteful pools of inventory in the OM system.

Kanban eliminates the need for traditional paperwork like sheafs of orders or long lists of due dates. Each worker produces whatever the Kanbans dictate. Kanban is also a simple system to use and understand, eliminating the need for complex computer technology for order tracking and scheduling.

Benefits of Kanban. As practiced at companies such as Hewlett-Packard and Toyota, Kanban systems have resulted in significant benefits:

---

[11]Steven A. Melnyk and Phillip L. Carter, "Viewing Kanban as an (s,Q) System: Developing New Insights into a Japanese Method of Production and Inventory Control," in *Management by Japanese Systems,* ed. by Sang M. Lee and Gary Schwendiman (New York: Praeger, 1982), pp. 165–180.

[**E X H I B I T   9 . 9**]

Kanbans in Operation

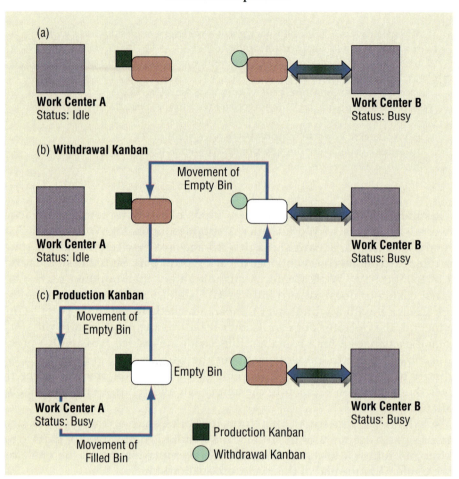

- Reduced inventory levels
- Less confusion over sequences of activities
- Less obsolescence of inventories while in storage
- Smaller floor-space requirements for storing inventory
- Reduced lead times
- Improved quality
- Higher employee productivity
- Greater system flexibility

Level, Mixed-Model Scheduling

To build what customers want in the desired amounts at the correct times, a firm must change how it schedules operations every day. This change begins with Kanban or pull scheduling so that every activity in a transformation process responds to the demands of its internal or external customer. However, a pull scheduling system must conform to a larger scheme for scheduling end product production. Allen-Edmonds might develop an overall schedule for shoe production, while organizing a pull scheduling system to produce components and combine them, one by one.

To accomplish this larger goal, an operations manager prepares a **master production schedule** (MPS). This scheduling tool identifies for a given period of time, usually a month, the number of units of each specific end product that an OM process will build and when it will build each product. The master production schedule serves as a critical interface between the OM system and the rest of firm. It tells people throughout the firm what they can expect to receive from the OM system and when. Based on this information, marketing can make promises to customers, purchasing can plan for material needs, finance can arrange funding for working capital needs, etc. The concept of master production scheduling, while briefly introduced here, is discussed in greater detail in the chapter on resource planning.

The master schedule is critical to purchasing since the production goals that it contains help the purchasing manager plan, place, and evaluate purchases from suppliers. For logistics management, the master production schedule indicates when shipments to and from the operations management system have to be made. To the human resources management people, the master schedule is critical in determining the employee capacity requirements for the future. For marketing, the master production schedule indicates what the firm will deliver and when. This information is very useful when communicating with customers.

The goals of JIT encourage development of a master production schedule that produces some units of every end product every day. The MPS should also set a uniform flow of work over the month (or other planning period) to balance the competing demands of marketing and operations management. Marketing would like to set new schedules every few minutes to respond immediately to customer demand, but the OM system would find this variability almost impossible to sustain. Operations managers can more easily change production from month to month in response to changes in customer demand, but within each month they need to keep production essentially frozen.

Similarly, a smooth, predictable flow of work requires an identical schedule for each day. In this situation, planning one day's production gives a master production schedule for the entire month, since it simply repeats the daily schedule for the number of working days in the month.

Load Leveling.   Just-in-time manufacturing tries to develop a daily schedule through **load leveling**, a technique for balancing the rate of production with the rate at which the market wants products. Ultimately, this method tries to set a schedule that generates products at exactly the rate that customers want them. For example, suppose that a firm makes four different end products, A, B, C, and D, with the following sales levels:

Model	Sales (units)
A	16,000 per month
B	8,000
C	4,000
D	2,000
Total sales	30,000 per month
Capacity	20 days of planned production
	8 hours of production planned per day

master production schedule

A periodic (usually monthly) statement of the number of units of each specific end product that an OM process will build and when it will build each product

load leveling

A JIT scheduling technique that balances the rate of production with the rate at which the market wants produced

A level, daily load would produce 1,500 units per day; this breaks down to 187.5 units per hour or 1 unit every 19.2 seconds. This critical rate of 19.2 seconds is the **cycle time**.[12] If the MPS matches the rate of production to the cycle time, then it synchronizes the rate of output with the rate of demand. In this way, JIT helps the OM system to produce at exactly the rate of customer demand.

Load leveling generates one daily schedule that produces 800 units of Model A, 400 units of Model B, 200 units of Model C, and 100 units of Model D. The OM system then repeats this schedule every working day of the month.

To make this schedule feasible, operations managers must ensure a match between available capacity in the OM system and the capacity demanded by daily production goals. To correct insufficient capacity, they must add work hours or other resources to make extra capacity; if the system has more capacity than it needs to meet the goals, the managers must reduce capacity by either limiting work hours or divesting other resources. Load leveling does not ask whether production fully exploits available resources; rather, it asks whether the output rate is coordinated with the demand rate. In this way, it treats daily demand as fixed and adjusts capacity to match.

Mixed-Model Scheduling.   With a daily schedule that identifies how many units of each model an OM system will produce per day, operations managers must decide how to distribute this production over the day. For one option, they could run all units of Model A in one batch, followed by three more batches for all units of Model B, Model C, and then Model D. This schedule would create very uneven demand for components during the day, as the system would have to supply everything needed to produce each model in a single, large batch or lump. This lumpy demand encourages the system to build in large lots, creating wasteful inventory and variation in shop-floor activities.

As an alternative, **mixed model scheduling** tries to set a production sequence for end products that creates the smoothest possible set of demands on all activities within the master production schedule. The MPS for Models A, B, C, and D would build the following mix each day:

Model	Output per day
Model A	800 units
Model B	400
Model C	200
Model D	100

The OM system has 8 hours (28,800 seconds) of capacity available each day, and it should build 1 unit of Model A every 19.2 seconds. Since it must build twice as many units of A as B, it should set the cycle time between units of B at 38.4 seconds. Similarly, 153.6 seconds should elapse between units of C, and 307.2 seconds between units of D. These cycle times suggest a mixed-model schedule with the sequence:

A-B-A-C-A-B-A-D-A-B-A-C-A-B-A-D-A-B-C-A-B-A-D-A-B-C

The schedule continuously repeats this sequence, producing 1 unit of D, 2 units of C, 4 units of B, and 8 units of A in each repetition. This gives a smooth demand on system resources with no variation.

[12]Kenneth A. Wantuck, *Just in Time for America* (Southfield, Mich.: KWA Media, 1989), p. 230.

Benefits of Level, Mixed-Model Scheduling.   As one of its major goals, just-in-time manufacturing works to simplify activities. Level, mixed-model scheduling promotes this goal by organizing potentially complex production activities through relatively simple methods. The technique offers other benefits, as well:

- *Smoother response to market demand*   This scheduling system produces some units of every product every day, so customers need not wait for later completion of large batches to get the products that they want. The firm can meet customer demand without holding large finished-goods inventories.
- *Simpler coordination of supply*   Because each day's schedule is identical over the month, operations managers can coordinate the flows of supply once and then repeat the same arrangements each day. Kanban, or pull scheduling, works very well in this setting.
- *Flatter learning curves*   Because operators produce every product and component frequently, the needed techniques and skills remain fresh.
- *Less inventory*   Continuous production synchronized to demand frees the firm from storing large quantities to meet demand between runs. If it were to build all units of A at once, it would have to make enough units to last until the next production run, creating a need to store a lot of inventory.

Setup Reduction

To produce just what customers want in the desired amounts, an OM system must build in small lot sizes, ideally in order quantities of 1 unit. High setup costs make this impossible in many OM systems. Setup costs capture all of the time requirements to prepare a system to build a part, including:

1. *Process preparation time*   The most obvious component of setup time covers needed alterations to a piece of equipment to run a new lot, including such activities as finding needed tools and accessories, changing the equipment, and testing and adjusting the new setup to ensure that it can produce good quality consistently. Consistency is important because it takes time to prepare a system to produce the good outputs that JIT requires.
2. *Process teardown time*   At the end of the run, workers must remove the setup to allow later adjustments to the equipment to process a new batch.
3. *Learning time*   Before running the new order, the equipment operator must know how to do the work. This may require pulling up instructions for either preparing the equipment or processing the outputs. Setup includes any time required to learn how to process an order.

For example, think about the task of making pancakes. You might begin this process by looking for a recipe. After finding the recipe, you read it over, noting the needed ingredients. You spend time gathering the ingredients and then begin heating the griddle. While the griddle heats, you mix the ingredients, but before you can cook any pancakes, you have to make sure that the griddle is hot enough. You burn one test pancake because the griddle is too hot. You throw away the burned pancake and turn down the heat, then repeat this process until you get a good pancake. If you have more batter than you need for one breakfast, you might cook extra pancakes and store them to reheat later. After cooking the pancakes you want, you must clean up the stove, the dishes, and the utensils. This little example illustrates all three elements of setups:

Setup Element	Activity
Process preparation time	Finding the ingredients
	Heating the griddle
Process teardown time	Cleaning up the stove, dishes, and utensils
Learning time	Finding and reading the recipe
	Testing the first few pancakes to adjust heat

Making pancakes requires a lot of time for setups. In fact, setup costs often strongly influence time requirements and lot sizes for economical production. A high setup cost increases the lot size because this allows the firm to spread the cost over a larger number of units. To meet customer demand for 1 unit, an OM system can either produce the unit to order (as with the pancakes) and absorb the setup costs or take the item from inventory accumulated through earlier excess production. This decision must balance the setup cost against the cost of holding inventory, including the carrying cost (storage, bookkeeping, etc.) and the opportunity cost. Opportunity cost reflects the gain that the firm could have earned in some alternative investment for the money it spent on inventory. The sacrifice of this best alternative investment represents a cost of holding inventory.

[**PROBLEM 9.1**]

Setup–Inventory Trade-off

Suppose that an operations manager has measured the setup cost for an order at $10. Inventory carrying cost is $2 per unit per month, and demand is 10 units per month. A table helps to show the trade-off between total inventory carrying cost and total setup cost:

Order Size (units)	Total Setup Cost[a] (per month)	Total Inventory Carrying Cost[b]	Total Costs
1	100.00	1.00	101.00
2	50.00	2.00	52.00
3	33.33	3.00	36.33
4	25.00	4.00	29.00
5	20.00	5.00	25.00
6	16.67	6.00	22.67
7	14.30	7.00	21.30
8	12.50	8.00	20.50
9	11.11	9.00	20.11
10	**10.00**	**10.00**	**20.00**
11	9.10	11.00	20.10
12	8.30	12.00	20.30
13	7.69	13.00	20.69

[a](Customer demand/Order quantity) × Setup.
[b]Order quantity (Q) × Carrying costs × ½ (since ½Q defines the total inventory carrying costs).

The setup cost for a given order size reflects the setup cost per order times the number of orders of that size needed to meet customer demand. The inventory carrying cost reflects one-half of the number of units held in stock for each order size times the order quantity. (Average inventory is generally calculated by adding beginning and ending inventories and dividing by 2.)

To achieve the lowest total cost, the operations manager would set an order quantity of 10 units. At this level of output, total setup cost equals total inventory carrying cost. For any order quantity less than 10, the setup cost exceeds the inventory carrying cost; for any order quantity greater than 10, the total inventory carrying cost exceeds the setup cost.   [■]

The large lots resulting from large setup times generate several benefits and costs. For the benefits, setup time takes a smaller portion of total processing time, reducing the apparent cost of operating labor-hours.[13] Inventory can help to level loads on the operations management system by absorbing extra production and feeding extra demand, especially for unexpected rush orders. It also acts as a cushion, as explained early in the chapter, helping to soften disruptions due to defective products or equipment breakdowns.

The costs of larger lots begin with the resources that inventory consumes. This includes both financial capital invested in producing it and the physical space it occupies without adding real value. Inventory storage costs money for racks, pallets, and storage areas and for stockroom personnel. Transportation and storage of stock increases handling, raising labor-hours to move products to stockrooms and then to customers or other work stations, rather than moving the products directly to their destinations. Larger lots require longer lead times. They also increase the risk of obsolescence, which forces the firm to dispose of outdated stock after a model change, either by selling old products at discount prices or by discarding them. Finally, inventory quality deteriorates over time; steel products might rust, for example, and few people would want to eat a microwaved, three-week-old pancake.

Besides the costs of large lot sizes, setups raise other concerns. While necessary to prepare for operations, setups consume capacity without really adding value. They also introduce variation into an OM process due to differences in time requirements to locate needed tools, materials, and instructions; variation in the time required to calibrate or adjust equipment, such as the time spent testing the temperature of the pancake griddle; and time requirements for testing output to evaluate the accuracy of the setup.

Reducing Setup Times.   Any just-in-time manufacturing system works hard to reduce setup times. An effective setup-reduction program should pursue four major objectives:[14]

- *Evolve toward lot sizes of 1 unit.* This requires setups that take no longer than the time to produce a single unit of output. We can support the policy of building to order when setup costs are less than or equal to the time it takes to make one unit of production. Such a system can effectively build what customers want when they want it.
- *Run every part every day.* This keeps the schedule level.
- *Make the first piece right every time.* Effective setup reduction must not only reduce the time it takes to change over from one part to another; it should also eliminate any need for testing and adjustment, ensuring that every piece emerges from the process perfect the first time.

[13]Shigeo Shingo, *A Revolution in Manufacturing: The SMED System* (Cambridge, Mass.: Productivity Press, 1985), pp. 16–17.
[14]Wantuck, *Just in Time*, p. 188.

[**EXHIBIT 9.10**]

Auto Hood and Fender Setups for an 800-Ton Press

	Toyota	United States	Sweden	Germany
Setup time	10 minutes	6 hours	4 hours	4 hours
Setups per day	3	1	—	½
Lot size	1 day	10 days	1 month	—

SOURCE   Kenneth A. Wantuck, *Just in Time for America* (Southfield, Mich.: KWA Media, 1989), pp. 186–188.

- *Keep setup times to 10 minutes.* Ideally, the time it takes to change over equipment should never take more than 10 minutes. Evidence confirms that this ambitious goal is very feasible. (See Exhibit 9.10.)

To achieve these four goals, any setup reduction program can draw on several procedures, some familiar and some quite new.

Process Flow Analysis of Setup Times.   Setup time can increase if operations managers fail to carefully document the steps of the procedure. As a first step in understanding, controlling, and reducing setups, they must examine current procedures, perhaps using tools such as process flow charts or assembly charts. They might also videotape setup procedures and then study the tapes.

Housekeeping.   An efficient setup should look like a pit stop at the Indianapolis Speedway. Good housekeeping and careful organization help to smooth the process, placing every tool, worker, and material container in a specified place and returning everyone and everything to the proper place at the finish of the procedure. In addition, good housekeeping should emphasize cleanliness, since a clean, neat area allows setups to proceed as planned. Clutter causes unplanned delays and variance.

Practiced Teamwork.   Like a pit stop at the Indianapolis Speedway, an efficient setup requires people to work together as an experienced team in which each member knows and carries out certain responsibilities and tasks. Workers must practice setups so that the members can carry out their tasks quickly, almost without thinking, and without error.

single-minute exchange of dies
A three-stage method for reducing setups by separating internal and external setups, converting internal setups to external setups, and streamlining all setup procedures

Single Minute Exchange of Dies (SMED).   **Single-minute exchange of dies** (SMED) is a systematic procedure for reducing long setups developed by Shigeo Shingo.[15] This technique traces the origins of long setups to several causes:

- Preparation, after-process adjustment, checking of material, etc.
- Mounting and removing tools and fittings
- Measurements, settings, and calibrations
- Trial runs and adjustments.

SMED tries to reduce the impact of these causes in a three-stage process.

---

[15]Shingo, *Revolution in Manufacturing.*

Stage 1 separates internal and external setups. An **internal setup** includes any setup procedure that occurs while the equipment sits idle. For example, if a pancake cook were to wait for the griddle to heat up before mixing the batter, the mixing step would represent an internal setup. In contrast, an **external setup** is any setup activity that workers complete while the equipment operates. An external setup would mix the batter while waiting for the griddle to heat. Stage 2 responds to this distinction by converting internal setups to external setups.

Stage 3 in the SMED process works to streamline all activities in a setup. Specifically, it advocates eliminating any activities for adjustments, calibrations, elaborate positioning, unnecessary tightening, or trial runs. For example, workers might mount tools in the correct positions on guides or back plates and then place the entire units during setup. Standardizing setups can help to flatten learning curves by eliminating the need for relearning. Technology can also contribute to this effort, as when a laser level helps workers judge alignment of dies; perhaps a pancake griddle could include a light that would turn green to indicate the right temperature.

Benefits of Reduced Setups.   Reducing setups can bring many benefits. Quicker setups increase capital turnover rates, earning a higher return on the firm's investment in equipment by maximizing its productive time. Smaller inventory requirements use plant space more efficiently and reduce nonvalue-adding operations such as stock handling, further enhancing productivity. Also, low inventory requirements minimize losses due to unusable stock after model changes or demand forecast errors. Eliminating setup errors improves both quality and safety. Less complicated setups simplify housekeeping and lower operating expenses, as well.

Poka-Yoke (Fool-Proofing)

Just-in-time practitioners try to develop OM systems that produce output with perfect quality every time. Unfortunately, processes can obstruct this goal by creating opportunities for error and confusion. Assembly workers may insert components upside down due to poor understanding of which end goes up; setup workers may mount dies onto machines incorrectly due to ignorance of the correct orientation. A pancake cook might make errors due to uncertainty about when the griddle reaches the right temperature.

To produce perfect quality the first time every time, operations managers must identify all of these opportunities for error and eliminate them. They must design parts and processes that make the desired results inevitable. This goal guides **poka-yoke** or fool-proofing.[16]

Opportunities for error arise for many reasons. An incomplete process may leave workers to supply missing pieces. Poor markings may allow confusion about how to combine parts. Poor communication about the exact sequence of activities may lead to variance when workers follow conflicting procedures. OM systems come to rely on the experience and accumulated knowledge of employees, but they often gain this knowledge and experience only at the cost of making errors. Furthermore, they may forget previously learned skills, leading to further errors.

---

internal setup
Any setup procedure that occurs while the equipment sits idle

external setup
Any setup activity that workers complete while the equipment operates

poka-yoke
A just-in-time method to design parts and processes in ways that make desired results inevitable, based on a Japanese term

---

[16]Kiyoshi Suzaki, *The New Manufacturing Challenge: Techniques for Continuous Improvement* (New York: Free Press, 1987), pp. 98–101; Shigeo Shingo, *Zero Qualtity Control: Source, Inspection, and the Poka-Yoke System* (Norwalk, Conn.: Productivity Press, 1986), pp. 99–261.

When any system must depend on the experience of employees, operations managers often feel the need for inspections and quality control checks, recognizing that people do make mistakes.

Poka-yoke tries to change either the process or its resources to eliminate the need to rely on human experience and accumulated knowledge. Business process reengineering, discussed in Chapter 5, can be viewed as a form of poka-yoke. Other poka-yoke methods might:

- Color code similar parts to help workers distinguish them (e.g., right is red, left is green).
- Set up counters to detect the number of welding operations on an assembly and compare this number with the standard. A warning signal sounds whenever the two numbers do not match.
- Place templates over an assembled component to show operators the differences between parts and how to insert them.

Examples of poka-yoke abound in everyday life. For example, a standard electrical plug fits into an outlet in only one way because one of the two prongs is larger than the other. This ensures that people will insert the plug properly to create a grounded circuit.

Poka-yoke can yield a number of important benefits for an OM system. It reduces the cost of relearning and simplifies production scheduling. By strictly limiting the opportunity for worker errors, and the associated frustration, it often helps to improve employee morale.

Poka-Yoke and Human Discretion.   Poka-yoke may seem likely to make a work setting boring for employees. Why, some critics ask, would anyone want to work in a system that leaves no opportunity to think about operations? In fact, however, employees want to use some skills more than others. People, in general, do not perform especially well in tasks that involve monitoring, data recording, and checking. These are the tasks that poka-yoke tries to eliminate by replacing them with fool-proof mechanisms. In contrast, people excel at recognizing patterns and differences and at problem solving. By eliminating the need for people to monitor data and check operations, poka-yoke tries to free employees to focus on solving more stubborn problems.

Quality at the Source

To achieve the objectives of JIT, a firm must develop new ways to view customers and to identify and solve problems. It can no longer merely catch problems after they occur through inspections. Rather, improvement must focus on the sources of products. The quality of a product is determined at the instant that the OM system makes it, and no amount of inspection will ever make it any better.[17] Just-in-time manufacturing relies heavily on this concept of **quality at the source**.

Quality at the source forces every person involved in a transformation process to recognize his or her role as a supplier to one or more internal or external customers. The quality of the outputs of later stages of production depends substantially on the quality of their inputs. Allen-Edmonds' final assembly operations can produce a quality shoe only if makers of components like leather uppers and soles produce acceptable quality through processes that are under control.

quality at the source
An orientation within JIT manufacturing toward targeting efforts to improve quality at the activities that produce it

[17]Wantuck, *Just in Time*, p. 39.

Input from factory workers like these is key to successful implementation of quality at the source.
SOURCE   T. Crosby/Liaison International

Human input is the key to successful implementation of quality at the source. Human workers must study, identify, analyze, uncover, and correct quality problems in the process. The operations manager, in turn, must support these human activities by providing sufficient training (e.g., in the problem-solving tools) and by implementing technology to help support human contributions. Quality at the source reinforces the major principle of just-in-time manufacturing that promotes respect for humans through three techniques: jidoka (autonomation), stop-and-fix/line-stop systems, and andon (trouble lights).

Jidoka.   Jidoka, Japanese for *autonomation,* describes technological features of equipment and processes that detect problems while the systems run and flag these problems to operators.[18] A jidoka system tries to eliminate the need for the operator to spend time monitoring routine activities of a process. For example, a limit switch on a machine might monitor the contents of a feeding bin and light a signal or sound a tone when the bin becomes nearly empty to alert the operator to refill it. A counter might track the number of parts produced and light a signal or sound a tone when this number equals the amount needed.

Stop-and-Fix/Line-Stop Systems.   A stop-and-fix or line-stop system works on a simple premise that an operator should stop the process and immediately fix any significant problem that arises rather than allowing it to continue making poor-quality output. Besides guarding against low quality, such a system causes serious discomfort at the source of the problem since its failure has shut down the process in a highly visible way, perhaps disrupting other operations that depend on the problem activity. This creates a powerful motivation to find a solution.

Stop-and-fix systems differ from jidoka, in which the equipment sends the signal and stops itself. In contrast, stop-and-fix empowers the operator to stop the system as needed, as the next "On the Job" box shows.

---

[18]Suzaki, *New Manufacturing Challenge,* pp. 91–93.

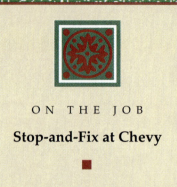

ON THE JOB

Stop-and-Fix at Chevy

Implementing a stop-and-fix system can be a very cost-effective move, but it can also yield some unintended results. On the first day such a system was installed in a Chevrolet engine plant, an operator stopped the line because a piston-and-ring assembly had scored the cylinder wall on one of the engines. This old, recurring problem resulted from sharp edges and burrs left on the rings during manufacturing. The people on the shop floor could identify no quick fix, so they called the product engineer at another building across town. The engineer immediately saw the reasons for the problem and offered to write a change order to add a little chamfer (sloped shoulder) to eliminate the sharp edges. This pleased the plant workers, but they wondered why engineering had not addressed their earlier complaints about the same problem. The product engineer replied that, "I didn't know you had the problem." The old system suffered due to lack of a needed communication link between the plant, where the problem surfaced, and engineering, which held authority to make the necessary changes.

SOURCE   Kenneth A. Wantuck, *Just in Time for America*, (Southfield, Mich.: KWA Media, 1989), pp. 57–58.

Andons/Trouble Lights.   Programs to enhance quality at the source may rely on visual signals to identify the exact locations of problems in OM systems. JIT systems often combine these **andons**, or trouble lights, with jidoka and stop-and-fix systems to make problems highly visible, allowing workers to develop visual control of a process. For example, the Chevrolet engine plant might have placed a light over the work station where the piston was inserted to act as an andon and shine when the worker noticed the problem. This light would communicate the problem to everyone on the shop floor, and it would identify the exact location of the problem. This would allow supervisors and engineers to go to the right place without wasting time finding it.

Flexible/Cross-Trained Workers

To produce the products that customers want at the rate that they want them, a just-in-time system requires a new understanding of capacity. Instead of treating capacity as a certain quantity fixed by current levels of workers and equipment, JIT assumes that operations managers can vary capacity to match customers' needs. This, in turn, requires a change in the way that they look at their tasks of scheduling and training the work force.

A worker who can perform only one task does not fit well into a just-in-time manufacturing environment, which requires a more flexible resource. A flexible work force can move from one area where the firm experiences low demand to more active areas. By cross-training employees, that is, by training workers to perform more than one operation or task, a firm can more easily develop such a flexible work force.

This move toward a flexible work force has several important implications for management and compensation of employees. It places more demands on workers, requiring them to move beyond the role of simple problem-solvers to become multiskilled resources. JIT programs want to hire and retain people who are interested in doing many things within the firm, so pay and job security can no longer be linked solely to seniority. Instead, they reflect the number and types of an individual employee's skills. Some firms refer to programs to pay people according to the range of their job skills as *pay for skill.*

Group Technology

Many firms organize their transformation systems along functional lines. For example, Allen-Edmonds might gather all equipment for cutting leather in one work center and all sewing equipment in another. A shoe in process would move from area to area to allow completion of needed operations. This arrangement makes production extremely flexible, since any work center can process any part that requires its function. However, this flexibility comes at a price.

A functionally organized system must allow for a great deal of physical movement of work in process between diverse work centers. The organization scheme may not define an efficient sequence for completion of a particular order. Such an order would travel back and forth across the shop floor.

Further, orders often sit idle in queues for extended periods in a functionally organized OM system. When an order reaches a work center, it has to wait for a machine to become available and for workers to set up the equipment. All of these activities take time, and an order can spend from 75 percent to 90 percent of its total lead time simply waiting in queues.

Finally, functionally organized work centers make learning critical. Because the system's product mix changes every day, employees can forget how to build certain parts that they have not made for a while. This need for relearning may raise the cost of the order.

These traits of functional OM systems interfere with the goals of just-in-time manufacturing, but another organizing principle can improve performance. **Group technology** gathers all of the equipment necessary for complete production of a family of similar parts to link all operations in a particular process.[19]

A later chapter explains the concept of group technology in greater detail as part of the discussion of product and process design. Within JIT manufacturing, group technology is based on the concept of part families, or groups of similar parts. These similarities could reflect common design features or manufacturing needs. After grouping parts into families that share some important characteristics, the operations managers organizes a work cell for each family that gathers together all of the equipment and facilities needed to build that set of parts. The physical layout arranges facilities in the optimum sequence to produce the parts in the family. Typically such a layout forms a *U*-shaped sequence like that in Exhibit 9.11. From a position in the middle, the operator performs all of the operations needed to build each unit of output.

Group technology work cells shrink physical distances between operations as compared to functional layouts, so they often sharply reduce lead times. In addition, they smooth the flow of orders, leaving less work in process between work centers or waiting in queues than in functionally organized facilities. Since the operator can often move parts between nearby operations by hand, group technology may eliminate the need for automated material-handling equipment. Also, by building similar parts in a single work cell, this system can produce orders with fewer setups than a functionally organized system, which promotes progress toward the JIT goal of building what customers want in the amounts they want

group technology
An equipment layout dedicated to the complete production of a family of similar parts by linking together all operations in a particular process

[19]Wantuck, *Just in Time*, p. 139.

[**EXHIBIT 9.11**]

Example of a Group Technology Layout

| Raw Materials | Saw | Lathe | Mill |

Start of Production

Worker Motion

| Finished Parts | Press | Lathe | Heat Treat |

SOURCE   Kenneth A. Wantuck, *Just in Time for America* (Southfield, Mich.: KWA Media, 1989), p. 145.

with minimum lead times. As a group technology work cell builds a single set of outputs continuously, workers become intimately familiar with the system's outputs and processes, avoiding the need for expensive relearning and helping them to identify opportunities for improvement. Finally, a work cell can improve quality by providing an opportunity for visual inspection after each operation as the operator moves a part from one machine to the next.

Focused Factories

The discussion of group technology shows why JIT systems frequently abandon efforts to build many, diverse products in single, large systems. Instead, such a system tends to organize production into a series of smaller, more focused systems.

In traditional manufacturing, a large factory produces every one of a firm's products in one location to take advantage of economies of scale. However, large plants are more difficult to manage than smaller facilities. In general, managing more people requires more rigid, bureaucratic methods. Also, a large plant often must produce wide varieties of products to achieve the volume of production it needs to justify its fixed costs. This output variety complicates worker training, and it can spread confusion and increase variance even with fully trained employees.

A large auto component plant might try to produce similar parts for both auto manufacturers and the repair and replacement part market. Car manufacturers want low-cost components delivered on time, so they provide suppliers with demand schedules for large orders several weeks in advance. In contrast, small distributors buy replacement parts only to meet their customers' repair needs. These buyers need speedy service on comparatively small orders, and demand is difficult to predict because no one knows how many of a particular part will break.

Despite the functional similarity of the parts, a single factory cannot serve both markets without chaos and frustration. The two markets require the firm to compete on different order winners, order losers, and order qualifiers. To satisfy the first group of customers, the plant would have to run large lots with few schedule vari-

[**E X H I B I T   9 . 1 2**]

Sample Focused Factory Layout

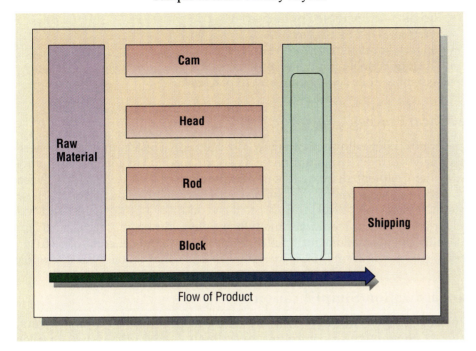

Cam

Head

Raw Material

Rod

Shipping

Block

Flow of Product

ations and relatively high levels of capacity utilization. To satisfy the second group of customers, it would have to respond quickly to changing demand, frequently shifting production from one component to another. This variability would interfere with the system's work to meet the demands of the first group of customers.

To resolve this conflict, the plant's managers might replace the single process with a series of linked, focused factories. A focused factory organizes an OM system to meet the needs of a specific target market rather than trying to achieve many, potentially inconsistent objectives with a single system.[20] In other words, a focused factory structures its capabilities to be consistent with one market's order winners, order qualifiers, and order losers.

By focusing attention on a limited set of skills and requirements, focused factories reduce the confusion and variance caused by product variety. They also allow better organization of the transformation process to encourage short, quick movements through the system. A focused factory might organize production into a line flow, as in Exhibit 9.12. This would reduce the space between operations, bringing workers close together so they can talk and interact to share information and ideas for improvements. By assigning workers to specific tasks, a focused factory can justify investments in special-purpose equipment. This may also reduce the variety of skills that employees need, making employee training simpler and less costly. The familiar stream of work also helps workers to remember what they have to do and enhances their opportunities to study the process and identify opportunities for adding more value. Focused factories can also reduce the need for storage space.

[20]Terry Hill, *Manufacturing Strategy* (Homewood, Ill.: Richard D. Irwin, 1989); and Wickham Skinner, "The Focused Factory," *Harvard Business Review,* May/June 1974, pp. 113–121.

Ferro Manufacturing, a supplier of door mechanisms and latching systems to the auto industry, has reaped many significant benefits by implementing focused factories:[21]

- Productivity increased by 46 percent.
- Scrap rates fell by 67 percent.
- Rework hours fell by 93 percent.
- The total cost of quality fell by 47 percent.
- Assembly floor space shrank by 15 percent.

Statistical Process Control

To generate output with perfect quality, the people in a just-in-time system need to apply analytical tools to monitor process performance and evaluate their control of the process. Chapter 8 discussed many of these types of tools, which form the basis of statistical process control. Techniques such as run charts, control charts, and scatterplots enable employees to measure their control of a process and identify any need for intervention. Traditional manufacturing might assign specialists to apply these tools, but JIT manufacturing places them in the hands of employees to move decision-making authority to the lowest levels and achieve quality at the source.

Standardization/Simplification

At the beginning of this chapter, we described the focus of just-in-time manufacturing on eliminating or controlling two closely linked OM system problems: waste and variance. Variance can arise from inconsistency in operations as every operator performs tasks in a different way, usually in honest efforts to improve performance. These individual improvements can make both lead times and quality levels inconsistent, and they may contribute to waste.

Variance can also arise from inconsistent or nonstandard tools such as shipping or storage containers. Suppose, for example, that a work station receives six containers of parts with 41, 38, 42, 45, 40, and 48 units inside, respectively. The differences in unit counts may seem more of an annoyance or inconvenience than a major problem, but consider how they would complicate an inventory count. If every container holds a different number of parts, workers would have to physically count every part in every container. This time-consuming activity bores workers, and it creates no value.

simplification

A JIT initiative to identify and eliminate any unnecessary process steps through process analysis techniques

standardization

A JIT initiative to replace inconsistent methods with standard routines for process tasks

To reduce amount of time spent in such routine tasks, a JIT practitioner relies on the process analysis techniques of Chapter 5 to identify and eliminate any unnecessary process steps in a **simplification** effort. In a related practice, **standardization** replaces inconsistent methods with standard routines for process tasks. By defining a single method for all workers who perform any activity, standardization helps operations managers to identify problems with equipment, materials, or worker capabilities. Also, it allows employees to spend less time learning how to carry out an activity so they can spend more time identifying and correcting problems. The result is a cycle of improvement, as illustrated in Exhibit 9.13. This technique promotes continuous improvement in much the same way as the plan-do-check-act cycle or Deming wheel.

This emphasis on standardization can carry beyond individual tasks to address the overall layout of the work place. A common or standard layout can

[21]Wantuck, *Just in Time*, pp. 136–137.

[**E X H I B I T   9 . 1 3**]

Cycle of Improvement

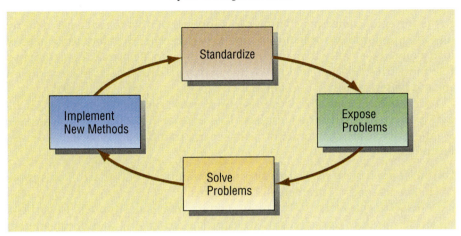

reduce the amount of time that workers spend looking for tools and inputs in unfamiliar surroundings. This also reduces the burden of training workers who move from one work center to another.

Standardization of shipping and storage containers could vastly simplify the task of maintaining accurate inventory records in the earlier example by filling every container with 40 units arranged in five layers of eight units each. To evaluate inventory, workers could then count the full containers and multiply the number by 40 to arrive at the number of units inside. They could then count the number of full layers in any partially full containers and multiply by 8, then add the few units in any partial layers.

Supplier Partnerships

JIT techniques cannot stop at the internal boundaries of an operations management system. Suppliers play critical roles by feeding necessary inputs to the transformation process that it cannot make effectively for itself. For example, Allen-Edmonds might rely on outside suppliers to provide leather, dye, thread, and metal eyelets. It may also buy inputs that the transformation process consumes in its operation like machine lubricants or repair parts and cleaning solutions for facility maintenance.

Suppliers influence the performance of a JIT transformation process since it depends on them to deliver inputs that meet or exceed quality requirements on time in the right quantities. If suppliers fail to feed inputs in accordance with these requirements, they can bring a just-in-time manufacturing system to a stop, since it cannot draw inputs from inventory while waiting for suppliers to meet expectations.

Effective just-in-time manufacturing needs the support of suppliers in four roles:

- Sources of problem-solving expertise
- Practitioners of quality at the source principles
- Timely communicators
- Participants in cost reduction programs

Suppliers as Sources of Expertise.   JIT systems often benefit from suppliers' expertise. Through its extensive work with a specific product or process, the supplier may have come to understand a particular product or process better than its customer. For example, Chrysler decided not to design the radio for its LH car (e.g., the Intrepid), deferring that task to suppliers that were real experts in radio design. A supplier may apply new technology and other developments in its own industry more effectively than its customers, which focus primarily on other markets or industries. Specialized knowledge may help suppliers to make more intelligent and better-informed decisions.

To draw on this valuable expertise, and operations manager under JIT must forge a partnership with the supplier. This partnership calls on the supplier to take a more active and prominent role in several traditionally internal activities of its customers:

- *Problem solving at the buyer's site*   A JIT manufacturer may call on suppliers to join its internal problem-solving teams.
- *Product design advice*   A JIT manufacturer may ask suppliers to participate on its product design teams to improve designs by identifying potential problems or opportunities for improvement in advance.
- *Product design completion*   Under certain conditions, a JIT manufacturer, recognizing a supplier's product expertise, may simply turn over the task of designing parts that meet preset functional specifications to the supplier. Chrysler might define size and performance characteristics it wants in a radio and hire a supplier's design engineers to design and build a product that meets or exceeds those specifications.
- *Problem solving at the supplier's site*   In this two-way partnership, the buying organization may also expect attention and responsiveness to its own input about the supplier's operation.

In these interactions, a JIT manufacturer seeks to benefit from a supplier's accumulated knowledge and skills. Such partnerships breach barriers that separate customers from suppliers, bringing organizations closer together to work together to add value for customers.

Suppliers as Practitioners of Quality at the Source Principles.   Ideally, a JIT system needs suppliers to supply parts with 100 percent quality levels. This standard eliminates the need for inspections of incoming shipments; all inputs move directly from the receiving dock to the process activities. High quality also reduces the need for inventory control and material handling at shipping and receiving.

Of course, perfect quality outputs should come from uniform, tightly controlled processes rather than 100 percent inspection, in which the supplier physically checks every part to make sure that it meets quality requirements. To achieve this ambitious goal, the buying organization must work closely with its suppliers to make their processes reliable and compatible with its own internal processes.

supplier certification
A buyer demand that suppliers demonstrate that their processes can consistently deliver inputs of acceptable quality in timely and appropriate lots

Some just-in-time manufacturers institute **supplier certification** programs as part of this effort. They require suppliers to demonstrate that their processes can consistently deliver inputs of acceptable quality in timely and appropriate lots. A buying organization should never need to check the parts it receives from a certified supplier. Should it encounter some problem with those inputs, it would monitor future shipments to watch for any recurrence or for other indications of some persistent problem that might call for an active response.

Suppliers as Timely Communicators.   As part of its support of its customer's JIT system, a supplier must help to maintain on-going communication between the organizations. Well-timed communication helps the buyer coordinate supplier shipments with the needs of its OM system. Ultimately, routine contacts should act as a form of Kanban or pull scheduling system. This flow of information should also cover current and future production schedules, product designs and changes, and perceived problems.

Suppliers as Participants in Cost Reduction Programs.   Many just-in-time manufacturers insist, often through contract provisions, that suppliers work continuously to reduce the costs of the goods and services that they deliver. They expect suppliers to apply the JIT tools and techniques described in this section to improve their own internal processes. In particular, they expected suppliers to distinguish activities that contribute to value from those that do not. To help suppliers to achieve cost-reduction goals, JIT manufacturers usually follow several guidelines for their supplier relations.

Long-Term Contracts.   A JIT buyer may offer the security of a long-term contract as an incentive for the supplier to make the long-term changes necessary for an effective JIT relationship. This commitment assures the supplier that future orders will reward its efforts.

Narrow Supplier Bases.   A JIT manufacturer may offer to buy more input from fewer suppliers as another incentive for cooperation. Besides encouraging willing suppliers, a narrower supplier base brings definite cost savings.[22] It also gives the buyer more influence over suppliers' decisions because they rely on it for larger shares of their business. This increase in business reinforces the suppliers' incentives to keep control over their processes and reduce costs. Finally, a firm can develop closer ties with fewer suppliers and maintain more frequent communications.

Stable Production Plans.   As part of its contribution to a stable relationship, the buyer must commit to stable production plans. Avoiding large, last-minute changes helps to keep requirements on suppliers reasonable.

Partnerships with suppliers develop a strong mutual interdependence between both organizations. Each depends on the other to do its job well. This helps the buyer by gathering inputs from financially sound suppliers with well-developed and carefully managed processes. This interdependence also helps suppliers by ensuring relationships with dependable customers that provide valuable schedule information, work cooperatively, and respect the expertise of the suppliers.

Kaizen/Continuous Improvement

As discussed in Chapter 7, the Japanese discipline of *kaizen* unites everyone within the organization from top managers and operations managers to operating workers in pursuit of the goal of ongoing improvement.[23] This concept reinforces the emphasis in just-in-time manufacturing on continuing activity to add value to the transformation process and reduce waste. Together, these principles try to inspire

[22]Keki R. Bhote, *Strategic Supply Management: A Blue Print for Revitalizing the Manufacturer-Supplier Partnership* (New York: American Management Association, 1989), pp. 45–55.

[23]Masaaki Imai, Kaizen: *The Key to Japan's Competitive Success* (New York: Random House, 1986), p. xxix.

everyone in the company to improve one aspect of the operations management system, major or minor, every day. At Caterpillar of Peoria, Illinois, for example, employees suggested dispensing soft drinks in cans rather than paper cups, since the cups were likely to split and create housekeeping problems and they were more difficult to carry, store, and use on the shop floor. Instead, workers could easily carry cans to their work stations and set them aside until they wanted a drink. The combined effects of even tiny changes result in large overall improvements.

CORPORATE IMPLICATIONS OF JUST-IN-TIME MANUFACTURING

A catalog of JIT methods may create the false impression that operations managers can implement self-contained just-in-time programs within their OM systems. If fact, such a program brings wide-ranging changes that make it a comprehensive corporate system. This system has startling implications, both for the firm as a whole and for individual functional areas.

Marketing

Just-in-time manufacturing makes valuable contributions to the firm's marketing effort, but it also imposes strict discipline. Marketers find the constant stream of low-cost, high-quality products delivered consistently on time to be highly attractive. Also, reductions in order lead times through JIT allow quick responses to market trends.

At the same time, marketing must recognize some concrete limits on the responsiveness of the JIT operations management system. JIT requires extremely stable short-term schedules. Once operations managers set monthly schedules and plan process activities and supplier inputs, they can make no changes until the next scheduling cycle. Marketing can no longer expect to honor customers' requests for last-minute changes and rush orders. Sales representatives and others must encourage customers to plan ahead and educate them about orders that the firm can and cannot accept. Marketers may even have to turn down orders or schedule changes that they know would disrupt the OM system's near-term schedules.

Marketers may also have to decide how to distribute available production among customers. For example, if customers order more of a certain product than the OM system will produce, the firm cannot supply everything that everyone wants. Marketers might decide to partially fill every order, or to fill certain orders completely and wait until the following month before filling the remaining orders. They may even decide not to accept the excess orders at all.

Just-in-time manufacturing can also affect product options that the firm offers. Such options allow buyers to customize products, but they also introduce variance to the OM system. The exact demand for specific options often defies predictions, with customers frequently requesting some options and only occasionally asking for others. Options also create a need for inventory, since the OM system can seldom make them available exactly when customers request them.

To see why, consider the potential options on a bicycle. A manufacturer can make a bike frame out of three types of steel, and it might offer 12 different paint schemes. The customer might choose among five saddles, four types of pedals, six types of wheels, and eight packages of shifting and braking components. Multiply the numbers of options to discover that an operations manager would have to manipulate 35,560 different combinations. A requirement to schedule production for so many combinations of options could derail any JIT program.

To solve the problem, JIT manufacturing might simply identify options with weak demand and drop them. Alternatively, the firm might group individual options together into packages. For example, a premium-performance package might include the firm's best saddle, a specific pedal type, a performance wheel set, and a choice between two packages of components rather than eight. To make the packages attractive to customers, the firm might offer price reductions on the packages as compared to purchasing options separately. As a third option, the firm might offer some options only as later modifications by bicycle dealers.

Just-in-time manufacturing might affect marketing in more profound ways by determining much about how the firm competes. While JIT can improve quality, lead time, cost, and reliability, it does sacrifice some short-term flexibility. In some markets, a firm may have to offer flexibility to really satisfy customers.

Product Engineering

To make JIT work effectively, engineers must provide accurate designs and specifications that the firm can build using existing capacity. Product designs should exploit any possible commonalities in processing methods or components. Common processing or component parts can reduce setups and promote the success of focused factories and group technology.

Whenever possible, engineers should avoid introducing unique parts or processes, which ultimately increase variance. Like marketing, product engineering must practice discipline under JIT manufacturing. This discipline challenges engineers' creativity to design new products that use existing processes and tools, often by drawing on previous product designs. Engineers must work closely with operations managers through design teams and concurrent engineering.

Human Resource Management

Just-in-time manufacturing depends heavily on human contributions for its success. Therefore, it has powerful implications for recruitment and selection, training, and performance evaluation and compensation.

Recruitment and Selection. The JIT environment suits curious, self-motivated employees who want to improve operations. It relies on constant questions about why a system works like it does and why it does not work better. Recruiters should look for employees who want interesting, proactive roles. Workers should know how to identify and solve problems, work effectively with others in teams, and learn new skills quickly.

Not every applicant can offer these traits, so the human resource management function must attract the right applicants and then choose carefully among them. Education is one indicator of an employee's abilities to learn new skills quickly and to solve problems effectively. In general, a higher level of education indicates that an applicant will likely learn quickly and solve problems effectively. As a result, just-in-time manufacturing systems tend to have above-average numbers of college-educated employees.

After recruiting suitable applicants, the human resource management function must rigorously screen and evaluate them. Rather than simply interviewing candidates and hiring the one who seems best, JIT systems require extensive testing to answer some critical questions:

- Can the person add structure to an unstructured problem and then solve it?
- Can the person work well in a group?
- How quickly can the person learn to carry out certain tasks?
- Can the person identify examples of waste?
- How does the person respond to a potential problem that no one else seems to notice?

This testing can range from laboratory experiments to classroom simulations. The process is time-consuming, perhaps occupying from 3 to 8 days.

Training.   Many American firms offer training only when a new employee enters the company or when a current employee changes jobs or assumes new tasks. Training also tends to focus specifically on individual tasks. JIT requires training in the tools and process of problem solving, including statistical process control charts, cause-and-effect diagrams, Pareto analysis, and process flow analysis. Furthermore, this training tends to continue as long as the employee keeps working in the system. For example, Japanese auto assembly plants located in the United States give new employees, on average, 370 hours or just over 9 weeks of training. In contrast, the average American auto maker gives each new employee about 46 hours of training. Until recently, Saturn, one of a few exceptions, gave its employees about 350 hours of training.

Performance Evaluation.   JIT systems cannot evaluate employees simply on such measures as number of hours spent per job, cost variance data, or numbers of good parts produced. A JIT system requires employees to perform effectively housekeeping duties and safety monitoring; they must master different skills and identify and solve problems that they encounter on the job. To judge this kind of performance, a JIT manufacturer needs a new, more comprehensive set of performance measures. Exhibit 9.14 provides an example of one such evaluation form currently in use in an American just-in-time manufacturing system.

Because they need to reward teamwork, JIT systems tend to replace individual performance measures such as piece-rate systems with rewards for entire teams. For these and other reasons, a JIT system imposes unusual demands on employees, so it must manage them in unusual ways.

Cost Accounting

Like other organizational practices, cost accounting procedures must change to accommodate the new realities under JIT. For one change, cost standards must deemphasize the distinction between direct labor and total labor. JIT blurs the distinction between direct and indirect labor, as when machine operators (direct labor) take over many housekeeping tasks previously assigned to indirect labor. Many JIT manufacturers may decide to follow Hewlett-Packard's lead and drop the division between direct and indirect labor from their cost reports in favor of a single cost category—labor.

In fact, JIT reduces the importance of direct labor as a component of cost. In many firms, labor now accounts for less than 5 percent of total costs, creating a problem for traditional cost accounting systems that allocate overhead costs in

[**E X H I B I T   9 . 1 4**]

Performance Appraisal Form for a Factory Position

Evaluation Form

Name _____   Time in Position _____

Job Description _____

Supervisor _____

	Rating	Comments
Employee's Results		
A. Quality of Work		
B. Quantity of Work		
C. Makes Work-Related Decisions with Minimum Supervision		
D. Safety		
E. Housekeeping		
Job Knowledge		
A. Knowledge of Job and Skills		
B. Versatility		
Diligence		
A. Start and End of Shift		
B. Attendance		
C. Length of Breaks		
Contribution to Team		
A. Contribution to Team Objectives		
B. Willingness to Express Ideas, Innovate		

Trend

Has Employee Improved His/Her Performance since the Last Appraisal?

Same ☐   Better ☐   Worse ☐

Supervisor's remarks _____

Interview date _____

Employee's comments and suggestions _____

Signatures

Supervisor _____

Business Leader _____

Employee _____

Rating Criteria

Marginal: Provisional, below acceptable

Competent: Fully trained and experienced

Commendable: Exceeds in time, quality, or scope many, if not all, major job requirements

SOURCE   Reprinted with the permission of APICS, Inc., from James Fishbein, "Performance Appraisal in a JIT Plant," *APICS 33d Conference Proceedings*, New Orleans, La., October 8–12, 1990, p. 355.

[**EXHIBIT 9.15**]

Single Plant-to-Plant Logistics Routes

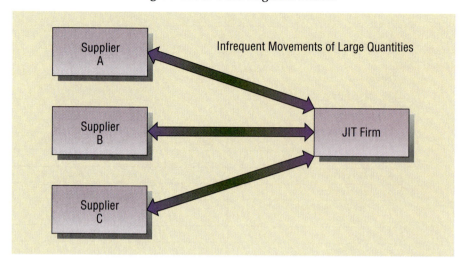

proportion to labor requirements. The decreased importance of direct labor has also reduced the need for detailed labor-cost reports, which most cost accounting systems still produce.

Finally, JIT systems have pushed firms away from standard costing and toward other methods of costing. The search for new cost drivers has encouraged firms to look at new methods of accounting for costs and allocating overhead. For example, activity-based costing (ABC) tries to identify the most appropriate cost drivers on which to base assignment of costs to particular activities, and then it assigns the costs of the activities to products that emerge from those activities. (ABC costs are discussed in Chapter 3.) An alternative to ABC, throughput costing, assigns overhead on the basis of the time a product spends in the process; a product that takes longer to pass through the system must carry a greater share of total overhead.[24]

Logistics

Many traditional OM systems organize transportation links between buyers and suppliers as series of single plant-to-plant routes (Exhibit 9.15). The supplier produces enough output to fill a truck or a railway car (because full shipments reduce shipping costs) and sends the shipment to the buyer. At the buyer's plant, the load waits at a shipping dock until an inspector verifies acceptable amounts and quality levels. The inputs then move to inventory stores, which act as buffers for infrequent movements of large quantities between supplier and buyer.

JIT practitioners see enormous waste in these logistical arrangements. They prefer frequent deliveries of small quantities directly to work stations without complicated shipping and receiving procedures. Therefore, they must rethink the logistics network. Instead of moving each supplier's output on a separate truck, they move goods from several suppliers on a single truck that makes frequent, regular trips. The truck picks up a partial load at one supplier's facility and then

---

[24]Brian H. Maskell, *Performance Measurement for World Class Manufacturing* (Cambridge, Mass.: Productivity Press, 1991), Chapter 12.

[**EXHIBIT 9.16**]

Mixed-Load, Multiple-Plant Transportation

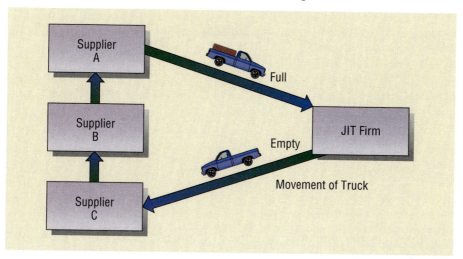

moves on to the next. By the time it picks up all of the loads on its route, the truck can return with a full load. This system, known as either **mixed-load, multiple-plant transportation** or the **milk-run system**, makes frequent deliveries of small quantities from several suppliers (Exhibit 9.16).[25] In this way, it keeps inventories low, since the truck moves only enough inputs to satisfy the immediate needs of the JIT system.

Other logistical changes include sending trucks past traditional receiving docks straight to the production line. Workers immediately take inputs from trusted, perhaps certified, suppliers for use in production. These inputs bypass storage areas, drastically reducing material inventories. Even the truck designs show the influence of JIT manufacturing. Loading trailers only from the rear is a very inefficient practice. JIT system trailers have been redesigned to allow access from the sides to make loading and unloading quick and flexible.

Finally, because JIT systems suffer serious disruption from late deliveries and missed shipments, the ability to track orders in transit becomes important. Increasingly, shipping companies are outfitting their trucks and railroad cars with tracking devices such as global positioning systems (GPS) or cellular phones that allow JIT buyers to determine immediately the status and location of any shipment.

mixed-load, multiple-plant transportation (milk-run system)
A JIT logistical system based on frequent, regular transportation of partial loads from many suppliers

Corporate Strategy

The earlier sections have hinted at a close, two-way link between JIT manufacturing and corporate strategy. Initially, corporate strategy triggers a firm's movement to just-in-time manufacturing in an effort to eliminate waste and enhance value for customers. These views of value and waste influence the specific tools and techniques that organization members use during the implementation of JIT. However, as implementation proceeds and managers and employees gain experi-

[25]The name *milk run* comes from practices in the dairy industry. Once every day, a tanker truck visits all of the farms on its route. At each stop, it picks up a partial load of milk and then returns to the dairy plant with a full load at the end of the route.

[**EXHIBIT 9.17**]

Link between JIT and Corporate Strategy

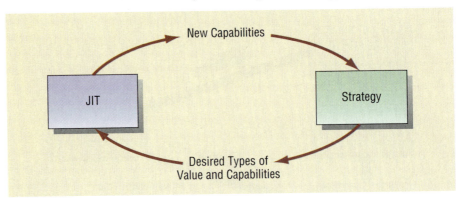

ence with it, they develop or uncover new capabilities of the firm. These capabilities may affect how top managers decide to compete in the marketplace, giving the JIT system a strong influence on corporate strategy (Exhibit 9.17).

LIMITS TO JUST-IN-TIME MANUFACTURING

Any organization can implement what we might call Big JIT. Small and large firms, manufacturers, and service providers can develop organizationwide systems aimed at identifying and eliminating waste and enhancing value for customers. All must foster certain conditions, however, to make organizationwide JIT work effectively. First, everyone in the system must understand clearly what constitutes value and waste.

Next, the firm must build trust between management and operating employees to allow effective sharing of decision-making power. Workers must see JIT as a way to enhance the firm's ability to compete rather than simply as a management ploy to increase their work loads and burdens of responsibility. On the other hand, managers must trust employees' decision-making abilities to honor their choices and challenge only obviously flawed decisions. The firm must also trust the decisions and product/process expertise of its suppliers. To build trust, everyone within the JIT system, both within and outside the firm, must recognize their mutual interdependencies.

Cooperation must accompany this trust. Employees must participate vigorously, for example, in any program to enhance quality at the source. They must cooperate in all JIT problem-identification and problem-solving efforts, a major commitment that some workers may not be willing to accept. Suppliers must cooperate to work with the firm as a partner and as a source of expertise.

In contrast with the wide applicability of Big JIT, the tools and techniques associated with Little JIT (i.e., setup reduction, group technology, mixed-model level scheduling, Kanban scheduling) apply only in more narrow circumstances, both on the shop floor and within the supply chain. In general, these tools suit products in the late growth to mature stages of the product life cycle most effectively. Exhibit 9.18 summarizes the applicability of JIT methods in the various stages of the product life cycle.

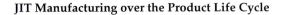

JIT Manufacturing over the Product Life Cycle

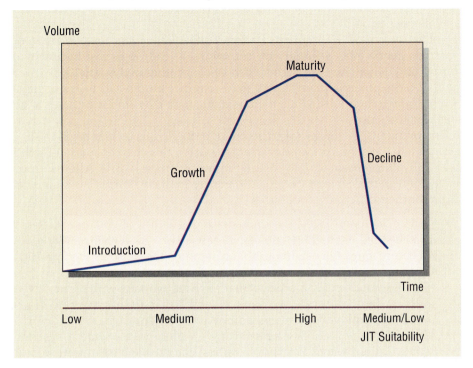

Stable product families facilitate the reorganization of functional layouts to define work cells. JIT methods do not require absolute stability with no change at all in product families. Over time, the systems can accommodate changes, dropping or modifying some parts and adding new ones. Planning for smooth production flows does require at least short-term stability, though.

JIT methods work most effectively for production at volumes in the medium to high range. Operations managers measure production volume by evaluating frequency, the number of units of an output that the system builds over time, and repetition, the number of units it builds per order. Many of the techniques of Little JIT, especially Kanban or pull scheduling, require rather high production volumes. Medium to high production volumes also give employees sufficient exposure to the products to flag sources of waste and develop changes to eliminate them.

Workers must be able to develop labor skills for JIT systems over relatively short periods. A just-in-time system relies heavily on flexible workers who can carry out many tasks. A custom furniture or cabinet-making shop would have trouble implementing JIT methods because each cabinet is unique and product quality depends on the skill of the cabinet maker more than anything else. Similarly, Steinway, the world's leading manufacturer of fine pianos, might encounter obstacles if it were to apply just-in-time techniques in its production. JIT systems cannot easily duplicate the effects of craftsmanship that workers develop over extended apprenticeships and long careers.

Compensation in a JIT system should center on salaries or time-based wages. Salary and straight time pay workers for attendance rather than output, so they do not distract from the goal of building what customers want when they want it.

Consider, for example, a worker in a piece-rate pay scheme who can earn more by producing more. Just-in-time manufacturing would control this worker's output and perhaps threaten his or her earnings. The worker may resist implementation of just-in-time manufacturing, fearing that it would take money out of her or his pocket.

Finally, successful JIT implementation requires that everyone perceive a need for change. People may willingly try something as radical as just-in-time manufacturing only when they see higher costs of continuing in the same way. A company that faces potential bankruptcy may convince employees to try something different to save their jobs, while a more stable firm may find it difficult to overcome the status quo.

The conditions for successful JIT manufacturing in this section begin to suggest a resolution to the paradox introduced at the start of this chapter. Harley-Davidson successfully implemented just-in-time manufacturing while Allen-Edmonds achieved only partial success. Several differences in the two firms' situations could account for their different experiences:

- Harley-Davidson faced the immediate possibility of collapse. Unless the firm changed its methods, managers saw a very good chance that it would fail before long. Allen-Edmonds faced no such threat, so its workers did not feel the same urgent need for change.
- Allen-Edmonds made a product that required workers with higher levels of skills. Allen-Edmonds workers resembled craftsmen, while Harley-Davidson employed mainly assembly-line workers.
- Allen-Edmonds paid workers through a piece-rate payment system. Its people did not want to support a radical change like just-in-time manufacturing that might reduce their take-home pay.

JUST-IN-TIME MANUFACTURING AND LEAN PRODUCTION

lean production

An organizationwide OM system orientation to design and develop higher value products while consuming fewer resources for both direct costs and overhead

While just-in-time manufacturing is a relatively new development in North America, recent research has suggested the potential for development of a new stage in the move toward waste control and elimination. Called **lean production** by Womack, Jones, and Roos, the idea for the new method grew out of a research project at the Massachusetts Institute of Technology (MIT) that compared OM systems of the auto industries in North America, Japan, and Europe.[26] This study identified a new category of performance that exceeded the goals set by JIT manufacturing. The first two columns in Exhibit 9.19 list performance data for lean production.

Lean producers made more output with less input than competitors. They consumed fewer resources to generate more value for customers. These firms needed less labor, less material, less energy, less time, less floor space, and less overhead. This last cost has become critical, since it represents the single largest component of cost for most firms.

[26]James P. Womack, Daniel T. Jones, and Daniel Roos, *The Machine That Changed the World* (New York: Rawson Associates, 1990).

[**EXHIBIT 9.19**]

Performance Characteristics for Lean Production

	Japanese in Japan	Japanese in North America	Americans in North America	All Europe
Performance				
Productivity (hrs/vehicle)	16.8	21.2	25.1	36.2
Quality (assembly defects/100 vehicles)	60.0	65.0	82.3	97.0
Layout				
Space (sq. ft./vehicle/yr.)	5.7	9.1	7.8	7.8
Size of repair areas (percentage of assembly space)	4.1	4.9	12.9	14.4
Inventories (days for eight sample parts)	0.2	1.6	2.9	2.0
Work Force				
Percentage of work force in teams	69.3	71.3	17.3	0.6
Job rotation (0 = none; 4= frequent)	3.0	2.7	0.9	1.9
Suggestions/employee	61.6	1.4	0.4	0.4
No. of job classes	11.9	8.7	67.1	14.8
Training of new production workers (hours)	380.3	370.0	46.4	173.3
Absenteeism	5.0	4.8	11.7	12.1
Automation				
Welding (percentage of direct steps)	86.2	85.0	76.2	76.6
Painting (percentage of direct steps)	54.6	40.7	33.6	38.2
Assembly (percentage of direct steps)	1.7	1.1	1.2	3.1

SOURCE   Reprinted with the permission of Rawson/Scribner, an imprint of Simon & Schuster from *The Machine That Changed the World*, p. 92, by James P. Womack, Daniel T. Jones, and Daniel Roos. Copyright 1990 James P. Womack, Daniel T. Jones, Daniel Roos, and Donna Sammons Carpenter.

Characteristics of Lean Production

Lean production builds three major traits into an OM system: aggressive efforts to satisfy customers, lean operations throughout the entire delivery system, and tight integration of resource networks.

Aggressive Customer Satisfaction Effort.   Once a lean producer earns a customer's business, it wants to keep that customer indefinitely. For example, Toyota collects extensive sets of data about its customers, their buying patterns, and their needs. The company works vigorously to anticipate customers' future needs and to build cars that will meet or exceed these needs as they emerge. The lean producer strives always to delight its customers.

Rather than building standard cars for large markets, the MIT study found that lean producers try to break down markets in smaller, more focused niches. Sharp images of cohesive groups of customers allow the firms to accurately describe those people's needs and to match their products closely to those needs. As a result, these firms have developed valuable reputations for sensitivity to customers, and

Just-in-Time Manufacturing to Support Lean Production

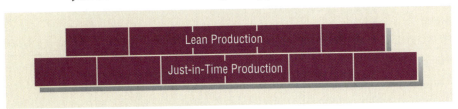

they have reinforced their market images by providing products faster and with higher quality levels than competitors. Their aggressive sales programs treat customers not as obstacles or objectives to capture but rather as partners in close, ongoing relationships for mutual satisfaction and growth.

Lean Operations throughout the Delivery System.   Lean producers attack the two major components of costs: variable or direct costs and overhead. Drawing heavily on JIT techniques and procedures, these firms focus all of their efforts on producing the outputs that customers want with the minimum possible direct costs for labor, materials, and tools. In this way, lean production builds on the foundation laid down by just-in-time manufacturing (Exhibit 9.20).

Lean producers also question the need for any activity that either creates overhead or is unnecessary. Through JIT techniques, they attack overhead costs for shipping, receiving, inspection, and rework. In this process, they recognize the limits of their own expertise and do not try to perform every activity necessary to build a product. For example, Chrysler contracted with outside suppliers to design and manufacture components such as seats and radios that lay outside the limits of its expertise, focusing its internal investments on areas critical to its success. This gave the firm the inputs it needed while trimming overhead required for their production from its cost structure.

As a result, lean production significantly affects the firm's break-even point in two ways: by increasing the contribution margin (the difference between the price that customers pay and the firm's direct costs) and by reducing its overhead costs. The contribution margin grows as the firm charges a higher price to deliver a better product faster while it reduces direct costs at the same time (Exhibit 9.21). Together, these changes drive the break-even point downward, enhancing the firm's flexibility. It can afford to produce smaller quantities, allowing niche marketing, and it can change outputs more quickly in response to changes in customer demand. Compared with mass producers with lower contribution margins and higher fixed costs, the lean producer seems quite agile, leading some to favor the term *agile competitor* over *lean producer.*

Tightly Integrated Network of Resources.   Like JIT manufacturers, lean producers find opportunities for improvement outside their own internal transformation processes. The managers of these firms try to coordinate all of the resources that contribute to the design, production, and delivery of products to their customers, both within the firm and outside it. They try to actively manage their networks of suppliers, distributors, shippers, and even customers as external resources. They work hard to integrate these inputs through extensive use of technology (e.g.,

[**EXHIBIT 9.21**]

Changes in Cost Structure under Lean Production

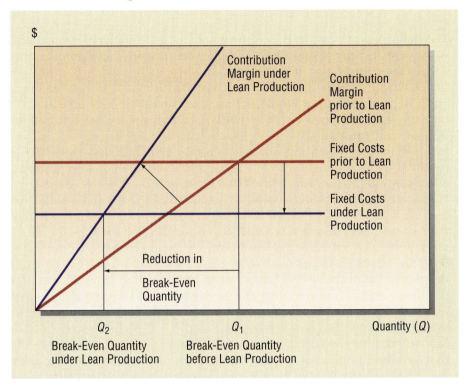

electronic data interchange, bar coding, and automated identification) and coordinating mechanisms such as simultaneous engineering or concurrent design.

Lean production creates a firm that consumes the minimum possible resources to produce the maximum possible value for customers. This organizationwide effort makes the term somewhat inaccurate since the firm seeks to move beyond a lean production system to develop a lean corporation.

CHAPTER SUMMARY

Despite its relatively recent emergence in North America, just-in-time manufacturing has now become an integral element of operations management. In this chapter, we have examined this set of principles and management tools and its prescriptions for a value-driven OM system:

1. Just-in-time manufacturing is a system that works continuously to identify, control, and eliminate all sources of waste within the firm. In a goal closely linked to waste reduction, JIT seeks to make the OM system more predictable by reducing variance at all levels of the firm.
2. Just-in-time manufacturing operates as an organizationwide system and as a set of analytical tools for operations managers. Corporate or Big JIT recognizes

many causes of waste, indicated by long lead times, high scrap rates, low quality, and frequent inspection. Some causes originate within the OM system, and many others come from outside. In contrast, Little JIT or shop-floor JIT deals with the analytical techniques and tools that managers use to achieve larger, strategic goals.

3. The definition of *waste* varies with customers' definitions of *value*. Because waste is related to value, each firm implements just-in-time manufacturing in a way that suits its specific customers.

4. In this chapter, we defined *just-in-time manufacturing* as an organizationwide quest to produce output within the minimum possible lead time and at the lowest possible total cost by continuously identifying and eliminating all forms of waste and variance.

5. Just-in-time manufacturing makes a central distinction between waste as a residual effect and its cause. Waste is a symptom of some process problem. To effectively eliminate waste, a firm must identify and correct its cause.

6. While most people associate just-in-time manufacturing with Japanese industrial firms, specifically Toyota, this system has two parents: Henry Ford and the American supermarket. Henry Ford helped develop the tools for JIT while the supermarket provided the vision of a continuous stream of desired products from suppliers to customers.

7. People play critical roles in the successful implementation of JIT, identifying problems and recommending and implementing improvements. In JIT, respect for people moves beyond a desirable attitude to become a necessity of life.

8. Just-in-time manufacturing continuously strives to achieve seven major objectives: produce only what customers want, produce products only at the rate that customers want them, produce with perfect quality, produce with minimum lead times, produce only the features that customers want, produce without wasting resources, and produce with methods that support people's development.

9. To achieve these seven objectives, just-in-time manufacturing draws on a number of tools and techniques: Kanban or pull scheduling; level, mixed-model scheduling; setup reduction; total productive maintenance; poka-yoke (fool-proofing); quality at the source; flexible, cross-trained workers; group technology; focused factories; statistical process control; standardization; supplier partnerships; and *kaizen* or continuous improvement.

10. Just-in-time manufacturing becomes an organizationwide system because its implementation affects operations of functions throughout the firm, including marketing, product engineering, human resource management, cost accounting, logistics, and corporate strategy.

11. Any firm can implement just-in-time principles to reduce waste and variance, including manufacturers and service providers of all sizes. However, the tools and techniques of Little JIT work best in environments characterized by trust, cooperation, common understandings of value and waste, stable product families, time-based compensation systems, and clear recognition of needs for change.

12. Just-in-time manufacturing can be viewed as a step in the evolution of operations management toward the principles of lean production, an organizationwide system that links all operations even more closely to the concepts of value and waste.

[KEY TERMS]

just-in-time manufacturing 386

Big JIT 401

Little JIT 401

Kanban 402

withdrawal Kanban 402

production Kanban 402

master production schedule 405

load leveling 405

cycle time 406

mixed-model scheduling 406

single-minute exchange of dies 410

internal setup 411

external setup 411

poka-yoke 411

quality at the source 412

group technology 415

simplification 418

standardization 418

supplier certification 420

mixed-load, multiple-plant transportation (milk-run system) 427

lean production 430

total productive maintenance 439

[DISCUSSION QUESTIONS]

1. What parts of the American food distribution systems inspired the Japanese to develop just-in-time manufacturing?

2. Describe the two major things that Taichi Ohno saw at Ford's huge car manufacturing complex that led, in part, to the development of the Toyota just-in-time manufacturing system. Why were these two things unacceptable to the Japanese? Why had American manufacturers so willingly accepted them?

3. Explain what you think are the underlying principles of JIT.

4. Exhibit 9.2 uses the analogy of a boat hitting rocks as the level of water falls. Why is water a good analogy for inventory? Is the sequence in which rocks are encountered a good way to prioritize inventory reduction activities? How might this prioritization scheme differ from one used in an accounting department?

5. Why is achievement of the following goals critical to the success of JIT?
   a. Setup time and cost reduction
   b. A relatively stable shop load
   c. Employee empowerment
   d. Statistical quality control
   Give an example of how each area contributes to the success of a JIT program.

6. Is it possible to apply JIT to service organizations? Cite instances of organizations applying JIT elements.

7. Why is the concept of waste such an important part of the JIT philosophy?

8. You work in the marketing department of a firm that sells mountain bicycles and related gear. Its manufacturing division has decided to wholeheartedly adopt the JIT philosophy. Will this affect your ability to delight your customers? Make a list of the potential pluses and minuses of this JIT decision.

9. Your boss asks you how many kanban cards each location within your plant needs. What factors should go into your answer? Create a formula to answer this question.

10. How does the concept of system variance impact your ability to drive inventory out of a plant when a JIT approach has been adopted? Create an electronic spreadsheet model to show how a reduction in demand variance impacts inventory in a two-stage manufacturing process.

11. Discuss how JIT might apply to a fast-food hamburger stand. How will it have to be modified to deal with daily demand variation?

12. Discuss how lead time reduction impacts a Kanban system.

CAUTION

[CRITICAL THINKING REQUIRED]

1. Can the JIT approach enhance a worker's quality of life? Discuss how it might or might not.
2. How could you apply JIT principals and practices to product design?

CASE 9.1

Good Guy Hospital $upply

Good Guy Hospital $upply (GGH$) was founded in the 1960s to serve the hospital and nursing home industry. Over the past 35 years, its sales have grown an average 26 percent per year, through both geographical expansion and increased existing-market penetration. Key to GGH$'s success is service. It prides itself that it is able to fill 99.4 percent of all requests within 24 hours and many requests actually are delivered more quickly.

In 1996, GGH$'s quality service coordinator developed a plan to improve service levels. The new system uses a just-in-time approach to the medical supply needs of GGH$'s clients.

GGH$'s clients had been using personal computers in their hospital medical supply stockrooms to place GGH$ orders. While these clients could still purchase from other supply houses, the GGH$ order entry system made it much easier for the clerical staff to place an order with GGH$.

The new JIT plan, however, eliminates supplies going through GGH$'s clients' medical supply stockroom. Now the medical facility's staff and GGH$ would determine the type and desired level of supplies at each stocking point. GGH$ plans to place supplies at each of these stocking points; and a GGH$ sales representative will tour the medical facility, identify items that have been used, and immediately restock them using inventory in the sales representative's van. Using barcoded stock and a mobile sales register, GGH$ will give the hospital a detailed invoice for the items consumed each day. These reports will be designed to support each facility's medical cost control system.

GGH$'s quality service coordinator argues that the increased distribution costs of this proposed system will be offset by increased product and service pricing and by the increased share of each hospital's business, and GGH$ will become the vendor of choice for all items covered by its system. She argues that the hospitals will find this system attractive because it will greatly reduce their costs for stocking, ordering, and distributing medical supplies within the medical facility.

QUESTIONS

1. Is Good Guy's plan an appropriate application of JIT? Why or why not?
2. Identify each of the stakeholders in this situation. What will each give up and get if the proposed system is accepted by GGH$'s clients?

CASE 9.2

Roboworks, Inc.

An engineering student at MIT, Roberta Reese created an all-purpose household robot for her senior project. Her project attracted a venture capitalist's interest.

The initial product line included three battery-powered robots code-named Red, Blue, and Yellow. Red uses vacuum technology to clean carpets and dust shelves. Blue uses water-jet technology to clean dishes, toilet bowls, bath tubs, and the like. Yellow can do Red's work and Blue's work.

The material used for these three models is shown below.

Red

A. Vacuum system
   Sensing System
   Vacuum kit
B. Mobile platform R
   Wheel Set
   R Batteries

Blue

A. Cleaning system
   Sensing system
   Washer/Dryer kit
B. Mobile platform B
   Wheel set
   B Batteries

Yellow

A. Vacuum system
   Sensing System
   Vacuum kit
B. Cleaning system
   Sensing system
   Washer/Dryer kit
C. Mobile platform C
   Wheel set
   R Batteries
   B Batteries

Reese has hired Taiichi O'Brien as the production manager to design the production system. O'Brien has extensive experience with just-in-time manufacturing. JIT appeals to Reese because she has limited capital. Taiichi decided on a two-stage system. The cleaning, vacuum, and mobile platforms would be assembled in the first stage. The second stage consists of the final assembly and testing.

O'Brien sets up the following manufacturing floor plan:

Finished Goods	Subassembly Units	Raw Materials
Red	Vacuum systems	Vacuum kit
	Cleaning systems	Cleaning kit
		R-Base
Blue	Red base	B-Base
		Wheels
	Blue base	R-Batteries
Yellow	Yellow base	B-Batteries

Production moves from raw materials through the subassembly department to finished goods. Reese estimates the daily demand for each product to have the following distributions:

Red	Discrete Uniform	Range: 1 thru 6
Blue	Discrete Uniform	Range: 1 thru 6
Yellow	Unsure	

Yellow has a strange distribution demand. Reese estimates demand for Yellow as the difference between the demand for Red and Blue—the demand for Yellow is the larger of the demands for Red and Blue minus the smaller of the demands for Red and Blue.

O'Brien needs to determine the number of kanban cards for each stocking point. Given the plant's ample capacity, both the finished goods and the subassembly unit departments can live with a one-day lead time. Reese's suppliers all demand 5 days to deliver goods (goods ordered on day 1 are delivered at the start of day 6). Vacuum and cleaning kits can be ordered individually, whereas all other products must be ordered in quantities of 10.

QUESTION

How many kanban cards does Roboworks need to avoid stockouts?

[S E L E C T E D   R E A D I N G S   ]

Abegglen, James C., and George Stalk, Jr. *Kaisha: The Japanese Corporation.* New York: Basic Books, 1985.

Bhote, Keki R. *Strategic Supply Management: A Blue Print for Revitalizing the Manufacturer-Supplier Partnership.* New York: American Management Association, 1989.

Ford, Henry. *Today and Tomorrow.* Cambridge, Mass.: Productivity Press, 1989.

Gardner, James A. *Common Sense Manufacturing.* Homewood, Ill.: Business One-Irwin, 1992.

Grieco, Peter L., Michael W. Gozzo, and Jerry W. Claunch. *Just-in-Time Purchasing: In Pursuit of Excellence.* Plantsville, Conn.: PT Publications, 1988.

Hall, Robert W. *Zero Inventories,* Homewood, Ill.: Dow Jones-Irwin, 1983.

Imai, Masaaki. Kaizen: *The Key to Japan's Competitive Success.* New York: Random House, 1986.

Keane, Patrick T. "Harley-Davidson Motor Company: Material as Needed (MAN) and Manufacturing Revitalization," in *Just-in-Time, Not Just in Japan,* ed. by Mehran Sepehri. Falls Church, Va.: American Production and Inventory Control Society, 1986, pp. 151–174.

Keane, Patrick T., and James P. King. *Failing in the Factory: A Shop Floor Perspective on Correcting America's Misunderstanding and Misuse of Just-in-Time.* Wilton, Conn.: Brown House Communications, 1990.

Maskell, Brian H. *Performance Measurement for World Class Manufacturing.* Cambridge, Mass.: Productivity Press, 1991.

Monden, Yasuhiro. *Toyota Production System.* Norcross, Ga.: Industrial Engineering and Management Press, 1983.

Nakajima, Seiichi. *TPM: Introduction to TPM, Total Productive Maintenance.* Cambridge, Mass.: Productivity Press, 1988.

Shingo, Shigeo. *A Revolution in Manufacturing: The SMED System.* Cambridge, Mass.: Productivity Press, 1985.

Sugimori, Y., K. Kusunoki, F. Cho, and S. Uchikawa. "Toyota Production System and Kanban System—Materialization of Just-in-Time and Respect-for-Human System." *International Journal of Production Research* 15, no. 6 (1977), pp. 553–564.

Suzaki, Kiyoshi. *The New Manufacturing Challenge: Techniques for Continuous Improvement.* New York: Free Press, 1987.

Wantuck, Kenneth A. *Just-in-Time for America: A Common Sense Production Strategy.* Southfield, Mich.: KWA Media, 1989.

Womack, James P., Daniel T. Jones, and Daniel Roos. *The Machine that Changed the World.* New York: Rawson Associates, 1990.

APPENDIX 9A

Total Productive Maintenance

At any point in time, equipment may break down, potentially seriously disrupting a firm's entire operations. In the early 1980s, for example, Chrysler was struggling even to survive with an equipment uptime ratio of 36 percent, although managers like Richard Dauch pointed out that the company was paying for 100 percent of the equipment.[27] In other words, workers could use the equipment to produce output only 36 percent of the time; breakdowns, maintenance, and readjustments occupied the rest of the time.

Breakdowns contribute to variance within an OM system, disrupting carefully planned JIT relationships. They also contribute to six major types of losses:[28]

1. Downtime due to equipment failure
2. Downtime for setups and adjustments such as exchanges of dies in injection molding machines, etc.
3. Speed losses due to idling and minor stoppages caused by abnormal operations of sensors, blockages, etc.
4. Speed losses due to discrepancies between designed and actual speeds of equipment
5. Defect losses due to process defects that cause scrap and quality problems
6. Defect losses due to reduced yields in the time between machine startup and stable production

Total productive maintenance (TPM) is a JIT method designed to eliminate these six forms of loss by identifying and attacking all causes of equipment breakdowns and system downtime.

Originally developed in Japan, TPM can viewed as the latest development in the evolution of maintenance methods. This sequence began with corrective maintenance, which followed some simple advice: if it ain't broke, don't fix it. A corrective maintenance system performs no maintenance on any piece of equipment if it can run without attention. Once equipment breaks, someone comes to repair it. This casual attitude exposes an OM system to extreme uncertainty and risk because no one knows when or where equipment will break down. To protect against disruption, operations managers must rely on redundant equipment to provide excess capacity or flexible, multipurpose machines to keep production moving during repairs.

Preventive maintenance, the next step in the evolution of maintenance techniques, assumes a more proactive stance, establishing maintenance routines to take care of equipment. Maintenance workers regularly oil and clean equipment and perform other periodic maintenance. Car owners perform preventive maintenance by changing the oil every 3 months or 3,000 miles. While preventive maintenance improved reliability as compared to corrective maintenance, it ignored many causes of breakdowns in equipment.

Productive maintenance, or predictive maintenance, extended preventive maintenance to try to reduce the chances of breakdowns through modern monitoring and analysis techniques such as computer-aided monitoring and forecasting

total productive maintenance

A JIT method designed to identify and attack all causes of equipment breakdowns and system downtime

---

[27]Richard E. Dauch, *Passion for Excellence* (Homewood, Ill.: Business One-Irwin, 1993), p. 176.

[28]Seiichi Nakajima, *TPM: Introduction to TPM, Total Productive Maintenance* (Cambridge, Mass.: Productivity Press, 1988), p. 14.

that diagnoses the condition of equipment during operation. In using these techniques, productive maintenance tries to identify signs of equipment deterioration or imminent failure and to take corrective action before actual equipment failure.

TPM, the fourth stage in the evolution of maintenance techniques, works much more broadly to identify and correct all potential causes of breakdowns to achieve an ambitious goal of zero breakdowns. Five principles guide TPM programs:[29]

1. Maximize equipment effectiveness (i.e., reduce downtime to zero).
2. Establish a thorough system of preventive maintenance for the entire life span of equipment, from design and acquisition to disposition.
3. Implement maintenance programs in all organizational areas (engineering, operations, facility management, maintenance) to spread TPM throughout the system.
4. Involve every single member of the organization, from top managers to workers on the shop floor.
5. Assign responsibility for preventive maintenance to small, autonomous groups of employees rather than managers.

Like JIT, TPM grew from North American roots. People in the trucking industry noticed that drivers who had responsibility for maintaining their own trucks, especially owner-operators, posted better uptime records than drivers who followed maintenance schedules for procedures carried out by maintenance centers. Drivers who owned their own trucks, it seemed, recognized the link between their incomes and the availability of the trucks. This gave them built-in incentives to keep the trucks in top operating condition.

TPM is a comprehensive system of equipment maintenance that encompasses all activities with any influence on equipment uptime:[30]

1. *Regulating basic conditions*   TPM advocates keeping a well-organized shop floor. A Japanese term translates as *parlor factory,* suggesting that an entire shop should be so clean that workers feel they should walk around in stocking feet to avoid making messes.
2. *Adhering to proper operating procedures*   The most significant cause of chance breakdowns is a failure to follow proper operating procedures. When operators deviate from procedures, they introduce errors and variance into the process.
3. *Restoring deterioration*   TPM requires diligent effort to discover and predict deterioration in equipment and then to follow standard repair methods designed to eliminate any sources of variation in the system.
4. *Improving weaknesses in design*   TPM tries to identify and correct any defects in equipment designs that contribute to breakdowns or complicate maintenance. This feature is evident in modern computers by several manufacturers that produce modular designs. When a part breaks down, the computer shows a code to indicate the location of the problem. The user reports the code through a toll-free telephone support line, and a company representative identifies the defective part and sends a new one along with instructions for replacing it. The user need not resort to specialized service people or repair facilities.

[29]Ibid., p. 10.
[30]Ibid., p.40.

5. *Improving operation and maintenance skills*   Equipment users contribute to TPM by learning and following correct operating procedures to prevent errors that may cause chance breakdowns. Also, sharp skills help to prevent repair errors and correct any problems on the first try. TPM enhances the skills of both users and maintenance workers through education and training.

Through these activities, TPM attacks variance and waste created by breakdowns by preventing problems and eliminating causes of defects.

C H A P T E R   T E N

Demand Management and Demand Forecasting

C H A P T E R   O U T L I N E

TAKING IT IN THE SHORTS

Demand Management in Operations Management

Demand Management

Demand Management in Service Organizations • Demand Management in Manufacturing Organizations • Demand Management and Product Development • Market Information Systems for Demand Management

Demand Forecasting

Five-Step Demand Forecasting Process • Forecasting as a Process • Qualitative Demand Forecasts • Quantitative Forecasting

Demand Tracking

Naive Forecasts • Weighted Averages • Exponential Smoothing • Adaptive Forecasting • Forecast Error

Understanding Final-Product Demand and Demand for Components

CHAPTER SUMMARY

Case 10.1 HAPPINESS EXPRESS

On the Job COMPAQ'S CRYSTAL BALL

On the Job MOTHERS WORK QUICK STEP

By the Way… GOVERNMENT AS RECORD KEEPER

Appendix 10A FORECASTING LEARNING LAB

C H A P T E R   O B J E C T I V E S

[At the end of this chapter, you should be able to]

- Explain the role of demand management in an OM system and the larger organization.
- Describe differences in managing demand for service providers and manufacturers.
- Discuss methods of qualitative demand forecasting.
- Show how managers derive meaning from time-series data through quantitative forecasts, including adjustments for seasonal variations.
- Apply several common demand-tracking models, including naive forecasting, weighted averages, exponential smoothing, and adaptive forecasting.
- Demonstrate methods to measure and correct forecasting error.
- Relate demand for a finished product to component demand.

Scott R. Goodwin, Inc.

Taking It in the Shorts

THE FRUIT OF THE LOOM CORPOR-ation is blessed with the best known brand in America. Lately, howev-er, they seem to have some problems. Late in 1993, they misread the market demand for their end products. Demand turned out to be sub-stantially lower than anticipated. Their inventories ballooned. In response, they significantly cut back their planned production for the 1994 season.

Demand during the first half of 1994 turned out to be substantially more than Fruit of the Loom management had projected. While they scrambled to get more raw materials from their suppliers, their inven-tories began to run out. Fruit's management estimated that they lost $20 million in sales so far in 1994.

Fruit of the Loom's woes in 1994 were not unique. IBM seemingly guessed wrong with some of its Thinkpad sub-compacts. It ended up selling a large number of them on Home Shopping Channel for $800, which was close to cost. In the summer of 1995, Apple Computer had a similar problem because it apparently underestimated the demand for its PowerPC computer models. As a consequence, its PowerPC chip supplier was unable to make sufficient quantities to meet demand. This in turn meant that it could not introduce a lower-cost model as planned to compete with Pentium chip computers selling for less than $2000.

SOURCE
Susan Chandler,
Business Week,
issue 3375, June 6,
1994, p. 38.

Supply limitations were also slowing down the introduction of Radius's Macintosh clone models, thereby reducing the customer base that software developers wanted to support Macintosh system application software.

All for the want of a decent forecast!

Forecasting problems are not unique to business. In 1948, the *Chicago Tribune,* which proclaimed itself the "world's greatest newspaper," sought to gain a competitive advantage by conducting a telephone survey to predict the outcome of the presidential election. Based on those results, the paper's editors ran an election-day special edition proclaiming "Dewey Wins." When a final count of votes revealed that Democrat Harry Truman won the election over Republican Thomas E. Dewey, the misfortune of the *Tribune* taught the world a graphic lesson about the dangers of basing forecasts on inaccurate information. The survey's sampling plan ignored the bias introduced by telephone polling when more Republicans than Democrats owned telephones.

Such bitter experience can flavor events years later. For the 1952 election, CBS engaged the ENIAC, one of the first electronic computers, to help it predict the winner of the first Eisenhower-Stevenson contest. Within 30 minutes after the final polls closed, this early-day mainframe computer spit out a prediction that Eisenhower would win by an electoral vote landslide. This information proved accurate, giving CBS a distinct advantage over its competitors, but no one in charge was willing to risk believing it after the *Chicago Tribune* debacle. Thus, CBS failed to exploit its competitive advantage over rival networks.

A business firm can better serve its customers by learning what its customers want and then designing and delivering a good or service that meets those needs. The first step in this process requires operations managers to forecast demand. Accurate forecasts tell the firm what products customers will demand in some future time period, how many units of those products customers will want, and when they will expect delivery. The basic understanding of demand forecasting methods developed in this chapter will provide the basis for later discussions of product and process development and more detailed production planning. This chapter's coverage begins with a discussion of the differences among the operations manager's tools to measure and influence customer demand: demand management, demand forecasting, and demand tracking.

DEMAND MANAGEMENT IN OPERATIONS MANAGEMENT

Rather than simply reacting to emerging market desires, both business executives and politicians would prefer to manipulate demand. Business organizations routinely try to achieve this goal through effective marketing. An operations management business process to achieve some influence over customer demand is **demand management**. Operations managers first seek to discover product characteristics that drive customer demand. With this knowledge, they can explore

demand management

An operations management initiative to achieve some influence over customer demand ways to influence the timing pattern of demand by certain customers to benefit both them and the producing firm.

Demand management seeks to control demand in two ways. First, it tries to influence the pattern of customer orders, as when JIT firms seek to level the work loads on their OM systems. Second, it tries to reduce the uncertainty of its demand pattern. Ideally, operations managers would prefer constant, fully predictable demand. If they cannot make actual demand conform to this rigid requirement, however, they can still do their jobs more effectively if they know with reasonable certainty what pattern customer orders will display.

If they cannot actively manage demand, then operations managers work toward their next most desirable alternative—to accurately predict it. The **demand forecasting** process tries to develop a reliable statement about the amounts, timing, and pattern of future customer orders. A successful demand forecast provides an organization's decision makers with timely, reasonably accurate information. The value of a forecast depends on how effectively it supports management decisions.

Demand forecasting relies on either intrinsic or extrinsic inputs. Forecasts based on **intrinsic inputs** predict future events based on the past, as when a ballpark concessionaire evaluates past hot dog sales to predict sales for a future game. **Extrinsic inputs** represent conditions independent of the OM system's activities that affect customer demand. The hot dog vendor might adjust a demand forecast based on the predicted temperature and attendance for an upcoming game.

Even if we cannot effectively forecast demand, it still is helpful to track demand. Knowing what has happened is valuable if the firm can make a quick response. Knowing what just has happened may also be valuable input to the learning process—it provides fresh data to discover factors that influence customer behavior.

If uncertainty about intrinsic or extrinsic inputs prevents operations managers from developing demand forecasts that they can present with confidence, they may try to gain more insight through demand tracking. Systematic evaluation of past trends and patterns in customer orders may provide valuable input for management decisions if the firm keeps lead times short enough so that it can respond quickly to emerging information. Demand tracking may also help operations managers to accumulate knowledge that gives insight into customer behavior.

Exhibit 10.1 summarizes the management contributions of demand management, demand forecasting, and demand tracking. The exhibit divides tracking activities between finished-product demand and demand for materials or components. It describes the customers for resource-demand information as "materials planners," referring to organization members responsible for either production or purchasing of tangible inputs that the OM system needs to produce a finished good or service. A manufacturer's transformation process needs parts and subassemblies that become part of its end product. Retailers and distributors need finished products of suppliers to replenish their stocks and sell to their customers. A service provider needs tangible goods to support its offering of an intangible product such as the Big Mac buns, clown balloons, and napkins.

In this chapter, we present the topics from Exhibit 10.1 in the same order. We start by covering proactive demand management and conclude with the most passive demand-tracking tools. The early sections of the chapter present mostly managerial concepts, while the later sections detail some common analytical tools. We conclude the chapter with a business forecasting laboratory designed to provide students with some hands-on experience manipulating demand information from hypothetical data.

demand forecasting

An effort to develop a reliable statement about the amounts, timing, and pattern of future customer orders

intrinsic input

Information that helps demand forecasters to predict future events based on the record of similar phenomena in the past

extrinsic input

Information about conditions independent of an OM system's activities that affect a forecast of customer demand

Demand Management, Demand Forecasting, and Demand Tracking

	Demand Management	Demand Forecasting	Demand Tracking	
			Finished-Product Demand	Resource Demand
Level of detail	Aggregate to unit	Aggregate to unit	Aggregate to component	Part or component
Planning horizon	Short to long	Short to long	Short	Short
Operations-level planning customers	Marketing and operations	Marketing and operations	Sales, planners, and management	Materials planners
Strategic planning use	Long-range resource planning	Mid-range to long-range planning	Plan feedback	Data for planning
Management posture	Proactive	Mostly reactive	Reactive	Reactive

DEMAND MANAGEMENT

Demand management is a business process that seeks to coordinate and influence all sources of demand for the firm's products to help operations managers target their system's resources efficiently to promote implementation of the firm's competitive strategy. Demand management requires coordination because people throughout the organization may be seeing only parts of the overall demand picture. Somewhere within the management structure, some process must develop a holistic image of the firm's product characteristics and the customer needs that drive them. Demand management must try to influence customer orders rather than control them. A firm with a scarce product may dictate to customers when they can get its good or service, but most firms must compete vigorously with rivals by treating consumers like the monarchs of commerce. Operations managers try to influence customer decisions by packaging product characteristics and options in ways that convince customers that the firm can most effectively satisfy their needs.

An operations management function should not blindly accept the passive role of receiving orders or other information about demand from either internal or external customers. Instead, active pursuit of demand information and education about process capabilities can influence the stream of work demanded of the OM system. This may help to enhance its efficiency and, quite possibly, its overall effectiveness. Of course, a narrow focus on efficiency risks failing to delight customers if the OM system produces the wrong products or features, however efficiently it works. The cartoon in Exhibit 10.2 hangs in almost every North American factory, displaying a common contempt between the sales department and the OM department, which must answer customer requests relayed by sales personnel to be effective. Demand management efforts can contribute to a better relationship and help to solve internal coordination problems that result when orders reach a plant in an unmanaged stream.

Firms must recognize the consequence of failure to manage the rate at which work demands reach the operations management function. Unregulated demand forces an OM system to sacrifice either efficiency or effectiveness in one of four ways:

Symptom of a Problem

1. By maintaining sufficient extra resources to expand and contract capacity to meet variable customer needs
2. By backlogging certain orders to buffer against demand fluctuations
3. By tolerating dissatisfaction of either internal or external customers with the system's delivery reliability
4. By buffering the system from demand fluctuations, either by stocking inventory or by permitting incoming orders to be backlogged.

Too many firms misunderstand the limitations of their OM systems' abilities to manage capacity and satisfy fluctuating demand. Resulting failures frustrate company personnel and alienate customers. Both groups may begin looking for the opportunities to flee to better-managed rivals.

Demand Management in Service Organizations

Service providers face serious demand-management problems because they cannot inventory their products to meet customer demand when it arises. To delight its customers, such a firm must choose among three responses:

1. Maintain sufficient capacity to satisfy every need immediately.
2. Try to influence the pattern of customer arrivals in some way to make it match the firm's capacity.
3. Develop a flexible pricing strategy to stimulate demand during slack periods when capacity sits idle.

To match capacity to likely demand, operations managers need both good forecasts and flexible resource bases. Without good forecasts, they need extremely flexible resources to add or subtract capacity at will. Otherwise, profit margins will suffer from the cost of maintaining underutilized capacity.

Rather than trying to match capacity to the pattern of demand, service providers may look for a mutually beneficial way to influence customer arrivals so

The number of a flight's discount seats is dependent upon how many full-fare seats have been sold. Airlines use this "ripe banana" pricing strategy to avoid profit loss caused by empty seats.

SOURCE: Jim Pickerell/Stock Boston

" We would rather turn you down than let you down. "

Bekins Moving Company motto

they match the OM system's capacity. As one way to do this, an organization may provide information about its slow and busy periods. A chart hanging near the queue in a local Post Office may show when the office typically experiences its most and least active demand. One household moving company uses its well-advertised corporate motto to influence the pattern of demand. Since moving household goods requires skilled operators using special-purpose vans, the firm tries to manage the pattern of the work flowing into its system. Knowing about these limitations, customers modify their behavior by contracting for the firm's services well before they need to move.

As another method for influencing the pattern of demand, a service provider may invite customers to book appointments. This mechanism benefits both parties. It helps the service providers like doctors, lawyers, and hair stylists allocate capacity to demand, and customers the reduced waiting times and lower prices than they would have to pay to cover the costs of excess capacity.

Rather than adjusting capacity or influencing the overall pattern of demand, a service provider may set prices to stimulate demand in slack periods and avoid leaving idle capacity. Firms that bid for service contracts often adjust prices to regulate sales. Supermarkets often start advertised sales on Thursdays, the day before the payday-driven bring demand. A make-to-order business may well bid for work at lower prices simply to keep key personnel busy. When the same firm's workload approaches capacity, it may not bid or offer a bid high enough to justify the higher cost of working above capacity or securing additional resources.

Airlines and other fixed-capacity service firms routinely practice a so-called *ripe-banana pricing strategy* to sell services that will lose any value if they go unsold by a specific time. An unsold airline ticket on yesterday's flight to Chicago has no value, so an airline's price structure may try to maximize ticket sales to high-paying business customers while still collecting marginal revenues by selling tickets with travel restrictions at low prices to economy-minded customers who would not fly at regular fares. Airlines carefully manage the number of low-fare tickets available on particular flights to maximize expected revenue. Their computer systems periodically compare the expected revenue of keeping a seat at the normal

$400 fare against the revenue from offering it as a $259 super saver fare. As the date of a flight approaches, airlines increase the number of unsold tickets offered at lower fares. To avoid annoying full-fare customers, airlines often sell the bargain tickets through third-party agencies like cut-rate ticket services that advertise in newspapers.

For a fourth, potentially dangerous option, a firm can practice **service-delay management** and simply require customers to wait for service. Only by providing such superb service that people seem willing to wait can a company prosper in these conditions. Car buffs may tolerate long waits to get their classic E-types tuned up by the best Jaguar mechanic in three states. Clients of Henri, Bakersfield's premier hairdresser, may not mind a 3-week wait, believing that, "He makes me look *fabulous!*" Firms can expect customers to accept long waits only when they deliver value that more than offsets the bother they experience. Price-conscious buyers expect minimal customer service and long checkout lines at deep-discount retailers, but they wait only as long as the price benefits justify.

Service-delay management exposes the firm to serious danger because managers cannot really tell when the combination of wait and benefit no longer delights customers and begins straining their patience. Customers who have begun merely to tolerate the wait may listen to competitors' appeals. The firm may discover the problem only after they leave, exclaiming "Henri? He is okay, but Andrew is *just fabulous!*"

To think about the service-delay strategy in another way, a firm might redefine it as a **waiting-management program**. In many instances, zero-wait performance may not be economically feasible. In such a case, operations managers must find ways to delight customers while they wait. Early OM research literature described an innovation that placed a mirror near an elevator to make waiting for the elevator more tolerable. Some car washes try to make the wait for service pleasant by offering a coffee shop with pastries and free morning newspapers. Before cellular phones, one car wash placed a courtesy telephone in each booth of its adjacent coffee shop to allow customers to conduct business while they waited. Service organizations must always remember that the totality of the experience determines whether the customer leaves delighted.

Demand Management in Manufacturing Organizations

Manufacturers must confront many of the same demand-management issues as service providers, but in more complex settings. Service organizations often place fewer levels of workers between decision makers and customers than manufacturers' organizations. Specific demand patterns normally have more visible impacts on service operations than on manufacturing operations. Sometimes, manufacturer's sales representatives (or other employees who deal most closely with customers) either do not understand or do not care about the effects of an order on the firm's OM system. Such an attitude may reflect compensation incentives that stress short-term gains. Similarly, manufacturing workers may seem to care only about keeping their system flowing smoothly, whether or not they satisfy customers. Most often both sales reps and OM system workers want to help the firm profitably delight customers. Both need effective communications to assure that the OM system has sufficient resources to deliver goods as promised.

Pressure to stretch production capacity may come from sources other than sales reps. Desire to generate "good numbers" in a financial report for some period, usually a fiscal quarter, also places excessive demands on manufacturing operations. Top managers and finance professionals may urge operations managers to

service-delay management
The practice of making delays as short as possible under the best possible conditions, to minimize adverse customer reaction (e.g., offering complementary wine to restaurant patrons while they wait for a table)

waiting-management program
Arrangements to delight customers while they wait for service

"A smile does not cost much but usually pays handsome dividends."

Old Norwegian Proverb

speed up shipments at the end of a month or a quarter in order to transform existing orders into billable transactions. These pressures distort demand management in services, too, but those firms don't have as many options as manufacturers to influence the timing of a billable transaction.

Demand management is one activity that crosses traditional corporate boundaries. The marketing function has traditionally worked to identify existing and latent customer demands and to craft product strategy. The responsibilities of marketing have also overlapped with those of operations management in the course of managing ongoing selling and promotional activities. These should remain the responsibilities of marketing, although they affect demand management within the OM system.

Initially, the demand-management activities of the operations management function sought to facilitate cooperation between the sales efforts of marketing and the OM department's order entry function. Businesses that experienced erratic demand often sought to protect their OM systems from this system variance by building buffers in the form of inventory or long product lead times.

promised delivery date
The date when operations managers, sales representatives, and the customer agree for delivery of an order

In a make-to-order situation, the **promised delivery date** represents one buffer against variations in demand. When a customer places an order, someone must estimate when the firm can expect to fill it. This employee may calculate a due date based on a static process, or the date may vary depending the current work load, anticipated resource availability, and the customer's needs. If sales representatives trust the process for setting promised delivery dates, they may report the result to the customer unchanged. Otherwise, they may quote a later due date in order to provide a cushion to guard against disappointment if the OM system misses the date. If the customer finds the promised due date unacceptable, sales reps may work with operations managers to ask for an earlier order completion date. Worse, sales reps may just quote an earlier due date and then pressure the OM system to fulfill the promise.

In a make-to-stock situation, the demand-management process begins by checking for a desired product in finished-goods inventory. If this search fails at one site, it may extend to other sources of supply within the firm's system. An automobile dealer will first try to sell you a car off its lot; if it does not have the car that you want, it will search other dealers of the same model to see if they have a car in stock with the desired options. Many firms maintain multiple inventory sites, and they often follow similar intrafirm search procedures to try to satisfy their customers' demands.

If the seller cannot find the desired product anywhere in its existing stock, operations managers may hear a call: "How quickly can you make one of these?" The exchange may result in a rush order. This example shows how information systems can add value, both for the customer who wants a desired product as quickly and easily as possible and for operations managers who want to keep the production schedule free of unnecessary variance due to rush orders.

final build schedule
The planned timing and sequence of specific orders scheduled to be completed by the final assembly process

In an assemble-to-order situation, demand management involves trying to find an open, parts-feasible slot in the **final build schedule** that satisfies the customer's desired due date. The term *parts-feasible* means that the firm can build the order from uncommitted components in inventory or from components that it can acquire before the build schedule calls for production to begin. The inventory and product procurement processes provide input to guide this demand-management decision. In a later chapter, we will discuss how the materials requirements planning system can help the order-entry process to set realistic delivery dates based on the current shop work load, incoming orders, planned resources, and existing inventory.

This skateboard manufacturer strives to meet customer demand by stocking plenty of finished product.
SOURCE: Lawrence Migdale/Stock Boston

Since some customers have more urgent needs than others, operations managers should maintain some slack in the final build schedule in order to respond to the short-term needs of preferred customers. Too many order-entry systems automatically place every incoming order in the earliest feasible slot in the build schedule. Sales representatives may appreciate the help making their sales quotas, but this policy can hurt the firm's competitiveness by limiting its ability to respond quickly when an order really needs a short delivery date. Worse yet, a firm may respond to unnecessarily tight limits by rescheduling other orders, disrupting the final build schedule. Operations managers often quip, "We don't schedule work, mostly we reschedule work!" This introduces variance and waste.

In many make-to-order systems, the demand management process requires the operations managers to estimate the most-likely production lead time capabilities for a pending order given the current shop load and resources. The process of setting due dates starts with the customer's question: How soon can you make this for me? The firm should answer with another question: How soon do you need it? If the customer's desired date fits within the firm's current capabilities, it becomes the order's due date. If not, then the demand-management process must decide whether the customer's business justifies extraordinary measures. Some customers demand more than the firm can profitably satisfy.

This decision must also consider the costs of assigning a high priority to orders from a marginal customer. How will such a rush order affect performance for other customers in the queue? If this analysis suggests adverse consequences, then operations managers must decide which customers they value most. If the firm feels pressure from competing demands of several worthy customers, it might well consider augmenting capacity.

In each of these manufacturing situations, the difficulty of the due-date estimation process varies with the complexity of the OM system and the capabilities of the planning process. An estimate in a multistage manufacturing system requires a more complex process than an estimate in a system with fewer stages. The estimation process also becomes more complex for a system in which many components can be used in many different end products. When this occurs, the manufacturing planning and control system must keep track of components promised for existing orders. For any set of OM system characteristics, however, an effective operations planning system helps managers to give better estimates than even simple estimates from poor operations planners.

Demand management occupies much of an operations manager's attention in any manufacturing system. Like just-in-time manufacturing, which requires a level work load to succeed, many OM systems rely on a controlled release of work to the shop for efficient operation. Highly variable demand encourages a plant manager to build buffers against this uncertainty, increasing inventories, lead times, and extra capacity to guard against surprises. Ironically, this effort to make the OM system flexible reduces the flexibility of the firm as a whole. To avoid this destructive result, marketing and operations management must work hard to promote understanding of the best way to add value for worthy customers.

Demand Management and Product Development

Both manufacturers and service providers feel powerful market pressure for fast-to-market competition. To meet this challenge, many firms have assigned product development projects to cross-functional teams, further encroaching on traditional marketing decisions. Product and process engineers now activity participate in projects to design products that meet customer needs.

The rapid pace of many business environments has forced product-development strategy to the center of many firms' strategic plans. The vice president of marketing for Compaq's desktop PC division recently commented, "It used to be every new product had six months of uniqueness. Now it's a long weekend." The "On the Job" box relates more of the story of Compaq's response.

Market Information Systems for Demand Management

To plan for its new Pentium-based microcomputer, Compaq needed information about the likely behavior of major players in the PC industry. For a firm that elects to compete based on a fast-to-market strategy, success depends on projecting customer demand for new products or features to achieve both fast-to-market and fast-to-product leadership. To reach the market first with the right product, a firm's marketing function must intimately understand both existing and latent demands of the targeted market segment.

The fashion-driven clothing industry vividly demonstrates this principle. Predicting the reception of a new line of merchandise by retail customers resembles the process of predicting election outcomes. To begin, product planners need to know what customers are likely to buy. Once the firm launches a product line, it needs quick information about the market's response to the new goods. Without a good idea of which items are selling and which are not, buyers might order goods that the firm will later have to mark down and sell at a loss.

Similarly, a manufacturer of fashion-driven merchandise must know what customers want to buy to avoid misdirecting expensive manufacturing resources. A supply chain with quick-response capabilities may allow the firm to make more of profitable, fast-moving items. Accurate, timely marketing information can help to prevent wasteful investment of manufacturing resources to make more of the slow-moving items that distributors will probably not reorder. The "On the Job" box discusses the solution of Mothers Work to this problem.

This kind of rapid response blurs the distinctions among demand management, demand forecasting, and demand tracking discussed earlier in the chapter. As a firm develops the ability to respond more quickly, its need to forecast

ON THE JOB

Compaq's Crystal Ball

During the early 1990s, Compaq Computer had earned the reputation for being first to market with new computer technologies. But in March 1995, Michael Parides nervously watched the latest sales returns, since he had persuaded his bosses that it was in Compaq's best interest not to be early to market with a computer using Intel's Pentium chip. How had he done this? With the help of an elaborate computer model of the competition within the PC market—a model Compaq likened to a "SimCity" for the entire PC business. Compaq claims that its model can "simulate conditions, such as component price changes, fluctuating demand for a given feature or price, and the impact of rival models." So, rival and customer forces had been combined into one all-inclusive model. Compaq even claimed that their model had anticipated HP's 22 percent price reduction in March of 1995.

Competitive models are not new to Compaq. But this one really had the firm out on a limb. Industry pundits decried Compaq's sluggish new product strategy. Sales personnel and the distribution channel screamed that they needed "fresh" goods. He met with a lot of "You don't understands" or "We've seen all this before" from certain elements of Compaq's management. But Parides was able to convince top management that an early introduction of the Pentium-based line would wreak havoc on the pricing of Compaq's 486-based units. His model indicated that a delayed product introduction strategy would boost the firm's profits by $50 million.

When you are a pioneer, it pays to have a little luck. Intel's "minor" bug in its Pentium chip probably caused many potential customers to hold back. True to the model's prediction, Intel slashed Pentium chip prices, which in turn enabled Compaq to introduce its machines with a $2,300 to $4,500 price range. Furthermore, the delay enabled Compaq to include in its Desktop line network diagnostic features that would save corporate customers thousands in after-sale system maintenance.

Profits in the last quarter of 1994 were up 61 percent, in part because Compaq avoided markdowns it does due to product changeover. Compaq's new products and pricing are being well received. Now the model is the star. Management indicates that "within 12 months, all of Compaq's computers will be designed with the help of Parides' new simulation tool."

SOURCE   "At Compaq, A Desktop Crystal Ball," *Business Week*, March 20, 1995.

diminishes. Mothers Work did not need a forecast as much as a slower competitor because it could determine by the following morning what products had sold the previous day. Through point-of-purchase queries, the firm learned what each purchaser wanted, telling managers what styles and colors would sell actively and which would stay on the rack. Mothers Work suggests a system that developed beyond demand management to allow its resupply system to react almost instantly to concrete knowledge from the field.

 ## DEMAND FORECASTING

At the start of this chapter, we distinguished between among management, demand forecasting, and demand tracking. In this section, we discuss the objectives and

ON THE JOB

Mothers Work Quick Step

When Rebecca Matthias started Mothers Work in 1985, she admits that she really did not know what she was doing. As a pregnant architect, she was frustrated by the lack of fashionable clothing for professional women. The choice seemed to be the "dress for success look" or something from Omar the tent maker's one-size-fits-all. Dior-like fashion could not be found. So Rebecca started her own firm, which she called Mothers Work. Today, her firm dominates the high end of the mothers-to-be market.

When confronted with the task of knowing what to make, Dan, Rebecca's engineering-trained husband, commented, "This nothing but a pattern recognition problem." Thus, they set out to create an information system that would provide the firm with the most up-to-date information of what is selling and of what customers said they would have purchased if it had been available. The customer sale transaction became a one-person focus group. And since these customers were not likely to remain long in this market , Mothers Work knew that it needed to be both fast to market and fast to product. Lacking industry experience, the Matthiases didn't know this was not possible—and no one told them.

Today, Mothers Work has a system in place that is the envy of the industry. Given a new fashion idea, it can make that item within three weeks. If an item is sold out in one of its 184 company-owned stores, it can replenish that item in two days if the item is in stock and within one week if a new batch needs to be made. This permits Mothers Work stores to maximize the amount of expensive space allocated to product display. In 1994, Mothers Work had sales of just under $60 million. In 1995, it acquired its main competitor, Pea in a Pod, for $23.9 million. The upscale maternity market never has been more agile.

SOURCE   *Pinnacle,* Cable News Network, February 18, 1995.

techniques of demand forecasting. Two quotes from Oliver Wight guide our priorities in this discussion:

> There is no such thing as a reliable forecast.[1]

> Unless the system is 100 percent reliable, it must be made simple enough so that the people who use it will know how to use it intelligently.[2]

The first quote gives a useful reminder for decision makers to avoid basing conclusions on unrealistic forecasts. Surely, demand forecasters should try constantly to improve their processes and provide more reliable predictions. Still, decision makers must keep their systems flexible enough to adjust for reasonable forecasting errors.

Wight's second quote urges demand forecasters to identify the users of their forecasts, explain the strengths and weaknesses of the analytical tools that developed the forecasts, and then work to delight their internal customers who rely on accurate demand forecasts. Effective employee involvement in demand forecasting requires accessible analytical models that help users to understand and take ownership of the forecasting process. When demand forecasting becomes a user-operated

[1]Oliver W. Wight, *Production and Inventory Management in the Computer Age* (Boston: CBI, 1974), p. 147.
[2]Ibid., p. 149.

business process, the continuous improvement processes discussed in Chapter 5 can flourish.

Five-Step Demand Forecasting Process

Guided by Oliver Wight, we propose a five-step process for demand forecasting:

1. Identify the internal customer and decision-making processes that the forecast will support. More than one user may rely on the information, so look carefully to find all of them.
2. Identify likely sources of the best data inputs.
3. Select forecasting techniques that will most effectively transform available data into timely, reliable forecast information over the most appropriate planning horizon.
4. Apply the proposed technique to data gathered for the appropriate business process. State assumptions explicitly in writing.
5. Monitor the performance of the forecasting process, as for any continuous-improvement or quality-management process. Periodic reviews of the basic assumptions that underlie forecasts help to keep the process for future forecasts on target.

No forecasting process, however well-conceived and carefully implemented, can consistently provide perfect information. Indeed, any forecast that perfectly predicts subsequent events must raise serious suspicions. Investigation may reveal demand management by some upstream process. If the organization considers this control desirable, it eliminates the need for the demand forecast. A perfect forecast may also indicate more sinister developments like someone "cooking the books" or reporting performance data that shows conformance with plans rather than actual events.

In Step 1, the forecaster evaluates the the needs of the internal customers for a forecast. The specific organizational situation must dictate the choice of forecasting process to align it with the information needs of decision makers. Makridakis and Wheelwright have summarized six characteristics of the forecasting environment that drive this decision.[3]

Time Horizon.   The forecasting process should suit the period of time over which the decision maker's current actions will affect business performance. As discussed earlier, the time horizon of an operations management forecast depends on the OM system's lead time. If a system takes 10 weeks to build an ordered product, then its forecast demand is 10 weeks from the current date or longer. A system that can respond in 2 weeks can work with a shorter, probably more accurate forecast. This suggests yet another benefit of fast-to-market production.

Level of Detail.   The level of detail in a forecast also depends on the user's need for information. Demand data aggregated over many products, markets, or time periods may make a forecast more reliable as variations offset one another; this smooths the process, as long as users do not need data for more specific segments of demand. In fact, attempts to force data sources to provide more precise inputs may jeopardize cooperation by busy participants, especially when the data reporting system provides only aggregated information to them.

[3]S. Makridakis and S. A. Wheelwright, *Forecasting Methods for Management* (New York: John Wiley & Sons, 1989), p. 27.

Before pressing for more detailed input, forecasters should assess the stability of the mix of demand. If the variables that drive an aggregate time series behave consistently, more detailed data may give no significant benefit. With inconsistent demand for specific segments in a mix, however, aggregation could either help or diminish the value of the forecast to its intended users. Offsetting moves by randomly fluctuating variables will stabilize a composite time series. Obviously, combining the data makes the forecasting process easier, but it may mask changes in particular segments of demand that would affect decision making.

A lumber company vice president made this point vividly, saying, "I don't want to know the aggregate price of lumber. I need to know the price of 2x4s and 2x6s down the road so I can tell my people how to cut up the logs." Clearly, this operations-level manager saw little value in a forecasting process for higher-level corporate planning based on cumulative data.

Number of Demand Segments.   The amount of effort to devote to a forecast clearly depends on the range of demand covered by the forecast. To forecast demand for a single, critical product, a firm may want to expend considerable resources to get the best possible forecast. A demand forecast for 1,000 products should rely on methods for manipulation of mass data to exploit economies of scale in computation; a detailed forecast for each product would raise costs more than its addition to value.

Control versus Planning.   A forecasting process should meet users' needs for management control or planning functions. Control requires management by exception methods to generate early-warning signals when some aspect of operations exceeds acceptable performance limits. This function requires forecasts to detect variations in patterns of performance. In contrast, planning often assumes that current patterns will continue, so it needs forecasts to identify significant patterns that seem likely to continue in the future.

Constancy.   Extremely constant performance permits a forecaster to extrapolate past patterns to predict the future. Without constancy, the forecaster needs to adjust projections based on judgments of likely variations. A fluid forecasting process can help the firm to modify its actions to reflect the most recent information.

Existing Business Processes.   Current users of demand forecasts should provide strong input about any changes to the system. Organizational inertia often dictates continued reliance on familiar tools.

Another influence on the choice of a demand forecasting process comes from the conflicting demands of system design and system-use planning. System design normally needs broader, longer-term forecasts to support resource management and capacity planning. Aggregate information helps firms to determine a configuration of people, plant, and equipment that provides suitable capabilities and capacity to serve customers in the targeted market segment. Demand forecast errors in this area usually leave the firm with underutilized or over-extended operational resources.

Systems-use planning, on the other hand, needs forecasts that support more detailed intermediate and short-range decisions about staffing, initiating production or purchase orders, and routine production scheduling. Demand forecast errors create excess inventory, lost sales, high expediting costs, and ultimately larger buffers in the form of safety stocks, slack capacity, or planning lead times.

By collecting and sending data via modem, this sales representative immediately updates the company's market database.   SOURCE: Bob Daemmrich/Stock Boston

After forecasters resolve all of these questions to identify internal customers for their demand forecasts, they continue the five-step process with Step 2, determining the sources of input data. The forecasters must evaluate potential sources of information based on the insight they offer about past and current activities and their input for timely predictions about future developments. This process should screen good sources of information to assure that the organizational benefits will justify the time they will take away from their other activities to participate. Often, the busy schedules of a firm's best-informed managers do not allow them time to provide detailed inputs. The least-informed information sources, often found at corporate headquarters, may seem quite willing to undertake this effort, but their inputs may make the forecast irrelevant.

Information-age technology helps to solve this problem. For example, an interactive dialog between business planners and line personnel can help them collaboratively come up with a better forecast. Marketing guided by sales data has enhanced the selling capabilities of some companies. In the same way, emerging sources of market-level information can enhance the operations manager's database to improve demand forecasting. Further processing can transform input data into critical nuggets of both detailed and aggregate demand data that satisfy the needs of decision makers. Never before have companies brought together so much data with such powerful analytical capabilities to provide such meaningful, timely information to managers in such useful formats.

Effective use of this technology will, however, require designers of information systems and forecasting processes to understand the needs and capabilities of working managers. The human-resource management function must support this potential by training corporate and field managers in techniques for mining the firm's information database. The ideal image of such a data-rich forecasting system shows a regional sales manager sitting in a motel room each night feeding the latest market-level insights back to headquarters and reflecting on the current state of the firm's database with a focused, analytical mind. Technology may replace frank discussions over martinis with in-depth interactions over the Internet.

After defining users' information needs and scouting sources of demand information during the first two steps, in Step 3 the forecaster selects the most appropriate demand forecasting tool. The criteria for this choice must, of course, reflect the needs and comfort levels of the internal users of the forecasts. Gene Woolsey, the noted management iconoclast, has warned that forecasters should avoid technology overkill, advising forecasters that, "A manager would rather live with a problem that he cannot tolerate than use a solution that he cannot understand."[4] If a manager must make this choice, the designers of the forecasting system have not completed their jobs. They may have failed to understand their internal customer's needs or to provide enough training to make the user comfortable with the forecasting process and its output. As always, the customer determines value.

In Step 4, the forecaster applies the chosen forecasting tool to develop data that will support management decisions. As in the application of the Deming wheel or any scientific method, the process must track and study the accuracy of its output and continually help users to refine the forecasting process. This fifth, systems-review step must explicitly state the assumptions that underlie the forecasts. Otherwise, forecasting becomes strictly a numerical exercise because users cannot judge the applicability of its output to their routine decisions. For the same reason, the forecasting process must allow managers' judgments to influence its results.

Forecasting as a Process

Forecasting can be described as a process that transforms historical time-series data and/or qualitative assessments into a prediction of future events. This process can yield either quantitative or subjective projections. Familiar numerical forecasts include news reports of economic data such as, "Sales of automobiles in 1998 will be 14.5 million cars." Another forecast could just as easily predict the occurrence or timing of some event, such as when the civil aviation industry will commit to composite-fiber aircraft fuselages.

As Exhibit 10.3 implies, the forecasting process combines quantitative, analytical data with qualitative, subjective inputs. The most effective blend produces forecasts that meet decision makers' needs for accurate and timely information. Qualitative or subjective inputs suggest likely environmental conditions such as people's opinions about whether it will rain today. This simple information may meet a manager's needs, as when someone wants to predict attendance at the community swimming pool. However, a farmer may prefer a quantitative, analytical projection such as a predicted rainfall of 1.2 inches today. Indeed, the farmer might well prefer a mix of qualitative and quantitative data such as an expectation for 1.2 inches of steady rain over a 3-hour period this afternoon. Once again, effectiveness begins with a clear image of the user and the use of the forecast.

Qualitative Demand Forecasts

Qualitative forecasts reflect people's judgments or opinions. Some people base their judgments of future events on historical data. Others seem to draw conclusions supported by little more than tea leaves. Demand forecasters must identify sources of reliable judgments as they gather inputs for projections of important phenomena or characteristics.

---

[4]R. E. D. Woolsey and H. F. Swanson, *Operations Research for Immediate Application: A Quick and Dirty Manual* (New York: Harper & Row, 1975).

[**E X H I B I T   1 0 . 3**]

Basic Forecasting Process

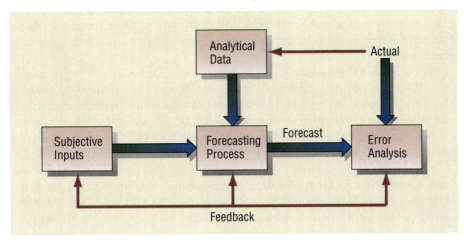

These inputs support five qualitative business forecasting techniques: grass-roots forecasting, focused forecasting, historical analogy, market research methods, and the Delphi method.

Grass-Roots Forecasting. **Grass-roots forecasting** seeks input from people at the level of the organization that gives them the best contact with the phenomenon under study. A marketing study might ask sales representatives for their readings of current market conditions. Evaluation of these inputs must watch for short-term perspectives. Some people willingly offer forecasts based only on their most recent experiences.

grass-roots forecasting

A qualitative forecasting method that seeks input from people at the level of the organization that gives them the best contact with the phenomenon under study

Focused Forecasting. First proposed by Bernie Smith about 10 years ago, **focused forecasting** combines a common-sense, grass-roots investigation with a computer simulation process to assess the effectiveness of the respondents' decision rules.[5] The computer simulation augments analysis of judgments as quirky as this store manager's statement: "To estimate daily sales, I count the number of cars entering my parking lot by 10 a.m., multiply by $50 and then add $300 if it is a payday." Smith contends that his methods give better forecasts for finished-goods inventory management than some of the traditional, rigorous statistical techniques covered later in this chapter.

Smith's approach to forecasting merits attention because front-line personnel can often provide more valuable information than most organizations expect from them. Thus, development of a business forecasting process should consider both its intended users and grass-roots members of the organization. This review might not find a simple cure for a complex forecasting problem, but it will at least show front-line employees that managers respect their experience and insights.

focused forecasting

A qualitative forecasting method that combines a common-sense, grass-roots investigation with a computer simulation process to assess the effectiveness of the respondents' decision rules

Historical Analogy. Forecasting based on **historical analogy** explores the possibility that past events can give insights into prediction of related future develop-

historical analogy

A qualitative forecasting method that evaluates past events as part of predictions about some related future development

[5]B. T. Smith, *Focused Forecasting: Computer Techniques for Inventory Control* (Boston: CBI, 1984).

ments. This method assumes that the future events will show a pattern of behavior similar to that of some set of past events. For example, the sales pattern of black-and-white television sets may have helped the developers of color television sets for forecast sales. Economists have relied extensively on this kind of model to forecast business cycles and related developments. News reports frequently cite economists' comparisons of current economic trends with similar stages of past business cycles.

This method risks inaccuracy if the forces that drove past events might no longer affect present developments in the same way. Someone who forecasted market acceptance of citizens-band radio sets based on that of color television sets would have been stuck with a warehouse full of CB radios. Even a forecast of future sales of CB radio sets based on actual sales from the first year or two of this fad product would have resulted in large, unwanted inventories.

Market Research Forecasting Tools.   Marketers have developed a wide range of tools developed for evaluating the purchasing patterns and attitudes of current or potential buyers of a good or service. Marketing texts explain in detail how to develop, conduct, and analyze consumer surveys, interviews, and focus groups. Designers of goods and services use these tools to understand their current customers and the buyers they would like to serve.

panel consensus

A qualitative forecasting technique that gathers knowledgeable people to craft a forecast by engaging in an open dialogue over a relatively short period of time

One marketing research method, **panel consensus**, invites a panel of knowledgeable people to craft a forecast by engaging in an open dialogue over a relatively short period of time. This technique assumes that no single group or person is likely to have access to all of the key inputs in a demand-forecasting process. Instead, a group of individuals from sales, marketing, engineering, etc., perhaps meeting regularly, might make better forecasts jointly than an isolated staff person at corporate headquarters could produce.

Delphi method

A qualitative forecasting method that gathers information through sequential, independent responses by a group of experts to a series of questionnaires

Delphi Method.   The **Delphi method** compiles forecasts through sequential, independent responses by a group of experts to a series of questionnaires. The forecaster compiles and analyzes the respondents' input and develops a new questionnaire for the same group of experts. This sequence works toward a consensus that reflects input from all of the experts while preventing any one individual from dominating the process.

The choice to base decisions on these qualitative forecasting techniques depends on the firm's situation. If a manager needs a forecast too quickly to allow time for a detailed, quantitative analysis, then qualitative methods may support timely decision making. Qualitative study may also fill a gap when forecasters lack sufficient data to conduct a thorough quantitative analysis. However, even when they have sufficient time and data, forecasters may deeply suspect that for one reason or another, information about the past may not support good decisions for the future. Qualitative may even prove superior to quantitative ones after fruitless exploration of the known analytical tools.

Quantitative Forecasting

Quantitative forecasting techniques transform input in the form of numerical data into forecasts using methods in one of three categories:

1. Historical time-series studies, which use past data as inputs for analysis to infer future events

[**EXHIBIT 10.4**]

Three Time-Series Patterns

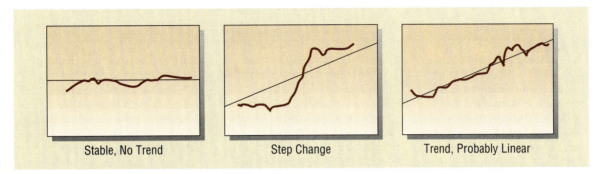

| Stable, No Trend | Step Change | Trend, Probably Linear |

2. Causal studies, which look for causal relationships between leading variables and forecasted variables
3. Mathematical or simulation models, which try to represent past behavior in a valid mathematical relationship and then alter data to project future events

Each category of methods assumes that past events provide a good basis for understanding the future.

People's daily routines involve many time series. News reports include some especially familiar ones:

- Today's weather is expected to be 85°F, which is 2° below average.
- In June, the nation's seasonally adjusted unemployment rate fell to 6.9 percent.
- By the first of October, the nation's supply of home heating fuel inventories had risen to 140 million barrels, but this level remained below normal.
- Hewlett-Packard's third-quarter earnings rose 40 percent over last year's period, but fell 12 percent from this year's second-quarter results.

Each statement enhances the meaning of the numbers by placing them in a historical context. A temperature of 85° is hot, but still not above the historical average. The "By the Way" box reports on government-calculated time series for economic data and hints at the complexity of deriving meaning from quantitative data.

Rough Cut Analyses of Time Series.   Graphing the data makes a good first step in any time-series analysis. An informal pattern-recognition process can then ask questions such as:

- Does any characteristic of the curve draw immediate attention?
- Does the time series appear to represent output of a stable process?
- Does the curve reveal any step changes in the time series?
- Does current information suggest causes of observed shifts?
- Does the curve suggest some trend, cycle, or other relationship that seems likely to lead to a reasonably accurate forecast?

Exhibit 10.4 shows some common patterns and their meanings. The straight lines represent the analyst's approximation of averages for the data. (Statistical analysis would perform least-squares regression to position these lines accurately.)

[BY THE WAY... GOVERNMENT AS RECORD KEEPER]

After the Great Depression, people came to believe that the nation's leaders needed better information for fiscal planning. Thus, the U.S. National Bureau of Economic Research (NBER) set out to create a national accounting system to better understand the extent and nature of changes in the nation's economy. The NBER and several government agencies that later assumed similar tasks developed time series designed to measure both total economic activity and more specific patterns of economic activity in the consumer, business, and government sectors. The numbers were designed to be the best apolitical assessment of economic data.

As anyone knows, however, liars find that numbers make ready tools. To guard against distortion, economists quickly found that they needed to adjust their data to remove the impact of recurring factors, such as weather conditions, agricultural practices, and the annual back-to-school surge in spending. They developed methods to decompose time-series variations into changes attributable to unknown factors and those that recurring factors fail to explain. Further analysis may yield some explanation, but the changes remain independent of normal seasonal factors, secular trends, or business-cycle effects.

One common method for analyzing time series related to national economic activity, the X-11 method, was developed by Julius Shiskin of the Census Bureau. In essence, this method transforms raw time-series data into a residue of unexplained variations. The process can be described schematically as shown in the chart below.

The time series of unexplained variations is often called the *irregular component*. A consistent pattern in this irregular component may reflect changes in one of the traditional factors or the effects of some other recurring factor not yet included in the analysis.

Over the past 20 years, such time series have revealed less predictable trends in the cyclical changes in the nation's economy. Both the lengths and the amplitudes of patterns have become somewhat less regular. We will leave that problem to the economists.

Decomposition of Raw Time Series Data

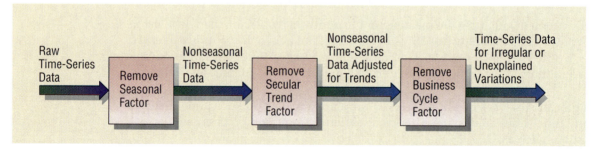

Nonlinear patterns may indicate that some other systematic force is influencing the data. This justifies further analysis to understand the process that generated the time series.

In Exhibit 10.5, the curved line illustrates a time series with both a trend and a seasonal variation. The straight line represents a rough approximation of a least-squares average. The gap between the straight line and the curved one is often called the *forecast error,* as discussed in more detail later in the chapter. During each cycle, the time series shows a pattern of approximately equal positive and negative

[**E X H I B I T   1 0 . 5**]

Seasonal Time Series with a Trend

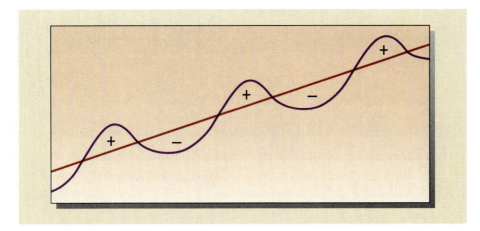

forecast errors. This may indicate a predictable variation that would support a good forecast based on both seasonal and trend information.

A trained statistician would find this discussion a little sloppy, but we do not need a rigorous statistical explanation here. Instead, an operations manager should think about the data in the analytical arsenal. The concept of forecast error also has value at this point, since it signals the variation that demand forecasting needs to explain.

Seasonal Adjustments.   Seasonal variations in raw data may mask the effects of other, more interesting causes. Demand forecasters filter out these seasonal effects to clarify the picture of underlying process steps. For example, the retail sales figures in the top row of Exhibit 10.6 make December look quite strong. To evaluate these figures intelligently, however, the forecast must adjust for the effects of Christmas season sales. An effective, quick-and-dirty method might compare a month's sales with sales over the same period in the prior year.

Another, more rigorous analytical technique would develop seasonal adjustment factors for each month. Exhibit 10.6 expresses these seasonal factors as percentages of annual sales that normally occur in specific months. The store typically generates 19.2 percent of its annual sales in the month of December, so a forecaster could divide that month's sales by 0.192 to find a deseasonalized annual sales rate implied by the monthly data. Dividing by 12 gives a monthly sales figure

[**E X H I B I T   1 0 . 6**]

Seasonal Adjustment of Retail Sales Data

Month	October	November	December
Sales	$120,329	$130,295	$260,391
Seasonal factor	8.2%	9.1%	19.2%
Deseasonalized sales	$122,285	$119,262	$113,017

[**EXHIBIT 10.7**]

Quarterly Sales and Seasonal Adjustment Factors, 1990–1995

Year	1st Qtr	2nd Qtr	3rd Qtr	4th Qtr	Total
1990	52	63	40	29	184
Percentage of annual total	28.3%	34.2%	21.7%	15.8%	
1991	50	64	42	30	186
Percentage of annual total	26.9%	34.4%	22.6%	16.1%	
1992	54	66	41	31	192
Percentage of annual total	28.1%	34.4%	21.4%	16.1%	
1993	56	63	43	29	191
Percentage of annual total	29.3%	33.0%	22.5%	15.2%	
1994	50	67	42	31	190
Percentage of annual total	27.3%	35.3%	22.1%	16.3%	
1995	51	64	40	30	185
Percentage of annual total	27.6%	34.6%	21.6%	16.2%	
5-year average	27.7%	34.3%	22.0%	16.0%	

adjusted for seasonal effects. The deseasonalized data in the exhibit seems to indicate declining sales in November and December, despite the increases shown by the raw data.

Forecasters can calculate seasonal adjustment factors in two ways. The first and easiest is appropriate for a time series that shows no significant trend. It would not accurately portray the time series in Exhibit 10.6 because the trend would overstate sales in the late months of the year. If data for a time series over 3 to 6 years show no trend, the forecaster follows a four-step procedure:

1. Calculate each period's figure (perhaps monthly sales) as a percentage of that year's total.
2. Check for stable seasonal patterns in data for successive years. Monthly proportions should not vary significantly from one year to another. If the time series shows isolated unusual proportions, investigate likely causes during that period or year. If this study uncovers some logical, nonrecurring abnormality, throw out the data for that year to prevent corruption of the calculation.
3. Average the seasonal adjustment factors for each period in successive years with acceptable data.
4. Adjust the past year's data for the average seasonal adjustment factors to remove seasonal effects; continue to adjust new statistics as they occur.

At each step in the procedure, the forecaster must judge how well the results achieve the intention to yield reliable data for decision makers.

The pattern of seasonal adjustment factors in Exhibit 10.7 suggests that the causes of seasonal variations appear to recur in a stable sequence. The data shows little change from one year to the next. The consistent figures for deseasonalized quarterly sales in Exhibit 10.8, graphed in Exhibit 10.9, form a solid base for a forecast of future demand.

A trend in the time series disrupts this method for calculating seasonal adjustment factors. For data that show some trend or frequent irregular events, a

Deseasonalized Quarterly Sales, 1990–1995

1990	46.9	45.9	45.5	45.4
1991	45.1	46.6	47.8	47.0
1992	48.7	48.1	46.6	48.6
1993	50.5	45.9	48.9	45.4
1994	45.1	48.8	47.8	48.6
1995	46.0	46.6	45.5	47.0

centered moving average method gives more reliable results. To calculate a centered moving average for a time series with an odd number of periods in a cycle, such as weekly data, the forecaster simply averages the values for an equal number of periods before and after the current period. This process might estimate deseasonalized sales for a particular day by taking a 7-day moving average for data beginning 3 days earlier and ending 3 days later.

$$\mathbf{d_4} = (d_1 + d_2 + d_3 + d_4 + d_5 + d_6 + d_7)/7 \qquad (10.1)$$

The **bold print** in the equation denotes the estimate based on the past data. In this case, the estimate represents the deseasonalized sales rate for period four.

The forecaster needs a slightly more elaborate formula to calculate a centered moving average for a cycle with an even number of periods, as for quarterly and monthly data. To see why, consider an example. The average of sales data for four quarters of a year represents a forecast for a point between the end of the second quarter and the start of the third, as shown in the bottom line of Exhibit 10.10. Likewise, a 4-quarter average running from the second quarter of Year 1 through the first quarter of Year 2 yields a forecast for a point at the end of the third quarter, indicated by the middle line of Exhibit 10.10. An average of these two averages gives a centered average for the third quarter, indicated by the top line in the exhibit.

centered moving average

A technique for adjusting data for seasonal variation by averaging figures for equal periods before and after the period under study

Bar Graph of Quarterly Sales Patterns, 1990–1995

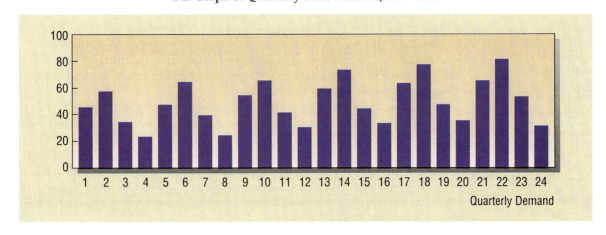

[**EXHIBIT 10.10**]

Centered Moving Averages for Time Series with Even Periods

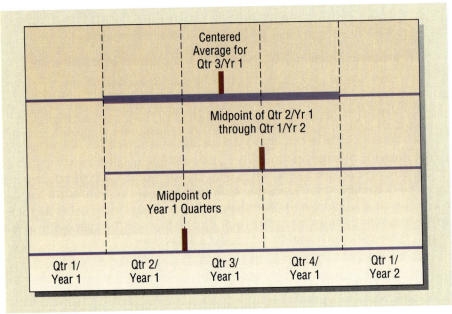

For quarterly data, the forecaster calculates a centered moving average by the formula:

$$d_3 = (d_1 + 2d_2 + 2d_3 + 2d_4 + d_5)/8 \qquad (10.2)$$

A longer expression gives the centered moving average for the seventh month in a 12-month period:

$$d_7 = [d_1 + 2(d_2 + d_3 + d_4 + d_5 + d_6 + d_7 + d_8 + d_9 + d_{10} + d_{11} + d_{12}) + d_{13}]/24 \qquad (10.3)$$

This may seem like a lot of work for a single month's seasonally adjusted data, but computer spreadsheets greatly reduce the burden of this highly repetitive task.

Exhibit 10.11 presents a quarterly time series of sales data for a highly seasonal product. Equation 10.2 can give centered moving averages beginning in the third quarter of 1988 based on raw sales data for first quarter in 1988 through the first in 1989. Dividing the centered moving average into the raw sales for the same period gives a statistic that forecasters often call a **seasonal index**. Dividing a quarterly seasonal index by 4 gives the equivalent of the seasonal adjustment factor discussed earlier in the section. The seasonal index for the third quarter of 1988, (1.4375/4) or 0.359, represents a point estimate of the proportion of sales that normally occur in the quarter of the year.

The data in Exhibit 10.11 supports seasonal index calculations for the third quarters in seven years. The average of these seven figures, 1.4086, gives a seasonal adjustment factor of 35.2 percent. Since the numbers seem quite stable over this 8-year period, a forecaster could use them to transform actual sales data to remove seasonal variations and gain insight into underlying changes. In addition, the forecaster can apply the average seasonal index figures in the next to last row of Exhibit 10.11 to transform raw sales data to deseasonalized numbers for reliable quarter-to-quarter comparisons.

seasonal index

A statistic that allows forecasters to adjust for seasonal variations found by dividing a centered moving average into raw data

[**E X H I B I T   1 0 . 1 1**]

Sample Calculation of Centered Moving Average

	Qtr.	Sales	4-Qtr. Moving Average	Seasonal Index 1st Qtr.	2nd Qtr.	3rd Qtr.	4th Qtr.
1988	1	$60.7					
	2	97.8					
	3	147.3	$102.4			1.4375	
	4	102.0	104.0				0.9809
1989	1	64.8	105.7	0.6134			
	2	106.0	106.5		0.9952		
	3	152.4	106.6			1.4298	
	4	103.8	106.9				0.9712
1990	1	63.5	107.4	0.5910			
	2	109.6	109.2		1.0040		
	3	152.8	111.7			1.3677	
	4	117.9	112.9				1.0439
1991	1	69.9	114.6	0.6103			
	2	112.3	115.6		0.9715		
	3	163.5	115.4			1.4159	
	4	115.7	116.1				0.9970
1992	1	70.7	117.9	0.5994			
	2	116.4	119.3		0.9754		
	3	174.2	119.5			1.4578	
	4	116.5	121.0				0.9626
1993	1	71.0	122.1	0.5818			
	2	128.4	122.9		1.0445		
	3	170.4	124.6			1.3674	
	4	127.3	125.1				1.0179
1994	1	73.8	126.0	0.5856			
	2	129.0	127.0		1.0157		
	3	177.4	128.2			1.3840	
	4	128.4	129.3				0.9930
1995	1	82.0	132.3	0.6199			
	2	130.0	136.7		0.9514		
	3	199.8					
	4	141.1					
Average seasonal index				0.6002	0.9940	1.4086	0.9952
Average seasonal factor				0.1500	0.2485	0.3521	0.2488

For example, suppose that a forecaster receives a report of a sales total of $85,200 for the first quarter of 1996. This latest sales number indicates a seasonally adjusted increase of 3.8 percent in sales for the first quarter 1996. Using the average seasonal index figures from Exhibit 10.11, the forecaster can calculate deseasonalized sales figures over the previous 5 quarters:

1995	Qtr. 1	$ 82.0/0.6002 = 136.6
	Qtr. 2	130.0/0.9940 = 130.8
	Qtr. 3	199.8/1.4086 = 141.8
	Qtr. 4	141.1/0.9952 = 141.8
1996	Qtr. 1	85.2/0.6002 = 141.9

[**EXHIBIT 10.12**]

Common Nonlinear Trends

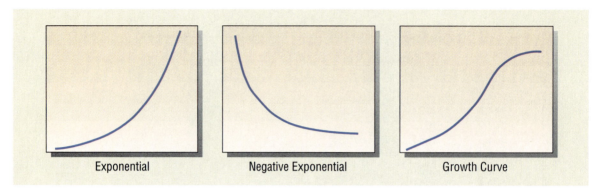

| Exponential | Negative Exponential | Growth Curve |

Note that the table repeats the first-quarter average seasonal index to deseasonal-ize first-quarter sales for both 1995 and 1996 .

The deseasonalized numbers indicate flat sales over the last 3 quarters. This might suggest that the store owner should work more aggressively on creating demand and spend cash more cautiously on purchases like inventory and capaci-ty expansion. The same numbers might result from a cash-conscious buyer cutting back on purchases, eroding demand over that period. These possibilities reinforce the message that numbers cannot answer questions by themselves; they can only contribute to management investigation and judgment of causes and effects.

Determining Trend Factors. The trend component of a time series normally results from some force that causes a general rise or decline in values over time. In the United States, the number of people smoking cigarettes has declined each year for some time as has the number of 1980 Ford LTD cars needing replacement front left fenders. The number of people over 65 has increased each year. Different causes have created these long-term trend effects.

A linear trend results when data remains constant or rises or falls at a constant rate, describing a straight line on a graph. Exhibit 10.12 shows graphs of exponen-tial trends and the traditional sales-growth trend for a new product. Of course, nothing dictates that any long-term trend must follow any of these familiar curves.

As in seasonal analysis, the forecaster should begin a trend analysis by graph-ing the data. To keep computation simple, one may hope for a straight line, giving a linear equation to represent the trend with the form:

$$T_t = a + bt \tag{10.4}$$

where

T_t = trend value for period t
t = number of periods from the origin
a = y-axis intercept at the origin
b = slope of the line

The forecaster then tries to find values for the constants, a and b, that will equate the independent variable, t, and the dependent variable, T_t.

Assume that we have the four years of quarterly sales shown in Exhibit 10.13. The value of the independent variable runs from 1 to 16 which is shown in the fifth

[**EXHIBIT 10.13**]

Least-Squares Calculation

	Qtr.	Sales	Seasonal Index	t	Deseasonalized Sales	$t \times x$	$t \times t$
1992	1	$70.7	0.6002	1	117.8	118	1
	2	116.4	0.9940	2	117.1	234	4
	3	174.2	1.4086	3	123.7	371	9
	4	116.5	0.9952	4	117.1	468	16
1993	1	71.0	0.6002	5	118.3	591	25
	2	128.4	0.9940	6	129.2	775	36
	3	170.4	1.4086	7	121.0	847	49
	4	127.3	0.9952	8	127.9	1023	64
1994	1	73.8	0.6002	9	123.0	1107	81
	2	129.0	0.9940	10	129.8	1298	100
	3	177.4	1.4086	11	125.9	1385	121
	4	128.4	0.9952	12	129.0	1548	144
1995	1	82.0	0.6002	13	136.6	1776	169
	2	130.0	0.9940	14	130.8	1831	196
	3	199.8	1.4086	15	141.8	2128	225
	4	141.1	0.9952	16	141.8	2268	256
Totals				136	2,031	17,769	1,496

column. If we use the deseasonalized sales as our actual data points, x_t, we can then use the least-squares method to minimize the expression:

$$\sum_{t-1}^{t=n} \left(T_t - x_t \right)^2 \tag{10.5}$$

where n = number of periods.

The forecaster can calculate the values of the constants in Equation 10.4 using an expression for the slope of the graph line:

$$b = \frac{\sum_{t-1}^{t=n} t x_t - \left(\sum_{t-1}^{t=n} t \sum_{t-1}^{t=n} x_t \right)/n}{\sum_{t-1}^{t=n} t^2 - \left(\sum_{t-1}^{t=n} t \right)^2 / n} \tag{10.6}$$

Another expression gives the y-axis intercept:

$$a = \sum_{t-1}^{t=n} x_t \Big/ n - b \sum_{t-1}^{t=n} t \Big/ n \tag{10.7}$$

Fortunately, most spreadsheet programs have functions designed to perform this repetitive task. Exhibit 10.13 illustrates the input and results.

The forecaster would find the slope of the trend line as:

$$b = \frac{\sum_{t-1}^{t=n} t x_t - \left(\sum_{t-1}^{t=n} t \sum_{t-1}^{t=n} x_t \right)/n}{\sum_{t-1}^{t=n} t^2 - \left(\sum_{t-1}^{t=n} t \right)^2 / n} = [17{,}769 - (136)(2{,}031)/16]/[(1{,}496) - (136)^2/16]$$

[**EXHIBIT 10.14**]

Forecast Errors

t	Deseasonalized sales	Forecast	Error
1	117.8	115.8	−2.0
2	117.1	117.3	0.2
3	123.7	118.8	−4.9
4	117.1	120.3	3.2
5	118.3	121.8	3.5
6	129.2	123.3	−5.9
7	121.0	124.7	3.8
8	127.9	126.2	−1.7
9	123.0	127.7	4.8
10	129.8	129.2	−0.6
11	125.9	130.7	4.8
12	129.0	132.2	3.2
13	136.6	133.7	−2.9
14	130.8	135.2	4.4
15	141.8	136.7	−5.2
16	142.8	138.1	−4.7

This yields a slope of $b = 1.4882$ per quarter. The forecaster would then calculate the y-intercept:

$$a = \sum_{t=1}^{t=n} x_t \Big/ n - b \sum_{t=1}^{t=n} t \Big/ n = (2{,}031/16) - (1.4882)(136)/16 = 114.33$$

Finally, the linear formula gives a forecast of demand in each period:

$$y_t = a + bx_t = 126.78 + 0.0176\,t$$

As a final step in the analysis, the forecaster must evaluate the accuracy of the quarterly demand forecasts based on the linear equation.

An informal analysis of the forecast error information in Exhibit 10.14 indicates slight variation of actual deseasonalized sales data from forecasts, perhaps because seasonal index values for the 4-year period are not quite accurate. Overall, however, Exhibit 10.14 shows errors with small magnitudes and no consistent pattern, and Exhibit 10.15 confirms this conclusion graphically. Together, the exhibits support the assumption of a linear trend.

The least-squares method offers a valuable, if rather rigorous, tool for demand forecasting. It helps the forecaster to adjust the results of quantitative methods like rough cut analysis and seasonal adjustment to evaluate the effects of any trend. Together these methods, perhaps in combination with qualitative methods reviewed early in the section, can help operations managers to develop reliable forecasts of demand in stable, predictable situations. In less stable situations, however, clear images of the future may remain elusive. Even then, however, operations managers can try to trace the broad outlines of short-term conditions by applying demand-tracking methods.

This section deals with two types of tools. The first tool allows the business forecaster to adjust time series to factor out any seasonal influences. The second,

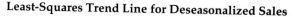

[**E X H I B I T   1 0 . 1 5**]

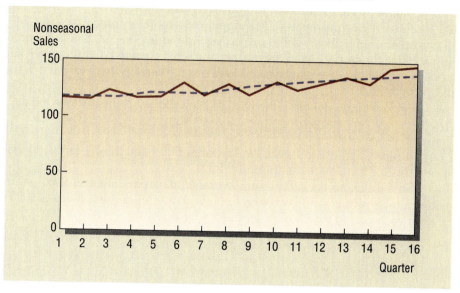

Least-Squares Trend Line for Deseasonalized Sales

the least squares method, helps the business forecaster understand the relationship between the times series under study and time. Together, they help answer two questions. The first is, "Are these two factors stable enough to enhance our numbers?" The next logical question is, "Now that we have adjusted the time series for seasonal and trend factors, how is the business doing?" Management can now direct its resources to real problems rather than to a normally recurring phenomenon.

DEMAND TRACKING

Most short-range forecasting models amount to demand-tracking models. They primarily support near-term operations management decisions such as inventory ordering and resource scheduling. They make basic assumptions that seasonal variations, trends, and cyclical pressures have negligible effects. If these disruptions to continuing operations seem important in a situation, then an operations manager should seriously question the applicability of these models.

Naive Forecasts

This almost trivial practice assumes the current results as the next period's forecast. If a store sells 10 units of a product one day, then its manager forecasts sales of 10 units for the next day. Naive short-term forecasting implies that other bits of past data can add little to the analysis. This method is easy to explain and apply, and, it may perform reasonably well in some situations.

Weighted Averages

The discussion of demand forecasting applied moving averages to decompose data into the NBER's traditional time series components, i.e. seasonal, trend, cyclical, and irregular variations. For short-range forecasting or demand tracking, operations managers often ignore these distinctions and rely on eclectic weighting mechanisms that simply seem to make sense for rather casual reasons.

For example, a naive forecast might leave an uneasy feeling that the future could catch the firm unprepared. Managers may more willingly base near-term forecasts on actual results over the preceding 3 periods. This adjustment would at least minimize the impact of a single, uncharacteristic period. On the other hand, such a limited weighted average would lack enough sensitivity to capture changes in direction or major shifts in the time series.

A 3-period weighted average would give a forecast for the next period as:

$$\mathbf{d_t} = (d_{t-1} + d_{t-2}d_{t-3})/3 \tag{10.8}$$

The term d_t represents the forecasted value for period t and the d_{t-n} terms represent actual results for the designated periods.

To plan a quick-and-dirty moving average, managers must set two parameters: the number of periods over which to calculate the moving average and the weight for each period's data. The general equation is:

$$\mathbf{d_t} = (a_1 d_1 + a_2 d_2 + a_3 d_3 + \ldots + a_n d_n) \tag{10.9}$$

where

$$a_1 + a_2 + a_3 + \ldots + a_n = 1.00$$

Equation 10.8 gave a special case of this one with n specified as 3 and equal values of 0.33 for each of the coefficients. In general, increasing the size of n reduces the impact of atypical results in isolated time periods, but it also reduces the sensitivity of the moving average to significant shifts in the time series. To compensate for this weakness, managers can assign disproportionate weights to results for the most recent time periods. The 3-period moving average might have just as easily assigned weights of $a_1 = 0.50$, $a_2 = 0.30$, and $a_3 = 0.20$ to emphasize data for the most recent periods.

Exponential Smoothing

exponential smoothing

A short-range tracking tool for time series that balances recent data against longer-term patterns by adjusting weighting coefficients in a weighted average

R. G. Brown, a consultant with the Arthur D. Little Company, has developed a more elaborate short-range tracking tool for time series, **exponential smoothing**. The name reflects the negative exponential decline of the weighting coefficients for more distant data in Equation 10.9. Each weight is smaller by a fixed percentage than the weight assigned to data for the previous period:

$$\mathbf{F_{t+1}} = \alpha d_t + \alpha(1-\alpha)d_{t-1} + \alpha(1-\alpha)^1 d_{t-2} + \alpha(1-\alpha)^2 d_{t-3} + \alpha(1-\alpha)^3 d_{t-4} + \ldots \tag{10.10}$$

where

$\mathbf{F_{t+1}}$ = the forecast for the next period, $t + 1$
α = constant, normally called a *smoothing coefficient*
d_t = actual result in Period t

The simple exponential smoothing equation usually takes a different form. To make this conversion, recall the forecast for Period t:

$$\mathbf{F_t} = \alpha d_{t-1} + \alpha(1-\alpha)d_{t-2} + \alpha(1-\alpha)^2 d_{t-3} + \alpha(1-\alpha)^3 d_{t-4} + \alpha(1-\alpha)^4 d_{t-5} + \ldots \tag{10.11}$$

Multiply both sides of Equation 10.11 by $(1 - \alpha)$ to get:

$$(1-\alpha)\mathbf{F_t} = \alpha(1-\alpha)d_{t-1} + \alpha(1-\alpha)^2 d_{t-2} + \alpha(1-\alpha)^3 d_{t-3} + \alpha(1-\alpha)^4 d_{t-4} + \alpha(1-\alpha)^5 d_{t-5} + \ldots$$

Substitute $(1-\alpha)F_t$ for the last four terms in Equation 10.10 to get:

$$\mathbf{F_{t+1}} = \alpha d_t + (1-\alpha)\mathbf{F_t} \tag{10.12}$$

Rearrange terms:

$$\mathbf{F_{t+1}} = d_t + \alpha(d_t - \mathbf{F_t}) \tag{10.13}$$

Both equations offer convenient simplicity. Equation 10.12 states the forecast for the next period as a linear combination of this period's results, d_t, and the most recent forecast, $\mathbf{F_t}$. A manager sets the smoothing coefficient to $\alpha = 0.10$ to base one-tenth of the new forecast on recent results and the remaining nine-tenths on the past forecast.

Equation 10.13 states the new forecast as the prior forecast plus a fraction to compensate for forecast error. The term $(d_t - \mathbf{F_t})$ does not represent an error that justifies any blame, since all forecasts miss actual results by at least a little bit. The language of business forecasting calls these differences *forecast errors,* however, and later discussion will show how they function as variables subject to process-control techniques.

[**PROBLEM 10.1**]

Exponential Smoothing to Track Sales

During this month, actual sales of 115 units exceeded the forecast of 110 units. With a smoothing constant of 0.10, the next month's forecast is:

$$\mathbf{F}_{\text{next month}} = \alpha d_{\text{current month}} + (1-\alpha)\mathbf{F}_{\text{current month}}$$

$$\mathbf{F}_{\text{next month}} = 0.10(115) + (1 - 0.1)(110) = 11.5 + 99 = 110.5 \text{ units} \quad [\blacksquare]$$

To see the effect of the smoothing constant, α, compare the differences in weights with two different values, reported in Exhibit 10.16. After the first period, each period's weight equals the prior period's weight times $(1-\alpha)$. By the 20th period, the period weights become negligible. Note that the cumulative period weights of both smoothing coefficients converge to 1.0, but the higher coefficient value emphasized more recent events more strongly. Hence, to make an exponential smoothing forecast more sensitive to recent events, managers increase the smoothing constant. For stable time series, firms commonly specify smoothing constants between 0.05 and 0.10.

Practitioners have identified two additional benefits of the simplified version of the exponential smoothing model shown in Equation 10.12. First, the term *exponential smoothing* sounds impressive. Hence, consultants have found that it enhances their ability to justify their billing rates. Plant level employees also like to drop the term to create an aura of sophistication.

The second benefit comes from the reduced computer storage and computation requirements, an important consideration in the 1950s but less critical today. Equation 10.12 requires much less input data than a 12-period moving average, and it generates a forecast with fewer arithmetic operations. The difference became vastly more significant over thousands of stock-keeping units, attracting eager converts in the early days of the exponential-smoothing model.

Some may wonder why exponential smoothing remains popular when the cost and availability of computer storage and processing capacity have become so much less important. The simplicity and effectiveness of this method warrant its

[**E X H I B I T   1 0 . 1 6**]

Data Weights and Smoothing Coefficients

	Smoothing Coefficient = 0.10		Smoothing Coefficient = 0.25	
Period	Period Weight	Cumulative	Period Weight	Cumulative
1	0.1000	0.1000	0.2500	0.2500
2	0.9000	0.1900	0.1875	0.4375
3	0.0810	0.2710	0.1406	0.5781
4	0.0729	0.3439	0.1055	0.6836
5	0.0656	0.4095	0.0791	0.7627
6	0.0590	0.4686	0.0593	0.8220
7	0.0531	0.5217	0.0445	0.8665
8	0.0478	0.5695	0.0334	0.8999
9	0.0430	0.6126	0.0250	0.9249
10	0.0387	0.6513	0.0188	0.9437
11	0.0349	0.6862	0.0141	0.9578
12	0.0314	0.7176	0.0106	0.9683
13	0.0282	0.7458	0.0079	0.9762
14	0.0254	0.7712	0.0059	0.9822
15	0.0229	0.7941	0.0045	0.9866
16	0.0206	0.8147	0.0033	0.9900
17	0.0185	0.8332	0.0025	0.9925
18	0.0167	0.8499	0.0019	0.9944
19	0.0150	0.8649	0.0014	0.9958
20	0.0135	0.8784	0.0011	0.9968
21	0.0122	0.8906	0.0008	0.9976
22	0.0109	0.9015	0.0006	0.9982

continued use in many industrial settings, even though history has diminished some of the reasons for its early significance.

The simple exponential-smoothing model in Equation 10.12 is really just a special case of the weighted moving-average method. It cannot anticipate the effects of cyclical variations, trends, or irregular shifts in a time series. In each of these cases, Exhibit 10.17 shows that the simple model will lag the actual time series. In each case, the forecaster can reduce the lag effect by increasing the value of the smoothing constant, but this also increases the risk of disruption due to a quirky number.

Exponential Smoothing with Trend Effects. Early users of the exponential-smoothing model soon started to augment the simple model to accommodate non-standard data. Common sense suggests changing each period's forecast to include an increment as an adjustment for a known trend:

$$FIT_{t+1} = F_{t+1} + T_{t+1} \tag{10.14}$$

where

FIT_{t+1} = forecast including trend for Period t
F_{t+1} = forecast for Period t from the simple model
T_{t+1} = current forecast of the period trend increment

Behavior Pattern of a Simple Exponential Smoothing Model

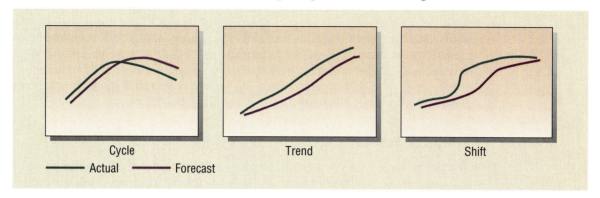

Cycle   Trend   Shift

───── Actual   ───── Forecast

$$F_{t+1} = FIT_t + \alpha(d_t - FIT_t) \tag{10.15}$$

This expression implicitly assumes that the past trend will continue in the future. An exponential-smoothing model for trend can indicate the validity of this assumption:

$$T_{t+1} = T_t + \partial(d_t - FIT_t) \tag{10.16}$$

where ∂ is the transsmoothing coefficient.

[**P R O B L E M   1 0 . 2**]

Exponential Smoothing to Track Sales with Trend Effects

Assume a forecast for the current period, **FIT_t**, predicted sales of 250 units and recent experience suggested a likely sales increase of 10 units each period. Actual sales for the period reached 270 units. Assuming a smoothing coefficient of $\alpha = 0.10$ and a trend smoothing coefficient of $\partial = 0.05$, determine a forecast for the next period.

$$T_{t+1} = T_t + \partial(x_t - FIT_t) = 10 + 0.05(270 - 250) = 10 + 1 = 11$$

and

$$F_{t+1} = FIT_t + \alpha(x_t - FIT_t) = 250 + 0.10(270 - 250) = 252$$

hence

$$FIT_{t+1} = F_{t+1} + F_{t+1} = 252 + 11 = 263$$

If actual demand in Period $t+1$ turned out to be 265, then the forecast for Period $t+2$ would be:

$$T_{t+2} = T_{t+1} + \partial(x_{t+1} - FIT_{t+1}) = 11 + 0.05(265 - 263) = 11 + 0.1 = 11.1$$

then

$$F_{t+2} = FIT_{t+1} + \alpha(x_{t+1} - FIT_{t+1}) = 263 + 0.10(265 - 263) = 263.2$$

hence

$$FIT_{t+2} = F_{t+2} + T_{t+2} = 263.2 + 11.1 = 273.3 \quad [\ \blacksquare \ ]$$

Selecting Smoothing Coefficient Values.   Since exponential smoothing models are essentially linear combinations of the most recent event and a prior forecast, the value of the smoothing constant must fall between 0 and 1.0. For this reason, Exhibit 10.16 showed cumulative weighting factors that approached 1.0. The final choice of a value depends on management judgment. If the model tracks a fairly stable variable free of extreme seasonal effects, trends, or shifts, then a smoothing coefficient between 0.05 and 0.10 seems appropriate. A more volatile time series may require a larger value in the 0.15 to 0.50 range, however. At the extreme, one might set $\alpha = 1.0$ if last period's results seem like the best guess for the current period. By this time, this choice should sound rather naive.

Adaptive Forecasting

Short-term forecasting procedures such as exponential smoothing often form part of management strategies based on the principle of keeping models simple, but adapting to unforeseen change. Exponential-smoothing models can emphasize recent events by increasing the smoothing coefficients, but some managers may look for a more rigorous procedure.

adaptive forecasting

A method of tracking a time series that sets smoothing coefficients based on observed forecast errors

Adaptive forecasting techniques base the choice of smoothing coefficients on observed forecast errors. One simple and effective approach adjusts the smoothing constant to reflect the magnitude of the most recent forecast error. While errors remain small, the forecast includes a small smoothing coefficient; large errors call for large coefficients.

Other proponents of adaptive forecasting have developed more elaborate procedures for adjusting projections to reflect forecast errors. Differences between them come from two basic decisions: when to make adjustments and how large to make the adjustments. All of these models balance simplicity against model performance.

Some models reflect cumulative forecast errors. Others project even near-term demand through complex, three-coefficient exponential-smoothing models that indicate the success of the forecasting procedure at tracking real and significant shifts in the time series. To accomplish this analysis, the equations include a tracking signal based on an exponentially smoothed actual error divided by the exponentially smoothed absolute error. Clearly, this area invites input from inventive minds eager for the challenge of fine-tuning short-term forecasting techniques.

Forecast Error

Earlier discussions have mentioned forecast errors as possible disruptions in the forecasting process. These errors also function as inputs to the quality-improvement process for forecasts. Formally defined, **forecast errors** represent differences between actual outcomes and forecasts for the same periods, that is, the difference between d_t and F_t.

forecast error

The difference between an actual outcome and a forecast for the same period

A stream of such differences creates a time series of error terms:

$$e_t = d_t - F_t \qquad \text{where } t = 1, 2, 3, 4, \dots n \qquad \textbf{(10.17)}$$

A positive value for e_t indicates that actual data exceeded the forecast; a negative value indicates an overly optimistic forecast. Runs of like-sign errors indicate some bias in the forecasting tool, a shift in the behavior of the process, or some cyclical variation.

Operations managers must use the information supplied by forecast errors, along with pertinent external information, to improve their service to the internal customers of the forecasts. To guide their actions, managers must determine the performance characteristics that they should reasonably expect of their forecasting tools. The decision often centers on four traits of effective forecasts:

1. Accuracy sufficient to support the decision-making process
2. Reasonably timely indications of major shifts in process performance
3. Simplicity in use
4. Understandable to users

Obviously, this list forces tradeoffs, for example, between accuracy and simplicity. As always, the customer's preference should guide the operations manager's decision.

The problem of measuring forecast accuracy resembles the process-control problem discussed in Chapter 8. Instead of having to judge overall characteristics based on the statistical attributes of a series of small samples, however, forecasting accuracy reflects the attributes of streams of forecast errors.

Recall that the early users of control charts in quality management considered range as a shortcut for a measure of the dispersion of values within a sample rather than calculating the standard deviation of the sample's data. The early practitioners of forecast error measurement made the same choice. They created a new statistic called the **mean absolute deviation** (MAD), defined as:

mean absolute deviation
A measure of forecast accuracy that averages the absolute value of forecast errors for a sample

$$MAD = \sum_{t-1}^{n} \left| d_t - F_t \right| \Big/ n \qquad \textbf{(10.18)}$$

where

d_t = actual demand for period t
F_t = forecast for period t
n = number of periods

Note that this equation sums the absolute value of the forecast errors, so negative values do not offset positive ones and hide variation of the forecast from actual data. Many forecasters prefer MAD over standard deviation because it is easier to use, involving only a subtraction operation.

MAD and Standard Deviation. For normally distributed forecast errors, 1.00 standard deviation equals 1.25 the mean absolute deviations, or 1.00 MAD equals 0.80 standard deviations. Thus, 3.75 MADs are equivalent to 3.00 standard deviations in a normal process.

The originators of MAD were concerned that this measure of accuracy would miss major forecast errors, so they created another term, the **mean squared error** (MSE):

mean squared error
A measure of forecast accuracy that averages the square of total forecast errors for a sample

$$MSE = \sum_{t-1}^{n} \left(d_t - F_t \right)^2 \Big/ (n-1) \qquad \textbf{(10.19)}$$

The terms represent the same variables as in the MAD expression, Equation 10.18. The MSE looks like a formula for the variance of forecast errors, but such a formula would use the actual forecast errors (e, e_t) and the mean of the forecast errors:

$$\text{Forecast error variance} = \sum_{t-1}^{n} \left(e_t - \bar{e} \right)^2 \Big/ (n-1) \qquad \textbf{(10.20)}$$

While the MSE does not correctly state the standard deviation of the forecast errors, many practitioners use it as a decent approximation.

[**PROBLEM 10.3**]

MAD and MSE for Forecast Error Detection

To see how to calculate MAD and MSE, consider the data in Exhibit 10.18. Applying Equations 10.15 and 10.16 gives these values:

$$MAD = 63/10 = 6.3 \quad MSE = 589/9 = 65.4$$

Either of these statistics can give an estimate of the standard deviation of the forecast errors. The first estimate, 1.25 times the MAD statistic, gives a value of 6.30×1.25, or 7.78. The square root of the MSE gives a second estimate of 8.08. Both approximate 8.00.   [▪]

To interpret a MAD or MSE value, or an implied standard deviation, recall the four traits of an effective short-term forecasting process. Simple forecasting models such as exponential smoothing and moving averages satisfy the desire for a tool that is easy to use and explain. Forecast error statistics like MAD and MSE emphasize forecast accuracy and indicators of major shifts in demand. The choice of a single short-term forecasting tool should probably involve a tradeoff of simplicity against accuracy. Forecasters need a simple and efficient model because they have to prepare thousands of forecasts; they also need a reliable model, or perhaps a mechanism to indicate inaccuracy in the simple model. This choice applies management by exception to target management attention on deviations from expected performance.

For another tool, control charts, discussed in Chapter 8 as signals of possible lapses in process control, can also contribute to business forecasting systems. A forecast error control chart might specify upper and lower bounds at ± 3 standard deviations above and below an assumed mean error of zero (Exhibit 10.19). Continuing the example from Problem 10.3, the standard deviation estimate of 8.0 would imply control limits at ± 24.0 for the data in Exhibit 10.18.

Just as in quality management, the rules that signal an out-of-control situation apply here. The forecast error analysis must ask whether an unbiased forecasting

[**EXHIBIT 10.18**]

Data for Forecast Error Calculations

Period	Actual	Forecast	Forecast Error	|Actual − Forecast|	Error Square
1	345	340	5	5	25
2	328	341	−13	13	156
3	335	339	−4	4	18
4	330	339	−9	9	78
5	334	338	−4	4	16
6	340	338	2	2	6
7	338	338	0	0	0
8	328	338	−10	10	96
9	345	337	8	8	67
10	350	338	12	12	153
Total			−16	63	589

[**E X H I B I T   1 0 . 1 9**]

Forecast Error Control Chart

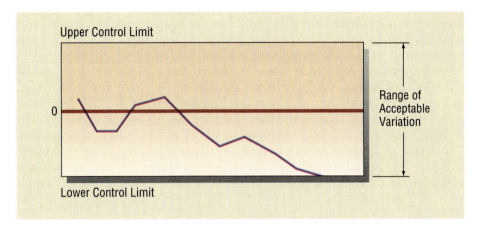

tool under the assumed conditions would produce forecast errors with the observed values or pattern. Unfortunately, there may not be a value outside the 3 standard deviation control limit to signal an error.

In addition, practitioners objected that it would take too long to analyze the pattern of forecast errors for every stock-keeping unit. The creators of the MAD and MSE statistics reacted to this criticism by creating a new tool that helped users of these statistics to remember forecast error conditions in previous periods. This **tracking signal** records each product's cumulative forecast error, eliminating the need to maintain a control chart for each item in stock. Mathematically, they expressed this signal as:

tracking signal
An indicator of cumulative forecast error implied by MAD and MSE statistics for an individual product or item in inventory

$$\text{Tracking signal} = \sum_{t=1}^{t=n}\left(d_t - F_t\right)\Big/MAD \qquad \textbf{(10.21)}$$

For each period, the forecaster recalculates each product's tracking signal and compares that value with a control limit, normally set somewhere between ±3 and ±8 standard deviations. The smaller limit gives a more sensitive indicator, perhaps signaling a problem when the data shows only minor variation. The larger limit allows wide latitude for forecast performance, perhaps waiting to signal a problem until the process produces extreme variation.

The earlier discussion of adaptive forecasting hinted at a similar attempt to automate signals for management intervention. Rather than simply indicating poor forecast accuracy, adaptive forecasting automatically increases the value of the smoothing constant, anticipating the forecaster's reaction to make data more manageable. This approximates the effect of a much more complex computerized expert system.

Such automatic correction for unpredictable data can simplify the life of the manager, but when a particular demand forecast routinely misstates actual results, it warrants some sort of management intervention. This intervention should include some assessment of the real effects of poor forecasts on organization operations. For example, consistently low forecasts may suggest a need for additional production of the popular product. Managers may also decide to raise the safety stock level to keep more inventory as a buffer against the continuing uncertainty.

Forecasters should also review the pattern of forecast errors to study the process that generates actual demand. Past patterns of forecast errors may suggest sources of variation. This knowledge may help managers to focus resources either to eliminate the causes of undesirable errors and improve forecasting accuracy or to find the causes of favorable forecast errors and exploit them as market opportunities. Clearly, if actual sales far exceed forecasted sales, the firm should not try to eliminate the cause of the forecast error and bring actual sales down to match the forecast.

Finally, forecasters should review the model and parameters of a forecasting tool that fails to capture actual demand accurately. They may discover a need to upgrade a simple model to accommodate seasonal influences. They may need to make a simple model more sensitive by increasing the value of the smoothing coefficient. They might even learn something about their business environment by reviewing the assumption of every short-term forecasting model that past performance provides a good basis for predicting the future. Routine variations of actual results from forecasts may suggest that this basic assumption has lost validity.

UNDERSTANDING FINAL-PRODUCT DEMAND AND DEMAND FOR COMPONENTS

Demand for components ultimately depends on demand for the final products that use them. The patterns of part usage often differ from final product assembly schedules because manufacturing schedules often do not follow product sales closely. Operations managers schedule production in batches and time production runs to maximize efficiency. They ship truckloads of products to distribution centers in order to achieve economies. These sources of system variance force demand forecasts for components to consider likely needs of production runs rather than cumulative demand for end products.

Even the method of transmitting customer orders through the distribution system can transform a relatively stable end-product demand pattern into an intermittent, lumpy part usage pattern within the manufacturing process. Suppose that you run an egg-manufacturing process composed of several single-hen work stations. Your only customer is Louie's Diner, a small breakfast nook in Hope, Arkansas. Each day, Louie's only customer routinely orders two eggs over easy. The hens could easily meet this need, but Louie does not communicate his needs daily. Instead, he orders a dozen eggs about once a week. Thus the hens face a lumpy demand pattern of 0-0-0-0-0-12-0-0-0-0-0-12, etc. If Louie would buy two eggs every day, you could satisfy him by simply hiring two reliable hens. His demand for eggs in dozens, however, forces you to create products in 12-unit batches, perhaps by accumulating stock or hiring temp-hens about once a week.

This simple example illustrates a problem that most manufacturing organizations face every day. Some simple communication between customer and producer could help to smooth operations for both. Still, structural problems within manufacturing complicate patterns of component demand. Any economies of scale create requirements for batch sizes that transform relatively uniform final-product demand into a rather lumpy and erratic pattern of component needs.

Exhibit 10.20 illustrates a relatively stable stream of orders for finished goods and the intermittent orders of components designed to feed the resulting production. The structural problem that sets the component production schedule could result from a warehouse ordering in truckload quantities or some downstream department that requires large, infrequent lots of inputs for a batch production

Economies of Scale and Component Demand

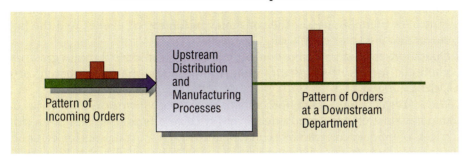

process. Clearly, this problem is one that the just-in-time approach to operations management tries to solve. A decision to use smaller trucks or smaller egg cartons can be justified if it provides higher value to the next-stage customer.

CHAPTER SUMMARY

At the start of this chapter, Fruit of the Loom struggled to schedule production without a good forecast of demand to suggest how many of its products to make and how much raw material to buy. Mothers Work needed to know what was selling to take advantage of its quick response capabilities.

1. Demand management seeks to influence demand in a way that helps the OM system to function effectively. Demand forecasting tries to anticipate future demand based on observed patterns of past customer orders. Demand tracking works to accurately measure actual demand. The choice of methods for each of these tasks begins with the internal customer's need for information as an input to some business process.

2. Demand management in service industries creates appointment systems or other scheduling methods to match customer needs to OM system capacity. Some firms set up flexible pricing systems to attract customers during periods of slack demand. Without these two methods, the service provider can simply force customers to wait.

3. Demand management in make-to-order manufacturing centers on methods for setting promised delivery dates. In assemble-to-order manufacturing, operations managers coordinate promised delivery dates with component manufacturing schedules to compile parts-feasible final build schedules. Make-to-stock manufacturers often maintain elaborate inventory management systems to move finished goods to the locations where customers want them.

4. Demand management creates a compelling need for cross-functional cooperation to speed product development. Accurate input from market information systems supports and guides this process.

5. The five-step process of demand forecasting begins by identifying the internal customer for the forecast. It continues by identifying the best sources of necessary information inputs and selecting and applying appropriate forecasting models to generate timely, reliable forecasts over the correct time period. The process concludes with a step to monitor the accuracy of forecasts.

6. The choice of a forecasting process depends on six conditions in the OM environment: the time horizon for management decisions, the level of detail that the user of the forecast needs to support decisions, the number of products for which the process must generate forecasts, the decision makers' emphasis on control or planning needs, the constancy of forecasted events, and the firm's current methods for developing forecasts.

7. Operations managers derive qualitative demand forecasts through grass-roots methods, focused forecasting, historical analogy, market research, or the Delphi method.

8. They develop quantitative forecasts to decompose historical time-series data into seasonal effects, trend effects, and cyclical effects to reveal the residual effects of unique, current forces on demand. Rough-cut analysis looks for obvious repeating changes in a time series, usually by graphing it. To adjust for seasonal effects, forecasters calculate centered moving averages based on seasonal adjustment coefficients and seasonal index values. To evaluate trend effects, forecasters employ the statistical least-squares method, often with the aid of computer spreadsheet software.

9. In demand tracking, operations managers may develop naive forecasts or employ more sophisticated weighted-average methods. Exponential smoothing refines weighted averages to control the emphasis on the most recent data in a time series by varying the smoothing coefficient and adding a term for forecast error. Adaptive forecasting adjusts these coefficients for cumulative experience based on actual results.

10. Two measures of forecast error, mean absolute deviation and mean squared error, try to approximate a statistical standard deviation without too much complex calculation. A tracking signal based on these measures indicates when forecast error exceeds tolerable limits based on cumulative evaluations of deviations of forecasts from actual results for each product in a firm's inventory.

11. Economies of scale and other structural problems in an OM system can decouple demand for components from final-product demand.

Many readers may feel relieved of a heavy weight of theoretical discussions and mathematical symbols after completing this complex chapter. The forecasting learning lab in Appendix 10A invites more practical applications to encourage a more comprehensive understanding of the detailed information discussed throughout the chapter. The lab format saves readers from entering the data, freeing them to focus on the more interesting challenge of matching the tools discussed in this chapter to real-world scenarios. Please feel free to modify the templates. Unlike a chemistry laboratory, a mistake won't blow up anything.

[KEY TERMS]

demand management 444
demand forecasting 445
intrinsic input 445
extrinsic input 445
service-delay management 449

waiting-management program 449
promised delivery date 450
final build schedule 450
grass-roots forecasting 459

focused forecasting 459
historical analogy 459
panel consensus 460
Delphi method 460
centered moving average 465
seasonal index 466

[DISCUSSION QUESTIONS]

1. Think of four instances in your life when you confronted sellers' demand management practices. List the tradeoffs that determined scheduling in each case. As a value-conscious customer, do you think that each of the four sellers served you well?

2. Prepare a list of your service purchases that involved customer scheduling. What did you gain as a customer by tolerating this scheduling? What did you lose? Interpret this analysis in light of the value equation.

3. Research results that imply that golf balls warmed to between 105 and 128 degrees Fahrenheit travel about 15 to 25 meters farther than unwarmed balls if properly hit. Based on this exciting research, your firm has developed a new product—a golf ball warmer. How would you estimate the demand pattern for this product?

4. Your boss has less training than you have in business statistics. She asks you to explain the logic of the least-squares method for determining a trend line. What would you tell her?

5. Now that you have proved yourself such a useful source of information, your boss wants you to explain the term *exponential smoothing*. How do you reply?

6. Your firm is considering reducing staff and your business forecasting department has been mentioned as a prime candidate for this treatment. Outline a brief to defend the value of your department's services to the firm. How could you quantify your claims?

7. Explain the management principles inherent in short-term demand forecasting models.

8. Recall a poor decision that you made without a correct assessment of recent events. What information systems could you implement to avoid repeating the same mistake?

9. Someone in your organization suspects a causal relationship between statistics on corrugated board shipments reported in *Business Week* and your company's shipments using the boxes. How would you test this assertion? If you were to verify the relationship, how could you use it in your business?

10. Your firm manufactures a laser-processed identification card for the hospital market. Each patient carries a card imprinted with his or her entire medical history to be read by an optical scanner. Health-care reform proposals in Congress are considering distributing such cards as integral parts of a proposed national health program. Currently your plant has a capacity of 24 million cards a year, and your firm has patent protection on the technology. How would you estimate demand over the next 5 years? Draw a decision tree describing your company's options.

11. The morning newscast reports that this month's seasonally adjusted unemployment rate fell from 7.1 percent to 6.8 percent, while the number of unemployed rose by about 600,000. Your English-major friend does not understand how this could be so. Explain the calculation process.

12. What is a seasonal adjustment factor or seasonal index? When can a calculation safely use them?

13. If a simple model assumes no trend and makes no allowance for seasonal variations, how will it behave when applied to a time series with:
   a. Significant long-term trend
   b. Significant seasonal effects

c. Significant random shifts in the demand function, either upward or downward

d. Significant random, temporary surges in demand like those produced by offering customers a two-for-one deal

14. Assume that you are the regional operations manager responsible for 27 Burger Queen restaurants. What types of demand forecasts do you think you would need for your short-term planning? What decisions would each forecast support? Identify the internal customer of each forecast?

15. As the regional manager of 27 Burger Queens, you are thinking about expanding the number of outlets in your area. What types of forecasts would you want to help solve this systems-design problem?

16. You have become concerned about the amount of copier paper used in your office after repeatedly running out of supplies. Your assistant keeps track of the number of reams (packages of 500 sheets) for 24 weeks:

Week	1	2	3	4	5	6	7	8	9	10	11	12
Reams of paper	232	263	271	248	235	261	207	243	237	293	243	260

Week	13	14	15	16	17	18	19	20	21	22	23	24
Reams of paper	253	270	230	253	238	272	222	243	289	238	262	234

a. Compare the effectiveness of 2-week, 4-week, and 12-week moving averages. Which should you use to forecast copier paper use during the next week.

b. Compare the performance of the simple exponential smoothing model with smoothing constants of 0.01, 0.05, and 0.25. Assume a forecast for Week 1 of 230 reams. Which constant worked best?

c. Create your own adaptive forecasting model. How accurately did it forecast each week's paper use? Why do you think that it did better or worse than the best model discovered in Questions 16a and 16b?

d. How could you use this information to solve the paper shortage problem?

e. How would you try to dissolve this problem?

C A U T I O N

[C R I T I C A L   T H I N K I N G   R E Q U I R E D]

1. Exponential smoothing became popular, in part, because computers had limited memory capacity and computing resources were expensive. How will demand forecasting change when both are virtually free commodities?

2. Describe the likely effects of the following business trends on demand forecasting processes:

   a. Just-in-time manufacturing

   b. Fast-to-market product design

   c. Division of many markets into isolated niches

   How would you modify your firm's demand management or demand forecasting processes in response to these trends?

C A S E   1 0 . 1

Happiness Express

Top management at Happiness Express has a problem. In June 1995, *Business Week* listed this relatively new marketer of accessory toys at the top of its Hot Growth Companies list. In fiscal 1995, Happiness Express posted the following results:

Sales	$49.5 million (up 111.8 percent)
Earnings	$6.4 million (up 439.2 percent)
Return on capital	68.2%
Market value	$78 million
Price-earnings ratio	11

The company's managers worry, however, because it has achieved these results by marketing accessories to hot toys. It fills a niche producing toys and accessories based on popular licensed characters like Walt Disney's Little Mermaid, Fox's popular Simpsons cartoon, and, of course, Barney the Dinosaur.

This market has shown serious instability, however. Barney-related gadgets accounted for 55 percent of fiscal 1994 sales. The following year, Barney contributed less than 1 percent to sales. In fiscal 1995, Happiness Express earned 75 percent of both its sales and its revenue from Power Rangers merchandise.

Wall Street toy-industry analysts observe that every company that has derived more than 50 percent of its profits from a single hot product faces financial difficulty when that product cools off. One stock analyst as already projected a 33 percent drop in earnings to $5 million for Happiness Express this year. On Wall Street, you are only as good as your last hit product.

Happiness Express management has responded to this threat by diversifying its product base by acquiring many new licenses. It also has added experienced toy-industry executives from Tyco and Hasbro to strengthen its management team. The firm has focused its strategy on taking a position in front of each potential new fad and then acting quickly enough to ride that wave to the marketplace. To do this, Happiness will have to excel at fast-to-product design and astute demand forecasting.

QUESTIONS

1. Is Happiness Express a promising candidate for a demand-management program? Why?
2. What type of demand-forecasting program should the firm adopt?
3. What other business processes should Happiness strengthen?

SOURCE   "Happiness Is a Hot Toy," *Business Week,* May 22, 1995, p. 40.

[SELECTED READINGS]

Box, G. E. P., and G. M. Jenkins. *Time Series Analysis Forecasting and Control*, rev. ed. San Francisco: Holden-Day, 1976.

Brown, R. G. *Smoothing, Forecasting, and Prediction.* Englewood Cliffs, N.J.: Prentice-Hall, 1963.

Makridakis, S., and S. C. Wheelwright. *Forecasting Methods for Management*, 5th ed. New York: John Wiley & Sons, 1989.

Shiskin, J., A. H. Young, and Y. C. Musgrave. *The X-11 Variant of the Census II Method, Seasonal Adjustment Program.* U. S. Bureau of the Census, Technical Paper 15.

Woolsey, R. E. D., and H. F. Swanson. *Operations Research for Immediate Application: A Quick and Dirty Manual.* New York: Harper & Row, 1975.

Winters, P. R. "Forecasting Sales by Exponentially Weighted Moving Averages." *Management Science,* April 1960, pp. 324–342.

APPENDIX 10A

Forecasting Learning Lab

In earlier studies, you may have taken a chemistry laboratory class where you received a specimen of some substance with the assignment of identifying it. This appendix seeks to replicate that kind of discovery-based learning. It provides a time series and some additional data for each of several situations. Some numbers will seem abstract, but most problems will provide additional information that may help you. Beware: all data is not useful.

In the interest of economy, these problems save you the trouble of entering the data; the student disk includes all time-series data. The data will be the same in each template. This template also allows us to avoid overloading this chapter with long, expensive tables, enhancing the value of this text by reducing its retail cost.

Data Set 1 [File DS1]

Profile.   This time series reports demand over a 260-week period. You found the data at the bottom of a drawer, so you know nothing about the business, its industrial sector, or the manner in which it has been collected.

Assignment 1A.   Determine whether or not this time series exhibits either seasonal or trend effects.

Assignment 1B.   Select three of the short-term forecasting models discussed in this chapter. Use the data for the first 156 weeks to determine the needed parameters for each model, then use these parameters in each of the three short-term forecasting models to test their effectiveness over the last 104 weeks of this time series.

Based on your analysis of each model's forecast error patterns, which one would you recommend? Why?

Data Set 2 [File DS2]

Profile.   This data set includes a 260-week time series for a variable of considerable interest to your firm—employee absenteeism. It also provides numbers over the same period for five other variables that represent potential causes of fluctuations in absenteeism.

Assignment 2A.   Use data for the first 208 weeks to test the assumption that variables 1 through 5 have significant effects on the dependent variable (absenteeism).

Assignment 2B.   Use this information to develop a model capable of forecasting the dependent variable. Test the performance of your model on data for the last 52 weeks. How good is your model?

Data Set 3 [File DS3]

Profile.   This data set comes from the federal government's Department of Labor Statistics, which collects state and national unemployment statistics. The data set includes monthly data for the last 20 years for the number of jobless people and the total number of people in the work force. It also includes the deseasonalized coefficients currently in use.

Assignment.   Review the seasonal effects implied by the data and evaluate the accuracy of the current coefficients. What problems do you foresee with using these numbers?

Data Set 4 [File DS4]

Profile.   As a demand analyst at a fast-food corporation's headquarters, you are asked to study the within-day pattern of demand for its burger product. The data set represents the sales for a representative company operation for the last 20 Tuesdays. The number of burgers sold in each 15-minute interval is listed.

Assignment.   Estimate the seasonal factors for burger demand within a day. Who within the corporation might be interested in this data? How might they use it?

Data Set 5 [File DS5]

Profile.   In training classes for the above fast-food corporation, the impact of weather on sales is frequently discussed. Some possible winter-related factors are:

- Whether the outlet has a drive-up window
- The nature of foul weather
    light rain
    heavy rain
    light snow
    heavy snow
- The geographic region of country (in some regions, bad weather is the norm)
- The location of outlet
    stand-alone
    within a store, such as Wal-Mart
    within a school

Assignment.   Analyze how weather might impact sales, using this data.

Data Set 6 [File DS6]

Profile.   The manager of plant maintenance is trying to figure out how many maintenance personnel to schedule through a day. As part of his analysis, he has recorded the number of calls for service his department has received in each hour over the past ten weeks; the plant works one eight-hour shift.

Assignment.   Analyze the nature of service-call demand.

Data Set 7 [File DS7]

Profile.   Is it more valuable to forecast detailed demand or aggregate demand? Sales figures for five portable radio models for each week over the past year are provided. This is shown in file DS7.

Assignment.   What can you tell about demand for this product? What short-term forecasting approach would you recommend to track demand? What managerial implications do you find? What additional data might you want?

Data Set 8 [File DS8]

Profile.   The blood technician at a central city hospital is alarmed by the number of times the hospital has run out or nearly run out of units of blood. The demand for blood is driven largely by the number and type of emergencies the hospital experiences—many of which are the result of violence. You have data for daily blood usage at the hospital's emergency department for the last calendar year, including factors such as day of week, weather conditions, and full moons.

Assignment.   Can you provide a reasonably good forecasting model? What do the data say?

Data Set 9 [File DS9]

Profile.   Pep Girls, an auto parts store for working women, can buy low-priced battery jumper cables from an offshore source. However, the vendor requires a one-time purchase in May for delivery in October. You have data for store-by-store sales for the last 10 years. Not all stores have been open for the full 10 years.

Assignment.   How many sets of jumper cables should Pep Girls buy to assure only a 5 percent chance of running out of stock?

Data Set 10 [File DS10]

Profile.   Your firm uses a simple exponential smoothing model to track demand for the 4,000 units in its warehouse. The stocked items are food items with fairly stable demand. Two factors account for the major portion of forecast errors.
   The first factor that affects the forecast is a promotion for that item—a food chain may run an ad running an item at a hot price. Knowing about these promotions beforehand is not possible.
   The second type of demand shift occurs when a chain decides either to add or to drop an item. In this case, the actual mean of the demand function has shifted, but the warehouse is not usually informed of these decisions either.
   Your data set concerns a product with the above characteristics, including daily demand for this item over the past year.

Assignment.   Determine the proper smoothing constant and an appropriate tracking signal scheme that can help spot the significant changes that have occurred in this item's demand function. What would you recommend?

CHAPTER ELEVEN

Product-Innovation Process

CHAPTER OBJECTIVES

[At the end of this chapter, you should be able to]

- Describe the effects of target markets on a firm's product line.
- Discuss how technology and social forces affect product development.
- List key elements of product design and development of market leaders.
- Explain the tradeoffs that drive standardization decisions.
- Outline the contributions of emerging organizational structures to processes for designing new products for change-driven markets.
- Trace the cross-functional links among marketing, engineering, and operations management that facilitate product innovation.

3M Scours the Market for New Ideas
—and Cleans Up at the Supermarket

WHEN LIVIO DESIMONE TOOK OVER as CEO of 3M in 1991, the $14-billion-a-year Minnesota corporation already had a strongly entrenched culture of innovation. For years 3M had spent 6 to 7 percent of its revenues on research and development—double the industry average. Its 8,000 researchers spent 15 percent of their time "bootlegging"—brainstorming and working on projects of their own choosing.

But as DeSimone looked over the idea factory's recent accomplishments, he was discouraged to see mostly variations of old themes, such as neon versions of 3M's once-revolutionary Post-it notes. Sales figures more than hinted at creative stagnation: 3M's growth had almost completely stalled.

DeSimone decided to crank up 3M's innovation machine, with a target of gleaning 30 percent of its annual revenues from products less than four years old. He reorganized the firm to create more cross-functional teams, moving marketing staff closer to scientists and involving inventors in overall product strategy. He also improved communication with the firm's potential customers, assessing customer preferences at each stage of a product's development. Finally, DeSimone instituted a so-called "pacing program," calling on his managers to focus on only the best new ideas and rush them from the lab to the market.

DeSimone's strategy of scouring for new ideas has paid off, inspiring products like Scotch-Brite Never Rust soap pads, which hit the market in record time. Steel wool pads like Brillo and SOS can leave tiny metal splinters in consumer's hands and rust stains on the sink. Not only is 3M's new webbed plastic pad immune to these defects, but it's made from recycled plastic beverage bottles, appealing to consumers' environmental consciousness. Within eighteen months of its introduction, the pad had cleaned up at the supermarket, capturing a whopping 22 percent of the $100-million-a-year U.S. market.

Thanks largely to new products like this, 3M's net profits increased 5 percent in 1994 to $1.3 billion. Some $1 billion of 3M's $15.1 billion revenues in 1994 came from products launched during the year, and analysts expect things to go even better for 3M in the future. Experts attribute most of the turnaround to 3M's new chairman and his goal of watching for ideas for new products which consumers did not even know they wanted.

SOURCES

Shawn Tully, "Why to Go for Stretch Targets," *Fortune,* November 14, 1994, pp. 148–150.

"The Mass Production of Ideas, and Other Impossibilities," *The Economist,* March 18, 1995, p. 72.

In Chapter 5, we stressed the importance of OM processes. While these operational details have important effects on organizational effectiveness, the product that the firm delivers still determines whether or not it delights its customers. Customers are demanding continuing improvements in quality and more customized products. Further, they want quick delivery and a pleasant smile. They compare the performance of each product offering with its costs to assess value.

In this chapter, we discuss organizational arrangements for creating goods and services that meet or exceed customers' expectations. We describe key attributes of the goods and services that a firm delivers to its customers and the business process by which it creates and enhances them, called the *product-innovation process.* As an overall objective for this chapter, we want to develop a framework to help business students learn to work effectively with key members of cross-functional product-development teams.

GOODS, SERVICES, AND PRODUCTS

Marketers define a **product** as anything that an organization can offer to a market for attention, acquisition, use, or consumption that might satisfy a want or a need.[1] They also distinguish the three levels of a product shown in Exhibit 11.1.

The **core product** represents the essential benefit or service that the customer experiences. The product designer must create a bundle of goods and services to meet or exceed the expectations of the firm's target customers. The **actual product**

product

Anything that an organization can offer to a market for attention, acquisition, use, or consumption that might satisfy a want or a need

core product

The essential benefit or service that the customer experiences

actual product

The unit that sits on a shelf or in a showroom display

[1]P. Kotler and G. Armstrong, *Principles of Marketing,* 5th ed. (Englewood Cliffs, N.J.: Prentice-Hall, 1991), p. 253.

Three Levels of a Product

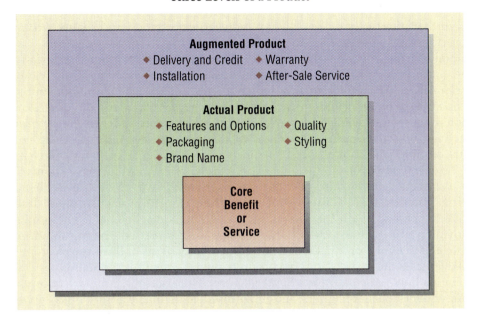

is the unit that sits on a shelf or in a showroom display. Recall from a discussion early in the book that goods are tangible parts of products designed to satisfy some customers' needs.

The **augmented product** represents the intangible component or service that a product provides. In the auto industry, the augmented product includes after-sale customer service, routine maintenance and repair services, financing, and the 3-year/36,000 mile warranty. McDonald's augmented product includes a cheerful greeting when a customer approaches the counter, a neat children's play area, clown images, and clean rest rooms. Some products may consist almost entirely of augmented services. A life insurance policy may include a tangible document, but the core benefit to the customer comes from the assurance of financial security for the buyer's beneficiaries.

augmented product
The intangible component or service that a product provides

Basis for Competition among Products

To survive the intense competition among products, a firm must provide what customers want. The square labeled *core benefit or service* in Exhibit 11.1 is small. Product designers face a harder challenge than dart players because changes in technology, consumer preferences, and competitive conditions force them to aim at moving targets. The risk of missing a dynamic target cannot free the firm from the need for product innovation. Instead, it forces the firm to develop a product design and development process smart enough to anticipate market shifts and agile enough to follow them. Chapter 10 described such a system at Mothers Work. Later in this chapter, we will describe some management tools that can help firms to make their product-innovation processes more nimble.

Managing Customer Expectations.   The most successful competitors often move beyond systems that respond to observed desires and begin working to manage customer expectations. The familiar goal of meeting or exceeding customers' expectations dominates the product-innovation process. A firm with a product design that effectively closes the gap between expectation and reality will out-compete rivals in the race to satisfy customers.

Some firms intentionally work to raise customer expectations, especially if they can meet or exceed those higher expectations while competitors cannot. Alaska Airlines advertises superior inflight meals, and it need not provide four-star cuisine to beat other airlines' food quality. Another firm may try to reduce expectations of amenities while raising expectations of low prices if it can compete most effectively on price. Southwest Airlines encourages customers to expect safe, courteous, on-time transportation, but not much more, at lower fares than rivals charge.

To effectively manage customer expectations, a firm must not only know what the customers want but also how they are likely to behave. This requires the marketing function to provide a thorough understanding of customers' latent demands, perhaps with the assistance of operations management. The product-innovation process must identify the set of tradeoffs that will permit the firm to create and deliver a product that exceeds the expectations of the target customers, while it meets the expectations of corporate management for profitability.

In his book, *Manufacturing Strategy,* Terry Hill used the familiar concepts of order winners, order qualifiers, and order losers to define necessary links between a firm's stated objectives and the output it needs from its OM process to achieve those objectives. In the following sections, we will apply this concept to the process of designing competitive products, first for service organizations and then for manufacturers of tangible products.

Competitive Strengths in Services

The task of managing customer expectations requires difficult choices among seemingly infinite ways to please customers. One-size-fits-all solutions common in make-to-stock manufacturing also appeal to some service organizations. That is how McDonald's got its start. Other service providers favor the virtual-enterprise model (described in greater detail in Chapter 13) that tries to provide a highly customized service for an individual customer, any time, any place, and at prices not significantly higher than standardized offerings—and probably on credit with a no-questions-asked return policy.

In its purest form, a service firm delivers an experience or a set of events that make customers say "Wow!" These might include a fantastic meal, a soccer match that excites you, and a 300 bowling score that you will never let your friends forget. Service firms also deliver some experiences that are not so delightful—a root canal from your dentist, a negative credit report on a nice couple who had offered to buy your house.

Services seem harder to define than goods because they vary so much in form. Some analysts try to distinguish services by the nature of their activities. Fitzsimmons breaks services into five subgroups:[2]

- Business services (banking, advertising, finance, insurance)
- Trade services (retailing, wholesaling, maintenance and repair)
- Infrastructure services (trucking, communications, etc.)

---

[2]J. A. Fitzsimmons, *Service Management for Competitive Advantage* (New York: McGraw Hill, 1994), p.170.

- Social/personal services (restaurants, health care, gardening)
- Public services (education, police protection, garbage removal)

Following our earlier discussion on services, we return to this topic here. These operations share certain traits:

1. *Intangibility*   Service providers deliver products that customers cannot touch or grasp. An ad agency delivers a radio commercial. A publisher of romantic novels delivers desirable feelings. These product offerings may also include components that customers can touch (i.e., books), but customers actually buy the experiences.
2. *Perishability*   Most services, but not all, are perishable. A Broadway play exists only in the memory of the audience after the curtain falls. Videotape may capture part of the experience, but not everything that the audience felt, saw, and sensed in the theater.
3. *Simultaneity*   Customers or something of theirs must be present to undergo the service. Hair cuts, back rubs, and eye exams require the presence of the customer. Firms cannot store these services for future consumption as they can store manufactured goods. Although a gardener can mow a customer's lawn while no one is home, the object of the service (the lawn) still must be present.
4. *Heterogeneity*   Individual preferences and perceptions of particular customers often determine the nature and content of a service. The service provider may not know exactly what product it will deliver until the customer asks for specific help. A waiter asks diners what they will order. Local telephone installers can plan specific actions only after arriving on site. This trait requires a service delivery system to prepare for a wide range of possible encounters.

Some operations management theorists believe that services differ so much from goods that they require separate treatment. This appeal for separation of service management from operations management hinges on the cross-functional nature of service management. We point out that effective operations management for a manufacturer also crosses functional boundaries, especially during product-innovation projects.

Product-Innovation Challenge

General Electric CEO Jack Welch once stated that a successful firm needs satisfied customers, satisfied employees, and an adequate cash flow to perpetuate survival. Of these three tests, satisfying customers is the most difficult, and this focuses critical attention on the effort to design products that exceed customers' expectations. Efficient producers of merely satisfactory products often will not survive.

Three American giants, IBM, General Motors, and Sears, learned this lesson through painful experience. Exhibit 11.2 illustrates the changes in the relative stock market rankings of these former industrial leaders over the past 20 years. By 1992, other well-known American firms like Wal-Mart, Merck, and Coca-Cola had surged ahead of these slumping giants. Also, 8 of the top 20 firms in worldwide stock market value have come from Japan.

These declining giants truly seem like dinosaurs since each appears unable to adjust to changing economic conditions or to revise its image of what its markets want. This has happened before, but in the 1990s, it is occurring at a faster pace. In your lifetime, many one-time industry leaders have lost stature under the

Stock Market Values of Three Industrial Giants

Firm	1972		1992	
	Rank	Sales ($ billions)	Rank	Sales ($ billions)
IBM	1st	$46.8	26th	$29.0
GM	4th	23.2	40th	22.0
Sears	6th	18.2	81st	16.0

SOURCE   Adapted from Carol Loomis, "Dinosaurs," *Fortune*, May 3, 1993, p. 37.

competitive assault of new goods and services. These might include Chuck E. Cheese Pizza Time Theaters, Pong (the early home video game), and the Ford Country Squire station wagon. Only Coca-Cola, Elvis, and the Barbie Doll seem likely to live forever.

This need to innovate creates a dilemma. History confirms that most new products fail. Some are not innovative enough, while others exceed the innovative skills of their producers. Despite this risk, failure to innovate increases the chance that competitors' products will take a firm's customers, leaving it to fade over time. The challenge of product innovation demands a blend of old and new that supports stable prosperity in an ever-changing marketplace.

Long-term winners recognize changing business conditions and nurture the organizational skills they need to influence and respond to market demands. Some will respond to new demands with entirely new products. Some will employ new technologies that enable them to make, deliver, or service an existing product better. Some winners will manage to defend successful products against new competitive threats.

Even makers of viable, mature products like Classic Coca-Cola and Jell-o must listen to the marketplace. This task can become frustrating because meaningless noise often drowns out important information. Still, all markets are dynamic, some more than others, so all require continuous monitoring to spot new conditions and continuing trends.

Trends in Product Innovation

Trends provide change that seems likely to continue in the future. Less predictable surprises also complicate product development, but much of a firm's market analysis can project future developments based on known conditions. Most firms must anticipate the effects of some important external forces in today's business environment.

Shift toward a Service Economy.   For much of North American history, economies have shifted away from agriculture and toward manufacturing. Late in the 20th century, the economy has been shifting away from manufacturing and toward the service sector. For example, early meat packing and refrigeration technology enabled fresh meat to reach stores far away from agricultural regions. Product innovation transformed some fresh meat into processed products like cured bacon, hot dogs, and Spam™ with longer shelf lives. As the economy moved

The Reebok Pump shoe is an example of how innovation is a key factor in competitive marketing.
SOURCE: Elizabeth Sher Goodwin

toward services, more consumers bought their processed bacon as part of Denny's $1.99 breakfast special. By the 1990s, trade in services accounted for over 70 percent of the U.S. gross domestic product and an even larger percentage of jobs.

Globalization of Markets.   Global competition has overshadowed local markets for many products. General Electric had long dominated the U.S. market for light bulbs before 1983, when the Dutch electronics giant Philips bought Westinghouse's lamp business. Suddenly, GE faced foreign competitors in its home market while it had no real presence in theirs. To counter the threat from Philips, GE had to acquire light-bulb makers in Hungary and Britain.

Firms can gain cost advantages by selling in foreign markets because they can spread product design and development costs over larger unit sales. Ford will ultimately sell its new Contour model in 70 countries with the same platform design, engine, and transmission in each market, reducing the contribution that each unit's price must make to the model's $6 billion product development cost. To gain such an advantage, a firm needs a product design robust enough to sell vigorously in foreign markets.

Firms may fear the additional work of international operations, but they may have no choice as the continuing free trade movement opens up national borders ever more widely to foreign products. Consumers may not even know which products come from foreign producers, perhaps through domestic final-assembly operations processing foreign-made components. If you doubt this, just look inside your personal computer.

Rise of Consumerism.   One author recalls asking his father why the family had to buy an unfashionable Nash. "It had the shortest waiting period," was the reply. Consumers clamored for scarce manufactured goods after World War II, as car buyers flocked to showrooms to snap up new models in the first week after introduction. Sellers could peddle anything they could make.

The service sector was not much better. Fashion critics predicted 1 inch longer hems and fashion-conscious women dutifully toiled at their Singer sewing machines to make their skirts and dresses conform. At mealtime, highway travelers could choose between reliable, so-so food at Howard Johnson's or infamous greasy-spoon diners.

In the mid-1950s, however, fashion designers in Paris fawned over the chemise, a dress that only a pear-shaped woman could love, and Ford introduced its Edsel. The public greeted both innovations with a yawn, indicating a major change in the marketplace. Consumers began questioning the need to base their purchase decisions on the whims of fashion trendsetters and mass manufacturers. The mass markets began to fragment, and marketers began chasing the pieces. Sellers of goods and services must now listen to customers before deciding what to offer. In fact, industrial buyers tell their suppliers what they want, when they want it, and often how to make it, as when they demand ISO 9000 certification.

Critical Importance of Time.   Just about everyone in the business world must move faster than ever before. Consumers no longer want to wait for products. In days of old, for example, an amateur photographer snapped a roll of film in a Kodak Brownie camera and took the film down to the drugstore to be developed. Sometime during the next week, the drugstore shipped the film to a central processing facility which made pictures and negatives and returned them to the drugstore about a week later, long after Aunt Gertie has gone home to Buffalo.

Today, a photographer can get prints and negatives from an in-store processing center within an hour. If that seems too long, another camera will provide pictures instantly, or a digital camera can display the shots immediately on the television screen or home computer, perhaps after manipulating the image to remove Aunt Gertie's tattoo.

Time has come to dominate the product design and development process. Firms can no longer indulge in long product-development lead times and take higher risks through longer-term forecasts of customer demand and the possibility of technologies becoming obsolete. Being faster to market allows a firm to increase the likelihood of getting the right product to the right customer at the right time and quite likely at the targeted cost. Time is still money, but many operations must revise this conventional wisdom to say, "Time instead of money."[3]

Quality Rules.   The quality revolution has transformed most firms' business strategies. Firms must treat quality often as an order qualifier rather than an order winner, and poor quality is almost always an order loser. Product designers must know even more about targeted customers than ever before to judge how they will assess product quality. A poor understanding of customers almost guarantees failures in design quality in addition to potential failures in quality of conformance through poor control of OM processes. Shortcomings in either of these areas will diminish the quality of a product's overall benefits, disappointing customers.

Litigation.   Product designers used to practice so-called *Detroit engineering*, initially over-designing parts to assure that they would perform satisfactorily. After early success, they would reduce a part's over-design buffer systematically until the part began to fail too frequently. They would then strengthen the design marginally to create a part with an acceptable failure rate.

In an era when colleges graduate more lawyers than engineers, this is no longer a wise practice. Designers must envision every possible way that customers

---

[3]J. D. Blackburn, *Time-Based Competition* (Homewood, Ill.: Business-One/Irwin, 1991).

[**E X H I B I T   1 1 . 3**]

Goods and Services in the Product Bundle

100 percent Good	100 percent Service

Supermarket groceries
　　Levi's 501s
　　　　McDonald's Big Mac
　　　　　　Office photocopier
　　　　　　　　Jiffy-Lube car care
　　　　　　　　　　Four Seasons gourmet meal
　　　　　　　　　　　　Airbrushed wedding picture
　　　　　　　　　　　　　　Supercut 6 haircut
　　　　　　　　　　　　　　　　Hotel concierge service

might misuse a product. In particular, they must make children's toys fire-proof, swallow proof, batter-proof, etc. Juries no longer seem to care whether injuries result from unreasonable uses.

Green Movement.   Manufacturers used to stop worrying about their products after shipping them. Now customers expect a firm to operate in an environmentally responsible manner. Good corporate citizenship requires product designers to consider the impact of a product from the raw materials in its components to its fate after customers consume it. Designers of consumer products must give special attention to the ecological consequences of their packaging methods. In the past, firms often made product packages for products like laundry detergents, lawn fertilizers, candy bars, and compact disks larger than necessary because customers often confused size with value.

This and other trends help to drive product design and development decisions, requiring careful attention from all operations managers. In addition, new demographic and technological forces continually emerge within specific industries. Listening to customers may not reveal these powerful forces completely or quickly enough. Leading-edge competitors, many of whom will remain obscure until their success brings them notoriety, are working vigorously to gain advantages by reaching the market first with truly innovative products.

DESIGNING GOODS AND SERVICES

The early part of the chapter described most products as mixes of goods and services. Exhibit 11.3 lays out a representative mix of tangible and intangible product benefits in the marketplace. For each product listed, some competitor offers a variation with either a higher or lower service component. (Mr. Andre, this month's stylist to the stars, offers so much more than just a hair cut!) In each case, however, the customer receives an experience; the total package of benefits to the customer determines the value of the product.

Entrepreneurs succeed by targeting and meeting specific consumer needs. The *San Jose Mercury Times* recognized and met its customers' need for on-line access to its newspaper, which increased circulation and profits.   SOURCE: Mark Richards/PhotoEdit

Design of Services

Most services start with an idea, perhaps when an existing or potential customer states an unmet need. "What I'm really looking for is a computer software store where I can see what is in those packages and try the the software." This statement expresses dissatisfaction with the presentation of computer software in the marketplace. The entrepreneur must then determine how many other potential customers have similar desires. If many people share this view, the entrepreneur can develop processes to profitably satisfy this stated need.

vector marketing

Service based on an understanding of customers so complete that the organization can anticipate latent demands

Ideas for new services may emerge within a firm. The concept of **vector marketing** calls for a firm to understand its customers so completely that it can anticipate latent demands. The innovation to satisfy these demands could simply extend or improve an existing service. For example, many people see great promise in a service to customize a newspaper to suit the interests of each customer. A particular buyer could ask for expanded local coverage, more financial news, fewer want ads, television listings based on a specific cable hookup, and a personalized comics section. Organizations have already begun to provide this service with processes based on flexible printing presses and home computer videotext services.

service delivery system

The network of processes designed to fulfill identified customer needs

The firm's **service delivery system** sets up processes designed to fulfill identified customer needs. This system specifies the activities in these processes and their sequence, and it deploys productive resources to carry out organization plans. This network of processes must include some means of measuring the performance of the system. Its arrangements for human resources must include carefully designed and implemented training processes to ensure that customers always interact with well-trained and motivated workers. Chapter 12 covers the design of delivery systems in more detail.

Continued success requires an up-to-date understanding of current and potential customers. Consumer marketers have long used psychological profiles of targeted customers, and service buyers fit into similar schemes. Fitzsimmons modified the consumer model to describe four types of service buyers:[4]

[4]Fitzsimmons, *Service Management*, p. 170.

[**E X H I B I T   1 1 . 4**]

Four Pizza-Service Strategies

Customer Type	Order Winner	Chain	Strategic Programs
Economizers	Price/volume	Little Caesar's	Two for the price of one, low-cost sites
Convenience Seekers	Delivery speed	Domino's	Speedy delivery (but not speeding drivers)
Personalized Care Seekers	Friendly service, custom pizzas	Cloverdale Pizza	Long-term employees, customized orders
Ethical/Loyal Buyers	Loyalty	Hawkeye Pizza	Sponsorship of local bowling teams, sports bar ambiance

- *Economizers*   These people want maximum value for their expenditures of time, money, or effort. Jiffy-Lube tailors its car-care outlets to meet this need.
- *Personalized Care Seekers*   These people seek interpersonal gratification from recognition by workers, pleasant conversations, and attentive, individual service. They want a friendly greeting by name and a regular order waiting on their usual table.
- *Convenience Seekers*   These people treat delivery speed and goods and/or services with minimum fuss as order winners.
- *Ethical/Loyal Customers*   These people choose services based on some moral obligation. One person might patronize fellow Rotarians. Charles chooses his fast food because he likes the clown.

Knowledge of customers targets a firm's services at the bull's eye of core product benefits.

Exhibit 11.4 details how several firms respond to the needs of the four segments of the pizza market. Little Caesar's and Domino's have built nationwide businesses through their strategies. Local firms like Tacoma's Cloverdale Pizza and Hawkeye Pizza serve just about every town. Their customers went to high school with the owners, who know the names of spouses and kids and the toppings they like on their pizzas. Pizza Hut, another national chain, has tried to imitate this kind of personalized service by displaying callers' phone numbers and previous orders on computer screens. The firm's customers will determine whether high-tech gimmicks can duplicate the benefits of personal relationships.

Consumers' attitudes toward service products also depend somewhat on the options available in the market. This range of available choices helps both product designers and marketers to understand previously identified order winners as starting points for their own product-innovation programs. Existing services fit in one of five classifications.

Zero-Say Services.   People must accept these services, often from government agencies, whether they want them or not. Examples include fluoridation of water supplies, refuse-collection services, student-activity fees, etc. Some customers strongly resent buying these services, but they lack the authority to refuse to participate. Often people must pay for such services whether or not they derive any benefits.

Minimum-Say Services.   These services give customers a single option of buying or voting with their feet (or their television remote controls). Many customers would like more input into the characteristics of these products, especially if they are paying for product attributes that they do not want while doing without desirable attributes. English-speaking cable television customers can understand the value of some Spanish-language channels, but they may resent the loss of C-Span to make room among the available channels. Government regulation, technology, and economic forces currently deny cable subscribers the possibility of customized service, but that soon will change.

Mandated Services with Options.   Government or other social institutions mandate purchases of minimum levels of some services, such as automobile insurance. Most customers can choose among vendors, however, such as State Farm or Farmers Insurance, and perhaps select other service attributes. In the commercial market, firms make choices to suit mandated fire insurance, workers' compensation, employee health-care plans, and annual boiler inspections to their particular needs.

Elective Services.   These most common services include jobs that people could do themselves, but they find that others can do the jobs more cheaply or more effectively. Many customers buy services to cut their hair, mow their lawns, handle public relations, or even design products. Note that this category covers both commercial and consumer services.

In each case, the customer must decide whether to make something, hire someone else to make it, or buy a standard product. This decision becomes particularly important in services related to business infrastructure, such as owning a fleet of trucks or shipping with common carriers, owning computing facilities or contracting with time-share providers, and hiring guards or contracting for plant security. Outside suppliers' core competencies may allow them to do better work more cheaply. Together with personal laziness, this fact has defined a trend in both business and personal life toward hiring others to perform services that people used to provide for themselves.

Luxury Services.   Most customers admit that they don't really need these services, but they enjoy the treat. Like the area of product design, this category is dynamic. People used to view trips to the hair stylist as luxuries, but now many view them as elective necessities. Personal bodyguards formerly seemed like luxuries for movie stars and mob bosses, but now many businesses feel the need to protect their key executives.

Designers of service products need thorough knowledge of the core benefits that targeted customers want. Services in the first two categories may generate feelings of frustration in customers. Despite the mandates or other requirements for certain services, providers have no valid reason to treat ultimate consumers disrespectfully. Increasingly, government, private, and volunteer service agencies are re-engineering their processes to excel at even the most menial tasks. Well-run organizations have vividly demonstrated the possibility of constructing world-class service delivery systems. Servicemaster, for example, empowers employees to dignify their work servicing restrooms, corridors, and other facilities and make it a source of personal pride. The City of Austin, Texas, has reoriented its service processes to increase the satisfaction of both customers and workers. Workers often take the blame for poorly designed service processes that cause them to deliver substandard service. Ultimate users of these systems share some of the blame for this dissatisfaction if they continue to tolerate it.

[**E X H I B I T   1 1 . 5**]

Matrix of Service Processes

Customization

	Low	High
Low	**Service Factory** Airlines Trucking Firm Hotel Resort and Recreation Firm	**Service Shop** Hospital Auto Repair Firm Other Repair Services
Labor Intensity **High**	**Mass Service** Retailer Wholesaler School Retail Banking	**Professional Service** Doctor Attorney Accountant Architect

SOURCE   Reprinted from "How Can Service Businesses Survive," by Roger Schmenner, *Sloan Management Review* (vol. 27: Spring 1986), p. 25, by permission of the publisher. Copyright 1986 by the Sloan Management Review Association. All rights reserved.

Types of Service Processes.   The kinds of systems that create service quality vary by labor intensity and the level of customization of the service product. Schmenner developed a classification scheme based on these criteria to create a matrix of four typical service providers, as illustrated in Exhibit 11.5. The vertical axis measures labor intensity based on the ratio of labor costs to capital costs. Service organizations with high costs for plant assets, equipment, or franchising fall in the upper panels. The horizontal axis measures the degree of customization, including changes that customers dictate through their involvement with the service.

The upper, left panel defines **service factories**. Their managers focus on efficiency to succeed selling predefined services to cover their high capital costs. An airline cannot operate efficiently without expensive airplanes and standard schedules, to which customers must adapt their needs. Many fast-food outfits also fit this mold. McDonald's workers prepare Big Macs to meet standard requirements in regimented systems that replace human labor with equipment operations as much as possible. Even the courteous service is standardized.

Heterogeneous customer needs force hospitals to customize their services, since patients do not arrive with standard illnesses. Hence health-care organizations fit the category of **service shops**, providing customized services in a capital-intensive environment, the most expensive combination of these traits. Much of the health-care reform debate in the 1990s represents an attempt to contain costs (i.e., enhance efficiency) without unduly detracting from the quality of the custom services.

Mass service organizations seek to provide routine or standardized services through labor-intensive processes. Mass service systems tend to employ less well-trained workers than other service firms, in part because they seek to offer

service factory

An organization that provides a standardized service through a process low in labor intensity

service shop

An organization that provides a customized service through a process low in labor intensity

mass service

An organization that provides a routine or standardized service through a labor-intensive process predictable, undifferentiated services. This rule has created an opportunity for competitive advantage for one such firm, Nordstrom's, which has provided extensive training for its relatively unskilled workers to personalize the services they offer to customers.

The lower, right panel of the exhibit defines operations that offer highly customized services through processes with high labor costs relative to their capital investments. These **professional service** systems create much of their customization through customer/server interactions. A builder conceives a house design to fulfill a dream and, together with an architect, creates a building plan to realize the dream.

A similar matrix compares the object of the service with its location (Exhibit 11.6). Some service systems allow flexible guidelines for the best location in which to serve customers. Evolving technology soon will permit customized home delivery of services previously available only at servers' sites. The information highway will soon carry movies, educational services, and financial analysis on demand to any suitably equipped television set. Rapid advances are erasing limits on technical feasibility of many services. The remaining limits depend on what consumers want.

Design of the Product Bundle

Through these kinds of analyses of customer demands and process characteristics, service designers formulate recommendations for a bundle of goods and services to satisfy and delight the organization's targeted customers. That **product bundle** must include some standard components:

1. The product bundle contains a definition of the **supporting facilities** that the service delivery system will need. These physical resources, such as theaters, golf courses, medical facilities, restaurants, etc., allow the organization to offer a product with the features that customers want.
2. The product bundle also specifies **supporting goods** that customers will purchase or consume along with the primary product. The list for a burger joint might include buns, soda, cups, napkins, tables, playground equipment, etc.
3. The product bundle defines the **explicit services** that the firm intends to provide as part of its delivery of core benefits or services to customers. These essential or intrinsic components define important characteristics of the product bundle, such as the pain relief that a root-canal procedure ultimately yields, a smoother running air-conditioning system provided by a repair service, etc.
4. Finally, the product bundle specifies the **implicit benefits** of a good or service, many of them psychological benefits. A college student might appreciate the security of narrow distribution of grade reports or keeping his or her telephone numbers, GPA, or weight out of the university directory. The same student might value the pride of attending a prestigious school, in addition to the educational benefits that the college provides.

Customers, of course, determine the value of each component of the product bundle. Product designers must understand the firm's target customers well enough to choose to add only those features that contribute to the competitive strength of the product bundle. Adding a turbocharger to a tiny commuter car might not score many points with customers; they might respond more positively to a solid warranty.

---

professional service

An organization that offers a highly customized service through a labor-intensive process

product bundle

The set of product and organizational characteristics that combine to delight customers

supporting facility

A physical resource that allows the organization to offer a product with the features that customers want

supporting good

A physical good that customers purchase or consume along with the primary product

explicit service

A service that the firm provides as part of its delivery of core benefits or services to customers

implicit benefit

A benefit, frequently a psychological feeling, that accompanies the core benefits of a product

[**EXHIBIT 11.6**]

Object and Location of a Service Process

	What is Serviced?	
Where Is It Serviced?	Person	Thing
Customer's Site	TV Viewing Employee Training Swim Lessons Pizza Delivery Police Protection	Horse Shoed Lawn Care Computer Repair Catering Garbage Pickup
Server's Site	Exercise Clinic Loan Deal Legal Services Movie Theaters Health Care Services Beauty Salons	Dry Cleaning Tax Preparation Stock Sales Pizza Preparation Goods Transportation

Note that the first components listed for the product bundle do not appear in the Actual Product ring of Exhibit 11.1. This reveals a conceptual limitation in the marketer's perspective of a product. That diagram showed only what customers see; operations managers must also deal with the supporting processes through which the firm delivers its goods and services. In Chapter 12, we will discuss supporting facilities and other supporting structures within the service delivery system in greater detail.

Design of the Actual Product

The physical goods that form part of an actual product are tangible items that intermediaries purchase, stock, and transport to the point where final customers assume control of the goods. Retail chains like Wal-Mart and Target perform little design work on physical products. Instead, they mostly develop service delivery systems that procure, transport, and market goods designed by other organizations.

More typical manufacturing firms transform raw materials into goods with more useful forms. Such a firm might saw logs into lumber, process sugar beets to make table sugar, forge and machine metal into car parts, and assemble car parts into finished vehicles. A few years later, another firm disassembles the spent vehicle to recover recyclable materials.

Some of these firms really do little product design. How frequently must a saw mill redesign its 2 × 4 lumber? This has occurred once within the past 20 years, when the lumber industry convinced regulatory agencies that an improved, thinner piece of wood worked just as well as a thicker piece. Many firms need not revise their product designs every day.

Just as in services, the process of designing a new good or a modification of an existing one begins in the inner circle of Exhibit 11.1 with the product's core benefit or service. The essence of the product design process for a good closely resembles that for a service. It differs in two important ways. First, production of a physical good generally involves a more complex process with many more steps and often longer lead times. Second, an organization can inventory physical products, adding a layer of complexity to the design of the order-fulfillment process.

Service management theorists sometimes cite a third difference. They argue that physical product design differs from service design because customers often experience the product bundles for goods remotely. Makers of goods have less direct contact with final consumers, so they must work harder to gather feedback. They cannot design their products based only on input from returned warranty cards. This distinction raises the importance of after-sale customer service in product-innovation processes for physical goods.

To begin the process of designing an actual product with its core benefit to customers, an organization must evaluate the motivations of those customers. Categories of buyers like those introduced in the discussion of service product design may offer useful insights for designers of physical goods, as well:

- *Economizers*   These customers favor low prices as order winners, provided products meet other order qualifiers. Customers for raw materials and other bulk commodities often look at price before anything else, as do designers of more complex products who need component parts that fulfill minimum functional requirements. They may hold their ultimate products to higher standards, but they can buy noncritical components based mostly on price. Finally, buyers may act like economizers when they evaluate one type of merchandise but demonstrate other traits when buying other items. For example, someone might evaluate the purchase of a lawn rake as an economizer while paying less attention to price in purchases of personal attire.

- *Convenience Seekers*   These buyers want physical products that are easy to use, operate, or consume. They prefer prepared foods, preassembled components, and packaging that facilitates quick use. They want goods with features that make their lives easier.

- *Customizers*   These buyers want goods made specifically to meet their unique needs. They want it their way! Some might resent this kind of behavior as picky, but most of these people are really just informed buyers who clearly understand what they need and the adverse consequences of buyer goods that fail to meet these specifications. A firm can satisfy some customizers by offering a wide variety of selections. Others will accept only truly custom-made products.

- *Functionists*   Buyers in this new category value efficiency and functional performance above all. They buy goods that earn the most favorable reports from *Consumers Union* and develop strange attachments to boxy, reliable cars. These people eagerly study product reviews and other analytical information to justify their purchases based on superior performance in core benefits.

- *Style-Driven Consumers*   These buyers look at form rather than substance. They buy cars, clothing, and kitchen utensils that look good, often reacting strongly to brand influences such as a well-placed alligator on a garment or an endorsement from Barney the dinosaur or a popular sports figure. They may target aesthetics as order winning criteria, but these buyers normally set above-average quality as an important qualifier.

[**EXHIBIT 11.7**]

Three-Ring Customer-Fulfillment Process

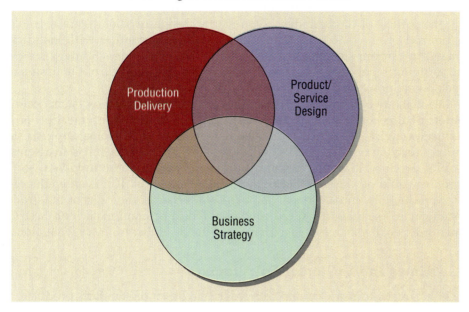

- *Ethical/Loyal Customers*   Some people buy products with only passing consideration of cost, convenience, quality, or variety. Some avoid products made in China, with child labor, or in nonunion shops. Others insist on environmentally sound goods. Some are just loyal, such as the football fans who wore Oakland Raider T-shirts for all the years the team played in Los Angeles. (Given the inflated Oakland Raider ticket price, this customer loyalty was not rewarded.)
- *Otherwise Driven Customers*   Only the most egocentric operations manager could believe that customers select products based entirely on OM-related criteria. Other reasons, such as credit availability, may affect customers' product selections, sometimes decisively. Product designers should consider any such forces to avoid basing important decisions on false assumptions.

Information about a product's appeal, or lack of appeal, to a customer is a key input to the product-innovation process. Marketing research offers key inputs to the firm's cross-functional effort to define an actual product and the other components of the product bundle. Focus groups and other research tools can provide important feedback to product designers as they work to discover what capabilities or features customers will receive favorably.

 CUSTOMER-FULFILLMENT PROCESS

A comprehensive image of product development comes from an understanding of customers' normal interactions with an organization that offers them a bundle of goods and services. Exhibit 11.7 represents this interaction as a three-ring, interlocking **customer-fulfillment process**.

customer-fulfillment process

A series of interlocking subprocesses that describe customers' normal interactions with an organization that offers them a bundle of goods and services

The Production/Delivery area captures the customer's order and receipt of the firm's product. In the Product Design area, the firm designs the actual and augmented products and combines features into the product bundle that the customer experiences. The firm may repeat this process periodically for a standard product or at the request of the customer. Requests for design revisions usually result in customized products, but they may affect standard products with insufficient demand to warrant stocking revised versions. In the Business Strategy area, the firm formulates policies that direct its actions, including those of the design and development processes.

In a make-to-stock situation, the customer's contact with the system occurs at the left of this diagram. The response occurs within the intersection of the Production/Deliver and the Product Design circles. If the customer orders a standard product, the response occurs at the left of this intersection. If it is an assemble-to-order product, a limited amount of design work may be involved, so this response would be closer to the right of this intersection. If it is an engineer-to-order product, the initial system response will occur at the right of the Product Design circle. The amount of lead time required to respond to each of these customer orders will, of course, be a function of the flexibility of the organization.

Lead Times and Customer Fulfillment

For either make-to-stock or make-to-order purchases of standard products, the product design cycle periodically creates new products or revised versions of existing offerings. The frequency of this design revision process is a major decision in a firm's product-innovation strategy.

For a make-to-order purchase of a customized product, the customer's request triggers the design and development process. Since most firms want to keep their design personnel busy, the new order may have to wait a long time for delivery. This process may include a product estimate step to assess the actual needs of the customer before setting a price. At any point, the customer may become dissatisfied with the design, the price, or the promised delivery date. The parties resolve these uncertainties through negotiations, contributing to the considerable increase in management resources required for customized product design as compared to the process of designing standard offerings.

This discussion does not imply that no firm can ever escape the need for long product design lead times. Some firms arrange their OM processes to deliver customized offerings by quickly combining modules to offer wide ranges of options. Customers at Baskin-Robbins do not buy previously made ice cream cones, but the firm can quickly satisfy just about anyone's cravings by stuffing a scoop of a favorite flavor into a cone and perhaps tossing some chocolate sprinkles on top. An earlier chapter described the process by which Japan's Panasonic can turn out a highly customized bicycle in less than 2 days through its computerized order-entry system and flexible automation. Lenscrafters has set up its OM process to complete an eye examination and make a new set of customized glasses extremely rapidly.

The nature of the customer's request, however, may not allow a firm to exploit quick-response capabilities. A customer who wants a custom-built home must wait longer than someone who is willing to buy a standard design. Someone who places a special order for a Rolls Royce must wait longer than a customer at a Chevy dealer. The product design lead time for a complex, make-to-stock product, such as a new car model, can take a long time, perhaps as long as 6 years, but the firm completes most of this work before the customer places an order.

Business Strategy and Customer Fulfillment

Business strategy provides critical guidance for the customer-fulfillment process. It defines the basis for the firm's competitive advantage, the amounts and types of resources it deploys, and the scope of the promises it makes to its potential customers. Business strategy evaluates how much it wants to serve particular customers and whether new product ideas really suit the specific company. No firm should expect to exceed every customer's expectations at every time throughout the marketplace. Bekin's slogan, "We would rather turn you down, than let you down" illustrates a clear, well-understood choice, embodied in a business strategy, that helps to guide product design decisions.

Employees from three functional areas within the organization, marketing/sales, design engineering, and operations management, staff this three-ring customer-fulfillment process, and these groups often pursue conflicting goals. Engineers often seem more determined to express their creative urges and solve intricate problems than to address customers' needs. Both engineers and operations management personnel often resent the perceived willingness of marketing to respond to every real and imagined whim of any customer, regardless of the demands of the resulting product variety. Operations management personnel often seem overly devoted to building a stable, well-organized environment in their pursuit of higher efficiency. Business strategy bridges the gaps between these functions to establish guidelines for resolving disputes.

 ## PRODUCT ARCHITECTURE

After firming up the specifications of their product idea, product designers must make some key decisions. The resulting **product architecture** establishes essential limits for all subsequent design decisions based on answers to some critical questions:

product architecture
Broad guidelines for designing a product and the OM system to produce it that establish essential limits for all subsequent design decisions

- How well can a standardized product meet the core needs of targeted customers?
- How well can a standard product comprised of a flexible set of optional functional modules satisfy the core needs of buyers who want customized products?
- How effectively can product designers divide the functions of the product among separate modules?
- How should these modules interface with each other?
- How much technical risk should the design of each module take?
- How much reserve capacity should the designs of the overall product and each module include?
- Which of these modules should designers develop in-house and which should they contract out to outside designers and/or manufacturers?

None of these decisions affect marketers' portrayal of a product. Acting within the boundaries of the firm, they have important effects, not only on the design quality of the product, but also on the efficiency of the product-innovation process. A careful product architecture process can help designers to develop products more quickly and more cheaply, as this section's discussion of the six product architecture issues will explain.

The product architecture clearly affects some of the decisions in the firm's customer fulfillment system, such as whether to make a standardized product to stock or a customized product to order. We will consider these issues in the next chapter, where we will discuss the tradeoffs associated with a product or a service delivery system. Remember, however, that the two areas remain closely intertwined.

Product Standardization

Many operations managers would prefer to make and sell standardized products. Most organizations must rely on a single set of equipment and communications channels, so they assume a need for some degree of standardization. A single system can more easily turn out a stable set of products, and the heritage of mass manufacturing emphasizes the value of standardization for efficient and effective operations.

To modern ears, however, this may sound like excuses based on entrenched beliefs that try to justify stubborn resistance to change. In reality, the OM system exists only to delight customers. Several arguments for and against standardization contribute to a better understanding of the tradeoffs that any business must make.

Lower Product-Design Costs.   The product-design cycle naturally creates a number of economies of scale. An earlier section mentioned the benefits of spreading the cost of designing and developing a product over a large number of units. The organization can realize these economies of scale only if it can satisfy a significant number of potential customers with a common design. Firms develop mass manufacturing systems believing that sufficient numbers of customers are willing to buy the standardized products that those systems produce.

Unfortunately, in trying to develop a single good or service that will please many customers, designers may include features in the product that some customers do not want. A stoic newspaper subscriber flips past an unwanted comic section. A hearing-impaired car buyer must pay for an unwanted car radio. Many kids would prefer Campbell's vegetable soup without the lima beans. An individual customer may perceive flaws in a standard product design that forces people to pay for unwanted features.

Lower Component-Design Costs.   Incorporating standard components in a product can also lower its overall cost. This decision allows the organization to provide product features without paying for new engineering work. An outside vendor of a good or service may offer a better product or process more cheaply than the firm could develop on its own. By taking advantage of this expertise, it can lower its production costs.

Lower Production Costs.   A firm can make standardized products or parts in batch sizes that maximize economies of scale. Large batches spread setup costs over large numbers of units in each production run. In addition, batches of standardized products often justify investments in larger-capacity, more efficient machines and production processes. By producing a standard good or service, a firm can organize its OM process in a manner that allows it to staff the system with less skilled employees, creating efficiencies from the division of labor in both manufacturing and service industries.

A firm that builds a standard, nonperishable product to stock can accumulate finished goods in inventory in anticipation of demand. This decouples production from demand. Outside considerations need not drive production, freeing

Companies like John Deere install standard components throughout their product lines. This production practice lowers overall design costs.   SOURCE: Courtesy of Deere & Company

operations managers to enhance the efficiency of the plant through optimum utilization of its people and equipment.

Lower Delivery Costs.   The opportunity to inventory standard products may also create economies of scale in transportation. Shipments of goods from the factory to either warehouses or retail outlets can take advantage of economical truckload transportation rates.

Quicker Deliveries.   A firm can also move its inventories of standard products to sites near customers. This facilitates a rapid response to any order, helping to delight a time-conscious customer. This decision must balance the higher cost of deploying stocks across larger distances due to requirements for physical storage facilities and human resources to staff them.

Recognition of Known Standard Products.   **Known products** assure consumers that their purchases will meet their expectations. A thirsty person knows what a Pepsi Cola or a Coors Lite will taste like. People find this familiarity reassuring when they do not feel adventurous. Quality of conformance becomes an order qualifier, and often an order winner, for a standardized product.

known product
A good or service with standardized and widely recognized features

Simplified Value Comparisons.   Standardized goods and services help consumers to shop for the best price or product performance. People can easily compare Wal-Mart's price for a certain grade of Quaker State motor oil with the price of the same product at Kmart. This familiarity can become extremely important in mail-order purchases from catalog offerings.

Stronger Consumer Protection.   In today's litigious society, a few standard products offer government agencies and lawyers conspicuous targets for consumer protection scrutiny. Food regulations assure McDonald's customers that their Quarter Pounders will contain 0.25 pounds of approved meat. Regulators cannot keep such a close eye on the local burger joint.

Recall from Chapter 7, however, that Deming argued against product standards as "prescriptions for mediocrity." Some firms have cited conformance with existing government standards to defend against product liability suits. General Motors can correctly say that its pickup trucks with side-mounted gas tanks met every government standard in effect at the time the trucks were built. While the company may have argued from firm legal ground when it refused the federal government's request to recall the trucks, it is not likely to delight people who have lost loved ones in fiery side-collision crashes.

product interface

The place where functional capabilities meet

Quicker Design through Standardized Product Interfaces.   A **product interface** is the place where functional capabilities meet. Interactions between two ill-suited capabilities create dysfunctional interfaces. Someone who tries to plug an American appliance into a British electrical socket will encounter a dysfunctional interface. This always imposes some cost to reconcile the conflict, as when the traveler must spend time and money to acquire a special electrical adapter.

Operations managers rely on standardized interfaces to avoid these problems. We deal with them daily. Air-traffic controllers worldwide agree to communicate with pilots in a well-understood variant of the English language. Every personal computer employs one of a few well-understood architectures with standard interfaces so that hard-disk manufactures know what types of connection cables they should supply. By following standards for these interfaces, product designers can avoid spending time and money dealing with individual differences.

Enhanced Design Agility in an Industry.   Standardized product features and interfaces in microcomputers permit designers of components and software to enhance their offerings without risking incompatibility as long as they stay within the parameters specified by the standards. This open-architecture environment frees firms to compete on value-added product features rather than basic functionality. If nearly all competing products are composed of the same brands of standardized components, however, firms may face serious difficulty making their products seem unique. Even today's homogeneous microcomputer market has not become quite that simple, but as customers have become more knowledgeable, they have lost their willingness to pay premium prices for particular brands of a rather standard product composed largely of other vendors' branded components. As Compaq learned after painful losses, computer buyers have come to understand that low-overhead assemblers can offer products that are functionally identical to those of more prestigious firms for lower prices.

Standards as a Communications Tool.   At a coffee shop, you might make a request like, "I'll have a large cup of fresh-brewed French roast coffee, please." You have just defined the product you want using three well-understood terms. You want about 12 ounces of coffee made recently (perhaps within the last 30 minutes) from a specific type of bean. Similarly, many effective organizations are emphasizing product standards more prominently in their communications systems to simplify the jobs of manufacturing, marketing, and management control. They want to avoid an unfortunately common response to a product request: "What did you say you wanted?" Explicit statements of product standards greatly reduce the communication efforts required to respond to questions.

One negative effect of standardized parts on the product-innovation process may escape attention. Most product engineers feel the need to indulge their creative urges. Sometimes they feel frustrated when an organization wants a well-designed, low-cost product instead of the best product that the designers can conceive. The authors share this frustration, as do most students of engineering, and these common feelings often challenge the skills of managers who must guide product-development projects. In resolving this conflict, they must remind engineers that they work as part of a business function that exists only to serve the needs of the firm's customers.

Mass Customization

As discussed in Chapter 3, mass customization is a product-development strategy that seeks to satisfy a market's desire for a customized product while retaining the economies of scale of mass production. In his book, *Mass Customization*, Joseph Pine argues that a firm can achieve this ambitious goal by several fundamental methods or combinations of them:[5]

- Customize services offered with standard basic packages of goods and services
- Create customized goods and services
- Customize standard goods and services at the point of delivery
- Organize the customer-fulfillment process to provide quick responses
- Assemble standard, modular components to customize final goods and services

Each of these techniques works to achieve low-cost, individualized products. Pine explains each one fairly straightforwardly, beginning with definitions of key links in a **value chain**. This is a sequential process for development, production, marketing, and delivery of a product.

value chain

A sequential process for development, production, marketing, and delivery of a product

Modular Product Designs

The design of a product with a simple structure need not consider in much detail the location of some function within the overall product. Such a product requires solutions to rather easy questions like whether to make the buttery taste of popcorn an integral part of the corn kernel or to spray it on after popping. The design of a more complex product must carefully define which parts will perform which key functions. The product architect might imagine meeting with a system's modules and asking, "Okay now, who is going to do what?"

At one extreme, the architecture could concentrate all functions in a single, special-purpose unit. This would avoid the need to deal with interfaces between modules. For this reason, among others, people often buy dedicated electronic devices that can accomplish only limited applications.

At the other extreme, the architecture can develop a module to perform each essential function, perhaps including existing, off-the-shelf components for some functions. This decision may speed up product development and lower its cost. It also requires careful attention to the designs of interfaces, however, such as cables that connect the functional units. Also, the collection of modules might occupy more space or consume more power or some other critical resource. Within any system, a modular design invariably loses some performance as compared to a single, integrated set of functions, measured either by component efficiency, systemwide efficiency, or both. Each interface imposes a cost; electrons can only travel so fast, mechanical interfaces invariably lose some performance to friction, etc. Finally, a modular architecture will likely encounter some difficulty matching the

[5]J. B. Pine, *Mass Customization* (Cambridge, Mass.: Harvard Business School Press, 1993), Chapter 8.

capabilities of off-the-shelf components well enough to get optimum performance from all of them.

Modular design offers a major advantage when the technologies of the different modules are changing at uneven rates. Within a microcomputer, the central processing unit (CPU) reaches obsolescence most rapidly. A modular design may allow the owner to upgrade the microprocessor to gain a state-of-the-art machine relatively cheaply. Modular architecture also offers valuable benefits if the demands on one function cause its components to wear out faster than the other components. Flashlights with replaceable batteries allow users to keep part of their equipment while replacing only the worn out components.

The product-design architect must fully understand the tradeoffs associated with each of these issues and then try to find the best set of compromises between their demands. This decision must allow for the possibility that this set will turn out to be a null set, that is, the situation may dictate that comprises aren't worth the sacrifice. Effective product innovation requires designers to take as much time and make as much effort as necessary to build a product in the right way for a particular situation.

Modular Design Interface Decisions

Within a modular product, designers must weigh the benefits of an open architecture. Along with the other benefits of standard interfaces, they open the opportunity to supply components that perform the stated missions of the modules to many vendors. One common standardized interface, a 110-volt electrical outlet, assures home appliance designers of a known, reliable connection to an electricity supply.

When it dominated the computer market, IBM periodically changed the interfaces between functional modules of its systems to foil competitors. When the firm saw Memorex making substantial inroads into its disk-drive business, IBM changed the interface on its next model to render its competitor's products unusable. While this tactic may secure customers' expenditures, those people may resent paying more for products as a result. A similar battle is now raging among Intel, Microsoft, telecommunications companies, and applications software developers (see the "On the Job" box).

Technical Risk in Product Architecture

This decision can spark controversy in a high-technology firm because willingness to assume risk varies throughout an organization. Design engineers often express frustration over the apparent unwillingness by both marketing and operations personnel to push technological innovations to the limit. If customers do not want or need these innovations, more cautious organization members may have a valid argument to justify their go-slow strategy. An excessively risk-averse firm may start losing customers, however, if competitors can offer successful innovations. The organization must make this choice as a business decision—not an engineering decision.

In the past, some market leaders have not prospered by following risk-adverse product-innovation strategies. Caterpillar let other firms take the lead in new products, believing that its strong market position would allow it to successfully introduce new ideas that proved viable. The rapid rise of Komatsu caused the firm to review this strategy. Similarly, IBM waited for others to develop the personal computer market before storming in with its PC. The strategy worked for a while, but agile competitors ultimately hurt IBM in this key market segment.

ON THE JOB

**The Battle for
Standardized Interfaces**

■

The question of who will set standards for emerging computer and electronic technologies in the future remains open. Software makers who compete with Microsoft say that the industry giant has gained enormous power by controlling personal computer standards. Developers of applications software want industrywide control over the interface between the Windows 95 operating system and other vendors' software. So far, Microsoft has refused to yield that control, maintaining that "it is playing fair."

Whether industrywide committees should rein in cowboys like Bill Gates may soon become a moot question, however. Some argue that technologies are developing too quickly for this kind of control. For years, standard-setting committees labored to develop an elaborate framework for computer networking called *Open Systems Interconnection*. They scrambled to react when this process was blindsided by companies selling new, Internet-style networking software. The Defense Department sponsored the development of the Internet in the 1970s to maintain nationwide communications after a nuclear attack through a highly decentralized system that could route messages around disruptions. Today, this ad hoc system has grown in size and scope far beyond its creators' dreams. Although no one agency controls the Internet, the Internet Engineering Task Force, a small corps of cowboy-techies, influences its evolving structure.

The need for standardized interfaces may continue to diminish as the enormous capabilities of today's microchips expand further. Cheap computing power could allow systems to translate between protocols as needed through appropriate software or microprocessors dedicated to the task. This possibility allows product designers to proceed with their plans even without agreements on established protocols. As one high-tech cowboy put it, "Innovate now, clean up later."

SOURCE   "Cowboys versus Committees," *Business Week*, April 10, 1995, pp. 104–106.

Reserve Capacity Considerations

The chapters on just-in-time manufacturing introduced the concept of reserve capacity to ensure that a process can move output according to plan. More traditional manufacturers heavily emphasized the highest possible utilization rate for equipment. Efficiency drove these decisions. JIT practitioners measured effectiveness instead by how quickly a system or a machine could respond to a need.

The placement of reserve capacity in a modular design requires an understanding of the impact of capacity shortfalls on the system. This decision requires answers to fairly straightforward questions about the locations and timing of capacity bottlenecks. If a specific bottleneck occurs, how will it affect the flow of work through the OM system? Computer simulation offers an extremely powerful tool for this kind of analysis.

In-House versus Outside Module Development

Chapter 13 on supply management will cover this make-or-buy decision more extensively. It does have a strategic effect on the product-innovation process, however. Some people believe that a firm should make and/or design only those components for which it has a strategic advantage. If other manufacturers can make disk drives as well as IBM can, it may risk diluting its resources by working in this area instead of buying another firm's product. For an end product approaching maturity, however, the firm may need to resort to selective vertical integration to achieve or maintain cost competitiveness.

Benefits of Product Architecture

Clearly, product architecture decisions have powerful strategic consequences. Just as business strategy provides a general direction for organizational activities, product architecture provides broad guidelines for the work of product-design teams. Further, just as people in each functional area can develop a myopic perspective that blinds them to influences outside their department, members of design teams may also focus too narrowly on their own contributions to product development. In defining a product architecture, a design team must think through many issues that can become sources of conflict, cost overruns, project delays, and/or inferior product designs without careful attention.

 ## MANAGING THE PRODUCT-INNOVATION PROCESS

Any organization's effort to conceive and implement a formal process for product innovation, like all critical decisions, should begin with a clear understanding of the customers that those products should please. Who will buy these products? What are those people buying now? Who sells it to them? What would induce them to switch to a new product? Is the appeal of this offer certain? If not, how can designers test the hypothesis? If so, beware of false security! These basic elements of the organization's image of its customer can ultimately develop into an informed vision that can guide the process for product innovation.

As in much of the early part of the chapter, these questions sound more like subjects for marketers than for operations managers. In today's organization, however, these decisions stretch beyond the boundaries of any single business function. The problems of the American automobile industry attest to the need to keep customers at the front of product decisions. In the sections that follow, we discuss two different ways to implement this process: as a sequential series of activities or through an innovative system called *concurrent engineering*.

Sequential Process for Product Development

Most American firms have organized their product design and development processes sequentially, as shown in Exhibit 11.8. The sequence typically emerges as each functional area completes its part of the project before passing on the results to the next operation. In recent years, mounting criticism of this disjointed process has argued for an interactive product design process that brings together all of the necessary functions to develop offerings capable of exceeding customer expectations while generating sufficient cash flow for the firm to survive.

Example.   Executives of an auto manufacturer approve a bold proposal to develop a new automobile model called a *minivan*. This new vehicle looks like a small van, drives like a car, and fits in a standard garage.

Before this project can start, the design process must establish certain key parameters to guide later decisions. A target price will dictate a target cost for the

[**EXHIBIT 11.8**]

Sequential Product Development

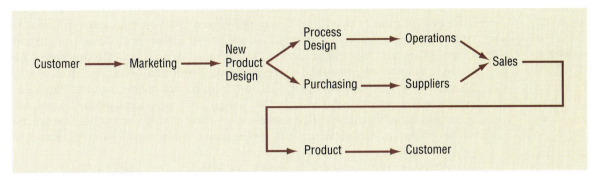

vehicle. A prospective launch date governs schedules of all phases of the project. Extensive initial market research can help to focus the design and development process on the features that customers want.

The styling department then builds clay models to refine the image of the product. Engineering then takes over and starts to define required parts for a vehicle with the intended capabilities and features. Representatives of the styling and engineering departments meet to work out any problems that emerge. Sometimes higher-level managers must step in to reconcile differences.

Suppliers and process engineers then receive the component designs with instructions to figure out how to make and assemble the parts. More problems emerge. More meetings follow to continue the search for parts and processes capable of producing a vehicle that fulfills the initial vision within targeted costs.

Finally, manufacturing begins the task of making a few test units of the new model. More problems arise and department representatives hammer them out in more meetings. As the new model launch season approaches, manufacturing schedules production of the minivan design with most of its problems resolved. Marketing needs quick boosts in volume to meet an announced product launch date. Dealers have placed firm orders so that they will have models to sell during the kickoff advertising program.

Shortcomings of Sequential Product Development.   This example illustrates some of the problems that arise in a sequential-innovation process. First, it often takes too much time. A long design lead time may result in a product that appears outdated at its introduction alongside the products of quicker rivals. Long design lead times also push the time horizon for demand forecasts far into the future, seriously complicating that process, as Chapter 10 explained. A 5-year design lead time requires demand forecasts beginning 5 years into the future and stretching over the life of the product, perhaps as long as 10 years. No one can accurately predict conditions in the firm's market so far in the future.

Also, sequential product development may cost too much. Japanese car makers invest substantially less to create new car models than their American or European competitors. Conventional wisdom solemnly affirms that rush jobs cost more, and this assumption pervades many project planning programs. Many critical path methods, for example, automatically assign higher costs to tasks or activities performed over shorter periods of time. Many manufacturing systems charge high rates to expedite work, believing that this will reduce their overall efficiency. Sequential product design achieves the worst of both worlds—it takes too long and it costs too much.

Sequential product development also inhibits proactive quality management. The **design quality** produced by an innovation process reflects the inherent value that customers place on product features. One measure of design quality is the number and timing of engineering changes needed to refine the product. As compared to Japanese firms, the more sequential product development processes of American firms tend not to make similar numbers of engineering changes, but those changes tend occur later in the design process when they cost more. Worse yet, sequential processes often make engineering changes after the product launch dates, imposing inestimable costs on the company by weakening its relationships with customers.

Product recalls are the hallmarks of poor product design. They amount to unpaid advertisements heralding product-development mistakes. Injudicious handling of publicly recognized design failures can have disastrous effects on firms' reputations that last much longer than most executives realize. However, expert handling of such disasters can turn them into public-relations victories. When Johnson & Johnson learned of product tampering with its best-selling Tylenol™ pain reliever, it conducted what is now considered the textbook example of a product-recall program. The firm's quick response spared no expense to reaffirm in its customers' minds the firm's commitment to their well-being. Despite initial losses, Johnson & Johnson ultimately regained its lost market share and actually improved its reputation.

The problem with sequential product development is a problem of communication, but also of perspective. The process in Exhibit 11.8 permits people to work comfortably within the confines of their niches in the functional hierarchy. Engineers spend most of their time with like-trained engineers, and they expect performance evaluations as engineers by other engineers. To allow necessary exchanges between departments, sequential design processes often establish time-consuming committees. Worse yet, people may address written memos to nearly every living soul with any remote connection to a project, adding more to already mountainous piles of paper than to cross-functional understanding as a basis for action.

Sequential product development creates larger problems than ineffective communication. It creates a problem of perspective. People responsible for product development need to know more than what the next internal customer needs; they need to understand the needs of ultimate customers and how those people will use the new product. Lack of this ultimate customer perspective often leads to flawed product designs. The infamous Chevy Monza, built in the 1970s, required owners to lift the engine from its mounts simply to change its spark plugs, a classic case of failure to understand buyers' uses of a product. Bright and well-meaning engineers missed an obvious design flaw because they lacked the ultimate consumer perspective.

Origins of Disjointed Product Development.   American manufacturers did not always do such a poor job of interfunctional cooperation in product design. During the early stages of the U.S. industrial revolution, product innovators like Thomas Edison succeeded in part because they maintained cross-functional perspectives. Edison created his "innovation factory," joining engineers with other workers in multidisciplinary teams.

---

design quality

The inherent value that customers place on product features

The Menlo Park labs created an environment in which these teams could quickly test and refine ideas. An engineer could take a product design idea down the hall to secure the needed materials from a well-supplied stock room, and then go a little farther to a machine shop to build a prototype or supervise its fabrication by skilled workers. Edison encouraged exploration and experimentation, viewing failures as additions to the body of knowledge. He built pilot plants for potentially successful products within walking distance of the innovation labs. Within the limits of acceptable logistics, he even built full-scale manufacturing plants next to his innovation factory in order to facilitate communications between production and engineering.

This system and similar ones at many other American businesses succeeded, in part, by minimizing the problems of perspective and communication. The business planner and the product designer, often the same person, shared an understanding of the technology and economics of their joint endeavor.

Unfortunately, the remarkable success of Henry Ford's automobile assembly line led him to expand the division of labor concept to the organization as a whole. Ford tried to copy his principles of interchangeable, unskilled workers assembling standardized parts, and apply it to most functions of management. Industrial engineers specialized in narrow aspects of products and processes, limiting careers within narrow boundaries and eliminating the cross-functional training of Thomas Edison's innovation factory. As the product became more complicated, the areas of specialization narrowed further and management hierarchies became steeper. Communications among product design participants disintegrated.

Also, engineers began to learn less about practical information in school. Many colleges dropped practical courses in machine-shop, metal-fabrication, and foundry techniques in favor of more theoretical information. At the same time, decay in the nation's system of vocational training schools widened the knowledge gap between production workers and designers. The success of unions widened this communications gap in many cases.

Mass producers like the auto makers could tolerate these conditions throughout the years after World War II because no competitors offered any better deals. The Big Three prospered turning out standardized cars each year and making major model changeovers every 3 to 5 years. This permitted them to spread the high cost of new product designs over several years' production, and badge engineering further increased the volume of production for components. Standard models and components kept costs low by fully exploiting economies of scale.

This made a lot of economic sense to the number-crunchers in Detroit, but customers became dissatisfied. GM reacted with surprise when Oldsmobile buyers, who grew up hearing about the superiority of the division's so-called "Rocket" engines, complained about the substitution of Chevrolet engines. Car dealers understood the problem, but the auto makers thought they knew better. This communication gap originated in the same division of labor as the firms' internal divisiveness.

The plight of American automobile manufacturers illustrates the shortcomings of sequential product design. Similar problems appear in most organizations that have failed to make a needed adjustment away from rigidly segmented mass manufacturing/mass marketing strategies to more flexible methods designed to better serve fragmented markets. Not all firms need to make this adjustment, however; some stable markets, such as table salt and corn flakes, still permit deliberate, sequential processes for product innovation.

Customer Responsiveness in Product Innovation

Using the following basic value-adding strategies:
1. Provide top quality, as perceived by the customer.
2. Provide superior service/emphasize the intangibles.
3. Achieve extraordinary responsiveness.
4. Be an internationalist.
5. Create uniqueness.

Which employ the following four capability building blocks:
1. Become obsessed with listening.
2. Turn manufacturing into a marketing weapon.
3. Make sales and service forces into heroes.
4. Pursue fast-paced innovation using as a guiding premise:
   1. Invest in applications-oriented small starts.

Using the following four key strategies:
1. Pursue team product/service development.
2. Encourage pilots for everything.
3. Practice creative "swiping."
4. Make word-of-mouth marketing systemic.

Employing the following innovation-encouraging tactics:
1. Support committed "champions."
2. Model innovation/practice purposeful impatience.
3. Support fast failures.
4. Set quantitative innovation goals.

Which yields the desired new look:
1. A corporation with a capacity for innovation.

SOURCE   Adapted from Tom Peters, *Thriving on Chaos: Handbook for a Management Revolution* (New York: Alfred A. Knopf, 1987).

Rediscovery of Concurrent Engineering

A catalog of the obvious faults of sequential product-design processes does not solve those problems. Similarly, anyone can easily spot the appropriate goal—to delight the firm's target customers—or advocate better teamwork. Unfortunately, these simple statements fail to solve complex problems in product development. The ultimate solutions begin with these principles, but most large organizations need more complex systems to achieve simple goals.

Chapter 9 described the role of one such tool, concurrent engineering, in just-in-time manufacturing systems. Recall that this method sets up a comprehensive process for completing the steps in process design through continuing involvement of cross-functional teams of organization members. By completing many steps at once, such a team can drastically reduce the time from product idea to commercially viable product, dramatically enhancing an organization's fast-to-market capabilities. This has become a critical organizational skill in many rapidly changing company environments.

In *Thriving on Chaos*, Tom Peters maintains that winners need organizations that can quickly adapt to "shifting circumstances." While the universal applicability of Peters's manifestoes remains questionable, Exhibit 11.9 summarizes his valuable guidelines for the product-innovation process. One need not fully understand

ON THE JOB

Thermos Teamwork Keeps Innovation Sizzling

The revolutionary Thermos Electric Grill provides a good example of how a corporation can use its core competency to develop new products. When Monte Peterson assumed control of the $225 million company, he realized that innovation provided the key to its survival. Thermos had already made significant inroads into the $1 billion outdoor barbecue grill market, but Peterson knew he needed new products to stimulate sales. He reorganized his marketing, manufacturing, and engineering staff into interdisciplinary teams and gave them a daunting task: to design an electric grill capable of "expanding the boundaries of Thermos's business."

Extensive research, including a month on the road interviewing backyard chefs, revealed several surprising clues to the market. More and more, women were doing the grilling, and they weren't as fond of messy charcoal. Consumers were also becoming more concerned about safety and environmental issues. All this pointed toward electric grills, but there was also a perception that they did not get hot enough to sear food with that distinctive outdoor flavor.

That's where Thermos's core competency came in. Engineers used Thermos's vacuum technology to design a grill with a domed vacuum top, which tightly focused the heat into the same patterns a charcoal- or gas-fired grill makes. As a result, a hamburger off the new Thermos grill looks and tastes the same as one cooked on a charcoal grill, complete with grill lines. But Thermos grill users also enjoyed the intangible benefits of knowing they were making less pollution and less mess.

Not only did the new high-end Thermos grill ignite the market, but it swept up eight design awards as well for its aesthetics and ease of use. Along with other new Thermos products, the grill contributed to an overall 13 percent increase in revenues in 1993, and managers project that the grill will eventually capture 20 percent of its market.

The product also proves Peterson's reorganization a sizzling success. "We needed to reinvent our product lines, and teamwork is doing it for us," said Peterson.

SOURCE Brian Dumaine, "Payoff from the New Management," *Fortune,* December 13, 1993, p. 103–116.

the meaning of each statement in the outline; notice, however, that Peters advocates an extremely inclusive set of principles that underlie an innovative product-development organization that can effectively cope with and thrive on change.

Product Innovation in the Learning Organization

In Chapter 6, we discussed Peter Senge's concept of the learning organization and the difficulty that an existing organization faces when it tries to empower cross-functional teams to carry out product design and development among other organizational functions. Senge also offers a conceptual framework for understanding what an organization must do to develop a team-oriented management style. His five disciplines make sense, but attracting participants among organization members often requires champions of those disciplines to unlearn much that has helped them to survive in the past. This is the essence of the learning organization.

The "On the Job" box discusses one company's experience with a move toward a more participative product-innovation process. How many of either Peters's or Senge's points can you see in operation? Success stories like the

Thermos experience have become common in North American industry, in part because businesses have organized themselves better to design and develop products and services that their customers want. In the next section, we will discuss how firms have changed their organization structures to achieve revolutionary strides in product development.

 # ORGANIZING FOR WORLD-CLASS PRODUCT DEVELOPMENT

Effective product innovation requires a number of business processes dedicated to allocating the firm's resources wisely within the Business Strategy component of the customer-fulfillment process illustrated in Exhibit 11.7. As one major output, a business strategy must produce a framework for deciding what types of markets the firm wants to serve and with which products. As a second major output, it must generate a statement about the technologies through which it intends to produce those products. Thermos reverted to vacuum technologies, one of its core competencies, to solve a product design problem. Together, these business strategy choices define the firm's product-innovation stance, determining whether it will try to reach the market first with a new feature or let others innovate and follow only if sufficient numbers of customers want this feature.

product-development strategy
A component of business strategy that coordinates all of the major business activities that contribute to product innovation

In their book titled *Revolutionizing Product Development*, Wheelwright and Clark argue that most firms should develop explicit **product-development strategies** to coordinate all of the major business activities that contribute to product innovation. They cite several critical driving forces for this need: intense international competition; fragmented, demanding markets; and diverse, rapidly changing technologies. While these forces may be more active in young, technically dominated industries, the Thermos story demonstrated their impact in stable markets like outdoor grills. Recall the fate of a two-wheeled dinosaur named Schwinn when it dismissed the bicycle market as mature and immune to innovation.

Infrastructure for Innovation

Wheelwright and Clark invoke the image of a funnel, illustrated by the dotted lines in Exhibit 11.10, to depict the activities that support a fast-cycle product development activity. At the front end of the funnel, two ongoing business processes must begin the process.

Technology assessment and forecasting predicts technological developments that a business should anticipate. This function evaluates new process technologies that will emerge from research and development endeavors to find practical applications in the marketplace. An important question involves the extent to which various firms will benefit from these technologies. Boeing Aircraft might ask how fast composite fibers will replace metals in airplane frames. A cable television operator might wonder how quickly the information highway will take shape and which technologies will determine success in its operation.

This technology assessment then continues by weighing the benefits of acquiring essential capabilities from outside suppliers, perhaps through some kind of strategic alliance or a simple purchase, or developing them internally. Technology strengths might well determine which outside firms the cable industry might enter. As part of strategy development, some business process needs to assume the

[EXHIBIT 11.10]

Product-Development Strategy

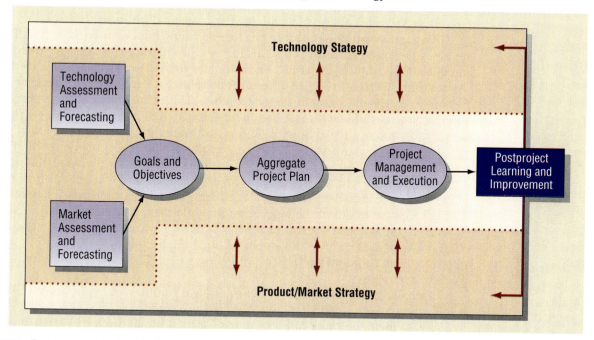

SOURCE   Reprinted/adapted with the permission of The Free Press, an imprint of Simon & Schuster, from *Revolutionizing Product Development*, p. 35, by S. C. Wheelwright and K. B. Clark. Copyright 1992 by Steven C. Wheelwright and Kim B. Clark.

responsibility of asking these questions and then search both inside and outside the firm to get the best answers.

In addition to information about trends in technology, product-development strategy needs an assessment of the firm's current markets and those that it would like to enter. This analysis should go beyond merely forecasting unit sales or their dollar value by product and region. This market assessment and forecasting effort should seek to form the basis for understanding and managing customers' expectations through the tools discussed in Chapter 10. Important questions concern customers' satisfaction with the market's current offerings, potential changes in their order winners and qualifiers, outlines of likely opportunities, and vulnerabilities in the firm's current offering mix.

Assessments of both the marketing and technology situations can come either from organizationwide business processes or more decentralized efforts. That decision should reflect the organization architect's assessment of the best resources to assign to the work. In the past, firms tended to complete these activities as corporate functions. More recent trends have led toward smaller corporate headquarters and more resources deployed among divisions or even product lines.

Technology and Product/Market Strategies.   However the firm completes these assessment processes, their outputs become major inputs to the firm's **technology strategy** and **product/market strategy**. Both of these component strategies specify directions and rates for introductions of innovations into the marketplace. The technology strategy determines whether the company will introduce new technology in small increments or whether the nature of the technology warrants a major

technology strategy

A component of product-development strategy that guides plans for introducing technological innovations

product/market strategy

A component of product-development strategy that guides the type, scale, and timing of innovations in product features or market targeting breakthrough strategy. Of course, these decisions depend on the firm's overall willingness to take risks. Similarly, the marketing strategy determines whether the firm introduces large-scale, blockbuster innovations or sequences of incrementally enhanced models. The technology and product/market strategies must also create internal consistency with the firm's general business strategy.

These formal processes cannot produce anything on their own, however. They require substantive ideas or proposals for new products to enter into the development strategy funnel. Listening to customers provides essential clues to their desires, but this free advice requires deft handling. A firm may well appoint one person to receive all externally generated ideas. This person must insure a gracious reception for any idea to keep existing business as well as stimulating new products. Processing of such an idea should include a review by an attorney to advise about ownership rights to resulting new products. Legal disputes often flare up over valuable product ideas. Recently, an inventor successfully sued the major automobile manufacturers claiming that they had "improperly used" his invention of the multispeed windshield wiper. Some firms take the extraordinary step of certifying someone as out of the loop by routinely returning all unsolicited product ideas to guard against later claims for compensation. Now there's a dead end job! Relations over new product development must carefully balance the need to share information and continue to satisfy customers against the desire to avoid divulging plans to competitors.

Internally generated ideas create fewer legal troubles, but workers' creativity needs careful management, too. Employment agreements often require individuals to assign to their employers all patent and/or intellectual property rights to ideas generated while employed by the firm. Some firms maintain in-house reward systems for new ideas. While these programs have some merit, they risk diverting people's focus away from team-oriented organization. Other firms follow Senge's principle of Building a Shared Vision, advocating pride of membership in a successful team as its own reward. This permits the organization to focus on what needs to be done rather than on who does what and the size of any reward. In particular, money awards can become downright divisive!

Project Management Planning

Newly received or discovered product ideas should pass through some formal screening process to identify and target resources on those with the most commercial promise. Two additional parts of the product-development strategy process affect this screening process, however, so they require prior consideration. First, product development needs a clear statement of the goals and objectives of product and process development. This statement specifies process development, as well, because it competes with product development for the firm's innovation-related funds. The firm's process for selecting development projects should coordinate the overall investment pattern to ensure internal consistency.

The statement of goals and objectives within the product-development strategy should guide and direct any developmental activities. According to Wheelwright and Clark:

> At the aggregate level, the goals and objectives need to be made explicit and then juxtapositioned to examine their compatibility and complementability. The purpose of this process is to provide integration both in the aggregate and at the level of the individual projects. Typically, the goals range from market share (by customer segment and channel) to revenues and profits, and from dates for platform

[**E X H I B I T   1 1 . 1 1**]

Performance Metrics for Product Innovation

Performance Criterion	Performance Metric

Cost	Actual versus plan
	  Total number of engineering hours
	  Outside service expenditures

Time to market	Actual versus plan
	  Elapsed time from conception to launch
	  Time required to recover investment

Quality	Design—actual versus plan
	  Design-measured customer satisfaction
	  Conformance—actual results versus specs

General	Number started versus number completed Number started versus number successful Production yields—actual versus plan Percentage of sales from new products Market share—actual versus plan Number of patents secured

generation introductions and technology achievement to new product/process performance directors.[6]

This should seem somewhat familiar. In coverage of quality function deployment in Chapter 8, the development of the central part of the house of quality addressed efforts to make a product's engineering characteristics compatible with and complementary to customers' requirements. The function of developing quantitative statements of goals also plays an integral role in business planning.

Statements of goals and objectives focus the product-development strategy process. Business planning often includes projections of how much growth in sales an existing product should provide, leaving a gap to allow for new business. Effective planning takes this process a step further by estimating how much and when each product-innovation project will contribute to the firm's achievement of its overall goals and objectives.

Performance measurement must have a place as an integral part of this planning process. Beyond the routine sales and profit objectives, the product and process innovations should be evaluated based on three additional criteria: cost (or productivity), time to market, and quality. Exhibit 11.11 lists some typical performance metrics for each criterion.

Aggregate Project Plan.   After setting and quantifying goals and objectives, the innovation infrastructure continues with development of an aggregate project plan. This critical reality check ensures that proposed projects described in the statement of goals and objectives are resource feasible. It helps the firm to plan its deployment of resources to direct the right amount of resources of the right type to each project at the right time to maximize the likelihood of its success.

[6]S. C. Wheelwright and K. B. Clark, *Revolutionizing Product Development* (New York: Free Press, 1991).

To create an aggregate project plan, even the most modern product-development process needs to complete some old-fashioned project planning. This activity begins by breaking down the project into specific tasks. It then estimates the type and the amount of resources that each task requires. Although this estimate is subject to considerable uncertainty, failure to quantify, at least approximately, the distribution of resources risks allowing the project to run out of control. In a sequential product-development system, this planning produces a sequence of tasks that form the project network.

Based on more general project-planning as input, commercial project-management software packages can help operations managers to determine the likely length of a project, its critical path (i.e., the sequence of tasks that cannot suffer delay without delaying the entire project), and the timing of resource needs. Resource planning must also consider the needs of other projects. Unless the project can rely on resources dedicated exclusively to its activities, it may seem feasible by itself while other projects plan to use the same resources, leading the organization as a whole to take on many more projects than it can complete. Unfortunately, similar situations arise quite regularly.

At some point, any project proposal must state what workers or other resources it will need and when and for how long it will need them. These are difficult questions. No two projects seem alike, so past experience may not help much with an estimate of current needs. Some involve extensive technical support while others need mostly marketing resources.

Wheelwright and Clark present a classification scheme of four primary types of developmental projects to help clarify resource needs for project planning (Exhibit 11.12). By fitting even widely varying projects into these four types, planners can produce reasonably good approximations of resource needs.

Research and Advanced Development Projects.   Companies undertake these ambitious projects to find new core products or processes, for example, a project by General Motors to develop an electric car. Such a complex task requires an advanced mix of skills, perhaps provided by people without experience with past products or processes to encumber their progress. A firm needs a special type of organization to nurture such a team and to protect it somewhat from the realities of the marketplace. Schedules are important, but project managers must not try to force such basic innovation to occur on their schedule.

Breakthrough Development Projects.   These projects seek to develop products or processes that will employ some entirely new technology, itself perhaps developed through an advanced development project. Ford based some breakthrough projects on its V8 engine. In the same way, GM developed its Corvair around a rear-drive, aluminum, air-cooled engine. Some breakthroughs succeed, some don't. Sony developed its Betamax video recorder based on both new core products and new core processes. Polaroid's Land Camera created a new core product and process. Breakthrough products often become beachheads in their markets for entire families of products.

Platform or Generational Development Projects.   These projects develop platforms from which the firm can launch later, derivative products. Apple Computer's development of its Powerbook line of laptop computers and its Newton personal digital assistant are good examples of such projects. If successful, these innovations will provide starting points for entire sequences of related products. These products do

[**E X H I B I T   1 1 . 1 2**]

Primary Types of Development Projects

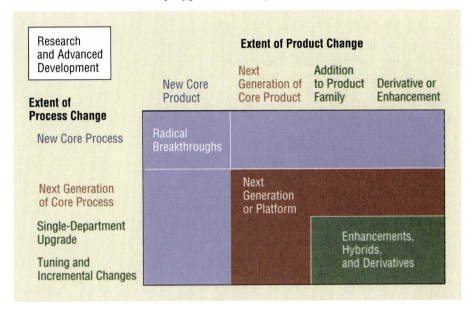

SOURCE   Reprinted/adapted with the permission of The Free Press, an imprint of Simon & Schuster, from *Revolutionizing Product Development,* p. 49, by S. C. Wheelwright and K. B. Clark. Copyright 1992 by Steven C. Wheelwright and Kim B. Clark.

not represent breakthroughs, however, which deploy formerly unknown products or processes.

Derivative Development Projects.   These projects refine and improve selected features of existing products. Adding a CD-ROM drive to an existing computer or adding a peanut butter flavor to M&Ms would amount to derivative projects, as would a sequel to a successful motion picture. The scope of such a project is much narrower than the other, more ambitious innovations.

The labels along the left side and top of Exhibit 11.12 suggest strategic implications of this classification scheme. Clearly, a sweeping project to develop a new core process or product or both requires more resources and more organizational flexibility. In particular, participants must expect to engage more vigorously in Senge's systems thinking perspective than participants in a project to build a derivative of some successful current product or process. Small projects with limited scopes in the lower right corner of Exhibit 11.12 probably do not require cross-functional product-innovation teams.

Project Management for Concurrent Engineering

Concurrent engineering carries out product-innovation projects through cross-functional teams that complete the multistage process detailed in Exhibit 11.13. This process relieves the engineering department of sole responsibility for the design stage, instead spreading the work among many departments, as Thermos did. Senge's book has provided valuable help for practitioners of concurrent engineering.

[**EXHIBIT 11.13**]

Activities and Responsibilities in Concurrent Engineering

Conceptual Design

Marketing: Proposes and investigates product concepts
Engineering: Proposes new technologies and simulates performances
Operations: Proposes and investigates manufacturing/delivery processes

Product Design

Marketing: Defines markets and specifies objectives
Engineering: Chooses components and key suppliers
Operations: Defines process architecture and estimates costs

Product and Process Engineering

Marketing: Conducts customer tests on prototypes
Engineering: Builds full-scale prototypes for evaluation and refinement
Operations: Builds system to manufacture prototype, plans full-scale system, tests tooling and new procedures

Pilot Development And Testing

Marketing: Prepares for market roll out, trains sales force
Engineering: Evaluates and tests pilot unit
Operations: Builds pilot units in commercial processes, refines the system, trains personnel, checks suppliers

Volume Production and Launch

Marketing: Fills distribution channel, sells and promotes, gains feedback from target customers
Engineering: Evaluates customers' experience with product
Operations: Builds up plant to volume targets, refines quality, yield, and cost performance

Post-Sale Service

Marketing: Gains customer feedback
Engineering and Operations: Study warranty data

The Gantt chart in Exhibit 11.14 illustrates the time-to-market advantage that concurrent engineering gains by overlapping product-development activities, despite its pattern of devoting more time to the work of each stage. Each bar represents the beginning and completion dates of a project stage. The bar for each sequential engineering activity begins at the point where the preceding bar ends because functional specialists complete all tasks within a stage before they pass on responsibility for the next stage to other specialists. When product designers complete their tasks, they hand the project to product and process engineers.

Concurrent engineering, on the other hand, permits a single team to start working on each stage before finishing work on the earlier stage. This overlap both relies on and reinforces the broad perspective that members bring to cross-functional teams. Note that the chart shows longer bars for concurrent engineering stages, indicating that this method requires more elapsed time per stage. In later sections, we will discuss the reasons for this relationship.

The Thermos story illustrated a typical concurrent engineering effort to complete all of the functional tasks listed in Exhibit 11.13 within a single cross-functional

[**E X H I B I T   1 1 . 1 4**]

Sequential versus Concurrent Engineering

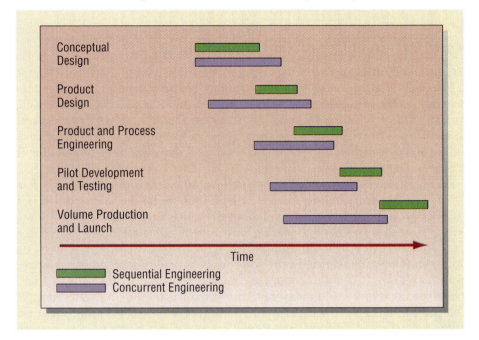

team. A core group of key team members stay with the team throughout all stages of product innovation, joined periodically by new members with specific skills who act more or less as consultants. In this way, the team can expand and contract its skill base, making it both efficient and flexible. The core team members provide critical leadership, commitment, and perspective to a project.

As mentioned earlier, concurrent engineering does complicate resource planning somewhat. Aggregate project planning gains importance for its assurance that the the firm can complete all projects it undertakes with its existing resource base. This involves a complex plan to assign multiple resources, including equipment, engineers, market researchers, etc., to competing tasks in a feasible, timely manner. Fortunately, computer software for project management helps an organization to coordinate multiple projects with varying resource requirements reasonably efficiently.

Even the most automated planning system still needs inputs, however, like estimates of time requirements for each resource. Rough-cut estimates usually will suffice, as long as planning remains flexible. If it demands rigid adherence to every due date for each individual design-process activity, a firm risks trouble when designers sacrifice design criteria to meet the milestone, endangering the firm's achievement of its overall design quality objectives.

Even with these difficulties, a team-driven multiple-project environment may in fact simplify resource management as compared with a more centralized, hierarchical system. The core members of a cross-functional product-design team can effectively plan their use of dedicated resources. They may still need to interact with an organizationwide resource-allocation process to plan for discretionary resources, but planners can distribute limited stocks of shared resources much more easily than they can allocate all organizational resources among multiple products over each period in the planning horizon. This is a perfect example of dissolving a major problem, or at least greatly diminishing its scope, by redefining its limits. Never try to solve a big problem with one large decision when a series of small decisions can do just as well!

Success Record of Concurrent Engineering

Two seminal studies of the global automobile industry by Clark and Fujimoto and Womack et al. provide good illustrations of the impact of cross-functional concurrent engineering on product and process innovation. These field studies have gathered convincing empirical data on the actual business practices of the auto industry. We will generalize their findings to build a structure for understanding and extending their lessons for product design and development to other industries.

The Clark and Fujimoto study evaluated product-development activities based on cost, quality, and time-to-market, all problem areas in sequential product design. They measured cost by evaluating the funds that firms spent to develop products from idea inception to market launch, with adjustments for differences in the car models. American car companies, with their sequential methods, used about 3.0 million engineering hours to produce a new model, whereas Japanese companies required 1.7 million hours to complete the same activities concurrently.[7]

The researchers' second measure of performance, quality, indicated how well developed products met the expectations of target customers, covering both design quality and quality of conformance. Practitioners of concurrent engineering implemented programs such as quality function deployment and design for manufacture, discussed later in this chapter, to ensure that their product designs accurately reflected the needs of both internal and external customers.

The researchers' measurement of time to market evaluated the elapsed times of various product-development efforts from idea inception to product launch. They found that Japanese firms took 46 months on average while American firms took 60 months.[8]

These findings imply that time can cost money. Again, this defies the teachings of conventional wisdom that faster action costs more. Data from poor resource-management systems confirm the old ideas while hiding possibilities for improvement.

The Womack et al. study confirmed the conclusions of Clark and Fujimoto. Its evaluation of car designs identified four major differences that can partially explain the differences in performance between mass manufacturers and what the study called *lean manufacturers*.

Leadership.   The study found strong project-leadership organization structures in the Japanese lean producers. In the Toyota system, this strong leader is called a *shusa*. Some American firms have built similarly successful product-development processes; they advocate the leadership of innovation champions whose vision and power drive product design. Peters called these people *committed champions*. Whatever the name, this leader brings many strengths to the product-innovation process, including vision, broad product knowledge, skillful handling of organizational relationships, and an ability to inspire team members with diverse perspectives.

[7]Clark and Fujimoto.
[8]Ibid.

Toyota employees prize any opportunity to act as shusas, since the position traditionally carries great power and job satisfaction. This leader's personal power and organizational skills give the design team the necessary resources to design, develop, justify, and launch newly designed products. Unlike American design teams, the core members of Japanese teams often stay with their projects long after successful launches pursuing the ultimate goal of building a satisfied customer base rather than just a successful product.

In Western firms, by contrast, product-development leadership brings less organizational esteem. Team members often view their roles as temporary assignments within career paths that depend largely on relations with fellow functional specialists. Leaders must work harder to coordinate these weakly committed team members and to gain needed cooperation among functional areas, often in competition with other major responsibilities of team members. Such an assignment often represents a short-term staff outside the organization's prime career-advancement tracks. As launch date approaches, product design and development teams often disband or shrink.

Teamwork.   Japanese car manufacturers built their organizations to encourage active teamwork among both individuals and functional departments, and the shusa's role contributes to this strength. While individual employees maintain links to their functional departments, the shusa's evaluation determines the organization's assessment of individual performance and subsequent job assignments. Teamwork can grow over time as core members remain committed for the entire life of the project.

Most Americans serve on product-development teams as short-term diversions from their primary positions in their functional departments. Their workspace often remains within those departments, reinforcing their identification with their functional areas rather than the new team. Relocation can become important in such a new project, as one successful team at a Midwestern company learned when it lost its perfect off-site location because real-estate experts found it uneconomical. Team members scattered among their individual functional departments and team effectiveness dissipated.

Teamwork influences cost effectiveness, as well. Clark and Fujimoto found that about 900 engineers participated in a typical project at a U.S. firm while the Japanese firms "enlisted about 485."[9] The most committed practitioners of the shusa system reduced team membership to only 333. These lower numbers reflect more efficient organizations and lower turnover within Japanese product design teams. Conversely, U.S. firms often reassign key team members prematurely to new projects.

Communications.   Womack et al. discovered more than just the expected differences in patterns of communication between Japanese and American auto makers. Rather than simply communicating through different channels, American firms seemed to fail to communicate effectively. In their sequential process activities, they frequently overlooked critical design issues early in a project's life. Functional specialists seemed to make vague commitments only to rescind them to avoid the real consequences of the projects, perhaps complaining that insufficient access to upstream decision making prevented them from contributing.

In contrast, Japanese teams spend more time early in the process fleshing out design problems and then formally pledging to make agreed upon contributions to

---

[9]Ibid.

Product Development Performance: Japan vs. American Automakers

	Japanese Producers	American Producers
Average engineering hours per new model	1.7 million	3.1 million
Average development time per new model	46.2 months	60.4 months
Number of employees in project team	485	903
Number of body types per new model	2.3	1.7
Average ratio of shared parts	18%	38%
Supplier share of engineering	51%	14%
Engineering change cost as share of total die costs	10–30%	30–50%
Ratio of delayed parts	1 in 6 late	1 in 2 late
Die development time	13.8 months	25.0 months
Prototype lead time	6.2 months	12.4 months
Time from production start to first sale	1 month	4 months
Return to normal production after new model	4 months	5 months
Return to normal quality after new model	1.4 months	11 months

SOURCE   Reprinted with the permission of Rawson/Scribner, an imprint of Simon & Schuster, from *The Machine That Changed the World: The Story of Lean Production,* p. 118, by James P. Womack, Daniel T. Jones, and Daniel Roos. Copyright © 1990 by James P. Womack, Daniel T. Jones, Daniel Roos, and Donna Sammons Carpenter.

the group. Early in a project's life, the shusa involves a wide variety of perspectives to force the team to confront as many foreseeable problems as possible. These initial agreements reduce the need for later communication.

Simultaneous Development.   Through vigorous project leadership, committed teamwork, and active early communications, Japanese auto makers and their suppliers complete much of their component and process designs at the same time. The shusa's coordination helps team members to define their tasks and relationships with other members' tasks, encouraging teamwork and communication to help members take shared risks.

An American designer of a stamped, metal part, say a fender, maintains an arm's-length relationship with the die maker. Since this supplier pays severe penalties if the die fails to meet specifications, the firm waits for a final design before starting the job.

A Japanese product-development process would invite the die maker to join the team. This early involvement both helps the part designer to plan for the manufacturing process and allows the die maker to start machining work as soon as preliminary specifications become available. More detailed work must wait for later refinements, but the initial operations can carry on without precise dimensions. This early involvement can both improve the product design and save some revisions. Also, the die maker offers expertise without increasing the design team's engineering burden or cost. This win-win situation reduces costs, improves quality, and shortens lead times.

Much of the celebrated competitive advantage of Japanese auto makers in the 1980s began in the 1960s and 1970s with concurrent engineering to overcome a reputation for poor quality and to produce fuel-efficient cars at economical prices. Exhibit 11.15 lists the advantages that the Japanese producers built. In the 1980s

[**EXHIBIT 11.16**]

Fragmentation of the American Car Market

	1955	1973	1986	1989
American products				
Number of products on sale	25	38	47	50
Sales per product[a]	309	322	238	219
Japanese products				
Number of products on sale	0	19	41	58
Sales per product[a]	0	55	94	73

[a]Including sales of vans and light trucks

SOURCE   Reprinted with the permission of Rawson/Scribner, an imprint of Simon & Schuster, from *The Machine That Changed the World: The Story of Lean Production*, p. 125, by James P. Womack, Daniel T. Jones, and Daniel Roos. Copyright © 1990 by James P. Womack, Daniel T. Jones, Daniel Roos, and Donna Sammons Carpenter.

and 1990s, these firms' marketing strategies set out to extend the benefits of their superior product-development capabilities by offering wider varieties of products to fragment the North American market.

Exhibit 11.16 illustrates dramatic changes in unit sales for individual models. Japanese producers have systematically increased the numbers of models they offer, selling fewer units per model. American car manufacturers have had to respond by offering larger varieties of their own models, causing a 50 percent decline in average unit sales per model. Japan's car manufacturers have continued to earn profits selling no more than 300,000 units per year of a single model with an average age of 2 years. Their American rivals have labored to keep pace despite losses or marginal profits selling models that averaged 5 years old. (The 1994 Dodge Ram pickup truck replaced an 18-year-old model!) In fact, Toyota has become so good at economically introducing new models that in 1993 the Japanese government asked the firm to slow down its product-innovation process in order to relieve the competitive pressures on Detroit and certain weaker Japanese competitors.

In the 1990s, Detroit seems to have heard the message. Chrysler designed and developed its successful LH model through a new team process (LH stands for last hope). Chrysler also spent $1 million building its Chrysler Technology Center, ironically bringing many of the same capabilities of Thomas Edison's turn-of-the-century innovation factory under a single roof. Most recently in the spring of 1994, Chrysler introduced its Neon model, illustrating the benefits of the firm's concurrent-engineering program as described in the "On the Job" box.

Within Chrysler, success seems to have become contagious. The firm's macho new pickup truck will help it to gain market share in this uniquely American market segment and the LH line has reestablished Chrysler's presence in the more lucrative market for medium-sized cars. Its minivans continue to hold market share, and its Cherokee and Grand Cherokee lines remain competitive players.

ANALYTICAL TOOLS FOR PRODUCT INNOVATION

The continuing discussion of sequential horror stories and concurrent solutions may seem somewhat theoretical. To anchor the principles of the earlier sections in

ON THE JOB

Chrysler Lights Its Future with Neon

■

Chrysler had successfully started down the road to becoming a "learning organization" with the development of its LH line in the early 1980s. But as Chrysler weighed its options for developing its next subcompact car, it found itself out of cash, so many of its top executives were leaning toward joint development.

Robert Marcell, head of Chrysler's small car division, helped turn the tide in a dramatic meeting with Lee Iacocca in July of 1990. Marcell was painfully aware that joint development would probably mean a loss of more jobs for his native Michigan. He made an emotional pitch to Lee Iacocca, suggesting that Chrysler could not afford to lose its small-car production capabilities. "If we dare to be different, we could be the reason the U.S. auto industry survives," Marcell told Iacocca. He proposed that Chrysler risk producing a daring new design using concurrent engineering.

In April of 1991 Marcell got his way, and the Neon model got the go-ahead. Everything depended on the bottom line, and Marcell knew that headquarters would pull the plug if he couldn't keep costs rock bottom. With a target base price of $8,600, the Neon couldn't be a cheap car—it had to be a better car that cost less.

After careful market research, design teams cut away extra features like power windows and four-speed transmission and worked to improve overall quality. In the earliest stages, Chrysler's suppliers worked closely with in-house engineers to design components in an unprecedented new "partnership" arrangement. Chrysler also entered into another unprecedented "partnership" arrangement with its workers, inviting United Auto Workers union members to take part in the design process. Chrysler asked for UAW input in designing a car and parts that were easy to build, and UAW workers helped assemble the first production prototypes. This partnership enabled Chrysler to significantly improve its assembly procedures, adding to the Neon's overall quality at less cost.

In the spring of 1994, the Neon rolled off the line with a total development cost of about $1.3 billion—about $500 less per car than any comparable subcompact. Marcell triumphantly ensured his $8,600 base price, buying a little more time for Chrysler's future and the future of Michigan in the bargain.

SOURCE   "Chrysler's Neon," *Business Week,* May 3, 1993.

operations management practice, in this section we discuss some practical, analytical tools for product innovation. Each practical problem discussed here begins with a lack of interfunctional perspective. Each potential solution offers some kind of cross-functional response.

Design for Manufacture

design for manufacture
A product-innovation tool that integrates the activities of product designers with those of the designers of the manufacturing or service delivery processes that make the product

Design for manufacture (DFM) seeks primarily to integrate the activities of product designers with those of the designers of the manufacturing or service delivery processes that make the product. Design for manufacture does not require complete unification of these activities on one team. They must simply coordinate their efforts to produce the cooperation of team members. DFM gives representatives from manufacturing a forum for providing inputs about the strengths and limitations of the OM process during a product's design phase.

The early development of design for manufacture responded to friction created by product designs that did not fit existing production systems. These responses often implemented systems theory, as when firms created expert systems to constrain engineers' choices early in the design process. These systems essentially codified the insight of shop-floor workers to provide automatic input to designs. Other DFM systems created standards that specified the best manufacturing practices. One firm reduced the number of hole sizes that designers could expect a shop to drill from hundreds down to 27. An engineer could still specify a nonstandard size, but only after filling out a seven-page form to justify the variation.

While changes like these may have simplified life for manufacturing engineers, they ignored the root cause of the problem—poor cooperation between two functional areas. Even when manufacturing representatives joined product-development teams, they often took advantage of the desire for unanimity to seize a sort of veto power. "Since you ask," the argument went, "do it my way." Design engineers responded predictably: "We knew it would not work."

American industry often produced a traditional response to this dismal situation—they hired consultants to recommend obvious solutions. This produced simple guidelines, such as:

- Minimize the number of parts, including fasteners.
- Minimize the number of fabrication or assembly operations.
- Discover customers' functional requirements and match the design to them.
- Determine process capabilities and design products to match them.
- Specify standard components with proven quality levels whenever possible.
- Design multifunctional modules and combine them.
- Create designs that simplify fabrication, assembly, and servicing.
- Design products to allow one-way assembly with no wasteful backtracking.
- Avoid special-purpose fasteners or those that require special tools.
- Make parts strong enough to withstand inevitable mishandling.
- Anticipate potential misuse by the dumbest possible customer and create a design that prevents it.

This list may seem to state no more than basic common sense, but the "On the Job" box illustrates the novelty of these ideas to many product designers.

Design for Assembly

The discussion of design for manufacturing hinted at the principles of **design for assembly** (DFA). As the name implies, DFA focuses on reducing assembly costs and indirectly increasing the quality of conformance by creating designs that fit well with assembly operations. This simple strategy begins by reducing as much as possible the number of parts needed to assemble the product. It then works to ensure that the remaining parts fit together as easily as possible.

These simple guidelines compare to the advice of a swimming instructor who said to a struggling student, "Don't sink!" These goals are easier to state than to accomplish. To help solve this problem, Geoffrey Boothroyd and Peter Dewhurst, two entrepreneurial engineering professors, created a quantitative scoring method for part features that identifies areas for potential savings. They begin by scoring an initial design, either a prototype design for an new product or the current design for an existing one, assigning penalty points for each feature of the design. The DFA team then seeks to redesign the product to improve this design score.

Some DFA methods actually produce designs to assess their scores. Others simulate the performance of new designs through computer models. All DFA scoring mechanisms reflect organizations' experience and many spark heated arguments.

design for assembly
A product-innovation tool that reduces assembly costs and indirectly increases the quality of conformance by creating designs that fit well with assembly operations

ON THE JOB

Mattel's Serious Approach to DFM for Toys

The creator of Barbie dolls and other children's toys should be in a fun business. In reality, it's a cut-throat, mature business that requires a cost minimization strategy to remain competitive. Hence, Mattel Toy manufactures in twelve low-labor-cost countries.

Because there are limits to the benefits of cheap labor, Mattel created a "Design for Competitive Advantage" program to streamline costs. They started off right by setting up a training program to teach DFM principles to their engineers. To begin, they created a computerized data bank to help them identify similar or redundant parts. This system also helped them establish standardized part tolerances. The result? Lower costs and a shorter product design cycle.

To illustrate their new approach, Mattel selected Color Spin, an existing product that helps a toddler develop "visual awareness and action-reaction motor skills." The product retails for about $13 and is designed for babies six months and older. The existing product design called for 55 parts to be made, purchased, and assembled. The schematic of the parts and their location in the final product is shown to the right. After applying simple DFM principles, the Mattel team was able to halve the part counts and increase the toy's quality and performance. The improved product also is shown to the right. How did they do it? Mostly by redesigning parts to snap together. In other cases, plastic welding replaced fasteners. An in-house software system analyzed the cost effectiveness of design alternatives.

Mattel was able to shave 38 percent from the cost of Color Spin—an annual savings of $700,000. When asked what advice they would give to others, they responded:

- Make sure its a team effort, with designers aboard as allies.
- Choose a leader who has experience on both sides, design and manufacturing.
- Get support from as high up in the company as possible.
- Assure recognition for DFM achievements and stimulate continued interest.
- Maintain an understanding of what the customer wants, and exceed their expectations.

Mattel expected to save $40 million using DFM in 1992.

SOURCE   D. Gardner, "DFM Adds Sparkle to Toy Line," *Design News*, July 7, 1991, pp. 62–64.

The DFA method proposed by Boothroyd and Dewhurst provides an excellent example of the benefits of quantification, even with extremely subjective numbers. It forces entrenched organization members to rethink their positions, often with impressive results as one happy user, Ford Motor Company, attests. Although no one can accurately measure the relative contribution of DFA, Ford has reportedly achieved a cost advantage over GM in the range of $1,500 per vehicle.

Design for Post-Sale Service

design for service
A product-innovation tool that incorporates features to help owners and repair technicians maintain products

A similar discipline, **design for service**, requires less explanation, though it is no less important than DFM or DFA. Just about everyone has experienced frustration over poor instructions in a service manual or heard a mechanic angrily mutter, "Who designed this?" Design for service simply requires product designers to incorporate features that help owners and repair technicians to maintain products; designers should serve these people as customers that they hope to see again and again.

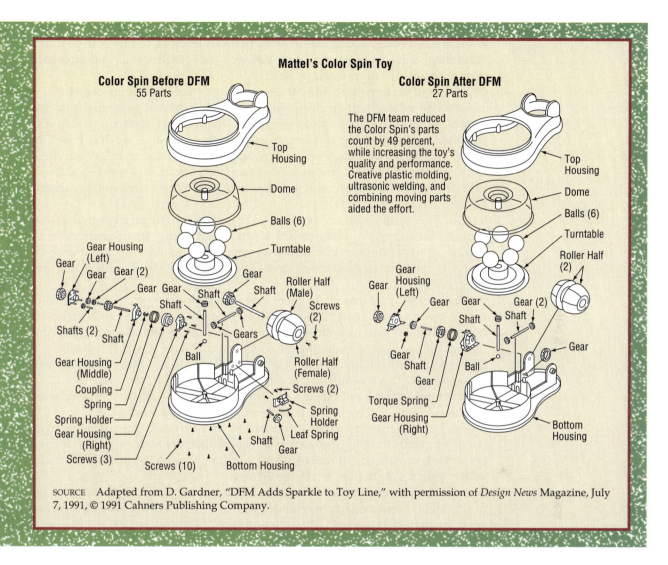

Mattel's Color Spin Toy

SOURCE   Adapted from D. Gardner, "DFM Adds Sparkle to Toy Line," with permission of *Design News* Magazine, July 7, 1991, © 1991 Cahners Publishing Company.

Design for Recycling

Another somewhat self-evident discipline, design for recycling, has only recently received attention. For example, many people feel that designers of nuclear-power facilities should work to facilitate the ultimate disposal of both the plant and its spent fuel rods. This principle extends to less lethal products, as well, including personal computers, dry-cell batteries, disposable diapers, and cars. In the final chapter, we discuss in greater detail the impact of this and other issues involved in the green movement.

CHAPTER SUMMARY

In this chapter, we considered the process by which an organization creates products that meet or exceed the expectations of target customers.

1. A customer views any product, either a good or a service, as a core benefit with certain distinguishing features that define the actual, or physical, product. Additional features like warranties, delivery and credit terms, and after-sale service define the augmented product.

2. Designers of services face difficulties in defining their products because services differ substantially in form, but those products fall generally into five groups: business services, trade services, infrastructure services, social/personal services, and public services. Another system classifies services based on options available to customers as zero-say services, minimum say services, mandated services with options, elective services, and luxury services. All service products share the characteristics of intangibility, perishability, simultaneity, and heterogeneity.

3. Several important social and commercial trends affect the product-innovation process, including the shift toward a service economy, the globalization of markets, the continuing rise of consumerism, the increasing importance of time, the emergence of quality as an order qualifier, the threat of litigation, and the green movement.

4. Product designers cluster customers into viable groups with the help of marketing specialists to create markets with sufficiently similar demands to permit the development of an appropriate product. One system characterizes customers for services as economizers, personalized, care seekers, convenience seekers, and ethical/loyal customers. Customers for physical goods include these groups, plus customizers, functionists, and style-driven consumers.

5. The customer-fulfillment process combines production/delivery systems with product-design systems under the direction of business strategy.

6. Product architecture provides a framework and direction for participants in the product-innovation process. A product architecture forces product designers to look outside the limits of their own functional specialties to discover wider, systems influences on design issues.

7. Standardization, one kind of product architecture, provides substantial savings in production and design costs, and it reduces lead times. It may also please some customers, but others may demand more flexibility in product features.

8. Mass customization, a newer product architecture, combines standard modules to provide products with custom features at competitive costs. The interfaces between modules become critical in such a system.

9. The theoretical limitations of sequential product-development processes have become disturbingly real in the world market for automobiles. Today's organizations can no longer expect to succeed, or even survive, by selling products developed over lengthy and disjointed sequential processes.

10. Concurrent engineering provides a more effective model for product innovation, in which a cross-functional team combines the efforts and expertise of diverse members, including suppliers, to carry a product-innovation project from initial idea through successful launch and after-sale service. U.S. auto manufacturers and other firms have begun to follow Japanese firms in implementing this method to meet the challenge of product innovation in today's fragmented markets.

[**KEY TERMS**]

product   492
core product   492
actual product   492
augmented product   493
vector marketing   500
service delivery system
   500
service factory   503
service shop   503
mass service   503
professional service   504

product bundle   504
supporting facility   504
supporting good   504
explicit service   504
implicit benefit   504
customer-fulfillment
   process   507
product architecture   509
known product   511
product interface   512
value chain   513

design quality   518
product-development
   strategy   522
technology strategy   523
product/market strategy
   523
design for manufacture
   534
design for assembly   535
design for service   536

[**DISCUSSION QUESTIONS**]

1. Think back to your childhood, and make a list of ten or so products that seemed to be market leaders. What happened to them? Why?
2. Name three American products or firms that have maintained top market positions over the past 10 or 20 years. What have these firms done to maintain their supremacy?
3. Can you name five female inventors? If so, in what types of organizations did they work? If not, why do you think this is so? Are there things you think American businesses could do to increase their numbers?
4. You must create a new technology assessment and forecasting department for a textbook publisher. What scope of technologies should the new department follow?
5. Now you must create a market assessment and forecasting department for a textbook publisher. What market forces should the system study?
6. As a student, define the ideal textbook for this course. Would something other than a textbook suit your needs better?
7. Describe the product architecture of your college curriculum. What difficulties do you encounter in completing this analysis?
8. A clever employee of a pharmaceutical firm has an idea for a new product. A new substance called *degarlic* placed in an existing inhaler package can reduce the measurement of the garlic content of a person's breath with a single shot before going on a date. What kind of team would you put together to investigate this idea?
9. You are reading over the shoulder of the ghost of Ray Kroc, the person who made McDonald's famous. In your reading about his creation, you come across this passage:

> No one buys a Big Mac for the simple reason of eating it. Instead the behavior is part of the entire "gestalt" in which the consumer participates on a subliminal level. The purchase of a Big Mac involves a deep interior perception of self, family, country, and socioeconomic status. Along with the Big Mac, a

consumer "buys" a vision of [a person] at leisure on a well-desired break, a vision of family cohesiveness, … [and] a particular type of patriotism.

Does Kroc's ghost seem delighted, concerned, or perplexed?

10. List five products you have encountered that resulted from mass customization processes. How does each implement mass customization? How would you convert the service aspect of the product to be made in a service factory?

11. Think of your journey through higher education as a personal product-development adventure. In what ways do you think the concepts discussed in this book could be applied to your school's curriculum to enhance your educational process? What are the tradeoffs involved for the other institutional stakeholders?

12. In what ways might design for manufacturing enhance and detract from products on the market? How could DFM enhance the value of two products? How could it diminish the value of two products?

13. Think of five products that you currently own or use that show poor attention to post-use disposal. If government were to demand a redesign to make each product more environmentally responsible, what additional costs would you and/or the vendor incur?

14. In the 1950, George Romney, the president of American Motors, promoted a compact model called the *American* by promising that its outer appearance would not change for at least 5 years. What tradeoffs did the product designers make? To which types of consumers were they trying to appeal? Did you think that a similar design would work today?

15. Which decisions discussed in this chapter depend heavily on product-delivery system issues? How might a firm address both product-innovation and delivery-system design issues at the same time?

C A U T I O N

[C R I T I C A L   T H I N K I N G   R E Q U I R E D]

1. New currency designs are in the works for the United States. What product specifications are important here? How might the new designs be used to deter counterfeiting?

2. You are having dinner with a Czech student who is visiting at your university. After reading this chapter, she asks you whether time-based competition has improved the quality of your life. How would you respond? Why might she ask?

CASE 11.1

Dayglo® Field of Dreams

Several years ago, a talented homemaker started a home-grown business in which she created attractive, hand-painted casual wear for women using Dayglo® paints. This hobby quickly grew into a small business in which the owner and a close friend produced the goods for sale at nearby craft bazaars.

As the cash flowed in, the entrepreneur's engineer husband had a vision: "If we make them by the thousands, people will buy them. We will hire more creative people, sales reps to market our creations, accountants to count the money, and I'll be able to quit my job as an engineer. We'll become the Mrs. Fields of women's wear."

Exhibits 11.17 and 11.18 show the existing and proposed business processes. The transformed

business would build additional manufacturing capacity by hiring more neighbors to make the items. A newly hired sales rep would sell this output to small women's clothing stores throughout the western states. The husband envisioned himself handling administrative duties while his wife would run the creative side.

In pursuit of higher productivity, this husband-and-wife team agreed to be a living case for an undergraduate operations management class. The class quickly discovered that the existing business processes could not fulfill the partners' dream. One student asked whether the sales rep would sell samples or actual merchandise. The owners responded that the sales reps would ask store buyers what they wanted and the production

[EXHIBIT 11.17]

Existing Process

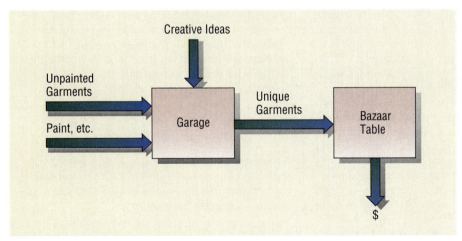

[E X H I B I T   1 1 . 1 8]

Envisioned Process

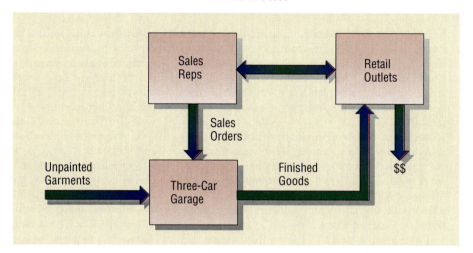

function would send them a set of like products in the requested sizes. A student with some retail experience objected, "Sounds like the customers would be buying a pig-in-a-poke." A finance major then commented, "What a wonderful excuse for not paying an invoice! Just say that this is not what I had ordered." An operations management major then asked, "How will the process replicate like goods? What if twin sisters wanted identical outfits?"

The owners realized that they would have to make some standardized items. This disturbed the creative half of the team, since she was quite proud of the individuality of her output. "No two items are alike—that is what I am selling." As she reluctantly saw the need to create a standard product, the pair encountered a number of new problems. How could they produce copies of creative designs in large numbers? Which markings or irregularities represented products of the creative process and which represented failures to achieve quality of conformance? How could the partners assure the stores that they would deliver products that would match the representative products?

Clearly, this new enterprise needed to focus even more attention on how to standardize the manufacturing processes rather than just the product.

Q U E S T I O N

As the entrepreneurs in this case, how would you answer the questions posed by the students? (Remember these questions as you read the next chapter on process innovation.)

CASE 11.2

General Electric's Revolutionary Product

In 1986, General Electric's large-appliance division thought that it had a breakthrough product in a new high-end, side-by-side refrigerator powered by a revolutionary compressor. In 1981, GE had conducted surveys to assess the status of its large-appliance business. Its market share and profits were falling. Its methods for refrigerator production were so antiquated that making a single piston for its compressor took 220 steps and making a compressor took 65 minutes of labor. The study estimated that rivals in Japan and Italy needed less than 25 minutes per compressor and paid lower labor rates. As a result, GE recognized a competitive disadvantage because its compressors cost approximately twice those of its rivals.

GE's top managers were not known for complacency. After the strategic review, they knew that the firm needed a bold plan to reinvigorate its large-appliance business to avoid the same fate as GE's *former* small-appliance business. The resulting strategy led to the development of a rotary compressor that would both give the firm a performance advantage and eliminate its cost disadvantage. In May 1982, division managers created a team to design the new rotary compressor and to show the world that America still could be a leader in manufacturing.

In September 1983, Division Manager Roger Schipke and two top engineers flew to GE's corporate headquarters to present their bold plan for investing $120 million in a new factory to make a newly designed compressor. They told GE Chairman Jack Welch that building a rotary compressor "wasn't a moonshot" since they had built 12 million units for GE's air conditioners. At first glance, the project did not seem like a completely new undertaking. The newly designed unit weighed less, consumed less energy, and required one-third as many parts as the old reciprocal com-

pressors. The new factory and design would enable GE to cut the cost of its compressors in half.

Through extensive experience with rotary compressors, however, GE had learned that they tend to run hotter than traditional compressors. This caused no problem in most air conditioners since fast-flowing coolant reduced the heat. Other initial problems arose, but by the mid-1970s, the designers had worked out solutions, while maintainingreciprocal compressors for large models to solve a tendency to break down in hot climates such as Arizona's. Also, some concern remained about the high-pitched whine from these units. Nonetheless, GE's design team anticipated placing rotary compressors in all future refrigerators.

Another concern focused on the firm's ability to manufacture key parts that required machining with precision equivalent to one-hundredth the width of a human hair. GE had never produced such fine machining in mass production. The design team felt that they could overcome these problems and achieve the division's design mission. They just needed to make one small change in the newly designed machine, which closely resembled the compressor from GE's time-tested air conditioner. They wanted to fabricate two small but important parts out of powdered metal rather than machining them from hardened steel. This process would fuse the powered metal into the desired shapes under pressure, which would achieve both tight engineering tolerances and the division's cost reduction goals.

In 1982, GE began limited testing of the prototype refrigerators with their rotary compressors. By the fall of 1984, life-cycle tests of about 600 compressors did not produce a single documented failure. The firm's management gave final approval to proceed with the new line of refrigerators, and full-scale production had begun on schedule by

March 1986. Just 2½ years after board approval, the new compressor plant was cranking out rotary compressors at a rate of one every 6 seconds.

GE's fast-to-market success was matched by a marketing success. Consumers snapped up the new $2,000 side-by-side models, which offered other innovations, as well, such as a refreshment center in the door. GE's market share shot up 2 full points to about 30 percent, its best showing in years.

In July 1987, one of the new models failed. The unit had operated in an unventilated closet in Philadelphia's summer heat. Designers wondered whether they could dismiss that incident as just a fluke. Additional reports of failure came in from Puerto Rico. Over the next few months, GE's management sensed that it had a real problem as the toll of failed units mounted. A team of field technicians confirmed that the powdered metal fabricated parts caused these failures.

To the firm's credit, GE's managers acted fast. They quickly sought out alternate suppliers of compressors, even persuading one former compressor manufacturer to return to the business. In desperation, the firm purchased some compressors from the Japanese. This reaction ignored cost since GE's reputation in the refrigeration business was at stake. The firm committed itself to compensating and satisfying customers, installing new compressors in their refrigerators before they knew that they had problems. By the end of 1988, GE had replaced the compressors on 1.1 million units, taking a $450 million pretax charge. Worse yet, thousands of units remained in the market that the firm could not locate.

The management review of this fiasco revealed some interesting facts:

1. Early in the design phase, a consultant had suggested that GE form a joint venture for the endeavor with a Japanese firm that already had a rotary refrigerator on the market. This recommendation was rejected.
2. The firm had declined an offer of consulting help from a former GE design engineer with extensive experience designing rotary compressors for the air conditioning division.
3. Design team leaders felt that their experience in the aerospace area could translate to compressor design. One said that the chief test engineer felt that, "you don't need previous compressor design experience to design a new compressor."
4. While none of the tested prototypes had failed, the copper windings on the compressor motor had indicated discoloration, often a symptom of excessive heat.
5. The individual who oversaw these tests had worked under four supervisors in 3 years and believed that his supervisors "didn't relay these findings up the chain of command" in part because they lacked sufficient technical expertise to ask the right questions. Furthermore, he felt that supervisors did not want to do anything that might jeopardize "so big a project."

QUESTION

How would you change GE's organizational design to avoid another premature rush to market?

[SELECTED READINGS]

Abernathy, W. J., K. B. Clark, and A. M. Kantrow. *Industrial Renaissance: Producing a Competitive Future for America*. New York: Basic Books, 1983.

Albrecht, Karl and Ron Zemke. *Service America: Doing Business in the New Economy*. Burr Ridge, Ill.: Dow Jones-Irwin, 1995.

Blackburn, J. D. *Time-Based Competition: The Next Battle Ground in American Manufacturing*. Homewood, Ill.: Business-One/Irwin, 1991.

Hammer, M., and J. Champy. *Reengineering the Corporation*. New York: Harper Business, 1993.

Heskett, J. L. *Managing in the Service Economy*. Cambridge, Mass.: Harvard Business School Press, 1986.

Hill, Terry. *Manufacturing Strategy: Text and Cases*. Homewood, Ill.: Richard D. Irwin, 1989.

Martin, W. B. *Quality Service: The Restaurant Manager's Bible*. Ithaca, N.Y.: Cornell University Press, 1986.

Melnyk, S. A., and R. Narasimhan. *Computer-Integrated Manufacturing: Guidelines and Applications from Industrial Leaders*. Homewood, Ill.: Business One/Irwin, 1991.

Muhlemann, A., J. Oakland, and K. Lockyer. *Production and Operations Management*, 6th ed. London: Pitman, 1992.

Ohmae, K. *The Borderless World: Power and Strategy in the Interlinked Economy*. New York: Harper Business, 1990.

Peters, T. *Thriving on Chaos: Handbook for a Management Revolution*. New York: Alfred A. Knopf, 1987.

Pine, B. J. *Mass Customization: The New Frontiers in Business Competition*. Cambridge, Mass.: Harvard Business School Press, 1993.

Rosenthal, S. R. *Effective Product Design and Development: How to Cut Lead Time and Increase Customer Satisfaction*. Homewood, Ill.: Business One-Irwin, 1992.

Savage, C. M. *Fifth Generation Management: Integrating Enterprises through Human Networks*. Boston: Digital Press, 1990.

Senge, P. M. *The Fifth Discipline: The Art and Practice of the Learning Organization*. New York: Doubleday, 1990.

Smith, P. G., and D. G. Reinertsen. *Developing Products in Half the Time*. New York: Van Nostrand Reinhold, 1991.

Stalk, G., Jr., and T. M. Hout. *Competing against Time*. New York: Free Press, 1990.

Wheelwright, S. C., and K. B. Clark. *Revolutionizing Product Development*. New York: Free Press, 1992.

Womack, J. P., et al. *The Machine that Changed the World: The Story of Lean Production*. New York: Harper-Collins, 1990.

CHAPTER TWELVE

Designing the Delivery Process

CHAPTER OBJECTIVES

[At the end of this chapter, you should be able to]

- Detail the decision-making processes through which operations managers design product-delivery systems.
- Describe the forces that influence the designs and management routines for service-delivery systems.
- List some common categories of service-delivery systems and their appropriate applications.
- Define the role of automation in improving the efficiency and effectiveness of service-delivery systems.
- Explain the forces that influence manufacturing systems.
- Apply a product/process matrix model to determine the appropriate implementations of particular manufacturing systems.
- Illustrate the role of automation in improving the efficiency and effectiveness of manufacturing systems.

Arco Strikes It Rich with Innovative Service Delivery

LARGE MULTINATIONAL OIL COMPANIES like Arco make most of their profits from the recovery and refinement of crude oil. For years these companies considered retail gasoline stations a necessary evil and focused their stratagems for growth elsewhere.

That's not to say the corner gas station hasn't undergone a lot of changes since the 1950s, when getting your car filled with gas was an elaborate ritual, and gas station attendants fell over themselves to please by pumping the gas, checking the oil, and wiping the windshield. As consumers became more economy-minded, this rather elegant service-delivery system gave way to the ubiquitous self-serve pumps. Now electronic communications technology has taken this self-serve concept even further by enabling consumers to pay for their gas without ever going inside the service station. Consumers can now swipe their credit cards through the gas station equivalent of an automated teller machine. Among other targets, this system strongly appeals to parents who hate leaving their small children alone in the car while they go in to pay for gas.

In the midst of all these changes, Arco has kept pace with its competitors, but in the 1980s it did them one better. Arco changed the name of the game by transforming its service stations into 7-Eleven-style mini-markets.

Actually, it was the 7-Eleven chain which really did the innovating by selling gas outside its convenience stores. By the 1980s 7-Eleven had become the largest merchandiser of gasoline in the United States. Taking its cue from 7-Eleven's success, Arco moved in on this niche market and began selling convenience items. In 1991 Arco sold about $500 million of 49-cent flash-frozen hamburgers and became the world's largest vendor of Reese's Peanut Butter Cups. As an added benefit, the availability of all those last-minute eggs, milk, and Twinkies now gave Arco a crucial edge, luring customers away from its competitors. Sales of gasoline went up, with the average store selling about 225,000 gallons a year in 1991, or double the industry average.

Arco's success just goes to prove that the new rules of the nineties are now in effect. It's no longer enough for companies to constantly improve the quality of their products. They have to constantly look for ways to improve the way their products and services are delivered as well.

SOURCE
"Atlantic Richfield Co. Is Winning the West by Breaking the Mold," *Wall Street Journal*, August 7, 1991, p. 1.

No doubt should remain that an organization must provide a good product to achieve business success. Without an effective means of making, distributing, and selling that product, however, customers will ignore the valuable contributions of the product design team. Marketers can then undertake the selling task, while operations managers concentrate on the production and distribution activities within a firm's value chain.

Throughout the early chapters, we stressed the need to change OM processes to accomplish a change in the value that an organization delivers to customers. In Chapter 11, we discussed the contribution of the product-innovation process to this goal. In this chapter, we develop an equivalent understanding of methods for designing business processes to make and deliver those innovative new goods and services. We begin by considering the process-innovation needs of service providers, and then turn to a similar discussion for manufacturers of physical goods.

In Chapter 13, we will continue with a related discussion of supply chain management to show how external OM processes contribute to a firm's customer-satisfaction goals.

PROCESS INNOVATION IN SERVICE-DELIVERY SYSTEMS

In Chapter 5, we presented a number of tools for analyzing existing or proposed business processes. In this section, we will apply these tools to the important work of designing new service-delivery systems or enhancing the performance of existing systems.

Initial Analysis

Like any customer-pleasing endeavor, process innovation must begin by identifying targeted customers and discovering as much information as possible about their needs, expectations, and latent desires. The innovation process can then continue with an assessment of the services that the organization can offer to satisfy those customers. This initial analysis must resolve a number of important questions about potential customers, the objects of the new service, and other issues.

Customers for Services.   Will the organization serve a person, a group, or another organization? To identify potential customers, the service provider needs answers to several questions:

- Can the organization categorize service recipients by customer types like those introduced in Chapter 11 (economizers, convenience seekers, etc.)? If not, then it will need a flexible service-delivery process to satisfy heterogeneous service demands.
- What order winners, order qualifiers, and order losers drive customer decisions?
- Can the organization build a detailed customer profile specifying numbers of customers of various types and where they live, shop, and use the service?

Marketing makes significant contributions to this inherently cross-functional effort to detail customer descriptions and determine methods of collecting information for buying decisions.

Objects of Service Delivery.   Do customers want services for themselves or another person or organization (like haircuts or temporary office help) or for some physical thing (like lawn mower repair)? The organization might deliver its service to several direct recipients, including humans, machines, or intangible things like information files.

- Services to machines include maintenance and repair of watches, washing machines, and industrial equipment.
- Services to information files include input, maintenance, and backup of bank accounts, credit files, order files, databases, and computer software.

Interactions of Service Dispensers with Customers.   The term **service dispenser** describes the business processes through which the organization provides its service. Several characteristics define this interaction:

service dispenser
The business processes through which the organization provides its service

- The organization might dispense the service through humans, machines, or communications media.
- The organization might dispense the service at the customer's site or some other place.
- The preferred form of communication for the service-delivery process could range from verbal to visual or written.
- The service process might involve other human senses, as well, such as smell, touch, fear, etc.

Existing Service Delivery Systems.   The organization cannot ignore an opportunity to save the cost of needlessly duplicating someone else's work by dispensing its service through existing channels. Another organization like McDonald's, Nordstrom's, or Federal Express might provide an outlet through which to dispense some service. Determining this opportunity should help the service system manager envision the level of service and whether it needs to be custom designed or a modification of an existing system.

Search for a Suitable Existing System

The last part of the initial analysis intends simply to avoid reinventing the wheel. If an existing service-delivery system can help an organization to meet the needs of its customers, then it should consider adopting that system as a good starting point for the process-innovation project.

A project to deliver pizza to residential customers might look for an existing service that provides home delivery of some other product; perhaps it could deliver the pizza, as well. The search should reach beyond the limits of existing pizza delivery services. White Castle, a Midwestern hamburger chain, will deliver its popular burgers via Federal Express. While this solution may seem a bit extreme, process innovators may find valuable solutions two or three standard deviations away from the norm.

This search should compare the attributes of potential service-delivery systems, perhaps scoring them in a format like the one in Exhibit 12.1. While many of the terms seem similar to those from the initial analysis, remember that this evaluation focuses exclusively on the benefits of the service-delivery system. Combining these results with the understanding of the customer developed earlier can lead to a well-designed system with attributes that mirror the demands of the targeted customers.

Upon identifying an existing service-delivery system that can meet a specific customer need, the planner should study and document in detail the business processes that provide this capability. An entire system may not fit particular needs, but certain parts may provide useful contributions to a system that can meet customers' needs. This system, either new or adapted from existing capabilities, will probably display one of several classic forms.

Classic Forms of Service-Delivery Systems

Operations managers can often simplify the work of process innovation by duplicating or adapting types of systems that have succeeded in the past. In manufacturing, such familiar models result from the requirements of equipment layouts and work flows between stations. Besides moving the innovation effort forward quickly, these models simplify communications; operations managers understand immediately that specifications for a paced assembly line will define a system that delivers components to workers in some regulated fashion, usually via a conveyor system of some kind.

Some characteristics of service processes complicate the effort to identify such representative models of delivery systems. First, service systems often perform less visible work than manufacturing systems, and the tasks and their patterns may vary much more than in manufacturing systems. Operations managers describe this diversity by saying that service processes are *heterogeneous*. Despite these difficulties, the typical persistence of operations managers has led to the development of some representative forms of service-delivery systems.

To illustrate these forms, the following paragraphs describe their adaptations to three familiar types of service enterprises. The first type, food-dispensing services, ranges all the way from vending machines to upscale restaurants. The second type, cash-disbursing services, can include parents, bank tellers, ATMs, etc. The third group, retail merchandisers, spans the market from upscale department stores such as Nordstrom's to minimum-service, discount outlets such as Kmart. By comparing service-delivery models for these sample organizations, we intend to illustrate the application of attribute-mapping methods to understand the merits of each model.

[**EXHIBIT 12.1**]

Attribute Map for Existing Service Systems

Nature of Interaction		Importance		
Personal	Physical	Extremely	Not	NA
Labor Intensity				
High	Low	Extremely	Not	NA
Customization				
Custom	Adaptation	Standard	Extremely	Not	NA
Method of Payment				
Credit	Cash	Extremely	Not	NA
Nature of Service		*Comments*		
Intangible	Tangible	_____		
Simultaneity of Consumption				
Much Later	Later	Immediate	_____	
Number of Customers				
Few	Many	_____		
Number of Service Dispenser Locations				
Few	Many	_____		
Number of Transactions/Location				
Few	Many	_____		
Perishability of Product				
Highly Perishable	Nonperishable	_____		

Food-Dispensing Systems. To cope with the wide reach of this diverse group of services, we take three examples: vending machines, fast-food outlets, and traditional restaurants. Exhibit 12.2 indicates the positions of these systems on an attribute map with letters, beginning with *V* for vending machines.

Customers bring few expectations to these machines. They want the mechanisms to dispense the chosen food in reasonably edible condition and not to take their money without dispensing anything. The slot for paper money should accept moderately wrinkled bills, and the change mechanism should not run out of coins. The map shows a heavy physical weighting for the nature of the interaction, low labor intensity, standard products, and cash payment. The nature of the service is entirely tangible, consumption usually occurs immediately after the transaction, and the number of customers and transactions per location varies. Vending machines normally sell rather nonperishable goods, but some have temperature-control capabilities that allow them to store products with shorter shelf lives like sandwiches.

Fast-food chains, such as McDonald's and Burger King (*M* and *B*, respectively, in Exhibit 12.2), typify what Ted Levitt calls **production-line service delivery**. Just as Henry Ford revolutionized manufacturing with his assembly line, Ray Kroc of

production-line service delivery

A standardized, carefully ordered system for rapidly delivering uniform, high-quality service products

[**E X H I B I T   1 2 . 2**]

Attribute Map for Food Service Systems

Nature of Interaction

Personal ——————————————————— Physical   *Importance*
  R   M B   V   R

Extremely ——————— Not NA
 MB   V

Labor Intensity

High ——————————————————— Low   *Importance*
 R   M B   V

Extremely ——————— Not NA
 R   MB   V

Customization

Custom ———— Adaptation ———— Standard
   R   B   M V

Extremely ——————— Not NA
   R   B   MV

Method of Payment

Credit ——————————————————— Cash
R   B M V

Extremely ——————— Not NA
   R   BMV

Nature of Service

Intangible ——————————————————— Tangible
  R   M B   V

Comments

The show matters at
Reynaldo's.

Simultaneity of Consumption

Much Later ———— Later ———— Immediate
   R   M B   V

Reynaldo's customers savor
their food; others just eat.

Number of Customers

Few ——————————————————— Many
   R   MB   V

Vending machine volume
varies with location.

Number of Service Dispenser Locations

Few ——————————————————— Many
R   V   B M

Number of Transactions/Location

Few ——————————————————— Many
R   V   B   M

Vending machine volume
varies with location.

V = Vending machine; M = McDonald's; B = Burger King; R = Reynaldo.

McDonald's pioneered development of a standardized service system that could offer "rapid delivery of a uniform, high-quality mix of prepared foods in an environment of obvious cleanliness, order, and cheerful courtesy."[1] At either McDonald's or Burger King, customers expect workers to take their orders politely and efficiently, but the transaction doesn't become more personal than that. Both offer rather standard products, although Burger King's system allows for some modifications. Both follow standard food preparation procedures, and they

[1]Theodore Levitt, "Production-Line Approach to Services," *Harvard Business Review,* September–October 1972, pp. 41–52.

automate those procedures where possible to assure uniform quality with low labor intensity. Actual food preparation may take place well in advance of purchase, much of it at other locations as suppliers deliver preshredded lettuce and precut, frozen French fries. Most customers pay with cash, though some restaurants now accept credit cards.

The process at Reynaldo's, a hypothetical upscale restaurant, differs substantially from those of vending machines or fast-food stands. Reynaldo seeks to please his customers by providing a pleasant setting, competent servers who fuss over their customers, and a superb chef. Customers willingly pay Reynaldo's high prices because his service exceeds their expectations based on his reputation. They like to go to the one and only Reynaldo's, designated by the letter *R* in Exhibit 12.2.

Cash-Dispensing Systems.   These services illustrate another representative model for delivering services. In an earlier time, someone who needed cash had to go into the bank and wait in line to present a check to a teller. The teller surveyed the check, reviewed the current account balance, checked identification, and then disbursed the requested funds. To avoid this daunting hassle, many customers withdrew large amounts of cash infrequently.

The automated teller machine (ATM) changed this system. Plastic ATM cards or credit cards have replaced checks in cash-withdrawal transactions, and the electronic terminal and computerized information system replaced the teller. The new system has automated both the account-balance review and the disbursement of funds. Customers have taken over the rest of the work. Exhibit 12.3 presents an attribute map of these two systems for delivering the same service.

A service process in which customers complete many of the tasks that servers might otherwise perform is called **customer-involvement service delivery**.[2] This method represents a growing trend. At Burger King, a counter worker hands over a paper cup and directs customers to the soft-drink dispenser. Many restaurants fill salad bars with vegetables and invite customers to fit as much as they can on their plates. In California, some personal computer retailers provide work benches, testing equipment, advice, and component parts and invite customers to build their own customized units. The familiar slogan "have it your way" has transformed to "do it your way."

This is not a new concept, of course. Urban neighborhoods have offered coin-operated laundromats for years, but the customers thought of them as new locations for old drudgery rather than innovative new customer-involvement service systems. The economizers among a firm's customers may welcome the chance to act as unpaid employees if it gives them a better value; convenience seekers may turn up their noses at the same opportunity. ATM machines satisfy both of these groups, however, by increasing efficiency and lowering costs for the bank and reducing hassle for the customer.

Retailing Systems.   The services offered by retail stores illustrate the third representative model of service-delivery systems. In traditional merchandise retailing, customers travel from store to store searching for desired tangible objects. The customer experience can range from a fun, delightful activity to an indifferent, variably efficient commercial exercise. At the delightful extreme, customers value the trained and motivated sales staff at Nordstrom's, an upscale department store noted for highly personalized customer service. Within these large stores, salespeople create

customer-involvement service delivery

A service process in which customers complete many tasks that form part of the service

[2]C. H. Lovelock and R. F. Young, "Look to Customers to Increase Productivity," *Harvard Business Review,* vol. 57, no. 2, pp. 168–178.

[**EXHIBIT 12.3**]

Attribute Map for Cash Disbursement Systems

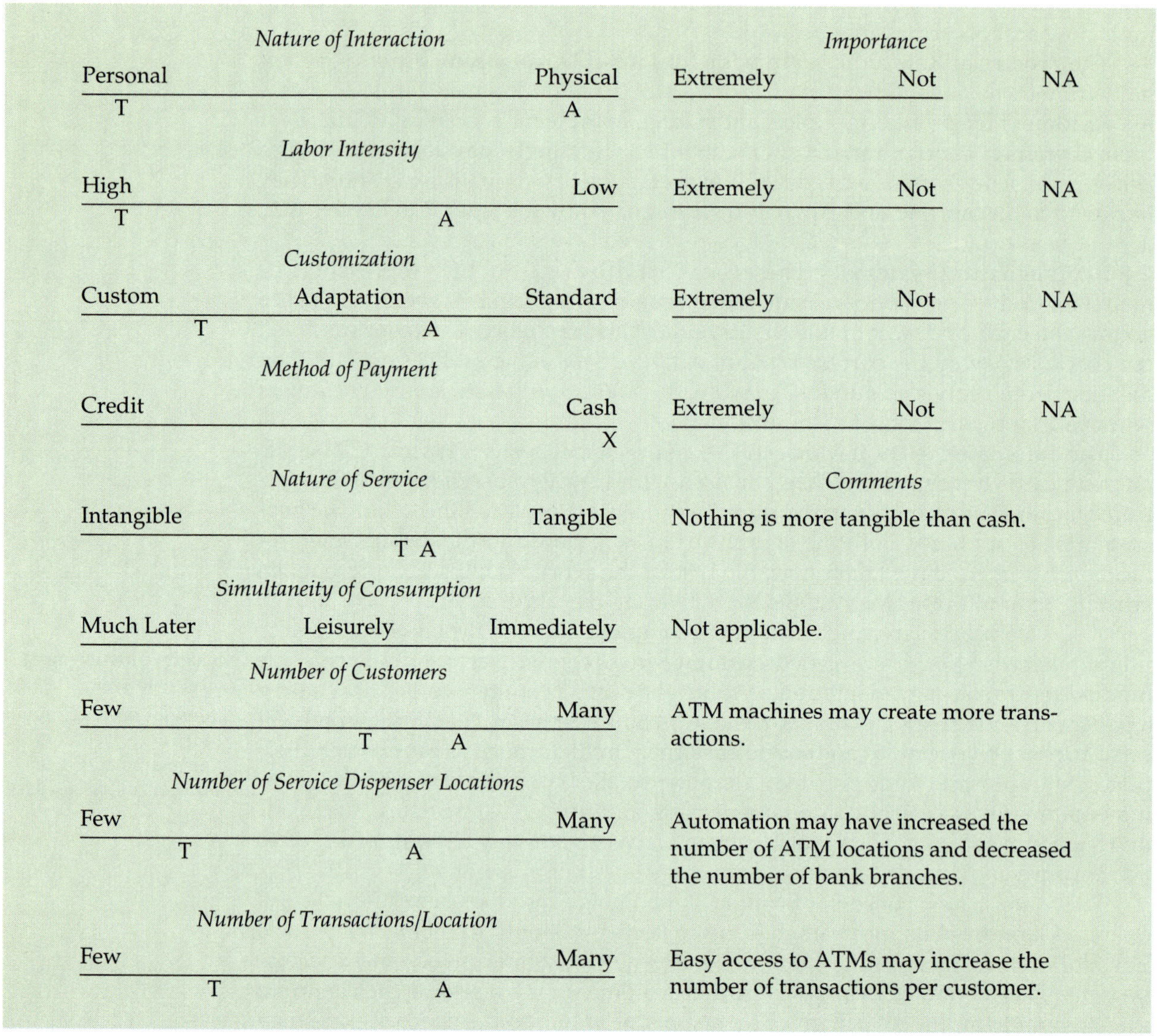

Nature of Interaction			*Importance*		
Personal		Physical	Extremely	Not	NA
T		A			

Labor Intensity					
High		Low	Extremely	Not	NA
T	A				

Customization					
Custom	Adaptation	Standard	Extremely	Not	NA
	T	A			

Method of Payment					
Credit		Cash	Extremely	Not	NA
		X			

Nature of Service			*Comments*		
Intangible		Tangible	Nothing is more tangible than cash.		
	T A				

Simultaneity of Consumption					
Much Later	Leisurely	Immediately	Not applicable.		

Number of Customers					
Few		Many	ATM machines may create more trans-actions.		
	T A				

Number of Service Dispenser Locations					
Few		Many	Automation may have increased the number of ATM locations and decreased the number of bank branches.		
	T A				

Number of Transactions/Location					
Few		Many	Easy access to ATMs may increase the number of transactions per customer.		
	T A				

T = Teller disbursement; A = ATM disbursement.

an atmosphere of clusters of intimate boutiques by knowing the preferences of their customers. They track these preferences not in high-tech, computerized data-bases, but in old-fashioned notebooks. Using basic tools, this system motivates salespeople to win one new personal customer each day, even at the cost of extra-ordinary measures like personally delivering items to their homes. This kind of service comes from **personal-attention service delivery**.

At the other extreme, Kmart attracts swarms of shoppers with its blue-light specials. Over the past few years, Kmart has worked systematically to squeeze personal-selling costs out of its retail establishments. By staffing stores mostly with part-time employees, the chain minimizes its overhead costs for human

personal-attention service delivery

An individualized system that seeks to delight customers by catering to their specific needs resources. This step creates a bare-bones shopping experience with only minimal product information available. Workers can stock shelves and direct shoppers to the locations of desired merchandise, but they cannot help much with purchase decisions. Sears has addressed this problem by offering an 800 number to call for product information. If the store runs out of stock, future availability remains doubtful because the firm lacks the necessary distribution infrastructure to keep stores predictably stocked.

As always, customers determine whether Nordstrom's or Kmart provides the best value. Both stores fill their parking lots, but Kmart seems to recognize a problem with its system. Each year, its annual reports talk about new beginnings, massive restructuring of its existing stores, and so forth. No similar travails seem to disrupt the calm at Nordstrom's. Its major problem seems to center on claims by the retail clerks' union, which protests that Nordstrom's does not pay its nonunion employees for the additional services that they provide for customers. Few organizations would complain about employees doing more than customers ask.

Nordstrom's and Kmart would have obvious positions on the attribute map for retailers. Equally obviously, the personal-attention service system of the former requires active support from the firm's organizational design to align the interests of employees with its customer-service goals. The cross-functional process for building such a successful system begins with a vision of the ideal employee. Human resource management recruiters then carefully attract and screen applicants for the needed attitudes and skills. For years, Disneyland has succeeded in this effort by searching for cheerful applicants and then training them to become "service actors" who accept responsibility for ensuring that every guest of the park has a pleasant visit.

The division of the discussion so far among food-delivery systems, cash-disbursement systems, and retail systems has merely illustrated three representative models for service-delivery systems: production-line service, customer-involvement service, and personal-attention service. Of course, firms in different industries can employ each of these models; a bank can offer personal attention to its customers. Also, some systems may differ from these models, and the models that underlie the systems of particular organizations may not be obvious. Remember that service-delivery systems complicate classification schemes.

Service Blueprinting

In addition to attribute mapping, operations managers can return to process flow analysis to evaluate a proposed or existing design for a service-delivery system. Lynn Shostack has developed a variation of process flow analysis especially for service systems that she calls **service blueprinting**. This procedure involves four steps:

service blueprinting
An analytical tool to identify and eliminate potential failures and set time and cost standards for service-delivery systems by process flow analysis

1. *Identify processes.* Map all business processes that perform essential roles in delivering the service-oriented product.
2. *Isolate the fail points.* Scrutinize the process flow diagrams and identify points at which the system can fail to meet or exceed the expectations of customers, then design fail-safe procedures to eliminate these potential defects. Since service quality often depends on employees, training may be more important than designing poka-yoke mechanisms like those in manufacturing systems.
3. *Establish a time frame.* Since time is an essential part of a service's value package, the system designer should establish standard execution times.

Service Blueprint for a Video Rental Business

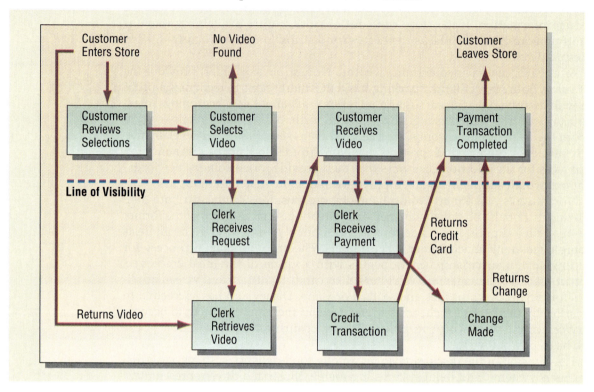

This also helps to control costs since the labor components of total execution time determine much about the cost equation.

4. *Analyze profitability.* Complete a pro forma income estimate early in the design stage to serve as a reality check throughout the analysis. This step requires reasonable estimates for what customers will pay for the envisioned service, how many customers it will serve and how often, and the likely cost structure.

line of visibility

A marker on a service blueprint that distinguishes which process activities occur within sight of customers

Service blueprinting establishes a **line of visibility** to distinguish which process activities occur within sight of customers. In the video rental business blueprinted in Exhibit 12.4, one line of visibility would identify the point at which customers interact with employees. This exhibit presents a rough sketch of the customer's interactions with the process activities of the store. The solid lines represent physical movements, and the dotted lines indicate communication flows.

The line of visibility also allows a second interpretation of the service-delivery process by focusing attention on customer interactions with employees. This line could mark a point of physical separation in the system; perhaps a new system could save customers the trouble of completing the activities above the line, primarily selecting videos and paying the rental fees. Clearly, a new system could not complete these activities cost effectively by assigning store personnel to verbally describe available titles over a telephone, however. A catalog could provide this information, but customers want the most recent releases, so the store would have to print expensive new catalogs too frequently. Through emerging communications networks, however, the store soon could offer a current video catalog on line. Customers could dial up on their home computers to survey the available offerings and then make selections; store workers would then charge the rental fees to customers' accounts and hold the videos for pickup, or perhaps deliver them at additional cost.

This example illustrates an important advantage of service blueprinting. It forces process designers to describe an existing or proposed system and then encourages them to rethink activities to discover potential improvements. For each envisioned system, it also presents a framework for estimating both the cost to the organization and the value received by customers.

Automation in Service Processes

Many people recognize automation as a system of intelligent machines performing physical work in place of human employees. They often overlook similar innovations in the service sector, however. Vending machines replace store clerks who would otherwise sell sodas and candy. In Australia, sheep ranchers have worked on robots to shear wool from temporarily immobilized animals. In Belgium, smart robots are milking cows—and the cows seem to like it. Even in human medicine, doctors are using robots to perform certain surgical procedures with more precision than human hands could achieve. In particular, miniaturized robotic systems with remote monitoring capabilities allow doctors to perform less invasive surgery.

Automation to Involve Customers in Service Delivery.   Automation also has affected more traditional service-delivery systems, often with important customer involvement. Users of ATMs provide information and data input that enable banks to replace human tellers. Power lawn mowers automate some yard maintenance chores with active human involvement. Wash-and-wear clothing and automatic washing machines with delicate fabric cycles have reduced the burden of laundry chores, and HBO and microwave popcorn have significantly reduced the role of movie theaters in people's lives. In each case, customers seem to accept the trade-offs of automating customer-involvement services.

Automation through Digital Information Storage.   Automation has had its most important effects on information-processing services. Human providers of information services are quickly giving way to information machines. In telephone services, for example, today's retirees remember speaking the phrase "information please" into the phone to attract the attention of human operators who specialized in quick access to telephone directory data. Now, automated, preprogrammed systems play recorded instructions to guide callers through decision-tree structures to find needed information, usually starting off with a phrase like, "Press 1 if you are calling from a touch-tone telephone." A customer can check on an up-to-date credit balance without ever speaking to a person.

Service automation also has advanced information control by storing digital descriptions of people, objects, and transactions in huge databases, often with input and output through bar-coding systems. In the United States, a citizen's Social Security number quickly is approaching the status of a national identification number. Employees commonly wear bar-coded badges that identify them, their permissible activities, and often permit access to certain rooms, computer facilities, and databases. In Marin County, California, veterinarians insert microchips into the necks of dogs and cats to facilitate their identification. Within this lifetime, some less invasive means may emerge to imprint infants at birth

Service Automated Information is used in processes as diverse as dog-sled racing. Veterinarians and race officials identify dogs from information stored on implanted microchips.   SOURCE   William Johnson/ Stock Boston

with identification that supports still more encompassing service-delivery automation. In the classroom of the future, professors will scan DNA scents and brain waves to detect the presence and mental preparedness of students.

Bar coding has already transformed information systems at retail stores. Firms might extend these systems to supplement the knowledge base of retail clerks. A chain of auto parts stores like Kragen, for example, needs employees who understand both cars and customer service, and competitive pressure prevents the company from paying large salaries for these rare workers. An automated system that involves the customer in the transaction may help to resolve this dilemma.

Welcome to our Kragen Car Care Information Kiosk

Please answer the following questions so that we may better serve you:

What is the make of your vehicle?

Your vehicle's model number and year?

Which of the following parts do you need?

    Ignition System
      Spark plugs
      Distributor points
      Electrical wiring
    Transmission
    Braking System
      Brake pads
      Brake fluid

A computerized kiosk could identify the needed part based on customer input of the year, make, model, and special equipment and indicate the cost of the part and the stock number at the store or distribution center. To buy the part, the customer would direct the system to print out an order card with retrieval instructions for store personnel. The top of the document carries a code that triggers an information-system update. The bottom half goes to the cashier.

Further study might question the need for the kiosk to require so much input. The information system could recognize a customer as a member of the Kragen Car Club based on a bar-coded identification number and assume the stored description of that person's car and any previously purchased parts. Information technology seems likely to continue to enhance retail transactions beyond any foreseeable limits. Indeed, car manufacturers might provide buyers with CD-ROMs or digitized cards that store all pertinent information about a vehicle. Before long, these and other innovations will become commonplace, perhaps at the cost of a human smile over the counter.

Automation to Span Long Distances.   Automation frees service systems from geographic limits by allowing them to transmit goods and information quickly and cost effectively between customers and the service provider. On a small scale, 7-Eleven benefits from the ability to monitor gasoline transactions remotely. Initially, the information traveled only 50 feet or so. Once the gas pumps started to accept ATM or credit cards, however, the information transaction started to span continents. Checking the credit limit on a customer's MasterCard now may involve an inquiry to a computer in Chicago. A call to a local Pizza Hut may reach an operator in Chicago, displaying a local telephone number, the location of the nearest pizza outlet, and a preference for double cheese and anchovies.

Automation for Distribution Efficiencies.   Automation has also influenced the distribution capabilities of service-delivery systems. In the past, time delays and economies of scale in transportation forced many service systems to maintain large inventories. Mothers Work, described in Chapter 10, increased customer choices, minimized stockouts, and achieved high asset utilization rates through effective information systems and rapid shipments of small parcels.

American mail-order retailers have discovered that they can mail catalogs to customers in Japan more cheaply than Japanese rivals can distribute catalogs of the same size domestically. Global toll-free telephone numbers allow L.L. Bean and Lands' End to efficiently market their wares to customers around the globe. Future developments of electronic money, or e-money, will further reduce the difficulties of distant transactions. The global scope of operations of UPS and other carriers allows firms to deliver goods cheaply and quickly enough to outcompete Japan's inefficient domestic distribution system. Automation is making the world a smaller place.

Automation changes the capabilities of both customer and service provider in many profound ways. One of the authors learned as a third-grader how to use a dial telephone from a local telephone company representative. Today, grade-school students use computers to find library books and cruise worldwide networks to complete their science projects. As the 21st century dawns, American businesses can anticipate a stream of new customers and employees who have grown up expecting the benefits of automation. The "On the Job" box illustrates how one service organization has integrated information technology into its world-class delivery system.

ON THE JOB

Quality Service at the Ritz-Carlton

The Ritz has built an enviable business by dazzling both customers and employees. Mr. Roa, the firm's Director of Quality, attributes its success to a system in which "employees are trained to 'actively notice' guest preferences daily, which are then entered into our customer database on a national level." The day before a customer's scheduled arrival, a report prints out his or her preferences. Employees can then make sure that Mrs. Robinson receives the feather pillows that she prefers, more oranges and no apples in the fruit basket, and herbal tea with honey. The firm employs a guest-history coordinator whose sole job is to analyze guest preferences and the performance of hotels in the chain at meeting these customer expectations.

In addition, each day, a defect report identifies internal and external customer service failures. This report focuses on the nature of the defect rather than the employee responsible to emphasize improving the service-delivery system rather than assigning blame. Mr. Roa states that employees rely so heavily on this report that some have even asked others to fax it to them on vacation.

This information provides a powerful tool, but the hotel chain must also get its employees to care. Through another simple system, the firm recognizes superior employee efforts to surpass customer expectations through several awards:

- *Five Star Awards* Five or more employees each quarter earn benefits like extra vacation days, cash, airline tickets, and free lodging at any Ritz-Carlton hotel in the United States. In addition, quarterly winners are eligible to win larger annual awards. Ritz staff members nominate and select winners.
- *Lightning Strikes Awards* General managers give these discretionary awards of cash or tickets to concerts, theater performances, or sports events to employees who have gone out of their way to help customers.
- *First Class Cards* Any employee or manager can thank another staff member for special service by writing out one of these cards. Copies of the cards go to the employees, their managers, and their personnel files.
- *Cash Certificates of Good Ideas* For each valuable suggestion they submit, employees earn $5 and another $10 if the firm implements the idea. Idea of the Month winners receive an additional $25. In 1994, the New York hotel paid $5,000 to employees for their suggestions—a small price for valuable process improvements.
- *Team Recognition* When a team of employees solve some problem, they earn rewards like candy, pizza parties, or some other gesture of organizational appreciation.

The Ritz-Carlton is so committed to its goal of providing Six Sigma quality service that it empowers any employee to rebate up to $2,000 per day on any guest's bill in order to provide "instant pacification" without seeking hotel management approval. This organization has developed a truly unique blend of superior information technology and world-class service delivery.

People-Driven Service-Delivery Systems

Automation, especially information systems, may seem to have pushed human employees out of service organizations. As in more familiar examples from manufacturing, these systems have reduced or eliminated the most repetitive jobs, such as old-style telephone operators who plugged in cords to make desired connections. More intelligent and flexible automation systems are now eliminating or affecting even more complex jobs. Workers whose accumulated knowledge provided a valuable resource for customers have lost their positions to automated systems that incorporate the humans' knowledge. Personal computers now help library users to perform the more routine tasks of research librarians. Other systems free customer-service representatives from the burdens of simple tasks like looking up credit balances. Some systems have entirely taken over such jobs. Of course, computer-assisted surgery systems have not replaced surgeons, but they have improved the quality of medical care and have raised its cost.

Overall, however, the Ritz-Carlton story illustrates how automation has expanded the role of humans in service-delivery systems. Although it has taken over many menial jobs, it has also propelled many job enlargement and job enrichment programs that have improved the quality of work within service-delivery systems.

At the same time, the rise of consumerism has imposed new requirements for better prepared and motivated service-system employees to ensure effective performance at the moment of truth. Customers no longer tolerate lazy responses like "I'll get back to you" or "That's not my department." People within service systems need the motivation and training to handle heterogeneous activities.

Automated service-delivery systems may employ fewer people to perform activities, but the remaining jobs challenge workers to become effective resources for customers. A well-trained, empowered work force remains a key element of any world-class service delivery system.

 ## PROCESS INNOVATION IN MANUFACTURING SYSTEMS

Manufacturing processes differ from service processes in three ways. First, they include more visible activities due to the tangible nature of goods. Second, those activities normally occur beyond the view of the customer. Third, they often repeat the same activities over and over again. These traits make manufacturing processes easier to understand than service processes.

In Chapter 11, we classified potential buyers of goods as economizers, convenience seekers, customizers, functionalists, style-driven consumers, ethical/loyal customers, or motivated by something else. An understanding of the idiosyncrasies of these customer types becomes the starting point of most product and process design.

The word *most* allows for exceptions, primarily the production of commodity products, such as gold bullion, plywood, steel, and road salt. Buyers and producers understand and accept universal standards for these goods, so firms cannot really identify a direct customer to delight because economizers dominate the market segment. Specifications set by an industry association or other agency define order qualifiers for commodity goods. Price usually acts as the order winner, but availability becomes critical in times of scarcity.

A manufacturer of commodity goods must focus on a single process design goal—to make those goods at the lowest possible price. To make joint products, such as a wide range of wood products from a pile of logs, a special version of this process design goal focuses on producing the mix of products with the highest value. Such a firm decides whether to process primary products further into secondary products, as when a lumber company decides whether to fabricate doors, roof trusses, etc., by judging whether the subsequent processing adds enough value to warrant the additional costs.

The designers of manufacturing processes for goods other than commodities should actively participate in the firm's drive to delight its customers. The word *should* recognizes that this does not always occur, especially for firms that compete in businesses characterized by mass manufacturing, distribution, and marketing. In Chapter 11, we described the traditionally sequential product-design process for such markets. Such systems often reduce the role of operations managers to simply implementing other people's designs, but more active involvement remains possible and desirable.

The process-design work of operations managers need not end at a company's boundaries. A Hewlett-Packard engineer participated on Motorola's core-product development team for its Bandit pager. Solectron issues beepers to its production personnel so customers can directly contact key people to resolve quality or product-design issues quickly. Solectron also empowers its shop-level workers to directly contact any customer to clear up any possible problem at the earliest point in the value-adding process.

All too often, however, manufacturing personnel work simply to survive by promising the best possible response to a particular set of circumstances. They act only to resolve immediate problems, often repeatedly. Without a last line of defense in manufacturing against disappointing value, customers might receive less than they expect, which could cost the firm its competitive position in the market. Of course, statements like these indicate symptoms of a bigger problem.

In the 1970s, Terry Hill, a British professor of management, developed a scheme designed to break down communications barriers between functional departments. This method integrated operations management input into marketing strategy by adapting Hill's familiar order winner/order qualifier analysis of product value to apply to cross-functional communications within a firm. To do this, Hill created a five-column table designed to help marketing and manufacturing managers translate their perspectives into customer-driven actions (Exhibit 12.5). In the first column, the participants clearly state the corporate or strategic business unit's objectives, whether handed down from top management or democratically determined. In the next column, marketing outlines a strategy for achieving those objectives based on a clear understanding of the firm's target customers and their values and idiosyncrasies. These first two steps record the results of routine communications between top managers and marketing specialists. They often state goals as dollar amounts (or amounts of other currencies).

The two right-hand columns define the firm's manufacturing priorities. The fourth column addresses physical plant issues while the fifth states specifications for organizational design. Some analysts have implied a completely erroneous time distinction, claiming that plant issues reflect long-term decisions while infrastructure may vary over the short term. In fact, infrastructure determines the climate and culture within the organization, and these characteristics profoundly affect its physical processes. Operations managers often find that they can change machinery more easily than the way employees work or the control systems by which the firm motivates employees and evaluates their performance. Indeed, some management control software, a critical part of today's manufacturing infrastructure, costs more than some machines and other physical equipment and takes at least as much training and experience to master.

The central column of the table, the key to Hill's analysis, joins manufacturing and marketing in a unified effort to delight customers. This initiative assumes that

Framework of Integrating Manufacturing and Marketing Strategies

Corporate Objectives	Marketing Strategy	Orders Winners	Manufacturing Strategy	
			Process Choice	**Infrastructure**
Growth	Product markets	Price	Alternative process	Function support
Survival	and segments	Quality	categories	Manufacturing planning
Profit	Range	Delivery speed	Process-choice	and control system
Return on	Mix	Delivery reliability	tradeoffs	Quality assurance and
investment	Volume	Color range	Process positioning	control
Other financial	Standard versus	Product range	Capacity	Manufacturing systems
measures	customized	Design leadership	size	engineering
	Levels of innovation	Technical support	timing	Clerical procedures
	Leader versus		location	Payment system
	follower		Role of inventory	Work structuring
				Organizational structure

SOURCE   Terry Hill, *Manufacturing Strategy: Text and Cases.* Burr Ridge, Ill.: Irwin, 1989, p.33.

manufacturing personnel will offer proactive, energetic input based on customer expectations. If marketers identify price as the order winner, for example, then operations managers should structure their processes to keep costs as low as possible.

Such a plan often leads manufacturing to choose among General Electric's three infamous options: automate, emigrate, or evaporate. Each choice eliminates certain possibilities. Traditionally, automation has required less product variety or batch production processes that rely on high work-in-process inventories. Emigrating to a location with relatively low costs normally reduces the firm's ability to respond quickly to market needs. Evaporation need not involve a complete shut down; instead, the firm can drastically reduce its manufacturing capabilities by outsourcing to supply needs that it previously met through in-house processes. As we will explain in a subsequent section, new management techniques and manufacturing technologies allow operations managers to escape these three no-win options.

Hill encourages manufacturing to educate marketing about the necessary tradeoffs in OM process decisions. No reasonable customer demands that a single product offer minimum costs, maximum product flexibility, state-of-the-art product design, and Six Sigma quality. Together, the functional specialists must decide which of these priorities to emphasize based on those that appeal most to customers. Likewise, marketing must convince manufacturing to surrender dreams of simple, repetitive mass manufacturing. To survive in a competitive marketplace, both must carefully follow shifts in market behavior, evolving technologies, and potential new entrants into the marketplace.

Terry Hill's framework enhances innovation in two specific areas: product design and process design. In Chapter 11, we described the value of order winners and order qualifiers as guidelines for cross-functional product innovation. Even if a firm maintains a sequential product-development process, Hill's framework builds a convenient bridge across communication gaps that separate functions.

The five-column table may need modification when technological change drives the product and process innovation. We will shore up this weakness in the following section.

Components of Manufacturing Processes

As in service-system design, operations managers group manufacturing systems into categories that represent typical solutions to common problems. This initial analysis guides their choices of tools and equipment that suit the work and the process for completing it. Just as a golfer seldom succeeds by hitting drives with a putter, manufacturing managers introduce waste into their OM systems when they try to perform tasks with improper equipment. To describe the typical categories of manufacturing processes, however, we need to present the components that make up those processes. Each process combines people, machines, information systems, and other resources to perform unique roles within individual limitations to produce the required output.

Beginning at the lowest possible level, a manufacturing process needs **actual tools**, that is, implements that physically interact with raw materials, parts, and subassemblies to make necessary transformations. This class of resources includes simple things like a nail or a screw along with highly engineered products like lasers or carbide drills. Some may view a discussion of such basic tools as trivial, but careful study of the system's need for tools and their arrangement can save the firm significant sums. From another perspective, failure to deal with manufacturing technology at this level most certainly will result in processing inefficiencies and excessive investment in tools.

The second component of manufacturing processes, **fixtures**, hold work pieces during processing. A simple system may require no fixtures or make them integral parts of machines. A simple drill press may drill holes in work pieces clamped to a stationary work table or even held by hand. In a more complex operation, some fixture external to the machine holds the work, allowing the machine and the operator to work simultaneously. While the machine processes one part, the operator affixes the next to a jig or an extra work table. When the machine finishes one piece, the operator removes the fixture and places the next one to repeat the operation. This sequence becomes even more complex in a flexible manufacturing system which moves the part loading operation even farther from the site of the machining operation.

The third component of manufacturing processes, the **machines** or **machining centers**, are equipment that complete processing tasks. The simplest machines include hand-held drills, paint sprayers, and nailing guns. At the other extreme, highly automated, special-purpose work centers can perform highly varied tasks without human intervention. On a modern car assembly line, welding robots perform long sequences of carefully choreographed operations on a wide range of passing car bodies with different configurations.

The designs of special-purpose machines limit them to performing certain tasks. Conversely, general-purpose machines are designed to complete wider ranges of activities, often less efficiently than special-purpose machines. Operators may control machines manually or by placing templates to guide them. **Numerically controlled machines**, or nc machines, read computer code which directs their operations. Normally, a computer might direct an nc machine to move 3.75 inches along the x-axis and 2.75 inches along the y-axis and then drill a hole 2.50 inches deep with its 0.50-inch drill. Since some machines stock more than one tool, nc

actual tool
An implement that physically interacts with raw materials, parts, and subassemblies to make necessary transformations

fixture
An implement that holds work pieces during processing

machine (machining center)
A piece of equipment that completes processing tasks

numerically controlled machine
A machine that reads computer code which directs its operations

programs also specify tools for particular operations. Numerical control works almost like a robotic nurse handing surgical instruments to a mechanical doctor.

Manufacturing processes rely heavily on a fourth component, humans. A process may not employ many workers if a few have sufficient skills to capably perform all necessary tasks. For a low volume of work, a single highly skilled person may suffice. If the volume of work exceeds one person's capacity, then management must hire another worker and then decide whether each will perform all tasks in parallel or if the two employees will split the tasks and perform them sequentially. This division of labor may increase efficiency as compared to each worker completing all phases of production for a single job.

As a manufacturing organization grows and spreads over a larger geographic area, the designers of the organization must decide which type of infrastructure will best serve its goals. They must determine the points at which a process needs skilled workers and how to make key decisions, through a coordinated, centralized system or a decentralized system. Operations managers face their most difficult challenge in managing the human components of their systems.

A fifth component of manufacturing processes, **transporters**, move materials, parts, subassemblies, tools, and other resources between activities. In the simplest system, human transporters may carry resources from station to station or some gravity-driven system may move them. More elaborate systems may automate the work of the transporters. To move work in routine patterns, a process may employ simple conveyors. If the work routine varies from piece to piece, then flexible human transportation might do a better job. Some conditions warrant investments in smart conveyance systems directed either by computers or human intervention. Finally, a process may benefit from a flexible form of automation such as **automated guided vehicles** (AGVs), which move around the system based on pre-programmed instructions. AGVs routinely deliver tools, paperwork, work in process, and even coffee in many manufacturing operations. Some hospitals distribute medical records via AGVs, but none have yet entrusted patients to them.

transporter
A component of a manufacturing process that moves resources between activities

automated guided vehicle
A transport device that moves around an OM system based on preprogrammed instructions

The last tangible component of a manufacturing process, inventory, acts to enable or disable activities. The discussion of JIT manufacturing in Chapter 9 described common suspicions of inventory as a symptom of wasteful OM practices. Any thorough description of a manufacturing system must specify the roles that inventory plays, however, both to add value and to add waste.

The last major component of manufacturing processes, information systems, provide the intelligent stimuli to guide the work of humans and machines. Through operations charts, a firm's information system tells either humans or machines what to produce and how to produce it. The information system tells transporters where to take work next, and it details the types, amounts, and locations of inventory in storage throughout the production and distribution system. It tracks the use of materials and labor in each step of the transformation process and compares these figures with established standards. In this way, the information system provides the basis for performance evaluations of humans, groups, departments, and even machines.

Success in any manufacturing process depends on an effective information system. Computers and application software have become integral parts of most effective manufacturing infrastructures, but they cannot provide needed coordination by themselves. Just as a person needs the right tool to do a job the right way, a company needs to the right information system to make its OM process truly effective. The information system must gather and distribute data in a way that supports the firm's organizational design. The following sections will explain how several typical categories of manufacturing processes combine information with other resources to profitably generate products that delight customers.

Overview of Traditional Process Categories

The categories in Exhibit 12.6 illustrate a continuum of process types rather than a set of discrete alternatives. No two manufacturing systems match exactly or fit any category's criteria in exactly the same way. Based on certain key similarities, however, operations managers generally recognize five classical forms of manufacturing processes ranging from one-of-a-kind projects to high-volume, repetitive continuous operations.

The exhibit differentiates these categories based on their average order sizes. The large ellipse for batch production signifies its status as the predominant form of production in North America. These zones overlap because clear distinctions do not always separate process choices. While the exhibit depicts them as discrete entities, they really represent stages along a continuum.

Projects

project

A category of manufacturing processes that completes a single job at a site other than the firm's facilities

Operations managers organize a manufacturing process as a **project** to complete a single job at a site other than the firm's facilities. A construction company must bring its production resources to the river to build a dam, for example.

Typical Applications.   The large size of the individual job, that is, the large number of tasks it requires, distinguishes a project. Middle-level to high-level operations managers accept responsibility for securing and scheduling the necessary resource mix for cost-effective and timely completion of a project. At the end of the project, the organization redeploys the resources devoted to that job or releases them.

Sometimes firms use the term *project* for large manufacturing jobs within one of the other categories of manufacturing processes. For example, Boeing treats production of each 777 as a separate project within the routine operations of its Everett, Washington, final-assembly plant. Multiproject management tools help operations managers to keep each project moving toward completion in an orderly, timely manner. This avoids starving the final-assembly line as upstream processes produce parts and resolve schedule conflicts over shared production resources.

Businesses often treat other activities besides manufacturing orders as projects. Chapter 11 described the product-innovation process as a project for which managers coordinate completion of many activities, often in different parts of an organization. A firm might manage development of an employee safety program as a project. Management of these activities may involve some of the logic and management tools developed for project management, but this section focuses primarily on manufacturing and assembly projects.

Order Winners.   Firms with project-oriented manufacturing processes often compete on the basis of price or capability to complete a specialized job technically correct on time. Many firms (and people, as well) can do technically competent work, but only at a slow pace; most businesses cannot tolerate much delay, however. Capability acts at least as an order qualifier, and perhaps as an order winner for an especially technical job. Price often acts as an order winner for a project, perhaps through a competitive bidding process, especially if the customer is an economizer. Even the most price-conscious economizer knows, however, that project costs

[**EXHIBIT 12.6**]

Process Category Matrix

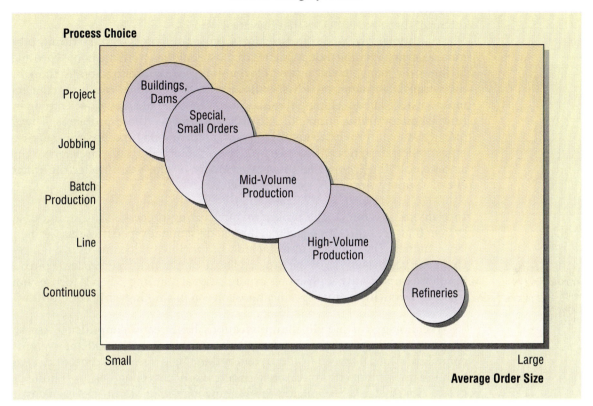

can balloon if the manufacturer lacks necessary capabilities to complete the work correctly on schedule.

Physical Resource Mix.   The particular characteristics of a project determine the physical resource needs of the manufacturing process, but many projects share some common requirements. To finish a unique job, a firm usually need not permanently acquire special-purpose machines unless later projects will also call for those capabilities. Instead, the firm can rent or lease equipment for the appropriate period of time.

Projects also generally must complete many tasks far from the firm's headquarters. This need for remote production places a premium on equipment reliability since most projects can ill afford delays due to equipment down time. Project managers are risk adverse when it comes to acquiring equipment, and prefer the tried-and-true to minimize uncertainty. They can usually attribute waste and overruns in costs or time to some unforeseen circumstance.

Human Resource Mix.   The unique demands of a project and its remoteness from headquarters also strongly influence human resource practices in the manufacturing process. Project managers often rely on short-term employees and known, reliable subcontractors to complete their work. This places a premium on the ability to attract the best subcontractors, which depends, in turn, on their perception of the firm as a valuable customer. In fact, the capabilities of subcontractors may well become an important part of the order winners for a project. To maintain these critical relationships, for example, some construction companies intentionally submit unusually low bids during slack periods simply to keep subcontractors working and happy. On the other hand, unreliable or deceptive project managers often get the subcontractors that they deserve.

The human resource practices for a project-oriented manufacturing process must also consider the independence of most activities from the home base and its facilities for management oversight. Employees or subcontractors at the job site must translate unique project specifications into functional reality. Engineers do make mistakes in developing these specifications, so field crews need strong interfunctional communication skills to spot and resolve these problems. They frequently must improvise to get the job done right and on time, and this requires an organization design that fosters employee responsibility and competence. Unlike an assembly line, project employees normally do not work under the watchful eye of a supervisor.

Information System.   The project manufacturing process needs an information system that does three things. First, it must disseminate specifications for the project activities. This function must include a capability of documenting engineering changes over the course of the project. The documentation serves legal purposes, but more importantly it promotes organizational learning when it focuses not on tracking errors in original specifications, but on promoting early communications and cross-functional understanding.

Technology for mobile communications has greatly simplified these tasks. Beepers, mobile telephones, and portable computers with modems have made communications between headquarters and the field simple and productive. This technology has moved project management closer to techniques for routine batch production; just as a McDonald's knows how many Big Mac it sells each day, project managers can update progress reports daily, including detailed information about any necessary engineering changes.

In its second important role, a project management information system must support a planning system to help managers track progress and recognize deviations from schedule. Information about daily progress helps the project manager to schedule resources in a cost-effective manner and to redeploy them as necessary from nonessential activities or those that are ahead of schedule to those that seem likely to endanger the timely completion of the project. Software for both mainframes and personal computers now offers project management tools such as PERT and CPM.

Finally, the information system must track actual expenditures for labor and materials and compare them against initial cost estimates. In particular, this function must document any additional costs due to revisions requested by customers to support changes in project billing. Many projects call for partial payments based on progress to date, so the manufacturer needs some tracking system to document progress and support billing statements. In addition, key personnel may earn part of their compensation by achieving certain project objectives. This adds another reason for carefully evaluating true measures of performance.

Inventory.   Work in process accounts for most of a project's inventory. To support production at a remote site, project managers may want to schedule the arrival of inventory as the need for it arises. In addition to conserving working capital, this tactic prevents problems due to lack of secure storage areas at remote sites. Out in the open, materials tend to degrade or even to disappear. Thieves frequently plunder construction sites, for example.

Of course, a project does not accumulate finished-goods inventory because the final product is the completed project, which changes immediately from an inventory account to an account receivable at the conclusion of the sale. Completion of a project ahead of schedule or some problem that holds up acceptance may lead to a considerable total for finished-goods inventory, however.

Adaptability to Change.   Projects offer the most flexible opportunities of all manufacturing processes to adapt to change. Minimal long-term investment in equipment frees the firm to explore new technologies. Flexible staffing practices allow some control of production volume, although too much variability in employment may alienate key employees and subcontractors.

These details hide a major source of resistance to change, however: the organization's knowledge base. Since familiar technologies reduce system variance, many firms prefer to stick to doing what they know best. Consistent performance also enhances the value of traditional capabilities as order winners. For these reasons, the apparent flexibility due to limited long-term commitments for equipment and people may overstate the true potential to adapt to change.

Jobbing

Another category of manufacturing processes, **jobbing**, irregularly produce relatively few units of a product, but they produce more units more frequently than a project would produce.

jobbing
A manufacturing process that irregularly produces single or small lots in a shop characterized by flexible machines and skilled workers.

Typical Applications.   Jobbing is most effective for processing small or unique orders. In its simplest form, one or two individuals in a small garage or shop may perform all of work involved with processing a single order. A larger jobbing process called a *job shop* can process many jobs at the same time.

Job shops can operate make-to-stock and make-to-order systems. In a make-to-stock job shop, some mechanism indicates that the process should make more of some stocked item. A Kanban card may trigger this order, or a demand forecast may project more orders than existing inventory can supply.

A make-to-order job shop manufactures a product to fill an order for a standard product for which the firm does not maintain inventories. Following the existing production process, employees pull the bill of material to check availability of parts. If the shop has all of the needed parts on hand, production proceeds. If not, purchasing or component subprocesses acquire or make the needed parts. Many job shops hold needed raw materials for make-to-order goods in kits, which they assemble in response to specific orders.

When a make-to-order shop receives a request to manufacture a part that it has never made before, the process becomes more complicated. First, such requests often come in as requests for bids rather than firm orders. To answer this request, operations managers must complete a bid estimation process like the one diagrammed in Exhibit 12.7 to evaluate the product's specifications and estimate the cost of filling the order.

If the customer eventually places a firm order, the operations manager releases it to the job shop with instructions for routing through the process activities. Most products pass through machine processing in specific sequences of work centers, perhaps following instructions in the form of numerical-control data or a

[**E X H I B I T   1 2 . 7**]

Bid Estimation Process

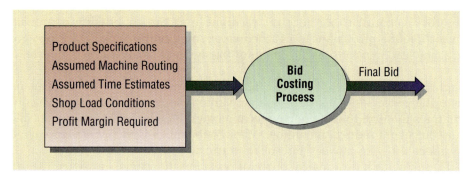

simple chart that breaks down the job into a set of tasks, i.e. drill a 1-inch hole completely through the steel plate at a specific location.

As the job flows through the job shop, it routinely encounters queues at each work center because it is just one of many parts in the system, each with its own set of unique requests. In effect, the system tells the part, "Get in line, I'll get to you as soon as possible." If a part could comment on customer-service standards upon leaving a job shop, it probably would complain that the process had wasted too much of its time, forcing it to sit waiting in queues. In fact, job shops commonly place parts in queues for 95 percent of the total production time because they focus primarily on efficiency at work centers by making sure that their workers never run out of work.

By operating in this manner, job shops can produce small orders more cheaply than other categories of manufacturing processes could achieve. Thus, job shops control most small or unique orders for widely varying products.

Order Winners.   Job shops base their competitive success on a number of strengths. They compete with large-scale producers like batch or line processes by stressing their capabilities to fabricate wide varieties of products. These higher-volume processes could produce a given output more cheaply, but only at order quantities large enough to provide economies of scale. Smaller job shops compete with larger ones by offering lower costs and often quicker delivery times; larger job shops compete with smaller ones by offering better, more productive equipment or better order-entry systems. Individual firms may stress superior reputations for quality, delivery reliability, or other specific strengths. As discussed in Chapter 9 on JIT manufacturing, increasing numbers of customers now select and certify suppliers, including job shops, based on process capabilities rather than price.

Physical Resource Mix.   Job shops accumulate physical resources to achieve and maintain process flexibility because their varied work flows do not allow them to keep equipment that can perform only limited types of work. Job shops keep their work centers flexible by equipping them with standard, general-purpose machines, tools, and fixtures. The makers of this equipment sell their models in large numbers to widely varied users, spreading product-development costs over many units and making general-purpose machines less costly than special-purpose machines. These machines also can perform more tasks, but they cannot match the production rates of dedicated, special-purpose machines outfitted with job-specific tools and fixtures.

[**EXHIBIT 12.8**]

Job Shop with a Process Layout

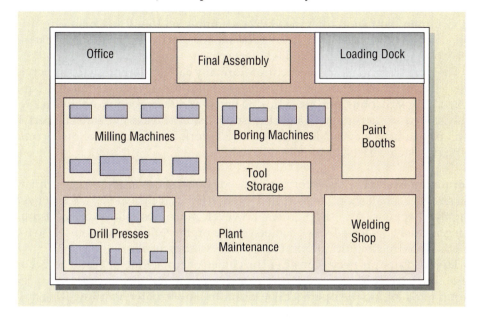

The layout of job shop equipment also maximizes flexibility. Since operations managers cannot determine ahead of time the machine requirements and route of each incoming job, they normally define **process layouts**, as shown in Exhibit 12.8. Also called *functional layouts,* these arrangements group similar machines or work centers in clusters, and all of the people who work in a particular area specialize in those machines. If workers encounter problems, with those machines or their output, they know where on the shop floor to go for help. If one job requires more capacity than a single machine can offer, the operations manager can split it between two machines without creating a difficult control problem.

Physical resources define some typical classifications for job shops. A measure of size normally reflects the number of machines or the average number of jobs in the shop at one time, though it may also indicate numbers of workers or annual billings. These measures need not match. A **labor-limited job shop** employs significantly fewer workers than it would need to operate each machine. The capacity of such a shop is based on worker output rather than machine output. To measure work of such varied types, operations managers normally express capacity in some general unit of measure like dollars, pounds of output, or number of jobs per year.

The physical resources of a job shop, especially one with a functional layout, must allow for a flexible materials handling system. Such shops build in few conveyors because most work flows follow unpredictable routes. As a result, work-in-process inventory clutters the shop floors of most of these systems while it waits for processing or for transportation to the next work station. Some plants do move goods with conveyor systems by shuttling every completed lot back to a central storage point where it waits for movement out to the next operation. Such a system can become fairly expensive. Other job shops have relied on AGVs for more flexibility, but most use manual labor or fork lifts to haul work in process.

process layout

An arrangement of physical resources that groups similar machines or work centers in clusters

labor-limited job shop

A job shop that employs significantly fewer workers than it would need to operate each machine

Human Resource Mix. Flexible machines and layouts require flexible workers. A job shop needs employees who can evaluate the requirements of new jobs and initiate procedures to fulfill those requirements without continual instructions from supervisors. These employees must know how to read blueprints. In addition, for a labor-limited job shop, they need cross-training so they can operate multiple machines, and other shops can gain important benefits from this training. Like projects, job shops require highly skilled workers.

Their organizational infrastructures normally call for decentralized supervisory styles. Operations managers provide the right tools, well-maintained equipment, clear instructions, and realistic due dates, and then get out of the way. Such highly skilled workers do not need close supervision or extensive staff support. Job shops pay hourly wages, since their varied work loads do not allow practical incentive systems based on production volume.

Information System. The information needs of job shops seem to vary primarily with size. In a small shop, workers and supervisors can easily keep track of everything that happens. As a shop grows, however, more jobs follow different routes through widely dispersed work centers, so the organization needs some systematic method for tracking the location and progress of each job.

To illustrate this need, consider the choice of a machine operator to process one of five jobs, A,B,C,D, and E. Job A arrived first. Job B resembles the recently completed job, so the operator could minimize setup by handling it next. Job C is a short job that the machine can complete by the end of the shift. Job D requires careful attention to tight tolerances. The salesperson who took the order for Job E happens to be the plant manager's daughter. Each of these jobs has its own due date, and each needs a different amount of machine time. In Chapter 18, we will look at procedures for making this decision; for now, notice the job shop's need for an elaborate information system to guide and support operating decisions.

The firm's customer service manager has a similar problem. A customer wants to know the status of an overdue job that turns out to be Job C, the short job described earlier. The machine operator could finish it quickly, but the job needs additional processing by two other work centers. What should the customer service manager tell the customer? How could the system expedite the job within the shop? Without a decent information system, no one can answer these questions, except perhaps to bully the job through the shop. This can be costly, especially if it delays the plant manager's daughter's job.

Besides reporting on the current status and priority of the work in a job shop, its information system should include a good database with accurate records of costs for past jobs to help with estimates for bids. Group technology methods look for similarities between tasks in a new job and those that the shop has performed in the past. This information contributes essential background for job routing and bid estimating if the firm can duplicate or adapt a successful process from the past rather than inventing an entirely new one.

A job shop's information system must also help with job costing. To evaluate the costs for its variable jobs, the shop needs a system for tracking the contributions of labor, materials, and specialist support to each job. A transaction-tracking system reads a bar-coded identification tag for each job and assigns time for each worker and each machine that help to process it. Each time a part moves from an input queue to a work center, the system starts charging costs to the job and extending credit for work completed to both the work center and its operator. The same system charges material usage to the job.

At the completion of the job, the information system can report on its usage of production resources, and it can compare those figures to estimates made for the bid. This helps operations managers to target their analysis on significant variances to ascertain the causes of potentially important problems; they will respond differently if the problem resulted from a flawed bid or poor shop-floor performance. At the end of a period, the information system provides input for evaluation of work loads on workers and machines to help production planners distribute work efficiently. In a labor-limited shop, managers can redeploy workers at unused work centers with a queue of waiting jobs. In this way, accumulating information facilitates systemwide learning.

Once again, information becomes a key input to job shop planning and control systems. Small shops we can get away with informal information systems, but the information needs in any job shop with 20 or more work centers demand a formal system.

Operations managers must avoid using information system reports to justify repressive judgments of employees. If they do not like the use of those reports, they can easily manipulate work flows enough to erode the validity of the numbers. Smart workers can beat any information system!

Inventory.   As for a project, work in process represents the vast majority of a job shop's inventory. Obviously, long queues and slow production increase work in process, while quicker work flows reduce it. As mentioned earlier, ample work in process maximizes the efficiency of work centers by ensuring that they will stay busy.

A make-to-order job shop should accumulate little finished-goods inventory, except when the shop completes a job early and the buyer will not accept the goods until the due date. A make-to-stock job shop should also keep little finished-goods inventory, instead shipping completed orders on to buyers. Inventories of raw materials in a job shop depend on their importance in reducing lead times. If the shop can quickly acquire raw materials as needed, then it should hold little in inventory. If raw materials orders require long lead times and the shop can reasonably expect to need those materials, then it should hold limited amounts of them in inventory. If the operations managers have no idea what raw materials the shop will need, they would be foolish to stock raw materials. Inventory levels depend on individual situations.

Adaptability to Change.   Job shops succeed based on their flexibility. Their structures suit new-product development extremely well, as they can quickly acquire new tooling as needed and they maintain adaptable, general-purpose equipment and machines. The suppliers of this equipment can always offer additional units from their stocks of standard products, so the shop can add capacity in relatively small increments by purchasing new equipment and hiring new workers.

Job shops may face a tougher challenge in responding to volume flexibility than design flexibility, though. Most job shops prize their skilled workers, so they tend to respond to falling demand first by reducing their order backlogs. Instead of having 2 months of work waiting for processing, this total may drop to 6 weeks of work. Recognizing this decline, the firm may bid more aggressively for new work by promising shorter lead times and perhaps lower prices that will provide lower profit margins. A usually busy shop might eliminate all overtime or, in extreme circumstances, switch to a 4-day work week. Since job shops often don't keep much finished-goods inventory, they may lack buffers against slowdowns and feel the effects more quickly than batch producers or other manufacturing processes.

Batch Production

When a firm manufactures a product routinely in moderate volumes, operations managers may see an opportunity to eliminate some of the variability of a jobbing system by grouping orders into larger quantities and running them in longer batches. This creates a process system known as **batch production**.

Typical Applications.   The decision to choose batch production hinges on the definition of *moderate* volume. Operations managers base this assessment on the capacity of the process equipment. Batch production makes sense when a situation calls for order sizes significantly smaller than a dedicated process can turn out running continuously, but large enough to justify longer production runs than a job shop typically plans.

For example, suppose that a process can produce 50,000 units of a particular product per week, while weekly demand consumes 20,000 units. The firm's operations managers can respond to this situation in four ways:

1. Live with the mismatch and run the process at 40 percent of capacity, or 2 days per week.
2. Reduce process capacity to match existing demand.
3. Urge marketing to sell more of the product.
4. Produce another product on the same process.

The cost of retooling the system to make another product may eliminate the second and fourth options for the short term, leaving only the first and third. A longer-run response would have to include redesigning the process to reduce part changeover costs.

Most production by North American manufacturers calls for moderate volumes. In fact, 75 percent of all production runs manufacture lots of 50 units or less. Clearly, job shops could handle smaller orders, but for orders of moderate volumes, batch production offers significant economies of scale through several streamlining measures:

1. *Reductions in setup times*   Batch production runs fewer, larger orders than jobbing, spreading the costs of preparing the operator, the machine, and its fixtures over larger numbers of units.
2. *Reduction of costs due to production startups*   These costs include lower levels of productivity or higher levels of scrap that commonly occur at the start of a new production run.
3. *Cost benefits of designing and/or acquiring special-purpose equipment*   Production at moderate volume often justifies the cost of machines, tools, or fixtures that increase output rates and efficiency.
4. *Labor-rate savings*   Specialized equipment for batch production reduces labor intensity, allowing the firm to replace skilled job-shop workers with less-skilled production line workers who command lower wages.
5. *Lower production overhead for preparing bids and supporting new job releases*   This cost benefit comes from bidding and tracking fewer, larger jobs than a job shop typically must accommodate.

Batch production effectively manufactures standardized products, usually to fill recurring orders. This streamlines or even eliminates many planning activities of job shops. Less frequently, it may suit production of unique orders for unusually large lot sizes, perhaps 50 units or so. Batch production finds its ideal conditions in make-to-stock systems.

[**E X H I B I T   1 2 . 9**]

Batch Production with a Product Layout

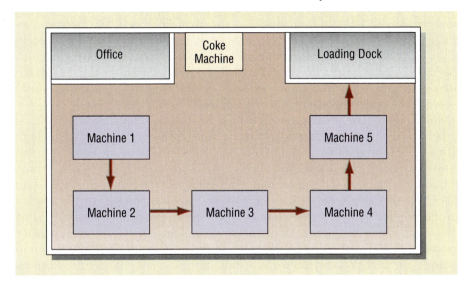

Order Winners.   Batch producers match their competitive strategies to rivals' weaknesses. In competition against job shops, batch producers must usually overcome disadvantages in speed of response and product flexibility. Normally, they base their success on cost advantages. Job shops can make products in batches of moderate volume, but uncharacteristically long runs often back up such systems, as when retail bank customers must wait while a scoutmaster buys traveler's checks for every member of the troop.

To compete against high-volume, production-line systems, batch producers stress their relative advantages in flexibility and often cost. These larger-scale competitors require long periods of down time and expensive setups to change over from one moderate-volume run to another, so batch producers can often beat their schedules and their prices.

Physical Resource Mix.   The physical resource needs of batch processes vary widely depending upon the nature of the firm's products, production technology in the industry, and the competitive environment. For moderate lot sizes, most batch producers need flexible equipment. They may find more specialized machines, tools, and fixtures appropriate if they decide to sacrifice some flexibility to focus their strategies narrowly on certain products.

Such a focus may justify **product layout**, in which the system arranges equipment to match the typical flow of work, as illustrated in Exhibit 12.9. This layout requires a stable pattern of processing for similar components in which production begins at one work center and proceeds predictably through the rest.

A predictable flow of production tasks creates a number of opportunities to reduce waste. First, if parts normally flow in one direction, the simple decision about task sequences minimizes the need for a system to track work in process. In particular, organizing batch production in *U*-shaped cells brings substantial advantages through economical use of space and close arrangements of work stations to facilitate communication between workers. Stable production flows may also allow

product layout

An arrangement of physical manufacturing resources in a configuration that corresponds to a routine flow of production tasks simple material-handling devices, such as conveyors, to move parts from one machine to the next.

Product layouts like the one in Exhibit 12.9 work well if the capacities of the machines match one another. Recall from Chapter 5 that the capacity of such a configuration equals that of the machine with the smallest capacity. If operations managers can combine machines with minimal setup times, nearly identical capacities, and low variability of operating times, then the batch process can function almost like a high-volume production line. Few batch operations can establish such stable routines, so they must decouple machines or work centers and buffer variance between them with work-in-process inventories.

Multistage batch processes can adjust for uneven machine capacities in a number of ways. If the system does not need the additional capacity of the higher-volume machines, then its problem centers on potentially wasteful investment in excessive capacity rather than the imbalance. If, however, it can benefit from the additional capacity, then the problem focuses on relieving pressure at the bottleneck. To do this, the bottleneck work center or machine might work more hours than the others. Many plants schedule bottleneck operations to work a second shift specifically to complete operations for which they need additional capacity. A firm might also divert some of the work at the bottleneck operation to another machine with slack capacity or to a subcontractor. As a last resort, operations managers should consider acquiring an additional machine, though many seem to jump at this obvious response before they consider more economical alternatives.

Human Resource Mix.   Batch production can often proceed effectively with less-skilled workers than job shops require, but this does not make the staffing decision automatic. Limited requirements for relatively simple setups do not require highly skilled workers. To complete more challenging setups, operations managers may hire skilled specialists for that work while assigning less-skilled operators for routine production tasks, which might well bore the skilled workers. Highly variable tasks may require skilled operators, however, to avoid producing entire batches of poor-quality goods. Operations managers must carefully match human resources to process requirements.

They must also supervise batch production more closely than they would oversee tasks in a job shop. To maintain effective connections between tasks, employees within a batch process must work effectively together. At one plant in Silicon Valley, workers observed a cardinal rule never to make a downstream team member look bad by swamping him or her with work. When they they saw their output piling up, they suspended production and performed other work, preferably helping out at the backed up work center.

Information System.   Batch production requires most of the same information systems as job shops, but less detailed reporting may suffice. While a batch process may manipulate more parts, for example, its materials handling procedures group them into lots to correspond to batch sizes. The information system can then track specific lots rather than individual parts. On a college campus, such a system might track the schedules of classes rather than the more varied movements of individual students.

Since the system records transactions by batch, it records far fewer transactions each day. More predictable part flow reduces the need to keep track even of batches. If the regular schedule specifies that an order should reach a particular work station at a certain time, someone who needs information, perhaps to respond to a customer question, can simply ask the workers at that station about the order.

Also, parts flow through batch production more quickly than through a job shop, shrinking work-in-process inventory and reducing the burden of tracking it.

The information system for a batch production process must provide production specifications to the shop floor, just as in a job shop, but it must do so less often. Further, if specialists perform production setups, they can assume responsibility for this information, easing the load on the information system.

Batch production also simplifies performance tracking. The firm relies on familiar cost-tracking procedures to evaluate costs for specific orders, but with fewer, larger orders than in a job shop, it can do so with significantly fewer cost-entry transactions. Some firms elect to track productivity and costs using **process costing** procedures. By comparing aggregate data about resource inputs like labor and materials with data about product outputs, operations managers can measure the performance of a batch production system or its subsystems over a time period; a job shop cannot effectively evaluate skilled workers based solely on cost data gathered for a highly variable process. Some firms base group wage incentive systems on periodic productivity statistics.

process costing
Performance-evaluation procedures based on aggregate data about resource inputs and product outputs

Inventory.   Batch production frequently generates large inventories. Predictable work flows simplify scheduling of inputs, so batch production does not need excessive stocks of raw materials. Once it launches a job, however, work-in-process inventory often balloons, especially if the firm allows it to accumulate as a way of adjusting for capacity differences between subprocesses. Without extremely tight scheduling, each following job must wait while a work center processes moderately large jobs ahead of it.

The late Taiichi Ohno, the founder of JIT, spotted this problem when he visited facilities of the Ford Motor Company following World War II. Ford's highly specialized equipment produced at a rate much faster than later processes could use its output, so managers arranged the equipment for batch production, despite its high setup costs. To minimize overall costs in this system, Ford had to produce in large batches, making enough to cover the system's needs until economies of scale justified another production run.

In a one-stage production process, this inventory would represent finished goods. In a multistage batch production process, however, an order can wait in a series of long lines. As it does, inventory costs add up continually, raising the investment in work in process, floor space to store it between subprocesses, and infrastructure to manage it.

If a batch-production operation could complete orders exactly on their delivery dates, it would accumulate little finished-goods inventory. Normally, however, batch scheduling calls for completion far in advance of shipping dates. This inflates finished-goods inventory. In addition, a make-to-stock producer plans to keep goods available whenever a customer calls. The production scheduler must maintain sufficient inventory to last until the scheduled completion of the next order, and this amount varies with customer demand and the sometimes-variable timing of process output, especially when shop work loads vary. Schedulers hate risk, so they order a little extra, and stacks of costly inventory rise.

Adaptability to Change.   Batch production may range from extremely flexible to rather rigid, depending upon the details of its layout and the standards for comparison. Clearly, a decision to arrange specialized equipment, tools, and fixtures in a product layout must accept some reduction in flexibility as compared to a job shop. Compared to a production line, however, batch production can seem highly adaptable.

The ability to produce more than one product allows a batch-production facility to adjust its volume to sales demand, provided that customers' desire for all of its products does not fluctuate in unison. If demand for one product rises while demand for another falls, then the batch process can redeploy capacity away from weak sellers to more popular products. This product mix flexibility is a major strength of batch-production systems.

In addition, a flexible mix of resources may allow the firm to introduce compatible new products without significant expenditures for new production capacity. This potential to maximize the return from the firm's investment in equipment encourages product designers and manufacturing engineers to work closely in the product-innovation process.

Line Production

Everyone has seen assembly lines. Charlie Chaplin fell into one in the classic film *Modern Times*, and many other cultural media since have illustrated the concept. **Line production** usually comes to mind when people think of manufacturing.

Typical Applications.   In reality, the line form of production is not used as often as most people think. It is only applicable to production situations in which a large volume of a standard product needs to be made. The process category matrix in Exhibit 12.6 indicated its applicability with low part variety and high-volume production of each part.

The category of line production includes three variants. The first and most obvious fabricates or assembles a single model at a time. Henry Ford loved this mode so much that he offered to paint a Model T any color the customer wanted, as long as it was black. The second type of production line, called a **mixed-model production line**, can produce more than one model as long as the variations fall within a single part family. This raises questions about what constitutes a different model. Does the model change when the color changes or when some units get optional radios, convertible tops, two extra doors, etc.? Strictly speaking, any of these variations create a mixed-model line, but in practice operations managers usually apply the term to lines that mix basic configurations of products rather than features within a single configuration. Adding a radio or changing the color does not really make a mixed-model line, though workers in the painting department may think that it does.

After single-model and mixed-model lines, batch operations define the third form of production lines. As the last section explained, a batch line makes a moderate volume of one item and then switches to another item.

Although most people tend to think first of assembly lines, the category also includes fabrication lines. Such a line might start with a hard-boiled egg at one end and pass it down a line where a series of semiskilled artisans paint portions of a design. After the last work station, a customer can buy a hand-painted egg. Tourists and others buy many Chinese works of art "hand-crafted" in just this way.

The machining equivalent of the Chinese egg line is called a **transfer line**. Such a system introduces raw material, perhaps chunks of metal, at one end and moves it on conveyors past work stations that process it into something useful like an engine block. At each stage, the unit of work stops in a set position and fixtures secure it to a rigid base so special-purpose machines can perform operations according to some predetermined plan, usually under numerical control. This

line production
A category of manufacturing processes that arranges special-purpose machines and equipment in a rigid sequence to perform repetitive tasks for large orders

mixed-model production line
A production line that can produce more than one model as long as the variations fall within a single part family

transfer line
A production line that carries raw materials on conveyors past work stations that process it into something useful

single-minded dedication proves marvelously productive, provided only that the firm can generate enough demand to consume the output. The main drawback comes from the same rigidity, which prevents such a system from making more than a few parts, perhaps only a single part. When the business declines, this kind of equipment makes an interesting artifact.

Order Winners.   With sufficiently large volumes, production lines enable manufacturers to make standardized products more cheaply than any other process choice. In a cost-competitive market for products that do not vary much, this can provide a key competitive strength. This possibility depends, however, on the determination of sufficiently large volumes. In general, single-mode lines generate lower costs than mixed-mode lines for the same product. If the product mix must include significant variations, however, only careful, detailed analysis will reveal the most cost-effective choice.

Critics have often blamed the assembly line manufacturing process as a root cause of America's quality problems, especially in the automotive industry. Any poorly run operation can cause quality to decline, however. The cars that won accolades for their quality came from assembly lines, as well, often staffed with American workers. Even an assembly line can compete on the basis of quality, provided the firm organizes and implements the process effectively.

In addition to cost, a production line can compete on the basis of delivery speed if its structure supports the strategy. At an auto show room, a customer might want a car that no dealer has in stock; the manufacturer could make that car within 1 day, although delivery might take longer, of course, depending upon the customer's location. This assumes an extremely flexible schedule for the auto maker's final assembly line. Quite naturally, operations managers would prefer a little more time. No auto maker has implemented such a system, perhaps because both the dealer and the auto maker would prefer to sell cars presently in stock. Still, assembly lines do not assume complete rigidity; for sufficiently standardized products, these operations can compete on the basis of speed more effectively than batch producers or job shops.

Physical Resource Mix.   The physical resources of a production line cover an extremely wide range. They can perform both transformation and transportation activities manually or add many levels of automation up to computer-controlled robots. Humans work more flexibly, but they do not always perform tasks as accurately as well-designed and carefully programmed robots. As production lines have become more sophisticated, however, their machines, tools, and fixtures have moved rapidly toward specialization, as the "By the Way" box describes. Developments in smart automation promise systems that are both accurate and flexible.

Transfer lines invariably include specialized machines, tools, fixtures, and materials-handling equipment. These resources often allow them to produce goods at mind-boggling speeds. A line can make crown caps for bottles at a rate in excess of 10,000 per minute. Soft-drink can lines run at similar rates. At such high rates of production, output can easily outstrip demand, forcing a conversion to batch production. Zapata, a manufacturer of crown caps, finds it necessary to switch products about once every hour.

With its standardized products and special-purpose equipment, line production suits a product layout like that in Exhibit 12.10. The fixed flow of parts enables such a firm to thoroughly automate its materials-handling activities.

[BY THE WAY... CHRYSLER'S ARGUMENTS WITH ROBOTS]

When Lee Iacocca left Ford to join Chrysler, he wanted to make an immediate change to jazz up the product line. As one quick way, he decided to reintroduce a convertible model.

Years earlier, all three American manufacturers had discontinued these models, partly for safety reasons, but most because they thought that the availability of reliable air conditioning systems would reduce demand. This created an after-market industry to buy new cars, cut off their roofs, and install convertible tops.

As Iacocca hurried to return to this market, he encountered an intractable robot. Rigid programming left the device capable only of welding on a roof, and no one, not even Iacocca, could change its mind. To introduce the new convertible quickly, Chrysler took cars from the production line after the robot had done its work. Workers cut off the roof from each car and added the new top.

Despite the terrible waste, the premium prices for the new cars made the move a financial success. It also reinforced Iacocca's reputation for understanding the buying public.

Human Resource Mix.   When Henry Ford introduced his assembly line, one important attraction came from its ability to assign unskilled workers immediately to meaningful work, since each employee needed to know how to do only a few tasks. One job might require a worker to lie in a pit and tighten two bolts that attached the bottom of the right fender to the chassis of a car as it passed overhead.

[**E X H I B I T   1 2 . 1 0**]

Simplified Crown Cap Transfer Line

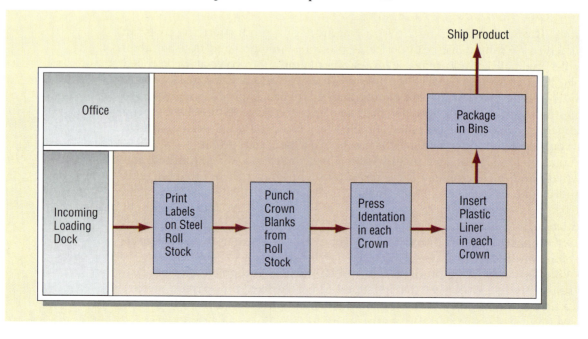

ON THE JOB

Different Assembly Line at Caterpillar

■

In Lafayette, Indiana, Caterpillar has created an unusual assembly line to make some of the largest diesel engines in the world. These engines power giant earth-moving machines, ships, and backup electrical-power systems. These applications allow no tolerance for recalls. The first two applications make it difficult for customers to return malfunctioning engines for service. Failure of a power-backup system may threaten someone's life in a hospital, and it could have consequences almost as dire for a commercial operation like a credit-card network.

To guarantee reliable products, Caterpillar has organized its assembly line in an unusual way. The line employs only certified mechanics. These skilled workers earn wages comparable to those of a diesel mechanic in a service department. To eliminate boredom, workers routinely rotate assignments. They can do this because each worker knows how to do every job on the line. To make the work still less repetitive, Caterpillar sets the part cycle time (i.e., the time allocated to perform a work station's task on a particular engine) at a much longer period than the typical time for automobile final assembly lines.

This limited activity probably bored workers, but it provided steady work for grateful employees, many of them newly arrived immigrants. These workers did not even have to learn English because the plants often segregated workers by nationality, in part to aid communications, but quite possibly also to maintain control.

After a while, despite their desire for stable jobs, workers began to resent the boring, repetitive tasks. They began to listen to union organizers, absenteeism increased, and, quite naturally, boredom led to an unwitting or intentional decline in quality. These problems did not really matter much to early auto makers because American consumers did not have anything better to buy.

As described in Chapter 6, this attitude toward human resources spread throughout Ford, leading to a premium on the division of labor and an erosion of the value on broad training. This has changed dramatically in recent years. Ford and Chrysler now express the intention of hiring better-educated workers for their assembly lines. Chrysler plans for an increase in the span of control from 25-to-1 to 50-to-1. Production lines now require workers to accept responsibility for carrying out their assignments using their brains as well as their hands. NUMMI, the GM-Toyota joint venture, continues to rely on empowered teams to perform and enhance shop-floor activities. Respect for workers has become an important organizational value, and supervisors no longer earn rewards simply for domination of their teams. The "On the Job" box discusses another company, Caterpillar, in which workers must ensure quality from the outset.

Information System.   Much of the information system for a production line revolves around the final build schedule. These systems need to perform two functions: (1) tell line workers what to do to each subassembly that comes down the line, and (2) tell purchasing staff and upstream manufacturing processes about the component needs of the final assembly line. Suppose that a simple line makes a single product in a set quantity each shift; its information system need only indicate to final assembly workers what each one should do to every unit during a shift. For suppliers, internal and external, the information system must state how many units of which inputs it needs; this amounts to the bill of materials for the final product.

The information system for a production line that performs batch processing needs some mechanism to warn both workers and suppliers of a change to a new end product. Besides this additional requirement, the system performs like that for the simple production line.

For a mixed-model assembly line, the information system must specify differences for each item coming down the line. In an automotive line, a large-font computer printout taped to the hood may tell workers what to do to that car to provide the correct options and features. A materials-handling system for such line must ensure that workers have the parts they need, preferably in the right order. Production lines do not leave workers enough time to search for things. The supply system needs detailed information about the exact mix of the final build schedule in order to notify suppliers of expected deliveries for each shift over the planning horizon. In order to improve stability within the supply chain, a manufacturer may commonly freeze its orders for a fixed period. For big-ticket manufactured goods like jet aircraft, the freeze period might extend throughout a year; for an auto-assembly line, it might cover 3 weeks; for a personal-computer line, it might be as short as a few days.

Supply management critically influences the ability of a production line to compete on the basis of delivery speed. A supply network that responds rapidly to short-term changes allows a firm to respond quickly to customer demand, although these changes often raise operating costs within the supply network. For this reason, many production lines make mature products for which change remains limited. These kinds of producers need suppliers that offer high-quality, low-cost components, so they must carefully avoid sending conflicting messages. No supplier can offer both low-cost components and quick responses to unstable demand.

The accounting systems of most production-line manufacturers rely on process costing. They carefully measure the inputs of labor hours, materials, and components and compare this information against the total output produced. These inputs go into the classical variance analysis form of control.

When designing an assembly line or adjusting the configuration of an existing line for a desired level of output, operations managers must know what tasks the OM system must complete to finish each unit. They break down each job into minimum rational work units and estimate the time requirements of each task. When they finish cataloging all necessary tasks, the time requirements of each one, and their necessary sequence, operations managers have solved the **assembly line balancing problem**.

assembly line balancing problem

Detailed analysis to catalog all necessary tasks in a production line, the time requirements of each one, and their necessary sequence

[**P R O B L E M   1 2 . 1**]

Balancing a Production Line

To assemble a finished car, a production line must complete a set of tasks, t_i in which $i = 1, 2, 3, ..., n$ represents the time it takes to perform each task. Suppose, also, that some of the tasks must observe known precedence constraints, i.e., t_2 must occur before t_8. How should a production line assign tasks to produce output at a specified rate of M units per shift? A four-step process provides the answer:

1. Determine the total number of hours of work required to make 1 unit:

$$\text{Total hours per unit} = \sum_{i=1}^{n} t_i$$

2. Determine the unit cycle time by dividing effective minutes per shift by the parts required per shift:

$$\text{Unit cycle time} = (8 \text{ hours} \times 50 \text{ minutes per hour})/M \text{ units}$$

   For example, if a line must produce 400 cars per 8-hour per shift, then it must produce 50 cars an hour. Working 50 minutes per hour, the line needs to produce a car each minute. In the jargon of industrial engineering, this amounts to a unit cycle time of 1 minute. This implies that each worker must complete all assigned tasks within 1 minute to avoid slowing down the rest of the line.

3. Determine the minimum number of work stations required by dividing the total hours per unit by the unit cycle time:

   Minimum number of work stations = Total work per unit/Unit cycle time

   If the tasks to produce a car sum to 87 minutes, to find the minimum number of work stations for the line:

   Minimum number of work stations = 87 min. work per unit/1 min. per station
   = 87 stations

   Under ideal conditions, the production line needs at least 87 work stations to produce the required output.

4. Assign the minimum number of rational work units, t_i, to the work stations in a manner that satisfies precedence requirements and cycle time limitations. No work station should have more than 1 minute of work to do.   [■]

Adaptability to Change.   Clearly, production lines do not offer the maximum flexibility of any process category. Operations managers' control of output volumes may face limits under union contracts or informal resistance by workers. Strong unions have negotiated contracts that require production lines to run at full capacity or not at all. To increase output volume, a production line may have to run on Saturday shifts or in overtime hours during the week. To reduce output volume, the line may simply shut down or feed finished goods into inventory to feed later demand (or so managers hope).

In settings that allow more flexibility, operations managers can adjust the rate of production by speeding up and slowing down the part cycle time. To produce more units of output per shift, they will have to add work stations and reallocate the extra work to the expanded capacity. To reduce output, they remove workers from the line and reallocate the smaller volume of work to the remaining work stations.

In certain industries, unions have sought to protect members from employment uncertainty by negotiating contracts that guarantee significant parts of workers' wages. For example, in the automobile industry, Big Three management can curtail production if they want, but the workers still make most of their guaranteed wages.

This discussion does not imply that a production line can never adapt to change. One rather flexible production line bagged potting soil. During the busy season, four workers ran the line: one operator filled the bags, a second sealed the tops closed by guiding them through a heat sealer, and two more workers removed the sealed bags and positioned them on pallets. On a good day, a four-person crew could complete 4,000 1-cubic-yard bags. When business slowed down, the sealer operator moved to other work and one operator both filled and sealed the bags, which traveled down the line to the other two workers, who stacked them on pallets as before. This three-person crew could finish about 2,700 bags. If one of the bag stackers moved to a different job, the remaining two-person crew could complete about 1,900 bags per shift. Finally, when business really slowed down, one person could fill the bags, walk them down the line past the sealer, and place them on a pallet, finishing about 900 to 1,000 bags per shift. A production line can indeed achieve volume flexibility.

To change a production line to allow product mix flexibility, operations managers must sacrifice some efficiency. If a line allots time for a work station to install a car CD player, each order that does not call for a CD player will cause a loss of efficiency because the worker earns the same money and the investment in tools does not decline, but the process adds less value to the car as it passes. Some lines try to offset these inefficiencies by adjusting the sequences of jobs. Automobile assembly lines seldom carry station wagons in succession because the special features of this model tend to stress certain work stations. This kind of adjustment can solve some problems created by differences in units, but it adds one more constraint to the final assembly schedule.

Transfer lines tend to be less flexible than assembly lines because the designs of their special-purpose machinery often assume production of goods at the rated line speed. The volume flexibility characteristics of such a line resemble those of an assembly line with a rigid union contract.

Cellular Manufacturing

While students may not recognize manufacturing cells as readily as assembly lines, those who have eaten in cafeterias have acted as operators in food-serving cells. At noon, customers enter a cafeteria looking for a wide variety of foods, though just about all want some combination of an entree, perhaps a salad, a beverage, and dessert. Within each of these food groups, customers desire considerable mix flexibility.

cellular manufacturing

A category of manufacturing processes that produces a family of similar outputs, one at a time, by linking together all possible operations in the required process

product family

A group of similar outputs

Cellular manufacturing offers this kind of choice by laying out equipment dedicated to the production of a family of similar outputs, one at a time, by linking together all possible operations in the required process. All of cellular manufacturing revolves around **product families**, or groups of similar outputs. The similarities could reflect common design features or manufacturing traits. A cafeteria's product family includes the range of food choices it offers for lunch.

Typical Applications.   Recall that line production effectively manufactures substantially identical output from a limited set of parts. Cellular manufacturing stretches that system's criteria for similarity of outputs and components. It relies on identifying a group of parts that require many of the same operations that employ essentially the same set of machines. An ideal cellular manufacturing system would define a constant sequence of manufacturing tasks for all of its outputs and a single set of quality standards. Closely comparable functional characteristics, as for a line of low-horsepower water pumps, also simplify processes in this category, though these systems do not require it. For example, a shoe manufacturer's cellular process

More and more companies are using manufacturing cells to increase production efficiency and accuracy.
SOURCE: Steve Dunwell/The Image Bank

may treat each shoe size as a different product; despite differences in size and shape, the process can still make them all in the same way.

Manufacturing cells try to achieve efficiency similar to that of line production while preserving some of the mix flexibility of job shops. Cellular manufacturing employs the concept of group technology, introduced in Chapter 9, to combine a subset of a plant's jobs with similar manufacturing requirements. If the firm finds sufficient demand for these outputs, it can redeploy some equipment from a job shop to create a product layout that resembles a small production line. The rest of the job shop's machines can remain in a more typical functional layout, taking input from the manufacturing cell as needed. Within that cell, orders can flow smoothly in sequence, avoiding some of the physical movement around the shop floor that the job shop would require.

If operations managers identify several families of outputs within their process, they can arrange a work cell for each one that includes all of the equipment and facilities needed to make products in that family. The physical layout of a cell reflects the requirements of its particular output. One typical layout creates a *U*-shaped production flow like the one in Exhibit 12.11. Operators work in the middle of the layout, where they perform all tasks necessary to build a unit.

Order Winners.   Cellular manufacturing can achieve both economies of scale comparable to those of a production line and product mix flexibility comparable to that of a job shop. Production can speed through a manufacturing cell in times close to those for a production line, helping a firm to compete on the basis of delivery time more effectively than most jobbing operations. Also, cellular manufacturing offers a number of potential cost savings that may help the firm to compete on the basis of cost, as well.

Physical Resource Mix.   Like most compromises, cellular manufacturing involves certain tradeoffs. Since cells need machines that perform their functions on all or most units of output, they often employ general-purpose equipment. This requirement limits their efficiency as compared to a transfer line with special-purpose equipment, but the cell offers an advantage over a job shop since output

[**EXHIBIT 12.11**]

Manufacturing Cell Layout

similarities limit the mix of production tasks and reduce setup costs. In fact, really similar operations may require no significant changeover or setup time or just minor adjustments. The narrow scope of operations may also justify investments in fixtures that reduce setup times. Also, workers gain process knowledge as they continuously produce similar outputs, and this practice helps them to make changeovers more efficient and reliable. The first unit comes off the line ready for the customer every time.

Because manufacturing cells reduce physical distance between operations, they accumulate less work in process between work stations than a functionally organized shop. Work cells tend to improve quality by offering an opportunity for a visual inspection and verbal communication among cell workers. Also, operators often move parts across these short distances by hand, eliminating the need for extensive materials-handling equipment.

A manufacturing cell needs much less floor space than a job shop to accomplish the same work. In switching to cellular setups, job shops commonly reduce their floor space requirements by 75 percent. One firm in Cedar Falls, Iowa, actually closed one of its two buildings and built a full-court basketball facility for workers in an idle part of its remaining factory. This dramatic reduction in the need for space comes from savings in storage of work-in-process inventory. Recall that a job shop may leave work sitting in queues waiting for processing for 95 percent of its production lead time. Cellular manufacturing dramatically reduces this unproductive time.

Human Resource Mix. Cellular manufacturing often involves job enlargement that calls on operators to perform multiple tasks within the cell. In making the same class of parts over and over again, employees can learn their work thoroughly, or perhaps forget less of it. Most important, however, a worker or a small group of workers gain pride in the cell's workmanship. Work within a cell often enhances the interpersonal skills and team identity of employees. They may meet after work for the cell's own bowling team.

Finally, work cells change the amount and mix of indirect labor in a job shop. Self-directed teams staff many cells, and they need little supervision. Cells need few materials-handling workers because so much movement stays within their boundaries. They need few workers for inventory and production planning because cellular processes accumulate little inventory to track and the production routines make much scheduling automatic. Lastly, cellular manufacturing employs few industrial engineers since it empowers operators within the cells to carry out continuous-improvement programs.

Information System.   Cells do not need elaborate information support. Within the confined area of the cell, workers can easily keep track of orders and equipment, and they can immediately report to others as needed. In a job shop, resources travel throughout the facility and orders move in many patters, producing similarly complicated information flows. Also, workers' familiarity with their processing tasks minimizes their need for instructions. Finally, cellular manufacturing suits process costing which simplifies the task of cost accounting as compared to job-lot cost accounting.

Inventory.   Earlier discussions have described the remarkably small need for work-in-process inventory within a manufacturing cell. High quality and extensive worker knowledge also minimize the need to hold inventory just in case. However, some operations that do not practice JIT may turn out products in advance of need to keep cells busy during lulls in demand. This may result in work-in-process and/or finished-goods inventory.

Adaptability to Change.   Manufacturing processes do not provide gains without costs. Cellular manufacturing can improve mix flexibility within a product family, but the firm must accept some risk of dedicating physical resources to produce outputs that generate insufficient demand. Still, cellular manufacturers often can finance needed additional equipment from savings through reductions in floor space and inventory needs. The "On the Job" box describes some real-world examples in which cellular manufacturing has improved flexibility and helped firms to meet increasingly fragmented customer expectations.

Continuous-Flow Processes

A production line can offer some opportunity to customize a standard base product by adding specific configurations of options. Highly standardized commodity goods do not require even this limited flexibility, however, so a firm can employ an extremely efficient **continuous-flow process** to produce such output. Unlike the processes to produce identical, discrete units of some basic product, continuous-flow processes usually produce streams of undifferentiated materials like liquids, gases, and minerals. Operations managers typically view a production line as a string of connected work stations; they think of continuous processes as a single entity.

continuous-flow process
A category of inflexible manufacturing processes that produces an undifferentiated stream of a highly standardized product

Such a process often divides up its output into discrete chunks. Sugar lines package the product in bags, and chemical manufacturers fill barrels or railroad tank cars. Some continuous-flow processes move their finished goods to market through continuous-flow transportation, as when a refinery pumps processed oil products through a pipeline. A pipeline can, however, transport goods in batches, as well.

Typical Applications.   Clearly, a continuous-flow process can manufacture only a completely standardized good. Such a process might transform one input flow

ON THE JOB

New Assembly Lines in Japan

At a Sony plant in Japan, workers are dismantling conveyor belts on which 50 or so workers had assembled camcorders. Sony is replacing this assembly line with tables arranged in "a snail shaped" configuration. Within each cell, four workers walk through this spiral line, each performing all assembly operations required for an entire camcorder themselves. They are trained to do everything from soldering to product testing. Sony claims that the spiral line has been able to reduce the time required to assemble a camcorder from 70 to 15 minutes.

Cellular manufacturing is emerging as the new industrial standard. In a recent survey by Paul Swamidass of Auburn University, "34 percent of the 1,042 American plants said that they are using assembly cells with 'moderate' or extreme success."

In the era of mass manufacturing, paced assembly lines were hard to beat. Today, in many markets "persnickety consumers and persistently tough competition are pushing companies to add niche items and shorten production cycles." NEC now makes 19 models of cellular and cordless phones, up from 3 ten years ago. The product life cycle of their phones has shrunk from three years to one.

Traditional assembly lines just could not produce this increased product mix variety in an ever-changing environment.

Cellular manufacturing offers firms the capability of making only those items for which orders exist. The goal is to eliminate the need to forecast demand and the investment in WIP and finished goods inventory. Achieving these goals will require major investment in humans. NEC's workers go through one week of intensive training to teach them all 12 manufacturing operations. Compaq requires its computer assemblers to go through 100 hours of training before starting to work in manufacturing cells. It estimates that worker training costs now amount to 5 percent of their annual cost. And it's worth it!

SOURCE   "Some Plants Tear Out Long Assembly Lines and Switch to Craft Work," *The Wall Street Journal,* October 12, 1994, p. 1.

into a series of output flows. Crude oil enters a refinery and removes any number of grades of oil products through the distillation process. Another continuous-flow process might blend together several inputs to produce one output. The U.S. Treasury's printing presses combine ink, magnetic fibers, and paper to feed out continuous sheets of crisp, smudge-free $100 bills.

Order Winners.   These processes produce commodities that normally compete based on price, though some offer unique properties. The Treasury works hard to keep others from duplicating its unique output. Somewhat similarly, a glass manufacturer might generate a product with special properties, and some steel manufacturers compete by developing unique abilities to meet specialized metallurgical needs. Suppliers of silicon to the semiconductor industry compete on the basis of quality since minute defects can make a chip worthless. Within the limits of acceptable product characteristics, however, the firm with the lowest processing cost usually prospers most in such a market.

Physical Resource Mix.   Continuous-flow processes tend to be the most capital intensive of any manufacturing systems. These facilities often employ narrowly specialized processing equipment designed to achieve carefully balanced through-put rates from specified inputs to fill specified storage capacities. An oil refinery design seeks to efficiently process a specific type of crude oil into a targeted blend of outputs; the same process may fail to correctly process crude from a different source with a different chemical composition, or it may process the input only with a substantial drop in efficiency. If the inputs to such a process are changed, the resulting capabilities mismatch will normally result in system performance below the plant's design capacity.

Continuous-flow processes use product layouts that arrange equipment to facilitate the flow of raw materials through processing steps into the finished product or products. The locations of continuous-flow processes often depend on the locations of raw materials sources, transportation economics, or environmental issues.

Human Resources Mix.   Continuous-flow processes need employees with training in their particular technology. Most rely extensively on automated processing steps, so they need few workers with specialized product and process knowledge to keep things running smoothly. These characteristics define a centralized organization structure with bureaucratic management styles.

Information System.   Managers of a continuous-flow process collect information that helps them to maintain process control. Often, they monitor conditions at stages throughout the process from a single, centralized facility; if instruments indicate some deviation from the routine, they can intervene to maintain quality. Automation influences this process through closed-loop systems that automatically adjust operations based on automatic readings and responses, frequently under computer control.

Such an information system must also document product and process characteristics over time. Buyers often demand documentation of the conditions under which a process generates a given product. Process documentation may also demonstrate compliance with environmental standards, as when a firm must show air-quality regulators how much of a given pollutant it has released over a period of time.

Adaptability to Change.   Continuous-flow processes cannot tolerate much variance. They perform limited, specialized functions to produce standardized product mixes. To recover the investment in expensive equipment, they generally operate at close to capacity at all times.

AUTOMATION IN MANUFACTURING PROCESSES

Manufacturing processes and service systems alike rely increasingly on one or more forms of **automation**. John Diebold and D. S. Harder coined this term in 1947 to refer to any self-powered and self-guiding or self-correcting mechanism. In its earlier development, operations managers viewed automation primarily as a replacement for human labor much as machines had done during the industrial revolution. Early robots took over routine materials-handling functions such as moving subassemblies between machines.

automation

A self-powered and self-guiding or self-correcting mechanism

Initially, automation seemed to offer a partial solution to acrimonious labor relations by replacing unionized workers with nonunionized robots and by reducing the skill levels of remaining employees to weaken craft unions, which represented the most skilled members of the work force. In the same way, applications of numerical-control technology sought to encode the skills of the machinist and teach them to more pliable machines. This attempt to reduce labor intensity created a need for some new programming skills, but nonunionized, white-collar systems analysts performed this work. This led to widespread resentment of automation and a perception that it posed a threat to workers' jobs.

While this attitude remains active today, wider perceptions of automation have expanded the limits of this thinking. For one important change, many manufacturing processes now need to maintain extremely flexible product and process capabilities. Fortunately, technological advances have fueled development of vastly more flexible automation systems than earlier systems would allow. Today's flexible automation can provide many cost advantages that firms could achieve previously only through high-volume, hard automation systems; at the same time, modern systems maintain much of the product and process flexibility of a job shop.

Besides replacing less efficient types of processes, automation offers the potential to significantly enhance the capabilities of existing ones. As their understanding of the causes of process variability improves, many process designers see automation as one tool for controlling or eliminating those causes. For example, products continually get smaller, severely challenging the abilities of the human hand to perform detailed tasks, especially in the world of electronics. Automated systems can perform many such tasks more effectively than human workers, unionized or not.

Preautomation

preautomation

An effort to simplify process activities sufficiently to prepare the workplace for effective automation

Automation offers one alternative for solving problems with process variability, but it is neither the only one nor the most important. Actually, process designers should try automation only after considering other, cheaper alternatives to redesign or reinvent a business process. A blind rush toward automation may lead only to costly investments that efficiently automate existing wasteful practices. To prevent this mistake, a rigorous **preautomation** effort should seek to simplify process activities sufficiently to prepare the workplace for effective automation.

Preautomation seeks to reduce waste in two ways. First, it tries to place all process resources as close together as possible. Effective automation should provide both humans and automatons with everything they need to do their jobs within a small area. In particular, process designers should look at any proposal to automate existing materials-handling activities with an extremely skeptical eye. Careful consideration of the reasons for moving materials and subassemblies should reveal the root causes for transportation activities. Moving machines and processes might more effectively solve the same problems.

Preautomation reduces waste in a second way suggested by an old proverb: "Everything has its proper place." An automation initiative will have to give instructions to tell robots where to find everything they need. People are flexible enough to tolerate sloppy instructions that would completely confound robots. This step often leaves operations managers stunned by the amount of waste that they have unwittingly tolerated.

Richard Schonberger cautions against rushing to automate processes before identifying and exploiting opportunities to reduce waste. He suggests a step after preautomation that he calls *low-grade process automation.* As an ardent advocate of just-in-time manufacturing, Schonberger refers to low-grade automation as a "problem pull rather than a technology push strategy." He defines this step as an incremental method of implementing automation that proceeds "step-by-step via installation of one low-grade device after another." Throughout this process, the firm should celebrate the vitality of shop-floor operators—often the very employees whose jobs risk elimination in fast-track automation projects.

A skeptic might see this process as a request that workers participate in planning the elimination of their jobs or massive enlargement of their duties without comparable enhancements in their pay. This criticism highlights a weak point of many automation projects: they seek to solve organization-design problems simply by investing more money. The remaining humans in the system will still determine much about its effectiveness. In such a horse race, a wise bettor would place money on a blue-collar nag rather than a stallion with an MBA.

"People have one attribute that makes them superior to any machine: brain power. Without brain power in the workplace, further process improvement would come to a halt."

Richard J. Schonberger

Flexible Manufacturing through Automation

A more productive attitude looks for opportunities to enhance effectiveness through automation, and effectiveness requires flexibility in today's market. Process designers no longer choose whether or not to employ flexible technology, but how to build flexibility into an envisioned system. They cannot automatically pursue this goal either, however; cost still governs many choices, and process flexibility can be costly. To justify this cost, a system needs focused flexibility, that is, flexibility that serves a real business need.

A history of the development of flexible manufacturing over the last 20 years illustrates this application of automation to combine advances in computer control on the shop floor with automated methods for materials handling and setup reduction. In the 1960s, the Air Force wanted to advance state-of-the-art machining practices. A Michigan inventor, Fred Harris, proposed a system to control machining operations by a paper tape, much as perforated rolls of paper had run player pianos. The Air Force took this idea to MIT, which seemed to offer the necessary process capability to refine and develop it further. The resulting numerically controlled lathe excited the Air Force but stimulated little interest in the civilian sector.

At about the same time, industrial engineers were developing automated materials-handling systems. With fixtures that held parts much like a saucer holds a cup, these systems offered another way to make setups external to machining centers. Workers could affix subassemblies to fixtures at a setup area and send them to machining centers on automated guided vehicles; these vehicles transferred the fixtures to a shuttle queue that delivered them to the machine for processing. A reference point on either the subassembly or the pallet indicated to the machine the proper positioning, confirmed by automated measuring devices. Humans take for granted their ability to spot errors before they occur, but early automation systems needed elaborate precautions to spot mistakes as astutely as humans.

Up to this point, automation amounts to no more than an advanced transfer line. Under the guidance of Schonberger's principle of low-grade automation, development of flexible methods might have stopped at this point. A new innovation propelled it further, however, by routing parts to machines in a flexible manner so that jobs could follow any possible route from any one machine to any

Two Major Components of an FMS

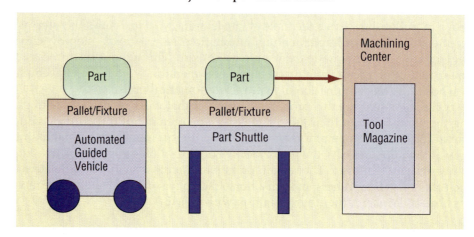

other. This system promised the same capabilities as a job shop, except for the ability to change tools.

This final ingredient of a truly flexible automation system arrived when a number of machine suppliers started to build what they called *machining centers.* These new machines offered the critical ability to switch tools, much as a surgical nurse hands instruments to the doctor during an operation.

Together, the automated materials-handling, measuring, and tool-changing systems completed what became known as a **flexible manufacturing system** (FMS). Exhibit 12.12 shows a sketch of two of these major components. The automated guided vehicle carries the fixture with the mounted subassembly to the machining center. The part shuttle positions this fixture at the machining center. The tool magazine holds an inventory of drill bits, cutting tools, etc. that define that center's capabilities.

Exhibit 12.13 shows the continuing process. The line around the perimeter of the work area indicates a track that guides the AGVs between the load/unload stations and the machining centers. After Machining Center 2 completes its job, the AGV picks up the completed part and heads to a load-station queue to wait until Machining Center 3 becomes free. It then carries the part there for further processing and continues with its next programmed task.

This FMS achieves flexible automation in a number of ways. First, the materials-handling system can take a part from any machine to any other machine. The example assumed that the automated guided vehicles followed a track. In another system, AGVs might follow wires in the floor or even a navigational guidance system. Other flexible manufacturing systems replace these AGVs with smart conveyors. As for any emerging technology, an FMS can move materials in many ways.

The equipment at the machining centers provides a second source of flexibility. An FMS tends to employ general-purpose equipment that can perform a wide variety of operations. This choice requires a tradeoff between the machining efficiencies of special-purpose equipment against the ability to produce a wider range of part types.

This flexibility allows many variations of parts designs within a single **parts family design envelope** defined by the limits of the FMS. Manufacturing and

flexible manufacturing system

An automation system with capabilities to process work as varied as a job shop with minimal direct human intervention

part family design envelope

A set of characteristics required of new parts for production within a flexible manufacturing system

[**E X H I B I T   1 2 . 1 3**]

Flexible Manufacturing System

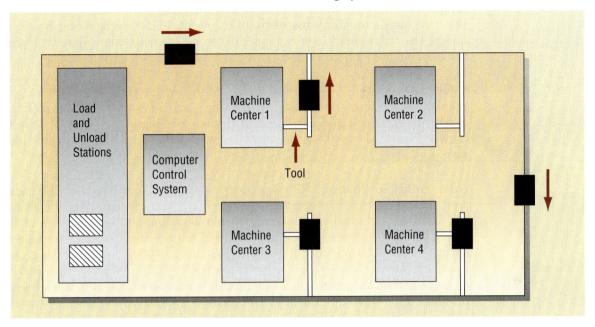

engineering standards require new part designs that conform to the machining and transportation capabilities of the FMS.

Typical Applications.   Flexible manufacturing systems work best for processes that must produce in moderate volumes, as the process category matrix in Exhibit 12.6 indicated. Such systems produce parts as needed because demand volume creates few economies of scale. Makers of farming and industrial equipment pioneered the development of FMS, along with aerospace manufacturers. More recently, high-volume manufacturers have implemented these systems as part of just-in-time strategies to add flexible capacity to their supply chains.

An FMS might offer a strong potential to produce replacement parts. Those parts must fit within the appropriate part family, however, so they fit the fixtures of the FMS. Redesigning fixtures and other equipment proves prohibitively expensive, so the part designs must reflect this limitation.

Order Winners.   A flexible manufacturing system helps a firm to compete on the basis of design flexibility and speed. An FMS can generally complete processing of an order in around 5 times the actual duration of machining operations. This compares very favorably with the usual standard for job shops of 20 or more times.

Human Resource Mix.   Flexible manufacturing systems pose their own problems for human resources management. They may contribute to the reduction in skill levels of machine-operator positions, transferring control to central systems operators. These systems may complicate employee relations further by placing red, yellow, and green lights above machining centers to indicate throughout the plant when someone's machine quits functioning.

Part of this problem began with the designs of early systems. Systems operators quite commonly worked in air-conditioned control rooms, supervising operations via phone like absentee landlords. This attitude is changing. Most new systems limit the scale of control and assign more responsibility to machine operators. These workers know what their equipment needs. In fact, recognizing employees' insight into the best match between work and assignment, one successful FMS site actually had the work force decide who would staff a new installation.

Information System.   A flexible manufacturing system resembles a job shop, and it has similar information needs. If anything, such a system needs simpler information because the computer control routine automatically records all system transactions. Most installations collect too much data and perform too little analysis of it.

Adaptability to Change.   Of all process categories, flexible manufacturing systems should offer the best opportunity for adjusting to new conditions. They often fall short of this ideal because investment decisions limit the ranges of their responses. Early systems commonly included fixtures that held only a single part each. Such special-purpose fixtures could cost $10,000 each, so firms resisted buying too many. As a result, a typical system could build only eight different types of parts. One retired plant manager did not resent this limit since the FMS performed the work that the firm needed much more cheaply that its other alternative: building three separate transfer lines.

Cost accounting also limits the adaptability of some flexible manufacturing systems. To avoid high startup costs for fixtures, programming, etc., some plants send new jobs to job shops that can fill the orders more cost effectively over the short term. To solve this problem, operations managers must design process flexibility into the system from the onset. Computer-integrated design capabilities can bridge product innovation and engineering to avoid excessive costs for redesigning parts to accommodate fixtures and other FMS requirements. A single system should integrate design, prototype production, and final manufacturing to make the optimum choices at every stage, but this requires extensive cross-functional communication and cooperation between designers and engineers.

As flexible manufacturing systems have evolved, they have implemented their principles with more flexibility. They have developed from space-age investments that try to automate every movement. Newer, smaller FMSs tend to create modular operations to make standardized components. Some firms no longer use the term *flexible manufacturing system;* instead, they set up automated manufacturing cells.

 ## PROCESS CATEGORIES AND THE PRODUCT LIFE CYCLE

The practical choice of a process model depends on available technology and customer needs, for two important criteria. It also depends on the characteristics of the product.

The discussion of product innovation in Chapter 11 outlined the changing needs of a product as it matures. Early in its product life cycle, its design and production volume may change drastically with engineering changes and market developments. Demand forecasts may fail to predict the many unknown developments with any accuracy. Operations managers regard new products as moving targets; they respond by keeping options open and waiting to invest in special-purpose equipment unless they have no choice.

During this early stage, the firm must often invest heavily to establish the service component of the product. It must arrange to answer questions raised by both end users and members of the distribution channel. If they fail, poor customer-service response times may negate the value of an otherwise high-quality product. When they introduce new products, firms must listen carefully to customers to recognize the need for small but important refinements.

As products mature, market action resolves these uncertainties. The firm can judge the advisability of process investments based on hard information. Early requirements for technical support give way to needs for process development and refinement. A product will make the most money at this stage, while production costs should decline.

After a product matures, marketers begin predicting declining demand. The pattern of the decline depends, of course, on the actions of the firm and its competitors. This creates a classic forecasting problem, as manufacturing managers start thinking carefully about whether or how to make a part. They may begin to abandon investments in special-purpose systems for high-volume production in favor of processes that better suit lower-volume production. This may require production in a job shop, someone else's job shop, or even an FMS.

CHAPTER SUMMARY

Product innovation and process innovation involve closely related activities. We have covered them in separate chapters, but firms actually conduct these activities in parallel. Both start with a well-defined understanding of what the firm must do to delight its target customers.

1. To create an OM system that provides a service, process designers must carefully evaluate the characteristics of the customers for that service, the object that will receive service, the system's interactions with customers, and the possibility of implementing the new system through existing delivery channels.
2. The intangible nature of services complicates analysis and focuses attention on the service-delivery transaction. The total service experience determines how well the firm delights its customers.
3. In developing either a service-delivery system or a manufacturing system, process designers often begin with some well-known models of typical OM systems. Production-line service delivery provides a standardized, carefully ordered system for rapidly delivering a uniform, high-quality service product. In customer-involvement service delivery, customers complete many of the tasks that form part of the service. In personal-attention service delivery, an individualized system seeks to delight customers by catering to their specific needs.
4. Attribute mapping and service blueprinting, among many other analytical techniques, help process designers to understand the needs of their customers and the best methods by which to satisfy them.
5. Automation and information technology have enhanced many service delivery systems, especially those that invite customer involvement, but employee performance still determines service quality.
6. The tangible products, less visible operations, and repetitive activities of manufacturing systems add clarity to process design, although specific organizations

adapt these models to suit individual circumstances. These systems consist of typical arrangements of standard types of resources, including tools, fixtures, general-purpose and special-purpose machines, workers, transportation devices like AGVs and conveyors, inventory, and information systems.

7. The project form of manufacturing completes a single job at a site other than the firm's facilities. Jobbing operations, including large job shops, irregularly produce relatively few units of their products, usually through process layouts. Batch production groups orders together and produces them in extended batches, often through product layouts. Line production arranges special-purpose machines and equipment in a rigid sequence, such as a familiar assembly line, to perform repetitive tasks for large orders. Cellular manufacturing produces a family of similar outputs, one at a time, by linking together all possible operations in the required process. Finally, continuous flow processes produce undifferentiated streams of highly standardized products.

8. Automation tries either to replace workers with sophisticated, usually computer-controlled machines or to enhance process capabilities by adding these machines to existing system resources. Flexible manufacturing systems adapt the second form of automation to create processes that combine the adaptability of job shops with the efficiency of production lines.

[**KEY TERMS**]

service dispenser 549
production-line service delivery 551
customer-involvement service delivery 553
personal-attention service delivery 554
service blueprinting 555
line of visibility 556
actual tool 564
fixture 564
machine (machining center) 564
numerically controlled machine 564

transporter 565
automated guided vehicle 565
project 566
jobbing 569
process layout 571
labor-limited job shop 571
batch production 574
product layout 575
process costing 577
line production 578
mixed-model production line 578
transfer line 578

assembly line balancing problem 582
cellular manufacturing 584
product family 584
continuous-flow process 587
automation 589
preautomation 590
flexible manufacturing system 592
part family design envelope 592

[**DISCUSSION QUESTIONS**]

1. What problems do you encounter when you separate the product innovation process from the process design process, i.e., that part of the operations management system that is responsible for designing the product delivery process? Discuss.

2. How does the process design process differ between a service delivery system and a manufactured goods delivery system?

3. Discuss the interaction points between operations and marketing in the process design process. Should marketing be more or less involved when the product bundle leans in the direction of the service component?

4. For each of the following situations, classify the following typical customers. Speculate on the nature of the typical customer's value equation.
   a. A person who searches for garage sales
   b. A person who shops on Home Shopping Channel
   c. A person who routine reads the newpaper want ads
   d. A person who buys college textbooks for a course

5. Forty years ago, the Automat, a revolutionary form of food establishment, was created in Manhattan. Customers viewed food behind glass windows. They inserted nickels in a slot to the right of items they wanted to buy. The door was unlocked so that the food could be removed. Automats today are either closed or replaced by fast-food restaurants. What changes in technology and customer values might have caused the decline and demise of Automats?

6. Many years ago, the head of General Motors said, "If you want a cheap car, buy a used one." Analyze used-car business processes. List some of the likes and dislikes of the typical customer shopping for a used car. Can this merchandise be moved to profitably delight customers? How would you propose doing this?

7. Prepare a service blueprint of each of the following service experiences:
   a. You take your car to a Jiffy-Lube to have its oil changed.
   b. You take your car to your insurance agent to show the extent of recent vandalism.
   c. You go to your nearest Chevy dealer to buy a new Monte Carlo.
   d. You take a midterm examination in your local POM course.

8. Cite five automated forms of service that you routinely receive and five personalized forms of service that your receive. How does your value set influence the extent to which these services satisfy your needs? Did a lack of personal attention influence your response?

9. A classic problem at the grade school level is a lack of communication between parent and teacher. Apply one or more of the concepts discussed in this chapter to this problem. Can you think of a solution to this problem? Be specific.

10. Discuss the demands each of the classic forms of production have on each of the following corporate resources:
    a. Staffing, i.e., amount and skill profile
    b. Finished goods warehouse capacity
    c. Cost accounting
    d. Manufacturing plant square footage required
    e. Post-sale customer support

11. Describe an unpleasant experience that you have recently had with both a service and a manufactured good. What flaws in the product delivery system may have caused these unpleasant experiences? What remedial steps would you recommend?

12. On a recent multiple-choice exam, you were asked to classify the following question as being either true or false: "The job shop is the most costly process choice." Is this generalization true or false? Under what conditions might it be true, and under what conditions might it be false?

CAUTION

[CRITICAL THINKING REQUIRED]

1. This chapter has discussed the decline of mass manufacturing, an approach that made America the envy of the world thoughout many of the postwar years. What product markets is it still the best approach for? To manufacturing or providing services? What attributes do these markets have?
2. In what business circumstances would the voice of the customer not always be constructive? Why?

CASE 12.1

Best Bank in America

In 1995, *Money* magazine named an unusual bank as the best in America. To earn this distinction, the bank offered:

- Rock-solid safety
- Free checking services regardless of account balance
- Market-leading credit card deals, with no annual fees and low interest rates (13.04 percent on May 1, 1995, with a national average of 18.00 percent)
- Five withdrawals per month free of service charges from any ATM
- Generous yields on CDs and savings accounts
- Bargain interest rates on car loans and mortgages
- Nationwide service

Customers found this fine service at a bank located in San Antonio, Texas. This location did not deter customers across the country from opening accounts there, however, because virtually all of them conducted business over the telephone or personal computer links. Retail banks assumed that they needed well-placed branches to serve their customers' needs, but this bank had no physical locations. In another sense, however, every touch-tone telephone amounted to a branch. For $14.95, the bank sold software that would permit customers to pay bills, check account balances, and transfer funds via computer.

The institution, USAA Federal Savings Bank, grew from the business of USAA Corporation, an auto insurance provider that served current and former members of the military. Since these customers moved frequently from base to base, the company needed capabilities to serve them at their remote and changeable locations. Over the years, USAA expanded the scope of its service to its unique market by offering property and casualty insurance, life insurance, no-load mutual funds, and discount stock brokerage service. Ultimately, the firm added a federally chartered savings bank to this list. Today, this bank handles 30,000 calls each day on 150 toll-free phone lines staffed by 370 customer-service reps.

The capabilities that USAA developed to serve its far-flung insurance customers gave it a cost advantage over rivals for those people's banking business. IDC Financial Publishing has reported that USAA Federal generated operating expenses as a percentage of revenue 40 percent lower than the average bank. The institution's president, Jack Antonini, said, "We offer customers low prices because we don't have to spend a lot on marketing or brick and mortar."

While USAA has beat its competitors at the business of electronic banking, it faces a stiff challenge to retain the loyalty of its customers. No-nonsense, nationwide service has delighted military personnel and veterans, but most of the bank's 142,000 customers now come from civilian life. These less mobile people may not need a bank to follow them around the country, reducing the competitive advantage of USAA's customer-service system. Each week customers hear appeals from firms that offer unusual benefits like credit toward car purchases based on credit-card purchase volume, free air-travel miles, etc. USAA must try to maintain its competitive edge as other firms try to duplicate its success via the information highway.

QUESTIONS

1. As a civilian customer, how would you value the banking services that USAA offers?
2. Prepare a service blueprint of the firm's banking operations with as much detail as the case information allows.
3. What new forms of competition will USAA face in the future?
4. What changes should USAA make to its service-delivery system?

SOURCE   Vanessa O'Connell, "The Best Bank in America," *Money*, June 1995, p. 126.

CASE 12.2

Multimedia Mary

This semester, you are taking a managerial accounting course from Professor Mary Kern, one of the most remarkably prepared persons that you have ever had—that's the good news. The bad news is that Kern is a multimedia guru. All communications with her outside of class must take place in a prerecorded interactive environment. In class, she is live and a teaching pro. But outside of class, she uses an elaborate Internet-based system to perform all of her other classroom-related matters. She has prerecorded a response to almost every question that you might have. If her expert system cannnot respond to a question, she will respond via Internet within 24 hours.

Kern's exams are essay questions. An expert system grades them and transmits a meaningful response to the course's Internet home-page within 24 hours. (Each student has a password that assures student privacy.) While this procedure seems cold, the critiques provide far more feedback than some other instructors supply. You can challenge responses using the home-page grievance procedure, and Kern responds in one week via the network. Homework solutions and trial exam exercises are also available on the home-page.

QUESTIONS

1. What do you see as the pros and cons of Kern's educational process?
2. Would you recommend Kern to your friends? Why?
3. What can Kern do to make her course a more meaningful learning experience?

[SELECTED READINGS]

Fitzsimmons, J. A. *Service Management for Competitive Advantage*. New York: McGraw-Hill, 1994.

Hall, Robert. *The Soul of the Enterprise*. New York: Harper Business, 1993.

Hill, Terry. *Manufacturing Strategy*. Homewood, Ill.: Richard D. Irwin, 1989.

Melnyk, S. A., and R. Narasimhan. *Computer-Integrated Manufacturing*. Homewood, Ill.: Business-One/Irwin, 1992.

Skinner, Wickham. "The Focused Factory." *Harvard Business Review*, May–June 1974.

CHAPTER THIRTEEN

Supply Chain Management

CHAPTER OBJECTIVES

[At the end of this chapter, you should be able to]

- Explain the concepts of a supplier, a firm's supply base, and supply chain management.
- Outline the supplier's contributions to the value-driven OM system.
- Differentiate the internal factory from the external factory.
- Trace the interactions among purchasing managers, suppliers, and operations managers.
- Describe the increasingly important role of a firm's supply chain in its OM system.
- Illustrate the shift in buyer-supplier relationships due to outsourcing to outpartnering.
- Apply four major process tools—make-buy analysis, supplier scheduling, value analysis/value engineering, and supplier certification/evaluation—to supply chain management situations.

Elizabeth Sher
Goodwin

Chrysler Unseats Its Competition with Supplier Partnerships

WHEN LEE IACOCCA GAVE THE GO-ahead to Chrysler's Neon project in 1990, he was taking a big risk. Until that time, no American subcompact car had been able to turn a profit for its manufacturer. But Chrysler's Neon ultimately reversed this trend, thanks largely to the unprecedented partnerships Chrysler entered into with its suppliers in the earliest stages of the Neon project.

Robert Marcell, head of Chrysler's small-car division, knew that such partnerships held the key to Chrysler's success. In order to make a profit, Marcell had to meet stringent production deadlines, and that meant bringing suppliers on board early. After all, outside companies would be furnishing 70 percent of the value of the car in the form of tires, seats, suspension, and other components.

In an unprecedented move, Marcell allowed engineers from key potential suppliers to drive the first Neon prototype during an October 1990 meeting. His team then issued a cost challenge, inviting suppliers to make use of sensitive Chrysler financial data and ideas in a mutual effort to cut costs.

Companies that signed on to this unique partnership soon found that collaborating with Chrysler was a two-way street. For example,

Johnson Controls, Inc., was initially able to make the Neon's seats within Chrysler's price targets, but Chrysler was unhappy with their safety, weight, and comfort. Before Johnson Controls engineers knew it, ten Chrysler engineers had virtually moved into their glass-and-brick building west of Detroit to work out these issues. After working five long days together the partners agreed on new weight, cost, and performance standards that were so on target that they didn't need to be changed again.

This unique partnership also allowed Chrysler to accept higher component costs from Johnson Controls because they translated into savings overall. At Chrysler's request, Johnson designed some rear seats with the capability of folding down to expand trunk space. But Chrysler engineers insisted that Johnson design the special seats so they could be installed in the same way as other seats. This made each seat cost more, but Chrysler ended up saving about $1 million overall in final assembly costs. Thanks to its successful partnership with Johnson Controls and other major suppliers, Chrysler met its stringent cost and time deadlines for the Neon—and came out with Detroit's first profitable subcompact car in the bargain.

SOURCE

David Woodruff and Karen Lowry Miller, "Chrysler's NEON: Is This the Small Car Detroit Couldn't Build?" *Business Week,* May 3, 1993 (Number 3317), pp. 116–126.

In developing and building Chrysler's Neon model, the firm's operations managers abandoned the traditional boundaries of their own factories, called the *internal factory* by some, to draw critical input and commitment from suppliers. They integrated their work with that of suppliers so closely that the outside firms' facilities came to function as *external factories* within a larger system developed specifically to produce a car that would delight customers. To borrow phrases from Tom Peters, Chrysler moved from outsourcing, buying inputs from other firms instead of making them in-house, to outpartnering, or building intimate relationships with suppliers for the mutual benefit of all.[1]

Many organizations have joined Chrysler in this pursuit, including Motorola, Ford, Intel, Xerox, Apple Computers, Kingston Technologies, Marriott Hotels, and Nintendo.[2] Some view this trend as evidence of a fundamental change in the corporate structure of business. They call the resulting hybrid organizations *virtual corporations.*[3]

In this chapter, we present a management framework for supply chain management, including an overview of the contributions that suppliers make to the OM system and the firm as a whole. They bring unique core competencies that can complement the firm's own capabilities to enhance overall value. As part of this discussion, we compare the traditional and emerging roles of supplier management and identify the causes of this transformation, which culminates in the development of virtual corporations. In addition, we discuss several analytical tools for

[1]Tom Peters, *The Tom Peters Seminar: Crazy Times Call for Crazy Organizations* (New York: Vintage Books, 1994), p. 144.

[2]Richard Brandt, "Is Nintendo a Street Fighter Now?" *Business Week,* August 29, 1994, p. 35.

[3]William H. Davidow and Michael S. Malone, *The Virtual Corporation: Structuring and Revitalizing the Corporation for the 21st Century* (New York: Harper Business, 1992).

[**EXHIBIT 13.1**]

Supplier Contributions to the OM System

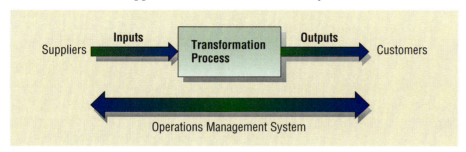

effective supply chain management, including total cost analysis (as introduced and discussed in Chapter 4), make/buy analysis, value engineering, and supplier certification.

OVERVIEW OF SUPPLY CHAIN MANAGEMENT

Every OM system operates a transformation process that changes inputs to make its products (Exhibit 13.1). Ultimately, every operations manager for any firm, service organization or manufacturer, public or private, must obtain materials, expertise, and services from organizations outside the firm. These **suppliers** contribute wide varieties of inputs, as Exhibit 13.2 illustrates.

supplier
An organization outside the firm that provides essential inputs of materials, expertise, and services to an OM system

Benefits from Suppliers

Even if a company could internally generate all of the inputs it would need to make its product, it should consider buying some from suppliers instead for several compelling reasons.

Lower Costs.   No firm can produce every good and service that it needs at a lower cost than other, more specialized firms. For example, to become the lowest-cost producer of computer chips, Compaq would have to make significant investments in research and development and in equipment and technology. Also, it would have to produce higher volumes than its internal demand could consume to justify these investments. Instead, Compaq and other microcomputer manufacturers can save money by purchasing chips from a supplier like Intel that has the specialized resources, facilities, and expertise to produce them at the lowest possible cost.

Better Flexibility.   To supply all inputs through internal production, the firm would have to invest heavily in additional resources, and these expenditures would limit its ability to adapt to change. The costs of new facilities and equipment, supporting infrastructures like information systems, and additional skilled personnel all increase overhead (fixed costs). The firm would have to divest and redeploy all of these resources to respond quickly to changes in the quantity demanded or product mix, slowing its reaction time. Instead, it might simply purchase different inputs from suppliers to make the same adjustments.

[**E X H I B I T   1 3 . 2**]

Range of Supplier Inputs

Items Provided	Examples
Goods	
Raw materials	Steel for Chrysler cars
Components	Intel computer chips for Compaq
Maintenance, repair and operating (MRO) items (e.g., oil, grease, gloves, paper clips)	Pads of paper from an office supply store
Equipment	Cincinnati Milacron milling machines for Chrysler
Energy	Consolidated Edison electricity
Packaging	Dart disposable coffee cups
Services	
Custodial/maintenance services	Plant care for office foliage
Waste disposal	Waste Management recycling collections
Food processing	Catering
Data processing	Time sharing
Temporary employees	Kelly Temporary Services®
Consulting	Andersen Consulting
Expertise/Knowledge	
Concurrent engineering	Johnson Controls, Inc., design for Neon seats
Problem solving	

Higher Quality.   Suppliers can frequently provide better inputs for an OM system than a firm could make on its own. The supplier of a car radio specializes in that product, so it can learn to produce a reliable model with attractive features. For this reason, Chevrolet buys Bose sound systems for its Corvettes and Saab installs Clarion radios in its cars.

Market Perceptions of Higher Quality.   In addition, inputs from suppliers with strong reputations for quality lead customers to attribute the same value to products that include those components. Microcomputer buyers confidently purchase machines from local manufacturers that lack the resources of Compaq or IBM because those buyers recognize the value of components from Intel, Seagate, and Sony. By including these high-quality components, a manufacturer can give its product a strong quality image.

Easier Availability of Excess Capacity.   To react to a change in demand, a self-sufficient firm would have to adjust its internal capacity to match. By subcontracting for inputs from suppliers, however, it can simply buy more or less, as needed. In effect, it can use suppliers' OM systems as sources of quick excess capacity in times of strong demand without the burden of paying for wasted capacity when demand declines. Finally, the ability to meet excess demand quickly may reduce the risk of potential customers buying from competitors, instead.

Newer Technology.   A supplier's specialized focus and large production volume justifies investments in the most recent technology and processes. That supplier's customer benefits from these advances without the risk of costly investments in rapidly obsolete equipment. For example, microcomputer producers buy microchips from Intel because it offers products created in state-of-the-art processes and technologies.

Broader Access to Technical Expertise.   Suppliers often develop expertise in their businesses that can improve the products of their customers. For example, Chrysler contracted with Johnson Controls Inc. (JCI) to improve its Neon model by tapping the supplier's widely acknowledged expertise in the design and manufacture of car seats.

Better Market Information.   Suppliers often serve multiple customers and work in many markets, giving them access to a great deal of information. Suppliers can provide a firm with valuable intelligence about new technological developments, its competitors' actions, labor-management relations, and customer behavior, both in its own markets and in more distant but related ones.

Sharper Focus on Core Competencies.   Operations managers face a daily challenge of making the most efficient use of their system's resources. Success often depends on targeting investments to enhance certain critical skills and capabilities, or core competencies, as we discuss later in this chapter. These capabilities determine how well the firm provides and redefines value for its customers, and spreading efforts among less important activities risks dissipating the firm's energies and weakening its critical skills. For this reason, operations managers often look to suppliers for inputs outside their firm's core competencies.

Wider Perspectives.   Along with its products, a supplier can provide an image of the firm from an outside perspective. Activities that make sense to people inside the firm may look quite different to outside observers. Some firms actively seek this kind of criticism of current processes and practices from suppliers. Apple Computer asks certain suppliers for input to avoid complacency and self-satisfaction among employees who feel pride in their achievements that may obscure opportunities for further improvement.[4]

More Active Social Roles.   Finally, as part of every firm's social responsibilities and obligations, it must encourage the success of minority-owned businesses. It can fulfill this obligation in part by buying products from minority-owned suppliers.

Spectrum of Supplier Relationships

The spectrum in Exhibit 13.3 illustrates the range of activities, services, and functions for which a firm relies on suppliers. At one end, through **product buys**, or **capacity buys**, suppliers provide access to low-cost, high-quality inputs that can enhance a firm's own name recognition and excess production capacity. These purchases essentially substitute external inputs for internal production. At this end of the spectrum, economic considerations drive the purchase decision; the firm buys from suppliers when they can provide inputs more cheaply than it could make them itself through internal processes.

   At the other end, **process buys**, or **capability buys**, bring many important benefits to the purchaser, including better flexibility, newer technology, broader

product (capacity) buy
A relatively low-cost, high-quality purchase of inputs from external suppliers as a substitute for internal production

process (capability) buy
A purchase that results from an intimate relationship between the knowledge bases, capabilities, and processes of two firms

[4]Peters, *Seminar*, Chapter 4.

[**EXHIBIT 13.3**]

Spectrum of Supplier Activities

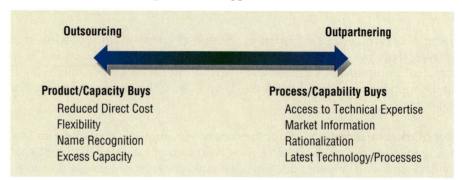

technical expertise, better market information, sharper focus on core competencies, a wider perspective on internal activities, and a more active social role. These intimate involvements between the knowledge bases, capabilities, and processes of two firms make the relationship far more complex and difficult to manage than a simple product buy.

A product buy creates an arm's-length relationship in which the operations manager identifies the OM system's need and shops for it among suppliers. For example, a Chrysler manager might determine that the current schedule of car production creates a need for 20,000 tires next week. The manager communicates this requirement to a supplier which arranges for delivery of the tires without much interaction beyond the placement of orders and receipt of products.

In contrast, a process buy results from a close relationship between the OM system and the supplier. The supplier must understand in detail the needs of its customer, including the exact nature of the problems and symptoms that its personnel encounter. In turn, the operations manager must clearly understand the capabilities and limitations of the supplier. Awareness of conditions throughout both firms' processes help them to work together in a trusting relationship like the one that developed between Johnson Controls, Inc., and Chrysler during the development of the Neon.

Today's operations managers describe product buys with the term **outsourcing**. They describe process buys as **outpartnering**. Supplier relationships in many organizations are moving rapidly from the first toward the second.

outsourcing

The practice of buying inputs from suppliers without much involvement beyond ordering and receiving procedures

outpartnering

The practice of buying inputs from suppliers as part of a deep and continuing relationship between two firms

purchasing

The organizational function that acts as an intermediary between the OM system and its suppliers

 ## PURCHASING: THE LINK BETWEEN SUPPLIERS AND THE OM SYSTEM

In practice, just about any OM system develops close links with its suppliers, and each becomes highly dependent on the other (Exhibit 13.4). As part of this relationship, however, almost all operations managers must work with suppliers through intermediaries in the **purchasing** function.

Purchasing staff members usually manage all relationships with suppliers and arrange all orders for OM system inputs. They make final decisions about what the firm buys, from whom it buys, and the terms and conditions of payment. In this

[EXHIBIT 13.4]

Interdependence between OM System and Supplier

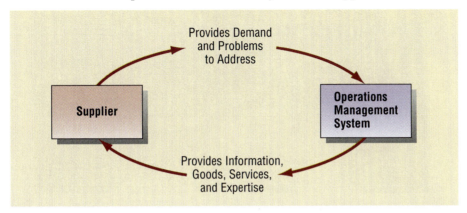

work, these organization members manage an important asset—knowledge of the firm's needs and the capabilities of various suppliers.

These statements do not imply dictatorial control of input purchases, though. Operations managers, suppliers' representatives, and purchasing agents or managers work together to ensure productive interactions between the firm and its suppliers (Exhibit 13.5). These people form a sort of cross-functional team that expands this familiar concept to reach across the boundaries of both organizations.

Purchasing contributes to this effort by representing the firm as a customer. The organization needs this help because it spends much more money than individuals, and it needs vastly different products which it buys in different ways. This work requires specialists who develop and master specific skills and capabilities. If nothing else, organizational purchases create many detailed tasks such as clerical work and information exchanges that require dedicated staff members for effective management.

[EXHIBIT 13.5]

Major Players in Supply Management

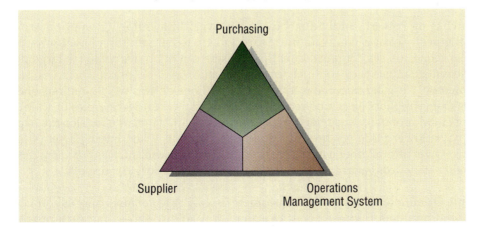

Companies like Wal-Mart use their purchasing power to stock huge volumes of product, and remain competitive by offering customers significant savings.   SOURCE   Gary Moss

Organizational versus Personal Purchasing

Every day, consumers choose among numerous purchasing opportunities from small decisions like buying a can of coffee or a pen to relatively large ones like buying a car or a house. Other people influence some individual purchases, as when an instructor chooses the textbook that students buy for a class. Still, individual needs and desires drive most personal purchases.

This wealth of experience with suppliers like grocery stores, car dealers, and book stores may lead individuals to assume that they could easily handle organizational purchasing. Reality teaches otherwise. A number of important differences create an important organizational need for purchasing expertise to manage relationships with suppliers.

Differences in Needs.   Most individuals buy what they need when they need it; organizational purchases often meet longer-term needs. Purchasing agents contracted for today's supplies long ago. Today they work to fulfill needs that will emerge in the next month or the next year, and those needs will emerge outside the purchasing function in the OM system.

Purchasing Power.   Individual buyers have very little influence on prices, as you will quickly learn if you walk into Sears and try to bargain for a lower price on a color television set. Organizational purchasers can often negotiate for large price discounts because they routinely buy huge volumes of products worth vast sums of money. Chrysler negotiates to purchase millions of tires worth millions of dollars from suppliers like Goodyear. Such large orders create economies of scale and large total profits for suppliers, so the purchasing manager at Chrysler can expect to pay a lower price per tire than an individual pays when buying a set of four. This power affects other aspects of the transaction as well, such as payment terms, quality standards, warranty provisions, and customer service support.

Time Orientation.   Individual customers usually regard stores only as sources of desired products. Someone goes to a shoe store to buy shoes, and each purchase may come from a different retailer. In contrast, organizational purchasers try to develop long-term relationships with suppliers.

For one benefit, continuing relationships help purchasers to negotiate lower prices since suppliers value the reduction in uncertainty that comes from a long string of regular orders. The likelihood of strong demand for future products reduces risk and therefore costs for suppliers. It also simplifies scheduling, demand forecasting, and production planning. A reliable, long-term relationship encourages a supplier to invest with confidence in technology and equipment to expand capacity, and it reassures banks and other lending institutions of the supplier's ability to repay loans. These attractive features induce suppliers to exchange lower prices for longer-term relationships and contracts.

Besides lower prices, the purchasing organization benefits from the commitment that a long-term relationship demonstrates. Suppliers reinforce this commitment, in turn, by ensuring prompt delivery and good service, at the expense of the needs of one-time customers, if necessary. This reduces risk for the purchasing organization.

In addition, both parties enhance their knowledge through long-term relationships with capable suppliers. As supplier personnel learn what the buying organization wants and the problems that it faces, they can begin to anticipate needs and suggest appropriate products or improvements in current practices. Purchasers learn about the capabilities, strengths, and limitations of suppliers, so they can set the right balance of orders among them. They can identify and eliminate weak, ineffective, or inefficient suppliers and buy more from suppliers that perform well or that offer certain critical capabilities.

Purchasing personnel have the time and skills to develop and maintain important long-term relationships with suppliers. This vital service alone justifies their role in the organization.

Judging the Effectiveness of Purchases. Individual buyers typically base purchase decisions on price. People drive long distances and scour sale ads in daily newspapers in their eternal search for bargains. Corporate purchasers evaluate more than just price.

Purchasing personnel accept responsibility for maintaining a reliable flow of inputs into the OM system. More than anything, they fear a shutdown of the transformation process for lack of needed supplies. Operations managers care little for low prices if unreliable supplies expose the firm to the cost of idle production facilities.

To avoid this dismal development, purchasing personnel judge a supplier based on many nonprice criteria, including product quality and procedures for assuring continued good quality, past performance, location, warranty, service, desire for business, labor/management relations, management structure, manufacturing processes, housekeeping procedures, and general conditions in plants and facilities. Most purchasing managers compare suppliers' prices only after satisfying themselves that those firms offer acceptable performance, and their skill at this work makes them important members of the organization.

Price governs organizational purchases only for standard, commodity-type products. OM systems can substitute such products from different suppliers fairly easily. Multiple suppliers often make things like screws, paper clips, and diskettes to stock to meet industrywide standards for quality.

Cost Impact of Purchase Decisions. Individual choices for large purchases may significantly affect personal finances, but organizational purchasing has a major impact on the prosperity of people throughout an organization and outside it. The decisions of purchasing personnel determine much of a firm's cost of goods sold and, ultimately, the profits that it earns for stockholders and the value that it offers to customers. Many North American firms spend between 50 and 80 percent of their total cost of goods sold on purchases of inputs from suppliers. Suppliers provide over 70 percent of all components from which Chrysler assembles its cars. By paying too much, purchasers can significantly erode the performance of the entire organization; on the other hand, a small reduction in input costs under such conditions can boost performance substantially.

Major Responsibilities of Purchasing

Clearly, purchasing personnel do more than simply arrange deliveries of needed supplies. A formal list of the responsibilities of this department covers a wide range of topics that require specialized skills and knowledge.

Setting the Terms and Conditions of Purchases.   Representatives from purchasing negotiate the terms when the firm buys any input. Sales contracts must specify myriad details like prices per unit, quantity discounts, terms of purchase, warranty provisions, return policies, and penalty clauses for late delivery or failure to meet quality or performance standards.

Supplier Selection.   In conjunction with internal customers from operations management and other functions, purchasers identify candidates to fill orders and choose among them. This decision often hinges on such factors as supplier capacity, past experience with the supplier, the supplier's eagerness for the firm's business, the supplier's specific strengths and limitations, and the price it offers.

Supplier Scheduling.   Purchasing agents share production schedules and other information with suppliers to coordinate the flow of inputs so that supplies arrive exactly when the OM system needs them. Operations managers often contribute to this effort.

Supplier Education.   To assure an integrated flow of inputs and orders, purchasing personnel must educate new suppliers about the buying organization's routines. Suppliers must understand their new customer's purchasing policies and procedures and how to interpret shared information, including planning documents. Rigorous supplier education can reduce the potential for confusion and friction over later orders.

Supplier Evaluation and Feedback.   An important part of purchasing work involves providing regular, timely, and meaningful feedback to suppliers about the performance of their products and any problems that arise. Purchasing must tell suppliers what they have done well and what they can improve to increase buyer satisfaction.

Supplier Certification.   In supplier certification programs, purchasing personnel conduct extensive reviews of sellers' processes and systems to evaluate their ability to consistently generate quality products in a timely fashion.[5] Certification confirms that a supplier has its system under control, so future orders can assume

[5]Keri R. Bhote, *Strategic Supply Management* (New York: AMACOM, 1989), Chapter 18.

conformance with applicable standards and move directly to work stations without detailed receiving procedures or inspections. This eliminates the bottleneck at the receiving dock, reducing inventory and the resources that it consumes, including floor space for storage, stock room clerks, and inspectors. In a later section of the chapter, we will explain the procedures for conducting this important evaluation.

Supplier Development.   Under certain conditions, purchasing staff must actively develop new sources of supply rather than simply evaluating the offers of potential sellers. This process, also called **reverse marketing**, may become necessary when:[6]

reverse marketing
Active efforts by purchasing personnel to develop new sources of supply rather than simply evaluating the offers of potential sellers

- The firm needs a new product that no supplier currently provides
- The firm wants a more convenient and less costly source of a product available only with difficulty, perhaps from a foreign supplier
- The firm wants to avoid overreliance on a single supplier
- A current supplier lacks sufficient capacity to meet the firm's demand
- The firm finds a supplier with compatible attitudes toward quality, timeliness, or flexibility that does not currently make a desired input
- The firm becomes dissatisfied with continuing poor performance by current suppliers and no other firm offers an alternative

In such cases, purchasing agents may search for potential suppliers and convince them to meet the firm's need.

Supplier Advocacy.   Besides representing the firm as a buyer to outside organizations, purchasing personnel often present the points of view of suppliers in conflicts with the firm's own procedures. For example, purchasing representatives may complain if frequent changes to internal schedules interfere with suppliers' efforts to schedule their production effectively and efficiently. When requirements change frequently, supplier personnel cannot decide in advance what to produce next. They often respond to this uncertainty by relying on higher levels of inventory, longer lead times, or excess capacity, all of which raise their costs and the price to the buyer.

A supplier of automotive seals, gaskets, and similar components faced such a problem with one of the Big Three auto makers. The customer supplied future production schedules 6 weeks ahead of need specifying in detail exactly what products it would need at which plants and in what quantities. Unfortunately, the schedule was completely useless because of constant, often daily revisions and updates. To a question about how production was scheduled in such a variable situation, the supplier's scheduler answered, "Well, it isn't. We receive the production schedule for the day at 6:00 a.m. and we make exactly what we have to for that day and no more. It is on the truck by 8:00 a.m. But, boy, are those *buyers* paying for the confusion and chaos that they create."[7]

A purchasing manager may try to protect the supplier in such a situation by educating the internal customers of purchasing (operations managers and others) about any limitations on the supplier's available capacity or conflicting commitments. As part of supplier advocacy, purchasing personnel may also actively solicit suggestions for potential improvements in the buying organization's own practices.

---

[6]Michiel R. Leenders and David L. Blenkhorn, *Reverse Marketing: The New Buyer-Supplier Relationship* (New York: Free Press, 1989).

[7]The scheduler actually used a less complimentary word than *buyers* to refer to personnel of the buying organization.

[**E X H I B I T   1 3 . 6**]

Total Transformation System: Internal and External Factories

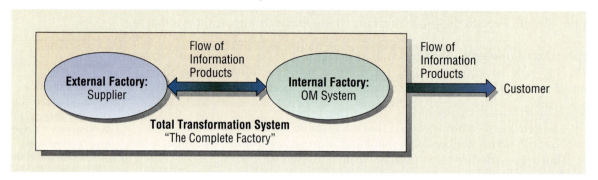

Increasing numbers of firms have tried to generate such feedback through **supplier councils**, in which influential managers from buying firms meet with key executives from their suppliers.[8] Such a council meets regularly, often between two and four times per year, to discuss and resolve supplier and buyer concerns and expectations and to measure performance by both supplier and customer. Supplier involvement in such a council often leads to full-fledged outpartnering like the relationship between Chrysler and Johnson Controls, Inc.

supplier council

A group of representatives from a buyer and a supplier who meet regularly to discuss and resolve supplier and buyer concerns and expectations and to measure performance by both parties

 ## MANAGING THE EXTERNAL FACTORY

An OM system depends on suppliers for many kinds of support, ranging from paper clips to new product ideas and solutions for internal problems. Because their operations become so completely integrated with the OM system of the buying organization, suppliers often function as external plants or factories, as discussed in Chapter 2. Together with an internal factory, or the buyer's own OM processes, they complete a total transformation process, as Exhibit 13.6 illustrates.

When suppliers function as extensions of internal processes rather than simply making necessary inputs, a buying organization may begin to expect the same management practices of suppliers that it employs in its own OM system. Just as operations managers must develop feasible plans for the firm's internal transformation process, they must work with purchasing managers to ensure that suppliers base their schedules on workable plans. Internal planning must reflect detailed information about suppliers' capabilities:

- Capacity levels
- Other customers' demands on that capacity
- Bottlenecks in internal processes
- Manufacturing lead times
- Plans for future capacity expansions
- Potential threats to supplier production (e.g., due to strikes either by that firm's workers or those of its suppliers)

[8]Bhote, *Strategic Supply Management,* p. 67–68.

conformance with applicable standards and move directly to work stations without detailed receiving procedures or inspections. This eliminates the bottleneck at the receiving dock, reducing inventory and the resources that it consumes, including floor space for storage, stock room clerks, and inspectors. In a later section of the chapter, we will explain the procedures for conducting this important evaluation.

Supplier Development.   Under certain conditions, purchasing staff must actively develop new sources of supply rather than simply evaluating the offers of potential sellers. This process, also called **reverse marketing**, may become necessary when:[6]

- The firm needs a new product that no supplier currently provides
- The firm wants a more convenient and less costly source of a product available only with difficulty, perhaps from a foreign supplier
- The firm wants to avoid overreliance on a single supplier
- A current supplier lacks sufficient capacity to meet the firm's demand
- The firm finds a supplier with compatible attitudes toward quality, timeliness, or flexibility that does not currently make a desired input
- The firm becomes dissatisfied with continuing poor performance by current suppliers and no other firm offers an alternative

In such cases, purchasing agents may search for potential suppliers and convince them to meet the firm's need.

Supplier Advocacy.   Besides representing the firm as a buyer to outside organizations, purchasing personnel often present the points of view of suppliers in conflicts with the firm's own procedures. For example, purchasing representatives may complain if frequent changes to internal schedules interfere with suppliers' efforts to schedule their production effectively and efficiently. When requirements change frequently, supplier personnel cannot decide in advance what to produce next. They often respond to this uncertainty by relying on higher levels of inventory, longer lead times, or excess capacity, all of which raise their costs and the price to the buyer.

A supplier of automotive seals, gaskets, and similar components faced such a problem with one of the Big Three auto makers. The customer supplied future production schedules 6 weeks ahead of need specifying in detail exactly what products it would need at which plants and in what quantities. Unfortunately, the schedule was completely useless because of constant, often daily revisions and updates. To a question about how production was scheduled in such a variable situation, the supplier's scheduler answered, "Well, it isn't. We receive the production schedule for the day at 6:00 a.m. and we make exactly what we have to for that day and no more. It is on the truck by 8:00 a.m. But, boy, are those *buyers* paying for the confusion and chaos that they create."[7]

A purchasing manager may try to protect the supplier in such a situation by educating the internal customers of purchasing (operations managers and others) about any limitations on the supplier's available capacity or conflicting commitments. As part of supplier advocacy, purchasing personnel may also actively solicit suggestions for potential improvements in the buying organization's own practices.

reverse marketing
Active efforts by purchasing personnel to develop new sources of supply rather than simply evaluating the offers of potential sellers

---

[6]Michiel R. Leenders and David L. Blenkhorn, *Reverse Marketing: The New Buyer-Supplier Relationship* (New York: Free Press, 1989).

[7]The scheduler actually used a less complimentary word than *buyers* to refer to personnel of the buying organization.

[**EXHIBIT 13.6**]

Total Transformation System: Internal and External Factories

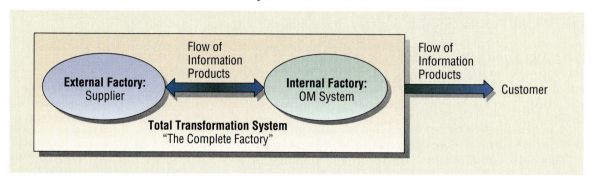

supplier council

A group of representatives from a buyer and a supplier who meet regularly to discuss and resolve supplier and buyer concerns and expectations and to measure performance by both parties

Increasing numbers of firms have tried to generate such feedback through **supplier councils**, in which influential managers from buying firms meet with key executives from their suppliers.[8] Such a council meets regularly, often between two and four times per year, to discuss and resolve supplier and buyer concerns and expectations and to measure performance by both supplier and customer. Supplier involvement in such a council often leads to full-fledged outpartnering like the relationship between Chrysler and Johnson Controls, Inc.

MANAGING THE EXTERNAL FACTORY

An OM system depends on suppliers for many kinds of support, ranging from paper clips to new product ideas and solutions for internal problems. Because their operations become so completely integrated with the OM system of the buying organization, suppliers often function as external plants or factories, as discussed in Chapter 2. Together with an internal factory, or the buyer's own OM processes, they complete a total transformation process, as Exhibit 13.6 illustrates.

When suppliers function as extensions of internal processes rather than simply making necessary inputs, a buying organization may begin to expect the same management practices of suppliers that it employs in its own OM system. Just as operations managers must develop feasible plans for the firm's internal transformation process, they must work with purchasing managers to ensure that suppliers base their schedules on workable plans. Internal planning must reflect detailed information about suppliers' capabilities:

- Capacity levels
- Other customers' demands on that capacity
- Bottlenecks in internal processes
- Manufacturing lead times
- Plans for future capacity expansions
- Potential threats to supplier production (e.g., due to strikes either by that firm's workers or those of its suppliers)

[8]Bhote, *Strategic Supply Management*, p. 67–68.

First-Tier Suppliers

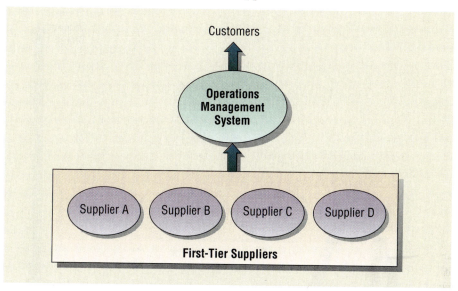

Customers

Operations
Management
System

Supplier A   Supplier B   Supplier C   Supplier D

First-Tier Suppliers

External Factories in the Supply Chain

The notion of external factories extends beyond the relationships with direct suppliers who provide immediate inputs, as Johnson Controls, Inc., supplies seats for Chrysler cars. These direct suppliers, or first-tier suppliers (Exhibit 13.7), form only one layer of interdependencies. To assure timely delivery of good quality materials and components in the right quantities, an operations manager must look beyond these first-tier suppliers to anticipate and prevent problems that might result from operations of *their* suppliers.

Movement from managing first-tier suppliers to second-tier and even more distant suppliers follows the supply chain. The **supply chain** spans all stages of processing from raw materials (e.g., iron ore and other components of steel) to final consumers (e.g., buyers of Neon cars). Each step in the supply chain forms links between buyers and sellers (Exhibit 13.8). Johnson Controls, Inc., sells seats to Chrysler that it makes from fabric, foam, steel, plastic, and thread purchased from suppliers.

Activities at each stage in the supply chain influence activities elsewhere along its length. As a result, operations managers must effectively control activities at every link. The buying firm's own manufacturing planning and control system makes it relatively easy to control the internal factory. Operations managers can decide on their own to replace inadequate equipment and retrain or replace ineffective employees. They cannot act so directly to control the external factory. Instead, they must either undertake a vertical integration program or rely on each supplier in the chain to control the actions of its own suppliers.

Vertical Integration.   By practicing vertical integration, a firm tries to establish direct control over the supply chain by purchasing controlling ownership interests in all suppliers. Suppliers must listen to the demands of this customer because it

supply chain
The sequence of suppliers and organizational buyers that spans all stages of processing from raw materials to final consumers

Links in the Supply Chain

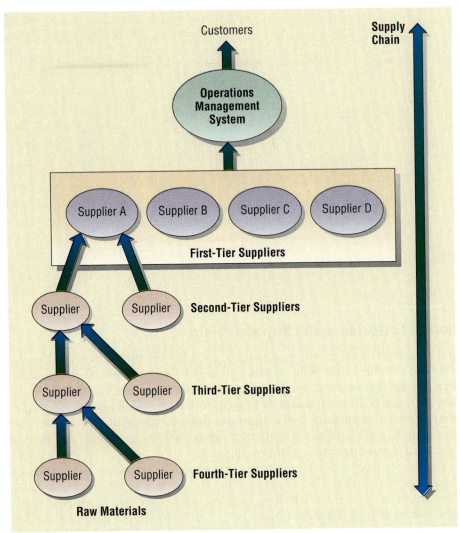

owns their firms and can replace personnel who fail to respond as desired. The "On the Job" box gives an example of vertical integration to control a supply chain.

At first glance, vertical integration seems like an attractive option, since ownership gives undisputed control. However, several major problems accompany this benefit. Purchases of suppliers require extensive financial resources, and they increase overall fixed costs. Before a purchase, suppliers' prices represent variable costs; afterward, their expenses become fixed costs of the larger organization. If demand drops, the buyer can no longer respond simply by buying fewer inputs. It must cover the continuing costs of the supplier out of a declining overall income. With vertical integration, a firm pays for increased control by reduced flexibility.

Finally, control can become a burden as much as a benefit. The new owner must establish systems and processes to coordinate activities throughout the larger organization. This often creates a bureaucracy that increases fixed costs and

In a 1926 book entitled *Today and Tomorrow,* Henry Ford summarized many of the lessons he had learned in managing the Ford Motor Company. One of these lessons involved the importance of the supply chain and the need to control it. By the early 1910s, Ford had developed a transformation process that ran like clockwork. In Ford's system, every form and source of variance had been identified, analyzed, and eliminated or controlled. Yet, Ford was still unable to create a system that was totally under control. Why? Because the transformation system was still susceptible to the problems originating at the various suppliers.

Ford assigned managers to study the problem of his suppliers. What they found greatly bothered him. Although Ford's factories were models of efficiency, in which housekeeping was emphasized and employees well paid, the factories of the suppli-

ON THE JOB

Vertical Integration for Supply Chain Control at Ford Motor Company

■

ers were often poorly organized, poorly run, and chaotic. Worse yet, workers were frequently poorly paid, poorly trained, and overworked.

To solve this problem, Ford took the radical step of acquiring all suppliers in the supply chain between his factories and the raw materials. By the mid 1920s, the supply chain linking Ford to the sources of raw material was almost totally owned by Ford and managed by Ford-appointed managers.

The result was total control. Iron ore was mined from Ford mines. It was then hauled by Fordson tractors to Ford-owned docks. There, it was loaded onto Ford ships and delivered to River Rouge, Michigan. At River Rouge, the ore was unloaded by Ford equipment and moved to a Ford steel plant, where it was converted into iron and steel. From the steel plant, the steel sheets were moved into the Ford Assembly plants, where it was used to build Ford cars and trucks and Fordson tractors. The finished cars when then shipped to Ford dealers for final delivery. Ultimately, the entire supply chain was controlled by decisions made at Ford headquarters in Dearborn, Michigan. Ford used to boast that it would take no more than 48 hours from the time iron ore was unloaded at the River Rouge docks until it found its way into a car rolling off the assembly line.

SOURCE   Henry Ford, *Today and Tomorrow* (Cambridge, Mass.: Productivity Press, 1988; reprint of 1926 edition).

reduces flexibility still further. The problems of vertical integration frequently outweigh the benefits.

Supplier Control.   Rather than direct control through ownership, a more persuasive, less commanding system of supplier control emphasizes the need for each member of the supply chain to accept responsibility for the performance of its suppliers. For example, Chrysler would expect Johnson Controls, Inc., to guarantee the performance of steel, fabric, plastic, and thread that it buys from suppliers. Supplier control offers several important incentives to induce suppliers to accept its requirements, including promises of increased business and special opportunities to bid on new orders. Suppliers who decline to assure the compliance of their own suppliers risk losing orders to more responsible competitors.

A supplier control program creates a single set of values to guide suppliers, purchasing personnel, and operations managers throughout the supply chain. Everyone involved works to implement the same vision of value through a dynamic, cooperative process that requires little investment in overhead. Supplier control recognizes the qualifications of each manager in the supply chain to manage direct suppliers instead of handing on that work to a distant bureaucracy. Finally, supplier control lays the foundation for full supply chain management that moves the firm from outsourcing to outpartnering.

 ## CONFRONTATION VERSUS PARTNERSHIP WITH SUPPLIERS

Different suppliers interact with an OM system in different ways. Some work through relatively formal, structured procedures in which they receive orders and fill them. Others integrate their procedures with those of the buying organization from initial product or process design through routine deliveries of standing orders.

Widely varying supplier relationships break down into four basic types:[9]

1. Confrontation
2. Arm's-length relationship
3. Acceptance of mutual goals
4. Full partnership

Exhibit 13.9 places these four stages of supplier involvement along a spectrum. At one end, **confrontation** represents the traditional relationship in which buyers and suppliers approach each other with strong distrust. At the other end, **partnership** represents a relatively new type of relationship characterized by close working relations, implicit trust, mutual respect, and dramatically redefined OM systems. Exhibit 13.9 recalls Exhibit 13.3 since confrontation corresponds to traditional views of outsourcing while partnerships result in outpartnering. In this section, we will focus on these two extremes in the spectrum.

Confrontation

Until the mid-1980s, confrontation pervaded most firms' contacts with their suppliers. Just-in-time manufacturing brought an emphasis on closer relationships, and the increasing importance of lead time and total cost analysis reinforced these new ties. Some firms still conduct business in traditional ways, however, treating suppliers and even organizational customers as adversaries. This type of relationship risks several serious obstacles to effective operations management.

Supplier Design Input.   A confrontational purchasing system ignores any expertise that suppliers might offer. The buying firm assigns internal personnel to design everything that it needs so that it can maintain complete control over its products, inviting no input from suppliers. It treats any offers of advice warily unless they promise lower prices. Suppliers act only to make and deliver requested products.

Criteria for Purchase Decisions.   Price dominates confrontational purchasing decisions. It often outweighs other considerations such as enhanced quality, reduced lead time, and improved flexibility. It is easy to measure. We can evaluate performance using dollars, and cost is directly attributable to purchasing. Some purchasers emphasize price so strongly that they consciously accept bids for lower-quality products.

confrontation

The traditional purchasing relationship in which buyers and suppliers approach each other with strong distrust

partnership

A relatively new type of purchasing relationship characterized by close working relations, implicit trust, mutual respect, and dramatically redefined OM systems

---

[9]Ibid., Chapter 2

[E X H I B I T   1 3 . 9]

Spectrum of Buyer-Supplier Relationships

Number of Suppliers.   Confrontational purchasing usually results in lower quality with longer and less predictable lead times because it bases buying decisions primarily on price. To guard against these problems and variations, buying firms frequently seek safety in numbers by recruiting multiple suppliers. If one supplier cannot meet a delivery schedule or quality standard, the buyer can simply order more inputs from the others.

As another tactic, it might hold large quantities of inventory. The ability to take needed inputs from safety stock protects the OM system from serious disruptions due to late or rejected supplier shipments. This system may include a program of extensive inspection of incoming products. Inspectors can catch poor-quality inputs before they reach production, but they also create bottlenecks on receiving docks, stretch overall lead times, and increase overhead costs for inspectors' salaries and facilities.

Routine Interactions.   Confrontational purchasing creates little significant interaction between buyer and suppliers. Neither would consider visiting the other's plant to share information and suggestions for improvement. Interaction usually centers on formal procedures for order placement or problems like late or incomplete orders. Precisely worded legal contracts often lay out provisions of confrontational business relationships and specify remedies for either party if the other fails to live up to the agreement. Exhibit 13.10 illustrates an extreme case of such a relationship.

Overall, confrontational relationships suffer from a general lack of trust. This lack of trust may begin when the buying organization evaluates purchasing personnel based strictly on how cheaply they obtain needed inputs. This leads them to emphasize low prices on all purchase decisions, placing severe pressure on suppliers' profit margins. Even when they can agree on a price, both sides may leave the negotiation worrying that the other took advantage of them.

Duration of the Relationship.   Lack of trust and loyalty typically limits confrontational relationships to the short term, frequently only 1 to 3 years. If the buyer can get a lower price from a new supplier, an existing relationship ends. Similarly, suppliers eagerly abandon old buyers for new ones willing to pay higher prices. Price competition and other factors such as high stress levels make for high supplier turnover in confrontational relationships, typically 100 percent over 10 years by one estimate.

[**EXHIBIT 13.10**]

Fictional Confrontational Response

Products Incorporated
P.O. Box 000, Avondale Estates, Georgia 30002
Metropolitan Atlanta Area
Phone: 404/000-0000

Attn: Mr. Stanley Dean
        Purchasing Agent

UNIVERSAL CORRECTION ACTION

In accordance with company policy, we wish to inform you that you received merchandise of the same quality that every other customer gets, and we think you are pretty chicken for sending this garbage back to us. We can't use it either. We ship whatever the hell comes off the production line, and whether or not it meets specifications, we are certain that it contains the right part number most of the time, which is what you ordered. Concerning your statement with regard to late delivery, which incidentally was only 3 months overdue, what the hell do you want? You did better than most of our customers. Next time, order a bigger dollar volume and we will give it our red carpet, extra-special-attention treatment. It might even be only 2 months late then! (Note the improvement).

For corrective action, per your chicken request, we will also investigate future orders more carefully so that we will ship so late that you will be in such a bind that you will accept whatever we send you.

Oh, about that little note which says "Cancel this order"—too late! As you can see, we are doing everything in our power to be cooperative and force this garbage on you, and if you are too stupid to deviate and use it as is, we want to remind you that we have your money and you're stuck with it.

                    Hoping for Future Orders,

                    Your Friendly Supplier

P.S.:   With regard to your statement that our part doesn't resemble your drawing, we
        wish to point out that you are in error. Your drawing does not resemble our part,
        which we hastened to point out to our salesman 2 weeks after we accepted your
        order. Don't blame us if you were negligent enough not to inquire about this
        minor detail, because everybody else knows about it.

SOURCE   Reprinted, with permission of the publisher, from *Strategic Supply Management* by Keri R. Bhote, p. 26. © 1989 AMACOM, a division of American Management Association. All rights reserved.

Implications of Confrontation.   Confrontation may suit purchases of inputs in mature and stable markets where numerous suppliers compete for limited sales. It may also keep the buying firm's short-term costs low, although it may have other effects on long-term costs.

[**E X H I B I T   1 3 . 1 1**]

Confrontational Pressures on Supplier Prices

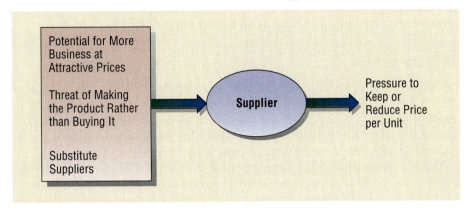

Exhibit 13.11 illustrates three forces in confrontational relationships that pressure suppliers to keep prices lower than their competitors. First, the buying organization could make the needed input in its own OM system rather than buying it from any outside supplier. Confrontation frequently reminds suppliers that they must compete with the firm's own potential capabilities as well as existing rival firms. When buyers will switch suppliers quickly in pursuit of lower prices, the threat of existing competitors pushes prices as low as possible. Finally, every supplier watches for opportunities to cut its own prices to take away business from rivals.

Partially offsetting low prices, however, confrontational relationships tend to keep the buying firm's fixed costs high. These relationships rely heavily on expensive, unproductive inspections, and buying firms spend large amounts to manage their numerous suppliers, including bid evaluation and performance monitoring procedures. Also, such buying firms design all products and components internally, so they must invest substantial sums in engineering staff, office space, and other resources for this work. All of these costs add to the burden of overhead expenses.

In addition to its price and cost effects, lack of trust and strict contract provisions force both parties to maintain rigid attitudes. Neither feels much incentive to react flexibly to maintain such a short-term, low-profit relationship. No contract can ever anticipate everything that might occur, however, and rigid attitudes can complicate any solution to the impasse.

In addition, quality and delivery problems often arise because suppliers cannot suggest ways to prevent them in the early stages of product and process design. Defects frequently become apparent only when designs enter production at suppliers' sites, after corrections become expensive. Both buyers and suppliers frequently respond, not by working together to resolve the problem, but by trying to assign blame. Suppliers predictably trace causes to defects in buyers' designs and deny responsibility for the costs of correcting the problems; buyers claim that suppliers ruin sound designs by trying to cut costs, so they must pay to correct any problems. Production ceases until arduous negotiations reach mutually acceptable solutions and assign costs. This time-consuming process resumes when another problem arises.

With lower quality, higher overhead costs, longer delivery lead times, and far less flexibility than more cooperative relationships, confrontational purchasing fails to meet the demands of dynamic business environments. While confrontation may well keep prices of inputs low in a stable environment, it does not encourage productivity gains that active partnerships can provide. Instead, it treats the external factory as just another source of some input. Chrysler managed to successfully develop and launch its new Neon model only through intimate outpartnering arrangements with Johnson Controls and other suppliers.

Full Partnership

Firms began forging partnerships widely in the middle to late 1980s to integrate suppliers' capabilities with those of the buying organization's. These systems have contributed to the success of companies such as Nike, Apple Computers, and Kingston, a maker of memory and CPU upgrades for microcomputers. In nearly every way, partnerships contradict the principles of confrontation.

While confrontation emphasizes survival of the fittest firms that can offer the lowest prices, partnerships stress mutual survival through unified operations. While confrontation encourages firms to struggle against one another as enemies, partners coordinate their activities as allies bound by common interests and goals. Confrontation treats suppliers as substitutes for internal production; partnerships treat suppliers as complements to internal capabilities. Finally, confrontation works narrowly to reduce direct dollar costs of purchases; partnerships take broad steps to maximize value for the buying organization and its customers, to reduce risk, to reduce total costs, and to improve the overall competitive position of the buying firm.

This revolutionary effort to draw on suppliers' capabilities and expertise requires a firm to develop new paradigms for working with them. Partnerships join representatives from buying organizations with those from suppliers as equal collaborators. This relationship requires several changes from the methods of confrontation.

Supplier Design Input.   Partnerships invite suppliers to participate in product or process design efforts, frequently through formal early supplier involvement (ESI) or simultaneous engineering programs. Suppliers may even act as equal partners in formulating the initial product concept, contributing insights based on long experience in specific areas.

Chrysler even included offices for supplier representatives when it laid out the design facilities in its new corporate headquarters in Auburn Hills, Michigan. The facilities organize work space around design conference rooms to encourage frequent meetings so design teams can resolve problems as soon as they arise.

Criteria for Purchase Decisions.   A buying organization forges partnerships with suppliers whose specific skills can fill some critical gap in its knowledge. These priorities helped Apple Computer to accelerate its early development.[10] In coping with the overwhelming success of its Apple II microcomputer, management decided against making all of the microchips, boxes, monitors, cables, and keyboards that the product would need. Instead, they deliberately decided to recruit suppliers that could provide the skills and expertise they lacked and to avoid building internal bureaucracies for those functions.

As a result, Apple developed partnerships with Frogdesign to supply external cases, Tokyo Electric to supply printers, and Regis McKenna to supply marketing services. Apple employees identified market needs that the components should

[10]James Brian Quinn and Frederick G. Hilmer, "Strategic Outsourcing," *Sloan Management Review,* Summer 1994, pp. 43–55.

satisfy while supplier representatives explained technically feasible solutions and then made the products that the teams had designed. Apple focused its internal resources on its own disk operating system and the supporting software that made its products unique. These close relationships with suppliers helped Apple to generate three times the average capital turnover of major computer producers and the highest ratio of market value to fixed investment throughout the 1980s.

Partnerships often look beyond immediate price differences to evaluate suppliers based on total costs.[11] A supplier may have to make significant initial investments to produce a component that it can recover only over extended future sales. Through total cost analysis, the buying organization accepts these costs as the price of a particular supplier's exceptional skills and capabilities, recognizing that it would ultimately spend more to make the same component internally or to buy it from another, less expert supplier.

Number of Suppliers.   To build and maintain partnerships, a buying organization deals with limited numbers of suppliers. Rather than dealing with many suppliers with varying qualifications, it identifies and works with a handful of competent, qualified, and cooperative partners. As W. Edwards Deming once pointed out, "We need fewer suppliers. ...It's difficult enough to find one supplier who can supply the quality you need, much less two, three, or half a dozen."[12]

By dealing with only a few suppliers, the buyer places large orders with each one, so it exercises strong influence over their decisions. This may seem risky, since production could suffer if a single supplier were to fail to meet its obligations, but in fact a typical firm buys from a small handful of very competent suppliers and many more average or less capable ones. Problems with delivery schedules or quality usually come from the many poor suppliers rather than the few good ones, so a firm can significantly improve its quality, lead time, cost, and flexibility by concentrating its orders with the best suppliers. This also reduces its administrative costs for managing suppliers.

More generally, fewer, more detailed relationships with suppliers stimulate the development of mutual learning and trust. Each firm learns about the needs and expectations, the strengths and limitations of the other. Such familiarity helps suppliers to spot and fill latent demands that customers can describe only vaguely. The growing commitment between organizations fosters trust and nurtures shared efforts to add value for ultimate customers. Exhibit 13.12 illustrates the compelling benefits of reducing a firm's supplier base.

Routine Interactions.   A partnership requires close, open, and informal interactions. They focus on dealing with problems that arise, and no contract can set out the terms and conditions of every possible development. Partners must approach problem solving with open and informal attitudes to facilitate necessary give and take.

Interactions in an effective partnership also require mutual respect. The members of the buying organization recognize and value suppliers' expertise and respect their opinions. Both parties listen when someone proposes a new idea, as Chrysler's management demonstrated when people from Johnson Controls, Inc., made recommendations about the design and manufacture of the Neon's rear seat. In the same way, suppliers must accept the insight of the buying organization into the demands and expectations of its internal and external customers. They do not

---

[11]Chapter 4 discussed total cost analysis.

[12]Bhote, *Strategic Supply Management*, p. 45.

[**E X H I B I T   1 3 . 1 2**]

Results of Supplier Base Reduction

Company	Percentage Reduction	Relative results
Allen-Bradley	20 percent in 2 years	Poor
Ford	45 percent in 3 years	Modest
3M	64 percent in 3 years	Acceptable
Motorola	70 percent in 3 years	Acceptable
Hewlett-Packard division	47 percent in 4 months	Spectacular
Xerox	90 percent in 1 year	Spectacular

SOURCE   Reprinted, with permission of the publisher, from *Strategic Supply Management* by Keri R. Bhote, p. 48. © 1989 AMACOM, a division of American Management Association. All rights reserved.

waste time worrying about the completeness and accuracy of the information that the buyer provides.

Representatives of buyers and the suppliers have very frequent contact, often working together on-site to solve a problem. In many cases, this contact extends beyond the professional level and includes social interactions. For example, a partnership between a Big-Three auto maker and a major first-tier supplier located in western Michigan developed every mode of communication from face-to-face conversations, on-site visits, and electronic messages through barbecues and picnics.

Partners often share both information and decision-making authority. They frequently exchange schedules, information and specifications for new product designs, and cost data, along with any other information that either party needs to solve a problem. Many buying organizations allow suppliers direct access to their computer systems.

The routine interactions of suppliers and a buying organization work to benefit all parties. By working together, partners expect to create better solutions than they could produce by working separately.

Duration of the Relationship.   A partnership needs a long time to build such a spirit of cooperation, so it limits turnover among suppliers by eliminating the causes that encourage them to look elsewhere for customers. Partnership fosters long-term loyalty, ultimately becoming the organizational equivalent of a marriage.

Implications of Partnership.   Partnerships suit the needs of organizations that must accommodate frequent design/process changes. They also match the needs of products that are critical to the success of the firm and those in the early stages of their life cycles. The movement toward partnership with suppliers has some important implications for the transformation process and the operations manager, however, that require careful attention and control.

Every partnership emphasizes common goals and values. A firm may try to develop a close working relationship by associating with suppliers that share its goals and values. A system designed to deliver the highest-quality product in the shortest lead time needs inputs from suppliers that also emphasize quality and lead time. Both respond to the same or similar types of value for customers, and both act in identical or similar ways to produce that value.

[**EXHIBIT   13.13**]

Traditional Transformation Process

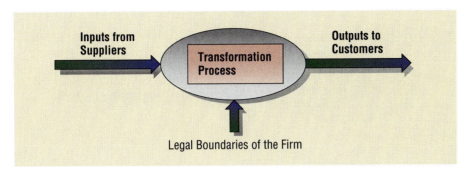

To accomplish this difficult goal, a partnership must redefine the transformation processes of the organizations. A traditional transformation process accepts outside inputs only when suppliers can offer them more cheaply than internal processes can make them (Exhibit 13.13); a partnership organizes a transformation process with internal activities that perform work central to the firm's own skills and knowledge, subcontracting the rest to a few trusted suppliers (Exhibit 13.14).

In subcontracting out activities, the operations management task changes from controlling internal activities to sharing authority, decision-making power, and planning responsibilities to integrate activities of suppliers with those of the firm. For example, Chrysler asked Johnson Controls, Inc., not only to design the seats for the Neon, but also to schedule production and build them. Separating work between suppliers' and buyers' facilities requires teamwork for effective management. Members bring different skills and capabilities. No one gives orders; rather, everyone listens to others and contributes to common decisions that guide OM system activities in both firms. This teamwork blurs the boundaries that separate the firm and its OM system from the supplier (Exhibit 13.15). Partners must identify everyone's responsibilities through open, trusting negotiations.

[**EXHIBIT   13.14**]

Partnership Transformation Process

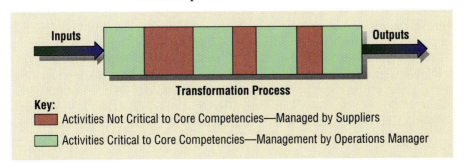

[**EXHIBIT 13.15**]

Blurring of Corporate Boundaries

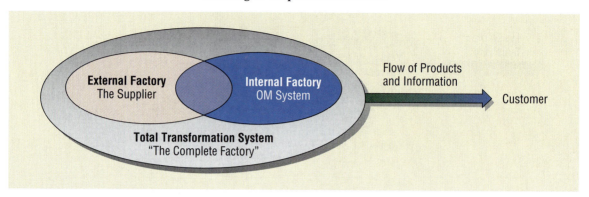

Trend from Confrontation to Partnership

Exhibit 13.16 summarizes the many differences between confrontation and partnership. Like the other developments discussed in this book, the emergence and growth of partnerships represent strategic and value-driven responses triggered by customer demand, advances in technology, and recognition of core competencies.

Customer Demand for the Benefits of Partnership.   In today's marketplace, customers want more then ever before and they want it now. As Ross and Kay, two consultants who address issues of organizational structures, observe, "Increasingly, corporations need to respond quickly. Like 3-year-olds, customers want what they want when they want it. ...In today's environment, what's needed is a new kind of organization, one that responds faster and is flexible."[13]

Partnerships ideally suit the demands of this new environment. Instead of hiring internal workers who can help it respond to a new demand, the firm now looks for suppliers that offer needed skills, systems, and capabilities. It forms a partnership with those suppliers that lasts as long as the need to satisfy new demands.

As needs change, however, the firm responds by changing suppliers and forming new partnerships. If current suppliers lack necessary skills or capabilities, even a loyal buyer must look for new ones. Most firms can find needed skills among existing suppliers, though, and the resulting partnership gives them flexibility and speed. It also reduces the need for investments in the firms' own systems.

Advances in Technology.   In the last 10 years, explosive advances in technologies for communications, computers, and graphics have facilitated the growth of partnerships by allowing extensive connectivity. In the early 1970s, for example, computer power was limited and people passed information either by telephone or by mail, leaving information flows disjointed. Today's computer networks, electronic data interchange (EDI) systems, and graphics standards allow people working in different areas of the country or around the world to maintain constant contact. Someone working in Germany can communicate with others in San Jose, California, or Calgary, Alberta, Canada. These technologies allow continuous communications.

[13]Gerald Ross and Michael Kay, *Toppling the Pyramids: Refining the Way Companies Are Run* (New York: Times Books, 1994), p. 15.

[**E X H I B I T   1 3 . 1 6**]

Differences between Confrontation and Partnership

Traits	Confrontation	Partnership
Basis for placing orders	Price, price, price!	Expertise, capabilities, problem-solving skills
Supplier design input	Uninvolved outsider	Active participant in the design process
View of the supplier	Outsourcing; substitute for internal capacity	Outpartnering, complement to internal skills and capabilities
Number of suppliers	Large for safety in numbers	Very limited
Duration of relationships	Short	Long-term marriage
Supplier turnover	High	Low
Routine interactions	Arm's length, formal, based on legal contracts	Close, handshake commitments based on trust
Mutual view of the relationship	Win-lose struggle for advantage	Win-win relationship, cooperation for mutual benefit
Frequency of contacts	Limited to exchanges of orders and problem solving	Constant
Views of information sharing	Tight control of information to guard advantages in negotiations	Open sharing of critical information
Degree of trust or respect	Little or none	Very high

Computers shut down only for system malfunctions, so they can exchange information across time zones almost as easily as across the street.

EDI systems link computers, allowing suppliers and buyers to exchange all forms of information continuously. A buyer's computer system can now release a schedule to the supplier's computer system without human intervention. In turn, a supplier can access routine updates simply by browsing through the buyer's computer system, reserving important communications for problems that require everyone's attention. EDI facilitates real-time scheduling, monitoring, and payment systems.

Graphics standards simplify sharing of design information that older systems captured and described using blueprints. The old practices inhibited flexibility because changing blueprints required redrawing plans, which someone had to physically carry from one place to another. Today's product designers draw diagrams on computer systems with software like CADAM or AutoCAD that employ standards like IGES (initial graphics exchange standards). The resulting electronic images of designs can travel immediately to a supplier's computer for display in a remote design system. Both partners' designers can review the design and make needed changes electronically. The quick and easy flow of images between suppliers and buying organizations helps a firm to generate better designs more quickly and at lower costs.

Recognition of Core Competencies.   In the past, firms oriented their decisions toward markets and products. For example, RCA saw itself as a manufacturer of televisions for the mass market; General Motors built cars for style-conscious buyers. Honda confused and confounded this thinking by successfully competing in a number of different markets—motorcycles, power generators, lawn mowers,

[**EXHIBIT 13.17**]

Link between Core Competencies and Markets

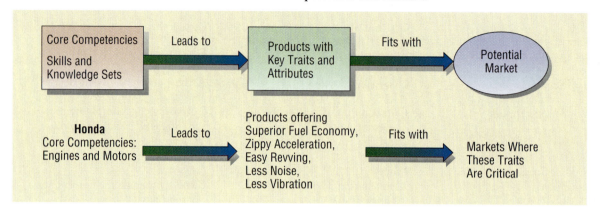

and cars. Honda further defied the conventional wisdom of the time by relying heavily on its suppliers to take over certain traditionally internal tasks. It survived and prospered following this innovative strategy, moving from outsider to major player in its industries, as did other companies including Yamaha, Hewlett-Packard, and 3M.

Careful study of these successes revealed that they prospered by recognizing and acting on their **core competencies**, or uniquely effective business processes. Honda exploited its core competencies in production of engines and motors, concentrating on markets (lawn mowers, automobiles, generators) in which success depended on good motors. Other firms provide numerous examples of such core competencies in action. Sony excels at producing small electronic products (e.g., the Walkman, the Walkman TV) because its core competencies lie in the area of miniaturization. FedEx became an industry leader in rapid delivery services by focusing on core competencies in logistics management.

A particular firm can identify the critical feature of its operation that defines its core competency based on several typical criteria:

Skills or Knowledge Sets.   Core competencies result from skills or knowledge sets that create streams of successful products rather than from the products themselves. These skills can range from expertise in processes, customer service, logistics management, specific market segments, or product design, among other areas. Managers identify product traits that suit their firm's core competencies and then center their competitive efforts on markets that prize those traits (Exhibit 13.17).

A unique set of skills confers a competitive advantage because rival firms cannot easily duplicate those capabilities, although they can easily reverse engineer a successful product. Honda bases its strategy on the core competency of producing good engines and motors. Chrysler has developed a fast and effective process for identifying a market segment, describing the traits that appeal to the segment (its order winners, order qualifiers, and order losers), and designing a car with the most appealing traits.

Value for Targeted Customers.   To base organizational success on core competencies, they must provide value for the firm's customers. This link between core competencies and customer value may seem indirect, but customers must appreciate the

core competency

A firm's uniquely effective business process on which its strategic success depends

features that the firm's unique capabilities add to its product. When Honda redesigned its Accord model for 1994, writers and reviewers praised its fuel economy, zippy acceleration, and quiet, smooth operation while almost ignoring the firm's dealer network and other product characteristics. Similarly, many people like the relatively quiet, smooth-running engines of Honda lawn mowers. The firm's core competency adds value for both sets of customers.

Resistance to Duplication.   A core competency must also prevent competitors from easily duplicating it, forming a competitive advantage that acts as a potential barrier to entry. To build such an advantage, the firm may rely on skills developed over a long period, forcing a rival to make the same investment over a similar period. It may also base its success on an extensive infrastructure that would cost rivals large sums to copy. Finally, the firm may develop core competencies that combine its personnel, systems, and past history.

Limited Focus.   Any single firm must focus on a few core competencies that identify what it does best. It can then target investments of scarce resources on assets that reinforce its core competencies, trusting that these investments will generate the highest rates of return. Further, by limiting its focus to a few core competencies, a firm can avoid spreading resources too widely in an effort to develop too many skills. This reduces a serious risk of stretching lead times and harming its position in the marketplace.

Also, by identifying limited processes as its core activities, a firm knows which functions it must carry out internally. Honda would never hire subcontractors to build its engines, even if they could produce the same designs more cheaply; this would teach the subcontractor about Honda's core skills, creating a potential competitor with the same capabilities. Honda might, however, contract with outside suppliers to provide any product or service outside its core competencies, especially if their core competencies give them special advantages those areas. Nike has applied the concept of core competencies extremely effectively to guide its management of both internal operations and subcontractors, as the "On the Job" box illustrates.

Extending Skills to New Markets.   Core competencies based on broad skills may apply outside the narrow limits of a single product market. Creative application of specific skills may allow a firm to move easily from one market to another.

Dynamic Skills.   Core competencies must change to follow mobile customers with developing expectations. Despite past success based on particular skills, many strong competitors continuously reinvent themselves by developing new skills or moving to new markets. Suppliers often fuel this change by introducing skills or knowledge sets of their own. By building a partnership with a recognized leader in some business process, a firm can begin to understand the requirements of that process and see how someone else has successfully applied it. Ford Motor Company, for example, found that many of its internal suppliers could not match the quality, practices, and costs of external suppliers; in working closely with these suppliers, Ford began to improve its own internal processes and practices.

Potential Disadvantages of Partnerships.   This discussion has described partnerships as important new sources of competitive success. It cannot ignore some potential problems that may limit applicability of these relationships.

There is one potential difficulty: partnerships take time to develop. Partners must build trust and mutual respect over time. Operations managers must also

ON THE JOB

Nike Manages Its Supplier Base

■

Nike is the largest supplier of athletic shoes in the world. Yet it outsources all of of its shoe production and manufactures only key technical components of its "Nike Air" system. Athletic footwear is technology and fashion intensive, requiring high flexibility at both the production and marketing levels. Nike creates maximum value by concentrating on preproduction (research and development) and postproduction activities (marketing, distribution and sales) linked together by per- haps the best marketing information system in the business. Using a carefully developed, on- site "expatriate" program to coordinate its foreign-based suppliers, Nike even outsourced the advertising component of its marketing program to Wieden & Kennedy, whose creative efforts led Nike to the top of the product-recognition scale. Nike grew at a compounded 20 percent growth rate and earned a 31 percent return on equity for its shareholders through most of the past decade.

SOURCE   James Brian Quinn and Frederick G. Hilmer, "Strategic Outsourcing," *Sloan Management Review*, Summer 1994, pp. 43–55.

spend considerable time assessing the unique strengths and capabilities of suppliers to identify those that seem best able to meet their firm's needs and to fulfill the promise of the new relationship. It takes time to train internal staff members in needed skills and to develop appropriate performance measures.

If time requirements do not derail a drive toward partnership, the threat of vulnerability might. With limited numbers of suppliers in a closely linked extended OM system, people in the buying organization may feel too dependent on a supplier. This sense of dependency may create concern if a supplier suddenly develops financial problems, forcing the buying organization to decide whether to support the troubled supplier or look for alternatives. While this possibility poses a real threat, the buyer can limit the danger by carefully evaluating potential suppliers before committing to them. This evaluation should consider financial stability, management structure, management personnel, and planning and control systems, among other criteria.

Virtual Corporations

virtual corporation

A partnership so close that two partners become for all operational purposes a single firm

In a partnership, a buying organization and its suppliers develop close relationships that recognize their mutual interdependence, respect, and trust to encourage shared risks and knowledge. At the logical extreme of this concept, partnerships become **virtual corporations**.[14] This relationship becomes close enough to obscure the boundary between the supplier's responsibilities and those of the buyer. Over the life of such a relationship, the two partners become for all operational purpos-

[14]Davidow and Malone, *Virtual Corporation.*

Walden Paddlers created a virtual corporation by contracting the design and manufacture of its kayaks to qualified outside suppliers, who complement the company.   SOURCE: Henry Horenstein

es a single firm. The terms of the relationship changes in response to dynamic customer needs, but the commitment remains solid.

Organizing the Virtual Corporation.   The buying organization in a virtual corporation relies on few suppliers, each of which offers important complementary skills and capabilities that others lack. The buyer's OM system focuses on the firm's core competencies, supplying capabilities in other areas through inputs from suppliers. The strength of these relationships depends on the needs of ultimate customers and the specific requirements of the product. As these requirements change, certain relationships become more important, while others lose importance.

For example, to guarantee access to well-designed seats for its Neon, Chrysler strengthened its ties with Johnson Controls, Inc. The Viper model, Chrysler's high-performance sports car, needs a powerful engine and agile handling, so the OM system emphasizes different types of partnerships for that model. Another firm entirely may supply Viper seats. This diversity forces Chrysler's operations managers to work seamlessly with different suppliers.

Exhibit 13.18 illustrates the impact of the virtual corporation on the OM system and its suppliers. Cy Olsen, an expert in virtual organizations, has described this altered transformation process as the *virtual factory*.

Supply Chain Management and Customer Value

Relations with suppliers and supply chain management raise some compelling managerial issues. Today's OM systems must reach beyond their own capabilities to call on suppliers to help them add value for customers. As a result, these firms now view themselves less as opponents than as partners, recognizing that customers want different benefits than they have wanted in the past. To satisfy these new demands, operations managers must embrace new ways of working with suppliers. For example, the virtual corporation represents the leading edge of supply chain management techniques.

[**EXHIBIT 13.18**]

Operations Management in the Virtual Corporation

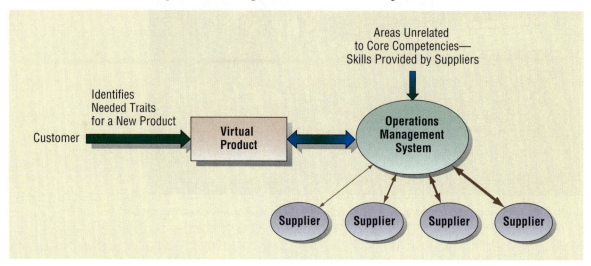

NOTE   Arrows indicate relationships; thicknesses of the arrows indicate the current importance of the skills provided by specific suppliers.

 ## PROCESS TOOLS FOR SUPPLY CHAIN MANAGEMENT

Any supply chain management effort, from confrontational purchasing to a virtual corporation, relies on certain process tools to evaluate resource flows between suppliers and the transformed OM system. Among many such tools, we will focus on four:

- Make-buy analysis
- Supplier scheduling
- Value analysis/value engineering
- Supplier certification/evaluation

Make-Buy Analysis

The most basic supply chain management decision requires the operations manager to choose whether to make a given product internally or buy it from a supplier. Early supplier management began and ended with this analysis for all products, even those related to the core competencies of the firm. As partnerships and virtual factories have become more prevalent, however, this decision has centered on commodity inputs that do not affect core competencies.

Make-buy analysis implements total cost analysis techniques to support OM decisions.[15] This tool guides operations managers toward the lowest-cost suppliers of needed products, including both internal and external factories. This process includes a number of well-defined steps that produce a final decision recommendation.

[15]See the discussion of the Operations Management Toolkit in Chapter 4 for a detailed discussion of total cost analysis.

Assess the Relationship of the Product to the Firm's Core Competencies.   Make-buy analysis begins with an evaluation of a product's relationship to the firm's current or future core competencies. Cost analysis is irrelevant for such a product, because strategic considerations dictate internal production rather than outsourcing. The analysis simply assumes that the risk of losing an important competitive advantage outweighs cost differences.

Despite the firm's core competency, a supplier may offer lower costs for several reasons. First, it may willingly make the products at a loss simply to learn about the buyer's core competency. For example, Samsung Electronics of South Korea bid for a contract to make microwave ovens under private label for Montgomery Ward.[16] Samsung managers knew that the company would lose money on every unit it sold, but they considered this loss an acceptable cost of gaining access to the U.S. market. They thought that their ovens could compete against those of more established firms, but they lacked a good knowledge of the market. Montgomery Ward taught Samsung about the features of a successful microwave oven, and this knowledge allowed Samsung to move beyond private-label production to compete head to head with other major manufacturers.

A supplier may also offer lower costs because it makes a product more efficiently than the potential buyer can, despite its core competency. Rather than subcontracting for the product, the buyer's operations managers should try to learn why the supplier can beat their own costs and upgrade their internal processes. Benchmarking provides one method for this kind of study.

If this step in the analysis determines that a needed input bears no significant relationship to the firm's core competencies, then later steps can evaluate the benefits of outsourcing.

Evaluate the Suitability of Product Characteristics for Outsourcing.   Make-buy analysis usually centers on products in the mature stages of their product life cycles. Firms also consider subcontracting for commodities, products with well-defined traits and design requirements and that multiple suppliers can readily provide. Firms typically do not consider purchasing products in the early stages of their life cycles (introduction and growth), because these types of products require more cooperation and joint problem solving than simple purchases allow.

Evaluate the Reasons for Outsourcing.   If the product seems appropriate for a supplier purchase, the make-buy analysis continues by judging the validity of the reasons for purchasing. For example, outsourcing might free up internal capacity to produce other, more profitable components if the current load on that capacity exceeds what it can produce. However, if subcontracting would free up capacity that would then sit idle, the buyer may not reduce its overall costs.

Assess All Relevant Quantitative Costs.   If previous steps indicate that outsourcing makes sense, the analysis proceeds by classifying costs as fixed or variable, relevant or irrelevant, direct or hidden. Recall that the total cost analysis procedures introduced in Chapter 4 compare quantitative costs before proceeding to evaluate qualitative costs. Exhibit 13.19 shows an example of this classification of fixed and variable costs.

A detailed breakdown of costs to make and buy an input highlights relative advantages for the supplier and for the buying organization. A supplier's cost

[16]When a company makes a product under private label, it builds that product for sale under another company's name. For example, Solectron builds the PowerPC for Apple.

[**EXHIBIT 13.19**]

Make-Buy Analysis for an Electronic Timer

Cost Elements	Make		Buy
	Initial Fixed Cost	Variable Cost	
Incoming inspection	—	$5.55	$5.81
Cost of quality; scrap, repair, inspection, testing	—	0.10	0.02
Direct labor overhead	—	0.33	0.04
Administrative overhead	—	0.11	0.03
Technical, managerial labor invested	$1.51	0.26	0.03
Freight, materials handling	—	0.06	0.03
Inventory costs	—	0.04	0.07
Tool investments	2.30	0.10	0.12
Total costs	3.81	6.93	6.24

SOURCE   Reprinted, with permission of the publisher, from *Strategic Supply Management* by Keri R. Bhote, p. 74. © 1989 AMACOM, a division of American Management Association. All rights reserved.

advantages might reflect either its own superior efficiency or the buyer's cost-allocation procedures. An accounting system may allocate overhead costs in a way that reduces the value of internal production. Knowledge of both the supplier's and buyer's cost structures also reinforces preparation for any negotiations.

Analysis of fixed investments, such as tools, must accommodate two types of fixed costs along with variable costs:

- *Fixed cost per contract*   The potential buyer would incur an initial, one-time cost to acquire fixed assets like tools at the outset of production.
- *Fixed cost per order*   It would incur on-going costs to inspect and maintain assets for individual production runs.
- *Variable cost*   Finally, production would consume some of the value of the assets for each unit produced through wear and tear.

In addition, make-buy analysis must calculate the cost of quality, that is, the cost of guaranteeing the required number of good units in a production run. This cost depends primarily on the proportion of acceptable units in the overall output of the production run.

[**PROBLEM 13.1**]

Cost of Quality in Make-Buy Analysis

Suppose that a firm needs 1,000 units of a component over a year. Past experience suggests that internal production usually generates 92 percent acceptable units, while a supplier can achieve 95 percent acceptable quality. How many units should the firm make or buy to get 1,000 good ones?

A batch of 1,000 units would include 92 percent or 920 good units and 80 defective ones. Simply adding 80 more units to the batch size would not solve the problem, however, because only 92 percent of the additional units would meet specifications. To get 1,000 good units, the firm would have to make a batch of 1,087:

$$\text{Batch size} = \frac{\text{Desired number}}{\text{Percentage acceptable}} = \frac{1,000}{0.92} = 1,086.9565 \qquad [\ \blacksquare\ ]$$

To calculate the cost of quality for inputs from suppliers, operations managers must complete a more complex analysis. Suppliers' warranty policies and any shipping costs associated with returns typically affect the total cost, for example. Suppliers can respond to problems with defective units in a number of different ways. Exhibit 13.20 describes some options and their impacts on purchase quantities and costs.

Thorough analysis reveals the quantitative costs to produce a needed input internally and to buy it from a supplier. This information may make the cheaper option seem like the better one, but total cost analysis must also include qualitative costs.

Assess All Qualitative Costs.   Subjective assessments of qualitative costs affect the choices implied by quantitative differences, although imprecise concepts can complicate measurement. Numerous qualitative features affect the make-buy decision, including:

- Loss of control by releasing work to a supplier
- Risk of dealing with a new supplier
- Importance assigned to a supplier's location and the convenience of site visits
- Quality of the supplier's management team
- Value structures of the two organizations, as when a quality-oriented buyer wants to deal with a quality-oriented supplier

[E X H I B I T   1 3 . 2 0]

Calculating Quantities and Costs with Different Return Policies

Terms for Defective Products	Units Bought – Quantity $	Shipping Costs	Comments
Buying organization absorbs costs	1,000/0.95 = 1,052.63 or 1,053 units, $10,530	1,053 × $1 = $1,053	Buyer must pay both acquisition and shipping cost for 53 extra units
Supplier absorbs costs	1,000 units, $10,000	1,000 × $1 = $1,000	Buyer fills need and returns defective units at the supplier's expense
Supplier replaces defective units; buyer pays return shipping	1,000 units, $10,000	1,053 × $1 = $1,053	Buyer pays to return 53 defective units
Supplier replaces defective units; buyer pays shipping both ways	1,000 units, $10,000	1,106 × $1 = $1,106	Buyer pays to return 53 defective units and to ship replacements (106 units shipped at $1 per unit)

NOTE   All figures assume 95 percent acceptable units, a need for 1,000 total units, a price of $10 per unit, and one-way shipping costs of $0.25 per unit.

- Supplier's willingness to remain flexible and accommodate changes in production schedules
- Loss of internal skills in building outsourced products
- Supplier's labor-management climate
- Supplier's warranty, repair, and support systems

Qualitative costs become particularly important in increasingly common decisions whether or not to buy from international suppliers. Foreign suppliers can often promise high quality, innovative products that domestic firms do not offer, low prices, and advanced design and production capabilities. However, some important qualitative costs offset these benefits:

- *Time differences*   At least, seven time zones separate a buyer in California from a potential supplier in Germany. The buyer may dislike having to make phone calls at 5 a.m. to reach the German supplier at 2 p.m. local time.
- *Cultural/linguistic differences*   Most Canadian and American firms feel most comfortable dealing with other Canadian and American firms. Everyone understands English, and they share many cultural characteristics. A Malaysian supplier may not speak English well, complicating communication, or understand the practices of a North American firm. For example, representatives of many North American firms may routinely drink wine or beer during a business lunch, potentially offending people from Malaysia, a Moslem country that does not tolerate consumption of alcohol.
- *Lead times*   An order takes longer to travel to a foreign supplier than to a domestic one. This increases order lead time, and it may decrease flexibility. For example, in the recession of the mid-1980s, one American buyer of steel suffered a setback when demand declined after the firm committed to purchase from Japanese suppliers which had lead times of 6 months and longer. American steel makers were quoting lead times of weeks or days, so the buyer could have avoided the long-term commitment.
- *Hidden costs*   Costs for transactions with foreign suppliers may change due to exchange-rate fluctuations, tariffs, duties, and high inventories to compensate for long lead times.
- *Training/technical support*   Foreign suppliers may have trouble providing essential training and technical support to distant buyers. Further complications can arise from instructional materials, as when they give measurements in centimeters to service personnel who normally measure in inches.
- *Returns and repairs of defective products*   If a batch of inputs from a foreign supplier fails to meet quality standards, the buyer may have to document problems, store defective units, pay for return shipments, deal with customs, and accommodate long lead times. The cost of quality rises for purchases from foreign suppliers.

Many qualitative costs can influence the trade-offs identified in quantitative analysis. A risk-averse decision maker may resist buying from a supplier, despite substantial cost advantages, to avoid qualitative costs.

Review the Capabilities of Current Suppliers.   After fully assessing the total quantitative and qualitative costs of both making and buying a needed input, the analysis must determine whether current suppliers can realistically handle any planned increases in orders. This decision requires a review of the technical, financial, manufacturing, and quality-related capabilities of those firms to evaluate their likely future strengths rather than their past performance.

Evaluate New Suppliers.   To decide whether to purchase from new suppliers, the buying organization must compare their capabilities against those of the best current suppliers or industry leaders. This benchmarking seeks to clearly position new suppliers relative to appropriate standards as an indication of the real value added by lower prices for inputs. A low price offered by a weak supplier does not represent any real bargain.

Make and Implement a Decision.   After extensive study, the buying organization's managers must make a decision based on their available information. If they decide to buy the input, they designate a particular supplier and document the anticipated benefits of outsourcing; if they decide to make the input internally, they document the reasons for this decision. In implementing the decision, they negotiate the terms of the purchase contract or acquire assets to initiate internal production.

Monitor the Decision and Revise It as Necessary.   Make-buy analysis does not end with the start of production or a purchase. In one more step, operations managers must compare the actual results of the decision against estimates and identify potential problems. This information may indicate a need for corrective action such as terminating the contract of an inferior supplier and reassigning it to another firm. The following example illustrates the application of this important technique.

Make-Buy Analysis: An Example.   Advanced Alliance Manufacturing (AAM) designs and fabricates intricate metal components for small orders (typically less than 100 units). In less than 10 years of operation, this firm has developed a reputation in its industry for quality, speed, and expertise. AAM has been able to develop this capability through heavy investments in advanced, computer-driven design and production systems, emphasis on recruiting highly skilled operators, extensive employee training, and systems for extensive, on-going communications among designers, customers, and shop-floor workers. These unique capabilities give AAM a significant competitive advantage that rivals cannot duplicate.

Rapidly growing demand has begun to exceed AAM's total capacity, and its operations managers cannot expand the system fast enough to keep pace. The firm needs to free up capacity soon, perhaps by subcontracting some of the parts it currently builds in-house. As one possible candidate for subcontracting, managers have chosen a flanged bracket, a relatively simple, commodity-type component, versions of which appear in products throughout the industry, including many of AAM's products. The firm began to build this part internally because it kept existing workers and equipment busy.

AAM has received a bid to supply the flanged bracket from MGT Industries, a past supplier located about 25 miles away that has provided responsive service and quality products. AAM has also received a bid from Keng Specialties of Hong Kong, a firm AAM has not dealt with before, but which has provided first-rate product samples. AAM managers have compiled the information in Exhibit 13.21 from the potential suppliers' bids and other sources.

Top managers want to avoid unnecessary risk in this make-buy decision. Therefore, operations managers must decide whether to make or buy the flanged bracket, and which supplier to choose if they decide to buy. (They cannot split the order between two or more suppliers.) They expect to need 20,000 units over the following year.

[**EXHIBIT 13.21**]

Data for Make-Buy Analysis for the Flanged Bracket

Criterion	Make	Buy from MGT Industries	Buy from Keng Specialties
Cost per unit	$1.75/unit	$1.63/unit	$1.20/unit (all purchases in lots of 2000)
Delivery cost	$0.05/unit	$0.09/unit	$0.20/unit (10000 minimum ship quantity)
Tool cost (dies, fixtures, etc.)	$15,000	$12,500	$10,000
Reliability[a]	95%	98%+	98%
Return policy		100% replacement with reimbursement for all transportation costs	100% replacement, after buyer pays transportation costs to Hong Kong
Order lead time	3 weeks	2 weeks	8 weeks
Duration of contract		2 years	1 year
Other details		5 years' experience as a supplier	New supplier, AAM liable for tariffs and duties
Desire for business	Not applicable	High	High
Primary language	English	English	Chinese, though English spoken

[a]Percentage acceptable.

The operations managers must compare three different alternatives: making the flanged bracket internally (the base case), buying it from MGT Industries, or buying it from Keng Specialties. To do this, they apply the make-buy analysis procedure.

Assess the Relationship of the Product to the Firm's Core Competencies.   AAM's core competencies center on quick fabrication of small quantities of complex metal components. The flanged bracket plays no critical role in this process.

Evaluate the Suitability of Product Characteristics for Outsourcing.   The flanged bracket is a standard, readily available product. In fact, AAM has built it internally in the past only to occupy idle capacity. This product represents a good candidate for outsourcing.

Evaluate the Reasons for Outsourcing.   AAM's short-term demand crunch has created the need to free up capacity. If the firm buys the flanged bracket from a supplier rather than producing it, it can devote that capacity to other products that influence its core competencies.

Assess all of the Relevant Quantitative Costs.   This step lays out the costs for each option, as in Exhibit 13.22. Clearly, internal production represents the most expensive option. Buying from Keng Specialties seems like the cheapest option, but AAM's operations managers must recognize that the exhibit understates the total costs of that option. Keng requires such large order quantities that AAM would have to buy at least half a year's requirements at a time, so it would incur significant storage and inventory carrying costs.

[**E X H I B I T   1 3 . 2 2**]

Quantitative Costs for the Flanged Bracket

Criterion	Make	Buy from MGT Industries	Buy from Keng Specialties
Order size to ensure 20,000 good units	20,000/0.95 = 21,053 units	20,000 units	20,000 units
Cost of 20,000 good units	21,053 × $1.75 = $36,842.75	20,000 × $1.63 = $32,600	20,000 × $1.20 = $24,000.00
Shipment size and cost for 20,000 good units	21,053 × $0.05 = $1,052.65	20,000 × $0.09 = $1,800	(20,000/0.98) × $0.20 = $4,210.53
Tool costs	$15,000.00	$12,500.00	$10,000.00
Other costs			Storage costs[a]
Total costs	$52,895.40	$46,900.00	$38,210.53
Savings by buying from lowest-cost supplier	$14,684.87	$8,689.47	$0

[a]Requirement to ship a minimum of 10,000 units, or 6 months' demand, creates inventory carrying cost

Assess All Qualitative Costs.   Exhibit 13.23 summarizes the subjective, qualitative costs that affect each option. In weighing these factors, AAM determines whether the cost savings of dealing with Keng Specialties ($8,700) justify the additional risks or whether MGT Industries offers a better deal. It would buy from MGT Industries only if it valued the intangible benefits of that option at more than $8,700. The risk-averse managers of AAM favor the bid from MGT Industries.

[**E X H I B I T   1 3 . 2 3**]

Qualitative Costs for the Flanged Bracket

Criterion	Make	Buy from MGT Industries	Buy from Keng Specialties
Advantages	Good past experience Lowest risk through direct control	Good past experience Local supplier Similar emphasis on speed and quality Low cost of quality Strong desire for business Shortest delivery lead time	Lowest total costs (excluding inventory carrying costs) Shortest contract period
Disadvantages	Highest total cost Requires capacity needed elsewhere Not a core competency	Longest contract (2 years) Above lowest costs	Uncertain inventory carrying costs No past experience Uncertain costs for tariffs and duties Distant location Different language and culture
Potential assessment[a]	−−	++	−

[a]Subjective assessment of attractiveness, where −− means strongly unattractive and ++ means strongly attractive.

Review the Capabilities of Current Suppliers.   Before finally deciding to buy from MGT Industries, AAM must evaluate its capabilities. If MGT has sufficient capacity to supply the inputs that AAM needs, both today and into the future, that supplier gets the order.

Evaluate New Suppliers.   Before more risk-tolerant managers would award the contract to Keng Specialties, they should carefully evaluate its systems and capabilities to verify that it can provide needed levels of quality and support.

Make and Implement a Decision.   Having collected all necessary information and completed the required analysis, AAM awards a 2-year contract to make the flanged bracket to MGT Industries. It can immediately begin converting the capacity with which it produced that product to make other products. Only subsequent monitoring of the results of the decision will demonstrate a need to revise the contract.

Supplier Scheduling

supplier scheduling

A system that controls releases of orders and continuing communications of priorities, needs, and quantities between suppliers and the buying organization's OM system

Once operations managers have completed make-buy analysis, they must develop systems for controlling outside production of outsourced products. **Supplier scheduling** controls releases of orders and continuing communications of priorities, needs, and quantities between suppliers and the buying organization's OM system. Supplier scheduling activities ensure that suppliers always support their customer's transformation system with the quality goods that it needs when and where it needs them in the correct quantities and at appropriate prices.

Supplier scheduling techniques can create a number of different systems. A list of orders released periodically, perhaps weekly or monthly, by the buyer may drive a supplier schedule. The orders indicate the products that each supplier should provide along with quantities, deadlines, and delivery locations. Suppliers then accept responsibility for filling these orders.

In practice, such a system tends to encourage accumulation of inventories to buffer processes against disruption by lapses from schedules. To guard against disappointing a valued customer, the supplier fills a finished-goods inventory, from which it distributes products in response to an order. This arrangement decouples its OM system from that of the customer, as shown in Exhibit 13.24. Without a stock of finished goods, the supplier may have to change its current master production schedule regularly to accommodate surprises in the customer's routine orders. These changes ripple through existing orders for components, forcing work stations to abandon some jobs and expedite or change others and creating massive confusion on the shop floor.

As an alternative, the buying firm can establish direct links between its own OM system and those of its suppliers through some computerized production planning and scheduling system such as materials requirements planning (MRP). Operations managers then provide up-to-date production schedules to all suppliers for the components that they provide, either through the mail or through some electronic system. This becomes especially effective when suppliers can tie into the buyer's computer system through EDI or by logging in directly and downloading schedule information. Suppliers benefit from this transfer of knowledge in several ways.

Detailed Knowledge of Buyer Needs.   Advanced supplier scheduling systems provide in-depth data about customer needs both currently and in the future. The forecasts help suppliers to manage their own operations by follow-up

Supplier Scheduling: Inventory as a Buffer

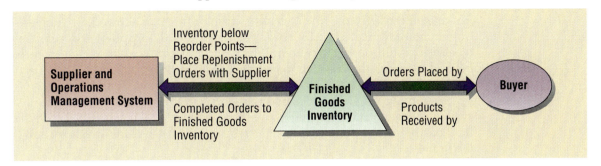

communications to determine the temporary or long-term nature of a perceived change in demand. They can begin responding to any long-term change early by building inventories, adding extra shifts or overtime production, or even expanding the physical capacities of their systems.

Simplified Internal Supplier Scheduling.   Detailed supplier schedules can enter directly into suppliers' systems for developing their master production schedules. This matches customer needs directly to internal production flows.

Improved Communications.   Since supplier scheduling systems like MRP produce and distribute reports regularly (e.g., weekly), they encourage continuous flows of communications between the buyer and its suppliers. Current information about buyer needs helps suppliers to set priorities, expediting some orders and setting aside others. In addition, representatives of the buyer and suppliers can share reactions to the MRP reports and discuss the impact of changes on both. This discussion educates each about the other's capabilities, helping both to plan for the future. To see the impact of supplier scheduling systems, especially MRP, consider a detailed example.

Supplier Scheduling at Steelcase.   Steelcase, a manufacturer of office furniture and office environments, quickly realized the importance of MRP as a supplier scheduling system in the early 1980s.[17] As the firm implemented MRP internally, the purchasing department began exploring the possibilities of sharing MRP-generated information with suppliers. They began training suppliers to use and interpret Steelcase's MRP system and its reports, which then served as a basis for negotiating supplier production and buyer commitments.

MRP really enhanced the firm's procedures for ordering fabric. Steelcase's production of office chairs created widely varying needs for fabric in different colors and with different textures. Steelcase wanted quick delivery of fabric in a rainbow of colors, while suppliers preferred to make the fabric and dye it after receiving orders to avoid carrying large, expensive inventories of individual colors.

When Steelcase buyers reviewed this dilemma with their fabric suppliers, they discovered that those firms took 3 to 5 weeks to generate raw fabric which they

[17]Phillip L. Carter and Robert M. Monczka, "Steelcase, Inc.: MRP in Purchasing," in *Case Studies in Materials Requirements Planning,* ed. by E. W. Davis (Falls Church, Va.: American Production and Inventory Control Society, 1978).

dyed in the last week. Based on this knowledge, Steelcase agreed to provide suppliers with MRP reports that projected future requirements for 13 weeks. Suppliers could safely make raw fabric for all orders in the first 8 weeks of a schedule; the buyers committed to buying this material. Of these first 8 weeks' orders, both parties treated those for the first 4 weeks as firm orders that allowed no changes. The buyers communicated exact color requirements to suppliers 2 weeks before Steelcase would need the material, leaving an extra week in which to respond beyond the week they needed to dye the fabric. MRP reports included projections for 5 additional weeks to outline trends in future demand.

By relying on supplier schedules derived from Steelcase's internal MRP system, suppliers have improved the coordination of their schedules with that of their customer. In addition, they have reduced their needs for inventory and their lead times.

Limitations of Supplier Scheduling.   When scheduling suppliers, operations managers must remember that their firm represents only one source of demand for a supplier. An individual firm influences its suppliers in proportion to the sizes of its orders and their importance as compared with those of other customers. Recall that an earlier section cited this fact to support the trend toward concentrating orders among few suppliers.

Also, a supplier scheduling system must do more that simply project future requirements. Suppliers need stability just as buying organizations do. A firm's own shop floor has difficulty coping with constant schedule changes, and suppliers experience the same problems. As a result, supplier schedules must designate some period before an order's due date when no more changes are allowed. The Steelcase system prevented changes over the 4 weeks following a schedule's issue date.

Value Analysis/Value Engineering

value analysis (value engineering)

A structured process that seeks to improve a product's design while maintaining its functional characteristics and marketing appeal to customers

Suppliers can contribute to product design efforts through **value analysis**, also called **value engineering**. This structured process seeks to improve a product's design while maintaining its functional characteristics and marketing appeal to customers. Typical value engineering projects combine internal personnel in cross-functional teams that bring together critical information about the product, its function, its marketing appeal, and its production methods. This technique is most effective during the early stages of product design.

Many companies now invite supplier input during product design by enhancing their value engineering functions to include suppliers on project teams. These initiatives often form part of comprehensive early supplier involvement (ESI) programs mentioned in the earlier discussion of the benefits of partnership (Exhibit 13.25).

Value engineering projects often begin structured product design reviews to make products easier to produce without sacrificing performance. A redesign of housings for electric drills replaced cast steel housings with plastic ones. While steel housings were very durable, they also raised production costs and stretched lead times. Value engineering teams identified the purpose of the housing as protecting the user from the inner workings of the drill and providing a convenient way to hold it. While plastic proved less durable than steel, it was easier and cheaper to make, took less lead time, and made the drill lighter. This last change pleased users who worked with the drill for long periods. Also, plastic did not conduct electricity reducing the safety risk of electrical shock as compared to steel housings and eliminating the need for grounding the tool.

[**E X H I B I T   1 3 . 2 5**]

Value Analysis with Simultaneous Engineering, and ESI Programs

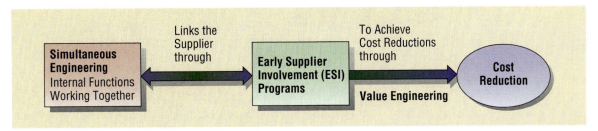

Such projects usually involve significant commitments of corporate resources, time, and effort. Many firms willingly make these investments to achieve attractive potential benefits:

- *Reduction in average purchasing costs of 25 percent*   As a general rule, a firm can reduce costs at least 10 percent without really trying; reductions of up to 75 percent are not uncommon.
- *Significant rate of return*   Value engineering programs usually yield returns on the resources invested ranging between 10 to 1 and 100 to 1.
- *Improved customer satisfaction*   Properly applied value engineering techniques enhance all elements of customer satisfaction (cost, quality, lead time, and flexibility) while improving the performance to cost ratio (i.e., value).
- *Lucky discoveries*   In exploring new technologies and materials, designers often discover ways to simultaneously enhance performance and reduce costs, as when manufacturers of electric drills made their products safer for users as they tried to make them lighter and cheaper to produce.
- *Higher employee morale*   Value engineering encourages and fosters teamwork and creativity. As people look at old problems in new ways, they often come to view the cost reduction as an intriguing game rather than as a difficult task.

Techniques for Value Engineering.   Product designers can deliver these benefits through a relatively simple process to understand, learn, and apply. Value engineering requires no complex techniques or procedures.

Value engineering begins by trying to improve functional characteristics rather than to reduce cost. An initial focus on cost tends to result in lower quality and reduced performance due to cheaper materials. Instead, reduced costs emerge as a by-product of the value engineering process.

By starting with functional characteristics, designers describe what the product does, not what it is. A paper clip, for example, is a method for marking pages or keeping papers together. Designers can then separate functions into two categories, those that make the product work and those that make it sell. For example, a drill's housing protects the user from the motor and gears; this helps to make it work. A housing with an especially comfortable handle makes the drill easier to use, which helps to sell the product.

Value engineering proceeds by describing each function in a two-word phrase (one verb and one noun). It then categorizes these phrases according to a typical customer's assessment of the importance of the function and the cost to

Value Engineering Responses for Functional Characteristics

Function's Worth[a]	Function's Cost	Action Required
High	Low	Emphasize
High	High	Reduce cost
Low	Low	Improve worth
Low	High	Eliminate

[a]Rated by end user.

the manufacturer of providing that function. Value engineering of the electric drill's housing might produce the following phrases:

Functions that Make the Product Work	Functions that Make the Product Sell
Provide grip	Reduce fatigue
Protect user	Allay fears
Ensure safety	Simplify use

Exhibit 13.26 shows some likely responses by the value engineering team to the results of these categories.

Some important questions can guide the assessment of the benefits and costs of product functions:[18]

- Can value engineering eliminate the function entirely?
- Can it eliminate the product that provides the function and provide the function in some other way?
- Can it simplify the product?
- Can it alter the product design to accommodate a faster method of production?
- Can it employ standard components or materials?
- Can it change specifications in beneficial ways?
- Would a higher-cost material simplify design and/or production enough to offset its cost?
- Can value engineering reduce the costs of tight tolerances or product finishes, tests, or packaging?
- Can it add other features that customers value (e.g., service, safety, flexibility)?

Value engineering produces a very value-intense product design. It generates a product that provides only those functions that customers want at the lowest possible total cost.

Supplier Certification and Evaluation

After linking suppliers to their own OM system, operations managers need some way to manage these linkages easily so that they can focus on running the internal factory without worrying about inputs from external factories. To guarantee reliable inputs without concentration, many firms maintain supplier certification and

[18]Bhote, *Strategic Supply Management*, p. 334.

[**EXHIBIT 13.27**]

Links between Certification and Evaluation of Suppliers

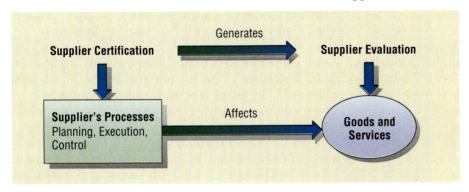

supplier evaluation programs. Certification verifies that suppliers operate effective processes, while evaluation focuses on the outputs of those processes, especially their quality levels. Exhibit 13.27 illustrates this relationship.

Techniques for Supplier Certification. Recall that practitioners of just-in-time manufacturing employ certification procedures to identify and develop small groups of good suppliers with reliable processes. They look for clearly documented sequences of activities under tight management control. Certified suppliers can demonstrate clearly and objectively to any outside observer their success at identifying, reducing, and controlling variations in products, processes, and materials using the tools of total quality management (TQM), just-in-time manufacturing, and the Operations Management Toolkit. Certification identifies suppliers that can reliably meet quality, delivery, cost, and flexibility targets because their processes support those objectives. They reduce the risk to the OM system so that operations managers need not continuously inspect or monitor supplier performance.

Supplier certification programs often conduct site visits. Teams with representatives from operations management, purchasing, engineering, and cost accounting visit the supplier's facilities and study first-hand such processes as:

- Materials-handling systems
- Capacity and production-planning systems
- Scheduling and shop-floor control systems
- Preventive maintenance programs
- Product-design systems
- Quality-control methods
- Database-management procedures
- Housekeeping routines

Certification teams evaluate these processes by reviewing available documentation for completeness and accuracy, assessing control procedures, and evaluating specific statistics, and judging employees' knowledge of processes and corrective procedures. A team member might spend time with a supplier's machine operator asking questions like how the firm would react to a machine breakdown or discovery of defective components. Such visits often provide detailed insights into suppliers' processes and management methods.

As an alternative, the buying organization can accept inputs only from externally certified suppliers. Earlier chapters have discussed quality certification/evaluation programs like ISO 9000 and the Malcolm Baldrige National Quality Award. These programs set out well-defined criteria for OM processes. Xerox and Motorola, among other firms, judge their suppliers against these exacting standards.

Supplier Evaluation. A complement to certification requirements, supplier evaluation provides essential feedback about the performance of the firm's inputs. This formal communication tells suppliers how well their products have performed relative to specific standards and indicates any problems that require management attention.

In many ways, supplier evaluation resembles classroom tests. Like student evaluation procedures, supplier evaluation gives easily comprehensible scores. A firm's scores may reflect conformance to some minimum criteria (e.g., percentage of deliveries within 1 day after due dates) or relative to other suppliers. Evaluation scores facilitate improvement by directing attention to critical weaknesses that the supplier must improve.

Supplier evaluation also clarifies expectations. Any evaluation process must begin by defining the desired results. Supplier evaluation sets specific criteria for both acceptable and superior performance to guide suppliers' efforts to change their systems. To help suppliers to understand these criteria and their implications for company management, the evaluation system should specify a few simple standards that reflect the competitive values of the buying organization. These standards should set difficult but attainable goals for suppliers and emphasize potential positive achievements rather than just thresholds to avoid negative sanctions.

More generally, supplier evaluation facilitates communication. Evaluations often stimulate discussions with customers about perceived problems, recent developments, and anticipated future changes. The evaluations also direct attention toward product characteristics that need improvement, leaving good performance to continue. This information becomes especially important when buyers trade with fewer suppliers, each of which must know without question what its customer wants. By meeting at least the minimum criteria, a supplier can usually ensure a continuing stream of orders.

The results of such rigorous evaluations provide rapid and timely feedback. To gain the most significant benefits, supplier evaluation should become a regular feature of supply chain management. Many firms initiate such reviews either periodically, perhaps quarterly or monthly, or after the buyer encounters some problem with the supplier's products. In general, more frequent evaluations improve performance because the actions and events that cause certain scores remain fresh in the minds of supplier personnel.

Finally, supplier evaluation creates an audit trail as periodic reviews document suppliers' performance over time. If a supplier receives repeated poor evaluations and does not demonstrate sufficient corrective action, then the stream of orders will stop. Formal evaluations justify such decisions and reinforce the buyer's commitment to good suppliers.

CHAPTER SUMMARY

Chrysler faced a critical challenge to design and build a subcompact car quickly, effectively, and efficiently. To meet this challenge, the firm redefined its transformation system to implement close outpartnering relationships with selected suppliers that involved them in the product from the initial design stage through manufacturing and delivery. Along the way, Chrysler encountered a number of important principles of supply chain management:

1. Every OM system combines two components: the internal factory over which the operations manager has responsibility and the external factories of suppliers. Operations managers can extend many of the same principles and practices for managing the internal factory to control activities in the external factory.

2. Suppliers provide essential goods and services and critical expertise and knowledge to a buyer's OM system. Capably managed suppliers can provide several important benefits, including reduced costs, enhanced flexibility, and name recognition.

3. The buying organization's purchasing function plays a crucial role in effective management of the supply chain.

4. To achieve the goals of adding value for customers by controlling and eliminating variance, operations managers must manage the entire supply chain from first-tier suppliers down to producers of raw materials.

5. Supply chain management relationships fall along a spectrum from confrontation to partnerships. Confrontation typically characterizes outsourcing relationships, which suit purchases of mature products in stable markets. Partnerships create outpartnering systems like the one Chrysler developed in building its Neon. These systems create new transformation processes that intertwine elements of both internal and external factories.

6. Outpartnering assigns tasks according to partners' core competencies, or critical skills or knowledge sets through which they generate value for customers. Each firm's core competencies determine the central processes on which it should concentrate its resources and those that it can safely subcontract.

7. At its logical extremes, outpartnering creates virtual corporations and virtual factories which blur the boundaries between the responsibilities and decisions of a buying firm and its suppliers.

8. One tool for supply chain management, make-buy analysis, bases subcontracting decisions on the results of total cost analysis.

9. Another tool, supplier scheduling, distributes detailed information among suppliers to coordinate their production activities with those of the buyer's OM system.

10. A third tool, value analysis/value engineering, works to reduce cost and improve value by identifying the critical functions of a product, determining the costs to provide those functions, and formulating strategies for improving functions while reducing costs. Operations managers can apply this tool most effectively during the early stages of product design as part of an early supplier involvement (ESI) program.

11. Finally, supplier certification and evaluation provides feedback about the performance of input processes and products. Supplier certification identifies suppliers that have demonstrated control of their processes to reduce variances in materials, process activities, and products. Supplier evaluation generates feedback about past performance.

Supply chain management is a dynamic process driven by value. As new value-driven requirements emerge, operations managers must implement new methods of controlling suppliers and entire supply chains.

[K E Y   T E R M S]

supplier 603	outpartnering 606	partnership 616
product (capacity) buy 605	purchasing 606	core competency 626
	reverse marketing 611	virtual corporation 628
process (capability) buy 605	supplier council 612	supplier scheduling 638
	supply chain 613	value analysis (value
outsourcing 606	confrontation 616	engineering) 640

[D I S C U S S I O N   Q U E S T I O N S]

1. You receive an assignment to join your firm's supplier-certification team. What supplier activities would you study? Name specific functions and procedures that you would analyze to assess the overall reliability of supplier's systems and processes.

2. How does supplier certification relate to the concept of poka-yoke discussed in Chapter 8?

3. Identify the core competencies of the following companies:
   a. McDonald's
   b. Wal-Mart
   c. Taco Bell
   d. Compaq

4. Complete a value engineering study of the following products:
   a. paper clip
   b. tie clip

5. In what ways did Chrysler's decision to involve its suppliers early in Neon's development contribute to its ability to produce a quality car in a timely manner? What definition of quality is most appropriate? How would you define *quality*?

6. A firm decides to move its supplier relationships toward "full blown partnerships." List five actions the buying company could take to signal this change. What might be initial reactions of the firm's suppliers? Why?

7. What are the conceptual linkages between JIT's emphasis on a limited number of suppliers and the concepts discussed in this total supply management chapter?

8. Discuss the evolving role of information technology in total supply management. List five technological innovations that have had a major impact on the way leading edge firms manage their supply chains. List five information technology innovations that will impact this function in the future. In what ways will these enable the firm to enhance the value of the goods and services it offers its customers?

9. Discuss the evolving role of the purchasing manager in the supply chain management process. List five changes that have impacted the purchaser's role. What changes in organization design did each necessitate?

10. Even though it is against corporate policy, certain suppliers routinely send gifts to your company's purchasing manager each year. Discuss ways in which your firm can deal with the problem to avoid both offending its suppliers and giving an appearance of impropriety. Would your recommendations be different for buyers working at your firm's offshore operations?

11. Discuss how total supply chain management contributes to each element of the value equation:
   a. Time base competition
   b. Quality
   c. Flexibility
   d. Cost

12. What do suppliers receive in return for engaging in closer ties with their major firms?
13. List five firms that you think have achieved a competitive advantage through vertical integration. Then cite five firms that you think are at a competitive disadvantage because of vertical integration. Compare and contrast the end product market and raw material sourcing conditions of each. What can you infer?
14. Discuss the linkages between a firm's demand management and demand forecasting activities and its supply chain management function. Cite five instances in which a firm has caused problems for its suppliers because it was unable to provide reasonably accurate demand projections.
15. Discuss the role electronic data interchange, EDI, has played in the supplier-buyer relationship. What decisions are implicitly made when one decides to utilize EDI? What does the firm get? What does it give up?
16. Given the increasing importance of environmental concerns, how would you incorporate these issues into the make-buy process?

C A U T I O N

[C R I T I C A L   T H I N K I N G   R E Q U I R E D]

1. Partnerships are attractive for both suppliers and buyers because of the close ties that they create, but they also require changes in the behavior of both the buying and supplying organizations. This is not hard to achieve if the buying organization is larger than the supplier. How do you bring about such changes if the supplying organization is larger than the buying organization? Why would there be problems?
2. Supply chain management crosses international borders. As we integrate our OM systems with those of suppliers located in the Far East and Europe, what types of problems and opportunities do these linkages create both for our firms and for the OM system?
3. Given the attractiveness of virtual factories, under what conditions does it make sense to vertically integrate (i.e., buy our suppliers)?

C A S E   1 3 . 1

Trail Frames Chassis

Trail Frames Chassis (TFC) of Elkhart, Indiana, is a major manufacturer of chassis for the motor home and van markets. Since it was founded in 1976 by two unemployed truck manufacturing engineers, TFC has grown into one of the major suppliers in this market. Success in the motor home and van markets is difficult because of the constant rate of change. Buyers in their late 40s to 60s want motor homes that ride like cars. They are willing to pay for innovations such as anti-lock braking systems, power-assisted steering, and computer-balanced suspension.

TFC produces a pusher type of chassis, that is, one powered by a diesel engine located at the rear. While costly to build, this design offers many advantages over front-engine designs (no tunnel for the transmission, reduced engine noise, better handling). However, these chassis make motor homes very expensive ($100,000 and up). TFC builds its chassis for large manufacturers such as

Winnebago, Airstream, and Gulf Air. In general, these companies order small quantities (5 to 10 in a batch), with many units customized to a specific customer's requirements.

TFC has become successful by developing new designs quickly. These designs build on TFC's extensive experience with motor home users, its knowledge of technological advances, and its ability to incorporate these advances in its designs. As a result, TFC has become the technology leader in its market. It is generally recognized that no one in the industry can match TFC's design and marketing knowledge. Until recently, TFC could design and build a chassis in less than 30 days, but lead times have been growing.

Recently, increasing demand and limited capital have stressed TFC. No longer able to keep up with demand, managers, led by president John Stickley, have studied the problem and identified the design department as the major bottleneck where demand exceeds capacity. While managers pondered this problem, they received an offer from Computer-Images, a design house located in Grand Rapids, Michigan, to take over the design responsibilities for the low end of the firm's product line. Comparing its terms with current design costs make the bid seem very attractive. Furthermore, Computer-Images has offered to work with TFC as a virtual corporation receiving specifications by electronic communications from TFC and generating new drawings with copies to TFC. The proposal would free up TFC staff to focus demand for medium to high-end chassis.

The table below lays out the details of the proposed make-buy decision. TFC can choose only one option. You must make a recommendation to the president that should cover both short-term and long-term considerations.

Criterion	Computer-Image Proposal	TFC Make Option
Contract period	3 years with option to cancel after first year with 45 days' warning	Not applicable
Cost per design	$225 per chassis	$490 per chassis (arrived at by summing direct labor computers and including corporate overhead)
Number of chassis per year	1,000 minimum to 2,500 maximum (1,250 expected), commitment to 1,250 designs per year	2,000 chassis maximum (assuming stable growth in other chassis lines)
One-time setup costs	$300,000[a]	$200,000[b]
Lead time[c]	< 2 working days	5 to 10 working days
Quality	All designs tested via computer simulation and certified feasible	Feasibility of designs based on expertise of designers
Time until delivery of first design	3 months	Immediately
Other terms and conditions	Computer-Images would be free to work with any other chassis builder. All designs generated by Computer-Images would become the property of Computer-Images. Computer-Images requires a training period of 6 months for TFC to teach critical design tasks.	To significantly expand design capacity would require a period of 6 to 8 months.

[a]Computer systems, training, etc.
[b]To expand design capacity
[c]From transmission of specifications to receipt of new design

CASE 13.2

Apple Computer

Throughout 1995, Apple Computer had a problem. Even though the firm's sales had been increased by 25 percent, the firm continued to lose market share. Rumors of the firm's sale or decline were common. Executives seemed to be leaving at an ever-increasing rate. One key executive was rumored to have sold all of his stock.

One cause of Apple's problem lay in its supply chain. Until 1995, Apple had a superbly designed product. Its renowned operating system had long been the envy of users in the Windows environment. The much ballyhooed and long-delayed arrival of Microsoft's Windows 95 really did not do much more than give the so-called IBM compatibles group the capabilities that Apple users long had had. But the advent of Windows 95 cast a negative pall over Apple's future and that of its loyal suppliers.

It was against this backdrop that suppliers were being asked to increase their capacity to meet Apple's growing needs for certain key components. It was true that Apple's sales were increasing. It was true that Apple finally had agreed to license its proprietary operating systems. But all this talk about Apple's future was beginning to cause certain cracks in supplier relationships.

The problem was further confounded by a product design decision that Apple made for some of its 1995 product introductions. Prior to this, Apple had used proprietary connections in its computers to interface with Apple-compatible computer accessories, such as printers, monitors, multimedia boards, etc. Its suppliers had to invest to make components for which there were few alternate corporate customers. But they dutifully made these investments.

Now, Apple had decided to adopt some connection devices that were standard for most other personal computers. The reason given for this design decision was logical: Apple users would have access to a wider range of products. No longer would Apple users need to wait for a company to make an Apple version of a neat new accessory. No longer would the Apple user have to pay a higher price for an Apple version. In short, this design change increase the value of the future Apple products.

It also made it somewhat easier for Apple to procure components for its final assembly plants. This was good news for Apple's production planners. It provided its purchasing managers additional supplier options. But for Apple's existing supply chain network, it may have seemed like a betrayal.

QUESTIONS

1. As Apple's chief corporate strategist, evaluate the pros and cons of this product design change.
2. Would it be in Apple's strategic interest to become less committed to its existing supplier-buyer partnerships?
3. How would you answer that same question if you were a major Apple supplier?
4. What type of program would you recommend to assuage Apple's existing supplier base?

[SELECTED READINGS]

Bhote, Keri R. *Strategic Supplier Management: A Blueprint for Revitalizing the Manufacturer-Supplier Partnership.* New York: AMACOM, 1989.

Byrne, John A., Richard Brandt, and Otis Port. "The Virtual Corporation." *Business Week,* February 8, 1993, pp. 98–102.

Cavinato, Joseph L. *Purchasing and Materials Management.* St. Paul, Minn.: West, 1984.

Davidow, William H., and Michael S. Malone. *The Virtual Corporation: Structuring and Revitalizing the Corporation for the 21st Century.* New York: Harper Business, 1992.

Dobler, Donald, David Burt, and Lamar Lee. *Purchasing and Materials Management,* 5th ed. New York: McGraw-Hill, 1990.

Emmelhorne, Margaret A. *Guide to Purchasing: Electronic Data Interchange.* Oradell, N.J.: National Association of Purchasing Management, 1986.

Hamel, Gary, and C. K. Prahalad. "Corporate Imagination and Expeditionary Marketing," *Harvard Business Review,* July–August 1991.

———. "Strategy as Stretch and Leverage." *Harvard Business Review,* March–April 1993.

———. *Competing for the Future: Breakthrough Strategies for Seizing Control of Your Industry and Creating the Markets of Tomorrow.* Cambridge, Mass.: Harvard Business School Press, 1994.

Leenders, Michiel R., and David L. Blenkhorn. *Reverse Marketing: The New Buyer-Supplier Relationship.* New York: Free Press, 1989.

Leenders, Michiel R., Harold Fearon, and Wilbur England. *Purchasing and Materials Management,* 9th ed. Homewood, Ill.: Richard D. Irwin, 1989.

Maskell, Brian. *Performance Measurement for World Class Manufacturing.* Cambridge, Mass.: Productivity Press, 1991.

Peters, Tom. *The Tom Peters Seminar: Crazy Times Call for Crazy Organizations.* New York: Vintage Books, 1994.

Prahalad, C. K., and Gary Hamel. "The Core Competence of the Corporation." *Harvard Business Review,* May–June 1990, pp. 79–91.

Quinn, James Brian, and Frederick G. Hilmer. "Strategic Outsourcing." *Sloan Management Review,* Summer 1994, pp. 43–55.

Schorr, J. E., and T. F. Wallace. *High Performance Purchasing.* Brattleboro, Vt.: Oliver Wight, 1986.

Sproull, Lee, and Sara Kiesler. *Connections: New Ways of Working in the Networked Organization.* Cambridge, Mass.: MIT Press, 1993.

Womack, James P., Daniel T. Jones, and Daniel Roos. *The Machine that Changed the World.* New York: Rawson Associates, 1990.

PART FIVE

Planning Issues in
Value-Driven OM Systems

CHAPTER FOURTEEN

Resource Management

CHAPTER OBJECTIVES

[At the end of this chapter, you should be able to]

- Explain the role of the resource-management process in strategic business planning.
- Trace the links between the resource-management process and other facets of operations management.
- Describe the differences between resource management for service operations and manufacturing operations.
- Illustrate the ties among long-term, intermediate, and short-term resource-management processes.
- State the conditions that favor planning based on aggregate and disaggregated product demand.
- Establish the length of the planning horizon.
- Outline the tradeoffs in classic methods for aggregate production planning.
- Demonstrate master operations scheduling techniques for both services and manufacturing operations.
- Show the influences of the resource-management process on capacity management.

Pink Floyd to Go

ATRAVELER APPROACHING THE Phoenix airport marveled at the work invested to construct a monstrous stage on the ground below for a Pink Floyd concert in Arizona State's football stadium. A night in a hotel adjacent to that stadium provided an unsolicited secondary experience with the spectacle of the show. Kaleidoscopic lights and laser beams lit the sky above the stage's 130-foot, McDonald's-like arch. Hotel windows pulsed with quadraphonic sounds from 300 speakers that spread the music far beyond the boundaries of the stadium. The aging British rock group gave fans a truly ear-pleasing, eye-popping experience.

The next morning, busy crews dismantled the stage that they had built only days earlier for just a single night's performance. The band played next in El Paso on Tuesday and then moved on to Dallas for a Thursday-Friday night gig. How could the crews tear down the entire set and have it ready for another show in only 2 days? the traveler wondered.

It turns out that they don't. The 700-ton Phoenix set was just one of three hopscotching the country for the 22-show tour, each accompanied by a crew of 200 to get everything ready for the traveling rock stars and their show. Besides preparing the stage, this team had to hire people and service firms to perform all of the other business processes that a successful rock concert requires. These varied responsibilities include printing, selling, and taking tickets; providing security for the set and the audience; hiring food and beverage vendors; and cleaning up postconcert litter. The tour's operations managers even hired a group of traveling doctors to administer to fans overcome by the excitement of the day.

This service organization relies on successful operation of all of these business processes on the night of the concert to delight its customers. Each concert represents a subproject within the larger project of the 22-show tour. To assure success for these projects, managers must secure the necessary resources to efficiently and effectively complete the tasks of each key business process. Based on their work, each customer will form an opinion of the total concert experience. Did the band still have it? Did the food and drink meet expectations? Were the portable personal relief facilities ample in number and acceptably clean? In short, was the show fun and worth the hassle?

Managers' criteria for success begin with profits. In addition, a successful concert hinges on efficient and effective accomplishment of all or most of the necessary business activities. The technical aspects of the sound and light systems should leave fans amazed. News reports should focus on the fulfillment of promised experience rather than the antics of beer-stained rowdies. The fans, the town, and local suppliers should be saying, "See you next year." Good resource-management processes help an organization to accomplish this satisfying result.

S O U R C E
"Pink Floyd's Retrogressive Progress," *USA Today,* April 25, 1994, p. 1D.

The fans leaving the stadium after the Pink Floyd concert probably understood little of the integral role that the band's resource-management process played in creating a delightful product experience. In fact, that process should remain in the background; fans came to the show not to witness a world-class OM function, but to watch and hear the band's performance. If the music had failed to satisfy them, no amount of operations-management skill could have saved the experience.

In a sense, good resource managers are unseen heroes in the rock-concert industry. Both customers and band members expect flawless implementation of effective plans, but lack of proper planning can mar otherwise pleasing events, as festivals around the town of Woodstock periodically demonstrate. In this chapter, we focus on planning and control, a key operations management process that enables rock stars and other operating workers to give world-class performances. These planning activities employ some specialized concepts, tools, and systems that define the resource-management process.

Recall that a process is a sequence of activities that takes one or more inputs and creates an output that customers value. Resources represent the capacity, labor, tools, and materials that become inputs to the transformation process. Management is the process of directing resources and organizing activities to achieve organizational objectives. This management process involves five interlinked functions: planning, analyzing, organizing, directing/implementing, and controlling. Combining these individual terms, then, the **resource-management process** is the business process that assures that other process activities have the

resource-management process

The business process that assures that other process activities have the inputs they need to contribute to a transformation process that satisfies customers in a way that promotes achievement of the strategic objectives of the organization

A travel agent successfully manages available resources, by planning for changes in consumer demand and resource availability.   SOURCE   Tom Tracy/The Stock Market

inputs they need to contribute to a transformation process that satisfies customers in a way that promotes achievement of the strategic objectives of the organization.

 ## ORGANIZATIONAL ROLE OF RESOURCE MANAGEMENT

The resource-management process requires its own inputs. It processes information inputs about OM system characteristics, including:

1. Actual and/or anticipated customer demand for the outputs of the transformation process
2. Types and scopes of business activities that will satisfy internal or external customers
3. Customer-service objectives established by larger organizational objectives
4. Profitability and resource-utilization objectives
5. Capabilities of the transformation process, which determine the amount of resources the firm needs to produce each unit of output

The resource-management process also produces its own outputs in the form of plans for actions that allow operating workers to efficiently and effectively serve the firm's target customers.

Activities in the Resource-Management Process

To transform information inputs into planning outputs, the resource-management process completes its own sequence of activities.

Planning.   This forward-looking activity anticipates specific arrangements for converting inputs into outputs in order to satisfy projected levels of demand. This activity also compares demands on resources with current and projected levels of available resources. In this way, planners identify any mismatches in which demand will either exceed OM system capabilities with planned levels of resources or fail to fully utilize those capabilities.

Acquisition.   Whenever planning activities identify a potential resource shortage, this activity works to cover the shortage by acquiring additional resources. Short-term acquisition might increase capacity by calling for overtime work or expediting materials shipments from suppliers. Long-term acquisition might expand current facilities or build a new plant.

Scheduling.   Scheduling activities assign resources to specific processes in sufficient quantities to satisfy anticipated demands. To allocate scarce resources, schedulers must set priorities for competing demands. After determining which customers the process should satisfy and in what order, scheduling assigns resources to individual orders based on those priorities.

Implementation.   Implementation activities carry out the plans developed by earlier activities. This function may also release orders to the OM system subprocesses.

Activities in Supporting Processes.   Several supporting business processes help firms to carry out resource-management activities:

- *Human resources planning*   This specialized process compares the expected number and skill mix of human workers to the planned rate of operations. We discuss these activities in Chapter 6.
- *Capacity planning*   Another supporting process evaluates the ability of the firm's long-term factors of production to complete planned activities. We cover this subject in Chapter 15.
- *Inventory planning*   This process projects the firm's need for inventories to support its planned production. We take up this question in Chapter 16.
- *Materials/components requirements planning*   A final supporting process evaluates the availability of physical inputs to complete planned activities. We say more about this work in Chapter 17.

In addition to the activities listed so far, some manufacturing organizations may need tool-planning processes to project needs for scarce tools and fixtures. Finally, every resource-management process must include an execution activity. This refers, not to the execution of actual product transformations, but to specific decisions that create detailed plans and supply appropriate resources to support implementation.

Planning Overview

Since many of these activities involve planning, a quick review of some of the concepts introduced in Chapter 4 may simplify the discussion. Planning is the process of deciding what to do. Pink Floyd's planners had to define all of the activities needed to put on a rock concert. Based on demand forecasts (projections of the size of the audience), they had to estimate the amounts of many resources that they would need to please the crowd, including how much beer to order, how many security guards to hire, etc.

After completing these projections, planners perform analysis to determine the best ways to meet anticipated needs. They then organize the resources selected in the analysis phase. The planning process continues with directing and implementing activities, which acquire or allocate needed resources. Finally, controlling activities measure the performance of the OM system in meeting the needs of customers and identify any gaps between desired and actual outcomes. This information, in turn, becomes an input to the next iteration of the planning process. Without plans, operations managers cannot achieve any control!

A specific organization's resource-management process adapts this general planning process to its own situation by asking some detailed questions:

- *What does the organization have to do?* Planning establishes goals and objectives that direct actions of OM system personnel.
- *When must the organization achieve these goals?* Planning defines the time period over which the OM system must achieve its goals.
- *Who must perform specific tasks?* Planning identifies individuals or groups who have roles in implementing plans. The answers to this question determine how broad or narrow a scope the plan's boundaries encompass.
- *How will the organization achieve its objectives?* Planning identifies actions the firm must take to achieve its goals.
- *How will the organization measure progress?* Finally, planning establishes performance measures against which to judge the effectiveness of people and processes to guide adjustments to current plans and development of future plans.

Within so many new and emerging techniques for operations management, resource management is not a new process. A long time ago, Oliver Wight, a pioneer of operations management methodology, wrote:

> To understand what production and inventory control should be, it is necessary to consider four basic functions it tries to perform:
>
> 1. Planning priorities
> 2. Planning capacities
> 3. Controlling priorities
> 4. Controlling capacities
>
> The production control/inventory control distinction becomes lost when the functions are categorized in this way. In fact, the functions in practice are more logically broken down into planning functions and control functions, since the people who plan priorities are in the best position to plan capacities. The people responsible for "controlling" capacity are in the best position to "control" priorities. Note that they control by monitoring progress against plan and by calling significant deviations to the attention of those responsible.[1]

Wight also noted that if you don't know what materials are needed and when they are needed (priority planning), it will be impossible to determine what capacity will be needed to make this material. Planning must precede control. There can be no control without valid planning. Priority planning must work well or none of the other functions can.

Wight's words neatly sum up the discussion in this chapter, although we expand his coverage to include service organizations. Also, we emphasize the links to other business processes that integrate resource management with the organization's overall operations strategy.

---

[1]Oliver Wight, *Production and Inventory Control in the Computer Age* (Boston, Mass.: CBI, 1974), p. 11.

[**EXHIBIT 14.1**]

Interrelationships of Resource Management

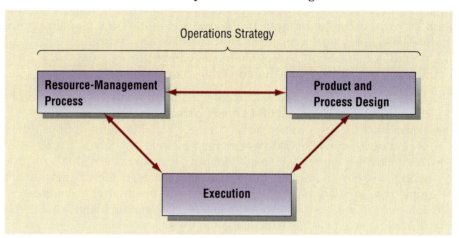

Resource Management and Operations Strategy

Exhibit 14.1 illustrates the role of resource management within the larger scheme of operations management. At the top of the diagram, operations strategy amounts to a functional expression of the firm's overall business strategy; it encompasses all of the firm's OM activities. As we described in Chapters 11 and 12, the operations strategy begins with the needs of customers and designs products and processes to satisfy those needs.

The product and process design box contains all of the tools that operating employees can apply to accomplish the firm's stated goals. These include systems for developing new product designs, existing product designs, transformation and distribution processes, employees and their skills, and infrastructure that supports the management of these processes. These tools determine many of the capabilities of the firm.

The resource-management process box contains tools for securing resources and generating plans that guide the efforts of operating workers to achieve organizational goals. The link to execution implies that the firm should issue no plan that it cannot expect to fulfill. If it lacks sufficient resources to accomplish projected activities, then it must either secure more inputs (money, inventory, equipment, or workers) or scale back the plan. In the second option, it must release less work to the OM system.

The execution box, which is discussed in Chapter 18, contains organizational tools that actually transform inputs. These activities make the tires, deliver the products, serve the drinks, or prepare the credit reports for clients. They produce the tangible things and the intangible experiences that customers buy.

Type A and Type B are simply generic titles used to describe two very different classes of customer and two very different types of buying behaviors. Type A, for example, could be a corporate OEM (Original Equipment Manufacturing) customer. These customers often develop a plan identifying their long-term needs and their purchases are driven by such plans. In contrast, a Type B could be an individual end user, typically not driven by long-term plans but by immediate needs. If they cannot buy what they originally wanted, they buy an acceptable substitute.

Schematic Relationships of Resource Management

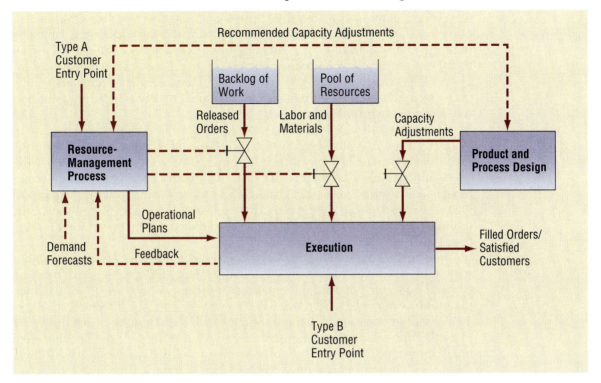

Exhibit 14.2 adds some detail to these interactions to illustrate the interface of the resource-management process with the customer-service function. Customers can enter the system at two points. Type A customers place orders that the firm will fill at some later date. A manufacturing organization with a make-to-order process serves customers in this way. A service organization handles such customers by scheduling them for later service or by providing some customized service such as designing a building or preparing a credit profile.

Type B customers come to the producer's site to obtain goods or services immediately. This group includes walk-in customers at a fast-food restaurant, people browsing at a retail store, or orders at the counter of a distributor of industrial parts. These customers expect the firm to offer the products they want at the time of purchase. Failure to fulfill this need normally harms an establishment's reputation.

Exhibit 14.2 shows three control valves that control resource flows. By manipulating the valve on the right, resource managers can make short-term adjustments to the process capacity of the organization. This represents actions like renting or acquiring additional equipment.

By adjusting the control valve in the center, managers can allocate more or less labor and material to shop-floor activities. This adjustment represents actions like scheduling overtime shifts and redeploying labor between parts of the organization to ensure that processes have the right amounts and mixes of materials and labor to do their jobs.

By adjusting the control valve on the left, resource managers regulate the rate at which they release work to the shop floor. This represents extending or reducing an order backlog or applying some demand-management tool like a schedule. A make-to-order business may practice resource management by releasing work to the production line in a steady stream that avoids either clogging the system with excessive work in process or leaving work stations idle.

Success in this setting requires close cooperation between the OM system and other functions within the firm (specifically marketing). Marketing must work with the OM system to know what amount of capacity is available and when. It then must try to help balance the demand for this capacity with the level of capacity available, by giving the customer realistic due dates. It also means telling the OM system what orders are really important and what orders are not as important (i.e., the relative priority of orders).

Exhibit 14.2 also illustrates the roles of demand forecasting and demand management. Type A customers interact with the organization at a distance from its execution systems. They may schedule appointments or place orders in advance of need, anticipating a lag before the firm can deliver their products as occurs in most make-to-order business. Type B customers expect to receive their good or service when or soon after they arrive. These retail buyers, walk-in restaurant patrons, or emergency-room patients may leave dissatisfied if they encounter any serious time lag.

In a business dominated by Type A customers, the current backlog of orders may influence prices and promised delivery dates. High prices or extended delivery lead times may discourage some cost-sensitive or time-sensitive customers to take their orders elsewhere. Managers may consciously set prices and control availability to make a product more exclusive if they think these actions will promote the firm's long-term interests. If they want to capture the fleeing orders to increase production volume, however, they need to find some way to increase short-term capacity and reduce the backlog. Feedback from execution systems helps to maintain consistency between promises to customers and the current capabilities of the transformation process.

In a business dominated by Type B customers, resource managers must provide a mix of resources that maximizes the likelihood of satisfying target customers. In a service business, this usually involves staffing decisions. Hiring too many servers raises costs, but too few reduce customer service. Clearly, a good tradeoff depends on reasonably accurate forecasts of demand along with flexible workers who are willing to come in on short notice or for short periods during peak load conditions. The firm may also manage to influence some Type B customers to accept service delays. The price structures of many electric utilities influence selected customers to forgo heavy use of electricity during peak hours.

In Chapters 16 and 17, we will discuss some similar methods of managing inventory to enhance customer service. Here, too, the decision-making process must make tradeoffs based on a sound understanding of customers' views of the value equation.

The "By the Way" box gives an example of a restaurant's demand management system based on reservations and customer wait times. Clearly, restaurant patrons experience resource-management techniques and, to a certain extent, system variance for a number of possible reasons. Some sources of variation simply lie outside the control of OM personnel. Differences in customer service times in a restaurant can cause variance because some meals take longer to prepare and some customers just like to linger over their meals. In an earlier time, patrons used to have a leisurely chat. Employees at a fine French restaurant have been known to ask patrons to leave tables so other customers with reservations could take their places. Such an event defines the total customer experience in a service

[BY THE WAY... RESOURCE MANAGEMENT IN ACTION]

The host at a fancy restaurant must practice resource management with a smile. You and your guest arrive promptly for your reservation. The host takes your name, acknowledges your reservation, and politely informs you of a short delay before your table is ready. You view the invitation to wait in the lounge somewhat cynically as a ploy to sell drinks with high gross profit margins. You can see empty tables, but you move to the bar, as instructed.

A look on the other side of the line of visibility (from the service blueprinting technique) reveals an error in your assumption of ulterior motives. A restaurant functions as a labor-limited service organization. Its capacity depends not on the number of tables, but on the serving capacity of its staff. The host could seat you at an empty table, but the server for that area could not deliver the fine service you expect from such an establishment. The restaurant's correct short-term solution is to manage your wait in a way that is least unpleasant to you, either in the lounge or at the table.

While you wait impatiently for a table, the host and the server discuss the status of the work load. The people at Table 2 have just taken their seats. Those at Table 7 have just gone up to the salad bar; their entrees will be ready in about 10 minutes. People at Table 6 are enjoying desserts and coffee, but these regular customers are never in much of a hurry. Table 1 is empty, but the server cannot handle another table just yet. You have to wait another 5 minutes.

organization. Diners might at least expect staff members to offer some enticement to relocate to the cocktail lounge!

Rather than making customers wait, an organization might maintain reserve capacity. The restaurant might keep extra servers on call in case of unexpectedly brisk business or simply keep one or more extra workers in the restaurant and run the process below its actual capacity. The second option would raise the firm's cost of labor (and it might make employees resent dividing tips among more people than necessary). Good servers, and other kinds of employees, are hard to find, however, and a staff of unskilled workers would quickly erode a firm's reputation.

To avoid both customer dissatisfaction and wasteful labor spending, operations managers could change the process to reduce variance. The restaurant's salad bar represents a customer-involvement technique to replace the need for internal capacity by shifting tasks to customers, as described in Chapter 12. To extend the concept, customers might place their orders upon arrival at an order-entry station and then take seats in a lounge where servers would inform them when their meals were ready. At an extreme, one Iowa restaurant invites customers to pick out cuts of meat, cook them at a common grill, and carry them to available tables. Patrons also serve themselves from salad bars, dessert tables, and drink dispensers. This limited service, apparently targeted at Economizer couples, offers not much more than facilities outside home for cooking and eating.

Operations managers should not make serious decisions about process standards alone because those decisions involve customers' total product experiences. Such decisions should pass reviews at least as high as the operations-strategy level and more likely by high-level organizational managers, since they significantly change the firm's product and therefore its competitive strategy.

Despite this wide involvement in decision making, execution-level personnel bear the brunt of customers' irritation over mismatches between customer expectations and delivered products. For a restaurant server and job-shop manager alike, failure of the resource-management process to control both demand and OM system resources invariably results in service shortfalls, wasteful expenditures, and workers' ulcers.

Operations Planning Hierarchy

Much resource-management activity centers on planning. Chapter 4 described planning at different levels in the organization, and Exhibit 14.3 shows how these levels form an integrated planning hierarchy. Careful, accurate planning provides necessary support for execution and achievement of organizational goals. Later sections of the chapter apply the principles of this hierarchy to OM systems for service organizations and then for manufacturers.

 ## RESOURCE MANAGEMENT IN SERVICE SYSTEMS

Service providers formulate plans at each of the levels outlined in Exhibit 14.3. Like any business planning process, these resource-management activities apply common principles to situation-specific details to yield plans tailored to the organization's individual needs.

Long-Term Resource Management

To plan for long periods, resource managers must answer strategic questions about significant forces that affect the resources that the firm can employ to carry out its operations management mission. This analysis focuses on three important areas.

Customer Demands.   Long-range planners assess the likely effects of evolving customer requirements on the firm's resource requirements. They want to know whether the firm will need more or different resources. Continuing market fragmentation may well require a more flexible OM process with varying resource needs.

Technological Developments.   Evolving technologies affect the ability of almost any firm's resource-management process to serve both internal and external customers. In particular, information technology powerfully influences today's operating methods and the resources they employ. Advances in bar-coding technology enhance the ability of monitoring systems to track the results of operational plans, for example. Technologies that allow nearly instantaneous assessments of on-going events can help a system to respond flexibly. Through market information systems, firms can collect valuable information about customers and their needs.

Population Characteristics.   Demographic trends change the attributes and availability of employees, and planners must anticipate these trends to determine how the organization will respond to them. McDonald's needs to know whether it can expect to find enough teenagers to flip its burgers in coming years. More detailed assessments of potential employees' technical and social skills help planners to develop training systems to assure that the firm will continue to delight its customers.

[E X H I B I T   1 4 . 3]

Operations Planning Hierarchy

Planning Horizon	Units of Measure	Nature of Activity
Long-Term Planning		
Long (Years)	Equivalent units or $	Largely strategic decisions about new product and process developments and major investments in plant and capacity
		Projects long-term customer requirements, technological advancements, and social and political trends
Aggregate Planning		
Midrange	Product families	Division-level decisions about human-resources planning (i.e., hiring, firing, overtime, and part time versus permanent employment)
		Addresses secondary issues like inventory planning, materials acquisition, and incremental expansions and contractions in facility capabilities
Master Scheduling		
Short (weeks to months)	Specific products	Operation-level decisions about when and where to make specific products
		Develops plans for inputs to support end-product production
Operations Planning and Control Systems		
Daily	Resources required Labor Material Capacity Tooling	Execution-level decisions about daily schedules for workers, equipment, and other resources

Note that these resource-management issues overlap with the questions that product and process designers ask. This similarity may tempt planners to try to combine these tasks, but wise operations managers hesitate to pigeon-hole forward thinking into a single process. The cross-functional nature of any long-term decision forces planning at this level to cut across many business processes, creating many potential overlaps with essential functions.

Intermediate Resource Management

As the restaurant example demonstrated, the key resource in a typical service operation is its staff. Employees perform most services, so their availability determines much about the capacity of the OM system. Intermediate resource management seeks to develop and maintain a pool of human resources sufficient to support the firm's needs over the following 6-month to 8-month period.

This process starts with five types of specifications for human-resources needs:

- Pattern of skills required to effectively serve customers over the planning horizon
- Human-resources need patterns within individual months, weeks, and days over the planning horizon

- Mix of skilled and unskilled employees that best serves the mutual interests of customers and other stakeholders
- Mix of full-time and temporary employees that best serves the mutual interests of customers and stakeholders
- Availability of workers with needed traits over the planning horizon

The detailed specifications for a particular situation depend on conditions. Service systems with methods that resemble a production line will employ higher proportions of unskilled workers. Skill-driven service operations, such as medical clinics, may need to focus more on how to attract workers with critical skills.

Obstacles to Intermediate Resource Management.   Service organizations often face some common problems:

1. Demand variability often stresses a firm's ability to either project variations or adjust capacity to meet accurately projected variations.
2. Differences in the times an OM system needs to serve individual customers often introduces serious variance.
3. Employees often resist working where and when the firm needs them.

These problems require attention in either long-range or intermediate plans. An operations manager should not confront these problems without support from other functions.

Demand variability and measures to control it have arisen in earlier chapters, especially in Chapters 9 and 10. Demand management provides a valuable starting point. Standard responses like booking appointments often help service firms to schedule their work flows evenly. Creative marketing can provide another powerful tool for smoothing uneven demand. The firm may try to attract customers who need or want to consume its service during its current slack periods, for example. Price structures frequently try to divert demand away from peak times.

To address problems with differences in service times, resource managers should begin by applying process flow analysis. They must determine whether customer expectations or process activities cause service-time variations. With the problem accurately diagnosed, they can look for ways to influence expectations or redesign the process to gain control of service times. Other organizations' solutions to similar problems may suggest a good response. Such a problem may well suit analysis by one or more of the tools in the Operations Managers' Toolkit.

Some specific tools include:

- Check sheets to identify what customers want from the service times and when
- Process flow analysis
- Pareto analysis
- Cause and effect diagrams

If resource managers cannot solve or dissolve problems with variability of demand or service times, then the analysis should shift to methods for resolving the problems using one of the tools from operations research. If a particular problem meets the conditions assumed by queuing theory models, then those models may help managers to estimate the server resources that their systems need to perform as desired. If queuing theory does not fit the practical conditions, then a simulation model can illustrate the economic and service tradeoffs. While this method does not guarantee an optimal response, it should at least provide some new insight into process characteristics that may spark an idea.

Problems with employee resistance to service system needs require solutions based on human-resources management principles. Resource managers must either redesign the service-delivery system to satisfy workers' expectations or alter the firm's compensation package to induce employees to accept the demands of the existing system. Again, benchmarking may reveal another firm's solution to a similar problem that might meet current needs.

Short-Term Resource Management

Short-term resource management differs from scheduling workers. It amounts to making sure that the OM system has all of the resources that it needs to do the job. Scheduling, on the other hand, arranges previously allocated resources to perform a given set of tasks as effectively as possible. As its key task, a service organization's short-term resource-management function modulates the flow of work to the employees who will perform it.

The timing of resource requirements normally becomes more important in services than in manufacturing. If, however, the service includes a perishable tangible good, such as sourdough bread, then the effectiveness of the manufacturing system also depends on the timing of demand.

The "On the Job" box describes the efforts of one service provider to meet its resource-management challenges.

 ## RESOURCE MANAGEMENT IN MANUFACTURING SYSTEMS

Manufacturing operations tend to require more complex resource-management processes than service operations because planners must control more resources from more categories at more locations and often over longer time horizons. As Exhibit 14.3 explained, the level of detail increases as resource managers move from long-term to short-term planning. Exhibit 14.4 illustrates another way of looking at the hierarchy of production planning developed by Bitran, Haas, and Hax of MIT. They advocate production planning based on a mathematical formulation of top-down planning. We will not fully lay out the entire production-planning method of these authors, but their conceptual framework illustrates the setting for resource management in manufacturing.

This model begins with fundamental planning principles. First, it produces no more detail than organizational decision makers need. Exhibit 14.4 shows the level of detail appropriate for each organization level on the right side. The second fundamental planning principle defines a planning horizon only as long as the lead time needed to make changes. If planners want to increase or decrease the level of production, they should look ahead far enough to make the necessary adjustments but no further. The last principle calls for aggregating and disaggregating data in a way that follows organizational lines.

This hierarchical planning model starts by assigning products to factories. In Chapter 12, we discussed guidelines for determining the location, processing technology, and size of a facility. Most of these decisions act as constraints on long-term resource-management decisions. An auto maker could not easily reverse a major decision to assemble minivans at a given site; it would consider making such a fundamental change only to correct a major mismatch. Resource managers lack the organizational authority they would need to reverse product

ON THE JOB

Managing the Flow of Service in the Restaurant Industry

A food-service operation creates a complex OM system composed of numerous subsystems, including the kitchen, the dining room, the cocktail lounge, and the front desk. Each of these parts must work well to assure smooth operation of the entire system. Service should flow continuously, steadily, and incrementally to customers.

As a key to this operational efficiency, particularly in a busy restaurant, resource management must maintain an even flow of service despite enormous potential for breakdowns. A problem in the kitchen soon spreads to disrupt the dining room. A properly designed system carefully balances the capacities of these subprocesses to promote overall efficiency. In addition, to achieve its potential for customer-pleasing effectiveness, this delicately balanced system requires skillful management.

Servers and hosts must effectively manipulate the flow of service. The host at the front desk develops a service strategy that routes a manageable stream of work to servers. Demand management tactics include scheduling arrivals through a reservation system and shunting surges in the flow into some holding area such as a cocktail lounge. Without a reservation system, the host may simply give realistic estimates of wait times to potential customers in an effort to modulate demand.

Servers exercise strong control over the timing of certain functions at each table. The service cycle in a typical restaurant creates at least 13 contact points at which servers influence the timing of service:

1. When the server initially greets newly seated customers
2. When any before-meal wants such as appetizers or cocktails reach the customers
3. When customers give their dinner orders
4. When the server passes on the dinner order to the kitchen
5. When salads reach the table
6. When entrees reach the table
7. When the server checks for any additional desires
8. When dinner plates are cleared
9. When customers order desserts and after-dinner drinks
10. When desserts and after-dinner drinks reach the table
11. When the server presents the check
12. When the server picks up the payment
13. When the server returns change or a credit card and receipt

Many customers pay more attention to times between these contact points than to their total elapsed times at their tables. No customer should ever wait so long for the server to complete any step that doubts emerge about the system simply abandoning him or her. Sometimes a simple gesture or comment acknowledging the pending step will reduce anxieties, but not for long.

SOURCE   *Quality Service, the Restaurant Manager's Bible* (Ithaca, N.Y.: Cornell University, 1992).

and process design decisions, but they should provide inputs to these design processes.

Aggregate Production Planning

charter

The assignment of product families to a specific plant or subprocess within a plant

Once planners have developed **charters** for each plant, and perhaps for subprocesses with plants, stating what each should make, each site needs its own aggregate production plan for fulfilling its charter. The **aggregate production plan** specifies planned rates of production, inventory levels, and employee staffing rates and policies. Aggregate planning reflects the influence of several inputs, including

[**EXHIBIT 14.4**]

Alternative Hierarchical Planning Model

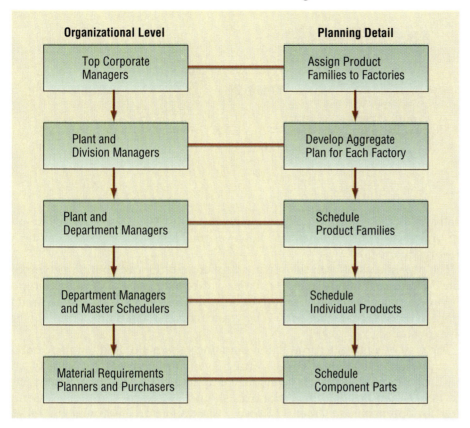

Organizational Level	Planning Detail
Top Corporate Managers	Assign Product Families to Factories
Plant and Division Managers	Develop Aggregate Plan for Each Factory
Plant and Department Managers	Schedule Product Families
Department Managers and Master Schedulers	Schedule Individual Products
Material Requirements Planners and Purchasers	Schedule Component Parts

SOURCE   Reprinted by permission, G. D. Bitran, R. A. Haas, and A. C. Hax, "Hierarchical Production Planning: A Two-Stage System," *Operations Research,* Vol. 30, No. 2, March–April 1982, pp. 232–251. Copyright 1982, the Operations Research Society of America (currently INFORMS), 290 Westminster St., Providence, RI 02903 USA.

the firm's overall business strategy, human resource policy, financial profile, product/plant charters, and short-term marketing plan.

The assumptions that underlie an organization's budget often become inputs to the aggregate planning process. If business conditions materially change during the course of a fiscal year, however, updates should incorporate recognized deviations. Planners should communicate any such change to the key individuals in sales, marketing, and finance since major shifts in an aggregate plan significantly affect their operations. Exhibit 14.5 describes the inputs to the aggregate production plan.

The level of detail for an aggregate production plan often covers a single product family. For example, Ford's truck plant needs an aggregate plan for its pickup models rather than separate plans for individual combinations of features. This plan might direct the process to make 4,350 F150 pickup trucks rather than 872 red F150 pickup trucks with specific options and other numbers of trucks with different packages of features.

The planning horizon for aggregate production planning often matches that for annual business planning, although it may range from 6 to 18 months. Planners

aggregate production plan

A plan that specifies planned rates of production, inventory levels, and employee staffing rates and policies to fulfill the charter of a plant or subprocess

[**EXHIBIT 14.5**]

Aggregate Production Plan Inputs

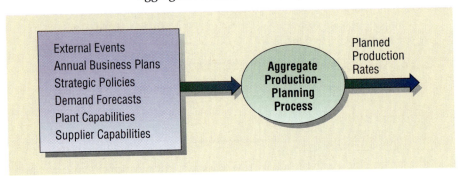

External Events
Annual Business Plans
Strategic Policies
Demand Forecasts
Plant Capabilities
Supplier Capabilities

Aggregate
Production-
Planning
Process

Planned
Production
Rates

usually break this information down to give monthly data. Some aggregate-planning processes give further detail, however, making weekly projections for the following quarter.

The capabilities of both the plant, supplier, and the distribution network are defined along part family lines. Since these are constraints, the production planning process may elect to focus more heavily on those which are likely to limit the options of the aggregate planners. Why waste management time focusing on non-active constraints?

The goal of aggregate production planning centers on defining the combination of production rates, employee staffing levels, and inventory patterns that satisfies the needs of the firm. This statement emphasizes the search for a satisfactory plan rather than an ideal one; planners should not waste resources in a futile search for optimal arrangements for every resource in an environment subject to change. Others argue that the goal of minimizing costs should guide aggregate planning. This can improve a plan as long as it does not jeopardize the other elements of the value equation: quality, flexibility, and time.

Mathematical Formulas for Aggregate Production Planning.   Increasing process variance raises the difficulty of aggregate production planning. To understand this relationship fully, it is useful to express the aggregate production planning problem in mathematical terms. To simplify the model, we assume that a plant produces only one product family. We also focus the analysis on cost minimization, although it could pursue some other objective.

With this background, the problem amounts to this: Given F_t, the demand forecast for Period t in the T-period time horizon, determine the feasible production rate, P_t, for each corresponding Period t that will result in the lowest possible cost.

The aggregate production plan usually includes several relevant costs.

Basic Production Costs.   This category covers both fixed and variable costs to manufacture the product. Since this planning deals with aggregate product information, it takes an aggregated unit cost, V, and a period cost, F. The basic production cost incurred in Period t is:

$$PROD_t = F + VP_t \qquad \text{for } t = 1, 2, 3, 4, ..., T$$

Costs of Changes in the Production Rate.   Certain production processes may experience costs when their rate of operation changes. These costs normally result from hiring and firing workers. Aggregate production planning usually assumes that the number of workers needed to produce one unit of equivalent product changes in a linear way. The number of workers needed in Period t is:

$$W_t = aP_t$$

Then the number of people hired in Period t is:

$$HIRE_t = W_t - W_{t-1} \quad \text{if } W_t > W_{t-1} \quad 0 \text{ otherwise}$$

Likewise, the number of people fired in Period t is:

$$FIRE_t = W_{t-1} - W_t \quad \text{if } W_{t-1} > W_t \quad 0 \text{ otherwise}$$

If the firm incurs a cost of C_h to hire one employee and a cost of C_f to fire one, then the cost of changing the rate of production is:

$$CHANGE_t = C_h(HIRE_t) + C_f(FIRE_t)$$

Inventory Holding Costs.   The firm also incurs costs to hold and maintain inventory, also frequently assumed to vary in a linear relationship with the production rate. A conservation of mass equation can give the amount of inventory at the end of Period t:

$$I_t = I_{t-1} + P_t - F_t$$

This states nothing more than beginning inventory plus the amount that the process will produce minus what forecasts indicate that the firm will sell. The rate charged to hold one unit of inventory, C_i, is:

$$INVCOST_t = C_i I_t$$

Backlogging Costs.   These costs challenge planners' estimating techniques. Make-to-stock producers may incur these costs when inventory drops to levels near or below zero. In this case, they reflect the loss of customer goodwill or the costs of wasteful practices to expedite particular orders.

Make-to-order plants normally operate in some optimum range of backlog. Too little backlog can cause production inefficiencies as capacity sits idle, waiting for more work. Too much can cause deterioration in customer service, and it may even drive away sales. The following illustration will omit backlogging costs to keep the formulas simple.

Planners can restate the aggregate production planning problem as:

$$\text{Minimize } z = \Sigma \ (PROD_t + CHANGE_t + INVCOST_t + BACKCOST_t) \quad \text{for } t = 1, 2, 3, \ldots, T$$

Subject to:

$$I_t = I_{t-1} + P_t - F_t \quad \text{for } t = 1, 2, 3, \ldots, T \qquad \text{Conservation of mass constraints}$$
$$P_t < PMAX \qquad \text{Production capacity constraints}$$
$$I_t < IMAX \qquad \text{Warehouse capacity constraints}$$
$$HIRE_t < HIREMAX$$
$$\qquad \qquad \qquad \qquad \text{Human resource policy constraints}$$
$$FIRE_t < FIREMAX$$

Clearly this model could become more complex. It might include additional variables to reflect the costs and capacity of overtime production. It might add some lower limit on inventory to minimize the chances of stockouts and expediting. This relatively simple model should suffice, however, to illustrate the tradeoffs of aggregate production planning.

Aggregate Production Planning with Variance.   Such a formal statement of costs and their relationships may tend to oversimplify aggregate production planning. System variance quickly scatters these neatly aligned numbers into a confusing jumble. If planners can easily and accurately forecast the patterns of demand without any significant seasonal variations to disrupt the data, then they face a relatively simple problem. (Of course, this statement also assumes that they find factors of production readily available throughout the planning horizon.) Without complications, the production plan can mirror the demand pattern.

Some difficulty may cloud the picture if planners cannot rely on the availability of a major factor of production, such as labor or a raw material, throughout the planning horizon. The production plan must then reflect the effect of this fact. For example, planners for a winery clearly must schedule crushing operations to follow grape harvesting patterns.

If planners question the accuracy of their demand forecasts, they may face more complex problems. The firm may want to keep investments in inventory low to avoid significant risk of holding more than it needs. In general, production planners should accumulate inventory to help level production rates only if the expected cost savings from smoother production exceed the expected costs of holding the stock. Estimates of inventory costs should include:

1. *Excess product costs*   The costs of making more than customers want
2. *Product obsolescence costs*   The costs of holding old stock after product designs or fashions change
3. *Product deterioration costs*   The costs of reductions in quality of stock before the firm can sell it

The firm can smooth production by accumulating inventory most effectively when it incurs minimal losses due to these costs. Unfortunately, planners cannot know most of these costs. Accounting data may provide a good starting point for calculating the cost of inventory, but this function collects data for reasons other than planning. Planners must expect to massage accounting numbers considerably to translate them into meaningful aggregate cost coefficients.

Along with resource availability and inventory levels, demand seasonality contributes to system variance. Operations managers like to produce at level rates, but customers lack the training to see the benefits of steady demand. They arrive when they want the firm's product. While demand management might solve this problem completely in some dream world, planners for real markets will need to devise strategies to accommodate seasonal variations in demand patterns.

Production Planning Strategies

Resource managers develop individual solutions to planning problems caused by system variance. These firm-specific arrangements generally represent one of three pure strategies for accommodating mismatches between demand and production capabilities:

- *Chase strategy*   This strategy sets the production rate equal to the demand rate. It then increases and decreases the firm's pool of human resources as needed, usually through hiring or firing permanent staff, perhaps supplemented by temporary workers.

- *Level-production strategy*   This strategy sets the production rate equal to the average demand rate. It then accumulates inventory during slack demand and distributes goods from inventory during peak demand periods. Human resources remain at a constant level.
- *Variable-hours strategy*   This strategy sets the production rate equal to the demand rate and keeps staffing levels stable. It compensates for demand variations by adjusting the number of hours that individuals work to make capacity match. Clearly, the success of this strategy depends on the extent of demand variability and the willingness of workers to accept uncertainty in their incomes.

Individual firms devise infinite combinations of these three pure strategies to suit their own circumstances.

Each of these pure strategies has its strengths and weaknesses. The **chase strategy** minimizes the costs of holding inventory, including the risk of investing scarce resources to accumulate the wrong products. The firm gains this benefit at the cost of potentially alienating employees. They may well return the firm's weak commitment to them, leading to low morale, high absenteeism, and uncaring attitudes.

Some firms succeed using this strategy by selecting employees who care little about employment uncertainty; any warm body will do. To reduce the risk of poor quality with such casual employees, they may automate their production processes to eliminate virtually any possibility of a mistake as McDonald's has done in designing its French-fry cookers. Firms may also try to vary the flow of work to match demand by adjusting orders from subcontractors. This merely downloads the problem to suppliers, but they may handle the variance by filling gaps with orders from other customers.

The **level-production strategy** is an operations manager's dream. It ignores the priorities of JIT manufacturing, however, and invests in inventory as a buffer. This may not create unduly high risk if a significant percentage of the firm's work load comes from mature products for which resource managers can easily forecast demand. They must answer a key question to judge the suitability of this strategy: will the benefits of a stable work force more than offset inventory holding costs? These benefits depend, of course, on the firm's ability to hire skilled employees or to economically train new employees in needed skills.

The **variable-hours strategy** tries to achieve the best of both worlds. It seeks to keep its key human skills while avoiding the costs and risks of holding large inventories. Lincoln Electric, the manufacturer of welding rods and equipment, uses a variation of this strategy. It guarantees 4 days of work per week to permanent workers, even during slow periods. To make this strategy work, the firm builds some inventory during slow periods and it hires temporary workers to meet peak demand without any guarantees of work hours.

The trend among American manufacturers to rely increasingly heavily on temporary workers reflects in part the attraction of a modified variable-hour strategy with its combination of volume flexibility and stable core of skilled, committed employees. If anyone doubts this phenomenon, note that Manpower, the temporary employment agency, had over 742,000 individual placements in 1994 in the United States alone.

A cynic might state a simple rule of thumb for balancing permanent and temporary workers: If a firm can easily find workers and the work does not require

chase strategy

A method of matching production to variable demand by setting the production rate equal to the demand rate and varying the pool of human resources as needed

level-production strategy

A method of matching production to variable demand by setting the production rate equal to the average demand rate and using inventory as a buffer

variable-hours strategy

A method of matching production to variable demand by setting the production rate equal to the demand rate and adjusting the work hours of stable groups of employees highly polished skills, it should hire temps; if good workers are scarce and the work demands strong skills, it should hire permanent employees. A quantitative problem might make this decision rule more concrete.

[**PROBLEM 14.1**]

Application of Production-Planning Strategies

Based on past data, a resource manager projects the following bimonthly demand pattern:

Period	Forecasted Demand	Number of Working Days
January–February	3,600 units	41
March–April	3,400	43
May–June	2,200	44
July–August	1,800	42
September–October	2,600	40
November–December	4,400	40
Total	18,000	250

Further labor-intensive study has yielded the following cost estimates:

Labor hours required per unit	5 hours
Cost of labor (including fringe benefits)	$10 per hour
Overtime premium	30 percent
Hiring and training costs	$450 per hire
Firing costs	$250 per fire
Beginning inventory	1,200 units
Beginning employment level	50 employees
Inventory holding costs	$10 per period
Material cost per unit	$100

The number of work days per month varies, in part because months have different numbers of days and in part because the number of weekend days per month varies.

Exhibit 14.6 presents a resource-management worksheet for the chase strategy. Inventory remains constant to a cost to the firm of $72,000 per year. The number of workers required equals the hours that the OM process must run to satisfy demand divided by the number of worker hours per month based on 8-hour days. The firm must adjust its staff over a range from 50 workers initially to a low of 27 in July–August. The total cost for the chase strategy comes to $1,008,360.

Based on the same data, Exhibit 14.7 shows the results of a level-production strategy that features a level work force. This strategy drops total costs to $998,043. Most of the savings come from lower hiring and firing costs. Inventory carrying costs rose only $6,000.

Exhibit 14.8 presents the results of the variable-hours strategy. To approximate this situation, the exhibit assumes that workers would be willing to accept a 4-day work week during a period of slow demand. During the summer months, the exhibit shows only 32 workers; actually, this gives an equivalent labor cost for the firm's true staffing level of 40 workers putting in 80 percent of the normal work week. The exhibit shows no hiring and firing costs after the downsizing at the start of the year, and total costs decline another $7,831 as

[**E X H I B I T   1 4 . 6**]

Resource-Management Worksheet for the Chase Strategy

```
                    The Chase Strategy Worksheet

            Beginning                       Hours       Work    Inventory
   Period   Inventory  Demand  Production  Required     Days      Cost
 Jan.-Feb.    1,200    3,600     3,600      18,000       41     $12,000
 Mar.-Apr.    1,200    3,400     3,400      17,000       43     $12,000
 May-Jun.     1,200    2,200     2,200      11,000       44     $12,000
 Jul.-Aug.    1,200    1,800     1,800       9,000       42     $12,000
 Sep.-Oct.    1,200    2,600     2,600      13,000       40     $12,000
 Nov.-Dec.    1,200    4,400     4,400      22,000       40     $12,000
                                                                $72,000

                        Regular
            Workers      Time    Overtime    Labor      Hiring   Firing
   Period   Required   Workers   Workers     Cost        Cost     Cost
 Jan.-Feb.    54.9       55         0       $180,400    $2,250      $0
 Mar.-Apr.    49.4       50         0       $172,000       $0   $1,250
 May-Jun.     31.3       32         0       $112,640       $0   $4,500
 Jul.-Aug.    26.8       27         0       $ 90,720       $0   $1,250
 Sep.-Oct.    40.6       41         0       $131,200    $6,750      $0
 Nov.-Dec.    68.8       69         0       $220,800   $12,600      $0
                                            $907,760   $21,600   $7,000

            Inventory   Labor    Hiring     Firing
Total Cost=  Cost +    Cost +    Cost +      Cost
            $72,000   $907,760   $21,600    $7,000    =$1,008,360
```

compared to costs for the level-production strategy. Most of these savings reflect lower inventory carrying costs.

The firm might reduce total costs still further by hiring temporary workers during months when the 40 permanent workers put in 8 hours of overtime per week each. For every 2-month period that requires overtime shifts, the firm's costs rise by approximately $1,900:

10 workers × 8 hour/week × 8 week/period × $3.00 premium/hour = $1,920/period

Since this occurs in four of the six 2-month periods, temporary workers could reduce total costs by about $8,000 per year.   [■]

Resource managers must weigh this gain against the potential for alienating workers who want to earn extra money from overtime after taking home smaller paychecks in slow periods. This illustrates the dangers of focusing too narrowly on the numbers in spreadsheets. Spreadsheets are tools. Like any tools, they become dangerous when people use them without thinking. Resource managers, and all managers, should always step back and assess the consequences of any decision that escape spreadsheet models.

[**EXHIBIT 14.7**]

Resource-Management Worksheet for the Level-Production Strategy

The Level Strategy Worksheet

Period	Beginning Inventory	Demand	Production	Hours Required	Work Days	Inventory Cost
Jan.–Feb.	1,200	3,600	3,000	15,000	41	$12,000
Mar.–Apr.	600	3,400	3,000	15,000	43	$6,000
May–Jun.	200	2,200	3,000	15,000	44	$2,000
Jul.–Aug.	1,000	1,800	3,000	15,000	42	$10,000
Sep.–Oct.	2,200	2,600	3,000	15,000	40	$22,000
Nov.–Dec.	2,600	4,400	3,000	15,000	40	$26,000
						$78,000

Period	Workers Required	Regular Time Workers	Overtime Workers	Labor Cost	Hiring Cost	Firing Cost
Jan.–Feb.	45.7	45	0.7	$150,585	$0	$1,250
Mar.–Apr.	43.6	45	0.0	$154,800	$0	$0
May–Jun.	42.6	45	0.0	$158,400	$0	$0
Jul.–Aug.	44.6	45	0.0	$151,200	$0	$0
Sep.–Oct.	46.9	45	1.9	$151,904	$0	$0
Nov.–Dec.	46.9	45	1.9	$151,904	$0	$0
				$918,793	$0	$1,250

Total Cost=	Inventory Cost +	Labor Cost +	Hiring Cost +	Firing Cost		
	$78,000	$918,793	$0	$1,250	=$920,043	

After deciding which production-planning strategy best suits their firm, planners can then determine its resource needs over the planning horizon. These projections help the procurement process to forge cost-effective supplier relationships. Suppliers appreciate reasonably accurate estimates of a customer's future needs, so sharing this information can enhance these ties.

Aggregate figures for individual periods over the planning horizon often fail to provide enough specific information to support production planning. Operations managers need to know specific demands like the dimensions of lumber to buy, the option packages to install on pickup trucks, the types of beer and container sizes to make in a brewery, and so forth. The master production schedule provides this information.

master production schedule

A document that defines the goods that specific shops will produce in definite quantities at definite times over a short-term planning horizon to carry out aggregate plans

 MASTER PRODUCTION SCHEDULING PROCESS

Resource management moves from general, aggregate plans for entire plants or large subprocesses to detailed specifications for near-term production. The **master production schedule** (MPS) transforms inputs from marketing and operations management into a document that defines the goods that specific shops

[**EXHIBIT 14.8**]

Resource-Management Worksheet for the Variable-Hours Strategy

The Flexible Work Hour Strategy Worksheet

Period	Beginning Inventory	Demand	Production	Hours Required	Work Days	Inventory Cost
Jan.–Feb.	1,200	3,600	3,280	16,400	41	$12,000
Mar.–Apr.	880	3,400	3,440	17,200	43	$8,800
May–Jun.	920	2,200	2,253	11,264	44	$9,200
Jul.–Aug.	972.8	1,800	2,150	10,752	42	$9,728
Sep.–Oct.	1,323.2	2,600	3,200	16,000	40	$13,232
Nov.–Dec.	1,923.2	4,400	3,200	16,000	40	$19,232
	723.2					$72,192

Period	Workers Required	Regular Time Workers	Overtime Workers	Labor Cost	Hiring Cost	Firing Cost
Jan.–Feb.	50.0	40	10	$173,840	$0	$2,500
Mar.–Apr	50.0	40	10	$182,320	$0	$0
May–Jun.	32.0	32	0	$112,640	$0	$0
Jul.–Aug.	32.0	32	0	$107,520	$0	$0
Sep.–Oct.	50.0	40	10	$169,600	$0	$0
Nov.–Dec.	50.0	40	10	$169,600	$0	$0
				$915,520	$0	$2,500

Total Cost=	Inventory Cost +	Labor Cost +	Hiring Cost +	Firing Cost		
	$72,192	$843,328	$0	$2,500	=$918,020	

---

will produce in definite quantities at definite times over a 6-week to 8-week planning horizon. The master production schedule represents the most important plan in the resource-management system because it becomes an agreement between marketing and manufacturing that defines the execution activities of the OM system over the short term. This agreement is particularly important in make-to-order systems since it reflects the firm's commitment to deliver products by the dates promised to customers.

The master production scheduling process deals with more detailed information than aggregate planning in part because operations managers need precise information about what the firm expects of them. To generate the necessary detail, planners disaggregate higher-level production plans to transform them into master production schedules. We will focus the discussion on master production scheduling for a bottling plant that produces 2-liter containers of soft drinks. This example assumes that aggregate planners define demand for product families while master schedulers define production routines for three distinct flavors, as illustrated in Exhibit 14.9.

Exhibit 14.10 shows that the aggregate production plan anticipates making 1,200, 800, and 600 2-liter bottles of soda over the 3-month planning horizon. Shop-floor workers need a more detailed plan to achieve this goal. To plan their work, they need a week-by-week schedule that specifies what flavors to make and when.

[EXHIBIT 14.9]

Soft-Drink Product Family

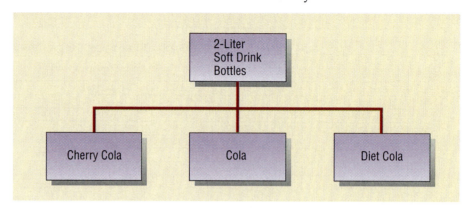

The master production schedule shown in the bottom half of the exhibit provides this information. It tells workers on the shop floor how much of each end product to make in each period, or *time bucket*.

In the real world, the master production scheduling process becomes more complicated. A manufacturing system with only a fair degree of complexity might process components through seven or eight manufacturing stages, including fabrication operations and assembling steps that join numerous parts into subassemblies. The process probably integrates parts purchased from outside vendors. It culminates in a final-assembly operation that combines numerous internally manufactured components, purchased components, and subassemblies into end products that delight customers.

[EXHIBIT 14.10]

Disaggregating Demand

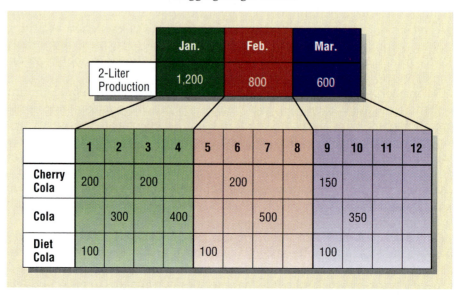

	Jan.	Feb.	Mar.
2-Liter Production	1,200	800	600

	1	2	3	4	5	6	7	8	9	10	11	12
Cherry Cola	200		200			200			150			
Cola		300		400			500			350		
Diet Cola	100				100				100			

[BY THE WAY... HYPOTHETICAL DEMAND PROJECTION]

On April 1, you are planning production for the next 2 months. Marketing has informed you of firm orders for 15 units of your firm's product for April delivery and 10 units so far for May delivery. Earlier demand forecasts projected sales of 25 units in each of these months. In the past, some customers have purchased units on short notice. You have 5 units in inventory.

What demand figures would you assume for the master scheduling process? What other information would you want?

Complex Control System for a Complex Manufacturing Environment

The resource-management process must provide operations managers with a plan that ensures delivery of quality products as promised to customers. The OM system needs a feasible plan that it can execute with its available resources of people, parts, and plant capacity. To achieve this task, a firm needs an effective manufacturing planning and control system along the lines shown in Exhibit 14.11. This may seem like a Rube Goldberg scheme, but complex operations normally require complex control systems. The exhibit reinforces the attraction of the alternative—systems simplification like that practiced in just-in-time manufacturing.

Not every production planning and control system includes every process shown in Exhibit 14.11. This framework sets comprehensive boundaries for a complete discussion. In this chapter, we discuss the upper part of this exhibit. In the next chapter, we discuss capacity-planning processes that appear in the lower part. This discussion must introduce certain key concepts of materials requirements planning (MRP), but a more detailed discussion of this technique will have to wait until Chapter 17, which deals with materials management.

The system in Exhibit 14.11 begins with long-term and intermediate planning for aggregate production levels discussed earlier in this chapter. The demand-management function processes inputs about product needs of both Type A customers (those that place orders and wait for delivery) and Type B customers (those that demand product upon arrival at the firm's site). Aggregate plans usually forecast and define demand for product families. To support the master production scheduling process, demand management must disaggregate its forecasts to provide detailed projections of demand for specific end products. These near-term projections often specify output based on a mix of firm orders and assumed demand. The "By the Way" box outlines such a situation.

Observe that a double arrow links the master production scheduling process with rough-cut capacity planning. Before committing to an MPS, the master scheduler evaluates the likelihood of implementing the proposed plan with current manufacturing resources. This quick-and-dirty assessment of capacity needs is called rough-cut capacity planning.

Once the master scheduler becomes reasonably comfortable with the feasibility of the proposed master production schedule, then the planning process continues with detailed material planning. This set of decisions reflect current inventories, the projected timing of completion of work in process, current shop-floor capacity,

[**EXHIBIT 14.11**]

Framework for a Manufacturing Planning and Control System

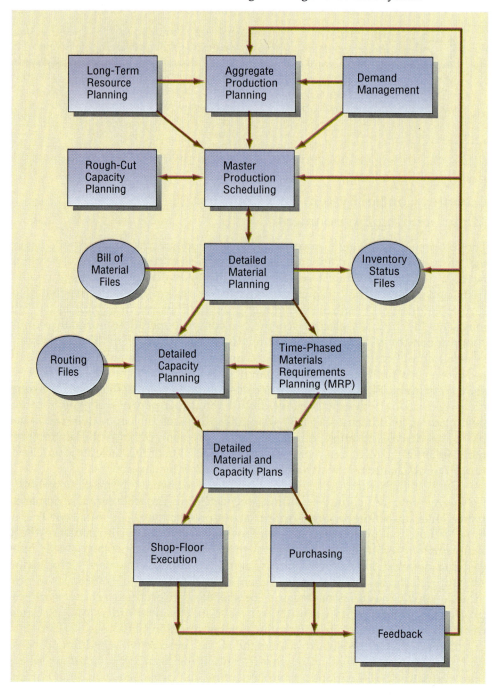

and the likely response of shop workers. The middle section of Exhibit 14.11 illustrates the functions that specify these criteria. For example, the inventory status files tell the master scheduler how much of finished goods and components wait in stock rooms to supply the OM process.

[**E X H I B I T   1 4 . 1 2**]

Simple Bill of Material

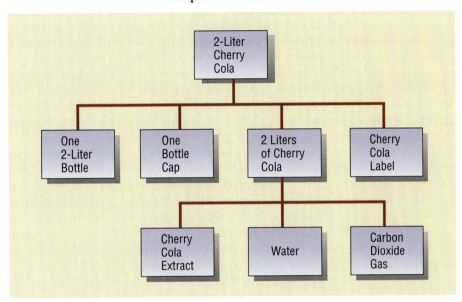

In addition, the **bill of materials** disaggregates end-product demand to specify the materials that the OM system needs to make projected volumes of each end product (Exhibit 14.12). When planners know the current inventory level of each item in the bill of materials, they can deduct these inventories from the gross requirements of the process to determine how much more they must acquire of each input. In addition, they must specify when the process will need each input.

They really cannot answer this question until they determine how and where each part is made. A **routing file** indicates the recommended sequence of processing steps to transform raw materials into each finished part. This file also specifies the capacity that the process needs for every operation to produce every part. Using this information, planners can calculate how much and which types of plant capacity the proposed master schedule will demand.

Shop-floor workers want more, however. Schedulers must indicate to them when all of this production should take place. To solve this problem, many manufacturing planning and control systems plug in **planned lead times**, or prespecified amounts of time scheduled for production operations to make individual parts. Planned lead times exceed the actual time that work centers take to process those parts. A part that requires only 1 hour of machine time may wait in a queue for a week, giving a 1-week long planned lead time. By knowing that a part passes through four operations, each with a 2-day planned lead time, resource managers can create a time-phased schedule for that part:

bill of materials

A list of process inputs that disaggregates end-product demand to specify what the OM system needs to make projected volumes of each end product

routing file

Planning information that indicates the recommended sequence of processing steps and the capacity required to transform raw materials into each finished part

planned lead time

A prespecified amount of time scheduled for production operations to make an individual part

Operation	Machine	Machine Time	Operation Due Date[a]
1	A	0.50 hours	Day 2
2	B	0.75	Day 4
3	D	1.50	Day 6
4	B	0.80	Day 8

[a]An operation due date is the time which the part is due to be completed by that work station.

If this referred to a job shop, the numbers would dictate the lengths of queues waiting in front of the work centers. Machine A might have seven jobs waiting, each with a different due date. Which one should the operator process next?

The ability of the shop to produce parts according to plan provides an essential measure of management effectiveness in a manufacturing system. Planned lead times solve the problem of specifying detailed timing of individual steps. The scheduler can divide the planning horizon into time buckets, normally by shifts, days, or weeks. Shorter time buckets speed parts more quickly through the system. Extremely detailed schedules have a down side, however, because they leave shop-floor workers less flexibility to define an efficient sequence of individual jobs. Also, any disruption can thoroughly upset an extremely tight schedule, increasing the likelihood that process activities will miss scheduled due dates.

Planned lead times allow schedulers to create time-phased materials-management systems. Working backward from end products, these systems calculate the overall input requirements to support production in each period over the planning horizon. Subtracting existing inventory gives the additional stock of each component that the process needs to produce according to the proposed schedule. These are the net input requirements. To make the master production schedule feasible, supporting activities must create sufficient units of the right inputs at the right times to satisfy net requirements.

Of course, each step in this production has its own set of resource needs. In turn, the bills of materials for those inputs define additional material needs, and machine time estimates for those inputs define additional machine capacity requirements. Once again, inventory may include some of these materials, and subtracting those amounts determines the net requirements of each input. This process carries backward to fully specify the production necessary to provide both manufactured and purchased parts.

At the end of the process, schedulers produce either a feasible master schedule or an indication of some shortage in materials or processing capacity. Either shortage calls for remedial action prior to the release of the master production schedule. Schedulers can respond in three ways:

1. Secure more resources
2. Release less work to the plant
3. Encourage the plant to achieve extraordinary results

The last option is not as unreasonable as it seems. Everyone can achieve higher productivity when circumstances demand extraordinary efforts. Manufacturing plants often prove this statement to make production reports look better at the ends of fiscal quarters. Students routinely exceed normal production of learning at the ends of semesters. As a routine practice, however, operations managers should avoid demanding such extreme efforts.

With a feasible master production schedule in hand, resource managers can give instructions to shop-floor personnel and purchasing representatives. Purchasing and operations decisions cycle back to update the inventory status file through two types of messages. First, firm production orders or purchase orders tell inventory managers that goods will arrive on estimated delivery dates. Materials-management systems rely on timely fulfillment of these promises. A second type of messages tell inventory managers that the internal or external factory has satisfied early commitments to make or deliver manufactured goods. Upon arrival of these goods, the system updates inventory files and records of outstanding orders.

Simplified View of the Master Scheduling Process

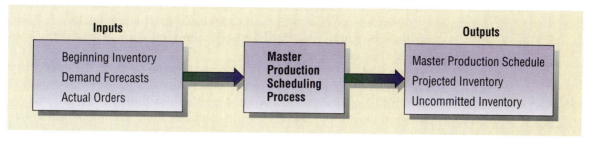

All of the planning iterations and information flows make master production scheduling seem quite complex. Exhibit 14.13 presents a simplified view of this process.

Besides making the flow of production activity predictable, a reliable master production scheduling process helps the firm to communicate effectively with customers. Information about the commitments of actual and planned inventory levels to actual orders tell company representatives what inventories they have available to promise to customers. This information provides strong support for an effective customer service system.

Best Practices in Master Production Scheduling

Late in the 1970s, three professors at Indiana University sought to determine the best practices of master production scheduling practices among leading-edge American manufacturers. The resulting field studies and industry/academic seminars identified certain widely effective scheduling practices. This study led to publication of master scheduling principles, as summarized in the following paragraphs.[2] Remember that scholars formulated these principles at a time in which markets placed fewer demands on manufacturing organizations to offer customized products in wide varieties based on fast-to-product capabilities.

General Management Responsibility for Master Production Schedule.   An organization's general managers must forge agreements among functional managers to achieve effective production planning and execution. Leading-edge companies shared a preference for a simple division of responsibilities. Operations managers bear responsibility for making products and preparing them for shipment according to plan; marketers bear responsibility for selling products as planned and often for controlling finished-goods inventory; finance keeps score. This principle emerges from an assumption of the need for a single, consistent forecast.

Coordination between Master Production Schedule and Production Plan.   This principle seems obvious, but organizations probably observe it less carefully than any other principle. Salespeople ask too often for special favors outside preset plans, disrupting efforts to maintain an orderly system. Scheduling for make-to-

[2] W. L. Berry, T. E. Vollmann, and D. C. Whybark. *Master Production Scheduling: Principles and Practice.* Washington, D.C.: American Production and Inventory Control Society, July 1979.

order or engineer-to-order producers must maintain agreement between the length of the production lead time and that of the order lead time. If customer expectations or market conditions allow effective sales efforts with a firm's current production lead time, then schedulers do not face a serious problem. If the market demands an order lead time shorter than the normal production lead time, however, the master scheduling process must begin production in advance of orders based on demand forecasts.

This requirement exposes the firm to certain risks, including the possibility that orders will exceed planned production. In such a case, the order-entry process must first try to fill pending orders from uncommitted units in the production plan. If the plan does not include enough extra units, then schedulers must perform some "what if" analysis through a computerized production planning and control system to look for a way to accommodate the orders without creating a material breach of the master production schedule. If planners cannot easily accommodate additional sales within the current production schedule, the general manager must weigh the gains from additional sales against the costs of disrupting shop-floor operations to fill those orders.

These risks are inherent whenever we are dealing with a forecast. When the demand lead time is shorter than the actual lead time, the firm must forecast the number of products to be demanded. If the forecast is low (which can occur when a product is in the growth phase of its life cycle), then demand will exceed production. Apple Computer is in a similar position. Because of past experiences where the amount produced exceeded the amount consumed, Apple took a conservative approach. However, the demand for Apple computers exceeded its 28 percent growth forecast. As a result, Apple now cannot meet its demand. The issues being discussed in this section are exactly the problems currently facing Apple's management.

Manufacturing Driven by the Master Production Schedule.   This principle essentially restates a basic management saying: "You plan your work, then you work your plan." Still, it contributes to organizational success by focusing the master production schedule on feasible plans. Unrealistic planning quickly spreads contempt throughout the organization. Shop-floor personnel soon disregard the MPS as an irrelevant top management exercise. Marketing, purchasing, and finance then feel free to promote their parochial interests. Effective execution of a feasible MPS builds respect for the OM function since it demonstrates its ability to manufacture goods in a cost efficient manner, on time, and with appropriate quality characteristics.

Organizational Role of the MPS.   Since the master production schedule serves as a key interface among marketing, purchasing, finance, and operations management, planners need a job description that outlines organizationwide policies and standards of performance for master scheduling. Besides clear lines of authority, a scheduler needs a thorough understanding of the capabilities of the manufacturing and procurement systems, a sixth sense of the needs and idiosyncrasies of the market and the sales organization, and behavioral skills to function smoothly within the organization. After picking the right person for this critical job, top managers must implement a suitable organizational design that encourages the cross-functional cooperation that a master production schedule needs.

The arrangements for compiling the master production schedule should set up a transparent process and build understanding by all organization members who use the plan. Without a fundamental understanding of the MPS and the process for developing it, shop-floor personnel will develop informal subsystems to make the same decisions. These adaptations normally add costs and confusion within the organization. If workers develop such an informal system, organization designers must uncover the reasons that the MPS failed to inspire confidence. Additional training of shop-floor personnel may integrate the MPS more effectively into the work routine, or workers may feel a real unmet need that requires a different remedial action.

Effect of All Known Requirements on the MPS.   The MPS process must assess every influence on production to assure that it develops a feasible production plan. In reality, literal interpretation of this statement would probably introduce too many facts into production planning, unnecessarily raising the cost of the process. If a factor of production never limits process activities, then the production planning process need not invest resources in controlling it. Coors planners need not check the availability of water to support a master production schedule. The firm may evaluate the availability of this resource as part of long-term planning, but it likely has no significant influence on the feasibility of an MPS.

Minimal Inclusion of Components in the Master Production Schedule.   Firms must control different numbers of parts as part of planning their manufacturing processes. A lumber mill transforms a log into many different end products; at the other extreme, Henry Ford transformed 500 or so parts into one Model T car. A graphic illustration would show a triangle with a log at one point and a broad range of products at the opposite side; the picture of Ford's production would start with a range of inputs at its base leading to a single end product. Mass customization creates a third possibility in which production transforms many individual parts into a small number of subassemblies that the firm can then assemble into many different end products to satisfy customers' preferences. A graphic illustration would show an hourglass shape. A diagram of an engineer-to-order system would have the same shape.

This principle urges planners to grasp the process at the best available control point. If process can produce many end products from a small number of component parts, then planners may decide to base the master production schedule on a forecast of component usage. Some forecasts reflect final assembly schedules; others come from aggregate demand forecasts for end products and representative planning bills. **Planning bills** are fictitious bills of materials for unbuildable dummy items that facilitate component scheduling. For example, a planning bill may list components of a representative mix of 1,000 2-liter bottles of various cola products. For the first week of July, planners might create a planning bill for 1,000 2-liter bottles, labels for 600 bottles of cola, 300 cherry cola labels, 100 diet cola labels, and the ingredients needed to make that specific mix of products. Clearly, each specific end product does not use all of these components, but the total list provides a good estimate for planning the resources that the plant will need during that week.

planning bill
A fictitious bill of materials for an unbuildable dummy item that facilitates component scheduling

Planning bills may also help schedulers for a process that produces many variations of a few designs that share similar configurations. For example, an automobile plant may produce cars with many different configurations of options, but much of this variation represents simple differences like paint color and easily installed options. System designers must determine how much detail an MPS needs to define the proper flow of materials for final assembly. A fairly stable mix may allow planners to develop a planning bill of a representative mix of cars to drive the production-planning process.

This bridal gown manufacturer uses time fences in the production schedule to guarantee the customer a finished product for her wedding.   SOURCE   Chuck Fishman/Woodfin Camp & Associates

firm planned order

A specification in the master production schedule that freezes the quantity and timing of a set of outputs in production

Master Production Schedule as a Set of Firm Planned Orders.   A **firm planned order** freezes the quantity and timing of a set of outputs in production. Master schedulers can change these specifications, but only by an overt act. Treating the MPS as a set of firm planned orders promotes essential organizational stability.

To understand this need for stability, suppose that your professor decides to lecture on material other than the assigned reading for the class session. This may lead you to decide that the syllabus (a classroom MPS) gives you little support in your preparations. Workers for most manufacturers react similarly to routine changes in the MPS. Schedulers cannot prevent necessary changes, but they should allow it only as a last resort. Instability leads people to disregard the scheduling process and devote their energies to probable rescheduling.

Stability of the Master Production Schedule.   Planners work to ensure the stability of the production process by developing a reliable MPS that leaves sufficient flexibility to satisfy the expectations of customers. This work begins with efforts to manage the expectations of customers through their interactions with sales representatives. Unless they get input from operations managers, salespeople frequently focus narrowly on pleasing customers at any cost, promising just about any desired delivery terms or order modifications that customers want. In many instances, this flexibility benefits the organization overall, but the decision normally should involve people other than first-line sales reps.

time fence

A point within the MPS that segments the planning horizon into time periods with well-defined provisions for changing orders

Make-to-order firms often set up **time fences** to manage the tradeoff between a stable master production schedule and needed flexibility. Time fences segment the planning horizon into three or more sections, each with well-defined provisions for changing orders, as Exhibit 14.14 illustrates.

Everyone in the organization can count on this system to deny any requests for changes on orders due prior to the first time fence. Short of an executive decision, orders due within 8 weeks remain frozen. Organization members will negotiate with customers who want to change orders with due dates between the first and second time fences. The MPS can easily accommodate change requests on orders due more than 16 weeks into the future. The locations of time fences depend on the

[**E X H I B I T   1 4 . 1 4**]

Time Fences in the Master Production Schedule

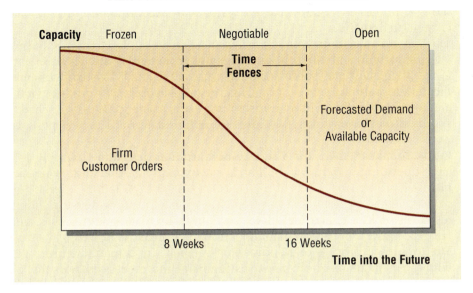

firm's marketing strategy and product structure. Long lead times like that for a Boeing 777 airplane require widely spaced time fences; production of a customized birthday cake can offer much shorter intervals.

A firm does not create time fences to punish customers, and responsible, caring customers do not find them especially troublesome. Besides stabilizing the master production schedule, time fences also defuse potential conflicts between OM personnel and salespeople performing their roles as customer advocates. Without well-defined criteria for changes, operations managers may even suspect salespeople of submitting so-called *soft orders* to get production started before customers make final decisions. Such practices might help marketing people sell products, but at a high cost of disruption in production planning systems.

CHAPTER SUMMARY

This chapter presents an overview of resource-management techniques for both service and manufacturing organizations.

1. Resource management controls the flow of inputs to an OM process through planning, acquisition, scheduling, and implementation activities. This work forms interconnections with several subprocesses discussed in other chapters, including capacity planning, materials requirements planning, human resources planning, and inventory planning.
2. Within the organization's operations strategy, resource management interacts with product and process design to ensure that those processes produce feasible plans that do not encounter unforeseen problems during execution. Demand forecasting and demand management provide decisive support for

this process by predicting the output that the OM system must produce to satisfy customers.

3. An organization can either maintain reserve capacity or involve customers in the OM process to assure that its system can accommodate unpredictable changes in demand.

4. The operations planning hierarchy lays out a series of planning activities with varying planning horizons, measurement units, activities, and levels of detail. Long-range plans may specify dramatic changes in an OM system with implementation spanning several years; aggregate plans relate to product families and focus primarily on human-resources needs; master production schedules specify production runs to fill orders for individual products over periods of weeks or months.

5. Resource management for a service organization determines staffing levels and supporting system capabilities to satisfy expected demand. Long-range planning projects the effects of changes in customer expectations, technological developments, and demographic trends; aggregate planning develops human-resources policies to accommodate variability in demand and in service-delivery procedures; short-term planning creates staffing schedules.

6. The top-down process of resource management for a manufacturer begins with top management decisions to assign plant and process charters that allocate production among the firm's facilities. Aggregate production planning adapts budgeting information to calculate basic production costs, costs of variability in the rate of production, inventory holding costs, and backlogging costs.

7. A manufacturer's production plan can accommodate variability in demand in three ways. It can adopt a chase strategy by matching production to variable demand; it can implement a level strategy by producing steadily and accumulating inventory as a buffer; it can follow a variable-hours strategy by holding staffing rates stable and adjusting employees' work hours as needed.

8. A firm's master production schedule disaggregates demand to designate resource requirements and timing to make individual products. A complex manufacturing system requires a complex resource-management system that develops an MPS based on long-term plans, aggregate plans, and demand management arrangements.

9. Rough-cut capacity planning provides a general idea of the feasibility of the MPS to allow early adjustments, if necessary. Detailed material planning compares the bills of materials for products and their components with available inventory and arranges to acquire additional resources. Planned lead times simplify the potentially massive detail of production schedules for components by specifying standard time requirements.

10. A study of the best practices throughout industry has identified several principles for master production scheduling. General management has responsibility for overall production planning, and subsequent planning must maintain coordination between the MPS and higher-level production plans. The MPS should drive all manufacturing activities and spread production information throughout the organization. It should cover all known resource needs, but it should also minimize detail by aggregating individual resource planning where possible through planning bills of materials. To keep production running smoothly and steadily, the MPS should represent a set of firm planned orders, and time fences should set limits for any changes.

[**KEY TERMS**]

resource-management
  process 654
charter 666
aggregate production
  plan 667
chase strategy 671

level-production strategy
  671
variable-hours strategy
  671
master production
  schedule 674

bill of materials 679
routing file 679
planned lead time 679
planning bill 683
firm planned order 684
time fence 684

[**DISCUSSION QUESTIONS**]

1. Assume that you have a summer internship as a management trainee for Pink Floyd's Touring Unit Number 2.
   a. Prepare a list of the business processes that you would need to manage to support a successful tour.
   b. Which processes should you handle internally, and which should you subcontract? Why?
2. As a management consultant, you have been asked to develop a system to evaluate the performance of Pink Floyd's three touring stage units. What would you recommend?
3. Assume each of the following roles and then define what you would expect the resource-management process to do for you:
   a. New car salesperson at a local BMW dealer
   b. Shift manager at a local fast-food restaurant
   c. Golf pro at a local country club
   d. University professor
4. Why would a firm pay part-time or temporary workers higher wage rates than it would pay similarly skilled full-time employees?
5. How does a production schedule influence the resource-management process? What tradeoffs does this constraint force customers to make?
6. List some examples of demand forecasting and demand management in the resource-management process. Consider these settings: a local restaurant, a campus book store, a travel line managing its fleet of cruise ships, and a company building a line of micro-computers.
7. Using the scenarios in the previous problem, list some example of the impacts of system variance on the resource-management process.
8. Your firm's top managers have stated a goal of serving all customers within 10 minutes of their arrival. How would you begin to work toward achieving this goal for the following customers:
   a. Spare parts buyer at Caterpillar's industrial tractor division
   b. Retail bank customers cashing checks
   c. Customers at a Pizza Hut outlet
   d. Customers at a local Midas Muffler shop
9. Discuss the tradeoffs that govern a decision to rely heavily on part-time employees and temporary workers rather than full-time employees to make resource management sufficiently flexible. What does the employer gain by this choice? What does it sacrifice?
10. Cite three applications of automation in resource management. How has each influenced the flexibility of the resource-management process?

11. Discuss the role of the master scheduler in production planning. What skills and knowledge would you expect to find in a job description for a master scheduler? Why?

12. What consequences would an organization face if the OM system were to fail to fulfill the promises set out in the master production schedule? Would these consequences differ from those for running over budget? Why?

13. Why must planners handle more details as they complete long-term production planning and begin short-term planning? How do the needs of the users of these plans differ?

14. Describe the resource-management process at your local Burger King restaurant. What decisions must this process make?

15. Describe the resource-management processes for:
    a. Final assembly line of an automobile manufacturer
    b. Job shop
    c. Three-stage batch manufacturer
    d. Project

C A U T I O N

[C R I T I C A L   T H I N K I N G   R E Q U I R E D]

1. How would the resource-management function of your school's dean change if the college's trustees were to demand that all students should be able to graduate in 4 years?

2. How should top managers evaluate a firm's resource managers? What performance measures should they choose? Describe some possible consequences of judging performance in this way.

CASE 14.1

Cedar Rapids Corporation

The Cedar Rapids Corporation, a manufacturer of road-paving equipment, must satisfy some demanding customers. Since road-paving firms usually sell their services to units of federal, state, or local government, the market demands equipment that can create roads that meet exacting specifications. The equipment manufacturers must maintain make-to-order systems since they cannot keep such customized equipment in stock.

Over the years, Cedar Rapids had developed a master scheduling process with well-understood planning lead times and time fences. The MPS permitted no changes within the last 3 weeks of an order's 10-week lead time. This period allowed the shop to achieve essential efficiencies while still leaving sufficient flexibility for marketers to serve road builders' needs.

Both Cedar Rapids and its road-contractor customers had experienced slow demand in the mid-1980s, but business started to improve early in 1987. The contractors initially ordered flexible and relatively inexpensive single-width pavers. In March, however, these customers recognized a stronger upward trend than they had anticipated; many asked to change their orders to double-width pavers that would prove more cost-effective on large jobs despite their higher prices. Of course, these customers wanted Cedar Rapids to make the double-width pavers by the original orders' delivery dates, and most change orders arrived after the 3-week time fence. The firm normally completed final assembly and testing during this period.

The stress of these changes started to break down the long-standing master scheduling process at Cedar Rapids. Production controllers indicated that they could accommodate the desired order changes, but not by the original due dates. Customers howled that weather left them only lim-ited windows of opportunity. Late delivery could prevent them from completing jobs on time and at estimated costs.

Marketing suggested that customers choose between two alternatives: accept the single-width pavers on time or accept the double-width pavers some time in May. Finding both alternatives unacceptable, the irate customers complained to top management, threatening to order from competitors unless the double-width pavers were delivered by the original delivery dates. The company president sided with the customers, fearing loss of sales and market share.

OM personnel dutifully responded to the president's order, tearing down partially completed pavers to convert them to double-width machines. The two machines shared many common parts, but not all, so planners released rush orders for component fabrication and purchasing. By the end of April, partially completed double-width pavers clogged the shop floor while they sat awaiting a few critical parts. The final-assembly department worked overtime to both disassemble and assemble pavers. Expedited work became routine and the old master schedule lost any meaning.

Worse yet, the customers the president so desperately wanted to please still furiously called for their orders. Top managers could have learned a valuable lesson about time fences. Rather, they fumed that the firm lacked a "world-class production scheduling system."

QUESTION

How could Cedar Rapids solve, resolve, and dissolve its scheduling problem? Give specific actions for each type of response.

CASE 14.2

Super Jungle Magic

Super Jungle Magic manufactured and marketed the leading potting soil in the California market for lawn and garden products. The firm sold most of its products directly to retailers, which resold them in their plant and garden departments. After seasonal demand faded every year, many retailers reallocated floor and shelf space for this product. Seasonal products related to Halloween, Thanksgiving, and Christmas often replaced Super Jungle Magic's products from October through mid-January.

Based on these trends, the firm anticipated sales for 1997 of:

Units Sales (000)

	Jan.	Feb.	Mar.	Apr.	May	Jun.	Jul.	Aug.	Sept.	Oct.	Nov.	Dec.	Total
Large bags[a]	20	40	100	150	140	120	50	40	60	30	10	10	770
Small bags[a]	10	15	15	20	15	15	10	10	15	20	10	10	165

[a]1-cubic-foot bags; small bags hold 8 quarts, sold in corrugated cartons with six bags per carton.

The Super Jungle Magic plant has the following capacities, depending upon the number of workers:

Number of People

	1	2	3	4
Large bags (bags per day)	800	1,800	3,000	4,000
Small bags (6-bag cases per day)	200	400	600	800

The firm's planning process assumes 20 work days in each month and 4 weekend days each month. During the peak season, planners expect the crew to work 10-hour shifts, with overtime pay for 2 hours. A four-person crew could produce 80,000 one-cubic-foot bags or 16,000 cases of 8-quart bags of potting soil per month working regular shifts.

The cost of labor at the SJM plant averages $7.50 per hour plus another $2.50 per hour for fringe benefits. The firm must spend approximately $750.00 to hire a worker and about $250.00 per discharge to lay off a worker. After training, workers can staff either production line for small or large bags without loss of productivity. Overtime work costs the firm $15.00 per hour.

Planners estimate direct costs, including labor, at $1.00 per 1-cubic-foot bag and $2.00 per case of 8-quart bags. They estimate the cost of inventory at approximately 3 percent of the direct cost of that product per month. The plant has indoor storage capacity for 40,000 cases and outdoor storage capacity for 80,000 bags. The firm cannot store corrugated containers of small bags outside, and it should not store large bags for more than 2 months because both the potting medium and the plastic bag start to deteriorate.

QUESTION

How should the firm schedule production in order to minimize its total costs for labor, hiring and firing, and inventory holding costs? (Use the template SJM.XS to facilitate your analysis.)

[<mark>S E L E C T E D   R E A D I N G S</mark>]

Berry, W. L., T. E. Vollmann, and D. C. Whybark. *Master Production Scheduling: Principles and Practice.* Pittsburgh, Pa.: American Production and Inventory Control Society, July 1979.

―――. *Manufacturing Planning and Control Systems,* 3d ed. Homewood, Ill.: Business One/Irwin, 1992.

Burbidge, J. L. *Production Planning.* London: Heinemann, 1971.

―――. *Production Flow Analysis for Planning Group Technology.* Oxford: Clarendon Press, 1989.

Fitzsimmons, J. A., and M. J. Fitzsimmons. *Service Management for Competitive Advantage.* New York: McGraw-Hill, 1994.

Fogarty, D. W., J. H. Blackstone, and T. R. Hoffmann. *Production and Inventory Management,* 2d ed. Cincinnati, Oh.: South-Western, 1991.

Niland, P. *Production Planning, Scheduling, and Inventory Control.* London: Macmillan, 1970.

Orlicky, J. *Materials Requirements Planning: The New Way of Life in Production and Inventory Management.* New York: McGraw-Hill, 1975.

Wight, Oliver W. *Production and Inventory Control in the Computer Age.* Boston, Mass.: CBI, 1974.

CHAPTER FIFTEEN

Capacity Management

CHAPTER OBJECTIVES

[At the end of this chapter, you should be able to]

- Discuss the detailed characteristics of an organization that determine its capacity.
- Apply capacity-management tools to regulate the flow of work to a service or manufacturing facility.
- Evaluate capacity-acquisition decisions for single machines, work cells, and plantwide investments.
- Describe the influence of capacity choices on the strategy-formulation process.

Elizabeth Sher
Goodwin

More Thunderzords, Please!

Super heroes face some treacherous situations, and so do the operations managers that make their plastic replicas. In 1994, Saban Enterprises expected a good year marketing toys based on its popular Power Rangers show, in which five teenagers rescue the town of Angel Grove from daily threats by evil space invaders led by villainous Rita Repulsa and Lord Zed. The pace of demand stunned even the most optimistic observers, however, and the company scrambled to find capacity to supply clamoring retailers.

Bandai, the Japanese manufacturer of the toys, had expected an increase in sales over the previous year, but not the tenfold increase that it experienced. In order to expand capacity, the firm's plant in Bangkok, Thailand, hired 600 additional workers to staff 24-hour production. The plant's 2,000-person work force boosted production from 150,000 to 725,000 toys a month, and other plants added to that total.

Nine plants in China, three in Thailand, two in Japan, one in Taiwan, and one in Mexico turned out Power Rangers merchandise. To gain maximum benefits from a division of labor, one plant makes Dragonzords while another makes Thunderzords. By the end of the 1994 season, Bandai expected to sell $300 million of these toys in United States alone. The uproar seemed likely to continue as the Power Rangers stormed into Europe and Canada. What havoc has Rita Repulsa wrought?

An important part of operations management involves acquiring productive resources to meet the firm's sales and customer-service goals. In the previous chapter, we described the resource-management process, in which operations managers estimate the amounts and types of resources that their transformation process needs to achieve these goals. That discussion emphasized the firm's need for human resources.

In this chapter, we focus on capacity-management decisions, which plan for physical resource needs. This analysis evaluates the requirements of a firm's transformation process for physical factors of production, such as plant facilities and equipment, to produce the volume of output specified by short-term and long-term business plans. A broader interpretation would include all process capabilities and intellectual capital that a firm needs to effectively implement its strategic plans. In the next chapter, we will focus on additional physical inputs to the OM process like materials, which fall under the category of inventory.

Capacity management mirrors the firm's overall planning processes and contributes to the effort to introduce a feasible flow of work to the OM system. The process for short-term capacity management can include activities to regulate the flow of work to the system. The nature of demand in a specific situation may make this impossible, however, increasing the importance of accurate demand forecasts. The process for long-term capacity management seeks to match the sizes and timing of adjustments in physical plant and equipment to OM system loads over the firm's long-term planning horizon. These decisions rely heavily on long-term business forecasts.

In this chapter, we start by developing three concepts of capacity that help operations managers to decide how much capacity their system will need to complete anticipated operations. We then use these concepts to discuss some analytical tools that support capacity-management decisions like sizing and locating individual pieces of equipment or service centers.

Finally, we will deal with capacity strategy, or the sequence of capacity decisions over time that combine to give the system capabilities that it needs to achieve its goals and objectives. A firm bases such decisions on strategic audits of capacity-enhancing investments that evaluate their contributions to the firm's progress toward its long-term objectives. Strategic audits carefully evaluate the sizes, timing, and locations of capacity expansions or contractions and the ability of planned technology to meet or exceed customers' expectations. In short, capacity strategy extends a firm's planning process beyond a single-stage analysis of individual moves like those in checkers to a chess game of multiple actions with networks of interconnections.

OVERVIEW OF THE CAPACITY-MANAGEMENT PROCESS

The opening story described the capacity-management challenge to marketers and manufacturers of Power Rangers merchandise. Bandai's OM effectiveness hinged on its ability to accelerate production quickly to help Saban Enterprises fully exploit an unexpected runaway marketing success. The ability of a firm or its suppliers to meet these challenges has become an essential core competency in the fast-moving market for fad toys. A more stable market requires similar capacity-planning responses, though it may present new requirements at a less frantic pace, as the "On the Job" box on Weyerhauser illustrates.

ON THE JOB

More Douglas Fir, Please!

■

Weyerhauser is a highly integrated producer of wood products that harvests trees, largely from its own 11-million-acre timberland holdings, and processes them into pulp, paper, lumber, and other forest products. The biological lead times to grow trees determine the length of Weyerhauser's capacity-planning horizon.

Capacity planning starts with a biological tree-growth model that establishes the maximum sustainable flow of wood fiber from each of the firm's forests. The model implicitly assumes that Weyerhauser expects to continue to grow and harvest trees forever.

Over the firm's extremely long 80-year planning horizon, its managers must make a number of related decisions about long-term capacity. They must separate trees that they will sell as logs from those that they will convert into forest-product commodities. They must plan the types and locations of new investments in tree-growing and log-processing facilities. In short, they must plan for raw-material flows and conversion facilities that will serve the firm's goal of extracting the highest value from its finite fiber resources.

Bandai and Weyerhauser face conceptually similar capacity-management problems, although the timing and complexity characteristics of those problems differ. To feed the ravenous market for Power Rangers, Bandai's operations managers must address limits on supply capacity in conditions of volatile demand, intense labor economics, and global logistics. They can rely on fairly straightforward manufacturing operations, although they must quickly train large numbers of unskilled workers.

Weyerhauser's capacity-management problem gives operations managers ample time to think through alternative capacity arrangements. (Trees don't grow

To obtain the greatest value from available resources, paper manufacturers manage capacity within a larger-than-average time period.   SOURCE   Mark C. Burnett/Stock Boston

as fast as the demand for the newest Power Ranger, and they normally stay put.) Furthermore, this commodity producer converts about the same volume of wood fiber each year, so its capacity-planning process relies less heavily than Bandai's process on accurate short-term demand forecasts. Weyerhauser managers must make much more complex decisions about the firm's mix of end products, however. They use large-scale mathematical models to route projected flows of wood-fiber inputs through conversion facilities in a way that optimizes the firm's profitability.

Criteria for Capacity-Management Decisions

Five shared criteria define the capacity-management problems in these two vastly different situations:

1. Number of units that internal and external factories must satisfy
2. Timing of demand:
   a. Ability or desirability of postponing demand
   b. Seasonal or cyclical variations in the demand pattern
   c. Effects of the product life cycle on demand
   d. Ability to forecast total market demand
   e. Stability of market share
3. Locations to expand or contract capacity in the customer-service system, including production, distribution, and retailing operations
4. Timing of capacity adjustments:
   a. Time required to expand or contract capacity
   b. Feasible increments of expansion or contraction
   c. Capacity adjustments to lead or lag anticipated changes in demand
5. Value tradeoffs for these decisions

To treat the capacity-management process as a system for delivering value, operations managers must include all four components of the value equation in capacity decisions. Bandai would gain little from additional capacity for Dragonzord production if it could not deliver the products on time according to specifications. Likewise, Weyerhauser would gain little from a revolutionary process for converting logs to wood fiber if customers cared little for the quality improvements that the new method might offer. Buyers of commodities may appreciate higher quality, but they normally decline to pay higher prices for it. Capacity-management decisions, like all organizational decisions, should reflect the values and needs of a firm's customers.

A service organization faces a more acute need than a manufacturer to establish the right amount of capacity in an advantageous location, since customers often expect immediate response from a service system. Insufficient server capacity can spoil the experience at a restaurant despite excellent food. A bank's service reputation often depends entirely on its ability to keep customers moving rapidly through queues. Increasingly, customers expect royal treatment (although they may prefer to avoid the flashes of tabloid photographers' cameras). If a firm does not or cannot manage its customers' expectations, then it must unfailingly maintain sufficient capacity to accommodate anticipated demand. Customers do not care whether they have to wait due to a shortage in human or equipment capacity; they evaluate their personal experience of the service. The next "By the Way" box shows how one bank eases its customers' expectations.

The discussion so far has assumed the preliminary definition of *capacity* from Chapter 1: what the firm can do effectively and efficiently. More rigorous analysis

requires some refinement of this concept. Operations managers need to know exactly how to evaluate capacity to avoid failures of their systems to produce expected outputs. The cause of such a mistake may originate in an imprecise understanding of the term.

Defining *Capacity*

Capacity is the rate of output from an OM system per unit of time, or the rate at which the firm withdraws work from the system. Each definition specifies capacity based on the output that a system can produce, store, and transport. Operations managers can measure capacity as an amount of resources available (i.e., number of machine hours, number of labor hours, number of tools, square feet of floor space) or an amount of potential output (i.e., number of products that can emerge from the process, dollar value of products).

To measure capacity for an operation with a varied output, operations managers must sometimes develop a standard unit of measure. Saban Enterprises might evaluate Bandai's capacity to produce all Power Rangers merchandise by measuring in equivalent Thunderzord units. Weyerhauser might measure the capacity of its various mills and other facilities in thousands of board feet of lumber. Pizza Hut might count sales of all products in equivalent pizza rounds. Dollar value may seem to offer an easier basis for measuring disparate streams of output, but it becomes a problem if the price of one end product fluctuates significantly, as lumber prices do. In such a situation, the value of a plant's output would vary without any change in its capacity, forming an unsteady basis for operations planning.

Operations managers frequently specify system capacities based on two terms: input rates and system loads. As shown in Exhibit 15.1, an input rate describes the speed of the flow of new jobs into a process. Different OM systems might state input rates as numbers of new orders for Power Rangers or thousands of board feet of logs entering a sawmill. The input rate of a process creates the demands on its capacity. In turn, capacity determines the rate of output of the process, or the speed at which the firm can pull completed work out of the process. More available capacity supports a faster potential rate of output.

[**EXHIBIT 15.1**]

Input Rate, Load, and Capacity

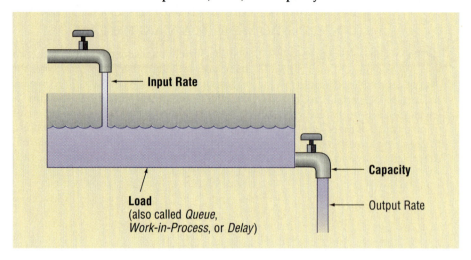

load

The volume of work that remains for a process to complete at any time

Load is the volume of work that remains for a process to complete at any time.[1] Load depends on the input rate of a process, its capacity, and perhaps lags in process activities. Generally, an input rate in excess of capacity increases load; an input rate less than capacity decreases load.

The flows into and out of the pool in Exhibit 15.1 can result from uncontrolled or managed streams of work. Each flow is affected by different factors in the system. For example, the incoming flow is influenced by the operation of the systems feeding the work center or machine (e.g., the planning system, which is releasing jobs to the system, or the work centers providing orders for this work center). The flow out of the backlog pool is influenced by the capacity at the work center and how it is used, as well as the state of the work centers using this output. For example, if these work centers are blocked, then the job may wait at this work center instead of moving to the next. Capacity determines the upper limit of the flow of completed work out of the system. At any time, the load is the difference between the cumulative flows into the system and the cumulative flows out of it, adjusted for any increases due to lags in transformation-process activities. If capacity exceeds the input rate, load can approach zero when the system immediately commences work on incoming jobs and transforms them into outputs without delay. Maytag commercials show an extreme case of this situation as a repair technician wistfully awaits an incoming service call. Load has some positive value when the nature of the transformation process demands that incoming jobs spend certain amounts of time in the system. This occurs in wineries, French restaurants, many manufacturing processes, and so-called *four-year* colleges, where delays can add unplanned semesters of education work to system loads.

Some systems partition existing load into two pools: orders awaiting release to the shop floor and orders currently in production. Operations managers often use the term **backlog** for the pool of orders awaiting shop-floor processing. They describe backlogs at work centers as *queues,* although operators also commonly express concern about the backlog or work load at a work center. An unusually

backlog

The pool of orders awaiting shop-floor processing

---

[1]John H. Blackstone, Jr., *Capacity Management* (Cincinnati, Oh.: South-Western, 1989), p. 7.

small queue often signals lack of work, and it may threaten the employment security of the operator. An unusually large queue may imply poor performance by the operator, again threatening someone's job tenure, or it may indicate a need for overtime or weekend work, threatening attendance at kids' soccer matches. These differences in terminology illustrate some imprecision in the meanings of the terms *load, work load,* and *backlog.*

A backlog may seem like a sign of inefficiency, but a firm may well expect to hold an order for a time before beginning processing. A manufacturer from the defense industry might emphasize its healthy status in its annual report by claiming, "Business in 1996 was quite good. Our backlog increased from $1.4 billion to $1.7 billion." In fact, a make-to-order business may need to maintain backlogs to keep key productive resources working steadily rather than waiting idle for completion of upstream activities. A declining backlog in such a make-to-order business often leads to personnel layoffs; a significant increase in such a firm's backlog often triggers capacity expansions to avoid extending promised delivery dates for new business or even endangering deadlines for existing jobs.

In a make-to-stock business, the size of a backlog often indicates the closeness of the match between current capacity and current demand. If existing demand propels a stream of orders faster than the internal and external factories can supply products, then a rising backlog will stretch product-replenishment times, usually with destructive consequences. Slow product replenishment often allows demand to deplete finished-goods inventories at the point of sale or distribution. This generally causes stockouts and customer dissatisfaction. Retailers and distributors try to anticipate delays in order lead times by ordering goods even earlier, so the factory receives its usual orders plus those that customers would have submitted later if they could expect normal lead times. In this way, a high plant load leads to an even higher load, exacerbating the problem for both the producer and the customers.

Through their capacity management activities, operations managers help the firm to balance demand with available productive resources in a way that adds value for customers. By maintaining appropriate levels of backlog and inventory, operations managers assure that the firm provides service that suits its target customers' values. To achieve this balance, however, they must understand and anticipate variations in measurements of various kinds of capacity.

TYPES OF CAPACITY

Some mismatches between demand and capacity result from frustrating gaps between the output rates that operations managers assume in planning and the rates that their plants actually generate. Such a gap often seems to infer some problem with management methods, but it may actually indicate an incomplete understanding of capacity. When operations managers state process capacities, they must clearly indicate which of three types of capacity they intend to specify:

- Maximum capacity, or design capacity
- Effective capacity, or planned capacity
- Demonstrated capacity

Each type of capacity describes a specific way of measuring the potential output of a process. Each gives useful insight into the appropriate response of the process to changes in demand.

Maximum Capacity

maximum capacity

A measure that defines the highest rate of output that a process or activity can achieve

Maximum capacity defines the highest rate of output that a process or activity can achieve. It specifies a theoretical upper limit above the usual rate for routine operations.

Operations managers calculate the maximum or design capacity of a process based on the number and durations of available shifts, the number of available machines and employees per shift, and the work days in the period of the calculation. This calculation requires some very important simplifying assumptions:

- *Equally skilled workers*   This assumption eliminates the need to account for differences in efficiency due to individual workers' training or abilities.
- *No loss of time to product changeovers or differences in products*
- *No loss of capacity due to machine breakdowns, worker problems, scrap, and salvage* This eliminates real-world disruptions like employees asking for time to rest or eat and problems with products that operations managers correct without changing equipment.
- *No loss of capacity due to preventive maintenance or planned downtime*
- *No overtime work or heroic efforts by employees*

These rather impractical assumptions limit maximum capacity to describing an upper limit for the regular output rate of a process or activity.

Operations managers can increase a maximum capacity only by increasing physical resources. They can do this over the long term by building new facilities, adding more or better equipment, or hiring more workers. They can increase maximum capacity over the short term or intermediate periods by adding a second or third shift. Overtime work provides a strictly short-term boost. Most of these options take time to implement, except simply scheduling overtime shifts.

Alternatively, managers can increase either short-term or long-term capacity by eliminating current process activities. Outsourcing or outpartnering relationships provide popular methods for doing this, as the discussion of supply chain management in Chapter 13 explained.

Effective Capacity

effective capacity

A measure that defines the output rate that managers expect for a given process or activity

Effective capacity identifies the output rate that managers expect for a given activity or process. They base production plans and schedules on this measure of output. Effective capacity normally falls short of maximum capacity by some amount, as Exhibit 15.2 illustrates.

Operations managers often plan to operate their systems at less than 100 percent of maximum capacity for several good reasons:

- *Accommodate unexpected demand*   No realistic shop-floor scheduler expects to receive all orders with normal lead times. Important customers often submit rush orders, with or without apologies, that require rapid responses. Firms have found that a little free capacity can add value.
- *Allow time for preventive maintenance and other activities that support capacity* Preventive maintenance reduces the chances of disruptions due to unplanned breakdowns. Scheduling downtime for this purpose can reduce system variance.
- *Correct unexpected breakdowns*   Despite careful maintenance, breakdowns reduce effective capacity.

Maximum and Effective Capacity

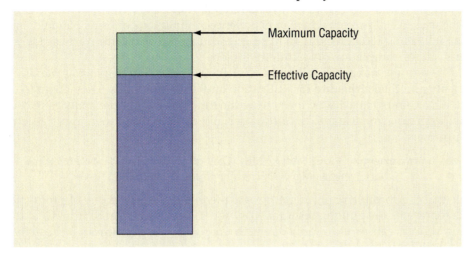

- *Employ capacity efficiently*   Running at maximum capacity can severely strain equipment and people. Operations managers often consciously run their plants at lower capacity levels to avoid harm to people and equipment.

Since effective capacity represents the output rate that a planner should realistically expect, the methods for developing this measure of capacity become important. One method expresses effective capacity as a percentage of maximum capacity. This is called a *top-down* calculation because top managers often set standards for it in advance. If a process has a maximum capacity of 840 hours per week and management wants to maintain a 20 percent cushion, then effective capacity equals 840 hours times 0.80, or 672 hours. Operations managers would then plan to run the process productively for 672 of 840 total hours.

Another method calculates effective capacity based on rates of utilization and efficiency. **Utilization** is the percentage of a resource's maximum capacity for which plans expect active involvement in production. For example, a shop-floor supervisor does not expect an employee to spend every minute of an 8-hour shift actively working. Even devoted workers need time for scheduled breaks and unplanned interruptions. Mathematically, utilization can be expressed as:

utilization

The percentage of a resource's maximum capacity for which plans expect active involvement in production

$$\text{Utilization} = \frac{\text{Actual hours}}{\text{Scheduled available hours}}$$

The efficiency rate measures the relationship between planned resource allocation for a process or activity and the actual resources that the process or activity consumes.[2] Capacity managers express an efficiency rate as a ratio of needed resources (labor time, machine time, tools, etc.) to some standard amount of resources. Mathematically, they calculate:

$$\text{Efficiency} = \frac{\text{Standard time}}{\text{Actual time}}$$

[2]Thomas Bihun and John Musolf, *Capacity Management Certification Review Course* (Falls Church, Va.: American Production and Inventory Control Society, 1985).

Operations managers often assume both efficiency and utilization rates as they work to develop feasible plans. They base estimates of actual times on workers' experience, the condition of plant equipment, the familiarity of workers with planned jobs, and the quality of raw materials. Unlike the utilization rate, efficiency can exceed 100 percent when an experienced employee performs planned tasks; it can fall below 100 percent if an inexperienced employee performs those tasks or plans call for completion of an unfamiliar job.

Operations managers calculate effective capacity by measuring maximum capacity and then adjusting for utilization and efficiency rates. They begin to calculate maximum capacity by measuring the time interval for the analysis in order to express capacity as a rate of output per unit of time. They then apply a general formula:

$$\text{Maximum capacity} = \text{Hours/Shift} \times \text{Shifts/Day} \times \text{Days/Week} \times \text{Planned overtime percentage} \times \text{Output/Hour for the critical resource}$$

Note that this formula requires planners to identify the critical factor of production. This represents the limiting resource in a process or activity. Recall from Chapter 5 that a process can produce only as much output as can pass through the activity with the lowest capacity.

After establishing the maximum capacity of a process, planners adjust for both efficiency and utilization to find the likely practical capacity of the process:

$$\text{Effective capacity} = \text{Maximum capacity} \times \text{Efficiency} \times \text{Utilization}$$

An example may help to demonstrate the practical application of this calculation.

[**P R O B L E M   1 5 . 1**]

Effective Capacity in Practice

A small plant processes jobs through eight machines with one operator per machine, running two 8-hour shifts a day for 5 days a week. The plant normally schedules no overtime production. Machine utilization rates average 80 percent, and overall plant efficiency averages 95 percent.

This information suggests several limits for the effective capacity problem. First, the link between each machine and a single employee allows planners to focus on machine capacity. The capacity calculation covers 80 hours per week (two shifts per day × 8 hours per shift × 5 days per week).

Maximum capacity equals 640.0 machine hours (80.0 hours per machine × 8 machines). Effective capacity equals:

486.4 machine hours =
  640.0 machine hours × 0.80 (utilization rate) × 0.95 (efficiency rate)

Operations managers can reasonably expect 486.4 machine hours of productive work from the plant every week. This calculation of effective capacity gives a critical limit for the plant's production schedule.   [■]

Demonstrated Capacity

demonstrated capacity
The actual level of output for a process or activity over a period of time

Planners calculate theoretical values for maximum and effective capacity to guide their arrangements for production. **Demonstrated capacity**, in contrast, deals with

[**EXHIBIT 15.3**]

Averaging Observed Results to Find Demonstrated Capacity

Work Center 123

Observation Period: 5 weeks beginning July 8, 1996

Week	Observed Output
1 (beginning July 8)	620 hrs.
2 (beginning July 15)	580
3 (beginning July 22)	635
4 (beginning July 29)	570
5 (beginning August 5)	550
Total hours (capacity)	2,955 hrs.
Average hours (demonstrated capacity)	591 hrs./week

actual rather than planned production. It measures the actual level of output for a process or activity over a period of time.

Operations managers calculate demonstrated capacity simply by averaging recorded figures for actual output over a period of time. Exhibit 15.3 shows this calculation for a work center that performs some process operation. Over a 5-week period, this work center produced output for an average of 591 hours per week, ranging from a high of 635 hours in Week 3 to a low of 550 hours in Week 5.

Demonstrated capacity may differ from both maximum and effective capacity for many reasons.

Product Mix. The number of different products that a process must generate affects its demonstrated capacity through requirements for setup times. Whenever a process switches production from one product to another, it must set up equipment for the new output. Setups may make changes to equipment (new tools or layouts), and they may require operators to relearn methods for making the new product. A diverse product mix requires many such changes, and these setups reduce demonstrated capacity.

Operator Skill and Experience. Operator skill differs from operator experience in important ways. Operator skill refers to abilities of individual workers. Some people naturally excel at work that requires great precision; the natural abilities of others suit them to physically demanding work. Excellent vision gives a person one essential requirement for work as a test pilot. Physical or natural attributes like these may help an individual to develop certain skills.

In contrast, experience comes from learning, training, and executing tasks. If an instructor shows someone how to do a task, then the trainee gains experience. Someone who makes something every day accumulates more experience than someone who has never made that product. In general, skill and experience both increase the efficiency of a worker and the demonstrated capacity of a process.

Condition of Equipment. The abilities of equipment also affect demonstrated capacity. Improving the capabilities or condition of equipment and tools raises demonstrated capacity. The condition of equipment and tools depends on operation, storage, and maintenance practices.

Types of Jobs.   Important differences between the work required for specific jobs often affect processing methods and efficiency. In particular, production of prototypes must proceed without guidance from established production standards or requirements. A process may turn out prototypes and other demanding jobs less efficiently than routine production, reducing demonstrated capacity, if workers have to spend more time doing each job.

Inaccurate Production Standards.   Demonstrated capacity may differ from effective capacity not because of inefficiencies in actual processing, but because of poor standards for process performance. If effective capacity inaccurately identifies the amount of time that a process should take to make 1 unit of output or the number of units of output it should make per period of time, then effective capacity will misstate real capacity and demonstrated capacity will differ.

Quality of Materials.   Demonstrated capacity also depends on the quality of the materials that a process handles. Poor-quality materials inhibit efficiency because the process must either work around defects or spend time inspecting finished products to ensure compliance with final-quality standards.

Other Factors.   Several additional causes can contribute to differences between demonstrated capacity and maximum or effective capacity for a process:

- *Starvation*   Capacity may disappear between two or more linked activities. If one work station sits idle waiting for inputs from either internal or external suppliers, then demonstrated capacity falls.
- *Blockage*   Like starvation problems, blockage problems inhibit efficiency when a downstream activity fails to keep pace with upstream activities. Also like starvation, a blockage in the activities of either internal or external customers can inhibit the smooth flow of work through the process.
- *Production yield problems*   Effective capacity plans for production of acceptable units of output. Demonstrated capacity does not count any units with quality defects, so scrap, rework, and salvage all reduce it.
- *Time spent on training*   Any unplanned training for employees can reduce demonstrated capacity by reducing either utilization or efficiency rates.

This list is not comprehensive. Demonstrated capacity often falls for other reasons like power failures and seasonal drops in efficiency. Still, these causes account for the most significant influences on demonstrated capacity.

Planning Effects of Capacity Types

By comparing maximum, effective, and demonstrated capacity, operations managers can identify potential improvements and decide how to implement them. These measures of capacity help to clarify several types of problems with capacity.

Insufficient Capacity.   Some physical obstacle such as lack of adequate machines, facilities, or tools may keep the capacity of a process below the level that the firm needs to satisfy demand. Capacity managers can overcome this obstacle only by adding new physical capacity. They can construct new facilities, buy more

Gaps among Maximum, Effective, and Demonstrated Capacities

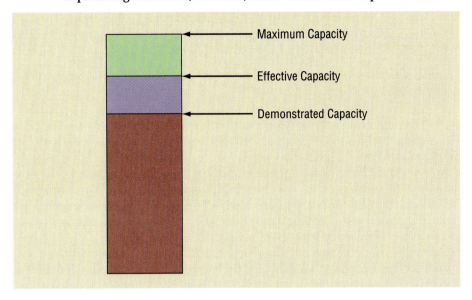

equipment, draw more heavily on the capacity of suppliers, or hire more employees. Each of these actions raises the maximum capacity of the process.

Excess Capacity.   A firm that can produce more output with existing resources than customers demand finds its OM process underutilized. The cost of maintaining this excess capacity forces the firm to spend more than necessary to produce its desired output. A manufacturer may incur costs for idle personnel or machines. A service organization incurs costs for idle personnel, and it risks loss of product appeal if customers sense that few people share their enthusiasm for the service. Restaurant customers may begin to doubt their choice for dinner if they notice that no one else has joined them in the dining room. Both manufacturers and service organizations experience large gaps between their effective and demonstrated capacities if they maintain excess capacities.

Uses of Existing Capacity.   A capacity problem may result from the current organization of productive resources rather than a mismatch between demand and the amount of capacity. Such a problem may result from unnecessary tasks in the current process or from equipment breakdowns, poor-quality inputs from suppliers, late deliveries, employee absenteeism, or inferior process design. Operations managers could increase the amount of capacity available to process activities without additional investments in resources by identifying and eliminating the impediments to current capacity.

To solve a capacity problem, managers must first diagnose its cause as either a mismatch between demand and capacity or simply a misuse of existing capacity. They do this by comparing planned levels of capacity (i.e., maximum and effective capacity) with the actual level of output from the system (i.e., demonstrated capacity). Exhibit 15.4 illustrates the relationship of these three measures of capacity. Gaps among these three types of capacity often help operations managers to evaluate capacity problems.

They encounter three different types of imbalances:

- Case 1: Demonstrated capacity < Effective capacity < Maximum capacity;
- Case 2: Effective capacity < Demonstrated capacity < Maximum capacity
- Case 3: Effective capacity < Demonstrated capacity = Maximum capacity

Each type of imbalance requires a different response since it results from different capacity-related problems.

Case 1. Demonstrated capacity falls short of effective capacity when the process produces less than it should produce. This occurs when problems arise with inputs or with amounts of available capacity.

An input problem would appear in Exhibit 15.1 as a restriction in the flow of orders into the process or its activities. If the process receives fewer orders than plans expect, the slow input reduces the load on the process and, eventually, its output. For this reason, demonstrated capacity falls short of effective capacity. Improvements in demand forecasts may correct the difference.

Starvation might reduce the input to a specific activity. This would reduce the output and demonstrated capacity of the process by depriving it of necessary physical or human resources. An insufficient number of workers would cause this kind of problem, as would a problem with deliveries from a supplier. Correcting the problem should restore demonstrated capacity to the level of effective capacity.

Besides these input problems, a capacity problem can keep demonstrated capacity from meeting planned standards. The effective capacity calculation indicates that the process has enough capacity, so operations managers must look for problems in the organization of its activities. Several process characteristics can drag down demonstrated capacity:

- Problems with the product mix that require too many setups
- Deficiencies in operators' skills or experience
- Machine breakdowns or problems with tools
- Processing prototypes or unfamiliar jobs
- Problems with materials
- Inaccurate or excessively tight standards
- Blockages
- Scrap, salvage, and rework
- Disruptive events like holidays, strikes, and power failures

Once operations managers understand why their system fails to perform at its effective capacity, they can begin to reduce the waste implied by this gap. Recall, however, that the gap between maximum and effective capacity may represent value-adding excess capacity rather than waste. The operations manager must determine the appropriate sizes of these gaps and eliminate waste while leaving the capacity cushion that promotes the firm's long-term interests.

This requires accurate diagnosis of either input or capacity problems. Two general guidelines help to target this initial evaluation of a shortage of demonstrated capacity as compared to effective capacity:

- If the capacity-limiting activity seems to sit idle a good deal of the time, then look first at input problems.
- If the capacity-limiting activity appears overloaded, as when it requires unplanned overtime to keep pace, then look first at capacity problems.

Case 2.   In general, operations managers seldom address problems when effective capacity falls short of demonstrated capacity. Several situations may cause a process to produce more than the plans demand:

- Favorable product mix limits setups
- Jobs well-suited to process characteristics
- Surprisingly experienced or skilled operators
- Unusually good quality of materials
- Lower than expected scrap, rework, and salvage

Operations managers seldom complain about such pleasant surprises. They may, however, decide to spend some time looking for the causes of these favorable conditions to try to duplicate them in the future. This analysis may trigger some rethinking about processes and management methods or some adjustment in effective capacity calculations. If we have, over time, high demonstrated capacity levels, our estimates are too low. If prolonged, we will create capacity imbalances because of excess capacity from this work center.

When demonstrated capacity exceeds effective capacity, the output rate may rise above the input rate, as work flows into the system according to plan and even more quickly out of it. This reduces the shop's load and its backlog. This reduces delays and production lead times, but it may also reduce the efficiency of a make-to-order system, as discussed earlier in the chapter, and cause some employee apprehension.

Case 3.   When demonstrated capacity exceeds effective capacity and begins to approach maximum capacity, the system may face an imminent lack of capacity. Such a system produces more than plans demand using nearly all of its available capacity. If this situation persists for long, operations managers must address an important threat of insufficient capacity. They can respond in three ways:

- *Adding capacity*   By adding resources to the OM process, managers can raise the limit imposed by maximum capacity. Short-term changes might add an overtime or weekend shift; long-term changes would add physical resources.
- *Changing the process*   Managers can try to change the process so that it uses less capacity. They may do this by subcontracting activities to suppliers or by reorganizing activities to eliminate some, perhaps with the help of process flow analysis methods described in Chapter 5.
- *Reducing the input rate*   Finally, managers can reduce the rate at which orders enter the process. They may refuse to accept new orders or quote longer delivery times. This response works best in make-to-order and engineer-to-order businesses. These actions may alienate our customers and greatly frustrate our marketing personnel. The operations manager should try to explain the problems to these groups, and with them work on exploring alternatives, assessing the implications of these alternatives, and identifying and implementing the alternatives that create the lowest costs.

These responses do not represent mutually exclusive choices; managers can combine two or all three options to resolve problems with insufficient capacity.

The discussions of these responses should not imply that demonstrated capacity can never exceed maximum capacity. In fact, operations managers encounter this situation when they improve their process by combining or eliminating unnecessary steps. The revamped process can then create more output than the old maximum capacity would suggest. Employees may also achieve this goal when their heroic efforts beat existing standards for units produced per hour.

CAPACITY MANAGEMENT TOOLS

In this section, we will discuss a number of detail-oriented tools that operations managers use to manage capacity within existing facilities. In the next section, we take a broader view of the strategic implications of capacity management.

Guidelines for Calculating Capacity

OM processes depend on capacity to generate output and satisfy customers. Operations managers influence this relationship by planning and implementing process activities based on measures of capacity, but they need a methodology for evaluating capacity and the activities that determine it in specific situations. The steps in this analysis form a process for calculating capacity.

Step 1: Describe the General Flow of Activities within the Process.   Process flow tools are discussed in Chapter 5. Operations begin evaluating the capacity of a process by identifying and describing the activities involved in the process and the organization of those activities. In particular, they want to assess the sequential or parallel organization scheme of process activities. As we will discuss later, this difference influences methods for calculating the overall capacity of a process.

Step 2: Establish the Time Period.   As pointed out before, operations managers measure capacity over some period of time. This evaluation should measure the capacity of every activity in the process over the same time period (e.g., year, month, week, or day). By mixing time periods, perhaps calculating the capacity of one activity for a week and the capacity of another for a day, the analyst risks introducing differences that prevent meaningful comparisons. This complicates analysis.

Step 3: Establish a Common Unit.   After choosing a time period, operations managers have to identify a common unit of measurement for the entire process. For example, they might find several measures for the capacity of activities in a process for manufacturing circuit boards. They might state the capacity of one machine based on the number of chips it inserts in a board per minute. Those units do not apply, however, to the capacity of a machine that solders the assembled board; the number of boards soldered per hour might make a more suitable measure for that activity. Subsequent analysis cannot compare such different units of measurement, however, so managers must identify a common unit of measurement for the capacity of every process, perhaps boards processed per hour.

Step 4: Identify the Maximum Capacity for the Overall Process.   Next, operations managers determine the overall maximum capacity for the entire process in two steps. First, they determine the maximum capacity for every individual activity, and then they combine this information to identify the overall capacity of the process. The first step is relatively straightforward, but the second requires careful study.

   The maximum capacity of a set of activities depends on their arrangement in sequence or in parallel. The capacity of a sequentially organized process equals that of the activity with the lowest maximum capacity. This activity, called the *bottleneck* in Chapter 5, constrains the flow of work to later stages of the process. The process can handle only as much work as will pass through the bottleneck activity, as Exhibit 15.5 illustrates.

[**EXHIBIT 15.5**]

Maximum Capacity of a Sequentially Organized Process

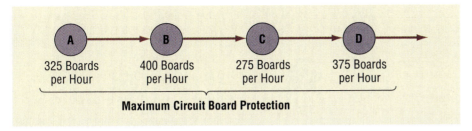

The bottleneck at Activity C has a capacity of only 275 boards per hour. Operation B can produce 400 boards per hour, but the process loses the excess capacity of 125 boards that Operation C cannot handle. Similarly, Activity D could turn out 375 boards an hour, but C can feed it only 275. As a result, the overall maximum capacity of this process is 275 boards per hour.

These statements assume that C consumes 1 unit of output from B to produce 1 unit of its own output and that all four operations work the same number of hours. If work-in-process inventory could accumulate between sequential operations, however, the firm might balance the capacities of the activities by working the bottleneck activity more hours than the others. In this way, operations managers could achieve high utilization rates despite mismatches in capacities of sequential operations. Despite its profligate reputation, inventory does add value in certain manufacturing situations.

The calculation of maximum process capacity changes for activities organized in parallel (Exhibit 15.6). If the parallel activities perform the same task, then they affect the capacity of the process based on the sum of their capacities. Activities B, E, and F perform the same task to complete the second activity of the process. Notice that Activity F performs this work twice as quickly as Activity B.

Not all parallel processes duplicate activities like this. In Exhibit 15.6, Activities B, E, and F might manufacture three different circuit boards that Activity C combines to produce a single subassembly. In this process, the second set of activities would have a capacity of 90 boards per hour because Activity B, the one with the smallest capacity, would limit the input rate to Activity C. This limit would set the overall capacity for the entire process, in turn, to 90 boards per hour, making Activity B the new bottleneck.

Step 5: Identify the Effective Capacity for the Overall Process.   After calculating the maximum capacity, operations managers determine the effective capacity, as described earlier in the chapter. Top managers can set this value by a top-down mandate, or operations managers can calculate it based on utilization and efficiency rates, as previously discussed. Sequential and parallel organization of activities have the same effects on the effective capacity of a process as they have on its maximum capacity.

Step 6: Determine the Demonstrated Capacity.   Operations managers calculate the demonstrated capacity for the entire process based on observed results over time.

[EXHIBIT 15.6]

Maximum Capacity of a Process Organized in Parallel

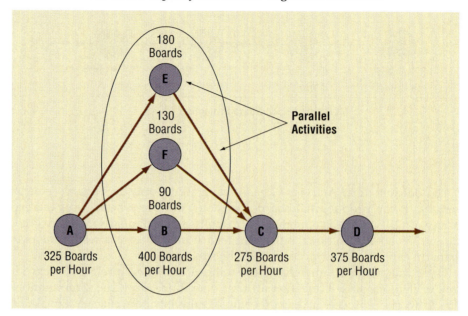

Step 7: Compare the Demonstrated, Effective, and Maximum Capacities and Take the Appropriate Actions.   In the final step of the capacity-calculation process, operations managers compare the three different measures of capacity and decide how to respond. They may choose to:

- Reduce the input rate
- Increase the upper limit on process capacity by adding resources
- Evaluate the current uses of capacity
- Do nothing

By applying this seven-step process, operations managers can assess the causes and scope of any capacity problem. In the next three sections, we will discuss possible applications of these concepts to support capacity management decisions.

Input/Output Control

input/output control

A tool for capacity management that manages work flows to match the demonstrated capacity of process

After developing a fairly good idea of the demonstrated capacity of a process, operations managers can control the flow of work, either throughout the process or to selected activities, to avoid overwhelming or wasting available capacity. **Input/ output control** manages work flows to match the demonstrated capacity of process. This method adjusts the valves at each end of the pool of work in Exhibit 15.1 to maintain stable relationships among inputs, outputs, and load on the process. Input/output control recalls the load-management methods of JIT manufacturing in its methods for buffering the system from erratic work flows.

As its underlying premise, input/output control assumes that bad things happen when either too much or too little work enters a shop. Too much work congests work stations and reduces the efficiency of production resources. At the other extreme, too little work can starve essential activities and reduce efficiency.

[**EXHIBIT 15.7**]

Input/Output Control Chart

		Week				
	1	**2**	**3**	**4**	**5**	**6**
Planned input	15	15	10	10	10	15
Actual input	13	14	14	12	10	13
Cumulative deviation	–2	–3	+1	+3	+3	+1
Planned output	12	14	14	14	12	12
Actual output	10	13	14	15	13	12
Cumulative deviation	–2	–3	–3	–2	–1	–1
Load 30	33	34	34	31	28	27

Shop-floor managers need to manipulate a certain amount of load to arrange work in efficient groups or sequences. Certain key machines or employees perform some tasks most effectively, and a moderate load allows operations managers to route jobs in a way that maximizes these benefits while still completing orders by their due dates.

Workers may respond to a light load by slowing down to seem busy and avoid potential layoffs. This will affect capacity significantly only if workers' experience of employment uncertainty makes them extremely hesitant to work themselves out of their jobs.

Input/output control prevents these problems by applying the classic management saying: you plan your work and then work your plan. It sets a production plan that indicates the amount of work that should flow into and out of the system for each period in the planning horizon. Exhibit 15.7 shows an example. It states planned and actual inputs and outputs in some common unit of measure. Weyerhauser measures the flow of work through its processes in cubic feet of wood. Another firm might measure the dollar value of orders received and shipped, subject to the warnings mentioned earlier about the disruptive effects of unstable prices. A firm might also state these quantities in standard labor hours.

This system releases work to the shop equal to the cumulative difference over time between the inflow of work released in earlier periods and the outflow of completed work. The top row in the exhibit indicates units of work to release over a 6-week period. In each of the first 3 weeks, actual flows differed from planned flows and from each other. In the first 2 weeks, the shop received less input than planned, but it received more than planned in the third and fourth weeks. The cumulative deviations in the third row do not seem too bad. The overall plan called for releasing 75 units of work and the actual data indicate only a 1-unit overall discrepancy.

To understand how I/O Control (IOC) works, explore the various rows to see how they are set and their implication for both the work center and the operations management system. Initially, the operations manager begins with three rows: planned input, planned output, and load. The planned input describes the amount of work that is intended to be released to the work center at given points in time. These amounts can be determined in a number of ways, ranging from taking the amount of work to be released for the month and dividing it by 4 to working with the people in the system to determine a realistic inflow rate. (All figures are stated in hours of capacity.) The planned output indicates the amount to process at the work center over each point in time. This can also be calculated or negotiated with the people working at the work center. The difference between the planned input and the planned output is the change to the amount of work waiting in the backlog pool (the load). As a result, in week 1, we plan to release 15 hours of work, but we only complete 12 hours. Therefore, the load should increase by 3 hours, from 30 to 33. By week 3, we are producing more than is being released. This should result in a planned decrease in load.

We can now compare our actual performance against these plans. In week 1, we planned to release 15 hours of work, but we actually released 13 hours, resulting in a 2-hour reduction in work load. However, over the 6-week time horizon, we ultimately released only 1 hour more than we had planned to. On the output side, we have a persistent problem in meeting planned output rates. At the end, we have produced 1 hour less than planned.

In terms of the actual impact on the load (or actual hours in the queue), in week 1, we increased the load by 3 hours (13–10). Week 2 increased the work load by an extra hour (14–13). Week 3, no change (14–14); week 4 saw the work load fall by 3 hours (12–15). We can compare the actual and planned rates to determine where the problems are, and we can compare the actual loads with the planned loads. The result can help us determine if we have a problem with the input side, the output side, or both. This tool is based on the simple premise that if we can control both the input and output side, we can control lead times and queue times.

Operations managers gain little by releasing work to a busy shop, unless some new job has a higher priority than the current ones. If the backlog becomes too large, workers feel the same anxiety that students experience in the weeks before final exams. If the backlog drops too low, the flow of work may have to follow inefficient routes through the system, just as light studying loads leave students to work haphazardly during the first two weeks of a semester.

In Chapter 14, we described the methods by which resource managers allocate human resources within a system to match short-term capacity with the current load. Input/output control does the same thing for either an entire process or a specific work center. If a few key work centers form bottlenecks that determine process capacity, this method helps managers to direct attention to these facilities.

Input/output control provides a useful tool by which operations managers can quantify work loads for processes and activities and plan smooth flows of work throughout their system. They release orders based on an understanding of the best load size for that system. While they could develop complex simulation models to estimate that load, most shop-floor managers probably rely on intuition and experience to judge this important quantity.

Capacity Sizing Tools

In addition to on-going operation of established processes, operations managers apply analytical tools for capacity management to help them design new OM systems. As part of these process-design decisions, they determine the sizes and locations of physical facilities. In this section, we discuss an application of total cost analysis to address the effects of capacity utilization and economies of scale on process design. In the next section, we discuss capacity location issues. In the final section of this chapter, our general discussion of the strategic effects of capacity management integrates both concepts.

By measuring maximum, effective, and demonstrated capacity, operations managers can realistically project the likely output rates of proposed configurations of productive resources. Based on these output rates, they can then estimate the impact of the utilization rate on the cost component of the value equation. The total cost per unit of production in some proposed system equals:

$$C = V + F/R \tag{15.1}$$

where:

C = Average unit production cost
F = Fixed costs of the system
V = Variable production cost
R = Planned capacity rate

Actually, this simple analysis needs some adjustment for the cost of operating a system without a sufficient cushion of excess capacity. As a plant's utilization rate increases, output rises beyond demonstrated capacity. This has some good effects and some bad ones. The benefits of high utilization include intensive scheduling that draws high returns from investments in facilities and equipment. A tight schedule creates a compelling need to prevent starvation and blockages as well as breakdowns and absenteeism; a small problem due to any of these causes can seriously disrupt the work flow throughout a shop. If human resources constrain output, increasing attention on motivating workers can coax additional output out of a tightly stretched system. Like students during finals week, operating employees can perform above theoretical standards over the short term.

Overutilization of plant resources has some undesirable longer-term consequences, however:

- Premium labor costs, including expenses for overtime or temporary help
- Costs to rush production, including expenses for expediting orders, a high cost of quality, and express freight services
- Threats to customer service, including incomplete and backlogged orders
- Excessive wear on factors of production, including overtaxed workers and machines that suffer from infrequent maintenance
- Limits on time for management initiatives, including continuous improvement

Equation 15.1 focuses only on costs, so it allows operations managers to ignore the other three elements of the value equation. To supplement their cost analysis, they need some means to approximate the impact of overextended production on their system's ability to provide the quality, speed, and product variety that delight its customers. One form of this analysis tries to develop a conceptual picture of the links between capacity utilization and the costs of overutilization, as in Exhibit 15.8.

Equation 15.1 quantifies the effect on a firm's average unit cost of a particular plant utilization rate, but no simple analysis can accurately state the costs of overutilization. All experienced plant managers recognize some diseconomies of scale, but they seldom can give precise cost estimates. The best information on this effect may come from prior cost accounting data. A less rigorous analysis might ask experienced plant personnel to estimate this curve. This tactic would produce less detail than careful managers want, but it would certainly improve decision making as compared to methods that ignore costs of overextending plant resources.

Capacity-Related Production Tradeoff Costs

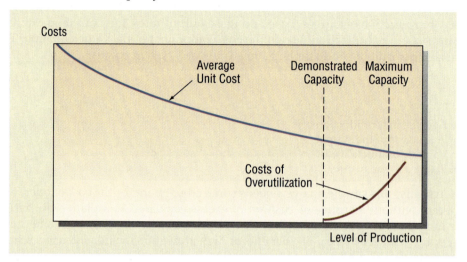

Operations managers might compare a number of seemingly feasible plant-size alternatives by developing sketches of economic effects like those in Exhibit 15.9. The curves present the general effects on average total costs of three potential plant sizes. Each shows a declining average total cost as the utilization rate increases until the process reaches its demonstrated capacity. Beyond the optimal point, diseconomies of scale due to overextended resources drive up costs, offsetting the incremental benefits of additional production.

The final choice of a plant size depends on its expected volume of production over time. If operations managers expect orders in Range 1, they should establish the smallest plant. They should plan for the medium-sized or large plant to

Economics of Plant-Size Alternatives

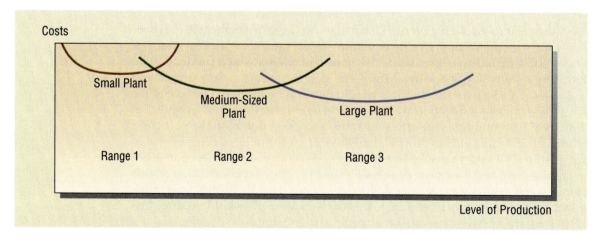

Bausch & Lomb's decision to build a new facility in Rochester, New York, involved extensive research and site analysis.   SOURCE   Peter Steiner/The Stock Market

handle volume in Ranges 2 or 3, respectively. If they expect growing or declining demand, a complete analysis would project production volume and costs for multiple time periods.

If operations managers have enough reliable information, they may construct a mathematical model of the effect of production volume on plant size. The lack of precision in the input data may cast doubt on the reliability of the model's conclusions, however. In practice, a spreadsheet based on the judgments of experienced personnel should usually suffice.

Analysis for a complex system with multiple plant sites raises additional issues that involve an organization's overall strategy, as we will discuss in a later section. Plant location also affects the economic effects of process design decisions.

Capacity Location Tools

Locating the best site of a facility is another important capacity decision. Saban's decision about sites for production of Power Ranger merchandise hinged on labor economies; Bandai won the contract based on its plants in areas with low labor costs. Weyerhauser controls transportation costs by locating its processing facilities near its forests and on waterways, if possible.

The competitive success of a service operation often depends on a location near customers. Other services can rely on telephones, computer networks, and overnight parcel services to maintain physical ties to customers. In both services and manufacturing, operations managers make location decisions on criteria that help the firm to deliver its product in a manner that profitably delights customers.

The competitive situations of individual firms create extremely specialized criteria, so their decisions require extended study and complex tradeoffs. In general, however, firms locate their facilities to gain the best available combination of methods and considerations:

1. Locations of customers or shipping points
2. Customers' expectations and value-equation priorities
3. Competitors' locations and operating methods
4. Projections of service levels and appeals to the latent demands of existing and potential customers
5. Actual or estimated relevant costs, perhaps through total cost analysis
6. Feasible alternatives for capacity adjustments
7. Projected consequences on all four elements of the value equation
8. Models to compare OM system consequences with customer desires
9. Effect on the firm's long-term objectives
10. Effect on the firm's profitability

Like many other decisions in operations management, location choices have shown the effects of powerful changes. In the past, firms treated plants and equipment as completely stationary resources. In many heavy industries, this remains true, but rapid mobility has become common in service, distribution, and high-technology businesses. Hence plant location decisions may move from long-term planning toward shorter-term processes.

Operations managers employ some sophisticated mathematical modeling techniques to determine the optimal solution to location problems.[3] Personnel who understand the economics of the firm's production and distribution systems can formulate good candidate solutions to most location problems and develop spreadsheets to compare the effects of site location scenarios. By calling on the expertise of other members of the organization, operations managers can conduct quick-and-dirty analysis of difficult questions. Better yet, the request for input often encourages a sense of ownership of eventual solutions throughout the organization.

 ## CAPACITY STRATEGIES

The detail of individual capacity decisions can begin to obscure their wider organizational effects. A firm's capacity strategy links together isolated capacity decisions into a time-sequenced pattern. In this section, we discuss how a firm can formulate its capacity strategy to ensure that it adds value for customers.

A firm's on-going process for capacity planning should include routine, systemwide reviews of the performance of all facilities. This information facilitates a long-term strategic perspective for decisions to add or subtract capacity. If operations managers decide instead to make significant adjustments in system capacity without guidance by a sound strategy, they often create systems that fail to serve customers' needs. In particular, a lack of effective strategic planning often results in overly large, unmanageable plants that suffer from diseconomies of scale, poorly located plants, or plants that struggle to do things that no longer suit their capabilities. When mounting problems force managers to evaluate such facilities comprehensively, they often wonder how they got into such a mess. All too often, they get there one decision at a time.

---

[3]These methods often involve mixed-integer programming since each facility location alternative requires a separate zero-one variable. See John O. McClain, L. Joseph Thomas, and Joseph P. Mazzole, *Operations Research: Production of Goods and Services* (Englewood Cliffs, N.J.: Prentice-Hall, 1992).

Customers in Capacity Strategy

The first priority for a capacity strategy focuses on the service that the firm offers to its customers. The values of its target market segments must drive any capacity strategy. Cost is an important part of the value equation, but it serves as a criterion for choosing between ways of meeting customers' needs for quality, flexibility, and speed rather than as a dominant consideration by itself.

The value equation guides a firm's investments throughout its value chain. Every addition to capacity should enhance one or more of cost, quality, flexibility, or speed. Vertical integration may help a firm to add value for Economizer customers by cutting costs and reducing prices. Even when cost dominates buying decisions, however, domestic or foreign vendors might provide inputs at least as cheaply as internal processes could without investments in capacity expansion.

Many firms ignore the other three elements of the value equation by defining capacity strictly in units of output and evaluating investments in capacity based only on easily quantified costs. Numbers capture economic tradeoffs in capacity plans, but a truly accurate capacity profile portrays the firm's overall ability to satisfy its target customers. If the firm serves customer groups other than Economizers, its managers must look beyond cost to evaluate the effect of a capacity investment on other elements of the value equation. Through some creative analysis, they can quantify quality, flexibility, and speed as well as cost.

Capacity reviews should evaluate the capabilities that the firm will need to serve customers in the future, as well. For example, advances in technology can affect each of the four elements of the value equation. Automated production equipment can lower labor costs and improve quality. Programmable equipment can enhance flexibility and speed. Swiss watch manufacturers learned a hard lesson about the risk of failing to keep capacity up to date. They lost market share to Timex when they failed to develop capacities to produce low-cost pin-lever mechanisms. Likewise, Timex initially lost ground to the Japanese when it reacted slowly in building a capacity to make electronic watches.

In the past, market leaders often could wait and observe product innovators before switching to new or improved product/process technologies. Time-based competition places a premium on rapid developments of new capacity, however. Any firm pays a high price to watch progress in markets where world-class competitors survive based on their fast-to-market capabilities.

Capacity strategy must also acknowledge that the capabilities of production facilities follow life cycles just as goods and services do. This does not imply that planners should accept the ultimate death of a plant or service center. Instead, they should focus the firm's capacity strategy on the dynamic needs of its customers and adjust the plant's capabilities to maintain high performance despite changing standards. Firms that fail to keep their capacities up to date risk following the Sears & Roebuck mail-order catalog onto the scrap heap.

Suppliers in Capacity Strategy

A firm can build a capacity strategy that serves customers well without owning every machine and hiring every worker. Before building new internal capacity, operations managers should ask how the potential investment will contribute to their strategic competitive advantage. Clearly, a capacity decision should favor any investment that would enhance the firm's core competency. The strategy-formulation process should judge any other investment to expand capacity based on its contribution to the firm's strategic goals and objectives.

To make this judgment, operations managers must decide how to involve their firm at each link in the value chain. An auto manufacturer's management must target direct, equity investments to specific areas of its business:

1. Automobile and component design
2. Raw materials (steel, rubber)
3. Inbound transportation of inputs
4. Primary component manufacturing (engines, chassis)
5. Secondary component manufacturing (electronics, seats, etc.)
6. Final assembly (assembly of finished cars)
7. Outbound transportation of finished vehicles
8. Dealers of new and used cars
9. Finance companies for car purchases (GMAC, Ford Motor Credit)
10. Car-rental agencies (Avis, Budget, etc.)
11. Post-sale service (repair shops)

Henry Ford sought to control all of the first seven elements in the early days of the auto industry. For years, General Motors was perceived to have a competitive advantage because it made so many more components for its cars than its competitors made for theirs. In more recent times, Chrysler has built a perceived competitive advantage, in part, by making so little of its cars. It sought to divest manufacturing of virtually all of its secondary components, although it relented under pressure from the United Automobile Workers union.

Participants in other industries target their investments on other kinds of capacity. Both Pepsi and Coca-Cola have changed their capacity structures to gain more control over their products' distributors. Fast-food companies continue to tinker with their mixes of company-owned and franchised outlets. Firms set up different combinations of internal and external factories for varying reasons, but they all pursue a general goal of gaining competitive advantage.

In pursuit of this common goal, many firms encounter some typical capacity choices. The choice of a site, or several sites, at which to construct capacity often powerfully influences an organization's success. In addition, firms must carefully time their investments in capacity in relation to demand patterns in the markets that they serve.

The decision of plant location has multiple dimensions. First, as we have seen in the preceeding section, there is a question of whether to locate this capacity within the internal factory or the external factory (using the terminology and frameworks of Chapter 13). Second, the internal factory setting raises several other issues, which are examined in this section—such as whether we want one central plant or multiple smaller plants, and should capacity come on line in advance of demand, coincide with demand, or lag behind demand.

Plant Site and Relocation Strategies

American firms have long looked for lower-cost sites where they could relocate their manufacturing facilities. The New England textile industry declined substantially in the middle part of this century when firms shifted production facilities to Southern locations with lower labor costs. This phenomenon continues today, but with a few new wrinkles.

Chrysler's Mexican assembly plants require management systems that recognize the unique demands of doing business in an increasingly borderless world.   SOURCE   Steven Starr/Stock Boston

Telecommunications technology has allowed firms to move many service jobs to new, often lower-cost, locations. Southwest Airlines relocated its customer-service center to Oklahoma City, and Citibank moved much of the clerical work for its credit cards to South Dakota. Many U.S. insurance firms have relocated clerical functions offshore to other English-speaking countries such as Ireland and Jamaica. Some firms actually maintain floating customer-service departments that route calls around the globe 24 hours a day.

The site relocation phenomenon is not limited to North America. In 1995, Hong Kong paging services moved much of its back-office work to provinces in mainland China. Indeed, European and Japanese firms can often manufacture certain goods more economically in the United States than in their home countries.

The North American Free Trade Agreement has accelerated the shift of labor-intensive processing functions to Mexico that started in 1965 with the bilateral maquiladora agreement between that country and the United States. Small border factories began as ideal sites for certain component-assembly activities, but the value chain within Mexico has expanded to include final-assembly operations. Detroit's Big Three auto makers all have quietly made major investments in final-assembly plants. Ford's Escort and Tracer models, products of one such facility, have received high quality ratings, proving that well-managed Mexican workers can indeed produce to world-class standards.

Operations managers increasingly work in a borderless world. The combined effect of information technology and government trade agreements allows firms to spread capacity easily across political boundaries and between outpartnering organizations. A call to a local GM Card inquiry service will equally likely ring in either of its Bethesda, Maryland, or Salinas, California, offices depending on the time of day and telephone backlog at each location. Through worldwide links between customer-service operations, firms have developed around-the-clock service capabilities. Soon a North American customer might receive answers to technical questions about an HP printer as easily from the firm's Shanghai staff as from an office around the corner.

ON THE JOB

United Biscuits for All the Tea in China

The thought of 1 billion people munching its product would attract just about any business. In 1986, this image enticed Sir Hector Laing, the chairman of Britain-based United Biscuits, Ltd., to consider the merits of investing £7 million to establish a biscuit-making facility in China. In 1989, United Biscuit made its first crackers in the Shenzhen Special Economic Zone just over the Hong Kong border.

The brutal crackdown in Tienanmen Square shortly after that time stirred some doubt at corporate headquarters about the wisdom of Sir Hector's move. Startup operations suffered setbacks due to local customs and a woefully weak logistics infrastructure. Local authorities had to learn that the firm would buy them dinner and let them sing karaoke, but it would not offer cash payments or other considerations, nor would it pay five people to do the work of one. In 1993, UB was paying its staff of 580 about £50 a month, about 20 percent above the national average. In Hong Kong, the same workers would earn 10 times that amount. Chris Strachan, UB's managing director in China summed up the experience as follows: "At the start, a good day was when we took three steps forward and only two back—often it was the reverse."

Still, the firm has reached Sir Hector's dream of a billion-biscuit market. In 1993, the plant was cranking out 5,000 biscuit packets per hour and considering an expansion. Unfortunately, the Chinese don't consume nearly as many biscuits as the British hoped they would, only half a kilo each per year on average. (The British consume 25 times that amount.) Nonetheless, Mr. Strachan noted that "if each Chinese person would consume just 5 biscuits per year, that would sustain two medium-sized biscuit factories."

SOURCE   K. Cooper, "Biscuits for All the Tea in China," *Daily Telegraph Business News*, November 20, 1993, p. 2.

The strategic implications of a decision to expand foreign capacity depend on the goals that the move serves. Firms undertake many investments in foreign countries to gain market proximity. Maintaining capacity within a company gives a firm access to its markets and may help it to avoid tariffs. Multinational firms make offshore investments to get close to customers by developing knowledge of local customs and tastes. If market proximity drives an investment in foreign capacity, then firms try to extend their value chains to reach closer to customers.

The "On the Job" box describes the pursuit by United Biscuit of a massive offshore market. It shared the difficulties that have plagued traders since Marco Polo who have tried to crack the Chinese market. Companies seeking customers for standard manufactured goods need additional lessons in getting close to their customers.

Most people believe that firms make offshore capacity investments primarily in pursuit of lower costs. Many firms invest abroad for this reason, but many others have other goals. Operations managers need a systemwide outlook to assess the real cost effectiveness of making a good or providing a service at some location remote from either internal or external customers. Once again, the value equation promotes this analysis by introducing wide-ranging gains and losses from moving a facility either closer to or farther away from adjacent steps in the value chain. Clearly, reliance on a foreign supplier can endanger delivery speed and product quality, including service quality. Conversely, a firm can enhance its product-mix flexibility if labor economics and different manufacturing economies of scale allow production of a wider range of goods.

In 1962, a local newspaper reporter asked the president of United States Steel at a mine-opening ceremony if the firm had decided to mine iron ore in Missouri to take advantage of the state's favorable business climate. "No," the executive responded, "We like to locate mines where the ore is." Availability of raw materials has long drawn firms to locate facilities close to oil, minerals, forests, and agricultural crops, crossing national boundaries to find these resources when necessary. The linkages between these operations may simply carry the materials back to the parent companies' home markets. As firms become truly multinational, however, raw materials, intermediate products, and finished goods will flow in many directions through complex networks like those of global oil companies.

Increasingly, firms are locating facilities offshore to gain access to **intellectual capital** in other countries. Many high-tech firms have built facilities in Israel, and computer software firms get high-quality computer code from workers in India and China. Xerox credits its joint venture in Japan for the rejuvenation of its manufacturing capabilities in the 1990s. Indeed, more restrictive immigration policies may force many high-tech firms to create foreign research facilities in order to gain access to these critical human resources.

intellectual capital
Critical human resources skills and capabilities

Lastly, political and ecological factors may influence the decision to build capacity in a foreign country. German pharmaceutical firms located research laboratories in the United States to avoid a widespread fear of genetic research among their own citizens. Regrettably, some firms have exploited differences in regulatory standards by relocating operations or exporting wastes to third-world countries with less restrictive environmental rules and enforcement practices.

Multiple-Site Options.   In an earlier time, all major breweries made all of their products at one location. As they gained larger shares of the national market, two facts influenced them to adopt multiple-site strategies. They could ship ingredients relatively cheaply, but transportation economics for the heavy products, composed mostly of water, justified building smaller plants close to major markets. Improvements in water purification technologies enabled them to do this without sacrificing product quality. Breweries and other firms need some criteria to guide planning for the locations of OM facilities. The value equation provides such a framework.

Customer service or cost drive most multiple-site capacity location decisions. Customer-service priorities dominate these decisions when markets demand especially rapid delivery or convenient accommodations. Market proximity becomes critical in such a market. The 7Eleven convenience store chain recognizes site location as the essential variable that determines store traffic. Marketers bear primary responsibility for locating sites that promote good customer service. In some circumstances, however, the locations of unique inputs of human or physical resources may significantly influence the customer-service potential of certain sites.

Cost-driven decisions about multiple-site OM networks can create product-distribution systems for either homogeneous or heterogeneous products. The design of a system to distribute some homogeneous product, like facilities for generating and distributing electricity, creates a network of site locations that moves the product through the system at the lowest possible cost. Components of total cost often include inbound freight, plant conversion costs, distribution center operating costs, and outbound freight costs. Increasingly, government agencies seek to attract new plants or distribution centers to their jurisdictions by offering tax

ON THE JOB

Y'All Build Fine Vehicles

■

Nashville's Johnny Paycheck sang about frustration with the auto industry in his hit song, "Take this job and shove it!" His neighbors throughout the Mid-South have ignored those complaints, however, and welcomed car makers from around the world. Plants in six southern states—Georgia, Kentucky, Louisiana, Texas, Tennessee, and Virginia—will make about a quarter of the cars and light trucks in America. While many see Japanese transplants behind this trend, Ford and General Motors are also major players.

The growth of auto capacity in the South reflects the changing economic and environmental realities in America. Government agencies have made the newcomers offers they couldn't refuse. South Carolina built a $350-million, 1.2-million-square-foot building to attract BMW. BMW cited four major reasons for its decision to accept this fine offer to locate in Spartanburg:

- *Work force* Right-to-work laws in South Carolina discourage union organizing efforts by the United Automobile Workers. Most foreign transplants pay near-union wages, but they want freedom from troublesome work rules.
- *Transportation* BMW wanted a plant with good access to rail, truck, air, and sea transportation.
- *Business-government relations* An active Chamber of Commerce helped BMW to work with government agencies to clear hurdles in a timely manner.
- *Incentives* The state offered to train workers and build the plant facility, but BMW indicated that competing states had offered similar benefits.

BMW's deal resembled those offered to Toyota in Georgetown, Kentucky; Nissan in Smyrna, Tennessee; and General Motors in Spring Hill, Tennessee. These firms received lucrative offers because economic analysis indicates that each automotive job contributes $100,000 a year to a local economy. Also, government agencies hope that just-in-time manufacturers will attract suppliers' plants to still more new facilities.

Just about all of these plants have been able to achieve higher levels of productivity than their rust-belt counterparts. Ford's unionized plants in Atlanta are considered among the most efficient in the world. Compared to traditional auto plants, it features less-restrictive work rules, a younger and better-trained work force, and more relaxed relationships among workers, management, and government agencies.

Y'all come on down!

SOURCE   M. Nauman, "That Is What They Like about the South," *Mercury News*, August 1, 1993, p. E1.

breaks and other financial incentives to companies, as the "On the Job" box illustrates. Incentives can benefit a firm, but they increase the risk of making bad choices to achieve short-term gains.

To design an effective heterogeneous product-distribution system, operations managers must complete a more complex analysis. They must decide how much of a number of different products to make and distribute from which locations. The first step in formulating such a capacity strategy involves assigning activities and roles to specific processing, storage, and transportation resources. For example, a tire manufacturer might place distribution centers in carefully defined regions and assign specific roles to each. Its Atlanta warehouse might stock replacement truck and automobile tires for distribution to retailers in 11 states across the southern United States. It might ship original equipment tires to auto manufacturers directly from its Akron factory and distribute tires for farm equipment and motorcycles through third-party firms. This arrangement gives a clear charter for the Atlanta distribution center; personnel there know exactly what they should do and not do.

A firm with multiple production plants also needs clear charters. Each location's plant charter should clearly designate the types of activities that the firm wants to perform at that location. Widely varied assignments run the risk of confusing the plant design, its personnel, and its equipment choices. In revising or renewing a plant's charter, operations managers compare the proposed assignments for plant processes with their original functions. Managers can trace the causes of this change to an evolving product mix and customer base.

This kind of plant profiling usually reveals mismatches between resource capabilities and the assignments that firms expect those resources to complete. Operations managers may decide to reassign work within a multiple-site network to improve the coordination of task requirements and facility capabilities. In some cases, they may dissolve mismatches by dropping the products or subcontracting the production work to better-qualified suppliers. In other cases, they may invest in new capacity or modify existing capacity to minimize the adverse effects of mismatches.

If production needs and process capabilities differ significantly and reassignment of plant charters seems inconvenient, the firm may want to consider a plant-within-a-plant configuration. By subdividing the physical and organizational resources of a diversified plant, operations managers may create a set of smaller subplants, each with a clearly defined charter, a focused work force, and facilities well-suited to its tasks.

Transportation Issues.   The popularity of just-in-time manufacturing practices has led many firms to relocate facilities in order to enhance their abilities to quickly and economically serve their customers. Suppliers of components to the automobile industry normally set up facilities within 450 miles of their customers' final-assembly lines. This permits 1-day deliveries, quite often in less than truckload quantities. In other industries, firms have moved warehouses closer to customers to improve their service.

On the other hand, efficient electronic communications and rapid shipping capabilities have drastically reduced the need for spare parts depots and other inventory centers throughout the country. Some companies have located warehouses next to Federal Express's Memphis facility. This location permits customers to place orders in small quantities as late as 10 p.m. for delivery the following morning.

Response Time in Capacity Strategy

The timing of a capacity-expansion project depends on a simple relationship between the time that the firm needs to make a significant adjustment in capacity and the advance warning it has of the need for change. Exhibit 15.10 illustrates this relationship.

Saban Enterprises had to expand its capacity to make Power Rangers merchandise in less than 1 year. At the spring toy trade show, retailers place orders for new and existing toys that they expect to sell. They plan for delivery in November. While retailers can place orders later, they risk losing the chance to receive hot items in time for the Christmas season. Saban Enterprises and its Pacific Rim suppliers began in early 1994 to secure additional plant space and injection-molding equipment, buy the injection molds, order the packaging, and train an unskilled

Capacity Planning Timing Zone

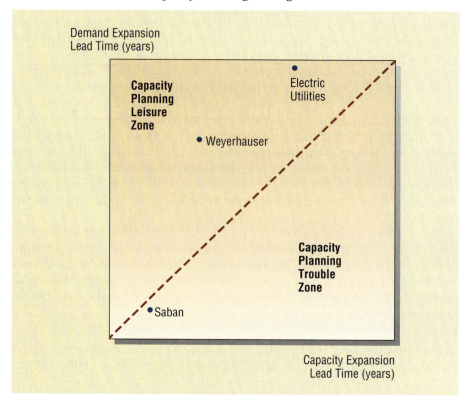

work force. Bandai's ability to add plant capacity quickly became a value-adding core competency in this time-driven environment.

Firms that fall above the diagonal line in Exhibit 15.10 have sufficient notice of new demand conditions to adjust capacity; those that fall below the line lack either timely information about demand or the ability to expand capacity as quickly as needed. The unlucky firms can do little to improve their condition. All firms base capacity decisions on the best available information, and the potential for error contributes significantly to total business risk. The markets for fad toys and fashion goods for teenagers fall into this capacity planning trouble zone.

Customers in other markets behave in more predictable ways. For years, demand forecasts for electricity showed fairly stable growth that doubled demand every 5 years. This approximately matched the lead time that electric utilities needed to build conventional generating plants; nuclear plants took even more time. Similarly, Weyerhauser's consistent demand allows it to add plant capacity at a relatively leisurely pace.

Examples of such deliberate capacity planning processes have become more rare over the last decade. Increasingly, firms build plants to make specific products. Demand for individual products, which can vary wildly as compared to demand for entire product lines, now drives many capacity decisions. Intel built its new plant in New Mexico to make Pentium chips, and Chrysler redesigned its Ontario, Canada, plant to make its LH line of cars. Unfortunately for GM, its

Arlington, Texas, plant is uniquely suited to assemble Chevy Caprices. Any such mismatch between demand and planned capacity creates either unsatisfied customers, who cannot get the products they want, or an unsatisfactory bottom line, when the firm cannot sell products that it can produce.

Fortunately, the same management practices that enable firms to rapidly design and develop new products also support rapid adjustments of process capacities. Computer-assisted systems for plant design and simulation modeling enable industrial engineers to conceive and refine new plant layouts extremely rapidly. Firms involve suppliers in the early stages of anticipated capacity expansions to seek input on both product features and plant equipment. The trend away from vertical integration, which may complicate planning throughout an extended system, also has facilitated this reduction in capacity-expansion lead time.

To a certain extent, improvements in market research have extended demand-expansion lead time, as well. Database marketing and improved product-demand forecasts permit some firms to anticipate market reactions that determine hot sellers. Still, fad products will likely remain in the capacity planning trouble zone.

Besides the pace of changes in demand and capacity-expansion lead time, the timing of capacity decisions depends on one more condition—customers' patience. Customers for Power Rangers did not want to wait long. A slow response by Saban would have resulted in lost sales, unhappy kids, and the possible destruction of Angel Grove. Retailer concern would have created a slightly less pressing problem. Unlike children, experienced retailers expect hot demand and short supplies of some popular products every year; still, they do not like to send customers away to buy from someone else.

Customers for many services and manufactured goods seem willing to wait, though. Customers with routine needs for the services of hair stylists, medical doctors, dentists, and BMW mechanics seem quite willing to accept schedule-driven service. Customers for either customized goods or unusual standard goods expect to wait for reasonable lengths of time. Patient customers help process designers to resolve their short-term demand-management problems, but they still need longer-term forecasts to make capacity-expansion decisions.

Timing Capacity-Expansion Strategies.   In an expanding market, each competing firm either implicitly or explicitly adopts one of three basic capacity-expansion strategies, as shown in Exhibit 15.11. A firm chooses the tradeoffs associated with each strategy based on managers' understanding of the needs of the firm's customers and its business strategy for meeting those needs.

The exhibit simplifies the behavior of real-world markets, which often diverge from the linear pattern of capacity expansion. Market demand for mature products and commodities may exhibit a linear growth trend, but newer products often grow in rising and falling patterns driven by the product life cycle. Actual expansion decisions depend on product differences, which may create steady, rapid growth, as for audio CD-ROM players, or spurts in demand followed by rapid declines, as for CB radios. Clearly, technological innovations can influence capacity-expansion plans, as well.

A firm employs a **capacity lead strategy** when it invests in capacity in advance of demand to eliminate the chance of losing sales to competitors. The economic tradeoff requires incremental profits from making those sales to exceed the incremental costs of operating the facility below full capacity. As an alternative, the firm may value its current customers so highly that it invests in the extra capacity despite the cost to protect its customer-service reputation.

capacity lead strategy
A method for timing capacity expansion that invests in new capacity in advance of market demand to eliminate the chance of losing sales to competitors

[EXHIBIT 15.11]

Three Pure Capacity Expansion Strategies

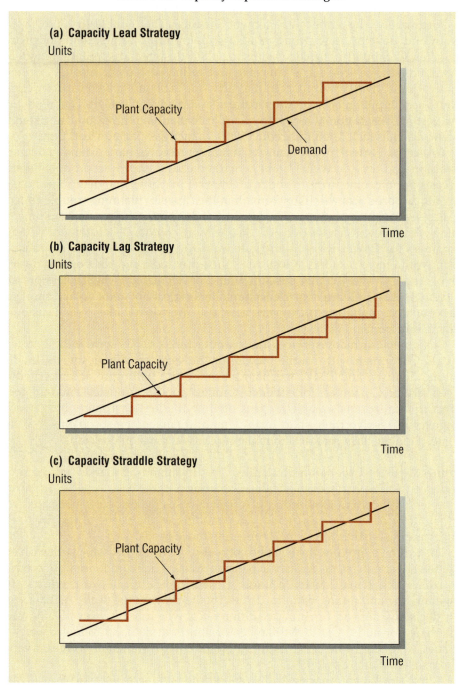

(a) Capacity Lead Strategy
Units

Plant Capacity

Demand

Time

(b) Capacity Lag Strategy
Units

Plant Capacity

Time

(c) Capacity Straddle Strategy
Units

Plant Capacity

Time

capacity lag strategy
A method for timing capacity expansion that calls for expansion investments only after confirmation of rises in demand in order to maintain a high utilization rate

A **capacity lag strategy** calls for expansion investments only after confirmation of rises in demand in order to maintain a high utilization rate. If a plant produces either a homogeneous commodity or a standard product that appeals to customers based primarily on cost, then this strategy will maximize profits by minimizing

O N   T H E   J O B

Meltdown at M&M

In the highly competitive global candy business, Mars Inc. has built a reputation over time as a fierce competitor. This privately held $13-billion firm is run by two billionaire brothers whose aversion to publicity rivals that of the late Howard Hughes. Headquartered in McLean, Virginia, some consider Mars as secretive as its neighbor, the CIA. Recent events imply that it may maintain superior security.

The company's top managers seem obsessed by the goal of maximizing the firm's asset utilization rate. They have conducted extensive research to find ways to squeeze more produc-

tion of M&Ms, Snickers, and the like out of company plants. Sales reps can sell beyond capacity, even in peak sales periods. As a result, Mars has developed a reputation for a bad fill rate. This doesn't refer to its methods for pouring candies into small bags,

but to the percentage of orders that production cannot fill completely, shipping either fewer goods or smaller quantities than customers order.

Insufficient excess capacity may help to explain the decline in domestic market share for Mars, which has lost 3 percent of its $10-billion domestic market. Unlike potential buyers of Power Ranger toys, few candy customers will postpone satisfaction of their desires long enough to wait for the next shipment of M&Ms. This problem illustrates the dangerous consequences of tying management performance more to return on assets than to continuing satisfaction of customers.

SOURCE   B. Saporito, "The Eclipse of Mars," *Fortune*, November 28, 1994, pp. 82–92.

---

operating costs. This choice makes the important assumption that customers will return after buying from competitors when the firm cannot fill their needs. This assumption may prove valid in markets for commodity products and those dominated by Economizers.

A **capacity straddle strategy** tries to keep abreast of growing demand by matching average capacity to average demand. It calls for capacity expansions only when managers expect that they can sell at least some of the additional output, but before they know that they can sell it all. Clearly, this strategy has some of the advantages and disadvantages of the two extreme choices. Success depends on the critical choice of how long to wait before building capacity.

The "On the Job" box discusses the effects on performance of capacity problems at Mars Inc. This story illustrates the essential strategic role of capacity timing decisions. Many operations managers rely on total cost analysis methods to balance the extra cost of operating below maximum capacity against the risk of stockouts and disappointing customers by keeping capacity below demand. To solve more complex problems over multiple time periods, they often formulate mixed-integer programming models with algorithms that indicate both the timing and sizes of any expansions. These techniques give valuable quantitative information, but managers must carefully evaluate the tradeoffs of every decision and its contributions to the firm's strategic objectives.

This discussion has implied that every firm times its investments in capacity based on internal considerations. In some business situations, however, collaborative arrangements with suppliers or even competitors can help to solve capacity-timing problems. Cooperation with competitors becomes particularly attractive for commodity products manufactured in capital-intensive facilities.

capacity straddle strategy
A method for timing capacity expansion that seeks to match average capacity to average demand

For example, a manufacturer of corrugated containers would have to spend $250 million to $300 million to expand its process capacity to manufacture liner-board, and the resulting increase in capacity would far exceed the firm's internal need. It might build the plant and hope to sell the excess output in the spot market. At the same time, a competitor might make the same plans, leaving both firms with expensive capacity to produce much more linerboard than either needs. To avoid this problem, the competitors could forge a long-term product swapping agreement in which Company A would build the plant first and sell linerboard to Company B at the posted market price. Company B would then time its next plant expansion for a time when the combined needs of the both companies would warrant additional capacity. Clearly, this strategy would work only in commodity markets where the firms could exchange essentially identical products.

Flexible outsourcing provides a similar solution that adjusts the flow of a company's work by mixing in some inputs from suppliers. When capacity becomes scarce, a firm may divert some of its internal work to the external factory rather than building new internal capacity. When it does expand capacity, it can take some of this work back within the internal factory. This would raise the firm's capacity utilization rate over a period of years while controlling the threat of stock-outs and poor fill rates. This practice would require careful planning and implementation to avoid alienating the firm's relationships with its suppliers.

Capacity Rejuvenation Decisions

Firms in many North American industries try to compete despite mismatches between their capacities and market demands. These firms maintain ample unit capacity, but their capabilities poorly suit the current competitive environment. Kmart has plenty of stores, but their old, worn-out appearances fail to delight customers. General Motors had ample capacity to produce its rear-drive Chevrolet Caprice and Buick Roadmaster models, but the market did not want enough of them to keep its Arlington, Texas, plant busy. Even market leaders must contend with such mismatches; Ford had surplus car-making capacity while its light-truck plants struggled to keep up under full loads.

Redeploying capacity within a firm can create costly problems. In 1995, Chrysler announced a $242 million expense to cover the costs of converting some of the capacity of its Newark, Delaware plant from car to light truck and van production.

Projects to make long-term adjustments in plant capacity often raise questions about the disposition of existing capacity. Many executives envy the attractive appearances of other firms' plants and wish to rebuild their own plants to different designs. They usually want more than shiny, new buildings and equipment and better plant layouts. Quite often, they wish that they could escape the cumulative human resources and labor-management practices of their current facilities. Prior to speaking at Stanford's 1993 Manufacturing Management conference, Donald Peterson, then the CEO at the Ford Motor Company, expressed envy of John Young, then the president of Hewlett-Packard, because he did not have to overcome the history of bad human-resources management practices Mr. Peterson had inherited at Ford.

Still, scrapping existing facilities creates problems with social responsibility, since current workers would lose their jobs. Additional sound business reasons support many major projects to rejuvenate existing facilities. These projects strain management resources, but they bring organizationwide payoffs that may justify the cost. In particular, such a project reassures workers, whose fear of losing their

[**EXHIBIT 15.12**]

Plant Rejuvenation Tradeoffs

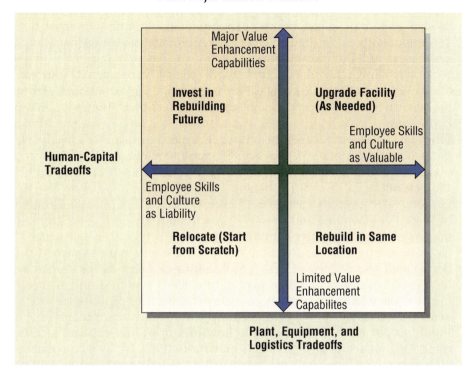

jobs contributes to divisive employee insecurity and morale problems. Closing a plant spreads this fear throughout the firm.

Chrysler undertook such an effort when it built its new Grand Cherokee assembly line at the site of its former Jefferson Avenue plant in Detroit. The new plant employed many of its former UAW employees, including older workers from central Detroit who might have brought old, inefficient habits and attitudes. The project succeeded, though. The plant makes cars of exceptional value with high productivity rates. The cumulative knowledge of its experienced work force has provided a hidden benefit in a work environment increasingly characterized by empowerment.

This option might not work in every case, but Exhibit 15.12 illustrates a framework for comparing tradeoffs in a rejuvenation effort. Decision makers could quantify these questions only with difficulty, but they may easily understate the value of the skills of current workers. Before scrapping a plant and moving to a greener pasture, a company should benchmark other firms, such as Chrysler, to identify the best practices by which they have transformed existing capacities and organizational cultures into world-class plants.

CHAPTER SUMMARY

In this chapter, we supplemented the coverage from the last chapter of resource management, primarily the management of human resources, by dealing with management of physical capacity.

1. Capacity is the rate of output of a process per unit of time. This definition requires considerable elaboration because imprecision in such subjects causes many capacity-management problems.
2. The difference between the input rate and output rate of a process determines its load. Load must match process capacity for stable, long-term operation.
3. The amount of work waiting to enter the system represents backlog. Many OM systems, especially make-to-order systems, need certain minimum levels of backlog to allow schedulers to route work efficiently to system resources.
4. Maximum capacity is a theoretical measure of the largest amount of work a process can handle. No process can sustain production at its maximum capacity for long.
5. Effective capacity measures the output that managers can reasonably expect the process to generate in practice. Operations managers find this proportion by adjusting maximum capacity for utilization and efficiency rates below 100 percent.
6. Demonstrated capacity measures the actual output of a process. Differences between demonstrated and effective capacity indicate divergence from plans that may require corrective action.
7. Operations managers apply some analytical tools to manage capacity. This begins with a seven-step process for calculating capacity: define process activities, establish a standard time period, establish a standard unit of measure, measure the maximum capacity, measure the effective capacity, measure the demonstrated capacity, and compare the measures and take appropriate action.
8. Input/output control regulates the flow of work to an existing facility by comparing its actual and planned input and output. In this way, operations managers control process load and match it to market demand to keep backlog in balance.
9. Capacity sizing decisions make tradeoffs between reductions in unit cost and increases in costs due to excessive utilization rates. Like on-going capacity management for an existing system, these decisions seek to balance capacity with market demand.
10. Facility location decisions vary for service providers and manufacturers and for individual firms. Despite wide variations in relevant criteria, several concerns commonly drive these choices: customers' locations and desires, locations of suppliers and raw materials, competitors' actions, and their effects on the firm's value equation.
11. Firms develop integrated capacity strategies to ensure that capacity-management actions support other efforts to please customers. Supply chain management also affects capacity actions.
12. Site relocation accounts for a critical part of capacity strategy. As part of this analysis, operations managers develop explicit plant charters for all facilities in a multiple-site OM system, often based on suppliers' capabilities and transportation concerns.
13. Operations managers must control capacity expansion response times in light of the pace of change in the markets that they serve. Options include capacity lead strategies, capacity lag strategies, and capacity straddle strategies.
14. Firms can often gain significant benefits, especially in human-resources management, by rejuvenating current facilities instead of scrapping old ones and building new ones.

In the next chapter, we cover techniques for managing another type of organizational resources: physical objects called inventory.

[KEY TERMS]

load   698

backlog   698

maximum capacity   700

effective capacity   700

utilization   701

demonstrated capacity
702

input/output control   710

intellectual capital   721

capacity lead strategy   725

capacity lag strategy   726

capacity straddle strategy
727

[DISCUSSION QUESTIONS]

1. Define the three measures of capacity and discuss the role of each in capacity management.

2. Discuss the process you would recommend to determine the capacity of your school of business.
   a. Which resource(s) might create bottleneck(s)?
   b. How could management relieve these bottlenecks?

3. For the capacity of your school of business, discuss how to implement each of the following OM concepts to improve efficiency:
   a. Value equation
   b. Demand management
   c. Process flexibility (including instruction)
   d. Automation
   In each case, be prepared to discuss tradeoffs between system efficiency and effectiveness.

4. What tradeoffs would affect the decision of a small firm, such as Snapple or Ben & Jerry's, to subcontract production to contract manufacturers as part of plans to expand into national and international markets? Name a corresponding example in high-tech industries. Are the tradeoffs the same there?

5. Compare and contrast the short-term capacity management processes for service providers and manufacturers. Cite an example of each to illustrate your points.

6. Review back issues of *Fortune, Forbes,* and *Business Week* to identify articles that illustrate these capacity-management problems:
   a. Lost market share when a firm lacked sufficient capacity to meet demand
   b. Too much excess capacity because a firm misjudged short-term demand
   c. Too much excess capacity as a result of a long-term shift in industry demand
   d. Reliance on contract manufacturing by a high-tech firm to achieve product-development goals

7. Visit a public library, then use its OM system to illustrate the concepts of capacity efficiency and effectiveness. How should the library's customers help set policy to govern these tradeoffs?

8. A firm is considering two capacity-expansion projects. The first alternative calls for plant expansion adjacent to the firm's major plant site in Bloomington, Indiana. The second calls for a new plant located near the firm's major West Coast market. Outline the procedures for evaluating the pros and cons of each alternative.

9. Apply the value-chain concept to explain the capacity siting strategies of the following firms:
   a. Coca-Cola
   b. Ford Motor Company
   c. Apple Computer
   d. Your local newspaper

10. Discuss the implications of a decision by a firm to accommodate outpartnering relationships in its plant/office location decisions.
11. A firm is considering building two small plants or one large plant to serve five industrial customers for a new product. The table gives the costs for these two alternatives:

Cost of small plant	$1 million
Cost of large plant	1.5 million
Fixed annual overhead at small plant	$150,000
Fixed annual overhead at large plant	250,000

Annual Transportation Costs

Destination	Plant Site 1	Plant Site 2
Customer 1	$20,000	$40,000
Customer 2	25,000	42,000
Customer 3	30,000	30,000
Customer 4	30,000	15,000
Customer 5	15,000	10,000

a. Based strictly on costs, which option should the firm choose?
b. What factors should management consider in addition to cost?

12. Your electricity firm, a public utility, has had a captive market. In recent years, the costs associated with small scale electric power plants have dropped so much that large users of electric power threaten to build their own plants. Furthermore, state and federal regulations may make it possible for low-cost producers of electricity to sell their product selectively in your market, and you would be able to sell in their markets. How do you determine a long-term capacity plan in light of these changes? How might they influence the way your firm will operate?
13. How would you measure the capacity of the Internet? Who is handling its capacity management function?

C A U T I O N

[C R I T I C A L   T H I N K I N G   R E Q U I R E D]

1. Throughout this text, we have said that operations management decisions must be driven by value. Which elements of the value equation are most important in helping an organization determine the amount and type of capacity it needs?
2. Envision a situation in which a firm has either too much or the wrong type of capacity for the market conditions expected over the next 5-year period. What alternatives should the firm consider? Is the value-driven approach helpful?
3. In November 1995, the Cleveland Browns announced that they were moving to Baltimore for economic reasons. A hardy, loyal fan asks you how a team playing in a stadium with a capacity of approximately 70,000, which is typically sold out, could be at a disadvantage. What is your response? (Hint: Consider what the critical capacity of a stadium is.)

CASE 15.1

Intel's Capacity Gamble

Capitalists long have sought to dominate markets through economies of scale. Early American industrial leaders like Henry Ford, Andrew Carnegie, and John D. Rockefeller achieved monopolistic powers within their industries by building such large-scale operations that potential competitors with limited capital resources could not hope to challenge them. About 50 years later, IBM achieved a similar dominant position in the mainframe computer business, and early in the 1980s, Japanese semiconductor manufacturers drove Intel and Texas Instruments from the world market for memory chips with aggressive capital-investment and product-pricing strategies.

More recently, Intel has come to completely dominate the microprocessor segment of the worldwide semiconductor market:

1993 Worldwide Microprocessor Market Share ($ millions)

Rank	Company	Revenue	92–93 Growth	Market Share
1	Intel	$6,569	73%	74%
2	Motorola	705	65	8
3	Advanced Micro Devices	511	–10	6
4	Texas Instruments	200	213	2
5	National Semiconductor	118	42	1
6	Cyrix	95	252	1
7	IBM	88		1
8	NEC	87	12	1
9	Hitachi	79	7	1
10	Toshiba	68	39	1
	All other companies	343	1	4
	Total Microprocessor Market	$8,863	61%	100%

SOURCE *San Francisco Sunday Examiner and Chronicle,* October 2, 1994. © *The San Francisco Examiner* 1994. Reprinted with permission.

Based on first-quarter 1995 results, market analysts expected that Intel would earn $3.55 billion on annual revenue of $15.8 billion.

At the rate Intel was growing, it seemed quite likely to become the most profitable company in America. Among high-profit firms, Exxon, GM, Ford, AT&T, and General Electric earn around $5 billion, but they all envy Intel's growth potential. Intel's 5-year average growth rate of 37 percent will vault it past these giants some time in 1997, if all goes well.

The company has not maintained this phenomenal growth rate by cheap investments. Intel invested more than $11 billion from 1991 to 1995. Its latest plant in Rio Rancho, New Mexico, cost about $1.8 billion, 600 times the $3 million that the firm spent on its first microprocessor plant. From another perspective, this number seems truly awesome: $1.8 billion exceeds the combined 1993 revenue from microprocessor production of Intel's eight largest competitors.

Early in 1995, the Semiconductor Industry Association, a U.S. industry trade group, spread some bad news. For 1995 and the ensuing years, it forecast worldwide sales growth of all types of chips of "only 15 percent." Most industries would welcome such an announcement as good news. Intel, whose microprocessors power 80 percent of all personal computers, saw problems ahead if this forecast were to prove true.

QUESTIONS

1. Discuss Intel's capacity-expansion strategy and relate it to the firm's overall corporate strategy.
2. To what risks does this planned capacity expansion expose Intel?

CASE 15.2

Class of 1962: Kmart versus Wal-Mart

In 1962, two retailing stars were born. Innovative Kmart discount stores transformed the venerable Kresge chain of five-and-dime variety stores into America's largest retailer. When Michael Antonini became president of Kmart in 1987, his chain's $25-billion revenue made it seem invincible. It had made good progress toward its goal of having a Kmart within 5 miles of 95 percent of the U.S. population.

The king of the hill experienced some problems, though. Some of its stores were 17 years old, and the chain's blue-light specials made it the butt of comedians' jokes. Still, the firm's name and reputation as a low-cost retailer gave it great visibility. A teacher in Bakersfield reported asking a 6 year old to name something that began with the letter *k*. "Kmart!" the child quickly responded. The company had achieved name recognition comparable to that of McDonald's, Coca-Cola, and Levi's.

That second retail star, Wal-Mart, still seemed far behind by most industry yardsticks, but it quickly had become the darling of the stock market. Most Americans had never bought anything from these back-woods merchants, who stuck to small, noncompetitive markets. Company insiders have reported that Mr. Antonini dismissed Wal-Mart executives as "snake-oil salesmen." By 1990, those despised competitors sold $32.6 billion a year in 1,721 stores, overtaking Kmart's $29.7 billion in 2,330 stores.

In the ensuing years, Kmart sought to rise to this challenge to its supremacy. It invested $3.5 billion to renovate, expand, and replace its older stores. It also sought to bolster its marketing and merchandising strengths by investing heavily in national television ad campaigns featuring Jaclyn Smith, a television star. Kmart also spent large sums to diversify its retailing chain by buying specialty retailers of books, office supplies, and sporting goods.

Wal-Mart traveled a different path. To reinforce its low-cost strategy, it targeted investments toward its distribution network. It built well-placed distribution warehouses in rural locations and equipped them with efficient materials-handling systems and effective store/warehouse information systems. It routed company-owned trucks efficiently between suppliers' plants to save freight costs by running full trucks. Its buyers became known as some of the tightest in America because they sought every available discount, including those normally extended only to independent distributors. Wal-Mart buyers also solicited the expertise of suppliers in helping them to buy the right merchandise. As a result, the firm achieved a 1 percent to 2 percent advantage in product distribution costs in an industry where low profit margins governed success.

Wal-Mart also started to experiment with different store sizes in preparation for an eventual invasion of Kmart's suburban turf. Its 230,000-square-foot hypermarket in Kansas City proved unwieldy to manage. Over time, the firm developed a store about half that size called a *supercenter*. The construction of a slick, new, 125,000-square-foot Wal-Mart supercenter next to one of Kmart's refurbished, 60,000-square-foot units had devastating effects on the aging giant. By contrast, Wal-Mart's low costs allowed it to prosper in brutal suburban competition.

Somehow, Kmart's management missed the significance of the threat. In the fall of 1993, Mr. Antonini proudly toured one of Kmart's new superstores. As he munched a sandwich, he commented that he might follow Sam Walton's lead and write a book detailing his retail success story. Observers wondered about this attitude from a manager who had watched his firm's share of the total discount-store market slide from 34.5 percent to 22.7 percent. During the same period, Wal-Mart's share had doubled to 41.6 percent.

QUESTION

Compare and contrast the concept of capacity that each firm implemented in investing its funds to maintain and/or achieve a competitive advantage.

[S E L E C T E D   R E A D I N G S]

Berry, W. L., T. E. Vollmann, D. C. Whybark. *Master Production Scheduling: Principles and Practice.* Falls Church, Va.: American Production and Inventory Control Society, July 1979.

————. *Manufacturing Planning and Control Systems,* 3d ed. Homewood, Ill.: Business One/Irwin, 1992.

Blackstone, J. H. *Capacity Management.* Cincinnati, Oh.: South-Western, 1989.

Burbidge, J. L. *Production Flow Analysis for Planning Group Technology.* Oxford: Clarendon Press, 1989.

Fitzsimmons, J. A., and M. J. Fitzsimmons. *Service Management for Competitive Advantage.* New York: McGraw-Hill, 1994.

Fogarty, D. W., J. H. Blackstone, and T. R. Hoffmann. *Production and Inventory Management,* 2d ed. Cincinnati, Oh.: South-Western, 1991.

Hayes, R. H., and S. C. Wheelwright. *Restoring Our Competitive Edge: Competing through Manufacturing.* New York: John Wiley & Sons, 1984.

Orlicky, J. *Materials Requirements Planning: The New Way of Life in Production and Inventory Management.* New York: McGraw-Hill, 1975.

Senge, Peter. *The Fifth Discipline: The Art and Practice of the Learning Organization.* New York: Doubleday, 1990.

Wight, Oliver W. *Production and Inventory Control in the Computer Age.* Boston, Mass.: CBI, 1974.

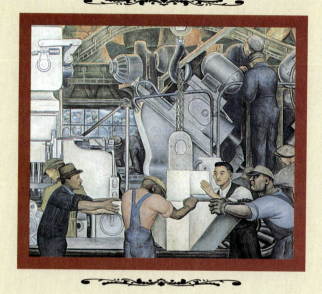

PART SIX

Execution in
Value-Driven OM Systems

CHAPTER SIXTEEN

Inventory Management

CHAPTER OBJECTIVES

[At the end of this chapter, you should be able to]

- Define the concept of inventory and understand the major reasons for having inventory in terms of the functions provided.
- Identify and examine the micro and macro issues which are integral to inventory management decisions.
- Describe the basic economic order quantity (EOQ) model and some of the major EOQ variants.
- Understand the analytical approaches used in modeling inventory decisions.
- Examine the application of inventory models and approaches within some very specific settings (e.g., retail and service).

Information Technology to the Rescue at Levi Strauss

With 144 years of experience, Levi Strauss in 1994 thought it knew how to make jeans. It takes only eight minutes to stitch denim into a pair of Levi's 501s, but managing the flow of materials from a mill in North Carolina, to a sewing plant in New Mexico, to Texas for stone washing, to Kentucky for warehousing and distribution was the Achilles' heel of this fashion giant. The entire trek from raw material to distribution involves 3,286 miles and 61 days.

Early in the 1990s, Levi's was being hobbled by an inventory control system that routinely lost sight of its stock. Its LeviLink system, which was installed in 1980, worked well as a basic communications network—as long as nobody needed to know at any one time where the goods were in the supply chain. When Levi's orders shirts from a supplier in Asia, staff members admit that "we don't know where they are until they show up on our loading dock." Worse yet, Levi's admits that it "doesn't have a clue" what really is on its retailers' shelves. This point was driven home when a corporate account representative boasted, "Give us your point-of-sale data and we'll tell you what is left in your inventory." When this statement was tested, Levi's estimates were proven to be off by more than 30 percent.

As long as Levi's was riding the blue jean boom, few retailers could take their business elsewhere. Broadway Department Stores' vice-president of sportswear noted, "Levi Strauss used to ship late to us, and they didn't seem to care. They had a pompous attitude." The immediate consequences of Levi's unreliability was that retailers overordered and warehoused merchandise to preserve their stores' customer service reputation. But because demand had been taxing its capacity, Levi Strauss could take the attitude that "retailers should consider themselves lucky with the clothes they got, when they got them."

An old proverb states that "you meet the same people on the way down that you met on the way up." Today, Levi's is experiencing the down side. Industry sales are slumping, and its major competitor, VF, is beating the pants off Levi's with its new product-distribution system. It can take up to a month to get an order from Levi's; VF can get you its Lee and Wrangler blue jeans usually within three days.

How does VF do it? VF hooked its own computers up to those of its major customers. Each night, VF customers, such as Wal-Mart, send data from smart, point-of-purchase cash registers straight to VF, which automatically places an order to restock that item. If VF has that item in stock, it ships it the next day. If the item is not in stock, VF's production system is able to ship it within a week. In 1995, about half of VF's jean business was handled through its quick response system. Tom Cole, the logistics chief at Federated Department Stores, commented that VF "gives the customer what the customer wants." John Freudenthal, the executive vice-president of the 59-unit Carson Pirie Scott chain commented, "We don't even classify Levi's as a so-called quick response supplier."

In 1995, Levi Strauss apparently got the message because it embarked on a $500 million customer service initiative. It is buying an IBM ES9000-960 mainframe computer to support its new information system to track each article of clothing from the fabric supplier to the store. But to truly serve the customer, Levi Strauss needs store-level inventory information. It needs advance notice from retailers about promotions, not by chain, but by store. In return, Levi's is offering

1. To ship 95 percent of all orders on the day and within an hour of request.
2. To customize a store's order by shipping "floor ready" merchandise (i.e., goods that are folded, priced, and packed as the customer wants).
3. To ship new clothing items to market in one month.
4. To fulfill 95 percent of all orders completely (i.e., all items ordered will be shipped).

Will the retailers buy in? Levi's hope so, because in 1994, it saw its share of the market slip to 17 percent while VF's market share rose to 30 percent. Retailers indicate that this decline was in part the result of Levi's slowness in replenishing stock.

S O U R C E

George Harrar, "Levi's Cool Brand, Lousy Distribution, IT to the Rescue," *Forbes,* September 12, 1994, pp. 140–142.

Joseph Weber, "Just Get It to the Store on Time," *Business Week,* March 6, 1995, pp. 66–67.

Inventory management seems easy to some—buy or make something that people want, just before they want it. In most business settings, this simple advice collapses under the weight of complex details. As Rick Lack, Levi's vice president of information resources, said, "We're guessing at demand. We end up with plenty of inventory, but it is all the wrong sizes."

Too many managers overlook the intricacies and assume that inventory management is easy. In Exhibit 16.1, Melden suffers from a common complaint. The boss assumes that inventory is equivalent to waste. Inventories may well represent the largest chunk of the firm's assets on its balance sheet, and they form a highly visible target for critics of efficiency. Inventories fill warehouses and clutter the shop floor, and many employees spend much of their time just keeping track of it. Despite these extensive stocks, however, the firm often faces shortages of needed resources in the right locations at the appropriate times. Frustrated managers find plenty of inventory, but it includes the wrong items.

The fashionable emphasis on just-in-time manufacturing reinforces the assumption that all inventory represents a symptom of waste, as discussed in Chapter 9. As in most crusades, however, some advocates of JIT become overzealous in their drive to eliminate inventories. In this chapter, we present an overview of the roles that inventories play in the OM processes of both service and manufacturing organizations. By the end of this chapter, we hope to refine the idea of

[**E X H I B I T   1 6 . 1**]

Inventory Management Trap

inventory management and show how to distinguish between a symptom that shows up in inventories and a real inventory problem. Equally importantly, we want to add some analytical methods to the Operations Management Toolkit to help managers frame and solve real inventory problems.

NATURE OF INVENTORY

Inventory is created when over a period of time more is made than is consumed. As a result, inventory is a stock, as compared to the flow concepts discussed in Chapter 5. This imbalance can occur as a reslut of two sets of actions. First, we can deliberately decide to make more than we need. We may do so because the cost of having excess inventory is far less than the cost of not having inventory (and thus being unable to satisfy an order). Alternatively, we may have inventory because of mistakes. We did not plan to have inventory, but perhaps a customer cancelled an order, or our forecasts exceeded actual demand.

inventory

A physical resource that a firm holds in stock with the intent of selling it or transforming it into a more valuable state

Simply put, **inventory** is a physical resource that a firm holds in stock with the intent of selling it or transforming it into a more valuable state. Firms measure inventories both in units of currency, i.e. dollar value, or well-understood physical quantities, i.e. units, cases, tons, gallons, etc. Large-scale statements of diverse inventories often convert physical quantities to dollar values to provide a common measure and avoid problems with incompatible units. This system assigns values to units of inventory based on either acquired cost or some form of standard cost.

The general category of inventories includes several more specific types of inventories:

raw materials inventories

Resources purchased as inputs to the transformation process that have not yet begun that process

work-in-process inventories

Resources currently undergoing transformation into more valuable states

finished goods inventories

Completed products held for later sale to customers

- **Raw materials inventories** hold resources purchased as inputs to the transformation process that have not yet begun that process.
- **Work-in-process inventories**, or WIP inventories, hold resources currently undergoing transformation into more valuable states.
- **Finished goods inventories** hold completed products for later sale to customers. Firms hold finished goods at various locations: at the plants that make them, at a warehouse or distribution center, in vehicles while in transit, and at retail outlets. In some cases, a firm may maintain finished goods at a customer's site to await sale on consignment.
- Maintenance, repair, and operating (MRO) inventories also include incidental resources purchased to support ongoing activities. Firms also call these inventories *supplies* or *consumables*.

Operations managers classify inventories relative to their locations in the supply chain. The finished goods for one operation often become raw materials for the next level. Intel produces a Pentium microprocessor and places it in finished goods inventory, perhaps to become raw material for Packard Bell's personal computer assembly plant. The microprocessor would remain in the finished goods category if Intel were to sell it to a computer retailer, such as CompUSA, for resale to an upgrading computer owner. The assignment of these classifications varies depending upon individual circumstances.

Whether or not an item of inventory appears as an asset on a firm's balance sheet also depends on circumstances. In some instances, accountants treat supplies as expenses and charge their costs to the accounting periods in which the firm purchased them. As we will discuss later, negotiation may determine the ownership of inventory assets. This chapter does not resolve questions about whether inventory shows up as an asset on the balance sheet. Operations managers manage inventory not to assign costs, but to assure that they provide the right resources in the right locations at the right times in order to best serve the needs of the firm and its customers.

Functional Roles of Inventory

Recall the definition of *value* from the early chapters. Those discussions pointed out that a well-run organization identifies a purpose for every action and an action for every purpose. To avoid wasting organizational resources on unneeded inventories, operations managers must set out a specific role for each type of inventory. A functional classification scheme can aid this process by defining a number of general roles for inventories.

Transit Inventory.   Items count as inventories as they move from one physical location to another, usually in trucks, rail cars, ships, barges, aircraft, or pipelines.

Buffer Inventory.   Despite the principles of just-in-time manufacturing, many firms hold inventory to protect against disruptions due to unplanned events like unexpectedly high demand, delayed shipments, or equipment breakdowns. Firms also position stocks to meet expected customer service needs. Retail stocks and spare-parts inventories fall into this category.

Seasonal Inventory.   Through careful planning, operations managers try to accommodate mismatches between when they want to provide goods and when buyers need them. A potato chip manufacturer makes fresh chips all year, but it can buy raw materials only at harvest time. At the other end of the value chain, a Christmas wreath maker must build up its finished goods stocks in anticipation of its peak December sales. In a sense, seasonal inventory is a special case of anticipatory inventory.

Decoupling Inventory.   This inventory accommodates differences between the rate or pattern of production and the rate or pattern of demand. A machine may produce 5,000 units a day, while daily demand averages only 50 units. It may make sense to decouple production from demand in this case and run the machine for 1 day to accumulate stock to supply demand for 100 days.

Similarly, economies of scale in purchasing or shipping may justify holding some decoupling inventory. You can buy beer most cheaply by the case, but you might consume only two bottles a night. A wheat buyer can economically purchase wheat only by the truckload to fill a need for only 400 bushels a day. Both the beer drinker and the wheat buyer hold inventory to decouple their supply rates from their consumption rates.

Speculative Inventory.   Some conditions may justify purchasing goods prior to need to avoid likely future price increases or supply shortages. In periods of high inflation, a firm may wisely invest surplus funds in tangible commodities that will probably increase rapidly in value. For another example, suppose that the release of Windows 95 seemed likely to create a shortage of aftermaket DRAM chips as personal computer owners rushed to upgrade their systems to meet the memory needs of the new software; a savvy retailer might stock up on chips prior to the potential shortage or price increase. This is also known as anticipatory inventory.

Lot Sizing or Cycle Function.   Although the operations manager would typically build only what is needed, in many cases this is not possible. Significant changeover or setup costs may be incurred. For example, we have an order for only five units. Each unit takes only five minutes to make; our total processing time is 25 minutes. However, it takes three hours to set up the equipment. Rather than make only five units, we make enough units so that the costs associated with having excess units in stock (i.e., inventory holding costs) are equal to the costs of setting up for the orders. The resulting order quantity using this logic is our lot size. We implement this logic later in this chapter when we deal with the economic order quantity.

This function is also known as the cycle function because of the pattern that the inventory exhibits. We make an order at the start and put the items into inventory. Over time, the items are consumed, and the amount in inventory falls until it is near or at zero. At this point, we reorder and the total inventory moves back up to its original position. The cycle is now repeated.

Mistakes.   Almost all systems accumulate goods as a result of poor decisions. Demand forecasts sometimes prove too high. Operations managers may produce a component as engineers bring them a new design. Completed products may not quite meet quality specifications, but staff members still hope to find uses for them. Mistakes are easy to spot in stock rooms, often by the layers of dust that gather on them.

Retail businesses deal effectively with their mistakes; they send the goods back, if they can, or they mark down the prices until someone buys the unneeded products. Many manufacturers act like pack rats, though. An operations manager may explain unused stocks by claiming that the last time the shop disposed of its obsolete parts, someone wanted one the following week.

Junking a part also has a direct impact on the firm's bottom line: old stock may stay in inventory to avoid making the business unit look bad. Managers rationalize as much to explain excessive inventories as in any area of their responsibilities. The next "By the Way" box shows how one company is "forced" to carry a special inventory item.

Adding Value through Inventories

Operations managers must carefully evaluate the merits of holding inventory to fill any of the functional roles discussed so far. They should base this judgment on the values of the customers whose needs the inventory will support. The functions of inventory can powerfully influence the four elements of the firm's value equation.

Quality.   The quality of many goods depends on freshness, which often varies with age. Bread and beer are best served fresh, while wine and steaks benefit from controlled periods of aging. In manufacturing, extensive work-in-process inventories may mask real quality problems. The trail of causes gets cold while an item sits awaiting processing at the next stage, decreasing the chances of finding out what went wrong to generate the defect. Recall that one advantage of cellular manufacturing comes from the ease of assigning personal responsibility within a small group of activities and workers. Also, a smaller investment in inventory makes it easier to declare goods defective.

With lower inventory, we cannot afford poor quality. With large levels of inventory, we can live with poor quality—if a part taken from inventory is found to be inadequate, we take another item. There is no urgency to correct the problem.

[BY THE WAY... THERE'S GOLD IN THAT THERE]
[COPPER—ON THE BALANCE SHEET]

Junking inventory is treated as an expense within the accounting system—the cost of goods sold increases and profits drop. In contrast, all inventory is considered to be an asset. For example, a Milwaukee company made copper couplings, which never rust, and never spoil. The firm had manufactured $2 million dollars of couplings for the U.S. Army during the Korean War (1950–1953). The army couldn't use them, but the firm's manager was convinced that eventually the firm would be able to sell the couplings. Thirty years later, they were still in inventory, even though they used a fair bit of production space for storage, and were expensive. Whenever anyone considered junking them, an accountant would immediately calculate the impact on cost of goods sold and point out that the action would turn the company's profit into a loss. As a result, the couplings were still around. In fact, there was a serious discussion within the plant that these couplings deserved their own pension plan since they had been around so long.

With less inventory, we cannot just take another item. We must either live with the poor quality, which will stop production later, or we can correct the problem. With this second line of action, our level of quality improves over time because we are constantly working to bring the process under control.

Speed.   The ability to quickly and reliably serve a customer is greatly influenced by the location of inventory within the value chain. A well-stocked retail outlet can quickly satisfy a customer's need for a standardized good. Likewise, properly positioned stocks of components can help a make-to-stock or assemble-to-order system to fill customer orders in a timely manner. In each case, the firm wins the bet if it invests in the inventory that customers eventually want; it loses if the value of the inventory declines or is destroyed before demand emerges.

Flexibility.   Anticipatory inventory can help a firm to match its mix of product offerings to changing customer needs. Success depends on the tradeoff between customer service and product obsolescence. A well-positioned inventory of standardized components or subassemblies can enable a firm to supply customized products that meet the expectations of individual customers within reasonable production lead times. For example, Burger King inventories its partially cooked patties, buns, and condiments. When there is a demand, the server puts the burger into a microwave and finishes cooking it. The burger can now be configured to the specific needs of the customer.

Cost.   Inventories affect both direct and indirect costs. The firm incurs direct costs to purchase, deliver, and manufacture a product. By building up and drawing down seasonal and decoupling inventories, it can more easily achieve economies of scale within its purchasing, logistics, and manufacturing functions. Savvy buyers fill speculative inventories when they seize opportunities to acquire goods on favorable terms; of course, a poor speculative purchase may place the firm at a disadvantage.

Companies like FAO Schwartz can't always maintain enough stock to meet customer demand for popular toys, but they try. Failure to do so can result in lost sales and consumer ill-will.
SOURCE   Robert Brenner/PhotoEdit

inventory holding costs

The funds, physical resources, and personnel that a firm ties up by maintaining inventories

stockout cost

A measure of the effects of failure to provide the products that customers want, leading to lost sales and reductions in goodwill

Inventory decisions also affect indirect costs. The funds and physical resources that a firm ties up by maintaining inventories contribute to its **inventory holding costs**. These costs also include expenses for people and systems to track and manage inventories. The chance to avoid spending large sums on inventory management provides one important advantage of JIT manufacturing.

Another major class of indirect inventory costs, often called **stockout costs**, measure the effects of failure to provide the products that customers want, leading to lost sales and reductions in goodwill. Firms have trouble accurately quantifying stockout costs. A lower-bound estimate would state the difference between the flow of funds that a transaction would have created and the direct cost of making, selling, and delivering the product that the firm would have sold.

This calculation records the one-time loss due to a stockout. Failure to satisfy a customer may cost a firm more than a single sale, though. The firm may lose its image as a reliable supplier, an important order qualifier for many customers. To accommodate this possibility, an upper-bound estimate of stockout cost would measure the loss of profits from the stream of purchases that a dissatisfied customer would have made but will not out of fear of another stockout. These purchases may affect far more than the single product that went out of stock.

An indirect cost of inventory closely related to stockout cost is the cost of unplanned back orders. If a make-to-stock firm must back order a customer request, it incurs a number of indirect costs. First, it must cover the incremental costs of ordering the item, expediting its production or purchase, and then notifying the customer when it becomes available. Second, expediting production or purchasing usually raises production costs. Most importantly, the back order may erode the goodwill of the customer who must wait. Customers may recognize a firm's heroic effort to supply desired products, but the total experience will still fall short of expectations.

The final major effect of inventory on costs results from setup costs for manufacturing or ordering. The discussion of JIT manufacturing illustrated why operations managers must not accept these costs as given. They drive efforts to achieve economies of scale. Eliminating or materially reducing setup costs greatly reduces the need for decoupling inventory.

[**BY THE WAY... INVENTORY MANAGEMENT IN YOUR KITCHEN**]

Your household probably shares many inventory problems with Melden's workplace. Take a good hard look in your pantry or kitchen cupboards. Divide everything you find there into three categories: food that you plan to consume within a week, food that you expect to consume within a month, and food that you may never consume. Without starting a family argument, ascertain who acquired the items in the last category and why.

The second part of this experiment is more dangerous.

Try to see how long you can go without buying any item that you normally stock in your pantry or freezer. By the third week, you will thoroughly understand the danger of Melden's tactic of cutting inventories by limiting inflows.

Guidelines for Inventory Decisions

By evaluating the functional roles of inventories and their effects on the firm's value equation, an operations manager like the unfortunate Melden from Exhibit 16.1 can address inventory decisions in an orderly manner. The functions of inventories within the value chain determine whether they contribute to the firm's achievement of its strategic goals or represent symptoms of operating problems. An audit of the effects of inventories on value can identify the reasons for holding stocks at each link in the value chain.

The merits of holding inventory at any point in the value chain depend on the needs and expectations of the internal and external customers at that stage. Mail-order customers seem willing to wait to acquire desired products in exchange for low prices or convenient delivery ("Please allow 6 to 8 weeks for delivery"). A firm with sufficiently patient customers might not even need to make or acquire finished products prior to customer orders. On the other hand, some customers prefer to see, feel, or experience finished products before they decide to buy. The values of a firm's customers dictate its inventory policies. Like other OM decisions, stocking practices must support the strategic goals of the firm.

If they do not, Melden and other operations managers might respond in a way that maximizes their own comfort in the daily routine of the organization. When pressed to eliminate inventory, they can comply most easily by selling it or using it in some way in the transformation process. They probably cannot influence what the firm makes or sells, however, so they will most likely choose the next-best response and reduce the inflow of stocks by curtailing buying. This may actually reduce value and disrupt the progress of the OM process by causing stockouts of raw materials, components, and finished products.

Melden personifies the inventory dilemma. How much stock is too much? What should the OM function stock and where should it hold stocks? These questions require answers in the form of system design decisions rather than daily operating decisions. A system usually produces counterproductive results when it reflexively tries to minimize inventories simply by pressuring Melden to eliminate them. The "By the Way" box translates this problem into more familiar, domestic terms.

DESIGN OF INVENTORY MANAGEMENT SYSTEMS

The design of a system to manage inventories must define formal links between inventory decisions and the firm's stated strategic goals. This requires a clear understanding of the firm's markets, the expectations of customers in those markets, and the inherent characteristics of the items in inventories throughout the value chain. This information guides answers to a number of critical questions, which we discuss in this section. We have grouped them into categories for macro issues and micro issues, although this distinction is not always clear in practice.

Macro Issues in Inventory Management Systems

When dealing with inventory, the operations manager must work at two levels. At the *micro* level, emphasized to this point, we are making item-by-item decisions; it is very detailed. The second *macro* level is much broader and deals with issues that have strong implications for both the type of value delivered by our system and the strategic stance of the company. At this level we are concerned with the amount of overall inventory to have, its position in the supply chain, and its profile (the relative size of finished goods, work-in-process, and raw material). We now turn our attention to this level of inventory management.

Need for Finished Goods Inventories.   In reality, this issue raises two questions. First, operations managers must decide whether the firm needs to maintain inventory to satisfy internal or external customers. Like mail-order buyers, they may willingly wait for their products. This basic system-design question determines whether the firm can succeed by making standardized products to stock.

Patrons of a classy French restaurant expect to wait while the chef prepares a fine meal from basic ingredients. Indeed, they might lower their estimation of the restaurant's quality if they suspect that the chef fills their orders by assembling to order some ready-made components. Customers who want highly customized goods also expect to wait, since the firm cannot possibly anticipate their unique requests. To meet the speed, quality, and flexibility expectations of these market segments, firms might decide not to stock finished goods inventories at all.

The second, closely related question asks whether someone else in the value chain might carry needed inventory. For years, Volkswagen dealers convinced VW Beetle owners that they should carry spare fan belts just in case. Industrial equipment salespeople commonly urge each new equipment owner to buy a set of spare parts that the equipment will likely need. These tactics reduce the response time required to meet a customer's need and influence the speed element of the customer's value equation. In a sense, these sellers practice a form of demand management. They do not diminish the overall volume of spare parts demand, but they do reduce the load on the firm's product lead time.

Ownership of Inventories.   Transferring ownership of inventories may relieve the firm of the financial burden of maintaining stocks, but not the responsibility for managing them. For example, Stern's Miracle-Gro has created an image as a maker of plant fertilizers through TV commercials in which actor James Whitmore reports on horticultural award winners with their 7-pound tomatoes. In the 1980s, this firm owned neither a factory nor a warehouse; it contracted out its manufacturing and distribution functions, leaving its operations managers to perform only inventory planning activities.

Advances in information-processing technologies enhance the ability of retail establishments to carry goods on consignment. This keeps these assets on the books of suppliers until the final sale. Major chains like Wal-Mart and Kmart have enough clout to induce some suppliers to own the goods stocked in their stores until end users purchase them. In one arrangement, 3M Company receives nightly payments from Wal-Mart for each day's sales of its Scotch brand tapes. No such relationship could function without bar-code readers and an efficient electronic data interchange network.

Customers for Miracle-Gro fertilizer and Scotch tape remain unaware that the firm that takes their money does not own the goods it sells them. Wal-Mart clearly benefits from savings on inventory investments in 3M products; this cost to 3M is partly offset by Wal-Mart's quick payments. Each party must weigh the cost trade-offs with individual consignment deals and similar shifts of inventory ownership.

Specific Contents of Inventories.   The choices of materials, components, and products that the firm holds in inventory normally hinge on the speed, flexibility, and quality expectations of customers. Service organizations must resolve three issues to make this choice. First, they must determine what items targeted customers will likely want based on knowledge of their customers. Some supplement their information by actively asking, "Did you find everything you needed?" Others use database marketing to extend their knowledge of the customers in their marketing areas. For example, Pep Boys, a major retailer of auto parts, tracks car registrations in each market to help it decide what to stock in each store.

The second issue in the choice of what products to stock involves the variety of products that customers expect to find in stock. If a firm sells a product in more than one size, it must decide which sizes to carry in inventory. If a store sells more than one comparable brand for a product, it must determine which ones to keep in stock. In retailing, store classifications often reflect customer expectations. Customers in a 7-Eleven store do not expect a wide selection of sizes or brands for convenience goods like shampoo; they expect a broader variety of products in a supermarket, and a major drug chain outlet should carry every available product and size. In these product-stocking decisions, economies of scale for both the buying and distribution functions carry considerable weight. To maximize these cost savings, most chains tend to centralize control over decisions about what to stock.

Customers' willingness to wait is the third determinant of what a service firm chooses to stock. How much longer will customers wait to receive customized products? Will the quality of the service improve or deteriorate if the firm asks customers to wait? Burger King invites fast-food customers to "Have it your way" because the company believes that they will accept slightly longer waits to get slightly customized burgers. They will not wait too long, however, so Burger King par-broils its beef patties, and workers subsequently cook them to order and smother them with the chosen gastric accessories.

Order lead time may depend less on customer impatience than on how long it will take to get desired stocks. A number of years ago, the National Whole Blood Resources arm of the National Institutes of Health funded research to determine how to manage blood-bank inventories. At the time, approximately 20 percent of donated units were outdated (i.e., spoiling) before use. In one sense, the program was flawed because it sought to manage donated blood rather than donor visits. Scandinavian countries chose instead to manage blood donors, recognizing that the best place to store blood is in a prescreened donor's body. The success of this system depended on quick responses by willing donors to calls for blood. Scandinavian blood banks had to stock some units to handle emergencies, but they did not need nearly as many units as American repositories routinely held. The response of these service organizations amounted to tradeoffs among speed, cost, and quality.

Manufacturers have to make similar tradeoffs. Often, they must make goods immediately available, so they set up make-to-stock systems to produce standard goods. In other instances, customer preferences vary too widely for firms to anticipate specific product requests. If a particular firm can meet this need by selling customized combinations of standard components, then an assemble-to-order system may work well, especially if customers seem unwilling to wait while the firm builds fully customized products from raw materials. In each case, the design of the inventory management system will need to understand the tradeoffs that will permit the firm to profitably satisfy the needs of its customers.

Of course, aspects of the operations management function other than inventory management also influence the ability of the firm to quickly satisfy a customer's need. For example, order lead time and design lead time affect the time between the request for a customized product and its delivery. The customer cares only about the total lead time, though. Operations managers must grapple with the processes for introducing an order, designing the product, and making it.

Locations of Inventories.   Retail customers often hear store employees say, "If it's not on the shelf, we don't have it." This statement reflects a policy decision by store management to keep only one level of inventory. All goods flow directly from suppliers or the warehouse through the stock room to the store's shelves. The term *stock room* serves only as a quaint reminder of the traditional function of that facility.

Catalog showroom retailers like Service Merchandise and Best share a different strategy. They fill shelf space with product samples and supply purchased products from adjacent stock rooms. These systems presume that customers will sacrifice a little time at the store in exchange for low costs. Printed catalogs and television shopping channels save consumers time and possibly money, provided they will accept slightly slower product delivery. Note that these consumers make a tradeoff between shopping time and delivery time. Emerging technologies will soon permit couch-potato shoppers to control the display of products on a television or computer monitor and possibly to interactively haggle on price. In each case, the expectations and demands of a firm's specific customers drive its inventory strategy.

Manufacturers encounter two special questions when planning inventory locations. For one, they often must decide where to store spare parts inventories. In the days before quick-delivery services, such as Federal Express, firms sought to position warehouses in locations from which they could cost effectively deliver spare parts and other goods within acceptable time periods. A firm that maintains a few large warehouses can achieve low outbound freight costs, but this centralization may place resources far from customers, impairing the firm's ability to make speedy deliveries. Many small warehouses may respond more quickly, but they sacrifice economies of scale in inventory operations.

An equipment opertor needs spare parts quickly to keep its resources productive; this customer may judge the value of the equipment purchase by how quickly the manufacturer supplies those parts. Caterpillar, the manufacturer of earth-moving equipment, understands that most of its customers value machine uptime, so it promises to deliver a spare part anywhere in the United States within 2 days, or to provide it free of charge. This promise integrates Caterpillar's inventory management system for spare parts with its marketing strategy to convince potential customers that its parts stocking system and field service will assure high rates of machine utilization. In construction, where time is money, many customers value this product attribute, and they pay premium prices for Caterpillar's products to get it.

Manufacturers also need careful plans for the locations of raw materials and work-in-process inventories. Operations managers justify a location of an inventory stocking point for internal customers by two arguments:

1. The location enables activities at earlier and/or later stages of a process to improve operating efficiency enough to offset incremental inventory holding costs.
2. The location reduces product lead time over the entire system enough to support the firm's quick-response goals.

For example, transportation economies might force an assembly line to accept 30,000-unit shipments from a distant supplier even though the line uses only 1,000 units per day. At much higher freight costs for less-than-truckload shipments, the firm could have 1,000 units delivered each day. Full-truckload freight rates may save enough on inbound freight costs to offset the higher holding costs of an average inventory of 15,000 units. Once again, operations managers must decide what arrangements give their firm the most competitive combination of quality, delivery speed, product variety, and cost.

Tracking Inventory. A firm's ordering and stock replenishment process needs key inputs to specify the current level of inventory and the number of units on order. In the past, retailers counted inventories periodically to determine how much stock they had on hand. Many actually sacrificed sales by closing down their stores at fixed intervals to take physical inventory counts because they could not cost effectively maintain accurate, ongoing inventory records. Bar-coding technology and intelligent point-of-sale terminals now help retailers to maintain up-to-date, accurate inventory records. A firm must justify an investment in such technology by comparing the benefits of timely inventory decisions and the cost savings of less frequent physical counts of inventory against the cost of the transaction-tracking system. The inability of Levi Strauss to quickly and correctly identify rapidly selling products put the firm at a competitive disadvantage in its battle with VF for market share.

Manufacturers face similar but more complex problems, since they must track inventory through elaborate networks of work stations. To keep track of work-in-process inventory, a manufacturer must develop an efficient process for recording transactions within the plant. It needs a current, accurate record of the status of each work order and its location of the shop floor. Once again, bar-coding technology provides an easy way to accomplish this goal in combination with shop-floor data entry terminals, but such a system can be expensive. A manufacturer may also have more trouble assessing the specific value of the system's contribution to information about conditions in the shop because other business processes, such as the cost accounting function, may use the same data. A job-lot cost accounting system would duplicate some of the functions of a shop-floor inventory tracking system, for example.

However, the operations manager is interested in issues such as the location of the inventory and the number of units in stock while the accounting system is interested in the amount of money tied up in inventory. One system may not be able to serve both needs, and will result in compromises that may adversely affect the operations of the transformation system.

Both service and manufacturing organizations need to base inventory decisions on accurate information, especially when decision makers work at a site remote from the actual inventories, as users of computerized inventory management systems do. This need often raises the importance of maintaining accurate inventory records to make it a key business process. Many firms take physical inventory counts to assure this essential accuracy, but not without risk of mistakes. A department store once paid a local church for time spent by volunteers to perform a physical inventory count. Despite the benefits of this innovative bit of charity, a trained operations manager might well wonder if the store could run a more effective system by keeping one or two competent people busy year round verifying inventory rather than recruiting many inexperienced people to do it all at once.

Many manufacturing firms prefer ongoing programs over periodic physical counts to verify inventory records. To keep their records current, these firms often practice **cycle counting**, a procedure to systematically take physical counts of some items in inventory each day and reconcile any differences that emerge. A cycle counting plan specifies a group of items to check over some period of time (per day or week) and the procedures for reconciling any differences. This method allocates inventory tracking resources in a way that resembles Pareto analysis, checking the most important inventory items regularly while counting the least critical items only infrequently, perhaps once a year. If a firm demonstrates that its tracking system maintains extremely accurate inventory records, accounting standards permit it to substitute end-of-year records for the more traditional physical inventory count.

A cycle counting program does not eliminate the need for everyone who works in an inventory tracking system to maintain rigorous accuracy. Even the newest retail sales clerk must understand the importance of a simple transaction like exchanging a large-size shirt for an identical shirt in an extra-large size. The clerk must record the return of the large-size shirt to inventory and the removal of the extra-large. Fortunately, bar coding makes this a simple task. The department manager must accomplish a more difficult task—training everyone on staff to recognize the significance of these seemingly inconsequential transactions.

Responsibility for Key Inventory Decisions.   A firm's organizational design should specify who makes operating decisions about inventories. The choice depends on who has the best information about market conditions, staff workers at corporate headquarters or managers in the field or on the shop floor. Of course, this varies with different markets, the availability of timely information about demand and inventory status, and the quality of operating managers.

This choice must also weigh the best use of a manager's time. The manager of a retail store might spend 60 percent of the work day taking inventory and processing paperwork for orders. The chain might decide instead to assign these duties to headquarters staff to free store managers for duties supervising and training subordinates and serving customers.

In fact, someone entirely outside a retail organization may well handle inventory management, usually a vendor as discussed in the "On the Job" box. Vendor representatives cruise down the aisles of many drugstores carrying portable bar-code readers similar to the one in the photo on page 753. Upon reading a product's bar code, the unit displays a preset stock level for that stock keeping unit (SKU). If the store should stock 10 units of a particular SKU and only 4 units remain on the shelf, the vendor rep enters an order for 6 units using bar-coded information. At the end of the visit, he or she downloads the total order to a file server which automatically sends the information to store management and the vendor's distribution center.

cycle counting
A procedure to systematically take physical counts of some items in inventory each day and reconcile any differences that emerge

ON THE JOB

Wal-Mart Changes Its Diaper Policy

■

For years, Wal-Mart's distribution system did a brisk business shipping Procter & Gamble's highly successful Pampers line of disposable diapers. Since the bulky product required extensive storage space, the retailer wanted to hold system inventory to a minimum. On the other hand, it did not want to risk stockouts that would threaten its ability to satisfy brisk demand for this highly popular end-use product.

Wal-Mart managers determined that P&G probably knew more about the flow of Pampers through its distribution system than its own managers knew. They asked P&G to assume responsibility for telling Wal-Mart when to order Pampers and how much to order. Wal-Mart would then review the recommendation and issue a purchase order.

The system worked so well that Wal-Mart eventually eliminated the purchase order review. Besides saving storage space, the arrangement with P&G enhances Wal-Mart's cash flow. Its traditional payment practices take longer than the average time for a shipment of Pampers to flow through the retail/distribution system. The retailer still owns the merchandise, but it now pays for shipments shortly after selling the products. Few retailers enjoy the luxury of paying for goods with the cash receipts from sales of those goods.

SOURCE   Hammer and Champy, *Reengineering the Corporation* (New York: Harper & Row, 1993), pp. 61–62.

In a manufacturing organization, a computer program can handle inventory management, placing orders through an EDI system, or an authorized buyer can do this work. Anyone from an hourly, operating employee to a designated member of headquarters staff may act as an authorized buyer. The nature of the ordering transaction dictates the best distribution of authority. An automatic order entry system can simplify inventory management for repetitive purchases in a

Tracking inventory with portable bar-code scanners enables vendors to download merchandise orders directly to distribution centers.   SOURCE   Courtesy of Symbol Technology

stable setting without disruptions due to exogenous information. This arrangement suits many high-volume final assembly systems for which prior arrangements specify suppliers and prices.

More complex inventory decisions in manufacturing organizations require more active human intervention. Production planning triggers the decision to initiate an order, which moves to staff members in the purchasing function for completion. To avoid disputes between the OM and purchasing functions, everyone must understand the criteria for acceptable tradeoffs among cost, quality, speed, and flexibility. The discussion of total supply management in Chapter 13 explains this important point in detail.

Micro Issues in Inventory Management Systems

Most reviews of inventory control techniques emphasize three basic micro issues: how much to order, when to place orders, and how to select suppliers. The choice of suppliers can be either a micro or a macro decision. In the past, purchasers outsourced needed materials and components by contracting with suppliers that offered the best terms. In practice, "best terms" usually meant lowest cost.

More recently, many firms have opted for longer-term supplier relationships. Often, they look for a supplier not for a single product, but for everything in a particular product family. A restaurant may look for the best terms for all of its bakery needs rather than just burger buns. Chapter 13 described this trend toward long-term, partnering relationships. Partnerships with suppliers become important in a JIT manufacturing system, as well, as the firm seeks to deal with as few suppliers as possible.

Order Quantity Decisions.   In the operations management literature, Harris addressed this issue first as early as 1913.[1] He focused on the familiar problem of balancing the cost of setting up for production runs against the cost of holding the inventories that large production runs create. Today's operations managers deal with this tradeoff by applying the classic economic order quantity formula discussed in the next section.

Order Timing Decisions.   Timing orders becomes important when a significant time interval elapses before delivery. If a supplier can fill an order immediately, the purchaser simply places orders when stocks run out. To allow for significant order lead time, however, the purchaser must estimate demand during that lead time. With constant demand, the purchaser sets a reorder point by multiplying the demand rate by the lead time.

If demand during the order lead time remains uncertain, then the reorder point must balance the cost of holding additional buffer inventory against the expected cost of a stockout. The next section will cover this adjustment in more detail.

Since World War II, scholars have published hundreds of articles describing the optimal values for key inventory parameters. While much of this work helped to improve actual practices and procedures for inventory management, almost all of the resulting systems shared a flawed goal of optimizing inventory models for existing OM systems. Recall from Chapter 9 that the Japanese pioneers of just-in-time manufacturing elected instead to attack defects in their manufacturing

[1]D. Erlenkotter, "Ford Whitman and the Economic Order Quantity Model," *Operations Research* 38, no. 6 (November–December 1990), p. 937.

environments. Instead of resolving inventory management problems, they dissolved them by eliminating their causes.

 ## BASIC MODELS FOR INVENTORY MANAGEMENT

Operations managers for an organization address the macro and micro issues of inventory management by designing a specific process that meets the needs of internal and external customers. They generally apply some standard models, making changes as necessary to adapt them to individual circumstances.

They begin by gaining an overall perspective of the firm's inventory problem and how inventory decisions affect other business functions. Inventory system analysis suits the conditions for the five-step analysis process discussed in Chapter 4: (1) size up and describe the problem, (2) state the problem, (3) analyze the problem, (4) prescribe a solution, (5) implement recommended changes.

To size up and describe the problem, operations managers can perform an **inventory audit** to answer seven questions:

1. What existing systems control inventory? A thorough description would specify the current arrangements for inventory management based on attributes like those listed in Exhibit 16.2.
2. What resources support existing levels of inventory? Clearly, a system handles different categories of inventories, distinguished by locations, functions, and product characteristics. Exhibit 16.3 shows one way to break down total inventories into smaller classifications to begin to identify the resource requirements they create.
3. What internal and external customers must an inventory management system serve?
4. What functions do inventories perform at each location, or how do inventories add value for internal and external customers? Of course, the system should add value in ways that reinforce the firm's competitive combination of speed, quality, flexibility, and cost.
5. What business practices, technologies, or other structural conditions cause the firm to stock larger quantities in inventory than might otherwise be prudent? These could include volume discounts, minimum order quantities, shipping practices, etc.
6. What decisions or events led the firm to hold unproductive inventories? To answer this question, perform a **dead stock audit**. First, identify dead or slow-moving stock at each location. Then, without assessing blame, try to learn why the firm came to hold these unproductive assets and what operational and fiscal consequences it could expect if it were to purge the system of them.
7. How much overhead does each location's inventory-management system consume? The firm's policies for assigning overhead affect this answer. A firm can easily answer this question if its cost accounting system, such as activity-based costing, specifically identifies activities that generate overhead. Most firms would struggle to find such detailed information.

The first six questions should form essential parts of any inventory audit. The seventh, to identify the contribution of inventory to overhead, may involve too great an effort. Still, even a gross estimate of the hidden costs of inventory and

inventory audit
A study to size up and describe a firm's inventory management system

dead stock audit
A review of unproductive inventories that identifies dead or slow-moving stock at each location and discovers why the firm came to hold that stock

[**EXHIBIT 16.2**]

Attributes for an Inventory Audit

Product attributes
  Value risks
    Cost stability
    Product perishability
    Product obsolescence
    Risk of theft
  Storage needs
    Amount, location, and purpose of inventory in system
    Specialized environment requirements (refrigeration)
    Packaging/storage economies of scale, case count, palletized, etc.
Demand attributes
  Independent versus dependent demand
  Customer patience
  Pattern of arrival (continuous, lumpy, seasonal, cyclic, etc.)
System management practices
  Continuous versus perpetual review
  Single-item versus multiple-item review
  Integrity/accuracy of database
  Degree of information automation (universal product codes, bar coding, etc.)
  Organization's willingness to decentralize decision making
Product/part replenishment attributes
  Sources (internal and external factory)
  Source performance attributes
    Transportation model and economics
    Delivery speed
    Delivery reliability
Sources of system instabilities
  Demand uncertainty
  Process yield uncertainty
  Source lead time uncertainty
Cost attributes
  Inventory holding costs
  Setup/product ordering costs
  Stockout costs and/or unplanned back-ordering costs
  Service level goals

its management may reveal much of the waste traditionally associated with excessive stocks.

The inventory audit reveals the present system for managing stocks, but how can a firm logically develop a better system? A traditional, top-down manager might simply order that such a system must come to pass and leave Melden to work out the details under a threat of termination. More effective managers have developed better ways, however, as we explained in Chapter 4. Several methods might suggest improvements or the characteristics of an entirely new system:

1. Pareto analysis might help to identify the locations of common stock shortages.
2. Benchmarking might suggest the best practices of similar operations.

[**E X H I B I T   16 . 3**]

Resource Requirements by Inventory Classification

Type	Amount ($)	Inventory Turns	Comments
Raw materials		12×/year	
Work in process		4×	
Finished goods		6×	

3. Cause-and-effect analysis might point out the root causes of stockouts or other inventory problems.
4. Total cost analysis or incremental cost analysis might offer a model of the economic tradeoffs associated with alternative inventory stocking policies.
5. A queuing model might help to determine the most economic buffer stock policy.

Designers of an inventory management system should take care not to rush too quickly through the problem description phase. As with most other real-life problems, the search for the root causes for inventory problems may lead in many directions throughout the organization. Only after thorough study can operations managers really understand the situation.

After sizing up and describing the inventory management problem, the problem statement specifies the relationships between observed symptoms and the stated problem. A clear statement of the problem targets operations managers' efforts toward appropriate activities and protects them from wasting resources working on the wrong problem. Most importantly, the problem statement process should foster agreement among key participants about the nature of the problem that a new inventory management system should solve.

In the Levi Strauss problem described at the start of this chapter, the problem statement would identify whether the problem was one of communication (we need a better system of recording, storing, and transmitting information), system stockkeeping (we need to improve our systems for getting, recording, and maintaining highly accurate inventory counts), inventory profiling (too much of our inventory is in finished goods which, if not exactly what the customer wants, cannot be changed to meet customer demand), lot sizing (we did not use the "right" order quantity when building or filling orders) or demand management (we really don't understand what the customer wants). The problem, once set down and agreed to, begins the focal point for determining what tools to use and the general approach to be taken.

After crafting a problem statement that clearly identifies the scope of the problem, problem analysis can begin to trace the relationships among the problem, its symptoms, and the constraints that limit the decision maker's courses of action. To facilitate this study, the problem statement should distinguish between controllable variables and those that decision makers cannot control.

From the problem statement, we can derive the model of the decision-making process, to identify constraints or limitations. The presence of significant constraints or limitations determines our general approach to solving the problem. For example, if Levi Strauss operations managers feel that they are faced by a simple lot sizing problem with no significant limitations, they would solve the problem using simple

> "The less you understand the problem, the bigger you make the model."
>
> Old Operations Research Proverb

procedures and techniques. They might develop a solution for identifying the best lot size using a spreadsheet program such as Excel. Alternatively, they might be able to develop an answer analytically using mathematical tools such as calculus.

In other cases, the model may identify whether the variables are deterministic (known with certainty in advance), or random/stochastic (there is variation in the variables which can be predicted or described using a distribution). In most cases, unconstrained cost minimization models often indicate solutions to relatively simple inventory problems.

However, if there are random/stochastic variables identified in the model, the task of generating an answer becomes more complex. Because of uncertainty, we move from trying to solving a stochastic problem. As a result, we can no longer generate a solution that maximizes the overall solution, but rather one that maximizes or minimizes some expected value (i.e., on average, using this lot sizing logic, we can expect that our costs should be...). Again, the solution becomes more complex if we have constraints (e.g., all orders must be fulfilled within 48 hours, and we promise that the customer will expect 95 percent of all orders filled within one hour of the order being received).

In this book, we will focus on the relatively simple formulations of the inventory problems. The more complex problems (e.g., the model tries to accommodate more than two decision variables with one or more constraints), we will leave for other more advanced texts. Realize, however, that most of the models presented in this text represent gross simplifications of real-world problems. They produce local decision rules that serve the decision-making process well, but users should always view these results with a skeptical eye. At the very least, users should always ask whether or not a resulting policy recommendation makes sense. Would a savvy inventory planner be seen using these results?

If models do not seem to offer insight into a stated inventory problem, then experimentation may suggest some ways to improve system effectiveness. TQM techniques like Deming's plan-do-check-act method, described in Chapter 4, help to systematically focus employee attention on identified inventory problems. They intend not to find optimal solutions, but to guide continuous improvement. These methods of improving a system through employee involvement, unlike analytical models, draw on the expertise of the people closest to the problem; these people will most likely understand why a proposed solution offers the best available response.

" Every solution creates another problem. "

Old Swiss Proverb

After complete analysis of the problem, the prescription phase evaluates alternative solutions. Analytical models or experiments can provide insights into the criteria for a solution, but not the solution itself. The prescription for an inventory problem translates the insights about what the inventory management system should do into specific processes and activities that will do it. In this phase, operations managers must also assess any possible negative consequences of proposed solutions.

The final step implements prescribed changes. The prescription should close the gap between observed inventory conditions and desired conditions. To fully achieve the objective of building an effective inventory management system, its key participants must accept the problem statement and agree that the proposed prescription will likely solve the problem. Uncommitted employees will not successfully implement any solution.

Classic Economic Order Quantity Model

One of the most fundamental inventory management problems is lot sizing. Here we are interested in identifying the order quantity that will result in the lowest

[**EXHIBIT 16.4**]

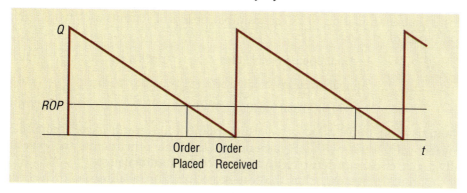

EOQ Inventory Cycle

total cost. The simplest form of the total cost equation involves only two major components. The first is the cost of having inventory—we have inventory to avoid setting up every time that we receive an order. The second cost is the cost of setup—in setting up for each order, we avoid the costs of carrying inventory. We want to identify that order quantity that minimizes the sum of these two costs. The **economic order quantity (EOQ) model** addresses the inventory-management question of how much to order of an item with independent demand to minimize the total cost of holding this inventory. The problem statement assumes constant annual demand and instantaneous replenishment. In these conditions, it asks how much to order at one time to meet annual demand D with fixed ordering or setup costs C_0 and a cost of holding a unit of inventory C_h. Inventory costs vary with the average level of inventory. Exhibit 16.4 illustrates the behavior of inventory over time for this problem.

economic order quantity model

A basic inventory-management model that determines how much to order of an item with independent demand to minimize the total cost of holding this inventory

Analysis of this problem reveals only one decision variable, Q, the quantity to order. The assumption of constant demand simplifies a second potential decision variable, *ROP*, the reorder point; inventory managers set this quantity simply by multiplying the order lead time (the time they will have to wait for delivery) by the demand rate.

With the terms defined, a formula states the total annual cost function of Q:

$$TC(Q) = \text{Total annual setup cost} + \text{Total annual inventory holding cost} \quad \textbf{(16.1)}$$

$$TC(Q) = \text{Number of orders/year} \times \text{Setup cost} + \text{Average inventory} \times \text{Holding cost} \quad \textbf{(16.2)}$$

$$TC(Q) = (D/Q) \times C_o + (Q/2) \times C_h \quad \textbf{(16.3)}$$

To solve the problem, inventory managers find the quantity that gives the minimum total cost using a chart, a spreadsheet, or calculus.

[**PROBLEM 16.1**]

Economic Order Quantity

A firm estimates annual demand for an item at 1,000 units. Setup costs are approximately $200 per production run. Holding costs are estimated to be $25 per unit per year. How much should the firm order to minimize total setup and holding costs?

To solve this problem graphically, simply plug values of Q into the total cost equation (Equation 16.1). For example, orders of 10 units each would give total costs of:

$$\text{Annual setup cost} = (1{,}000/10) \times 200 = \$20{,}000 \tag{16.4}$$

$$\text{Annual inventory holding cost} = (10/2) \times 25 = \$125 \tag{16.5}$$

$$\text{Total cost } (Q = 10) = \$20{,}125 \tag{16.6}$$

Plotting these three values gives three points on a graph like Exhibit 16.5. Further calculations with larger values of Q indicate other points and eventually define curves for setup costs, holding costs, and total costs.

Exhibit 16.5 shows that the total cost function declines as order size increases until the point where incremental savings in setup costs no longer offset incremental increases in inventory holding costs. This analysis suggests an order quantity in the range of 120 to 130 units.

A simple spreadsheet can also suggest a solution to this problem, as shown in Exhibit 16.6. Once again, the minimum cost order quantity seems to be around 130 units. A more detailed spreadsheet could target the quantity more accurately, but this refinement might require more effort than additional cost savings would justify, especially since the graph showed a rather flat total cost curve in the range of the minimum cost solution, so a small change in order quantity in either direction would have little effect on total cost.

[**E X H I B I T   1 6 . 5**]

Total Annual Inventory Costs

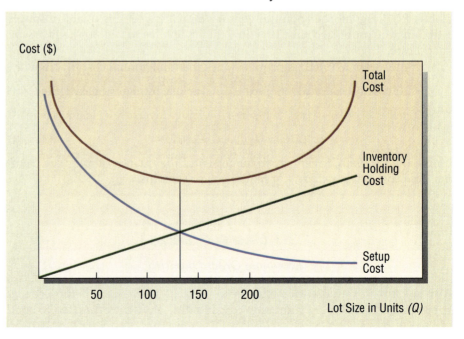

Spreadsheet Solution to Problem 16.1

Lot Size (Q)	Orders/ Year	Setup Costs	Average Inventory	Holding Costs	Total Cost
10	100	$20,000	5.0	$125	$20,125
20	50	10,000	10.0	250	10,250
30	33	6,667	15.0	375	7,042
40	25	5,000	20.0	500	5,500
50	20	4,000	25.0	625	4,625
60	17	3,333	30.0	750	4,083
70	14	2,857	35.0	875	3,732
80	13	2,500	40.0	1,000	3,500
90	11	2,222	45.0	1,125	3,347
100	10	2,000	50.0	1,250	3,250
110	9	1,818	55.0	1,375	3,193
120	8	1,667	60.0	1,500	3,167
130	8	1,538	65.0	1,625	3,163
140	7	1,429	70.0	1,750	3,179
150	7	1,333	75.0	1,875	3,208
160	6	1,250	80.0	2,000	3,250
170	6	1,176	85.0	2,125	3,301
180	6	1,111	90.0	2,250	3,361
190	5	1,053	95.0	2,375	3,428
200	5	1,000	100.0	2,500	3,500
210	5	952	105.0	2,625	3,577
220	5	909	110.0	2,750	3,659
230	4	870	115.0	2,875	3,745

To solve the EOQ model using calculus, inventory managers would take the first derivative of the total cost equation with respect to the decision variable, Q:

$$\frac{d}{dQ}TC = \frac{d}{dQ}\left(\frac{1,000}{Q}\right) \times C_o + \frac{d}{dQ}\left(\frac{Q}{2}\right) \times C_h \qquad (16.7)$$

$$(-1,000/Q2)C_o + C_h = 0$$

This yields an order quantity of:

$$Q = \sqrt{2DC_o/C_h} = \sqrt{2(1,000)(200)/25} = 126.5 \text{ units} \qquad (16.8) \quad [\blacksquare]$$

The classic EOQ model made some restrictive assumptions. More elaborate models relax those assumptions to accommodate more variable real-world inventory-management situations.

Production Lot Scheduling Model

The classic EOQ model assumes that the activity of producing and consuming inventory is sequential in nature—all of the units in the lot size are produced or

[**EXHIBIT 16.7**]

Production Lot Scheduling: EOQ with Consumption

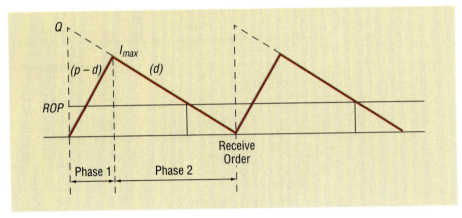

delivered in one batch. No consumption of this inventory is allowed until *all* of the units in the order quantity have been produced. Once completed, these items are then made available. As a result, we can see that the act of making the inventory is separate and distinct from the act of consuming the inventory. This situation is most appropriate for purchasing situations or for internal production settings where we make units for multiple users (and we are not linked to these users). However, in many settings, the act of making inventory and the act of consuming it overlap—as we make the units, they are being consumed. This situation is most frequently encountered internally on the shop floor when the process that fills the order is located near the operation that will use the order as inputs.

production lot scheduling model

An inventory-management model that accommodates consumption of units from an order while the supplying process works to complete the rest of the order

To deal with this situation, the **production lot scheduling model** adds two more variables. Let p represent the rate at which an upstream work center makes goods, and let d be the constant rate at which a downstream work center consumes them.

An inventory cycle in this model consists of two phases. During the first phase, the supplying process makes goods at a rate of p units an hour and its customer consumes them at a rate of d units per hour. The difference between production and consumption ($p - d$ units per hour) accumulates in inventory. During the second phase, no production occurs and consumption depletes the inventory at a rate of d units per hour. The length of phase one is Q/p. Thus, the maximum amount of inventory buildup is the production run time multiplied by the buildup rate, or:

$$I_{max} = (Q/p) \times (p - d)$$

Exhibit 16.7 illustrates this situation. Note that the production lot scheduling model shares a condition with the classic EOQ model that demand for the item remains independent of the demand of the other items in the system.

This change to the model assumptions requires a change in the total cost equation:

$$\text{Annual } TC = \text{Annual setup cost} + \text{Annual holding cost} \tag{16.9}$$

$$\text{Annual } TC = (D/Q) \times C_o + (I_{max}/2) \times C_h \tag{16.10}$$

$$I_{max} = (Q/p) \times (p - d) \tag{16.11}$$

Substituting I_{max} into the total cost equation yields:

$$TC = (D/2) \times C_o + [Q/p] \times (p-d) \times C_h \qquad (16.12)$$

Calculus gives a solution for the minimum value of Q, the economic order or production quantity:

$$Q_{min} = \sqrt{2DC_o/C_h} \times \sqrt{(p/(p-d))} \qquad (16.13)$$

Note that as d approaches the value of p, the order quantity approaches infinity. This makes sense; if the consuming work center uses up the input at a rate close to the supplying work center's production rate, then the supplying work center can work continuously solely to produce that item. Conversely, if p is much larger than d, then Equation 16.13 approaches the classic economic order quantity model. This, too, seems reasonable, since the assumptions of that model correspond to a situation with p in excess of d.

[**PROBLEM 16.2**]

Applying Production Lot Scheduling

Return to Problem 16.1, but assume that the supplying work center runs at a production rate of 40 units per week, and weekly demand equals 20 units (i.e. 1,000 units per year divided by 50 weeks per year). This gives an economic order or batch size of:

$$Q_{min} = \sqrt{(2)(1,000)(200)/25} \times \sqrt{(40)/(40-20)} = 126 \times 1.41 = 178 \text{ units} \qquad (16.14)$$

The production lot size model gives a larger order quantity than the classic economic order quantity formula. The columns in Exhibit 16.8 for average inventory and holding costs explain the upward shift from 126 to 178. The maximum inventory, I_{max}, equals only one-half of the average order quantity, Q. Therefore, inventory carrying costs run only half as high as those of the basic EOQ model with instant replenishment of inventory. [■]

Quantity Discount Model

Another real-world complication affects the economic order quantity model: suppliers often give quantity discounts to induce customers to place larger orders than they might otherwise desire. Suppliers normally offer price discounts to raise the quantities of their manufacturing, marketing, or product distribution activities and take advantage of economies of scale. Inventory managers must carefully evaluate any quantity discount to understand why the supplier offers a lower price and how it affects the low-cost order quantity.

This analysis becomes especially important for a discount based on marketing economies of scale. Either purchasing agents or salespeople may see efficiency gains in higher-volume orders. These gains may reduce costs by raising the quantities of purchase transactions without affecting the timing of deliveries. The supplier may give a discount for a large order to be delivered in smaller lots.

The potential cost savings from a quantity discount include a lower purchase price and lower transaction costs to process fewer purchase orders and invoices. The buyer may also incur lower inbound freight costs and fewer receiving expenses. Such a discount normally raises costs for working capital and warehousing, and some degradation of product quality may also contribute to higher costs. As for

[**EXHIBIT 16.8**]

Spreadsheet for Order Quantity with Consumption

Lot Size (Q)	Orders/ Year	Setup Cost	Average Inventory	Holding Costs	Total Cost
10	100	$20,000	2.5	$ 63	$20,063
20	50	10,000	5.0	125	10,125
30	33	6,667	7.5	188	6,854
40	25	5,000	10.0	250	5,250
50	20	4,000	12.5	313	4,313
60	17	3,333	15.0	375	3,708
70	14	2,857	17.5	438	3,295
80	13	2,500	20.0	500	3,000
90	11	2,222	22.5	563	2,785
100	10	2,000	25.0	625	2,625
110	9	1,818	27.5	688	2,506
120	8	1,667	30.0	750	2,417
130	8	1,538	32.5	813	2,351
140	7	1,429	35.0	875	2,304
150	7	1,333	37.5	938	2,271
160	6	1,250	40.0	1,000	2,250
170	6	1,176	42.5	1,063	2,239
180	6	1,111	45.0	1,125	2,236
190	5	1,053	47.5	1,188	2,240
200	5	1,000	50.0	1,250	2,250
210	5	952	52.5	1,313	2,265
220	5	909	55.0	1,375	2,284
230	4	870	57.5	1,438	2,307

quantity discount model
An inventory-management model that accommodates price discounts for large orders

earlier inventory models, inventory managers develop a **quantity discount model** by capturing all relevant costs in a total cost equation.

To illustrate this process, we will revise Problem 16.1 from the discussion of the classic EOQ model. All conditions remain the same, except the seller offers these quantity discounts:

Quantity	Price per Unit
100 or fewer units	$100 each
101 to 300 units	90
301 units or more	85

If the firm were to purchase 150 units, for example, each would cost $90.

[**PROBLEM 16.3**]

Order Sizes with Quantity Discounts

The total annual cost function once again depends solely on the purchase quantity, *Q:*

$TC(Q)$ = Annual purchase cost + Annual setup cost + Annual inventory holding cost

$TC(Q)$ = Annual usage × Price (Q) + (Number of orders/year) × Order cost +
         Average Inventory × Holding Cost

$$TC(Q) = D \times \text{Price }(Q) + (D/Q) \times C_o + (Q/2) \times C_h \qquad (16.15)$$

The term $D \times$ Price (Q) has been added because the price is now dependent on the quantity, and how much we pay per year is influenced by how much we buy per order. This problem requires a more difficult solution than the EOQ or production lot size models because the cost function is discontinuous. This does not seriously impede a graphic solution, though. Exhibit 16.9 shows only one more curve than the earlier section required, and two curves are disjointed.

The setup cost curve declines exponentially, as it did in the earlier models. The inventory carrying cost curve behaves much as it did in those models, except that it drops at the quantities that trigger price discounts, the price break points, creating discontinuities. This assumes that inventory holding costs depend on the average dollar amount of inventory. Since the price declines from $100 to $90 a unit for orders above 100 units, the slope of the inventory holding cost line becomes a little less steep to reflect the lower dollar investment per unit.

The major difference in this chart comes from the addition of the annual purchased cost function. It is level up to an order quantity of 100 units. After that point, it drops down to reflect the annual savings from the first price break. A similar discontinuous drop occurs at the next price break point of 250 units. The total cost equation simply sums these three cost curves.

[E X H I B I T   1 6 . 9]

Total Inventory Cost with Quantity Discounts

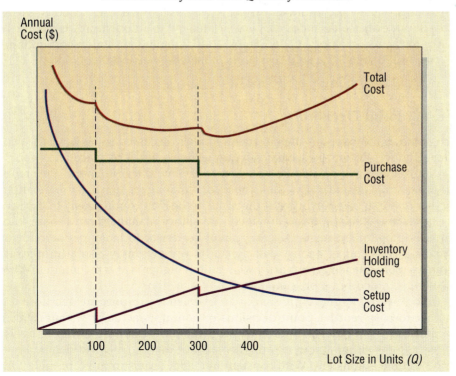

Each price break defines a region for costs. For each price break, we would like to pick a quantity that results in lowest total cost. Ideally this would be the EOQ. However, in many cases, as we move to price breaks consistent with larger order quantities, the EOQ is often less than the minimum quantity that we need to buy to justify the new lower price. For example, the price break is $47.50 if we buy 250 or more. However, when we use $47.50 in our EOQ, we get 83.4 units. But if we buy only 83.4 units, we must pay $50 per unit, the price for any order less than 100 units (for any order between 100 and less than 250 we would pay $48). In this case the minimum order quantity consistent with this price break is 250 units.

Some study of the total annual cost equation suggests that the optimum solution with a quantity discount can occur only at the order size generated by the classical EOQ model or at one of the price break points above this amount. To solve the problem analytically, then, follow a four-step procedure:

1. Write the total cost equation.
2. Solve the classical EOQ model assuming the highest price without any discounts.
3. If Q_{min} falls in a quantity range with a lower purchase cost, recalculate the EOQ assuming the inventory holding cost for that range. Label this number Q_2.
4. Evaluate the total cost equation at an order quantity of Q_2 and at the next highest price break point.

The optimal solution occurs at the value of Q with the lowest total cost. Technically, you should evaluate the total cost equation at all price breaks above Q_2, since a really large price break at some higher quantity might give an even lower total cost. Most quantity discount programs do not give such generous price breaks, though.

Spreadsheets offer another tool to solve the order quantity problem with discounts. This works in much the same way as in the earlier sections, except that the spreadsheet includes a logical *if* statement to automatically calculate the price for a given value of Q. In Exhibit 16.10, the new minimum cost quantity occurs at 250 units. The total cost starts to increase beyond that point.   [■]

Reorder Point Decisions

Each of the above inventory-management models discussed so far has indicated an order quantity. Recall the second micro question—when to place an order. This question also raises a related issue: when to review. If a firm checks the status of inventory only periodically, then inventory managers may also logically ask whether or not to place an order at that time. If the firm continuously tracks inventory levels and stock on order, however, inventory managers can choose to continuously monitor for items that they should order or to make periodic reviews, perhaps at the end of each week. Periodic reviews may use administrative resources more efficiently, but they will result in higher buffer inventories. We will discuss this tradeoff in more detail later in this section.

Inventory managers must make an even more important decision about whether to base reorder point decisions on amounts actually withdrawn from inventories or estimates of future withdrawals. Most simple ordering decision models assume either that demand is constant or that the mean of demand over a period of time is constant. With constant demand, order timing can safely follow

[**EXHIBIT 16.10**]

Spreadsheet for Order Quantity with Price Discounts

Annual usage = 1,000   Setup cost = $200   Holding Cost = $25/year

Lot Size (Q)	Price	Purchase Cost	Orders/ year	Setup Cost	Average Inventory	Holding Cost	Total Cost
10	100	100,000	100	$20,000	5	$ 125	$120,125
20	100	100,000	50	10,000	10	250	110,250
30	100	100,000	33	6,667	15	375	107,042
40	100	100,000	25	5,000	20	500	105,500
50	100	100,000	20	4,000	25	625	104,625
60	100	100,000	17	3,333	30	750	104,083
70	100	100,000	14	2,857	35	875	103,732
80	100	100,000	13	2,500	40	1,000	103,500
90	100	100,000	11	2,222	45	1,125	103,347
100	100	100,000	10	2,000	50	1,250	103,250
110	90	90,000	9	1,818	55	1,375	93,193
120	90	90,000	8	1,667	60	1,500	93,167
130	90	90,000	8	1,538	65	1,625	93,163
140	90	90,000	7	1,429	70	1,750	93,179
150	90	90,000	7	1,333	75	1,875	93,208
160	90	90,000	6	1,250	80	2,000	93,250
170	90	90,000	6	1,176	85	2,125	93,301
180	90	90,000	6	1,111	90	2,250	93,361
190	90	90,000	5	1,053	95	2,375	93,428
200	90	90,000	5	1,000	100	2,500	93,500
210	90	90,000	5	952	105	2,625	93,577
220	90	90,000	5	909	110	2,750	93,659
230	90	90,000	4	870	115	2,875	93,745
240	90	90,000	4	833	120	3,000	93,833
250	90	90,000	4	800	125	3,125	93,925
260	85	85,000	4	769	130	3,250	89,019
270	85	85,000	4	741	135	3,375	89,116

actual usage; with lumpy or irregular demand over time, orders should anticipate variations in inventory requirements. This helps the production planning system to allow for known disruptions to a stable work flow such as a need to ship a large order at the end of the fourth week in May. Simple inventory reordering models ignore this kind of information, so they require some form of human intervention.

Reorder Points with Constant Demand.   With an assumption of constant demand, as in the classic economic order quantity model, inventory managers should place an order when remaining stocks will just satisfy requirements for an item over the order lead time:

$$\text{Reorder point} = \text{Demand during lead time} = D \times LT \qquad \text{(16.16)}$$

where

D = demand rate per period
LT = lead time in periods

All terms must be stated using the same units of analysis. This is, the demand must be stated in the same units as the lead times. For example, if we sell 5,200 units a year but our lead time is 3 weeks, the demand is stated in years and the lead time in weeks. We must convert both to a common unit—weeks, in this case. Our demand converts to 100 units per week, and our lead time is three weeks. As a result, the reorder point is 300 units.

If demand equals 40 units per week and it takes 3 weeks to receive an order, the reorder point occurs at:

$$ROP = D \times LT = 40 \text{ units/week} \times 3 \text{ weeks} = 120 \text{ units} \qquad \textbf{(16.17)}$$

Whenever demand depletes stocks to leave only 120 units, inventory managers should order Q units.

If demand remains exactly constant and lead time equals precisely 3 weeks, then the new shipment will arrive just as production uses the last unit in stock. Of course, this flawless timing also assumes that the order goes out the instant that available stock plus units on order hits 120 units. If the inventory level reaches the reorder point on Monday and no one places an order until Friday, the firm will need safety stock to prevent a stockout. The size of this buffer depends on how much risk the firm wants to take. To prevent a stockout with absolute certainty, safety stock should hold enough to satisfy demand for 1 week since inventory could reach the reorder point early on the first day of the ordering cycle.

This safety stock adds to the cost of placing orders only once a week. The weekly review makes sense if the firm saves more by consolidating ordering tasks and paperwork that it must spend to maintain an additional week's worth of inventory. Once again, inventory issues require cost tradeoffs.

Reorder Points with Uncertain Demand.   Just as safety stock protects against stockouts with periodic reordering, it can also protect against uncertainties in demand. Inventory managers conduct careful analysis to determine how much buffer stock to hold to avoid stockouts caused by unexpectedly high demand, as Exhibit 16.11 illustrates. Two major variations cause uncertainty in demand for inventories: fluctuations in demand rates and fluctuations in delivery times.

To set an order quantity, inventory managers must balance setup costs against inventory carrying costs. To set a reorder point, they must manage the tradeoff between the cost of carrying buffer inventories and the cost of stockouts and/or poor service. In some cases, firms incur a third cost—the direct and indirect cost of rescheduling work to avoid stockouts. These expediting costs cover disruptions of planned production, unplanned overtime, and premium prices paid to acquire or deliver orders with short lead times.

Most companies really do not know how much stockouts cost them. To estimate the elusive cost of a stockout, inventory managers need to project a customer's reaction. As one component of this cost, they might assume that the customer would award all future orders to another vendor. The cost of a stockout then equals the lost unit profit from the current sale plus the profits from all future sales to that customer. The unit profit loss equals the difference between the selling price and the direct costs to manufacture, sell, and distribute the product.

Another component of the cost of a stockout comes from its influence on the behavior of key people within the organization. Failure to deliver a product harms salespeople, both financially if their compensation is based on an incentive system, and more generally by detracting from their overall selling effectiveness.

[E X H I B I T   16.11]

Safety Stock for Uncertain Demand

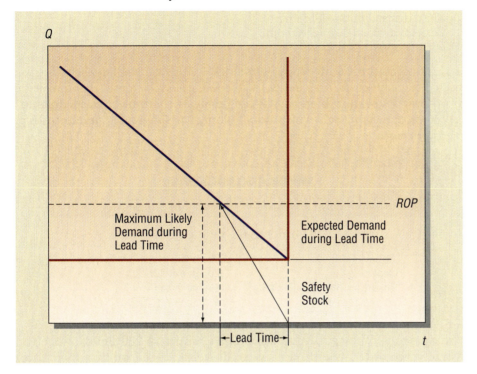

Salespeople's reactions may harm operations planning, as when they inflate sales forecasts to assure themselves that planners will make at least enough stock. They may even turn in phony sales orders, known as *soft orders,* to start production based on tentative demand that may later disappear.

If inventory managers can accurately estimate the cost of a stockout, they can set reorder points based on a total cost function. However, incremental cost analysis often proves easier to understand. This method adds units to safety stock until the expected increase in inventory holding cost exceeds the expected reduction in stockout cost. For the first unit of safety stock, the inventory holding cost is:

$$\text{Unit safety stock cost per order cycle} = C_h/\text{Number of orders per year} \qquad \textbf{(16.18)}$$

For Problem 16.1 (the classic EOQ model problem), this cost would equal:

$$\text{Unit safety stock cost} = \$25.00/(1{,}000/126) = \$3.15/\text{order cycle} \qquad \textbf{(16.19)}$$

This cost per unit of safety stock does not vary; the second, third, and fourth units would each add the same amount to the overall inventory holding costs.

The expected stockout cost for a given reorder point diminishes with additional units of safety stock. If demand displays a normal distribution over the appropriate lead time, then the probability of a stockout without any safety stock case would equal 0.50. Adding a unit of safety stock increases the reorder point by 1 unit as it diminishes the probability of a stockout. Then the expected savings in stockout costs for each unit added to the reorder point equals:

$$E[\text{Stockout cost from } n\text{th item of safety stock}] = C_s \times \text{Pr} \{D_{LT} > [E(\mu_{LT}) + n]\} \qquad \textbf{(16.20)}$$

where

C_s = unit cost of a stockout
D_{LT} = actual demand during lead time
μ_{LT} = expected demand during lead time
n = nth unit of safety stock

Clearly, the first unit added to safety stock will cause the largest reduction in expected stockout costs. As n increases, the likelihood decreases that the next unit will prevent a stockout. Incremental cost analysis continues to add units to the safety stock until a unit raises inventory holding costs more than it reduces expected stockout costs.

[**P R O B L E M   1 6 . 4**]

Incremental Analysis of the Level of Safety Stock

To illustrate, suppose that a firm has the following attributes:

Annual demand	1,000 units per 50 week year
Order cost (C_o)	$200 per order
Inventory holding cost (C_h)	$10 per year
Stockout cost (C_s)	$30 per unit short
Order lead time	3 weeks

The classic EOQ formula gives an order quantity of 200 units, so the firm would place orders about once every 10 weeks. Based on incremental cost analysis, the firm needs safety stock of:

$$ROP = 3 \text{ weeks} \times 20 \text{ units/week} + \text{Safety stock} = 60 \text{ units} + SS \qquad \textbf{(16.21)}$$

Assume that demand displays a normal distribution during the 3-week order lead time with a mean of 120 and a standard deviation of 10 units. This gives an inventory holding cost per cycle of:

$$(\$10/\text{year})/(1{,}000 \text{ units/year}/200 \text{ units per order}) = \$2.00 \text{ per order cycle}$$

A single unit of safety stock gives a probability that demand will exceed 61 units of:

$$\text{Pr}\{\text{Demand} > 61\} = 0.5 - \text{Pr}\{0 < z < 1/10\} = 0.50 - 0.038 = 0.462 \qquad \textbf{(16.22)}$$

Therefore, the expected cost of a stockout equals:

$$E[\text{Stockout cost}] = \$30 \times 0.462 = \$13.86 \qquad \textbf{(16.23)}$$

The first unit of safety stock costs $3.15 in inventory holding costs and saves $13.86 in estimated stockout costs. Exhibit 16.12 shows that the 16th unit of safety stock fails to reduce expected stockout cost enough to warrant its inventory holding cost.

Finally, the reorder point is:

$$ROP = D \times LT + \text{Safety stock} = 20 \times 3 + 15 = 75 \text{ units} \qquad \textbf{(16.24)}$$

Recall that this method relies on an assumption of a normal distribution of demand during the appropriate lead time with a mean of 120 and a standard deviation of 10.   [■]

[**E X H I B I T   1 6 . 1 2**]

Determining Optimum Safety Stock Using Incremental Analysis

Units of Safety Stock	Holding Costs	Pr(Stockout)	Stockout Costs	Incremental Savings
1	$2.00	0.4602	$13.81	$11.81
2	2.00	0.4207	12.62	10.62
3	2.00	0.3821	11.46	9.46
4	2.00	0.3446	10.34	8.34
5	2.00	0.3085	9.26	7.26
6	2.00	0.2743	8.23	6.23
7	2.00	0.242	7.26	5.26
8	2.00	0.2119	6.36	4.36
9	2.00	0.1841	5.52	3.52
10	2.00	0.1587	4.76	2.76
11	2.00	0.1357	4.07	2.07
12	2.00	0.1151	3.45	1.45
13	2.00	0.0968	2.90	0.90
14	2.00	0.0808	2.42	0.42
15	2.00	0.0668	2.00	0.00
16	2.00	0.0548	1.64	−0.36

Reorder Points Based on Service Levels.   Inventory managers must rely on a complex and hazy estimate of stockout costs to set a reorder point with uncertain demand. Many firms avoid this problem by substituting service level standards for stockout costs in the reorder point calculation.

The first of two basic types of service level standards, a **Type I service level**, sets a reorder point to give a specified probability that the firm will have enough units in stock, including safety stock, to meet demand during the order lead time. In Problem 16.4, inventory managers could apply a table of values in the normal distribution (Appendix A) to determine the most appropriate safety stock level.

Type I service level

A method of calculating a reorder point to give a specified probability that the firm will have enough units in stock, including safety stock, to meet demand during the order lead time

Suppose that the service level requires stock to satisfy 90 percent of orders. In the table, the shaded area under the curve should equal 45 percent, which occurs at a standard deviation of 1.645. To get a reorder point, apply the formula:

$$z = (x - \mu_{LT})/\partial_{LT} \tag{16.25}$$

where ($z = 1.645$), ($\mu_{LT} = 60$), ($\partial_{LT} = 10$), then solve for the reorder point:

$$x = (1.645)(10) + 60 = 16.45 + 60 = 76.45 \text{ units} \tag{16.26}$$

The ROP of 77 will result in a safety stock of 17 units. This sets a service level with less than a 5 percent chance of a stockout during any ordering cycle. (This ROP roughly equals that from the prior section only by coincidence; a different service level standard would have given a different reorder point.) Note that the reorder point calculation based on the Type I service level requires no cost information.

Another type of service level standard, a **Type II service level**, seeks to give safety stocks that assure that inventory will meet at least 95 percent of all demand. Stated another way, this standard will allow stock to run short by no more than 5 percent of total demand. Again, in Problem 16.4, a Type II 95 percent service level would supply at least 950 units on time out of the annual demand of 1,000 units.

Type II service level

A method of calculating a reorder point to give safety stocks that assure that inventory will meet at least 95 percent of all demand

This allows stock to run no more than 50 units short annually, so the maximum expected stockout per ordering cycle would equal:

$$E[\text{Short per cycle}] = E[\text{Short per year}]/(\text{Annual demand}/Q) \qquad (16.27)$$

In Problem 16.4, this would give:

$$E[\text{Short per cycle}] = 50 \text{ units per year}/(1{,}000/200) = 10 \text{ units per cycle} \qquad (16.28)$$

Inventory managers must then determine a level of safety stock that will run no more than 10 units short per cycle.

In the reorder-point expression $ROP = D \times LT + SS$, the decision variable is SS. The expected number of units short per cycle comes from the expression:

$$\sum_{x=ROP+1}^{\infty}(x - ROP)\Pr\{x\} \leq 10 \text{ units} \qquad (16.29)$$

If the expected stockout exceeds the standard, inventory managers raise the ROP by increasing SS until the expression on the left is equal to or less than the number on the right.

This requires messy and tedious calculations! Fortunately, a table can reduce the drudgery. Exhibit 16.13 assumes a normal distribution, normalized with a mean of zero and a standard deviation of 1.0. To normalize Problem 16.4 to meet the same criteria, divide by the standard deviation of the demand during the order lead time:

$$E[z] = E[n]/\partial_{LT} = 10/10 = 1.00 \qquad (16.30)$$

where

$E[z]$ = standardized number of units short per cycle
$E[n]$ = expected number of units short per cycle
∂_{LT} = standard deviation of demand during lead time

To use Exhibit 16.13, follow three steps:

1. Locate the previously calculated value of $E[z]$ in the table.
2. Read across the row to find the appropriate z value.
3. Calculate the ROP using the formula from Equation 16.25:

$$z = (ROP - \mu_{LT})/\partial_{LT} \qquad (16.31)$$

Exhibit 16.13 gives a z value of −90 for an $E[z]$ of 1.00. Now solve for ROP:

$$ROP = z\partial_{LT} + \mu_{LT} = (-0.90)(10) + 60 = -9 + 60 = 51 \qquad (16.32)$$

Equation 16.32 suggests that a Type II service standard requires a reorder point 9 units below the expected demand during the order lead time. This may seem to leave a possibility of significant stockouts. Indeed, the row of Exhibit 16.13 for $E[z]$ = 1.00 indicates that this reorder-point policy will result in stockouts 81 times out of 100 cycles (0.3159 + 0.5000). It seems to suggest that the OM process must tolerate stockouts that average approximately 2.5 units on four out of five orders.

To help clear up this confusion, recall from Exhibit 16.11 that an order risks a stockout only at the end of an order cycle. Also, the economic order quantity equals 200 units. Normally distributed demand during the order lead time has a mean of 60 units and a standard deviation of 10. Therefore, even with a Type II service standard reorder point of 51 units, the vast majority of arriving customers experience little risk of shortages.

To emphasize the potential risk, assume extreme conditions. Arbitrarily increase the order quantity to equal the annual demand, so the firm would order

Expected Stockouts by Standard Deviation of Demand

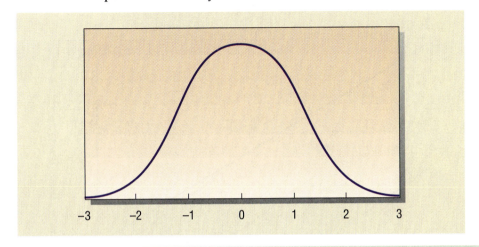

$E[z]$	z	$E[z]$	z	$E[z]$	z	$E[z]$	z
4.500	−4.50	0.399	0.00	2.205	−2.20	0.004	2.30
4.400	−4.40	0.351	0.10	2.106	−2.10	0.003	2.40
4.300	−4.30	0.307	0.20	2.008	−2.00	0.002	2.50
4.200	−4.20	0.267	0.30	1.911	−1.90	0.001	2.60
4.100	−4.10	0.230	0.40	1.814	−1.80	0.001	2.70
4.000	−4.00	0.198	0.50	1.718	−1.70	0.001	2.80
3.900	−3.90	0.169	0.60	1.623	−1.60	0.001	2.90
3.800	−3.80	0.143	0.70	1.529	−1.50	0.000	3.00
3.700	−3.70	0.120	0.80	1.437	−1.40	0.000	3.10
3.600	−3.60	0.100	0.90	1.346	−1.30	0.000	3.20
3.500	−3.50	0.083	1.00	1.256	−1.20	0.000	3.30
3.400	−3.40	0.069	1.10	1.169	−1.10	0.000	3.40
3.300	−3.30	0.056	1.20	1.083	−1.00	0.000	3.50
3.200	−3.20	0.046	1.30	1.000	−0.90	0.000	3.60
3.100	−3.10	0.037	1.40	0.920	−0.80	0.000	3.70
3.000	−3.00	0.029	1.50	0.843	−0.70	0.000	3.80
2.901	−2.90	0.023	1.60	0.769	−0.60	0.000	3.90
2.801	−2.80	0.018	1.70	0.698	−0.50	0.000	4.00
2.701	−2.70	0.014	1.80	0.630	−0.40	0.000	4.10
2.601	−2.60	0.011	1.90	0.567	−0.30	0.000	4.20
2.502	−2.50	0.008	2.00	0.507	−0.20	0.000	4.30
2.403	−2.40	0.006	2.10	0.451	−0.10	0.000	4.40
2.303	−2.30	0.005	2.20	0.339	0.00	0.000	4.50

SOURCE   R. G. Brown, *Decision Rules for Inventory Management* (New York: Holt Reinhart & Winston, 1967), pp. 95–103

new supplies only once a year. With the Type I service standard, the *ROP* equals 77 units, as determined in Equation 16.26. This *ROP* assures that demand during the order lead time will not exceed stock more than 5 percent of the time. This probability applies only during the time that the order remains outstanding, however, once a year in the extreme situation. Exhibit 16.14 shows the level of inventory over

[**EXHIBIT 16.14**]

Stockout Risk over the Order Cycle

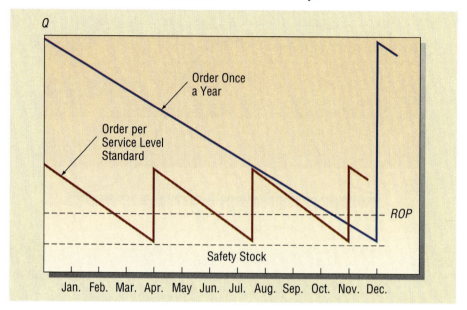

the year. Notice that inventory holds enough units to satisfy the vast majority of customers at the high reorder point.

Orders of 200 units expose customers to much more risk, though. The firm still faces only a 5 percent risk of running out in each order cycle, but this risky period occurs five times a year. The difference between Type I and Type II service levels centers on the higher threat of stockouts when a firm waits longer to place orders.

The choice between these standards depends on the firm's inventory management goals. Type I service level policies appeal to stock room personnel, who want to set reorder points high enough to avoid the grief of telling customers that they will have to wait. This protection comes at the cost of more safety stock than a Type II service level requires. A Type II service standard tries instead to maximize customer service, the most important goal of any firm.

The firm may have to supply more than a single product to satisfy those customers, however. Suppose that a customer normally purchases ten different products at once. A 95 percent Type II service level leaves a 5 percent chance of a stockout on each product. Thus, the probability that this customer will receive everything in an order equals $(0.95)^{10} = 0.60$. A firm may regret completely satisfying a customer only 60 percent of the time, especially if the customer needs all ten products to perform an important task, such as rebuilding a motor or making a batch of home brew.

[**PROBLEM 16.5**]

Setting a Reorder Point with Safety Stock

A firm purchases an essential input that requires a lead time of 15 days. A review of consumption over the last year indicates that the firm uses 4 units of the input in each of its 250 work days, or 1,000 units per year. Thus, the average demand during the order lead time equals 4×15, or 60 units. The firm sets an order quantity of 200 units.

Further analysis indicates that the standard deviation of demand during the 15-day lead time is 50 units. Inventory managers set a service standard of 95 percent, so customers will experience stockouts that total no more than 50 units during a year.

To calculate the reorder point, apply Equation 16.33:

$$ROP = z\partial_{LT} + \mu_{LT} = z(50) + 60 = 54 \tag{16.33}$$

Now calculate the standard deviation of the cushion necessary to assure a 95 percent service level. Equation 16.31 gives the expected number of units out of stock per ordering cycle:

$$E[z] = E[n]/\partial_{LT} = (1 - 0.95)(200)/50 = 10/50 = 0.20$$

Exhibit 16.13 does not include a row for $E[z] = 0.20$, but interpolation yields $z = 0.49$, or a negative 0.9 standard deviations.

$$ROP = (0.49)(50) + 60 = 24.5 + 60 = 84.5 \text{ units} \approx 85 \text{ units}.$$

The inventory managers arrive at a policy of ordering 200 units whenever the number on hand and on order falls below 85 units.

To check the validity of this answer, note that the expected number of units out of stock during the year should equal the expected number out of stock per order cycle times the number of cycles in a year:

$$E[\text{Short}/\text{year}] = E[z] \times \partial_{LT} \times \text{Annual demand}/\text{Lot size}$$
$$= 0.20 \times 50 \times 1,000/200 = 10 \times 5 = 50 \text{ units short}/\text{year}$$

The firm will supply 950 of the 1,000 units it needs from stock. [■]

Order Quantities with Dynamic Demand

The classic EOQ model assumes stable demand. It encounters difficulty when sales display a lumpy pattern, even when inventory managers know with certainty the amounts and timing of variations in demand. For example, Exhibit 16.15 shows the effect of applying the EOQ model to a variable demand pattern. The table assumes a setup cost of $200 per order and a monthly inventory holding cost of $2. Averaging demand over the 9-month period would equate the demand to a constant rate of 111 units per month. The EOQ model would give a quantity of 149 units to minimize total costs:

$$EOQ = \sqrt{2DC_o / C_h} = \sqrt{2(111)(200)/2} = 149$$

An attempt to apply the EOQ (rounded off to 150 units) runs into two problems. Production must exceed the standard lot size in February, June, and September to satisfy surges in demand. In leaner months, however, the firm ends up with excess inventories. Production generates 150 units in January, but the firm needs only 100, so 50 units sit unused in inventory. Despite this extra stock, however, the firm needs to run 200 units to satisfy high February demand.

Beyond the mismatch, a larger question arises: Why plan to carry any beginning inventory at all into a month when the firm knows that it will need to make another batch? It may seem logical instead to make 100 units in January and 250

[**EXHIBIT 16.15**]

EOQ with Lumpy Projected Demand

	Jan.	Feb.	Mar.	Apr.	May	Jun.	Jul.	Aug.	Sep.	Total
Beginning inventory	0	50	0	125	75	50	0	100	75	
Demand	100	250	25	50	25	225	50	25	250	1,000
Production	150	200	150			175	150		175	
Ending inventory	50	0	125	75	50	0	100	75	0	
Setup cost	200	200	200	0	0	200	200	0	200	1,200
Inventory holding cost	100	0	250	150	100	0	200	150	0	950
Total costs	300	200	450	150	100	200	400	150	200	2,150

units in February, unless some capacity constraint prevents the firm from producing 250 units in a single month. This would meet expected demand while eliminating the inventory holding cost of carrying over 50 units.

Dynamic programming can reveal the optimal solution to this problem, but shop-floor personnel seldom understand the method. Instead, inventory managers have developed a number of reasonably good heuristics to schedule work to satisfy dynamic demand. We will discuss three: the periodic time interval method, the part period balance method, and the Silver-Meal heuristic.

periodic time interval method

A technique for inventory management with uneven demand that adjusts the timing of orders based on the ratio of the average order quantity to average demand

Periodic Time Interval Method.   The **periodic time interval method** begins by simply averaging expected demand for a product over the planning horizon. For Exhibit 16.15, this gave an average demand of 111 units per month. Based on this monthly average demand, the method calculates a hypothetical level-demand EOQ; this procedure gave an EOQ of 149 units.

The method diverges from the classic EOQ model by finding a time interval that matches the order quantity. The formula for this economic time interval is:

$$\text{Economic time interval} = EOQ/\text{Average demand} = 149/111 = 1.34$$

The result indicates that the firm should order either every week or every 2 weeks. Exhibit 16.16 illustrates the effects of ordering every week. Note that total costs fall from $2,150 to $1,800. A student who accepts the challenge of adjusting the time interval more carefully might do even better.

part period balancing method

A technique for inventory management with uneven demand that satisfies demand for subsequent periods through economical, combined production runs

Part Period Balancing Method.   The **part period balancing method** sets order quantities in multiples of single-period demands. It decides the number of future periods to supply in a given period by continuing to combine production until the incremental inventory holding cost exceeds the setup cost for a new production run.

To see how this works, consider a planning sequence for Exhibit 16.17:

1. A production lot for January would require a setup cost of $200.
2. Total the inventory holding costs to fill February's demand in the January production run and store the units until needed:

$$C_{1+2} = 250(1)(\$2) = \$500 > \$200 \text{ Setup cost}$$

This exceeds the cost of another setup, so it clearly pays to plan another production run in February.

[**E X H I B I T   1 6 . 1 6**]

Periodic Time Interval Method with Lumpy Demand

	Jan.	Feb.	Mar.	Apr.	May	Jun.	Jul.	Aug.	Sep.	Total
Beginning inventory	0	0	0	0	0	0	0	0	0	
Demand	100	250	25	50	25	225	50	25	250	1,000
Production	100	250	25	50	25	225	50	25	250	
Ending inventory	0	0	0	0	0	0	0	0	0	
Setup cost	200	200	200	200	200	200	200	200	200	1,800
Inventory holding cost	0	0	0	0	0	0	0	0	0	0
Total costs	200	200	200	200	200	200	200	200	200	1,800

3. Now consider the merits of combining subsequent months' demand with the February production run:

$$C_{2+3} = 25(1)(\$2) = \$50 < \$200$$
$$C_{2+3+4} = 25(1)(\$2) + (50)(2)(\$2) = \$50 + \$200 = \$250 > \$200$$

It would pay to make products for both February and March in a single run, but it would be cheaper to set up for a separate run to meet April's demand.

4. Should the firm add subsequent months' demand, starting with that for May, to the April production run?

$$C_{4+5} = (25)(1)(\$2) = \$50 < \$200$$
$$C_{4+5+6} = (25)(1)(\$2) + (225)(2)(\$2) = \$50 + \$900 = \$950 > \$200$$

Again, the firm could produce what it needs for May most economically by combining those products with the April production.

5. The demand for June justifies another production run, perhaps to include the demand for July and August:

$$C_{6+7} = (50)(1)(\$2) = \$100 > \$200$$
$$C_{6+7+8} = (50)(1)(\$2) + (25)(2)(\$2) = \$100 + \$100 = \$200$$

[**E X H I B I T   1 6 . 1 7**]

Part Period Balancing Method with Lumpy Demand

	Jan.	Feb.	Mar.	Apr.	May	Jun.	Jul.	Aug.	Sep.	Total
Beginning inventory	0	0	25	0	25	0	75	25	0	
Demand	100	250	25	50	25	225	50	25	250	1,000
Production	100	275	0	75	0	300	0	0	250	
Ending inventory	0	25	0	25	0	75	25	0	0	
Setup cost	200	200	0	200	0	200	0	0	200	1,000
Inventory holding cost	0	50	0	50	0	150	50	0	0	300
Total costs	200	250	0	250	0	350	50	0	200	1,300

[**EXHIBIT 16.18**]

Silver-Meal Heuristic with Lumpy Demand

	Jan.	Feb.	Mar.	Apr.	May	Jun.	Jul.	Aug.	Sep.	Total
Beginning inventory	0	0	100	75	25	0	75	25	0	
Demand	100	250	25	50	25	225	50	25	250	1,000
Production	100	350	0	0	0	300	0	0	250	
Ending inventory	0	100	75	25	0	75	25	0	0	
Setup cost	200	200	0	0	0	200	0	0	200	800
Inventory holding cost	0	200	150	50	0	150	50	0	0	600
Total costs	200	400	150	50	0	350	50	0	200	1,400

The firm could meet September's demand most economically by scheduling a separate production run.

Following the part period balancing method, the firm would make enough in January, February, April, June, and September to cover the demand over the entire period. Exhibit 16.17 illustrates cost savings of $500 over the costs of the periodic time interval method, which was itself cheaper than the classic EOQ model.

Silver-Meal heuristic

A technique for inventory management with uneven demand that combines demand for subsequent periods until the average cost per period starts to rise

Silver-Meal Heuristic. The **Silver-Meal heuristic**, developed by Edward Silver and Harlan Meal, conducts an incremental analysis similar to that of the part period balancing method, but its decision rule continues to combine demand for subsequent periods until the average cost per period starts to rise.[2] Note that this method measures average cost per period rather than average unit cost.

Exhibit 16.18 illustrates the resulting order quantity decisions:

$$\text{Avg. } P_{1+2+3} = \$200$$

$$\text{Avg. } P_{1+2} = [\$200 + (250)(1)(\$2)]/2 = \$700/2 = \$350 > \$200$$

$$\text{Avg. } P_2 = \$200$$

$$\text{Avg. } P_{2+3} = [\$200 + (25)(1)(\$2)]/2 = \$250/2 = \$125 < \$200$$

$$\text{Avg. } P_{2+3+4} = [\$200 + (25)(1)(\$2) + (50)(2)(\$2)]/3 = \$450/3 = \$150 < \$200$$

$$\text{Avg. } P_{2+3+4+5} = [\$200 + (25)(1)(\$2) + (50)(2)(\$2) + (25)(3)(\$2)]/4 = \$600/4 = \$150 < \$200$$

$$\text{Avg. } P_{2+3+4+5+6} = [\$200 + (25)(1)(\$2) + (50)(2)(\$2) + (25)(3)(\$2) + (225)(4)(\$2)]/5$$
$$= \$2,400/5 = \$280 > \$200$$

$$\text{Avg. } P_6 = \$200$$

$$\text{Avg. } P_{6+7} = [\$200 + (50)(1)(\$2)]/2 = \$300/2 = \$150 < \$200$$

$$\text{Avg. } P_{6+7+8} = [\$200 + (50)(1)(\$2) + (25)(2)(\$2)]/3 = \$400/3 = \$133 < \$200$$

$$\text{Avg. } P_{6+7+8+9} = [\$200 + (50)(1)(\$2) + (25)(2)(\$20) + (250)(3)(\$2)]/4$$
$$= \$1,900/3 = \$833 > \$200$$

[2]E. Silver, and H. C. Meal, "A Heuristic for Selecting Lot Size Quantities for the Case of a Deterministic Time-Varying Demand Rate and Discrete Opportunities for Replenishment," *Production and Inventory Management* 14, no. 2 (1973), pp. 64–74.

The Silver-Meal heuristic would schedule production runs in January, February, June, and September. The cost of this scheme would exceed the cost under part period balancing by $100.

Better performance by one method over another does not necessarily mean that one will always outperform the other. Results for particular examples may vary. Over the years, many researchers have applied simulation methods to compare the effectiveness of these methods against so-called *optimal solutions.*

These solutions come from many sources. Some attempt to improve on the results by using alternative formulations of the lot-sizing logic. The goal of these alternative formulations is to improve on the underlying logic. Some draw on dynamic programming and introduce certain simplifications. Others recast the nature of the costs. Still others use the concept of a look forward-look back. Instead of setting each order quantity and forgetting about it, the rules (specifically part period balancing) ask "Is it better from a total cost perspective for the order to cover one more period? To cover one less period?"[3]

The results of this research show an overall advantage for the Silver-Meal heuristic:

Heuristic Method	Increase over Optimal Solution
Classic EOQ model	30 percent higher
Part period balancing method	7 percent higher
Silver-Meal heuristic	2 percent higher

SOURCE   J.R. Evans, *Applied Production and Operations Management,* 4th Ed., Minneapolis: West, 1990, p. 475.

The discussion in this section suggests many ways to model inventory problems, and it omits many more of them. Modeling does not solve an inventory problem, though. People solve real inventory problems based on their fundamental understanding of the true problem and their analytical ability to understand its tradeoffs. Models provide tools to help them gain insights into causes and measures most likely to enhance system effectiveness. Still, problem solvers must always complete the first step of understanding the problem. They must also carry through to the last step—assuring that workers fully accept the proposed solution and that they can implement it. Workers care little about the intermediate process; they care only whether it solves their problem!

TYPES OF INVENTORY SYSTEMS

Throughout this text, we discuss three basic types of inventory control systems. In Chapter 9, we explained how pull mechanisms, such as kanbans, trigger production or purchasing decisions in JIT manufacturing systems. These systems work well in highly repetitive environments with little business turbulence, but more variable situations require more flexible control systems.

In this section, we will describe another group of methods called *independent demand inventory systems.* These systems assume that inventory managers can consider the actual demand for each product in isolation. Control decisions assume that the demand for a product and the cost of making it do not depend materially on arrangements for other items.

[3]These rules and their underlying logic are found in Joseph Orlicky, *Material Requirements Planning,* New York: McGraw-Hill, 1975, Chapter 6 (pp. 120–138).

[**E X H I B I T   1 6 . 1 9**]

ABC Classification Scheme

Item	Annual Demand	Unit Cost	Annual Volume ($000)	Percentage of Total
1	1,000	$4,300	$4,300	39.3%
2	5,000	720	3,600	32.9
3	1,900	500	950	8.7
4	1,000	710	710	6.5
5	2,500	250	625	5.7
6	2,500	192	480	4.4
7	400	200	80	0.7
8	500	100	50	0.5
9	200	210	42	0.4
10	1,000	35	35	0.3
11	3,000	10	30	0.3
12	9,000	3	27	0.2

During the 1960s, some people began to suspect the validity of this assumption of independence. In many manufacturing situations, final assembly schedules clearly influence demand for component parts. To accommodate this demand dependency, inventory managers developed a third method for managing production and inventories known as *materials requirements planning* (MRP). Chapter 17 discusses this method of planning the purchases and production of component parts based on knowledge of the requirements of final assembly and end products.

Classifying Inventory Systems by Degree of Control

Besides the continuum from dependence to independence, one can also classify inventory control procedures by the degree of control or intensity of management effort that they require. Since items in stock vary in importance, inventory managers should not devote equal attention to everything. Many firms group inventoried items according to their relative importance and manage them based on these classifications.

One common method, the ABC method, classifies items into three groups based on some measure of importance. These systems most commonly measure importance based on annual dollar usage, which multiplies the annual usage rate in units by the cost per unit. In this way, this variant of Pareto analysis seeks to isolate the vital few items in stock from the trivial many. Recall that Pareto analysis normally makes this distinction in the form of an 80/20 split. Most ABC applications assign A status to the 20 percent of all items that account for 65 percent of the firm's annual dollar usage. The B classification normally includes the 30 percent of items, which account for 25 percent of the firm's annual dollar usage. C items are the remaining 50 percent that normally account for only 10 percent of the annual dollar usage.

To illustrate this approach, consider the example in Exhibit 16.19. To make the distinction, the table must list the items in stock in decreasing order by importance. A spreadsheet application can easily accomplish this by sorting with respect to the fourth column.

[BY THE WAY... HAMLET AND THE TWO-BIN SYSTEM]

The two-bin system describes exactly what we expect to see in practice. In the past, our order consisted of only two bins. We used the first bin (which was frequently labeled "use first"). When we finished with this bin, we opened the second bin. On top we found an order form, which we would deposit to release a replenishment order.

The quantity in the second bin was the amount we needed over the replenishment lead. This time-honored system leads some to ask, "Two-bin or not two-bin? That is the question."

The far-right column indicates that the first two items account for around 72 percent of the dollar usage. These obvious A items deserve the tightest management control. Items 3 through 6 seem to fall into a second cluster, while Items 7 through 12 all have annual usages below 1 percent of the total. Note that this analysis does not rigidly enforce the 65/25/10 percent split. The classification scheme should emphasize shared management control characteristics among clusters of items. ABC analysis seeks to determine some logical basis for establishing the appropriate degree of control for everything in inventory.

This example measures importance based on total annual dollar volume. In other situations, highly perishable items or those subject to long lead times may fit the high priority classification. Inventory managers should choose their classification systems to suit the results that they need.

Classifying Systems by Their Procedures

Inventory managers have devised many systems with common and unique procedures. Some are as simple as the **two-bin system**, which triggers an order when someone takes the last bin, opens the last box, uses the last check book, or whatever. The next "By the Way" box describes the two-bin system. Others are much more complex. Just about every inventory system is driven by three basic micro questions:

two-bin system

An inventory management system that orders stock whenever someone takes the last bin, opens the last box, etc.

1. When to review the status of the system (decision variable—t)
    A. Perpetual
    B. Periodic
    C. When triggered by an internal event (such as when a related item is under review) or an external event (such as when something happens outside the firm)
2. When to place an order (decision variables—R or s)
    A. At every review (R)
    B. When the inventory level falls below the reorder point (s)
    C. Upon ordering something else
    D. When dramatic changes might happen
3. How much to order (decision variable—Q or S)
    A. Economic order quantity (Q)
    B. Enough to restore inventory to a set level (S)
    C. Enough to supply future needs

Two or three of these attributes describe a current or potential system. For example, an [s,Q] system would order Q units whenever the amount on hand and on order would fall below s. For example, when you get to 25 units (R), order 100 units (Q). The absence of a t attribute often implies a perpetual system. While this classification scheme could add many categories, these can accommodate 36 possible combinations.

The attribute combinations indicate management priorities. A [t,S] system would periodically review inventory status every t periods and order enough every review period to bring the inventory up to a set level, S. This system would make economic sense if the firm could benefit from no significant economies of scale in either production or purchasing and when inbound freight costs would warrant ordering a number of items at the same time. This is analogous to asking other members of the household, "Should I get anything else while I am at the store?"

The models discussed earlier for single-item, independent-demand inventory management systems suggest general values for the three decision variables. In more specific applications, inventory managers should first evaluate the parameters that characterize their system, or that they think their system should display. They should then test the effectiveness of their classification. (One way to do this is to develop a simple simulation model. In each case, four different streams of random demands are available to test the robustness of each set of decision variable values.)

Inventory ordering decisions could also consider the inventory levels of other items, but this would complicate the decision-making process. Most inventory control decision rules are **local rules**; they consider the cost tradeoffs for individual items. At the other extreme, global rules solve inventory problems by controlling the broadest possible set of circumstances. Globally formulated solutions may add significant value, but an inventory management system should address real, pressing problems first.

local rule

A decision principle based on the cost tradeoffs for individual items

Inventory Systems in Service Industries

At the start of this chapter, we began our examination of inventory by focusing on the problems of retailers—specifically, Levi Strauss. We used these problems to develop a general understanding of the broad issues and challenges which are integral to inventory management. We now return to the challenges facing retailers with the objective of understanding the tools, procedures, and approaches that have been developed to help this group meet their unique challenges. Managing retail inventories requires a delicate tradeoff between the need to stock a mix of products that delight customers and the need to turn over that stock rapidly to assure an adequate return on investment. Retailers control this balance based on thorough knowledge of their customers. They know how much customers value convenient locations and product variety. They judge customers' willingness to forego some variety to get lower costs. They evaluate the level of quality that customers expect and how much extra customers will pay for better quality.

The success of inventory management in retailing often hinges on who in the organization makes these decisions. In a fairly stable market with little variability between locations, a centralized system may produce effective buying decisions. The major function of such an inventory system then focuses on tracking goods and providing signals to trigger appropriate actions.

Centralized buying can lead to bad decisions when markets exhibit significant differences. In such a system, a central, computerized inventory-tracking system may simply provide decentralized buyers with key feedback about sales

In contrast to the retailer management system, distribution centers can employ push or pull systems to accurately forecast product and system requirements.   SOURCE   Chris Jones/The Stock Market

trends. It may also perform record keeping functions to support the efforts of local decision makers.

Bar coding and intelligent point-of-sale terminals have enhanced this function of retail inventory systems. Advanced information technologies now tell retail planners what each store sold the previous day. This function enables centralized buyers to relocate slow-selling merchandise to more receptive outlets. It also provides useful information to guide future orders, helping firms to avoid buying more of unwanted merchandise. In this way, a central inventory-tracking system promotes a major objective of all retail firms—to minimize product markdowns.

In some retail operations, the local manager can most effectively judge what stock to order. Even a relatively centralized system may empower a store manager as a mini-entrepreneur, allocating some funds for discretionary purchases. Such an open-to-order system gives a manager authority to invest company funds in a certain amount in inventory that promotes the stated mission of the store. Each month, this authority to spend equals the gap between the store's authorized inventory level, which may change seasonally, and the projected actual amount after monthly sales. This may lead to difficult decisions like whether to accept special discounts on large purchases, leading to a higher profit margin on a specific item, or to place smaller orders and invest discretionary funds in additional stock.

Distribution system capabilities play a key role in a retail inventory system because they control the order lead time. A quick-response distributor minimizes the amount of safety stock the retailer must hold. Supported by timely daily transaction data, such a system amounts to a pull system, much like kanbans in JIT manufacturing, for staple products. By carrying fewer units of a product, a retailer frees up shelf space and working capital to expand the variety of the store's product offering. Quick-response information systems also enable chains that perform both retailing and distribution functions, such as Wal-Mart, to better manage their promotional products by transporting slow-moving goods to other stores that will more easily sell them.

In the past, retailers tended to accept shipments sent to them by their suppliers. These suppliers, like Levi Strauss, often felt that they were in a better position to determine what the retailer needed. Retailers now recognize that their task is to coordinate the flow of products from the suppliers with the consumption of these products by the customer. The better these two flows are coordinated, the less inventory is needed and the more likely that the supplier will essentially finance the inventory levels of the retailer.

Wal-Mart has been very successful in developing this idea. From the time Wal-Mart places an order with a vendor until Wal-Mart sells the order to a customer takes on average 22 days. Yet, Wal-Mart pays its vendors on a 45-day cycle (a supplier receives payment 45 days after it ships the order), which is common for the industry. As a result, the supplier—not Wal-Mart—essentially finances Wal-Mart's inventory.

One way to develop this coordination is to use the pull techniques described in Chapter 9 and to apply that logic at the distribution center level.

Rapid distribution and transportation systems have also greatly altered end-user firms' inventories. Now that parts suppliers can deliver goods overnight anywhere in the country, end users can carry smaller spare-parts inventories. Some firms are even locating warehouses next to the hubs of Federal Express or United Parcel Service in order to eliminate the lead time for source-to-hub transportation.

Distributors' inventory-management systems differ from retailers' systems because they handle orders with less personal interaction. Retail transactions enhance the store manager's insight into the true needs of customers. Distributors more often receive orders through electronic communication media, so they gain less personal understanding of customers through routine transactions. Hence, most distributors' inventory control systems rely more heavily on computerized control.

Distribution centers can employ either push or pull inventory-control systems. In a pull system, the distribution center determines its requirements based on known or forecasted customer requirements. It then pulls inventory into the warehouse by placing orders with manufacturers. Some common pull systems in use in distribution centers are order point systems, base stock systems, and distribution requirements planning.

With a pull system, the distribution is constantly sending the vendors signals that indicate the need for replenishment. These signals are based either on forecasts or on the actual demand at the store level. The vendor cannot ship unless a signal or order for replenishment is received. Once the order is received, the vendor must respond as fast as possible. These types of pressures are being applied to Levi Strauss by its customers.

Order Point Systems.   These $[R,Q]$ systems place orders whenever the inventory level for a given product at the distribution center falls below the reorder point. The system features little or no coordination with other distribution centers, so manufacturers often experience erratic demand for many items.

Periodic Review Systems.   These $[t,Q]$ or $[t,S]$ systems periodically review warehouse inventories every t periods and replenish stocks by ordering either fixed quantities, Q, or, to restore desired stocking levels, S. These distributors must normally carry significant safety stocks to avoid stockouts during delays between periodic reviews. They can benefit, however, from economies of scale in inbound freight and purchasing by combining orders for different products. This arrangement may allow the firm to order smaller quantities of specific products without sacrificing transportation efficiencies, as the "On the Job" box illustrates.

Base Stock Systems.   In this inventory-management system, each stocking location within the a distributor's system establishes a base stock level for each product

R obert Furtado, vice president of operations for Ingram Micro, claims to have achieved a competitive advantage through the firm's inventory-management procedures. This integrated system ties together all aspects of the business, including purchasing, warehousing, accounts receivable, accounts payable, and shipping.

The Santa Ana, California, distributor of electronic goods saves still more money by redirecting all inbound shipments through its northern California

ON THE JOB

Ingram Micro Combines and Saves

freight-consolidation center. Instead of shipping goods separately to Ingram's seven ware-

houses, vendors send single, large shipments to the new center, which breaks them down and then transfers them to individual warehouses. In addition to lower inbound freight costs, Ingram saves on subsequent transportation because the trucks going to its regional warehouses carry full loads, lowering overall cost per pound shipped. These steps, along with its centralized, UPS-centered freight-management system, should save about $2 million per year.

SOURCE   T. H. Garretson, "Tight Margins Put the Squeeze on Inventory," *Computer Sources*, December 1992.

in inventory. These locations, along with retail operations, routinely file daily or weekly reports on their sales of each product rather than placing orders only when they want more. The factory then uses this information to plan production and coordinate more cost-effective shipments. The factory also smooths scheduling by basing planning decisions on the combined requirements for each item at each destination rather than reacting to individual orders. Advanced telecommunication technologies allow for more frequent contact among retailer, distributor, and manufacturer, supporting improved production planning.

Distribution Requirements Planning.   In Chapter 17, we will discuss dependent demand inventory control systems. In manufacturing, such a system is often called *materials requirements planning.* Its distribution-system counterpart is distribution requirements planning (DRP). Thorough coverage of these systems will have to wait until Chapter 17 introduces the underlying concepts.

All kinds of organizations create different types of inventory-management systems, in part because each operation seeks a unique application for its individual situation. Indeed, they probably do need to adapt inventory-control measures to local conditions, but they probably waste resources developing new systems from scratch instead of adjusting one of the good commercial inventory-control systems on the market. Most commercial systems permit users to supplement standard functions with customized subroutines, so each firm can meet its own needs.

 ## CHAPTER SUMMARY

In this chapter, we have described how inventory supplies independent demand in service and manufacturing operations. In the next chapter, we will present materials requirements planning, a method for managing inventory in complex manufacturing systems when demand for individual products depends on that for other products.

1. The chapter clarified the common perception that all inventory contributes to waste. In fact, inventories frequently contribute to the competitive strength of the firm by adding value for customers. Inventory becomes waste when it does not help the firm to achieve its blend of speed, quality, flexibility, and cost.

2. To design an inventory-management system, operations managers must address several macro issues that determine the effect of inventories on long-term, strategic decisions. These include whether or not to stock finished goods in inventory, who in the value chain should own inventories, what products those inventories should include, where in the value chain to hold inventories, how to track the movements of products into and out of inventories, and who should make decisions about inventories.

3. Micro issues in designing an inventory-management system affect repetitive decisions. These issues include order quantities, the timing of orders, and the choice of suppliers from which to buy products.

4. The classic economic order quantity model guides many organizations' decisions. It balances the cost of holding inventories against the setup costs for a new production run.

5. One common variant, production lot scheduling, adjusts the classic EOQ model for consumption of units in an order before completion of production.

6. Another variant, the quantity discount model, adjusts the EOQ model for price breaks offered by suppliers for large orders.

7. Reorder point decisions must weigh the risk and cost of stockouts against the cost of holding safety stock to prevent them. Inventory managers may set service level standards to avoid the difficult and uncertain analysis of stockout costs.

8. Dynamic demand complicates order quantity or lot sizing decisions. To set order quantities in such uncertain conditions, inventory managers employ the periodic time interval method, the part period balancing method, and the Silver-Meal heuristic. Individual circumstances should guide the choice among these methods.

9. Inventory-management models invoke several basic microeconomic concepts such as marginal cost and marginal revenue, among others.

10. Spreadsheet software provides a valuable tool for solving inventory management models.

11. One can classify types of inventory systems by the degree of control that individual products require; an ABC system provides one method for doing this. One can also classify inventory systems by their procedures for reviewing stock levels, placing orders, and setting order quantities. Retailers control inventories through order point systems, periodic review systems, base stock systems, and distribution requirements planning.

[**KEY TERMS**]

inventory 742	finished goods inventories 742	cycle counting 752
raw materials inventories 742	inventory holding cost 746	inventory audit 755
work-in-process inventories 742	stockout cost 746	dead stock audit 755
		economic order quantity model 759

[DISCUSSION QUESTIONS]

1. How does inventory contribute to the value-adding activities of a firm? When should inventory be considered a symptom of waste? Why?

2. What activities contribute to the cost of carrying inventory? Who are the internal customers for these activities?

3. It has been noted that dust is often a symptom of a prior decision gone wrong. What types of mistakes might contribute to a firm's dusty inventory? What can inventory managers do to minimize the amount of dead stock in their inventory?

4. Discuss how the following have impacted inventory management practices:
   a. Advances in information technology
   b. Increased market segmentation
   c. Premium small-package services (i.e., FedEx, UPS, etc.)
   d. Global manufacturing operations

5. Your firm asks you to benchmark some firms with leading edge inventory management systems. What criteria would you use to decide which firms had the best practices? List five or more performance measures and then indicate why each contributes to the value generation goals of your organization.

6. Why is the classic EOQ model still being used in textbooks and in the industrial environment?

7. Your industrial engineering department has a highly effective setup and order cost reduction program. As a result, it has reduced the lump sum costs associated to nearly zero dollars. How should the firm determine the number of units to order at a time? What factors went into your recommendation?

8. Why is there a 2 in the classic economic order quantity model?

9. It has been said that if all other factors are the same, the economic order quantity model with usage will always recommend lot sizes equal to or larger than the classic EOQ model. Why?

10. Your firm buys goods from a certain vendor once a month. How would this fact influence the inventory model that would be useful? What type of inventory ordering procedure would you suggest?

11. Your trucking company charges according to the number of pounds being shipped, with one rate for deliveries under 5,000 lbs., another for deliveries in the 5,000 to 25,000 lb. range, and so forth. How does this system influence which inventory model is used? Why?

12. Use the Classic EOQ spreadsheet to determine how each input parameter would have to change in order to increase the model's lot size by 10 percent, i.e., before the total cost equation is 110 percent of the optimal amount.
   a. Inventory holding costs
   b. Setup costs
   c. Stockout costs

d. The constant demand assumption (if this is not possible, suggest an alternative sensitivity test)

What are the managerial implications of this?

13. A firm has an item with a constant demand of 2,000 units per month. It believes that the inventory costs for this item are

Setup costs	$25 per setup
Inventory holding costs	40 percent per year
Unit selling cost	$20.00
Purchase cost	$12.00

a. Write a total cost equation for this problem.
b. Determine the optimal lot size.
c. Determine cost of the minimum cost solution.

14. Along with the above data, the warehouse has a static inventory stocking policy, i.e., a given item has a fixed amount of storage space allocated to it. For the above product, the additional data is:

Cubic feet per unit	4 cu. ft.
Maximum space allowed per product	10,000 cu. ft.

What is the most economically feasible inventory order amount? How does it change the total cost equation?

15. You have been asked to prepare an ABC analysis of your department's stocks. Classify the following items into A items, B items, and C items according to dollar usage.

Part Number	Estimated Annual Usage	Unit Cost
1	7,000	$ 10
2	2,000	30
3	80	800
4	50	1,200
5	300	20
6	150	45
7	80	150
8	10	1,800
9	15	40
10	450	50

How would you use this information?

16. Your company has been buying an item from Vendor A for $5.00 each. Vendor B is offering you a reduced price if you purchase the item in higher quantities. Vendor A says that it too could offer volume discounts. Now you must choose from the following two price lists:

Quantity	Vendor A	Vendor B
1 to 999	$5.00	$5.05
1,000 to 4,999	4.75	4.78
5,000 or more	4.50	4.45

Ordering costs are $50 per order. Inventory holding costs are $5.00 per unit per year. Monthly demand is expected to be about 1,000 units.

a. Which vendor is the lower cost source?
b. Given the above demand estimate, how many units would you order?
c. What would the annual costs be for selecting each vendor?
d. How much will you save if you switch?

17. An item's weekly demand is normally distributed with a mean of 40 units and a standard deviation of 5. This item's vendor requires a four-week lead time.
    a. What will be the distribution of demand during lead time, i.e., what will its mean, standard deviation, and shape be?
    b. What should the reorder point be if the company wants 95 percent service level?
18. Visit (a) a food supermarket, (b) a food distributor, and (c) a manufacturer of branded foods that can produce far more output than demand normally would consume.
    a. What types of inventories exist throughout each firm's value chain? How do the levels of each type of inventory compare with the levels of other types of inventory within that firm?
    b. What functions do the types of inventory within each firm perform?
    c. How might each firm manage its inventories?
19. Visit a chain auto parts store, such as Pep Boys, and an independently owned auto parts store. How does each store manage its inventory? Are the independent stores at a disadvantage? Why and why not?
20. Visit an automobile junk yard and an antique shop. Compare and contrast their inventory control systems. How do they differ? How are they alike?
21. Design a plan to increase the turnover rate of your food inventory to 52 times a year. How will your plan affect the other facets of your life?
22. Visit a book superstore and a small, local book store (other than your friendly college book store). How do they determine which books to stock and what are their reordering criteria? How does each deal with unpredictable best-sellers?
23. Visit a regional warehouse. How does it communicate with suppliers and customers? What types of inventory control systems does it use?

C A U T I O N

[**C R I T I C A L   T H I N K I N G   R E Q U I R E D**]

1. Most auditors zero in on how a firm measures the volume of inventory and the procedures used to calculate its value. Why?
2. Prepare a list of businesses that created products that increased in value or grew in volume over time. How would this trait influence your inventory management practices?

C A S E   1 6 . 1

International Semiconductor

International Semiconductor is a worldwide manufacturer of semiconductor chips, with $2 billion in revenue and 20,000 employees. It manufactures semiconductor chips for three markets: automotive, telecommunications, and computer manufacturers. It sells no product directly to the public. It has component fabrication plants in California, Oregon, Texas, Scotland, Malaysia, and the Philippine Islands. The final step in its manufacturing processes is the somewhat labor intensive step called "packaging." The volume production for most of its items is done in lower-cost Southeast Asian countries. The finished product is then sent back to the company's seven customer service centers strategically located in the United States, Europe, and Japan.

Early in 1995, Federal Express Logistics Services approached the company with a proposal. Now that it had located its Asia hub at a former U.S. air base in the Philippines, FedEx proposes to ship all finished goods from its Asian hub. Its proposed integrated logistics system would provide the following benefits for International:

Reliable, short, dock-to-dock delivery

Condensed order cycle time

Expedited customer clearance

Reduced inventory carrying costs

Real-time product shipment visibility

Central freight billing and reporting

FedEx's teleservices link

Management dedicated to logistics

FedEx's tentative analysis indicated that they could provide International's customers two-day delivery anywhere in the industrialized world and still produce substantial inventory holding and transportation costs savings for International.

At first glance, this proposal seems unbelievable to Vance Pinion, International's vice-president of logistics. In 1995, International shipped slightly more than 2 million boxes containing 7 billion parts to almost 5,000 customer locations in over 60 countries. Total outbound freight cost International almost $60 billion in 1995, or approximately 2.9 percent of total corporate sales.

Speed was also a consideration. International's customers increasingly were demanding quicker product deliveries. A survey of its customers indicated that they wanted a 25-day total cycle time from the time an order was made to product delivery. An internal survey revealed that International's cycle time was under 45 days 95 percent of the time. The other 5 percent could be as long as 90 days. Because International and its customers cannot be sure which 5 percent would be late, both keep buffer stock to make up for inconsistent supply. The hidden costs of product expediting and premium freight costs were not known.

When International studied how a typical order spent its 45 days in the system, it found

Step	Percent of Total Cycle Time
Sales and Order Entry	15%
Scheduling/Manufacturing	15
Manufacturing	40
Transit to Regional Distribution Centers	5
Order Picking at Regional Distribution Centers	15
Delivery from Regional Distribution Centers	10

In addition to the five regional distribution centers, this study indicated that the firm had ten other warehousing locations in which significant finished product was stored. The number of people involved in creating packing lists and shipping was estimated to be approximately 750 employees—almost 4 percent of the firm's total.

These initial studies indicated that an incremental approach was not likely to result in the total cycle time being reduced from an unreliable 45 days to a dependable 25 days. Pinion formed a task force of key transportation individuals from each of International's major divisions. Anna Hilterhouse has been invited to be the Analog Device Division's (ADD) representative on this team. She asks you to brief her on how this proposal might work for ADD. As a start, she needs the following data:

1. Total inventory investment by location throughout ADD's value chain
2. Total intersite transportation costs for material flowing within ADD
3. Total outbound freight on finished goods shipping

This report is needed by a week from Monday—eight calendar days away.

QUESTIONS

1. What additional factors do you think Hilterhouse and ADD should consider?
2. Can you propose a systematic plan to investigate the FedEx alternative?

CASE 16.2

The Cash Crunch Game

May Gardenia suspected that there was more to inventory control than the classic economic lot size formula. As a buyer in a local garden store, she now sees that the world is slightly more complex. She does not have enough working capital to adequately stock the store. Her budget is $5,000 and she is supposed to stock sufficient product to delight her customers. Fortunately, only the four items listed below need to be purchased; the rest is placed in the department on consignment by vendors.

Product	Purchase Price	Weekly Demand	EOQ
Lawn mowers	$100	30	25
Mulchers	$100	20	20
Snowblowers	$100	10	14
Chippers	$100	5	10

The EOQ were determined using an assumed $10 order cost and a $1 per week inventory holding cost.

Demand is not constant—it can be anywhere from 5 below the mean to 4 above the mean. For example, the range of demand for lawn mowers is equally likely to be any number from 25 to 34 units. When the department is out of stock, customers go elsewhere to buy the product. The result is a loss of goodwill and a cost of $200 per unit of demand unmet.

All customers, for some unknown reason, arrive at the start of the month and pay cash. Gardenia immediately uses $100 of the sale price to rebuild the cash account, and the remaining part of the sales goes to a store account.

The supplier of these goods is reliable but only ships to your store on a cash-on-delivery basis. While it is quite reliable, the supplier requires two weeks of lead time, i.e., goods ordered in week one are delivered at the start of week three. If Gardenia is out of cash, the vendor charges double the purchase price, which in this case is $100 per unit.

Gardenia's task is to devise an inventory policy capable of minimizing total inventory holding costs, vendor penalty costs, and loss of goodwill costs. Use the CASHCRUNCH template to simulate performance over a 50-week period.

[SELECTED READINGS]

Brown, R. G. *Decision Rules for Inventory Management.* New York: Holt, Rinehart and Winston, 1967.

Buffa, E. S., and J. Miller. *Production-Inventory Systems: Planning and Control,* Rev. Ed. Homewood, Ill.: Richard D. Irwin, 1979.

Eilon, Samuel. *Elements of Production Planning and Control.* New York: Macmillan, 1962.

Haley, G., and T. M. Whitin. *An Analysis of Inventory Systems.* Englewood Cliffs, N.J.: Prentice-Hall, 1963.

Naddor, Eliezer. *Inventory Systems.* New York: John Wiley & Sons, 1966.

Plossl, George W. *Production and Inventory Control,* 2d ed. Englewood Cliffs, N.J.: Prentice-Hall, 1985.

Vollman, Thomas. "The Hidden Factory." *Harvard Business Review,* May–June, 1981.

Vollmann, T. E., W. L. Berry, and D. C. Whybark. *Manufacturing Planning and Control Systems.* Homewood, Ill.: Richard D. Irwin, 1992.

Whitin, Thomson M. *The Theory of Inventory Management,* 2d ed. Princeton, N.J.: Princeton University Press, 1957.

CHAPTER SEVENTEEN

Materials Management

CHAPTER OUTLINE

CHAPTER OBJECTIVES

[At the end of this chapter, you should be able to]

- Explain the fundamental task of materials management.
- Describe the mechanics of materials requirements planning (MRP),
  its input requirements, and the reports that it generates to aid
  operations planning and control.
- Differentiate the logical premises of materials requirements planning from those of JIT and independent-demand inventory systems
  like the EOQ model.
- Identify conditions that favor successful application of MRP.
- Trace interactions between the materials-management function and
  line managers, marketing personnel, and the firm's management
  information system.
- Discuss the further development of MRP into manufacturing
  resources planning (MRPII) to expand the range of support services that materials management provides to other business
  processes.

Elizabeth Sher
Goodwin

More Green Toothbrushes?

A FEW YEARS AGO, ONE OF THE authors visited Oral B's toothbrush manufacturing plant at the invitation of its production planning and control manager. The manager wanted help diagnosing a cause for the failure of a recently introduced materials requirements planning system to meet top management's expectations.

After a briefing, the author toured the plant. At one injection-molding machine, an operator worked busily turning out green, plastic toothbrush handles. A brief look at the work orders for jobs waiting for access to the machine indicated a serious problem. Despite a queue with work orders for jobs more than 3 weeks past due, the operator was filling an order with a due date 2 weeks into the future. The worker explained, "When I have the machine set up for green toothbrush handles, I do all the green handle orders together."

That simple initial comment indicated the cause of the plant's planning problem. Workers pursued the plant manager's goal of maximizing efficiency rather than the goals outlined by the MRP system. This led them to base decisions on the priority of minimizing production setup time. The plant manager later explained a predictable reaction to the new MRP system: "Oh, it's just another bureaucratic hassle imposed on us by corporate headquarters."

T his brief story sets the stage for this chapter, with major themes. First is the overall importance that managers and firms assign to the materials management system. The top management of Oral B hired a consultant when they wanted to know what was happening to their Materials Requirements Planning (MRP) system. They felt that the successful operation of this system was critical to the effective operation of their materials management system. Furthermore, management had implemented MRP. This is not a minor undertaking—the implementation of an MRP system ranges from $50,000 to $2,000,000. Yet, in spite of the importance assigned to MRP systems and the cost of implementation, the rate of successful implementations remains relatively low at between 5 and 20 percent.

In this chapter, we examine the concept of the materials management system. We also explore the reasons for its importance to the effective and efficient operation of the value-driven operations management system, focusing on MRP. This procedure is most effective when used within the context of a dependent demand setting. MRP is also very widely used as the heart of many materials management systems in North America. This chapter ends with a discussion of the factors influencing the successful implementation of an MRP system and future developments in MRP.

materials management
A plant-organizing function that assures a predictable flow of components and other inputs through a transformation process

Materials management is a plant-organizing function that assures a predictable flow of components and other inputs through a transformation process. This set of operations management tasks evolved into an integrated organizational function to meet a recognized need for a predictable flow of components and other inputs. The materials management system focuses primarily on material needs as compared to the capacity concerns raised in Chapter 16. It sits between the planning systems described in Chapter 14 and the execution and scheduling systems of Chapter 18.

The American Inventory and Control Society defines materials management as, "the grouping of management functions supporting the complete cycle of material flow from the purchase and internal control of production materials to the planning and control of work in process to the warehousing, shipping, and distribution of the finished parts."[1] By this definition, materials management begins after completion of the product design and ends before post-sale customer service.

In Chapter 13, we saw an example of a material management system used by Steelcase. In this chapter, we expand on this theme. Materials management is one part of the integrated manufacturing planning system. This system consists of production planning, master production scheduling, and planning (Chapter 16); supply chain management (Chapter 13); shop floor control (Chapter 18); and materials management. The system coordinates the activities of both the internal and external factory so that the flow of products (goods and services) meets the needs of the customers as reflected in the master production scheduling. Each system deals with a different aspect of the overall planning and control problem. For example, supply chain management deals with the selection and integration of suppliers into the value-driven operations management system while capacity planning deals with the planning, management, and control of capacity. The material management system deals with the identification of what materials are needed to meet production and customer needs as well as when these items must be ordered. These materials can come from either our suppliers or internally from our process in the form of components.

---

[1]James F. Cox III, John H. Blackstone, Jr., and Michael S. Spencer, *APICS Dictionary*, 8th ed. (Falls Church, Va.: American Production and Inventory Control Society, 1995), p. 50.

This system is different from inventory management (Chapter 15) in that inventory systems focus primarily on how much, when, and what within the independent demand setting (i.e., a setting where the demand must be forecasted). Materials management deals with these same questions but in the context of dependent demand (where demand is derived or calculated). The materials management system relies on a different approach to deal with this type of demand than that described in Chapter 15. This approach is referred to as material requirements planning, or MRP.

MATERIALS REQUIREMENTS PLANNING

MRP is used to manage components where the demand for the items is linked to another demand. For example, the demand for car wheels is linked to the demand for cars. To determine the number of wheels that we need, we start by determining the number of cars that we will build and when. In this setting, the demand for wheels is dependent on the demand for cars (the notion of dependent is discussed in greater detail later on in the chapter). This setting is typically encountered when dealing with transformation processes and when dealing with suppliers who provide components such as wheels.

"Getting the right quantity at the wrong time does not accomplish anything."

Oliver Wight, MRP pioneer

In the past, most manufacturing systems relied on independent-demand inventory control models, like the order point/order quantity, to trigger production of both final products and component parts along with orders for components from outside vendors. These systems frequently resulted in situations where there was simultaneously too much and not enough inventory, because of several factors. First, these systems treated each item as if it were independent. As a result, they did not take advantage of the interrelationships between items to reduce the amount ordered and to better coordinate orders. Second, these systems looked to the past when determining what to order and when. They assumed that the future would be like the past, and they used this information to generate the forecasts for each item that drove, in turn, the schedule of orders. Furthermore, these systems could not use information about future demand that was contained in the master production schedule. As a result, they tried to replenish stocks depleted by past production rather than providing inputs for future production. To remedy these deficiencies, MRP was developed. **Materials requirements planning** (MRP) determines what final products the firm will make for a future period, and then it specifies production of needed inputs to make those products.

For each final product, the MRP system maintains a recipe of necessary inputs to make 1 unit. Essentially, it multiplies the number of units of finished products planned for production by the number of parts needed to make each unit to determine the OM system's total input needs, or its **gross requirements**.

What makes MRP so attractive is its simple and straightforward logic. It makes sense. In practice, MRP is not quite that simple. The final production schedule depends on current inventories and inputs on order that suppliers have not yet delivered. Planners must also determine when the transformation process will need each component. If they plan to assemble 50 units of a final product in Week 6, they should also plan to provide necessary components prior to the start of that week. Of course, these inputs could arrive immediately as production begins in Week 6, but any disruption could destroy the plan. Still, the early proponents of MRP reasoned that firms could significantly cut WIP inventories by timing the arrival of components to coincide with the beginning of final assembly.

materials requirements planning
A system that determines what final products the firm will make for a future period and then specifies production of needed inputs to make those products

gross requirements
The total input needs of the OM system in MRP, found by multiplying the units of finished products planned for production by the number of parts needed to make each unit

History of Materials Requirements Planning

Faced with the problem during World War II of greatly increasing production to meet a suddenly increased demand, managers recognized that the old procedures were not adequate. They turned to new procedures to get more out faster. This was the promise that techniques such as linear programming delivered on.

The early proponents of MRP championed an innovative form of manufacturing organization which they called the *materials-management approach*. These pioneers envisioned a production planning and control system in which production-planning staff would coordinate the flow of materials throughout the OM system to deliver the right products to the right locations at the right times. The materials-management approach became a sort of crusade, and its advocates wielded MRP as a weapon for change.

Systems Approaches versus Functional Thinking.   Materials management implementation led to disagreement about who in the organization would determine the right answer. The materials management approach required an integrated approach. The various functions affected by it (purchasing, logistics, and operations management) had to work together and be willing to share both power and decision-making authority. This requirement ran counter to firms strongly organized along functional lines that defined each group's realm of power.

At Oral B, line managers viewed the firm's new MRP system as a mechanism for distant production planning staffers to dictate operations at their factory. The line managers' goal was to increase utilization and decrease down-time, not to meet customer due-dates if these due-dates caused reduced utilization due to increased setups. As a result, a potential conflict was created.

This potential for conflict extended to the other functional groups. In many firms, purchasing saw its task as keeping costs down through "better" purchasing and ensuring that the operations management system never stopped because of the lack of purchased material. As a result, they tended to buy in large quantities. They also worked closely with their suppliers. They felt that the materials management people unfairly restricted them and affected their ability to get the best deals for the firm. However, since purchases account for about two-thirds of the cost of the goods sold, the purchasing function and its knowledge could not be ignored. They had to play an important role within the material management function (the exact structure and form of this fit will vary from firm to firm).

Transportation and distribution had long been responsible for making logistics decisions that had reduced the transportation costs for the firm, such as delaying orders completed by operations management and holding them until a full truck- or carload could be accumulated. They had never had to consider trade-offs so that the needs of the customer could be better met. Warehouse managers felt that their understanding of customer needs would be lost if centralized into a company-wide materials management system. They also expressed concern that these new methods would overshadow their own professional discipline of business logistics, which is the art and science of obtaining and distributing materials and products.

Developing an integrated materials management system was a difficult task. Each function had to stop optimizing its performance at the expense of overall corporate performance. Implementing such a system has been for most firms a long and costly undertaking.

The "By the Way" box reprints one author's reaction to all of this disagreement.

Exhibit 17.1 suggests the causes behind the organizational politics that have surrounded the materials-management movement. The changes involved in that

[BY THE WAY... POETRY OF PRODUCTION CONTROL]

To parody the conflict over materials management in many organizations, Oliver Wight wrote a takeoff on John Godfrey Saxe's poem "The Blind Men and the Elephant":

It was six men of management
To learning much inclined
Who discoursed on production control
And the answers they did find
—from experience, and the lessons
That reward an inquiring mind.

"Order to mins and maximums,"
The first was heard to say,
"You'll have neither too much nor too little
When production's controlled this way."

"But the answer lies in a forecast,"
Said the second in line,
"Just anticipate your sales,
And everything will be fine."

"I doubt it" said the third one,
"you've forgotten the EOQ.
With balanced setups and inventories,
What problems can ensue?"

The fourth one said: "Use order points
To get the desired control.
When you order materials soon enough,
You'll never be 'in the hole.' "

"But you really need a computer."
Said the fifth—"P.C.'s a dream
With loads run from last week's payroll cards
And exception reports by the ream."

Said the sixth, "Materials management
Is a concept to which "I'm devoted—
Instead of learning production control,
I've escaped by getting promoted."

So study each book and seminar,
Attend every one you can, sir!
You'll find a thousand experts
—each with PART of the answer!

SOURCE   G. W. Plossl and O. W. Wight, *Production and Inventory Control: Principles and Techniques* (Englewood Cliffs, N.J.: Prentice-Hall, 1967), p. 190. Reprinted by permission of Prentice-Hall, Inc., Upper Saddle River, N.J.

movement might well revise the firm's organization chart to resemble the second half of the exhibit. Clearly, the vice president of operations and similar line managers had good reasons to view these changes as threats to their authority.

Within the past decade, new practices and attitudes have moved into the territory that the materials-management movement established earlier. Proponents of just-in-time manufacturing and total quality management have demanded roles in OM decision making through urgent assertions like "quality is free" and "delight the customer." The best practices of materials management have changed in response. We will discussion the impacts of these new forces on the materials-management function in a later section of this chapter.

Emergence of Quarterly Ordering Systems.   Many changes in the organizational environment contributed to the development of MRP systems. Out of World War II came the confidence in applications of mathematics to industrial problems. The use of linear algebra and later introduction of fledgling electronic computers simplified solutions of complex allocation problems. Computer-based project-management systems began to incorporate Gantt's scheduling logic, confirming the significant new role of computers in business planning. The rush of pent-up demand following World War II created large backlogs at many American businesses. In

[**EXHIBIT 17.1**]

Two Ways to Organize the Materials Management Function

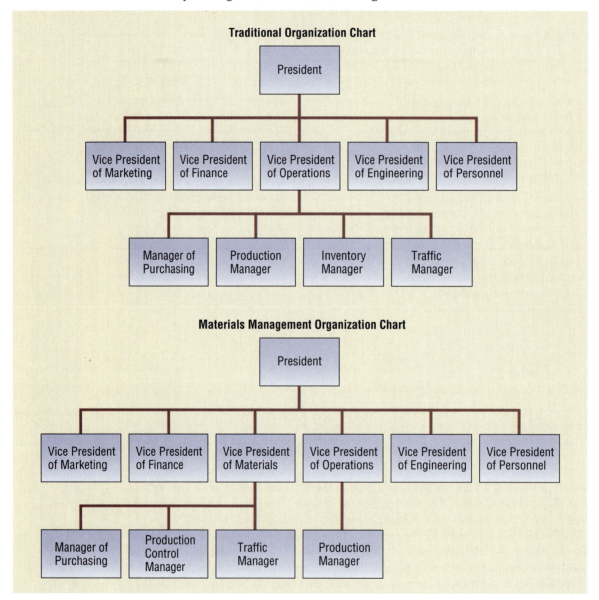

addition, customers had grown accustomed during the war to waiting for products. As a consequence, inadequate capacities in many businesses kept production 12 to 18 months behind demand as measured by firm customer orders.

Early materials-management practitioners developed the quarterly ordering system to control production in this stable environment. Starting with a promised delivery date for each order in the backlog, a firm's production planners built a **final-assembly schedule** (FAS) which set a feasible, multiquarter plan based on capacity constraints imposed by the final-assembly process. For each component and subassembly, planners repeated a formal process to assure that they could

final-assembly schedule

A feasible, multiquarter production plan based on capacity constraints imposed by the final-assembly process make or procure needed inputs in a timely fashion. Within a quarterly plan, they set a final-assembly date for each order and then worked backward to determine requirements for components and subassemblies to meet that date. They allowed ample lead times for fabrication or assembly of components to set start dates that would satisfy the timing of final assembly.

Production planners felt no need to forecast demand since backlogs of orders and this backward-planning logic told the factory and its purchasing agents exactly what to supply and when. The quarterly ordering system began to encounter problems, however, as continuing production began to satisfy the pent-up wartime demand. Rather than change their familiar and once-reliable process, production planners began to base scheduling decisions on demand forecasts. Detailed monthly forecasts of sales for final products came to replace data about firm customer orders awaiting completion, and the former make-to-order system quietly evolved to function primarily as a make-to-stock system. (Demand management did keep some well-trained customers dutifully placing orders far in advance, however.)

Failure of Quarterly Ordering Systems.   Two new problems further complicated quarterly ordering. First, salespeople needed to know how much planned production they could promise to new customers. To find this amount, they had to subtract units committed to firm customer orders and likely orders from total planned production. They must have wished for the simplicity of a pure make-to-order or make-to-stock business.

Finally, forecast-based production planning yielded increasingly unreliable results. When managers knew demand with certainty, they could plan their work and then work their plan. Forecasts invariably misstated actual demand due to unanticipated orders or cancellations. To accommodate adjustments to demand forecasts, planners had to revise their schedules.

The quarterly ordering system is very manual and time-consuming. Its outputs were only momentarily valid. If someone changed an order or one of the part counts was wrong, the accuracy of the overall system was completely off. We then had to go back through the quarterly ordering system's recalculations—a time-consuming, major undertaking.

Flat production systems with relatively short production lead times often allowed enough flexibility to deal effectively with inaccuracies in forecasts. However, systems that lacked flexibility suffered from instability due to frequent demand forecast changes. Really extensive instability often induced informal organizations to disregard formal planning systems. Workers dismissed production planning as an activity for someone else and devised their own systems to deal with the daily realities of their jobs. This kind of adaptation reduced production planning to a wasteful, theoretical exercise.

Lack of timeliness proved the greatest weakness of the quarterly ordering system. Planners had to spend a long time manually breaking down a final product to determine its component needs. If nothing changed, the benefit probably justified the effort, but the business environment became more dynamic. As the environment got more dynamic and customers wanted their orders done quickly, managers would often compromise the quarterly ordering system. Orders were taken out of their schedule positions that had been carefully coordinated and calculated. The resulting components orders based on these schedules now became equally meaningless.

Materials Requirements Planning as a Solution.   In the 1950s, the emergence of electronic computers stimulated the development of MRP. A handful of pioneers saw these new capabilities as an opportunity to improve and transform production planning systems. They spent their professional lives developing, refining, and promoting the techniques of materials requirements planning. Indeed, many people view the 1960s and 1970s as the era of the MRP crusade.

One of these pioneers, Joe Orlicky, earned a reputation as the father of MRP while working as a director of production control at J. I. Case, a major manufacturer of farm implements. Case ran a system with extensive vertical integration that required systems for purchasing and manufacturing many components. Orlicky observed that classical methods for setting reorder points and reorder quantities resulted in poorly timed orders. These methods led Case to make parts based on what it had used rather than what it needed to complete planned production.

Orlicky responded by developing a production planning system that would supply components just before assembly required them. The system, which he called *materials requirements planning*, started with a schedule detailing final products that the firm wanted to make by period. It then worked backward to determine how many component parts it needed and when it needed them. This resembled the procedures of the quarterly ordering system, but MRP made planning much more dynamic by determining weekly quantities rather than quarterly ones.

By 1960, Joe Orlicky, Oliver Wight, George Plossl, and a few other practitioners had developed computer-based systems for materials requirements planning. They encountered skeptics, as most pioneers do, in both managerial and academic ranks when they introduced their early applications. After observing the lack of success of early attempts to apply computers in factories, Orlicky complained that, "there were probably fewer manufacturing people who were optimistic about the potential for computer applications in manufacturing in 1968 than there had been in 1958."[2] Many industrial practitioners saw the systems as Rube Goldberg apparatuses made of punch cards. Most operations researchers scorned MRP's lack of optimal scheduling criteria.

By the mid-1960s, Orlicky had left J. I. Case and moved on to IBM, where he served as manufacturing industry education manager. At IBM, he approached his work as a practitioner who saw the computer as an organizing tool. This attitude conflicted with the prevalent belief of the company's applied mathematicians that the computer represented a tool for optimizing mathematical models. Orlicky's style and practical perspective resulted in a communication gap between these two camps that persists to a certain extent to this day.

MRP pioneers held little more regard for OM educators. In his book, *Production and Inventory Management in the Computer Age,* Oliver Wight recognized Ed Davis, then at MIT, as someone who had "restored [his] faith that there *are* educators who are concerned about the relevance of business education."[3] This statement reveals the contempt of early MRP pioneers for business-school professors, whom they correctly regarded as allies of operations researchers focused on optimization over practical application.

A key breakthrough occurred in 1968 when Orlicky met with William Berry and Clay Whybark, two young business professors at Purdue University. This meeting established a bridge, albeit a shaky one, between the crusading MRP practitioners and the academic community. The following year, IBM sponsored a conference at Pougkeepsie where a number of academics confronted heavy doses of MRP theory and practice. By the 1970s, the MRP crusade had developed a

---

[2]Oliver W. Wight, *Production and Inventory Management in the Computer Age* (Boston: CBI, 1974), p. vii.
[3]Ibid., p. xi.

powerful momentum that did not fade until the JIT movement overcame it a decade later.

Nature of the Materials Requirements Planning Problem

Materials requirements planning attacked the dual problems of too much inventory and not enough inventory. Conditions within many industrial settings contradicted two of the basic assumptions of the classic EOQ model, a key component of the order point/order quantity inventory system. This dual problem created waste and reduced value for the customer. Too much inventory meant that costs were increased and lead time reduced in building and storing items that were not really needed. Too little inventory meant that items were not available when needed. Both problems created costs, which the customer was no longer willing to tolerate.

Dependent Demand.   The demand for many items is not independently generated and does not have to be forecasted. The demand for many items used to make the final assembly item is driven by the final assembly schedule, as discussed in Chapter 14. The demand for hot dogs drives the demand for wieners, buns, mustard, and relish.[4] Within the operations management system, similar linkages occur. Operations managers do not need to forecast component demand—we know this demand with greater certainty because it is calculated.

Exhibit 17.2 presents a simplified representation of the requirements to make a bicycle. Demand for front-wheel subassemblies depends on the final-assembly schedule's plans for every bicycle that the firm intends to build with the same front-wheel subassembly. Similarly, the demand for rims and spokes depends on the planned production of front-wheel subassemblies, and the demand for hoops and wire depends on the plans for rims and spokes.

Note the hierarchical designations for parts in Exhibit 17.2. Level 0 usually represents a final product, such as a particular bicycle model. Level 1 parts normally represent discrete components of a Level 0 item, and so forth. These level designations emphasize the hierarchical nature of production planning in MRP. They point out the top-down planning, beginning with known or forecasted demand for the final product, which determines the need for Level 1 parts. The structure also points the bottom up nature of execution. While we plan from the top when managing material, we build from the bottom up.

This important feature of MRP eliminates the need to forecast demand for any outputs except Level 0 products. It may seem strange to think about higher-level parts having smaller level numbers. Level 0 items are the highest-level parts, and Level 1, Level 2, and Level 3 items are sequentially lower-level parts.

Level numbers clarify **parent-component relationships** in MRP. A parent product is one made from components. Unlike in biology, the demand of a single parent can create demand for its components, called **dependent demand**. More than one parent may drive dependent demand for a component; the demand for flour in a bakery equals the sum of the flour used to make each of the bakery's final products.

parent-component relationship
The need for lower-level parts to make a higher-level product

dependent demand
Demand for components that results from demand for a higher-level product

---

[4]Hot dogs are sold in packs of ten while hot-dog buns are normally sold in packs of eight. Observers have long attributed this mismatch to a failure to maintain links between levels of demand through the supply chain.

[**EXHIBIT 17.2**]

Components of a Bicycle

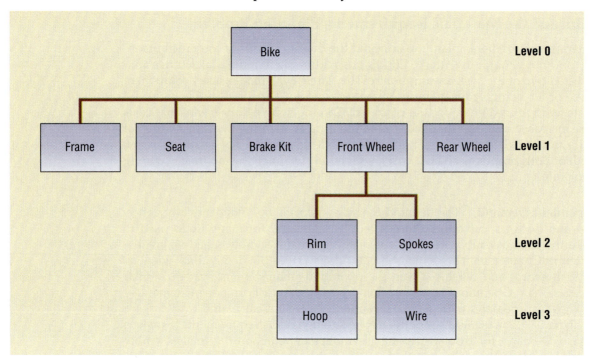

Lumpy Demand.   Real-world OM systems often violate a second basic assumption of the EOQ model because demand may not remain constant. Instead, firms often need to make final products and components in discrete, irregular groups. The bicycle manufacturer may need to produce particular models in batches. The firm would then encounter lumpy demand for each subassembly driven by the timing of the final-assembly schedule.

For example, look at Exhibit 17.3. Final Product A includes two parts, B and C. Even if the firm can rely on fairly constant demand for A, the demand for B displays a lumpy pattern. Panel b, which resembles the production lot scheduling model from Chapter 16, indicates the reason. The firm needs B only when it assembles A. The bases of the highlighted triangles indicate these time intervals. At other times, the firm needs no B because the final-assembly line is not making A.

Exhibit 17.4 displays the contrast between the traditional reorder point EOQ model's response to demand for B and the MRP model's response. (This comparison requires two simplifying assumptions: B has the same EOQ as A and the reorder point and lead time equal zero.) Panel a depicts the lumpy usage pattern for B that results when the process needs this part only when it makes A, the Level 0 product. Panel b shows the EOQ model inventory level for B; it starts off at a level needed for one batch of A. The inventory level falls at a rate appropriate to support production of A. The inventory of B runs out just as the process completes production of A, triggering the reorder point. The system automatically reorders inventory of B without determining when it will need more.

Exhibit 17.4c demonstrates the benefits of forward planning. MRP schedules production of B only when the process needs the inventory to support assembly of

[**E X H I B I T   1 7 . 3**]

Waste Due to Lumpy Demand

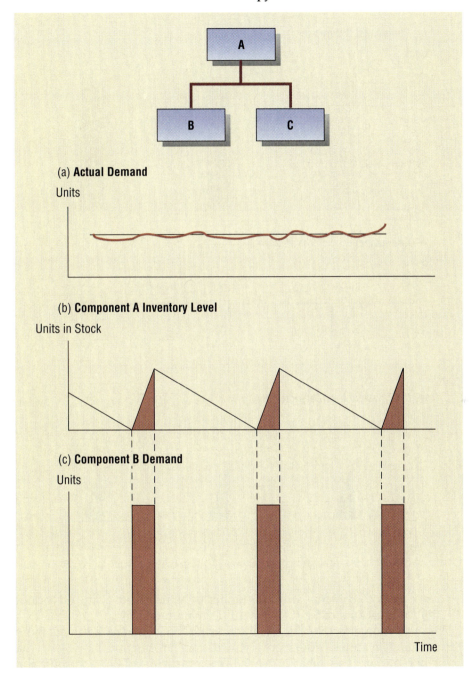

(a) **Actual Demand**

Units

(b) **Component A Inventory Level**

Units in Stock

(c) **Component B Demand**

Units

Time

A and only in the amount that it needs to support planned production of A. The production run of A leaves no inventory of B, and stocks remain empty until just before new orders for A need more B.

In practice, MRP does not perform as well as Exhibit 17.4 implies. Still, the exhibit illustrates a key capability of MRP to plan for production and purchasing of

[**EXHIBIT 17.4**]

EOQ Model versus MRP Model with Lumpy Demand

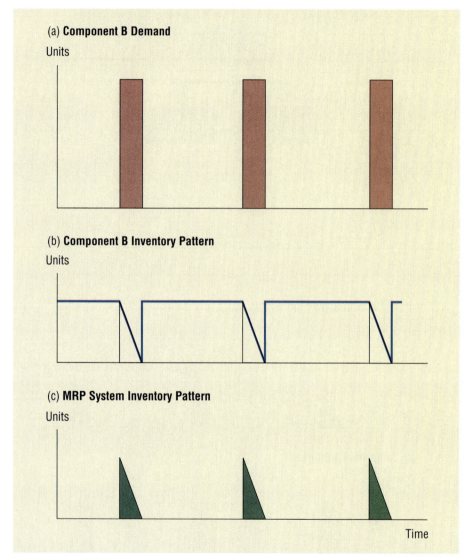

(a) **Component B Demand**

Units

(b) **Component B Inventory Pattern**

Units

(c) **MRP System Inventory Pattern**

Units

Time

component parts to coincide with the timing of actual need. Some advocates of MRP promote it as a more flexible form of JIT manufacturing.

This discussion illustrates the observation of Orlicky that a traditional reorder-point mechanism times orders poorly, ordering production based on what a process uses rather than what it needs. This practice leads to accumulation of wasteful inventory, as shown in Exhibit 17.4b, where inventory levels remain high despite a lack of demand for B.

The solution in Exhibit 17.4c seems almost too simple, but it captures the essence of MRP. This method intends to deliver inputs as needed, subject to a firm's strategic objectives. These objectives usually try to achieve a desired service level at the lowest possible cost or to keep costs as low as possible while maintaining some minimum service level. The design of the production planning system must honor the firm's choice of a method for gaining its competitive advantage through a unique combination of speed, quality, flexibility, and cost.

Planning and scheduling production should also be consistent with how we compete in the marketplace. If our strategic strength is flexibility, we should plan for small lot sizes, medium levels of capacity utilization, short lead times, and finished components for assembly into configured end items. If we emphasize cost, then we plan for long runs, few changeovers, and high levels of capacity utilization.

The timing of demand affects a firm's purchasing function as much as its OM function, as discussed in Chapter 13 on supply chain management. Whether the firm purchases or fabricates a component, it must provide that input in the right amount at the right location and the right time. The internal and external factories need much the same information about future demand far enough in advance to allow them to complete their own planning.

Cost of Poor Timing

Joe Orlicky observed this waste at J. I. Case when traditional EOQ logic led the OM process to make products without considering the timing of its need for them. To illustrate the cost of poor timing, Orlicky referred to an example.

[**PROBLEM 17.1**]

Waste Due to Poorly Timed Production

An OM process needs an average of 6 units of a component per week. Its manufacturing costs give an economic order quantity of 50 units based on the classic EOQ formula. Exhibit 17.5 specifies the demand and costs over a 10-week period.

Clearly, production in lots of 50 generates needless inventory carrying costs in Weeks 2 through 8. If the firm were to produce in lots of 40 units, it would save 19 percent on these costs over the 10-week period. (See Exhibit

[**EXHIBIT 17.5**]

Demand and Costs with an EOQ of 50

	Week 1	Week 2	Week 3	Week 4	Week 5	Week 6	Week 7	Week 8	Week 9	Week 10
Demand	20	0	20	0	0	0	0	0	20	0
Beginning inventory	0	30	30	10	10	10	10	10	10	40
Production	50	0	0	0	0	0	0	0	50	0
Ending inventory	30	30	10	10	10	10	10	10	40	40
Setup cost[a]	$50.00	$0.00	$0.00	$0.00	$0.00	$0.00	$0.00	$0.00	$50.00	$0.00
Inventory holding cost[b]	6.92	6.92	2.31	2.31	2.31	2.31	2.31	2.31	9.23	9.23
Total cost	$56.92	$6.92	$2.31	$2.31	$2.31	$2.31	$2.31	$2.31	$59.23	$9.23

Overall total cost = $145.16

[a]Setup cost = $50 per setup
[b]Inventory holding cost = $12 per unit per year, or $0.231 per unit per week

[**EXHIBIT 17.6**]

Demand and Costs with an EOQ of 40

	Week 1	Week 2	Week 3	Week 4	Week 5	Week 6	Week 7	Week 8	Week 9	Week 10
Demand	20	0	20	0	0	0	0	0	20	0
Beginning inventory	0	20	20	0	0	0	0	0	0	20
Production	40	0	0	0	0	0	0	0	40	0
Ending inventory	20	20	0	0	0	0	0	0	20	20
Setup cost[a]	$50.00	$0.00	$0.00	$0.00	$0.00	$0.00	$0.00	$0.00	$50.00	$0.00
Inventory holding cost[b]	4.62	4.62	0.00	0.00	0.00	0.00	0.00	0.00	4.62	4.62
Total cost	$54.62	$4.62	$0.00	$0.00	$0.00	$0.00	$0.00	$0.00	$54.62	$4.62
Overall total cost = $118.46										

[a]Setup cost = $50 per setup

[b]Inventory holding cost = $12 per unit per year, or $0.231 per unit per week

17.6.) This simple example shows the extreme sensitivity of inventory costs to lot-sizing and timing decisions in conditions of lumpy demand.   [■]

IMPLEMENTATION OF MATERIALS REQUIREMENTS PLANNING

time bucket

A discrete time interval in a larger MRP production schedule

net requirements

The difference between total units required and units available in inventory and incoming orders that defines the minimum production goals for a period in MRP

The earlier overview laid out the simple logic of MRP. Practical implementation begins with an estimate of units needed to satisfy customer demand. This states the gross requirements for a schedule period, and further analysis breaks down the total into requirements for discrete time intervals, called **time buckets**. Before scheduling new production, the process must determine how many units it can draw from inventory and firmly scheduled deliveries in future time buckets. These **net requirements**, the difference between total units required and units available in inventory and incoming orders, define the minimum production goals for the period.

An MRP system normally defines demand for final products (often in the form of a master production schedule or a final assembly schedule), but in a later section we will discuss situations when component demand forecasts should drive an MRP system. We prefer to keep the presentation simple for now.

Once production planners for a bicycle manufacturer know how many units of each model they need to make in each time bucket, they figure out how many units of each component they must supply to satisfy that schedule. This simple determination depends on the recipe for each bicycle model, although MRP replaces this home-economics language with the term *bills of materials*. Known production of Level 0 units in each time bucket yields the number of Level 1 units through simple matrix multiplication. If planners need to make 10 units of a bicycle model in the first time bucket, then they need 10 units of each component in the model's bill of materials, including the frame, seat, brake kit, front-wheel assembly, and rear-wheel assembly.

Planners then need to specify when in the first time bucket to supply those components. While this much detail may seem picky, it really does matter. Consider your reaction if your employer were to tell you that payday would come some time in June. To avoid this kind of confusion and distress, early MRP users established conventions for timing designations. An MRP system requires planners to specify gross requirements at the start of a time bucket. Producers of a component can then make it any time during the time bucket, allowing them to schedule operations efficiently within individual time buckets.

Lower-level scheduling requires information about how long it takes individual departments to make their assigned components. This time requirement determines how far in advance an upstream department needs to know net requirements in order to supply rims to the front-wheel assembly process when it needs them. MRP includes a planned lead time value for each component to state the length of time that planners should allow for a department to make it. Recall from Chapter 14 that planned lead time does not specify the actual processing time to make a component. A component that requires only 1 hour of processing time may have a planned lead time of 2 days. The difference represents a buffer that permits the producing department to define efficient production lots and work flows.

For the same reason a professor might give a student 6 weeks to do a report that requires 15 or so hours of actual work. The student would probably begin scheduling this work by trying to make all required inputs to complete the report available at the start of the assignment in order to fit the work in with other activities scheduled during the time bucket. This scheduling exercise would require an estimate of the latest possible start date that would allow timely completion of the assignment, again depending on the existing backlog of other activities in the time bucket. Of course, the student might also wait until shortly after that latest start date and then recognize the report as a rush job to be completed by a version of the just-in-time system.

Production planners follow this rather simple logic to implement a materials requirements planning system. They need several key inputs:

1. A master schedule, which specifies the firm's requirements for final products by time period
2. A bill of materials for each final product in the master schedule, which defines the components that the final-assembly process needs to complete that product
3. Accurate information about the inventory status of all final products and components
4. Accurate information about the status of all scheduled incoming components
5. The planned lead time of every required process

In the following sections, we will describe each input and its role in the overall MRP process. Then we will work through an example problem to illustrate how to integrate the inputs to complete a production schedule. In later sections, we will build upon this firm understanding of the logic of MRP to show how it contributes to a larger system for manufacturing planning and control.

Master Production Schedule

The master production schedule (MPS), discussed in Chapters 9 and 14, plays a key role in MRP, as well. It serves as an information buffer between the demands

[E X H I B I T   1 7 . 7]

Environment of the Master Production Schedule

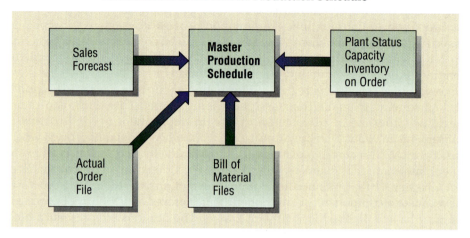

of marketing to satisfy customer orders and the production that the OM process can achieve with its current resources. Exhibit 17.7 illustrates the inputs into the master schedule. The task of the master production schedule typically falls to the master scheduler.

A firm's business plan usually expresses performance targets in aggregate terms, such as dollars or units sold. Those numbers generally also determine the budgets and the standards of performance for key executives and departments. Operations managers also need to pay attention to the firm's performance goals, but they need to know exactly what products to make to fulfill their roles in the organization. The master scheduler translates aggregate performance targets into production in units during specific periods.

This process begins by breaking down annual business plan numbers to produce sales forecasts by model. A comparison with actual orders may reveal a difference between intentions and real-world performance, and the master scheduler must resolve the question to fully specify planned production.

If actual orders fall significantly short of planned sales, the scheduler must evaluate the impact of slowing production on the OM process. The firm loses the return to its investment in production capacity if it cannot keep the plant running at a steady pace. On the other hand, it may face serious business risk if it produces a product for which it has no existing orders. Anything that it makes but cannot sell becomes inventory—often slow-moving inventory at that!

The master production schedule must find answers for these hard questions. This essential role makes the MPS a key input to the materials requirements planning process. Its importance also extends outside the MRP process, making it a joint agreement between marketing, manufacturing, and financial management on short-run production and output.

To do this job well, the master scheduler needs accurate information. This requirement includes inventory records that correctly indicate stock levels and the amounts and timing of current production and outstanding purchase orders. The scheduler needs up-to-date bills of materials that reflect any planned engineering changes. Marketing must supply clear information about existing customer requirements, current orders, and the most recent sales forecast.

The master production schedule depends critically on the comparison between the sales forecast for a final product and current orders for that product. A scheduler for a make-to-stock producer normally cannot rely on existing orders and must work entirely from forecasts. If, however, a firm makes all or a significant portion of its sales to order, then the master scheduler can test the assumptions of the forecast against current orders.

This comparison might take the form of a table:

	Week 1	Week 2	Week 3	Week 4	Week 5	Week 6	Week 7	Week 8
Units forecasted	40	30	10	10	50	40	10	10
Actual order file	30	35	5	0	5	0	0	3

How many units should the master production schedule require? Orders for Week 1 seem to fall 10 units below the forecast, but those for Week 2 exceed the forecast by 5 units. Did customers wait to place some orders planned for Week 1 until Week 2? The table gives no more information, but the scheduler might inquire further, perhaps asking someone close to those customers what happened. At the same time, the scheduler might try to determine whether the dearth of orders in Weeks 3 through 8 seemed normal. Perhaps customers usually do not commit until 1 or 2 weeks prior to delivery, so new orders will push actual orders closer to the forecast over time.

Schedulers frequently encounter this problem. They may try to solve it by relying on forecasts from marketing. If those forecasts seem questionable, however, the schedule could simply assume that sales will equal the larger of the two numbers. This would give rather conservative estimates of demand on which to base the master production schedule:

	Week 1	Week 2	Week 3	Week 4	Week 5	Week 6	Week 7	Week 8
Units forecasted	40	30	10	10	50	40	10	10
Actual order file	30	35	5	0	5	0	0	3
Assumed demand	40	35	10	10	50	40	10	10

Any error would tend to create too much production rather than too little. In this way, the MPS protects the firm from the significant cost of stockouts, although it may drive inventories slightly higher than actual sales justify.

Bill of Materials (BOM)

Recall from Chapter 14 that a bill of materials is an engineering document that specifies the physical requirements to make a product, including assemblies, subassemblies, parts, and raw materials. Exhibit 17.2 divided these requirements for production of a bicycle into a four-level diagram called a *product structure tree*. Actually, that exhibit did not represent a complete BOM; it showed only the Level 1 subassemblies and lower-level detail only for the front-wheel assembly. The exhibit truncated that product structure tree to avoid clutter due to unnecessary detail. For much the same reason, production planners often compile **single-level bills of materials** which show the subordinate components only one level down to indicate the immediate requirements to manufacture the product. A *multi-level bill* shows every item needed and when needed. This bill is very information-dense and somewhat redundant. A *single-level bill* shows only immediate items needed to

single-level bill of materials

A document that lists subordinate components only one level down to indicate the immediate requirements to manufacture the product build the part—for a wheel, it would show the rim, rim strip, tube, tire, hub, stokes, skewers, and nipples, but would not show the components that make up the components. For example, a spoke consists of a portion of wire. The single level bill for the spoke will include its components.

A single-level bill of materials for a bicycle would look like this:

- Bicycle
-    Frame
-    Seat
-    Brake kit
-    Front-wheel assembly
-    Rear-wheel assembly

It would not show the lower-level components that make up the Level 1 components. This format for a BOM would be most helpful to final assemblers, who do not need to know what goes into a wheel assembly or a brake kit.

Others within the firm, such as cost accountants, might need more detailed information. To meet this need without spreading confusion, planners often compile **indented bills of materials:**

indented bill of materials

A list of product components that indents all products at the same level within the product structure by the same amount

- Bicycle(Model 154A)
-    1-Frame (Part F345)
-    1-Seat (Part S1267)
-    1-Brake kit (Part B498)
-    1-Front-wheel assembly (Part FW100)
-       1-Rim (Part R23)
-          1-Hoop (Part H76)
-       36-Spokes (Part S0145)
-          2.0-Wire (Part W45)
-    1-Rear-wheel assembly (Part RW103)

This listing indents all products at the same level within the product structure by the same amount. The Level 0 bicycle starts at the left with Level 1 components like the front-wheel assembly. Level 2 components of that assembly indent farther, and Level 3 components indent farther still.

This bill of materials provides additional information beyond the names of components. First, and perhaps most importantly, it states **part numbers**. Statements in English or any other language leave the system open to confusion and mistakes. MRP systems specify components by their part numbers to guarantee the unambiguous information that the manufacturing environment requires.

part number

An unambiguous, numerical designation for each component within an OM process

The example also added quantities. Planners in a biscuit manufacturing plant cannot do their jobs knowing only that workers will combine flour, shortening, baking powder, and water. They need to know how much of each and the units of measurement by which to specify quantities. The bicycle manufacturer would always specify wire for spokes in lineal feet; the 2.0 units of wire would tell planners that the process would use 2.0 linear feet of wire to make each spoke. They could then determine that it would need 72 feet of wire to make spokes for a single front-wheel assembly.

If a firm's product structure remains relatively stable, then it can manage its bill of materials files through a fairly straightforward process. However, if numerous engineering changes affect the components of a firm's products, the it needs a systematic method for managing these changes. Many firms have software packages called *bill of materials processors* to create flexible organization routines for

When generating a bill of materials, companies like this bike manufacturer detail units of measure as well as quantities required, in order to maintain an adequate stock of production supplies.
SOURCE   Henry Horenstein/Stock Boston

product-structure information to facilitate adjustments for engineering changes and to provide appropriate output reports to management.

These companies also rely on a disciplined engineering change request (ECR) system, where engineering changes are reviewed. Typically the ECR process involves a cross-functional group with representatives from engineering, operations management, purchasing, production and inventory control, finance, and safety. This committee meets frequently. For example, a spoke manufacturer has identified a structural defect in part number S0155 and identified a replacement (S0156). The ECR process would immediately replace S0155 with S0156 in the appropriate bills. It would also authorize the immediate disposal of the remaining stocks of S0155. Such immediate changes often involve safety reasons or customer-initiated changes. In other cases, the engineers have identified a better component. Instead of implementing the change immediately, the committee might indicate that the effectivity date is dependent on when the inventory runs out.

Plant managers often rely on **where-used reports**. A bill of materials presents information about the product structure of a final product. Managers often need to evaluate the applications of a particular component or subassembly in the larger product structure, however. For example, if managers at a bicycle manufacturer were to learn of a strike against a supplier of a specific brake kit, they might want to know which bike models used that kit. The where-used report gives that information. Identifying linkages between parents and components is also referred to as "pegging" or "drilling." When we look at a component and are interested in determining the parents affected by its use, we are said to be pegging up or drilling up. In contrast, when we try to determine the components affected by a parent schedule, we are said to be pegging down or drilling down.

where-used report
A report from an MRP system that states the applications of a particular component or subassembly in the larger product structure

Inventory Record Files

To be successful, MRP requires up-to-date inventory records that state how much of what items are located where because it relies on information rather than actual stocks. The better the quality of the information, the greater the probability of a successful MRP system. People often assume that firms can easily keep track of inventories. This assumption often proves incorrect. Inventory record accuracy becomes critical in a computer-driven MRP system because production planning decisions hinge on stock counts. Managers must decide whether to order more units of an input or whether they have enough in stock to carry out planned production. They can make a reliable judgment only if records accurately report the number of units in inventory and if each unit is a usable input.

In the past, firms generally held plenty of inventory so that production could continue if some inventory counts misstated true, usable stocks. In smaller manufacturing systems, production planners could stay familiar with changing conditions, so informal controls often sufficed. For example, one production planner in Iowa knew that a certain plastic component would shrink every year when winter approached. Units in stock at that time could no longer become inputs to production, although they made good windshield scrapers during icy weather. When the firm centralized its MRP system at corporate headquarters, that piece of informal system knowledge probably did not survive the transition.

Centralized or not, however, a materials requirements planning system needs to maintain inventory records accurately so that planners can be sure that those records exactly match the numbers of units in stock. North American managers no longer simply assume a difference between these two numbers, thanks to lessons from the Japanese. They have developed a number of ways to maintain accurate inventory records.

This conceptually simple task begins with the design of a system for inventory-transfer transactions. This system should define fail-safe, easy-to-use procedures and provide for careful employee training. Bar coding provides a key enabling technology to combine accuracy with simple operations.

After designing a transaction-tracking system, MRP practitioners conduct an ongoing audit of inventory accuracy, called *cycle counting* as discussed in Chapter 16. The "By the Way" box highlights the value of this practice. Many firms conduct physical inventory counts at the ends of fiscal periods, but some have managed to convince their auditors that accurate cycle counting can fully replace year-end inventory audits. In this way, they have eliminated another wasteful practice.

Order Status File

Commuters know the frustration of stopping on the way home after a long day to buy milk or some other necessity only to discover when they get home that someone else in the household did the same thing. Production planners face the same problem. They need to maintain production-control systems to keep track of inputs on order and avoid placing duplicate orders.

Since MRP plans for potential events rather than tracking actual ones, it also must distinguish between orders that purchasing personnel have actually placed and those that planners have considered placing. MRP practitioners have a specific term for orders for which the firm has issued legally binding paperwork: scheduled receipts. Scheduled receipts may represent incoming supplies from outside vendors, or they may reflect firm production orders issued to internal processes. While a firm may simply hold the output from these firm orders in stock and absorb the inventory holding cost, MRP often tries to time delivery to coincide with need. Because planners interpret scheduled receipts as fixed quantities, they

[BY THE WAY... PICK YOUR POISON]

Many periodic inventory audits rely on casually hired, poorly trained staff. Production planners have to choose between infrequent inventory counts by large numbers of incompetent people and continuing counts by smaller numbers of competent people.

Many stockrooms are staffed by employees who are not well paid or well trained. In a costly paradox, however, these people are responsible for managing large amounts of the company's assets. Their inventory counts are often wrong, but other companies recognize the importance of the stock-

room and staff it with qualified, well-trained, intelligent people who see their jobs not as inventory management but as resource management. As a result, these people provide the companies with continuing counts and significantly higher levels of inventory accuracy.

often define a separate row in MRP documents for this quantity. (A later section will explain these documents in detail.)

Since production processes count on scheduled receipts to arrive at specific times, vendors must clearly understand that successful MRP requires adherence to promised due dates. We discuss the importance of reliable vendor deliveries later in the chapter as part of the supplier certification process.

Planned Lead Times

As we explained in an earlier section, operating workers need to know more than how many components they must produce to support assembly of the final products specified on the master production schedule. They need to know when they must supply those parts, as well. Subprocesses could simply maintain steady rates of production to meet a master schedule for level production of a stable product mix. However, any irregularities in the rate of production and/or the product mix create irregular usage rates for parts from the lower levels of the product structure tree. Batch production exacerbates these irregularities enough that component production schedules can vary, even with fairly level demand for a final product. Exhibit 17.3 illustrated the reasons for this variation.

MRP tries to control timing based on planned lead times. Work centers organize their activities within time buckets to achieve these planned lead times. Suppose that a bicycle manufacturer must ship 10 units of a particular model at the start of Week 11. If each subprocess has a planned lead time of 2 weeks, production planners work backward based on these offsets to specify production of all subassemblies and components. Exhibit 17.8 shows the resulting Gantt chart.

The final-assembly department expects to receive all of the components it needs at the start of Week 9. It has 10 working days to fit the 10 bikes into its existing schedule as efficiently as possible. Likewise, the front-wheel assembly department expects to receive 10 rims and 360 spokes at the start of Week 7. It, too, can schedule this job any time within its 10 days of planned lead time. The same process carries the schedule down through the bill of materials.

MRP's time-phased planning mechanism permits each department to arrange its work more or less independently of other departments. The operations manager

[**EXHIBIT 17.8**]

Bicycle Assembly Schedule

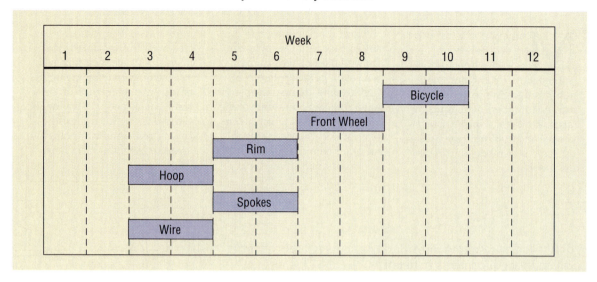

must now keep the actual lead time in line with the planned lead time. If the actual lead time exceeds the planned, then the order is late and the coordination promised by MRP is seriously affected. However, if the actual lead is less than the planned, we have orders done early and WIP building up.

Exhibit 17.9 illustrates a common complaint that MRP seems to take too long to get orders through the shop. The reason comes from other demands on workers who perform necessary operations. An individual production order represents just one of many jobs in a department's schedule, each with its own due date. By pulling orders that share setups and other arrangements from a backlog, the department can define an efficient arrangement for its work. The backlog also serves as a buffer against uneven work flows or uneven resource availabilities, perhaps due to employee absenteeism or machine breakdowns. This flexibility also permits the department to expedite a limited number of rush jobs without pushing other jobs behind schedule.

MRP Records

MRP record

A document on which planners enter information to track production activities for a single final product, subassembly, or individual component

Practitioners systematically enter and track all of the information discussed so far on a document called the **MRP record**. Exhibit 17.10 shows a sample. They can use the same record form to plan production at any level within the product structure for either manufactured or purchased inputs. A unique MRP record corresponds to each final product, subassembly, and component within the system. Even if a component has more than one parent (i.e., more than one higher-level product requires it as an input), planners still maintain only one MRP record for it.

Each cell in an MRP record holds a valuable piece of information. The upper, left-hand corner of the MRP record shows a part description or part number. The rest of the form provides space for information about important MRP quantities:

- *Gross requirements* Cells in this row report the total expected demand for the component during successive time buckets. The MRP record for a final product would fill in this row with numbers from the master production

[**EXHIBIT 17.9**]

One User's Opinion of MRP

EIGHT WEEKS!!
Well, I could have built them in 2 days.

schedule. The record for a lower-level product would report gross requirements as the total planned order releases for parent products that require the component times the number of units that each parent requires.

- *Scheduled receipts*   This row reports orders of the component that planners expect to receive from vendors or internal subprocesses. Planned order receipts (discussed later) can change, but law or policy requires the process to accept delivery of these already purchased products.
- *Projected available balance*   This row determines the number of units that planners expect to have on hand at beginning of a time bucket. This value equals the ending inventory from the prior period plus scheduled receipts.
- *Net requirements*   These cells report the actual number of units that the process needs in each period. The net requirements indicate the amount by which demand (gross requirements) exceed supply (project available balance + scheduled receipts) in any period. If this amount is positive, we have a potential shortage in that period and we need to receive units which equal at least the net requirements. If the amount is zero or negative, then we have sufficient supply to meet demand (no action has to be taken).

[**E X H I B I T   1 7 . 1 0**]

MRP Record Form

					Period				
	Late	Week 1	Week 2	Week 3	Week 4	Week 5	Week 6	Week 7	Week 8
Item: Bicycle Model B									
Gross requirements									
Scheduled receipts									
Projected available balance									
Net requirements									
Planned order receipts									
Planned order releases									
Lead time =									
Lot size =									

- *Planned order receipts*   This row states the number of units of the component that the process will receive from internal or external suppliers at the beginning of each period, assuming that planned orders lead to actual production. Scheduled receipts deal with actual orders which are placed; planned receipts deal with potential orders which have not yet been placed.
- *Planned order releases*   This row states the number of units of the component that the MRP system plans to order at the start of each period. This number should match the number for planned order receipts after *LT* periods, where *LT* equals the lead time.

Note that each cell value represents a quantity at the start of the period. The example in Exhibit 17.10 shows weekly time buckets, but another situation might call for data broken down by shifts, days, months, or any other unit of time. Problem 17.2 illustrates the process for filling in an MRP record to show how to calculate each value.

[**P R O B L E M   1 7 . 2**]

Application of an MRP Record

Exhibit 17.11 shows MRP records for some front-wheel assembly components from the product structure of the bicycle in Exhibit 17.2. The student disk contains records for the complete product structure under the filename MRP-BIKE.XXX.

Exhibit 17.11 assumes that the master scheduler has calculated a need for 120 Model B bicycles over a 2-month period. The first line of the MRP record for the final product (the top record in the exhibit) shows rather lumpy demand, perhaps due to unavoidable market conditions. The same record shows that the MRP process has already released a production order for delivery of 50 bikes at the start of Week 2.

[**EXHIBIT 17.11**]

Partial MRP Records for a Model B Bicycle

					Period				
	Past Due	Week 1	Week 2	Week 3	Week 4	Week 5	Week 6	Week 7	Week 8
Item: Bicycle Model B									
Gross requirements		0	10	0	40	40	0	30	0
Scheduled receipts		0	50	0	0	0	0	0	0
Projected available balance—5		5	45	45	5	0	0	0	0
Net requirements		0	0	0	0	35	0	30	0
Planned order receipts		0	0	0	0	35	0	30	0
Planned order releases		0	0	35	0	30	0	0	0
Lead time = 2 weeks									
Lot size = Lot-for-Lot									
Item: Front Wheel									
Gross requirements		0	0	35	0	30	0	0	0
Scheduled receipts		0	0	0	0	0	0	0	0
Projected available balance—5		5	5	0	20	20	40	40	40
Net requirements		0	0	30	0	10	0	0	0
Planned order receipts		0	0	50	0	50	0	0	0
Planned order releases	50	0	50	0	0	0	0	0	
Lead time = 2 weeks									
Lot size = 50 units									
Item: Front Rim									
Gross requirements		50	0	50	0	0	0	0	0
Scheduled receipts		50	0	50	0	0	0	0	0
Projected available balance—15		10	15	15	15	15	15	15	15
Net requirements		0	0	35	0	0	0	0	0
Planned order receipts		0	0	50	0	0	0	0	0
Planned order releases		50	0	0	0	0	0	0	0
Lead time = 2 weeks									
Lot size = 50 units									

Finished goods inventory holds 5 units of Model B. Planned lead times for all component-production and final-assembly processes equal 2 weeks. Finally, planners order finished goods from the final-assembly department in varying lot sizes, called a *lot-for-lot strategy*, but processes for manufacturing lower-level components run batch sizes of 50 units.

A review of the MRP record for the finished bicycle reveals that the scheduled receipts of 50 units will cover demand until Week 5. The 5 units in inventory will not cover the expected demand in that week, 40 units, so planners need to place an order to make up for the 35-unit shortfall. They must release the order at the start of Week 3 for delivery at the start of Week 5. A similar shortfall projected for Week 7 requires a 30-unit order for release at the start of

Week 5. Of course, plans made the start of Week 1 may require changes to reflect updated forecasts of demand; if analysis in Week 2 suggests different numbers, planners can change the quantities of the two planned order releases in Weeks 3 and 5.

Based on this information, planners need to evaluate required outputs from the front-wheel assembly process. The MRP record for this process (the middle record in Exhibit 17.11) shows the results of their work. Recall that planned order releases of parent products drive the gross requirements for lower-level parts. The MRP record for the single final product, the Model B bicycle, indicates that the final-assembly department will start assembling 35 of these bikes sometime in Week 3 or 4. The rules of MRP dictate delivery of all necessary components at the start of the appropriate time bucket, so the component-production subprocess must supply 1 lot (50 units) of front-wheel assemblies at the start of Week 3. This shows exactly how the planned order releases for Model B drive gross requirements for front-wheel assemblies.

Suppose for a moment that the revolutionary design of Model B actually required two front-wheel assemblies for each bicycle. This change to the bill of materials would cause a change in the gross requirements row in the MRP record to 70 of those assemblies in Week 3 and 60 in Week 5. Furthermore, the MRP records for other bike models that required the same front-wheel assembly might show planned order releases during the 8-week period. Gross requirements for that assembly would increase to reflect the additional demand for the component.

Through a similar link, planned order releases of front-wheel assemblies drive the gross requirements for front rims, reported in the bottom MRP record in Exhibit 17.11. The front-wheel department's batch size of 50 units has a different effect on the gross requirements for front rims, however. A positive value for net requirements of front-wheel assemblies in any week triggers a reorder 2 weeks earlier of one or more 50-unit lots of front rims. The planned order releases for front-wheel assemblies at the starts of Weeks 1 and 3 drive the gross requirements for front rims and, eventually, a planned order release of 50 units in Week 1, which will cover all needed supplies for the 8-week period. If the exhibit included the MRP record for spokes, it would show gross requirements for spokes of 50×35, or 1,800 spokes.   [■]

At this point, the reader may need a change of pace. Spreadsheets offer a fine tool for learning about the process of completing an MRP record. We recommend that you stop for a moment and bring up the spreadsheet MRPBIKE.xxx. Browse a bit, paying particular attention to the formulae. The same disk also contains a blank spreadsheet template with the filename MRPREC.xxx. Try to fill in this template to create an MRP record with formulae of your own.

CAPACITY REQUIREMENTS PLANNING

In all of the discussion of materials management so far, we have assumed that the plant would have enough capacity to fill any order that the production schedule would require. The process for filling in MRP records included no step to check, for example, whether the spoke-making department had enough manufacturing

[**E X H I B I T   1 7 . 1 2**]

Capacity Requirements in Final Assembly

	Week 1	Week 2	Week 3	Week 4	Week 5	Week 6	Week 7	Week 8
Final Assembly								
Model A		30						
Model B				70		60		
Model C					40			
Total Hours		30		70	40	60		

capacity or wire to make spokes for all of the wheels that the firm needed. **Capacity requirements planning** (CRP) corrects this omission by extending the logic of MRP to identify the work load that a proposed master production schedule imposes on each part of the production system.

Planners require two additional pieces of information to complete a CRP evaluation. First, they need to know how much capacity a process requires to make 1 unit of a product. Back in Exhibit 17.11, they would need to know how much capacity the final-assembly process would need to make each of the 35 Model B bicycles scheduled for delivery at the start of Week 5. If each bike would require 2 labor hours of final-assembly department work, then this demand would create a work load of 35×2, or 70 labor hours.

Planners also need to know when the process would need these hours of capacity. The answer to this question depends on other demands on the department's capacity and how it assigns labor. Exhibit 17.11 assumed that final-assembly process would need all of the inputs for 35 units at the start of Week 3 and that it would complete those units by the start of Week 5. When during the 2-week lead time would the process perform this work?

If the department had no other work scheduled, it would probably start on the order early in Week 3. Whether or not it would complete all 70 hours of work before the end of Week 3 would depend on how it assigned labor. If one person were to handle the order alone, the job would stretch well into Week 4, assuming that the department would work one 40-hour shift per week.

More likely, however, the new order would join a queue of other work in the final-assembly department. Students solve a similar problem when they decide how to fit large term papers into their schedules of other work. Most MRP systems assume that manufacturing processes, like many students, complete jobs during the latest time bucket within the planned lead time. Exhibit 17.12 shows the final-assembly process completing all 70 hours of work on the 35-unit order in Week 4. In addition, that process performs 60 hours of work in Week 6 to make the 30 units scheduled for delivery by the master production schedule at the start of Week 7. (See Exhibit 17.11.)

Exhibit 17.12 shows orders for Models A and C, as well as Model B, to illustrate the load on the final-assembly process due to orders for other bicycle models. CRP combines the labor requirements on a department from all sources in order to provide operations managers with an estimate of the combined labor-hour requirements for final assembly over the planning horizon.

capacity requirements planning
A procedure that extends the logic of MRP to identify the work load that a proposed master production schedule imposes on each part of the production system

Note that the component-production processes still expect to supply needed inputs for assembly of 35 Model B bicycles before the 2-week planned lead times for other processes begin. This lead time protects shop-floor level schedulers from excessive demands. If they can schedule only 40 labor hours of capacity for the 70-hour order, then they can complete 30 hours of the work in Week 3 and the remaining 40 hours in Week 4. Week 6 looks more difficult, however, because an order for Model C requires more than the 40 hours of available capacity. Fortunately, the department seems free of any load in Week 1 and it has 10 hours of extra capacity left in each of Weeks 2 and 3.

This example shows the problems of reconciling production requirements with capacity limits. The demand for capacity (the load as defined in Chapter 15) is greater than the amount of capacity available (as occurs in this case). The manager can change when the order is released to the shop floor by either releasing it earlier, to take advantage of capacity available in these periods, as was done in this case (this action is often referred as "pulling the order forward"). The manager can delay the release of the order if capacity is available in later periods (pushing the order back). Alternatively, the manager can increase the amount of capacity by using overtime, weekend shifts, or subcontracting (this action is discussed later in this chapter). The specific action will be influenced by such considerations as the costs of changing capacity.

This simple example clearly shows why shop-floor operations managers prefer planned lead times considerably longer than the actual processing times that jobs require. They need this flexibility to fit assembly of Model B in the department schedule with other final-assembly jobs. They will have to schedule some of the work detailed in Exhibit 17.12 early to complete both orders for Model B on time. As an alternative, they might try to create some additional capacity.

Overtime and Other Capacity-Expansion Techniques

Problems with insufficient labor, inadequate equipment, or unavailable raw materials can all destroy the feasibility of a master production schedule. The MRP record shows this kind of problem in a column headed "Late." (Review Exhibit 17.11.) Entries in this column signal the master scheduler that a department has not completed planned production on time. The remaining schedule may still be feasible, but only if some departments complete their work before the expiration of their entire planned lead times.

Operations managers often schedule overtime shifts when they need to expand capacity to solve a problem like this. Plants also employ expediters to cut lead times for selected orders. These people cajole or prod shop-floor workers to move a job to completion in less than the allotted lead time. Workers hear requests like, "Terry, my good friend, I know that you work hard to get these rims out in 2 weeks, but this is a special case." Terry remains a good friend only until the expediter puts too much strain on the goodwill in the relationship.

Limited patience and other potential problems often plague MRP systems with regular late signals. Such problems indicate infeasible master production schedules. In reality, workers may manage to deliver orders on time, but the organization often pays a high cost for nonroutine operations.

Capacity Requirements Planning for Component Production

Capacity requirements planning extends beyond final products to reach lower levels of the product structure. The schedule of front-wheel assembly production is feasible only if the department has enough capacity to support the final-assembly plan. The MRP records in Exhibit 17.11 implied that this department needed capacity to deliver its net requirements of 30 units by the start of Week 3. If the department lacks that capacity, then final assembly cannot begin production of the 35-unit batch of Model B bicycles at the start of that week.

Actually, the front-wheel assembly operation needs enough capacity to produce a 50-unit batch, its standard lot size, within its allotted 2-week planned lead time. The difference between the lot size and the component's net requirements becomes work-in-process inventory. Exhibit 17.11 shows that the process carries over 20 front-wheel assemblies into Weeks 4 and 5, and even larger amounts accumulate in subsequent periods.

To estimate the capacity requirements to produce front-wheel assemblies, planners need to know how much labor the department takes to make each assembly. If it spent 1 hour to assemble a front wheel, then the firm would have a capacity requirement of 50 hours of labor in both Week 2 and Week 4. (Once again, CRP assumes that the department will complete the work during the last time bucket in the planned lead time.) Clearly, the shop-floor managers could move up either of these jobs by 1 week to finish them within the 2-week planned lead times.)

Capacity requirements for rim manufacturing during the 8-week period remain low because the department has already completed 50 units at the start of Week 1. The MRP process must have placed an order 2 weeks earlier; if it had not, the 15 units of inventory would have failed to satisfy the gross requirements for rims at the start of Week 1. The MRP record would then have shown 35 units under the Late column in the planned order releases row, indicating a materials-management failure.

If units do show up in the late column, the planner must choose among three options: change the master production schedule to reduce the demand for Level 1 and higher parts, expedite an order's progress through departments downstream from the late process to complete it in less than planned lead times, or plead with upstream suppliers (either internal or external factory) to make or ship their inputs with shorter lead times. To guard against these unpleasant alternatives, MRP systems often maintain some safety stocks.

MRP AND THE PRODUCTION PLANNING PROCESS

Production planning must achieve two familiar objectives. MRP helps planners to assure that they schedule work through the shop floor in a way that meets the expectations of customers, as we have emphasized throughout the chapter. Planners must also schedule work in an efficient way, however, that meets the expectations of the firm's higher-level managers and owners.

So far, we have focused on constraints that might limit output below levels that internal and external customers need. MRP must also identify any work flows that do not justify the firm's investment in its current resources. When the master scheduling process finds underloading in a system, it must consider increasing the flow of work, either by acquiring more orders, increasing the proportion of work done within the internal factory, or prematurely introducing current orders. As an alternative, schedulers might redeploy manufacturing resources. This often requires a reduction in the firm's work force or the number of hours that current employees work.

CARE AND FEEDING OF THE MRP DATABASE

Up to this point, MRP may have seemed like a largely theoretical problem. The powerful effect of this method on the success of the organization and its members gives new importance to the need for a production planning system that can introduce, organize, and present information in a timely and useful manner. This system begins with MRP's need for information inputs, summarized in Exhibit 17.13.

This list highlights two characteristics of MRP: it requires planners to process a lot of data, and much of that data seems subject to frequent change. These facts spurred early users of MRP to become eager internal customers of their firms' data-processing departments, the precursors of information systems specialists. In turn, the processing needs of these departments made them major customers for keypunch cards. The limited data-processing capabilities of the time gave an image of unwieldy excess to early MRP processes. This alienated shop-floor personnel, who often made complaints like, "They produce more paperwork than we produce goods!" MRP pioneers needed thick skins.

New technology has simplified the care and feeding of the database, but MRP's information needs didn't end with solutions to technical data-processing problems. Just as in inventory-management systems, planners must communicate with MRP software regularly and follow correct protocols. Updates must correct computer files to reflect decisions made external to the MRP software. Managers must act on decisions recommended by MRP output reports. Poor maintenance of information resources can cause costly process breakdowns.

Output Reports for Materials Requirements Planning

Virtually all MRP output reports summarize data from MRP and CRP records. Many managers do not want to sort through complex information about routine operations to find exceptions that require their attention. "Just tell me what I need to do," they say. Planners can most effectively serve these internal customers by asking what decisions they might want to make. Most fall into four major categories.

Planned Order Releases.   MRP records give information about all planned order releases, but operating managers need to know about those that require action during the current decision period. MRP reports must transform planned order releases for inputs from the external factory into purchase orders. They must generate work orders for inputs made by the internal factory.

Orders that Need Expediting.   MRP system reports should emphasize any entries in the Late column of the MRP records. Managers need red flags to guide their heroic efforts to save the master production schedule from collapse. Without intervention, a process downstream from the late process will find insufficient quantities of necessary components to assemble its own output and complete its job.

Within the internal factory, the expediters may descend on the unfortunate Terry to take away some planned lead time. To speed inputs from the external factory, managers may need to prod the supplier's sales staff to ship on schedule or ask for a partial shipment to keep production moving while the supplier completes the order. They may also choose an alternative supplier or use a faster mode of transportation than that specified in original plans. If all of these actions fail to restore the feasibility of the plan, managers may have to revise the master production schedule.

[**EXHIBIT   17.13**]

Information Needs of Materials Requirements Planning

Sales and demand-related information
    Demand forecast by planning period for:
        Level 0 items
        Replacement parts
    Existing order files
        Level 0 products ordered by planning period
        Existing replacement part orders and due dates
Manufacturing resource data
    Resource availability by department and planning period
    Bill of materials data
        Bill of materials part structure
        Usage coefficients (hours used/units made)
Inventory status data
    Number of units in inventory
    Number and due dates of outstanding orders
Manufacturing process information
    Routing files for each product (how to make it)
    Status of work in process (what, where, and when)
    Shop-floor performance data (planned and actual)
        Yield data
        Costs
        Other relevant information
Internal control files
    Cost collection activities
        How, when, and where the firm incurs costs
        Standard cost data
    Performance measurement activities
        Production plan data
        Conformance to plan
        Performance variance analysis
Customer information
    Product shipping specifications (packaging and shipping mode)
    Invoicing data
    Special treatment file
Customer satisfaction information
    Source of components used
        Supplier certification, if any
        Part quality assurance data
    Manufacturing processes used
        Process certification, if any
        Part quality assurance data

Effectiveness of Capacity Allocation.   MRP reports indicate the need for some response to poor use of capacity by current plans. They guide planners' adjustments to the timing of planned production by moving jobs forward or back to improve the efficiency of the use of plant resources. They also indicate a need to adjust the planned level of capacity; managers might adjust the number of hours worked through overtime or shorter work days, or they might assign more or fewer workers to the affected process.

[**EXHIBIT   17.14**]

Planned Order Report

Item:	#22251	Date:	8-26-96
On hand:	112	Lead time:	2 wk.
On Order:	100	Lot Size:	100
Allocated:	50	Safety Stock:	50

Date	Order Number	Gross Required	Scheduled Receipts	Projected On Hand	Action Taken
				62[a]	
8-28	5513	30		32	
9-1	5514	25		7	
9-4	5528	30		(23)	
9-8	SR29	44	100	77	Expedite to 9-4
9-2	5531	30		47	
9-7	5540	35		12	
9-15	5548	30		(18)	Release PO 9-1

[a] Note that safety stock has been subtracted from projected on hand

Performance Evaluations.   Managers also use MRP reports to evaluate the performance of production planners, inventory managers, buyers, vendors, and the people who maintain the MRP database. They want to know the percentage of final products shipped on time and the percentage that pass through the system without expediting. They may want help investigating the reasons for expediting some orders, how much the firm has invested in resources for a process, and how inventory turnover has changed, among many subjects.

Planners must keep the information base of the MRP system accurate to keep it turning out reliable reports. MRP systems need accurate inventory counts, so most MRP systems include formal routines to assure the validity of inventory files. For similar reasons, planners monitor the number and types of data-entry and transaction-related errors. Like managers in JIT systems, MRP practitioners work hard to achieve error-free operations. Of course, this also requires thorough training of OM system personnel.

Space limitations do not permit examples of the myriad output reports that MRP systems typically generate. Exhibits 17.14 and 17.15 show examples. Note the austere, numerical formats. In the past, MRP generated rather cryptic reports. The new generation of MRP systems (e.g., Chess from MDIS, MRP9000 from Intuitive Manufacturing Systems, and ERPx from the J.D. Edwards Company), are designed to be easily read and understood. These systems employ a graphic user interface system with pull-down menus, push buttons, and easily customized reports.

The planned order report shows that the system released no purchase order when the projected stock on hand fell to a negative value the first time. Scheduled receipts of 100 units 4 days later probably accounts for this. Expediting efforts might well bring in that stock a little early; if not, the firm could draw from 50 units

[**E X H I B I T   1 7 . 1 5**]

MRP Action Report

				Date: 8-26-96

Item	Date	Order Number	Quantity	Action
22251	9-8	SR2944	100	Expedite to 9-4
42552	9-12		125	Release PO-2588
43491	9-12		150	De-expedite SR-2433
44216	9-12			Move forward WO-3351
26122	9-12			Move back WO-3356

of safety stock. That report does indicate a purchase order released on 9-1 to cover the anticipated shortage on 9-15.

Production planners evaluate the MRP action report by determining whether the specified responses would maintain the feasibility of the existing master production schedule. If not, they would go back to the drawing board, but only if they could find nothing else to do.

Besides these reports, production planners frequently use a **pegging report**. This document resembles the where-used report, which identifies the final products or lower-level parent products that require a particular component. Recall the discussion of the difficulty of judging the amount of available stock when a production plan combines firm customer orders with forecasted demand. The pegging report helps to solve this problem by identifying current orders that have contributed to gross requirements for a particular component. This information guides planners' choice between two potential responses to a problem with product availability:

pegging report
An MRP report that identifies current orders that have contributed to gross requirements for a particular component

1. They may free up available components or capacity to fill a particular order by deferring planned production of some less important order that requires the same resources.
2. They may find units of the required product in the master production schedule that the firm could sell to a new customer.

The pegging report tells planners which orders have claims to available products to help them make customer-driven rescheduling decisions.

Replanning in Materials Requirements Planning

The pioneers of MRP faced difficult problems implementing their systems through early mainframe computers with severely limited computing power and data-storage capacities. Also, they lacked simple systems for data entry such as bar-code readers. These defects in MRP tools forced planners to update their calculations rather infrequently, anywhere from monthly to weekly. Limitations on computer resources also forced them to plan for weekly time buckets over long planning horizons.

They set the MRP time horizon based on a simple formula:

Planning horizon length = Longest lead time + Number of weeks between decisions

Of course, the longest lead time must affect the planning horizon. To fulfill a plan to assemble and ship a final product by a certain date, planners must start production of components early enough to feed timely supplies to the final-assembly line. They determine when they must begin by identifying the component that takes the longest cumulative time to make. This gives the value for the longest lead time in the planning horizon formula.

That formula would not need to include the time between plans if processing activities were to begin immediately after the MRP system generated orders and set due dates. MRP systems often formulate plans after periodic reviews, however. They generate new master production schedules for a particular set of time buckets, often in monthly increments. Monthly updates of a master production schedule require a planning horizon long enough to accommodate delays before processing will begin on planned production orders that arrive in the last week of the master production scheduling cycle.

To illustrate this need to stretch planning horizons, suppose that a firm makes Final Product A from Components B and C. The final-assembly area requires 2 weeks of planned lead time. The supplier for Component B needs 2 weeks of lead time, while the supplier for Component C requires 3 weeks. This firm generates a new master production schedule every 4 weeks. Exhibit 17.16 illustrates this situation.

To ship an order of Final Product A at the start of Week 10, planners must order Component C (the one with the longest lead time) at the start of Week 5. This pushes the order back into the master scheduling cycle that started in Week 2. If planners wait until the next cycle, beginning in Week 6, to place this order, they will miss their due date for shipping the final product. They commonly avoid this problem by stretching their planning horizon to include the entire length of the scheduling cycle along with the lead times of final products.

Early MRP systems incurred large costs to recalculate production requirements and generate new master production schedules. Despite their limited processing capacities, they reviewed and updated all MRP records in one production run through a process called the **regeneration method**. Often, however, requirements changed little from one regeneration to another, especially in markets with stable demand. MRP practitioners responded by developing a more efficient procedure called the **net change method** that reconstructed MRP records only when changes in the schedule required adjustments. If 90 percent of a firm's MPS remained the same over successive planning periods, then planners needed to update the MRP records only for products in the 10 percent of the schedule that changed.[5]

During the last decade, three technological advances have powerfully enhanced the capabilities of MRP systems. Most obviously, the rapid acceleration in computing speeds and the drop in the cost of data-storage capacity allowed planning systems that had relied on expensive mainframe computers to run on personal computers. Also, bar-coding technology automated data entry for virtually all suppliers and every part of the internal factory. Third, communication links between plants and even continents helped to integrate planning activities throughout the supply chain.

regeneration method
A process for updating MRP records that revised all information in a single production run

net-change method
A process for updating MRP records that revised information only when changes in the schedule required adjustments

[5]Fans of multimedia computer programming may recognize an analogy between the net-change method and the processes by which the JPEG and MPEG graphics protocols present sequences of images by recording only changes in pixels from one frame to the next.

[**EXHIBIT 17.16**]

Minimum Planning Horizon

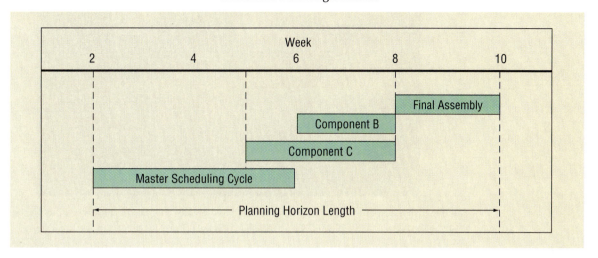

Today's MRP systems now allow bucketless planning, which takes advantage of computer power to immediately update MRP records whenever a transaction occurs, producing a continuous version of the net-change method. Planners have long suffered frustrating delays because they could schedule only one operation within a single planned lead time. If a component production activity turned out a bicycle rim early in its available lead time, planners still could not direct the front-wheel assembly operation to start its work until the beginning of the next time bucket. Bucketless planning transforms scheduling into an ongoing activity rather than a periodic exercise. Planners base decisions on fresh information rather than aging and potentially outdated snapshots of a changing system.

The value of a bucketless system depends largely on the amount of change in the environment. A firm with a static schedule may find that such a system may not add enough value to justify its substantial investment. Top managers must evaluate an investment in state-of-the-art MRP software just as they would evaluate any other outlay.

 ## EVOLUTION OF MANUFACTURING RESOURCES PLANNING

Planners can extend MRP to create a continuous process for managing OM activities, from the earliest suppliers to finished goods. Similarly, they can expand the role of MRP to integrate a wide variety of management processes within a single firm. In the following section, we will briefly discuss this evolution of materials requirements planning into **manufacturing resources planning** (MRPII).

Many organizational needs have propelled this evolutionary development, but three have become especially important:

1. *Integration of organization activities* In today's dynamic business environment, further elaboration of MRP methods helps firms to integrate the production planning and control function with all other major business

manufacturing resources planning
An OM system that expands the role of MRP to integrate a wide variety of management processes within a single firm

Satellite dishes and other technological advances have greatly enhanced business's ability to communicate between plants on a global level.   SOURCE   R. Gaillarde/Liaison International

processes, including accounting, quality management, product design, demand forecasting, resource management, and order entry.

In addition, the need for this integration has been emphasized by the recognition that to effectively implement these plans, all of the corporate resources have to be considered. This means not only those resources controlled or managed by the operations management system (inventory, machine capacity, plant capacity, tooling capacity, labor capacity), but also the capacity managed by the financial side of the firm (e.g., the financial resources in the form of cash and lines of credit). Both types of capacity have to be coordinated and managed within one integrated system.

2. *Time-based competition*   New planning and control techniques enable firms to reduce total planned lead times and satisfy customers, who no longer seem willing to wait while products snake through complex manufacturing systems. Powerful information technology carries timely, useful data to managers.

3. *Multiplant and multinational communications*   New applications of MRP techniques throughout the supply chain have reduced the frustration of tracking shipments. Operations managers found that they could not coordinate worldwide production and purchasing activities by faxing messages; they needed satellite-based communication systems that could display real-time information drawn from databases located throughout the world. Today, this capability enables production planners to react quickly, even in widely dispersed OM systems.

In response to the need for integration of organization activities, MRP expanded its functional scope. To facilitate time-based competition, MRP enhanced the speed of its replanning activities and the timeliness of its information flows. To promote wide-ranging communications, MRP expanded its geographic scope.

Recall the distinction in Chapter 9 between Big JIT and Little JIT. Materials requirements planning developed into a similar pair of methods for organization-wide materials management and narrower scheduling within functional divisions. The latter, MRP, represents the processes discussed earlier in this chapter for disaggregating the master production schedule (MPS) to define starting dates for individual component production. This created an effective program for manufacturing planning, but periodic reviews failed to establish desired large-scale organizational control.

Today, however, powerful computer systems with large storage capacities enable expanded MRP systems to support wide-ranging needs of organizations with timely information and decision making. Periodic planning routines have grown into ongoing, organizationwide replanning systems that continuously update status information for company activities and resources. These systems help decision makers to evaluate production planning alternatives and adjust schedules to enhance efficiency, both on the firm's own shop floor and in suppliers' facilities.

Expanding MRP Systems for Integrated Planning

As MRP systems gained enhanced capabilities, they began to integrate information from throughout the organization with an influence on the feasibility and effectiveness of production plans. These broad-based procedures became known as **closed-loop MRP systems**. Exhibit 17.17 shows an example.

In the upper third of the exhibit, double-headed arrows depict an interactive exchange between marketing and production to develop rough-cut plans with little detail. The engine of the MRP process then transforms the master production schedule into a detailed production plan. At this stage, the process verifies that the shop floor has enough components, capacity, and time to execute the plan. The resulting feasible MPS generates firm orders which show up as scheduled receipts on MRP records for affected components.

closed-loop MRP system
An expanded MRP system that integrates information from throughout the organization with an influence on the feasibility and effectiveness of production plans

Stabilizing MRP Systems

While enhancements enabled MRP practitioners to create feasible master production schedules, they also revealed shortcomings in the front end of the planning process. Shop floor managers gained little benefit from production plans, however detailed and practical, that showed repeated changes. Students would face similar disruption if a professor were to repeatedly change the sequence of topics in the course syllabus. On the shop floor level, workers described this instability, when they spoke in polite terms, as **nervousness**, defined as a pattern of significant changes in MRP records caused by apparently minor changes in the master production schedule or other inputs. Exhibit 17.18 shows a cause-and-effect diagram for nervousness in an MRP system.

JIT practitioners call this instability *system variance,* and they work to level system loads and standardize product mixes to stabilize conditions on the shop floor. While MRP system planners would also prefer stable front-end demand, they recognize that MRP offers an important advantage in its ability to deal more effectively than JIT with lumpy demand patterns. The developers of MRP sought means other than demand management to reduce system nervousness. Exhibit 17.19 lists some of these measures.

nervousness
A pattern of significant changes in MRP records caused by apparently minor changes in the master production schedule or other inputs

Operations managers judge the effects on value to make tradeoffs between potential responses to system instability. In the past, cost seemed to dominate the value equation, so planners resolved questions by choosing the lowest-cost solutions. As customers demanded more responsive OM systems with fast delivery speeds and flexible combinations of product features, MRP systems had to adapt to

Closed-Loop MRP System

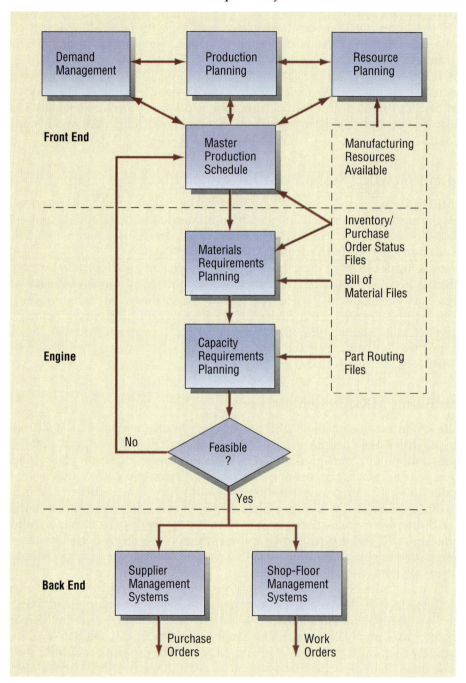

SOURCE   Adapted from Thomas E. Vollmann, William L. Berry, and D. Clay Whybark, *Manufacturing Planning and Control Systems* (Burr Ridge, Ill.: Richard D. Irwin, 1992), p. 5

Possible Causes of MRP System Nervousness

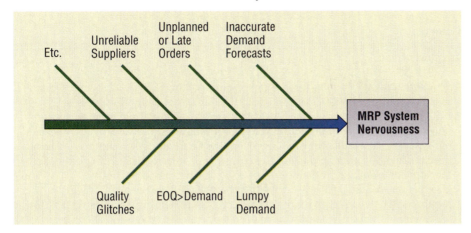

meet these evolving needs. While many of these changes have involved business processes for controlling production, ever more have required new arrangements for the actual transformation processes by which firms make their products.

Enhancing Control by Reducing Scale

Some firms have greatly reduced their need for elaborate MRP systems by converting their plants to cellular configurations. Group technology often allows the MRP system to treat five or so activities as a single cell. This eliminates a lot of detail, allowing planners to process fewer pieces of data and still retain control.

A traditional MRP system would schedule and track a component through each of the five stages shown in Exhibit 17.20. By combining them into a cell, planners can run data for a single, multistep process through the MRP engine instead of handling separate data for each stage. This shows the strong influence of decisions about transformation process arrangements on management processes.

To a certain degree, managers dissolve a control problem, rather than resolving or solving it, when they rearrange activities to define a cellular manufacturing system. Other firms have found a similar method to reduce the need for elaborate MRP systems by flattening their organizations. The "On the Job" box cites one example.

Expanding the Scope of Manufacturing Resources Planning

As the users of MRP moved down the learning curve, they saw new opportunities to add value by integrating other organization activities. Having mastered stable, closed-loop systems, they recognized the potential to expand the scope of computer-driven planning systems. Marketers saw advantages in working more closely with production planners to assure the best due dates for customers. MRP gave purchasers better information about projected component needs to help the external factory forecast demand. Human resource managers could use capacity planning data to estimate staffing levels. Accounting personnel recognized the

[**E X H I B I T   1 7 . 1 9**]

Methods for Reducing MRP System Nervousness

Method	Comments
Improve demand fore-casting process	An elusive goal
Eliminate lumpy demand	Begin with a review of sales force compensation methods. Is the customer's usage pattern lumpy, or are sales or transportation factors causing lumpiness?
Eliminate late orders	MRP systems often impose time fences that prohibit salespeople from accepting new orders with due dates within certain boundaries unless approved by some higher authority. Will a time fence prevent the firm from responding to customer needs? Can education help either the customer or sales personnel to understand the value of orderly purchasing?
Reduce production run sizes	If production economies of scale drive batch sizes far above the near-term gross requirements, then a setup reduction program could help. The firm could test the sensitivity of the EOQ quantity to small or moderate variations in the lot size.
Use firm planned orders	In a firm planned order, management overrides the normal process by which records trigger planned orders. The planned order releases in Exhibit 17.8 reflect a need for goods, a planned lead time, and some ordering mechanism. If this MRP process places an unacceptable load on a producing center, management can intervene by moving an order to another time bucket in order to create a smoother production plan. Before intervening, planners need to verify that the shop floor can accommodate unevenness by moving work around within planned lead times or by making short-term adjustments in capacity.
Improve training of materials-management planners	Users should master a materials-management system. It merely models real-world activities, which require careful implementation. MRP system planners must know how to trick the system to make it work for them and their internal customers. Both the MRP system and its planners exist to serve the firm and its customers. Planners in some of the more bureaucratic manufacturing planning and control systems often forget this fact.
Bucket changes	Instead of reacting to each change, put it into a "bucket" until the end of the period. Most changes will self-resolve before then.
Institute thresholds for change	Set up a threshold limit, beyond which changes will be ignored.

[**E X H I B I T   1 7 . 2 0**]

Cellular Manufacturing to Simplify MRP

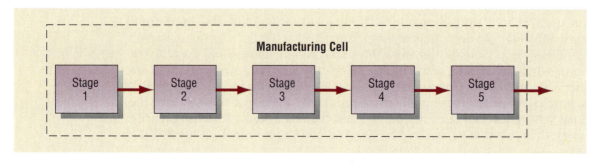

ON THE JOB

IBM Says "Have it Your Way—Now!"

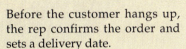

IBM did not gain its enviable position by speed. In North Carolina, however, its PC Direct operation is showing the world how to combine product customization with quick response through emerging technologies. A customer calls a toll-free number to reach one of rows of sales reps who can handle about 5,000 calls per day. As the customer talks, the sales rep enters specifications into an on-screen purchase order. An expert system automatically screens the order for violations of technical requirements to assure compatibility of the chosen blend of features. Another system checks component availability much as a travel agent checks seating capacity on a particular flight.

Before the customer hangs up, the rep confirms the order and sets a delivery date.

At the end of the call, the rep transfers the purchase order to a final assembly plant. The communication system routes the order via in-plant radio signals to a kitter holding a hand-held receiver with a bar coding wand. This worker immediately picks the necessary parts from inventory, following directions for the shortest route through the warehouse. At each stop, the worker adds a component to the kit and deletes the appropriate number of units from inventory records.

The completed kit moves to the PC assembly area where the set of bar coded parts is compared with the work order. Line workers snap together the PC and send it for automatic testing and packaging. If the customer requests the fastest possible service, PC Direct can ship the computer via Airborne Express for delivery the day after the order arrived. Clearly, Big Blue has changed!

SOURCE   Bob Sacha, "The Digital Factory," *Fortune*, September 14, 1994.

possibility of maintaining cost control systems for labor and materials based on the same transaction records by which MRP tracked orders within the system.

When an MRP system expands its functional scope to include related activities, it becomes a manufacturing resources planning (MRPII) system, as Exhibit 17.21 illustrates. What started out as a simple exercise in matrix algebra has evolved into a significant new computer software industry.

When an MRP system expands to include distribution, it is sometimes called *distribution requirements planning* (DRP). A master production schedule combines orders for like goods, so if two customers want 40 units and 60 units, respectively, of a bicycle model, then the MPS indicates a need for 100 units. DRP does essentially the same thing, but often for a smaller number of products. Abbott Laboratories includes about 750 final products on its MPS.

An MRPII system's scope includes marketing, finance, and accounting. It often is called *enterprise resources planning* (ERP), is enterprise-wide, and takes into account all resources and activities of the enterprise and integrates them for planning.

While these jazzy new terms connote a much broader role for computer-driven planning systems, operations managers must carefully avoid letting them set limits for the organization's strategic planning process. The allocation of corporate resources is one of the major functions of top management. Numbers alone do not make good strategic thinking. Indeed, if a firm's current information system comes to drive its comprehensive planning process, the lack of background on a completely new strategic alternative may prevent management from considering it.

[**EXHIBIT 17.21**]

Relationship between MRPII and MRP

A firm can add value by expanding its materials-management planning tools to support decisions in other functional areas, provided it restricts these limited tools to routine, short-term planning decisions. Rather than creating some all-inclusive decision-making process, successful extensions of MRP focus on specific applications.

Cost Accounting Applications.   Bar-coding technology has allowed planners to automate shop-floor transactions so completely that they can track each component, tool, and worker. This information easily translates into the amount of each of these resources that the process applies to a specific job. Accounting staff and operations managers use essentially the same transaction data to monitor performance within their systems. This led naturally to development of common software applications to support the needs of both areas. Even users of MDIS's package, Chess, can scarcely tell whether they contribute to accounting or operations management information. Microcomputer users can interface Misys's application software with ACCPAC accounting systems by Computer Associates. As seamless organizations emerge, seamless applications software follows.

Product Design Applications.   A product design team can find much of the information that they need already stored within the database of an MRPII system. When they develop that new product, much of the information that they generate will ultimately become part of the MRPII database. Designers and production planners can simplify their lives by sharing a database from the start.

Marketing Applications.   MRP and MRPII systems have long maintained links to marketing through order-entry functions. In make-to-order settings, these planners and marketers had to coordinate their activities to promise and meet feasible due dates that would satisfy customers. Planners verified availability of raw materials and slack capacity to fit in rush jobs requested by marketers. In formulating aggregate plans, the front end of the production-planning process has long included steps to assure that the firm secures appropriate resources for anticipated system loads.

Many MRPII systems include capabilities to simulate likely impacts of different business scenarios. Users can manipulate variables in computer models to assess the effects of losing a big order, moving a due date forward 3 weeks, and so forth. Simulation methods and "what if" analysis also enable the firm to evaluate the consequences of additions or contractions in plant capacity. In these and similar situations, decision makers deal with short-term or intermediate-term planning issues. They adjust existing systems. These tools may not help managers to evaluate alternatives that have little in common with existing operations.

As MRP has evolved into MRPII and expanded throughout organizations, it has also moved into smaller computers. An application that started out running on giant, punch-card chewing mainframes now occupies part of the capacity of a microcomputer. Some local divisions even maintain their own MRP-like systems to gain access to features that their larger organizational systems do not offer. With all of this change, some things continue. Shop-floor personnel still complain, "Those corporate types never quite understand our unique needs down here." Some still do not feel like internal customers.

 ## CHAPTER SUMMARY

Materials-management techniques for controlling the transformation process contrast with those of EOQ inventory management and JIT manufacturing. Chapter 9 described just-in-time methods which promote effective high-volume production of standardized products by triggering production orders to replace components as downstream activities consume them. Chapter 16 described inventory-management models which effectively handle independent demand for various components; these models assume that a process will need more of anything that it consumes, so they trigger reorders without projecting future demand.

1. Materials-management techniques thrive when demand for a final product drives demand for its components. These interrelationships create a complex network of production activities, so planners need a fairly complex system to manage those activities.

2. The development of materials requirements planning gave operations managers a tool for controlling production in the face of lumpy demand for final products and their components. In essence, MRP disaggregates expected final-product demand to project demand for components; it then schedules component production far enough in advance to complete final products on schedule.

3. The dependent demand that MRP practitioners seek to evaluate causes demand for components to display lumpy patterns, even with relatively constant demand for the final product. Therefore, materials requirements planning schedules production of lower-level products specifically to feed scheduled production of higher-level products. It times process activities to supply final assembly as needed without accumulating excessive inventories.

4. Practitioners begin to implement MRP by forecasting demand for a final product (a Level 0 product) for each time bucket. They then calculate gross requirements for each component in that product's bill of materials and subtract stock on hand to find net requirements. Similar analysis for components at successive levels of products gives scheduled receipts for all components, and planned lead times for these components indicate when production should begin in order to supply production at the next higher level in time to meet its schedule.

5. An MRP system requires the following: a master production schedule that reconciles the needs for final products from marketing with the production capacity of the OM system, as well as fixing the demand for the independent demand items; bills of material for each item in the product structure; and planned lead times that agree reasonably with actual lead times.

6. An MRP record for each component lists its gross requirements, scheduled receipts, projected available balance, net requirements, planned order receipts, and planned order releases by time bucket.

7. Capacity requirements planning (CRP) checks the feasibility of a production plan by comparing the shop load it implies with the capacity of the OM process, determined primarily by labor supply and available raw materials. Planners can try to expedite particular orders or expand capacity, perhaps by scheduling overtime, to address deficiencies in capacity; they can move orders forward in time, lay off shop-floor personnel, or reduce working hours to correct excesses of capacity.

8. Planners must work hard to maintain their MRP database. They generate several important output reports that specify planned order releases, orders that need expediting, how effectively the schedule uses plant capacity, and performance measures. The pegging report tells planners which specific orders create demand for a specific component's gross requirements.

9. Materials requirements planning has evolved into manufacturing resources planning (MRPII), a comprehensive production-control system that integrates contributions from all functional divisions throughout the organization, especially cost accounting, product design, and marketing. This development improves the responsiveness and stability of MRP systems, and it often reduces the scale of planning requirements by scheduling production of group-related activities that form manufacturing cells.

Advocates of materials management and MRP have created a powerful tool for operations managers. Unfortunately, they also have occasionally displayed the same resistance to change that they had to overcome in conflicts with line managers and other critics. They sometimes protect their beloved systems from incursions by proponents of JIT, empowerment, flat organization structures, and the quality revolution. In fact, all of these innovations can enhance an organization's effectiveness, but too few managers interrupt their personal crusades long enough to ask how they can best serve their customers.

[KEY TERMS]

materials management 794
materials requirements planning 795
gross requirements 795
final-assembly schedule 798
parent-component relationship 801
dependent demand 801
time bucket 806

net requirements 806
single-level bill of materials 809
indented bill of materials 810
part number 810
where-used report 811
MRP record 814
capacity requirements planning 819
pegging report 825

regeneration method 826
net-change method 826
manufacturing resources planning 827
closed-loop MRP system 829
nervousness 829

[DISCUSSION QUESTIONS]

1. What conditions enabled IBM to develop a quick-response capability to supply personal computers through its PC Direct program?

2. A young recruit to your MRP department has suggested summarily cutting all planned lead times in half in order to accurately reflect true processing times and reduce the factory's response time.
   a. What types of problems might you expect?
   b. Who would complain? Why?

3. The chart below illustrates a bill of materials for a final product, Part 100A. Numbers in parentheses represent units of particular components the parent products require. The final-assembly operation requires 1 week of planned lead time and all other operations require 2 weeks.

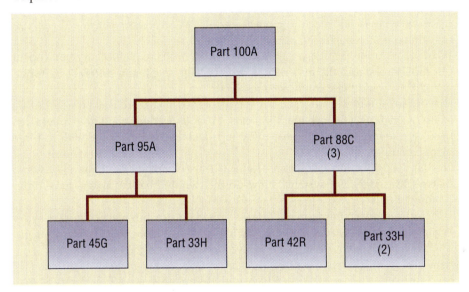

   a. If you need to produce 100 units of Part 100A by the start of Week 6, draw a Gantt chart to indicate the latest time bucket for each component.
   b. How many units of Part 33H does the factory need to make?
   c. If Part 33H requires 2 hours of processing time, how many hours of work will it require?
   d. In what week would the MRP system schedule that work?
   e. If the machine that makes Part 33H offers only 400 hours of capacity per week, when would the MRP system schedule this production?

4. Using the spreadsheet software of your choice, build MRP records for each component in the bill of materials for Question 3. Assume a 10-week planning horizon and beginning inventories and scheduled receipts as reported in the table:

Item	Beginning Inventory	Scheduled Receipts
Level 0		
100A	40	60 (week 1)
Level 1		
95A	20	60 (week 2)
88C	60	
Level 2		
33H	100	150 (week 2)
42R	80	
45G	70	100 (week 1)

Also assume that marketing has forecasted demand for Part 100A over the next 10 weeks as:

	Week 1	Week 2	Week 3	Week 4	Week 5	Week 6	Week 7	Week 8	Week 9	Week 10
Demand[a]	40	30	45	15	30	80	40	60	40	40

[a]Demand at the start of each week.

5. Why do materials requirements planning systems make better use of information than independent demand inventory control systems?
6. What are the objectives of: the master production schedule; materials requirements planning; and manufacturing resource management? How does each relate to each other?
7. If demand is known but lumpy, why are MRP systems superior to EOQ/ROP systems?
8. Under what conditions are MRP systems superior to just-in-time systems? How do these two types of manufacturing practices differ ? Can both systems work well together within one manufacturing distribution system?
9. What organization factors lead to the fact that an injection molding machine operator, the supervisors, and the materials managers have seemingly different performance goals? How could these conflicts be resolved?
10. One of the founders of MRP, Oliver Wight, argued that there was no need for safety stocks in materials management systems. What shop floor conditions might render this suggestion unrealistic? What if the firm had ample experience with just-in-time manufacturing?
11. Discuss the daily information transactions that are common to accounting systems and materials management systems. How do the two internal customers have different "control" needs?
12. Why is inventory counting so important for materials requirements planning systems?
13. What types of people problems are you likely to encounter in extending your plant's MRPII system to your firm's plants in Germany and Brazil? Why?
14. How can an MRP system contribute to a firm's quality management programs? Did MRP early practitioners deal effectively with the quality management process? Why or why not?
15. Bravo Valve makes two end products with the following bills of materials.

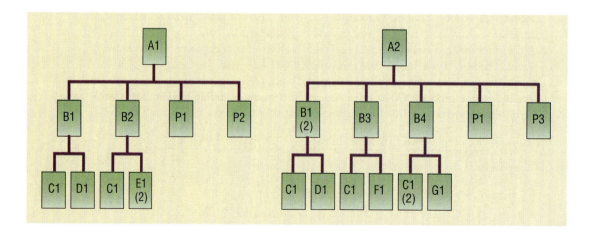

Parentheses indicate the number of units required to make the parent part.

A1 and A2 are assembled in Department 1. Parts B1, B2, B3, B4, C1, D1, E1, F1 and G1 are assembled or fabricated in Department 2. P1, P2, and P3 are purchased items. Each assembled or fabricated item requires one unit of plant capacity. Department 1 cannot work more than 40 hours per week.

The firm uses MRP to schedule production and purchases. All end items made in a week can be sold at the start of the next week. All Department 2 items require a 1-week lead time, i.e., items made in week 2 are available for assembly at the start of week 3. Purchased items require a 2-week lead time.

The demand for the two end items is:

	Week 1	Week 2	Week 3	Week 4	Week 5	Week 6	Week 7	Week 8
Projected A1 demand	10	15	10	50	15	10	20	10
Projected A2 demand	0	0	40	0	10	0	0	20

The beginning inventory position and the scheduled receipt status follow in the table:

Part	Beginning Inventory	Scheduled Receipts
A1	10	
A2	20	
B1	0	10 units at the start of Week 1
B2	10	10 units at the start of Week 1
B3	25	
B4	10	10 units at the start of Week 1
C1	40	
D1	10	20 units at the start of Week 1
E1	20	
F1	10	10 units at the start of Week 1
G1	10	
P1	20	30 units at the start of Week 1
P2	30	30 units at the start of Week 2
P3	10	25 units at the start of Week 2

If the firm uses a lot-for-lot approach to plan purchase and manufacturing operations, can it satisfy the project demand for A1 and A2 given these resources? Use the BravoMRP template to show your work.

16. Suppose the demand for A1 was increased from 50 to 60 in week 4. How much would the MRP records developed in Problem 15 change? Indicate each cell of the MRP records that have changed. Explain to your boss how the net change approach to MRP regeneration occurs.

17. The firm's new controller is concerned about the number of small lots being manufactured. She suggests to your boss that the plant should adopt a minimum lot size of 30 units in order to squeeze more capacity out of the plant. Modify the BravoMRP template to demonstrate the impact of going from lot-for-lot to the recommended minimum lot size model. What criteria would you use to measure the performance of each alternative? Why?

C A U T I O N

[C R I T I C A L   T H I N K I N G   R E Q U I R E D]

1. We can deal with the operations management system by applying either MRP or JIT procedures. These two systems take very different approaches. MRP can be reviewed as a passive mirror while JIT can be seen as being more proactive. How is this? In your answer, think about such areas as they want in which they approach lead times and setup times. Can we use MRP and JIT together? How?

2. How does an MRP system create "additional value" for its internal customers when it goes to being a real-time materials management system?

3. When information quality is poor, which system would you use in the short term to manage dependent items—an $[s,Q]$ system or an MRP system? Why?

CASE 17.1

Altman Alternator, Inc.

Altman Alternators, Inc. was a small manufacturer of replacement alternators for the industrial and construction equipment aftermarket. Over the years, it had developed a reputation as a reliable supplier of quality parts to distributors serving industrial forklift and earth moving contractors. Altman either had the item in stock or could get one made at a lower price than the original equipment manufacturers. Caterpillar was tough to beat, but most of the other OEMs were easy to best when it came to service. As a result, Altman's sales had been steadily increasing each year. In 1996, gross sales were expected to be almost $27 million—not bad for a few GI mechanics who had returned from Viet Nam with virtually no working capital.

Altman's best salesperson was Eddie Brown, or EB as he was called in the trade. EB was a real go-getter. If you needed something fast, Eddie was your man. EB's sales were almost twice that of Altman's second best salesperson.

While EB was a star in the field, he was a terror in the shop. Eddie realized that most of the workers in Altman's job shop hated picking parts for their orders, because it slowed them down and reduced their piece-work–driven paychecks. Eddie realized he could get quicker service from the shop if he picked the orders. He routinely secured the parts and tools needed to get his orders ready for machining and fabrication. EB knew the warehouse better than anyone in the plant. He was there so often that new employees thought that he was part of the warehouse crew.

The trouble with EB's routine was that he was interfering with the plant's production planning process. Altman had a fairly decent order entry system, which fed directly into the MRP system. With more than 60,000 part numbers, this system was necessary to keep control of Altman. But it couldn't control Eddie.

Because of EB's maneuvering, many of the other salespersons' orders were not getting done on time. The shop floor supervisors were undeservedly getting the reputation of not being able to get the work out on time.

As a former quality assurance inspector, Connie Steele, the new master scheduler understood what was going on. Eddie had tried many a time to "schmooze" her for jobs that he needed expedited. When that didn't work, he resorted to his early morning part-picking raids.

But EB had met his match. Steele announced that no materials would be released to the floor without a picking order and that all picking orders will be released through the MRP system. She boldly announced, "We will pick no order before its time!"

Eddie was perplexed and felt he was losing his competitive advantage, and wasn't going to take it any longer. Altman himself, the company founder, was going to hear about this.

As is the case with many business problems, in an attempt to resolve this problem, a meeting was called. Steele, the materials manager, the plant supervisors, and EB, were called to Altman's office. You, as an operations management intern, are invited as an observer. As a customer-driven manager, Altman knew that his firm couldn't tolerate this friction much longer.

QUESTIONS

1. How effective is Eddie as a manager? Since he gets the parts for his orders, he seems to be simplifying life for people on the shop floor and is getting orders filled early. How are his actions really affecting the overall operation of the MRP system?

2. How would you convince Eddie that he should not interfere in the operation of the MRP system and that he should follow the MRP-generated production schedules? What if he refuses?

[SELECTED READINGS]

Fogarty, Donald W., John H. Blackstone, and Thomas R. Hoffman. *Production and Inventory Management,* 2d ed. Cincinnati, Ohio: South-Western, 1991.

International Business Machines Corp. *Computer-Integrated Manufacturing.* White Plains, N.Y.: IBM, 1989.

Melnyk, Steven A., and Ram Narasimhan. *Computer-Integrated Manufacturing.* Homewood, Ill.: Business One-Irwin, 1992.

Melnyk, Steven A., Phillip L. Carter, David M. Dilts, and David M. Lyth. *Shop-Floor Control.* Homewood, Ill.: Dow Jones-Irwin, 1985.

Orlicky, Joseph. *Materials Requirements Planning.* New York: McGraw-Hill, 1975.

Vollmann, Thomas E., William L. Berry, and D. Clay Whybark. *Manufacturing Planning and Control Systems,* 3d ed. Homewood, Ill.: Richard D. Irwin, 1992.

Wight, Oliver W. *Production and Inventory Management in the Computer Age.* Boston, Mass.: CBI, 1974.

CHAPTER EIGHTEEN

Shop-Floor Control and Scheduling

CHAPTER OBJECTIVES

[At the end of this chapter, you should be able to]

- List the functions of the shop-floor control system.
- Describe the key role played by an order within a shop-floor control system.
- Discuss the five major activities of shop-floor control: order review/release, detailed scheduling, data collection/monitoring, control/feedback, and order disposition, and how they manage the five major resources of shop-floor control: people, tools, machine capacity, materials, and information.
- Explain detailed scheduling and its orientation toward people.
- Lay out the process by which combined planning and execution systems set and communicate order due dates.
- Apply scheduling procedures and tools to various operations.
- Explain how customer mix, planning techniques, facility layouts, and equipment/technology conditions influence shop-floor schedules.

A Day in the Life of a Scheduler

I T'S 6:30 A.M., AND BILL TAYLOR HAS already been at work for a half hour. He'll spend ten hours answering phones, handling crises, talking with dozens of people, and generally making sure that what must be done gets done. Each day he moves the schedules of 247 people around like the pieces of a large jigsaw puzzle. As the senior scheduler for the tool room at the General Motors Powertrain Division's Lansing plant, Taylor is responsible for assigning the right people to the right jobs on the right equipment at the right time in the right order—and dealing with emergencies along the way.

Taylor arrives at the tool room in Building 40 each day before 6 a.m. to plan 247 skilled craftspeoples' schedules around 24 different work centers. Each work center consists of one or more similar machines grouped together, such as lathes or grinders. All these work centers and workers depend on Taylor's actions and decisions to convert drawings and concepts to tools and parts.

Taylor looks over his work orders for the day, assigns priorities, and determines which orders should be released to the shop floor. Some of his staff already know their work for the day; they will continue building a model of a wheel well for the new Cadillac. Taylor plans out such long-term projects in conjunction with estimators, engineers, and machine operators well in advance of deadlines. Other craftspeople will work on standing orders for crib work, which means making equipment that is kept in inventory at the user site from standardized designs. While projects might last several months, a crib job usually takes only a week or two. With the projects and crib work assigned and under control—for the moment—Taylor turns his attention to troubleshooting.

After fielding phone calls to deal with questions and problems, Taylor tours the shop floor to track progress. He looks for bottlenecks and possible safety hazards. He also notes when some key craftspeople are absent. Although Taylor has been told about most of his shop's work way ahead of time, he also knows he might get hit with some surprises. He hopes they don't come while a key lathe operator is on vacation.

Sure enough, just as Taylor is starting to relax, someone runs in with an order for a Quick Response (QR) job. A machine on the plant floor is down. Unless Taylor and his crew can make a replacement part immediately, the plant will lose thousands of dollars. Taylor quickly writes out the specifications and puts them in a red folder, which is hand delivered to the shop floor. Machinists who receive the red folder know they must stop whatever they're doing and immediately shift their attention to the QR job.

Taylor looks at his watch as the red folder passes from machine to machine. The replacement part is hurried out the door in about six hours—not bad. At least there were no "walk-ins" today (emergency jobs that take longer than one shift to complete). It's almost 4 p.m. now and time for Taylor to head home, but first he gives the afternoon shift their schedule for the next eight hours.

By prioritizing orders, deciding when to start work on them, and tracking their progress, Bill Taylor is a one-man shop floor control system. Unlike the planners described in earlier chapters of this book, Taylor is the face of the execution side of operations management. And by 4 p.m. each day, he has a very tired face, indeed.

Operations managers at an industrial giant like General Motors and the dining room host at a local restaurant must both understand the importance of shop-floor control and scheduling. **Shop-floor control** is the primary operations management system for effectively executing production activities. This system breaks down into five distinct but interrelated activities. Procedures and techniques for scheduling, the most visible of these activities, identify the importance of individual jobs and determine a sequence that completes them by the times that customers need them. This work varies significantly between types of processing systems, including job shops, production lines, cellular manufacturing systems, and service systems.

shop-floor control

The primary operations management system for effectively executing production activities

OVERVIEW OF SHOP-FLOOR CONTROL

Every activity in an OM system either formulates or executes a plan. Planning answers several important questions:

Links between Planning and Execution

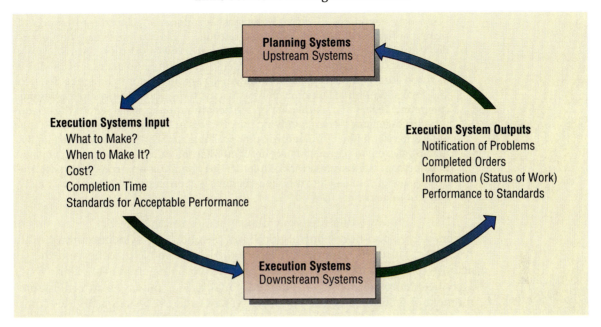

- *What* work should the OM system accomplish? The answer determines the outputs that the system should provide.
- *When* should it generate those outputs? The answer specifies activities to take immediately and those to defer for later action, and it separates essentially short-term activities from those that continue over longer terms.
- *Who* bears responsibility for performing specific activities at specific times? The answer gives assignments to people in the organization.
- *Where* should these people perform these activities? The answer assigns jobs to particular facilities.
- *How* should the OM process complete planned activities? The answer specifies processing steps and subprocesses and allots organizational resources to individual jobs.
- *Why* should the OM process perform certain activities? The answer matches the organization's actions to its objectives and indicates their contribution to value for customers.

Since planning must precede execution, operations managers often refer to planning systems as *upstream* systems. These systems combine inputs from multiple, interdependent subsystems (master production scheduling, inventory management, material requirements planning, capacity planning, aggregate planning and demand management), to project appropriate OM system activities over time. To execute plans, the shop-floor control system ranks orders by urgency of need and assigns resources such as labor, equipment, materials, and tools based on those rankings. Because the outputs of planning become inputs to shop-floor control, operations managers often call it the *downstream* system.

Exhibit 18.1 illustrates the substantial links and interdependencies between these systems. Clearly, effective execution depends on effective plans, and planning can be effective only if execution effectively completes assigned tasks.

Operations managers have coined a number of different names for shop-floor control (SFC), including *job-shop control, manufacturing activity planning,* and *production activity control.* By any name, SFC encompasses a:

> … group of activities directly responsible for managing the transformation of planned orders into a set of completed outputs. It governs the "very short term" detailed planning, execution, and monitoring activities needed to control the flow of an order from the moment that the order is released until that order is filled and its disposition completed. The SFC system is responsible for making the detailed and final allocation of labor, machine, capacity, tools, and materials to the various competing orders. It collects data on the activities taking place within the operations management system involving the progress of various orders and the status of resources and makes the information available to the planning system. Finally, the SFC system is responsible for ensuring that the orders released to the operations management system for completion are done in a way consistent with the firm's view of value. Often, this view requires that orders be completed in a timely and cost-effective manner.[1]

This definition identifies four major themes underlying SFC. First, customer orders drive shop-floor control decisions. Second, SFC systems control multiple resources. Third, the responsibilities of those systems extend beyond the single activity of scheduling to require comprehensive arrangements to ensure that OM activities complete orders as planned. Finally, SFC manages an order from the moment of its release by the planning system until processing activities complete the required output and return it to the planning system.

Orders in Shop-Floor Control

order

A statement that authorizes a firm's OM function to assign people, materials, tools, and equipment to build a predetermined quantity of a specific item

Every SFC system focuses on individual customer orders. In the simplest terms, an **order** authorizes OM personnel to assign people, materials, tools, and equipment to build a predetermined quantity of a specific item. An order also transmits important information such as a quantity, a due date for required outputs, a statement of urgency or priority in relation to other orders, and acceptable quality standards.

Operations managers deal with orders in many forms. They may receive individual orders or more comprehensive schedules that list all orders that the system must fill over a period of time, perhaps a day or a week. Orders can fulfill immediate needs of actual customers or anticipated needs of potential customers. Verbal orders often arrive by telephone; hard-copy orders come printed on paper or through computer records; customers or others may present orders in person. To appreciate the need to combine a wide variety of orders, consider Bill Taylor's job:

- A worker from an assembly line walks into the tool room's customer service area with a broken fixture that needs immediate repair to allow the line to restart production.
- The GM computer system generates a routine, weekly list of tool orders (called *crib orders*) to replace tools taken from inventory and used in production.
- A package of drawings, specifications, and example parts arrives from engineering to describe a new fixture for production of a car model scheduled for introduction in 3 years.

[1]Steven A. Melnyk and Phillip L. Carter, *Productivity Activity Control: A Practical Guide* (Homewood, Ill.: Dow Jones-Irwin, 1987), p. 1.

[**EXHIBIT 18.2**]

Different Forms of Orders

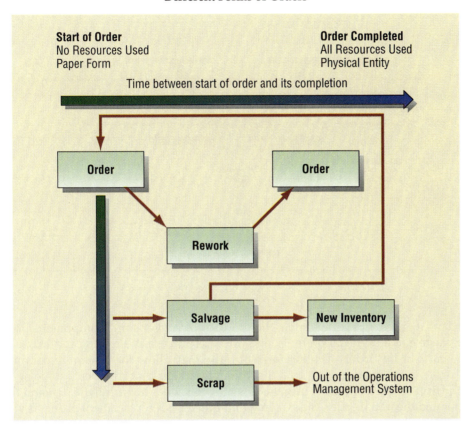

- A shop supervisor for a production line calls on the phone with news that one of the tools used on the line has broken and the supervisor needs a replacement within 48 hours. The order includes a part name and identifying number along with an account number to which to charge the cost.
- Conversations with maintenance workers reveal a list of tools and fixtures that will soon wear out and need replacement. This list becomes a stream of orders for the shop.

Orders express organizational intentions. Initially, an order represents a concept or idea of some particular finished goods. Shop-floor control assigns resources and schedules work to determine how workers transform the abstract order into a completed product. Along the way, it can take on one of four forms (Exhibit 18.2). An acceptable order moves routinely through the system to fulfill customer expectations for due date, quality, cost, and quantity. A **rework** order, or some portion of an order that becomes rework, requires special handling or extra processing to meet customer needs. These extra steps often correct problems with initial processing such as redrilling a hole that routine processing made too small to meet specifications. Rework represents a temporary order to bring products up to usual standards.

Salvage is an order or part of an order that the OM system cannot complete according to initial intentions, but for which the system can still find some use.

rework

An order or part of an order that requires special handling or extra processing to meet customer needs

salvage

An order or part of an order that the OM system cannot complete according to initial intentions, but for which the system can still find some use

[**EXHIBIT 18.3**]

Resources within Shop-Floor Control

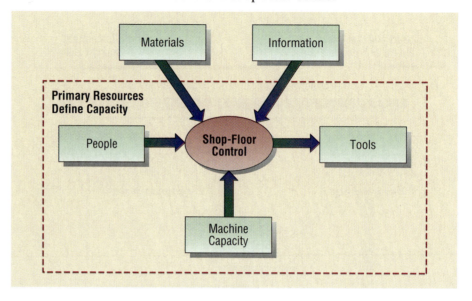

Perhaps workers can disassemble the product to recover some components, leaving waste equal to the labor, tools, and other resources invested to produce unusable parts of the order. Another form of reuse may allow the system to complete the order in a form different from the initial intentions that still meets some needs of the firm or its customers. Since the salvage order does not fulfill the demand that generated the initial order, the system often processes a replacement order, as well.

scrap

Any part of an order that the system cannot process into a usable product

Scrap is any part of an order that the system cannot process into a usable product. The system must dispose of such an order in some way. Despite its lack of value to the firm's own process, scrap may be very valuable to someone else. For example, a jeweler cannot use small diamond chips but a manufacturer of diamond-coated drills certainly can.

Of these four forms, only acceptable orders generate value. The other three forms indicate problems within the OM system. They attract the attention of process-control activities like just-in-time manufacturing and total quality management.

Resources Managed by the Shop-Floor Control System

To transform an order from a concept to a real product, the SFC system draws on five major resources (Exhibit 18.3). Of these five resources, the first three define the overall capacity of the SFC system.

People.   The human resources subject to shop-floor control include all people that the OM system needs to plan, process, or handle an order. This category covers overtime, employees transferred from other areas or locations, part-time help, multiple-shift operations, and people working flex-time schedules. SFC systems must account for both direct and indirect labor.

Tools.   This resource includes all of the equipment and special fixtures that help the OM system to complete setups and processing for a machine or other work center.

Machine capacity is just one resource that a shop floor manager must consider when designing an operation management system.   SOURCE   Donald Dietz/Stock Boston

Machine Capacity.   This resource reflects the total productive capacity offered by the equipment within the OM system. A shop's tool room, for example, includes machine capacity like drills, lathes, grinders, saws, and numerically controlled machines.

Materials.   An OM system's total stock of raw materials, processed materials, and components form part of the resources that its shop-floor control system allocates to complete an order. Materials requirements planning and other methods help operations managers to project needs for these resources.

Information.   The final SFC resource comes from information that guides efforts to complete an order. For each order, this resource includes a route that states needed processing steps and their sequence, time standards, a bill of materials, a due date, a quantity, and the customer's name. Also, a bill of labor and capacity lays out the needed capacities and their amounts.

"The planning system is held accountable for feasibility, the SFC system is held accountable for efficiency."

Anonymous

Altogether, these resources link the SFC system to the planning system. Planners determine the ultimate levels of capacity and materials available to the OM system by setting upper limits on the number of employees and the capacities of machines and tools. Since the planning system constrains the SFC system by determining resource levels, planners bear ultimate responsibility for the feasibility of any plan they release to the shop floor. The SFC system and its personnel remain accountable for applying resources efficiently to carry out the plans. (Chapter 17 discusses the material management system.)

◉ MAJOR ACTIVITIES OF SHOP-FLOOR CONTROL

In managing the efficient flow of orders through the execution system, the shop-floor control system completes several interrelated activities:

- Order review/release
- Detailed scheduling

- Data collection/monitoring
- Control/feedback
- Order disposition

Exhibit 18.4 illustrates the links between these steps and related planning and scheduling activities.

Order Review/Release

The order review/release (ORR) activity evaluates inputs from the planning system and prepares them for production by the transformation process. Through this activity, the shop-floor control system ensures that it releases only good orders to the floor and that it releases them in a sequence that helps the OM process to complete them on time in the correct quantities without creating unnecessary problems. ORR consists of four major steps: order documentation, material checking, capacity evaluation, and load leveling.

Order Documentation.   Order documentation adds information to orders received from the planning system to provide additional detail that will guide the transformation process. Typically, documentation specifies several important characteristics of an order:

- *Order identification*   The documentation step assigns a number or code to uniquely identify an order and allow subsequent tracking.
- *Routing*   Documentation also describes the various operations through which an order must pass and their sequence. An order's route helps to determine its resource requirements.
- *Time standards*   The time standards information identifies the expected amount of resources (machine and labor) that it requires at each stage. This information is useful for monitoring, scheduling, and capacity management.
- *Material requirements*   This information identifies the amount of components and other materials that the OM process will need to process an order.
- *Other*   Documentation may also state tool requirements, due dates for specific processing activities, anticipated levels of scrap, and special handling requirements.

This information becomes part of a packet that accompanies the order as it moves through processing steps. This packet can consist of a bundle of papers attached to the order sheet or a set of computer files that workers can call up by entering the order number or scanning a bar code.

Material Checking.   The order review/release activity allows an order to proceed only when the OM process can draw the components and materials it needs to complete processing. The material-checking step verifies this condition, perhaps by physically examining storage locations or by checking inventory status in a computerized materials requirements planning system. If the process lacks needed materials, this step orders them. The order waits in a file, often labeled "Orders Pending" or "Order Backlog," until the materials arrive.

Capacity Evaluation.   Besides essential materials, an OM process needs adequate available capacity to complete an order. The capacity-evaluation step of the order review/release activity compares the capacity requirements for an order with process capacity not currently occupied by other orders. If this analysis finds

[EXHIBIT 18.4]

Integrated Framework for Shop-Floor Control

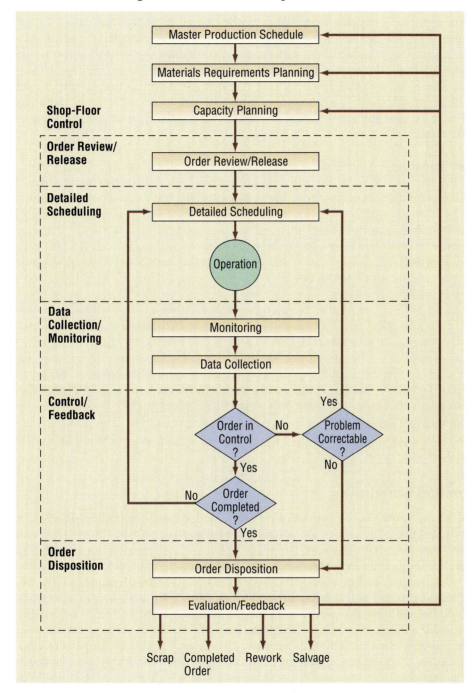

enough capacity, the activity can proceed with the next step, load leveling. If not, the release of the order may wait until the necessary capacity becomes available.

This step provides important protection against overloading the transformation system by releasing more work than it can complete. Without this safeguard, overloaded capacity would stretch lead times and make them more variable. Confusion would plague the transformation process as people wondered which orders they could fill and which they could not because of insufficient capacity.

This check may seem to duplicate efforts by the planning system to assure adequate capacity. Shop-floor control monitors actual capacity, however, while the planning system deals with advance information about expected capacity. At any time, the amount of available capacity can differ from an expected amount due to unanticipated influences such as changing priorities, employee absenteeism (perhaps due to illness, vacations, or jury duty), lack of equipment (perhaps due to unanticipated breakdowns or planned preventive maintenance), or inaccurate estimates of processing times (if earlier jobs take longer and consume more capacity than planned).

Load Leveling.   Many SFC systems regularly accumulate or backlog pending orders briefly, releasing them to the shop floor at a controlled rate to level the resulting load on the transformation process. This control reduces the peaks and raises the valleys of the load on capacity (Exhibit 18.5).[2] At peaks, a process has too much work so it suffers from long queues and lead times. At valleys, activities in the same process might sit idle, waiting for new work. Together, peaks and valleys create excessive variance in a process. **Load leveling** works to reduce this variance by rearranging work loads to move excess demand from the peaks to keep the shop busy during valleys.

Load leveling works by releasing orders early to fill valleys or by delaying orders in a backlog pool to trim peaks. In Exhibit 18.5, load leveling would focus on the workload scheduled for release between Weeks 11 and 25. Overall, the average load (100.23 hours per week) almost equals the amount of capacity available (100.00). Only the timing of the load creates potential problems. Load leveling would begin by releasing orders early to take advantage of available capacity in Weeks 1 to 10. It would then delay some subsequent orders to consume excess capacity available after Week 26. In this way, the pool of backlogged orders effectively decouples general needs of the planning system from detailed needs of the transformation process.

load leveling

A shop-floor control measure to rearrange work loads, moving excess demand from peaks to keep the shop busy during valleys

Detailed Scheduling

One of the most visible and action-oriented activities within shop-floor control, **detailed scheduling**, allocates specific OM resources at specific times to individual orders based on their priorities. After this activity sets priorities for orders, they wait for processing either in some central scheduling area or at individual work centers.

Detailed scheduling is essentially a process of matching demands on the transformation process with its resources. This matching process results in extremely detailed scheduling decisions, beginning with assignments of order priorities. To identify the exact sequence in which the transformation system meets competing demands, the detailed schedule must weigh the urgency of each order relative to others, the relative importance of each customer, the amount of processing that each order requires, the time remaining before each order's due date, and the reliability of due dates.

Based on these measures of priority, the detailed schedule allocates specific types and quantities of resources to each order. It also specifies the timing of pro-

detailed scheduling

A shop-floor control process that allocates specific OM resources at specific times to individual orders based on their priorities

---

[2]Peaks occur when arriving orders generate demand for processing activities in excess of available capacity; valleys occur when demand falls far short of available capacity.

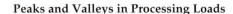

[**EXHIBIT 18.5**]

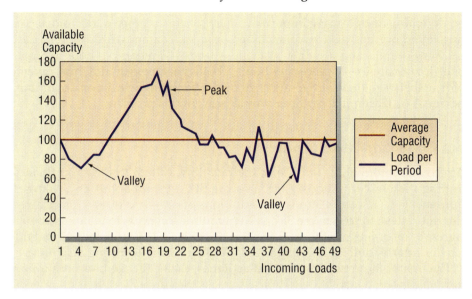

Peaks and Valleys in Processing Loads

cessing activities and resource commitments, including the times when resources become available for reassignment. If the process could supply needed resources from more than one location (for example, if more than one skilled operator could fill a given order), then the detailed schedule identifies the specific sources of necessary resources.

Detailed scheduling divides all of these allocations into three major categories: order sequencing/dispatching, scheduled maintenance, and other assignments.

Order Sequencing/Dispatching.   This process applies a prespecified set of decision rules to determine the specific sequence in which a facility will process a number of different orders. This process includes the corresponding assignment of workers, tools, and materials to selected jobs. These important decisions must support the predetermined goals of the SFC system and the vision of value that drives the OM system.

Based on decision guidelines commonly called *dispatching rules* or *priority rules,* the SFC system ranks orders from the most to the least important. A daily **dispatch list** typically communicates these priorities to employees on the shop floor, displaying all of the orders waiting for processing by a given machine or work center in rank order. This information guides the operator's choice of which order to fill next.

dispatch list
A daily document that communicates order priorities to shop-floor employees

Scheduled Maintenance.   Preventive maintenance is an important countermeasure against daily wear and tear on tools and equipment. Mechanical breakdowns temporarily eliminate the productive capabilities, usually when the process has the most urgent need for its machines and tools, according to some operations managers. Scheduled maintenance reduces the risk of machine breakdowns through routine lubrication and inspections of equipment along with periodic overhauls. Detailed scheduling must accommodate these preventive maintenance activities because they often compete with orders for access to tools and equipment.

Other Assignments.   Scheduled downtime and indirect labor also tie up productive resources. They help to level current loads by shutting down unneeded activities or diverting currently unneeded resources to ancillary activities such as counting stock or cleaning facilities. Just-in-time manufacturing has made scheduled downtime increasingly important, since it helps a process to avoid accumulating inventory between two machines or work centers with different output rates. For example, suppose that Machine A feeds 100 pieces per hour to Machine B, which can only use 80 pieces per hour. If both machines run full time, inventory builds up between them at the rate of 20 pieces per hour. Scheduled downtime for Machine A of 12 minutes per hour would prevent this problem.

Data Collection/Monitoring

Bidirectional information flows link the planning system to the shop floor. The planning system continuously updates the SFC system about any changes in requirements (e.g., cancellations and additions of orders, requests for changes in order due dates). In return, the SFC system routinely reports to planners about the progress of all orders in process. The shop-floor control process collects and maintains this information flow through its data collection/monitoring activities.

The first of these two interrelated activities, data collection, records information from shop-floor activities. It typically tracks the current locations of orders and their states of completion, actual consumption of resources by process activities, and any unplanned delays.

The monitoring activity then analyzes this accumulated information, often by comparing actual progress with planned progress. Shop-floor control can measure the progress of any order in several different ways: stage of processing, costs incurred to date, or time remaining until the due date. This analysis often includes comparisons against standards generated by people in engineering or accounting, records of past performance, or management expectations. Ultimately, monitoring works to identify the orders with the largest gaps between actual and desired performance. These orders become the targets for special attention from either operating employees or managers.

Control/Feedback

Every OM activity exhibits some variability. Operations managers tolerate this variability only until it begins to create problems and cause some part of the SFC system, from an entire process to a single order, to range out of control. To continue performing effectively and efficiently, the SFC system must reestablish control, often through direct intervention by either managers or employees. The control/feedback activity circulates information to others within the OM system or the firm to alert them to current conditions and potential problems. SFC analysts separate this activity into two linked procedures: control and feedback.

Control.   Problems or out-of-control processes require short-term adjustments that make changes in capacity. For example, a firm that competes on claims of timely delivery must respond quickly when an order falls behind schedule. As one response, a firm might call on subcontractors to help it handle excess work. More commonly, the shop-floor control system might allocate more capacity to a problem order by changing the work rate or scheduling overtime, part-time labor, or a second shift.

It may also assign **safety capacity**, or idle capacity that the firm keeps available for such emergencies, to the order. For example, a restaurant manager knows that Monday nights generally bring slow demand with only about 80 customers during the dinner rush from 5 p.m. to 8 p.m. Although the manager may know that four servers can keep these customers happy, he or she might decide to schedule five servers. The safety capacity of the extra server protects against service deficiencies if more than 80 people walk into the restaurant.

In addition to allocating additional capacity in some form, the SFC system can try to reestablish control by directing an order along some alternate route of process activities. Usually, some routine or preferred sequence of activities provides either the lowest cost, the fastest processing, or the best quality. Orders can follow other sequences, however, when something closes off part of the preferred route, as when a machine breaks down or another order keeps it busy. Alternate routes expose the system to some unusual costs in the form of longer setup times, higher scrap rates, or other differences, but they do allow the firm to meet its due dates.

A control system may also divide up a total system load into smaller lots to facilitate processing. Generally, operations managers try to process each order as one batch, so the first completed unit waits until a step finishes the rest of the units before moving to a later activity. To meet a critical due date, however, **lot splitting** may break up the order into several smaller batches that proceed separately through the shop. This method amounts to another way to complete an order more quickly by assigning more resources to it. Instead of processing a batch of 100 units through one machine, four smaller lots might run more quickly through four identical machines. Lot splitting reduces the calendar time to process an order, although it does increase setup time since several machines require identical adjustments. Overall, lead times fall (Exhibit 18.6).

An undesirable method of reestablishing control involves **expediting**, in which someone from the SFC system manually intervenes in the operation of the system to return an out-of-control order to an acceptable processing routine. Expediting frequently ties up a person to carry the critical order from machine to machine, pushing it through the process as quickly as possible. Operations managers often describe this response as "walking the order through the system."

In general, expediting fails to add value, or it can even create waste, for several reasons. First, it represents a reactive response that occurs only after an order ranges out of control rather than a proactive measure to maintain control. Second, expediting disrupts the progress of other jobs waiting in work-center queues. Someone who walks a job through the system delays other waiting orders, perhaps sending another job out of control that would otherwise have remained under marginal control. Finally, expediting corrects symptoms rather than the causes that send orders out of control in the first place.

Feedback.   The SFC system also transmits information about the progress of orders on the shop floor back to the planning system, as previously discussed. This link informs planners about events within the transformation process. It also identifies seriously troubled orders for which the SFC system cannot make sufficient capacity adjustments to restore control. The planning system may respond to feedback about orders too far behind schedule or too badly disrupted by problems with scrap or quality performance by taking one or more remedial actions:

- Changing the due date for the order, usually by pushing it further into the future
- Canceling the order

---

safety capacity

Excess capacity that the firm keeps available for unexpected demand; it acts as a buffer

lot splitting

A shop-floor control measure that breaks up an order into several smaller batches that proceed separately through the shop

expediting

A shop-floor control measure in which someone manually intervenes in the operation of the system to return an out-of-control order to an acceptable processing routine

[**EXHIBIT 18.6**]

Lot Splitting to Reestablish Control

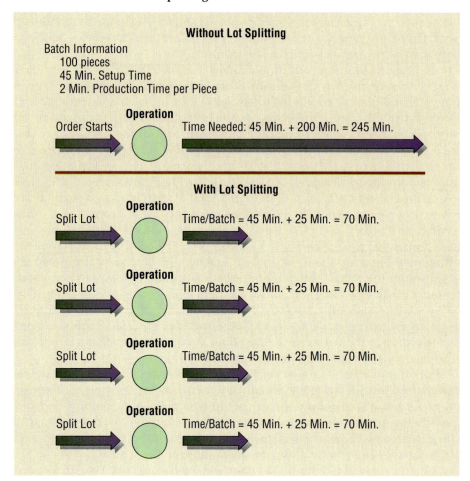

- Reducing the system's incoming load to free up extra capacity
- Reducing the order quantity

exception reporting

A shop-floor control measure that ignores noncritical jobs and focuses attention only on information that indicates a need for management intervention

Control/feedback rely on important **exception reporting** methods. Exception reporting focuses attention only on information that indicates a need for management intervention. Typically, this information involves critical or problem jobs. Exception reporting ignores noncritical jobs.

Order Disposition

The last activity within shop-floor control, order disposition, pursues two major objectives: to relieve the transformation system of responsibility for the order and to provide the rest of the firm with information to evaluate the performance of the transformation process and the recently completed order. At the completion of order disposition, operations managers and others can evaluate the performance of the transformation process against standards for several important measures:

- Resources used (perhaps measured in labor hours or machine hours)
- Materials consumed
- Hours of setup time
- Tools used
- Completion date
- Rework or scrap generated
- Units completed versus the number started

Finally, order disposition gives everyone a last chance to examine orders and to understand exactly what happened to them. People tend to forget quickly about closed-out orders. Before this point, order disposition creates an opportunity to study practical problems and their causes. Such a postmortem investigation may provide valuable information to support continuous-improvement activities.

Interactions between Shop-Floor Control Activities

Individually, the five shop-floor control activities give operations managers a lot to understand. Their effects and interactions should become more clear, however, through an example from the GM tool room.

At 7 a.m., activity in the tool room has settled into an established routine. Bill Taylor reviews a stack of forms, some of which represent orders from engineering for prototype tools. He pulls out some crib orders and sets them aside for the six process planners on the tool room staff. These planners convert each order into the necessary number of steps and operations, adding detail that operators need but that the initial orders omit. After setting out the exact work centers and their sequence for each order, the process planners determine what materials those activities will need. Internal stores hold much of these materials, and planners order the rest from external suppliers. Two filing cabinets hold all orders that must await either processing information or materials before release to the shop floor. All of these activities of process planners represent part of the shop-floor control system's order review/release function.

Bill Taylor immediately passes on any quick-response orders for management by area supervisors. More routine project and crib orders come out of their filing cabinets when the SFC system receives the necessary materials and information. They wait in numbered slots in six shelving areas for the completion of one more step, detailed scheduling, before their release to the shop floor for processing.

This scheduling process begins when Bill Taylor uses the computer system to assign a priority to each order. Often this priority reflects the time that the order arrived in the system. The overall urgency of an order may also affect this decision. The computer system then generates a sorted list of orders for every one of the tool room's 28 major work centers.

An order completes the order review/release activity and moves onto the shop floor once it enters the computer system and gains a spot in one of the five highest-priority slots for its first work center. Employees work only on the top five jobs for each work center as part of a load leveling procedure to control the amount of work released to the shop floor. This rule also helps to prevent the release of any problem orders, since the priority list carries an order only after planners have documented all of its steps and verified availability all of necessary materials.

Machine operators check the computer system before and after completing an operation for a part to make sure that they work on the right orders and also to identify the locations of those orders. Before working on a new order, they must complete several data collection/monitoring steps, including pulling the order, its materials, and documentation. They also enter information at a computer terminal to specify the order in process, the employee doing the work, and the time and date that processing begins.

Detailed scheduling in the tool room follows a fairly straightforward procedure. An employee checks the computer system and identifies the next job to process. If this job is not available, the operator looks down the list to find the next job.

When workers finish processing, they return the orders to customer service, where their status information receives updates to indicate completion of appropriate operations. Customer-service staff members (including Bill Taylor) identify any problems with the order at this time and determine the most appropriate action to take (control/feedback). They may modify the planned route for the order and release it back to the floor, or they may authorize overtime production for the order. If they find any problems that will affect the completion date of the order or its final quality level, they phone customers to discuss the problems. The information entered into the computer system by either operating employees or customer-service people helps the SFC system to track the progress and current locations of orders.

Once an order finishes the last operation in its detailed schedule, workers return it to the customer-service area to begin order disposition. To close out the order, staff members enter information into the computer indicating its completion. This process includes a check to verify complete information, including labor hours, material amounts, and the resolutions of any unexplained variances. Some projects pass through an additional step at this point to assemble several components, known as *details*, each of which follows its own route through the system up to this point.

Finally, the customer receives notice of completion of the order and arrangements for accepting delivery. A completed and evaluated job leaves the tool room, and Bill Taylor surrenders responsibility for it. In reaching this point, the order passes through every activity in the shop-floor control system.

BACKGROUND FOR SCHEDULING IN SHOP-FLOOR CONTROL

Many observers recognize little difference between scheduling and shop-floor control. This assumption may seem reasonable since scheduling is the most visible of the five SFC activities. Traditionally, it has drawn more attention than the other activities, from both managers and researchers.[3] In fact, the other activities may serve primarily to support effective scheduling.

Of the three objects of detailed scheduling—orders, preventive maintenance, and downtime—we will focus on scheduling procedures for orders. The same methods could simply treat maintenance and downtime as special kinds of orders.

Scheduling provides a controlled process through which people set and manipulate order priorities to determine the exact order in which a shop processes jobs. A particular sequence remains valid only as long as the priorities behind it continue to satisfy value-driven criteria communicated by other activities in the SFC system. To set these priorities, scheduling brings together people and analytical tools, as illustrated in Exhibit 18.7.

[3]Steven A. Melnyk, Phillip L. Carter, David M. Dilts, and David M. Lyth, *Shop-Floor Control* (Homewood, Ill.: Dow Jones-Irwin, 1985).

Roles in the Scheduling Process

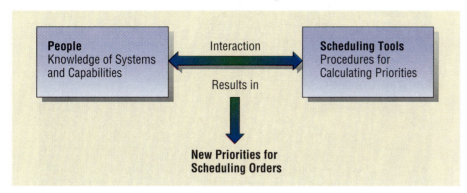

Three objectives drive the scheduling process. First, it seeks to ensure that the OM process completes orders in a manner that realizes the corporate vision of value for customers. A formal OM system tries to accomplish this objective by linking the SFC system to the planning system, primarily through the **order due date**. The planning system sets this date to inform the SFC system when it must return a finished product to the control of the planning system. An order due date sets a critical performance target because it powerfully affects the firm's success at satisfying its customers. In addition, early or late completion of a job exposes the firm to significant costs. Products completed ahead of schedule must wait in stock rooms, increasing inventory, costs, and waste. Of course, a late order disappoints a customer.

In addition to linking shop-floor control to the organization's vision of value, scheduling pursues a second objective of promoting overall efficiency on the shop floor. At a minimum, the planning system should generate feasible plans. However, the general information in these plans does not automatically equate to the most efficient schedule. Real efficiency comes when system personnel apply their insights and knowledge to arrange orders and schedules.

For example, one principle for improving efficiency argues for grouping together orders that share similar components, processing activities, or setups. Grouping orders with similar components can save time by allowing workers to withdraw many items at once from store rooms rather than making several trips. Processing similarities allow workers to perform tasks repeatedly, so speed increases. Similarities in setups save time spent to prepare work centers and machines. Efficiency also benefits when a schedule matches people with the types of orders that suit them. For example, Bill Taylor routes long, complex jobs to certain workers in GM's tool room, while others get relatively simple, multiple-piece orders.

In its third objective, scheduling seeks to develop and maintain conditions that limit variance in the transformation process. Variance comes from many causes such as peaks and valleys in the work load or orders with widely varying skill requirements or quantities. The detailed scheduling process should attempt to route work through a shop in a way that relieves or controls such sources of variance. For example, it might try to level variations in load by basing scheduling decisions on conditions at downstream work centers. The system might raise the priority levels of orders moving toward relatively idle work centers to keep that equipment busy while slowing the work flow to congested or bottlenecked work centers.

order due date

A performance target that informs the shop-floor control system when it must return a finished product to the control of the planning system

Despite a global increase in the use of computers in manufacturing, people remain the key to accurate scheduling of maintenance and repairs.   SOURCE   Gerd Ludwig/Woodfin Camp & Associates

Shop-floor controllers must resolve these objectives into a detailed schedule. They apply both human judgment and precise analytical tools to achieve these three objectives.

Human Judgment in Scheduling

Most modern SFC systems rely heavily on computers to complete their complex work. Computer terminals fill both the shop floor in GM's Lansing tool room and control stations in an oil refinery. Service systems such as car-repair garages make extensive use of computers.

Despite all of these computers, however, detailed scheduling still needs active involvement of people. People know much more than any computer could ever record, especially about qualitative process characteristics. Computer systems do not easily track subjective information like workers' relative skills at individual jobs and their ability to switch places without sacrificing efficiency. This vast storehouse of human knowledge provides a hidden agenda with a powerful influence on scheduling decisions.

For example, a scheduler for a job shop knows that a key employee has arranged to take a 3-week skiing vacation in a month's time. No one else in the shop can replace this worker, so scheduling decisions must anticipate the temporary loss of capacity. A thoughtful scheduler might review potential orders that the planning system will soon release and that will need the vacationing worker's skill and expertise. Perhaps planners could release some of these orders early to avoid delays.

Detailed scheduling typically involves dynamic, continuing interactions among three groups of people—dispatchers, department supervisors, and operating workers. Since each group can contribute important insights and information, each should influence scheduling priorities (Exhibit 18.8).

The dispatcher (also called the *scheduler* or *senior scheduler)* often acts as an interface between the planning function and the SFC system. This person looks for ways to satisfy both the objectives of the planning system (e.g., on-time delivery of a quality product) and the needs of the SFC system. The dispatcher controls the

[**E X H I B I T   1 8 . 8**]

Interactions within the Scheduling Process

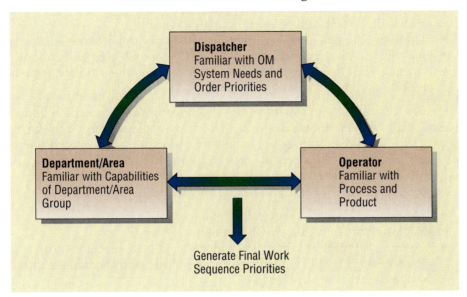

flow of work to various work centers and suggests order priorities to shop-floor personnel. As described earlier, a dispatch list often communicates these priorities.

At a minimum, the dispatch list should list jobs in a feasible order that reflects the potential capabilities of existing capacity. The dispatcher's specific responsibilities typically include:

- Keeping shop personnel aware of the status of work (e.g., orders due to arrive, orders in queues and ready for processing, orders assigned to work centers but not yet released, and orders released and behind schedule)
- Working with other dispatchers and department supervisors to ensure a timely and level flow of orders and materials to work centers without unnecessary congestion or work-in-process inventory
- Communicating any changes in order due dates and similar requirements of orders in process (e.g., quantities or product mixes)
- Regularly following and communicating needs for past-due orders and any other types of orders that require special attention
- Together with department supervisors, and operating workers when necessary, setting actual priorities for orders at various work centers

The second partner in the scheduling triangle, the department supervisor, allocates resources (e.g., equipment, employees, materials, and tools) to orders released to the department by the dispatcher. This work requires extensive knowledge of the department and the capabilities and limitations of its equipment and employees. Typically, the supervisor's specific responsibilities include:

- Assigning individual orders to specific equipment or operators
- Monitoring department capacity levels
- Evaluating the feasibility of orders released by the dispatcher in light of current conditions within the department

- Warning the dispatcher about any anticipated delays in order completion and their durations
- Ensuring timely and accurate reports of all transactions in the department involving performance standards like labor hours worked, scrap, salvage, rework, downtime, setup time, and material usage
- Identifying the causes of any problems within the department
- Ensuring that the department completes all work released to it on time
- Working with operating employees to determine the ultimate sequences of jobs

Finally, operating employees bring an important asset to the scheduling process—their detailed knowledge of the OM system, its products, and the capabilities of its work centers. Operators frequently make ultimate decisions about the exact sequences in which to process orders. In making these decisions, workers should strive to achieve efficiency without compromising due dates, quality, and flexibility. Typically, the operator's specific responsibilities include:

- Determining the actual processing sequence for orders
- Monitoring capacity at their work centers
- Reporting any problems and anticipated delays (e.g., machine breakdowns, excessive scrap, poor or suspect time standards, and incomplete information) to department supervisors
- Identifying and recording the causes of these problems to provide information to guide the SFC system's corrective actions and programs of continuous improvement and waste elimination
- Evaluating and commenting on the feasibility of scheduled work center loads
- Working with other operators and department supervisors to level shop loads by pulling work forward, when possible, to group orders with similar setups, component needs, or processing activities, as described earlier
- Monitoring the status of upstream and downstream work centers (Exhibit 18.9) and making appropriate changes in order priorities (e.g., increasing the priorities of orders going to idle work centers and decreasing the priorities of orders going to bottleneck operations)
- Keeping timely and accurate records of all transactions at their work centers
- Completing orders by scheduled due dates

Tools in Scheduling

Analytical scheduling tools help operations managers to resolve many technical requirements to generate a schedule and translate it into action. These tools require information inputs and an understanding of some basic definitions. In this section, we will discuss these needs along with some general scheduling principles. This will prepare for detailed discussions of some techniques and procedures that work in specific operating environments.

Physical flows of goods and services dominate scheduling decisions, and they often seem to divert attention away from critical information flows. The process draws on information from a variety of sources, including dispatch lists, input/output reports, order-location reports (also called *where-are reports*), and various status and exception reports. All of this information comes from estimates of order due dates, operation due dates, and scheduling calendars.

order due date

A performance target that informs the shop-floor control system when it must return a finished product to the control of the planning system

Order Due Dates.   As discussed earlier, an **order due date** is an internal due date. It specifies the time by which the OM system must complete all of the necessary

[**E X H I B I T   1 8 . 9**]

Downstream versus Upstream Work Centers

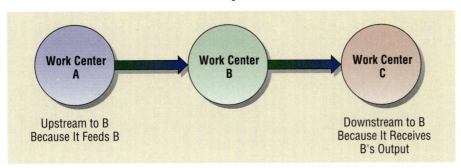

operations to make a finished product available. This date can be a calendar date or some specific time on a particular date. Differences in methods of setting order due dates often have important implications.

Customers specify their order need dates. For example, a customer can walk into GM's tool room with an order for completion no later than August 20. Bill Taylor must then determine whether or not the tool room can meet the desired date. If the order requires a longer lead time than the order need date will allow, Bill can (1) accept the order and hope everything works out, (2) try to negotiate the date, (3) refuse the order, or (4) assign extra capacity to meet the date.

Shop-floor control systems also assign some order due dates. This step begins when the dispatcher calculates the planned or estimated lead time for each new order in one of two ways. This calculation may apply a standard lead-time allowance. If standards call for a 3-week lead time for every order, then an order dated May 9 gets a due date of May 30 (21 days later). Alternatively, the scheduler or dispatcher might determine the number of operations needed to complete the order and the estimated time per operation. After adjustment for the current shop load, the sum of operation times determines the earliest possible order due date. The customer can then approve or reject it.

In a third method, a formal planning system such as materials requirements planning (MRP) can set order due dates. MRP systems often work backward from needed finished product dates to schedule orders for individual components. Time-phasing decisions move from a due date to a start date for each component in the bill of materials based on that component's standard lead time. The planning system can assume either a fixed lead time irrespective of order quantity and current shop load or a variable lead time.

Such a system may calculate variable lead times from formulas like the **total work content rule**, or TWK rule. This rule estimates lead time based on the amount of processing time needed for a specific job (setups plus operation or run times) adjusted for delays like time spent waiting in queues for equipment and transportation. Mathematically, TWK equals:

total work content rule
A method of calculating variable lead times that sums processing times for components in a specific job and adjusts for delays

$$TWK = k \times \sum_{i=1}^{n} \left(\text{setup}_i + \text{operation}_i \right)$$ **(18.1)**

where

k = multiplier
setup_i = setup time for Operation i
operation_i = total operation time for Operation i

[EXHIBIT 18.10]

Operation Lead Time Estimates

Operation	Description	Setup (hours)	Run Time per Piece (hours)
10	Rough turn	1.5	0.030
20	Finish turn	3.3	0.048
30	Mill face	1.8	0.025
40	Mill slots	0.6	0.010
Order quantity: 300 units		7.2	$0.113 \times 300 = 33.9$

Problem 18.1 illustrates this method for a hypothetical order that requires the processing steps listed in Exhibit 18.10.

[PROBLEM 18.1]

Order Lead Times through TWK

Summing the setup time and the total run time from the exhibit gives a total work content of 41.1 hours. Suppose that past experience suggests that k from the TWK equation equals 10, which means that the total lead time for processing an order tends average 10 times the length of the processing time.[4] This multiple reflects waiting time and time consumed by transportation and other activities such as inspections. The equation gives a total planned lead time for the order of 411 hours (10×41.1), and the planning system can use this value to set the order due date.   [■]

 Finally, customers and representatives of the shop-floor control system can negotiate order due dates through some combination of the previous methods. When a customer wants a different due date than the SFC system offers, they can seek a mutually acceptable compromise date. The customer may have to accept a later due date while the SFC system may have to reschedule some work to improve its original estimate.

Operation Due Dates.   An order due date tells the SFC system and its personnel when they must complete processing for a finished product. Operating employees usually need more detail, however. They need an individual **operation due date** that sets a completion time for every activity in the processing sequence for an order. Workers handling the order in Exhibit 18.10 would need four separate operation due dates for Operations 10, 20, 30, and 40. By meeting each one, the process would also meet the overall order due date. In many SFC systems, the operation due date for the last operation matches the overall order due date.

operation due date

A performance target that sets a completion time for every activity in the processing sequence for an order

---

[4]The planning system can set the k value in a number of different ways, including past experience and observation. Another method would run a linear regression with observed total lead time *(Y)* as the dependent variable and total processing time *(TWK)* as the independent variable. This equation should have the form $Y = k \times TWK$ (with no intercept). The slope of the regression line would give the k value.

[**E X H I B I T   1 8 . 1 1**]

Converting Hours into Days

	8-hour Shifts per Day		
	One Shift	**Two Shifts**	**Three Shifts**
Time per day	8 hours	16 hours	24 hours
Lead time in days for 411 hours	52 days	26 days[a]	18 days[b]

[a]$411/16 = 25.69$
[b]$411/24 = 17.125$

Scheduling Calendars.   In addition to order due dates, planned or estimated lead times help operations managers to determine when a process should start orders. This choice depends on the number of hours per work day allocated for production and the system's scheduling calendar. Recall that Exhibit 18.10 gave a planned lead time for a process of 411 hours. If the transformation system runs 8 hours per shift, that lead time translates into 52 work shifts ($411/8 = 51.375$). This calculation always rounds partial amounts upward to the next full shift. Exhibit 18.11 summarizes the relationships of shifts, hours per shift, and lead time estimates.

The number of work shifts for an order helps to determine both the due date and the starting date on which the SFC system should release the order to the shop floor. Schedulers compare this work-shift information with the firm's **scheduling calendar** to determine specific dates from lead-time data. Exhibit 18.12 illustrates three kinds of calendars for a process that runs 24 hours a day, 7 days a week.

scheduling calendar
A table for determining specific dates from lead-time data

[**E X H I B I T   1 8 . 1 2**]

Three Types of Scheduling Calendars

Sunday	Monday	Tuesday	Wednesday	Thursday	Friday	Saturday
1	**2**	**3**	**4**	**5**	**6**	**7**
171	172	173	174	175	176	177
121	122	123	124	125	126	127
8	**9**	**10**	**11**	**12**	**13**	**14**
181	182	183	184	185	186	187
128	129	130	131	132	133	134
15	**16**	**17**	**18**	**19**	**20**	**21**
191	192	193	194	195	196	197
135	136	137	138	139	140	141
22	**23**	**24**	**25**	**26**	**27**	**28**
201	202	203	204	205	206	207
142	143	144	145	146	147	148
29	**30**	**31**				
211	212	213	214	215	216	217
149	150	151	152	153	154	155

NOTE   For each day in the calendar, the first line lists the calendar date, the second line lists the numbered-week calendar representation, and the third line lists the M-day calendar representation.

By releasing the 52-shift order on Monday, May 2, the process could complete it 18 days later on Friday, May 20.

The second row in the exhibit illustrates a numbered-week calendar built on a week-numbering scheme like that of the formal materials requirements planning system. Within each week, this calendar identifies every production day, and sometimes every specific shift, with a three-number identifier. The first two numbers indicate the production week and the third character represents the specific day of that week. In Exhibit 18.12, schedulers would release the order on Day 172 (the 2nd day of the 17th week of production) and the order should reach completion on Day 196 (the 6th day of the 19th week). This type of calendar maintains a link between the calendars for the planning and SFC systems.

The third row illustrates an M-day calendar, which numbers work days consecutively without referring to the production week. The name comes from the practice of specifying up to 1,000 days and then beginning over again (so that the next day after Day 1,000 is Day 001). This calendar specifies a release date on Day 122 and a completion date of Day 140. This calendar simplifies adjustments for holidays. In the United States, the last Monday of May is the Memorial Day holiday. An M-day calendar would simply ignore this day, jumping from from Day 149 on Sunday to Day 150 on Tuesday. This adjustment highlights the importance of understanding the choice of a scheduling calendar in evaluating and communicating start dates and due dates.

General Scheduling Principles

To apply the concepts of order due dates, operation due dates, and scheduling calendars to a practical situation, operations managers must make two choices. The selection between forward and backward scheduling methods determines how they generate due dates and release dates. A second choice between push and pull scheduling affects more detailed movements of orders between work stations.

Forward versus Backward Scheduling.   Forward scheduling typically starts with the earliest date on which a process can begin working on an order. It adds lead times for individual activities needed to complete the order to find successive operation due dates. When the process reaches the last operation, its due date becomes the overall order due date. SFC systems typically employ forward scheduling methods to set due dates.

In contrast, backward scheduling starts with an order due date and works backward through the sequence of OM process activities, starting with the last operation and ending with the first. It subtracts successive activity lead times to determine individual operation due dates and ultimately the latest possible order start date. Customers and planning systems typically conduct this kind of analysis to evaluate the feasibility of desired due dates. An infeasible order due date results when the process gives an overall start date before the current date. Problem 18.2 describes the difference between forward and backward scheduling.

[**P R O B L E M   1 8 . 2**]

Forward and Backward Scheduling

Exhibit 18.13 shows time requirements for a set of process activities along with operation and order due dates determined by the two methods. This

[**EXHIBIT 18.13**]

Backward and Forward Scheduling Illustrated

Operation	Setup (hours)	Run (hours)	Operations (Days)	Queue	Transit
10			01		
20	1.5	0.030		02	01
30			05	02	01
40	3.3	0.048		02	01
50	1.8	0.025		02	01
60	0.6	0.010		02	01
95			03		
99			01		
Total	7.2	0.113	10	09	05

Operation and Order Dates—Forward Scheduling

Order quantity: 300
Due date: 320
Current date: 271

Operation	Hours	Days	Start	Operation Due Date
10		01	271	272
20	10.5	**04**	**273**	277
30		07	278	285
40	17.7	05	286	291
50	9.3	04	292	296
60	3.6	02	297	299
95		03	299	302
99		01	302	303
Total	41.1			

Operation and Order Dates—Backward Scheduling

Order quantity: 300
Due date: 320
Current date: 271

Operation	Hours	Days	Start	Operation Due Date
10		01	288	289
20	10.5	04	290	294
30		07	295	302
40	17.7	05	303	308
50	9.3	04	309	313
60	3.6	02	314	316
95		03	316	319
99		01	319	320
Total	41.1	27 days		

example assumes that the shop uses an M-day calendar and that it operates only one 8-hour shift per day. The exhibit lists setup times, run times, numbers of operations, queue times, and transit times for several activities. It shows a current date of Day 271 and an order due date of Day 320. The customer has ordered 300 units. Below this information, the exhibit shows the operation due dates for the order determined by both forward scheduling and backward scheduling.   [■]

The results with forward scheduling show a lead time for Operation 20 of 4 days (in bold type); this gives the sum of processing time for the activity (10.5 hours, or 2 days) and queue time (another 2 days). Also, the start date for Operation 20 (again, in bold type) reflects a 1-day delay after the due date of Operation 10 (Day 272) due to the 1-day transit time. Finally, notice that the operation due dates could slip by up to 17 extra days without compromising the final order due date of Day 320.

In turn, the backward-scheduling information indicates the latest possible operation due dates as well as the latest possible start date (Day 288) for the entire order. Both scheduling methods indicate a feasible order due date and processing sequence.

The two dates help the SFC manager understand how much slack there is and how it can be used. Using both procedures can show when is the latest start date and when is the earliest process date. The latest start date is important because the shop floor may be congested at the time of the required release date. Holding back the order can reduce the load at that time and ensure that the job is released when it can be done. To determine the slack (how long before the order must be released to meet its due date), backward scheduling can be used to calculate the latest start date. However, the customer may be willing to take an order completed early, and there may be excess capacity available on the shop floor. In this situation, forward scheduling can be used to determine when the order will be completed and the acceptability of this early completion. Forward and backward scheduling are not as much substitutes as they are complements.

Pull versus Push Scheduling.   The discussion of JIT manufacturing in Chapter 9 introduced the concept of pull scheduling. An alternative method, push scheduling, suggests very different guidelines for releasing work to the shop floor and moving it between operations.

Recall that pull-scheduling systems like kanbans transfer work between activities in response to demands from immediately adjacent downstream work centers. As in Exhibit 18.9, Work Center A feeds Work Center B which feeds Work Center C. Pull scheduling leaves Work Center A idle after completing an activity until Work Center B calls for more input. A signal from Work Center B that it needs components effectively pulls production from Work Center A. As an alternative, the work center might simply replenish stocks as calls from the downstream activity deplete them.

Pull scheduling provides several very attractive benefits. It simplifies scheduling because each activity builds just what its internal customers require when they require it. Only real demand drives orders from downstream activities, so unneeded inventories do not accumulate. Also, this system makes problems immediately apparent. A breakdown at Work Center C quickly idles Work Centers A and B, as well, drawing the attention of workers to correct the problem. Finally, pull scheduling automatically prevents additional load from piling up extra work at the bottleneck in the event of some problem.

Operations managers cannot implement pull scheduling easily, however. Success requires strong links between related work centers. Pull scheduling also demands good planning. The planning system should ideally release a level and balanced flow of work to the SFC system. After the system sets the schedule, everyone must agree to strictly control interventions by customers or marketing personnel to ask for changes in due dates, quantities, or product mixes.

In contrast, push scheduling moves an order to the next operation or work center in its route immediately on completion of the current activity whether or not that work center can begin processing it. As Work Center A pushes completed jobs to Work Center B, a large queue of work may accumulate.

Despite this potential drawback, push scheduling does offer benefits of its own. First, implementation is relatively simple—when a worker completes an order, it moves to the next work center and the worker proceeds with the next order on the priority list. This reduces the need for coordination of flows between work centers, and it eases requirements on both the planning system and the shop-floor layout. Push scheduling relaxes the connections between activities, so an order can move to a number of different operations from any point in the process. This enhances flexibility to deal with widely varying loads on different work centers. Finally, push scheduling keeps each work center busy as long as work remains in its queue.

Push scheduling does suffer from several important problems, as well. As described earlier, work-in-process inventory can build up as orders flow in while a work center processes current orders. Also, push scheduling makes a process prone to quality problems. If the processing steps at Work Center A go out of control, it may continue to produce defective parts until personnel at Work Center B notice the errors and inform others. This gives Work Center A a lot of time to produce defects. Also, a breakdown causes work to build up at the disabled work center. When it returns to production, workers may feel pressure to rush the activity to clear the waiting work, creating opportunities for quality problems. These queues also stretch lead times.

Furthermore, push scheduling tends to hide processing problems. Trouble in one part of the transformation system leaves other parts to function as normal. This creates an appearance of activity that can mask problems. Finally, push scheduling requires some form of dispatching rule to tell workers which orders to process next.

Both pull scheduling and push scheduling bring important trade-offs. The shop-floor control system should resolve these trade-offs in a way that enhances the firm's ability to add value for customers. It must also choose specific techniques and procedures for developing schedules that suit both customer needs and process characteristics.

SCHEDULING TECHNIQUES AND PROCEDURES

Scheduling techniques and procedures set guidelines for ranking pending jobs in order of urgency. Different procedures generate rankings in different ways to suit the organization's criteria for effective performance. A simple criterion might try to minimize the average flow time or the average amount of time that orders spend within the transformation process. Another might work to minimize the variability of order flow times, often measured by variance or standard deviation.

A related criterion might seek to maximize the number of orders completed during a period. This choice would focus attention on turning out the largest possible number of jobs whether or not the process completes them on time.

In contrast, another criterion might directly target a reduction in late orders. A system based on this criterion could measure the schedule performance of a process based on an actual number of late jobs or a percentage of jobs completed late. The organization may also need to control the average period of time between due dates and completion dates. Again, a refinement might target the standard deviation of orders' total delay to improve predictions of deviations from schedule and the overall reliability of the transformation system.

Similar criteria might target any variation from schedule to control both early and late orders. This would add value if customers needed their jobs delivered neither early nor late but right on schedule.

If setups account for a large percentage of the total lead time or cost, an organization might create scheduling criteria specifically to minimize setup time and cost. As discussed earlier, it might do this by grouping orders according to **sequence dependencies**, or similarities in setups or processing activities between two or more orders in a queue. When operators run such orders together, they eliminate the need to repeat setups. Orders that require the same tools can also benefit from this kind of coordination.

Finally, a firm's scheduling criterion might focus on minimizing work-in-process (WIP) inventory, that is, orders moving through the OM process but not yet completed. As a system carries more orders, its WIP rises and so do the costs of this stock of incomplete products. A firm might set schedules to control WIP in an effort to keep down costs.

Each criterion reflects a different view of value. For example, if a firm competes on speed, it should base scheduling rules on criteria like minimizing average flow time per job. If a firm creates value by delivering goods reliably, its scheduling rules should emphasize control variability of lead times or divergence from schedule, perhaps measured by variance or standard deviation. Similarly, a value equation centered on cost would justify scheduling rules that reduce WIP costs or setup costs. Firms that emphasize flexibility also might base scheduling decisions on setup times, which control many firms' flexibility levels.

Scheduling priorities also depend significantly on the specific traits of the firm's manufacturing environment. This distinction defines five general categories of scheduling procedures:

- *General-purpose procedures*   Some scheduling methods suit widely varying manufacturing settings, including short-interval scheduling (SIS), Gantt charts, and simulation.
- *Job-shop scheduling methods*   Dispatching rules and some other procedures suit the low volume and high variability of job shops.
- *Scheduling for bottlenecks*   A relatively new procedure called *optimizing production technology* (OPT) helps to identify and schedule bottleneck operations.
- *Service-delivery scheduling procedures*   Service organizations require their own kinds of scheduling procedures.
- *Production-line scheduling procedures*   Some methods prove especially suitable for high-volume processing and assembly lines.
- *Cellular-manufacturing scheduling procedures*   Firms that develop cellular-manufacturing layouts seek to merge the flexibility of the job shop with the short throughput time of the assembly line. This demanding environment requires special scheduling procedures to take advantage of its unique capabilities.

In this section, we look in turn at the first four categories of procedures. We cover the last two categories in Appendix 18A and Appendix 18B.

sequence dependency
A similarity in setup or processing activities between two or more orders in a queue

General-Purpose Procedures

Certain highly adaptable scheduling procedures contribute to scheduling decisions in a wide variety of settings—factories, warehouses, department stores, and offices among others. These include short-interval scheduling, Gantt charts, and simulation methods.

Short-Interval Scheduling.   Some consider short-interval scheduling (SIS) more as a general orientation toward scheduling than a specific technique. It guides scheduling decisions by a simple, straightforward principle: a company can improve its overall efficiency by controlling how it uses each hour of the work day.

In operation, SIS breaks down the capacity of a transformation system into small time units, usually 60 minutes or less. It then releases orders designed to take no more than the maximum size of the time unit. Certain rules guide people's work to schedule and complete these orders:[5]

- One individual, typically the operator, schedules the work for one work center.
- The schedule assigns a reasonable amount of work for each employee to complete in each specified time period.
- The schedule specifies all work loads in advance.
- Regular performance checks ensure that work centers complete jobs on schedule.

The schedule in Exhibit 18.14 defines a scheduling matrix for an 8-hour shift in a system with seven work centers. Each row represents a scheduling interval and each column represents a work center. Note that the exhibit sets intervals in military time, so 1400 represents 2 p.m. No production occurs during the lunch period (1200 to 1300), so the schedule omits this interval.

Each cell specifies an amount of work that the work center can complete within the interval, considering all demands of that work such as learning, setup time, and order quantity. The operator schedules jobs within the cell to complete this work within the hour. At the end of the hour, the department supervisor and the dispatcher receive reports on the status of all jobs (completed or in-progress) and the efficiency of each center and operator.

Gantt Charts.   Developed by H. L. Gantt in 1917, the **Gantt chart** is one of the oldest planning and scheduling procedures for OM systems. It applies equally well in manufacturing and service organizations, and it suits both computerized and manual applications. Also known as a *bar chart* because of its graphic displays of information, the Gantt chart lays out horizontal bars for activities related to specific jobs at individual work centers.

This chart helps operations managers to monitor the progress of each order through the process and the load on each work center in relation to available capacity. In conjunction with larger-scale scheduling techniques like critical path management (CPM) and the project evaluation and review technique (PERT), it also helps schedulers to evaluate the progress of an overall project. In each of these three tasks, the Gantt chart provides the user with a quick, visual indicator of the actual status of each order and its anticipated or planned status.

Gantt chart

A scheduling technique that lays out horizontal bars for activities related to specific jobs at individual work centers

---

[5]James H. Greene, *Production and Inventory Control: Systems and Control* (Homewood, Ill.: Richard D. Irwin, 1974), p. 386.

Short-Interval Scheduling Matrix

Interval/ Center	WC 1	WC 2	WC 3	WC 4	WC 5	WC 6	WC 7
Int 1 (0700–0800)							
Int 2 (0800–0900)							
Int 3 (0900–1000)							
Int 4 (1000–1100)							
Int 5 (1100–1200)							
Int 6 (1300–1400)							
Int 7 (1400–1500)							
Int 8 (1500–1600)							

Exhibit 18.15 shows a Gantt chart that spans six operations. Each row represents an operation, while each column represents 1 week of the order's overall estimated lead time. The inverted triangle indicates the current time (the beginning of Week 4). The light horizontal lines indicate the planned lead times for individual operations, while the heavy horizontal lines indicate actual progress.

The first operation, cut metal, proceeded without any problems, but the second began and ended behind schedule. The Gantt chart provides valuable and easily understood information about the progress of an order in relation to the schedule at every stage of the OM process. It also identifies the locations of any current problems. For example, Exhibit 18.15 shows that the Subassembly A operation has started late and it may require intervention to meet its due date at the end of Week 4.

Exhibit 18.16 shows how Gantt charts can help schedulers to control machine loads by comparing the anticipated demands on work centers or machines with actual demands. For this application, schedulers modify the Gantt chart so that each row represents a machine or work center, while each column represents a scheduling period measured in hours, shifts, weeks, or months. The light lines represent the projected loads on individual work centers by time period (days of the work week in the exhibit) while the heavy lines represent actual amounts of capacity consumed. The crossed-out box indicates an unavailable work center, perhaps because the lathe was down for maintenance on Monday. A comparison of planned and actual loads quickly identifies work centers with problems and those that run under control. Supervisors might investigate why the OD grinder has run continuously, although the schedule called for some down time.

Gantt Chart for an Electronic Component

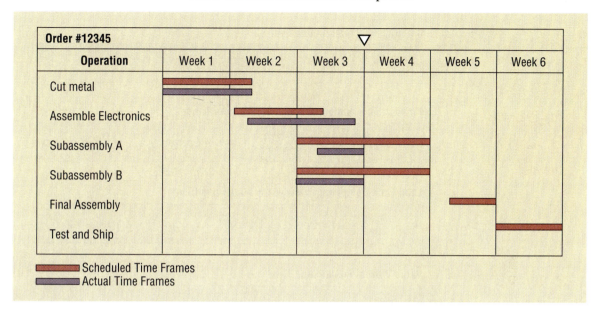

Gantt charts continue in widespread use due to their many advantages. They provide useful information in a format that is simple to develop and interpret. Schedulers can easily incorporate changes in timing, machine loads, and current status. Some common changes can make Gantt charts fairly flexible to apply. For

[**E X H I B I T 1 8 . 1 6**]

Gantt Chart for Machine Loading

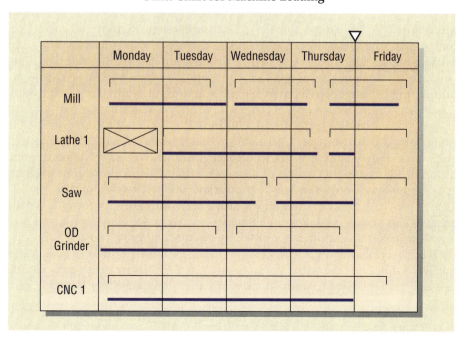

[**EXHIBIT 18.17**]

Breakdowns for Actual Time in a Gantt Chart

Initial View of Actual Lead Time

Process Flow Analysis View of Actual Lead Time

Operation Setup	Operation Processing	Inspection	Delay

Lead Time Component View of the Actual Lead Time

Setup Time	Processing Time	Inspection	Queue Time

Value View of Actual Lead Time

Necessary but Nonvalue-Adding	Value-Adding	Nonvalue Adding

example, Exhibit 18.15 indicated actual progress with heavy horizontal lines; a more detailed chart could show individual activities over this time period broken down by categories like those in Exhibit 18.17. Finally, Gantt charts suit the requirements of a wide range of media from ruled paper to mechanical devices such as the Sched-U-Graph™ and computer systems.

Simulations.   A simulation develops and implements a computer model of an actual system to evaluate alternative policies, schedules, or solutions. The simulation can model all kinds of arrangements like different dispatching rules, processing procedures, or assignments of orders to work stations. It proves especially valuable for projecting the impacts of changes in the amounts and timing of work loads.

Increasing numbers of organizations have adopted simulation methods to set and evaluate scheduling priorities, including GM, Ingersoll Milling of Rockford, Illinois, John Deere, and the U.S. Army's Watervliet Arsenal.[6] Simulation techniques have allowed these users to conduct complex "what if" experiments by comparing the results in models of alternative schedules. This kind of evaluation shows the user not only the most appropriate policy choice, but also the likely effects of that policy on the operation of the transformation process. Operations managers can know in advance whether excess work will build up anywhere in the system in certain conditions and where queues will grow most.

This powerful analytical method becomes even more popular as new computer software simplifies the work. Packages such as ARENA from Systems Modeling free users from the need to understand simulation languages. Rather, they simply

[6]"Manufacturing Arsenal Implements Scheduling System," *P&IM Review*, August 1990, pp. 40–41.

[E X H I B I T   1 8 . 1 8]

Scheduling Process for a Job Shop

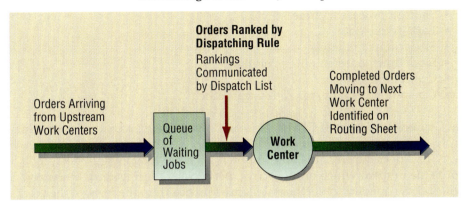

draw graphic representations of their transformation process and answer a few questions posed by the software to specify details like work order arrivals, processing-time distributions, and order routes. Based on this information, the software develops a simulation model that shows orders visually moving between work centers, machines becoming idle or busy, and workers moving between machines. Using such a software package, schedulers can easily produce accurate, comprehensible models.

Scheduling Rules for Job Shops

Scheduling can become quite complex in the variable environment of a job shop. This creates a need for more specific tools to supplement or replace the common, general ones. The routes of particular orders can vary significantly, as can order quantities, times between orders, processing times, and the frequency with which work centers receive and process orders for specific outputs. Job shops accommodate these variations through both pull scheduling and push scheduling; as we have already discussed pull methods, we will focus on push methods in this section.

To accommodate extreme variability in different parts of a job shop, schedulers direct separate work loads to individual work centers rather than aggregating a single load for the shop as a whole. Bill Taylor schedules 28 separate work centers rather than compiling a single, 28-step schedule for the entire tool room.

As orders arrive at a work center from various upstream activities, they accumulate in a queue or backlog of jobs competing for access to that center's equipment (Exhibit 18.18). As described early in the chapter, a dispatching rule sets priorities for these orders based on some formal logic or set of rules. When the work center completes its current job, the scheduling process reviews the priorities of all waiting orders to reflect the arrivals of new jobs and the passage of time. It moves the highest-priority order to the top of the dispatch list and directs the work center to take up that order. In this way, dispatching becomes an iterative process that sets priorities for orders in the queue, picks the highest-priority job for processing, and then resets priorities in the queue to repeat the cycle.

The importance of the scheduling process to performance in a job shop has inspired extensive research to develop, apply, and evaluate alternative dispatching rules. Of more than 100 different rules proposed by researchers and applied by practitioners, some have become common in OM systems:

- First come-first served
- Shortest processing time
- Earliest due date
- Slack time remaining
- Slack time per remaining operation
- Critical ratio rule
- Operation due date/operation start date

First Come-First Served (FCFS).   This rule, also known as *first in-first out* (FIFO), simply directs work centers to process orders in the exact sequence in which they arrive. This decision requires no computers or other technology; the system just records the times at which orders arrive, perhaps by placing cards at the end of a stack, and the operator pulls the orders in sequence from the front of the stack.

This rule brings benefits of simplicity in use, but it does suffer from a number of major shortcomings. It ignores important information like the order's due date, needed processing time, the relative importance of the customer, and any similarities in processing methods, setups, or components to other orders. Partly as a result of that deficiency, this rule tends to perform poorly on all performance criteria discussed earlier in this chapter.

In general, the first come-first served dispatching rule proves adequate only under certain important conditions. First, FCFS does effectively schedule essentially identical incoming orders. For example, McDonald's and similar service organizations rely on this principle, as do movie or theater box offices. In a homogeneous process, FCFS fairly distributes services among customers. FCFS can also function well with extremely short work queues, especially in just-in-time manufacturing systems.

Shortest Processing Time/Shortest Operation Time (SPT/SOT).   These methods set priorities for orders based on their requirements for processing time (setup plus operation time) or operation time (time per unit multiplied by order quantity). The most rapidly processed order gets the highest priority while the longest order gets the lowest priority.

This rule offers some important advantages. First, it effectively completes large numbers of jobs within relatively short periods of time. It also results in the smallest average time between due date and completion date. When a schedule sets either infeasible or highly suspicious due dates, SPT/SOT generally gives the most appropriate priority ranks. Finally, SPT/SOT also suits highly variable systems, as when a transformation process is either barely under control or out of control.

Despite these potential benefits, SPT/SOT is generally not recommended for several reasons. First, the method discourages fast processing of large jobs, leaving them to wait until the system finishes small jobs. Second, SPT/SOT ignores due dates when it sets priorities, so it does not support a goal of generating value by meeting due dates in a timely fashion. Finally, research has found that SPT/SOT adds variance to systems with little variability, reducing overall system predictability.[7]

---

[7]Steven A. Melnyk, David R. Denzler, and Larry D. Fredendall, "Variance Control versus Dispatching Efficiency," *Production and Inventory Management* 33, no. 3 (1992), pp. 6–13.

[**E X H I B I T   1 8 . 1 9**]

Problem with the EDD Dispatching Rule

Work center: 123
Current date: 137 (M-day calendar)

Scheduled Work

Order Number	Order Due Date	Remaining Processing Time (days)
13445AB	144	3
15667CX	148	11

Earliest Due Date (EDD).   This rule answers some criticisms of SPT/SOT by ranking orders by their overall completion dates. It sets the highest priority on the order with the earliest completion date, and it gives the lowest priority to the order with the latest overall due date. EDD supports any system that creates value by meeting due dates such as MRP. In addition, EDD encourages the on-time delivery of orders. It helps to minimize the time between due date and completion date for any order in the transformation process. EDD is most appropriate when orders follow a single route through the process and when the remaining processing time after completion of an activity does not constitute a critical component of total lead time.

However, EDD does suffer from several limitations. First, to work effectively, it requires attainable, realistic due dates. It performs poorly when handling excessively tight order due dates (e.g., when an order needs 100 hours of additional processing and only 105 hours remain before the due date) or infeasible due dates (e.g., when only 80 hours remain to complete the same order). Second, the EDD rule distorts the real urgency of an order because it fails to compare the need for additional processing time with the available time.

Exhibit 18.19 illustrates this problem for two orders. EDD would select the first job over the second. Note, however, that 7 days remain until the first job's due date (144 – 137 = 7 days). It needs 3 more days of processing so the system has a 4-day cushion for unexpected problems. The second job has 11 days left until its due date, and the system needs all of this time to complete processing. By delaying this order to process the first, EDD would deliver it late to the customer. Under such conditions, the firm needs a dispatching rule that favors the second order over the first.

Slack Time Remaining (SLACK).   This dispatching rule addresses the weakness uncovered in the discussion of EDD. It sets priorities to favor an order with relatively little slack, defined as the difference between the order due date and the current time adjusted for the amount of processing time remaining:

$$SLACK = \text{Order due date} - \text{Time now} - \text{Remaining processing time} \qquad (18.2)$$
$$= ODD - TNOW - RPT$$

The SLACK rule provides several important strengths. First, it considers both due dates and remaining processing time. Second, it creates a dynamic procedure for calculating priorities. All terms of the equation remain constant except the current time. As this changes, schedulers must recalculate priorities to update priority rankings.

[**EXHIBIT 18.20**]

SLACK and Remaining Operations

Work center: 123
Current date: 137 (M-day calendar)

Scheduled Work

Order Number	Order Due Date	RPT (Days)	Remaining Operations (ROP)
13446CD	149	6	1
17882MI	149	7	3

Like EDD, SLACK provides an appropriate dispatching rule for any system driven by due dates or for any system that seeks to generate value through reliable deliveries. Like EDD, SLACK depends on feasible and sufficiently distant order due dates. Because SLACK considers the amount of processing time remaining, it offers an improvement over EDD and a superior way to minimize the period between the due date and the order completion date for any order.

However, SLACK does present one important problem: it ignores the number of remaining operations. Exhibit 18.20 shows how this omission can distort priorities. Both orders have equivalent priorities under EDD, since they share a due date. SLACK would set a higher priority on the first order (SLACK = 6) than on the second (SLACK = 7). Note an important difference between these two orders: the first has reached its last operation while two more operations remain for the second. The second order must, therefore, wait in two more queues and pass through two more handling steps giving it a greater chance of falling behind schedule. To prevent this potential problem, the process should schedule the second job before the first.

Slack Time per Remaining Operation (S/OPN).   This dispatching rule corrects the shortcoming of the SLACK rule by dividing an order's slack by the number of remaining operations. A lower number justifies a higher priority. For example, returning to Exhibit 18.20, the first order would have S/OPN of 6 (SLACK/ROP = 6/1 = 6.0) while the second would have S/OPN of 2.3, giving it the higher priority. This rule shares many of the same strengths and limitations identified for the SLACK dispatching rule. In general, it offers a marginal improvement over the SLACK rule.

Critical Ratio Rule (CRR).   This rule, first proposed by IBM in the 1960s, solves the same problem as the S/OPN rule in a different way. It ranks jobs based on a critical ratio (CR) for each job equal to the time remaining until the due date divided by the remaining processing time or:

$$CR = \frac{(\text{Due date} - TNOW)}{RPT}$$

(18.3)

The resulting ratio indicates whether the order is ahead of schedule (CR > 1), on schedule (CR = 1), or behind schedule (CR < 1). All orders receive priority ranks in decreasing order from smallest to largest, so the job with the smallest CR gets the highest priority.

[**EXHIBIT 18.21**]

Calculations for OSD/ODD

Operation	Queue Time (Days)	Move Time (days)	Setup Time (hours)	Run Time (hours)
1	2	0	2	3
2	3	1	1	2
3	1	2	4	6
4	4	1	2	7
5	2	1	2	3
6	3	1	4	1

Due Date: 237 (M-day calendar)   Current time: 210   Quantity: 10

Until recently, CRR enjoyed wide acceptance as the most appropriate dispatching rule for many systems driven by due dates and reliability. Its popularity has begun to diminish, however, due to its expression of priorities as ratios. Most employees find weak intuitive appeal in this measurement; they prefer to think of numbers of days ahead of or behind schedule.

Operation Due Dates/Operation Start Dates (ODD/OSD).   This last, relatively new priority rule establishes a due date or start date for an individual operation for every order in a queue. It bases these dates on the backward or forward scheduling methods previously discussed. An order's OSD identifies the date on which it should begin processing at the work center. This date depends critically on the method for identifying the standard or expected queue time for every operation in the order's route. Most expected queue times come from work center standards. A higher standard queue time indicates greater demand for a work center.

Exhibit 18.21 assumes an 8-hour production day. For Operation 6, then, the sum of setup and run time translates into 1 shift (5 hours rounded up to 1 day); for Operation 4, the same calculation gives 9 hours or 2 days. Backward scheduling gives OSDs and ODDs for these operations, as Exhibit 18.22 shows.

[**EXHIBIT 18.22**]

Final OSD/ODD Data

Operation	Operation Start Date	Operation Due Date
1	213	214
2	215	216
3	219	221
4	226	228
5	231	232
6	236[a]	237[b]

[a]1 day of processing

[b]This date also becomes the order due date.

For example, the OSD for Operation 6 equals the ODD minus the processing time in days (237 – 1). To complete the order on time, the work center should start working on it no later than Day 236. The ODD for Operation 5 comes from subtracting the move time (1 day) and the queue time for Operation 6 (3 days) from the OSD for Operation 6, or Day 236 (236 – 1 – 3 = 232). The gap between the ODD for Operation 5 and the OSD for Operation 6 reflects time spent moving and in the queue between them.

In practice, the OSD/ODD method is becoming more common for several reasons. First, like the other priority rules based on due dates (EDD, SLACK, S/OPN, and CRR), ODD/OSD meshes well with date-driven systems such as MRP. Second, this rule considers the impact of the various components of lead time (run time, setup time, move time, queue time) on the appropriate timing for operations. Third, and most important, ODD/OSD states priorities in terms that prove meaningful for most people who work with the transformation process. For example, if an order has an operation start date of 229 and it has not yet started processing on Day 231, then everyone knows that the order is 2 days behind schedule.

Problem 18.3 summarizes the effects of the seven scheduling decision rules.

[**P R O B L E M   1 8 . 3**]

Order Scheduling Priorities

A scheduler must set priorities and compile a dispatch list for the orders listed in Exhibit 18.23. Each method gives its own judgment:

- *FCFS:* Process the orders in the exact sequence in which they arrive. *Dispatch List:* 132AB, 241GM, 117FD, 431AB, 332FM
- *SPT:* Process jobs in order of increasing processing time. *SPT by order:*

  117FD: 1.5 setup + 4.0 run = 5.5

  241GM: 1.0 + 8.0 = 9.0

  332FM: 3.0 + 7.0 = 10.0

  132AB: 2.0 + 10.0 = 12.0

  332FM: 0.5 + 11.5 = 12.0

[**E X H I B I T   1 8 . 2 3**]

Dispatching Rule Comparison

Work center: Lathe
Date today: 116 (M-day calendar)
Capacity per day: 8 hours

Job Number	Arrival Order	Setup Time (hours)	Run Time (hours)	ODD	Order Due Date	RPT (hours)	Remaining Operations
132AB	1	2.0	10.0	122	156	40	3
241GM	2	1.0	8.0	130	150	32	3
117FD	3	1.5	4.0	115	170	60	4
431AB	4	0.5	11.5	126	133	12	1
332FM	5	3.0	7.0	135	160	40	3

Dispatch List: 117FD, 241GM, 332FM, 132AB and 332FM tie. Note that the last two jobs tie because they have the same processing time. The scheduler might break the tie by comparing the importance of the customers, the importance of the jobs, whether one is behind schedule, or the operator's preference.

- *EDD:* Process jobs in sequence by increasing order due date. *Dispatch List:* 431AB (order due date = 133), 241GM, 132AB, 332FM, 117FD
- *SLACK:* Process jobs in order of increasing slack. *SLACK by job:*

$$132AB: 156 - 116 - (40/8) = 40 - 5 = 25.0$$
$$241GM: 150 - 116 - (32/8) = 34 - 4 = 30.0$$
$$117FD: 170 - 116 - (60/8) = 54 - 8 = 46.0$$
$$431AB: 133 - 116 - (12/8) = 17 - 2 = 15.0$$
$$332FM: 160 - 116 - (40/8) = 44 - 5 = 39.0$$

Dispatch List: 431AB, 132AB, 241GM, 332FM, 117FD
- *S/OPN:* Process jobs in order of increasing remaining slack per operation. *S/OPN by job:*

$$132AB: 25.0/3 = 8.33$$
$$241GM: 30.0/3 = 10.0$$
$$117FD: 46.0/4 = 11.5$$
$$431AB: 15.0/1 = 15.0$$
$$332FM: 39.0/3 = 13.0$$

Dispatch List: 132AB, 241GM, 117FD, 332FM, 431AB
- *CRR:* Process jobs in order of increasing critical ratio. *CRR by job:*

$$132AB: 40/5 = 8.00 \text{ (ahead of schedule)}$$
$$241GM: 34/4 = 8.50$$
$$117FD: 54/5 = 6.75$$
$$431AB: 17/2 = 8.50$$
$$332FM: 44/5 = 8.80$$

Dispatch List: 117FD, 132AB, 241GM and 431AB tie, 332FM
- *ODD:* Process jobs in order of increasing ODD. *Dispatch List:* 117FD, 132AB, 431AB, 241GM, 332FM   [■]

Categorizing Dispatching Rules.   The dispatching rules discussed so far share certain characteristics that define useful categories. For example, one group of dispatching rules, called *local rules,* base scheduling decisions on information from a current work center. Others, called *global rules,* consider activities elsewhere in the transformation system, especially at upstream or downstream work centers. In the past, limited computer power and inaccurate data forced schedulers to emphasize local rules. However, computer-based information systems allow today's shop-floor control systems to apply global rules to smooth work flows and reduce overall system variance.

From another point of view, dispatching rules fall into categories depending upon whether they assign static, unchanging priority numbers or dynamic numbers that may change over time. We have discussed a mix of static and dynamic rules. For example, FCFS, SPT, EDD, and OSD/ODD calculate a single priority number for each order. Arrival and completion of jobs at a work center do not affect the priorities of current orders. In contrast, the SLACK, S/OPN, and CRR dispatching rules, and any others based on slack, give dynamic priorities because each order's remaining slack changes as time passes. Dynamic rules require more work from schedulers, but they convey a useful indication of the time remaining for the system to complete an order.

Final Choice of a Dispatching Rule for a Job Shop.   The selection of a dispatching rule for a particular job shop depends on several considerations, beginning with simplicity of use. Because people must apply any dispatching rule, schedulers should choose one that is simple to use. As a rule of thumb, if it takes more than 5 minutes to explain a rule, workers will ignore it.

Workers also favor transparent and valid dispatching rules. Validity and transparency mean that the operation of the scheduling rule will be consistent with the approach they would have used, given the same task and need to generate a schedule. When the logic underlying any dispatching rule is transparent and valid, the users see it as logical and understand and accept the advantages it offers.

Dispatching rules should generate meaningful priorities that workers can readily interpret and understand. In systems driven by due dates, dispatchers, department supervisors, and operators immediately recognize the significance of the number of days that an order is ahead of or behind schedule. These priorities reinforce people's understanding of performance.

Despite their valuable contributions to scheduling efforts, dispatching rules can never replace effective capacity planning. Dispatching rules work best when a job shop maintains enough capacity to process waiting orders without compromising due-date performance on other orders. Dispatching rules cannot effectively ration inadequate productive resources among competing orders. This just causes frustration for everyone.

Techniques for Scheduling at Bottlenecks

Bottlenecks affect schedules in both job shops and process/assembly lines. (Appendix 18A discusses the second case.) They limit production and inhibit the OM system's drive to meet its value-based commitments for quality, lead time, cost, and flexibility. Bottlenecks often underlie any differences between what operations managers promise and what they deliver to internal and external customers.

Up to this point in the book, we have limited the discussion of bottlenecks to simplistic advice to note their locations and causes. We can now supplement those general guidelines with specific principles based on a body of knowledge that focuses directly on bottlenecks and management techniques to promote overall effectiveness and efficiency despite these limitations. In this section, we discuss practical methods for managing bottlenecks, including the theory of constraints, synchronous manufacturing, and optimized production technology (OPT). Together, these three methods describe a very broad system of operations management. They extend beyond scheduling to address planning, investment, and continuous improvement issues in a single system that resembles total quality management and just-in-time manufacturing.

Each of these practical methods focuses on a particular aspect of the problem of managing bottlenecks. The theory of constraints (TOC) provides a broad theoretical framework for evaluating the strategic importance of bottlenecks. OPT, supplemented by the drum-buffer-rope (DBR) procedure, provides process tools

[**EXHIBIT 18.24**]

Relationships of TOC, OPT, and Synchronous Manufacturing

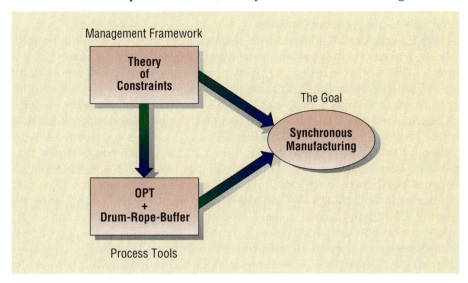

that help operations managers to implement the guidelines recommended by TOC. Finally, synchronous manufacturing describes the overall objectives that managers develop by applying TOC and OPT. Exhibit 18.24 illustrates the relationships of these elements.

Theory of Constraints.   The **theory of constraints** provides a basis for operations management that emphasizes the need to identify and manage constraints or bottlenecks within the OM system, the firm as a whole, or its network of external activities. An organization's information system might create constraints if the order-entry function takes longer to prepare an order for release than the transformation system needs to actually build the product. Other constraints could emerge in the market, the engineering system, or suppliers' functions. All of these constraints limit output.

TOC draws extensively from the work of Eli Goldratt, an Israeli physicist.[8] Although Goldratt has never worked in a manufacturing plant or even visited a U.S. facility, he has developed a complete framework for an effective transformation process and its management procedures.

The TOC framework begins with the premise that any OM system functions primarily to make money by delivering value to customers in the form of time, quality, cost, and flexibility benefits. One can measure its success in meeting these requirements by evaluating the amount of money that it earns. An OM system that more effectively delivers value should make more money for its owner. TOC advocates attacking bottlenecks and constraints because they significantly affect the firm's ability to make money by limiting the level of value that it can generate.

A second premise of TOC argues that variability occurs naturally in any process or system. Any attempt to balance shop loads must fail, therefore, because it does nothing to balance work flows. Operation A might produce a resource at a

theory of constraints
A basis for operations management that emphasizes the need to identify and manage constraints or bottlenecks

[8]Eliyahu M. Goldratt and J. Cox, *The Goal* (Croton-on-Hudson, N.Y: North River Press, 1984); and Eliyahu M. Goldratt and Robert E. Fox, *The Race* (Croton-on-Hudson, N.Y.: North River Press, 1986).

rate that just equals the average rate at which the Operation B consumes the resource. However, variations can quickly disrupt this perfectly balanced load. If A takes longer than expected to produce one order, then it creates a bottleneck at B. Rather than balancing load, TOC advocates balancing work flows in a way that accommodates unavoidable variance.

To do this, Goldratt's theory directs management attention toward identifying, managing, and eliminating bottlenecks or **capacity constrained resources** (CCRs). It assigns all system resources to one of two categories: bottlenecks and nonbottlenecks. A bottleneck resource constrains work flows and limits system throughput. Later activities then amplify problems that begin at the bottleneck, so improvements there benefit the system as a whole. In contrast, nonbottleneck operations do not constrain production, so investments there waste organizational resources because they do not increase the overall output of the system. These principles lead operations managers to focus attention primarily on bottlenecks. Effective planning and management of these capacity constrained resources creates an effective OM system.

In particular, planning must set realistic production goals in light of capacity constraints. Production plans, master production schedules, and all other plans should focus on bottleneck activities. If they create infeasible demands on bottleneck resources, then they create infeasible demands on the system.

To carry out those plans, operations managers should manipulate work flows to encourage effective utilization of capacity constrained resources. The theory of constraints distinguishes utilization of a resource from mere activation. Activating a resource simply sends it some materials to process or orders to fill; this could range from value-adding production of essential components to nonvalue-adding production of unnecessarily large lots to keep equipment busy. In contrast, utilizing a resource draws on its potential to contribute to corporate performance.

To achieve effective utilization of capacity constrained resources, operations managers must rethink current practices such as lot sizes and schedules. They should reduce nonproductive setups at bottlenecks by running the largest possible lot sizes. In contrast, nonbottleneck resources run small batches to fulfill their primary roles of feeding steady flows of inputs to support continuous operations at bottlenecks. Small batches consume significant capacity in frequent setups, but this lost capacity should not affect overall work flows because nonbottlenecks have excess capacity as compared to the capacities of bottlenecks.

The principles of the theory of constraints lead to a series of operating guidelines:

- Balance flows, not capacity.
- An hour lost at a bottleneck is forever lost.
- Time at a nonbottleneck resource has a negligible marginal value.
- The level of utilization at a bottleneck depends on some other constraint(s) within the system.
- Bottlenecks govern throughput, inventory, and quality.
- Utilize resources, do not simply activate them.
- The size of a batch that moves between work centers need not, and often should not, equal the size of the processing batch.
- Processing batch sizes may vary both along an order's route and over time.
- Schedules should simultaneously accommodate all constraints. Lead times result from scheduled sequences, so planners cannot determine them in advance.

The same guidelines underlie the comprehensive system of synchronous manufacturing and the tools of optimized production technology.

capacity constrained resource

An OM system resource that limits the capacity of the entire system

Synchronous Manufacturing.   The theory of constraints culminates in the development of a **synchronous manufacturing** system, defined by one pair of authors as "an all-encompassing management philosophy that includes a consistent set of principles, procedures, and techniques where every action is evaluated in terms of the common, global goal of the organization."[9] Synchronous manufacturing creates a highly coordinated system of activities designed to continuously enhance value. It coordinates work flows to reduce or eliminate nonvalue-adding resources like inventory and to protect current throughput and increase future throughput. By enhancing value, synchronous manufacturing tries to help managers generate more money for the firm.

Synchronous manufacturing organizes activities through a drum-buffer-rope (DBR) model. The drum represents the few critical constraints that determine the throughput of an entire system. These constraints pace overall throughput, in effect pounding out a drum beat that sets the pace for other activities.

Buffers in a DBR model represent slack that precedes critical resources and operations. This slack can take one of two forms: time buffers and inventory buffers. Time buffers introduce extra lead time at appropriate points within the process to protect it from unplanned variations.[10] For example, a 3-day time buffer in front of a work center would require upstream operations to complete necessary inputs for the work center and place them in its queue at least 3 days before it would actually need them. The extra supplies would allow the work center to keep running despite temporary problems at earlier stages of production. In contrast, an inventory buffer contains only enough materials to keep a work center busy for a single time interval (e.g., a week or a shift).

Synchronous manufacturing systems typically place time and inventory buffers before capacity constrained resources. This arrangement allows the CCRs to keep working despite variance elsewhere in the process. Additional buffers in front of the last shipping operation protect it from disruptions that could jeopardize final order due dates.

Along with drums and buffers, a DBR model includes ropes to represent coordinating links between activities. The rope stretches between a buffer before a CCR and the initial operation in its string of upstream activities, called the *gating operation.* Through this link, the DBR model manages the flow of material into the system and the inventories that accumulate along the way. The rope controls the rate at which the gating operation releases materials into production, providing a mechanism by which the CCR determines the overall pace of production. Similar ropes link all buffers to the gating operation. In practice, ropes function as a type of order review/release mechanism.

Exhibit 18.25 shows a sample application of DBR. The two time buffers control the rate of output of the gating work center through two ropes, one connected in front of the CCR and the other connected in front of assembly/shipping. DBR closely coordinates or synchronizes the production process.

Optimized Production Technology   Optimized production technology (OPT) is a complete information system for production planning and control through which operations managers create a detailed schedule for the transformation process. The procedures of OPT embody the premises of the theory of constraints.

synchronous manufacturing

A highly coordinated system of activities designed to continuously enhance value

---

[9]M. Michael Umble and M. L. Srikanth, *Synchronous Manufacturing* (Cincinnati, Oh.: South-Western, 1990), p. 129.

[10]Goldratt and Fox, *The Race*, p. 98.

[**EXHIBIT 18.25**]

Drum-Buffer-Rope Control

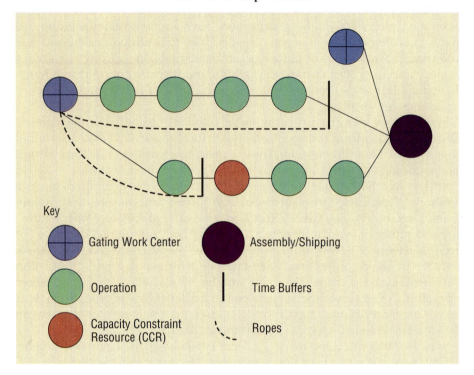

Key

Gating Work Center

Operation

Capacity Constraint Resource (CCR)

Assembly/Shipping

Time Buffers

Ropes

The formal software package for OPT combines four major modules: BUILDNET, SERVICE, SPLIT, and OPT. These modules help users to identify bottleneck resources. They then apply proprietary algorithms to plan resource needs (capacity, employees, tools, etc.) at those operations and generate schedules that move orders through needed work centers in an appropriate sequence.

OPT provides valuable help to operations managers as they try to generate a feasible master production schedule that accommodates constraints at bottleneck operations. In combination with DBR modeling, OPT also adjusts lot sizes to maintain work flows through the system. It reduces lot sizes at nonbottleneck operations to ensure a steady flow of inputs to the bottlenecks. Even if a nonbottleneck operation processes a large batch, OPT breaks down the total into smaller batches for transportation to downstream work centers. For example, it might move a lot of 150 units in packages of 25 units each. Lot sizes at the bottleneck operations, however, keeps batches as large as possible to consume the smallest possible amount of capacity in setups.

OPT has achieved impressive results in many cases, but it does suffer from one major limitation. The consultants who developed the software to get OPT out in the field will not reveal the proprietary algorithms by which OPT generates its output. Unfortunately, users may distrust the results if they do not understand the process for generating them. As Gene Woolsey of the Colorado School of Mines has put it to one of the authors, "A person would rather live with a problem that they see than use a solution that they don't understand."

The theory of constraints and the related concepts of synchronous manufacturing and optimized production technology have stirred powerful controversies in the operations management field. The elements of the techniques draw on several widely accepted principles of effective operations management:

- *Focus on the vital few rather than the trivial many.* These methods focus attention on the vital few bottlenecks in a transformation process.
- *Evaluate systems and activities based on their contributions to value.* These methods link measures of effectiveness to profits and the components of the value equation.
- *Successful operations management requires recognition and awareness of variance.* Variance occurs naturally in any OM system. The structure of an effective system must anticipate and allow for this problem.

SCHEDULING FOR SERVICE OPERATIONS

Techniques like placing time and inventory buffers before bottlenecks may help to guard against variance in a manufacturing environment, but they often lose effectiveness in service-delivery systems. Service organizations typically produce intangible outputs that they cannot hold in inventory, so buffers offer no protection against variance. Similarly, close customer contact may prevent a firm from applying dispatching rules when buyers exert their own ideas of scheduling priorities. Typically short lead times and definitions of value based on speed and flexibility leave schedulers with little opportunity for adjustment. Finally, the labor-intensive transformation processes of most service operations make highly variable human resources extremely important influences on the quality, performance, and output quantities of those systems.

Service operations pose some interesting challenges for shop-floor control systems, in general, and detailed scheduling procedures, in particular. We will discuss these challenges as they affect two interrelated scheduling problems: scheduling orders and scheduling employees (Exhibit 18.26).

[**E X H I B I T   1 8 . 2 6**]

Scheduling Decisions in Service Operations

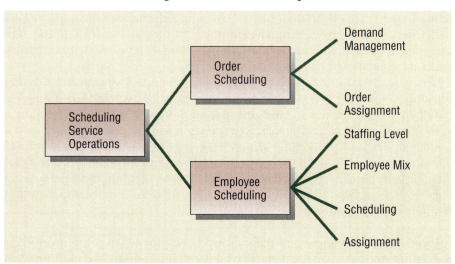

Scheduling Service Orders

Service firms schedule orders to ensure that employees complete them in appropriate sequences. These sequences must allow for the fact that orders take the form of people rather than slips of paper or computer displays. Like discussions of scheduling procedures in earlier chapters, this process begins with demand management to influence the flow of people into the system. (Demand management and forecast are covered in Chapter 10.) Familiar adaptations include reservation systems and off-peak price discounts among others. A firm may also try to actively shape the expectations of customers to match demand to current capacity. For example, a bank's branch manager might try to shape people's expectations of waiting times for services by placing an electronic sign that displays the current expected time in the teller queue. Customers may welcome this warning, and it may influence their reactions to the wait or lead them to choose to return at another time or patronize an automated teller machine.

After customers bring their order through the demand-management arrangements, order assignment must create a detailed schedule to control service delivery. Many of this chapter's dispatching rules (e.g., FCFS, SPT, and SLACK) and scheduling tools (e.g., Gantt charts, short-interval scheduling, and simulation) can help schedulers to determine the exact sequence in which to process competing service orders. For example, restaurant hosts often allot tables to customers in order of their times of arrival following the first come-first served dispatching rule.

Some organizations develop hybrid rules to separate critical jobs from less urgent ones. For example, calls to a 911 emergency-response system receive preference over routine calls to police station switchboards. This distinction creates a two-queue system that directs emergency orders to one queue for expedited service and routine orders to a more leisurely service process. Customers waiting in each queue receive priorities based on a first come-first served dispatching rule.

Scheduling Service Employees

Operations managers in a service organization must make critical decisions about scheduling employees along with detailed schedules for orders. They begin by setting an overall staffing level and then proceed to determine an employee mix, shift schedule, and job assignments.

Staffing Level.   This shop-floor control decision determines the capacity of a service-delivery system by setting the numbers of employees and shifts). These arrangements determine whether the firm maintains a level capacity or varies its capacity in response to changes in demand.

They also determine how it responds to unexpected variations in demand. For example, a restaurant manager might intentionally overstaff the dining room to maintain excess capacity to meet unexpected demand. This choice would suit a firm whose value equation emphasized a speedy response. Because the response to variations in demand powerfully affects the competitive success of a service firm and the exact type of value that it offers, the staffing-level problem becomes part of strategic planning. The production plan and master production schedule must specify this choice. The "On the Job" box discusses the use of pagers to handle customer demand fluctuations.

Employee Mix.   To choose a specific group of employees to combine in a single schedule, operations managers must weigh considerations like skill levels, the

Customer waiting time is unavoidable for service-based firms. In order to manage capacity and satisfy customer expectations, this bank might post approximate waiting times in the lobby.
SOURCE   Michael Newman/PhotoEdit

extent of any cross-training, and the ratio of part-time to full-time employees. These issues affect the overall flexibility of the firm's labor pool and the investments that it must make to develop the employees that it needs.

Managers must make important tradeoffs to determine an appropriate employee mix. To make employees more flexible, they could invest in cross-training. Of course, training costs money, so the decision must compare the benefits against the costs to justify the investment. The decision must also ensure that such investments support the type of value that the firm and its OM system intend to deliver to customers.

Shift Schedule.   Service-system operations managers must resolve very detailed questions to schedule employees for particular shifts. Schedulers can decide in a number of ways who works when with what days off. Gantt charts often help to suggest the best schedules.

Alternatively, a multiple-step scheduling heuristic might help to solve the problem:

1. Determine the number of employees needed to provide the desired level of service each day.
2. Determine the planned number of work shifts per period.
3. Sum up the results from Step 1 and divide by the number in Step 2, rounding partial values upward. The result indicates the number of employees that the firm needs.
4. Schedule days off by choosing two consecutive days that require the lowest total numbers of employees. In the case of ties, arbitrarily select a pair. Those consecutive days become a single employee's off days. That employee will then work the remaining days, so the scheduler reduces the number to staff needed for each shift by 1. This process repeats until it schedules every employee's off days.
5. Fit specific workers into the days-off slots created in Step 4 based on some criterion such as seniority or stated preferences, or rotate assignments among workers.

ON THE JOB

Paging Quality Service

■

It can be very difficult for service operations such as restaurants and retail shops to predict periods of high customer demand. Overstaffing costs money, but understaffing can result in bad service and lost customers. Flexible scheduling comes at a premium, and paging technology offers one way to make it affordable.

Restaurants started the trend of handing out pagers to customers so they could browse in nearby shops while they were waiting for a table. Chains such as the Outback Steakhouse have begun to do this as a matter of course, turning a customer irritation into an opportunity.

Now other service outlets such as pharmacies are beginning to experiment with this concept, handing out pagers to customers waiting for eyeglasses or medicine. At the time of this writing, pagers are currently being used on an experimental basis at pharmacies in Giant Food,

Eckerd Drug, CVS, and several large discounters, as well as at automotive repair shops and one-hour photo developers.

While pagers have already been used for some time as a way to relieve customer bottlenecks, some companies are developing new ways to use them for *predicting* bottlenecks. One supermarket has begun to use pagers in combination with a traffic counting system to alert management of an impending crunch at the checkout lanes. This concept could yield pro-

found applications for scheduling in the future.

Meanwhile, discount retail outfits can cut staffing levels by using pagers in conjunction with customer call boxes. Companies such as Kmart and Target have installed call boxes so that a customer can get help from an employee who might be stocking merchandise all the way across the store. Now at some Super KMart Centers, customers pressing the call button activate a pager instead of an overhead voice announcement, cutting down on noise pollution.

At the request of Mariott, JTech (a leading supplier of paging technology), is developing a more powerful system so that customers can page housekeeping and room service over an entire hotel complex. By using such technology, service operators can create more flexibility with scheduling, helping them make the "Moment of Truth" last just a little bit longer.

SOURCE   Gary Robins, "Paging Better Service," *Stores*, February 1995, pp. 46–47.

This heuristic does not ensure optimal results, but it usually tends to work well. Problem 18.4 illustrates an application of this method.

[**PROBLEM 18.4**]

Shift Scheduling in the GM Tool Room

Bill Taylor must develop work schedules for customer-service employees who accept orders from customers and then generate due dates and routing sheets for these orders. (Although this work occurs within a manufacturing operation, it really represents a service task.)

Exhibit 18.27 states the number of customer-service employees that Bill Taylor expects to need in the tool room for each day of the week (Step 1). He might have based these estimates on gut feel, past trends, or customer input. He has adjusted the results anticipating traditionally high demand on

Customer-Service Employees per Day

Monday	Tuesday	Wednesday	Thursday	Friday	Saturday	Sunday
11	8	8	11	12	6	6

Mondays and on Fridays and Thursdays as people try to get orders in before the weekend.

Summing up the requirements, Bill Taylor determines that he needs 62 work shifts for the week (Step 2). Since each employee works five shifts (40 hours per week), Bill needs 13 employees ($62/5 = 12.4$ employees, rounded up to 13) (Step 3).

He determines days off for each employee as illustrated in Exhibit 18.28. For the first days-off slot, Saturday and Sunday carry the lowest demand, so they become one person's off days. That worker will come to work the remaining 5 days, so Bill Taylor reduces the need for workers on those shifts by 1. Demand on Saturday and Sunday remains lowest, so another employee will have those days off and work the remaining days. Again, the scheduler adjusts the need for workers on Monday through Friday shifts, and then identifies the days with the lowest remaining demand. This process repeats until it specifies a pair of off days for each employee, indicated by horizontal boxes in Exhibit 18.28.

Notice that the tool room needs the 13th employee only to cover extra demand on Friday. The job skills require a full-time employee to justify training,

Scheduling Employees' Off Days

Employee Slot	Monday	Tuesday	Wednesday	Thursday	Friday	Saturday	Sunday
1	11	8	8	11	12	6	6
2	10	7	7	10	11	6	6
3	9	6	6	6	10	6	6
4	8	6	6	5	9	5	5
5	7	5	5	4	8	5	5
6	6	4	5	4	7	4	4
7	5	3	4	3	6	4	4
8	4	3	4	2	5	3	3
9	3	2	3	1	4	3	3
10	2	1	3	1	3	2	2
11	2	1	2	0	2	1	1
12	1	0	1	0	2	0	0
13	0	0	0	0	1	0	0

however, so this person's work on other days will provide excess capacity. Bill Taylor can allocate this excess capacity in any way that seems likely to serve the needs of his customers.

Finally, the scheduler must determine which specific employee gets which specific set of off days. The union contract or seniority may affect this decision. A seniority procedure would list all of the available off days and offer first choice to the most senior employee. The next most senior worker would choose next, followed by the remaining people in order.   [▪]

Assignment.   At the most detailed level, operations managers must control the assignments of employees to fulfill particular tasks that contribute to the total work of the service-delivery system. To keep that system flexible, they must determine when to move employees from one area to another. A number of simple heuristics or assignment rules can resolve these questions.

The judgment of shop supervisors often dominates these detailed assignments. In addition, simple rules about queue length may indicate the need to assign more people to a certain area. A supermarket manager might open a new check-out counter whenever more than five people wait in line. These workers come from other areas of the store or the manager calls in part-time help.

COMMON FORCES IN SCHEDULING AND SHOP-FLOOR CONTROL

Despite careful scheduling and thoughtful arrangements for shop-floor control, the dynamic organizational environment always demands flexibility. Operations managers must vary their arrangements to adapt to changes in their firm's customer mix, because these changes alter expectations and the components of the value equation. New technologies and other changes may require new shop-floor layouts to reorganize the transformation process; again, shop-floor control must adapt to the new situation. Different changes drive adaptations in different organizations, but four general forces influence scheduling and shop-floor control systems: customers, planning-system characteristics, shop layout, and technology.

A firm's customers determine the expectations of its SFC system and scheduling process. They set the criteria for any evaluation of scheduling effectiveness and efficiency. They can also disrupt a carefully crafted schedule by demanding changes in order priorities or due dates. This introduces external variance to the scheduling process.

Planning system characteristics significantly affect the scheduling and SFC systems by channeling customer demands to the shop floor. Customers usually interact with the planning system rather than directly with shop-floor employees. The planning system translates customers' orders into schedules of internal orders for release to the SFC system. In this process, planners try to smooth variances in customer orders to create conditions that favor a feasible schedule. In most service operations, however, no amount of planning can decouple customer orders from shop-floor schedules. As customers arrive at a bank, for example, they define not only the demand on the tellers and other OM resources, but also the schedule that the bank must meet.

The physical layout of a firm's equipment and work centers has a major impact on the scheduling process. The layout determines how far the system must transport orders between operations, and this distance in turn affects lead time. The layout also determines the amount of work that can accumulate between work centers, and it influences the overall sensitivity of the transformation system to bottlenecks and variances.

Finally, processing times and setup times both depend on the equipment or technology through which an organization transforms its inputs. These time variables in turn affect the critical decisions of lot sizes and order quantities. They can also influence choices of dispatching rules.

When we introduce a new technology such as group technology or flexibility manufacturing systems, we replace unique large setups with common setups and small unique setups. We must schedule by families to take advantage of this new feature. When we reduce setups through automation, we may want to consider another scheduling approach to take advantage of the new capabilities provided by the investment in automation.

CHAPTER SUMMARY

We began this chapter by looking at the problems encountered by Bill Taylor in managing daily activities in the GM tool room. He must create and implement a shop-floor control system that introduces orders from the planning system to the tool room's work centers. This system must also manage the flow of work in a way that produces finished goods in a timely and cost-effective manner while meeting or exceeding customers' quality requirements. In the course of the chapter, we explained Bill Taylor's specific responsibilities within the SFC system, including detailed scheduling, one of its major activities:

1. Operations managers execute their daily responsibilities through the shop-floor control (SFC) system. This system manages the flow of work from planning through execution to completion of finished products, including detailed assignments of resources to orders.
2. Ultimately, the SFC system carries out its activities in a way that supports the firm's vision of value, determined by its combination of speed, quality, flexibility, and cost.
3. Shop-floor control depends heavily on the planning system. Planners define the capacity that the SFC system controls. Without good planning, the SFC system cannot succeed.
4. Orders drive the SFC system. Nearly every activity and decision within the SFC system centers on the need to complete particular orders.
5. The SFC system consists of five major activities: order review/release, detailed scheduling, data collection/monitoring, control/feedback, and order disposition.
6. While schedulers apply may technical tools and procedures, scheduling remains primarily a human process. Dispatchers, department supervisors, and equipment operators draw on their knowledge and insights to determine and improve schedules. People choose appropriate scheduling tools and procedures and apply them to suit recognized needs.
7. Order due dates play critical roles in the success of any effective scheduling process. These dates indicate when the SFC system must complete all of the

operations that an order requires and return it to the control of the planning system. The crucial importance of these dates forces schedulers to clearly understand the procedures for setting them.

8. Because scheduling manipulates quantities of time, operations managers must understand the formats in which schedulers record and report dates. They specify dates on standard calendars, numbered-week calendars, and M-day calendars.

9. General-purpose scheduling procedures that suit most environments include short-interval scheduling, Gantt charts, and simulation.

10. To specify more detailed order sequences, schedulers often apply local dispatching rules such as first come-first served, shortest processing time/shortest operation time, and SLACK.

11. When capacity constrained resources, or bottlenecks, become important, the theory of constraints suggests some appropriate shop-floor control measures that target management attention on constraints that determine overall system capacity. Full implementation of this theory results in a synchronous manufacturing system. The drum-buffer-rope model helps managers to illustrate such a system.

12. Shop-floor control for a service operation requires careful schedules for labor capacity through order scheduling and employee scheduling measures. Employee scheduling must address four major problems: overall staffing levels, more detailed employee mixes, still more specific shift schedules, and very short-term assignments.

13. Every firm's scheduling process must adapt shop-floor procedures to customer demands, planning-system characteristics, work-center layout, and equipment/technology.

[**KEY TERMS**]

shop-floor control   844
order   846
rework   847
salvage   847
scrap   848
load leveling   852
detailed scheduling   852
dispatch list   853
safety capacity   855
lot splitting   855

expediting   855
exception reporting   856
order due date   862
total work content rule   863
operation due date   864
scheduling calendar   865
sequence dependency   870
Gantt chart   871

theory of constraints   883
capacity constrained resource   884
synchronous manufacturing   885

[**DISCUSSION QUESTIONS**]

1. A working student asks an operations management professor, "Why are you teaching scheduling procedures when most of the time we are rescheduling the line?" How would you respond to this person?

2. For which of the following activities would you recommend a backward-schedule? Why?
   a. Ordering a meal at McDonald's.
   b. Ordering dinner for four at an upscale French restaurant.
   c. Scheduling material deliveries for a large downtown building project.

    d. Scheduling material deliveries for a high-volume assembly line.
3. Give an example of scheduling solving, resolving, and dissolving problems.
4. What are the main shop-floor level scheduling activities in each of the following situations?

    a. A job shop

    b. A batch production operation

    c. A continuous flow operation

    d. A construction crew working on multiple projects

5. Discuss the role of information technology, including bar coding, on the above shop-floor scheduling.
6. What economic tradeoffs are associated with splitting a lot into two or more parts? Are they a problem or a symptom of a problem?
7. Some professionals, such as physicians, schedule their customers into fixed time slots. What does this scheduling logic assume? What type of system inefficiencies can it cause?
8. At a job shop's morning production meeting, the people present are the four department supervisors, the materials planner with the daily MRP status report, and the master scheduler. Speculate on the types of problems this group might be discussing and the types of decisions (or deals) they might be making.
9. How is scheduling different between manufacturing and service delivery systems?
10. Think of the due date setting as a business process. What are the inputs to this process? What are the outcomes? How should the performance of this process be measured? In what type of manufacturing processes is due date setting normally found?
11. Of the shop floor priority rules discussed in the text, which is the *fairest of them all?* Briefly state the reasons for your response. Is the validity of your response situation-specific?
12. How can you tell whether a production system is pushing or pulling product through the system? Give an example of each approach.
13. When and where are Gantt charts most useful? What are their limitations?
14. Describe the logic behind the theory of constraints. How might a TOC advocate criticize the MRP approach to production planning and control?
15. What is the implicit goal of the OPT approach to production scheduling? In what types of operating environments is it most appropriate? Least appropriate? Why?
16. How do many students inadvertently use the TOC to sequence courses?
17. Production control has decided to make the following product in the order shown. Use a Gantt chart to determine the make-span of this production run. All work on a given job must be completed by Station 1 prior to the job's start in Station 2.

	Estimated Processing Time	
Job	Station 1	Station 2
A	4 hrs	2 hrs
B	2 hrs	3 hrs
C	1 hr	4 hrs
D	4 hrs	1 hr

    Can you figure out a better production sequence? What was the basis for your logic?

18. On day 100, a contractor has two outstanding work orders. The first job calls for 16 days in Department A, sequentially followed by 8 days in Department B and 10 days in Department C. This job is due at the start of day 140. The second job requires 3 days in Department A, 12 days in Department B, and 12 days in Department C—all done in a sequential fashion. This second job is due on day 145. Only one job can be done in a department at a time.

    a. Draw a Gantt chart, using forward scheduling, to demonstrate how these two jobs can be completed by the scheduled due dates.

b. Then draw a Gantt chart of these two orders back scheduled

c. Is one procedure better than the other? Why?

19. The following data shows the current order file at a work center at the start of a 5-day work week. Jobs are given numbers in the sequence in which they arrive.

Order Number	Processing Time Required	Due Date
A	2 days	10
B	4 days	10
C	3 days	8
D	2 days	18
E	5 days	13

a. Sequence the orders using FCFS, SPT, EDD, and the CRR priority rules.

b. What performance metrics would you use to evaluate the effectiveness of these priority scheduling rules?

c. If Order C is most important, how would you change your scheduling procedures?

20. A nursing supervisor assigns nurses to shifts for the next week. The number of nurses required for each 4-hour time block is estimated as follows:

Shift	Mon.	Tues.	Wed.	Thur.	Fri.	Sat.	Sun
Morning							
6 to 10	10	10	10	10	8	6	6
10 to 2 PM	12	10	10	10	7	6	6
Afternoon							
2 to 6 PM	10	10	10	10	6	6	6
6 to 10	8	8	8	8	5	4	4
Night							
10 to 2 AM	4	4	4	4	3	3	3
2 to 6 AM	3	3	3	3	3	3	3

The nurses' contract calls for continuous 8-hours shifts for 5 consecutive days. What is the minimum number of full-time nurses needed to adequately staff this hospital department? How many hours of overstaffing exist? If the full cost of a nurse is $40 per hour, how much would the department pay if the work rules were relaxed in the following ways:

a. Nurses could be hired for 4-hour blocks, but still had to be scheduled for 40 hours a week.

b. The 5 consecutive day rule was required for only the 12 most senior nurses.

C A U T I O N

[C R I T I C A L   T H I N K I N G   R E Q U I R E D]

1. When it is necessary to utilize a real-time information system in scheduling system? By real-time, we mean that a central information system knows immediately whenever an entity or a resource has a change in status.

2. "All pigs are created equal, but some pigs are more equal than others" is a famous saying in George Orwell's *Animal Farm*. How can this fact be built into a job shop's order prioritization rules? Can you come up with a job prioritization rule that recognizes that some jobs are more important than others?

Uncle Otto's Wall

Uncle Otto started his plastic injection molding business forty years ago with a $450 loan from his father. Now, Marquis Plastics was a $40 million business specializing in the manufacture of tubs and lids for the butter substitute industry, like those used for the "I Can't Believe It's Not Butter!" brand. Even though the business is highly competitive, Uncle Otto eked out net profits from 3 to 5 percent through his tight-fisted management.

Uncle Otto always seemed to be focused on the past. His was not the type of business the Big Five accounting firm I worked for was likely to target. Uncle Otto used to call me "Little David," his slick nephew–management consultant. Thus, I was surprised to learn that he had named me managing director of the firm moments before he slipped into a coma. He died four days later.

Being a market-oriented person, the first thing I did was spend some time with Otto's sales force and his customers. I was struck by their loyalty, which was based on years of high quality, reliable service. On the other hand, the sales force seemed quite content simply to continue servicing the firm's existing customers. Most of Marquis's sales growth had been the result of its customers' growth.

The next stage of my orientation led me to the order entry department. This department seemed somewhat antiquated, but it had a fine record for accurately estimating each job's run times and production costs. When I asked how an order's due date was set, the order entry clerk just pointed to "The Wall."

"What is that?" I asked.

"It's our order board," she responded.

The wall consisted of 12 sliding panel doors, each representing one week's production schedule. It was the biggest Gantt chart that I had ever seen. Each machine in the plant was designated by a horizontal bar. Each bar was calibrated in hourly increments. As job inquiries were made, they were "tentatively scheduled" using a red felt marker on the order board. The earliest feasible due date was then communicated back to the customer. If the inquiry was converted into a firm purchase order, the color of the order was changed from red to blue on the wall.

The wall also served as a communications vehicle for the factory. When production wanted to know what was scheduled, they went "around the wall" to see their projected work load. When purchasing needed to know what and when plastic raw materials were needed, they too just checked the wall.

When I entered the production area, I was expecting to find antiquated equipment. Quite the contrary! What I observed was a neat, well-laid-out factory equipped with the most up-to-date equipment. The workers were qualified and well motivated, and they too were saddened by the unexpected death of Uncle Otto.

The production system was fairly simple. One line transformed plastic beads into tubs. The second stage printed the company's labels on the sides. Many of the orders used one of the five basic tub designs, but our customers increasingly elected to use distinctive tubs. The second line made the lids for the tubs, also printed. The final stage of the operation was packaging. To save space, lids and tubs were shipped separately in corrugated containers. Finished goods were stored by customers in the small but adequate warehouse adjacent to the loading dock. Most of the customers were local and picked up their supplies, usually on a weekly basis.

As I left to go home that night, I noticed my Porsche standing out in a sea of Chevy Caprices. Even Uncle Otto had driven a 5-year old Chevy wagon—just in case he had to make a rush pickup or delivery.

Most of all, I thought about that wall! How could Marquis control a $40 million business with 2 colors of felt pens and 12 sliding doors with Gantt charts?

My first instinct was to call one of my old systems analysis buddies. He would have a field day—Marquis was still using an old IBM system to do its accounting and payroll. But something in me told me to go slow; Uncle Otto's employees did not seem to welcome change. But then again, as a 38-year-old managing director, I was not looking forward to two decades making margarine tubs.

QUESTIONS

1. What additional information should "Little David" explore before taking on "The Wall"?
2. What type of production scheduling system would you recommend? Assume that as part of the firm's new mission statement, it has decided to expand both the product line and geographic sales regions in order to achieve a 25 percent annual sales growth goal.

CASE 18.2

Hawkeye Bottling Company

Hawkeye Bottling Company operates a soft-drink bottling line in Indianola, Iowa. It markets its returnable-bottle soft drinks throughout much of the Des Moines metropolitan area. It also manufactures canned soft drinks in St. Louis and ships them to its Indianola distribution center.

Hawkeye's production facilities consist of one bottling line that handles all of the firm's five flavors. Each time the line switches flavors, the line is down approximately one shift for a change to a cola product and two shifts for a change to the flavor-sensitive non-cola products.

How much this downtime costs the company is a function of how busy the plant is. It costs Hawkeye approximately $375 for each crew hour, but the firm has a no-layoff policy, so this cost is incurred whether or not the line is operating. Overtime work is always done on Saturday. The overtime rate is 150 percent of the regular time rate.

Hawkeye is wrapping up its fall quarter and now scheduling future production for the firm's nine-month production planning horizon. The demand for bottled soft drinks normally exceeds Hawkeye's capacity during the summer months, so the firm builds up seasonal inventories to be able to accommodate peak demand. For next year, it anticipates the following demand pattern:

Weekly Demand Rate

Product	Jan.	Feb.	March	April	May	June	July	Aug.	Sept.
Cola	10,000	12,000	14,000	20,000	28,000	34,000	40,000	45,000	35,000
Lemoncola	800	900	1,100	1,300	1,400	1,600	2,000	2,200	2,000
Diet cola	4,000	4,300	4,600	5,000	5,500	6,000	8,000	8,200	8,000
Mtnbrew	2,000	3,000	6,000	3,000	4,000	4,000	4,500	4,700	4,500
Gingerale	1,100	1,000	1,200	1,300	1,400	1,600	2,000	2,900	2,000
Total	17,900	21,200	26,900	30,600	40,300	47,200	56,500	62,400	51,500
Weeks per month	4	4	5	4	4	5	4	4	5
Monthly demand	71,600	84,800	134,500	122,400	161,200	236,000	226,000	249,600	257,500
Two-Shift Capacity	224,000	224,000	280,000	224,000	24,000	280,000	224,000	224,000	280,000

Regular-time capacity does not allow for time lost during product changeovers.

Two-shift production would result in substantially less product. For example, if a week's schedule called for each flavor to be made, the firm would incur three cola setups (24 hours) plus two non-cola setups (32 hours). Since there are only 80 regular hours per week, only 24 hours would be left to bottle the cola. Clearly, there are incentives to produce longer bottling runs. However, for each case carried over from one week to the next, the company incurs a $0.10 inventory holding cost.

QUESTION

Use Hawkeye template. Develop a feasible weekly production schedule that minimizes total labor and inventory holding costs. A feasible plan would have no stockouts (negative inventories) and schedule total hours of work (including setup time) at less than 96 hours a week. For the sake of simplicity, you may ignore paid holidays.

[SELECTED READINGS]

Baker, Kenneth R. *Introduction to Sequencing and Scheduling.* New York: John Wiley & Sons, 1974.
Blackstone, J. H., D. T. Phillips, and D. T. Hogg. "A State of the Art Survey of Dispatching Rules for Manufacturing Job Shop Operations." *International Journal of Production Research* 20, no. 1 (1982), pp. 27–45.

Conway, R. W., W. L. Maxwell, and L. W. Miller. *Theory of Scheduling.* Reading, Mass.: Addison-Wesley, 1967.

Fogarty, Donald W., John H. Blackstone, Jr., and Thomas R. Hoffmann. *Production and Inventory Management,* 2d ed. Cincinnati, Oh.: South-Western, 1991.

Goldratt, Eliyahu M., and J. Cox. *The Goal.* Norwich, Conn.: North River Press, 1984.

Goldratt, Eliyahu M., and Robert E. Fox. *The Race.* Croton-on-Hudson, N.Y.: North River Press, 1986.

Graves, S. C. "A Review of Production Scheduling." *Operations Research* 29, no. 4 (1981), pp. 646–675.

Greene, James H. *Production and Inventory Control.* Homewood, Ill.: Richard D. Irwin, 1974.

Melnyk, Steven A., Phillip L. Carter, David M. Dilts, and David M. Lyth. *Shop-Floor Control.* Homewood, Ill.: Dow Jones-Irwin, 1985.

Melnyk, Steven A., and Phillip L. Carter. *Production Activity Control: A Practical Guide.* Homewood, Ill.: Dow Jones-Irwin, 1987.

Melnyk, Steven A., and Phillip L. Carter. *Shop-Floor Control: Principles, Practices, and Case Studies.* Falls Church, Va.: American Production and Inventory Control Society, 1987.

Plossl, G. W., and O. W. Wight. *Production and Inventory Control.* Englewood Cliffs, N.J.: Prentice-Hall, 1967.

Smith, Martin R. *Short-Interval Scheduling: A Systematic Approach to Cost Reduction.* New York: McGraw-Hill, 1968.

Taylor, Sam G., Samuel M. Seward, and Steven F. Bolander. "Why the Process Industries Are Different." In *Process Industries Reprints.* Ed. by Sam G. Taylor, Robert E. Wickes, and Michael P. Novitsky. Falls Church, Va.: American Production and Inventory Control Society, 1984, pp. 1–16.

Taylor, Sam G., Samuel M. Seward, Steven F. Bolander, and Richard C. Heard. "Process Industry Production and Inventory Planning Framework: A Summary." In *Process Industries Reprints.* Ed. by Sam G. Taylor, Robert E. Wickes, and Michael P. Novitsky. Falls Church, Va.: American Production and Inventory Control Society, 1984, pp. 17–35.

Wassweiler, W. R. "Fundamentals of Shop-Floor Control." *23d Annual Conference Proceedings,* American Production and Inventory Control Society, Los Angeles, Calif., 1980, pp. 352–354.

Wight, Oliver W. *Production and Inventory Management in the Computer Age.* Boston, Mass.: Cahners Books, 1974.

Umble, M. M., and M. L. Srikanth. *Synchronous Manufacturing.* Cincinnati, Oh.: South-Western, 1990.

Vollmann, Thomas E., William L. Berry, and D. Clay Whybark. *Manufacturing Planning and Control Systems,* 3d ed. Homewood, Ill.: Business One-Irwin, 1992.

APPENDIX 18A

Scheduling for Process/Assembly Lines

Unique characteristics of common process/assembly lines, otherwise known as *flow shops,* create specialized scheduling needs. Most of these shops produce commodity products such as cement, paint, cattle feed, gasoline, and steel products.[11] They generate value by rapid times to product and low costs, usually in make-to-stock environments with few variations within a family of products. These systems allow few if any changes in product specifications, and they tend to produce in large volumes.

Typically, process/assembly lines carry materials flow over fixed routes between work centers via fixed-path materials-handling equipment like conveyors

---

[11]Sam G. Taylor, Samuel M. Seward, and Steven F. Bolander, "Why the Process Industries Are Different," in *Process Industries Reprints,* ed. by Sam G. Taylor, Robert E. Wickes, and Michael P. Novitsky (Falls Church, Va.: American Production and Inventory Control Society, 1984), pp. 1–16.

[**E X H I B I T   1 8 A . 1**]

Flow Shop Layout

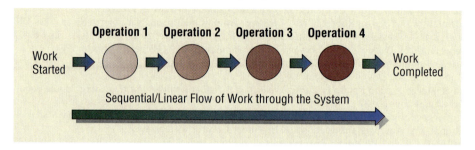

or pipes (Exhibit 18A.1). These system layouts create sequential work flows, and the specific processing activities and their sequence correspond directly to the requirements of the products. If the routing sheet requires a saw cut followed by a drilling operation followed by a CNC operation followed by another saw cut, then the shop floor lays out a saw linked, perhaps by conveyor, to a drill linked to a CNC work center linked to another saw. In this sequential process flow, the bottleneck operation determines the overall capacity of the line. As a result, shop-floor control emphasizes effective bottleneck scheduling.

The fixed routes and large production volumes justify investments in specialized, limited-capability equipment. As a result, any increase or change in capacity tends to require a long lead time as compared to similar changes in a job shop. Also, the relatively high fixed costs of these investments create incentives for operations managers to maintain relatively high utilization rates. In the flow shop, capacity, not materials, becomes the critical resource that requires intense management attention.

The effort to maintain a high and stable capacity utilization rate begins with master production scheduling. Operations managers must act by this relatively early point to ensure both the feasibility of the schedule and the complete and effective utilization of available equipment. The MPS must consider scheduling and sequences for individual orders because the system's finite capacity equals its output over typically continuous operations 24 hours a day, 7 days a week. To resolve scheduling conflicts within the confines of this available capacity, detailed scheduling must begin at this early stage.[12] This concern with capacity differentiates the shop-floor control systems of flow shops from those of job shops (Exhibit 18A.2).

The detailed schedule for a flow shop seeks primarily to arrange orders in a way that minimizes equipment downtime for changeovers and setups. Schedulers have developed several procedures to accomplish this task, some based on advanced mathematical procedures like linear programming. In this appendix, however, we examine a very simple but effective procedure—cyclical production scheduling.[13]

[12]William A. Thurwachter, "Capacity Driven Planning," in *Process Industries Reprints,* ed. by Sam G. Taylor, Robert E. Wickes, and Michael P. Novitsky (Falls Church, Va.: American Production and Inventory Control Society, 1984), pp. 136–154.

[13]Richard C. Heard, "Cyclical Production Scheduling," in *Process Industries Reprints,* ed. by Sam G. Taylor, Robert E. Wickes, and Michael P. Novitsky (Falls Church, Va.: American Production and Inventory Control Society, 1984), pp. 108–117.

[**EXHIBIT 18A.2**]

Planning Sequences in Flow Shops and Job Shops

Planning Sequence	Job Shop	Flow Shop
1	Product	Product
2	Material	Capacity
3	Capacity	Material

Cyclical Production Scheduling

This procedure helps with scheduling for parts within a product family when each product passes through similar operations or processes within the OM system. Sequence dependency has a critical effect on such a schedule since the time to run each product depends on the necessary adjustments to changeover from the previous product. For example, a system that processes orange juice must accommodate different grades of the product with different densities, which vary with the amounts of pulp. The system can hold down setup costs by scheduling various grades of juice in order of increasing density from light to heavy juices.

Cyclical production scheduling begins by generating a changeover time matrix. This table lists times required to change a system from producing one product to others. In Exhibit 18A.3, if a schedule were to call for production of A301 after production of A312, it would have to allow 7 hours for changeover time. The diagonal string of Xs reminds users that it makes no sense to measure the changeover time to run a product after another run of the same product.

After schedulers develop a changeover time matrix, they pick a product with which to start the schedule. They can do this in many ways. Orange juice production might automatically start with the lightest grade of juice. Another schedule

[**EXHIBIT 18A.3**]

Changeover Time Matrix

Time to Change from Product	To Product								
	A290	A301	A312	A293	A294	A305	A316	A307	A328
A290	X	6	1	2	5	4	7	8	3
A301	10	X	7	4	6	9	3	1	5
A312	2	7	X	3	4	5	6	8	
A293	4	6	2	X	7	3	5	6	5
A294	5	3	4	1	X	4	3	2	6
A305	6	3	2	5	7	X	4	1	8
A316	3	4	5	7	2	6	X	8	4
A307	1	3	6	8	4	5	7	X	3
A328	4	3	6	4	8	6	5	4	X

SOURCE Reprinted with the permission of APICS, Inc., from ichard C. Heard, "Cyclical Production Scheduling," in *Process Industries Reprints*, Sam G. Taylor, Robert E. Wickes, and Michael P. Novitsky, eds., The American Production and Inventory Control Society, 1984, p. 109.

[**E X H I B I T   1 8 A . 4**]

Single-Cycle Changeover Time Matrix

Time to Change from Product	To Product				
	A301	A312	A294	A305	A307
A301	X	7	X	9	1
A312	2	X	X	5	8
A294	3	4	X	4	2
A305	3	2	X	X	1
A307	3	6	X	5	X

might start with the product currently in production. Suppose that the firm with the changeover times from Exhibit 18A.3 decides to start with A294.

Schedulers X out its column and then proceed to the next step. They remove from the matrix any products for which they have no orders in the current production cycle, since they often need not produce every product in every cycle. Suppose that the planning system has submitted no orders for these products: A290, A293, A316 and A328. Removing them from the changeover time matrix gives a smaller table only for the current production cycle (Exhibit 18A.4).

The schedulers then adjust each row for the smallest changeover time in that row. After identifying the smallest changeover time in a row, they subtract that value from every other number in the row (Exhibit 18A.5).

The schedulers identify the next product in the schedule sequence. Beginning with the starting product, they identify the remaining product with the shortest changeover time from that initial product. The schedule begins with A294. Since A307 has the smallest changeover time from A294, it comes next on the schedule. The analysis then moves down to the row for A307 to find that the process can achieve the smallest changeover time by scheduling A301 next. On the row for A301, A307 has the smallest changeover time. Since the schedule already lists that product, however, the schedule places the remaining product with the next smallest changeover time (A312) in the following slot. Only A305 remains, so the

[**E X H I B I T   1 8 A . 5**]

Adjustment for the Smallest Changeover Time

Time to Change from Product	To Product				
	A301	A312	A294	A305	A307
A301	X	6	X	8	0
A312	0	X	X	3	6
A294	1	2	X	2	0
A305	2	1	X	X	0
A307	0	3	X	2	X

schedulers can write down the final production schedule: A294-A307-A301-A312-A305.

In most situations, this procedure should identify the optimal schedule. In this way, cyclical production scheduling helps operations managers in process/assembly line systems to minimize critical changeover costs.

APPENDIX   18B

Scheduling for Cellular Manufacturing Systems

Chapter 12 described the emergence of cellular manufacturing systems, which combine the flexibility of a job shop with the efficiency of an assembly line. Recall that this system dedicates OM resources in specific areas, called *manufacturing cells* or simply *cells,* to produce products and components in specific families through highly efficient miniature production lines. Often laid out in the shape of a *U,* manufacturing cells move orders in continuous flows from beginning to end. A cell houses all resources that workers need to produce products in one family. It arranges those resources in the order required to produce the designated outputs (Exhibit 18B.1).

The advantages of a cellular manufacturing system discussed in Chapter 12 also help operations managers to schedule production. A cellular layout can keep down lead times by gathering resources in a single location and dedicating them to specific tasks, which eliminates unnecessary setups. This layout also facilitates easy materials handling and controls work-in-process inventories because orders must travel only short distances and the system can run relatively small lot sizes.

[**E X H I B I T   1 8 B . 1**]

Cellular Manufacturing System Layout

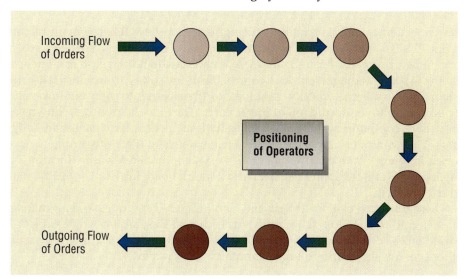

It simplifies planning and control through the combined effects of short lead times, low WIP inventories, and minimal setups. Schedulers for a manufacturing cell need to manage competition for system resources between far fewer orders than job shop schedulers must manage. Fewer jobs and setups simplify scheduling.

This process begins by separating staffed manufacturing cells from limited staffed cells. The difference determines the constraint on the schedule due to labor supply. A limited staffed system requires fewer employees than machines. The schedule for such a system must state rules to guide employees' choices of machines to operate after completing their current assignments.

In addition, a manufacturing cell can turn out varied flows of products. At one extreme, a cell's process can look very similar to that for an assembly line. An order enters at one end and moves sequentially through each work station until it reaches the other end as a completed product or component. Scheduling for such a cell closely resembles that for a process/assembly line, including the emphasis on the detailed master production schedule. The process sets the detailed schedule when it releases the order to the cell, and each machine simply works on the next batch or order that comes down the line.

At the other extreme, a manufacturing cell can generate highly variable work flows in which orders enter at multiple points, skip certain work centers, and backtrack to return to earlier work centers for further processing. Schedulers for such a cell apply modified versions of job-shop dispatching rules discussed in the body of the chapter. Rather than focusing on individual orders, however, they schedule product families or other groups of similar parts. First come-first served and shortest processing time tend to yield effective schedules for cellular manufacturing systems when schedulers apply them to product families rather than individual orders. FCFS would schedule production for the product family with the oldest order while SPT would assign the highest priority to the product family for which the cell has an order that would require the least amount of processing time.

Since cellular manufacturing has become popular only relatively recently, its detailed scheduling procedures have not yet fully developed. Certainly, however, one key to effective scheduling requires short setup times. Like FCFS and SPT for product families, detailed scheduling rules should sequence orders to minimize setups.

Scheduling for Flexible Manufacturing Systems

Closely related to cellular manufacturing, one can view flexible manufacturing systems (FMSs) as networks of manufacturing cells. The larger system joins together manufacturing cells through automated materials-handling systems, integrated systems for tool management and control, and integrated, computerized control systems. Such systems typically combine 2 to 15 machines to carry out low-volume to medium-volume production of metal parts. They can help to keep down setup times, since computer systems automatically issue orders for changes and adjustments. They can often reduce lead times from weeks to days, streamline work-in-process inventory, and control tool costs. A system that adds value through a mix of speed, cost, and flexibility can derive substantial benefits from a flexible manufacturing system.

These innovative, new systems have not operated for long, so their managers still struggle to develop scheduling procedures. Research on this subject has focused on the development and application of modified dispatching rules similar to those for job shops and cellular manufacturing systems.

PART SEVEN

The Strategic Audit

CHAPTER NINETEEN

Future Challenges for Operations Managers

CHAPTER OBJECTIVES

[At the end of this chapter, you should be able to]

- Describe the dynamic forces that drive the task of the operations manager.
- Outline the five major challenges likely to confront operations managers in the future: organizational vision, global activities, environmentally responsible operations, knowledge, and managing technology.
- List professional organizations and resource activities in which operations managers should participate to augment their ability to add value for their organizations.

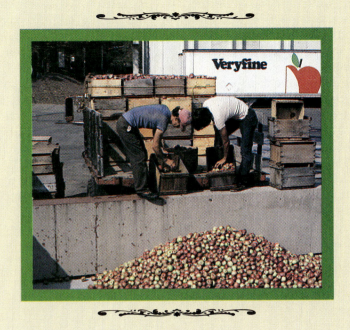

Meeting the Challenges at Commerce Clearing House and Veryfine Products

TWO VERY DIFFERENT FIRMS SUCCESS-fully met two different modern challenges to keep their market positions. Management was asleep at the wheel of Commerce Clearing House (CCH), a leading publisher of reports for accountants, lawyers, government agencies, and corporations. With the third best return on equity among 22 U.S. publishers and $53 million in earnings in 1987, CCH hugged tight to its print products and mainframes. But by 1992, losses mounted to a dramatic $64 million. What went wrong? "Management organization and our legacy computer systems were major impediments to our response to the market," says Oakleigh Thorne, whose family that controlled CCH since 1892 and still controls 56 percent of the stock. Thorne led a drastic shift to electronic publishing. "We were so wedded to the great revenue we were getting, we didn't have the courage to migrate to being a PC software company," says Thorne. "Also, instead of competing on quality of product, our competitors were emphasizing price at a time when the market was very receptive." Again a leader in its high-tech market, CCH is a warning to companies that relax into success.

Veryfine Products, Inc., a major producer of fruit juice, requires not only fresh fruit but also a great deal of water. It also generates a great

SOURCE

Patty de Llosa, "The Vision Thing," *Fortune*, November 14, 1994, p. 60.

Joel Makower, *Beyond the Bottom Line* (New York: Simon & Schuster, 1994), p. 129.

deal of waste, primarily the water and the waste that goes back to the ground water system under the town of Littleton, Massachusetts. To reduce the impact of these problems, the management of Veryfine worked very closely with the town to make sure the local water quality met not only local, state, and federal water-quality regulations but exceeded them.

To do that, the company built an $8 million water purification plant that returns to nature water that is often purer than it was when first taken from the ground. Equally important, Veryfine reduced its level of waste generation. By installing cooling towers for its can and bottle lines, the company reduced waste water by about 20 million gallons a year. The company made this investment even though it cost $500,000 and didn't generate any return on investment. Why? According to Samuel Rowse, Veryfine's president and grandson of the company's founder, the reason can be found in his belief that manufacturing firms must do more than jump on the environmental bandwagon. They must be in the driver's seat.

This last chapter presents five challenges to future operations managers. Its modular structure allows readers to cover each section separately, or all of them together, at any time during the course. Appendix 19A addresses future opportunities for personal development.

Two important premises underlie the discussion throughout this book: (1) operations management is a value-driven activity, and therefore (2) a firm's OM system must change continually to adapt to an inherently dynamic definition of value. Many of today's OM challenges emerge from the changes that will shape the operations management system of the future. In this chapter, we focus on five challenges:

- *Challenge of vision*   Reinventing the firm and its OM system
- *Challenge of global operations*   Buying and selling in global markets rather than local or domestic ones
- *Challenge of environmentally responsible operations*   Producing products that satisfy customers' needs without harming the natural environment
- *Challenge of knowledge*   Dealing with the new expectations and demands of the knowledge worker
- *Challenge of managing technology*   Adjusting OM process functions for changes in technology, since much of the novelty in operations management results from technological change, though not all technological changes are significant

Each of these challenges creates new opportunities and new dilemmas for operations managers. How they adapt to these new conditions will determine the structure, activities, and control systems of the OM system of the future.

Commerce Clearing House had to adapt to a shift toward microcomputer systems that made its mainframe-based system obsolete. To accommodate this new technology CCH had to change not only its own technology, but also the essential characteristics of its product. This threat also posed a challenge to the vision of

CCH management, which had not effectively anticipated and planned for the future. The firm's slow response had serious consequences. In 1987, CCH recorded the third-highest return on equity among U.S. publishers; by 1992, record losses had wiped out all of the profits earned in 1987.

Veryfine Products faced a challenge to operate in an environmentally responsible manner. Its management met this challenge, making Veryfine a leader in this emerging organizational responsibility.

Challenges should not alarm operations managers. In fact, they contribute to the dynamic, living character that enriches organizational life. They embody critical current events and likely future events that do not fit current frameworks, procedures, and systems. They demand new responses to new conditions. Operations managers can ignore challenges only at the risk of organizational success or even survival. Their responses to challenges often cause changes in their methods of managing the transformation process. Therefore, modern operations managers must confront the essential task of evaluating challenges, identifying those with the most critical effects, and then planning and implementing appropriate responses.

In this chapter, we discuss the implications of the five challenges for operations managers and responses of leading-edge firms. Specifically, this chapter will:

- Describe and define each of the five challenges and illustrate their importance to the operations manager and the firm as a whole.
- Identify the reasons behind the emergence of each of the five challenges.
- Identify the major issues and potential impacts that each challenge creates for operations managers.
- Describe tactics that help operations managers to maintain understanding and control of a dynamic OM system.

In this chapter, we try to orient the reader toward the future. To help the student stay current in a changing world, we not only discuss these five trends, but in an appendix we also present some guidelines to help prevent obsolescence of knowledge. Finishing this book and course should not mark the end of learning about operations management; rather, this step should mark the start.

CHALLENGE OF VISION

CCH foundered due largely to a lack of vision. Its managers assumed that the future would look very much like the past. They overlooked the impact of microcomputers, dismissing them as limited devices for word processing and graphics applications without a role in meeting the database management needs of CCH's large, organizational customers. The firm assumed that customers would continue to desire its reports and did not want direct access to data. To deter competitors, it relied on the high costs of acquiring, operating, and maintaining a mainframe network, the only way to provide comparable reports, according to management assumptions.

The development of microcomputers changed the rules of the game for CCH. Competitors could acquire these new machines relatively inexpensively and operate them relatively easily to create powerful, cost-effective systems. Microcomputers changed both the product and the transformation process in CCH's market. Microcomputers allowed users to process data themselves rather than revising and manually reprocessing data from CCH reports. This gave users the capability to generate their own highly customized reports to meet their own

[**EXHIBIT 19.1**]

Elements of an Organizational Vision

Today	5 to 10 Years in the Future
Which customers does the firm serve?	Which customers will the firm serve in the future?
With which firms does it compete?	With which firms will it compete in the future?
How does it deliver value to customers?	How will it deliver value to customers in the future?
What skills or capabilities make it unique?	What skills or capabilities will make it unique in the future?
In what end-product markets does it participate?	In what end-product markets will it participate in the future?
How does its transformation process work?	How will its transformation process work in the future?

SOURCE   Gary Hamel and C. K. Prahalad, *Competing for the Future: Breakthrough Strategies for Seizing Control of Your Industry and Creating the Markets of Tomorrow* (Boston, Mass.: Harvard Business School Press, 1994), pp. 16–17.

specific needs. As a result, they wanted a new product—a complete database that they could access through their own microcomputers—in place of expensive, generalized reports.

The drop in CCH's stock price in 1992 reflected the market's perception that the firm's service was becoming obsolete. To survive, it had to reinvent itself. Management had to adapt to the increased importance of price as a component of the value equation at the same time that they transformed the firm from a report publisher into a database publisher.

This dramatic change is not unique to CCH. Nearly every mature company faces the same challenge. Some reinvent themselves as part of forced responses to crises. However, others, such as British Air, Hewlett-Packard, and Compaq, have taken proactive steps to make changes in anticipation of potential developments. All such changes powerfully affect the firms' OM systems.

Also, vision drives every organization's efforts to reinvent itself. Successful corporate and industrial change emerges when managers develop and implement innovative visions of the future.

Vision—Defining the Concept

Vision changes the orientation of operations management decisions from the present to the future. It guides the firm's arrangements for the future and the transformation of the firm and the OM system over time. Managers form a vision for their organization by answering the two sets of questions listed in Exhibit 19.1. Their answers influence their vision of the organization's future.

vision
A strategic view of the organization, its products, and its processes that aims at creating and satisfying new forms of demand in a way that increases customer satisfaction and company market share and profits

We define **vision** as a strategic view of the organization, its products, and its processes that aims at creating and satisfying new forms of demand in a way that increases customer satisfaction and company market share and profits. These new forms of demand emerge from efforts to identify and challenge the existing mental mindsets of managers, employees, and external stakeholders. The vision materializes as a new view of the firm, its critical core competencies, and the value that it offers to customers. This definition emphasizes a number of important and interrelated traits.

Forward Looking.   Vision does not try to project present activities and competitive strengths forward into the future; that would be like driving a car looking only

[**EXHIBIT 19.2**]

Identifying New Demand

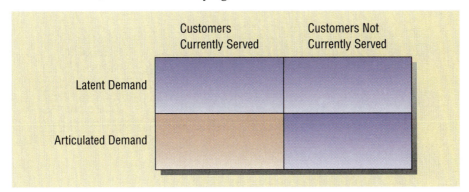

in the rear-view mirror. Rather, vision focuses on the road ahead and then tries to identify skills, resources, and processes that the organization must develop to navigate successfully in the future. Based on these elements, vision tries to create a sustainable competitive advantage for the future through one of three strategies.

First, the organization might try to change the rules of engagement, as LensCrafters did. Before this firm transformed the market, customers assumed that they would have to wait at least a week after placing an order to get eyeglasses. Firms maintained physical separation between the factories that ground lenses and assembled glasses and the sites where customers ordered and received the glasses. LensCrafters changed the rules of the game by merging the lens grinding-factory with the dispensing site.

As a second strategy for creating a sustainable competitive advantage, a firm might envision redrawing the boundaries between industries. AT&T and cable television providers are now racing to accomplish this kind of a transformation in telecommunications. If it can offer television programs over its fiber-optic lines, AT&T will blur the boundaries between cable entertainment companies and telecommunications carriers.

The strategy envisions creating an entirely new industry. The founders of Apple Computer foresaw a personal computer industry and worked to create it in the late 1970s.

Creating New Demand.   Recall from Chapters 1, 2, and 11 that at any point in time, a firm works to identify and satisfy a set of articulated customer demands. However, these demands do not define the entire market that it might serve. Latent demands create potential opportunities when customers feel an unmet need, but they describe how to satisfy that need. A firm could work to satisfy the latent and articulated demands of two types of customers: those that it currently serves and those that it does not currently serve. Vision looks beyond the articulated demands of current customers to identify three other types of new demand, as shown in the three purple areas of Exhibit 19.2. A thorough evaluation should explore the relative costs and benefits of trying to satisfy each type of demand.

Mental Maps.   Every firm and its management follow a **mental map**, a set of beliefs, relationships, and processes that link inputs to outputs and actions. Assumptions and untested beliefs also show up on mental maps, and they help to

mental map

A set of beliefs, relationships, and processes that link inputs to outputs and actions

Vision, Core Competencies, and the OM System

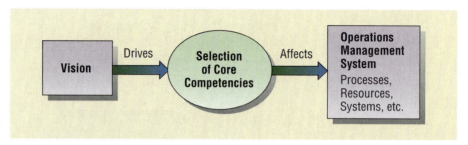

simplify decision making by outlining acceptable possibilities; at the same time, they obscure other possibilities.

Managers must often review and revise existing mental maps in the process of forming a new vision for the firm. In effect, they ask "what if" questions. For example, LensCrafters transformed the eyeglasses industry by asking, "What if we bring the lens-making facilities directly into the stores?" Apple had to redraw a mental map in developing its Macintosh computer. Earlier computer designs assumed that users would have to learn complex commands. The designers of the Macintosh asked, "What if a computer could accept user input in the form of icons selected by pointing and clicking a mouse without the need for cryptic commands?" The resulting graphical user interface (GUI) revolutionized computer operating systems through the Macintosh and later Windows.

Generating New Core Competencies.   Managers begin to develop a vision by defining likely future customer values. This forces them to define the core competencies that the firm will need to satisfy these new customer requirements. They may have to invest in new processes, systems, or capabilities if current core competencies cannot meet envisioned customer requirements. Exhibit 19.3 illustrates the sequence.

Managers temporarily ignore their understanding of current core competencies, since this information might restrict their view of the future to possibilities that conform with current capabilities. Management at CCH made this mistake in 1987 and failed to foresee the emerging dominance of the microcomputer.

Continuously Refining a Vision.   Once managers develop and implement a new vision that successfully challenges accepted conditions, that vision then becomes the new mental map. Over time, competitors copy it and try to improve on it as customers come to expect the promises of once-new definitions of value. To survive, the firm must repeat its successful innovation, continuously challenging existing orthodoxies. Competitors define some of these orthodoxies; others develop internally within the firm. By constantly mounting new challenges to a firm's current vision, managers try to identify old and outmoded features of the mental map and to replace them with newer and more attractive visions. All firms, including market leaders, must meet this requirement. The "On the Job" box reports on such a process at Boeing.

ON THE JOB

Boeing Reinvents the Design Process for the 777

Boeing of Seattle, Washington, is the world leader in designing and manufacturing jet aircraft for commercial travel. Despite its dominant position, however, changing conditions in the industry created serious challenges for the firm.

In the late 1980s, its management began to see the effects of intense profit pressure on the major airlines, resulting in weak demand for its aircraft. Boeing had expected the airlines to retire about 300 aircraft from service every year, but the actual number came closer to 100. The airlines could operate more cheaply by keeping older, relatively inefficient, but fully depreciated aircraft in service rather than spending millions for new aircraft.

Boeing management became convinced that their firm could survive in this new environment only by changing the entire process of designing and building aircraft to drastically reduce its costs and delivery time. By involving its entire work force in the project, Boeing committed itself to completely automating the design of new aircraft, reducing the build time on a new model by as much as 50 percent and by making even bigger cuts in inventory.

These activities centered on the development of Boeing's newest aircraft, the 777. If this project succeeds, it will reduce the overall costs of producing an airliner by over 25 percent. Boeing's competitors, such as Airbus, admit that Boeing will transform the industry if the 777 project meets its goals.

SOURCE   Gary Hamel and C. K. Prahalad, *Competing for the Future: Breakthrough Strategies for Seizing Control of Your Industry and Creating the Markets of Tomorrow* (Boston, Mass.: Harvard Business School Press, 1994), p. 69.

A set of fundamental questions can help managers to direct the process of continually reinventing the firm and constantly updating its vision:[1]

- *What is the firm's basic value proposition?* What kind of customers does it serve? What customers and needs does it currently ignore?
- *Where in the business system does the firm make a profit?* What activities generate its margins? What influences its costs and price? Could it extract profits at a different point in the value chain?
- *What does the firm know how to do well?* What kinds of skills prevail in the company? Might some alternative configuration of skills and assets more effectively serve customer needs?
- *How alertly does the firm watch for new value-delivery models?* How easily could it reconfigure its current system? Who within the firm would most vigorously resist change? What makes the firm vulnerable to new rules of the game?

Vision: The Operations Manager's Challenge

An organization's vision emerges from a strategic process with strong implications for the OM function. Several vision-driven changes will likely affect operations managers in the future.

[1]Gary Hamel and C. K. Prahalad, *Competing for the Future: Breakthrough Strategies for Seizing Control of Your Industry and Creating the Markets of Tomorrow* (Boston, Mass.: Harvard Business School Press, 1994), pp. 63–64.

Accept Change and Complexity.   When managers accept vision as a dynamic concept, they learn to deal with the probability of rapid change and complexity. Change accelerates when organizations anticipate performing different activities in the future than they currently perform. They often actively pursue rapid change, believing that early implementation brings substantial rewards.

Complexity may result from increasing segmentation of the market as the firm implements a new vision statement. Today's organizations usually move from serving larger market segments to smaller ones; some even treat individual customers as segments in their own right.

Operations managers must accept these developments as the new facts of life, despite the apparent paradox that they create. This paradox requires operations managers to simultaneously manage for stability and plan for change. To resolve this contradiction, they must emphasize stability in short-term plans because effective day-to-day functioning requires a degree of stability. A schedule does not mean much when the priorities of competing jobs change from moment to moment.

Over the long term, however, operations managers must plan for change. They must recognize that every system they might implement, no matter how well-conceived, will eventually become obsolete. New OM models will surely replace current systems such as just-in-time manufacturing. From the moment that they begin implementing a new system, operations managers must begin developing its successor. The process of building this successor benefits from detailed knowledge of the weaknesses of the current system.

Maintain Awareness of New Opportunities.   At first glance, vision seems to flow downward from top management. Only people at the top of the hierarchy have the authority to choose new demands to satisfy and services to provide in the future; managers at lower levels shape the OM system to support this new vision. This incomplete view ignores the influence of input and developments at lower levels through their effects on the feasibility of certain future choices. For example, a firm might not successfully compete on speed without effective computer skills among the work force. Operations managers influence the organizational vision by identifying technologies with strong potential strategic effects and communicating these benefits to top management.

For example, Boeing workers had to develop skills in computer-aided design (CAD) systems before the company's managers could form their vision of a new system to design and build the 777 airliner. The company first introduced CAD as an efficient tool for certain product-design tasks. Operations managers then educated top managers about the strategic potential of CAD systems. This task requires a formidable effort from the operations manager, whose activities usually focus on day-to-day events.

Further discouraging efforts to innovate, Richard Foster and Lowell Steele both noted that over 95 percent of all innovations either fail or have little or no real impact.[2] Only a small portion of the remaining 5 percent have any significant impact. At first glance, these statistics may seem to imply that operations managers should refrain from wasting time on innovations, since so many seem destined to fail. However, this ignores the pivotal impact of significant innovation successes for both the OM function and the firm as a whole.

---

[2]Richard Foster, *Innovation: The Attacker's Advantage* (New York: Summit Books, 1986), pp. 190–194; Lowell W. Steele, *Managing Technology: The Strategic View* (New York: McGraw-Hill, 1989), pp. 56–57.

Translate the Vision into Relevant Terms.   Before operations managers can implement a broadly worded organizational vision, they must restate it in terms that OM personnel can understand. Typically, these restatements specify activities and goals for capacity, processes, resource levels, inputs, outputs, and capabilities. For example, strategists at Boeing may have understood a statement that the firm needed to change the calculus of designing and building new airliners. However, this statement would have made little sense to a supervisor in the wing-assembly area. Operations managers had to perform a bridging function by translating that goal into objectives to reduce lead time, parts requirements, and inventory.

Maintain System Flexibility.   The new emphasis on change and complexity also complicates decisions about investments in the OM system. In general, they should favor investments that enhance the overall flexibility of the system. The discussion of knowledge later in this chapter explains further that investments in knowledge and learning provide critical enhancements to OM system flexibility.

Operations managers should also remember a caution from accountants: sunk costs are irrelevant. Once a firm makes a major investment in plant and equipment, the cost of that investment should not influence future decisions. Too much devotion to old investments in mainframe computers clouded decision-making processes at CCH, with near-disastrous results.

Maintain Awareness of Current Limits and the Need for Continual Learning. Vision demands change, and organization members will accept change only under two conditions. First, managers must recognize the effects, hidden assumptions, and limitations of their mental maps. They cannot afford unquestioning fidelity to any mental model, remembering that what worked in the past may not work today. The second condition for acceptance of change requires a recognition of the need for continual learning. To adapt to change, managers must remain open to new information and ideas. Curiosity should become a key component of the organizational character. Learning does not end with a college degree. Rather, it must be a life-long journey.

Vision: Summary Comments

The concept of vision presents a new and somewhat radical perspective on the firm, its mission, and the value that it offers to customers. Throughout this book, we have stressed the OM system's contributions to the firm's core competencies and capabilities, implying that strategies should maintain consistency with these OM strengths. When vision drives organizational decisions, however, operations management must become flexible and adapt to the strategic needs of the firm. As the organization's vision changes, its OM system must keep pace. The ultimate goal of both centers on consistently giving customers better value than competitors offer over time.

   ## CHALLENGE OF GLOBAL OPERATIONS

Today's operations managers manipulate global networks of resources. They integrate foreign suppliers into the supply chain, and they must make and deliver products that delight both local and foreign customers. This challenge is relatively new to North American firms, which operated primarily in domestic markets 40 years ago. They bought raw materials from neighboring suppliers and sold their products primarily to North American customers. Everyone often spoke the same language and few significant differences in culture complicated interactions.

Any international sales involved exchanges of the same products that firms made for their domestic markets. In some cases, this practice created problems, as when North American producers sold cars in England or Japan, where people drive on the left-hand side of the road. Foreign sales accounted for relatively minor proportions of overall business, however, so firms had little incentive to adapt. Often, they bought only raw materials from foreign suppliers; domestic sales of final goods produced internationally reached only small market niches that domestic producers did not value. For example, Honda developed its reputation in cars by selling primarily to college students who wanted low-cost, fuel-efficient, high-quality, basic transportation.

Today, firms build products for sale to both domestic and international markets. Some products have achieved consumer acceptance in foreign markets. For example, businesspeople in Japan prize Cross pens, made in Rhode Island, and frequently hand them out as gifts. Today's firms also buy from both domestic and international suppliers. Computers assembled in the United States may contain hard-disks produced in California and memory chips manufactured in Singapore, Malaysia, or Japan. Because firms now use so many foreign components, they have trouble setting criteria for identifying domestically produced products. A Toyota Camry has a stronger claim to status as a domestic car than a Ford Crown Victoria!

Value ultimately drives this movement from local to global operations. Firms buy inputs from foreign suppliers for several reasons. They often pay lower prices for the same features and quality; for the same price, they can get goods with higher quality or more features. They may even find components available from foreign sources that domestic suppliers do not yet offer. Firms sell to international markets because they can earn large profits there. These markets sometimes offer opportunities to expand and increase the rate of revenue growth, even when comparable domestic markets have reached maturity. Companies as diverse as Kentucky Fried Chicken, Motorola, and Cross pens have found success in global markets.

They do not reach the status of global organizations overnight, however. Before they operate globally, they have to begin to nurture global thinking. To understand how global competition can affect a firm's business, managers should begin by considering the effects on customers. This analysis should provide answers to several questions:

- Could the firm find significant markets for its products in regions of the world where it does not currently sell? Could it compete in those markets?
- If the firm were to decide to outsource all or part of the output of its current transformation process, would the change affect the value that current customers place on the product? Would they know? Could the firm ethically avoid informing them?
- Has any current competitor elected to carry out all or part of its transformation process offshore? If so, how has the arrangement affected its competitive methods?
- Do foreign firms seem likely to enter the domestic market? How would domestic customers value the products of those firms? How confidently can the firm answer this question?
- How do the firm's existing organizational traits limit its options to outsource or relocate all or part of its existing operations? Would the company's

Companies like 7UP have discovered the value of doing business in a global market. 7UP's manufacturing plant in Burma has increased company profits due to low production and supply costs.
SOURCE   Andy Hernandez/Liaison International

values tolerate such a decision? What impact would it have on the current
work force? Would any union contract allow foreign outsourcing? What
other consequences would such a decision have?

- Do global opportunities offer the firm a significant opportunity to enhance
the value of its products? For example, should Nordstrom's deny its customers the opportunity to buy less expensive and/or higher-quality shoes?

These questions point out numerous tradeoffs that operations managers
must consider when evaluating global alternatives. Any evaluation of a global
business alternative should begin with analysis of the effect on customers' assessment of value.

Primary Effects of Global Operations

In this section, we briefly discuss the ways in which global operations directly
affect an organization's operations. These effects create immediately apparent
tradeoffs that operations managers must resolve.

Offshore Outsourcing.   Any firm can buy raw materials and/or manufactured
components from offshore suppliers that offer better prices or quality than domestic suppliers. People normally attribute this kind of action to cost-reduction
motives, but firms have other reasons. Marco Polo went to China to acquire high-
quality ceramics rather than low-cost goods. Silicon chip makers buy raw materials
from Japanese sources mostly because those suppliers offer high quality. These
international arrangements help domestic firms to produce goods more efficiently
and often with higher quality.

Low-cost offshore suppliers can often help a firm to gain a competitive advantage, however. Ford achieves a 15 percent cost advantage over GM when it buys
brake shoes from Brazilian affiliates. The unions at GM's brake-shoe factories strive
to preserve American jobs by limiting this kind of outsourcing. Nike has built a
core competency by successfully contracting out virtually all shoe manufacturing,
mostly to Pacific Rim suppliers. These manufacturers probably do not make better
shoes than domestic firms could, but they do make less expensive shoes.

To gain these benefits from offshore outsourcing, a firm must sacrifice some flexibility. A supply network spread out over 5,000 miles would have to overcome serious obstacles to achieve a fast-to-product manufacturing capability. Such a network might well separate product design from process design, further inhibiting organizational flexibility. Operations managers have long tried to maintain close proximity between product and process design functions to speed product launches and design changes. This sacrifice may not trouble producers of mature products.

Offshore outsourcing can also increase system variance. For example, currency exchange-rate fluctuations can effect an OM system in a number of ways. Clearly, the costs of essential inputs rise and fall with exchange rates. Sometimes beneficial fluctuations further improve cost advantages. The same changes force losses on suppliers, however, who may want to renegotiate prices to compensate. During the 1995 peso crisis in Mexico, disadvantaged suppliers sought adjustments to existing supplier contracts. Since the value of the peso had fallen relative to the American dollar, these suppliers earned far less than they had anticipated from cross-border sales. Exchange rate uncertainty can significantly accelerate changes in the dynamic environment of operations management.

Offshore Operations.   Firms establish offshore operations for many reasons. Pursuit of a cost advantage is the most popular motive, for both manufacturing and service operations. The economic tradeoffs that govern offshore outsourcing also apply to offshore operations. The alternative of foreign production raises an additional issue, however—when to make a product or component and when to buy it. Vertical integration may allow a firm to earn the profits throughout the value chain, but this strategy can also affect how it manages its future growth. Today's low-cost locations will often face price competition from new directions tomorrow. A firm that establishes offshore manufacturing facilities to reduce its costs may end up chasing low wages around the world. The firm that moved from New England to South Carolina in the 1950s to take advantage of lower labor and material costs may have to follow these benefits to Vietnam within another decade.

When a firm establishes an offshore manufacturing facility, it must decide whether to transfer current management personnel or hire indigenous managers. Current managers would bring knowledge of the firm's products, processes, internal culture, and management style. These people may lack an understanding of the new labor and materials markets that local people could offer, however. The ability to manage local workers depends largely on a firm's ability to attract management talent. Native managers help to buffer foreign firms from the idiosyncrasies of the local labor force and government bureaucrats. Japanese firms learned this lesson when their management styles encountered resistance in some North American facilities.

A manufacturer can maintain control, however, when it expands operations to other countries. To preserve its core competencies while operating globally, a firm may have to assume a proprietary position. By relying, instead, on outsourcing to meet the same needs, a firm risks creating new competitors by teaching suppliers how to duplicate its own essential capabilities. For example, Savin Copiers came to regret its decision to rely on Ricoh to make its copiers. Ricoh prospered by mimicking Savin's methods, while Savin itself no longer exists.

This kind of exchange can become a benefit, however, if offshore manufacturing brings alternative perspectives into the domestic firm. Xerox learned what it needed to do to survive from its Japanese affiliate. General Motors and Ford have long drawn talent from the management ranks of their European operations. Ford used its ties with Mazda to learn about just-in-time manufacturing.

Offshore operations are becoming increasingly important in services, as well. This trend started when firms established out-of-region service centers. Citibank moved much of its credit-card processing work to South Dakota. Bank of America moved many of its operations out of California to areas with lower costs of living, such as Phoenix, Arizona. Lately insurance companies have pushed this trend one step further. Many of them process claims at facilities in Ireland, Jamaica, and other English-speaking countries via satellite-based communications systems. Hewlett-Packard has established global customer-service processes that might route problems to service reps in Hong Kong or Palo Alto for responses.

Offshore Product Innovation.   Within the past decade, the scope of offshore operations has broadened. While cost still drives much of this activity, international firms increasingly go to foreign lands in search of intellectual capital. U.S. firms locate facilities close to European centers of learning, and European firms look for similar benefits in the United States. For example, many German pharmaceutical firms have located research labs in the San Francisco Bay area, partly to place researchers near major research universities, but also for less obvious reasons. German firms could not engage in genetic research in their home country with its unfavorable political climate haunted by its Nazi past. That position has recently started to change.

Global Economies of Scale.   In the past, many domestic firms were content to compete largely in North American markets. The development of time-based competition has challenged the wisdom of this limitation for firms in dynamic markets that demand regular introductions of new products. These firms must rapidly recapture the costs of developing new products, since they can expect to sell those products only for short periods before even newer ones attract customers' attention. Firms that sell to large, international markets can generate needed returns more quickly than others that sell primarily to domestic markets. The world market often seems to consist of three large trading blocks plus the emerging nations; a firm can gain a competitive advantage by amortizing product-innovation expenditures over a sales base that spans more than one of these markets.

Even the most innovative firms have not always succeeded at developing products that satisfy global markets, however. Ford Motor Company tried to make its Escort a world car, but disagreements arose between its European and North American divisions. Ultimately, Ford sold different cars in the two markets, with only the ash tray as a common part. It has continued its effort to achieve a common design with its Mondeo/Contour/Mystique model. The success of the ambitious goal of designing a car that appeals to buyers on both sides of the Atlantic remains uncertain.

Software developers learned long ago that they must do more than translate their products' output into other languages to produce global successes. They have to develop computer code robust enough to accommodate significant adjustments to adapt the product to the mores of each nation's culture. Firms like Computer Associates involve European employees early in the product-development process to ensure than the result satisfies diverse customers.

American firms that want to understand global business could learn much from fast-food merchants, such as McDonald's. To succeed, they must understand what makes their products desirable in other markets. In some cases, such a firm can appeal directly to customers' desire to buy a American product. Many pop culture items sell well for this reason. In other situations, the values of foreign customers may lead in a different direction. Still, mass customizing techniques may allow a firm to provide the functional differences that distinct markets demand by combining common modules produced with significant economies of scale. For example, in Prague, you can buy a beer with your familiar Big Mac. McDonald's had to modify its domestic menu by adding beer to satisfy the expectations of its Czech customers. Of course, a firm may find it more economical to develop separate products for different markets or trading blocks.

Global Logistical Advantages.   As in domestic operations, firms place logistical support facilities close to foreign customers to achieve advantages based on either cost or delivery speed. Sometimes they can get the edge they need simply from overseas distribution facilities. In other cases, it makes economic sense to place all or part of their transformation processes offshore. Firms often maintain post-sales support processes close to foreign customers, but satellite-based communications systems may eliminate this necessity.

As in the domestic warehouse-location problem, a firm can keep down transportation costs by shipping in economical quantities. It can speed product delivery by stocking goods near foreign customers. These inventories may limit its ability to customize products to meet specific needs, however, unless those customers will wait for additional shipments from distant production facilities. As one way to solve this problem, a firm may include limited assembly capabilities in its production/logistics system so it can perform limited customizing nearer its foreign customers.

Secondary Effects of Global Operations

In addition to these five primary effects, the decision to operate globally raises a number of secondary issues. As a firm sets out to pursue the direct benefits of global operations, it must anticipate the indirect consequences of its activities. Some of these effects further enhance the firm's success, but others may create obstacles large enough to outweigh the value of the primary objectives.

Internationalizing Management.   The move into global markets often augments the firm's management with local people who understand the languages and cultures of its foreign customers. While difficult to quantify, this benefit is quite real. Foreign workers enhance their firms in several ways:

- In accommodating an international perspective, a firm learns to deal with its own diversity. Solectron and Amdahl Computer view the ability to communicate with employees in their native languages as a strategic strength of their organizations. While training costs money, inadequate communication often costs much more.
- A company's international perspective helps it to recognize and deal with the special characteristics of customers and suppliers.
- Evidence of a cosmopolitan, international outlook may even help a firm to attract quality employees and suppliers. The limited flow of new talent into the work force raises the importance of the firm's ability to attract young people. Some Midwestern firms already have difficulty attracting nonwhite job candidates from racially diverse areas, and firms located in rural areas face similar problems. Would you want to move to Bloomfield, Iowa?

Actually, you might like it there, but many good candidates refuse even to consider such a move.

Impact on Hourly Workers.   Workers fear losing their jobs more than any other employment calamity. Any discussion of offshore plants or foreign suppliers instantly deepens these fears and sparks controversy. North American hourly workers routinely hear and read horror stories about jobs traveling overseas. GM's employment is down in excess of 200,000! Mexican workers eagerly accept about $1 an hour, and Chinese workers envy that wage!

Domestic employees wonder how they can compete. Many others worry about the current $30-billion U.S. trade deficit and fear worse effects through continuing foreign expansion. These people have serious concerns, and they do not find comfort in calls to work smarter.

As a result, *outsourcing* has become a dirty word, especially for work transferred to a foreign site. For example, Lincoln Electric, a manufacturer of welding equipment and welding rod, gained a strong reputation as a good place to work through its renowned employee incentive program. Within the past decade this reputation suffered, however, when Lincoln built a plant in Mexico. While the move may have benefited corporate economics, workers in Cleveland asked whether the Mexican plant was taking away their work. They suspected arguments that the transfer of work would strengthen the company and create a bigger pie for everyone to share. These employees simply saw a decline in the size of their slice.

Global operations can also weaken the bargaining power of unions. When American members of the UAW began a walkout against Caterpillar, the firm's Far Eastern and European plants helped the firm to continue operating and blunted the effect of the strike. It also continued some domestic production by replacing striking workers with managers, new employees, and union workers who elected to cross the picket line. This problem will likely continue since no global unions seem poised to counterbalance the bargaining power of global corporations. In North America, for example, the once united UAW split into a Canadian union and an American one.

Indirect Impact on Product Innovation.   A global perspective can enhance the ability of the firm to develop niche-like products for increasingly fragmented markets. This requires a major change for North American manufacturers traditionally devoted to mass manufacturing. They dismissed overseas markets as too small and full of funny practices like measuring lengths in meters. Different laws, packaging requirements, and currencies further disrupted the mental maps of domestically oriented managers. When those managers did venture into foreign countries, they implemented one-size-fits-all strategies to peddle unmodified versions of products built for North American markets.

To delight customers in foreign countries, however, firms must learn to cater to requirements that seem odd to domestic observers. Global operations encourage and reward attitudes that accept the need to make some cars with steering wheels on the right, specific emissions equipment, subtle variations in colors, and special features like wipers on headlights for Swedish and German customers.

In developing a basic product that spans the entire global market, designers can make compromises that gain the approval of everyone on a committee but that erode value for individual customers; consensus often comes at the expense of value. In its global operations, a firm can develop insight that leads to common product features that do not amalgamate conflicting requirements into a poor marketing compromise. If the firm cannot make its product design look distinctly local, then it should consider developing a separate product for each market.

Besides the threat of overly generic product designs, global operations influence the product-innovation function by limiting the firm's fast-to-market capabilities. The adaptability of a team often diminishes as its membership increases. North American firms have just begun to learn about applications of cross-functional teams. When a foreign culture further complicates smooth interactions, global operations may compound this difficulty of teamwork.

To solve these problems that arise when global representatives join corporate product development teams, firms must change their management practices. They often decentralize the management of offshore subsidiaries, especially for local affairs like hiring, government relations, etc. The same method may solve some problems with product innovation. The central design function must produce a product architecture that captures the essence of a market need without precluding changes that tailor the product to a local market. This principle gives the best chance of combining the economies of scale of centralized product design and manufacturing with the agility of mass customization. Developing such a flexible system is a major challenge for global operations managers.

Financial Strength and Stability.   A successful expansion into global markets opens vast new opportunities for growth and spreads business risk among diverse markets. It brings access to superior suppliers who can help the organization to add new value to its products. Also, vast new markets offer the potential of large jumps in revenue. Finally, since the economies around the globe do not always expand and contract together, growth in one part of a firm's global operations can offset declines elsewhere, which helps to stabilize overall performance.

 ## CHALLENGE OF ENVIRONMENTALLY RESPONSIBLE OPERATIONS

Veryfine Products took a leadership position among today's organizations when it designed its transformation process to produce high-quality juice through a low-cost process that generated the minimum possible environmental waste. In the future, all operations managers will have to follow the example of this leading-edge firm to develop and implement environmentally responsible operations. This challenge marks a radical change in the way that organizations design, manage, and evaluate their OM systems. It also reflects a major change in the perceived compatibility of operations management and environmental preservation.

Interest in environmentally responsible operations (ERO) is not new. As long as people have operated transformation processes, they have dealt with the resulting waste streams. In the past, people outside operations management have championed environmentally responsible operations, with varying degrees of success. For example, many people associate ERO awareness with concerned private citizens and associations such as Greenpeace, the Sierra Club, and the Nature Conservancy. Most expressions of ERO priorities have emerged from political and social activities. This view is further reinforced by a common perception of a contradiction between effective and efficient operations management and ERO. Many people see waste as an inevitable by-product of the transformation process. They suppose that the process cannot make a product without creating environmental waste.

Companies like Dow Chemical recognize the importance of developing environmentally friendly products and applications. For instance, a Dow-developed process allows this minivan manufacturer to make bumpers that contain recycled plastics.   SOURCE   Courtesy of The Dow Chemical Company

This view is now changing. Many firms commit themselves to producing goods and services without unduly affecting the environment. Along with small firms such as Veryfine Juice, this list includes many large, internationally recognized companies such as Dow Chemical, Hermann Miller, Steelcase, 3M, Xerox, Motorola, The Gap, and Inter-Continental Hotels. These firms practice environmentally responsible operations not simply to generate good publicity, but because ERO makes sense. If implemented properly, the principle of ERO has been found to significantly reduce costs and to contribute directly to the bottom line.

In our discussion of the ERO challenge, we will focus on several questions:

- What are environmentally responsible operations?
- Why practice ERO now?
- What benefits does ERO bring?
- What major obstacles and paradoxes complicate the implementation and application of ERO?
- What challenges does ERO pose for operations managers?

Finally, we will discuss the scope of ERO to consider how to identify the boundaries of environmental problems. Despite new emphasis on ERO, a company is unlikely to please every environmentalist, in part because they often disagree among themselves.

Environmentally Responsible Operations—Defining the Concept

Simply put, the principle of **environmentally responsible operations** creates an economy-minded, systemwide, and integrated program to reduce or eliminate all environmental waste by revising product, process, and packaging designs to prevent its creation in any part of the transformation process. This section elaborates on aspects of the definition.

Waste as Waste.   The principle of ERO makes the fundamental recognition that byproducts, emissions, and other environmental waste represents another form of waste of organization resources. Just like product features that customers do not

environmentally responsible operations

An economy-minded, systemwide, and integrated program to reduce or eliminate all environmental waste by revising product, process, and packaging designs to prevent its creation in any part of the transformation process want, gas vented into the air consumes resources and increases costs without generating value for customers. By eliminating environmental waste, then, a firm can reduce costs, reduce lead times, increase quality, and improve both profitability and the value that customers receive.

ERO as a System Activity.   Waste is a symptom of OM system activities. Decisions made during product, process, and packaging design determine levels of waste such as sludge, discarded cardboard shipping containers, plastic wrapping materials, remnants of fabric trimmed from final products, HAP (hazardous air pollutants), and VOC (volatile organic compounds). In turn, several organizational functions influence design decisions; marketers identify what customers want, engineers actually design new products and processes, and accountants, suppliers, and human resource managers also contribute. To effectively reduce organizational waste, each of these groups should participate in any ERO initiative.

Prevention versus Remediation.   To deal with environmental waste, a firm can focus on cleaning it up (remediation) or on preventing the transformation process from creating it in the first place. When managers try to control waste currently created by the transformation process, they intervene too late. Despite vigorous clean-up efforts, the process continues to implement a wasteful design, generating still more waste. A firm may improve its waste-disposal functions, but it must revise underlying processes to really eliminate waste. This redesign often requires a substantial investment, but remediation usually costs more over the long run. Of course, the firm can avoid many of these expenses by addressing ERO concerns in initial product and process designs.

Economic Goals of ERO.   The balance between costs and benefits should justify any investments to reduce environmental waste and improve the overall efficiency and effectiveness of the design and transformation processes. Emotional reactions or government regulations often drive ERO efforts, and these forces can distort appropriate investments in the OM system. A requirement for economic justification for all investments forces decision makers to identify and quantify real costs and benefits and to limit expenditures to investments that will provide benefits in excess of their costs. Exhibit 19.4 summarizes this and the other components of the ERO concept.

To fully evaluate the costs and benefits of environmentally responsible operations, decision makers must identify the specific types of waste that the transformation process generates. This information determines the options of operations managers and the firm as a whole to reduce waste. Exhibit 19.5 summarizes types of waste and by-products that OM processes create as well as potential disposal methods.

New Urgency of Environmentally Responsible Operations

ERO concerns have moved from the fringes of operations management to the mainstream. Many developments have converged to cause this shift.

Government and Political Pressure.   Pollution has become an important political issue, and firms can seldom convince people to accept environmental waste near their homes. People who feel affected by atmospheric emissions or other waste streams often look for solutions within the political system. Nobody wants to breathe VOCs from a nearby plant or drink water contaminated by factory

[**EXHIBIT 19.4**]

Components of ERO

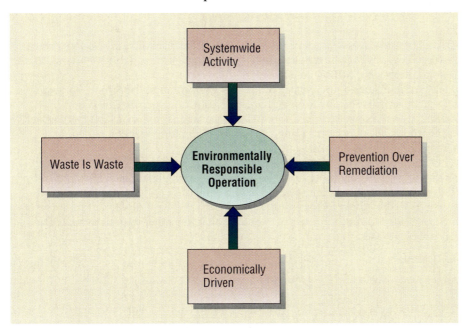

discharges. Within the firm, workers fear exposure to dangerous chemicals or wastes (e.g., asbestos) and may take action through political channels. Many politicians see opportunities to serve constituents (and attract votes) by attacking facilities that produce waste and pollution.

As a result, a vast and increasing set of laws and regulations govern production and disposal of environmental waste. One manager working in the office furniture industry had to comply with about 100 pages of regulations in 1980; in 1994, over 21,000 pages of regulations affected that person's work. Also, the penalties for failure to comply with these new regulations become more serious. In several recent cases, managers have served jail time for their firms' violations of pollution laws.

These laws often apply retroactively, as well. Their standards may govern both current actions and assessments of the effectiveness of and legal liabilities for past actions. A firm may face penalties for past actions that appear inadequate in light of today's laws and legal standards, despite its good-faith effort at the time to use the technology and follow the procedures then recognized as appropriate.

Introduction of New International Environmental Standards.   In Chapter 7, we introduced the ISO 9000 standards by which many industrial buyers certify potential suppliers. By 1996, a new set of standards, ISO 14000, will also detail criteria for judging the environmental responsibility of a firm. Initially, ISO 14000 will create voluntary guidelines and a certification program for three categories of organizational functions:[3]

---

[3]Mary Walter, "ISO Rushes to Set Global Environmental Standards," *Environmental Solutions,* September 1994, pp. 85–89.

[**E X H I B I T   1 9 . 5**]

Types of Waste and By-Products along with Disposal Options

Categories of Waste By-Products

Process By-products: The firm cannot find any use for many outputs of the transformation process so it must dispose of them in some fashion. This category includes such items as shavings, dust, fabric remnants, foam, and punchouts (remaining solid plates after cutting out shapes).

Hotsy, Slurry, Sludge: These are liquid or semi-liquid wastes produced when running a machine. For example, hotsy is a hot liquid run-off that often consists of water, coolant, and a lubricant such as Teflon or oil.

Packaging: Unwrapping components from suppliers leaves mounds of packaging materials. Often, this packaging material consists of cardboard, paper, plastic strapping, plastic wrapping film, wooden pallets, and Styrofoam. In many cases, these items go to landfills.

Volatile Organic Compounds (VOCs)/Hazardous Air Pollutants (HAPs): These are gases created by the transformation process. For example, when spray painting leaves excess spray that does not land on the product, or overspray. However, some of the spray goes into the atmosphere. These gases can be dangerous or poisonous.

Energy Costs: Some of the waste created by the transformation process can take the form of inefficient use of energy (e.g., electricity). If a machine requires more energy to operate than the other options available to the manager, excess energy consumed is waste.

Categories of Disposal Options Available

Dispose: Disposal simply throws away waste into the ground as landfill, into the water, or into the air (in which case, it can become a VOC).

Return to Sender: In some cases, a firm may simply return waste items to the senders. For example, firms located in Germany frequently return packaging to suppliers. Germany has very strict laws governing waste and waste management, so German firms do not want any disposal problems for packaging, so they want suppliers to ship goods with as little packaging as possible.

Reduce: Firms often try to reduce the amount of resources they use or the levels of waste they produce by redesigning their processes or products. They solve the problem by creating far less waste for disposal.

Consume Internally: In some cases, a firm can completely consume waste internally. For example, Hermann Miller has implemented an electrical cogeneration plant fed in part by packaging material from suppliers. These items are fed into a furnace that powers a generator to light Hermann Miller's plants and offices.

Remanufacture/Recycle: A product or process becomes waste when it reaches the end of its useful life. This disposal option tries not to throw away any component. Rather, it tries to take apart the product or process and rework the components to bring them up to original product/equipment/component standards. These reworked components can support other processes or products. Recycling converts the components back into a raw material form, which then becomes new input. For example, an obsolete microcomputer can yield silver, plastic, and gold as inputs for new computer chips or boards.

Process Further: A firm may first reprocess waste products and convert them into something with value to a specific customer. For example, processing turns fabric remnants into a hard material for the rear shelves in cars.

Reverse Disposal: A firm may also work with a third party to create a new market for the waste product. For example, a processor can convert rubber from tires into a matting under astroturf.

- *Management systems*   System development and integration and the introduction of environmental concerns into general business activities
- *Operations*   Consumption of natural resources and energy and incidents of waste discharges
- *Environmental systems*   Procedures for measuring and managing emissions, effluents, and other waste streams

Following on the success and visibility of ISO 9000 standards, the new standards seem likely to force many firms to incorporate the principles and practices of environmentally responsible operations into their OM processes.

O N   T H E   J O B

Leaders in Environmentally Responsible Operations

■

AT&T

The telecommunications giant has won 18 environmental awards since 1990. In 5 years, it reduced its total emissions 81 percent and cut disposal of manufactured waste in half. The firm recycles 60 percent of office papers after cutting its initial paper use by 10 percent through double-sided copying and switching to electronic memos. It offers financial incentives to employees who devise ways to improve environmental performance.

Church & Dwight

The maker of Arm & Hammer baking soda has a long history of environmental concern. It has used recycled packaging since 1907, and it made the first phosphate-free laundry detergent in 1970. It cut its already low releases of toxic chemicals by 45 percent from 1989 to 1992.

Dow Chemical

America's second-largest chemical company reduced its toxic releases by 32 percent between 1988 and 1991. Currently, it maintains release levels among the lowest in the industry. One of the first companies to put an environmental officer on the board of directors, it is also the first major corporation to organize an advisory council of outside experts to help set the company's environmental policy. Its WRAP program (for Waste Reduction Always Pays) has cut millions of pounds out of its hazardous and solid waste streams since 1986.

Hermann Miller

This furniture maker uses tropical wood only from sustainably managed forests. Its innovative manufacturing methods have reduced solid waste by 80 percent since 1982. The firm resells production scraps (e.g., fabric, foam, leather, plastic, vinyl) to auto and carpet makers. Herman Miller set a goal of zero discharge by 1996; that is, by 1996, it planned to eliminate *all* discharges (air, land, and water).

SOURCE   Faye Rice, "Who Scores Best on the Environment?" *Fortune,* July 26, 1993, pp. 114–122.

Opportunity for Publicity.   Publicity related to environmental responsibility has increasingly significant effects on organizational success. This impact can be either negative or positive. For example, Exxon suffered extended negative publicity as a result of the oil spill created when its tanker, the *Exxon Valdez,* ran aground in the Prince William Sound in Alaska. Exxon can never spend enough money cleaning up the waste to erase the television images of thick, black oil scum covering the shoreline and animals. In contrast, the "On the Job" box reports on positive publicity generated by the ERO performance of AT&T, Church & Dwight, Dow Chemical, and Hermann Miller. Each of these companies enjoys sales and marketing benefits based on its position as an acknowledged leader in the application and development of environmentally responsible operations.

Customer Demands.   Many customers want to buy from environmentally responsible suppliers. Companies such as Valley Plastics of California, Quad/Graphics of Wisconsin, and Hermann Miller of Michigan find that their ERO practices help them to sell their products, sometimes at premium prices. The Saturn Car Company emphasizes its environmental responsibility in appeals to its target market: women in their late 20s to mid-30s. People in this segment track environmental issues and want low-pollution cars produced with environmentally responsible processes.

Some controversy surrounds the real marketing value of ERO practices, however. Many people express their interest in environmentally friendly ("green") products, but their actual buying behavior may not bear out their statements. In response to surveys, many customers rank green practices (e.g., making toilet paper out of recycled paper) as a very important factor in buying decisions. When firms actually offer the products, however, they often meet with disappointing demand. Some customers balk at paying higher prices for recycled products, while others seem put off by their appearance. (Toilet paper made out of recycled paper does not look as clean and white as paper made of new wood pulp.)

Investment Attractiveness.   Besides people who buy their products, many firms also deal with another set of customers: people and groups that provide financial capital by buying their bonds and stocks. Traditionally, these investors have based investment decisions on strictly economic factors like profits, sales growth, and rates of return. Today, however, some emerging investment groups evaluate social issues along with financial performance. These investors buy securities issued by firms that combine good rates of return with adherence to environmental or social standards.

Interested organizations eagerly supply information to socially motivated investors. Although they do not invest directly, these organizations affect other people's investment decisions by highlighting firms with conspicuously good or bad environmental records. The Coalition for Environmentally Responsible Economies (CERES) is a not-for-profit organization of leading social investors and environmental groups. Every year, CERES produces a report that identifies environmental leaders along with a top-ten list of laggards. Finally, it publishes a list of firms that subscribe to the CERES principles. Environmentally and socially aware investors base investment decisions on this kind of information.

Benefits of Environmentally Responsible Operations

These and other external forces tend to drive organizations to recognize and implement the principle of ERO. In addition, they often find, however, that the change brings substantial internal improvements that help to justify the necessary investment.

Disaggregation of Overhead Costs.   The largest component of total cost for a typical firm today comes from overhead rather than materials or labor. In some firms, overhead accounts for over 60 percent of total costs. This figure includes expenses for handling, managing, storing, and disposing of environmental waste. Overhead also covers the cost of recruiting, training, and paying personnel to perform this work and the cost of elaborate, specialized equipment that these workers often need.

Finally, firms assign categorization costs to overhead. They incur categorization costs to analyze new forms of waste to determine how to dispose of it. For example, General Motors pays a categorization cost of $2,000 every time it must plan for disposal of a new item, irrespective of the size or quantity that the disposal function must handle. GM spends as much to categorize a single can of paint as to categorize a large bin of parts.

When an ERO program reduces environmental waste, it saves more than direct costs for materials. It also uncovers and attacks hidden but important overhead costs.

Influence over New Regulations.   Proactive implementation of ERO measures can actually help a firm to cope with the political ramifications of pollution and environmental waste. Legislators and regulators can find few concrete guidelines for acceptable practices on which to base environmental rules and standards. To identify appropriate limits, they often look at the policies and procedures of leading-edge firms as patterns for others to follow. For example, many of the policies and procedures for environmentally responsible operations within the chemical industry reflect the practices of Dow Chemical, an acknowledged ERO leader.

A firm can gain some influence over this otherwise unpredictable regulatory process by establishing itself as an ERO leader. Its own practices may then influence the laws and regulations under which it must operate.

Solutions to Disposal Problems.   A firm must find an acceptable way to dispose of any by-product or waste that it cannot recycle, reuse, or eliminate. This requirement presents a multifaceted problem for most operations managers. First, the current waste stream is rapidly filling available landfill space, and few new sites are opening to accept new waste, especially in such eastern American states as New Jersey and New York. Strong demand and limited supply drive charges for landfills steeply upward, leading many New York firms to pay to ship their garbage to the Midwest, where more available landfills charge lower rates.

Another problem complicates waste disposal options, as new standards govern what waste firms can dispose of and what they must reprocess. Foundries, for example, must make very expensive investments in scrubbers and other technology to satisfy requirements to recapture much of the pollution that they previously vented into the atmosphere.

Further, the responsibility of a firm that creates waste does not end with disposal. Many disposal sites in the United States face regulatory requirements to comply with current standards, even for waste they accepted and dealt with according to standards that applied at the time. To avoid the heavy financial burden of compliance, the owners of some sites have declared bankruptcy. The responsibility for cleaning up the waste then passes back to the firms that created it.

Finally, firms can choose between fewer options for disposal of waste. For example, some firms have considered exporting their pollution by moving their dirtiest operations to countries with far more lenient regulations. These countries, typically in the third world or less economically developed areas, desperately want industrialization, and they are willing to accept pollution as the cost of achieving that goal. However, provisions of the North American Free Trade Agreement (NAFTA) and the General Agreement on Tariffs and Trade (GATT) now prevent this action.

All of these problems with waste disposal increase the benefits of effective ERO practices that minimize waste in the first place. Firms can prevent waste disposal problems much more easily than they can solve them.

Improvements in Financial Performance.   Finally, many firms have discovered an important additional benefit of successful application of the principle of ERO: these firms tend to post exceptional financial performance. A recent study evaluated the overall business success of the firms with the best and worst ERO records. The study found many comparative strengths among ERO-conscious competitors:[4]

---

[4]Study by Steven E. Erfle and Michael J. Fratantuono of Dickinson College, cited in Joel Makower, *Beyond the Bottom Line*, p. 71.

- 16.7 percent higher operating income growth
- 13.3 percent higher sales-to-assets ratio
- 9.3 percent higher sales growth
- 4.5 percent higher earnings-to-assets ratio
- 3.9 percent higher return on investment
- 2.2 percent higher return on assets
- 1.9 percent higher asset growth

The study did not determine whether environmentally responsible operations cause improved business performance or good business performance causes better ERO performance. However, the correlation between these two dimensions of organization performance suggests that ERO is good business and good *for* business. The "On the Job" box illustrates the financial benefits of ERO for General Motors and 3M.

Major Obstacles to Environmentally Responsible Operations

If ERO offers such substantial benefits and other pressures compel managers so strongly toward implementing ERO systems, it may seem strange that more operations managers have not emphasized environmental responsibility. Certain paradoxes and other obstacles effectively discourage some firms from implementing ERO systems. Lack of enthusiasm for environmental responsibility usually reflects inability to overcome these obstacles.

Paradox of Top Management Support.   Our earlier discussion of new management initiatives like JIT and TQM repeatedly referred to the critical role of top managers in supporting organizational change. Top management must accept and champion any organizationwide development to build acceptance throughout the hierarchy.

Top managers may resist participating in an ERO program to avoid gaining detailed knowledge of environmental problems within the company. In this way, they reduce the risk of personal actions against them by regulatory agencies, such as the Environmental Protection Agency (EPA), which sometimes prosecute people at the highest level in an organization who have knowledge of failure to comply. A company president risks a personal fine or even a prison sentence if regulators can prove knowledge of violations. This leads people at the highest levels of the firm to prefer to remain ignorant of ERO conditions.

System Downtime.   To implement environmentally responsible changes, a firm often must shut down or curtail operations for a period of time. A busy production schedule may not leave enough time to introduce needed changes.

Unclear Criteria for Environmental Responsibility.   No well-defined criteria identify environmentally responsible practices and products. Managers may feel uncomfortable resolving tradeoffs to assess different degrees of environmental responsibility. For example, auto designers must decide whether to make an axle out of steel or graphite. Steel weighs more than graphite, so the firm consumes more resources to move and handle it and the car has lower gas mileage. Milling steel also creates more waste during the manufacturing process than molding graphite. However, car owners can recycle steel at the end of the product's life cycle, while the graphite axle becomes landfill. Which of these two options results in a more environmentally responsible car? Like consumers, many designers and

ERO at General Motors

General Motors creates much of its waste during the assembly process. In 1991, an internal audit noted that the firm created 88 pounds of waste and trash for every car it assembled. The company transported most of this waste to landfills or burned it. By 1992, GM had reduced its overall waste production to 31 pounds per vehicle, and by March 1994, assembly generated only 15 pounds per car. Some of the company's plants had become real ERO stars; the Fairfax, Kansas, plant generated about 1 pound of waste and trash for every Pontiac Grand Prix it assembled.

This reduction in waste had considerable consequences for General Motors. The firm paid dumping fees of $55 per ton of waste and trash. It assembled about 15,000 cars per day, 240 days a year. Just by reducing waste from 88 to 31 pounds per vehicle (a drop of 57 pounds), it cut its overall cost by over $5 million annually:

ON THE JOB

Real-World Gains from Environmentally Responsible Operations

■

(15,000 cars per day × 240 days/year × 57 pounds per car)/2,000 lb. per ton × $55/ton = $5,643,000

If the entire assembly operation could match the performance of the Fairfax plant and cut waste to 1 pound per vehicle, the company would save:

(15,000 cars per day × 240 days/year × 87 pounds per car)/2,000 lb. per ton × $55/ton = $8,613,000

The firm would enjoy these gains without significant capital outlays or investments. GM managers identified sources of waste using many of the analytical tools that we have discussed in this book.

ERO at 3M

Among all practitioners of ERO, 3M was among the earliest and has advanced as far as any. The company began to work seriously on reducing and eliminating waste and pollution in 1975 when it instituted its 3P, or Pollution Prevention Pays, program. This program provided financial incentives for employees to identify and eliminate waste. Employees had to demonstrate the financial impact of any suggestion on pollution prevention before the firm would consider implementing it. Since 1975, 3M has saved more than $600 million in reducing its output of pollution by half. It continues to pursue a goal of becoming a zero-discharge company.

SOURCE   General Motors cost information reprinted with permission of Simon & Schuster from *Beyond the Bottom Line*, p. 157, by Joel Makower and Business for Social Responsibility. Copyright © 1994 by Tildent Press, Inc., and Business for Social Responsibility.

managers express an appreciation of environmental responsibility, but complications limit practical implementation.

Good Business Practices versus Bad Investments.   Some leading management theorists have argued that a drive toward environmental responsibility ultimately enhances a company's efficiency and competitive strength. Introducing ERO systems forces the firm and its personnel to identify pollution and environmental waste along with other forms of waste. When they eliminate this drain on organizational resources that generate no corresponding value, workers reduce costs and increase value. They create a more competitive and more efficient firm.

Some recent research casts doubt on the real value of these supposed improvements. Financial evaluations of all forms of ERO investments have found negative returns. Furthermore, some evidence indicates that ERO investments do not promote the ultimate corporate goal of maximizing shareholder value. In other words, investments in ERO improvements can ultimately lower the value of the firm's securities. Any manager would hesitate to consider an investment under such conditions.

Short Product Life Cycles.   At first glance, a rapid turnover of new products should create many opportunities to improve ERO practices in the course of redesigning the product, process, or packaging. Short product life cycles, common in time-based competition systems, create just these conditions, so they may seem to encourage ERO development. When managers, engineers, and employees must cope with short product life cycles, however, they feel intense pressure to complete product development projects and start new ones. In the rush, ERO concerns often slip down the list of priorities. Employees plan to consider ERO practices after they finish everything else, but that day never comes.

Lack of Frameworks.   To successfully implement an ERO program, managers must develop new analytical frameworks (or mental maps) for the goals of the program, its components, and its impact on corporate performance. A great deal of the information about ERO comes phrased in legal jargon or from anecdotal stories and case studies. Managers would accept the concept more easily if they could refer to existing management models that would adequately explain the nature and scope of the project.

Lack of Measures.   Managers encounter a similar difficulty assessing the impact of an ERO program because they lack appropriate measures. The full impact of any ERO improvement depends on the cost of investments in equipment, training, and labor as compared to savings through reductions in waste disposal, processing, and storage requirements, along with other effects. Without clear measures, top managers may doubt the claims of potential benefits of the program. Therefore, advocates for ERO often state their arguments in ethical or moral terms, but these claims to company resources receive less attention than actions with obvious, direct impacts on the firm's competitive position within its marketplace or its bottom line.

Lack of Familiar Tools.   While managers can find analytical tools to help them solve ERO problems (e.g., life-cycle assessment), these tools tend to rely on logic and interpretation rather than quantitative techniques that many managers recognize and understand. Operations managers focus on the primary goal of producing a quality product on schedule at the lowest possible cost. They tend to ignore ERO tools that do not help them meet this objective, preferring more familiar methods. To really promote ERO, managers need new analytical tools that emphasize the practical perspective typical of operations managers. For example, if someone could modify the techniques of materials requirements planning, discussed in Chapter 17, to incorporate ERO issues, practicing managers might more willingly accept environmental responsibility.

Environmentally Responsible Operations— The Operations Manager's Challenge

As the principle of ERO gains increasing importance, it will force a number of critical tasks to the top of the operations management agenda. In this section, we review the most important of these tasks.

Choosing Compliance or Leadership.   Operations managers and other members of the organization must decide whether to emphasize simple compliance with legal requirements or to make the firm an industry leader in the development and application of ERO systems. Each choice has its own set of advantages and disadvantages.

Compliance recognizes the letter of the law as the firm's only responsibility. This level of practice minimizes the investments that the firm must make in its ERO activities. If managers believe that ERO interferes with their goal of maximizing shareholder value, then simple compliance may seem like a cost-effective option. However, compliance places the firm in a reactive position, leaving it vulnerable to surprises. This could become an especially dangerous position if it were to face some retroactive legal requirement. Compliance by today's standards may fall short of tomorrow's requirements. A series of tightening regulations could force the firm to spend continuously to bring itself back into compliance.

ERO leadership, in contrast, emphasizes doing more than legal requirements demand. Instead, operations managers and the firm as a whole try to establish a leading-edge ERO program. As discussed earlier, this effort can draw a great deal of positive publicity and even gain the firm some influence over regulations that govern its activities. However, this same visibility may raise expectations for future actions. Some future error with strong environmental implications would expose the firm to criticism for falling short of its own high performance targets. Also, regulatory agencies or decision makers in the industry may ultimately adopt different standards than those the firm champions and proactively implements. Weighing all of the advantages and disadvantages of both choices, leadership usually brings more benefits than compliance brings.

Creating Awareness.   Many managers and entire organizations still view publicity and ethical arguments as the primary motivations for environmentally responsible operations. They do not recognize ERO as a source of operational benefits, despite observed gains by leaders such as those chronicled earlier in the chapter. Many companies have demonstrated the potential for cost-effective improvements through ERO, but managers who understand this fact still must work to spread awareness among skeptical colleagues.

Efforts to create awareness of the benefits of ERO should first target top managers. They should then move to the shop floor and target operating employees whose efforts ultimately make ERO systems work.

To convince others, ERO advocates must identify and quantify the real but hidden costs of pollution and environmental waste. They can identify these costs in a number of ways. They can compare their own firms' cost and performance measures with those of other companies that have successfully implemented ERO programs. In addition, they can study and analyze current processes using the procedures and tools discussed in this book for such systems as just-in-time manufacturing and total quality management. Internal experts in financial tools and techniques such as the firm's accountants and financial analysts may provide valuable help in this effort. Finally, this analysis can compare the firm's current procedures and systems with those of ERO leaders. This application of benchmarking methods can reveal gaps between the firm's own practices and those of its role models.

Developing New Tools and Procedures that Users Understand.   While ERO advocates can apply many analytical tools and procedures to guide their strategy choices, the unfamiliar logic behind them leads most operating workers to suspect

Waste Streaming Diagram

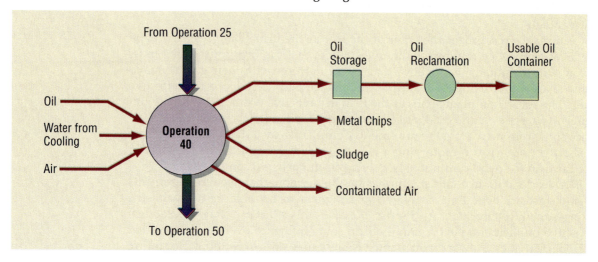

their conclusions. As a result, they rarely use or trust ERO tools. To encourage commitment to ERO, managers must develop tools based on more familiar principles. They may try to adapt procedures such as quality function deployment, house of quality, MRP, and process flow analysis. For example, General Motors has developed a modified version of process flow analysis, described in Chapter 5, specifically to study waste problems. This procedure, known as waste streaming, deserves more discussion because it clarifies ERO in a way familiar to most users.

Waste Streaming

waste streaming

An analytical method that applies process flow analysis to waste flows by graphically depicting the relationships between process inputs and waste outputs

As firms come to recognize the impact of polluting wastes and the need for better control over them, managers need better procedures to study and describe the waste outputs of their processes. **Waste streaming** applies the methods of process flow analysis to waste flows by graphically depicting the relationships between process inputs and waste outputs. Waste streaming also identifies how the process manages each type of polluting waste that it creates.

Exhibit 19.6 shows an example of waste streaming. Operation 40 uses three major inputs: oil, air, and cooling water. The operation produces four different types of waste: contaminated air, sludge, metal chips, and contaminated oil. The chart shows further details about the stream of contaminated oil; it goes first to storage and then to a reclamation activity that removes the contaminants from the oil. The chart does not show what happens to the contaminants, but the firm might dispose of them by burning them or transporting them to a disposal site. The process then returns the recycled oil to the usable oil container. A more detailed diagram would show similar steps for the other three forms of waste.

By carefully diagraming exactly what happens to the waste, process managers identify the exact costs of processing it. They also develop a clearer idea of the pollutant wastes that their processes produce, where they produce these wastes, and how they handle the wastes they create. Waste streaming then offers managers a valuable tool for both managing and eliminating such polluting types of wastes.

Environmentally Responsible Operations: Summary Comments

In the future, ERO will lose its optional character. Customers will take a broader view of the value that the OM system provides. In addition to their demands for low cost, rapid product design and production, high quality, and extensive variety, they will expect firms to offer products generated by environmentally responsible processes. Operations managers and their actions will powerfully affect the firm's success in meeting this new demand.

CHALLENGE OF KNOWLEDGE

The firm's view of its workers and their contribution to its success now focuses more on knowledge than on labor or time spent on the job. To better understand this profound change, consider some examples:

- *Canadian Imperial Bank of Commerce (CIBC)*   After a series of poor loans in the late 1980s, managers of this major North American lending institution decided to reevaluate their process for judging new loan applications. Their traditional loan application assessment had stressed the value of hard assets (buildings, land, equipment, cash, inventory), but loans that seemed strong by these standards often proved more risky than expected. Instead, the CIBC study found that knowledge assets formed a better basis for assessing the strength of a loan than hard assets. A firm rich in knowledge but poor in hard assets proved to offer a better credit risk than a firm with substantial hard assets but weak knowledge.[5]
- *Dow Chemical*   Dow Chemical bases its success on the output of a very active and productive research and development department. However, a review of this department's performance found a questionable rate of return on the research effort. In response, a Dow manager named Petrash developed a six-step process, for managing intellectual assets. This new process is starting to improve Dow's returns on its greatest asset—its knowledge.
    1. Define Strategy. Define the role of knowledge in the business.
    2. Assess competitors' strategies and knowledge assets.
    3. Classify the firm's portfolio of knowledge assets: What does it have? What does it use? Where do these assets belong?
    4. Evaluate the worth of intellectual assets. How much do they cost? How can the firm maximize their value? Should it keep them, enhance them, or divest them?
    5. Based on the inventory of knowledge assets, identify any gaps that the firm must fill to exploit this knowledge.
    6. Assemble a knowledge portfolio and repeat the process over and over again.[6]
- *American Express*   American Express found that it had to make changes in its workplace. It could no longer retain employees simply by offering them job security. Rather, they wanted greater individual challenges and opportunities for learning, and they wanted greater freedom. As a result, American

---

[5]Thomas A. Stewart, "Your Company's Most Valuable Asset: Intellectual Capital," *Fortune,* October 3, 1994, pp. 68–74.
[6]Ibid.

Express allowed many of its service agents and credit analysts to set their own work schedules. The firm began to treat employees as managers of themselves rather than as workers who carried out the orders of superiors according to externally imposed schedules.[7]

The rising importance of knowledge has created new criteria for success in each of these companies. CIBC discovered that it needed to emphasize customers that continuously invest in their knowledge bases over those that invest in hard assets. Dow gained new insight into the importance of managing its knowledge resources and linking them directly to strategy through a careful investment program. American Express learned that past benefits of security and stability no longer satisfy today's employees, and indeed few firms can really make those promises in the increasingly dynamic business environment. Instead, American Express attracts workers by offering jobs that present opportunities to learn and promote intellectual growth.

These companies share one important concern—to recognize, assess, and enhance knowledge. Operations managers of the future will encounter a difficult challenge to understand the nature of knowledge, its effect on OM systems, emerging knowledge-based developments, and tasks that the emphasis on knowledge create for operations managers.

Defining *Knowledge*

Since the late 1960s, North American institutions have transformed to create a knowledge society. Applications of energy, technology, and materials have given way to applications of intelligence, information, and knowledge. Many people incorrectly interpret knowledge and information as synonymous. Information amounts to the flow of data, meanings, and messages that become necessary inputs to develop knowledge.

In contrast, knowledge organizes the flow of information according to a person's mindset. Knowledge enhances and clarifies the mental map to help the person receive information inputs and draw new meanings to formulate internally consistent and logical action plans. In just-in-time manufacturing, the functional effects of knowledge begin when operations managers recognize high inventory levels (a flow of information). The mental map for an effective OM system characterizes high inventories as symptoms of problems in the system, so knowledge inspires and guides a search for sources of waste and other problems.

Components of Knowledge: Tacit and Explicit Knowledge

Knowledge combines two related components: explicit knowledge and tacit knowledge. The movement of information between them drives the process of creating knowledge. Exhibit 19.7 illustrates the relationship between these components.

explicit knowledge
Codified knowledge that people learn by reading or watching and communicate through formal, systematic languages

tacit knowledge
Knowledge that people gain by experience

Explicit knowledge is codified knowledge that encompasses anything that people learn by reading or watching. They communicate explicit knowledge through formal, systematic languages. In contrast, they obtain **tacit knowledge** through experience. People find it difficult to articulate their tacit learning to others. For example, an expert baker learns over time to judge whether a cake has finished baking by the color of its crust. The baker cannot tell an assistant how to make this evaluation; only experience will teach.

[7]Brian O'Reilly, "What Companies and Employees Owe One Another," *Fortune*, June 13, 1994, pp. 44–52.

[**E X H I B I T   1 9 . 7**]

Components of Knowledge

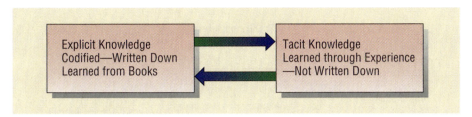

In Exhibit 19.7, when experience converts explicit knowledge into tacit knowledge, people complete the application of their learning. Many people have difficulty articulating tacit knowledge, but become better at it when they know it is available and also when they spend more time observing and testing it. When codification transforms tacit knowledge into explicit knowledge, people effectively create knowledge.

Knowledge creation begins with experience-based learning in which people apply current rules, mental maps, and rational frameworks to actual situations and observe results. Knowledge creation also includes a second activity, unlearning, in which people identify rules, mental maps, and frameworks that no longer work in practice and delete them from both the knowledge base and the shared mental map. Managers often overlook the extremely important step of unlearning. Managers at Commerce Clearing House (CCH) desperately needed to unlearn the firm's mental map with its emphasis on mainframe computers in order to adapt to the introduction of microcomputers.

Knowledge creation provides the critical mechanism by which people learn and adapt. It drives the emerging emphasis of commercial organizations on intellectual property and contributions to value. In many settings, knowledge provides the essential means by which the firm and its OM system continually develop, modify, and deliver value under rapidly changing conditions.

Knowledge and the Transformation Process

This recognition of knowledge as a critical corporate asset is now forcing managers to rethink their mental maps of the transformation process. Exhibit 19.8 shows the traditional and knowledge-based models of this process. Knowledge becomes a new output from the transformation process. Knowledge creation occurs within people and not within networks of equipment or computers. Individuals, groups, and organizations all create personal and shared knowledge, both by learning new principles and relationships and by unlearning old ones.

Transformation Process that Encourages Knowledge Creation.   The growth of knowledge as a component of value reshapes the routine tasks within operations management to place new emphasis on creating opportunities for knowledge creation. Success requires four conditions:

- *Autonomy*   By allowing workers to act on their own, operations managers create unexpected opportunities for learning as people encounter new situations and find ways to resolve them. Autonomy increases the probability that people will motivate themselves to create new knowledge.

[**EXHIBIT 19.8**]

Two Views of the Transformation Process

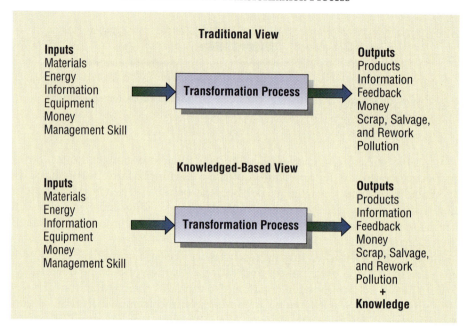

- *Fluctuation*   Fluctuations result from changing conditions based on changing environments. These fluctuations force people to explore new situations. Such an interaction may reveal a need to unlearn old ways.
- *Intent*   To create new knowledge, individuals must pursue opportunities for active intervention to achieve clear goals. Intent forces them to apply and test current beliefs, attitudes, and mental maps. Intent demands that workers become problem solvers rather than simply problem identifiers.
- *Variety*   Variety enlarges an individual's experience, creating new chances to integrate experiences into a broader perspective. This broader perspective leads to knowledge creation. Firms consciously try to increase variety through job rotation and job enlargement programs.

All together, these four conditions contribute to knowledge creation within a transformation process. To describe a transformation process enhanced in this way, operations managers have coined the term **knowledge factory**.

knowledge factory

A transformation process that combines autonomy, fluctuations, intent, and variety to establish conditions that favor knowledge creation

Knowledge Factory.   The concept of the knowledge factory has emerged in response to sweeping changes in today's workplace that are revolutionizing the role of shop-floor workers. A recent article in *Fortune* magazine cited six trends that are pushing firms toward establishing knowledge factories, listed in Exhibit 19.9.

The profound organizational effects of these changes include a need to accommodate a new type of employee—one interested in a job's contribution to personal learning and the strength of his or her resume rather than in security and short-term income gains. The "On the Job" box describes one employer that has made corresponding changes to emphasize the opportunities for learning and self-improvement that it offers to workers in lieu of any commitment to long-term employment.

[**EXHIBIT 19.9**]

Six Trends Reshaping the Workplace

1. The average company will become smaller, employing fewer people.
2. Traditional hierarchical organizations will give way to a variety of organizational forms, such as networks of specialists.
3. Technicians, ranging from computer repair techs to radiation therapists, will replace manufacturing operatives as the worker elite.
4. The vertical division of labor will give way to a horizontal division.
5. The paradigm of doing business will shift from making a good to providing a service.
6. Work itself will be redefined to emphasize constant learning, more higher-order thinking, and less 9-to-5 limitations.

SOURCE Walter Kiechiel III, "How We Work in the Year 2000," *Fortune,* May 17, 1994, pp. 38–52. © 1993 Time Inc. All rights reserved.

Knowledge: The Operations Manager's Challenge

Today and for the future, operations managers must adapt their goals and practices to the needs of the knowledge factory. Employee relations, organization structures, management styles, and training programs all require substantial learning and unlearning to adjust the contours of mental maps to reflect the new reality.

Accept the Knowledge Factory Employee. To create essential knowledge, a firm needs both systems that encourage new discoveries and applications and employees who function within those systems as independent, action-oriented problem solvers. Employees like Veronique Vienne, who loyally serve their own careers rather than the firm's continuing needs, pose a serious challenge to traditional management thinking. Operations managers may need to substantially revise their attitudes toward workers to accept the new type of employee without trying to force changes. Many firms follow the lead of John Sculley at Apple by explicitly accepting the value of this new category of employees and developing environments that recognize their short-term commitments.

New Management Styles. To manage knowledge factory employees, an operations manager must work more as a coach and facilitator than as a supervisor. The operations manager must distribute corporate information and direct workers to relevant resources. The manager must communicate the organization's vision to new employees and provide needed support, resources, and direction while allowing workers to control their activities.

Create Opportunities for Learning. Since many employees now expect to learn in their jobs, a firm must create opportunities for problem solving, decision making, and ongoing training and education. Traditional firms often limited training and education to short periods after new employees took their positions. The knowledge factory, however, requires ongoing education. As employees gain experience and familiarity, they need and can benefit from more and different types of education and training.

ON THE JOB

Corporations Respond to the "New Loyalty"

In an age of fierce global competition, corporate downsizing and outsourcing have become the norm, and most employees realize they can no longer expect their jobs to last a lifetime. Most corporations realize they can't pretend to offer such jobs either. While some firms continue to dance around the old, outworn etiquette of "job loyalty," other companies like Apple Computer are dealing with the issue more straightforwardly.

John Sculley, then Apple CEO, openly acknowledged that he couldn't promise his employees job security. But he could promise that a job with Apple would improve an employee's prospects in the long run, enabling him or her to learn and develop marketable skills for the wider job marketplace. He did this by making Apple a learning environment; a knowledge factory that would produce not only good products but good employees.

Increasingly the concept of "job loyalty" is yielding to the "new loyalty" of employees who now make their primary commitment to their career rather than to any one company. Prospective employees may care more about a job's opportunities for learning and growth than about the wages and prestige it offers. Training for the knowledge factory is ongoing, and jumping from job to job no longer carries the stigma it once had.

"My only career strategy is to plan what I can learn, specifically, from each job," explained Veronique Vienne, whose career in the fashion industry has spanned jobs as art director, marketing professional, and freelance writer. "I try to define very clearly two or three things that I can accomplish while I'm there." As a result of this strategy, Vienne has held seven different jobs over a ten-year period and often selects a job based on what she can learn rather than on how much it pays.

Sheryl Spanier, an outplacement consultant, agrees that the days of a steady career path are over. But that also leaves people more free to pursue their own personal growth and development as a priority. "The key is doing interesting, challenging things professionally, developing a uniqueness and expanding your skills," says Spanier.

SOURCE   Tom Peters, *The Tom Peters Seminars: Crazy Times Call for Crazy Organizations* (New York: Vintage Books, 1994), pp. 101 and 112.

Build Internal Attractiveness.   Many companies like Dow Chemical, Apple, Intel, and Hewlett-Packard recognize knowledge as a major organization asset. Because employees embody much of this knowledge, if they leave the firm, it loses the value of its investments in training. Today's firm and its operations managers must work consciously to enhance the attractiveness of continued employment as part of a strategy to retain the benefits of the knowledge that workers accumulate. These employees will not stay just to earn higher salaries; rather, operations managers must regularly demonstrate new benefits of continued employment to important employees. Many firms try to do this by continuously rotating job assignments to increase variety and the range of experiences. The sequence of assignments may follow a career path plan, and the firm assesses each employee's progress by measuring achievement against this career path.

Nonsalary perks help firms to attract and keep good employees. Some firms offer opportunities for sabbaticals as important perks. A sabbatical gives an employee paid time off from work for self-renewal and to spend time pursuing issues that interest him or her. In a similar perk, 3M allows employees to spend up to 15 percent of their time working on projects of their own that they think offer

[**EXHIBIT 19.10**]

Eight Keys to Career Self-Reliance for the Modern Manager

1. Think of yourself as a business.
2. Define your product or service.
3. Know your target market. To whom will you sell it?
4. Be clear on why customers buy from you. What is your value proposition? What do you offer that attracts the customer?
5. As in any business, drive for quality and customer satisfaction, even if your customer is someone else in your organization.
6. Know your profession and what is going on there. What constitutes best practices in your area? Is your entire profession becoming obsolete?
7. Invest in your own growth and development the way a company invests in R&D.
8. Be willing to consider changing your business or starting a new one. A person can have more than one successful career over the course of a professional lifetime. However, to succeed, you need three additional traits:
   a. Be a specialist. (You must be an expert in something.)
   b. Be connected. (You must be a team player.)
   c. Be a generalist. (You must know enough of different disciplines to mediate among them.)

SOURCE   Walter Kiechel III, "A Manager's Career in the New Economy," *Fortune,* April 4, 1994, pp. 68–72.

potential benefits. This policy has yielded some very innovative products. For example, Art Fry, an employee of 3M, wanted little adhesive papers to mark the places of the hymns he was going to sing at Sunday church services. This need led him to approach a fellow employee, Spence Silver, who had developed a light adhesive. Together, the two spent their free time perfecting Post-It™ notes. In 1994, 3M sold more than $100 million of them.[8]

Managers can try to make their firms' work environments attractive by giving employees access to resources to support creativity. Ritz-Carlton Hotels allows any employee to spend up to $2,000 to address any customer-related complaint. The employee need only account for the expenditure.

Finally, managers can try to create a work environment that exceptional employees find attractive by setting very high standards of performance. Ambitious performance standards may help to develop a sense of community among employees who share the satisfaction of achieving the highest goals. In the process, the firm may develop a reputation as a first-class organization that helps to attract people who value associations with leaders.

Of course, any activity to build the attractiveness of the firm's employment opportunities represents an investment of time. The firm must carefully direct this investment toward employees who offer it the greatest return for the investment. Not all employees justify the effort, but managers must invest the time and money to keep those who do within the firm. An effective policy requires procedures to identify these critical employees.

Recognize the Need for Continued Learning.   Both employees and managers need to continue to learn. Exhibit 19.10 lists one set of guidelines to promote learning by knowledge-driven employees.

[8]Marshall Loeb, "Ten Commandments for Managing Creative People," *Fortune,* January 16, 1995, p. 135.

[**EXHIBIT 19.11**]

Top Ten Technologies for 2005

Technology	Application
1. Genome mapping	Gene probes, predicting who will get what disease
2. Supermaterials	Rugged, adaptable service in communications, energy, transit
3. Compact energy sources	Powerful, long-lasting fuel cells and batteries
4. High-definition television	Digital video for better computer imaging
5. Handheld electronic devices	Phone, fax, computer together
6. Smart manufacturing systems	Sensor-driven assembly lines
7. Anti-aging products	Creams to erase wrinkles, gene tinkering to slow aging
8. Targeted medical products	Treatments for individual ailments, reduced side effects
9. Hybrid-fuel vehicles	Lower emission, high-mileage, high-performance transportation
10. Edutainment	Educational games, computerized simulations

SOURCE   Based on Battelle Technology Group; "Wonders of Tomorrow." Reprinted from March 6, 1995, issue of *Business Week* by special permission, copyright 1995 The McGraw-Hill Companies, Inc. All rights reserved.

Knowledge: Summary Comments

Every manager, both within the OM function and outside it, must cope with the growing importance of knowledge and the cycle of learning and unlearning. The firm sees the knowledge factory as a way to do more work with fewer resources. Employees see it as a source of interesting, challenging, and rewarding work opportunities. Operations managers see it as a set of new challenges.

 ## CHALLENGE OF TECHNOLOGY

Technology, like everything else in this world, is changing. Operations managers must understand the likely effect of technological change on a firm's economic viability to allow it to survive. The list of hot technologies in Exhibit 19.11 includes devices and skills that defy comparisons to earlier designs or mental models. Managers must develop entirely new mental maps to assess the impacts of these and the many other technological advances. Only by fully embracing innovation can they project the impact of technology on the firm's ability to design and deliver products that delight customers.

Exhibit 19.12 presents a questionnaire designed to clarify the needs for technology management in specific situations. Of course, different questions carry different weights for individual conditions. The assignment of responsibility to answer these and related questions also becomes important. Someone in the firm must accept responsibility to address the right issues, and he or she should perform a formal, annual review as part of this process. The review should not become so formal that it excludes questions that challenge the organization's mental map. The process needs careful protection from attacks by short-term thinkers. These requirements usually create a need for seasoned staff personnel to plan for the effects of technology. This choice does not, however, absolve top managers from their ultimate responsibility to think through long-term issues for themselves.

[**EXHIBIT 19.12**]

Technological Change Assessment

I. Source of Technological Change

List Technological Changes That Could Affect Your Existing Business:

Change 1.

_____

_____

How likely is this to occur? by: _____   ☐ Not Likely   ☐ Highly Likely

What impact is likely?   ☐ Minor Impact   ☐ Major Impact

How will this affect employee skills?   ☐ Require Major   ☐ Require Little
                                                    Retraining   Retraining

Change 2.

_____

_____

How likely is this to occur? by: _____   ☐ Not Likely   ☐ Highly Likely

What impact is likely?   ☐ Minor Impact   ☐ Major Impact

How will this affect employee skills?   ☐ Require Major   ☐ Require Little
                                                    Retraining   Retraining

[Add more questions as needed]

II. Potential New Business Opportunities

What new products might the firm offer customers?

_____

_____

_____

_____

_____

continued

[**EXHIBIT 19.12**]

Continued

II. Potential New Business Opportunities (continued)

What new features might the firm offer on existing products?

_____

_____

_____

What impact would the technological change have on existing features?

_____

_____

_____

III. Sources of New Competition

Technological Change: _____

What firms are likely to enter the market?

_____

_____

_____

What existing products are likely to attract new competition?

_____

_____

_____

[Add more sections as needed]

IV. Other Possible Consequences of Technological Change?

[No questionnaire can anticipate all possible consequences.]

_____

_____

_____

_____

_____

Managing for Technological Change

The essential goal of managing for technological change requires special management attention because imprecision clouds the discussion. One can cite examples of organizations that seem to do it well, but no distinct process contains all of the actions that made technology management succeed. The tendency among North American managers to evaluate products rather than processes complicates this judgment.

In this section, we would like to stimulate some initial thought about the process of managing technological change. The questionnaire is a good start, but it scarcely introduces the true dimensions of the task. As for any forecasting process, the development of a formal method should start with an acknowledgment that no firm can achieve perfect clairvoyance. Throughout business history, even industry greats have failed to understand the true impacts of their innovations.

To anticipate technological change, an organization should emphasize certain principles among its managers:

1. Technology exists only to promote the interests of the business and its customers. Terry Hill believes that since engineering is a business process, it should be managed as a business.

2. Effective managers must understand the effect of technology on the firm's current and desired future core competencies and its business strategy. They must find a way to synthesize the existing and latent needs of the business with emerging technologies.

3. Continuing education must maintain a broad understanding of existing and emerging technologies while it fosters managers' keen personal desire to master this knowledge. This principle presumes an innate desire for continuous learning and discovery.

4. Even outside formal education, organization members must closely monitor advances in intellectual property throughout the world within industry, government agencies, academia, and other research institutions. Increasingly, managers will have to navigate skillfully through information highways seeking wide-ranging, interactive associations with other people who share the same technology interests.

5. A fundamental understanding of management theory and practice, including both quantitative and qualitative business tools, underlies all of this exploration.

6. Finally, a technically competent manager must also recognize the importance of artfully predicting and manipulating change to his or her personal success. Some might deride this statement as support for unproductive office politics; in the real world, however, a manager needs organizational moxie or allies with that kind of skill to move the firm toward its goals.

Designing an organization to hire, train, and motivate technically capable people poses a significant challenge. Perceptions of a decline in organizational commitment to employees complicates this important work because necessary training places a company's intellectual property at risk. Even relatively successful high-tech giants such as IBM, Kodak, and Digital Equipment Corporation have found themselves unable to live up to promises of lifetime employment. To counterbalance the attraction of outside employment opportunities, a firm must nurture personal intellectual growth and economic security so that employees who embody the firm's intellectual property do not feel tempted to leave. Hewlett-Packard, among many other technology leaders, takes heroic steps keep the "HP family" intact rather than losing valued members to competitors.

A further complication results from need to manage technological change in the context of the moves toward global and environmental operations discussed in earlier sections of this chapter. Increasingly mobile intellectual resources bring

Russian scientists to work for American companies, while students take Ph.D. degrees from American institutions to create competitors in their home countries. American firms establish research labs in Japan and Europe to capture intellectual resources there.

These interconnections create new alliances. Firms accept the impossibility of maintaining leading-edge positions in all technologies. Therefore, they implement the concept of the focused factory to supplement their own expertise with the skills of other organizations. Recognizing the limits of their own technical skills, businesses have struggled to develop a new capability beyond fast-to-market product and process development; they now work to become fast to adopt, integrate, and apply technologies developed by others. In the process, they must root out any trace of the not-invented-here (NIH) syndrome to build truly borderless organizations that combine business functions from both internal and external sources. The first external extensions of a firm's technology base usually forge links to existing industrial customers and suppliers. Suppliers can often provide excellent technological insights, and they welcome invitations to incorporate their technological advances in the customer firm's products and processes.

Two firms may effectively serve both of their strategic interests by jointly developing some new technology. A supplier may need to draw on its customer's intellectual and/or fiscal resources to support development or simply to reduce risk and improve the project's focus. A joint-development project can accelerate both firms' drive toward sustainable competitive advantage by securing a proprietary position in a newly developed technology well ahead of competitors. A successful relationship requires a clear, legal expression of both parties' rights and responsibilities.

If a firm cannot control access to a new technology, it may still manage to derive some benefit from it by developing a capability to capitalize more effectively than competitors, more quickly, or both. For example, Microsoft's Windows 95 will change software development. The future success of software publishers will depend on their ability to make better use than their competitors of the capabilities of Windows 95.

A firm can also extend its technological span by making better use of its customers' intellectual property. Hewlett-Packard has based its long-standing competitive advantage in scientific instrumentation by involving customers so closely in its new designs that they in effect become integral members of the product-development team. In most cases, the firm works simply to develop an explicit understanding of their needs, but sometimes they actually transfer intellectual property back to HP.

A firm may also find technological expertise among researchers at universities and governmental agencies. Pharmaceutical firms have long maintained these relationships to extend their R&D budgets. As U.S. defense industries shrink, government think tanks, such as the Sandia and Lawrence Livermore National Laboratories, may begin offering technological expertise simply to survive budget cuts. Operations managers face a challenge adopt the expertise of these organizations without copying their bureaucratic management practices. The demands of time-based competition may outweigh some of the advantages of working with these labs.

The same shortcoming may also limit technology links between industry and academia. Advantages from the academic community's awareness of businesses needs for product or process innovation may prove too valuable to ignore, however, by supporting carefully targeted development programs. Firms have successfully mined the intellectual capabilities of the academic community by:

[**EXHIBIT 19.13**]

Technology-Management Process

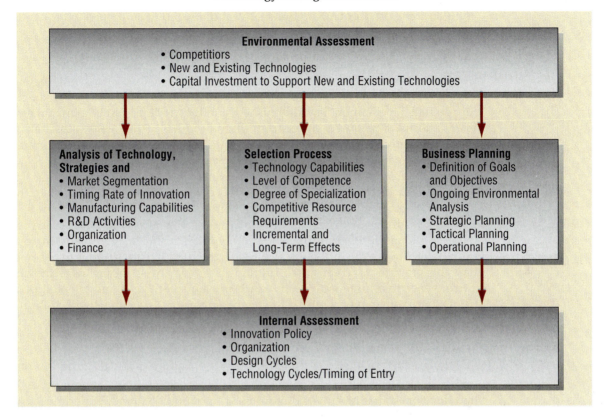

SOURCE   J. A. Edosomwan, *Integrating Innovation and Technology Management* (New York: John Wiley & Sons, 1989), p. 76. Copyright © 1989 John Wiley and Sons. Reprinted by permission of John Wiley and Sons, Inc.

- Extending long-term grants to individual academics or their schools
- Funding grants and scholarships to graduate students
- Employing faculty members as consultants

Unfortunately, an academic's need to publish research results may create a conflict with the sponsoring firm's desire to maintain secrecy.

Technology-Management Process

A formal technology-management process can help a firm to design and develop products and/or processes through which it can delight its customers. Since technology-related opportunities can come from many possible directions, every firm needs the most comprehensive technology-management process that it can maintain. Exhibit 19.13 illustrates the elements of this process.

Available space does not permit a full discussion of all aspects of the technology-management process, and we have discussed most of these issues elsewhere in this text. Remember, however, that the activities within this process represent essential parts of a firm's overall organization design. They provide valuable tools to help the firm maximize its ability to serve and satisfy its customers.

Technology and Product Maturity

Operations managers have long assumed that the need for product or process innovation declines as a product approaches maturity. While this premise may apply to some products, no organization should accept it as gospel. If the standard model had governed Schwinn's situation, its competitive threat would have come from cheap foreign imports and North Americans would have ended up pedaling Chinese bicycles; instead, unexpected technical innovations powered a new surge in the domestic industry. Similar comments could be made about the radio, television, and automobile markets. In each case, American firms assumed that the need for product development had diminished, and they redeployed both management talent and fiscal resources away from these products. Thus firms ultimately lost their competitive edges in these markets to upstart firms that saw opportunities to effectively reverse the life cycles of these products.

One could target blame in many directions for managers' failure to see these opportunities before competitors exploited them. For one possible cause, these firms could have relied on a flawed, but common strategic planning process. The Boston Consulting Group's well-known Strategic Business Unit (SBU) matrix typified the assumption that a firm should draw funds from its high market share-low growth divisions, called *cash cows*, to fuel growth in divisions with greater potential. This practice can create a self-fulfilling prophecy by stripping away the funds a firm needs to reinvigorate itself, which prevents both cash and talented people from stimulating new growth. If the firm assumes that customers will continue to accept the speed, quality, and flexibility of its existing products, then it invariably focuses on cost. Schwinn made this mistake without even wondering whether serious cyclists would pay for enhanced product performance.

American automobile manufacturers faced a similar experience. In the 1960s, they explored alternatives to the internal combustion engine, assuming that they had developed that technology about as far as it could extend. Experiments with gas-turbine, diesel, rotary, and electric motors failed to find a basis for new growth. Then Honda, the upstart motorcycle maker, introduced its CVCC engine which could meet new environmental standards. Detroit's Big Three struggled for years to catch up because they had let their skills with internal-combustion engines atrophy.

Information Technology and the Scope of Technology Management

Information technology provides a useful summary case to illustrate the nature of the operations manager's technology challenge. Computers, especially microcomputers, have dramatically changed the role of information. In former days, people used information technology for isolated tasks like calling for telephone numbers. Today, information has grown enormously to wash away most traces of analog experience in a flood of binary digits. People listen to digitized music, and they punch in personal identification numbers without hesitation. Within 10 years, family television sets will process digital signals controlled by CPUs as powerful as today's super computers.

The driving forces behind this digital revolution are microprocessors and dynamic random access memory chips. Once exotic innovations, these cheap, increasingly powerful, and surprisingly flexible bits of technology now control much of the flow of modern life, and they will not go away any time soon. Success will come to firms that design and develop products that capitalize on these new

Success in a growing technological society depends on a business's ability and willingness to utilize high tech products, like this notebook computer.   SOURCE   Charles Gupton/Stock Boston

components to satisfy the latent demands of customers. We emphasize latent demand because no one can really predict people's response to new products. As Deming once said, "No customer ever asked for the light bulb, the telephone, the radio." The challenge of technology management begins with such an intimate understanding of customers that managers can give them what they want before they know they want it. The future belongs to the organization that can discover the modern equivalent of Xerox's replacement for carbon paper.

Technology Paradox

The ongoing revolution driven by digital technology creates a paradox for today's organizations. The performance of such products accelerates, so they add ever higher levels of value, while their prices decline. To compute 1 million instructions per second, a firm spent about $100,000 in 1978; in 1995, that cost is approaching $10. Optical fibers have become so cheap that now makes sense to install enough capacity to last a lifetime. A *Business Week* article discussed this **technology paradox** in which organizations "can thrive at the very moment when their prices are falling the fastest."[9] According to Eastman Kodak Chairman George Fisher, "The only thing that matters is if the exponential growth of your market is faster than the exponential decline of your prices."[10] He further stated that companies will have to determine how to compete in a world with virtually free technology.

Consumers benefit from this paradox. They can buy HP inkjet printers that run faster and print more clearly than the firm's previous best-selling model, in the process adding color printing capabilities, all for a lower price than the earlier technology commanded. HP knows that if it does not offer its customers the benefits of this technology paradox, some other company will. Traditionally, new-product introductions allowed time for the firm to sell enough units to recover its investment; in the new process, firms must race so fast to beat competitors that they risk competing with their own products.

technology paradox

The surprising contradiction between the accelerating performance of technological products and the dramatic drops in their prices

[9]"The Technology Paradox," *Business Week*, March 6, 1995, p. 6.
[10]Ibid.

In short, the inverted economics of today's digital-technology revolution have stood business on its head. The new rules for survival demand "more than ingenuity, agility, and speed. They call for redefining value in an economy where the cost of raw technology is plummeting toward zero."[11] Value seems destined to depend on the ability of the firm to establish long-term relationships with customers. The advent of free technology will result in what *Business Week* called the *new rules of the game:*

1. *Products are most valuable when they're cheapest.* Niches for high-priced products shrink, and firms need lower prices and higher volumes to succeed. Just ask Compaq Computer.
2. *Make money by giving things away.* The high-tech market loves shaving economics—giving away the razor to sell blades. The creators of Mosaic, World Wide Web browsing software, introduced it free, and they started to sell the same package as Netscape.
3. *Teamwork conquers all.* The complexity of the latest electronic gadgets—such as digital satellite TV—requires the kind of collaborative systems design efforts that firms used to launch only for high value-added projects like aircraft, ships, and moon shots.
4. *Mass customize.* To avoid selling me-too products, firms need to develop agile manufacturing techniques that include unique features in each product off the line. That's how Dell sells PCs and Matsushita sells mountain bikes.
5. *Hurry up and waste.* Engineers still prefer efficiency and elegance in product design, but with cheap computing and communication resources and a critical need for fast-to-market capabilities, quick-and-dirty projects often post the best performance.
6. *Don't fear gluts.* Demand for individual products rises and falls, but hunger for basic capabilities like computer power remains insatiable over the long run. Memory chips have remained fantastically profitable despite moving from exotic specialty items to basic commodities.

In closing, the article observes that "information technology never will be literally free because someone will always come along and use so much of it that it will become scarce all over again. This will drive a need for more capacity and speed."[12]

Not all firms and markets will experience such rapid change, but virtually all of them must cope with technical change. Producers of rubber rafts use CAD/CAM systems to design and manufacture them out of space-age materials with amazing ruggedness so that adventurers can ply the Colorado River rapids through the ancient Grand Canyon.

CHAPTER SUMMARY

In this chapter, we have outlined four significant challenges that will complicate and enrich the work of operations managers in the future. These challenges will fill organization members' work lives with interesting people and technologies, demanding customers, and a host of government regulators watching intently to make sure that everyone abides by the letter of the law.

---

[11]Ibid.

[12]Ibid.

1. The challenge of vision requires operations managers to sustain a forward-looking effort to create new demand, keep their mental maps up to date, and generate new core competencies for their firm.

2. To master this challenge, operations managers must accept change and complexity, recognize new opportunities, maintain flexibility in their OM systems, and pursue continual learning throughout their careers.

3. The challenge of global operations forces operations managers to make decisions about offshore outsourcing, offshore OM processes, cross-border product innovation, global economies of scale, and logistical arrangements for overseas activities.

4. Global activities affect operations management indirectly, as well, by bringing international input and priorities to management practices, threatening the job security of hourly workers, increasing the demand for mass customized products to suit specific markets, and opening opportunities for dramatic financial growth.

5. The challenge of environmentally responsible operations forces operations managers to consider the effects of their activities on the natural environment. Process by-products and other unusable outputs constitute waste, and operations managers must constantly monitor and take economically justifiable steps to improve their systems to prevent production of these outputs rather than simply disposing of them after production.

6. Operations managers feel strong pressure to maintain environmentally responsible operations today because of pressure from government agencies and political organizations, new performance standards from internal sources and customers, opportunities for positive publicity, investor priorities, excessive overhead burdens, opportunities to influence the content of regulations, and disposal problems.

7. Certain obstacles and paradoxes complicate implementation of environmentally responsible operations. Top managers hesitate to involve themselves, fearing personal liability for organization practices; busy production schedules and short product life cycles leave little time to revise existing systems; ERO standards remain unclear, as do the likely effects on financial performance; operations managers lack mental frameworks, measures, and analytical tools to guide ERO decisions.

8. The ERO challenge forces operations managers to decide whether to set simple compliance or industry leadership as a goal. They must also work vigorously to spread awareness of ERO throughout their organization and to develop tools and procedures to clarify ERO activities to operating workers.

9. The challenge of knowledge forces operations managers to recognize and control knowledge as a critical organization asset. Through the transition from tacit to explicit knowledge, firms create new knowledge; in the process, managers must unlearn old ways before learning new ones.

10. Firms create conditions of autonomy, fluctuations, intent, and variety to stimulate new knowledge and create knowledge factories. Managers control knowledge factories by accepting changes in employees, developing collaborative styles of management, creating opportunities for learning, and keeping internal employment opportunities attractive.

11. The challenge of technology forces managers to adapt their operations and their mental maps to accommodate new threats and opportunities that technical advances create. They must monitor technological developments throughout the world and assess the effects of those developments on their own systems and organizations.

12. Often, organizations must form alliances with others, often suppliers and customers, specifically to gain access to new technologies. A fast-to-adopt strategy offers a new source of organizational capabilities based on internalizing developments pioneered elsewhere.

13. Rapid technological changes have accelerated the life cycles of many products, and they have fueled renewal and new growth in products that seemed to have reached maturity. Firms rely heavily on new information technologies to cope with the new, frantic pace of innovation.

14. Advances in technology have created a paradox in which product performance improves dramatically while prices show similarly abrupt drops. Success in this environment depends on rapid market growth to maintain profits despite falling prices.

Operations managers should avoid feeling too comfortable in their familiar OM environments. In the 21st century, organization will expect broad perspectives that managers cannot develop by spending their careers in single functions. Most operations managers will perform jobs in marketing, engineering, and other functional divisions. In this way, they can develop both technical and organizational literacy to become effective team players. This kind of diverse background may even lead to a position in top management. In any event, it encourages understanding and appreciation of the activities of colleagues, the organization, and society, in general.

[KEY TERMS]

vision   910
mental map   911
environmentally responsible operations
   923
waste streaming   934

explicit knowledge   936
tacit knowledge   936
knowledge factory   938
technology paradox   949

[DISCUSSION QUESTIONS]

1. Explain the role value plays in helping a firm define its vision and its operations management function. Use an example from the text and one of your own in your response.

2. About 15 years ago, citizen-band radios (aka CB radios) were the hot products. Sales rose rapidly and then rapidly declined. How might a flawed vision impair your ability to correctly forecast demand?

3. Explain how mastery of one of the operations management tools can be considered a core competency of a firm. Cite two examples.

4. Explain how value ultimately drives firms from local to global operations. Cite two or three examples of this transition. In each case, identify what elements of the value equation played the most significant roles.

5. Explain how a firm's global business perspective can help its internal employee-diversity management capabilities. Cite two examples.

6. Explain how product and process design flexibility contribute to a firm's ability to compete effectively in a global marketplace.

7. Define what being environmentally responsible means for the following types of business:
   a. A meat packing plant
   b. An oil refinery
   c. A bookstore with an adjacent coffeehouse
   d. A mushroom farm
   e. A child care center
   In each case, identify the types of activities and products that pose the greatest challenge.

8. In adopting an environmentally responsible position, define the stakeholders you use to define what is environmentally responsible.

9. You are not likely to improve a process unless you measure its performance. Discuss the problems of measurement that the ERO movement faces.

10. Does the concept of waste need to be redefined in an environmentally responsible world? If so, how? Why?

11. List five products that are damaging to the environment. In each case, what actions could be taken to resolve this problem? Who should be responsible for these actions? Who should bear the costs?

12. What role do higher-learning institutions play in a knowledge-driven world? How is your career affected?

13. List five professions that will be impacted by the challenge of knowledge. How can these professionals rise to this challenge?

14. How will the evolving knowledge base among workers impact the following operations management practices?
   a. Employee empowerment
   b. Labor-management relations
   c. Total quality management
   d. Cross-functional product development

15. How will the evolving knowledge base impact business globalization trends? Cite four important consequences.

16. Discuss the impact of powerful, relatively low-cost microcomputers and work stations on the ability of small manufacturers to participate in the technological revolution. Cite instances.

17. List 5 ways for new college graduates to maintain and expand their knowledge base after graduation. How can you enhance your value in this area, both to yourself and to the organization that hires you?

C A U T I O N

[C R I T I C A L   T H I N K I N G   R E Q U I R E D]

1. As the manager for a department in a large plant, you are considering replacing a piece of equipment which has created numerous environmental problems throughout the plant and the firm. According to corporate policy, you need to justify any investment by showing that the direct benefits accruing to the department requesting the investment exceed the costs. Using this criterion, you cannot justify the investment. However, if you can capture the benefits resulting to the other departments from your investment (e.g., the machining department will have to do less work on each part), you can justify the expense. The other departments, however, are not interested in participating in your project. How would you justify the investment? What could the corporation do to facilitate this process? (Hint: you might focus on performance review criteria, corporate decision making and investment policies, and the difficulty of assessing and justifying investments in environmentally responsible manufacturing activities.)

2. In the 1960s, the concept of "appropriate technology" was proposed. According to the supporters of this concept, the type of OM system (and its associated technology) introduced and used in a given setting should be appropriate or consistent with the resource and knowledge base of the setting. For example, if we have a great deal of well-educated workers, we will develop a system that makes use of them. What type of OM system, employing appropriate technology, would you develop for the following settings:
   a. China/India;
   b. Central America;
   c. East Germany, Poland, and the Czech Republic.

3. Companies today use resources from all over the world. What potential problems must the operations manager deal with in developing and scheduling production? In your answer, touch on such issues as: (1) scheduling; (2) capacity planning; (3) resource management; (4) quality control/management; and (5) warranty issues (both for incoming items and outgoing products).

4. Some of your components are supplied by firms located in Europe and the Far East. Can you apply just-in-time principles and practices discussed in Chapter 9? If so, how would you develop this JIT system?

C A S E   1 9 . 1

The Internet Child Care Center

Marsha Broom temporarily left her job in the CIA to have her first child. She and her husband knew that finding appropriate child care for their infant daughter would be a challenge. Their search for child care evolved into an unusual make-or-buy situation.

Broom knew from her CIA experience that surveillance technology had made significant advances. The Brooms already had wired their home nursery with a hidden camera to easily check on the well being of Ashley. Her ideal child-care situation would be one in which she could spy on the environment at any moment.

As she browsed the Internet one day, Broom realized that she could use this technology to answer her child-care prayers. Using relatively low-cost image transmissions, a child-care center could be subject to 100 percent surveillance. Parents could use the computer to dial the nursery's home page and then browse each room to check on their children. The nursery could also contact the parents: the children could even see and talk to their parents. Child-care personnel could also place constructive comments in each child's secure mail box about the child's progress, and the parents could use it to alert the child-care center about issues that needed to be addressed.

Broom discussed her dream with a friend who had owned a child-care center, who liked the idea for a different, more serious reason. Her friend had sold her business because she feared unfounded child abuse charges from the parents. Having all activities on videotape would enhance a center's ability to defend itself.

Broom also saw how the home page could enhance her communication with her daughter. She would know what had happened at the center each day: which stories were told. Did they watch an educational television program? What else had happened that day?

QUESTIONS

1. Define the type of value offered by this envisioned child-care center. To what type of parent would this child-care center be most appealing? What core competencies would this child-care center need?
2. What are the downside risks with the envisioned systems?

CASE 19.2

Southern Peru Copper

As a senior international business major, you have a most promising job interview. The interviewer thinks that you are an ideal candidate for Trans-Global Resources' Global Tigers management development program. This fast-track program provides international business majors with experience in each functional area of their business. After 18 months, most students are assigned to one of TGR's international operations.

The prospect of working for TGR causes you a personal dilemma. Two of your fraternity brothers participated in the program three years ago, and each has been rapidly promoted to responsible positions within TGR or one of its international affiliates. However, TGR's offshore operations have not always been environmentally responsible. Since you have always been a friend of the earth, the prospect of working for one of the big polluters of the world troubles you.

The day after your interview, you see a newspaper article about a company TGR owns part of. The headline reads, "U.S.-Owned Smelter Makes Residents Ill and Angry." Southern Peru Copper's smelting operations spewed 2,000 tons of sulfur dioxide into the air daily. The fog from this smelter, which was the eighth largest copper smelter in the world, was so heavy that drivers routinely had to use headlights during the day. Children were advised to play indoors. Law suits have been filed against SPC.

You are also concerned about the quotations of SPC's management. Many residents living near the smelter suffer from respiratory problems and cough up thick black mucus, but SPC officials claim that their smelter is not to blame for the town's health problems. Hans Flury, SPC's vice-president of legal affairs, states in the article that in the thirty years the company has operated in the town, it has never received a complaint from any of its 2,000 workers, proving that the environment is healthy.

The reporter, however, interviewed employees who said that they had reported to their supervisors the respiratory ailments that they and their families had suffered. When asked to account for the area's health problems, Flury said, "I don't live in Ilo so I don't know. I have not been there on one of those smoky days." Charles Preble, SPC's president, said, "We have a good relationship with the community, and I'd like to comment further but I can't because of the lawsuit."

Peruvian law does not specify emission limits. Local environmentalists say that was the problem—SPC complied with the law, even though its toxic releases are "10 to 15 times the limit for similar plants operating in the United States." Shutting SPC down would pose a serious economic problem for Peru. SPC's operations provide Peru 5,500 jobs and 17 percent of the country's export income. As a result, SPC has little to fear in the Peruvian courts. Up to this time, all previous lawsuits filed against SPC in Peru have been dismissed.

Nonetheless, Preble felt that his company had been a good corporate citizen "by providing workers with housing, education, electricity, water, medical care, and food." SPC built a village in the hills to house the families of its mostly American engineers and executives. As copper prices rose, the firm's economic shape improved sufficiently to permit it "to spend $151 million on environmental projects, including a $108 million sulfuric acid plant to reduce sulfur dioxide emissions and a dam and water treatment plant to keep waste from entering the Pacific."

Three American firms own 83 percent of SPC stock, the largest of which is Asarco's 51.8 percent share. In 1994, SPC's revenue increased to $677 million, up from $450 million the prior year. This growth was almost entirely due to increases in world copper prices. SPC earnings increased from $43.6 million in 1993 to $110 million in 1994. While Trans-Global Resources' share of SPC is only 15 percent, it routinely rotates Spanish-speaking engineers and executives to the SPC operation.

QUESTIONS

1. Discuss the pros and cons of a new college graduate with environmental sensitivities joining a firm such as Trans-Global Resources.
2. Although some multinational corporations have voluntarily adopted policies that require their overseas operations to comply with the same environmental standards they must follow in the United States, there are no legal agreements between nations to ensure compliance. What are some of the possible consequences of a GATT-like treaty to assure environmentally responsible operations? Who will benefit? Who will be disadvantaged? What is your position?

SOURCE   Calvin Sims, "In Peru, a Fight for Fresh Air: U.S.-Owned Smelter Makes Residents Ill and Angry." *The New York Times*, Tuesday, December 12, 1995, pages C1, C3.

[SELECTED READINGS]

Allenby, Braden. "Supporting Environmental Quality: Developing an Infrastructure for Design." *Total Quality Environmental Management* 2, no. 3 (1993), pp. 303–308.
"The Challenge of Going Green." *Harvard Business Review,* July-August 1994, pp. 37–43, 46–50.
D'Aveni, Richard A. *HyperCompetition: Managing the Dynamics of Strategic Maneuvering.* New York: Free Press, 1994.
Dimancescu, Dan. *The Seamless Enterprise.* New York: Harper Business, 1992.
Dretske, F. *Knowledge and the Flow of Information.* Cambridge, Mass.: MIT Press, 1981.
Drucker, Peter F. *The New Realities.* New York: Harper & Row, 1989.
Foster, Richard. *Innovation: The Attacker's Advantage.* New York: Summit Books, 1986.
Hamel, Gary, and C. K. Prahalad. *Competing for the Future.* Boston, Mass.: Harvard Business School Press, 1994.
Kiechel, Walter, III. "How We Work in the Year 2000." *Fortune,* May 17, 1994, pp. 38–52.
Labich, Kenneth. "Why Companies Fail." *Fortune,* November 14, 1994, pp. 52–68.
Loeb, Marshall. "Ten Commandments for Managing Creative People." *Fortune,* January 16, 1995, pp. 135–136.
Makower, Joel. *The E Factor: The Bottom-Line Approach to Environmentally Responsible Business.* New York: Times Books, 1993.
Makower, Joel. *Beyond the Bottom Line.* New York: Simon & Schuster, 1994.
Nonaka, Ikujiro. "A Dynamic Theory of Organizational Knowledge Creation." *Organization Science* 5, no. 1 (February 1994), pp. 14–37.

Peters, Tom. *The Tom Peters Seminars: Crazy Times Call for Crazy Organizations*. New York: Vintage Books, 1994.

Porter, Michael. "America's Green Strategy." *Scientific American,* April 1991, p. 168.

Sproull, Lee, and Sara Kiesler. *Connections: New Ways of Working in the Networked Organization*. Cambridge, Mass.: MIT Press, 1993.

Stewart, Thomas A. "Your Company's Most Valuable Asset: Intellectual Capital." *Fortune,* October 3, 1994, pp. 68–74.

Stack, Jack. *The Great Game of Business: The Only Sensible Way to Run a Company*. New York: Doubleday, 1992.

Walley, Noah, and Bradley Whitehead. "It's Not Easy Being Green." *Harvard Business Review,* May-June 1994, pp. 46–52.

Walter, Mary. "ISO Rushes to Set Global Environmental Standards." *Environmental Solutions,* September 1994, pp. 85–89.

APPENDIX 19A

Staying Current in a Changing Environment

Throughout this chapter, one theme emerges repeatedly. Operations managers must continue learning over their professional careers. The rapid change in OM systems will only accelerate. Without continuous learning, an operations manager risks letting essential skills become obsolete, leaving him or her unable to cope with emerging challenges. Fortunately, they can tap several resources to continue learning after leaving educational institutions. We discuss many of those resources in this appendix.

Relevant Literature

All managers should read published material that relates to their fields, including general information from daily editions of *The Wall Street Journal,* and weekly publications like *Business Week* and *The Economist*. Biweekly editions of *Fortune* supplement this list, as do monthly publications like *Forbes, Harvard Business Review, Manufacturing,* and *Production*. Each publication offers its own set of strengths. For example, *The Economist* provides excellent coverage of international issues. This British magazine reports thoroughly on events in Europe, South America, and the Far East, in addition to developments in North America.

Several journals provide essential information specifically for operations managers. The American Production and Inventory Control Society (APICS) publishes several valuable information sources, including quarterly editions of *Production and Inventory Management Journal* and its monthly *APICS: The Performance Advantage* which members receive free. The *Journal of Operations Management* offers valuable new information. The National Association of Purchasing Managers (NAPM) publishes its quarterly *International Journal of Purchasing and Materials Management* and members receive free copies of *NAPM Insights*.

If time pressures do not allow complete reading of these journals and magazines, managers can take advantage of commercially available abstracting services. CompuServe offers one of the most comprehensive, DIALOG, on-line at a reasonable cost. The service provides abstracts of an up-to-date and comprehensive listing of articles from a vast range of journals, including those listed earlier, from countries such as the United States, Canada, Australia, Germany, and Great Britain. A user can search the DIALOG database and display the results in several formats (titles, titles with abstracts, or full papers).

Professional Societies

Several professional organizations offer opportunities for continued learning to operations managers. The American Production and Inventory Control Society (address: APICS: 500 West Annandale Road, Falls Church, VA, 22046-4274, Phone: 1-800-535-5667) is the primary organization for practitioners in the field of production and inventory control. This national association organizes its 70,000 members into local chapters. Local chapters in many areas sponsor monthly dinner meetings, which often include plant tours followed by speeches. APICS also maintains special interest groups (SIGs) devoted to such topics as repetitive manufacturing.

Besides its publications listed in the previous section, APICS promotes the education of operations managers through annual conferences and certification programs. The program for Certification in Production and Inventory Management (CPIM) includes classes and examinations to certify competency in topics directly relevant to production and inventory management (e.g., capacity management, inventory control, forecasting, shop-floor control, just-in-time manufacturing). The program for Certification in Integrated Resource Management (CIRM) deals with a broad view of OM activities through a highly integrated curriculum that covers purchasing, logistics, marketing and customer service, and manufacturing processes.

The Society for Manufacturing Engineers (SME) (address: 1 SME Drive, P.O. Box 930, Dearborn, MI 48121, Phone: 1-313-271-1500) specifically targets managers working in manufacturing organizations. At present, about 72,000 professionals maintain memberships. While the name emphasizes manufacturing engineering, the society reaches beyond engineers to includes anyone involved in a firm's transformation process. Exhibit 19A.1 reprints the strategic plan of the SME. Like APICS, the SME maintains both local chapters and a national organization. It disseminates information through many channels, including monthly chapter meetings, the society's magazine (*Manufacturing Engineering),* and its blue-book series. These short (less than 50 page) books deal with current topics that interest members. In the past, installments in the blue-book series have covered green manufacturing, system simplification, and team building.

The National Association of Purchasing Managers (NAPM) (address: 2055 East Centennial Circle, P.O. Box 22160, Tempe, AZ, 85282-0960, Phone: 1-602-752-6276) focuses on generating and disseminating knowledge to meet the professional needs of people who work in purchasing and supply chain management. This society's 36,000 members work primarily as purchasing practitioners and educators. Like the other two societies, NAPM operates local chapters along with the national association. It distributes information primarily through local chapters' monthly dinner meetings. It also holds an annual conference that attracts well-known speakers, writers, and other participants; NAPM publishes transcripts of the proceedings. NAPM also publishes a monthly magazine, as discussed in the earlier section, and it runs a certification program for purchasing managers, who earn Certification in Purchasing Management (CPM) designations. This certification program, like the CIRM program run by APICS, provides broad-based instruction and competence testing in a varied range of topics.

[**E X H I B I T   1 9 A . 1**]

Society of Manufacturing Engineers Strategic Plan

Mission Statement

The mission statement defines the nature of SME's role and contribution in the achievement of its greater vision. SME's mission statement indicates why it exists, who it exists for and what it does.

Mission Statement:
The Society of Manufacturing Engineers serves its members and the international manufacturing community through the advancement of professionalism, knowledge and learning.

Long-Range Goals

The following represents SME's five long-range goals for the next six years. They encompass SME's vision and determine the direction the Society will pursue. They are outcome-oriented statements that represent what will constitute its future success. The achievement of each of these goals will move the Society toward the realization of what vision. All of the goals will need to be accomplished if SME is to fully achieve its vision.

Goals:
• SME will be acknowledged by its members and the international manufacturing community as a respected manufacturing engineering association driven by customer satisfaction.
• SME will be recognized as a premier source of learning and knowledge for the manufacturing community.
• SME will be a primary source for manufacturing information employing electronic media.
• SME will be viewed as a credible source of manufacturing information for those involved in the formation of public policy regarding science, technology and engineering related to manufacturing.
• SME will continue to be financially secure and stable.

SOURCE   Society of Manufacturing Engineers, *Strategic Plan.* Approved by the SME Board of Directors on November 14, 1994. Reprinted courtesy of Society of Manufacturing Engineers, Dearborn, Michigan, USA.

Professional societies offer opportunities to hear and talk with some of the leading practitioners and researchers in the operations management field. Local chapter meetings give access to networks of other operations managers so members can get to know people who have similar problems and interests. These people become resources for one another to help analyze problems and share feedback. Also, plant trips share information about practices in other organizations that help to stimulate learning. All of these society functions expose members to leading-edge concepts, systems, tools, and procedures. For example, much of the work on supply chain management discussed in Chapter 13 received financial support from the NAPM. APICS played a major role in the development and spread of MRP.

Participate on the Internet

The communications network dubbed the *Internet* provides a relatively new source of learning opportunities for nearly everyone. Users gain access to the Internet through university computer systems and fee-based on-line services like CompuServe, Delphi, America On-Line, and Genie. Internet connections forge two kinds of links between people interested in OM issues: mailing lists and World Wide Web (WWW) home pages.

A mailing list stores and distributes electronic mail messages posted by participants on a specific topic of interest.[13] When someone posts a question or comment

[13]To find information about the procedures for joining a mailing list, consult one of the many good books on the Internet available in most bookstores and libraries.

to the list, others receive the message and respond. This list distributes all messages to every participant, stimulating discussions that promote vigorous exchanges of ideas and information. Internet mailing lists bring together people from different parts of the United States and across the world to create a productive dialogue about ideas and new developments in the field. Among several mailing lists that apply to operations management, a few deserve special mention:

- *MFG-INFO@msu.edu*   This mailing list offered through Michigan State University targets manufacturing researchers, consultants, and practitioners. Access is free to anyone.
- *QUALITY@pucc.princeton.edu*   This mailing list, formally TQM in Manufacturing, deals with quality issues in various organizations, including government agencies and private-sector manufacturers and service firms. Run out of Princeton University, it promotes a fairly active exchange.
- *ISO9000@vm1.nodak.edu*   This mailing list, run from the University of North Dakota, focuses primarily on issues pertaining to ISO 9000 certification and the next-generation program, ISO 14000.
- *BPR-L@is.twi.tudelft.nl*   This mailing list with over 1,400 participants is run through Delft University in the Netherlands (although everyone communicates in English). It focuses primarily on business process reengineering and associated management and application issues.

In contrast to relatively simply mailing lists, home pages on the World Wide Web (WWW) provide potentially complex graphic catalogs of information about topics, including manufacturing, with automatic links to other, related resources. Access requires a graphics viewer such as Mosaic or Netscape. Each home page amounts to a virtual catalog or book full of information about new technical developments, products, or practices. A number of home pages should interest operations managers:[14]

- Business Information Resources
  (http://sashimi.wwa.com/~notime/eotw/business_info.html)
- AT&T Home Page
  (http://www.att.com/)
- Business Corporations
  (htpp://akebono.stanford.edu/yahoo/Business/Corporations/)
- Business Corporations: Manufacturing
  (http://akebono.stanford.edu/yahoo/Business/Corporations/Manufacturing/)
- Ernest & Young Home Page
  (http://www.worldserver.pipex.com/ernsty/)
- MAE Design Automation Lab, Arizona State University
  (htpp://asudesign.eas.asu.edu/)
- Manufacturers Information Net Home Page
  (htpp://mfginfo.com/home.html)
- Martin Marietta Energy Systems, Inc.
  (htpp://www.ornl.gov/mmes.html)
- Electronic Green Journal
  (htpp://www.lib.uidaho.edu/70/docs/egj/html)

---

[14]URLs, or home-page addresses, appear below the resource names in parentheses.

- The Phoenix Business Renewal Site
  (http://www.phoenix.ca/80/bpr/)
- WARIA—Workflow and Reengineering International Association
  (http://www.waria.com/WARIA/)
- IEEE Home Page
  (http://www.ieee.org/)
- The Society for Information Management
  (htpp://www.simnet.org/index.htm)
- Business Home Page
  (htpp://www.business.com.au/business/)
- Manufacturing Strategy Home Page
  (htpp://www.cranfield.ac.uk/public/mn/mr940715/)
- Lionheart On-Line (publisher of *APICS: The Performance Advantage*)
  (http://lionhrtpub.com/)
- Thomas Register Home Page
  (htpp://www.thomasregister.com/)
- MSN Shared Bookmark List (A listing of numerous other home pages)
  (http://web.msu.edu/sbm/sbmlist.html)
- Jet Propulsion Lab Technical Transfer Home Page
  (htpp://www.techtrans.jpl.nasa/conference.html)

Anyone interested in OM-related topics can access any of these home pages free.

Sabbaticals

As mentioned in the chapter text, many firms allow employees to take sabbaticals. This could provide a useful opportunity for an operations manager to learn about subjects that arise in the course of work, but that require more study than the daily routine allows.

Seminars

Practicing managers can learn about new developments and hone skills at seminars offered by universities, professional societies (both local chapters and national organizations), and consultants. Often these seminars bring experts to teach about topics of interest. Like meetings of local chapters of professional societies, seminars also provide opportunities for meeting other OM practitioners and networking.

College/University Faculty

Colleges and universities offer valuable educational resources, even after students graduate and take jobs. Faculty members often welcome contacts from working professionals. Also, students should maintain contact with past teachers. Both of these groups of faculty members keep current on new developments in their fields, and they willingly discuss these topics. They provide wonderful sounding boards for innovative new ideas that practitioners conceive.

Learning Resources Outside the OM Field

Rather than describing a specific resource, we want to sound a warning. Practitioners who limit their attention to OM-related issues risk ignoring new developments in other fields that will drive later changes in operations management. The challenge of vision requires operations managers to look outside their own field for events and ideas that will affect it in the future. They should occasionally read literature about strategy, human resource management (the initial source of many developments in teamwork), finance, logistics, and purchasing. The differences in perspective from these alternative sources of information force operations managers to rethink their own mental models, which often forces them to make productive changes.

Normal Distribution Tables

[**TABLE A**]

Areas under the Standard Normal Curve, 0 to z

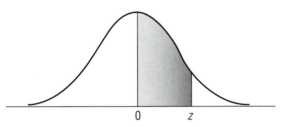

z	.00	.01	.02	.03	.04	.05	.06	.07	.08	.09
0.0	.0000	.0040	.0080	.0120	.0160	.0199	.0239	.0279	.0319	.0359
0.1	.0398	.0438	.0478	.0517	.0557	.0596	.0636	.0675	.0714	.0753
0.2	.0793	.0832	.0871	.0910	.0948	.0987	.1026	.1064	.1103	.1141
0.3	.1179	.1217	.1255	.1293	.1331	.1368	.1406	.1443	.1480	.1517
0.4	.1554	.1591	.1628	.1664	.1700	.1736	.1772	.1808	.1844	.1879
0.5	.1915	.1950	.1985	.2019	.2054	.2088	.2123	.2157	.2190	.2224
0.6	.2257	.2291	.2324	.2357	.2389	.2422	.2454	.2486	.2518	.2549
0.7	.2580	.2612	.2642	.2673	.2704	.2734	.2764	.2794	.2823	.2852
0.8	.2881	.2910	.2939	.2967	.2995	.3023	.3051	.3078	.3106	.3133
0.9	.3159	.3186	.3212	.3238	.3264	.3289	.3315	.3340	.3365	.3389
1.0	.3413	.3438	.3461	.3485	.3508	.3531	.3554	.3577	.3599	.3621
1.1	.3643	.3665	.3686	.3708	.3729	.3749	.3770	.3790	.3810	.3830
1.2	.3849	.3869	.3888	.3907	.3925	.3944	.3962	.3980	.3997	.4015
1.3	.4032	.4049	.4066	.4082	.4099	.4115	.4131	.4147	.4162	.4177
1.4	.4192	.4207	.4222	.4236	.4251	.4265	.4279	.4292	.4306	.4319
1.5	.4332	.4345	.4357	.4370	.4382	.4394	.4406	.4418	.4429	.4441
1.6	.4452	.4463	.4474	.4484	.4495	.4505	.4515	.4525	.4535	.4545
1.7	.4554	.4564	.4573	.4582	.4591	.4599	.4608	.4616	.4625	.4633
1.8	.4641	.4649	.4656	.4664	.4671	.4678	.4686	.4693	.4699	.4706
1.9	.4713	.4719	.4726	.4732	.4738	.4744	.4750	.4756	.4761	.4767
2.0	.4772	.4778	.4783	.4788	.4793	.4798	.4803	.4808	.4812	.4817
2.1	.4821	.4826	.4830	.4834	.4838	.4842	.4846	.4850	.4854	.4857
2.2	.4861	.4864	.4868	.4871	.4875	.4878	.4881	.4884	.4887	.4890
2.3	.4893	.4896	.4898	.4901	.4904	.4906	.4909	.4911	.4913	.4916
2.4	.4918	.4920	.4922	.4925	.4927	.4929	.4931	.4932	.4934	.4936
2.5	.4938	.4940	.4941	.4943	.4945	.4946	.4948	.4949	.4951	.4952
2.6	.4953	.4955	.4956	.4957	.4959	.4960	.4961	.4962	.4963	.4964
2.7	.4965	.4966	.4967	.4968	.4969	.4970	.4971	.4972	.4973	.4974
2.8	.4974	.4975	.4976	.4977	.4977	.4978	.4979	.4979	.4980	.4981
2.9	.4981	.4982	.4982	.4983	.4984	.4984	.4985	.4985	.4986	.4986
3.0	.4986	.4987	.4987	.4988	.4988	.4989	.4989	.4989	.4990	.4990

[TABLE B]

Areas under the Standardized Normal Curve from $-\infty$ to $-z$

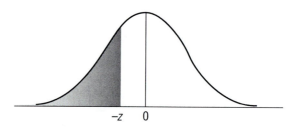

.09	.08	.07	.06	.05	.04	.03	.02	.01	.00	z
.0002	.0003	.0003	.0003	.0003	.0003	.0003	.0003	.0003	.0003	−3.4
.0003	.0004	.0004	.0004	.0004	.0004	.0004	.0005	.0005	.0005	−3.3
.0005	.0005	.0005	.0006	.0006	.0006	.0006	.0006	.0007	.0007	−3.2
.0007	.0007	.0008	.0008	.0008	.0008	.0009	.0009	.0009	.0010	−3.1
.0010	.0010	.0011	.0011	.0011	.0012	.0012	.0013	.0013	.0013	−3.0
.0014	.0014	.0015	.0015	.0016	.0016	.0017	.0018	.0018	.0019	−2.9
.0019	.0020	.0021	.0021	.0022	.0023	.0023	.0024	.0025	.0026	−2.8
.0026	.0027	.0028	.0029	.0030	.0031	.0032	.0033	.0034	.0035	−2.7
.0036	.0037	.0038	.0039	.0040	.0041	.0043	.0044	.0045	.0047	−2.6
.0048	.0049	.0051	.0052	.0054	.0055	.0057	.0059	.0060	.0062	−2.5
.0064	.0066	.0068	.0069	.0071	.0073	.0075	.0078	.0080	.0082	−2.4
.0084	.0087	.0089	.0091	.0094	.0096	.0099	.0102	.0104	.0107	−2.3
.0110	.0113	.0116	.0119	.0122	.0125	.0129	.0132	.0136	.0139	−2.2
.0143	.0146	.0150	.0154	.0158	.0162	.0166	.0170	.0174	.0179	−2.1
.0183	.0188	.0192	.0197	.0202	.0207	.0212	.0217	.0222	.0228	−2.0
.0233	.0239	.0244	.0250	.0256	.0262	.0268	.0274	.0281	.0287	−1.9
.0294	.0301	.0307	.0314	.0322	.0329	.0336	.0344	.0351	.0359	−1.8
.0367	.0375	.0384	.0392	.0401	.0409	.0418	.0427	.0436	.0446	−1.7
.0455	.0465	.0475	.0485	.0495	.0505	.0516	.0526	.0537	.0548	−1.6
.0559	.0571	.0582	.0594	.0606	.0618	.0630	.0643	.0655	.0668	−1.5
.0681	.0694	.0708	.0721	.0735	.0749	.0764	.0778	.0793	.0808	−1.4
.0823	.0838	.0853	.0869	.0885	.0901	.0918	.0934	.0951	.0968	−1.3
.0985	.1003	.1020	.1038	.1056	.1075	.1093	.1112	.1131	.1151	−1.2
.1170	.1190	.1210	.1230	.1251	.1271	.1292	.1314	.1335	.1357	−1.1
.1379	.1401	.1423	.1446	.1469	.1492	.1515	.1539	.1562	.1587	−1.0
.1611	.1635	.1660	.1685	.1711	.1736	.1762	.1788	.1814	.1841	−0.9
.1867	.1894	.1922	.1949	.1977	.2005	.2033	.2061	.2090	.2119	−0.8
.2148	.2177	.2206	.2236	.2266	.2296	.2327	.2358	.2389	.2420	−0.7
.2451	.2483	.2514	.2546	.2578	.2611	.2643	.2676	.2709	.2743	−0.6
.2776	.2810	.2843	.2877	.2912	.2946	.2981	.3015	.3050	.3085	−0.5
.3121	.3156	.3192	.3228	.3264	.3300	.3336	.3372	.3409	.3446	−0.4
.3483	.3520	.3557	.3594	.3632	.3669	.3707	.3745	.3783	.3821	−0.3
.3859	.3897	.3936	.3974	.4013	.4052	.4090	.4129	.4168	.4207	−0.2
.4247	.4286	.4325	.4364	.4404	.4443	.4483	.4522	.4562	.4602	−0.1
.4641	.4681	.4721	.4761	.4801	.4840	.4880	.4920	.4960	.5000	−0.0

[TABLE C]

Areas under the Standardized Normal Curve from $-\infty$ to $+z$

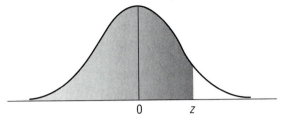

z	.00	.01	.02	.03	.04	.05	.06	.07	.08	.09
.0	.5000	.5040	.5080	.5120	.5160	.5199	.5239	.5279	.5319	.5359
.1	.5398	.5438	.5478	.5517	.5557	.5596	.5636	.5675	.5714	.5753
.2	.5793	.5832	.5871	.5910	.5948	.5987	.6026	.6064	.6103	.6141
.3	.6179	.6217	.6255	.6293	.6331	.6368	.6406	.6443	.6480	.6517
.4	.6554	.6591	.6628	.6664	.6700	.6736	.6772	.6808	.6844	.6879
.5	.6915	.6950	.6985	.7019	.7054	.7088	.7123	.7157	.7190	.7224
.6	.7257	.7291	.7324	.7357	.7389	.7422	.7454	.7486	.7517	.7549
.7	.7580	.7611	.7642	.7673	.7703	.7734	.7764	.7794	.7823	.7852
.8	.7881	.7910	.7939	.7967	.7995	.8023	.8051	.8078	.8106	.8133
.9	.8159	.8186	.8212	.8238	.8264	.8289	.8315	.8340	.8365	.8389
1.0	.8413	.8438	.8461	.8485	.8508	.8531	.8554	.8577	.8599	.8621
1.1	.8643	.8665	.8686	.8708	.8729	.8749	.8770	.8790	.8810	.8830
1.2	.8849	.8869	.8888	.8907	.8925	.8944	.8962	.8980	.8997	.9015
1.3	.9032	.9049	.9066	.9082	.9099	.9115	.9131	.9147	.9162	.9177
1.4	.9192	.9207	.9222	.9236	.9251	.9265	.9279	.9292	.9306	.9319
1.5	.9332	.9345	.9357	.9370	.9382	.9394	.9406	.9418	.9429	.9441
1.6	.9452	.9463	.9474	.9484	.9495	.9505	.9515	.9525	.9535	.9545
1.7	.9554	.9564	.9573	.9582	.9591	.9599	.9608	.9616	.9625	.9633
1.8	.9641	.9649	.9656	.9664	.9671	.9678	.9686	.9693	.9699	.9706
1.9	.9713	.9719	.9726	.9732	.9738	.9744	.9750	.9756	.9761	.9767
2.0	.9772	.9778	.9783	.9788	.9793	.9798	.9803	.9808	.9812	.9817
2.1	.9821	.9826	.9830	.9834	.9838	.9842	.9846	.9850	.9854	.9857
2.2	.9861	.9864	.9868	.9871	.9875	.9878	.9881	.9884	.9887	.9890
2.3	.9893	.9896	.9898	.9901	.9904	.9906	.9909	.9911	.9913	.9916
2.4	.9918	.9920	.9922	.9925	.9927	.9929	.9931	.9932	.9934	.9936
2.5	.9938	.9940	.9941	.9943	.9945	.9946	.9948	.9949	.9951	.9952
2.6	.9953	.9955	.9956	.9957	.9959	.9960	.9961	.9962	.9963	.9964
2.7	.9965	.9966	.9967	.9968	.9969	.9970	.9971	.9972	.9973	.9974
2.8	.9974	.9975	.9976	.9977	.9977	.9978	.9979	.9979	.9980	.9981
2.9	.9981	.9982	.9982	.9983	.9984	.9984	.9985	.9985	.9986	.9986
3.0	.9987	.9987	.9987	.9988	.9988	.9989	.9989	.9989	.9990	.9990
3.1	.9990	.9991	.9991	.9991	.9991	.9992	.9992	.9992	.9993	.9993
3.2	.9993	.9993	.9994	.9994	.9994	.9994	.9994	.9995	.9995	.9995
3.3	.9995	.9995	.9995	.9996	.9996	.9996	.9996	.9996	.9996	.9997
3.4	.9997	.9997	.9997	.9997	.9997	.9997	.9997	.9997	.9997	.9998

Glossary

absolutes for quality management Four laws proposed by Philip B. Crosby as fundamental elements of any effective TQM system

activity-based costing A method of allocating costs to specific products based on breakdowns of cost drivers

actual product The unit that sits on a shelf or in a showroom display

actual tool An implement that physically interacts with raw materials, parts, and subassemblies to make necessary transformations

adaptation A flexibility principle that emphasizes it more as uncertainty in the marketplace increases

adaptive forecasting A method of tracking a time series that sets smoothing coefficients based on observed forecast errors

aesthetics An attribute of quality that subjectively measures a product's appearance, feel, sound, taste, or smell

aggregate production plan A plan that specifies planned rates of production, inventory levels, and employee staffing rates and policies to fulfill the charter of a plant or subprocess

analysis A step in the problem-solving process that explains the development of the current situation

analyzing The process making sense of data that is often poorly structured, conflicting, inaccurate, or incomplete

As One/System Integration A strategy to reduce lead times by bringing together related activities, processes, and information flows

assemble to order A standard product assembled in response to a customer order to allow many user-specified options

assembly line balancing problem Detailed analysis to catalog all necessary tasks in a production line, the time requirements of each one, and their necessary sequence

assembly process chart A process flow analysis tool that depicts activities in subprocesses and how they flow together to form the overall process

At Once/Parallel Activities A strategy for reducing lead times by reorganizing sequential activities to occur in parallel, whenever possible

attribute data Data that indicates some qualitative condition of a process

augmented product The intangible component or service that a product provides

automated guided vehicle A transport device that moves around an OM system based on preprogrammed instructions

automation A self-powered and self-guiding or self-correcting mechanism

backlog The pool of orders awaiting shop-floor processing

banking A flexibility principle that tries to accumulate and reinforce it to meet future needs

batch production A mid-volume manufacturing process that routinely produces orders, usually in larger quantities than job shops do

benchmarking Comparing a company's own practices against similar practices of firms recognized as the most effective at some task

Better than/Automation A strategy for reducing lead times through technology or automation

Big JIT Just-in-time manufacturing as a large-scale, organizationwide philosophy

bill of materials A list of process inputs that disaggregates end-product demand to specify what the OM system needs to make projected volumes of each end product

bottleneck The lowest-capacity operation in a process

brainstorming A TQM tool that encourages people to envision and suggest any potential causes or relationships, reserving judgment about their accuracy for later analysis

business process reengineering A technique for implementing radical change in a process by defining the sequence of activities that most effectively deliver the output that customers want

C_p A TQM statistical tool that indicates the variability of a process

C_{pk} A TQM statistical tool of the variability of a process, adjusted for any deviation of the center of the distribution of process performance data from the midpoint of the specification width

capability A task that a particular OM system can perform effectively

capacity What the firm can do effectively and efficiently; people, information, and other resources that help to determine the capabilities of an OM process

capacity constrained resource An OM system resource that limits the capacity of the entire system

capacity lag strategy A method for timing capacity expansion that calls for expansion investments only after confirmation of rises in demand in order to maintain a high utilization rate

capacity lead strategy A method for timing capacity expansion that invests in new capacity in advance of market demand to eliminate the chance of losing sales to competitors

capacity requirements planning A procedure that extends the logic of MRP to identify the work load that a proposed master production schedule imposes on each part of the production system

capacity straddle strategy A method for timing capacity expansion that seeks to match average capacity to average demand

cause A condition that creates or contributes to a gap between the current and desired future situation

cause-and-effect diagram A problem-solving tool that visually represents relationships between symptoms and their root causes

cellular manufacturing A category of manufacturing processes that produces a family of similar outputs, one at a time, by linking together all possible operations in the required process

centered moving average A technique for adjusting data for seasonal variation by averaging figures for equal periods before and after the period under study

changeover flexibility The ability of an OM system to introduce a large variety of major design changes quickly within existing facilities

charter The assignment of product families to a specific plant or subprocess within a plant

chase strategy A method of matching production to variable demand by setting the production rate equal to the demand rate and varying the pool of human resources as needed

check sheet A widely used method for collecting data by defining categories and making a mark for each event in each category

closed-loop MRP system An expanded MRP system that integrates information from throughout the organization with an influence on the feasibility and effectiveness of production plans

coaching A management style that acknowledges and respects networks of relationships between individuals and the organization

common cause A systematic problem that produces variance in an OM process

concurrent engineering A TQM design tool that brings together representatives from all of the functions involved in designing, producing, delivering, and

selling a product to contribute to its initial design

confrontation The traditional purchasing relationship in which buyers and suppliers approach each other with strong distrust

continuous-flow process A category of inflexible manufacturing processes that produces an undifferentiated stream of a highly standardized product

control chart A TQM statistical tool that displays performance data as points across a set of limits for the upper and lower boundaries of acceptable process performance

controlled variance A variation from a standard process that a worker can correct or manage

controlling The process of measuring the results of previous decisions, comparing these results with expected results, and taking corrective action when necessary

core competency A uniquely effective business process on which a firm bases its strategic success

core product The essential benefit or service that the customer experiences

corporate culture The set of values that guide the decisions of a company's staff as they work to achieve its objectives

corporate goal A statement in concrete terms of what the company wants to achieve

corporate mission A statement that defines the firm both internally and externally

cost The denominator in the value equation that measures all costs (objective and subjective) that the customer incurs to acquire and use a product; also, the denominator of the value equation that indicates what the customer must pay for a given level of performance

cost of quality Juran's method of stating all of the costs associated with defective products in dollars and cents, including internal failure costs, external failure costs, appraisal costs, and prevention costs

critical path The sequence of activities that define the minimum lead time needed to complete a task or project

customer Anyone who consumes or is affected by the outputs of an OM system

customer-fulfillment process A series of interlocking subprocesses that describe customers' normal interactions with an

organization that offers them a bundle of goods and services

customer-involvement service delivery A service process in which customers complete many tasks that form part of the service

customer requirements planning matrix (Also called the *house of quality*) A tool of quality function deployment that identifies customer requirements and translates the requirements into a set of technical product features

customer service The firm's effort to define and implement its vision of value

cycle counting A procedure to systematically take physical counts of some items in inventory each day and reconcile any differences that emerge

cycle time The desired monthly time interval for production for each unit, which should match the sales time interval for the same month

dead stock audit A review of unproductive inventories that identifies dead or slow-moving stock at each location and discovers why the firm came to hold that stock

delay A process activity that results from interference with the process

Delphi method A qualitative forecasting method that compiles a forecast through sequential, independent responses by a group of experts to a series of questionnaires

demand forecasting An effort to develop a reliable statement about the amounts, timing, and pattern of future customer orders

demand management An operations management initiative to achieve some influence over customer demand

Deming cycle A sequence of plan-do-check-act designed to stabilize an OM system and identify opportunities for continuous improvement

Deming Prize Annual award by the Japanese government to recognize active contributions to development of quality management tools to promotion of quality improvement programs

demonstrated capacity The actual level of output for a process or activity over a period of time

dependent demand Demand for components that results from demand for a higher-level product

design for assembly A product-innovation tool that reduces assembly costs and indirectly increases the quality of conformance by creating designs that fit well with assembly operations

design for manufacture   A product-innovation tool that integrates the activities of product designers with those of the designers of the manufacturing or service delivery processes that make the product

design for service   A product-innovation tool that incorporates features to help owners and repair technicians maintain products

design lead time   The component of lead time devoted to producing a workable product design

design quality   The inherent value that customers place on product features

design tools   Statistical TQM tools that help employees to conceive and develop effective new processes

detailed scheduling   A shop-floor control process that allocates specific OM resources at specific times to individual orders based on their priorities

directing/implementing   The process of carrying out decisions made during planning, analyzing, and organizing

dispatch list   A daily document that communicates order priorities to shop-floor employees

distribution lead time   The component of lead time devoted to moving the product from the OM system to the customer

durability   An attribute of quality that measures performance under adverse conditions

economic order quantity model   A basic inventory-management model that determines how much to order of an item with independent demand to minimize the total cost of holding this inventory

effective capacity   A measure that defines the output rate that managers expect for a given process or activity

effectiveness   The extent to which the outputs of a transformation process satisfy the needs and expectations of customers in a way that contributes to the overall objectives and goals of the company

efficiency   A measure of costs incurred to deliver outputs

engineer to order   A unique product that allows extensive user customization or that has just begun its product life cycle

environmentally responsible operations   An economy-minded, systemwide, and integrated program to reduce or elimi-nate all environmental waste by revising product and process designs to prevent its creation in any part of the transformation process

exception reporting   A shop-floor control measure that ignores noncritical jobs and focuses attention only on information that indicates a need for management intervention

exciting quality   Quality that exceeds the customer's expectations, attracting favorable attention

expected quality   Quality that the customer expects and demands

expediting   A shop-floor control measure in which someone manually intervenes in the operation of the system to return an out-of-control order to an acceptable processing routine

explicit desire   A need that the customer recognizes and can describe

explicit knowledge   Codified knowledge that people learn by reading or watching and communicate through formal, systematic languages

explicit service   A service that the firm provides as part of its delivery of core benefits or services to customers

exponential smoothing   A short-range tracking tool for time series that balances recent data against longer-term patterns by adjusting weighting coefficients in a weighted average

external customer   Anyone outside the corporate boundaries of the producing firm who uses its output

external plant   Capacity of external suppliers

external setup   Any setup activity that workers complete while the equipment operates

extrinsic input   Information about conditions independent of an OM system's activities that affect a forecast of customer demand

fast to market   A competitive strategy based on reducing time to market

fast to product   A competitive strategy based on reducing time to product

final-assembly schedule   A feasible, multiquarter production plan based on capacity constraints imposed by the final-assembly process

final build schedule   The sequence of orders to pass through final assembly to become finished products

finished goods inventories   Completed products held for later sale to customers

firm planned order   A specification in the master production schedule that freezes the quantity and timing of a set of outputs in production

fitness for use   Joseph Juran's definition of *quality* which incorporates quality of design, quality of conformance, availability, safety, and field use

five deadly diseases and sins   Deming's list of bad practices that managers must address early in a TQM initiative

fixture   An implement that holds work pieces during processing

flexibility   A factor in performance that reflects the ease of changing the product to match the customer's needs; also, the ability of an OM system to respond quickly, measured by range and time, to externally and internally generated changes

flexibility responsiveness   The ability of the firm and its managers to change strategic objectives in response to changes in the marketplace

flexible manufacturing system   An automation system with capabilities to process work as varied as a job shop with minimal direct human intervention

flow chart   A graphic representation of process flows

focused forecasting   A qualitative forecasting method that combines a common-sense, grass-roots investigation with a computer simulation process to assess the effectiveness of the respondents' decision rules

forecast error   The difference between an actual outcome and a forecast for the same period

14 steps for quality improvement   A program of quality management that advocates a change in corporate culture to achieve a goal of zero defects

functionality   An attribute of quality that measures whether or not a product functions

Gantt chart   A scheduling technique that lays out horizontal bars for activities related to specific jobs at individual work centers

general process chart   A summary process flow analysis chart that indicates time required for and distance covered by activities in each category

good   A tangible product

grass-roots forecasting   A qualitative forecasting method that seeks input from people at the level of the organization that gives them the best contact with the phenomenon under study

gross requirements The total input needs of the OM system in MRP, found by multiplying the units of finished products planned for production by the number of parts needed to make each unit

group technology An equipment layout dedicated to the complete production of a family of similar parts by linking together all operations in a particular process

habit of quality An unwavering focus, routinely adjusted and reinforced, on the need for quality

histogram A TQM statistical tool that graphically displays data gathered during the operation of a process to show the extent and type of variance within the system

historical analogy A qualitative forecasting method that evaluates past events as part of predictions about some related future development

Hoshin management A TQM design tool that works toward dramatic, strategic breakthroughs for the organization

implementation A step in the problem-solving process that puts a chosen solution alternative into practice

implicit benefit A benefit, frequently a psychological feeling, that accompanies the core benefits of a product

indented bill of materials A list of product components that indents all products at the same level within the product structure by the same amount

indifferent quality Quality that the customer does not notice or appreciate

information flow An exchange of data that supports efforts to manage a process

input/output control A tool for capacity management that manages work flows to match the demonstrated capacity of process

inspection A process activity that checks or verifies the results of another activity

intellectual capital Critical human resources skills and capabilities

internal customer Anyone who uses the output of another area or department within the producing firm

internal setup Any setup procedure that occurs while the equipment sits idle

intrinsic input Information that helps demand forecasters to predict future events based on the record of similar phenomena in the past

inventory A physical resource that a firm holds in stock with the intent of selling it or transforming it into a more valuable state

inventory audit A study to size up and describe a firm's inventory management system

inventory holding cost The funds, physical resources, and personnel that a firm ties up by maintaining inventories

ISO 9000 A set of internationally accepted standards for business quality adopted in 1987 by the International Organization for Standardization

job design Assigning specific tasks and company resources to particular workers to create a system that effectively accomplishes the mission of the firm through daily contributions of indivdiuals

job enlargement A technique of enhancing a job by assigning more tasks to a single worker

job enrichment A technique of enhancing a job by expanding the scope of its activities to include tasks that require different skill levels

job rotation A technique of enhancing a job by cycling workers through different tasks during a shift

jobbing A category of manufacturing processes that irregularly produces relatively few units of a product in a flexible plant layout

just-in-time manufacturing An organizationwide quest to produce output within the minimum possible lead time and at the lowest possible total cost by continuously identifying and eliminating all forms of waste and variance

kaizen A quality enhancement principle of continuously introducing small improvements to an existing OM system

Kanban A system of control cards that govern material movements through an OM system within JIT (Also called *pull scheduling*)

key success factor Something that the firm must do well to accomplish its stated mission

knowledge factory A transformation process that combines autonomy, fluctuations, intent, and variety to establish conditions that favor knowledge creation

known product A good or service with standardized and widely recognized features

labor-limited job shop A job shop that employs significantly fewer workers than it would need to operate each machine

latent desire A need that the customer recognizes and understands only vaguely

lead time The interval between the start and end of an activity or series of activities

leadership An organizational quality that unifies members in pursuit of common goals and sustains vigorous motivation and commitment

lean production An organizationwide OM system orientation designed to design and develop higher value products while consuming fewer resources for both direct costs and overhead

Less of/System Simplification A strategy for reducing lead times that tries to identify steps that can be eliminated, combined, or repositioned to create a simpler system that takes less time

level-production strategy A method of matching production to variable demand by setting the production rate equal to the average demand rate and using inventory as a buffer

line of visibility A marker on a service blueprint that distinguishes which process activities occur within sight of customers

line production A category of manufacturing processes that arranges special-purpose machines and equipment in a rigid sequence to perform repetitive tasks for large orders

Little JIT Just-in-time manufacturing as a set of tactically oriented, analytical tools

load The volume of work that remains for a process to complete at any time

load leveling A JIT scheduling technique that balances the rate of production with the rate at which the market wants products; also, a shop-floor control measure to rearrange work loads, moving excess demand from peaks to keep the shop busy during valleys

local rule A decision principle based on the cost tradeoffs for individual items

lot splitting A shop-floor control measure that breaks up an order into several smaller batches that proceed separately through the shop

machine (machining center) A piece of equipment that completes processing tasks

make to order   A product that is built in response to a customer order following an existing design

make to stock   A standard product, often produced based on demand forecasts rather than known orders, that remains in inventory to await customer purchase

Malcolm Baldrige National Quality Award   Award administered by the Department of Commerce to recognize exceptional quality achievements by U.S. firms

management   The process of directing resources and organizing activities in achievement of corporate or organizational objectives

management tools for quality   Theoretical frameworks and mental models through which managers examine and influence OM processes to enhance quality

manufacturing lead time   The component of lead time devoted to producing the product within the firm's OM system

manufacturing resources planning   An OM technique that expands the role of MRP to integrate a wide variety of management processes within a single firm

mass customization   A corporate strategy designed to develop and maintain a sustainable competitive advantage by competing on the basis of flexibility

mass service   An organization that provides a routine or standardized service through a labor-intensive process

master production schedule   A document that defines the goods that specific shops will produce in definite quantities at definite times over a short-term planning horizon to carry out aggregate plans; also a periodic (usually monthly) statement of the number of units of each specific end product that an OM process will build and when it will build each product

material flexibility   The ability of the transformation process to adjust for unexpected variations in inputs

materials management   A plant-organizing function that assures a predictable flow of components and other inputs through a transformation process

materials requirements planning   A system that determines what final products the firm will make for a future period and then specifies production of needed inputs to make those products

maximum capacity   The largest amount of output that a process can generate; also called *design capacity*; also, a measure that defines the highest rate of output that a process or activity can achieve

mean   The expected value in a distribution

mean absolute deviation   A measure of forecast accuracy that averages the absolute value of forecast errors for a sample

mean squared error   A measure of forecast accuracy that averages the square of total forecast errors for a sample

mental map   A set of beliefs, relationships, and processes that link inputs to outputs and actions

minimum rational work unit   A single, continuous, and distinct motion of a worker or machine in a scientific management study

mission   The common, driving vision that underlies specific objectives and gives the organization its reason for existing

mix flexibility   The ability of an OM system to produce a wide range of products or variants with fast setups

mixed-load, multiple-plant transportation (milk-run system)   A JIT logistical system based on frequent, regular transportation of partial loads from many suppliers

mixed-model production line   A production line that can produce more than one model as long as the variations fall within a single part family

mixed-model scheduling   A method for setting a production sequence for end products that creates the smoothest possible set of demands on all activities within the master production schedule

model   An abstract representation of reality that simplifies actual events or situations

modification flexibility   The ability of the transformation process to implement minor product design changes

moment of truth   The customer's perception based on continuing assessments of the product's value. The customer's most recent experience determines to a large extent how that customer sees the company

More of/Excess Resources   A strategy to reduce lead times by deploying new resources in the form of extra labor, equipment, materials, or tools to overcome lead time increases due to resource shortages

MRP record   A document on which planners enter information to track production activities for a single final product, subassembly, or individual component

national culture   The set of shared assumptions and attitudes that guide the behaviors and beliefs of people from a particular country

nervousness   A pattern of significant changes in MRP records caused by apparently minor changes in the master production schedule or other inputs

net requirements   The difference between total units required and units available in inventory and incoming orders that defines the minimum production goals for a period in MRP

net-change method   A process for updating MRP records that revised information only when changes in the schedule required adjustments

nonstrict precedence   An order of process activities that allows more than one sequence

numerically controlled machine   A machine that reads computer code which directs its operations

one-dimensional quality   Quality that the customer expects, but that does not create an order loser when lacking

operating instruction   A statement in quality function deployment that translates critical process and product parameters into specifications for operations to be performed by plant personnel

operation   A process activity that causes a change or transformation to an input

operation due date   A performance target that sets a completion time for every activity in the processing sequence for an order

operations management   A field of study that tries to understand, explain, predict, and change the organizational and strategic effects of the transformation process

Operations Management Toolkit   A basic set of conceptual tools and techniques for completing the activities of operations management

order   A statement that authorizes a firm's OM function to assign people, materials, tools, and equipment to build a predetermined quantity of a specific item

order due date   A performance target that informs the shop-floor control system when it must return a finished product to the control of the planning system

order lead time The component of lead time consumed by links between the customer and the OM system

order loser A trait in which poor performance by the firm and its OM function can cause losses of current or future business

order qualifier A trait in which the firm and the OM function must perform acceptably to be considered as a candidate to fill an order

order winner A trait in which the firm and the OM function must perform well relative to competitors to win orders

organizational design The management task of defining relationships between jobs that help workers to accomplish the organization's objectives

organizational development An orchestrated, companywide process of revising procedures and relationships to close a gap between current and desired performance

organizing The process of developing structures for necessary tasks and assigning resources to them

outpartnering The practice of buying inputs from suppliers as part of a deep and continuing relationship between two firms

outsourcing The practice of buying inputs from suppliers without much involvement beyond ordering and receiving procedures

panel consensus A qualitative forecasting technique that gathers knowledgeable people to craft a forecast by engaging in an open dialogue over a relatively short period of time

paradigm A mental model or framework of thought

parent-component relationship The need for lower-level parts to make a higher-level product

Pareto analysis A problem-solving tool that sets management priorities based on the assumption that 80 percent of any gap between expected and actual performance results from 20 percent of an operation

part family design envelope A set of characteristics required of new parts for production within a flexible manufacturing system

part number An unambiguous, numerical designation for each component within an OM process

part period balancing method A technique for inventory management with uneven demand that satisfies demand for subsequent periods through economical, combined production runs

partnership A relatively new type of purchasing relationship characterized by close working relations, implicit trust, mutual respect, and dramatically redefined OM systems

pegging report An MRP report that identifies current orders that have contributed to gross requirements for a particular component

perceived quality An assessment of quality based on the reputation of the firm

performance A factor in the value equation that describes what a good or service does for the customer

periodic time interval method A technique for inventory management with uneven demand that adjusts the timing of orders based on the ratio of the average order quantity to average demand

personal-attention service delivery An individualized system that seeks to delight customers by catering to their specific needs

physical flow A movement of tangible inputs through the activities of a process to become outputs

physical link A tangible connection between related activities

planned lead time A prespecified amount of time scheduled for production operations to make an individual part

planning The process of deciding what to do

planning bill A fictitious bill of materials for an unbuildable dummy item that facilitates component scheduling

poka-yoke A just-in-time method to design parts and processes in ways that make desired results inevitable

postponement Deferring final assembly of a product to allow the customer to specify options

preautomation An effort to simplify process activities sufficiently to prepare the workplace for effective automation

predetermined motion-time measurement system A method for developing time standards based on a set database of elemental time standards for certain common motions

prescription/alternatives A step in the problem-solving process that develops potential solutions to a problem

price of conformance The cost of investments in training, product and process design, and buyer-seller relationships to improve quality

price of nonconformance The costs of poor quality in the form of rejected products, inspections, repairs, and unhappy customers

problem A perceived gap between a present situation and some desired situation

problem statement/diagnostics The stage in the problem-solving process in which managers state the current situation, listing symptoms, causes, and triggering events

process The sequence and organization of all activities needed to convert inputs into outputs; also, a collection of activities that transform inputs into an output that offers value to the customer

process (capability) buy A purchase that results from an intimate relationship between the knowledge bases, capabilities, and processes of two firms

process costing Performance-evaluation procedures based on aggregate data about resource inputs and product outputs

process flow analysis A technique for documenting activities in a detailed, compact, and graphic form to help the manager to understand the process and to highlight potential improvements

process flow chart A process flow analysis tool that categorizes each activity and details time requirements, briefly describes the activity, and presents other appropriate information

process flow diagram A process flow analysis tool in which the analyst draws physical flows through related activities

process layout An arrangement of physical resources that groups similar machines or work centers in clusters

process plan and quality control chart A quality function deployment tool that translates the columns of the technical features deployment matrix into critical process and product parameters and appropriate process control limits

process tools Statistical TQM tools that help employees to assess conditions in existing processes to detect problems and regain lost control

process width The interval between the lower and upper ends of the distribution of process performance data

product The output of any process (good or service); also, anything that an organization can offer to a market for attention, acquisition, use, or consumption that might satisfy a want or a need

product (capacity) buy A relatively purchase of inputs from external suppliers as a substitute for internal production

product architecture Broad guidelines for designing a product and the OM system to produce it that establish essential limits for all subsequent design decisions

product bundle The set of product and organizational characteristics that combine to delight customers

product family A group of similar outputs

product interface The place where functional capabilities meet

product layout An arrangement of physical manufacturing resources in a configuration that corresponds to a routine flow of production tasks

product-development strategy A component of business strategy that coordinates all of the major business activities that contribute to product innovation

product/market strategy A component of product-development strategy that guides the type, scale, and timing of innovations in product features or market targeting

production Kanban A card or other signal that accompanies an empty bin or other transportation option and authorizes a worker to produce parts to resupply a later stage of production

production lot scheduling model An inventory-management model that accommodates consumption of units from an order while the supplying process works to complete the rest of the order

production-line service delivery A standardized, carefully ordered system for rapidly delivering uniform, high-quality service products

professional service An organization that offers a highly customized service through a labor-intensive process

project A category of manufacturing processes that completes a single job at a site other than the firm's facilities

promised delivery date The date that operations managers, sales representatives, and the customer agree on for delivery of an order

purchasing The organizational function that acts as an intermediary between the OM system and its suppliers

quality A factor in performance that represents how well a product meets a customer's expectations

quality at the source An orientation within JIT manufacturing toward targeting efforts to improve quality at the activities that produce it

quality function deployment A set of methods to identify all of the major requirements of a firm's customers and to evaluate how well the designs of products and OM processes meet or exceed those requirements

quality trilogy The set of actions that encompass everything that the firm must do to define quality, including quality planning, quality control, and quality improvement

quality vaccine Crosby's image of a TQM regimen that improves the health of the firm and corrects its problems

quantity discount model An inventory-management model that accommodates price discounts for large orders

range An indicator of dispersion within a distribution that also indicates whether the distribution is open ended or closed ended

raw materials inventories Resources purchased as inputs to the transformation process that have not yet begun that process

redefinition A sudden, dramatic change driven by new methods of enhancing value; also, a flexibility principle that uses it to force competitors to react to one's own moves

reduction A flexibility principle that tries to reduce the need for it by identifying and eliminating causes of uncertainty

refinement An incremental improvement of existing practices

regeneration method A process for updating MRP records that revised all information in a single production run

reliability An attribute of quality that measures how long a product performs before it fails

rerouting/program flexibility The ability of the OM system to reduce uncertainty of equipment availability by quickly and easily changing the route (i.e., the sequence of machines) through which a job flows

resource-management process The business process that assures that other process activities have the inputs they

need to contribute to a transformation process that satisfies customers in a way that promotes achievement of the strategic objectives of the organization

reverse marketing Active efforts by purchasing personnel to develop new sources of supply rather than simply evaluating the offers of potential sellers

rework An order or part of an order that requires special handling or extra processing to meet customer needs

routing file Planning information that indicates the recommended sequence of processing steps and the capacity required to transform raw materials into each finished part

safety An attribute of quality that measures the likelihood of harm from a good or service

safety capacity Excess capacity that the firm keeps available for unexpected demands; it acts as a buffer

salvage An order or part of an order that the OM system cannot complete according to initial intentions, but for which the system can still find some use

Same as/Standardization A strategy to reduce lead times by trying to use standard processes or parts as much as possible, allowing people to focus on unique parts or process components

scatterplot A TQM statistical tool that graphically illustrates the relationship between two quantitative variables

scheduling calendar A table for determining specific dates from lead-time data

scrap Any part of an order that the system cannot process into a usable product

seasonal index A statistic that allows forecasters to adjust for seasonal variations found by dividing a centered moving average into raw data

sequence dependency A similarity in setup or processing activities between two or more orders in a queue

service An intangible product

service blueprinting An analytical tool to identify and eliminate potential failures and set time and cost standards for service-delivery systems by process flow analysis

service-delay management A strategy of matching demand to capacity by simply requiring customers to wait for service

service delivery system The network of processes designed to fulfill identified customer needs

service dispenser The business processes through which the organization provides its service

service factory An organization that provides a standardized service through a process low in labor intensity

service shop An organization that provides a customized service through a process low in labor intensity

serviceability An attribute of quality that measures a product's service-related traits

shape The symmetrical or asymetrical form of a distribution

shop-floor control The primary operations management system for effectively executing production activities

Silver-Meal heuristic A technique for inventory management with uneven demand that combines demand for subsequent periods until the average cost per period starts to rise

simplification A JIT initiative to identify and eliminate any unnecessary process steps through process analysis techniques

single-level bill of materials A document that lists subordinate components only one level down to indicate the immediate requirements to manufacture the product

single-minute exchange of dies A three-stage method for reducing setups by separating internal and external setups, converting internal setups to external setups, and streamlining all setup procedures

Six Sigma Motorola's TQM program which seeks to guarantee that 99.99966 percent of all products that the firm builds meet applicable standards

size-up/description The step in the problem-solving process at which managers gather information to accurately characterize a problem

sociotechnical systems perspective A method of studying the interfaces between humans and technology and emphasizing interactions outside formal organizational relationships

solution A set of actions designed to close the gap between the current and desired future situation by changing the conditions that created or contributed to the gap

sourcing lead time The components of lead time devoted to working with suppliers

spatial link The distance between two related activities

special cause A short-term source of variance in an OM process

specialization strategy Staffing narrow jobs with low-wage, quickly trained workers as part of a high-volume, repetitive manufacturing system

specification width The interval between the lower and upper limits on performance data for a product or process

speed A factor in performance that describes how quickly the firm can deliver a product to the customer or design and produce the product

stakeholder Any person or group with an interest in the functions of the operations management system or firm and its well-being

standard deviation A statistical indicator of variability within a distribution

standard of performance An indicator of organizational policy to guide the efforts of an individual manager

standardization A JIT initiative to replace inconsistent methods with standard routines for process tasks

statistical tools for quality Formal, scientific indicators through which managers assess their control of OM processes and identify problems and likely causes

stockout cost A measure of the effects of failure to provide the products that customers want, leading to lost sales and reductions in goodwill

storage A process activity that places an item under some kind of control

strict precedence A particular sequence of activities that a process needs to flow smoothly

supplier An organization outside the firm that provides essential inputs of materials, expertise, and services to an OM system

supplier certification A buyer demand that suppliers demonstrate that their processes can consistently deliver inputs of acceptable quality in timely and appropriate lots

supplier council A group of representatives from a buyer and a supplier who meet regularly to discuss and resolve supplier and buyer concerns and expectations and to measure performance by both parties

supply chain The sequence of suppliers and organizational buyers that spans all stages of processing from raw materials to final consumers

supporting facility A physical resource that allows the organization to offer a product with the features that customers want

supporting good A physical good that customers purchase or consume along with the primary product

symptom An indicator of some problem within a system

synchronous manufacturing A highly coordinated system of activities designed to continuously enhance value

system A goal-driven group of interrelated activities linked together by means of a network or structure

tacit knowledge Knowledge that people gain only by experience and that they cannot clearly communicate to others

technical features deployment matrix A tool of quality function deployment that translates the technical product features identified in the columns of the customer requirements planning matrix into design requirements for critical product components

technology paradox The surprising contradiction between the accelerating performance of technological products and the dramatic drops in their prices

technology strategy A component of product-development strategy that guides plans for introducing technological innovations

theory of constraints A basis for operations management that emphasizes the need to identify and manage constraints or bottlenecks

theory of variance Deming's central premise that variations from standard activities cause many problems for all OM processes and most firms

things gone wrong/things gone right Ford's quality framework based on errors and defects versus product benefits

throughput costing A method of allocating costs to products based on how long they spend in the OM system

time bucket A discrete time interval in a larger MRP production schedule

time fence   A point within the MPS that segments the planning horizon into time periods with well-defined provisions for changing orders

time to market   The total time that a firm takes to introduce a new product to the market or to revise an existing product

time to product   The time that the firm takes to respond to a customer order for an existing product

time-based competition   A strategy to enhance value by being faster to market or faster to product than competitors

total cost analysis   A decision-making technique in which managers identify all costs associated with a set of decisions and then choose the one with the lowest total cost

total product delivery lead time   The total lead time, including all components, needed to bring a product to market, assuming no inventory anywhere in the supply chain

total product experience   The combination of tangible and intangible product characteristics designed to win the customer's approval

total productive maintenance   A JIT method designed to identify and attack all causes of equipment breakdowns and system downtime

total quality environmental management   A technique that applies the tools and techniques of TQM to the problem of improving corporate environmental responsibility

total quality management   A culture that enfuses quality principles into every company activity; also, a program to focus all organizational activities on enhancing quality for customers by redirecting the corporate culture and implementing management and statistical tools

total work content rule   A method of calculating variable lead times that sums processing times for components in a specific job and adjusts for delays

tracking signal   An indicator of cumulative forecast error implied by MAD and MSE statistics for an individual product or item in inventory

trade-off analysis   A technique for choosing among decision alternatives based on the indifference point between them

transfer line   A production line that carries raw materials on conveyors past work stations that process them into something useful

transportation   A process activity that moves an object

transporter   A component of a manufacturing process that moves resources between activities

two-bin system   An inventory management system that orders stock whenever someone takes the last bin, opens the last box, etc.

Type I service level   A method of calculating a reorder point to give a specified probability that the firm will have enough units in stock, including safety stock, to meet demand during the order lead time

Type II service level   A method of calculating a reorder point to give safety stocks that assure that inventory will meet at least 95 percent of all demand

uncontrolled variance   A variation from a standard process due to the impact of some factor outside the control of the employee

unproductive fear   Concern for individual failure that causes waste by limiting the effectiveness of the group

utilization   The percentage of a resource's maximum capacity for which plans expect active involvement in production

value   The customer's subjective evaluation, adjusted for cost, of how well a good or service meets or exceeds expectations

value analysis (value engineering)   A structured process that seeks to improve a product's design while maintaining its functional characteristics and marketing appeal to customers

value chain   A sequential process for development, production, marketing, and delivery of a product

value equation   The mathematical expression of value as a ratio of performance to cost

variable data   Data that quantifies some process condition, allowing the analyst to count it and make comparisons

variable-hours strategy   A method of matching production to variable demand

by setting the production rate equal to the demand rate and adjusting the work hours of stable groups of employees

vector marketing   Service based on an understanding of customers so complete that the organization can anticipate latent demands

vendor scheduling   A system that controls releases of orders and continuing communications of priorities, needs, and quantities between suppliers and the buying organization's OM system

virtual corporation   A partnership so close that two partners become for all operational purposes a single firm

vision   A strategic view of the organization, its products, and its processes that aims at creating and satisfying new forms of demand in a way that increases customer satisfaction and company market share and profits

volume flexibility   The ability of the transformation process to accommodate variations in production quantities

waiting-management program   Arrangements to delight customers while they wait for service

waste   The opposite of value; also, any activity or action that adversely affects the value equation for the customer

waste streaming   An analytical method that applies process flow analysis to waste flows by graphically depicting the relationships between process inputs and waste outputs

Watch It/Variance Control   A strategy to reduce lead times by identifying and eliminating or controlling activities that create variance within lead times

where-used report   A report from an MRP system that states the applications of a particular component or subassembly in the larger product structure

withdrawal Kanban   A card or other signal that accompanies an order and authorizes a worker to take parts or materials necessary to fill the order

work sampling   A method of developing time standards based on statistically determined random observations of a worker or process

work-in-process inventories   Resources currently undergoing transformation into more valuable states

Name Index

Subject Index